The British Chambers of Commerce
Six Language Business Dictionary

"This multi-purpose dictionary will be of immense value to those companies already doing business in Europe and those preparing to break into the European market and beyond. Communication is an essential tool for business and the timely appearance of this dictionary is very welcome."

Sir Fred Catherwood, MEP
Vice-President of the European Parliament and former Chairman of the British Overseas Trade Board

The British Chambers of Commerce

Six Language
Business
Dictionary

Colt Books Ltd, Cambridge
with The Association of
British Chambers of Commerce

Colt Books Ltd
9 Clarendon Road, Cambridge CB2 2BH
Tel: 0223 357047   Fax: 0223 65866

with

The Association of British Chambers of Commerce
Sovereign House, 212 Shaftesbury Avenue, London WC2H 8EW
Tel: 071 240 5831   Fax: 071 379 6331

This edition first published by Colt Books Ltd, 1991
Reprinted 1991, 1992

This book was first published by Pan Books in 1978 as
A Multilingual Commercial Dictionary

© 1978 Laurence Urdang Associates Ltd

This revised edition: © Market House Books 1978
and © 1989 Econ Verlag GmbH; introduction © 1991 Colt Books Ltd

British Library Cataloguing in Publication Data
   Six language business dictionary
   1. Business enterprise
   I. Association of British Chambers of Commerce
   338.6

ISBN: 0 905899 03 2

Printed and bound in Great Britain by
Biddles Ltd, Guildford and King's Lynn

Introduction

British Chambers of Commerce, the UK's largest private sector providers of export and trade services, are delighted to be associated with the publication of this practical guide to the all important language of business. This dictionary covers the basic words and terms that are used in business in English, French, German, Italian, Portuguese and Spanish. It lists alphabetically the words in everyday business use in each language.

It is quick and easy to use, as each word is listed separately in all six languages with the equivalent word in the other five languages shown underneath. Where appropriate American terms are also given.

With the increasing emphasis on international trade, this dictionary will provide a useful tool for many people conducting business in a language with which they may not be entirely familiar. The difference between profit and loss may rest on a correct interpretation of the terms on which a particular deal has been negotiated.

This will be an invaluable aid for businesses throughout the European Community and well beyond.

This book was prepared for Pan Books Ltd by
Laurence Urdang Associates Ltd, Aylesbury.
Editor: Dr Alan Isaacs.
Contributors:
Hans Smith, MA, FCII, Dip Leg. Tr (French, German)
F. Garcia (Spanish)
A. Lauria Ll D (Italian).
Manolo B.R. Santos, BA MIL (Portuguese).

A

abandon *(m) n* Fr
De Abandon *(m)*
En abandonment
Es abandono *(m)*
It abbandono *(m)*
Pt abandono *(m)*

Abandon *(m) n* De
En abandonment
Es abandono *(m)*
Fr abandon *(m)*
It abbandono *(m)*
Pt abandono *(m)*

abandonment *n* En
De Abandon *(m)*
Es abandono *(m)*
Fr abandon *(m)*
It abbandono *(m)*
Pt abandono (m)

abandono *(m) n* Es, Pt
De Abandon *(m)*
En abandonment
Fr abandon *(m)*
It abbandono *(m)*

abbandono *(m) n* It
De Abandon *(m)*
En abandonment
Es abandono *(m)*
Fr abandon *(m)*
Pt abandono *(m)*

abbonamento *(m) n* It
De Abonnement *(n)*
En subscription (to a journal, etc.)
Es abono *(m)*
Fr abonnement *(m)*
Pt assinatura *(f)*

abbuono *(m) n* It
De Rabatt *(m)*
En allowance
Es bonificación *(f)*
Fr rabais *(m)*
Pt provisão *(f)*

Abfallprodukt *(n) n* De
En waste products
Es desperdicios *(m pl)*
Fr déchets *(m pl)*
It prodotto di rifiuto *(m)*
Pt desperdicios *(m pl)*

abgabenfrei *adj* De
En duty-free
Es exento de impuestos
Fr exempt de douane
It esente da dazio
Pt isento de impostos

abgabenpflichtig *adj* De
En dutiable
Es tasable
Fr taxable
It tassabile
Pt tributável

Abgangstag *(m) n* De
En sailing date
Es día de salida *(m)*
Fr date de départ *(f)*
It data di partenza *(f)*
Pt dia de saída *(m)*

ab Kai De
En ex quay
Es en muelle
Fr à prendre sur quai
It sulla banchina
Pt ex-cais

Abkommen *(n) n* De
En agreement; covenant
Es contrato; pacto *(m)*
Fr convention *(f)*
It accordo; convenzione *(m f)*
Pt acordo; pacto *(m)*

Ablauf *(m) n* De
En expiry
Es expiración *(f)*
Fr expiration *(f)*
It termine *(m)*
Pt expiração *(f)*

Ablehnung *(f) n* De
En disclaimer; rejection
Es renuncia rechazo *(f m)*
Fr déni; refus *(m)*
It rinunzia; rifiuto *(f m)*
Pt descante; rejeição *(m f)*

ablösbare Vorzugsaktien *(f pl)* De
En redeemable preference shares
Es acciónes preferentes amortizables *(f pl)*
Fr actions privilégiées amortissables *(f pl)*

It azioni preferenziali redimibili *(f pl)*
Pt acções redimíveis preferenciais *(f pl)*

abnehmend *adj* De
En diminishing
Es decreciente
Fr décroissant
It decrescente
Pt decrescente

abnehmender Ertrag *(m)* De
En diminishing returns
Es rendimientos decrecientes *(m pl)*
Fr rendements décroissants *(m pl)*
It proventi decrescenti *(m pl)*
Pt rendimentos decrescentes *(m pl)*

Abnehmerverein *(m) n* De
En consumer group
Es grupo de consumidores *(m)*
Fr groupe consommateur *(m)*
It gruppo di consumatori *(m)*
Pt grupo de consumidores *(m)*

aboard *adv* En
De an Bord
Es a bordo
Fr à bord
It a bordo
Pt a bordo

abogado *(m) n* Es
De Anwalt *(m)*
En lawyer; barrister; counsel
Am attorney
Fr avocat *(m)*
It avvocato *(m)*
Pt advogado *(m)*

abonnement *(m) n* Fr
De Abonnement *(n)*
En subscription (to a journal, etc.)
Es abono *(m)*
It abbonamento *(m)*
Pt assinatura *(f)*

Abonnement *(n) n* De
En subscription (to a journal, etc.)
Es abono *(m)*
Fr abonnement *(m)*

It abbonamento *(m)*
Pt assinatura *(f)*

abono *(m)* n Es
De Abonnement *(n)*
En subscription (to a journal, etc.)
Fr abonnement *(m)*
It abbonamento *(m)*
Pt assinatura *(f)*

à bord Fr
De an Bord
En aboard
Es a bordo
It a bordo
Pt a bordo

a bordo Es, It, Pt
De an Bord
En aboard
Fr à bord

above-mentioned *adj* En
De obenerwähnt
Es susodicho
Fr susmentionné
It suddetto
Pt supracitado

above par En
De über pari
Es a premio
Fr au-dessus du pair
It sopra la pari
Pt a prémio

Abrechnung *(f)* n De
En settlement (of accounts)
Es ajuste *(m)*
Fr règlement *(m)*
It quietanza *(f)*
Pt ajuste *(m)*

Abrechnungstag *(m)* n De
En settlement day; account day
Am due date
Es día de liquidación *(m)*
Fr jour de règlement *(m)*
It giorno della liquidazione *(m)*
Pt dia de liquidação *(m)*

Abrechnungszeitraum *(m)* n De
En accounting period
Es ejercicio *(m)*
Fr exercice *(f)*

It esercizio *(m)*
Pt exercício *(m)*

a breve scadenza It
De kurzfristig
En short-dated
Es a corto plazo
Fr à courte échéance
Pt a curto prazo

a breve termine It
De kurzfristig
En short-term
Es a corto plazo
Fr à court terme
Pt a curto prazo

Abriß *(m)* n De
En abstract
Es resumen *(m)*
Fr résumé *(m)*
It riassunto *(m)*
Pt resumo *(m)*

abroad *adv* En
De im Ausland
Es en el extranjero
Fr à l'étranger
It all'estero
Pt no estrangeiro

Absatzdirektor *(m)* n De
En marketing director
Es director mercantil *(m)*
Fr administrateur chef d'écoulement *(m)*
It direttore di mercato *(m)*
Pt director de comercialização *(m)*

Absatzübereinkommen *(n)* n De
En marketing agreement
Es acuerdo mercantil *(m)*
Fr accord de commercialisation *(m)*
It accordo di mercato *(m)*
Pt acordo sobre comercialização *(m)*

Abschätzung *(f)* n De
En appraisal
Es evaluación *(f)*
Fr évaluation *(f)*
It valutazione *(f)*
Pt avaliação *(f)*

ab Schiff De
En ex ship
Es en el buque
Fr ex ship
It ex ship
Pt ex-navio

Abschluß *(m)* n De
En deal
Es negocio *(m)*
Fr affaire *(f)*
It affare *(f)*
Pt negócio *(m)*

Abschreibtypistin *(f)* n De
En copy typist
Am transcriber
Es mecanógrafa *(f)*
Fr dactylo copiste *(f)*
It dattilografa *(f)*
Pt dactilógrafa *(f)*

Abschreibung für Abnützung (AFA) *(f)* De
En depreciation allowance
Es provisión para amortización *(f)*
Fr provision pour amortissement *(f)*
It quota di ammortamento *(f)*
Pt provisão para amortização *(f)*

Abschrift *(f)* n De
En copy
Es copia *(f)*
Fr copie *(f)*
It copia *(f)*
Pt cópia *(f)*

abscond *vb* En
De sich heimlich davonmachen
Es esconderse
Fr s'enfuir: décamper
It nascondersi
Pt ausentar-se para parte incerta

absenden *vb* De
En dispatch
Es expedir
Fr expédier
It spedire
Pt expedir

Absender *(m)* n De
En consignor
Es consignador *(m)*

Fr expéditeur *(m)*
It speditore *(m)*
Pt consignante *(m)*

(zur) Absendung empfangen De
En received for shipment
Es recibido para envio
Fr reçu pour envoi
It ricevuto per caricazione
Pt recebido para carregamento

Absendungserklärung
  (f) n De
En declaration of shipment
Es declaración de expedición
  (f)
Fr déclaration d'expédition *(f)*
It dichiarazione d'imbarco *(f)*
Pt declaração de expedição *(f)*

absentee n En
De Abwesende(r) *(m)*
Es ausente *(m)*
Fr manquant *(m)*
It assente *(m)*
Pt ausente *(m)*

absenteeism n En
De unerlaubte Abwesenheit *(f)*
Es ausentismo *(m)*
Fr absentéisme *(m)*
It assenteismo *(m)*
Pt absentismo *(m)*

absentéisme *(m)* n Fr
De unerlaubte Abwesenheit *(f)*
En absenteeism
Es ausentismo *(m)*
It assenteismo *(m)*
Pt absentismo *(m)*

absentismo *(m)* n Pt
De unerlaubte Abwesenheit *(f)*
En absenteeism
Es ausentismo *(m)*
Fr absentéisme *(m)*
It assenteismo *(m)*

abstain vb En
De seine Stimme enthalten
Es abstenerse
Fr s'abstenir
It astenersi
Pt abster-se

abstenerse vb Es
De seine Stimme enthalten
En abstain
Fr s'abstenir
It astenersi
Pt abster-se

s'abstenir vb Fr
De seine Stimme enthalten
En abstain
Es abstenerse
It astenersi
Pt abster-se

abster-se vb Pt
De seine Stimme enthalten
En abstain
Es abstenerse
Fr s'abstenir
It astenersi

abstract n En
De Abriß *(m)*
Es resumen *(m)*
Fr résumé *(m)*
It riassunto *(m)*
Pt resumo *(m)*

Abteilung *(f)* n De
En department; division
Es departamento; sección
  (m f)
Fr département; service *(m)*
It dipartimento; divisione
  (m f)
Pt departamento; secção *(m f)*

Abteilungsleiter *(m)* n De
En head of department
Es jeíe de departamento *(m)*
Fr chef de service *(m)*
It capo reparto *(m)*
Pt chefe de departamento *(m)*

Abtretungsvertrag *(m)* n De
En deed of assignement
Es titulo de asignación *(m)*
Fr acte attributif *(m)*
It atto di cessione *(m)*
Pt título de consignação *(m)*

a buon mercato It
De billig
En cheap
Es barato
Fr bon marché
Pt barato

abuso di influenza *(m)* It
De unzulässige Beeinflussung
  (f)
En undue influence
Es abuso de influencia *(m)*
Fr influence illégitime *(f)*
Pt influência imprópria *(f)*

abweichend adj De
En dissenting
Es disidente
Fr dissident
It dissidente
Pt dissidente

Abweichung *(f)* n De
En discrepancy
Es desacuerdo *(m)*
Fr écart *(m)*
It divergenza *(f)*
Pt discrepância *(f)*

ab Werk De
En ex works
Es de fábrica
Fr prise usine
It franco fabbrica
Pt na fábrica

Abwesende(r) *(m)* n De
En absentee
Es ausente *(m)*
Fr manquant *(m)*
It assente *(m)*
Pt ausente *(m)*

abwickeln vb De
En wind up (a business)
Es liquidar (un negocio)
Fr liquider (une entreprise)
It liquidare (una azienda)
Pt liquidar (um negócio)

abziehbare Unkosten *(pl)* De
En allowable expense
Es gastos deducibles *(m pl)*
Fr dépense déductible *(f)*
It spesa permessa *(f)*
Pt despesas deduzíveis *(f pl)*

abziehen vb De
En deduct
Es deducir
Fr déduire
It dedurre
Pt deduzir

acaparador *(m) n* Es
De Gewinnler *(m)*
En profiteer
Fr profiteur *(m)*
It profittatore *(m)*
Pt especulador *(m)*

acaparar el mercado Es
De den Markt beherrschen
En corner a market
Fr accaparer le marché
It accaparrare il mercato
Pt dominar o mercado

acção *(f) n* Pt
De Aktie *(f)*
En share
Es acción *(f)*
Fr action *(f)*
It azione *(f)*

acção judicial *(f)* Pt
De Prozeß; Klage *(m f)*
En legal action
Es pleito *(m)*
Fr action juridique *(f)*
It processo *(m)*

acção ordinária *(f)* Pt
De Stammaktie *(f)*
En ordinary share
Es acción ordinaria *(f)*
Fr action ordinaire *(f)*
It azione ordinaria *(f)*

acção preferencial *(f)* Pt
De Vorzugsaktie *(f)*
En preference share
Es acción preferente *(f)*
Fr action privilégiée *(f)*
It azione privilegiata *(f)*

accaparer le marché Fr
De den Markt beherrschen
En corner a market
Es acaparer el mercado
It accaparrare il mercato
Pt dominar o mercado

accaparrare il mercato It
De den Markt beherrschen
En corner a market
Es acaparer el mercado
Fr accaparer le marché
Pt dominar o mercado

accattatore *(m) n* It
De Kreditnehmer *(m)*
En borrower

Es prestatario *(m)*
Fr emprunteur *(m)*
Pt beneficiário de emprésti-
mo *(m)*

accelerated depreciation En
De beschleunigte Abschrei-
bung *(f)*
Es depreciación acelerada *(f)*
Fr amortissement accéléré
(m)
It deprezzamento accelerato
(m)
Pt depreciação acelerada *(f)*

accept *vb* En
De annehmen
Es aceptar
Fr accepter
It accettare
Pt aceitar

aceptación comercial *(f)* Es
De Handelsakzept *(n)*
En trade acceptance
Fr acceptation de commerce
(f)
It accettazione commerciale
(f)
Pt aceitação comercial *(f)*

acceptance *n* En
De Akzept *(n)*
Es aceptación *(f)*
Fr acceptation *(f)*
It accettazione *(f)*
Pt aceitação *(f)*

acceptance credit En
De Akzeptkredit *(m)*
Es crédito de aceptación *(m)*
Fr crédit par acceptation *(m)*
It credito d'accettazione *(m)*
Pt crédito de aceitação *(m)*

acceptance for honour En
De Intervention (bei Wechsel-
akzept) *(f)*
Es aceptación por interven-
ción *(f)*
Fr acceptation par interven-
tion *(f)*
It accettazione per interven-
to *(f)*
Pt aceitação por intervenção *(f)*

acceptance interval En
De Akzeptfrist *(f)*
Es intervalo de aceptación
(m)
Fr intervalle d'acceptation *(f)*
It intervallo dell'accettazione
(m)
Pt intervalo de aceitação *(m)*

accept an offer En
De ein Angebot annehmen
Es aceptar una oferta
Fr accepter une offre
It accettare una offerta
Pt aceitar uma oferta

acceptation *(f) n* Fr
De Akzept *(n)*
En acceptance
Es aceptación *(f)*
It accettazione *(f)*
Pt acetação *(f)*

acceptation conditionnelle
(f) Fr
De Annahme unter Vorbehalt
(f)
En qualifed acceptance
Es aceptación condicionada
(f)
It accettazione con riserva *(f)*
Pt aceitação com reservas *(f)*

acceptation de commerce
(f) Fr
De Handelsakzept *(n)*
En trade acceptance
Es acceptación comercial *(f)*
It accettazione commerciale
(f)
Pt aceitação comercial *(f)*

**acceptation par interven-
tion** *(f)* Fr
De Intervention (bei Wechsel-
akzept) *(f)*
En acceptance for honour
Es aceptación por interven-
ción *(f)*
It accettazione per interven-
to *(f)*
Pt aceitação por intervenção *(f)*

accepter *vb* Fr
De annehmen
En accept
Es aceptar
It accettare
Pt aceitar

accepter une offre Fr
De   ein Angebot annehmen
En   accept an offer
Es   aceptar una oferta
It   accettare una offerta
Pt   aceitar uma oferta

accettare vb It
De   annehmen
En   accept
Es   aceptar
Fr   accepter
Pt   aceitar

accettare una offerta It
De   ein Angebot annehmen
En   accept an offer
Es   aceptar una oferta
Fr   accepter une offre
Pt   aceitar uma oferta

accettazione (f) n It
De   Akzept (n)
En   acceptance
Es   aceptación (f)
Fr   acceptation (f)
Pt   aceitação (f)

accettazione commerciale
(f) It
De   Handelsakzept (n)
En   trade acceptance
Es   aceptación comercial (f)
Fr   acceptation de commerce
(f)
Pt   aceitação comercial (f)

accettazione con riserva (f) It
De   Annahme unter Vorbehalt
(f)
En   qualified acceptance
Es   aceptación condicionada
(f)
Fr   acceptation conditionnelle
(f)
Pt   aceitação com reservas (f)

accettazione per intervento
(f) It
De   Intervention (bei Wechsel-
akzept) (f)
En   acceptance for honour
Es   aceptación por interven-
ción (f)
Fr   acceptation par interven-
tion (f)
Pt   aceitação por intervenção (f)

accident du travail (m) Fr
De   Arbeitsunfall (m)
En   industrial accident
Es   accidente de trabajo (m)
It   infortunio sul lavoro (m)
Pt   acidente de trabalho (m)

accidente de trabajo (m) Es
De   Arbeitsunfall (m)
En   industrial accident
Fr   accident du travail (m)
It   infortunio sul lavoro (m)
Pt   acidente de trabalho (m)

acción (f) n Es
De   Aktie (f)
En   share
Fr   action (f)
It   azione (f)
Pt   acção (f)

acciones aplazadas (f pl) Es
De   Nachzugsaktien (f pl)
En   deferred shares
Fr   actions différées (f pl)
It   azioni postergate (f pl)
Pt   acções diferidas (f pl)

acciones auríferas (f pl) Es
De   Aktien von Goldbergwer-
ken (f pl)
En   gold shares
Fr   valeurs aunfères (f pl)
It   azioni aurifere (f pl)
Pt   acções de ouro (f pl)

**acciones con derecho de
voto** (f pl) Es
De   stimmberechtigte Aktien
(f pl)
En   voting shares
Fr   actions avec droit de vote
(f pl)
It   azioni con diritto di voto
(f pl)
Pt   acções com direito a voto
(f pl)

**acciones dadas como pri-
mas** (f pl) Es
De   Gratisaktien (f pl)
En   bonus shares
Am   stock dividend
Fr   actions d'attribution (f pl)
It   azioni di godimento (f pl)
Pt   acções de prémio (f pl)

acciones del fundador (f pl)
Es
De   Gründeraktien (f pl)
En   founder's shares
Fr   actions de fondateur (f pl)
It   azioni del fondatore (f pl)
Pt   acções de fundador (f pl)

**acciónes preferentes amor-
tizables** (f pl) Es
De   ablösbare Vorzugsaktien
(f pl)
En   redeemable preference
shares
Fr   actions privilégiées amortissables (f pl)
It   azioni preferenziali redimibili (f pl)
Pt   acções redimíveis preferenciais (f pl)

**acciones sin derecho de
voto** (f pl) Es
De   Aktien ohne Stimmrecht
(f pl)
En   non-voting shares
Fr   actions sans droit de vote
(f pl)
It   azioni senza diritto a voto
(f pl)
Pt   acções sem direito a voto
(f pl)

accionista (m) n Es, Pt
De   Aktionär (m)
En   shareholder, stockholder
Fr   actionnaire (m)
It   azionista (m)

acción ordinaria (f) Es
De   Stammaktie (f)
En   ordinary share
Fr   action ordinaire (f)
It   azione ordinaria (f)
Pt   acção ordinária (f)

acción preferente (f)
Es
De   Vorzugsaktie (f)
En   preference share
Fr   action privilégiée (f)
It   azione privilegiata (f)
Pt   acção preferencial (f)

acción por daños (f) Es
De   Schadenersatzklage (f)
En   action for damages
Fr   action en dommages et
intérêts (f)

It processo per risarcimento
(m)
Pt processamento pro danos
(m)

accluso *adj* It
De beiliegend
En enclosed
Es adjunto
Fr ci-joint; ci-inclus
Pt incluso

acções com direito a voto
(f pl) Pt
De stimmberechtigte Aktien
(f pl)
En voting shares
Es acciones con derecho de
voto *(f pl)*
Fr actions avec droit de vote
(f pl)
It azioni con diritto di voto
(f pl)

acções de fundador *(f pl)* Pt
De Gründeraktien *(f pl)*
En founder's shares
Es acciones del fundador
(f pl)
Fr actions de fondateur *(f pl)*
It azioni del fondatore *(f pl)*

acções de ouro *(f pl)* Pt
De Aktien von Goldbergwer-
ken *(f pl)*
En gold shares
Es acciones auríferas *(f pl)*
Fr valeurs aurifères *(f pl)*
It azioni aurifere *(f pl)*

acções de prémio *(f pl)* Pt
De Gratisaktien *(f pl)*
En bonus shares
Am stock dividend
Es acciones dadas como
primas *(f pl)*
Fr actions d'attribution *(f pl)*
It azioni di godimento *(f pl)*

acções diferidas *(f pl)* Pt
De Nachzugsaktien *(f pl)*
En deferred shares
Es acciones aplazadas *(f pl)*
Fr actions différées *(f pl)*
It azioni postergate *(f pl)*

**acções preferenciais cumu-
lativas** *(f pl)* Pt
De kumulative Vorzugsaktien
(f pl)

En cumulative preference
shares
Es valores privilegiados cu-
mulativos *(m pl)*
Fr actions de priorité cumulatives *(f pl)*
It azioni preferenziali cumulative *(f pl)*

**acções redimíveis prefe-
renciais** *(f pl)* Pt
De ablösbare Vorzugsaktien
(f pl)
En redeemable preference
shares
Es acciónes preferentes
amortizables *(f pl)*
Fr actions privilégiées amortissables *(f pl)*
It azioni preferenziali redimibili *(f pl)*

acções sem direito a voto
(f pl) Pt
De Aktien ohne Stimmrecht
(f pl)
En non-voting shares
Es acciones sin derecho de
voto *(f pl)*
Fr actions sans droit de vote
(f pl)
It azioni senza diritto a voto
(f pl)

accommodation bill En
De Gefälligkeitswechsel *(m)*
Es pagaré de favor *(m)*
Fr billet de complaisance *(m)*
It cambiale di favore *(f)*
Pt letra de favor *(f)*

accomplissement *(m)* n Fr
De Erfüllung *(f)*
En fulfilment
Es cumplimiento *(m)*
It adempimento *(m)*
Pt cumprimento *(m)*

acconto *(m)* n It
De Sofortzahlung *(f)*
En down-payment
Es pago de entrada *(m)*
Fr acompte *(m)*
Pt pagamento inicial *(m)*

acconto di dividendo *(m)* It
De vorläufige Dividende *(f)*
En interim dividend

Es dividendo provisional *(m)*
Fr dividende intérimaire *(m)*
Pt dividendo interino *(m)*

accord *(m)* n Fr
De Vereinbarung *(f)*
En settlement (agreement)
Es acuerdo *(m)*
It accordo *(m)*
Pt acordo *(m)*

**accord de commerce
bilatéral** *(m)* Fr
De bilateraler Handelsvertrag
(m)
En bilateral trade agreement
Es contrato comercial bilateral *(m)*
It accordo di commercio bilaterale *(m)*
Pt acordo comercial bilateral
(m)

**accord de commercialisa-
tion** *(m)* Fr
De Absatzübereinkommen *(n)*
En marketing agreement
Es acuerdo mercantil *(m)*
It accordo di mercato *(m)*
Pt acordo sobre comerciali-
zação *(m)*

accord en réserve *(m)* Fr
De Notvereinbarung *(f)*
En stand-by agreement
Es contrato de reserva *(m)*
It accordo di riserva *(m)*
Pt acordo a postos *(m)*

**Accord Général sur les
Tarifs Douaniers et le
Commerce** *(m)* Fr
De Allgemeines Zoll- und
Handelsabkommen *(n)*
En General Agreement on Ta-
riffs and Trade (GATT)
Es Acuerdo General sobre
Tarifas Aduaneras y Co-
mercio *(m)*
It Accordo Generale sulle
Tariffe Doganali e sul
Commercio *(m)*
Pt Acordo geral de Tarifas e
Comércio *(m)*

**Accord Monétaire Euro-
péen (AME)** *(m)* Fr
De Europäisches Währungs-
abkommen (EWA) *(n)*

En European Monetary
Agreement
Es Acuerdo Monetario Europeo (AME) *(m)*
It Accordo Monetario Europeo (AME) *(m)*
Pt Acordo Monetário Europeu (AME) *(m)*

accord mutuel *(m)* Fr
De gegenseitiges Einvernehmen *(n)*
En mutual agreement
Es acuerdo común *(m)*
It comune accordo *(m)*
Pt acordo mútuo *(m)*

accordo *(m)* n It
De Abkommen *(n)*
En agreement
Es contrato *(m)*
Fr convention *(f)*
Pt acordo *(m)*

accordo *(m)* n It
De Vereinbarung *(f)*
En settlement (agreement)
Es acuerdo *(m)*
Fr accord *(m)*
Pt acordo *(m)*

accord occulte *(m)* Fr
De Geheimvertrag *(m)*
En secret agreement
Es acuerdo secreto *(m)*
It accordo segreto *(m)*
Pt acordo secreto *(m)*

accordo di commercio bilaterale *(m)* It
De bilateraler Handelsvertrag *(m)*
En bilateral trade agreement
Es contrato comercial bilateral *(m)*
Fr accord de commerce bilatéral *(m)*
Pt acordo comercial bilateral *(m)*

accordo di mercato *(m)* It
De Absatzübereinkommen *(n)*
En marketing agreement
Es acuerdo mercantil *(m)*
Fr accord de commercialisation *(m)*
Pt acordo sobre comercialização *(m)*

accordo di reserva *(m)* It
De Notvereinbarung *(f)*
En stand-by agreement
Es contrato de reserva *(m)*
Fr accord en réserve *(m)*
Pt acordo a postos *(m)*

accordo di servizio *(m)* It
De Dienstvertrag *(m)*
En service agreement
Es contrato de servicio *(m)*
Fr contrat de service *(m)*
Pt contrato de serviço *(m)*

Accordo Generale sulle Tariffe Doganali e sul Commercio *(m)* It
De Allgemeines Zoll- und Handelsabkommen *(n)*
En General Agreement on Tariffs and Trade (GATT)
Es Acuerdo General sobre Tarifas Aduaneras y Comercio *(m)*
Fr Accord Général sur les Tarifs Douaniers et le Commerce *(m)*
Pt Acordo geral de Tarifas e Comércio *(m)*

Accordo Monetario Europeo (AME) *(m)* It
De Europäisches Währungsabkommen (EWA) *(n)*
En European Monetary Agreement
Es Acuerdo Monetario Europeo (AME) *(m)*
Fr Accord Monétaire Européen (AME) *(m)*
Pt Acordo Monetário Europeu (AME) *(m)*

accordo restrittivo *(m)* It
De einschränkende Bestimmung *(f)*
En restrictive covenant
Es convenio restrictivo *(m)*
Fr accord restrictif *(m)*
Pt obrigação restritiva *(f)*

accordo segreto *(m)* It
De Geheimvertrag *(m)*
En secret agreement
Es acuerdo secreto *(m)*
Fr accord occulte *(m)*
Pt acordo secreto *(m)*

accordo sui salari *(m)* It
De Lohnvereinbarung *(f)*
En wages agreement
Es acuerdo sobre salarios *(m)*
Fr convention des salaires *(f)*
Pt acordo sobre salários *(m)*

accordo sulla parola *(m)* It
De Kavaliersabkommen *(n)*
En gentleman's agreement
Es acuerdo sobre palabra *(m)*
Fr convention verbale *(f)*
Pt pacto de honra *(m)*

accordo tacito *(m)* It
De stillschweigendes Übereinkommen *(n)*
En tacit agreement
Es acuerdo tácito *(m)*
Fr convention tacite *(f)*
Pt acordo tácito *(m)*

accordo tariffario *(m)* It
De Zollabkommen *(n)*
En tariff agreement
Es acuerdo tarifario *(m)*
Fr accord tarifaire *(m)*
Pt acordo de tarifas *(m)*

accord restrictif *(m)* Fr
De einschränkende Bestimmung *(f)*
En restrictive covenant
Es convenio restrictivo *(m)*
It accordo restrittivo *(m)*
Pt obrigação restritiva *(f)*

accord tarifaire *(m)* Fr
De Zollabkommen *(n)*
En tariff agreement
Es acuerdo tarifario *(m)*
It accordo tariffario *(m)*
Pt acordo de tarifas *(m)*

account n En
De Konto *(n)*
Es cuenta *(f)*
Fr compte *(m)*
It conto *(m)*
Pt conta *(f)*

accountability *(n)* En
De Verantwortlichkeit *(f)*
Es responsabilidad *(f)*
Fr responsabilité *(f)*
It responsabilità *(f)*
Pt responsabilidade *(f)*

accountancy n En
De Buchhaltung (f)
Es contabilidad (f)
Fr comptabilité (f)
It contabilità (f)
Pt contabilidade (f)

accountant n En
De Buchhalter (m)
Es contador (m)
Fr comptable (m)
It contabile (m)
Pt contabilista (m)

account book En
De Kontobuch (n)
Es libro de cuentas (m)
Fr livre de comptes (m)
It libro di conti (m)
Pt livro de contas (m)

account day En
Am settlement date
De Abrechnungstag (m)
Es día de liquidación (m)
Fr jour de liquidation (m)
It giorno di liquidazione (m)
Pt dia de liquidação (m)

account executive En
De Kontaktgruppenleiter (m)
Es ejecutivo de cuenta (m)
Fr chef de comptes client (m)
It direttore conto cliente (m)
Pt chefe de conta de cliente (m)

accounting department Am
En accounts department
De Buchhaltung (f)
Es departamento de contabilidad (m)
Fr service de la comptabilité (m)
It ufficio contabilità (m)
Pt departamento de contabilidade (m)

accounting period En
De Abrechnungszeitraum (m)
Es ejercicio (m)
Fr exercice (f)
It esercizio (m)
Pt exercício (m)

account overdrawn En
De Konto überzogen (m)
Es cuenta en descubierto (f)

Fr compte découvert (m)
It conto scoperto (m)
Pt conta a descoberto (f)

account rendered En
De zur Begleichung vorgelegte Rechnung (f)
Es cuenta rendida (f)
Fr compte rendu (m)
It conto reso (m)
Pt conta remetida (f)

accounts department En
Am accounting department
De Buchhaltung (f)
Es departamento de contabilidad (m)
Fr service de la comptabilité (m)
It ufficio contabilità (m)
Pt departamento de contabilidade (m)

accounts payable En
De Kreditoren (m pl)
Es cuentas a pagar (f pl)
Fr comptes à payer (m pl)
It conti passivi (m pl)
Pt contas a pagar (f pl)

accounts receivable En
De Debitoren (m pl)
Es cuentas a recibir (f pl)
Fr créances (f pl)
It conti attivi (m pl)
Pt contas a receber (f pl)

accredited agent En
De Handelsbevollmächtigte(r) (m)
Es agente acreditudo (m)
Fr agent accrédité (m)
It agente accreditato (m)
Pt agente acreditado (m)

accréditif automatique-ment renouvelable (m) Fr
De automatisch sich erneuerndes Akkreditiv (n)
En revolving credit
Es crédito reponible (m)
It credito rotativo (m)
Pt crédito renovável (m)

accroissement (m) n Fr
De Erhöhung; Wertzuwachs (f m)
En increase; increment

Es aumento; incremento (m)
It aumento; incremento (m)
Pt aumento; incremento (m)

accroissement des coûts (m) Fr
De erhöhte Kosten (pl)
En increased costs
Es costes incrementados (m pl)
It costi aumentati (m pl)
Pt custos aumentados (m pl)

accrual (to an account) n En
De Zugang (m)
Es incremento (m)
Fr augmentation (f)
It incremento (m)
Pt acréscimo (m)

accrual (of interest) n En
De Auflaufen (n)
Es acumulación (f)
Fr accumulation (f)
It maturazione (f)
Pt acumulação (f)

accrue vb En
De auflaufen
Es acumular
Fr accumuler
It accumularsi
Pt acumular

accrued interest En
De aufgelaufene Zinsen (m pl)
Es interés acumulado (m)
Fr intérêts accumulés (m pl)
It interesse maturato (m)
Pt juro acumulado (m)

accumularsi vb It
De auflaufen
En accrue
Es acumular
Fr accumuler
Pt acumular

accumulation (f) n Fr
De Auflaufen (n)
En accrual
Es acumulación (f)
It maturazione (f)
Pt acumulação (f)

accumuler vb Fr
De auflaufen
En accrue

Es acumular
It accumularsi
Pt acumular

accusare ricevuta di It
De Empfang bestätigen
En acknowledge receipt of
Es acusar recibo de
Fr accuser réception de
Pt acusar a recepção de

accusé de réception *(m)* Fr
De Empfangsbestätigung *(f)*
En acknowledgment of receipt
Es aviso de recepción *(m)*
It avviso di recezione *(m)*
Pt aviso de recepção *(m)*

accuser réception de Fr
De Empfang bestätigen
En acknowledge receipt of
Es acusar recibo de
It accusare ricevuta di
Pt acusar a recepção de

aceitação *(f) n* Pt
De Akzept *(n)*
En acceptance
Es aceptación *(f)*
Fr acceptation *(f)*
It accettazione *(f)*

aceitação comercial *(f)* Pt
De Handelsakzept *(n)*
En trade acceptance
Es aceptación comercial *(f)*
Fr acceptation de commerce *(f)*
It accettazione commerciale *(f)*

aceitação com reserva *(f)* Pt
De Annahme unter Vorbehalt *(f)*
En qualified acceptance
Es aceptación condicionada *(f)*
Fr acceptation conditionnelle *(f)*
It accettazione con riserva *(f)*

aceitação por intervenção *(f)* Pt
De Intervention (bei Wechselakzept) *(f)*
En acceptance for honour
Es aceptación por intervención *(f)*

Fr acceptation par intervention *(f)*
It accettazione per intervento *(f)*

aceitar *vb* Pt
De annehmen
En accept
Es aceptar
Fr accepter
It accettare

aceitar uma oferta Pt
De ein Angebot annehmen
En accept an offer
Es aceptar una oferta
Fr accepter une offre
It accettare una offerta

aceptación *(f) n* Es
De Akzept *(n)*
En acceptance
Fr acceptation *(f)*
It accettazione *(f)*
Pt aceitação *(f)*

aceptación condicionada *(f)* Es
De Annahme unter Vorbehalt *(f)*
En qualified acceptance
Fr acceptation conditionelle *(f)*
It accettazione con riserva *(f)*
Pt aceitação com reservas *(f)*

aceptación por intervención *(f)* Es
De Intervention (bei Wechselakzept) *(f)*
En acceptance for honour
Fr acceptation par intervention *(f)*
It accettazione per intervento *(f)*
Pt aceitação por intervenção *(f)*

aceptar *vb* Es
De annehmen
En accept
Fr accepter
It accettare
Pt aceitar

aceptar una oferta Es
De ein Angebot annehmen
En accept an offer

Fr accepter une offre
It accettare una offerta
Pt aceitar uma oferta

achat *(m) n* Fr
De Kauf; Einkauf *(m)*
En purchase
Es compra *(f)*
It compra *(f)*
Pt compra *(f)*

achats *(m pl)* Fr
De Einkäufe *(m pl)*
En purchases
Es adquisiciones *(f pl)*
It acquisti *(m pl)*
Pt aquisições *(f pl)*

achat sur l'entrainement du moment *(m)* Fr
De Impulskaufen *(n)*
En impulse buying
Es compra espontánea *(f)*
It compra sullo stimolo del momento *(f)*
Pt compra impulsiva *(f)*

acheter *vb* Fr
De kaufen
En buy
Es comprar
It comprare
Pt comprar

acheteur *(m) n* Fr
De Käufer *(m)*
En buyer
Es comprador *(m)*
It compratore *(m)*
Pt comprador *(m)*

acidente de trabalho *(m)* Pt
De Arbeitsunfall *(m)*
En industrial accident
Es accidente de trabajo *(m)*
Fr accident du travail *(m)*
It infortunio sul lavoro *(m)*

acknowledge receipt of En
De Empfang bestätigen
Es acusar recibo de
Fr accuser réception de
It accusare ricevuta di
Pt acusar a recepção de

acknowledgment of receipt En
De Empfangsbestätigung *(f)*
Es aviso de recepción *(m)*

Fr accusé de réception *(m)*
It avviso di recezione *(m)*
Pt aviso de recepção *(m)*

a cobrar Pt
De anrechenbar
En chargeable
Es imputable; a cobrar
Fr imputable; imposable
It imputabile; imponibile

acompte *(m)* n Fr
De Sofortzahlung *(f)*
En down-payment
Es pago de entrada *(m)*
It acconto *(m)*
Pt pagamento inicial *(m)*

acompte *(m)* n Fr
De Rate *(f)*
En instalment
Es plazo *(m)*
It rata *(f)*
Pt prestação *(f)*

à concurrence de Fr
De hinauslaufend auf
En amounting to
Es ascendiendo a
It ammontante a
Pt no montante de

a condición Es
De vorausgesetzt
En on condition
Fr sous réserve
It a condizione
Pt sob condição de

acondicionamiento de aire
(m) Es
De Klimatisierung *(f)*
En air-conditioning
Fr climatisation *(f)*
It condizionamento dell'aria
(m)
Pt condicionamento do ar *(m)*

a condizione It
De vorausgesetzt
En on condition
Es a condición
Fr sous réserve
Pt sob condição de

à consignação Pt
De in Kommission
En on consignment

Es en consignación
Fr en consignation
It in conto deposito

a conto De
En on account
Es a cuenta
Fr à valoir
It in acconto
Pt por conta

acordo *(m)* n Pt
De Abkommen; Vereinbarung
(n f)
En agreement; settlement
Es contrato; acuerdo *(m)*
Fr convention; accord *(f m)*
It accordo; concordato *(m)*

acordo a postos *(m)* Pt
De Notvereinbarung *(f)*
En stand-by agreement
Es contrato de reserva *(m)*
Fr accord en réserve *(m)*
It accordo di riserva *(m)*

acordo comercial bilateral
(m) Pt
De bilateraler Handelsvertrag
(m)
En bilateral trade agreement
Es contrato comercial bilateral *(m)*
Fr accord de commerce bi-
latéral *(m)*
It accordo di commercio bilaterale *(m)*

acordo de tarifas *(m)* Pt
De Zollabkommen *(n)*
En tariff agreement
Es acuerdo tarifario *(m)*
Fr accord tarifaire *(m)*
It accordo tariffario *(m)*

**Acordo geral de Tarifas e
Comércio** *(m)* Pt
De Allgemeines Zoll- und
Handelsabkommen *(n)*
En General Agreement on Ta-
riffs and Trade (GATT)
Es Acuerdo General sobre
Tarifas Aduaneras y Co-
mercio *(m)*
Fr Accord Général sur les Ta-
rifs Douaniers et le Com-
merce *(m)*

It Accordo Generale sulle
Tariffe Doganali e sul
Commercio *(m)*

acordo irrevogável *(m)* Pt
De bindender Vertrag *(m)*
En binding agreement
Es obligación irrevocable *(f)*
Fr convention irrévocable *(f)*
It contratto vincolante *(m)*

**Acordo Monetário Europeu
(AME)** *(m)* Pt
De Europäisches Währungs-
abkommen (EWA) *(n)*
En European Monetary
Agreement
Es Acuerdo Monetario Euro-
peo (AME) *(m)*
Fr Accord Monétaire Eu-
ropéen (AME) *(m)*
It Accordo Monetario Euro-
peo (AME) *(m)*

acordo mútuo *(m)* Pt
De gegenseitiges Einverneh-
men *(n)*
En mutual agreement
Es acuerdo común *(m)*
Fr accord mutuel *(m)*
It comune accordo *(m)*

acordo secreto *(m)* Pt
De Geheimvertrag *(m)*
En secret agreement
Es acuerdo secreto *(m)*
Fr accord occulte *(m)*
It accordo segreto *(m)*

acordo sobre salários *(m)* Pt
De Lohnvereinbarung *(f)*
En wages agreement
Es acuerdo sobre salarios *(m)*
Fr convention des salaires *(f)*
It accordo sui salari *(m)*

acordo tácito *(m)* Pt
De stillschweigendes Über-
einkommen *(n)*
En tacit agreement
Es acuerdo tácito *(m)*
Fr convention tacite *(f)*
It accordo tacito *(m)*

a corto plazo Es
De kurzfristig
En short-term; short dated
Fr à court terme; à courte
échéance

It a breve termine; a breve
    scadenza
Pt a curto prazo

à courte échéance Fr
De kurzfristig
En short-dated
Es a corto plazo
It a breve scadenza
Pt a curto prazo

à court terme Fr
De kurzfristig
En short-term
Es a corto plazo
It a breve termine
Pt a curto prazo

acque territoriali (f pl) It
De Hoheitsgewässer (n pl)
En territorial waters
Es aguas territoriales (f pl)
Fr eaux territoriales (f pl)
Pt águas territoriais (f pl)

acquisition n En, Fr (f)
De Erwerb (m)
Es adquisición (f)
It acquisizione (f)
Pt aquisição (f)

acquisizione (f) n It
De Erwerb (m)
En acquisition
Es adquisición (f)
Fr acquisition (f)
Pt aquisição (f)

acquisti (m pl) It
De Einkäufe (m pl)
En purchases
Es adquisiciones (f pl)
Fr achats (m pl)
Pt aquisições (f pl)

acquitté adj Fr
De verzollt
En duty-paid
Es derechos pagados
It dazio pagato
Pt direitos pagos

acquitter une dette Fr
De eine Schuld begleichen
En discharge a debt
Es descargar una deuda
It estinguere un debito
Pt cancelar uma divida

acreedor (m) n Es
De Gläubiger (m)
En creditor
Fr créancier; créditeur (m)
It creditore (m)
Pt credor (m)

acreedores varios (m pl) Es
De Kreditoren (m pl)
En sundry creditors
Fr créditeurs divers (m pl)
It creditori diversi (m pl)
Pt créditos diversos (m pl)

acreedor no garantizado (m)
    Es
De nicht gesicherter Gläubi-
    ger (m)
En unsecured creditor
Fr créancier chirographaire
    (m)
It creditore non garantito (m)
Pt credor sem garantia (m)

acreedor privilegiado (m) Es
De bevorrechtigter Gläubiger
    (m)
En preferential creditor
Fr créancier privilégié (m)
It creditore privilegiato (m)
Pt credor preferencial (m)

acréscimo (m) n Pt
De Zugang (m)
En accrual
Es incremento (m)
Fr augmentation (f)
It incremento (m)

acta de disposición (f) Es
De Vergleichsabkommen (n)
En deed of arrangement
Fr contrat d'arrangement (m)
It atto di accordo (m)
Pt escritura de acordo (f)

actas (f pl) n Es
De Protokoll (n)
En minutes (of a meeting)
Fr procès-verbal (m)
It verbale (m)
Pt minutas de acta (f pl)

acte (m) n Fr
De Urkunde (f)
En deed; document
Es título; escritura (m f)
It atto (m)
Pt título; escritura (m f)

acte attributif (m) Fr
De Abtretungsvertrag (m)
En deed of assignment
Es título de asignación (m)
It atto di cessione (m)
Pt título de consignação (m)

acte de cession (m) Fr
De Übertragungsvertrag (m)
En transfer deed
Es escritura de transferencia
    (f)
It atto di trapasso (m)
Pt título de transferência (m)

acte défendu (m) Fr
De unerlaubte Handlung (f)
En tort
Es agravio (m)
It torto (m)
Pt agravo (m)

acte de vente (f) Fr
De Kaufvertrag (m)
En bill of sale
Es escritura de venta (f)
It contratto di vendita (m)
Pt escritura de venda (f)

actif (m) n Fr
De Aktivposten (m)
En asset
Es activo (m)
It attivo (m)
Pt valor (m)

actif adj Fr
De wirksam
En operative
Es operativo; activo
It attivo; operativo
Pt efectivo; em vigor

actif courant (m) Fr
De Umlaufvermögen (n)
En current assets
Es activo realizable (m)
It attivo liquido (m)
Pt bens no activo actual
    (m pl)

actif et passif (m) Fr
De Aktiva und Passiva (n pl)
En assets and liabilities
Es activo y passivo (m)
It attivo e passivo (m)
Pt activo e passivo (m)

actif immobilisé *(m)* Fr
De Vermögensanlage *(f)*
En capital asset
Am fixed asset
Es activo fijo *(m)*
It capitale fisso *(m)*
Pt bens de capital *(m pl)*

actif incorporel *(m)* Fr
De nicht greifbare Aktiven
(n pl)
En intangible assets
Es activo intangible *(m)*
It beni incorporali *(m pl)*
Pt bens intocáveis *(m pl)*

actif liquide *(m)* Fr
De flüssige Aktiven *(n pl)*
En liquid assets
Es activo líquido *(m)*
It disponibilità; attività liqui-
da *(f)*
Pt bens de activo líquidos
(m pl)

actif net *(m)* Fr
De Reinvermögen *(n)*
En net assets
Es activo neto *(m)*
It attivo netto *(m)*
Pt bens líquidos *(m pl)*

actifs défectibles *(m pl)* Fr
De kurzlebige Aktiva *(n pl)*
En wasting assets
Am depleting assets
Es activo gastable *(m)*
It attività in esaurimento *(f pl)*
Pt bens em uso ou deterio-
ração *(m pl)*

action *(f)* n Fr
De Aktie *(f)*
En share
Es acción *(f)*
It azione *(f)*
Pt acção *(f)*

action for damages En
De Schadenersatzklage *(f)*
Es acción por daños *(f)*
Fr action en dommages et
intérêts *(f)*
It processo per risarcimento
(m)
Pt processamento por danos
(m)

action juridique *(f)* Fr
De Prozeß; Klage *(m f)*
En legal action
Es pleito *(m)*
It processo *(m)*
Pt acção judicial *(f)*

actionnaire *(m)* n Fr
De Aktionär *(m)*
En shareholder
Am stockholder
Es accionista *(m)*
It azionista *(m)*
Pt titular de acções; accionista
(m)

action ordinaire *(f)* Fr
De Stammaktie *(f)*
En ordinary share
Es acción ordinaria *(f)*
It azione ordinaria *(f)*
Pt acção ordinária *(f)*

action privilégiée *(f)* Fr
De Vorzugsaktie *(f)*
En preference share
Es acción preferente *(f)*
It azione privilegiata *(f)*
Pt acção preferencial *(f)*

actions avec droit de vote
(f pl) Fr
De stimmberechtigte Aktien
(f pl)
En voting shares
Es acciones con derecho de
voto *(f pl)*
It azioni con diritto a voto
(f pl)
Pt acções com direito di voto
(f pl)

actions d'attribution *(f pl)* Fr
De Gratisaktien *(f pl)*
En bonus shares
Am stock dividend
Es acciones dadas como
primas *(f pl)*
It azioni di godimento *(f pl)*
Pt acções de prémio *(f pl)*

actions de fondateur *(f pl)* Fr
De Gründeraktien *(f pl)*
En founder's shares
Es acciones del fundador
(f pl)
It azioni del fondatore *(f pl)*
Pt acções de fundador *(f pl)*

**actions de priorité cumula-
tives** *(f pl)* Fr
De kumulative Vorzugsaktien
(f pl)
En cumulative preference
shares
Es valores privilegiados cu-
mulativos *(m pl)*
It azioni preferenziali cumulative *(f pl)*
Pt acções preferenciais cumulativas *(f pl)*

actions différées *(f pl)* Fr
De Nachzugsaktien *(f pl)*
En deferred shares
Es acciones aplazados *(f pl)*
It azioni postergate *(f pl)*
Pt acções diferidas *(f pl)*

**actions privilégiées amor-
tissables** *(f pl)* Fr
De ablösbare Vorzugsaktien
(f pl)
En redeemable preference
shares
Es acciónes preferentes
amortizables *(f pl)*
It azioni preferenziali redimibili *(f pl)*
Pt acções redimíveis preferenciais *(f pl)*

actions sans droit de vote
(f pl) Fr
De Aktien ohne Stimmrecht
(f pl)
En non-voting shares
Es acciones sin derecho de
voto *(f pl)*
It azioni senza diritto a voto
(f pl)
Pt acções sem direito a voto
(f pl)

active balance En
De Aktivsaldo *(m)*
Es saldo acreedor *(m)*
Fr balance excédentaire *(f)*
It saldo attivo *(m)*
Pt saldo credor *(m)*

active partner En
De aktiver Teilhaber *(m)*
Es socio activo *(m)*
Fr associé en nom *(m)*
It socio attivo *(m)*
Pt sócio activo *(m)*

activo *(m) n* Es
De Aktivposten *(m)*
En asset
Fr actif *(m)*
It attivo *(m)*
Pt valor *(m)*

activo e passivo *(m)* Pt
De Aktiva und Passiva *(n pl)*
En assets and liabilities
Es activo y pasivo *(m)*
Fr actif et passif *(m)*
It attivo e passivo *(m)*

activo fijo *(m)* Es
De Vormögensanlage; Anla-
    gevermögen *(f; n)*
En capital asset; fixed assets
Fr actif immobilisé; immobili-
    sations *(m; f pl)*
It capitale fisso; immobiliz-
    zazioni *(m; f pl)*
Pt bens de capital; bens fixos
    (m pl)

activo gastable *(m)* Es
De kurzlebige Aktiva *(n pl)*
En wasting assets
Am depleting assets
Fr actifs défectibles *(m pl)*
It attività in esaurimento *(f pl)*
Pt bens em uso ou deterio-
    ração *(m pl)*

activo intangible *(m)* Es
De nicht greifbare Aktiven
    (n pl)
En intangible assets
Fr actif incorporel *(m)*
It beni incorporali *(m pl)*
Pt bens intocáveis *(m pl)*

activo líquido *(m)* Es
De flüssige Aktiven *(n pl)*
En liquid assets
Fr actif liquide *(m)*
It disponibilità; attività liqui-
    da *(f)*
Pt bens de activo líquidos
    (m pl)

activo neto *(m)* Es
De Reinvermögen *(n)*
En net assets
Fr actif net *(m)*
It attivo netto *(m)*
Pt bens líquidos *(m pl)*

activo realizable *(m)* Es
De Umlaufvermögen *(n)*
En current assets
Fr actif courant *(m)*
It attivo liquido *(m)*
Pt bens no activo actual
    (m pl)

activos congelados *(m pl)* Es
De eingefrorene Guthaben
    (n pl)
En frozen assets
Fr fonds bioqués *(m pl)*
It attivo congelato *(m)*
Pt bens do activo
    congelados *(m pl)*

activo tangible *(m)* Es
De greifbare Aktiven *(n pl)*
En tangible assets
Fr biens immobiliers *(m pl)*
It beni materiali *(m pl)*
Pt bens visíveis *(m pl)*

activo y pasivo *(m)* Es
De Aktiva und Passiva *(n pl)*
En assets and liabilities
Fr actif et passif *(m)*
It attivo e passivo *(m)*
Pt activo e passivo *(m)*

actuaire *(m) n* Fr
De Aktuar *(m)*
En actuary
Es actuario *(m)*
It attuario *(m)*
Pt actuário *(m)*

actual cost En
De Gestehungskosten *(m pl)*
Es precio verdadero *(m)*
Fr prix de revient effectif *(m)*
It costo effetivo *(m)*
Pt custo verdadeiro *(m)*

actual total loss En
De wirklicher Totalverlust *(m)*
Es pérdida total efectiva *(f)*
Fr perte totale effective *(f)*
It perdita totale assoluta *(f)*
Pt perda total efectiva *(f)*

actuarial *adj* En, Es, Pt
De versicherungsmathema-
    tisch
Fr actuariel
It attuariale

actuariel *adj* Fr
De versicherungsmathema-
    tisch
En actuarial
Es actuarial
It attuariale
Pt actuarial

actuario *(m) n* Es
De Aktuar *(m)*
En actuary
Fr actuaire *(m)*
It attuario *(m)*
Pt actuário *(m)*

actuário *(m) n* Pt
De Aktuar *(m)*
En actuary
Es actuario *(m)*
Fr actuaire *(m)*
It attuario *(m)*

actuary *n* En
De Aktuar *(m)*
Es actuario *(m)*
Fr actuaire *(m)*
It attuario *(m)*
Pt actuário *(m)*

a cuenta Es
De a conto; auf Abschlag
En on account
Fr à valoir
It in acconto
Pt por conta

acuerdo *(m) n* Es
De Vereinbarung *(f)*
En settlement (agreement)
Fr accord *(m)*
It accordo *(m)*
Pt acordo *(m)*

acuerdo común *(m)* Es
De gegenseitiges Einverneh-
    men *(n)*
En mutual agreement
Fr accord mutuel *(m)*
It comune accordo *(m)*
Pt acordo mútuo *(m)*

**Acuerdo General sobre
Tarifas Aduaneras y
Comercio** *(m)* Es
De Allgemeines Zoll- und
    Handelsabkommen *(n)*
En General Agreement on
    Tariffs and Trade (GATT)

Fr Accord Général sur les
Tarifs Douaniers et le
Commerce (m)
It Accordo Generale sulle
Tariffe Doganali e sul
Commercio (m)
Pt Acordo geral de Tarifas e
Comércio (m)

acuerdo mercantil (m) Es
De Absatzübereinkommen (n)
En marketing agreement
Fr accord de commercialisa-
tion (m)
It accordo di mercato (m)
Pt acordo sobre comerciali-
zação (m)

**Acuerdo Monetario Euro-
peo (AME)** (m) Es
De Europäisches Währungs-
abkommen (EWA) (n)
En European Monetary
Agreement
Fr Accord Monétaire
Européen (AME) (m)
It Accordo Monetario Euro-
peo (AME) (m)
Pt Acordo Monetário Euro-
peu (AME) (m)

acuerdo secreto (m) Es
De Geheimvertrag (m)
En secret agreement
Fr accord occulte (m)
It accordo segreto (m)
Pt acordo secreto (m)

acuerdo sobre palabra (m)
Es
De Kavaliersabkommen (n)
En gentleman's agreement
Fr convention verbale (f)
It accordo sulla parola (m)
Pt pacto de honra (m)

acuerdo sobre salarios (m)
Es
De Lohnvereinbarung (f)
En wages agreement
Fr convention des salaires (f)
It accordo sui salari (m)
Pt acordo sobre salários (m)

acuerdo tácito (m) Es
De stillschweigendes Über-
einkommen (n)
En tacit agreement

Fr convention tacite (f)
It accordo tacito (m)
Pt acordo tácito (m)

acuerdo tarifario (m) Es
De Zollabkommen (n)
En tariff agreement
Fr accord tarifaire (m)
It accordo tariffario (m)
Pt acordo de tarifas (m)

acumulação (f) n Pt
De Auflaufen; Hortung (n f)
En accrual; hoard
Es acumulación; atesora-
miento (f m)
Fr accumulation; thésaurisa-
tion (f)
It maturazione; ammasso
(f m)

acumulación (f) n Es
De Auflaufen (n)
En accrual
Fr accumulation (f)
It maturazione (f)
Pt acumulação (f)

acumular vb Es, Pt
De auflaufen
En accrue
Fr accumuler
It accumularsi

acumular existencias Es
De Vorratslager anlegen
En stockpile
Fr stocker
It ammassare
Pt acumular existências

acumular existências Pt
De Vorratslager anlegen
En stockpile
Es acumular existencias
Fr stocker
It ammassare

acumulativo adj Es
De kumulativ
En cumulative
Fr cumulatif
It cumulativo
Pt cumulativo

a curto prazo Pt
De kurzfristig
En short-term; short-dated
Es a corto plazo

Fr à court terme; à courte
échéance
It a breve termine; a breve
scadenza

acusar a recepção de Pt
De Empfang bestätigen
En acknowledge receipt of
Es acusar recibo de
Fr accuser réception de
It accusare ricevuta di

acusar recibo de Es
De Empfang bestätigen
En acknowledge receipt of
Fr accuser réception de
It accusare ricevuta di
Pt acusar a recepção de

add vb En
De hinzufügen
Es añadir
Fr ajouter
It aggiungere
Pt adicionar

added value En
De Mehrwert (f)
Es valor agregado (m)
Fr valeur ajoutée (f)
It valore aggiunto (m)
Pt valor adicionado (m)

addieren vb De
En add up
Es sumar
Fr totaliser; additioner
It sommare
Pt somar

Addiermaschine (f) n De
En adding machine
Es máquina de sumar (f)
Fr machine à additionner (f)
It addizionatrice (f)
Pt máquina de somar (f)

adding machine En
De Addiermaschine (f)
Es máquina de sumar (f)
Fr machine à additionner (f)
It addizionatrice (f)
Pt máquina de somar (f)

addition n En, Fr (f)
De Aufschlag (m)
Es adición (f)
It addizione (f)
Pt adição (f)

addizionatrice *(f)* n It
De Addiermaschine *(f)*
En adding machine
Es máquina de sumar *(f)*
Fr machine à additionner *(f)*
Pt máquina de somar *(f)*

addizione *(f)* n It
De Aufschlag *(m)*
En addition
Es adición *(f)*
Fr addition *(f)*
Pt adição *(f)*

address n En
De Adresse *(f)*
Es dirección *(f)*
Fr adresse *(f)*
It indirizzo *(m)*
Pt endereço *(m)*

addressee n En
De Adressat *(m)*
Es destinatario *(m)*
Fr destinataire *(m)*
It destinatario *(m)*
Pt destinatário *(m)*

addressing machine En
De Adressiermaschine *(f)*
Es máquina de imprimir direcciones *(f)*
Fr machine à imprimer les adresses *(f)*
It macchina per stampare indirizzi *(f)*
Pt máquina de endereços *(f)*

add up En
De addieren
Es sumar
Fr totaliser; additioner
It sommare
Pt somar

adelanto *(m)* n Es
De Vorschuß *(m)*
En advance
Fr avance *(f)*
It anticipazione *(f)*
Pt adiantamento *(m)*

adempiere vb It
De erfüllen
En fulfil
Es cumplir
Fr remplir
Pt cumprir

adempimento *(m)* n It
De Erfüllung *(f)*
En fulfilment
Es cumplimiento *(m)*
Fr accomplissement *(m)*
Pt cumprimento *(m)*

adiamento *(m)* n Pt
De Vertagung *(f)*
En adjournment
Es aplazamiento *(m)*
Fr ajournement *(m)*
It aggiornamento *(m)*

adiantamento *(m)* n Pt
De Vorschuß *(m)*
En advance
Es adelanto *(m)*
Fr avance *(f)*
It anticipazione *(f)*

adiantar vb Pt
De vorschießen
En advance
Am prepay
Es anticipar
Fr avancer
It anticipare

adiante adj Pt
De Termin-
En forward
Es a término
Fr en avant; à terme
It a termine

adiar vb Pt
De vertagen; zurückstellen
En adjourn; defer
Es aplazar
Fr ajourner; différer
It aggiornare; differire

adição *(f)* n Pt
De Aufschlag *(m)*
En addition
Es adición *(f)*
Fr addition *(f)*
It addizione *(f)*

adición *(f)* n Es
De Aufschlag *(m)*
En addition
Fr addition *(f)*
It addizione *(f)*
Pt adição *(f)*

adicionar vb Pt
De hinzufügen
En add
Es añadir
Fr ajouter
It aggiungere

adjourn vb En
De vertagen
Es aplazar
Fr ajourner
It aggiornare
Pt adiar

adjournment n En
De Vertagung *(f)*
Es aplazamiento *(m)*
Fr ajournement *(m)*
It aggiornamento *(m)*
Pt adiamento *(m)*

adjudicación *(f)* n Es
De Verteilung *(f)*
En allotment
Fr attribution *(f)*
It ripartizione *(f)*
Pt aporcionamento *(m)*

adjudicar vb Es, Pt
De gerichtlich entscheiden
En adjudicate
Fr juger
It aggiudicare

adjudicate vb En
De gerichtlich entscheiden
Es adjudicar
Fr juger
It aggiudicare
Pt adjudicar

adjuger des dommages-intérêts Fr
De Schadenersatz zugestehen
En award damages
Es conceder daños
It concedere i danni
Pt conceder compensação

adjunto adj Es
De beiliegend
En enclosed
Fr ci-joint; ci-inclus
It accluso
Pt incluso

adjustment *(insurance)* En
De Regulierung *(f)*
Es reglamento *(m)*
Fr règlement *(m)*
It regolamento *(m)*
Pt ajuste *(m)*

admettre une caution Fr
De gegen Haftkaution
   freigeben
En grant bail
Es conceder fianza
It concedere la libertà prov-
   visoria su cauzione
Pt autorizar caução

administer *vb* En
De verwalten
Es administrar
Fr administrer
It amministrare
Pt administrar

administração *(f) n* Pt
De Verwaltung *(f)*
En administration
Es ministerio *(m)*
Fr gouvernement *(m)*
It governo *(m)*

administración *(f) n* Es
De Verwaltung *(f)*
En administration
Fr gestion *(f)*
It gestione *(f)*
Pt gestão *(f)*

administrador *(m) n* Es, Pt
De Verwalter *(m)*
En administrator
Fr administrateur *(m)*
It amministratore *(m)*

administrar *vb* Es, Pt
De verwalten
En administer
Fr administrer
It amministrare

administrateur *(m) n* Fr
De Direktor; Verwalter *(m)*
En director; administrator
Es director; administrador *(m)*
It amministratore *(m)*
Pt director; administrador *(m)*

**administrateur chef
   d'écoulement** *(m)* Fr
De Absatzdirektor *(m)*

En marketing director
Es director mercantil *(m)*
It direttore di mercato *(m)*
Pt director de comercialização
   (m)

administrateur délégué *(m)*
   Fr
De geschäftsleitender Direk-
   tor *(m)*
En managing director
Am president
Es director gerente *(m)*
It amministratore delegato
   (m)
Pt director geral *(m)*

administrateur dirigeant *(m)*
   Fr
De geschäftsführender Direk-
   tor *(m)*
En executive director
Am corporate officer
Es director ejecutivo *(m)*
It amministratore dirigente
   (m)
Pt director administrativo *(m)*

administration *(business) n*
   En
De Verwaltung *(f)*
Es administración *(f)*
Fr gestion *(f)*
It gestione *(f)*
Pt gestão *(f)*

administration *(government)*
   n En
De Staatsverwaltung *(f)*
Es ministerio *(m)*
Fr gouvernement *(m)*
It governo *(m)*
Pt administração *(f)*

administration *(f) n* Fr
De Vorstand *(m)*
En management
Es dirección *(f)*
It direzione; amministrazio-
   ne *(f)*
Pt gerência; direcção *(f)*

administrative assistant Am
En personal assistant (PA)
De persönlicher Assistent *(m)*
Es asistente privado *(m)*
Fr fonctionnel *(m)*
It assistente privato *(m)*
Pt secretário *(m)*

administrator *(of an estate) n*
   En
De Nachlaßverwalter *(m)*
Es administrador *(m)*
Fr curateur *(m)*
It curatore *(m)*
Pt curador *(m)*

administrator *(business) n* En
De Verwalter *(m)*
Es administrador *(m)*
Fr administrateur *(m)*
It amministratore *(m)*
Pt administrador *(m)*

administrer *vb* Fr
De verwalten
En administer
Es administrar
It amministrare
Pt administrar

admisión libre de impuestos
   (f) Es
De zollfreie Einfuhr *(f)*
En duty-free admission
Fr admission en franchise *(f)*
It ammissione in franchigia
   doganale *(f)*
Pt admissão livre de impostos
   (f)

admissão *(f) n* Pt
De Eintritt *(m)*
En entry
Es entrada *(f)*
Fr entrée *(f)*
It entrata *(f)*

admissão livre de impostos *(f)*
   Pt
De zollfreie Einfuhr *(f)*
En duty-free admission
Es admisión libre de im-
   puestos *(f)*
Fr admission en franchise *(f)*
It ammissione in franchigia
   doganale *(f)*

admission en franchise *(f)* Fr
De zollfreie Einfuhr *(f)*
En duty-free admission
Es admisión libre de im-
   puestos *(f)*
It ammissione in franchigia
   doganale *(f)*
Pt admissão livre de impostos
   (f)

admission free En
De Eintritt frei *(m)*
Es entrada gratuita *(f)*
Fr entrée gratuite *(f)*
It ingresso gratuito *(m)*
Pt entrada grátis *(f)*

adquisición *(f)* n Es
De Erwerb *(m)*
En acquisition
Fr acquisition *(f)*
It acquisizione *(f)*
Pt aquisição *(f)*

adquisiciones *(f pl)* Es
De Einkäufe *(m pl)*
En purchases
Fr achats *(m pl)*
It acquisti *(m pl)*
Pt aquisições *(f pl)*

Adressat *(m)* n De
En addressee
Es destinatario *(m)*
Fr destinataire *(m)*
It destinatario *(m)*
Pt destinatário *(m)*

Adreßbuch *(n)* n De
En directory
Es guía *(f)*
Fr répertoire *(m)*
It guida *(f)*
Pt guia *(m)*

adresse *(f)* n Fr
De Adresse *(f)*
En address
Es dirección *(f)*
It indirizzo *(m)*
Pt endereço *(m)*

Adresse *(f)* n De
En address
Es dirección *(f)*
Fr adresse *(f)*
It indirizzo *(m)*
Pt endereço *(m)*

adresse télégraphique *(f)* Fr
De Telegrammadresse *(f)*
En telegraphic address
Es dirección telegráfica *(f)*
It indirizzo telegrafico *(m)*
Pt endereço telegráfico *(m)*

Adressiermaschine *(f)* n De
En addressing machine
Es máquina de imprimir direcciones *(f)*

Fr machine à imprimer les adresses *(f)*
It macchina per stampare indirizzi *(f)*
Pt máquina de endereços *(f)*

aduana *(f)* n Es
De Zoll *(m)*
En customs
Fr douane *(f)*
It dogana *(f)*
Pt alfândega *(f)*

advance *(money) vb* En
Am prepay
De vorschießen
Es anticipar
Fr avancer
It anticipare
Pt adiantar

advance *(of money)* n En
Am prepayment
De Vorschuß *(m)*
Es adelanto *(m)*
Fr avance *(f)*
It anticipazione *(f)*
Pt adiantamento *(m)*

advance account En
De Darlehenskonto *(n)*
Es cuenta de anticipos *(f)*
Fr compte d'avances *(m)*
It conto anticipo *(m)*
Pt conta de adiantamentos *(f)*

advance in price *vb* En
De teurer werden; steigen
Es encarecer
Fr renchérir
It aumentare di prezzo
Pt encarecer

advance in price n En
De Preiserhöhung *(f)*
Es encarecimiento *(m)*
Fr renchérissement *(m)*
It rialzo *(m)*
Pt encarecimento *(m)*

advance payment En
De Vorauszahlung *(f)*
Es anticipo *(m)*
Fr paiement par anticipation *(m)*
It pagamento anticipato *(m)*
Pt pagamento adiantado *(m)*

adverse balance En
Am negative balance
De Passivsaldo *(m)*
Es saldo adverso *(m)*
Fr balance déficitaire *(f)*
It saldo passivo *(m)*
Pt saldo negativo *(m)*

advertisement n En
De Anzeige *(f)*
Es anuncio *(m)*
Fr annonce *(f)*
It annunzio *(m)*
Pt anúncio *(m)*

advertiser n En
De Anzeiger *(m)*
Es anunciante *(m)*
Fr annonceur *(m)*
It inserzionista *(m)*
Pt anunciante *(m)*

advertising n En
De Reklame; Werbung *(f)*
Es publicidad *(f)*
Fr publicité *(f)*
It pubblicità *(f)*
Pt publicidade *(f)*

advertising agency En
De Werbebüro *(n)*
Es agencia de publicidad *(f)*
Fr agence de publicité *(f)*
It agenzia pubblicitaria *(f)*
Pt agência de publicidade *(f)*

advertising brochure En
De Werbeschrift *(f)*
Es folleto publicitario *(m)*
Fr prospectus publicitaire *(m)*
It opuscolo pubblicitario *(m)*
Pt folheto publicitário *(m)*

advertising campaign En
De Werbefeldzug *(m)*
Es campaña publicitaria *(f)*
Fr campagne de publicité *(f)*
It campagna pubblicitaria *(f)*
Pt campanha publicitária *(f)*

advertising consultant En
De Werbeberater *(m)*
Es consultor de publicidad *(m)*
Fr conseil en publicité *(m)*
It consulente di pubblicità *(m)*
Pt perito de publicidade *(m)*

advertising copy En
De Werbetext (m)
Es material publicitario (m)
Fr copie publicitaire (f)
It testo pubblicitario (m)
Pt texto de publicidade (m)

advertising expenditure En
De Werbekosten (pl)
Es gastos publicitarios (m pl)
Fr dépenses de publicité (f pl)
It spese di pubblicità (f pl)
Pt despesa com publicidade (f)

advertising medium En
De Werbemittel (n)
Es medio de publicidad (m)
Fr support publicitaire (m)
It mezzo pubblicitario (m)
Pt meio publicitário (m)

advertising rates En
De Werbetarif (m)
Es tarifa para anuncios (f)
Fr tarifs de publicité (m pl)
It tariffa delle inserzioni (f)
Pt taxas de publicidade (f pl)

advertising schedule En
De Werbeplan (m)
Es plan de propaganda (m)
Fr programme des annonces (m)
It programma delle inserzioni (m)
Pt plano de campanha publicitária (m)

advice note En
De Anzeige (f)
Es aviso (m)
Fr lettre d'avis (f)
It lettera d'avviso (f)
Pt guia de remessa (f)

advisory adj En
De Beratungs-
Es consultivo
Fr consultatif
It consultivo
Pt consultivo

advisory board En
De Beratungsausschuß (m)
Es consejo consultivo (m)
Fr comité consultatif (m)
It consiglio consultivo (m)
Pt comité consultivo (m)

advogado (m) n Pt
De Anwalt (m)
En barrister; counsel
Am attorney
Es abogado (m)
Fr avocat (m)
It avvocato (m)

aérogare (f) n Fr
De Luftterminal (n)
En air terminal
Es terminal de aeropuerto (f)
It aerostazione (f)
Pt estação terminal aérea (f)

aérogramme (m) Fr
De Luftpostbrief (m)
En air letter
Es carta por avión (f)
It lettera aerea (f)
Pt carta por avião (f)

aéroport (m) n Fr
De Flughafen (m)
En airport
Es aeropuerto (m)
It aeroporto (m)
Pt aeroporto (m)

aeroporto (m) n It, Pt
De Flughafen (m)
En airport
Es aeropuerto (m)
Fr aéroport (m)

aeropuerto (m) n Es
De Flughafen (m)
En airport
Fr aéroport (m)
It aeroporto (m)
Pt aeroporto (m)

aerostazione (f) n It
De Luftterminal (n)
En air terminal
Es terminal de aeropuerto (f)
Fr aérogare (f)
Pt estação terminal aérea (f)

affaire (f) n Fr
De Abschluß (m)
En deal
Es negocio (m)
It affare (f)
Pt negócio (m)

affaire équitable (f) Fr
De anständige Abmachung (f)
En fair deal

Es trato equitativo (m)
It affare giusto (m)
Pt transacção razoável (f)

affaire qui marche (f) Fr
De gewinnbringendes Unternehmen (n)
En going concern
Es negocio en marcha (m)
It azienda in piena attività (f)
Pt negócio que vinga (m)

affaires (f pl) n Fr
De Geschäft (n)
En business
Es negocios (m pl)
It affari (m pl)
Pt negócios (m pl)

affare (m) n It
De Handel; Abschluß (m)
En bargain; deal
Es negocio (m)
Fr marché; affaire (m f)
Pt negócio (m)

affare giusto (m) It
De anständige Abmachung (f)
En fair deal
Es trato equitativo (m)
Fr affaire équitable (f)
Pt transacção razoável (f)

affari (m pl) n It
De Geschäft (n)
En business
Es negocios (m pl)
Fr affaires (f pl)
Pt negócios (m pl)

affectation (f) n Fr
De Zuführung (f)
En appropriation
Es apropiación (f)
It stanziamento (m)
Pt apropriação (f)

affidare vb It
De anvertrauen
En entrust
Es confiar
Fr confier
Pt confiar

affidavit n En
De beeidigte Erklärung (f)
Es declaración jurada (f)
Fr déclaration sous serment (f)

It dichiarazione giurata *(f)*
Pt declaração sob juramento *(f)*

affiliated company En
De Schwestergesellschaft *(f)*
Es compañia afiliada *(f)*
Fr société sœr *(f)*
It società affiliata *(f)*
Pt companhia subsidiária *(f)*

affittare *vb* It
De vermieten
En rent
Es alquilar
Fr louer; affermer
Pt alugar

affitto *(m) n* It
De Verpachtung *(f)*
En lease
Es alquiler *(m)*
Fr bail *(m)*
Pt aluguer; arrendamento *(m)*

affitto di terreno *(m)* It
De Grundpacht *(f)*
En ground-rent
Es renta del terreno *(f)*
Fr rente foncière *(f)*
Pt renda sobre o terreno *(f)*

affittuario *(m) n* It
De Mieter *(m)*
En tenant
Es inquilino *(m)*
Fr locataire *(m)*
Pt inquilino *(m)*

affrancatrice postale *(f)* It
De Frankiermaschine *(f)*
En franking machine
Es máquina de franquear *(f)*
Fr machine à affranchir *(f)*
Pt máquina de franquear *(f)*

affrètement *(m) n* Fr
De Befrachtung *(f)*
En chartering
Es fletamento *(m)*
It noleggio *(m)*
Pt fretamento *(m)*

affrètement à temps *(m)* Fr
De Zeitcharter *(f)*
En time charter
Es fletamento de tiempo *(m)*
It contratto di noleggio a tempo *(m)*
Pt fretamento de tempo *(m)*

affréteur *(m) n* Fr
De Befrachter *(m)*
En charterer
Es fletador *(m)*
It noleggiatore *(m)*
Pt fretador *(m)*

afloat *adv* En
De flott
Es a flote
Fr à flot
It flottante
Pt flutuante

à flot Fr
De flott
En afloat
Es a flote
It flottante
Pt flutuante

a flote Es
De flott
En afloat
Fr à flot
It flottante
Pt flutuante

agence *(f) n* Fr
De Agentur *(f)*
En agency
Es agencia *(f)*
It agenzia *(f)*
Pt agência *(f)*

agence de placement *(f)* Fr
De Stellenvermittlungsbüro *(n)*
En employment agency
Es agencia de colocaciones *(f)*
It agenzia di collocamento *(f)*
Pt agência de empregos *(f)*

agence de presse *(f)* Fr
De Nachrichtenbüro *(n)*
En news agency
Es agencia de prensa *(f)*
It agenzia d'informazioni *(f)*
Pt agência de notícias *(f)*

agence de publicité *(f)* Fr
De Werbebüro *(n)*
En advertising agency
Es agencia de publicidad *(f)*
It agenzia pubblicitaria *(f)*
Pt agência de publicidade *(f)*

agence de voyages *(f)* Fr
De Reisebüro *(n)*
En travel agent
Es agencia de viajes *(f)*
It agenzia di viaggi *(f)*
Pt agente de viagens *(m)*

agence immobilière *(f)* Fr
De Immobilienbüro *(n)*
En estate agency
Am real estate agency
Es correduría de fincas *(f)*
It agenzia immobiliare *(f)*
Pt agência de propriedades *(f)*

agencia *(f) n* Es
De Agentur *(f)*
En agency
Fr agence *(f)*
It agenzia *(f)*
Pt agência *(f)*

agência *(f) n* Pt
De Agentur *(f)*
En agency
Es agencia *(f)*
Fr agence *(f)*
It agenzia *(f)*

agência corretora de descontos *(f)* Pt
De Diskontbank *(f)*
En discount house
Es casa de descuentos *(f)*
Fr maison d'escompte *(f)*
It banca di sconto *(f)*

agencia de colocaciones *(f)* Es
De Stellenvermittlungsbüro *(n)*
En employment agency
Fr agence de placement *(f)*
It agenzia di collocamento *(f)*
Pt agência de empregos *(f)*

agência de empregos *(f)* Pt
De Stellenvermittlungsbüro *(n)*
En employment agency
Es agencia de colocaciones *(f)*
Fr agence de placement *(f)*
It agenzia di collocamento *(f)*

agência de notícias *(f)* Pt
De Nachrichtenbüro *(n)*
En news agency

Es agencia de prensa *(f)*
Fr agence de presse *(f)*
It agenzia d'informazioni *(f)*

agencia de prensa *(f)* Es
De Nachrichtenbüro *(n)*
En news agency
Fr agence de presse *(f)*
It agenzia d'informazioni *(f)*
Pt agência de notícias *(f)*

agência de propriedades *(f)*
    Pt
De Immobilienbüro *(n)*
En estate agency
Am real estate agency
Es correduría de fincas *(f)*
Fr agence immobilière *(f)*
It agenzia immobiliare *(f)*

agencia de publicidad *(f)* Es
De Werbebüro *(n)*
En advertising agency
Fr agence de publicité *(f)*
It agenzia pubblicitaria *(f)*
Pt agência de publicidade *(f)*

agência de publicidade *(f)* Pt
De Werbebüro *(n)*
En advertising agency
Es agencia de publicidad *(f)*
Fr agence de publicité *(f)*
It agenzia pubblicitaria *(f)*

agencia de viajes *(f)* Es
De Reisebüro *(n)*
En travel agent
Fr agence de voyages *(f)*
It agenzia di viaggi *(f)*
Pt agente de viagens *(m)*

agency *(commercial)* n En
De Agentur *(f)*
Es agencia *(f)*
Fr agence *(f)*
It agenzia *(f)*
Pt agência *(f)*

agency *(legal)* n En
De Vertretung *(f)*
Es mandato *(m)*
Fr mandat *(m)*
It mandato *(m)*
Pt mandato *(m)*

agenda n En
De Tagesordnung *(f)*
Es orden del día *(m)*
Fr ordre du jour *(m)*

It ordine del giorno *(m)*
Pt agenda *(f)*

agenda *(f)* n Pt
De Tagesordnung *(f)*
En agenda
Es orden del día *(m)*
Fr ordre du jour *(m)*
It ordine del giorno *(m)*

agenda da reunião *(f)* Pt
De Tagesordnung *(f)*
En business before the
    meeting
Am agenda
Es orden del día *(f)*
Fr ordre du jour *(m)*
It scopo dell'assemblea *(m)*

agent n En, Fr *(m)*
De Agent *(m)*
Es agente *(m)*
It agente *(m)*
Pt agente *(m)*

Agent *(m)* n De
En agent
Es agente *(m)*
Fr agent *(m)*
It agente *(m)*
Pt agente *(m)*

agent accrédité *(m)* Fr
De Handelsbevollmächtigte(r)
    (m)
En accredited agent
Es agente acreditudo *(m)*
It agente accreditato *(m)*
Pt agente acreditado *(m)*

agent attitré *(m)* Fr
De Handelsvertreter *(m)*
En appointed agent
Es agente nombrado *(m)*
It agente ufficiale *(m)*
Pt agente oficial *(m)*

agent d'assurances *(m)* Fr
De Versicherungsvertreter *(m)*
En insurance agent
Es agente de seguros *(m)*
It agenzia di assicurazioni *(f)*
Pt agente de seguros *(m)*

agent de commerce *(m)* Fr
De Handelsvertreter *(m)*
En mercantile agent
Am sales agent
Es agente mercantil *(m)*

It agente di commercio *(m)*
Pt agente comercial *(m)*

agent de recouvrement *(m)*
    Fr
De Inkassobeauftragte(r) *(m)*
En debt collector
Es agente recaudador *(m)*
It agente di ricupero crediti
    (m)
Pt cobrador *(m)*

agent ducroire *(m)* Fr
De Delkrederevertreter *(m)*
En del credere agent
Es agente del crédere *(m)*
It agente con del credere *(m)*
Pt agente del credere *(m)*

agente *(m)* n Es, It, Pt
De Agent *(m)*
En agent (commercial)
Fr agent *(m)*

agente accreditato *(m)* It
De Handelsbevollmächtigte(r)
    (m)
En accredited agent
Es agente acreditudo *(m)*
Fr agent accrédité *(m)*
Pt agente acreditado *(m)*

agente acreditado *(m)* Pt
De Handelsbevollmächtigte(r)
    (m)
En accredited agent
Es agente acreditudo *(m)*
Fr agent accrédité *(m)*
It agente accreditato *(m)*

agente acreditudo *(m)* Es
De Handelsbevollmächtigte(r)
    (m)
En accredited agent
Fr agent accrédité *(m)*
It agente accreditato *(m)*
Pt agente acreditado *(m)*

agente comercial *(m)* Pt
De Handelsvertreter *(m)*
En mercantile agent
Am sales agent
Es agente mercantil *(m)*
Fr agent de commerce *(m)*
It agente di commercio *(m)*

agente con del credere *(m)* It
De Delkrederevertreter *(m)*
En del credere agent

Es agente del crédere *(m)*
Fr agent ducroire *(m)*
Pt agente del credere *(m)*

agente de cargas e despachos *(m)* Pt
De Spediteur *(m)*
En shipping and forwarding agent
Es agente de embarques *(m)*
Fr agent metteur à bord *(m)*
It agente marittimo e di spedizione *(m)*

agente de embarques *(m)* Es
De Spediteur *(m)*
En shipping and forwarding agent
Fr agent metteur à bord *(m)*
It agente marittimo e di spedizione *(m)*
Pt agente de cargas e despachos *(m)*

agente del crédere *(m)* Es
De Delkrederevertreter *(m)*
En del credere agent
Fr agent ducroire *(m)*
It agente con del credere *(m)*
Pt agente del credere *(m)*

agente del credere *(m)* Pt
De Delkrederevertreter *(m)*
En del credere agent
Es agente de crédere *(m)*
Fr agent ducroire *(m)*
It agente con del credere *(m)*

agente delle imposte *(m)* It
De Schätzer *(m)*
En assessor
Es asesor *(m)*
Fr appréciateur *(m)*
Pt avaliador *(m)*

agente de patentes *(m)* Es, Pt
De Patentanwalt *(m)*
En patent agent
Fr conseil en brevets *(m)*
It agente di brevetti *(m)*

agente de seguros *(m)* Es, Pt
De Versicherungsvertreter *(m)*
En insurance agent
Fr agent d'assurances *(m)*
It agenzia di assicurazioni *(f)*

agente de viagens *(m)* Pt
De Reisebüro *(n)*
En travel agent

Es agencia de viajes *(f)*
Fr agence de voyages *(f)*
It agenzia di viaggi *(f)*

agente di assicurazioni marittime *(m)* It
De Seetransportversicherungsmakler *(m)*
En marine insurance broker
Es corredor de seguro marítimo *(m)*
Fr courtier d'assurances maritimes *(m)*
Pt corretor de seguros marítimos *(m)*

agente di borsa *(m)* It
De Börsenmakler *(m)*
En stockbroker
Es corredor de bolsa *(m)*
Fr courtier en bourse *(m)*
Pt corretor da bolsa *(m)*

agente di brevetti *(m)* It
De Patentanwalt *(m)*
En patent agent
Es agente de patentes *(m)*
Fr conseil en brevets *(m)*
Pt agente de patentes *(m)*

agente di commercio *(m)* It
De Handelsvertreter *(m)*
En mercantile agent
Am sales agent
Es agente mercantil *(m)*
Fr agent de commerce *(m)*
Pt agente comercial *(m)*

agente di ricupero crediti *(m)* It
De Inkassobeauftragte(r) *(m)*
En debt collector
Es agente recaudador *(m)*
Fr agent de recouvrement *(m)*
Pt cobrador *(m)*

agente di sconto *(m)* It
De Wechselmakler *(m)*
En bill broker
Es corredor de cambios *(m)*
Fr courtier de bons *(m)*
Pt corretor de câmbios *(m)*

agente exclusivo *(m)* Es, Pt
De Alleinvertreter *(m)*
En sole agent
Fr agent exclusif *(m)*
It rappresentante esclusivo *(m)*

agente expedidor *(m)* Es, Pt
De Spediteur *(m)*
En forwarding agent
Fr transitaire *(m)*
It spedizioniere *(m)*

agente marittimo e di spedizione *(m)* It
De Spediteur *(m)*
En shipping and forwarding agent
Es agente de embarques *(m)*
Fr agent metteur à bord *(m)*
Pt agente de cargas e despachos *(m)*

agente mercantil *(m)* Es
De Handelsvertreter *(m)*
En mercantile agent
Am sales agent
Fr agent de commerce *(m)*
It agente di commercio *(m)*
Pt agente comercial *(m)*

agente nombrado *(m)* Es
De Handelsvertreter *(m)*
En appointed agent
Fr agent attitré *(m)*
It agente ufficiale *(m)*
Pt agente oficial *(m)*

agente oficial *(m)* Pt
De Handelsvertreter *(m)*
En appointed agent
Es agente nombrado *(m)*
Fr agent attitré *(m)*
It agente ufficiale *(m)*

agente recaudador *(m)* Es
De Inkassobeauftragte(r) *(m)*
En debt collector
Fr agent de recouvrement *(m)*
It agente di ricupero crediti *(m)*
Pt cobrador *(m)*

agente sob comissão *(m)* Pt
De Kommissionär *(m)*
En commission agent
Es comisionista *(m)*
Fr commissionnaire en marchandises *(m)*
It commissionario *(m)*

agente ufficiale *(m)* It
De Handelsvertreter *(m)*
En appointed agent
Es agente nombrado *(m)*
Fr agent attitré *(m)*
Pt agente oficial *(m)*

agent exclusif *(m)* Fr
De Alleinvertreter *(m)*
En sole agent
Es agente exclusivo *(m)*
It rappresentante esclusivo *(m)*
Pt agente exclusivo *(m)*

agent metteur à bord *(m)* Fr
De Spediteur *(m)*
En shipping and forwarding agent
Es agente de embarques *(m)*
It agente marittimo e di spedizione *(m)*
Pt agente de cargas e despachos *(m)*

agente di assicurazioni *(f)* It
De Versicherungsvertreter *(m)*
En insurance agent
Es agente de seguros *(m)*
Fr agent d'assurances *(m)*
Pt agente de seguros *(m)*

Agentur *(f)* n De
En agency
Es agencia *(f)*
Fr agence *(f)*
It agenzia *(f)*
Pt agência *(f)*

agenzia *(f)* n It
De Agentur *(f)*
En agency
Es agencia *(f)*
Fr agence *(f)*
Pt agência *(f)*

agenzia di collocamento *(f)* It
De Stellenvermittlungsbüro *(n)*
En employment agency
Es agencia de colocaciones *(f)*
Fr agence de placement *(f)*
Pt agência de empregos *(f)*

agenzia d'informazioni *(f)* It
De Nachrichtenbüro *(n)*
En news agency
Es agencia de prensa *(f)*
Fr agence de presse *(f)*
Pt agência de noticias *(f)*

agenzia di viaggi *(f)* It
De Reisebüro *(n)*
En travel agent
Es agencia de viajes *(f)*

Fr agence de voyages *(f)*
Pt agente de viagens *(m)*

agenzia immobiliare *(f)* It
De Immobilienbüro *(m)*
En estate agency
Am real estate agency
Es correduría de fincas *(f)*
Fr agence immobilière *(f)*
Pt agência de propriedades *(f)*

agenzia pubblicitaria *(f)* It
De Werbebüro *(n)*
En advertising agency
Es agencia de publicidad *(f)*
Fr agence de publicité *(f)*
Pt agência de publicidade *(f)*

aggiornamento *(m)* n It
De Vertagung *(f)*
En adjournment
Es aplazamiento *(m)*
Fr ajournement *(m)*
Pt adiamento *(m)*

aggiornare *vb* It
De vertagen
En adjourn
Es aplazar
Fr ajourner
Pt adiar

aggiotatore *(m)* n It
De Börsenhändler *(m)*
En stockjobber
Es agiotista *(m)*
Fr marchand de titres *(m)*
Pt agiota *(m)*

aggiudicare *vb* It
De gerichtlich entscheiden
En adjudicate
Es adjudicar
Fr juger
Pt adjudicar

aggiungere *vb* It
De hinzufügen
En add
Es añadir
Fr ajouter
Pt adicionar

aggregate *adj* En
De gesamt
Es total
Fr global
It complessivo
Pt total

agio account En
De Agiokonto *(n)*
Es cuenta de agio *(f)*
Fr compte d'agio *(m)*
It conto d'aggio *(m)*
Pt conta de ágio *(f)*

Agiokonto *(n)* n De
En agio account
Es cuenta de agio *(f)*
Fr compte d'agio *(m)*
It conto d'agio *(m)*
Pt conta de ágio *(f)*

agiota *(m)* n Pt
De Börsenhändler *(m)*
En stockjobber
Es agiotista *(m)*
Fr marchand de titres *(m)*
It aggiotatore *(m)*

agiotista *(m)* n Es
De Börsenhändler *(m)*
En stockjobber
Fr marchand de titres *(m)*
It aggiotatore *(m)*
Pt agiota *(m)*

agotado *adj* Es
De ausverkauft
En sold out
Fr tout vendu
It tutto venduto
Pt esgotado

a granel Es, Pt
De in großer Menge
En in bulk
Fr en vrac
It alla rinfusa

agravio *(m)* n Es
De Beschwerde, unerlaubte Handlung *(f)*
En grievance; tort
Fr grief; acte défendu *(m)*
It lagnanza; torto *(f m)*
Pt agravo *(m)*

agravo *(m)* n Pt
De Beschwerde; unerlaubte Handlung *(f)*
En grievance; tort
Es agravio *(m)*
Fr grief; acte défendu *(m)*
It lagnanza; torto *(m)*

agreement *(written)* n En
De Abkommen *(n)*
Es contrato *(m)*

Fr convention (par écrit) *(f)*
It accordo *(m)*
Pt acordo *(m)*

agricoltura *(f) n* It
De Landwirtschaft *(f)*
En agriculture
Es agricultura *(f)*
Fr agriculture *(f)*
Pt agricultura *(f)*

agricultura *(f) n* Es, Pt
De Landwirtschaft *(f)*
En agriculture
Fr agriculture *(f)*
It agricoltura *(f)*

agriculture *n* En, Fr *(f)*
De Landwirtschaft *(f)*
Es agricultura *(f)*
It agricoltura *(f)*
Pt agricultura *(f)*

aguarde Pt
De am Apparat bleiben
En hold the line
Es espere al aparato
Fr ne quittez pas
It restare in linea

águas territoriais *(f pl)* Pt
De Hoheitsgewässer *(n pl)*
En territorial waters
Es aguas territoriales *(f pl)*
Fr eaux territoriales *(f pl)*
It acque territoriali *(f pl)*

à haute teneur Fr
De erstklassig
En high-grade
Es alta calidad
It di qualità superiore
Pt alto-nível

ahorrar *vb* Es
De aufsparen
En save
Fr épargner; économiser
It risparmiare; economizzare
Pt poupar; economizar

aiuto *(m) n* It
De Hilfe *(f)*
En help
Es ayuda *(f)*
Fr secours *(m)*
Pt ajuda *(f)*

air-conditioning *n* En
De Klimatisierung *(f)*
Es acondicionamiento de aire *(m)*
Fr climatisation *(f)*
It condizionamento dell'aria *(m)*
Pt condicionamento do ar *(m)*

air freight En
De Luftfracht *(f)*
Es flete aéreo *(m)*
Fr fret aérien *(m)*
It trasporto aereo *(m)*
Pt frete aéreo *(m)*

air letter En
De Luftpostbrief *(m)*
Es carta por avión *(f)*
Fr aérogramme *(m)*
It lettera aerea *(f)*
Pt carta por avião *(f)*

air line En
De Fluggesellschaft *(f)*
Es línea aérea *(f)*
Fr compagnie aérienne *(f)*
It linea aerea *(f)*
Pt companhia de aviação *(f)*

airmail *n* En
De Luftpost *(f)*
Es correo aéreo *(m)*
Fr poste aérienne *(f)*
It posta aerea *(f)*
Pt correio aéreo *(m)*

airmail receipt En
De Luftpostempfangsbe-scheinigung *(f)*
Es recibo aeropostal *(m)*
Fr récépissé de poste aérienne *(m)*
It ricevimento per posta aerea *(m)*
Pt recibo de via aérea *(m)*

airport *n* En
De Flughafen *(m)*
Es aeropuerto *(m)*
Fr aéroport *(m)*
It aeroporto *(m)*
Pt aeroporto *(m)*

air terminal En
De Luftterminal *(n)*
Es terminal de aeropuerto *(f)*
Fr aérogare *(f)*
It aerostazione *(f)*
Pt estação terminal aérea *(f)*

air traffic En
De Luftverkehr *(m)*
Es tráfico aéreo *(m)*
Fr trafic aérien *(m)*
It traffico aereo *(m)*
Pt tráfego aéreo *(m)*

air transport En
De Lufttransport *(m)*
Es transporte aéreo *(m)*
Fr transport aérien *(m)*
It trasporto aereo *(m)*
Pt transporte aéreo *(m)*

air waybill En
De Luftfrachtbrief *(m)*
Es carta de porte aéreo *(f)*
Fr lettre de transport aérien *(f)*
It nota di spedizione aerea *(f)*
Pt guia de porte aéreo *(f)*

ajournement *(m) n* Fr
De Vertagung *(f)*
En adjournment
Es aplazamiento *(m)*
It aggiornamento *(m)*
Pt adiamento *(m)*

ajourner *vb* Fr
De vertagen
En adjourn
Es aplazar
It aggiornare
Pt adiar

ajouter *vb* Fr
De hinzufügen
En add
Es añadir
It aggiungere
Pt adicionar

ajuda *(f) n* Pt
De Hilfe *(f)*
En help
Es ayuda *(f)*
Fr secours *(m)*
It aiuto *(m)*

ajuste *(m) n* Es, Pt
De Abrechnung *(f)*
En settlement
Fr règlement *(m)*
It quietanza *(f)*

Akkordarbeit *(f) n* De
En piecework
Es trabajo a destajo *(m)*
Fr travail à la tâche *(m)*

It lavoro a cottimo *(m)*
Pt trabalho por peça *(m)*

Akte *(f)* n De
En file
Es archivo *(m)*
Fr dossier *(m)*
It archivio *(m)*
Pt ficheiro *(m)*

Aktenschrank *(m)* n De
En filing cabinet
Es fichero *(m)*
Fr classeur *(m)*
It schedario *(m)*
Pt móvel ficheiro *(m)*

Aktie *(f)* n De
En share
Es acción *(f)*
Fr action *(f)*
It azione *(f)*
Pt acção *(f)*

Aktiengesellschaft (AG) *(f)*
De
En public limited company
Es Sociedad anónima (SA) *(f)*
Fr Société anonyme (SA) *(f)*
It Società anonima (SA) *(f)*
Pt Sociedade anónima (SA)
(f)

Aktienindex *(m)* n De
En share index
Es índice de las acciones *(m)*
Fr indice des actions *(m)*
It indice delle azioni *(m)*
Pt índice das acções *(m)*

Aktieninhaber *(m)* n De
En stockholder
Es accionista *(m)*
Fr détenteur de titres *(m)*
It azionista *(m)*
Pt accionista *(m)*

Aktienkapital *(n)* n De
En share capital
Am stock capital
Es capital en acciones *(m)*
Fr capital social *(m)*
It capitale azionario *(m)*
Pt capital em acções *(m)*

Aktienmarkt *(m)* n De
En share market
Am stock market
Es mercado de valores *(m)*

Fr marché des valeurs *(m)*
It mercato azionario *(m)*
Pt mercado de acções *(m)*

Aktien ohne Stimmrecht
(f pl) De
En non-voting-shares
Es acciones sin derecho de
voto *(f pl)*
Fr actions sans droit de vote
(f pl)
It azioni senza diritto a voto
(f pl)
Pt acções sem direito a voto
(f pl)

Aktien von Goldbergwerken
(f pl) De
En gold shares
Es acciones auríferas *(f pl)*
Fr valeurs aurifères *(f pl)*
It azioni aurifere *(f pl)*
Pt acções de ouro *(f pl)*

Aktienzertifikat *(n)* n De
En share certificate
Am certificate of stock
Es título de acción *(m)*
Fr certificat d'actions *(m)*
It certificato azionario *(m)*
Pt título de acções *(m)*

Aktionär *(m)* n De
En shareholder
Am stockholder
Es accionista *(m)*
Fr actionnaire *(m)*
It azionista *(m)*
Pt titular de acções; accionista
(m)

Aktiva und Passiva *(n pl)* De
En assets and liabilities
Es activo y pasivo *(m)*
Fr actif et passif *(m)*
It attivo e passivo *(m)*
Pt activo e passivo *(m)*

aktiver Teilhaber *(m)* De
En working partner; active
partner
Es socio activo *(m)*
Fr associé actif; associé en
nom *(m)*
It socio attivo *(m)*
Pt sócio actuante; sócio
activo *(m)*

Aktivposten *(m)* n De
En asset
Es activo *(m)*
Fr actif *(m)*
It attivo *(m)*
Pt valor *(m)*

Aktivsaldo *(m)* n De
En active balance
Es saldo acreedor *(m)*
Fr balance excédentaire *(f)*
It saldo attivo *(m)*
Pt saldo credor *(m)*

Aktivwert *(m)* n De
En asset value
Es valor en activo *(m)*
Fr valeur de l'actif *(f)*
It valore in attivo *(m)*
Pt valor do activo *(m)*

Aktuar *(m)* n De
En actuary
Es actuario *(m)*
Fr actuaire *(m)*
It attuario *(m)*
Pt actuário *(m)*

Akzept *(n)* n De
En acceptance
Es aceptación *(f)*
Fr acceptation *(f)*
It accettazione *(f)*
Pt aceitação *(f)*

Akzeptfrist *(f)* n De
En acceptance interval
Es intervalo de aceptación
(m)
Fr intervalle d'acceptation *(f)*
It intervallo dell'accettazione
(m)
Pt intervalo de aceitação *(m)*

Akzeptkredit *(m)* n De
En acceptance credit
Es crédito de aceptación *(m)*
Fr crédit par acceptation *(m)*
It credito d'accettazione *(m)*
Pt crédito de aceitação *(m)*

à l'acquitté Fr
De verzollt
En ex bond
Es fuera de aduanas
It sdoganato
Pt livre de alfândega

a largo plazo Es
De langfristig
En long-term
Fr à long terme; à longue
  échéance
It a lunga scadenza
Pt a longo prazo

a la vista Es
De bei Sicht
En at sight
Fr à vue
It a vista
Pt à vista

albacea *(m) n* Es
De Vollstrecker *(m)*
En executor
Fr exécuteur *(m)*
It esecutore *(m)*
Pt executor *(m)*

albergo *(m) n* It
De Hotel *(n)*
En hotel
Es hotel *(m)*
Fr hôtel *(m)*
Pt hotel *(m)*

alcista *(m) n* Es
De Haussespekulant *(m)*
En bull
Fr haussier *(m)*
It rialzista *(m)*
Pt altista *(m)*

alcista *adj* Es
De steigend
En bullish
Fr haussier
It rialzista
Pt altista

**al contado contra documen-
  tos** Es
De bar gegen Versandpapiere
En cash against documents
  (c.a.d.)
Fr comptant contre docu-
  ments
It contanti contro documenti
Pt em dinheiro contra docu-
  mentação

à l'étranger Fr
De im Ausland
En abroad
Es en el extranjero
It all'estero
Pt no estrangeiro

alfândega *(f) n* Pt
De Zoll *(m)*
En customs
Es aduana *(f)*
Fr douane *(f)*
It dogana *(f)*

algorithm *n* En
De Algorithmus *(m)*
Es algoritmo *(m)*
Fr algorithme *(m)*
It algoritmo *(m)*
Pt algorítmo *(m)*

algorithme *(m) n* Fr
De Algorithmus *(m)*
En algorithm
Es algoritmo *(m)*
It algoritmo *(m)*
Pt algorítmo *(m)*

Algorithmus *(m) n* De
En algorithm
Es algoritmo *(m)*
Fr algorithme *(m)*
It algoritmo *(m)*
Pt algorítmo *(m)*

algoritmo *(m) n* Es, It
De Algorithmus *(m)*
En algorithm
Fr algorithme *(m)*
Pt algorítmo *(m)*

algorítmo *(m) n* Pt
De Algorithmus *(m)*
En algorithm
Es algoritmo *(m)*
Fr algorithme *(m)*
It algoritmo *(m)*

alien *adj* En
De ausländisch
Es extranjero
Fr étranger
It straniero
Pt estrangeiro

alijar *vb* Pt
De über Bord werfen
En jettison
Es echar al mar
Fr jeter à la mer
It fare gettito

alimentation *(f) n* Fr
De Eßwaren *(f pl)*
En foodstuffs
Es comestibles *(m pl)*

It generi alimentari *(m pl)*
Pt géneros alimentícios *(m pl)*

alla pari It
De al pari
En at par
Es al par
Fr au pair
Pt ao par

alla rinfusa It
De in großer Menge
En in bulk
Es a granel
Fr en vrac
Pt a granel

allegato *(m) n* It
De Beilage *(f)*
En enclosure
Es anexo *(m)*
Fr annexe *(f)*
Pt anexo *(m)*

allège *(f) n* Fr
De Leichter *(m)*
En lighter (boat)
Es barcaza; gabarra *(f)*
It chiatta *(f)*
Pt barcaça *(f)*

alle Gefahren *(f pl)* De
En all risks
Es todos los riesgos *(m pl)*
Fr tous risques *(m pl)*
It tutti i rischi *(m pl)*
Pt todos os riscos *(m pl)*

Alleinvertreter *(m) n* De
En sole agent
Es agente exclusivo *(m)*
Fr agent exclusif *(m)*
It rappresentante esclusivo
  (m)
Pt agente exclusivo *(m)*

all'estero *adv* It
De im Ausland
En abroad
Es en el extranjero
Fr à l'étranger
Pt no estrangeiro

allestimento delle vetrine
  (m) It
De Schaufensterdekoration *(f)*
En window-dressing
Es preparación de escapara-
  tes *(f)*

Fr art de l'étalage *(m)*
Pt preparação de montras *(f)*

allgemeines Hauptbuch *(n)*
De
En general ledger
Es libro mayor general *(m)*
Fr journal général *(m)*
It libro mastro generale *(m)*
Pt livro-mestre geral *(m)*

allgemeines Pfandrecht *(n)*
De
En general lien
Es privilegio general *(m)*
Fr privilège général *(m)*
It privilegio generale *(m)*
Pt privilégio geral *(m)*

Allgemeines Zoll- und Handelsabkommen *(n)*
De
En General Agreement on Tariffs and Trade (GATT)
Es Acuerdo General sobre Tarifas Aduaneras y Comercio *(m)*
Fr Accord Général sur les Tarifs Douaniers et le Commerce *(m)*
It Accordo Generale sulle Tariffe Doganali e sul Commercio *(m)*
Pt Acordo geral de Tarifas e Comércio *(m)*

allgemeine Unkosten *(pl)* De
En general expenses
Es gastos generales *(m pl)*
Fr frais généraux *(m pl)*
It spese generali *(f pl)*
Pt despesas gerais *(f pl)*

allot (shares, etc.) *vb* En
De verteilen
Es asignar
Fr attribuer
It assegnare
Pt atribuir

allotment (of shares) *n* En
De Verteilung *(f)*
Es adjudicación *(f)*
Fr attribution *(f)*
It ripartizione *(f)*
Pt aporcionamento *(m)*

allotment letter En
De Verteilungsbrief *(m)*
Es letra de adjudicación *(f)*

Fr avis d'attribution *(m)*
It lettera da ripartizione *(f)*
Pt aviso de aporcionamento *(m)*

allow (a discount) *vb* En
De gewähren (einen Rabatt)
Es conceder (un descuento)
Fr consentir (une remise)
It concedere (uno sconto)
Pt conceder (um desconto)

allowable expense En
De abziehbare Unkosten *(pl)*
Es gastos deducibles *(m pl)*
Fr dépense déductible *(f)*
It spesa permessa *(f)*
Pt despesas deduzíveis *(f pl)*

allowance *n* En
De Rabatt *(m)*
Es bonificación *(f)*
Fr rabais *(m)*
It abbuono *(m)*
Pt provisão *(f)*

all risks En
De alle Gefahren *(f pl)*
Es todos los riesgos *(m pl)*
Fr tous risques *(m pl)*
It tutti i rischi *(m pl)*
Pt todos os riscos *(m pl)*

almacén *(m)* *n* Es
De Lager; Warenlager *(n)*
En store; warehouse
Fr magasin; entrepôt *(m)*
It magazzino *(m)*
Pt armazém *(m)*

almacenamiento *(m)* *n* Es
De Lagerung *(f)*
En storage
Fr emmagasinage *(m)*
It magazzinaggio *(m)*
Pt armazenamento *(m)*

almacenar *vb* Es
De lagern
En store
Fr emmagasiner
It immagazzinare
Pt armazenar

almacén de aduanas *(m)* Es
De Lager unter Zollverschluß *(n)*
En bonded warehouse
Fr entrepôt *(m)*

It magazzino doganale *(m)*
Pt armazém alfandegário *(m)*

a longo prazo Pt
De langfristig
En long-term; long-dated
Es a largo plazo
Fr à long terme; à longue échéance
It a lunga scadenza

à long terme Fr
De langfristig
En long-term
Es a largo plazo
It a lunga scadenza
Pt a longo prazo

à longue échéance Fr
De langfristig
En long-dated
Es a largo plazo
It a lunga scadenza
Pt a longo prazo

al par Es
De al pari
En at par
Fr au pair
It alla pari
Pt ao par

al pari De
En at par
Es al par
Fr au pair
It alla pari
Pt ao par

alquilador *(m)* *n* Es
De Mieter *(m)*
En hirer
Fr locataire *(m)*
It noleggiatore *(m)*
Pt alugador *(m)*

alquilar *vb* Es
De mieten; vermieten
En hire; rent
Fr louer; affermer
It noleggiare; affittare
Pt alugar

alquiler *(m)* *n* Es
De Verpachtung; Miete *(f)*
En lease; rent
Fr bail; loyer *(m)*
It affitto; pigione *(m)*
Pt aluguer; renda *(m f)*

als Gegenrechnung De
En per contra
Es en contrapartida
Fr contrepartie; par contre
It in contropartita
Pt em contrapartida

alta calidad Es
De erstklassig
En high-grade
Fr à haute teneur
It di qualità superiore
Pt alto-nível

alta mar (f) Es
De hohe See (f)
En high seas
Fr hautes mers (f pl)
It alto mare (m)
Pt alto-mar (m)

alteingeführtes Geschäft (n)
    De
En old-established business
Es casa sólida (f)
Fr maison solide (f)
It casa di vecchia fondazio-
    ne (f)
Pt empresa de há muito
    estabelecida (f)

alterations (to a building) n pl
    En
De Umbau (m)
Es reformas (f pl)
Fr travaux de transformation
    (m pl)
It modifiche (f pl)
Pt modificações (f pl)

alterations and renewals En
De Änderungen und Erneue-
    rungen
Es reformas y renovaciones
Fr réfections et améliorations
It modifiche e rinnovamenti
Pt modificações e renovações

alterations and repairs En
De Änderungen und Repara-
    turen
Es reformas y reparaciones
Fr transformations et répara-
    tions
It modifiche e riparazioni
Pt modificações e reparações

Altersversorgung (f) De
En old-age pension
Es retiro de vejez (m)

Fr pension de retraite (f)
It pensione per la vecchiaia
    (f)
Pt pensão (f)

altista (m) n Pt
De Haussespekulant (m)
En bull
Es alcista (m)
Fr haussier (m)
It rialzista (m)

altista adj Pt
De steigend
En bullish
Es alcista
Fr haussier
It rialzista

alto adj Es, It
De hoch
En high
Fr haut; élevé
Pt elevado

alto-mar (m) Pt
De hohe See (f)
En high seas
Es alta mar (f)
Fr hautes mers (f pl)
It alto mare (m)

alto mare (m) It
De hohe See (f)
En high seas
Es alta mar
Fr hautes mers (f pl)
Pt alto-mar (m)

alto-nível adj Pt
De erstklassig
En high-grade
Es alta calidad
Fr à haute teneur
It di qualità superiore

alugador (m) n Pt
De Mieter (m)
En hirer
Es alquilador; arrendador (m)
Fr locataire (m)
It noleggiatore (m)

alugar vb Pt
De mieten; vermieten
En hire; rent
Es alquilar
Fr louer; affermer
It noleggiare; affittare

aluguer (m) n Pt
De Verpachtung (f)
En lease
Es alquiler (m)
Fr bail (m)
It affitto (m)

a lunga scadenza It
De langfristig
En long-term; long-dated
Es a largo plazo
Fr à long terme; à longue
    échéance
Pt a longo prazo

ama de casa (f) Es
De Hausfrau (f)
En housewife
Fr ménagère (f)
It massaia (f)
Pt dona de casa (f)

amalgamación (f) n Es
De Fusion (f)
En amalgamation
Am merger
Fr fusion (f)
It fusione (f)
Pt amalgamento (m)

amalgamar vb Es, Pt
De fusionieren
En amalgamate
Am merge
Fr fusionner
It fondersi

amalgamate vb En
Am merge
De fusionieren
Es amalgamar
Fr fusionner
It fondersi
Pt amalgamar

amalgamation n En
Am merger
De Fusion (f)
Es amalgamación (f)
Fr fusion (f)
It fusione (f)
Pt amalgamento (m)

amalgamento (m) n Pt
De Fusion (f)
En amalgamation
Am merger
Es amalgamación (f)
Fr fusion (f)
it fusione (f)

amanhã *adv* Pt
De morgen
En tomorrow
Es mañana
Fr demain
It domani

à mão Pt
De vorrätig
En on hand
Es disponible
Fr disponible
It disponibile

am Apparat bleiben De
En hold the line
Es espere al aparato
Fr ne quittez pas
It resti in linea
Pt aguarde

amélioration *(f) n* Fr
De Verbesserung *(f)*
En improvement
Es mejora *(f)*
It miglioramento *(m)*
Pt melhoramento *(m)*

amende *(f) n* Fr
De Geldstrafe *(f)*
En fine
Es sanción; multa *(f)*
It multa *(f)*
Pt multa *(f)*

a mitad de precio Es
De zum halben Preise
En half price
Fr à moitié prix
It metà prezzo
Pt metade do preço

ammanco *(m) n* It
De Mangel; Fehlbetrag *(m)*
En deficiency
Es deficiencia *(f)*
Fr manque; insuffisance *(m f)*
Pt deficiência; defeito *(f m)*

ammassare *vb* It
De Vorratslager anlegen
En stockpile
Es acumular existencias
Fr stocker
Pt acumular existências

ammasso *(m) n* It
De Hortung *(f)*
En hoard

Es atesoramiento *(m)*
Fr thésaurisation *(f)*
Pt acumulação *(f)*

amministrare *vb* It
De verwalten
En administer
Es administrar
Fr administrer
Pt administrar

amministratore *(m) n* It
De Verwalter, Direktor *(m)*
En administrator; director
Es administrador; director *(m)*
Fr administrateur *(m)*
Pt administrador; director *(m)*

amministratore delegato *(m)*
It
De geschäftsleitender Direktor *(m)*
En managing director
Am president
Es director gerente *(m)*
Fr administrateur délégué *(m)*
Pt director geral *(m)*

amministratore dirigente *(m)*
It
De geschäftsführender Direktor *(m)*
En executive director
Am corporate officer
Es director ejecutivo *(m)*
Fr administrateur dirigeant *(m)*
Pt director administrativo *(m)*

**ammissione in franchigia
doganale** *(f)* It
De zollfreie Einfuhr *(f)*
En duty-free admission
Es admisión libre de impuestos *(f)*
Fr admission en franchise *(f)*
Pt admissão livre de impostos *(f)*

ammontante a It
De hinauslaufend auf
En amounting to
Es ascendiendo a
Fr à concurrence de
Pt no montante de

ammontare *(m) n* It
De Betrag *(m)*
En amount

Es suma *(f)*
Fr somme *(f)*
Pt quantia *(f)*

ammontare da riportare *(m)*
It
De Übertrag *(m)*
En amount carried forward
Am carry forward amount
Es suma y sigue *(f)*
Fr report à nouveau *(m)*
Pt importância transportada *(f)*

ammortamento *(m) n* It
De Amortisation; Entwertung *(f)*
En amortization; depreciation; redemption
Es amortización; depreciación *(f)*
Fr amortissement; dépréciation *(m)*
Pt amortização; depreciação *(f)*

à moitié Fr
De halb
En half
Es medio
It mezzo
Pt meio

à moitié prix Fr
De zum halben Preis
En half price
Es a mitad de precio
It metà prezzo
Pt metade do preço

amortir une créance Fr
De eine Schuld erlassen
En write off a debt
Es cancelar una deuda
It cancellare un credito
Pt cancelar um débito

amortir une perte Fr
De einen Verlust abschreiben
En write off a loss
Es cancelar una pérdida
It cancellare una perdita
Pt anular um prejuízo

Amortisation *(f) n* De
En amortization
Es amortización *(f)*
Fr amortissement *(m)*
It amortamento *(m)*
Pt amortização *(f)*

amortissement *(m) n* Fr
De Tilgung; Amortisation *(f)*
En redemption; amortization
Es amortización *(f)*
It ammortamento *(m)*
Pt amortização *(f)*

amortissement accéléré *(m)*
Fr
De beschleunigte Abschrei-
bung *(f)*
En accelerated depreciation
Es depreciación acelerada *(f)*
It deprezzamento accelerato
(m)
Pt depreciação acelerada *(f)*

amortização *(f) n* Pt
De Tilgung; Amortisation *(f)*
En redemption; amortization
Es amortización *(f)*
Fr amortissement; rembour-
sement *(m)*
It ammortamento *(m)*

amortización *(f) n* Es
De Tilgung; Amortisation *(f)*
En redemption; amortization
Fr amortissement; rembour-
sement *(m)*
It ammortamento *(m)*
Pt amortização *(f)*

amortization *n* En
De Amortisation *(f)*
Es amortización *(f)*
Fr amortissement *(m)*
It ammortamento *(m)*
Pt amortização *(f)*

amostra *(f) n* Pt
De Probe; Muster *(f n)*
En sample
Es muestra *(f)*
Fr échantillon *(m)*
It campione *(m)*

amostra avulsa *(f)* Pt
De Stichprobe *(f)*
En random sample
Es muestra aleatoria *(f)*
Fr épreuve au hasard *(f)*
It campione a casaccio *(m)*

amostra grátis *(f)* Pt
De kostenlose Probe *(f)*
En free sample
Es muestra gratuita *(f)*
Fr échantillon gratuit *(m)*
It campione gratuito *(m)*

amostra sem valor *(f)* Pt
De Muster ohne Wert *(n)*
En sample of no value
Es muestra sin valor *(f)*
Fr échantillon sans valeur *(m)*
It campione senza valore *(m)*

amount *n* En
De Betrag *(m)*
Es suma *(f)*
Fr somme *(f)*
It ammontare *(m)*
Pt quantia *(f)*

amount carried forward En
Am carry forward amount
De Übertrag *(m)*
Es suma y sigue *(f)*
Fr report à nouveau *(m)*
It ammontare da riportare
(m)
Pt importância transportada
(f)

amounting to En
De hinauslaufend auf
Es ascendiendo a
Fr à concurrence de
It ammontante a
Pt no montante de

amtlich *adj* De
En official
Es oficial
Fr officiel
It ufficiale
Pt oficial

añadir *vb* Es
De hinzufügen
En add
Fr ajouter
It aggiungere
Pt adicionar

**analisador de investimen-
tos** *(m)* Pt
De Investitionsanalyst *(m)*
En investment analyst
Es analizador de inversiones
(m)
Fr analyste d'investisse-
ments *(m)*
It analizzatore d'investimenti
(m)

análise *(f) n* Pt
De Analyse *(f)*
En analysis
Es análisis *(m)*

Fr analyse *(f)*
It analisi *(f)*

análise de custo *(f)* Pt
De Kostenanalyse *(f)*
En cost analysis
Es análisis de costes *(m)*
Fr analyse des coûts *(f)*
It analisi dei costi *(f)*

análise de custo e benefício
(f) Pt
De Gewinnanalyse *(f)*
En cost benefit analysis
Es análisis de costes y bene-
ficios *(m)*
Fr analyse des coûts et ren-
dements *(f)*
It analisi dei costi e benefici
(f)

análise de sistemas *(f)* Pt
De Systemanalyse *(f)*
En systems analysis
Es análisis de sistemas *(m)*
Fr analyse de systèmes *(f)*
It analisi di sistemi *(f)*

análise de variação *(f)* Pt
De Varianzanalyse *(f)*
En variance analysis
Es análisisde variaciones *(m)*
Fr analyse de la variance *(f)*
It analisi della variazione *(f)*

análise de vendas *(f)* Pt
De Verkaufsanalyse *(f)*
En sales analysis
Es análisis de ventas *(m)*
Fr analyse des ventes *(m)*
It analisi delle vendite *(f)*

**análise do tempo e
progresso** *(f)* Pt
De Arbeitszeit- und Ablaufstudie *(f)*
En time and motion study
Es estudio de tiempo y progreso *(m)*
Fr étude du temps et
mouvements *(f)*
It studio dei tempi e dei movimenti *(m)*

análise marginal *(f)* Pt
De Randanalyse *(f)*
En marginal analysis
Es análisis marginal *(m)*
Fr analyse marginale *(f)*
It analisi marginale *(f)*

analisi (f) n It
De Analyse (f)
En analysis
Es análisis (m)
Fr analyse (f)
Pt análise (f)

analisi dei costi (f) It
De Kostenanalyse (f)
En cost analysis
Es análisis de costes (m)
Fr analyse des coûts (f)
Pt análise de custo (f)

analisi dei costi e benefici (f)
It
De Gewinnanalyse (f)
En cost benefit analysis
Es análisis de costes y bene-
ficios (m)
Fr analyse des coûts et ren-
dements (f)
Pt análise de custo e be-
nefício (f)

analisi della linea critica (f) It
De Netzplantechnik (f)
En critical path analysis
(c.p.a.)
Es análisis de recorrido críti-
co (m)
Fr analyse du chemin critique
(m)
Pt análise de transcurso críti-
co (f)

analisi della variazione (f) It
De Varianzanalyse (f)
En variance analysis
Es análisis de variaciones (m)
Fr analyse de la variance (f)
Pt análise de variação (f)

analisi delle vendite (f) It
De Verkaufsanalyse (f)
En sales analysis
Es análisis de ventas (m)
Fr analyse des ventes (f)
Pt análise de vendas (f)

analisi di sistemi (f) It
De Systemanalyse (f)
En systems analysis
Es análisis de sistemas (m)
Fr analyse de systèmes (f)
Pt análise de sistemas (f)

analisi marginale (f) It
De Randanalyse (f)

En marginal analysis
Es análisis marginal (m)
Fr analyse marginale (f)
Pt análise marginal (f)

análisis (m) n Es
De Analyse (f)
En analysis
Fr analyse (f)
It analisi (f)
Pt análise (f)

análisis de costes (m) Es
De Kostenanalyse (f)
En cost analysis
Fr analyse des coûts (f)
It analisi dei costi (f)
Pt análise de custo (f)

**análisis de costes y benefi-
cios** (m) Es
De Gewinnanalyse (f)
En cost benefit analysis
Fr analyse des coûts et ren-
dements (f)
It analisi dei costi e benefici
(f)
Pt análise de custo e benefi-
cio (f)

análisis de sistemas (m) Es
De Systemanalyse (f)
En systems analysis
Fr analyse de systèmes (f)
It analisi di sistemi (f)
Pt análise de sistemas (f)

análisis de variaciones (m)
Es
De Varianzanalyse (f)
En variance analysis
Fr analyse de la variance (f)
It analisi della variazione (f)
Pt análise de variação (f)

análisis de ventas (m) Es
De Verkaufsanalyse (f)
En sales analysis
Fr analyse des ventes (f)
It analisi delle vendite (f)
Pt análise de vendas (f)

análisis marginal (m) Es
De Randanalyse (f)
En marginal analysis
Fr analyse marginale (f)
It analisi marginale (f)
Pt análise marginal (f)

analizador de inversiones
(m) Es
De Investitionsanalyst (m)
En investment analyst
Fr analyste d'investisse-
ments (m)
It analizzatore d'investimenti
(m)
Pt analisador de investimen-
tos (m)

an alle, die es angeht De
En to whom it may concern
Es a quien concierna
Fr à qui de droit
It a tutti gli interessati
Pt a quem disser respeito

Analogrechner (m) n De
En analogue computer
Am analog computer
Es computadora analógica (f)
Fr calculateur analogique (m)
It calcolatore analogico (m)
Pt computador analógico (m)

analogue computer En
Am analog computer
De Analogrechner (m)
Es computadora analógica (f)
Fr calculateur analogique (m)
It calcolatore analogico (m)
Pt computador analógico (m)

analyse (f) n Fr
De Analyse (f)
En analysis
Es análisis (m)
It analisi (f)
Pt análise (f)

Analyse (f) n De
En analysis
Es análisis (m)
Fr analyse (f)
It analisi (f)
Pt análise (f)

analyse de la variance (f) Fr
De Varianzanalyse (f)
En variance analysis
Es análisis de variaciones (m)
It analisi della variazione (f)
Pt análise de variação (f)

analyse des coûts (f) Fr
De Kostenanalyse (f)
En cost analysis
Es análisis de costes (m)

It analisi dei costi *(f)*
Pt análise de custo *(f)*

**analyse des coûts et ren-
dements** *(f)* Fr
De Gewinnanalyse *(f)*
En cost benefit analysis
Es análisis de costes y bene-
ficios *(m)*
It analisi dei costi e benefici
(f)
Pt análise de custo e benefi-
cio *(f)*

analyse des ventes *(f)* Fr
De Verkaufsanalyse *(f)*
En sales analysis
Es análisis de ventas *(m)*
It analisi delle vendite *(f)*
Pt análise de vendas *(f)*

analyse de systèmes *(f)* Fr
De Systemanalyse *(f)*
En systems analysis
Es análisis de sistemas *(m)*
It analisi di sistemi *(f)*
Pt análise de sistemas *(f)*

analyse du chemin critique
(m) Fr
De Netzplantechnik *(f)*
En critical path analysis
(c.p.a.)
Es análisis de recorrido críti-
co *(m)*
It analisi della linea critica *(f)*
Pt análise de transcurso críti-
co *(f)*

analyse marginale *(f)* Fr
De Randanalyse *(f)*
En marginal analysis
Es análisis marginal *(m)*
It analisi marginale *(f)*
Pt anállse marginal *(f)*

Analysenwerkzeug *(n)* De
En analytical tool
Es instrumento de análisis *(m)*
Fr instrument d'analyse *(m)*
It strumento d'analisi *(m)*
Pt instrumento de análise *(m)*

analysis *(n)* En
De Analyse *(f)*
Es análisis *(m)*
Fr analyse *(f)*
It analisi *(f)*
Pt análise *(f)*

analyste d'investissements
(m) Fr
De Investitionsanalyst *(m)*
En investment analyst
Es analizador de inversiones
(m)
It analizzatore d'investimenti
(m)
Pt analisador de investimen-
tos *(m)*

analytical tool En
De Analysenwerkzeug *(n)*
Es instrumento de análisis *(m)*
Fr instrument d'analyse *(m)*
It strumento d'analisi *(m)*
Pt instrumento de análise *(m)*

anbieten *vb* De
En offer
Es ofrecer
Fr offrir
It offrire
Pt oferecer

an Bord De
En aboard
Es a bordo
Fr à bord
It a bordo
Pt a bordo

anchorage *n* En
De Ankerplatz *(m)*
Es anclaje *(m)*
Fr ancrage *(m)*
It ancoraggio *(m)*
Pt ancoragem *(f)*

anclaje *(m)* *n* Es
De Ankerplatz *(m)*
En anchorage
Fr ancrage *(m)*
It ancoraggio *(m)*
Pt ancoragem *(f)*

ancoragem *(f)* *n* Pt
De Ankerplatz *(m)*
En anchorage
Es anclaje *(m)*
Fr ancrage *(m)*
It ancoraggio *(m)*

ancoraggio *(m)* *n* It
De Ankerplatz *(m)*
En anchorage
Es anclaje *(m)*
Fr ancrage *(m)*
Pt ancoragem *(f)*

ancrage *(m)* *n* Fr
De Ankerplatz *(m)*
En anchorage
Es anclaje *(m)*
It ancoraggio *(m)*
Pt ancoragem *(f)*

andar com serviço incluído
(m) Pt
De Etagenwohnung mit
Bedienung *(f)*
En service flat
Es piso con servicio incluido
(m)
Fr appartement avec service
(m)
It appartamento con servizio
(m)

andar independente *(m)* Pt
De Einfamilienwohnung *(f)*
En self-contained flat
Es piso independiente com-
pleto *(m)*
Fr appartement indépendant
(m)
It appartamento indipenden-
te *(m)*

andar mobilado *(m)* Pt
De möblierte Mietwohnung *(f)*
En furnished flat
Am furnished apartment
Es piso amueblado *(m)*
Fr appartement meublé *(m)*
It appartamento ammobilia-
to *(m)*

**Änderungen und Erneue-
rungen** De
En alterations and renewals
Es reformas y renovaciones
Fr réfections et améliorations
It modifiche e rinnovamenti
Pt modificações e renovações

**Änderungen und Reparatu-
ren** De
En alterations and repairs
Es reformas y reparaciones
Fr transformations et répara-
tions
It modifiche e riparazioni
Pt modificações e reparações

andeuten *vb* De
En imply
Es implicar
Fr impliquer

It implicare
Pt significar

anerkannter Streik *(m)* De
En official strike
Es huelga oficial *(f)*
Fr grève officielle *(f)*
It sciopero ufficiale *(m)*
Pt greve oficial *(f)*

anexo *(m) n* Es
De Beilage *(f)*
En enclosure
Fr annexe *(f)*
It allegato *(m)*
Pt anexo *(m)*

anexo *(m) n* Pt
De Beilage *(f)*
En enclosure
Es anexo *(m)*
Fr annexe *(f)*
It allegato *(m)*

Anfangs- De
En initial
Es inicial; primario
Fr initial; premier
It iniziale
Pt inicial

Anforderung *(f) n* De
En requisition
Es pedido; solicitud *(m f)*
Fr demande *(f)*
It richiesta; requisizione *(f)*
Pt pedido *(m)*

angeben (den Preis) De
En quote
Es cotizar
Fr coter
It quotare
Pt cotizar

Angebot *(n) n* De
En bid; tender
Es oferta *(f)*
Fr offre; soumission *(f)*
It offerta *(f)*
Pt oferta; proposta *(f)*

(ein) Angebot annehmen De
En accept an offer
Es aceptar una oferta
Fr accepter une offre
It accettare una offerta
Pt aceitar uma oferta

Angebot und Nachfrage De
En supply and demand
Es oferta y demanda
Fr offre et demande
It offerta e domanda
Pt oferta e procura

angegebener Preis *(m)* De
En quoted price
Es precio cotizado *(m)*
Fr prix coté *(m)*
It prezzo quotato *(m)*
Pt preço cotizado *(m)*

angegebener Zollwert *(m)*
De
En declared value
Es valor declarado *(m)*
Fr valeur déclarée *(f)*
It valore dichiarato *(m)*
Pt valor declarado *(m)*

angelernt *adj* De
En semi-skilled
Es semidiestro
Fr semi-qualifié
It semiprovetto
Pt semieespecializado

angemessener Ertrag *(m)* De
En fair return
Es beneficio razonable *(m)*
Fr rendement équitable *(m)*
It discreto profitto *(m)*
Pt rendimento justo *(m)*

angemessener Preis *(m)* De
En fair price
Es precio razonable *(m)*
Fr prix raisonnable *(m)*
It prezzo equo *(m)*
Pt preço razoável *(m)*

**angenommener Totalver-
lust** *(m)* De
En constructive total loss
Es pérdida total constructiva
(f)
Fr perte réputée totale *(f)*
It perdita presunta totale *(f)*
Pt perda total construtiva *(f)*

Angestellte(r) *(m) n* De
En (salaried) employee; clerk
Es empleado (a sueldo); ofici-
nista *(m)*
Fr appointé; employé; com-
mis *(m)*
It stipendiato; impiegato *(m)*

Pt assalariado; empregado
(de escritório) *(m)*

Ankerplatz *(m) n* De
En anchorage
Es anclaje *(m)*
Fr ancrage *(m)*
It ancoraggio *(m)*
Pt ancoragem *(f)*

Ankunft *(f) n* De
En arrival
Es llegada *(f)*
Fr arrivée *(f)*
It arrivo *(m)*
Pt chegada *(f)*

Anlage *(f) n* De
En installation; plant
Es planta; instalación *(f)*
Fr appareil; installation *(m f)*
It impianto; macchinario *(m)*
Pt instalação (fabril) *(f)*

Anlagegüter *(n pl) n* De
En capital goods
Es bienes de producción
(m pl)
Fr biens déquipement *(m pl)*
It beni strumentali *(m pl)*
Pt mercadorias de capital
(f pl)

Anlagevermögen *(n) n* De
En fixed assets
Es activo fijo *(m)*
Fr immobilisations *(f pl)*
It immobilizzazioni; attivo
fisso *(f pl; m)*
Pt bens fixos *(m pl)*

Anlaufhafen *(m) n* De
En port of call
Es puerto de escala *(m)*
Fr port d'escale *(m)*
It porto di scalo *(m)*
Pt porto de escala *(m)*

anlegen *vb* De
En invest
Es invertir
Fr investir; placer
It investire
Pt investir

Anleihe *(f) n* De
En loan
Es empréstito *(m)*
Fr emprunt *(m)*

It   prestito *(m)*
Pt empréstimo *(m)*

(eine) Anleihe begeben De
En float a loan
Am raise a loan
Es emitir un empréstito
Fr émettre un emprunt
It lanciare un prestito
Pt lançar um empréstimo

Anleihekonto *(n) n* De
En loan account
Es cuenta de préstamos *(f)*
Fr compte des prêts *(m)*
It conto anticipazioni *(m)*
Pt conta de empréstimos *(f)*

Anleihewerte *(m pl) n* De
En loan stock
Es títulos de préstamo *(m pl)*
Fr titres d'emprunt *(m pl)*
It titoli di prestito *(m pl)*
Pt títulos de empréstimo *(m pl)*

Anleitung *(f) n* De
En instruction
Es instrucción *(f)*
Fr instruction *(f)*
It istruzione *(f)*
Pt instrução *(f)*

Anmeldegebühr *(f) n* De
En registration fee
Es derechos de registro *(m pl)*
Fr droit d'enregistrement *(m)*
It tassa di registrazione *(f)*
Pt custas de registo *(f pl)*

Annahme unter Vorbehalt *(f)* De
En qualified acceptance
Es aceptación condicionada *(f)*
Fr acceptation conditionnelle *(f)*
It accettazione con riserva *(f)*
Pt aceitação com reservas *(f)*

année civile *(f)* Fr
De Kalenderjahr *(n)*
En calendar year
Es año civil *(m)*
It anno solare *(m)*
Pt ano civil *(m)*

année de base *(f)* Fr
De Grundjahr *(n)*
En base year

Es año de base *(m)*
It anno di base *(m)*
Pt ano base *(m)*

année en cours *(f)* Fr
De laufendes Jahr *(n)*
En current year
Es año en curso *(m)*
It anno in corso *(m)*
Pt ano corrente *(m)*

annehmen *vb* De
En accept
Es aceptar
Fr accepter
It accettare
Pt aceitar

annexe *(f) n* Fr
De Beilage *(f)*
En enclosure
Es anexo *(m)*
It allegato *(m)*
Pt anexo *(m)*

anno di base *(m)* It
De Grundjahr *(n)*
En base year
Es año de base *(m)*
Fr année de base *(f)*
Pt ano base *(m)*

anno fiscale *(m)* It
De Steuerjahr; Einkommensteuerjahr *(n)*
En tax year; fiscal year; income-tax year
Es año fiscal *(m)*
Fr exercice fiscal; exercice budgétaire *(m)*
Pt ano fiscal *(m)*

anno in corso *(m)* It
De laufendes Jahr *(n)*
En current year
Es año en curso *(m)*
Fr année en cours *(f)*
Pt ano corrente *(m)*

annonce *(f) n* Fr
De Anzeige *(f)*
En advertisement
Es anuncio *(m)*
It annunzio *(m)*
Pt anúncio *(m)*

annonceur *(m) n* Fr
De Anzeiger *(m)*
En advertiser

Es anunciante *(m)*
It inserzionista *(m)*
Pt anunciante *(m)*

anno solare *(m)* It
De Kalenderjahr *(n)*
En calendar year
Es año civil *(m)*
Fr année civile *(f)*
Pt ano civil *(m)*

annuaire des téléphones *(m)* Fr
De Fernsprechbuch *(n)*
En telephone directory
Es guía de teléfonos *(f)*
It elenco telefonico *(m)*
Pt lista telefónica *(f)*

annual *adj* En
De jährlich
Es anual
Fr annuel
It annuale
Pt anual

annual accounts En
De Jahresabschluß *(m)*
Es balance anual *(m)*
Fr bilan annuel *(m)*
It bilancio annuale *(m)*
Pt balancete anual *(m)*

annuale *adj* It
De jährlich
En annual
Es anual
Fr annuel
Pt anual

annual general meeting En
Am stockholders meeting
De Jahreshauptversammlung *(f)*
Es asamblea general anual *(f)*
Fr assemblée d'actionnaires annuelle *(f)*
It assemblea generale annuale *(f)*
Pt assembleia geral anual *(f)*

annualitá *(f) n* It
De Annuität *(f)*
En annuity
Es anualidad *(f)*
Fr annuité *(f)*
Pt anuidade *(f)*

annual rate En
De Jahreskurs *(m)*
Es tasa anual *(f)*
Fr taux annuel *(m)*
It tasso annuale *(m)*
Pt taxa anual *(f)*

annual report En
De Jahresbericht *(m)*
Es memoria anual *(f)*
Fr rapport annuel *(m)*
It relazione annuale *(f)*
Pt relatório anual *(m)*

annuel *adj* Fr
De jährlich
En annual
Es anual
It annuale
Pt anual

Annuität *(f)* n De
En annuity
Es anualidad *(f)*
Fr annuité *(f)*
It annualitá *(f)*
Pt anuidade *(f)*

annuité *(f)* n Fr
De Annuität *(f)*
En annuity
Es anualidad *(f)*
It annualitá *(f)*
Pt anuidade *(f)*

annuité différée *(f)* Fr
De Anwartschaft auf
  Leibrente *(f)*
En deferred annuity
Es anualidad aplazada *(f)*
It rendita vitalizia differita *(f)*
Pt anuidade diferida *(f)*

annuity n En
De Annuität *(f)*
Es anualidad *(f)*
Fr annuité *(f)*
It annualitá *(f)*
Pt anuidade *(f)*

annulation *(f)* n Fr
De Annullierung *(f)*
En annulment; cancellation
Es anulación; cancelación *(f)*
It annullamento *(m)*
Pt annulação; cancelamento
  (f m)

annuler *vb* Fr
De annullieren
En cancel
Es cancelar
It cancellare
Pt cancelar

annuler un chèque Fr
De einen Scheck rückgängig
  machen
En cancel a cheque
Am cancel a check
Es anular un cheque
It annullare un assegno
Pt cancelar um cheque

annullamento *(m)* n It
De Annullierung *(f)*
En annulment; cancellation
Es anulación; cancelación *(f)*
Fr annulation *(f)*
Pt anulação; cancelamento
  (f m)

annullare un assegno It
De einen Scheck rückgängig
  machen
En cancel a cheque
Am cancel a check
Es anular un cheque
Fr annuler un chèque
Pt cancelar um cheque

annullieren *vb* De
En cancel
Es cancelar
Fr annuler
It cancellare
Pt cancelar

Annullierung *(f)* n De
En annulment; cancellation
Es anulación; cancelación *(f)*
Fr annulation *(f)*
It annullamento *(m)*
Pt anulação; cancelamento
  (f m)

annulment n En
De Annullierung *(f)*
Es anulación *(f)*
Fr annulation *(f)*
It annullamento *(m)*
Pt anulação *(f)*

annunzio *(m)* n It
De Anzeige *(f)*
En advertisement
Es anuncio *(m)*

Fr annonce *(f)*
Pt anúncio *(m)*

ano base *(m)* Pt
De Grundjahr *(n)*
En base year
Es año de base *(m)*
Fr année de base *(f)*
It anno di base *(m)*

año civil *(m)* Es
De Kalenderjahr *(n)*
En calendar year
Fr année civile *(f)*
It anno solare *(m)*
Pt ano civil *(m)*

ano civil *(m)* Pt
De Kalenderjahr *(n)*
En calendar year
Es año civil *(m)*
Fr année civile *(f)*
It anno solare *(m)*

ano corrente *(m)* Pt
De laufendes Jahr *(n)*
En current year
Es año en curso *(m)*
Fr année en cours *(f)*
It anno in corso *(m)*

año de base *(m)* Es
De Grundjahr *(n)*
En base year
Fr année de base *(f)*
It anno di base *(m)*
Pt ano base *(m)*

año económico *(m)* Es
De Geschäftsjahr *(n)*
En financial year
Fr exercice *(m)*
It esercizio *(m)*
Pt ano financeiro *(m)*

año en curso *(m)* Es
De laufendes Jahr *(n)*
En current year
Fr année en cours *(f)*
It anno in corso *(m)*
Pt ano corrente *(m)*

ano financeiro *(m)* Pt
De Geschäftsjahr *(n)*
En financial year
Es año económico *(m)*
Fr exercice *(m)*
It esercizio *(m)*

año fiscal *(m)* Es
De Steuerjahr; Einkommen-
steuerjahr *(n)*
En fiscal year; tax year; in-
come-tax year
Fr exercice budgétaire; exer-
cice fiscal *(m)*
It anno fiscale *(m)*
Pt ano fiscal *(m)*

ano fiscal *(m)* Pt
De Steuerjahr; Einkommen-
steuerjahr *(n)*
En fiscal year; tax year; in-
come-tax year
Es año fiscal *(m)*
Fr exercice budgétaire; exer-
cice fiscal *(m)*
It anno fiscale *(m)*

anotação de diário *(f)* Pt
De Tagebuchsposten *(m)*
En journal-entry
Es asiento en el libro diario
(m)
Fr article d'un livre journal *(m)*
It registrazione a giornale *(f)*

anpassungsfähig *adj* De
En flexible
Es flexible
Fr flexible
It flessibile
Pt flexível

anrechenbar *adj* De
En chargeable
Es imputable; a cobrar
Fr imputable; imposable
It imputabile; imponibile
Pt a cobrar

Anreiz *(m)* n De
En incentive
Es estímulo; incentivo *(m)*
Fr incitation; stimulant *(f m)*
It incentivo *(m)*
Pt incentivo *(m)*

Anruf *(m)* n De
En telephone call
Es llamada telefónica *(f)*
Fr appel téléphonique *(m)*
It chiamata telefonica *(f)*
Pt chamada telefónica *(f)*

Anschaffungskosten *(pl)* De
En historic cost
Es coste primitivo *(m)*

Fr coût d'acquisition primitif
(m)
It costo primitivo *(m)*
Pt custo original *(m)*

Anspruch *(m)* n De
En claim; (legal) title
Es reclamación; título *(f m)*
Fr réclamation; titre; droit
(f m m)
It reclamo; titolo; diritto *(m)*
Pt reclamação; título *(f m)*

anständige Abmachung *(f)*
De
En fair deal
Es trato equitativo *(m)*
Fr affaire équitable *(f)*
It affare giusto *(m)*
Pt transacção razoável *(f)*

**anständige Handlungswei-
se** *(f)* De
En fair play
Es juego limpio *(m)*
Fr traitement juste *(m)*
It condotta leale *(f)*
Pt jogo limpo *(m)*

anstellen *vb* De
En engage; appoint
Am hire
Es apalabrar
Fr engager
It fissare
Pt empregar

anstiften *vb* De
En instigate
Es instigar; provocar
Fr provoquer
It provocare; istigare
Pt instigar

answer n En
De Antwort *(f)*
Es respuesta *(f)*
Fr réponse *(f)*
It risposta *(f)*
Pt resposta *(f)*

anteayer Es
De vorgestern
En day before yesterday
Fr avant-hier
It avantieri
Pt anteontem

antecipado *adj* Pt
De vorzeitig (bezahlt)
En anticipated
Es anticipado
Fr anticipé
It anticipato

anteilsmäßig *adj* De
En pro rata
Es pro porcionalmente;
a prorata
Fr proportionnellement au
prorata
It proporzionalmente pro
rata
Pt proporcionalmente pro
rata

anteontem Pt
De vorgestern
En day before yesterday
Es anteayer
Fr avant-hier
It avantieri

anteporto *(m)* n Pt
De Außenhafen *(m)*
En outer harbour
Es antepuerto *(m)*
Fr avant-port *(m)*
It avamporto *(m)*

antepuerto *(m)* n Es
De Außenhafen *(m)*
En outer harbour
Fr avant-port *(m)*
It avamporto *(m)*
Pt anteporto *(m)*

anticipado *adj* Es
De vorzeitig (bezahlt)
En anticipated
Fr anticipé
It anticipato
Pt antecipado

anticipar *vb* Es
De vorschießen
En advance (money)
Am prepay
Fr avancer (de l'argent)
It anticipare
Pt adiantar

anticipare *vb* It
De vorschießen
En advance (money)
Am prepay
Es anticipar

Fr   avancer (de l'argent)
Pt   adiantar

anticipated adj En
De   vorzeitig (bezahlt)
Es   anticipado
Fr   anticipé
It   anticipato
Pt   antecipado

anticipato adj It
De   vorzeitig (bezahlt)
En   anticipated
Es   anticipado
Fr   anticipé
Pt   antecipado

anticipazione (f) n It
De   Vorschuß (m)
En   advance (of money)
Am   prepayment
Es   adelanto (m)
Fr   avance (f)
Pt   adiantamento (m)

anticipé adj Fr
De   vorzeitig (bezahlt)
En   anticipated
Es   anticipado
It   anticipato
Pt   antecipado

anticipo (m) n Es
De   Vorauszahlung (f)
En   advance payment
Fr   paiement par anticipation
     (m)
It   pagamento anticipato (m)
Pt   pagamento adiantado (m)

Antrag (m) n De
En   application; motion
Es   solicitud; moción (f)
Fr   demande; motion (f)
It   domanda; mozione (f)
Pt   requisição; moção (f)

Antragsformular (n) n De
En   application form; entry
     form
Es   formulario de solicitud; so-
     licitud de inscripción (m f)
Fr   formulaire de demande;
     feuille d'inscription (m f)
It   modulo di domanda; bol-
     letta d'entrata (m f)
Pt   formulário de requisição;
     impresso de admissão (m)

Antwort (f) n De
En   answer
Es   repuesta (f)
Fr   réponse (f)
It   risposta (f)
Pt   resposta (f)

anual adj Es, Pt
De   jährlich
En   annual
Fr   annuel
It   annuale

anualidad (f) n Es
De   Annuität (f)
En   annuity
Fr   annuité (f)
It   annualitá (f)
Pt   anuidade (f)

anualidad aplazada (f) Es
De   Anwartschaft auf
     Leibrente (f)
En   deferred annuity
Fr   annuité différée (f)
It   rendita vitalizia differita (f)
Pt   anuidade diferida (f)

anuidade (f) n Pt
De   Annuität (f)
En   annuity
Es   anualidad (f)
Fr   annuité (f)
It   annualitá (f)

anuidade diferida (f) Pt
De   Anwartschaft auf
     Leibrente (f)
En   deferred annuity
Es   anualidad aplazada (f)
Fr   annuité différée (f)
It   rendita vitalizia differita (f)

anulação (f) n Pt
De   Annullierung (f)
En   anulment
Es   anulación (f)
Fr   annulation (f)
It   annullamento (m)

anulación (f) n Es
De   Annullierung (f)
En   annulment
Fr   annulation (f)
It   annullamento (m)
Pt   anulação (f)

anular um prejuízo Pt
De   einen Verlust abschreiben
En   write off a loss

Es   cancelar una pérdida
Fr   amortir une perte
It   cancellare una perdita

anular un cheque Es
De   einen Scheck rückgängig
     machen
En   cancel a cheque
Am   cancel a check
Fr   annuler un chèque
It   annullare un assegno
Pt   cancelar um cheque

anunciante (m) n Es, Pt
De   Anzeiger (m)
En   advertiser
Fr   annonceur (m)
It   inserzionista (m)

anuncio (m) n Es
De   Anzeige (f)
En   advertisement
Fr   annonce (f)
It   annunzio (m)
Pt   anúncio (m)

anúncio (m) n Pt
De   Anzeige (f)
En   advertisement
Es   anuncio (m)
Fr   annonce (f)
It   annunzio (m)

anúncios classificados (m pl)
     Pt
De   Kleinanzeige (f)
En   classified advertisement
Es   anuncio por palabras
     (m pl)
Fr   petite annonce (f)
It   piccola pubblicità (f)

anuncio por palabras (m) Es
De   Kleinanzeige (f)
En   classified advertisement
Fr   petite annonce (f)
It   piccola pubblicità (f)
Pt   anúncios classificados
     (m pl)

anvertrauen vb De
En   entrust
Es   confiar
Fr   confier
It   affidare
Pt   confiar

Anwalt (m) n De
En   lawyer; barrister
Am   attorney

Es abogado *(m)*
Fr avocat *(m)*
It avvocato *(m)*
Pt advogado *(m)*

Anwartschaft auf Leibrente
   (f) De
En deferred annuity
Es anualidad aplazada *(f)*
Fr annuité différée *(f)*
It rendita vitalizia differita *(f)*
Pt anuidade diferida *(f)*

Anzahlung *(f)* n De
En deposit; payment on
   account
Es desembolso inicial; pago a
   cuenta *(m)*
Fr arrhes; (versement d'un) à
   compte *(f pl; m)*
It caparra; pagamento in
   conto *(f m)*
Pt sinal; pagamento à conta
   (m)

Anzeige *(f)* n De
En advertisement; advice
   note
Es anuncio; aviso *(m)*
Fr annonce; lettre d'avis *(f)*
It annunzio; lettera d'avviso
   (m f)
Pt anúncio; guia de remessa
   (m f)

Anzeiger *(m)* n De
En advertiser
Es anunciante *(m)*
Fr annonceur *(m)*
It inserzionista *(m)*
Pt anunciante *(m)*

an Zollfreilager De
En ex warehouse
Es puesto en almacén
Fr à prendre en entrepôt
It franco magazzino
Pt no armazém

ao par Pt
De al pari
En at par
Es al par
Fr au pair
It alla pari

à ordem da alfândega Pt
De unter Zollverschluß
En in bond

Es en aduanas
Fr en entrepôt
It sotto vincolo doganale

apalabrar *vb* Es
De anstellen
En engage; appoint
Am hire
Fr engager
It fissare
Pt empregar

aparatos eléctricos de casa
   (m pl) Es
De elektrische Haushaltsgüter
   (n pl)
En household electrical
   goods
Fr electro-ménager *(m)*
It elettrodomestici *(m pl)*
Pt electro-domésticos *(m pl)*

apartamento *(m)* n Es, Pt
De Etagenwohnung *(f)*
En flat
Am apartment
Fr appartement *(m)*
It appartamento *(m)*

apartment n Am
En flat
De Etagenwohnung *(f)*
Es apartamento *(m)*
Fr appartement *(m)*
It appartamento *(m)*
Pt apartamento *(m)*

apartment house Am
En block of flats
De Wohnungsgebäude *(n)*
Es bloque de pisos *(m)*
Fr immeuble *(m)*
It fabbricato di appartamenti
   (m)
Pt edifício de andares *(m)*

aplazamiento *(m)* n Es
De Vertagung *(f)*
En adjournment
Fr ajournement *(m)*
It aggiornamento *(m)*
Pt adiamento *(m)*

aplazar *vb* Es
De vertagen; zurückstellen;
   aufschieben
En adjourn; defer; hold over
Fr ajourner; différer
It aggiornare; differire
Pt adiar

apoderado *(m)* n Es
De Bevollmächtigte(r); Stell-
   vertreter *(m)*
En attorney; proxy
Fr mandataire *(m)*
It mandatario; procuratore
   (m)
Pt procurador *(m)*

apólice (de seguro) *(f)* n Pt
De Police *(f)*
En policy
Es poliza *(f)*
Fr police *(f)*
It polizza *(f)*

apólice com participação
   nos lucros *(f)* Pt
De Police mit Gewinnberech-
   tigung *(f)*
En with-profits policy
Am participating policy
Es póliza con beneficios *(f)*
Fr police avec participation
   aux bénéfices *(f)*
It polizza con profitti *(f)*

apólice de seguro de in-
   cêndio *(f)* Pt
De Feuerversicherungsschein
   (m)
En fire insurance policy
Es póliza de seguro de incen-
   dios *(f)*
Fr police incendie *(f)*
It polizza d'assicurazione in-
   cendio *(f)*

apólice de seguros *(f)* Pt
De Versicherungspolice *(f)*
En insurance policy
Es póliza de seguro *(f)*
Fr police d'assurance *(f)*
It polizza di assicurazione *(f)*

apólice flutuante *(f)* Pt
De laufende Police *(f)*
En floating policy
Es póliza flotante *(f)*
Fr police flottante *(f)*
It polizza flottante *(f)*

apólice liquidada *(f)* Pt
De beitragsfreie Police *(f)*
En paid-up policy
Es póliza liberada *(f)*
Fr assurance libérée *(f)*
It polizza interamente paga-
   ta *(f)*

aporcionamento *(m) n* Pt
De Verteilung *(f)*
En allotment
Es adjudicación *(f)*
Fr attribution *(f)*
It ripartizione *(f)*

a porte debido Es
De Portonachnahme
En carriage forward
Am F.O.B. shipping point
Fr en port dû
It porto assegnato
Pt transporte a pagar

a porte pagado Es
De franko
En carriage paid
Am freight charges paid
Fr port payé
It franco di porto
Pt porte pago

aposentação *(f) n* Pt
De Rücktritt; Pensionierung
(m f)
En retirement
Es retiro *(m)*
Fr retraite *(f)*
It ritiro *(m)*

apostilla *(f) n* Es
De Fußnote *(f)*
En footnote
Fr apostille *(f)*
It postilla *(f)*
Pt nota de rodapé *(f)*

apostille *(f) n* Fr
De Fußnote *(f)*
En footnote
Es apostilla *(f)*
It postilla *(f)*
Pt nota de rodapé *(f)*

appareil *(m) n* Fr
De Gerät; Anlage *(n f)*
En appliance; plant (industrial)
Es aparato; planta *(m f)*
It apparecchio; impianto *(m)*
Pt aparelho; instalação *(m f)*

appartamento *(m) n* It
De Etagenwohnung *(f)*
En flat
Am apartment
Es apartamento *(m)*
Fr appartement *(m)*
Pt apartamento *(m)*

appartamento ammobiliato
(m) It
De möblierte Mietwohnung *(f)*
En furnished flat
Am furnished apartment
Es piso amueblado *(m)*
Fr appartement meublé *(m)*
Pt andar mobilado *(m)*

appartamento con servizio
(m) It
De Etagenwohnung mit Bedienung *(f)*
En service flat
Es piso con servicio incluido
(m)
Fr appartement avec service
(m)
Pt andar com serviço incluído *(m)*

appartamento indipendente *(m)* It
De Einfamilienwohnung *(f)*
En self-contained flat
Es piso independiente completo *(m)*
Fr appartement indépendant
(m)
Pt andar independente *(m)*

appartement *(m) n* Fr
De Etagenwohnung *(f)*
En flat
Am apartment
Es apartamento *(m)*
It appartamento *(m)*
Pt apartamento *(m)*

appartement avec service
(m) Fr
De Etagenwohnung mit Bedienung *(f)*
En service flat
Es piso con servicio incluido
(m)
It appartamento con servizio
(m)
Pt andar com serviço incluído *(m)*

appartement indépendant
(m) Fr
De Einfamilienwohnung *(f)*
En self-contained flat
Es piso independiente completo *(m)*
It appartamento indipendente *(m)*
Pt andar independente *(m)*

appartement meublé *(m)* Fr
De möblierte Mietwohnung *(f)*
En furnished flat
Am furnished apartment
Es piso amueblado *(m)*
It appartamento ammobiliato *(m)*
Pt andar mobilado *(m)*

appel (de fonds) *(m)* Fr
De Kündigung (von Geldern)
(f)
En call (for funds)
Es llamada (de fonds) *(f)*
It richiesta (di fondi) *(f)*
Pt chamada (de fundos) *(f)*

appel téléphonique *(m)* Fr
De Anruf *(m)*
En telephone call
Es llamada telefónica *(f)*
It chiamata telefonica *(f)*
Pt chamada telefónica *(f)*

appel téléphonique interurbain *(m)* Fr
De Ferngespräch *(n)*
En trunk call
Am long distance call
Es llamada interurbana *(f)*
It comunicazione interurbana *(f)*
Pt chamada inter-urbana (tronicas) *(f)*

applicant (for a post) *(n)* En
De Bewerber *(m)*
Es candidato *(m)*
Fr candidat *(m)*
It candidato *(m)*
Pt candidato *(m)*

application *n* En
De Antrag *(m)*
Es solicitud *(f)*
Fr demande *(f)*
It domanda *(f)*
Pt requisição *(f)*

application form En
De Antragsformular *(n)*
Es formulario de solicitud *(m)*
Fr formulaire de demande *(m)*
It modulo di domanda *(m)*
Pt formulário de requisição *(m)*

appoint *vb* En
De ernennen
Es nombrar

Fr nommer
It nominare
Pt nomear

appointé *(m)* Fr
De Angestellte(r) *(m)*
En salaried employee
Es empleado a sueldo *(m)*
It stipendiato *(m)*
Pt assalariado *(m)*

appointed agent En
De Handelsvertreter *(m)*
Es agente nombrado *(m)*
Fr agent attitré *(m)*
It agente ufficiale *(m)*
Pt agente oficial *(m)*

appointment (meeting) *n* En
De Verabredung *(f)*
Es entrevista *(f)*
Fr entrevue *(f)*
It appuntamento *(m)*
Pt encontro *(m)*

apportion *vb* En
De zuteilen
Es repartir
Fr répartir
It ripartire
Pt atribuir

appraisal *n* En
De Abschätzung *(f)*
Es evaluación *(f)*
Fr évaluation *(f)*
It valutazione *(f)*
Pt avaliação *(f)*

appreciate (in value) *vb* En
De im Wert steigen
Es subir (en valor)
Fr apprécier
It aumentare (di valore)
Pt aumentar; subir

appréciateur *(m)* *n* Fr
De Schätzer *(m)*
En assessor
Es asesor *(m)*
It agente delle imposte *(m)*
Pt avaliador *(m)*

appreciation (in value) *n* En
De Wertsteigerung *(f)*
Es subida (en valor) *(f)*
Fr appréciation *(f)*
It aumento *(m)*
Pt aumento *(m)*

appréciation *(f)* *n* Fr
De Wertsteigerung; Pla-
   nungsgewinn *(f m)*
En appreciation; betterment
Es subida (en valor); plusvalía
   (f)
It aumento; plus-valore *(m)*
Pt aumento; melhoria *(f)*

apprécier *vb* Fr
De im Wert steigen
En appreciate (in value)
Es subir (en valor)
It aumentare (di valore)
Pt aumentar; subir

apprendista *(m)* *n* It
De Lehrling *(m)*
En apprentice
Am trainee
Es aprendiz *(m)*
Fr apprenti *(m)*
Pt aprendiz *(m)*

apprenti *(m)* *n* Fr
De Lehrling *(m)*
En apprentice
Am trainee
Es aprendiz *(m)*
It apprendista *(m)*
Pt aprendiz *(m)*

apprentice *n* En
Am trainee
De Lehrling *(m)*
Es aprendiz *(m)*
Fr apprenti *(m)*
It apprendista *(m)*
Pt aprendiz *(m)*

apprenticeship *n* En
Am trainee period
De Lehre *(f)*
Es aprendizaje *(m)*
Fr apprentissage *(m)*
It tirocinio *(m)*
Pt aprendizagem *(f)*

apprentissage *(m)* *n* Fr
De Lehre *(f)*
En apprenticeship
Am trainee period
Es aprendizaje *(m)*
It tirocinio *(m)*
Pt aprendizagem *(f)*

appropriarsi indebitamente
   It
De unterschlagen

En embezzle
Es defalcar
Fr détourner
Pt desfalcar

appropriation *n* En
De Zuführung *(f)*
Es apropiación *(f)*
Fr affectation *(f)*
It stanziamento *(m)*
Pt apropriação *(f)*

appropriation account En
De Rückstellungskonto *(n)*
Es cuenta de apropiación *(f)*
Fr compte d'affectation *(m)*
It conto di stanziamento *(m)*
Pt conta de apropriação *(f)*

appropriazione indebita *(f)* It
De Unterschlagung *(f)*
En embezzlement
Es defalco *(m)*
Fr détournement de fonds
   (m)
Pt desfalque *(m)*

appuntamento *(m)* *n* It
De Verabredung *(f)*
En appointment
Es entrevista *(f)*
Fr entrevue *(f)*
Pt encontro *(m)*

a premio Es
De über pari
En above par
Fr au-dessus du pair
It sopra la pari
Pt a prémio

a prémio Pt
De über pari
En above par
Es a premio
Fr au-dessus du pair
It sopra la pari

aprendiz *(m)* *n* Es, Pt
De Lehrling *(m)*
En apprentice
Am trainee
Fr apprenti *(m)*
It apprendista *(m)*

aprendizagem *(f)* *n* Pt
De Lehre *(f)*
En apprenticeship
Am trainee period

Es aprendizaje *(m)*
Fr apprentissage *(m)*
It tirocinio *(m)*

aprendizaje *(m) n* Es
De Lehre *(f)*
En apprenticeship
Am trainee period
Fr apprentissage *(m)*
It tirocinio *(m)*
Pt aprendizagem *(f)*

à prendre en entrepôt Fr
De an Zollfreilager
En ex warehouse
Es puesto en almacén
It franco magazzino
Pt no armazém

à prendre sur quai Fr
De ab Kai
En ex quay
Es en muelle
It sulla banchina
Pt ex-cais

après demain Fr
De übermorgen
En day after tomorrow
Es pasado mañana
It dopodomani
Pt depois de amanhã

apresentar demissão Pt
De den Rücktritt einreichen
En hand in one's resignation
Es presentar la dimisión
Fr remettre sa démission
It rassegnare le dimissioni

apresentar letra para aceite
Pt
De einen Wechsel vorlegen
En present a bill for accept-
ance
Es presentar una letra para
aceptación
Fr présenter une traite à
l'acceptation
It presentare una cambiale
per accettazione

apropiación *(f) n* Es
De Zuführung *(f)*
En appropriation
Fr affectation *(f)*
It stanziamento *(m)*
Pt apropriação *(f)*

apropriação *(f) n* Pt
De Zuführung *(f)*
En appropriation
Es apropiación *(f)*
Fr affectation *(f)*
It stanziamento *(m)*

aguas territoriales *(f pl)* Es
De Hoheitsgewässer *(n pl)*
En territorial waters
Fr eaux territoriales *(f pl)*
It acque territoriali *(f pl)*
Pt águas territoriais *(f pl)*

aquecimento central *(m)* Pt
De Zentralheizung *(f)*
En central heating
Es calefacción central *(f)*
Fr chauffage central *(m)*
It riscaldamento centrale *(m)*

a quem disser respeito Pt
De an alle, die es angeht
En to whom it may concern
Es a quien concierna
Fr à qui de droit
It a tutti gli interessati

à qui de droit Fr
De an alle, die es angeht
En to whom it may concern
Es a quien concierna
It a tutti gli interessati
Pt a quem disser respeito

a quien concierna Es
De an alle, die es angeht
En to whom it may concern
Fr à qui de droit
It a tutti gli interessati
Pt a quem disser respeito

aquisição *(f) n* Pt
De Erwerb *(m)*
En acquisition
Es adquisición *(f)*
Fr acquisition *(f)*
It acquisizione *(f)*

aquisições *(f pl)* Pt
De Einkäufe *(m pl)*
En purchases *(pl n)*
Es adquisiciones *(f pl)*
Fr achats *(m pl)*
It acquisti *(m pl)*

Arbeit *(f) n* De
En work
Es trabajo *(m)*
Fr travail *(m)*

It lavoro *(m)*
Pt trabalho *(m)*

Arbeiter *(m) n* De
En worker
Es trabajador *(m)*
Fr ouvrier *(m)*
It lavoratore *(m)*
Pt trabalhador *(m)*

Arbeitgeber *(m) n* De
En employer
Es patrono *(m)*
Fr employeur *(m)*
It datore di lavoro *(m)*
Pt patrão *(m)*

Arbeit in der Ausführung *(f)*
De
En work-in-progress
Am work in process
Es trabajo en curso *(m)*
Fr travaux en cours *(m pl)*
It lavoro in corso *(m)*
Pt trabalho em curso *(m)*

Arbeitsaufgabe *(f) n* De
En job specification
Es especificación del trabajo
(f)
Fr donnée d'exécution *(f)*
It specifica del lavoro *(f)*
Pt especificação de obra *(f)*

Arbeitsbedingungen *(f pl) n*
De
En working conditions
Es condiciones de trabajo
(f pl)
Fr conditions de travail *(f pl)*
It condizioni di lavoro *(f pl)*
Pt condições de trabalho *(f pl)*

Arbeitsbeschreibung *(f) n* De
En job description
Es descripción del trabajo *(f)*
Fr description du travail *(f)*
It descrizione del lavoro *(f)*
Pt descrição da tarefa *(f)*

Arbeitsbewertung *(f) n* De
En job evaluation
Es valoracion del trabajo *(f)*
Fr évaluation du travail *(f)*
It valutazione del lavoro *(f)*
Pt avaliação de tarefa *(f)*

Arbeitsbeziehungen *(f pl) n*
De
En industrial relations

47 Arbeitszeit- und Ablaufstudie

Es relaciones humanas industriales *(f pl)*
Fr relations humaines dans l'entreprise *(f pl)*
It relazioni nell'industria *(f pl)*
Pt relações industriais *(f pl)*

Arbeitseinkommen *(n) n* De
En earned income
Es renta del trabajo *(f)*
Fr revenu du travail *(m)*
It reddito di lavoro *(m)*
Pt receita de trabalho *(f)*

Arbeitserlaubnis *(n) n* De
En work permit
Es permiso de trabajo *(m)*
Fr permis de travail *(m)*
It permesso di lavoro *(m)*
Pt carta de trabalho *(f)*

Arbeitskonflikt *(m) n* De
En industrial dispute
Es conflicto laboral *(m)*
Fr conflit ouvrier *(m)*
It vertenza operaia *(f)*
Pt conflito de trabalho *(m)*

Arbeitskräfte *(f pl) n* De
En labour force
Es mano de obra *(f)*
Fr main d'œuvre *(m)*
It mano d'opera *(f)*
Pt trabalhadores; mão de obra *(m f)*

arbeitslos *adj* De
En out of work
Es parado; sin trabajo
Fr en chômage
It disoccupato
Pt desempregado

Arbeitslosenunterstützung *(f) n* De
En unemployment benefit
Es subsidio de paro *(m)*
Fr secours de chômage *(m)*
It indennità di disoccupazione *(f)*
Pt subsídio de desemprego *(m)*

Arbeitslosigkeit *(f) n* De
En unemployment
Es desempleo *(m)*
Fr chômage *(m)*
It disoccupazione *(f)*
Pt desemprego *(m)*

Arbeitsmarkt *(m) n* De
En labour market
Es mercado de mano de obra *(m)*
Fr marché du travail *(m)*
It mercato della mano d'opera *(m)*
Pt mercado de mão de obra *(m)*

Arbeitsnachweisstelle *(f) n* De
En employment exchange
Am state employment agency
Es bolsa de trabajo *(f)*
Fr bureau de placement *(m)*
It ufficio di collocamento *(m)*
Pt centro de serviços de emprego *(m)*

Arbeitsplatzwechsel *(m) n* De
En labour turnover
Es movimiento de la mano de obra *(m)*
Fr fluctuations de personnel *(f pl)*
It movimento della mano d'opera *(m)*
Pt movimento de trabalhadores *(m)*

Arbeitspsychologie *(f) n* De
En industrial psychology
Es psicología industrial *(f)*
Fr psychotechnique *(f)*
It psicologia industriale *(f)*
Pt psicologia industrial *(f)*

Arbeitsschicht *(f) n* De
En shift; turn
Es turno *(m)*
Fr équipe de travail *(f)*
It turno di lavoro *(m)*
Pt turno *(m)*

Arbeitsstreitigkeit *(f) n* De
En trade dispute
Es conflicto laboral *(m)*
Fr conflit du travail *(m)*
It vertenza di lavoro *(f)*
Pt conflito comercial *(m)*

Arbeitsstudie *(f) n* De
En work study
Es estudio del trabajo *(m)*
Fr étude du travail *(f)*
It studio di lavoro *(m)*
Pt estudo sobre trabalho *(m)*

Arbeitsstunde pro Mann *(f)* De
En man-hours
Es horas-hombre *(f pl)*
Fr heures-homme *(f pl)*
It ore-uomo *(f pl)*
Pt horas-homem *(f pl)*

Arbeitstag *(m) n* De
En working day
Es día laborable *(m)*
Fr jour ouvrable *(m)*
It giornata lavorativa *(f)*
Pt dia de trabalho *(m)*

Arbeitsteilung *(f) n* De
En division of labour
Es división del trabajo *(f)*
Fr division du travail *(f)*
It divisione del lavoro *(f)*
Pt divisão do trabalho *(f)*

Arbeitsunfall *(m) n* De
En industrial accident
Es accidente de trabajo *(m)*
Fr accident du travail *(m)*
It infortunio sul lavoro *(m)*
Pt acidente de trabalho *(m)*

Arbeitsverhältnis *(n pl) De*
En labour relations
Es relaciones patrón-obrero *(f pl)*
Fr rapports du travail *(m pl)*
It relazioni con la mano d'opera *(f pl)*
Pt relações de trabalho *(f pl)*

Arbeitswoche *(f) n* De
En working week
Es semana laboral *(f)*
Fr semaine de travail *(f)*
It settimana lavorativa *(f)*
Pt semana de trabalho *(f)*

Arbeitszeit *(f) n* De
En hours of work
Es jornada laboral *(f)*
Fr durée du travail *(f)*
It ore lavorative *(f pl)*
Pt horas de trabalho *(f pl)*

Arbeitszeit- und Ablaufstudie *(f)* De
En time and motion study
Es estudio de tiempo y progreso *(m)*
Fr étude du temps et mouvements *(f)*

It studio dei tempi e dei movimenti *(m)*
Pt análise do tempo e progresso *(f)*

arbitrador *(m) n* Es
De Schiedsrichter *(m)*
En arbitrator
Fr arbitre *(m)*
It arbitro *(m)*
Pt árbitro *(m)*

arbitrage *n* En
De Kursvergleich *(m)*
Es arbitraje *(m)*
Fr arbitrage *(m)*
It arbitraggio *(m)*
Pt arbitragem *(f)*

arbitrage *(m) n* Fr
De Kursvergleich; Schiedsgerichtsverfahren *(m n)*
En arbitrage; arbitration
Es arbitraje; arbitramento *(m)*
It arbitraggio; arbitrato *(m)*
Pt arbitragem *(f)*

arbitragem *(f) n* Pt
De Kursvergleich; Schiedsgerichtsverfahren *(m n)*
En arbitrage; arbitration
Es arbitraje; arbitramento *(m)*
Fr arbitrage *(m)*
It arbitraggio; arbitrato *(m)*

arbitrager *vb* Fr
De sich decken
En hedge
Es cubrirse
It coprirsi
Pt cobrir-se

arbitraggio *(m) n* It
De Kursvergleich *(m)*
En arbitrage
Es arbitraje *(m)*
Fr arbitrage *(m)*
Pt arbitragem *(f)*

arbitraje *(m) n* Es
De Kursvergleich *(m)*
En arbitrage
Fr arbitrage *(m)*
It arbitraggio *(m)*
Pt arbitragem *(f)*

arbitramento *(m) n* Es
De Schiedsgerichtsverfahren *(n)*

En arbitration
Fr arbitrage *(m)*
It arbitrato *(m)*
Pt arbitragem *(f)*

arbitration *n* En
De Schiedsgerichtsverfahren *(n)*
Es arbitramento *(m)*
Fr arbitrage *(m)*
It arbitrato *(m)*
Pt arbitragem *(f)*

arbitration award En
De Schiedsspruch *(m)*
Es sentencia arbitral *(f)*
Fr sentence arbitrale *(f)*
It lodo arbitrale *(m)*
Pt decisão de arbitragem *(f)*

arbitration board (court) En
De Schiedsgericht *(n)*
Es tribunal arbitral *(m)*
Fr cour d'arbitrage *(m)*
It tribunale arbitrale *(m)*
Pt tribunal de arbitragem *(m)*

arbitrato *(m) n* It
De Schiedsgerichtsverfahren *(n)*
En arbitration
Es arbitramento *(m)*
Fr arbitrage *(m)*
Pt arbitragem *(f)*

arbitrator *n* En
De Schiedsrichter *(m)*
Es arbitrador *(m)*
Fr arbitre *(m)*
It arbitro *(m)*
Pt árbitro *(m)*

arbitre *(m) n* Fr
De Schiedsrichter *(m)*
En arbitrator
Es arbitrador *(m)*
It arbitro *(m)*
Pt árbitro *(m)*

arbitro *(m) n* It
De Schiedsrichter *(m)*
En arbitrator
Es arbitrador *(m)*
Fr arbitre *(m)*
Pt árbitro *(m)*

árbitro *(m) n* Pt
De Schiedsrichter *(m)*
En arbitrator

Es arbitrador *(m)*
Fr arbitre *(m)*
It arbitro *(m)*

architect *n* En
De Architekt *(m)*
Es arquitecto *(m)*
Fr architecte *(m)*
It architetto *(m)*
Pt arquitecto *(m)*

architecte *(m) n* Fr
De Architekt *(m)*
En architect
Es arquitecto *(m)*
It architetto *(m)*
Pt arquitecto *(m)*

Architekt *(m) n* De
En architect
Es arquitecto *(m)*
Fr architecte *(m)*
It architetto *(m)*
Pt arquitecto *(m)*

architetto *(m) n* It
De Architekt *(m)*
En architect
Es arquitecto *(m)*
Fr architecte *(m)*
Pt arquitecto *(m)*

archivar *vb* Es
De aufreihen
En file
Fr classer
It archiviare
Pt arquivar

archiviare *vb* It
De aufreihen
En file
Es archivar
Fr classer
Pt arquivar

archivio *(m) n* It
De Akte *(f)*
En file
Es archivo *(m)*
Fr dossier *(m)*
Pt ficheiro *(m)*

archivo *(m) n* Es
De Akte *(f)*
En file
Fr dossier *(m)*
It archivio *(m)*
Pt ficheiro *(m)*

archivo de fichas *(m)* Es
De Kartei *(f)*
En card-index file
Fr fichier *(m)*
It schedario *(m)*
Pt ficheiro com índice *(m)*

área de chão *(f)* Pt
De Bodenfläche *(f)*
En floor space
Es superficie de piso *(f)*
Fr surface de plancher *(f)*
It superficie di pavimento *(f)*

area indigente *(f)* It
De Notstandsgebiet *(n)*
En distressed area
Es región deprimida *(f)*
Fr région déprimée *(f)*
Pt zona deprimida *(f)*

argent *(m)* n Fr
De Geld *(n)*
En money
Es dinero *(m)*
It denaro *(m)*
Pt dinhero *(m)*

argent à vue *(m)* Fr
De Sichtgelder *(n pl)*
En money on call
Es dinero a la vista *(m)*
It denaro a vista *(m)*
Pt dinheiro à ordem *(m)*

argent bon marché *(m)* Fr
De billiges Geld *(n)*
En cheap money
Es dinero barato *(m)*
It denaro a basso interesse
    (m)
Pt dinheiro barato *(m)*

argent cher *(m)* Fr
De teures Geld *(n)*
En dear money
Es dinero caro *(m)*
It denaro ad alto interesse
    (m)
Pt dinheiro caro *(m)*

argent comptant *(m)* Fr
De Bargeld *(n)*
En cash
Es dinhero contante *(m)*
It denaro contante *(m)*
Pt dinheiro de contado *(m)*

arithmetic mean En
De arithmetisches Mittel *(n)*
Es media aritmética *(f)*
Fr moyenne arithmétique *(f)*
It media aritmetica *(f)*
Pt média aritmética *(f)*

arithmetisches Mittel *(n)* De
En arithmetic mean
Es media aritmética *(f)*
Fr moyenne arithmétique *(f)*
It media aritmetica *(f)*
Pt média aritmética *(f)*

armazém *(m)* Pt
De Warenhaus; Warenlager
    (n)
En department store; ware-
    house, store
Es grandes almacenes; al-
    macén *(m pl; m)*
Fr grand magasin; magasin;
    entrepôt *(m)*
It grande magazzino; ma-
    gazzino *(m)*

armazém alfandegário *(m)* Pt
De Lager unter Zollverschluß
    (n)
En bonded warehouse
Es almacén de aduanas *(m)*
Fr entrepôt *(m)*
It magazzino doganale *(m)*

armazenamento *(m)* n Pt
De Lagerung *(f)*
En storage
Es almacenamiento *(m)*
Fr emmagasinage *(m)*
It magazzinaggio *(m)*

armazenar vb Pt
De lagern
En store
Es almacenar
Fr emmagasiner
It immagazzinare

armed forces En
De Streitkräfte *(f pl)*
Es fuerzas armadas *(f pl)*
Fr forces armées *(f pl)*
It forze armate *(f pl)*
Pt forças armadas *(f pl)*

arquitecto *(m)* n Es, Pt
De Architekt *(m)*
En architect
Fr architecte *(m)*
It architetto *(m)*

arquivar vb Pt
De aufreihen
En file
Es archivar
Fr classer
It archiviare

arrears pl n En
De Rückstand *(m)*
Es atrasos *(m pl)*
Fr arrérages *(m pl)*
It arretrati *(m pl)*
Pt atrasos *(m pl)*

arrendador *(m)* n Es
De Vermieter *(m)*
En lessor
Fr bailleur *(m)*
It locatore *(m)*
Pt senhorio; arrendador *(m)*

arrendatario *(m)* n Es
De Mieter *(m)*
En lessee
Fr locataire *(m)*
It locatario *(m)*
Pt locatário; arrendatário *(m)*

arrérages *(m pl)* Fr
De Rückstand *(m)*
En arrears
Es atrasos *(m pl)*
It arretrati *(m pl)*
Pt atrasos *(m pl)*

arretrati *(m pl)* It
De Rückstand *(m)*
En arrears
Es atrasos *(m pl)*
Fr arrérages *(m pl)*
Pt atrasos *(m pl)*

arretrati di paga *(m pl)* It
De Lohnnachzahlung *(f)*
En back pay
Es pago atrasado *(m)*
Fr rappel de traitement *(m)*
Pt vencimento atrasado *(m)*

arrhes *(f pl)* n Fr
De Anzahlung *(f)*
En deposit
Es desembolso inicial *(m)*
It caparra *(f)*
Pt sinal *(m)*

arriéré adj Fr
De rückständig
En overdue

Es vencido
It scaduto
Pt vencido

arriesgar *vb* Es
De wagen
En hazard
Fr hasarder
It arrischiare
Pt arriscar

arrimage *(m)* *n* Fr
De Verstauung *(f)*
En stowage
Es estiba *(f)*
It stivaggio *(m)*
Pt estiva *(f)*

arrimer *vb* Fr
De verstauen
En stow
Es estibar
It stivare
Pt estivar

arriscar *vb* Pt
De wagen
En hazard
Es arriesgar
Fr hasarder
It arrischiare

arrischiare *vb* It
De wagen
En hazard
Es arriesgar
Fr hasarder
Pt arriscar

arrival *n* En
De Ankunft *(f)*
Es llegada *(f)*
Fr arrivée *(f)*
It arrivo *(m)*
Pt chegada *(f)*

arrivée *(f)* *n* Fr
De Ankunft *(f)*
En arrival
Es llegada *(f)*
It arrivo *(m)*
Pt chegada *(f)*

arrivo *(m)* *n* It
De Ankunft *(f)*
En arrival
Es llegada *(f)*
Fr arrivée *(f)*
Pt chegada *(f)*

art de l'étalage *(m)* Fr
De Schaufensterdekoration *(f)*
En window-dressing
Es preparación de escaparates *(f)*
It allestimento delle vetrine *(m)*
Pt preparação de montras *(f)*

art de vendre *(m)* Fr
De Verkaufsgewandtheit *(f)*
En salesmanship
Es arte de vender *(m)*
It arte della vendita *(f)*
Pt ciência de vender *(f)*

arte della vendita *(f)* It
De Verkaufsgewandtheit *(f)*
En salesmanship
Es arte de vender *(m)*
Fr art de vendre *(m)*
Pt ciência de vender *(f)*

arte de vender *(m)* Es
De Verkaufsgewandtheit *(f)*
En salesmanship
Fr art de vendre *(m)*
It arte della vendita *(f)*
Pt ciência de vender *(f)*

article d'un livre journal *(m)* Fr
De Tagebuchsposten *(m)*
En journal-entry
Es asiento en el libro diario *(m)*
It registrazione a giornale *(f)*
Pt anotação de diário *(f)*

articles de luxe *(m pl)* Fr
De Luxuswaren *(f pl)*
En luxury goods
Es artículos de lujo *(m pl)*
It articoli di lusso *(m pl)*
Pt artigos de luxo *(m pl)*

articles de marque *(m pl)* Fr
De Markenwaren *(f pl)*
En branded goods
Es artículos de marca *(m pl)*
It articoli di marca *(m pl)*
Pt artigos de marca *(m pl)*

articles of association En
Am articles of incorporation
De Gesellschaftsvertrag *(m)*
Es artículos de asociación *(m pl)*
Fr contrat de société *(m)*

It statuto sociale *(m)*
Pt escritura de sociedade *(f)*

articles of incorporation Am
En articles of association
De Gesellschaftsvertrag *(m)*
Es artículos de asociación *(m pl)*
Fr contrat de société *(m)*
It statuto sociale *(m)*
Pt escritura de sociedade *(f)*

articoli di lusso *(m pl)* It
De Luxuswaren *(f pl)*
En luxury goods
Es artículos de lujo *(m pl)*
Fr articles de luxe *(m pl)*
Pt artigos de luxo *(m pl)*

articoli di marca *(m pl)* It
De Markenwaren *(f pl)*
En branded goods
Es artículos de marca *(m pl)*
Fr articles de marque *(m pl)*
Pt artigos de marca *(m pl)*

articoli di spesa *(m pl)* It
De Aufwendungsposten *(f pl)*
En items of expenditure
Es artículos de gasto *(m pl)*
Fr postes de dépense *(m pl)*
Pt itens de despesa *(m pl)*

articoli fantasia *(m pl)* It
De Modeartikel *(m pl)*
En fancy goods
Es artículos de fantasía *(m pl)*
Fr nouveautés *(f pl)*
Pt artigos de fantasia *(m pl)*

artículos de asociación *(m pl)* Es
De Gesellschaftsvertrag *(m)*
En articles of association
Am articles of incorporation
Fr contrat de société *(m)*
It statuto sociale *(m)*
Pt escritura de sociedade *(f)*

artículos de fantasía *(m pl)* Es
De Modeartikel *(m pl)*
En fancy goods
Fr nouveautés *(f pl)*
It articoli fantasia *(m pl)*
Pt artigos de fantasia *(m pl)*

artículos de gasto *(m pl)* Es
De Aufwendungsposten *(f pl)*
En items of expenditure

Fr postes de dépense *(m pl)*
It articoli di spesa *(m pl)*
Pt itens de despesa *(m pl)*

artículos de lujo *(m pl)* Es
De Luxuswaren *(f pl)*
En luxury goods
Fr articles de luxe *(m pl)*
It articoli di lusso *(m pl)*
Pt artigos de luxo *(m pl)*

artículos de marca *(m pl)* Es
De Markenwaren *(f pl)*
En branded goods
Fr articles de marque (m pl)
It articoli di marca *(m pl)*
Pt artigos de marca *(m pl)*

artigos à consignação *(m pl)*
Pt
De Kommissionsgüter *(n pl)*
En goods on consignment
Es mercancías en consigna-
ción *(f pl)*
Fr marchandises en con-
signation *(f pl)*
It merce in conto deposito *(f)*

artigos de cabedal *(m pl)* Pt
De Lederwaren *(f pl)*
En leather goods
Es marroquinería *(f)*
Fr maroquinerie *(f)*
It pelletterie *(f pl)*

artigos de consumo per-
duráveis *(m pl)* Pt
De dauerhafte Konsumgüter
(n pl)
En consumer durables
Es bienes de consumo duraderos *(m pl)*
Fr biens de consommation
durables *(m pl)*
It beni di consumo durabili
(m pl)

artigos de fantasia *(m pl)* Pt
De Modeartikel *(m pl)*
En fancy goods
Es artículos de fantasía *(m pl)*
Fr nouveautés *(f pl)*
It articoli fantasia *(m pl)*

artigos de luxo *(m pl)* Pt
De Luxuswaren *(f pl)*
En luxury goods
Es artículos de lujo *(m pl)*
Fr articles de luxe *(m pl)*
It articoli di lusso *(m pl)*

artigos de malha de lã *(m pl)* Pt
De Strickwaren *(f pl)*
En knitted goods
Es géneros de punto *(m pl)*
Fr bonneterie *(f)*
It maglieria *(f)*

artigos de marca *(m pl)* Pt
De Markenwaren *(f pl)*
En branded goods
Es artículos de marca *(m pl)*
Fr articles de marque *(m pl)*
It articoli di marca *(m pl)*

artigos sujeitos a aprovação
(m pl) Pt
De Probegüter *(n pl)*
En goods on approval
Es mercancías sujetas a
aprobación *(f pl)*
Fr marchandises à condition
(f pl)
It merce soggetta ad appro-
vazione *(f)*

ärztliche Untersuchung *(f)*
De
En medical examination
Es examen médico *(m)*
Fr examen médical *(m)*
It visita medica *(f)*
Pt inspecção médica *(f)*

asalariado *(m)* Es
De Lohnempfänger *(m)*
En wage earner
Fr salarié *(m)*
It salariato *(m)*
Pt assalariado *(m)*

asamblea general *(f)* Es
De Hauptversammlung; or-
dentliche Versammlung *(f)*
En general meeting; statutory
meeting
Fr assemblée générale; as-
semblée ordinaire *(f)*
It assemblea generale *(f)*
Pt assemblea geral; assem-
bleia estatutária *(f)*

asamblea general anual *(f)*
Es
De Jahreshauptversammlung
(f)
En annual general meeting
Am stockholders' meeting
Fr assemblée d'actionnaires
annuelle *(f)*

It assemblea generale
annuale *(f)*
Pt assembleia geral anual *(f)*

asamblea general extraor-
dinaria *(f)* Es
De außerordentliche Generalversammlung *(f)*
En extraordinary general
meeting
Fr assemblée générale ex-
traordinaire *(f)*
It assemblea generale
straordinaria *(f)*
Pt assembleia geral extraordinária *(f)*

asamblea general ordina-
ria *(f)* Es
De ordentliche Generalver-
sammlung *(f)*
En ordinary general meeting
Am stockholders' meeting
Fr assemblée générale *(f)*
It assemblea generale ordi-
naria *(f)*
Pt assembleia geral ordinária
(f)

ascender *vb* Es
De befördern
En promote
Fr donner de l'avancement à
It promuovere
Pt promover

ascendiendo a Es
De hinauslaufend auf
En amounting to
Fr à concurrence de
It ammontante a
Pt no montante de

ascenseur *(m)* n Fr
De Aufzug *(m)*
En lift
Am elevator
Es ascensor *(m)*
It ascensore *(m)*
Pt ascensor *(m)*

ascenso *(m)* n Es
De Beförderung *(f)*
En promotion
Fr avancement; promotion
(m f)
It avanzamento; promozione
(m f)
Pt promoção *(f)*

ascensor *(m) n* Es, Pt
De Aufzug *(m)*
En lift
Am elevator
Fr ascenseur *(m)*
It ascensore *(m)*

ascensore *(m) n* It
De Aufzug *(m)*
En lift
Am elevator
Es ascensor *(m)*
Fr ascenseur *(m)*
Pt ascensor *(m)*

asegurable *adj* Es
De versicherbar
En insurable
Fr assurable
It assicurabile
Pt susceptível de ser objecto
de seguro

asegurado *(m) n* Es
De Versicherte(r) *(m)*
En insured
Fr assuré *(m)*
It assicurato *(m)*
Pt titular de seguro *(m)*

asegurador *(m) n* Es
De Versicherer *(m)*
En insurer; underwriter
Fr assureur *(m)*
It assicuratore *(m)*
Pt segurador *(m)*

asegurar *vb* Es
De versichern
En insure
Fr assurer
It assicurare
Pt segurar

asesor *(m) n* Es
De Schätzer *(m)*
En assessor
Fr appréciateur *(m)*
It agente delle imposte *(m)*
Pt avaliador *(m)*

asesor administrativo *(m)* Es
De Geschäftsführungsberater
(m)
En management consultant
Fr ingénieur-conseil en or-
ganisation *(m)*
It consulente di direzione
aziendale *(m)*
Pt perito de administração *(m)*

asiento *(m) n* Es
De Eintragung *(f)*
En entry
Fr inscription *(f)*
It registrazione *(f)*
Pt lançamento *(m)*

asiento en el libro diario *(m)*
Es
De Tagebuchsposten *(m)*
En journal-entry
Fr article d'un livre journal *(m)*
It registrazione a giornale *(f)*
Pt anotação de diário *(f)*

asientos saldados *(m pl)* Es
De Ausgleichsposten *(m pl)*
En balancing items
Fr postes rééquilibrants
(m pl)
It voci di pareggio *(f pl)*
Pt valores de equilíbrio *(m pl)*

asignar *vb* Es
De verteilen
En allot
Fr attribuer
It assegnare
Pt atribuir

asistente *(m) n* Es
De Assistent *(m)*
En assistant
Fr commis *(m)*
It assistente *(m)*
Pt assistente *(m)*

asistente privado *(m)* Es
De persönlicher Assistent *(m)*
En personal assistant (PA)
Am administrative assistant
Fr fonctionnel *(m)*
It assistente privato *(m)*
Pt secretário *(m)*

asociación *(f) n* Es
De Verband *(m)*
En association
Fr association *(f)*
It associazione *(f)*
Pt associação *(f)*

asociación comercial *(f)* Es
De Unternehmerverband *(m)*
En trade association
Fr association professionelle
(f)
It associazione commerciale
(f)
Pt associação comercial *(f)*

**Asociación de Mercado
Libre de América Latina**
(f) Es
De Lateinamerikanische Frei-
handelszone *(f)*
En Latin American Free Trade
Association (LAFTA)
Fr Association Latino-
Américaine de Libre-
Échange *(f)*
It Assoziazione di Libero
Scambio dell'America La-
tina *(f)*
Pt Associação do Comércio
Livre da América Latina *(f)*

assalariado *(m) n* Pt
De Lohnempfänger *(m)*
En wage earner
Es asalariado *(m)*
Fr salarié *(m)*
It salariato *(m)*

assay *n* En
De Probe *(f)*
Es ensayo *(m)*
Fr essai *(m)*
It saggio *(m)*
Pt verificação *(f)*

assegnare *vb* It
De verteilen
En allot
Es asignar
Fr attribuer
Pt atribuir

assegnatario *(m) n* It
De Zessionar *(m)*
En assignee
Es cesionario *(m)*
Fr cessionnaire *(m)*
Pt cessionário *(m)*

assegno *(m) n* It
De Scheck *(m)*
En cheque
Am check
Es cheque *(m)*
Fr chèque *(m)*
Pt cheque *(m)*

assegno al portatore *(m)* It
De Inhaberscheck *(m)*
En cheque payable to bearer
Am check payable to bearer
Es cheque al portador *(m)*
Fr chèque payable au porteur
(m)
Pt cheque ao portador *(m)*

assegno aperto *(m)* It
De Inhaberscheck *(m)*
En open cheque
Es cheque abierto *(m)*
Fr chèque ouvert *(m)*
Pt cheque em branco *(m)*

assegno falsificato *(m)* It
De gefälschter Scheck *(m)*
En forged cheque
Es cheque falsificado *(m)*
Fr faux chèque *(m)*
Pt cheque falsificado *(m)*

assegno garantito *(m)* It
De bestätigter Scheck *(m)*
En certified cheque
Am certified check
Es cheque certificado *(m)*
Fr chèque certifié *(m)*
Pt cheque certificado *(m)*

assegno in bianco *(m)* It
De Blankoscheck *(m)*
En blank cheque
Am blank check
Es cheque en blanco *(m)*
Fr chèque en blanc *(m)*
Pt cheque em branco *(m)*

assegno postdatato *(m)* It
De nachdatierter Scheck *(m)*
En postdated cheque
Es cheque a fecha retrasada
   (m)
Fr chèque postdaté *(m)*
Pt cheque post-datado *(m)*

assegno sbarrato *(m)* It
De Versicherungsscheck *(m)*
En crossed cheque
Es cheque cruzado *(m)*
Fr chèque barré *(m)*
Pt cheque cruzado *(m)*

assegno turistico *(m)* It
De Reisescheck *(m)*
En traveller's cheque
Am traveler's check
Es cheque de viajero *(m)*
Fr chèque de voyage *(m)*
Pt cheque de viajante *(m)*

assemblea dei creditori *(f)* It
De Gläubigerversammlung *(f)*
En meeting of creditors
Es reunión de acreedores *(f)*
Fr assemblée de créanciers
   (f)
Pt assembleia de credores *(f)*

assemblea generale *(f)* It
De Hauptversammlung; or-
   dentliche Versammlung *(f)*
En general meeting; statutory
   meeting
Es asamblea general *(f)*
Fr assemblée générale; as-
   semblée ordinaire *(f)*
Pt assembleia geral; assem-
   bleia estatutária *(f)*

**assemblea generale
annuale** *(f)* It
De Jahreshauptversammlung
   (f)
En annual general meeting
Am stockholders' meeting
Es asamblea general anual *(f)*
Fr assemblée d'actionnaires
   annuelle *(f)*
Pt assembleia geral anual *(f)*

**assemblea generale
straordinaria** *(f)* It
De außerordentliche Generalversammlung *(f)*
En extraordinary general
   meeting
Es asamblea general extraordinaria *(f)*
Fr assemblée générale ex-
   traordinaire *(f)*
Pt assembleia geral extraordinária *(f)*

**assemblée d'actionnaires
annuelle** *(f)* Fr
De Jahreshauptversammlung
   (f)
En annual general meeting
Am stockholders' meeting
Es asamblea general anual *(f)*
It assemblea generale annu-
   ale *(f)*
Pt assembleia geral anual *(f)*

assemblée de créanciers *(f)*
   Fr
De Gläubigerversammlung *(f)*
En meeting of creditors
Es concurso de acreedores
   (m)
It convocazione dei creditori
   (f)
Pt reunão de credores *(f)*

assemblée générale *(f)* Fr
De Hauptversammlung; or-
   dentliche Generalver-
   sammlung *(f)*

En general meeting; ordinary
   general meeting
Es asamblea general; asamblea general ordinaria *(f)*
It assemblea generale; assemblea generale ordinaria *(f)*
Pt assembleia geral; assembleia geral ordinária *(f)*

**assemblée générale
extraordinaire** *(f)* Fr
De außerordentliche Generalversammlung *(f)*
En extraordinary general
   meeting
Es asamblea general extraordinaria *(f)*
It assemblea generale
   straordinaria *(f)*
Pt assembleia geral extraordinária *(f)*

assemblée ordinaire *(f)* Fr
De ordentliche Versammlung
   (f)
En statutory meeting
Es asamblea general *(f)*
It assemblea generale *(f)*
Pt assembleia estatutária *(f)*

assembleia de credores *(f)*
   Pt
De Gläubigerversammlung *(f)*
En meeting of creditors
Es reunión de acreedores *(f)*
Fr assemblée de créanciers
   (f)
It assemblea dei creditori *(f)*

assembleia estatutária *(f)* Pt
De ordentliche Versammlung
   (f)
En statutory meeting
Es asamblea general *(f)*
Fr assemblée ordinaire *(f)*
It assemblea generale *(f)*

assembleia geral *(f)* Pt
De Hauptversammlung *(f)*
En general meeting
Es asamblea general *(f)*
Fr assemblée générale *(f)*
It assemblea generale *(f)*

assembleia geral anual *(f)* Pt
De Jahreshauptversammlung
   (f)
En annual general meeting

Am stockholders' meeting
Es asamblea general anual (f)
Fr assemblée d'actionnaires
annuelle (f)
It assemblea generale annuale (f)

assembleia geral extraordinária (f) Pt
De außerordentliche Generalversammlung (f)
En extraordinary general meeting
Es asamblea general extraordinaria (f)
Fr assemblée générale extraordinaire (f)
It assemblea generale straordinaria (f)

assembleia geral ordinária (f) Pt
De ordentliche Generalversammlung (f)
En ordinary general meeting
Am stockholders' meeting
Es asamblea general ordinaria (f)
Fr assemblée générale (f)
It assemblea generale ordinaria (f)

assembly line En
De Montageband (n)
Es linea de montaje (f)
Fr chaîne de montage (f)
It catena di montaggio (f)
Pt cadeia de montagem (f)

assente (m) n It
De Abwesende(r) (m)
En absentee
Es ausente (m)
Fr manquant (m)
Pt ausente (m)

assenteismo (m) n It
De unerlaubte Abwesenheit (f)
En absenteeism
Es ausentismo (m)
Fr absentéisme (m)
Pt absentismo (m)

assess damages En
De den Schadenersatzbetrag feststellen
Es evaluar daños
Fr fixer des dommages- intérêts

It valutare i danni
Pt avaliar os danos

assessment n En
De Besteuerung (f)
Es evaluación (f)
Fr imposition (f)
It imposta (f)
Pt balanço fiscal (m)

assessor n En
De Schätzer (m)
Es asesor (m)
Fr appréciateur (m)
It agente delle imposte (m)
Pt avaliador (m)

asset n En
De Aktivposten (m)
Es activo (m)
Fr actif (m)
It attivo (m)
Pt valor (m)

assets and liabilities En
De Aktiva und Passiva (n pl)
Es activo y pasivo (m)
Fr actif et passif (m)
It attivo e passivo (m)
Pt activo e passivo (m)

asset value En
De Aktivwert (m)
Es valor en activo (m)
Fr valeur de l'actif (f)
It valore in attivo (m)
Pt valor do activo (m)

assicurabile adj It
De versicherbar
En insurable
Es asegurable
Fr assurable
Pt susceptível de ser objecto de seguro

assicurare vb It
De versichern
En insure
Es asegurar
Fr assurer
Pt segurar

assicurato (m) n It
De Versicherte(r) (m)
En insured
Es asegurado (m)
Fr assuré (m)
Pt titular de seguro (m)

assicuratore (m) n It
De Versicherer (m)
En insurer; underwriter
Es asegurador (m)
Fr assureur (m)
Pt segurador (m)

assicurazione (f) n It
De Versicherung (f)
En assurance
Es seguro (m)
Fr assurance (f)
Pt seguro (m)

assicurazione contro i rischi di guerra (f) It
De Kriegsrisikoversicherung (f)
En war-risk insurance
Es seguro contra riesgo de guerra (m)
Fr assurance du risque de guerre (f)
Pt seguro contra risco de guerra (m)

assicurazione contro terzi (f) It
De Haftpflichtversicherung (f)
En third-party insurance
Es seguro contra responsabilidad civil (m)
Fr assurance responsabilité civile (RC) (f)
Pt seguro contra terceiros (m)

assicurazione corpo (m) It
De Kaskoversicherung (f)
En hull insurance
Es seguro del casco (m)
Fr assurance sur le corps (f)
Pt seguro do casco (m)

assicurazione credito (f) It
De Kreditversicherung (f)
En credit insurance
Es seguro crediticio (m)
Fr assurance crédit (f)
Pt seguro de crédito (m)

assicurazione di gruppo (f) It
De Gruppenversicherung (f)
En group insurance
Es seguro de grupo (m)
Fr assurance de groupe (f)
Pt seguro de grupo (m)

assicurazione domestica (f) It
De Wohnungsversicherung (f)

En household insurance
Es seguro de casa *(m)*
Fr assurance ménagère *(f)*
Pt seguro de casa *(m)*

assicurazione dotale *(f)* It
De Erlebensversicherung *(f)*
En endowment policy
Es póliza dotal *(f)*
Fr assurance à terme fixe *(f)*
Pt título de doação *(m)*

assicurazione incendio *(f)* It
De Feuerversicherung *(f)*
En fire insurance
Es seguro de incendios *(m)*
Fr assurance incendie *(f)*
Pt seguro de incêndio *(m)*

assicurazione malattia *(f)* It
De Krankenversicherung *(f)*
En health insurance
Es seguro de enfermedad *(m)*
Fr assurance maladie *(f)*
Pt seguro de doença *(m)*

assicurazione mista *(f)* It
De kombinierte Versicherung
(f)
En comprehensive insurance
Es seguro combinado *(m)*
Fr assurance combinée *(f)*
Pt seguro compreensivo *(m)*

assicurazione sulla vita *(f)* It
De Lebensversicherung *(f)*
En life assurance
Am life insurance
Es seguro de vida *(m)*
Fr assurance sur la vie *(f)*
Pt seguro de vida *(m)*

assiette de l'impôt *(f)* Fr
De Steuerveranlagung *(f)*
En tax base
Es base contributiva *(f)*
It ripartizione della
tassazione *(f)*
Pt base de imposto *(f)*

assignation *(f)* n Fr
De Vorladung *(f)*
En writ
Es auto; orden *(m f)*
It citazione *(f)*
Pt citação; ordem *(f m)*

assignee n En
De Zessionar *(m)*
Es cesionario *(m)*

Fr cessionnaire *(m)*
It assegnatario *(m)*
Pt cessionário *(m)*

assignment n En
De Übertragung *(f)*
Es cesión *(f)*
Fr cession *(f)*
It cessione *(f)*
Pt consignação *(f)*

assignor n En
De Überträger *(m)*
Es cesionista *(m)*
Fr cédant *(m)*
It cedente *(m)*
Pt cessionista *(m)*

assinatura *(f)* n Pt
De Unterschrift; Abonnement
(f n)
En signature; subscription
Es firma; abono *(f m)*
Fr signature; abonnement
(f m)
It firma; abonnamento *(f m)*

assinatura em branco *(f)* Pt
De Blankounterschrift *(f)*
En blank signature
Es firma en blanco *(f)*
Fr blanc-seing *(m)*
It firma in bianco *(f)*

assistant n En
De Assistent *(m)*
Es asistente *(m)*
Fr commis *(m)*
It assistente *(m)*
Pt assistente *(m)*

assistant manager En
De Unterdirektor *(m)*
Es sub-director *(m)*
Fr sous-directeur *(m)*
It vice-direttore *(m)*
Pt subdirector *(m)*

Assistent *(m)* n De
En assistant
Es asistente *(m)*
Fr commis *(m)*
It assistente *(m)*
Pt assistente *(m)*

assistente *(m)* n It, Pt
De Assistent *(m)*
En assistant
Es asistente *(m)*
Fr commis *(m)*

assistente privato *(m)* It
De persönlicher Assistent *(m)*
En personal assistant (PA)
Am administrative assistant
Es asistente privado *(m)*
Fr fonctionnel *(m)*
Pt secretário *(m)*

associação *(f)* n Pt
De Verband *(m)*
En association
Es asociación *(f)*
Fr association *(f)*
It associazione *(f)*

associação comercial *(f)* Pt
De Unternehmerverband *(m)*
En trade association
Es asociación comercial *(f)*
Fr association professionnel-
le *(f)*
It associazione commerciale
(f)

**Associação do Comércio
Livre da América Latina**
(f) Pt
De Lateinamerikanische Frei-
handelszone *(f)*
En Latin American Free Trade
Association (LAFTA)
Es Asociación de Mercado
Libre de América Latina *(f)*
Fr Association Latino-
Américaine de Libre-
Échange *(f)*
It Associazione di Libero
Scambio dell'America
Latina *(f)*

association n En, Fr *(f)*
De Verband *(m)*
Es asociación *(f)*
It associazione *(f)*
Pt associação *(f)*

**Association Latino-Améri-
caine de Libre-Échange**
(f) Fr
De Lateinamerikanische Frei-
handelszone *(f)*
En Latin American Free Trade
Association (LAFTA)
Es Asociación de Mercado
Libre de América Latina *(f)*
It Associazione di Libero
Scambio dell'America
Latina *(f)*
Pt Associação do Comércio
Livre da América Latina *(f)*

associazione commerciale
(f) It
De Unternehmerverband *(m)*
En trade association
Es asociación comercial *(f)*
Fr association profession-
nelle *(f)*
Pt associação comercial *(f)*

**Associazione di Libero
Scambio dell'America
Latina** *(f)* It
De Lateinamerikanische Frei-
handelszone *(f)*
En Latin American Free Trade
Association (LAFTA)
Es Asociación de Mercado
Libre de América Latina *(f)*
Fr Association Latine-
Américaine de Libre-
Échange *(f)*
Pt Associação do Comércio
Livre da América Latina *(f)*

associé *(m)* n Fr
De Teilhaber *(m)*
En partner
Es socio *(m)*
It socio *(m)*
Pt sócio *(m)*

associé actif *(m)* Fr
De aktiver Teilhaber *(m)*
En working partner
Es socio activo *(m)*
It socio attivo *(m)*
Pt sócio actuante *(m)*

associé en second *(m)* Fr
De jüngerer Teilhaber *(m)*
En junior partner
Es segundo asociado *(m)*
It socio giovane *(m)*
Pt sócio júnior *(m)*

assurable *adj* Fr
De versicherbar
En insurable
Es asegurable
It assicurabile
Pt susceptível de ser objecto
de seguro

assurance n En
De Versicherung *(f)*
Es seguro *(m)*
Fr assurance *(f)*
It assicurazione *(f)*
Pt seguro *(m)*

assurance *(f)* n Fr
De Versicherung *(f)*
En insurance; assurance
Es seguro *(m)*
It assicurazione *(f)*
Pt seguro *(m)*

assurance à terme fixe *(f)* Fr
De Erlebensversicherung *(f)*
En endowment policy
Es póliza dotal *(f)*
It assicurazione dotale *(f)*
Pt título de doação *(m)*

assurance combinée *(f)* Fr
De kombinierte Versicherung
(f)
En comprehensive insurance
Es seguro combinado *(m)*
It assicurazione mista *(f)*
Pt seguro compreensivo *(m)*

assurance crédit *(f)* Fr
De Kreditversicherung *(f)*
En credit insurance
Es seguro crediticio *(m)*
It assicurazione credito *(f)*
Pt seguro de crédito *(m)*

assurance de groupe *(f)* Fr
De Gruppenversicherung *(f)*
En group insurance
Es seguro de grupo *(m)*
It assicurazione di gruppo *(f)*
Pt seguro de grupo *(m)*

**assurance du risque de
guerre** *(f)* Fr
De Kriegsrisikoversicherung
(f)
En war-risk insurance
Es seguro contra riesgo de
guerra *(m)*
It assicurazione contro i
rischi di guerra *(f)*
Pt seguro contra risco de
guerra *(m)*

assurance incendie *(f)* Fr
De Feuerversicherung *(f)*
En fire insurance
Es seguro de incendios *(m)*
It assicurazione incendio *(f)*
Pt seguro de incêndio *(m)*

assurance libérée *(f)* Fr
De beitragsfreie Police *(f)*
En paid-up policy
Es póliza liberada *(f)*

It polizza interamente
pagata *(f)*
Pt apólice liquidada *(f)*

assurance maladie *(f)* Fr
De Krankenversicherung *(f)*
En health insurance
Es seguro de enfermedad *(m)*
It assicurazione malattia *(f)*
Pt seguro de doença *(m)*

assurance ménagère *(f)* Fr
De Wohnungsversicherung *(f)*
En household insurance
Es seguro de casa *(m)*
It assicurazione domestica
(f)
Pt seguro de casa *(m)*

assurance mutuelle *(f)* Fr
De Versicherung auf Gegen-
seitigkeit *(f)*
En mutual insurance
Es coaseguro *(m)*
It mutua assicurazione *(f)*
Pt seguro mútuo *(m)*

**assurance responsabilité
civile (RC)** *(f)* Fr
De Haftpflichtversicherung *(f)*
En third-party insurance
Es seguro contra responsabi-
lidad civil *(m)*
It assicurazione contro terzi
(f)
Pt seguro contra terceiros *(m)*

assurance sur la vie *(f)* Fr
De Lebensversicherung *(f)*
En life assurance
Am life insurance
Es seguro de vida *(m)*
It assicurazione sulla vita *(f)*
Pt seguro de vida *(m)*

assurance sur le corps *(f)* Fr
De Kaskoversicherung *(f)*
En hull insurance
Es seguro del casco *(m)*
It assicurazione corpo *(m)*
Pt seguro do casco *(m)*

assuré *(m)* n Fr
De Versicherte(r) *(m)*
En insured
Es asegurado *(m)*
It assicurato *(m)*
Pt titular de seguro *(m)*

assurer *vb* Fr
De versichern
En insure
Es asegurar
It assicurare
Pt segurar

assureur *(m) n* Fr
De Versicherer *(m)*
En insurer; underwriter
Es asegurador *(m)*
It assicuratore *(m)*
Pt segurador *(m)*

asta *(f) n* It
De Versteigerung *(f)*
En auction
Es subasta *(f)*
Fr vente aux enchères *(f)*
Pt leilão *(m)*

astenersi *vb* It
De seine Stimme enthalten
En abstain
Es abstenerse
Fr s'abstenir
Pt abster-se

astillero *(m) n* Es
De Schiffswerft *(f)*
En dockyard
Fr chantier de construction
de navires *(m)*
It cantiere *(m)*
Pt estaleiro *(m)*

a termine It
De Termin-
En forward
Es a término
Fr en avant; à terme
Pt adiante

a término Es
De Termin-
En forward
Fr en avant; à terme
It a termine
Pt adiante

atesoramiento *(m) n* Es
De Hortung *(f)*
En hoard
Fr thésaurisation *(f)*
It ammasso *(m)*
Pt acumulação *(f)*

a testa It
De pro Kopf
En per capita
Es por cabeza
Fr par tête
Pt per capita

at par En
De al pari
Es al par
Fr au pair
It alla pari
Pt ao par

atracagem *(f) n* Pt
De Kaigold *(n)*
En wharfage
Es muellaje *(m)*
Fr quayage *(m)*
It diritto di sosta *(m)*

atraso *(m) n* Pt
De Verzug *(m)*
En delay
Es retraso *(m)*
Fr retard; délai *(m)*
It ritardo *(m)*

atrasos *(m pl) n* Es, Pt
De Rückstand *(m)*
En arrears *pl n*
Fr arrérages *(m pl)*
It arretrati *(m pl)*

atribuir *vb* Pt
De verteilen; zuteilen
En allot; apportion
Es asignar; repartir
Fr attribuer; répartir
It assegnare; ripartire

at sight En
De bei Sicht
Es a la vista
Fr à vue
It a vista
Pt à vista

attache-papiers *(m) n* Fr
De Büroklammer *(f)*
En paper clip
Es sujetapapeles *(m)*
It fermacarte *(m)*
Pt grampo *(m)*

attività in esaurimento *(f pl)* It
De kurzlebige Aktiva *(n pl)*
En wasting assets
Am depleting assets

Es activo gastable *(m)*
Fr actifs défectibles *(m pl)*
Pt bens em uso ou deterio-
ração *(m pl)*

attivo *(m) n* It
De Aktivposten *(m)*
En asset
Es activo *(m)*
Fr actif *(m)*
Pt valor *(m)*

attivo *adj* It
De wirksam
En operative
Es operativo; activo
Fr actif
Pt efectivo; em vigor

attivo congelato *(m)* It
De eingefrorene Guthaben *(n
pl)*
En frozen assets
Es activos congelados *(m pl)*
Fr fonds bloqués *(m pl)*
Pt bens do activo congela-
dos *(m pl)*

attivo e passivo *(m)* It
De Aktiva und Passiva *(n pl)*
En assets and liabilities
Es activo y passivo *(m)*
Fr actif et passif *(m)*
Pt activo e passivo *(m)*

attivo liquido *(m)* It
De Umlaufvermögen *(n)*
En current assets
Es activo realizable *(m)*
Fr actif courant *(m)*
Pt bens no activo actual
(m pl)

attivo netto *(m)* It
De Reinvermögen *(n)*
En net assets
Es activo neto *(m)*
Fr actif net *(m)*
Pt bens líquidos *(m pl)*

atto *(m) n* It
De Urkunde *(f)*
En deed; document
Es título; escritura *(m f)*
Fr acte; titre *(m)*
Pt título; escritura *(m f)*

atto a tenere il mare It
De seefest
En seaworthy
Es marinero
Fr en état de navigabilité
Pt em condições de navega-
ção

**atto costitutivo e statuto
sociale** (m) It
De Statuten (f pl)
En Memorandum and Articles
of Association
Am articles of incorporation
Es estatutos; carta orgánica
(m pl; f)
Fr statuts; acte constitutif (m
pl; m)
Pt estatuto de associação (m)

atto di accordo (m) It
De Vergleichsabkommen (n)
En deed of arrangement
Es acta de disposición (f)
Fr contrat d'arrangement (m)
Pt escritura de acordo (f)

atto di cessione (m) It
De Abtretungsvertrag (m)
En deed of assignment
Es título de asignación (m)
Fr acte attributif (m)
Pt título de consignação (m)

atto di concordato (m) It
De Vergleichsabkommen (n)
En deed of composition
Es concordato (m)
Fr concordat (m)
Pt concordata (por escrito) (f)

atto di nazionalita (m) It
De Schiffsregister (n)
En ship's register
Es registro del barco (m)
Fr certificat d'immatriculation
(m)
Pt registo do navio (m)

atto di trapasso (m) It
De Übertragungsvertrag (m)
En transfer deed
Es escritura de transferencia
(f)
Fr acte de cession (m)
Pt título de transferência (m)

atto ipotecario (m) It
De Verpfändungsurkunde (f)
En letter of hypothecation
Es carta de hipoteca (f)
Fr lettre hypothécaire (f)
Pt carta de hipoteca (f)

attorney n En
De Bevollmächtigte(r) (m)
Es apoderado (m)
Fr mandataire (m)
It mandatario (m)
Pt procurador (m)

attorney n Am
En barrister
De Anwalt (m)
Es abogado (m)
Fr avocat (m)
It avvocato (m)
Pt advogado (m)

attribuer vb Fr
De verteilen
En allot
Es asignar
It assegnare
Pt atribuir

attribution (f) n Fr
De Verteilung (f)
En allotment
Es adjudicación (f)
It ripartizione (f)
Pt aporcionamento (m)

attuare vb It
De bewerkstelligen; ausfüh-
ren
En implement
Es hacer efectivo; ejecutar
Fr exécuter
Pt executar

attuariale adj It
De versicherungsmathema-
tisch
En actuarial
Es actuarial
Fr actuariel
Pt actuarial

attuario (m) n It
De Aktuar (m)
En actuary
Es actuario (m)
Fr actuaire (m)
Pt actuário (m)

a tutti gli interessati It
De an alle, die es angeht
En to whom it may concern
Es a quien concierna
Fr à qui de droit
Pt a quem disser respeito

at warehouse En
De auf Lager
Es en almacén
Fr en dépôt
It in deposito
Pt em armazém

au-dessus du pair Fr
De über pari
En above par
Es a premio
It sopra la pari
Pt a prémio

auction n En
De Versteigerung (f)
Es subasta (f)
Fr vente aux enchères (f)
It asta (f)
Pt leilão (m)

auctioneer n En
De Versteigerer (m)
Es subastador (m)
Fr commissaire-priseur (m)
It venditore all'asta (m)
Pt leiloeiro (m)

audio-dactilógrafa (f) n Pt
De Audiotypistin (f)
En audio-typist
Am dictaphone operator
Es audio-mecanógrafa (f)
Fr dictaphoniste (f)
It dittafonista (f)

audio-mecanógrafa (f) n Es
De Audiotypistin (f)
En audio-typist
Am dictaphone operator
Fr dictaphoniste (f)
It dittafonista (f)
Pt audio-dactilógrafa (f)

audio-typist n En
Am dictaphone operator
De Audiotypistin (f)
Es audio-mecanógrafa (f)
Fr dictaphoniste (f)
It dittafonista (f)
Pt audio-dactilógrafa (f)

Audiotypistin (f) n De
En audio-typist
Am dictaphone operator
Es audio-mecanógrafa (f)
Fr dictaphoniste (f)
It dittafonista (f)
Pt audio-dactilógrafa (f)

audio-visivo adj It
De audiovisuell
En audio-visual
Es audio-visual
Fr audio-visuel
Pt audio-visual

audio-visual adj En, Es, Pt
De audiovisuell
Fr audio-visuel
It audio-visivo

audio-visuel adj Fr
De audiovisuell
En audio-visual
Es audio-visual
It audio-visivo
Pt audio-visual

audiovisuell adj De
En audio-visual
Es audio-visual
Fr audio-visuel
It audio-visivo
Pt audio-visual

audit n En
De Bücherrevision (f)
Es revisión (examen) de cuen-
    tas (f)
Fr vérification comptable (f)
It revisione dei conti (f)
Pt fiscalização de contas (f)

audit vb En
De prüfen
Es revisar
Fr vérifier et certifier
It rivedere
Pt fiscalizar as contas

audited accounts En
De geprüfte Geschäftsbücher
    (n pl)
Es cuentas revisadas (f pl)
Fr comptes vérifiés et certi-
    fiés (m pl)
It conti verificati e certificati
    (m pl)
Pt contas fiscalizadas (f pl)

auditor n En
De Bücherrevisor (m)
Es revisor de conti (m)
Fr réviseur des comptes (m)
It sindaco (m)
Pt fiscal de contas (m)

auditor's report En
De Bericht des Abschlußprü-
    fers (m)
Es informe de los intervento-
    res (m)
Fr rapport des vérificateurs
    des comptes (m)
It relazione dei sindaci (f)
Pt relatório do fiscal de
    contas (m)

auf den Markt bringen De
En launch (a product)
Es lanzar (un producto)
Fr lancer sur le marché
It lanciare (un prodotto)
Pt lançar (um produto)

aufdringliches Verkaufen (n)
    De
En hard sell
Es venta insistente (f)
Fr vente débrouillarde (f)
It vendita facendo sforzo (f)
Pt venda insistente (f)

aufgeben vb De
En give up
Es renunciar
Fr céder
It cedere
Pt desistir

aufgelaufene Zinsen (m pl)
    De
En accrued interest
Es interés acumulado (m)
Fr intérêts accumulés (m pl)
It interesse maturato (m)
Pt juro acumulado (m)

aufgeschobene Schulden (f
    pl) De
En deferred liabilities
Es pasivo transitorio (m)
Fr passif différé (m)
It passività differite (f pl)
Pt passivo adiado (m)

auf Lager De
En at warehouse
Es en almacén

Fr en dépôt
It in deposito
Pt em armazém

auflaufen vb De
En accrue
Es acumular
Fr accumuler
It accumularsi
Pt acumular

Auflaufen (n) n De
En accrual
Es acumulación (f)
Fr accumulation (f)
It maturazione (f)
Pt acumulação (f)

auflegen (ein Schiff) vb De
En lay-up
Es desarmar
Fr désarmer
It disarmare
Pt desarmar

Auflösung (f) n De
En dissolution
Es disolución (f)
Fr dissolution (f)
It scioglimento (m)
Pt dissolução (f)

aufreihen vb De
En file
Es archivar
Fr classer
It archiviare
Pt arquivar

Aufruhr und innere Unruhen
    De
En riot and civil commotion
Es revueltas y conmociones
    civiles
Fr émeutes et désordres
It rivolte e moti civili
Pt motins e perturbações civis

aufschieben vb De
En hold over
Es aplazar; diferir
Fr différer
It differire
Pt diferir; adiar

aufschiebende Bedingung
    (f) De
En condition precedent
Es previa condición (f)

Fr condition suspensive *(f)*
It condizione sospensiva *(f)*
Pt condição prévia *(f)*

Aufschlag *(m) n* De
En addition
Es adición *(f)*
Fr addition *(f)*
It addizione *(f)*
Pt adição *(f)*

Aufseher *(m) n* De
En supervisor
Es supervisor *(m)*
Fr surveillant *(m)*
It supervisore *(m)*
Pt supervisor *(m)*

Aufsicht *(f) n* De
En control
Es control *(m)*
Fr contrôle *(m)*
It controllo *(m)*
Pt controlo *(m)*

Aufsichtsbeamte(r) *(m) n* De
En inspector
Es inspector *(m)*
Fr inspecteur; vérificateur *(m)*
It ispettore *(m)*
Pt inspector *(m)*

aufsparen *vb* De
En save
Es ahorrar; economizar
Fr épargner; économiser
It risparmiare; economizzare
Pt poupar; economizar

Auftrag durch die Post *(m)*
De
En mail order
Es pedido por correo *(m)*
Fr commande par lettre *(f)*
It ordine per corrispondenza *(f)*
Pt venda pelo correio *(f)*

Auftragsbuch *(n) n* De
En order book
Es libro de pedidos *(m)*
Fr livre de commandes *(m)*
It libro degli ordini *(m)*
Pt livro de encomendas *(m)*

auf Treu und Glauben De
En in good faith
Es de buena fé

Fr de bonne foi
It in buona fede
Pt de boa fé

auf Verlangen De
En on demand
Es a vista
Fr sur demande
It a vista
Pt à vista; sob demanda

Aufwendungsposten *(f pl) n* De
En items of expenditure
Es artículos de gasto *(m pl)*
Fr postes de dépense *(m pl)*
It articoli di spesa *(m pl)*
Pt itens de despesa *(m pl)*

Aufwertung *(f) n* De
En revaluation
Es revalorización *(f)*
Fr revalorisation *(f)*
It rivalutazione *(f)*
Pt revalorização *(f)*

Aufzug *(m) n* De
En lift
Am elevator
Es ascensor *(m)*
Fr ascenseur *(m)*
It ascensore *(m)*
Pt ascensor *(m)*

augmentation *(f) n* Fr
De Zugang *(m)*
En accrual
Es incremento *(m)*
It incremento *(m)*
Pt acréscimo *(m)*

augmentation de capital *(f)*
Fr
De Kapitalerhöhung *(f)*
En increase of capital
Es aumento de capital *(m)*
It aumento di capitale *(m)*
Pt aumento de capital *(m)*

augmenter *vb* Fr
De steigen; zunehmen
En increase; rise
Es aumentar; encarecer
It aumentare; crescere
Pt aumentar

au jour le jour Fr
De täglich
En day-to-day

Es día a día
It di giorno in giorno
Pt dia a dia

aumentar *vb* Es, Pt
De steigen; zunehmen
En increase; rise
Fr augmenter; hausser
It aumentare; crescere

aumentare *vb* It
De steigen; zunehmen
En increase; rise
Es aumentar; alzar
Fr augmenter; hausse
Pt aumentar

aumentare di prezzo It
De teurer werden; steigen
En advance in price; go up
Es encarecer
Fr renchérir
Pt encarecer

aumentato costo della vita
(m) It
De erhöhte Lebenshaltungs-
kosten *(pl)*
En increased cost of living
Es coste de vida más alto *(m)*
Fr renchérissement du coût
de la vie *(m)* .
Pt custo de vida mais eleva-
do *(m)*

aumento *(m) n* Es, It, Pt
De Erhöhung; Zunahme *(f)*
En increase; rise
Fr hausse; accroissement *(f)*

aumento de capital *(m)* Es, Pt
De Kapitalerhöhung *(f)*
En increase of capital
Fr augmentation de capital *(f)*
It aumento di capitale *(m)*

aumento di capitale *(m)* It
De Kapitalerhöhung *(f)*
En increase of capital
Es aumento de capital *(m)*
Fr augmentation de capital *(f)*
Pt aumento de capital *(m)*

au pair Fr
De al pari
En at par
Es al par
It alla pari
Pt ao par

ausbeuten *vb* De
En exploit
Es explotar
Fr exploiter
It sfruttare
Pt explorar

ausente *(m) n* Es, Pt
De Abwesende(r) *(m)*
En absentee
Fr manquant *(m)*
It assente *(m)*

ausentismo *(m) n* Es
De unerlaubte Abwesenheit *(f)*
En absenteeism
Fr absentéisme *(m)*
It assenteismo *(m)*
Pt absentismo *(m)*

Ausfailbürgschaft *(f) n* De
En letter of indemnity
Es carta de indemnización *(f)*
Fr cautionnement *(m)*
It lettera di garanzia *(f)*
Pt documento de garantia *(m)*

Ausfuhranreiz *(m) n* De
En export incentive
Es estímulo de exportación *(m)*
Fr motif d'exportation *(m)*
It incentivo alla esportazione *(m)*
Pt incentivo para a exportação *(m)*

ausführen *vb* De
En export
Es exportar
Fr exporter
It esportare
Pt exportar

Ausfuhrgenehmigung *(f) n* De
En export permit
Es permiso de exportación *(m)*
Fr autorisation d'exporter *(f)*
It permesso d'esportazione *(m)*
Pt licença de exportação *(f)*

Ausfuhrprämie *(f) n* De
En export bonus
Es subsidio a las exportaciones *(m)*

Fr prime à l'exportation *(f)*
It premio d'esportazione *(m)*
Pt subsidio de exportação *(m)*

Ausfuhrsonderrabatt *(m) n* De
En export rebate
Es descuento por exportación *(m)*
Fr remise sur les exports *(f)*
It sconto d'esportazione *(m)*
Pt desconto de exportação *(m)*

Ausfuhrverkäufe *(m pl) n* De
En export sales
Es ventas de exportación *(f pl)*
Fr ventes d'exportation *(f pl)*
It vendite per esportazione *(f pl)*
Pt vendas de exportação *(f pl)*

Ausgabedruck *(m) n* De
En computer printout
Es impresión *(f)*
Fr sortie sur imprimante *(f)*
It stampato d'uscita dell'elaboratore *(m)*
Pt informe impresso pelo computador *(m)*

Ausgabe junger Aktien *(f)* De
En new issue
Es nueva emisión *(f)*
Fr émission d'actions nouvelles *(f)*
It nuova emissione *(f)*
Pt emissão nova *(f)*

Ausgaben *(f pl) n* De
En expenditure
Es desembolso *(m)*
Fr frais *(m pl)*
It spesa *(f)*
Pt despesas *(f pl)*

Ausgaben- und Ertragskonto *(n)* De
En income and expenditure account
Es cuenta de ingresos y gastos *(f)*
Fr compte de revenus et dépenses *(m)*
It conto proventi e spese *(m)*
Pt conta de receitas e despesas *(f)*

ausgeben *vb* De
En issue
Es emitir
Fr émettre
It emettere
Pt emitir

ausgegebenes Kapital *(n)* De
En issued capital
Es capital emitido *(m)*
Fr capital versé *(m)*
It capitale emesso *(m)*
Pt capital emitido *(m)*

Ausgleich *(m) n* De
En settlement
Es satisfacción *(f)*
Fr règlement *(m)*
It regolamento *(m)*
Pt satisfação *(f)*

ausgleichen (eine Rechnung) De
En balance an account
Es saldar une cuenta
Fr balancer un compte
It pareggiare un conto
Pt equilibrar uma conta

Ausgleichsfonds *(m) n* De
En equalization fund
Es fondo de compensación *(m)*
Fr fonds de régularisation *(m)*
It cassa di compensazione *(f)*
Pt fundo de compensação *(m)*

Ausgleichsposten *(m pl) n* De
En balancing items
Es asientos saldados *(m pl)*
Fr postes rééquilibrants *(m pl)*
It voci di pareggio *(f pl)*
Pt valores de equilíbrio *(m pl)*

Ausgleichssaldo *(m) n* De
En balance due
Es balance vencido *(m)*
Fr solde dû *(m)*
It saldo dovuto *(m)*
Pt saldo em dívida *(m)*

Auskunft *(f) n* De
En information
Es información *(f)*

Fr information; renseigne-
ment *(f m)*
It informazione *(f)*
Pt informação *(f)*

Ausländer *(m) n* De
En foreigner
Es extranjero *(m)*
Fr étranger *(m)*
It straniero *(m)*
Pt estrangeiro *(m)*

ausländisch *adj* De
En foreign; alien
Es extranjero
Fr étranger
It straniero; estero
Pt estrangeiro

Auslandsanleihe *(f) n* De
En external loan
Es préstamo exterior *(m)*
Fr emprunt extérieur *(m)*
It prestito esterno *(m)*
Pt empréstimo externo *(m)*

Auslandskonto *(n) n* De
En external account
Am foreign currency account
Es cuenta exterior *(f)*
Fr compte transférable *(m)*
It conto estero *(m)*
Pt conta externa *(f)*

Auslandswechsel *(m) n* De
En foreign bill
Es letra sobre el exterior *(f)*
Fr lettre de change sur
l'étranger *(f)*
It cambiale sull' estero *(f)*
Pt letra de país a país (cam-
bial) *(f)*

Auslassung *(f) n* De
En omission
Es omisión *(f)*
Fr omission *(f)*
It omissione *(f)*
Pt omissão *(f)*

Auslegung *(f) n* De
En interpretation
Es interpretación *(f)*
Fr interprétation *(f)*
It interpretazione *(f)*
Pt interpretação *(f)*

Ausrüstung *(f) n* De
En equipment
Es equipo *(m)*
Fr équipement *(m)*
It equipaggiamento *(m)*
Pt equipamento *(m)*

ausschließen *vb* De
En exclude
Es excluir
Fr exclure
It escludere
Pt excluir

ausschließlicher Markt *(m)*
De
En exclusive market
Es mercado exclusivo *(m)*
Fr marché exclusif *(m)*
It mercato esclusivo *(m)*
Pt mercado exclusivo *(m)*

Ausschluß *(m) n* De
En exclusion
Es exclusión *(f)*
Fr exclusion *(f)*
It esclusione *(f)*
Pt exclusão *(f)*

Außenhafen *(m) n* De
En outer harbour
Es antepuerto *(m)*
Fr avant-port *(m)*
It avamporto *(m)*
Pt anteporto *(m)*

Außenhandel *(m) n* De
En foreign trade
Es comercio exterior *(m)*
Fr commerce extérieur *(m)*
It commercio estero *(m)*
Pt comércio externo *(m)*

Außenhandelsdefizit *(n) n* De
En trade gap
Es vacío comercial *(m)*
Fr déficit du commerce exté-
rieur *(m)*
It disavanzo della bilancia
commerciale *(m)*
Pt vazio comercial *(m)*

**außerordentliche General-
versammlung** *(f)* De
En extraordinary general
meeting
Es asamblea general extraordinaria *(f)*

Fr assemblée générale ex-
traordinaire*(f)*
It assemblea generale
straordinaria *(f)*
Pt assemblea geral extraordinária *(f)*

außer Steuer De
En excluding tax
Es impuesto no incluido
Fr hors taxe (HT)
It tassa esclusa
Pt impostos excluídos

Aussperrung *(f) n* De
En lock-out
Es cierre *(m)*
Fr lock-out *(m)*
It serrata *(f)*
Pt lockout *(m)*

ausstatten *vb* De
En equip; endow
Es equipar; dotar
Fr équiper; doter
It equipaggiare; dotare
Pt equipar; dotar

ausstehende Schulden *(m pl)*
De
En outstanding accounts
Es cuentas pendientes *(f pl)*
Fr comptes à percevoir *(m pl)*
It conti aperti *(m pl)*
Pt contas por saldar *(f pl)*

Aussteller *(m) n* De
En drawer; exhibitor
Es librador; exhibidor *(m)*
Fr tireur; exposant *(m)*
It traente; espositore *(m)*
Pt sacador; expositor *(m)*

Ausstellung *(f) n* De
En exhibition
Es exposicion *(f)*
Fr exposition *(f)*
It esposizione *(f)*
Pt exposicão *(f)*

ausverkauft *adj* De
En sold out; out of stock
Es agotado
Fr tout vendu
It tutto venduto; esaurito
Pt esgotado

Auszahlung *(f)* n De
En disbursement
Es desembolso *(m)*
Fr déboursement *(m)*
It esborso *(m)*
Pt desembolso *(m)*

aus zweiter Hand De
En second-hand
Es de segunda mano
Fr d'occasion
It di seconda mano
Pt de segunda mão

authority n En
De Vollmacht *(f)*
Es autoridad *(f)*
Fr mandat *(m)*
It autorità *(f)*
Pt autoridade *(f)*

authorized capital En
De genehmigtes Kapital *(n)*
Es capital autorizado *(m)*
Fr capital autorisé *(m)*
It capitale autorizzato *(m)*
Pt capital autorizado *(m)*

auto *(m)* n Es
De Vorladung *(f)*
En writ
Fr assignation *(f)*
It citazione *(f)*
Pt citação; ordem *(f m)*

Auto *(n)* n De
En car
Es coche *(m)*
Fr voiture; automobile *(f)*
It automobile; macchina *(f)*
Pt carro; automóvel *(m)*

auto-servicio *(m)* n Es
De Selbstbedienung *(f)*
En self-service
Fr libre service *(m)*
It servirsi da sè *(m)*
Pt self-service *(m)*

automation n En, Fr *(f)*
De Automation *(f)*
Es automatización *(f)*
It automazione *(f)*
Pt automatização *(f)*

Automation *(f)* n De
En automation
Es automatiazación *(f)*

Fr automation *(f)*
It automazione *(f)*
Pt automatização *(f)*

**automatisch sich erneu-
erndes Akkreditiv** *(n)* De
En revolving credit
Es crédito reponible *(m)*
Fr accréditif automatique-
ment renouvelable *(m)*
It credito rotativo *(m)*
Pt crédito renovável *(m)*

automatização *(f)* n Pt
De Automation *(f)*
En automation
Es automatización *(f)*
Fr automation *(f)*
It automazione *(f)*

automatización *(f)* n Es
De Automation *(f)*
En automation
Fr automation *(f)*
It automazione *(f)*
Pt automatização *(f)*

automazione *(f)* n It
De Automation *(f)*
En automation
Es automatización *(f)*
Fr automation *(f)*
Pt automatização *(f)*

automobile *(f)* n It
De Auto; Wagen *(n m)*
En car
Es coche *(m)*
Fr voiture; automobile *(f)*
Pt carro; automóvel *(m)*

autoridad *(f)* n Es
De Vollmacht *(f)*
En authority
Fr mandat *(m)*
It autorità *(f)*
Pt autoridade *(f)*

autoridade *(f)* n Pt
De Vollmacht *(f)*
En authority
Es autoridad *(f)*
Fr mandat *(m)*
It autorità *(f)*

autorimessa *(f)* n It
De Garage *(f)*
En garage

Es garaje *(m)*
Fr garage *(m)*
Pt garagem *(f)*

autorità *(f)* n It
De Vollmacht *(f)*
En authority
Es autoridad *(f)*
Fr mandat *(m)*
Pt autoridade *(f)*

autorização *(f)* n Pt
De Erlaubnis; Erlaubnisschein
(f m)
En permit
Es permiso *(m)*
Fr permis *(m)*
It permesso *(m)*

autorizar caução Pt
De gegen Haftkaution freige-
ben
En grant bail
Es conceder fianza
Fr admettre une caution
It concedere la libertà
provvisoria su cauzione

autorisation d'exporter *(f)* Fr
De Ausfuhrgenehmigung *(f)*
En export permit
Es permiso de exportación
(m)
It permesso d'esportazione
(m)
Pt licença de exportação *(f)*

available adj En
De verfügbar
Es disponible
Fr disponible
It disponibile
Pt disponível

avalar vb Es
De gegenzeichnen
En back
Fr avaliser
It avallare
Pt avalizar

avaliação *(f)* n Pt
De Abschätzung; Wertbe-
stimmung *(f)*
En appraisal; valuation
Es valuación; evaluación *(f)*
Fr évaluation *(f)*
It valutazione *(f)*

avaliação aproximada *(f)* Pt
De rohe Schätzung *(f)*
En rough estimate
Es presupuesto aproximado
   (m)
Fr estimation approximative
   (f)
It valutazione approssimati-
   va *(f)*

avaliação cautelosa *(f)* Pt
De vorsichtige Schätzung *(f)*
En conservative estimate
Es presupuesto prudente *(m)*
Fr évaluation prudente *(f)*
It valutazione prudente *(f)*

avaliação de tarefa *(f)* Pt
De Arbeitsbewertung *(f)*
En job evaluation
Es valoracion del trabajo *(f)*
Fr évaluation du travail *(f)*
It valutazione del lavoro *(f)*

avaliação excessiva *(f)* Pt
De Überschätzung *(f)*
En over-estimate
Es presupuesto por exceso
   (m)
Fr surestimation *(f)*
It valutazione eccessiva *(f)*

avaliação insuficiente *(f)* Pt
De Unterschätzung *(f)*
En under-estimate
Es presupuesto por defecto
   (m)
Fr sous-estimation *(f)*
It sottovalutazione *(f)*

avaliador *(m)* n Pt
De Schätzer *(m)*
En assessor
Es asesor *(m)*
Fr appréciateur *(m)*
It agente delle imposte *(m)*

avaliar *vb* Pt
De einschätzen; bewerten
En estimate; evaluate
Es estimar; evaluar
Fr estimer; évaluer
It stimare; valutare

avaliar os danos Pt
De den Schadenersatzbetrag
   feststellen
En assess damages
Es evaluar daños

Fr fixer des dommages- intérêts
It valutare i danni

avaliser *vb* Fr
De gegenzeichnen
En back
Es avalar
It avallare
Pt avalizar

avalista *(m)* n Es, Pt
De Gegenzeichner *(m)*
En backer
Fr avaliste *(m)*
It avallante *(m)*

avaliste *(m)* n Fr
De Gegenzeichner *(m)*
En backer
Es avalista *(m)*
It avallante *(m)*
Pt avalista *(m)*

avalizar *vb* Pt
De gegenzeichnen
En back
Es avalar
Fr avaliser
It avallare

avallante *(m)* n It
De Gegenzeichner *(m)*
En backer
Es avalista *(m)*
Fr avaliste *(m)*
Pt avalista *(m)*

avallare *vb* It
De gegenzeichnen
En back
Es avalar
Fr avaliser
Pt avalizar

à valoir Fr
De a conto; auf Abschlag
En on account
Es a cuenta
It in acconto
Pt por conta

avamporto *(m)* n It
De Außenhafen *(m)*
En outer harbour
Es antepuerto *(m)*
Fr avant-port *(m)*
Pt anteporto *(m)*

avance *(f)* n Fr
De Vorschuß *(m)*
En advance
Am prepayment
Es adelanto *(m)*
It anticipazione *(f)*
Pt adiantamento *(m)*

avancement *(m)* n Fr
De Beförderung *(f)*
En promotion
Es ascenso; promoción *(m f)*
It avanzamento; promozione
   (m f)
Pt promoção *(f)*

avancer (de l'argent) *vb* Fr
De vorschießen
En advance
Am prepay
Es anticipar
It anticipare
Pt adiantar

avantages accessoires *(m
   pl)* Fr
De Sozialleistungen *(f pl)*
En fringe benefits
Es beneficios suplementarios
   (m pl)
It vantaggi accessori *(m pl)*
Pt benefícios extras *(m pl)*

avant-hier *adv* Fr
De vorgestern
En day before yesterday
Es anteayer
It avantieri
Pt anteontem

avantieri *adv* It
De vorgestern
En day before yesterday
Es anteayer
Fr avant-hier
Pt anteontem

avant-port *(m)* n Fr
De Außenhafen *(m)*
En outer harbour
Es antepuerto *(m)*
It avamporto *(m)*
Pt anteporto *(m)*

avanzamento *(m)* n It
De Beförderung *(f)*
En promotion
Es ascenso; promoción *(m f)*

Fr avancement; promotion
   (m f)
Pt promoção *(f)*

avaria *(f)* n It, Pt
De Havarie *(f)*
En average (marine insur-
   ance
Es avería *(f)*
Fr avarie *(f)*

avaria generale *(f)* It
De große Havarie *(f)*
En general average (G.A.)
Es avería general *(f)*
Fr avaries communes *(f pl)*
Pt avaria grossa *(f)*

avaria grossa *(f)* Pt
De große Havarie *(f)*
En general average (G.A.)
Es avería general *(f)*
Fr avaries communes *(f pl)*
It avarie generale *(f)*

avaria particolare *(f)* It
De besondere Havarie *(f)*
En particular average
Es avería particular *(f)*
Fr avarie particulière *(f)*
Pt avaria particular *(f)*

avaria particular *(f)* Pt
De besondere Havarie *(f)*
En particular average
Es avería particular *(f)*
Fr avarie particulière *(f)*
It avaria particolare *(f)*

avarie *(f)* n Fr
De Havarie *(f)*
En average (marine insur-
   ance)
Es avería *(f)*
It avaria *(f)*
Pt avaria *(f)*

avarié *adj* Fr
De havariert
En with average (WA)
Es con avería
It con averia
Pt com avaria

avarie particulière *(f)* Fr
De besondere Havarie *(f)*
En particular average
Es avería particular *(f)*
It avaria particolare *(f)*
Pt avaria particular *(f)*

avaries communes *(f pl)*
   Fr
De große Havarie *(f)*
En general average (G.A.)
Es avería general *(f)*
It avaria generale *(f)*
Pt avaría grossa *(f)*

avaries de route *(f pl)* Fr
De Beschädigung beim
   Transport *(f)*
En damage in transit
Es daños en ruta *(m pl)*
It danno durante trasporto
   (m)
Pt danos em trânsito *(m pl)*

avec droit de recours Fr
De mit Rückgriff
En with recourse
Es con recurso
It con risorso
Pt com recurso

average n En
De Durchschnitt *(m)*
Es promedio *(m)*
Fr moyenne *(f)*
It media *(f)*
Pt média *(f)*

average (marine insurance) n
   En
De Havarie *(f)*
Es avería *(f)*
Fr avarie *(f)*
It avaria *(f)*
Pt avaria *(f)*

average bond En
De Havarieschein *(m)*
Es fianza de avería *(f)*
Fr compromis d'avarie *(m)*
It compromesso d'avaria *(m)*
Pt fiança de avaria *(f)*

average cost En
De Durchschnittskosten *(m
   pl)*
Es coste promedio *(m)*
Fr coût moyen *(m)*
It costo medio *(m)*
Pt custo médio *(m)*

avería *(f)* n Es
De Havarie *(f)*
En average (marine insur-
   ance)
Fr avarie *(f)*

It avaria *(f)*
Pt avaria *(f)*

avería general *(f)* Es
De große Havarie *(f)*
En general average (G.A.)
Fr avaries communes *(f pl)*
It avaria generale *(f)*
Pt avaria grossa *(f)*

avería particular *(f)* Es
De besondere Havarie *(f)*
En particular average
Fr avarie particulière *(f)*
It avaria particolare *(f)*
Pt avaría particular *(f)*

avião a jacto *(m)* Pt
De Düsenflugzeug *(n)*
En jet aircraft
Es avión jet *(m)*
Fr avion à réaction *(m)*
It aviogetto *(m)*

aviogetto *(m)* n It
De Düsenflugzeug *(n)*
En jet aircraft
Es avión jet *(m)*
Fr avion à réaction *(m)*
Pt avião a jacto *(m)*

avion à réaction *(m)* Fr
De Düsenflugzeug *(n)*
En jet aircraft
Es avión jet *(m)*
It aviogetto *(m)*
Pt avião a jacto *(m)*

avión jet *(m)* Es
De Düsenflugzeug *(n)*
En jet aircraft
Fr avion à réaction *(m)*
It aviogetto *(m)*
Pt avião a jacto *(m)*

avis *(m)* n Fr
De Benachrichtung *(f)*
En notice
Es aviso *(m)*
It avviso; preavviso *(m)*
Pt aviso *(m)*

avis d'attribution *(m)* Fr
De Verteilungsbrief *(m)*
En allotment letter
Es letra de adjudicación *(f)*
It lettera da ripartizione *(f)*
Pt aviso de aporcionamento
   (m)

avis de crédit *(m)* Fr
De Gutschriftanzeige *(f)*
En credit note
Es nota de crédito *(f)*
It nota di credito *(f)*
Pt aviso de crédito *(m)*

avis de débit *(m)* Fr
De Lastschrift *(f)*
En debit note
Es nota de débito *(f)*
It nota di addebito *(f)*
Pt aviso de débito *(m)*

aviso *(m)* n Es, Pt
De Anzeige; Benachrichtigung *(f)*
En advice note; notice
Fr avis; lettre d'avis *(m f)*
It avviso; lettera d'avviso *(m f)*

aviso de aporcionamento *(m)* Pt
De Verteilungsbrief *(m)*
En allotment letter
Es letra de adjudicación *(f)*
Fr avis d'attribution *(m)*
It lettera da ripartizione *(f)*

aviso de crédito *(m)* Pt
De Gutschriftanzeige *(f)*
En credit note
Es nota di crédito *(f)*
Fr avis de crédit *(m)*
It nota di credito *(f)*

aviso de débito *(m)* Pt
De Lastschrift *(f)*
En debit note
Es nota de débito *(f)*
Fr avis de débit *(m)*
It nota di addebito *(f)*

aviso de despacho *(m)* Pt
De Versandschein *(m)*
En despatch note
Es aviso de expedición *(m)*
Fr bordereau d'expédition;
bulletin d'envoi *(m)*
It bollettino di spedizione *(m)*

aviso de entrega *(m)* Es
De Lieferschein *(m)*
En delivery note
Fr bordereau de livraison *(m)*
It nota di consegna *(f)*
Pt guia de entrega *(f)*

aviso de expedición *(m)* Es
De Versandschein *(m)*
En despatch note
Fr bordereau d'expédition;
bulletin d'envoi *(m)*
It bollettino di spedizione *(m)*
Pt aviso de despacho *(m)*

aviso de recepção *(m)* Pt
De Empfangsbestätigung *(f)*
En acknowledgment of receipt
Es aviso de recepción *(m)*
Fr accusé de réception *(m)*
It avviso di recezione *(m)*

aviso de recepción *(m)* Es
De Empfangsbestätigung *(f)*
En acknowledgment of receipt
Fr accusé de réception *(m)*
It avviso di recezione *(m)*
Pt aviso de recepção *(m)*

aviso de seguro del riesgo *(m)* Es
De Deckungszusage *(f)*
En cover note
Fr lettre de couverture *(f)*
It nota di copertura *(f)*
Pt nota de cobertura *(f)*

aviso oficial *(m)* Es
De Inverzugsetzung *(f)*
En formal notice
Fr mise en demeure *(f)*
It intimazione *(f)*
Pt notificação formal *(f)*

a vista It
De bei Sicht
En at sight
Es a la vista
Fr à vue
Pt à vista

à vista Pt
De bei Sicht
En at sight
Es a la vista
Fr à vue
It a vista

avocat *(m)* n Fr
De Anwalt *(m)*
En lawyer; barrister; counsel
Am attorney
Es abogado *(m)*
It avvocato *(m)*
Pt advogado *(m)*

à vue Fr
De bei Sicht
En at sight
Es a la vista
It a vista
Pt à vista

avviamento *(m)* n It
De Geschäftswert *(m)*
En goodwill
Es valor de la clientela *(m)*
Fr bon vouloir *(m)*
Pt boa vontade *(f)*

avviso *(m)* n It
De Benachrichtigung *(f)*
En notice
Es aviso *(m)*
Fr avis; préavis *(m)*
Pt aviso *(m)*

avviso di recezione *(m)* It
De Empfangsbestätigung *(f)*
En acknowledgment of receipt
Es aviso de recepción *(m)*
Fr accusé de réception *(m)*
Pt aviso de recepção *(m)*

avvocato *(m)* n It
De Anwalt *(m)*
En lawyer; barrister; counsel
Am attorney
Es abogado *(m)*
Fr avocat *(m)*
Pt advogado *(m)*

award damages En
De Schadenersatz zugestehen
Es conceder daños
Fr adjuger des dommages-intérêts
It concedere i danni
Pt conceder compensação

ayer adv Es
De gestern
En yesterday
Fr hier
It ieri
Pt ontem

ayuda *(f)* n Es
De Hilfe *(f)*
En help
Fr secours *(m)*
It aiuto *(m)*
Pt ajuda *(f)*

azar *(m)* n Es
De Wagnis *(n)*
En hazard
Fr hasard; risque *(m)*
It rischio *(m)*
Pt risco; azar *(m)*

azione *(f)* n It
De Aktie *(f)*
En share
Es acción *(f)*
Fr action *(f)*
Pt acção *(f)*

azione ordinaria *(f)* It
De Stammaktie *(f)*
En ordinary share
Es acción ordinaria *(f)*
Fr action ordinaire *(f)*
Pt acção ordinária *(f)*

azione privilegiata *(f)* It
De Vorzugsaktie *(f)*
En preference share
Es acción preferente *(f)*
Fr action privilégiée *(f)*
Pt acção preferencial *(f)*

azioni aurifere *(f pl)* It
De Aktien von Goldbergwer-
    ken *(f pl)*
En gold shares
Es acciones auréferas *(f pl)*
Fr valeurs aurifères *(f pl)*
Pt acções de ouro *(f pl)*

azioni con diritto di voto
    (f pl) It
De stimmberechtigte Aktien
    (f pl)
En voting shares
Es acciones con derecho de
    voto *(f pl)*
Fr actions avec droit de vote
    (f pl)
Pt acções com direito a voto
    (f pl)

azioni del fondatore *(f pl)* It
De Gründeraktien *(f pl)*
En founder's shares
Es acciones del fundador *(f
    pl)*
Fr actions de fondateur *(f pl)*
Pt acções de fundador *(f pl)*

azioni di godimento *(f pl)* It
De Gratisaktien *(f pl)*
En bonus shares
Am stock dividend

Es acciones dadas como
    primas *(f pl)*
Fr actions d'attribution *(f pl)*
Pt acções de prémio *(f pl)*

azioni postergate *(f pl)* It
De Nachzugsaktien *(f pl)*
En deferred shares
Es acciones aplazadas *(f pl)*
Fr actions différées *(f pl)*
Pt acções diferidas *(f pl)*

**azioni preferenziali
    cumulative** *(f pl)* It
De kumulative Vorzugsaktien
    (f pl)
En cumulative preference
    shares
Es valores privilegiados cu-
    mulativos *(m pl)*
Fr actions de priorité cumula-
    tives *(f pl)*
Pt acções preferenciais cumu-
    lativas *(f pl)*

**azioni preferenziali
    redimibili** *(f pl)* It
De ablösbare Vorzugsaktien *(f
    pl)*
En redeemable preference
    shares
Es acciónes preferentes
    amortizables *(f pl)*
Fr actions privilégiées amor-
    tissables *(f pl)*
Pt acções redimíveis preferen-
    ciais *(f pl)*

azioni senza diritto a voto
    (f pl) It
De Aktien ohne Stimmrecht
    (f pl)
En non-voting shares
Es acciones sin derecho de
    voto *(f pl)*
Fr actions sans droit de vote
    (f pl)
Pt acções sem direito a voto
    (f pl)

azionista *(m)* n It
De Aktionär *(m)*
En shareholder
Am stockholder
Es accionista *(m)*
Fr actionnaire *(m)*
Pt accionista *(m)*

B

bac *(m)* n Fr
De Fährboot *(n)*
En ferry-boat
Es transbordador *(m)*
It nave traghetto *(f)*
Pt barco de travessia *(m)*

bacino carbonifero *(m)* It
De Kohlenrevier *(n)*
En coal field
Es yacimiento de carbón *(m)*
Fr bassin houiller *(m)*
Pt jazigo de carvão *(m)*

bacino di carenaggio *(m)* It
De Trockendock *(n)*
En dry dock
Es dique seco *(m)*
Fr cale sèche *(f)*
Pt doca-seca *(f)*

bacino di raddobbo *(m)* It
De Trockendock *(n)*
En graving dock
Es dique de carenas *(m)*
Fr bassin de radoub *(m)*
Pt doca de querenas *(f)*

back *vb* En
De gegenzeichnen
Es avalar
Fr avaliser
It avallare
Pt avalizar

backer n En
De Gegenzeichner *(m)*
Es avalista *(m)*
Fr avaliste *(m)*
It avallante *(m)*
Pt avalista *(m)*

back pay En
De Lohnnachzahlung *(f)*
Es pago atrasado *(m)*
Fr rappel de traitement *(m)*
It arretrati di paga *(m pl)*
Pt vencimento atrasado *(m)*

backwardation n En
De Kursabschlag *(m)*
Es prima de aplazamiento *(f)*
Fr déport *(m)*
It deporto *(m)*
Pt juro de mora *(m)*

bad debt En
De uneinbringliche Schuld *(f)*
Es deuda incobrable *(f)*
Fr créance irrécouvrable *(f)*
It credito inesigibile *(m)*
Pt dívida incobrável *(f)*

bad debt reserve En
De Dubiosenreserve *(f)*
Es reserva para deudas incobrables *(f)*
Fr provision pour créances douteuses *(f)*
It riserva per crediti inesigibili *(f)*
Pt reserva para dívidas incobráveis *(f)*

bagagem de mão *(f)* Pt
De Handgepäck *(n)*
En hand-luggage
Es equipaje de mano *(m)*
Fr bagages à main *(m pl)*
It bagaglio a mano *(m)*

bagages à main *(m pl)* Fr
De Handgepäck *(n)*
En hand-luggage
Es equipaje de mano *(m)*
It bagaglio a mano *(m)*
Pt bagagem de mão *(f)*

bagagliaio *(m)* n It
De Packwagen *(m)*
En guard's van
Es furgón *(m)*
Fr fourgon *(m)*
Pt furgão *(m)*

bagaglio a mano *(m)* It
De Handgepäck *(n)*
En hand-luggage
Es equipaje de mano *(m)*
Fr bagages à main *(m pl)*
Pt bagagem de mão *(f)*

bagaglio eccedente *(m)* It
De Übergepäck *(n)*
En excess luggage
Es exceso de equipaje *(m)*
Fr excédent de bagages *(m)*
Pt excesso de bagagem *(m)*

Bahnfrachtbrief *(m)* n De
En railway receipt
Es recibo ferroviario *(m)*
Fr bulletin de chargement *(m)*
It ricevuta ferroviaria *(f)*
Pt recibo ferroviário *(m)*

bail n En
De Haftkaution *(f)*
Es fianza *(f)*
Fr caution *(f)*
It cauzione *(f)*
Pt caução *(f)*

bail *(m)* n Fr
De Verpachtung *(f)*
En lease
Es alquiler *(m)*
It affitto *(m)*
Pt aluguer; arrendamento *(m)*

bailee n En
De Gewahrsaminhaber *(m)*
Es depositario *(m)*
Fr dépositaire *(m)*
It depositario *(m)*
Pt caucionado *(m)*

bailleur *(m)* n Fr
De Vermieter *(m)*
En lessor
Es arrendador *(m)*
It locatore *(m)*
Pt senhorio; arrendador *(m)*

baisse *(f)* n Fr
De Sturz *(m)*
En fall
Es baja; caida *(f)*
It caduta; ribasso *(f m)*
Pt baixa; queda *(f)*

Baissekonto *(n)* n De
En bear account
Es cuenta de especulaciones a la baja *(f)*
Fr compte des speculations à la baisse *(m)*
It conto di speculazioni al ribasso *(m)*
Pt conta de especulações baixistas *(f)*

Baissemarkt *(m)* n De
En bear market
Es mercado bajista *(m)*
Fr marché orienté à la baisse *(m)*
It mercato tendente al ribasso *(m)*
Pt mercado de tendência baixista *(m)*

baisser *vb* Fr
De stürzen
En fall
Es caer; bajar

It cadere; ribassare
Pt cair; baixar

Baissespekulant *(m)* n De
En bear
Es bajista *(m)*
Fr baissier *(m)*
It ribassista *(m)*
pt baixista *(m)*

baissier *(m)* n Fr
De Baissespekulant; Baissier *(m)*
En bear
Es bajista *(m)*
It ribassista *(m)*
Pt baixista *(m)*

baixa *(f)* n Pt
De Sturz *(m)*
En fall
Es baja, caida *(f)*
Fr baisse; chute *(f)*
It caduta; ribasso *(f m)*

baixista *(m)* n Pt
De Baissespekulant; Baissier *(m)*
En bear
Es bajista *(m)*
Fr baissier *(m)*
It ribassista *(m)*

baixista *adj* Pt
De flau
En bearish
Es bajista
Fr orienté à la baisse
It ribassista

baixo-nível *adj* Pt
De minderwertig
En low-grade
Es baja calidad
Fr de qualité inférieure
It di qualità inferiore

baja *(f)* n Es
De Sturz *(rn)*
En fall
Fr baisse; chute *(f)*
It caduta; ribasso *(f m)*
Pt baixa; queda (f)

baja calidad Es
De minderwertig
En low-grade
Fr de qualité inférieure
It di qualità inferiore
Pt baixo-nível

bajar de valor Es
De nachlassen
En fall off
Fr ralentir; baisser de valeur
It diminuire
Pt diminuir; decrescer

bajista (m) n Es
De Baissespekulant; Baissier
(m)
En bear
Fr baissier (m)
It ribassista (m)
Pt baixista (m)

bajista adj Es
De flau
En bearish
Fr orienté à la baisse
It ribassista
Pt baixista

balança (f) n Pt
De Waage (f)
En scales
Es balanza (f)
Fr balance (f)
It bilancia (f)

balança comercial (f) Pt
De Handelsbilanz (f)
En trade balance
Es balanza comercial (f)
Fr balance commerciale (f)
It bilancia commerciale (f)

balança de pagamentos (f)
Pt
De Zahlungsbilanz (f)
En balance of payments
Es balanza de pagos (f)
Fr balance des paiements (f)
It bilancia dei pagamenti (f)

balance n En
De Saldo (m)
Es balance; saldo (m)
Fr balance; solde (f m)
It bilancio; saldo (m)
Pt saldo (m)

balance (m) n Es
De Saldo; Bilanz (f)
En balance; balance sheet
Fr balance; solde; bilan
(f m m)
It bilancio; saldo (m)
Pt saldo; balancete (m)

balance (f) n Fr
De Saldo; Waage (m f)
En balance; scales
Es balance; saldo; balanza
(m m f)
It bilancio; saldo; bilancia
(m m f)
Pt saldo; balança (m f)

balance a budget En
De einen Haushaltsplan ins
Gleichgewicht bringen
Es balancear el presupuesto
Fr équilibrer un budget
It pareggiare un bilancio
Pt equilibrar um orçamento

balance a cuenta nueva (m)
Es
De Übertrag (m)
En balance brought down
Am balance carried forward
Fr solde à reporter (m)
It bilancio riportato (m)
Pt saldo transportado (m)

balance an account En
De Eine Rechnung ausglei-
chen
Es saldar una cuenta
Fr balancer un compte
It pareggiare un conto
Pt equilibrar uma conta

balance anual (m) Es
De Jahresabschluß (m)
En annual accounts
Fr bilan annuel (m)
It bilancio annuale (m)
Pt balancete anual (m)

balancear el presupuesto Es
De einen Haushaltsplan ins
Gleichgewicht bringen
En balance a budget
Fr équilibrer un budget
It pareggiare un bilancio
Pt equilibrar um orçamento

balance brought down En
Am balance carried forward
De Übertrag (m)
Es balance a cuenta nueva
(m)
Fr solde à reporter (m)
It bilancio riportato (m)
Pt saldo transportado (m)

balance carried forward En
De Saldovortrag (m)
Es saldo de entrada (m)
Fr report à nouveau (m)
It saldo da riportare (m)
Pt saldo transportado (m)

balance commerciale (f) Fr
De Handelsbilanz (f)
En trade balance
Es balanza comercial (f)
It bilancia commerciale (f)
Pt balança comercial (f)

**balance de comprobación
de saldos** (m) Es
De Probebilanz (f)
En trial balance
Fr bilan de vérification (m)
It bilancio di verifica (m)
Pt balancete de verificação
(m)

balance déficitaire (f) Fr
De Passivsaldo (m)
En adverse balance
Am negative balance
Es saldo adverso (m)
It saldo passivo (m)
Pt saldo negativo (m)

balance des paiements (f) Fr
De Zahlungsbilanz (f)
En balance of payments
Es balanza de pagos (f)
It bilancia dei pagamenti (f)
Pt balança de pagamentos (f)

balance due En
De Ausgleichssaldo (m)
Es balance vencido (m)
Fr solde dû (m)
It saldo dovuto (m)
Pt saldo em dívida (m)

balance excédentaire (f) Fr
De Aktivsaldo (m)
En active balance
Es saldo acreedor (m)
It saldo attivo (m)
Pt saldo credor (m)

balance in hand En
De verfügbarer Saldo (m)
Es sobrante (m)
Fr solde en caisse (m)
It saldo in cassa (m)
Pt saldo em poder (m)

balance of payments En
De Zahlungsbilanz *(f)*
Es balanza de pagos *(f)*
Fr balance des paiements *(f)*
It balancia dei pagamenti *(f)*
Pt balança de pagamentos *(f)*

balance of trade En
De Handelsbilanz *(f)*
Es balanza comercial *(f)*
Fr balance commerciale *(f)*
It bilancia commerciale *(f)*
Pt balança comercial *(f)*

balancer un compte Fr
De eine Rechnung ausglei-
chen
En balance an account
Es saldar una cuenta
It pareggiare un conto
Pt equilibrar uma conta

balance sheet En
De Bilanz *(m)*
Es balance *(m)*
Fr bilan *(m)*
It bilancio *(m)*
Pt balancete *(m)*

balancete *(m) n* Pt
De Bilanz *(f)*
En balance sheet
Es balance *(m)*
Fr bilan *(m)*
It bilancio *(m)*

balancete de verificação
(m) Pt
De Probebilanz *(f)*
En trial balance
Es balance de comprobación
de saldos *(m)*
Fr bilan de vérification *(m)*
It bilancio di verifica *(m)*

balance vencido *(m)* Es
De Ausgleichssaldo *(m)*
En balance due
Fr solde dû *(m)*
It saldo dovuto *(m)*
Pt saldo em dívida *(m)*

balancing items En
De Ausgleichsposten *(m pl)*
Es asientos saldados *(m pl)*
Fr postes rééquilibrants
(m pl)
It voci di pareggio *(f pl)*
Pt valores de equilíbrio *(f pl)*

balanço final *(m)* Pt
De Schlußbilanz *(f)*
En final balance
Es saldo final *(m)*
Fr solde net *(m)*
It saldo finale *(m)*

balanço fiscal *(m)* Pt
De Besteuerung *(f)*
En assessment
Es evaluación *(f)*
Fr imposition *(f)*
It imposta *(f)*

balanza *(f) n* Es
De Waage *(f)*
En scales
Fr balance *(f)*
It balancia *(f)*
Pt balança *(f)*

balanza comercial *(f)* Es
De Handelsbilanz *(f)*
En trade balance
Fr balance commerciale *(f)*
It bilancia commerciale *(f)*
Pt balança comercial *(f)*

balanza de pagos *(f)* Es
De Zahlungsbilanz *(f)*
En balance of payments
Fr balance des paiements *(f)*
It bilancia dei pagamenti *(f)*
Pt balança de pagamentos *(f)*

ballast *(marine) n* En
De Ballast *(m)*
Es lastre *(m)*
Fr lest *(m)*
It zavorra *(f)*
Pt lastro *(m)*

Ballast *(m) n* De
En ballast
Es lastre *(m)*
Fr lest *(m)*
It zavorra *(f)*
Pt lastro *(m)*

banca *(f) n* It
De Bank *(f)*
En bank
Es banco *(m)*
Fr banque *(f)*
Pt banco *(m)*

banca agricola *(f)* It
De Landbank *(f)*
En land bank

Es banco agrícola *(m)*
Fr banque agricole *(f)*
Pt banco d'agricultura *(m)*

**banca associata alla stanza
di comepensazione** *(f)* It
De Girobank *(f)*
En clearing bank
Es banco de compensación
(m)
Fr banque de virement *(f)*
Pt banco de compensação e
rateio *(m)*

banca commerciale *(f)* It
De Handelsbank *(f)*
En merchant bank
Es banco mercantil *(m)*
Fr banque commerciale *(f)*
Pt banco comercial *(m)*

banca di emissione *(f)* It
De Notenbank *(f)*
En issuing bank
Es banco emisor *(m)*
Fr banque d'émission *(f)*
Pt banco emissor *(m)*

banca d'investimenti *(f)* It
De Finanzbank *(f)*
En investment bank
Es banco de inversiones *(m)*
Fr banque d'affaires *(f)*
Pt banco de investimentos
(m)

banca di presiti *(f)* It
De Kreditbank *(f)*
En lending bank
Es banco de préstamos *(m)*
Fr banque de prêts *(f)*
Pt banco de empréstimos *(m)*

banca di sconto *(f)* It
De Diskontbank *(f)*
En discount house
Es casa de descuentos *(f)*
Fr maison d'escompte *(f)*
Pt agência corretora de des-
contos *(f)*

**Banca Europea d'Investi-
menti** *(f)* It
De Europäische Investitions-
bank *(f)*
En European Investment
Bank
Es Banco Europeo de Inver-
siones *(m)*

Fr Banque Européenne d'Investissement *(f)*
Pt Banco Europeu de In-
vestimentos *(m)*

**Banca Internazionale
per la Ricostruzione
e lo Sviluppo** *(f)* It
De Internationale Bank für
Wiederaufbau und Wirt-
schaftsförderung *(f)*
En International Bank for Reconstruction and De-
velopment
Es Banco Internacional para
Reconstrucción y Desar-
rollo *(m)*
Fr Banque Internationale
pour la Reconstruction et
le Développement *(f)*
Pt Banco Internacional de
Reconstrução Desenvolvi-
mento *(m)*

banca privata *(f)* It
De Privatbank *(f)*
En private bank
Es banco privado *(m)*
Fr banque privée *(f)*
Pt banco privado *(m)*

bancarotta *(f)* n It
De Bankrott *(m)*
En bankruptcy
Es bancarotta *(f)*
Fr faillite *(f)*
Pt bancarotta *(f)*

bancarotta *(f)* n Es, Pt
De Bankrott *(m)*
En bankruptcy
Fr faillite *(f)*
It bancarotta *(f)*

banca succursale *(f)* It
De Filialbank, Zweigbank *(f)*
En branch bank
Es sucursal del banco *(f)*
Fr banque succursale *(f)*
Pt filial de banco *(f)*

banchiere *(m)* n It
De Bankier *(m)*
En banker
Es banquero *(m)*
Fr banquier *(m)*
Pt banqueiro *(m)*

banchina *(f)* n It
De Kai *(m)*
En quay
Am pier
Es muelle *(m)*
Fr quai *(m)*
Pt cais *(m)*

banco *(m)* n Es, Pt
De Bank *(f)*
En bank
Fr banque *(f)*
It banca *(f)*

banco agrícola *(m)* Es
De Landbank *(f)*
En land bank
Fr banque agricole *(f)*
It banca agricola *(f)*
Pt banco d'agricultura *(m)*

banco comercial *(m)* Pt
De Handelsbank *(f)*
En merchant bank
Es banco mercantil *(m)*
Fr banque commerciale *(f)*
Pt banca commerciale *(f)*

banco d'agricultura *(m)* Pt
De Landbank *(f)*
En land bank
Es banco agrícola *(m)*
Fr banque agricole *(f)*
It banca agricola *(f)*

**banco de compensação e
rateio** *(m)* Pt
De Girobank *(f)*
En clearing bank
Es banco de compensación
(m)
Fr banque de virement *(f)*
It banca associate alla stan-
za di compensazione *(f)*

banco de compensación *(m)*
Es
De Girobank *(f)*
En clearing bank
Fr banque de virement *(f)*
It banca associata alla stan-
za di compensazione *(f)*
Pt banco de compensação e
rateio *(m)*

banco de empréstimos *(m)*
Pt
De Kreditbank *(f)*
En lending bank

Es banco de préstamos *(m)*
Fr banque de prêts *(f)*
It banca di prestiti *(f)*

banco de inversiones *(m)* Es
De Finanzbank *(f)*
En investment bank
Fr banque d'affaires *(f)*
It banca d'investimenti *(f)*
Pt banco de investimentos
(m)

banco de investimentos *(m)*
Pt
De Finanzbank *(f)*
En investment bank
Es banco de inversiones *(m)*
Fr banque d'affaires *(f)*
It banca d'investimenti *(f)*

banco de préstamos *(m)* Es
De Kreditbank *(f)*
En lending bank
Fr banque de prêts *(f)*
It banca di prestiti *(f)*
Pt banco de empréstimos *(m)*

banco emisor *(m)* Es
De Notenbank *(f)*
En issuing bank
Fr banque d'émission *(f)*
It banca di emissione *(f)*
Pt banca emissor *(m)*

banco emissor *(m)* Pt
De Notenbank *(f)*
En issuing bank
Es banco emisor *(m)*
Fr banque d'émission *(f)*
It banca di emissione *(f)*

**Banco Europeo de
Inversiones** *(m)* Es
De Europäische Investitions-
bank *(f)*
En European Investment
Bank
Fr Banque Européenne d'In-
vestissement *(f)*
It Banca Europea d'Investi-
menti *(f)*
Pt Banco Europeu de In-
vestimentos *(m)*

**Banco Europeu de
Investimentos** *(m)* Pt
De Europäische Investitions-
bank *(f)*
En European Investment
Bank

Es Banco Europeo de Inversiones *(m)*
Fr Banque Européenne d'Investissement *(f)*
It Banca Europea d'Investimenti *(f)*

banco fideicomisario *(m)* Es
De Treuhandgesellschaft *(f)*
En trust company
Fr société fiduciaire *(f)*
It società fiduciaria *(f)*
Pt empresa de investimentos
(f)

**Banco Internacional de Re-
construção e Desenvol-
vimento** *(m)* Pt
De Internationale Bank für
Wiederaufbau und Wirt-
schaftsförderung *(f)*
En International Bank for Reconstruction and Deve-
lopment
Es Banco Internacional para
Reconstrucción y
Desarrollo *(m)*
Fr Banque Internationale
pour la Reconstruction et
le Développement *(f)*
It Banca Internazionale per
la Riconstruzione e lo Sviluppo *(f)*

**Banco Internacional para
Reconstrucción y
Desarrollo** *(m)* Es
De Internationale Bank für
Wiederaufbau und Wirt-
schaftsförderung *(f)*
En International Bank for Re-
construction and Deve-
lopment
Fr Banque Internationale
pour la Reconstruction et
le Développement *(f)*
It Banca Internazionale per
la Ricostruzione e lo Svi-
luppo *(f)*
Pt Banco Internacional de
Reconstrução e Desenvol-
vimento *(m)*

banco mercantil *(m)* Es
De Handelsbank *(f)*
En merchant bank
Fr banque commerciale *(f)*
It banca commerciale *(f)*
Pt banco comercial *(m)*

banco privado *(m)* Es,Pt
De Privatbank *(f)*
En private bank
Fr banque privé *(f)*
It banca privata *(f)*

bandeira *(f)* n Pt
De Flagge *(f)*
En flag
Es bandera *(f)*
Fr pavillon, drapeau *(m)*
It bandiera *(f)*

bandeira de conveniência *(f)*
Pt
De billige Flagge *(f)*
En flag of convenience
Es bandera de conveniencia
(f)
Fr enseigne de convenance
(f)
It bandiera di convenienza *(f)*

bandeja *(f)* Es
De Palette *(f)*
En pallet
Fr palette *(f)*
It paletta *(f)*
Pt paleta *(f)*

bande magnétique *(f)* Fr
De Magnetband *(n)*
En magnetic tape
Es cinta magnética *(f)*
It nastro magnetico *(m)*
Pt fita magnética *(f)*

bandera *(f)* n Es
De Flagge *(f)*
En flag
Fr pavillon, drapeau *(m)*
It bandiera *(f)*
Pt bandeira *(f)*

bandera de conveniencia *(f)*
Es
De billige Flagge *(f)*
En flag of convenience
Fr enseigne de convenance
(f)
It bandiera di convenienza *(f)*
Pt bandeira de conveniência
(f)

bandiera *(f)* n It
De Flagge *(f)*
En flag
Es bandera *(f)*
Fr pavillon, drapeau (m)
Pt bandeira (f)

bandiera di convenienza *(f)* It
De billige Flagge *(f)*
En flag of convenience
Es bandera de conveniencia
(f)
Fr enseigne de convenance
(f)
Pt bandeira de conveniência
(f)

bank n En
De Bank (f)
Es banco *(m)*
Fr banque *(f)*
It banca *(f)*
Pt banco *(m)*

bank vb En
De einlegen
Es depositar (en el banco)
Fr déposer à banque
It depositare in una banca
Pt depositar (no banco)

Bank *(f)* n De
En bank
Es banco *(m)*
Fr banque *(f)*
It banca *(f)*
Pt banco *(m)*

bankable bills En
De diskontierbare Wechsel *(m
pl)*
Es efectos negociables *(m pl)*
Fr papier bancable *(m)*
It effetti scontabili *(m pl)*
Pt valores transaccionáveis
pelo banco *(m pl)*

bank account En
De Bankkonto *(n)*
Es cuenta bancaria *(f)*
Fr compte en banque *(m)*
It conto in banca *(m)*
Pt conta bancária *(f)*

Bankauftrag *(m)* De
En banker's order
Es orden bancaria *(f)*
Fr ordre bancaire *(m)*
It ordine bancario *(m)*
Pt ordem bancária *(f)*

bank balance En
De Bankguthaben *(n)*
Es saldo de banco *(m)*
Fr solde en banque *(m)*
It solda in banca *(m)*
Pt saldo no banco *(m)*

bankbook n Am
En passbook
De Bankbuch, Sparbuch (n)
Es libreta de banco (f)
Fr carnet de compte (m)
It libretto di conto (m)
Pt livrete de conta (m)

Bankbuch (n) n De
En passbook
Am bankbook
Es libreta de banco (f)
Fr carnet de compte (m)
It libretto di conto
Pt livrete de conta (m)

bank charges En
De Bankspesen (f pl)
Es gastos de banco (m pl)
Fr frais bancaires (m pl)
It spese di banca (f pl)
Pt taxas bancárias (f pl)

bank crash En
De Bankkrach (m)
Es quiebra de banco (f)
Fr krach d'une banque (m)
It crollo di banca (m)
Pt falência bancária (f)

bank credit En
De Bankkredit (m)
Es crédito bancario (m)
Fr crédit bancaire (m)
It credito bancario (m)
Pt crédito bancário (m)

bank credit card Am
En cheque card
De Scheckkarte (f)
Es tarjeta de cheque (f)
Fr carte de chèque (f)
It scheda per assegni (f)
Pt cartão de validação de
    cheques (m)

Bankdarlehen (n) n De
En bank loan
Es préstamo bancario (m)
Fr prêt bancaire (m)
It prestito bancario (m)
Pt empréstimo bancário (m)

bank deposit En
De Bankeinlage (f)
Es depósito bancario (m)
Fr dépôt bancaire (m)
It deposito bancario (m)
Pt depósito bancário (m)

bank discount En
De Diskont (m)
Es descuento bancario (m)
Fr escompte en dehors (m)
It sconto di banca (m)
Pt desconto bancário (m)

Bankeinlage (f) n De
En bank deposit
Es depósito bancario (m)
Fr dépôt bancaire (m)
It deposito bancario (m)
Pt depósito bancário (m)

banker n En
De Bankier (m)
Es banquero (m)
Fr banquier (m)
It banchiere (m)
Pt banqueiro (m)

banker's draft En
De Banktratte (f)
Es giro bancario (m)
Fr traite bancaire (f)
It tratta bancaria (f)
Pt letra de banco (f)

banker's indemnity En
Am banker's guarantee
De Bankgarantie (f)
Es garantía bancaria (f)
Fr garantie de banque (f)
It garanzia bancaria (f)
Pt garantia bancária (f)

banker's order En
De Bankauftrag (m)
Es orden bancaria (f)
Fr ordre bancaire (m)
It ordine bancario (m)
Pt ordem bancária (f)

banker's reference En
De Bankzeugnis (n)
Es referencia bancaria (f)
Fr référence de banquier (f)
It referenza bancaria (f)
Pt referência bancária (f)

Bankgarantie (f) n De
En banker's indemnity
Am banker's guarantee
Es garantía bancaria (f)
Fr garantie de banque (f)
It garanzia bancaria (f)
Pt garantia bancária (f)

Bankguthaben (n) n De
En bank balance
Es saldo de banco (m)
Fr solde en banque (m)
It saldo in banca (m)
Pt saldo no banco (m)

Bank Holiday En
Am legal holiday
De gesetzlicher Feiertag (m)
Es día de fiesta (m)
Fr jour férié (m)
It festività legali (f)
Pt feriado (m)

Bankier (m) De
En banker
Es banquero (m)
Fr banquier (m)
It banchiere (m)
Pt banqueiro (m)

Bankkonto (n) n De
En bank account
Es cuenta bancaria (f)
Fr compte en banque (m)
It conto in banca (m)
Pt conta bancária (f)

Bankkrach (m) n De
En bank crash
Es quiebra de banco (f)
Fr krach d'une banque (m)
It crollo di banca (m)
Pt falência bancária (f)

Bankkredit (m) n De
En bank credit
Es crédito bancario (m)
Fr crédit bancaire (m)
It credito bancario (m)
Pt crédito bancário (m)

bank loan En
De Bankdarlehen (n)
Es préstamo bancario (m)
Fr prêt bancaire (m)
It prestito bancario (m)
Pt empréstimo bancário (m)

banknote n En
Am bill
De Banknote (f)
Es billete de banco (m)
Fr billet de banque (m)
It biglietto di banca (m)
Pt nota de banco (f)

Banknote *(f)* n De
En banknote
Am bill
Es billete de banco *(m)*
Fr billet de banque *(m)*
It biglietto di banca *(m)*
Pt nota de banco *(f)*

bank rate En
De Diskontsatz, Banksatz *(m)*
Es tasa de descuento *(f)*
Fr taux d'escompte *(m)*
It tasso di sconto *(m)*
Pt taxa de desconto *(f)*

Bankrott *(m)* n De
En bankruptcy; failure
Es quiebra; insolvencia *(f)*
Fr failite *(f)*
It bancarotta, fallimento *(f m)*
Pt falência *(f)*

bankrupt n En
De Gemeinschuldner *(m)*
Es quebrada *(m)*
Fr failli *(m)*
It fallito *(m)*
Pt falido *(m)*

bankruptcy n En
De Konkurs, Bankrott *(m)*
Es quiebra *(f)*
Fr faillite *(f)*
It fallimento, bancarotta *(m f)*
Pt falência *(f)*

Banksatz *(f)* n De
En bank rate
Es tasa de descuento *(f)*
Fr taux d'escompte *(m)*
It tasso di sconto *(m)*
Pt taxa de desconto *(f)*

Bankspesen *(f pl)* n De
En bank charges
Es gastos de banco *(m pl)*
Fr frais bancaires *(m pl)*
It spese die banca *(f pl)*
Pt taxas bancárias *(f pl)*

bank statement En
De Kontoauszug *(m)*
Es extracto de cuenta *(m)*
Fr relevé de compte *(m)*
It estratto conto *(m)*
Pt extracto de conta bancária *(m)*

bank transfer En
De Banküberweisung *(f)*
Es transferencia bancaria *(f)*
Fr virement bancaire *(m)*
It trasferimento bancario *(m)*
Pt transfêrencia bancária *(f)*

Banktratte *(f)* n De
En banker's draft
Es giro bancario *(m)*
Fr traite bancaire *(f)*
It tratta bancaria *(f)*
Pt letra de banco *(f)*

Banküberweisung *(f)* n De
En bank transfer
Es transferencia bancaria *(f)*
Fr virement bancaire *(m)*
It trasferimento bancario *(m)*
Pt transferência bancária *(f)*

Bankzeugnis *(n)* n De
En banker's reference
Es referencia bancaria *(f)*
Fr référence de banquier *(f)*
It referenza bancaria *(f)*
Pt referência bancária *(f)*

banque *(f)* n Fr
De Bank *(f)*
En bank
Es banco *(m)*
It banca *(f)*
Pt banco *(m)*

banque agricole *(f)* Fr
De Landbank *(f)*
En land bank
Es banco agrícola *(m)*
It banca agricola *(f)*
Pt banco d'agricultura *(m)*

banque commerciale *(f)* Fr
De Handelsbank *(f)*
En merchant bank
Es banco mercantil *(m)*
It banca commerciale *(f)*
Pt banco comercial *(m)*

banque d'affaires *(f)* Fr
De Finanzbank *(f)*
En investment bank
Es banco de inversiones *(m)*
It banca d'investimenti *(m)*
Pt banco de investimentos *(m)*

banque d'émission *(f)* Fr
De Notenbank *(f)*
Es issuing bank

Es banco emisor *(m)*
It banca di emissione *(f)*
Pt banco emissor *(m)*

banque de prêts *(f)* Fr
De Kreditbank *(f)*
En lending bank
Es banco de préstamos *(m)*
It banca di prestiti *(f)*
Pt banco de empréstimos *(m)*

banque de virement *(f)* Fr
De Girobank *(f)*
En clearing-bank
Es banco de compensación *(m)*
It banca associata alla stanza di compensazione *(f)*
Pt banco de compensação e rateio *(m)*

Banque Européenne d'Investissement *(f)* Fr
De Europäische Investitionsbank *(f)*
En European Investment Bank
Es Banco Europeo e Inversiones *(m)*
It Banca Europea d'Investimenti *(f)*
Pt Banco Europeu de Investimentos *(m)*

Banque Internationale pour la Reconstruction et le Développement *(f)* Fr
De Internationale Bank für Wiederaufbau und Wirtschaftsförderung *(f)*
En International Bank for Reconstruction and Development
Es Banco Internacional para Reconstrucción y Desarrollo *(m)*
It Banca Internazionale per la Ricostruzione e lo Sviluppo *(f)*
Pt Banco Internacional de Reconstrução e Desenvol- . vimento *(m)*

banqueiro *(m)* n Pt
De Bankier *(m)*
En banker
Es banquero *(m)*
Fr banquier *(m)*
It banchiere *(m)*

banque privée *(f)* Fr
De Privatbank *(f)*
En private bank
Es banco privado *(m)*
It banca privata *(f)*
Pt banco privado *(m)*

banquero *(m) n* Es
De Bankier *(m)*
En banker
Fr banquier *(m)*
It banchiere *(m)*
Pt banqueiro *(m)*

banque succursale *(f)* Fr
De Filialbank, Zweigbank *(f)*
En branch bank
Es sucursal del banco *(f)*
It banca succursale *(f)*
Pt filial de banco *(f)*

banquier *(m) n* Fr
De Bankier *(m)*
En banker
Es banquero *(m)*
It banchiere *(m)*
Pt banqueiro *(m)*

barataria *(f) n* Pt
De Baratterie *(f)*
En barratry
Es baratería *(f)*
Fr baraterie *(f)*
It baratteria *(f)*

baratería *(f) n* Es
De Baratterie *(f)*
En barratry
Fr baraterie *(f)*
It baratteria *(f)*
Pt barataria *(f)*

baraterie *(f) n* Fr
De Baratterie *(f)*
En barratry
Es baratería *(f)*
It baratteria *(f)*
Pt barataria *(f)*

barato *adj* Es, Pt
De billig
En cheap
Fr bon marché
It a buon mercato

barattare *vb* It
De Tauschhandel treiben
En barter
Es trocar

Fr troquer
Pt trocar

baratteria *(f) n* It
De Baratterie *(f)*
En barratry
Es barateria *(f)*
Fr baraterie *(f)*
Pt barataria *(f)*

Baratterie *(f) n* De
En barratry
Es baratería *(f)*
Fr baraterie *(f)*
It baratteria *(f)*
Pt barataria *(f)*

Barbestand *(m) n* De
En cash in hand
Es efectivo en caja *(m)*
Fr espèces en caisse *(f pl)*
It pronti contanti *(m pl)*
Pt fundos à ordem *(m pl)*

barcaça *(f) n* Pt
De Lastkahn; Leichter *(m)*
En barge; lighter
Es barcaza; gabarra *(f)*
Fr péniche; allège *(f)*
It chiatta *(f)*

barcaza *(f) n* Es
De Lastkahn; Leichter *(m)*
En barge; lighter
Fr péniche; allège *(f)*
It chiatta *(f)*
Pt barcaça *(f)*

barco *(m) n* Es
De Schiff *(n)*
En ship
Fr navire *(m)*
It nave *(f)*
Pt naivo *(m)*

barco de contenedores *(m)*
     Es
De Containerschiff *(n)*
En container ship
Fr navire porte-containers
     (m)
It nave de contenitori *(f)*
Pt navio de contentores *(m)*

barco de travessia *(m)* Es
De Fährboot *(n)*
En ferry-boat
Es transbordador *(m)*

Fr bac *(m)*
It nave traghetto *(f)*

barco mercante *(m)* Es
De Handelsschiff *(n)*
En merchant ship
Fr navire marchand *(m)*
It nave mercantile *(f)*
Pt navio mercante *(m)*

barème *(m) n* Fr
De Tarif *(m)*
En scale (of fees, charges,
     etc.)
Es tarifa *(f)*
It tariffa *(f)*
Pt tarifa *(f)*

bargain (deal) *n* En
De Handel *(m)*
Es negocio *(m)*
Fr marché; affaire *(m f)*
It affaare *(m)*
Pt negócio *(m)*

bargain (cheap purchase) *n*
     En
De Gelegenheitskauf *(m)*
Es ganga *(f)*
Fr occasion *(f)*
It accasione *(f)*
Pt pechincha *(f)*

bargain *vb* Am
En haggle
De feilschen
Es regatear
Fr machander; chipoter
It mercanteggiare; cavillare
Pt regatear

bargain-hunting *n* En
De Jagd nach Sonder-
     angeboten *(f)*
Es caza de rebajas *(f)*
Fr chasse aux soldes *(f)*
It caccia alle occasioni *(f)*
Pt caça aos saldos *(f)*

bargaining position En
De Verhandlungslage *(f)*
Es situación de negociar *(f)*
Fr situation permettant de
     négocier *(f)*
It situazione permettente di
     trattare *(f)*
Pt situação de regatear *(f)*

bargaining power En
De Verhandlungsposition *(f)*
Es poder de negociación *(m)*
Fr pouvoir de négociation *(m)*
It potere di contrattare *(m)*
Pt poder de regateio *(m)*

bargain offer En
De Sonderangebot *(n)*
Es oferta de ocasión *(f)*
Fr offre exceptionelle *(f)*
It offerta d'occasione *(f)*
Pt oferta a preço excepcional
(f)

bargain price En
De Spottpreis *(m)*
Es precio de ocasión *(m)*
Fr prix de solde *(m)*
It prezzo d'occasione *(m)*
Pt preço excepcional *(m)*

barge *n* Es
De Lastkahn *(m)*
Es barcaza *(f)*
Fr péniche *(f)*
It chiatta *(f)*
Pt barcaça *(f)*

bar gegen Versandpapiere
De
En cash against documents
(c.a.d)
Es al contado contra docu-
mentos
Fr comptant contre docu-
ments
It contanti contro documenti
Pt em dinheiro contra docu-
mentação

Bargeld *(n)* *n* De
En cash
Es dinero efectivo *(m)*
Fr espèces *(f pl)*
It denaro *(m)*
Pt dinheiro *(m)*

**Bargeldauszahlungs-
automat** *(m)* *n* De
En cash dispenser
Es caja automática *(f)*
Fr distributeur d'argent
comptant *(m)*
It cassa automatica *(f)*
Pt caixa automática *(f)*

Bargeldvoraussage *(f)* *n* De
En cash forecast
Es previsión de fondos *(f)*

Fr prévision comptant *(f)*
It previsione contanti *(f)*
Pt previsão de fundos (em
dinheiro) *(f)*

Bargeschäft *(n)* *n* De
En cash deal
Es trata al contado *(m)*
Fr transaction au comptant
(f)
It operazione a contanti *(f)*
Pt negócio em dinheiro *(m)*

Barrabatt *(m)* *n* De
En cash discount
Es descuento de caja *(m)*
Fr escompte de caisse *(m)*
It sconto per pergamento a
contanti *(m)*
Pt desconto de contado *(m)*

barratry *n* En
De Baratterie *(f)*
Es bQatería *(f)*
Fr baraterie *(f)*
It baratteria *(f)*
Pt barataria *(f)*

barreira alfandegária *(f)* Pt
De Zollschranke *(f)*
En customs barrier
Es barrera aduanera *(f)*
Fr barrière douanière *(f)*
It barriera doganale *(f)*

barreira comercial *(f)* Pt
De Handelsschranke *(f)*
En trade barrier
Es barrera comercial *(f)*
Fr barrière commerciale *(f)*
It barriera commerciale *(f)*

barrel *n* En
De Faß *(n)*
Es barril *(m)*
Fr tonneau *(m)*
It botte *(f)*
Pt barril *(m)*

Barren *(m)* *n* De
En ingot
Es lingote *(m)*
Fr lingot; barre *(m f)*
It lingotto *(m)*
Pt lingote *(m)*

barrera aduanera *(f)* Es
De Zollschranke *(f)*
En customs barrier

Fr barrière douanière *(f)*
It barriera doganale *(f)*
Pt barreira alfandegária *(f)*

barrera comercial *(f)* Es
De Handelsschranke *(f)*
En trade barrier
Fr barrière commerciale *(f)*
It barriera commerciale *(f)*
Pt barreira comercial *(f)*

barriera commerciale *(f)* It
De Handelsschranke *(f)*
En trade barrier
Es barrera comercial *(f)*
Fr barrière commerciale *(f)*
Pt barreira comercial *(f)*

barreira doganale *(f)* It
De Zollschranke *(f)*
En customs barrier
Es barrera aduanera *(f)*
Fr barrière douanière *(f)*
Pt barreira alfandegária *(f)*

barrière commerciale *(f)* Fr
De Handelsschranke *(f)*
En trade barrier
Es barrera comercial *(f)*
It barriera commerciale *(f)*
Pt barreira comercial *(f)*

barrière douanière *(f)* Fr
De Zollschranke *(f)*
En customs barrier
Es barrera aduanera *(f)*
It barriera doganale *(f)*
Pt barreira alfandegária *(f)*

barril *(m)* *n* Es, Pt
De Faß *(n)*
En barrel
Fr tonneau *(m)*
It botte *(f)*

barrister *n* En
Am attorney
De Anwalt *(m)*
Es abogado *(m)*
Fr avocat *(m)*
It avvocato *(m)*
Pt advogado *(m)*

barter *vb* En
De Tauschhandel treiben
Es trocar
Fr troquer
It barattare
Pt trocar

base aurea *(f)* It
De Goldobligation *(f)*
En gold standard
Es patrón oro *(m)*
Fr étalon or *(m)*
Pt ouro-padrão *(m)*

base contributiva *(f)* Es
De Steuerveranlagung *(f)*
En tax base
Fr assiette de l'impôt *(f)*
It ripartizione della
tassazione *(f)*
Pt base de imposto *(f)*

base de imposto *(f)* Pt
De Steuerveranlagung *(f)*
En tax base
Es base contributiva *(f)*
Fr assiete de l'impôt *(f)*
It ripartizione della
tassazione *(f)*

base metal En
De unedles Metall *(n)*
Es metal no noble *(m)*
Fr métal vil *(m)*
It basso metallo *(m)*
Pt metal pobre *(m)*

base salarial *(f)* Pt
De Lohnsatz *(m)*
En wage rate
Es tarifa de salarios *(f)*
Fr taux des salaires *(m)*
It tariffa salariale *(f)*

base year En
De Grundjahr *(n)*
Es ano de base *(m)*
Fr année de base *(f)*
It anno di base *(m)*
Pt ano base *(m)*

basic pay En
Am base pay
De Grundlohn *(m)*
Es salario-base *(m)*
Fr salaire de base *(f)*
It salario fondamentale *(m)*
Pt salário-base *(m)*

bassin de radoub *(m)* Fr
De Trockendock *(n)*
En graving dock
Es dique de carenas *(m)*
It bacino di raddobbo *(m)*
Pt doca de querenas *(f)*

bassin houiller *(m)* Fr
De Kohlenrevier *(n)*
En coal field
Es yacimiento de carbón *(m)*
It bacino carbonifero *(m)*
Pt jazigo de carvão *(m)*

basso metallo *(m)* It
De unedles Metall *(n)*
En base metal
Es metal no noble *(m)*
Fr métal vil *(m)*
Pt metal pobre *(m)*

batch *n* En
De Stoß *(m)*
Es lote *(m)*
Fr lot *(m)*
It lotto *(m)*
Pt loto *(m)*

batch costing En
De Stapelkostenberechnung
(f)
Es fijación de precio por lotes
(f)
Fr évaluation du coût des lots
(f)
It valutazione del costo per
partita *(f)*
Pt fixação de preço por lote *(f)*

bateau à vapeur *(m)* Fr
De Dampfer *(m)*
En steamer
Es buque de vapor *(m)*
It vapore *(m)*
Pt vapor *(m)*

Baukredit *(m)* n De
En building oan
Es crédito de construcción
(m)
Es crédit de construction *(m)*
It prestito immobiliare *(m)*
Pt empréstimo para contrução
(m)

Bauland *(n)* n De
En building land
Es solares *(m pl)*
Fr terrain à bâtir *(m)*
It terreno edile *(m)*
Pt terreno para construção *(m)*

Bauunternehmer *(m)* n De
En building contractor
Es contratista de obras *(m)*
Fr entrepreneur de bâtiment
(m)

It impresa edile *(f)*
Pt construtor de obras *(m)*

Beamter *(m)* n De
En civil servant
Am government employee
Es funcionario del gobierno
(m)
Fr fonctionnaire *(m)*
It impiegato statale *(m)*
Pt funcionário público *(m)*

bear *n* En
De Baissespekulant; Baissier
(m)
Es bajista *(m)*
Fr baissier *(m)*
It ribassista *(m)*
Pt baixista *(m)*

bear account En
De Baissekonto *(n)*
Es cuenta de especulaciones
a la baja *(f)*
Fr compte des speculations
à la baisse *(m)*
It conto di speculazioni al ri-
basso *(m)*
Pt conta de especulações bai-
xistas *(f)*

bearer bond En
De Inhaberobligation *(f)*
Es título al portador *(m)*
Fr bon au porteur *(m)*
It titolo al portatore *(m)*
Pt título ao portador *(m)*

bearer debenture En
De Inhaberobligation *(f)*
Es obligación al portador *(f)*
Fr obligation au porteur *(f)*
It obligazione al portatore *(f)*
Pt obrigação ao portador *(f)*

bearer security En
De Inhabereffekten *(n pl)*
Es valor al portador *(m)*
Fr valeur au porteur *(f)*
It valore al portatore *(f)*
Pt título ao portador *(m)*

bearish *adj* En
De flau
Es bajista
Fr orienté à la baisse
It ribassista
Pt baixista

bear market En
De Baissemarkt *(m)*
Es mercado bajista *(m)*
Fr marché orienté à la baisse
  (m)
It mercato tendente al ribas-
  so *(m)*
Pt mercado de tendência
  baixista *(m)*

become operative En
De wirksam werden
Es entrar en vigor
Fr entrer en vigueur
It entrare in vigore
Pt entrar em vigor

bedingt *adj* De
En conditional
Es condicional
Fr conditionnel
It condizionale
Pt condicional

Bedingung *(f) n* De
En condition
Es condición *(f)*
Fr condition *(f)*
It condizione *(f)*
Pt condição *(f)*

Bedingungen *(f pl) n* De
En terms
Es condiciones *(f pl)*
Fr conditions *(f pl)*
It condizioni *(f pl)*
Pt condições (f pl)

beeidigte Erklärung *(f)* De
En affidavit
Es declaración jurada *(f)*
Fr déclaration sous serment
  (f)
It dichiarazione giurata *(f)*
Pt declaração sob juramento
  (f)

befördern *vb* De
En promote
Es ascender
Fr donner de l'avancement
It promuovere
Pt promover

Beförderung (eines Ange-
  stellten)*(f) n* De
En promotion
Es ascenso; promoción *(m f)*

Fr avancement; promotion
  (m f)
It avanzamento; promozione
  (m f)
Pt promoção *(f)*

Beförderung (Transport)*(f) n*
  De
En transport
Es transporte *(m)*
Fr transport *(m)*
It trasporto *(m)*
Pt transporte *(m)*

Befrachter *(m) n* De
En charterer
Es fletador *(m)*
Fr affréteur *(m)*
It noleggiatore *(m)*
Pt fretador *(m)*

Befrachtung *(f) n* De
En chartering
Es fletamentor *(m)*
Fr affrètement *(m)*
It noleggio *(m)*
Pt fretamento *(m)*

Befragte(r) *(m) n* De
En interviewee
Es persona entrevistada *(f)*
Fr personne interrogée *(f)*
It intervistato *(m)*
Pt entrevistado *(m)*

befreien *vb* De
En free
Es liberar
Fr libérer; affranchir
It liberare
Pt libertar; livrar

Befreiung *(f) n* De
En exemption
Es exención *(f)*
Fr exemption *(f)*
It esenzione *(f)*
Pt isenção *(f)*

Befugnis *(f) n* De
En warrant
Es mandato *(m)*
Fr ordonnance *(f)*
It mandato *(m)*
Pt mandato *(m)*

begebbar *adj* De
En negotiable
Es negociable

Fr négociable
It negoziabile
Pt negociável

begebbares Wertpapier *(n)*
  De
En negotiable instrument
Es titulo negociable *(m)*
Fr effet de commerce *(m)*
It titulo negoziabile *(m)*
Pt título negociável *(m)*

beglaubigte Abschrift *(f)* De
En certified true copy
Es copia auténtica *(f)*
Fr copie certifiée *(f)*
It copia conforme *(f)*
Pt cópia autenticada *(f)*

**(zur) Begleichung vorge-
  legte Rechnung** *(f)* De
En account rendered
Es cuenta rendida *(f)*
Fr compte rendu *(m)*
It conto reso *(m)*
Pt conta remetida *(f)*

Begünstigte(r) *(m) n* De
En beneficiary
Es beneficiario *(m)*
Fr bénéficiaire *(m)*
It beneficiario *(m)*
Pt beneficiário *(m)*

behalten *vb* De
En keep
Es tener; conservar
Fr tenir; maintenir
It tenere; mantenere
Pt manter; reter

Beilage *(f) n* De
En enclosure
Es anexo *(m)*
Fr annexe *(f)*
It allegato *(m)*
Pt anexo *(m)*

beiliegend *adj* De
En enclosed
Es adjunto
Fr ci-joint; ci-inclus
It accluso
Pt incluso

bei Nichterfüllung De
En in case of default
Es en caso de incumplimiento
Fr en cas de défaillance

It in caso di inadempienza
Pt em caso de não cumprimento

bei Sicht De
En at sight
Es a la vista
Fr à vue
It a vista
Pt à vista

Beitrag *(m)* n De
En contribution
Es contribución *(f)*
Fr contribution *(f)*
It contributo *(m)*
Pt contribuição *(f)*

beitragen *vb* De
En contribute
Es contribuir
Fr contribuer
It contribuire
Pt contribuir

beitragsfreie Police *(f)* De
En paid-up policy
Es póliza liberda *(f)*
Fr assurance libérée *(f)*
It polizza interamente pagata *(f)*
Pt apólice liquidada *(f)*

Belegschaft *(f)* n De
En work force
Es masa obrera *(f)*
Fr effectif *(m pl)*
It massa lavoratrice *(f)*
Pt massa trabalhadora *(f)*

Belegstück *(n)* n De
En voucher
Es pieza justificativa *(f)*
Fr pièce justificative; fiche *(f)*
It pezza d'appoggio *(f)*
Pt vale *(m)*

beliefern *vb* De
En supply
Es surtir
Fr fournir
It fornire
Pt fornecer

benachrichtigen *vb* De
En inform
Es informar; avisar
Fr informer; renseigner
It informare
Pt informar

Benachrichtigung *(f)* n De
En notice; communication
Es aviso; comunicación *(m f)*
Fr avis; communication *(m f)*
It avviso; comunicazione *(m f)*
Pt aviso; comunicação *(m f)*

Benannte(r) *(m)* n De
En nominee
Es nominatario *(m)*
Fr personne dénommée *(f)*
It persona nominata *(f)*
Pt nomeado *(m)*

bénéfice *(m)* n Fr
De Gewinn *(m)*
En profit
Es ganancia; beneficio *(f m)*
It utile; profitto *(m)*
Pt lucro; beneficio *(m)*

bénéfice brut *(m)* Fr
De Bruttogewinn *(m)*
En gross profit
Es ganancia bruta *(f)*
It utile lordo *(m)*
Pt lucro bruto *(m)*

bénéfice net *(m)* Fr
De Reingewinn *(m)*
En net profit
Es ganancia neta *(f)*
It utile netto *(m)*
Pt lucro liquido *(m)*

bénéfice par titre *(m)* Fr
De Gewinn pro Aktie *(n)*
En earnings per share
Es beneficios por acción *(m pl)*
It profitti per azione *(m pl)*
Pt proventos por acção *(m pl)*

bénéfices non répartis *(n pl)* Fr
De unverteilte Gewinne *(n pl)*
En undistributed profits
Es beneficios no distribuidos *(m pl)*
It profitti non distribuiti *(m pl)*
Pt lucros não distribuidos *(m pl)*

bénéficiaire *(m)* n Fr
De Begünstigte(r); Zahlungsberechtigte(r) *(m)*
En beneficiary, payee
Es beneficiario *(m)*

It beneficiario *(m)*
Pt beneficiário *(m)*

benficial interest En
De Nießbrauchsrecht *(n)*
Es usufructo *(m)*
Fr usufruit *(m)*
It usufrutto *(m)*
Pt usufruto *(m)*

benficial owner En
De Nießbrauchnutzer *(m)*
Es usufructuario *(m)*
Fr usufruitier *(m)*
It usufruttuario *(m)*
Pt usufrutuário *(m)*

beneficiario *(m)* n Es, It
De Begünstigte(r), Zahlungsberechtigte(r) *(m)*
En beneficiary, payee
Fr bénéficiaire *(m)*
Pt beneficiário *(m)*

beneficiário *(m)* n Pt
De Begünstigte(r); Zahlungsberechtigte(r) *(m)*
En beneficiary; payee
Es beneficiario *(m)*
Fr bénéficiaire *(m)*
It beneficiario *(m)*

beneficiário de empréstimo *(m)* Pt
De Kreditnehmer *(m)*
En borrower
Es prestatario *(m)*
Fr emprunteur *(m)*
It accattatore *(m)*

beneficiary n En
De Begünstigte(r) *(m)*
Es beneficiario *(m)*
Fr bénéficiaire *(m)*
It beneficiario *(m)*
Pt beneficiário *(m)*

beneficio *(m)* n Es
De Gewinn *(m)*
En profit
Fr bénéfice *(m)*
It utile *(m)*
Pt benefício *(m)*

benefício *(m)* n Pt
De Gewinn *(m)*
En profit
Es beneficio *(m)*
Fr bénéfice *(m)*
It utile *(m)*

beneficio razonable *(m)* Es
De angemessener Ertrag *(m)*
En fair return
Fr rendement équitable *(m)*
It discreto profitto *(m)*
Pt rendimento justo *(m)*

beneficios extras *(m pl)* Pt
De Sozialleistungen *(f pl)*
En fringe benefits
Es beneficios suplementarios
   (m pl)
Fr avantages accessoires
   (m pl)
It vantaggi accessori *(m pl)*

beneficios no distribuidos
   (m pl) Es
De unverteilte Gewinne *(f pl)*
En undistributed profits
Fr bénéfices non répartis
   (m pl)
It profitti non distribuiti *(m pl)*
Pt lucros não distribuidos *(m pl)*

beneficio sobre capital *(m)*
   Es
De Kapitalertrag *(m)*
En return on capital
Fr rémunération du capital *(f)*
It reddito del capitale *(m)*
Pt juro sobre o capital *(m)*

beneficios por acción *(m pl)*
   Es
De Gewinn pro Aktie *(n)*
En earnings per share
Fr bénéfice par titre *(m)*
It profitti per azione *(m pl)*
Pt proventos por acção *(m pl)*

beneficios sobre capital
   (m pl) Es
De Kapitalgewinn *(n)*
En capital gains
Fr gains en capital *(m pl)*
It plusvalore di capitale
   (m pl)
Pt lucros de capital *(m pl)*

beneficios suplementarios
   (m pl) Es
De Sozialleistungen *(f pl)*
En fringe benefits
Fr avantages accessoires
   (m pl)
It vantaggi accessori *(m pl)*
Pt benefícios extras *(m pl)*

Benennung des Bestim-
   mungshafens *(f)* De
En port mark
Es marca de destino *(f)*
Fr marque de destination *(f)*
It marche di destinazione
   (f pl)
Pt marca de porto *(f)*

beni di consumo *(m pl)* It
De Konsumgüter *(n pl)*
En consumer goods
Es bienes de consumo *(m pl)*
Fr biens de consommation
   (m pl)
Pt bens de consumo *(m pl)*

beni di consumo durabili
   (m pl) It
De dauerhafte Konsumgüter
   (n pl)
En consumer durables
Es bienes de consumo du-
   raderos *(m pl)*
Fr biens de consommation
   durables *(m pl)*
Pt artigos de consumo perdu
   ráveis *(m pl)*

beni di consumo non
   durevoli *(m pl)* It
De nicht dauerhafte Ver-
   brauchsgüter *(n pl)*
En consumer non-durables
Es bienes de consumo
   perecederos *(m pl)*
Fr biens de consommation
   non-durables *(m pl)*
Pt bens de consumo não
   duráveis *(m pl)*

beni durevoli *(m pl)* It
De langlebige Güter *(n pl)*
En durable goods
Es mercancías no perecede-
   ras *(f pl)*
Fr biens durables *(m pl)*
Pt mercadorias imperecíveis
   (f pl)

beni immobili *(m pl)* It
De unbewegliches Vermögen;
   Immobilien *(n; f pl)*
En real estate
Es bienes inmuebles *(m pl)*
Fr biens immeubles *(m pl)*
Pt propriedade imobiliária *(f)*

beni incorporali *(m pl)* It
De nicht greifbare Aktiven
   (n pl)
En intangible assets
Es activo intangible *(m)*
Fr actif incorporel *(m)*
Pt bens intocáveis *(m pl)*

beni materiali *(m pl)* It
De greifbare Aktiven *(n pl)*
en tangible assets
Es activo tangible *(m)*
Fr biens immobiliers *(m pl)*
Pt bens visíveis *(m pl)*

beni strumentali *(m pl)* It
De Anlagegüter *(n pl)*
En capital goods
Es bienes de producción
   (m pl)
Fr biens d'équipement *(m pl)*
Pt mercadorias de capital
   (f pl)

bens *(m pl)* n Pt
De Vermögen *(n)*
En estate; property
Es finca *(f)*
Fr bien; propriété *(m f)*
It proprietà *(f)*

bens de activo líquidos *(m pl)*
   Pt
De flüssige Aktiven *(n pl)*
En liquid assets
Es activo líquido *(m)*
Fr actif liquide *(m)*
It disponibilità; attività
   liquida *(f)*

bens de capital *(m pl)* Pt
De Vermögensanlage *(f)*
En capital asset
Am fixed asset
Es activo fijo *(m)*
Fr actif immobilisé *(m)*
It capitale fisso *(m)*

bens de consumo *(m pl)* Pt
De Konsumgüter *(n pl)*
En consumer goods
Es bienes de consumo *(m pl)*
Fr biens de consommation
   (m pl)
It beni di consumo *(m pl)*

bens de consumo não
   duráveis *(m pl)* Pt
De nicht dauerhafte Ver-
   brauchsgüter *(n pl)*

En consumer non-durables
Es bienes de consumo
    perecederos *(m pl)*
Fr biens de consommation
    non-durables *(m pl)*
It beni di consumo non
    durevoli *(m pl)*

bens do activo congelados
    (m pl) Pt
De eingefrorene Guthaben
    (n pl)
En frozen assets
Es activos congelados *(m pl)*
Fr fonds bloqués *(m pl)*
It attivo congelato *(m)*

bens fixos *(m pl)* Pt
De Anlagevermögen *(n)*
en fixed assets
Es activo fijo *(m)*
Fr immobilisations *(f pl)*
It immobilizzazioni; attivo
    fisso *(f pl; m)*

bens intocáveis *(m pl)* Pt
De nicht greifbare Aktiven
    (n pl)
En intangible assets
Es activo intangible *(m)*
Fr actif incorporel *(m)*
It beni incorporali *(m pl)*

bens líquidos *(m pl)* Pt
De Reinvermögen *(n)*
En net assets
Es activo neto *(m)*
Fr actif net *(m)*
It attivo netto *(m)*

bens mobiliários *(m pl)* Pt
De bewegliche Güter *(n pl)*
En movable assets
Es mobiliario *(m)*
Fr biens mobiliers *(m pl)*
It proprietà mobiliare *(f)*

bens no activo actual *(m pl)*
    Pt
De Umlaufvermögen *(n)*
En current assets
Es activo realizable *(m)*
Fr actif courant *(m)*
It attivo liquido *(m)*

bens visíveis *(m pl)* Pt
De greifbare Aktiven *(n pl)*
En tangible assets
Es activo tangible *(m)*

Fr biens immobiliers *(m pl)*
It beni materiali *(m pl)*

Berater *(m)* n De
En consultant
Es consultor *(m)*
Fr conseil *(m)*
It consulente *(m)*
Pt consultor *(m)*

Beratungs- De
En advisory
Es consultivo
Fr consultatif
It consultivo
Pt consultivo

Beratungsausschuß *(m)* n De
En advisory board
Es consejo consultivo *(m)*
Fr comité consultatif *(m)*
It consiglio consultivo *(m)*
Pt comité consultivo *(m)*

berechnen *vb* De
En calculate
Es calcular
Fr calculer
It calcolare
Pt calcular

Berechnung *(f)* n De
En calculation
Es cálculo *(m)*
Fr calcul *(m)*
It calcolazione *(f)*
Pt cálculo *(m)*

Bergegeld *(n)* n De
En salvage charges
Es cargos de salvamento
    (m pl)
Fr indemnité de sauvetage *(f)*
It spese di salvataggio *(f pl)*
Pt encargos de salvamento
    (m pl)

Bergung *(f)* n De
En salvage
Es salvamento *(m)*
Fr sauvetage *(m)*
It salvataggio *(m)*
Pt salvamento *(m)*

Bergwerk *(n)* n De
En mine
Es mina *(f)*
Fr mine *(f)*
It miniera *(f)*
Pt mina *(f)*

Bergwerkskonzession *(f)* n
    De
En mineral concession
Es concesión minera *(f)*
Fr concession minière *(f)*
It concessione mineraria *(f)*
Pt concessão mineira *(f)*

Bericht *(m)* n De
En report
Es informe, reportaje *(m)*
Fr rapport; compte-rendu
    (m)
It relazione; rapporto *(f m)*
Pt relatório *(m)*

Berichtigung *(f)* n De
En correction
Es corrección *(f)*
Fr correction *(f)*
It correzione *(f)*
Pt correcção *(f)*

bersaglio *(m)* n It
De Ziel *(n)*
En target
Es objetivo *(m)*
Fr but *(m)*
Pt objectivo *(m)*

Beruf *(m)* n De
En job; occupation
Es trabajo *(m)*
Fr occupation *(f)*
It lavoro; occupazione *(m f)*
Pt ocupação *(f)*

Berufsausbildung *(f)* n De
En vocational training
Es formación profesional *(f)*
Fr formation professionnelle
    (f)
It addestramento
    professionale *(m)*
Pt treino vocacional *(m)*

Berufsrisiko *(n)* n De
En occupational hazard
Es riesgo profesional *(m)*
Fr risque professionnel *(m)*
It rischio del lavoro *(m)*
Pt acidente próprio da
    profissão *(m)*

Berufungsgericht *(n)* n De
En court of appeal
Es tribunal de apelación *(m)*
Fr cour d'appel *(m)*
It corte d'appello *(f)*
Pt tribunal de apelação *(m)*

beschädigte Waren *(f pl)* De
En damaged goods
Es mercancías averiadas *(f pl)*
Fr marchandises avariées
   (f pl)
It merce avariata *(f)*
Pt mercadorias danificadas
   (f pl)

Beschädigung *(f)* n De
En damage
Es daño *(m)*
Fr dommage *(m)*
It danno *(m)*
Pt dano *(m)*

Beschädigung beim Transport *(f)* De
En damage in transit
Es daños en ruta *(m pl)*
Fr avaries de route *(f pl)*
It danno durante trasporto
   (m)
Pt danos em trânsito *(m pl)*

beschäftigen *vb* De
En employ
Es emplear
Fr employer
It impiegare
Pt empregar

Beschäftigung *(f)* n De
En occupation; employment
Es ocupación; empleo *(f m)*
Fr occupation; emploi *(f m)*
It occupazione; impiego *(f
   m)*
Pt ocupação; emprego *(f m)*

bescheinigen *vb* De
En certify
Es certificar
Fr certifier
It certificare
Pt certificar

Bescheinigung *(f)* n De
En certificate
Es certificado *(m)*
Fr certificat *(m)*
It certificato *(m)*
Pt certificado *(m)*

Beschlagnahme *(f)* n De
En embargo
Es embargo *(m)*
Fr embargo *(m)*
It embargo *(m)*
Pt embargo *(m)*

beschleunigte Abschreibung *(f)* De
En accelerated depreciation
Es depreciación acelerada *(f)*
Fr amortissement accéléré
   (m)
It deprezzamento accelerato
   (m)
Pt depreciação acelerada *(f)*

Beschluß *(m)* n De
En resolution; decision
Es resolución *(f)*
Fr resolution *(f)*
It deliberazione *(f)*
Pt resolução; proposta *(f)*

beschlußfähige Anzahl *(f)* De
En quorum
Es quórum *(m)*
Fr quorum *(m)*
It quorum *(m)*
Pt quórum *(m)*

beschränkt *adj* De
En limited
Es limitado
Fr limité
It limitato
Pt limitado

Beschreibung *(f)* n De
En description
Es descripción *(f)*
Fr description *(f)*
It descrizione *(f)*
Pt descrição *(f)*

Beschwerde *(f)* n De
En complaint; grievance
Es queja; agravio *(f m)*
Fr plainte; grief *(f m)*
It lagnanza *(f)*
Pt queixa; agrovo *(f m)*

besondere Havarie *(f)* De
En particular average
Es avería particular *(f)*
Fr avarie particulière *(f)*
It avaria particolare *(f)*
Pt avaria particular *(f)*

Bestandsaufnahme *(f)* n De
En stocktaking
Es inventario; balance *(m)*
Fr levée d'inventaire *(f)*
It compilazione dell'inventa-
   rio *(f)*
Pt inventário de existências
   (m)

bestätigen *vb* De
En confirm
Es confirmar
Fr confirmer
It confermare
Pt confirmar

bestätigter Kreditbrief *(m)* De
En confirmed letter of credit
Es carta de crédito confirma-
   da *(f)*
Fr lettre de crédit
   confirmée *(f)*
It lettera di credito confer-
   mata *(f)*
Pt carta de crédito confirma-
   da *(f)*

bestätigter Scheck *(m)* De
En certified cheque
Am certified check
Es cheque certificado *(m)*
Fr chèque certifié *(m)*
It assegno garantito *(m)*
Pt cheque certificado *(m)*

bestätigter unwiderruflicher Kreditbrief *(m)* De
En confirmed irrevocable
   letter of credit
Es carta de crédito irrevocable confirmada *(f)*
Fr lettre de crédit irrévocable
   confirmée *(f)*
It lettera di credito confermata e irrevocabile *(f)*
Pt carta de crédito irre-
   vogável confirmada *(f)*

Bestätigung *(f)* n De
En confirmation
Es confirmación *(f)*
Fr confirmation *(f)*
It conferma *(f)*
Pt confirmação *(f)*

bestechen *vb* De
En bribe
Es sobornar
Fr corrompre
It corrompere
Pt subornar

Bestechung *(f)* n De
En bribery
Es soborno *(m)*
Fr corruption *(f)*
It corruzione *(f)*
Pt suborno *(m)*

Bestechungsgeld *(n) n* De
En bribe
Es soborno *(m)*
Fr pot-de-vin *(m)*
It dono per corrompere *(m)*
Pt suborno *(m)*

bestellen *vb* De
En order
Es hacer un pedito
Fr commander; passer une
commande
It ordinare
Pt encomendar

Bestellformular *(n) n* De
En order-form
Es solicitud de pedido *(f)*
Fr bulletin de commande *(m)*
It foglio d'ordinazione *(m)*
Pt impresso de encomenda
(m)

Bestellung *(f) n* De
En order
Es pedido *(m)*
Fr commande *(f)*
It ordine *(m)*
Pt encomenda *(f)*

Besteuerung *(f) n* De
En taxation; assessment
Es tributación; evaluación *(f)*
Fr imposition *(f)*
It tassazione; imposta *(f)*
Pt tributação; balanço fiscal
(f m)

Bestimmungshafen *(m) n* De
En port of destination
Es puerto de destino *(m)*
Fr port de destination *(m)*
It porto di destinazione *(m)*
Pt porto de destino *(m)*

Bestimmungsort *(m) n* De
En destination
Es destino *(m)*
Fr destination *(f)*
It destinazione *(f)*
Pt destino *(m)*

beteiligen *vb* De
En participate
Es participar
Fr participer
It partecipare
Pt participar

beteiligt sein De
En hold shares
Es tener acciones
Fr détenir des actions
It tenere azioni
Pt reter acções

Betrag *(m) n* De
En amount
Es suma *(f)*
Fr somme; montant *(m)*
It ammontare *(m)*
Pt quantia *(f)*

Betriebsausgaben *(f pl) n* De
En operating costs
Es costes operacionales
(m pl)
Fr frais d'exploitation *(m pl)*
It spese di gestione *(f pl)*
Pt custos de exercício *(m pl)*

Betriebsgeheimnis *(n) n* De
En trade secret
Es secreto commercial *(m)*
Fr secret industriel *(m)*
It segreto commerciale *(m)*
Pt segredo commercial *(m)*

Betriebskapital *(n) n* De
En trading capital; working
capital
Es capital de explotación;
capital circulante *(m)*
Fr fonds de roulement *(m)*
It capitale d'esercizio *(m)*
Pt capital de exploração *(m)*

Betrug *(m) n* De
En fraud
Es fraude *(m)*
Fr fraude *(f)*
It frode *(f)*
Pt fraude *(f)*

betrügen *vb* De
En cheat
Es engañar
Fr tricher
It truffare
Pt enganar

betrügerisch *adj* De
En fraudulent
Es fraudulento
Fr frauduleux
It fraudolento
Pt fraudulento

betterment *n* En
De Planungsgewinn *(m)*
Es plusvalía *(f)*
Fr appréciation *(f)*
It plus-valore *(m)*
Pt melhoria *(f)*

Bevölkerung *(f) n* De
En population
Es población *(f)*
Fr population *(f)*
It popolazione *(f)*
Pt população *(f)*

Bevollmächtigte(r) *(m) n* De
Fn attorney
Es apoderado *(m)*
Fr mandataire *(m)*
It mandatario *(m)*
Pt procurador *(m)*

bevorrechtigter Gläubiger
(m) De
En preferential creditor
Es acreedor privilegiado *(m)*
Fr créancier privilégié *(m)*
It creditore privilegiato *(m)*
Pt credor preferencial *(m)*

bewegliche Güter *(n pl) n* De
En movable assets
Es mobiliario *(m)*
Fr biens mobiliers *(m pl)*
It proprietà mobiliare *(f)*
Pt bens mobiliários *(m pl)*

Beweglichkeit *(f) n* De
En mobility
Es movilidad *(f)*
Fr mobilité *(f)*
It mobilità *(f)*
Pt mobilidade *(f)*

Beweis *(m) n* De
En evidence
Es evidencia *(f)*
Fr preuve *(f)*
It prova *(f)*
Pt prova *(f)*

beweisen *vb* De
En establish; prove
Es demostrar; probar
Fr démontrer; prouver
It dimostrare; provare
Pt demonstrar; provar

Bewerber *(m) n* De
En applicant
Es candidato *(m)*

Fr candidat *(m)*
It candidato *(m)*
Pt candidato *(m)*

bewerkstelligen *vb* De
En implement; bring about
Es hacer efectivo; ejecutar
Fr exécuter
It attuare; effettuare
Pt executar

bewerten *vb* De
En evaluate
Es evaluar
Fr évaluer
It valutare
Pt availar

bezahlter Urlaub *(m)* De
En holidays with pay
Es vacaciones retribuidas
   (f pl)
Fr congés payés *(m pl)*
It vacanze retribuite *(f pl)*
Pt férias pagas *(f pl)*

Bezogene(r) *(m) n* De
En drawee
Es librado *(m)*
Fr tiré *(m)*
It trattario *(m)*
Pt sacado *(m)*

Bezüge *(m pl) n* De
En emolument
Es emolumento *(m)*
Fr émoluments *(m pl)*
It rimunerazione *(f)*
Pt emolumento *(m)*

bid *(n)* En
De Angebot *(n)*
Es oferta *(f)*
Fr offre *(f)*
It offerta *(f)*
Pt oferta *(f)*

bidder *(n)* En
De Bietende(r) *(m)*
Es ofertante *(m)*
Fr enchérisseur *(m)*
It offerente *(m)*
Pt proponete *(m)*

bien *(m) n* Fr
De Vermögen *(n)*
En estate; property
Es finca *(f)*
It proprietà *(f)*
Pt bens; propriedade *(m pl; f)*

bienes de consumo *(m pl)* Es
De Konsumgüter *(n pl)*
En consumer goods
Fr biens de consommation
   (m pl)
It beni di consumo *(m pl)*
Pt bens de consumo *(m pl)*

bienes de consumo
   duraderos *(m pl)* Es
De dauerhafte Konsumgüter
   (n pl)
En consumer durables
Fr biens de consommation
   durables *(m pl)*
It beni di consumo durabili
   (m pl)
Pt artigos de consumo
   perduráveis *(m pl)*

bienes de producción *(m pl)*
   Es
De Anlagegüter *(n pl)*
En capital goods
Fr biens de d'équipement
   (m pl)
It beni strumentali *(m pl)*
Pt mercadorias de capital
   (f pl)

bienes inmuebles *(m pl)* Es
De unbewegliches Vermögen;
   Immobilien *(n; f pl)*
En real estate
Fr biens immeubles *(m pl)*
It beni immobili *(m pl)*
Pt propriedade imobiliária *(f)*

biens d'équipement *(m pl)* Fr
De Anlagegüter *(n pl)*
En capital goods
Es bienes de producción
   (m pl)
It beni strumentali *(m pl)*
Pt mercadorias de capital
   (f pl)

biens de consommation
   (m pl) Fr
De Konsumgüter *(n pl)*
En consumer goods
Es bienes de consumo *(m pl)*
It beni di consumo *(m pl)*
Pt bens de consumo *(m pl)*

biens de consommation
   durables *(m pl)* Fr
De dauerhafte Konsumgüter
   (n pl)

En consumer durables
Es bienes de consumo
   duraderos *(m pl)*
It beni di consumo durabili
   (m pl)
Pt artigos de consumo
   perduráveis *(m pl)*

biens de consommation
   non-durables *(m pl)* Fr
De nicht dauerhafte
   Konsumgüter *(n pl)*
En consumer non-durables
Es bienes de consumo
   perecederos *(m pl)*
It beni di consumo non
   durevoli *(m pl)*
Pt bens de consumo não
   duráveis *(m pl)*

biens durables *(m pl)* Fr
De langlebige Güter *(n pl)*
En durable goods
Es mercancías no
   perecederas *(f pl)*
It beni durevoli *(m pl)*
Pt mercadorias imperecíveis
   (f pl)

biens immeubles *(m pl)* Fr
De unbewegliches Vermögen;
   Immobilien *(n; f pl)*
En real estate; tangible assets
Es bienes inmuebles *(m pl)*
It beni immobili *(m pl)*
Pt propriedade imobiliária *(f)*

biens mobiliers *(m pl)* Fr
De bewegliche Güter *(n pl)*
En movable assets
Es mobiliario *(m)*
It proprietà mobiliare *(f)*
Pt bens mobiliários *(m pl)*

biens saisis *(m pl)* Fr
De gepfändete Güter *(n pl)*
En distressed goods
Es mercancías embargades
   (f pl)
It merce sequestrata *(f)*
Pt mercadorias consumo *(f
   pl)*

Bietende(r) *(m) n* De
En bidder
Es ofertante *(m)*
Fr enchérisseur *(m)*
It offerente *(m)*
Pt proponente *(m)*

biglietto d'andata *(m)* It
De   einfache Fahrkarte *(f)*
En   single fare; single ticket
Am   one way fare
Es   pasaje de ida *(m)*
Fr   billet d'aller *(m)*
Pt   passagem de ida *(f)*

biglietto di andata e ritorno
    (m) It
De   Rückfahrkarte *(f)*
En   return fare; return ticket
Am   roundtrip fare
Es   pasaje de ida y vuelta *(m)*
Fr   billet d'aller et retour *(m)*
Pt   passagem de ida e volta *(f)*

biglietto di banca *(m)* It
De   Banknote *(f)*
En   banknote
Am   bill
Es   billete de banco *(m)*
Fr   billet de banque *(m)*
Pt   nota de banco *(f)*

biglietto gratuito *(m)* It
De   Freikarte *(f)*
En   free ticket
Es   billete gratuito *(m)*
Fr   billet de faveur *(m)*
Pt   bilhete gratuito *(m)*

bilan *(m)* Fr
De   Bilanz *(f)*
En   balance sheet
Es   balance *(m)*
It   bilancio *(m)*
Pt   balancete *(m)*

bilan annuel *(m)* Fr
De   Jahresabschluß *(m)*
En   annual accounts
Es   balance anual *(m)*
It   bialancio annuale *(m)*
Pt   balancete anual *(m)*

bilancia *(f)* n It
De   Waage *(f)*
En   scales
Es   balanza *(f)*
Fr   balance *(f)*
Pt   balança *(f)*

bilancia commerciale *(f)* It
De   Handelsbilanz *(f)*
En   trade balance
Es   balanza comercial *(f)*
Fr   balance commerciale *(f)*
Pt   balança comercial *(f)*

bilancia dei pagamenti *(f)* It
De   Zahlungsbilanz *(f)*
En   balance of payments
Es   balanza de pagos *(f)*
Fr   balance des paiements *(f)*
Pt   balança de pagamentos *(f)*

bilancio *(m)* n It
De   Saldo; Bilanz *(m f)*
En   balance; balance sheet
Es   balance; saldo *(m)*
Fr   balance; solde; bilan
    (f m m)
Pt   saldo; balancete *(m)*

bilancio annuale *(m)* It
De   Jahresabschluß *(m)*
En   annual accouts
Es   balance anual *(m)*
Fr   bilan annuel *(m)*
Pt   balancete anual *(m)*

bilancio di verifica *(m)* It
De   Probebilanz *(f)*
En   trial balance
Es   balance de comprobación
    de saldos *(m)*
Fr   bilan de vérification *(m)*
Pt   balancete de verificação *(m)*

bilancio preventivo *(m)* It
De   Haushaltsplan *(m)*
En   budget
Es   presupuesto *(m)*
Fr   budget *(m)*
Pt   orçamento *(m)*

bilancio riportato *(m)* It
De   Übertrag *(m)*
En   balance brought down
Am   balance carried forward
Es   balance a cuenta nueva
    (m)
Fr   solde à reporter *(m)*
Pt   saldo transportado *(m)*

bilan consolidé *(m)* Fr
De   konsolidierte Bilanz *(f)*
En   consolidated balance
    sheet
Es   hoja de balance
    consolidado *(f)*
It   bilancio consolidato *(m)*
Pt   folha de balanço
    consolidado *(f)*

bilan de vérification *(m)* Fr
De   Probebilanz *(f)*
En   trial balance

Es   balance de comprobación
    de saldos *(m)*
It   bilancio di verifica *(m)*
Pt   valancete de verificação *(m)*

bilan intérimaire *(m)* Fr
De   Zwischenbilanz *(f)*
En   interim financial statement
Es   extracto financiero
    provisional *(m)*
It   rendiconto finanziario
    provisorio *(m)*
Pt   extracto financeiro interino
    (m)

Bilanz *(f)* De
En   balance sheet
Es   balance *(m)*
Fr   bilan *(m)*
It   bilancio *(m)*
Pt   balancete *(m)*

bilateraler Handelsvertrag
    (m) De
En   bilateral trade agreement
Es   contrato comercial
    bilateral *(m)*
Fr   accord de commerce
    bilatéral *(m)*
It   accordo di commercio
    bilaterale *(m)*
Pt   acordo comercial bilateral
    (m)

bilateral trade agreement
    En
De   bilateraler Handelsvertrag
    (m)
Es   contrato comercial
    bilateral *(m)*
Fr   accord de commerce
    bilatéral *(m)*
It   accordo di commercio
    bilaterale *(m)*
Pt   acordo comercial bilateral
    (m)

bilden *vb* De
En   form; constitute
Es   constituir
Fr   constituer
It   costituire
Pt   constituir

Bildschirmeinheit *(f)* n De
En   visual-display unit (vdu)
Es   unidad de visualización *(f)*
Fr   unité de visualisation *(f)*

It unità di visualizzazione *(f)*
Pt móvel-montra de exposição de visuais *(m)*

bilhete de identidade *(m)* Pt
De Personalausweis *(m)*
En identity card
Es carnet de identidad *(m)*
Fr carte d'identité *(f)*
It carte d'identità *(f)*

bilhete gratuito *(m)* Pt
De Freikarte *(f)*
En free ticket
Es billete gratuito *(m)*
Fr billet de faveur *(m)*
It biglietto gratuito *(m)*

bill (account) *n* En
De Rechnung *(f)*
Es cuenta, nota *(f)*
Fr compte; note *(m f)*
It conto; nota *(m f)*
Pt conta *(f)*

bill (paper money) Am
En banknote
De Banknote *(f)*
Es billete de banco *(m)*
Fr billet de banque *(m)*
It biglietto di banca *(m)*
Pt nota de banco *(f)*

bill broker En
De Wechselmakler *(m)*
Es corredor de cambios *(m)*
Fr courtier de bons *(m)*
It agente di sconto *(m)*
Pt corretor de câmbios *(m)*

billet à ordre *(m)* Fr
De Schuldschein *(m)*
En promissory note
Es pagaré *(m)*
It pagherò *(m)*
Pt promissória *(f)*

billet d'aller *(m)* Fr
De einfache Fahrkarte *(f)*
En single fare; single ticket
Am one way fare
Es pasaje de ida *(m)*
It biglietto d'andata *(m)*
Pt passagem de ida *(f)*

billet d'aller et retour *(m)* Fr
De Rückfahrkarte *(f)*
En return fare; return ticket
Am roundtrip fare

Es pasaje de ida y vuelta *(m)*
It biglietto di andata e ritorno *(m)*
Pt passagem de ida e volta *(f)*

billet de banque *(m)* Fr
De Banknote *(f)*
En banknote
Am bill
Es billete de banco *(m)*
It biglietto di banca *(m)*
Pt nota de banco *(f)*

billet de bord *(m)* Fr
De Übernahmebescheinigung *(f)*
En mate's receipt
Es recibo de embarco *(m)*
Es recibo de ambarco *(m)*
It ricevuta d'imbarco *(f)*
Pt recibo de embarque *(m)*

billet de complaisance *(m)* Fr
De Gefälligkeitswechsel *(m)*
En accommodation bill
Es pagaré de favor *(m)*
It cambiale di favor *(f)*
Pt letra de favor *(f)*

billet de faveur *(m)* Fr
De Freikarte *(f)*
En free ticket
Es billete gratuito *(m)*
It biglietto gratuito *(m)*
Pt bilhete gratuito *(m)*

billete de banco *(m)* Es
De Banknote *(f)*
En banknote
Am bill
Fr billet de banque *(m)*
It biglietto di banca *(m)*
Pt nota de banco *(f)*

billete gratuito *(m)* Es
De Freikarte *(f)*
En free ticket
Fr billet de faveur *(m)*
It biglietto gratuito *(m)*
Pt bilhete gratuito *(m)*

billig *adj* De
En cheap; equitable
Es barato; equitativo
Fr bon marché; équitable
It a buon mercato; equo
Pt barato; equitativo

billige Flagge *(f)* De
En flag of convenience
Es bandera de conveniencia *(f)*
Fr enseigne de convenance *(f)*
It bandiera di convenienza *(f)*
Pt bandeira de conveniência *(f)*

billiger *adj* De
En cheaper
Es más barato
Fr meilleur marché
It meno caro
Pt mais barato

billiges Geld *(n)* De
En cheap money
Es dinero barato *(m)*
Fr argent bon marché *(m)*
It denaro a basso interesse *(m)*
Pt dinheiro barato *(m)*

bill of entry En
De Zolleinfuhrschein *(m)*
Es declaración de aduana *(f)*
Fr déclaration en douane *(f)*
It bolletta di entrata *(f)*
Pt declaração alfandegária *(f)*

bill of exchange En
De Wechsel; Tratte *(m f)*
Es letra de cambio *(f)*
Fr lettre de change *(f)*
It tratta cambiale *(f)*
Pt letra de câmbio *(f)*

bill of lading En
De Konnossement *(n)*
Es conocimiento (de embarque) *(m)*
Fr connaissement *(m)*
It polizza di carico *(f)*
Pt conhecimento *(m)*

bill of quantities En
De Kostenvoranschlag *(m)*
Es cubicación de obra *(f)*
Fr devis *(m)*
It preventivo *(m)*
Pt relação de quantidades *(f)*

bill of sale En
De Kaufvertrag *(m)*
Es escritura de venta *(f)*
Fr acte de vente *(f)*
It contratto di vendita *(m)*
Pt escritura de venda *(f)*

bill payable at sight En
De Sichttratte *(f)*
Es letra a la vista *(f)*
Fr effet exigible à vue *(m)*
It effetto pagabile a vista *(m)*
Pt letra à vista *(f)*

bill rate En
De Diskontsatz *(m)*
Es tasa de descuento (efectos) *(m)*
Fr taux d'escompte (traites) *(m)*
It tasso di sconto (cambiale) *(m)*
Pt taxa de desconto (letras) *(f)*

bills discounted En
De diskontierte Wechsel *(m pl)*
Es efectos descontados *(m pl)*
Fr effets escomptés *(m pl)*
It effeti scontati *(m pl)*
Pt letras descontadas *(f pl)*

bills for collection En
De fällige Wechsel *(m pl)*
Es efectos a cobar *(m pl)*
Fr effets en recouvrement *(m pl)*
It effetti all'incasso *(m pl)*
Pt letras a descontar *(f pl)*

bills payable En
De Wechselschulden *(f pl)*
Es letras pagaderas *(f pl)*
Fr effets à payer *(m pl)*
It effetti passivi *(m pl)*
Pt letras a pagar *(f pl)*

bills receivable En
De Wechselforderungen *(f pl)*
Es letras a cobrar *(f pl)*
Fr effets à recevoir *(m pl)*
It effetti attivi *(m pl)*
Pt letras a cobrar *(f pl)*

bindender Vertrag *(m)* De
En binding agreement
Es obligación irrevocable *(f)*
Fr convention irrévocable *(f)*
It contratto vincolante *(m)*
Pt acordo irrevogável *(m)*

binding agreement En
De bindender Vertrag *(m)*
Es obligación irrevocable *(f)*
Fr convention irrévocable *(f)*
It contratto vincolante *(m)*
Pt acordo irrevogável *(m)*

Binnenhandel *(m)* n De
En home trade
Am domestic sales
Es comercio interior *(m)*
Fr commerce intérieur *(m)*
It commercio interno *(m)*
Pt comércio interno *(m)*

bitte nachsenden De
En please forward
Es se ruega hacer seguir
Fr prière de faire suivre
It far proseguire
Pt é favor enviar

blacking *(n)* En
Am boycott
De Boykott *(m)*
Es boicoteo *(m)*
Fr boycottage *(m)*
It ostracismo *(m)*
Pt boicote *(m)*

black list En
De schwarze Liste *(f)*
Es lista negra *(f)*
Fr liste noire *(f)*
It lista nera *(f)*
Pt lista negra *(f)*

black market (securities) En
De schwarze Börse *(f)*
Es bolsa negra *(f)*
Fr bourse noire *(f)*
It borsa nera *(f)*
Pt bolsa negra *(f)*

black market (goods) En
De schwarzer Markt *(m)*
Es mercado negro *(m)*
Fr marché noir *(m)*
It mercato nero *(m)*
Pt mercado negro *(m)*

blanc-seing *(m)* n Fr
De Blankounterschrift *(f)*
En blank signature
Es firma en blanco *(f)*
It firma in bianco *(f)*
Pt assinatura em branco *(f)*

blank bill En
De Blankowechsel *(m)*
Es letra en blanco *(f)*
Fr traite en blanc *(f)*
It effetto in bianco *(m)*
Pt letra em branco *(f)*

blank cheque En
De Blankoscheck *(m)*
Es cheque en blanco *(m)*
Fr chèque en blanc *(m)*
It assegno in bianco *(m)*
Pt cheque em branco *(m)*

blank credit En
De offener Kredit *(m)*
Es crédito en blanco *(m)*
Fr crédit à découvert *(m)*
It credito in bianco *(m)*
Pt crédito em branco *(m)*

blank endorsement En
De Blankoindossament *(n)*
Es endoso en blanco *(m)*
Fr endossement en blanc *(m)*
It girata in bianco *(f)*
Pt endosse em branco *(m)*

blank form En
De Blankoformular *(n)*
Es formulario en blanco *(m)*
Fr formulaire en blanc *(m)*
It modulo in bianco *(m)*
Pt impresso em branco *(m)*

Blankoformular *(n)* n De
En blank form
Es formulario en blanco *(m)*
Fr formulaire en blanc *(m)*
It modulo in bianco *(m)*
Pt impresso em branco *(m)*

Blankoindossament *(n)* n De
En blank endorsement
Es endoso en blanco *(m)*
Fr endossement en blanc *(m)*
It girata in bianco *(f)*
Pt endosse em branco *(m)*

Blankoscheck *(m)* n De
En blank cheque
Am blank check
Es cheque en blanco *(m)*
Fr chèque en blanc *(m)*
It assegno in bianco *(m)*
Pt cheque em branco *(m)*

Blankounterschrift *(f)* n De
En blank signature
Es firma en blanco *(f)*
Fr blanc-seing *(m)*
It firma in bianco *(f)*
Pt assinatura em branco *(m)*

Blankowechsel *(m) n* De
En blank bill
Es letra en blanco *(f)*
Fr traite en blanc *(f)*
It effetto in bianco *(m)*
Pt letra em branco *(f)*

blank signature En
De Blankounterschrift *(f)*
Es firma en blanco *(f)*
Fr blanc-seing *(m)*
It firma in bianco *(f)*
Pt assinatura em branco *(f)*

Blitz *(m) n* De
En lightning
Es relámpago *(m)*
Fr foudre *(f)*
It fulmine *(m)*
Pt relâmpago *(m)*

blocage des dividendes *(m)*
Fr
De Dividendenstopp *(m)*
En dividend limitation
Es bloqueo de dividendos *(m)*
It blocco dei dividendi *(m)*
Pt limitação de dividendos *(f)*

blocage des salaires *(m)* Fr
De Lohnstopp *(m)*
En wage-freeze
Es bloqueo de salarios *(m)*
It blocco dei salari *(m)*
Pt congelação de salários *(f)*

blocco *(m) n* It
De Blockade *(f)*
En blockade
Es bloqueo *(m)*
Fr blocus *(m)*
Pt bloqueio *(m)*

blocco degli affitti *(m)* It
De Mietzinskontrolle *(f)*
En rent control
Es control de alquileres *(m)*
Fr contrôle des loyers *(m)*
Pt controlo de rendas *(m)*

blocco dei dividendi *(m)* It
De Dividendenstopp *(m)*
En dividend limitation
Es bloqueo de dividendos *(m)*
Fr blocage des dividendes
(m)
Pt limitação de dividendos *(f)*

blocco dei salari *(m)* It
De Lohnstopp *(m)*
En wage-freeze
Es bloqueo de salarios *(m)*
Fr blocage des salaires *(m)*
Pt congelação de salários *(f)*

bloc commercial *(m)* Fr
De Handelsblock *(m)*
En trade bloc
Es bloque comercial *(m)*
It unione commerciale *(f)*
Pt bloque comercial *(m)*

blockade *n* En
De Blockade *(f)*
Es bloqueo *(m)*
Fr blocus *(m)*
It blocco *(m)*
Pt bloqueio *(m)*

Blockade *(f) n* De
En blockade
Es bloqueo *(m)*
Fr blocus *(m)*
It blocco *(m)*
Pt bloqueio *(m)*

block diagram En
De Säulendiagramm *(m)*
Es diagrama de bloque *(m)*
Fr ordinogramme *(m)*
It schema a blocchi *(m)*
Pt organigrama *(m)*

blocked account En
De gesperrtes Konto *(n)*
Es cuenta bloqueada *(f)*
Fr compte bloqué *(m)*
It conto bloccato *(m)*
Pt conta bloqueada *(f)*

blocked deposits En
De gesperrte Einlagen *(f pl)*
Es depósitos bloqueados
(m pl)
Fr dépôts bloqués *(m pl)*
It deposito con vincolo
bloccato *(m)*
Pt depósitos bloqueados
(m pl)

blocked exchange En
De blockierte Devisen *(f pl)*
Es divisas bloqueadas *(f pl)*
Fr devises bloquées *(f pl)*
It valute bloccate *(f pl)*
Pt câmbio bloqueado *(m)*

blockierte Devisen *(f pl)* De
En blocked exchange
Es divisas bloqueadas *(f pl)*
Fr devises bloquées *(f pl)*
It valute bloccate *(f pl)*
Pt câmbio bloqueado *(m)*

block of flats En
Am apartment house
De Wohnungsgebäude *(n)*
Es bloque de pisos *(m)*
Fr immeuble *(m)*
It fabbricato di appartamenti
(m)
Pt edificio de andares *(m)*

blocus *(m) n* Fr
De Blockade *(f)*
En blockade
Es bloqueo *(m)*
It blocco *(m)*
Pt bloqueio *(m)*

bloque comercial *(m)* Es, Pt
De Handelsblock *(m)*
En trade bloc
Fr bloc commercial *(m)*
It unione commerciale *(f)*

bloque de pisos *(m)* Es
De Wohnungsgebäude *(n)*
En block of flats
Am apartment house
Fr immeuble *(m)*
It fabbricato di appartamenti
(m)
Pt edifício de andares *(m)*

bloqueio *(m) n* Pt
De Blockade *(f)*
En blockade
Es bloqueo *(m)*
Fr blocus *(m)*
It blocco *(m)*

bloqueo *(m) n* Es
De Blockade *(f)*
En blockade
Fr blocus *(m)*
It blocco *(m)*
Pt bloqueio *(f)*

bloqueo de dividendos *(m)*
Es
De Dividendenstopp *(m)*
En dividend limitation
Fr blocage des dividendes
(m)
It blocco dei dividendi *(m)*
Pt limitação de dividendos *(f)*

bloqueo de salarios *(m)* Es
De Lohnstopp *(m)*
En wage-freeze
Fr blocage des salaires *(m)*
It blocco dei salari *(m)*
Pt congelação de salários *(f)*

bloquer un chèque Fr
De einen Scheck sperren
En stop a cheque
Am stop a check
Es suspender el pago de un cheque
It fermare un assegno
Pt suspender o pagamento de um cheque

blotting paper En
De Löschpapier *(n)*
Es papel secante *(m)*
Fr papier buvard *(m)*
It carta assorbente *(f)*
Pt papel mata-borrão *(m)*

board meeting En
De Vorstandssitzung *(f)*
Es reunión del consejo de administración *(f)*
Fr réunion du conseil d'administration *(f)*
It riunione del consiglio d'amministrazione *(f)*
Pt reunião da administração *(f)*

board of directors En
De Vorstand *(m)*
Es consejo de administración *(m)*
Fr conseil d'administration *(m)*
It consiglio d'amministrazione *(m)*
Pt direção *(f)*

boa vontade *(f)* Pt
De Geschäftswert *(m)*
En goodwill
Es valor de la clientela *(m)*
Fr bon vouloir *(m)*
Pt avviamento *(m)*

bodega *(f)* n Es
De Laderaum *(m)*
En hold
Fr cale *(f)*
It stiva *(f)*
Pt porão *(m)*

Bodenfläche *(f)* n De
En floor space
Es superficie de piso *(f)*
Fr surface de plancher *(f)*
It superficie di pavimento *(f)*
Pt área de chão *(f)*

Bodmereibrief *(m)* n De
En bottomry bond
Es contrato de préstamo a la gruesa *(m)*
Fr contrat à la grosse aventure *(m)*
It contratto di prestito a cambio marittimo *(m)*
Pt título de bodemeria *(m)*

Bodmereidarlehenszinsen *(m pl)* n De
En bottomry interest
Es interés de préstamo a la gruesa *(m)*
Fr profit maritime *(m)*
It interessenza a cambio marittimo *(f)*
Pt juro de bodemeria *(m)*

bogus *adj* En
De falsch
Es falso
Fr faux
It falso
Pt falso

bogus company En
Am phantom operation
De Schwindelgesellschaft *(f)*
Es sociedad fantasma *(f)*
Fr société fantôme *(f)*
It società fasulla *(f)*
Pt sociedade fantasma *(f)*

boicote *(m)* n Pt
De Boykott *(m)*
En boycott; blacking
Es boicoteo *(m)*
Fr boycottage *(m)*
Pt boicottaggio; ostracismo *(m)*

boicoteo *(m)* n Es
De Boykott *(m)*
En boycott; blacking
Fr boycottage *(m)*
It boicottaggio; ostracismo *(m)*
Pt boicote *(m)*

boicottaggio *(m)* n It
De Boykott *(m)*
En boycott
Es boicoteo *(m)*
Fr boycottage *(m)*
Pt boicote *(m)*

boîte aux lettres *(f)* Fr
De Briefkasten *(m)*
En letter-box
Am mail-box
Es buzón *(m)*
It cassetta postale *(f)*
Pt caixa postal *(f)*

bolletta di entrata *(f)* It
De Zolleinfuhrschein; Antragsformular *(m n)*
En bill of entry; entry-form
Es declaración de aduana; solicitud de inscripción *(f)*
Fr déclaration en douane; feuille d'inscription *(f)*
Pt declaração alfandegária; impresso de admissão *(f m)*

bollettino di spedizione *(m)* It
De Versandschein *(m)*
En despatch note
Es aviso de expedición *(m)*
Fr bordereau d'expédition; bulletin d'envoi *(m)*
Pt aviso de despacho *(m)*

bollo *(m)* n It
De Stempel *(m)*
En stamp
Es sello *(m)*
Fr timbre *(m)*
Pt selo *(m)*

bolsa *(f)* n Es, Pt
De Börse *(f)*
En stock exchange
Fr bourse *(f)*
It borsa *(f)*

bolsa de trabajo *(f)* Es
De Arbeitsnachweisstelle *(f)*
En employment exchange
Am state employment agency
Fr bureau de placement *(m)*
It ufficio di collocamento *(m)*
Pt centro de serviços de emprego *(m)*

bolsa negra *(f)* Es, Pt
De schwarze Börse *(f)*
En black market (securities)

Fr bourse noire (f)
It borsa nera (f)

bom adj Pt
De gut
En good
Es bueno
Fr bon
It buono

bon (m) n Fr
De Obligation; Gutschein (f m)
En bond; voucher
Es bono; obligación (m f)
It buono; obligazione (m f)
Pt título; obrigação (m f)

bon (adj) Fr
De gut
En good
Es bueno
It buono
Pt bom

bonança (f) Pt
De Hausse (f)
En boom
Es bonanza (f)
Fr haute conjoncture (f)
It rialzo (m)

bonanza (f) n Es
De Hausse (f)
En boom
Er haute conjoncture (f)
It rialzo (m)
Pt bonança (f)

bon au porteur (m) Fr
De Inhaberobligation (f)
En bearer bond
Es título al portador(m)
It titolo al portatore (m)
Pt título ao portador(m)

bond (n) En
De Obligation; Pfandbrief (f m)
Es bono; obligación (m f)
Fr bon; obligation (m f)
It buono; obbligazione (m f)
Pt título; obrigação (m f)

bonded goods En
De Waren unter Zollverschluß
    (f pl)
Es mercancías en aduana
    (f pl)
Fr marchandises en douane
    (f pl)

It merci sotto vincolo
    doganale (f pl)
Pt mercadorias à ordem da
    alfândega (f pl)

bonded warehouse En
De Lager unter Zollverschluß
    (n)
Es almacén de aduanas (m)
Fr entrepôt (m)
It maggazzino doganale (m)
Pt armazém alfandegário (m)

bondholder n En
De Obligationär (m)
Es obligacionista (m)
Fr obligataire (m)
It portatore di obbligazioni
    (m)
Pt titular de obrigações (m)

bon du trésor (m) Fr
De Schatzwechsel (m)
En exchequer bond
Am treasury bond
Es bono de tesorería (m)
It buono del tesoro (m)
Pt título do tesouro (m)

bonificación (f) n Es
De Rabatt (m)
En allowance
Fr rabais (m)
It abbuono (m)
Pt provisão (f)

**bonificación por no-recla-
    mación** (f) Es
De Schadenfreiheitsrabatt (m)
En no-claims discount or
    bonus
Fr bonification pour non
    sinistre (f)
It sconto per assenza di
    sinistri (m)
Pt desconto por ausência de
    reclamações (m)

**bonification pour non
    sinistre** (f) Fr
De Schadenfreiheitsrabatt (m)
En no-claims discount or
    bonus
Es bonificación por
    no-reclamación(f)
It sconto per assenza di
    sinistri (m)
Pt desconto por ausência de
    reclamações (m)

bon marché Fr
De billig
En cheap
Es barato
It a buon mercato
Pt barato

bonne garde (f) Fr
De sichere Verwahrung (f)
En safe custody
Es custodia (f)
It custodia (f)
Pt custódia segura (f)

bonneterie (f) Fr
De Strickwaren (f pl)
En knitted goods
Es géneros de punto (m pl)
It maglieria (f)
Pt artigos de malha de lã (m pl)

bono (m) n Es
De Obligation; Gutschein (f m)
En bond; voucher
Fr bon; obligation (m f)
It buono; obbligazione (m f)
Pt título; obrigação (m f)

bono de tesorería (m) Es
De Schatzwechsel (m)
En exchequer bond
Am treasury bond
Fr bon du trésor (m)
It buono del tesoro (m)
Pt título do tesouro (m)

bons offices (m pl) Fr
De Freundschaftsdienste (m
    pl)
En good offices
Es buenos servicios (m pl)
It buoni uffici (m pl)
Pt bons serviços (m pl)

bons serviços (m pl) Pt
De Freundschaftsdienste (m
    pl)
En good offices
Es buenos servicios (m pl)
Fr bons offices (m pl)
It buoni uffici (m pl)

bonus (n) En
De Prämie (f)
Es prima; gratificación (f)
Fr prime; gratification (f)
It gratificazione (f)
Pt bónus; gratificação (m f)

bónus *(m) n* Pt
De Prämie *(f)*
En bonus
Es prima; gratificación *(f)*
Fr prime; gratification *(f)*
It gratificazione *(f)*

bonus shares En
Am stock dividend
De Gratisaktien *(f pl)*
Es acciones dadas como
primas *(f pl)*
Fr actions d'attribution *(f pl)*
It azioni di godimento *(f pl)*
Pt acções de prémio *(f pl)*

bon vouloir *(m)* Fr
De Geschäftswert *(m)*
En goodwill
Es valor de la clientela *(m)*
It avviamento *(m)*
Pt boa vontade *(f)*

book cost En
De Buchwert der Einkäufe
(m f)
Es coste contable *(m)*
Fr prix de revient
comptable *(m)*
It costo contabile *(m)*
Pt custo contabilizado *(m)*

book debt En
De Buchschuld *(f)*
Es deuda contabilizada *(f)*
Fr dette comptable *(f)*
It debito attivo *(m)*
Pt cébito contabilizado *(m)*

bookkeeper *n* En
De Buchhalter *(m)*
Es contable *(m)*
Fr commis-comptable *(m)*
It contabile *(m)*
Pt empregado de contabili-
dade *(m)*

book-keeping *n* En
De Buchhaltung *(f)*
Es contabilidad *(f)*
Fr comptabilité *(f)*
It contabilità *(f)*
Pt contabilidade *(f)*

books of account En
De Geschäftsbücher *(n pl)*
Es libros de cuentas *(m pl)*
Fr livres comptables *(m pl)*

It libri contabili *(m pl)*
Pt livros de contabilidade
(m pl)

book value En
De Buchwert *(m)*
Es valor contable *(m)*
Fr valeur comptable *(f)*
It valore d'inventario *(m)*
Pt valor contabilizado *(m)*

boom *n* En
De Hausse *(f)*
Es bonanza *(f)*
Fr haute conjoncture *(f)*
It rialzo *(m)*
Pt bonança *(f)*

bordereau d'achat *(m)* Fr
De Schlußschein *(m)*
En contract note
Es nota de contrato *(f)*
It nota di contratto *(f)*
Pt nota-contrato *(f)*

bordereau d'expédition *(m)*
Fr
De Versandschein *(m)*
En despatch note
Es aviso de expedición *(m)*
It bollettino di spedizione *(m)*
Pt aviso de despacho *(m)*

bordereau de livraison *(m)* Fr
De Lieferschein *(m)*
En delivery note
Es aviso de entrega *(m)*
It nota di consegna *(f)*
Pt guia de entrega *(f)*

borrador *(m) n* Es
De Konzept; Entwurf *(m n)*
En draft; rough copy
Fr projet; brouillon *(m)*
It bozza *(f)*
Pt rascunho *(m)*

borrow *vb* En
De entleihen
Es pedir un préstamo
Fr emprunter
It prestare
Pt contrair empréstimo

borrowed capital En
De Fremdkapital *(n)*
Es capital a préstamo *(m)*
Fr capitaux empruntés *(m pl)*

It capitale preso a prestito
(m)
Pt capital por empréstimo *(m)*

borrower *n* En
De Kreditnehmer *(m)*
Es prestatario *(m)*
Fr emprunteur *(m)*
It accattatore *(m)*
Pt beneficiário de
empréstimo *(m)*

borrowing power En
De Kreditfähigkeit *(f)*
Es facultad de crédito *(f)*
Fr capacité à avoir du crédit
(f)
It capacità creditizia *(f)*
Pt potencial de obtenção de
crédito *(m)*

borsa *(f) n* It
De Börse *(f)*
En stock exchange
Es bolsa *(f)*
Fr bourse *(f)*
Pt bolsa *(f)*

borsa nera *(f)* It
De schwarze Börse *(f)*
En black market (securities)
Es bolsa negra *(f)*
Fr bourse noire *(f)*
Pt bolsa negra *(f)*

Börse *(f) n* De
En stock exchange
Es bolsa *(f)*
Fr bourse *(f)*
It borsa *(f)*
Pt bolsa *(f)*

**(an der) Börse notierte
Wertpapiere** *(n pl)* De
En listed security
Es valores cotizables *(m pl)*
Fr valeurs admises à la
Bourse *(f pl)*
It titoli quotati (in Borsa)
(m pl)
Pt valor de Bolsa com cotação
oficial *(m)*

(die) Börse spielen De
En gamble on the stock
exchange
Es jugar a la Bolsa
Fr jouer à la Bourse

Börsenhändler

It   giocare in Borsa
Pt   jogar na Bolsa

Börsenhändler(m) n De
En   stockjobber
Es   agiotista (m)
Fr   marchand de titres (m)
It   aggiotatore (m)
Pt   agiota (m)

Börsenkurs (m) n De
En   stock-exchange
     quotation
Es   curso de bolsa (m)
Fr   cours de bourse (m)
It   quotatione di borsa (f)
Pt   cotação da bolsa (f)

Börsenmakler (m) n De
En   stockbroker
Es   corredor de bolsa (m)
Fr   courtier en bourse (m)
It   agente di borsa (m)
Pt   corretor da bolsa (m)

Börsentag (m) n De
En   market day
Es   día de bolsa (m)
Fr   jour de bourse (m)
It   giorno di borsa (m)
Pt   dia de bolsa (m)

botte (f) n It
De   Faß (n)
En   barrel
Es   barril (m)
Fr   tonneau (m)
Pt   barril (m)

bottega (f) n It
De   Laden (m)
En   shop
Es   tienda (f)
Fr   magasin (m)
Pt   loja (f)

bottle-neck n En
De   Engpaß (m)
Es   embotellamiento (m)
Fr   goulot d'étranglement (m)
It   strozzatura (f)
Pt   engarrafamento (m)

bottomry bond En
De   Bodmereibrief (m)
Es   contrato de préstamo a la
     gruesa (m)
Fr   contrat à la grosse
     aventure (m)

It   contratto di prestito a
     cambio marittimo (m)
Pt   titulo de bodemeria (m)

bottomry interest En
De   Bodmereidarlehenszinsen
     (m pl)
Es   interés de préstamo a la
     gruesa (m)
Fr   profit maritime (m)
It   interessenza a cambio
     marittimo (f)
Pt   juro de bodemeria (m)

bouche-trou (m) n Fr
De   Überbrückung (f)
En   stop-gap
Es   recurso provisional (m)
It   provvedimento
     temporaneo (m)
Pt   tapa-buracos (m)

bought ledger En
Am   purchase book
De   Einkaufsbuch (n)
Es   libro mayor de compras
     (m)
Fr   grand livre d'achats (m)
It   mastro acquisti (m)
Pt   livro-mestre de compras
     (m)

bourse (f) n Fr
De   Börse (f)
En   stock exchange
Es   bolsa (f)
It   borsa (f)
Pt   bolsa (f)

bourse noire (f) Fr
De   schwarze Börse (f)
En   black market (securities)
Es   bolsa negra (f)
It   borsa nera (f)
Pt   bolsa negra (f)

bout (m) n Fr
De   Ziel (n)
En   goal
Es   meta objetivo (f m)
It   scopo; traguardo (m)
Pt   meta; objectivo (f m)

boycott (n) En
De   Boykott (m)
Es   boicoteo (m)
Fr   boycottage (m)
It   boicottaggio (m)
Pt   boicote (m)

boycottage (m) n Fr
De   Boykott (m)
En   boycott; blacking
Es   boicoteo (m)
It   boicottaggio (m)
Pt   boicote (m)

Boykott (m) n De
En   boycott; blacking
Es   boicoteo (m)
Fr   boycottage (m)
It   boicottaggio (m)
Pt   boicote (m)

bozza (f) n It
De   Konzept (n)
En   draft copy
Es   borrador (m)
Fr   projet (m)
Pt   rascunho (m)

branch (n) En
De   Filiale; Zweigstelle (f)
Es   sucursal; filial (f)
Fr   succursale; filiale (f)
It   succursale; filiale (f)
Pt   filial (f)

branch bank En
De   Filialbank; Zweigbank (f)
Es   sucursal del banco (f)
Fr   banque succursale (f)
It   banca succursale (f)
Pt   filial de banco (f)

branch office En
De   Zweigbüro (n)
Es   sucursal (f)
Fr   succursale (f)
It   succursale (f)
Pt   sucursal (f)

branch n En
De   Handelsmarke (f)
Es   marca (de fábrica) (f)
Fr   marque de fabrique (f)
It   marca (di fabbrica) (f)
Pt   marca de fábrica (f)

Brand (m) n De
En   fire
Es   fuego; incendio (m)
Fr   incendie (f)
It   incendio (m)
Pt   fogo; incêndio (m)

branded goods En
De   Markenwaren (f pl)
Es   artículos de marca (m pl)

Fr articles de marque *(m pl)*
It articoli di marca *(m pl)*
Pt artigos de marca *(m pl)*

brand image En
De Warenimage *(n)*
Es imagen de marca *(f)*
Fr image de marque *(f)*
It immagine di marca *(f)*
Pt imagem apresentada pela marca *(f)*

brand leader En
De führende Marke *(f)*
Es marca directriz *(f)*
Fr marque de point *(f)*
It marca di punta *(f)*
Pt marca mais cotada *(f)*

brand name En
De Markenbezeichnung *(f)*
Es nombre comercial *(m)*
Fr marque de fabrique *(f)*
It marca *(f)*
Pt marca *(f)*

breach of contract En
De Vertragsverletzung *(f)*
Es incumplimiento del contrato *(m)*
Fr rupture de contrat *(f)*
It rottura di contratto *(f)*
Pt rotura de contrato *(f)*

breach of warranty En
De Verletzung der Gewähr- leistungspflicht *(f)*
Es incumplimiento de la garantía *(m)*
Fr rupture de garantie *(f)*
It violazione di garanzia *(f)*
Pt violação de garantia *(f)*

break-even point En
De Rentabilitätsgrenze *(f)*
Es punto de igualdad de ingresos y gastos *(m)*
Fr point de seuil *(m)*
It punto di pareggio *(m)*
Pt ponto de acerto *(m)*

breaking bulk En
De Löschen der Ladung *(n)*
Es fraccionamiento de la carga *(m)*
Fr rupture de charge *(f)*
It inizio scarico *(m)*
Pt retalhar a carga *(f)*

Brennerei *(f)* n De
En distillery
Es destilería *(f)*
Fr distillerie *(f)*
It distilleria *(f)*
Pt distilaria *(f)*

brevet *(m)* n Fr
De Patenturkunde *(f)*
En letters patent
Am patent
Es patente de invención *(f)*
It brevetto *(m)*
Pt patente de invenção *(m)*

brevet d'invention *(m)* Fr
De Erfindungspatent *(n)*
En patent
Es patente *(f)*
It brevetto *(m)*
Pt patente *(f)*

brevetto *(m)* n It
De Erfindungspatent; Patenturkunde *(n f)*
En patent; letters patent
Es patente de invención *(f)*
Fr brevet d'invention *(m)*
Pt patente de invenção

bribe n En
De Bestechungsgeld *(n)*
Es soborno *(m)*
Fr pot-de-vin *(m)*
It dono per corrompere *(m)*
Pt suborno *(m)*

bribe vb En
De bestechen
Es sobornar
Fr corrompre
It corrompere
Pt subornar

bribery n En
De Bestechung *(f)*
Es soborno *(m)*
Fr corruption *(f)*
It corruzione *(f)*
Pt suborno *(m)*

bridging loan En
Am bridge-over
De Vorschußkredit *(m)*
Es crédito provisional *(m)*
Fr crédit provisoire *(m)*

It credito provvisorio *(m)*
Pt crédito provisório *(m)*

Brief *(m)* n De
En letter
Es carta; letra *(f)*
Fr lettre *(f)*
It lettera *(f)*
Pt carta *(f)*

Briefkasten *(m)* n De
En letter-box
Am mail-box
Es buzón *(m)*
Fr boîte aux lettres *(f)*
It cassetta postale *(f)*
Pt caixa postal *(f)*

Briefkopf *(m)* n De
En letterhead
Es membrete *(m)*
Fr en-tête *(m)*
It intestazione *(f)*
Pt cabeçalho *(m)*

Briefmarke *(f)* n De
En postage stamp
Es sello de correos *(m)*
Fr timbre-poste *(m)*
It francobollo *(m)*
Pt selo postal *(m)*

Briefwechsel *(m)* n De
En correspondence
Es correspondencia *(f)*
Fr correspondance *(f)*
It corrispondenza *(f)*
Pt correspondência *(f)*

broker *(n)* En
De Makler *(m)*
Es corredor *(m)*
Fr courtier *(m)*
It sensale *(m)*
Pt corretor *(m)*

brokerage *(n)* En
De Maklergebühr *(f)*
Es corretaje *(m)*
Fr courtage *(m)*
It senseria *(f)*
Pt corretagem *(f)*

brouillon *(m)* n Fr
De Entwurf *(m)*
En rough copy
Am draft
Es borrador *(m)*
It brutta copia *(f)*
Pt cópia rascunho *(f)*

Bruchteil *(n)* n De
En fraction
Es fracción *(f)*
Fr fraction *(f)*
It frazione *(f)*
Pt fracção *(f)*

Brüsseler Verzeichnis *(n)* De
En Brussels Nomenclature
Es Nomenclatura de Bruselas
  (f)
Fr Nomenclature de
  Bruxelles (N. D. B.) *(f)*
It Nomenclatura di Bruxelles
  (f)
Pt Nomenclatura de Bruxelas
  (f)

Brussels Nomenclature En
De Brüsseler Verzeichnis *(n)*
Es Nomenclatura de Bruselas
  (f)
Fr Nomenclature de
  Bruxelles (N. D. B.) *(f)*
It Nomenclatura di Bruxelles
  (f)
Pt Nomenclatura de Bruxelas
  (f)

brut *adj* Fr
De brutto
En gross
Es bruto
It lordo
Pt bruto

bruto *adj* Es, Pt
De brutto
En gross
Fr brut; gros
It lordo

brutto *adj* De
En gross
Es bruto
Fr brut; gros
It lordo
Pt bruto

Bruttobetrag *(m)* n De
En gross amount
Es importe bruto *(m)*
Fr montant brut *(m)*
It importo lordo *(m)*
Pt importância total *(f)*

Bruttoeinkommen *(n)* n De
En gross income
Es ingreso bruto *(m)*

Fr rendement brut *(m)*
It reddito lordo *(m)*
Pt receita bruta *(f)*

Bruttogewicht *(n)* n De
En gross weight
Es peso bruto *(m)*
Fr poids brut *(m)*
It peso lordo *(m)*
Pt peso bruto *(m)*

Bruttogewinn *(m)* n De
En gross profit
Es ganancia bruta *(f)*
Fr bénéfice brut *(m)*
It utile lordo *(m)*
Pt lucro bruto *(m)*

Bruttoinlandsprodukt *(n)* n
  De
En gross domestic product
  (GDP)
Es producto interior bruto *(m)*
Fr produit intérieur brut *(m)*
It prodotto interno lordo *(m)*
Pt produto interno bruto *(m)*

Bruttoprämie *(f)* n De
En gross premium
Es prima bruta *(f)*
Fr prime brute *(f)*
It premio lordo *(m)*
Pt prémio bruto *(m)*

Bruttoregistertonne *(f)* n De
En gross register ton
Es tonelada de registro brutto
  (f)
Fr tonneau de jauge brute *(m)*
It tonnellaggio lordo di
  registro *(m)*
Pt tonelada de registo bruto
  (f)

Bruttosozialprodukt *(n)* n De
En gross national product
  (GNP)
Es producto nacional bruto
  (m)
Fr produit national brut *(m)*
It prodotto nazionale lordo
  (m)
Pt produto nacional bruto *(m)*

Bruttotonnage *(f)* n De
En gross tonnage
Es tonelaje brutto *(m)*
Fr tonnage brut *(m)*
It tonnellaggio lordo *(m)*
Pt tonelagem de peso bruto
  (f)

Bruttotonne *(f)* n De
En gross ton
Es tonelada bruta *(f)*
Fr tonne forte *(f)*
It tonnellata lorda *(f)*
Pt tonelada de peso bruto *(f)*

Bruttoverdienstspanne *(f)* n
  De
En gross margin
Es márgen bruto *(m)*
Fr marge brute de bénéfices
  (f)
It margine lordo *(m)*
Pt margem bruta *(f)*

Bruttozins *(m)* n De
En gross interest
Es interés bruto *(m)*
Fr intérêts bruts *(m pl)*
It interesse lordo *(m)*
Pt juro bruto *(m)*

Bücherrevision *(f)* n De
En audit
Es revisión de cuentas *(f)*
Fr vérification comptable *(f)*
It revisione dei conti *(f)*
Pt fiscalização de contas *(f)*

Bücherrevisor *(m)* n De
En auditor
Es revisor de cuentas *(m)*
Fr réviseur des comptes *(m)*
It sindaco *(m)*
Pt fiscal de contas *(m)*

Buchhalter *(m)* n De
En accountant; bookkeeper
Es contador *(m)*
Fr comptable *(m)*
It contabile *(m)*
Pt contabilista *(m)*

Buchhaltung *(f)* n De
En book-keeping; account-
  ancy; accounts depart-
  ment
Es contabilidad; departamento de contabilidad *(f m)*
Fr comptabilité; service de la
  comptabilité *(f m)*
It contabilità; ufficio
  contabilità *(f m)*
Pt contabilidade; departamento de contabilidade
  (f m)

Buchschuld *(f)* n De
En book dept
Es deuda contabilizada *(f)*
Fr dette comptable *(f)*
It debito attivo *(m)*
Pt débito contabilizado *(m)*

Buchwert *(m)* n De
En book value
Es valor contable *(m)*
Fr valeur comptable *(f)*
It valore d'inventario *(m)*
Pt valor contabilizado *(m)*

Buchwert der Einkäufe *(m)*
De
En book cost
Es coste contable *(m)*
Fr prix de revient comptable
(m)
It costo contabile *(m)*
Pt custo contabilizado *(m)*

budget n En, Fr *(m)*
De Haushaltsplan *(m)*
Es presupuesto *(m)*
It bilancio preventivo *(m)*
Pt orçamento *(m)*

budgetary control En
De Haushaltskontrolle *(f)*
Es control presupuestario *(m)*
Fr contrôle budgétaire *(m)*
It controllo a bilancio
preventivo *(m)*
Pt controlo orçamental *(m)*

bueno *adj* Es
De gut
En good
Fr bon
It buono
Pt bom

buenos servicios *(m pl)* Es
De Freundschaftsdienste *(m
pl)*
En good offices
Fr bons offices *(m pl)*
It buoni uffici *(m pl)*
Pt bons serviços *(m pl)*

Buffer-stocks *(m pl)* n De
En buffer stocks
Es existencias de
regularización *(f pl)*
Fr stocks de régularisation
(m pl)
It scorte di equilibrio *(f pl)*

Pt existências de
regularização *(f pl)*

buffer stocks En
De Buffer-stocks *(m pl)*
Es existencias de
regularización *(f pl)*
Fr stocks de régularisation
(m pl)
It scorte di equilibrio *(f pl)*
Pt existências de
regularização *(f pl)*

building contractor En
De Bauunternehmer *(m)*
Es contratista de obras *(m)*
Fr entrepreneur de bâtiment
(m)
It impresa edile *(f)*
Pt construtor de obras *(m)*

building land En
De Bauland *(n)*
Es solares *(m pl)*
Fr terrain à bâtir *(m)*
It terreno edile *(m)*
Pt terreno para contrução *(m)*

building loan En
De Baukredit *(m)*
Es crédito de construcción
(m)
Fr crédit de construction *(m)*
It prestito immobiliare *(m)*
Pt empréstimo para con-
strução *(m)*

built-in obsolescence En
De eingebautes Veralten *(n)*
Es decaimiento incorporado
(m)
Fr désuétude incorporée *(f)*
It decadimento incorporato
(m)
Pt obsolência pré-incorpo-
rada *(f)*

bulk cargo En
De Schüttgut *(n)*
Es carga en granel *(f)*
Fr cargaison en vrac *(f)*
It carico alla rinfusa *(m)*
Pt carga a granel *(f)*

bulk carrier En
De Massenfrachtführer *(m)*
Es transportador a grand *(m)*
Fr transporteur de marchan-
dises en vrac *(m)*

It trasportatore di merce alla
rinfusa *(m)*
Pt transportador de carga
geral *(m)*

bull n En
De Haussespekulant *(m)*
Es alcista *(m)*
Fr haussier *(m)*
It rialzista *(m)*
Pt altista *(m)*

bulletin de chargement *(m)*
Fr
De Bahnfrachtbrief *(m)*
En railway receipt
Es recibo ferroviario *(m)*
It ricevuta ferroviaria *(f)*
Pt recibo ferroviário *(m)*

bulletin de commande *(m)* Fr
De Bestellformular *(n)*
En order form
Es solicitud de pedido *(f)*
It foglio d'ordinazione *(m)*
Pt impresso de encomenda
(m)

bullion n En
De Gold- und Silberbarren
Es oro y plata sin acuñar
Fr barres d'or ou d'argent
It oro ed argento in verghe
Pt ouro ou prata em barra

bullish *adj* En
De steigend
Es alcista
Fr haussier
It rialzista
Pt altista

bull market En
De Haussemarkt *(m)*
Es mercado alcista *(m)*
Fr marché orienté à la hausse
(m)
It marcato tendente al rialzo
(m)
Pt mercado de tendência
altista *(m)*

Bummelstreik *(m)* n De
En go-slow strike
Am slow down
Es huelga de producción
lenta *(f)*
Fr grève perlée *(f)*
It sciopero a singhiozzo *(m)*

Pt greve de abrandamento
do ritmo de produção (f)

Bundes- De
En federal
Es federal
Fr fédéral
It federale
Pt federal

bunker n En
De Bunker (m)
Es carbonera (f)
Fr soute (f)
It carbonile (m)
Pt carvoeira (f)

Bunker (m) n De
En bunker
Es carbonera (f)
Fr soute (f)
It carbonile (m)
Pt carvoeira (f)

buona qualità media (f) It
De gute Durchschnittsqualität
(f)
En fair average quality (faq)
Es calidad media razonable (f)
Fr qualité commerciale
moyenne (f)
Pt qualidade média razoável
(f)

buoni uffici (m pl) It
De Freundschaftsdienste
(m pl)
En good offices
Es buenos servicios (m pl)
Fr bons offices (m pl)
Pt bons serviços (m pl)

buono (m) n It
De Obligation; Gutschein (f m)
En bond; voucher
Es bono; obligación (m f)
Fr bon; obligation (m f)
Pt título; obrigação (m f)

buono adj It
De gut
En good
Es bueno
Fr bon
Pt bom

buono del tesoro (m) It
De Schatzwechsel (m)
En exchequer bond

Am treasury bond
Es bono de tesorería (m)
Fr bon du trésor (m)
Pt título do tesouro (m)

buque de carga (m) Es
De Frachtschiff (n)
En cargo boat
Fr cargo (m)
It nave de carico (f)
Pt navio de carga (m)

buque de vapor (m) Es
De Dampfer (m)
En steamer
Fr bateau à vapeur (m)
It vapore (m)
Pt vapor (m)

bureau (m) n Fr
De Büro; Schreibtisch (n m)
En office; desk
Es oficina; mesa (f)
It ufficio; scrittoio (m)
Pt escritório; secretária (m f)

bureau de placement (m) Fr
De Arbeitsnachweisstelle (f)
En employment exchange
Am state employment agency
Es bolsa de trabajo (f)
It ufficio di collocamento (m)
Pt centro de serviços de
emprego (m)

bureau de poste (m) Fr
De Postamt (n)
En post office
Es oficina de correos (f)
It ufficio postale (m)
Pt estação de correios (f)

bureau sans cloisons (m) Fr
De Großraumbüro (n)
En open-plan office
Es oficina sin particiones (f)
It ufficio senza divisioni (m)
Pt escritório sem divisões (m)

Bürge (m) n De
En surety; guarantor
Es fianza; garante (f m)
Fr cautionnement; garant (m)
It cauzione; garante (f m)
Pt fiança; fiador (f m)

burglary n En
De Einbruchdiebstahl (m)
Es robo (m)
Fr vol avec effraction (m)

It furto con scasso (m)
Pt roubo (m)

Bürgschaft (f) n De
En surety
Es fiador (m)
Fr caution (f)
It garante (m)
Pt fiador (m)

Bürgschaft leisten De
En guarantee
Es garantizar; avalar
Fr garantir; avaliser
It garantire; avallare
Pt garantir; assegurar

Büro (n) n De
En office
Es oficina (f)
Fr bureau (m)
It ufficio (m)
Pt escritório (m)

Büroklammer (f) n
De
En paper clip
Es sujetapapeles (m)
Fr attache-papiers (m)
It fermacarte (m)
Pt grampo (m)

Bürovorsteher (m) n De
En office manager
Es jefe de oficina (m)
Fr chef de bureau (m)
It capu ufficio (m)
Pt chefe de escritório (m)

business (the occupation) n
En
De Geschäft (n)
Es negocios (m pl)
Fr affaires (f pl)
It affari (m pl)
Pt negócios (m pl)

business (firm) n En
De Firma (f)
Es casa de comercio (f)
Fr maison de commerce (f)
It casa commerciale (f)
Pt casa de comércio (f)

**business before the
meeting** En
Am agenda
De Tagesordnung (f)
Es orden del día (f)
Fr ordre du jour (m)

It scopo dell'assemblea (m)
Pt agenda da reunião (f)

business cycle En
De Konjunkturzyklus (m)
Es ciclo económico (m)
Fr cycle économique (m)
It ciclo d'affari (m)
Pt ciclo esconómico (m)

business expenses En
De Geschäftskosten (pl)
Es gastos de los negocios
(m pl)
Fr frais commerciaux (m pl)
It spese generali (f pl)
Pt despesas do exercício
(f pl)

business hours En
De Geschäftszeit (f)
Es horario de comercio (m)
Fr heures d'ouverture (f pl)
It orario d'apertura (m)
Pt horas de funcionamento (f
pl)

businessman n En
De Geschäftsmann (m)
Es hombre de negocios (m)
Fr homme d'affaires (m)
It uomo d'affari (m)
Pt homem de negócios (m)

business manager En
De Geschäftsführer (m)
Es gerente de negocios (m)
Fr gérant d'affaires (m)
It direttore commerciale (m)
Pt gerente de negócios (m)

Bußklausel (f) n De
En forfeit clause
Es cláusula de decomiso (f)
Fr clause de dédit (f)
It clausola di penalità per
inadempienza (f)
Pt cláusula de cedência (f)

busta (f) n It
De Umschlag (m)
En envelope
Es sobre (m)
Fr eneloppe (f)
Pt envelope (m)

busta con dinestra (f) It
De Fensterbriefumschlag (m)
En window-envelope

Es sobre de ventanilla (m)
Fr enveloppe à fenêtre (f)
Pt envelope de endereço
exposto (m)

but (m) n Fr
De Ziel; Zweck (n m)
En target; purpose
Es objetivo (m)
It bersaglio; scopo (m)
Pt objectivo (m)

buy vb En
De kaufen
Es comprar
Fr acheter
It comprare
Pt comprar

buyer n En
De Käufer (m)
Es comprador (m)
Fr acheteur (m)
It compratore (m)
Pt comprador (m)

buzón (m) n Es
De Briefkasten (m)
En letter-box
Am mail-box
Fr boîte aux lettres (f)
It cassetta postale (f)
Pt caixa postal (f)

by air En
De per Luftpost
Es por avión
Fr par avion
It per via aerea
Pt por avião

by-product n En
De Nebenprodukt (n)
Es producto derivado (m)
Fr sous-produit (m)
It sottoprodotto (m)
Pt produto derivado (m)

C

caballo de vapor (cv) (m) Es
De Pferdestärke (PS) (f)
En horse-power (hp)
Fr cheval-vapeur (ch-v) (m)
It cavallo (m)
Pt cavalo-vapor (m)

cabeçalho (m) n Pt
De Briefkopf (m)
En letterhead
Es membrete (m)
Fr en-tête (m)
It intestazione (f)

cabedal de imitação (m) Pt
De Kunstleder (n)
En imitation leather
Es piel de imitación (f)
Fr simili-cuir (m)
It finta pelle (f)

cable n En, Es (m)
De Kabeltelegramm (n)
Fr câblogramme (m)
It cablogramma (m)
Pt telegrama (m)

cablogramma (m) n It
De Kabeltelegramm (n)
En cable
Es cable (m)
Fr câblogramme (m)
Pt telegrama (m)

câblogramme (m) n Fr
De Kabeltelegramm (n)
En cable
Es cable (m)
It cablogramma (m)
Pt telegrama (m)

cabotage n En, Fr (m)
De Küstenschiffahrt (f)
Es cabotaje (m)
It cabotaggio (m)
Pt cabotagem (f)

cabotagem (f) n Pt
De Küstenschiffahrt (f)
En cabotage
Es cabotaje (m)
Fr cabotage (m)
It cabotaggio (m)

cabotaggio (m) n It
De Küstenschiffahrt (f)
En cabotage
Es cabotaje (m)
Fr cabotage (m)
Pt cabotagem (f)

cabotaje (m) n Es
De Küstenschiffahrt (f)
En cabotage
Fr cabotage (m)

It cabotaggio *(m)*
Pt cabotagem *(f)*

caça aos saldos *(f)* Pt
De Jagd nach Sonderangeboten *(f)*
En bargain-hunting
Es caza de rebajas *(f)*
Fr chasse aux soldes *(f)*
It caccia alle occasioni *(f)*

caccia alle occasioni *(f)* It
De Jagd nach Sonderangeboten *(f)*
En bargain-hunting
Es caza de rebajas *(f)*
Fr chasse aux soldes *(f)*
Pt caça aos saldos *(f)*

cadeia de montagem *(f)* Pt
De Montageband *(n)*
En assembly line
Es línea de montaje *(f)*
Fr chaîne de montage *(f)*
It catena di montaggio *(f)*

cadere *vb* It
De stürzen
En fall
Es caer; bajar
Fr baisser; tomber
Pt cair; baixar

caduta *(f)* n It
De Sturz *(m)*
En fall
Es baja; caida *(f)*
Fr baisse; chute *(f)*
Pt baixa; queda *(f)*

caer *(vb)* Es
De stürzen
En fall
Fr baisser; tomber
It cadere; ribassare
Pt cair; baixar

caer en quiebra Es
De Konkurs anmelden
En go bankrupt
Fr faire failite
It fallire
Pt falir

café *(m)* n Es, Fr, Pt
De Kaffee *(m)*
En coffee
It caffè *(m)*

caffè *(m)* n It
De Kaffee *(m)*
En coffee
Es café *(m)*
Fr café *(m)*
Pt café *(m)*

cair *(vb)* Pt
De stürzen
En fall
Es caer; bajar
Fr baisser; tomber
It cadere; ribassare

cais *(m)* n Pt
De Kai *(m)*
En quay; wharf
Am pier
Es muelle *(m)*
Fr quai *(m)*
It banchina; scalo *(f m)*

caisse *(f)* n Fr
De Kasse; Geldkassette *(f)*
En cash-desk; cash-box
Es caja *(f)*
It cassa; cassetta *(f)*
Pt caixa *(f)*

caisse d'épargne *(f)* Fr
De Sparkasse *(f)*
En savings bank
Es caja de ahorros *(f)*
It cassa di risparmio *(f)*
Pt caixa económica *(f)*

caisse d'épargne postale
(f) Fr
De Postsparkasse *(f)*
En Post Office Savings Bank
Es caja postal de ahorros *(f)*
It cassa di risparmio postale
(f)
Pt caixa económica postal *(f)*

caissier *(m)* n Fr
De Kassierer *(m)*
En cashier
Am teller
Es cajero *(m)*
It cassiere *(m)*
Pt caixa *(m)*

caixa *(f)* n Pt
De Kasse; Geldkassette *(f)*
En cash-desk; cash-box
Es caja *(f)*
Fr caisse *(f)*
It cassa; cassetta *(f)*

caixa *(m)* n Pt
De Kassierer *(m)*
En cashier
Am teller
Es cajero *(m)*
Fr caissier *(m)*
It cassiere *(m)*

caixa automática *(f)* Pt
De Bargeldauszahlungsautomat *(m)*
En cash dispenser
Es caja automática *(f)*
Fr distributeur d'argent comptant *(m)*
It cassa automatica *(f)*

caixa de cartão *(f)* Pt
De Karton *(m)*
En carton
Es cartón *(m)*
Fr carton *(m)*
It cartone *(m)*

caixa económica *(f)* Pt
De Sparkasse *(f)*
En savings bank
Es caja de ahorros *(f)*
Fr caisse d'épargne *(f)*
It cassa di risparmio *(f)*

caixa económica postal *(f)* Pt
De Postsparkasse *(f)*
En Post Office Savings Bank
Es caja postal de ahorros *(f)*
Fr caisse d'épargne postale
(f)
It cassa di risparmio postale
(f)

caixa postal *(f)* Pt
De Briefkasten *(m)*
En letter-box
Am mail-box
Es buzón *(m)*
Fr boîte aux lettres *(f)*
It cassetta postale

caixeiro viajante *(m)* Pt
De Handelsvertreter; Geschäftsreisende(r) *(m)*
En commercial traveller
Am salesman
Es viajante de comercio *(m)*
Fr commis-voyageur *(m)*
It viaggiatore di commercio
(m)

caja *(f) n* Es
De Kasse; Geldkassette
    (f)
En cash-desk; cash-box
Fr caisse *(f)*
It cassa; cassetta *(f)*
Pt caixa *(f)*

caja automática *(f)* Es
De Bargeldauszahlungsau-
    tomat *(m)*
En cash dispenser
Fr distributeur d'argent
    comptant *(m)*
It cassa automatica *(f)*
Pt caixa automática *(f)*

caja de ahorros *(f)* Es
De Sparkasse *(f)*
En savings bank
Fr caisse d'épargne *(f)*
It cassa di risparmio *(f)*
Pt caixa económica *(f)*

caja de seguridad nocturna
    (f) Es
De Nachttresor *(m)*
En night safe
Fr coffre de nuit *(m)*
It deposito notturno *(m)*
Pt cofre nocturno *(m)*

caja fuerte *(f)* Es
De Geldschrank *(m)*
En safe
Fr coffre-fort *(m)*
It cassaforte *(f)*
Pt cofre *(m)*

caja menor *(f)* Es
De kleine Kasse *(f)*
En petty cash
Fr petite caisse *(f)*
It piccola cassa *(f)*
Pt despesas de caixa *(f pl)*

caja postal de ahorros *(f)*
    Es
De Postsparkasse *(f)*
En Post Office Savings Bank
Fr caisse d'épargne postale
    (f)
It cassa di risparmio postale
    (f)
Pt caixa económica postal
    (f)

cajero *(m) n* Es
De Kassierer *(m)*
En cashier
Am teller
Fr caissier *(m)*
It cassiere *(m)*
Pt caixa *(m)*

calado *(m) n* Es, Pt
De Tiefgang *(m)*
En draught (of a ship)
Fr tirant d'eau *(m)*
It pescaggio *(m)*

calcolare *vb* It
De berechnen
En calculate
Es calcular
Fr calculer
Pt calcular

calcolatore *(m) n* It
De Rechner; Computer
    (m)
En computer
Es computadora *(f)*
Fr ordinateur *(m)*
Pt computador *(m)*

calcolatore analogico *(m)*
    It
De Analogrechner *(m)*
En analogue computer
Am analog computer
Es computadora analógica *(f)*
Fr calculateur analogique *(m)*
Pt computador analógico *(m)*

calcolatrice *(f) n* It
De Rechenmaschine *(f)*
En calculator
Es calculadora *(f)*
Fr machine à calculer *(f)*
Pt máquina de calcular *(f)*

calcolazione *(f) n* It
De Berechnung *(f)*
En calculation
Es cálculo *(m)*
Fr calcul *(m)*
Pt cálculo *(m)*

calcolo errato *(m)* It
De Rechenfehler *(m)*
En miscalculation
Es cálculo erróneo *(m)*
Fr erreur de calcul *(f)*
Pt erro de cálculo *(m)*

calcul *(m) n* Fr
De Berechnung *(f)*
En calculation
Es cálculo *(m)*
It calcolazione *(f)*
Pt cálculo *(m)*

calculadora *(f) n* Es
De Rechenmaschine *(f)*
En calculator
Fr machine à calculer *(f)*
It calcolatrice *(f)*
Pt máquina de calcular *(f)*

calculador de custos *(m)*
    Pt
De Kalkulator *(m)*
En cost accountant
Es contable de costes *(m)*
Fr comptable de prix de
    revient *(m)*
It contabile dei costi di
    produzione *(m)*

calcular *vb* Es, Pt
De berechnen
En calculate
Fr calculer
It calcolare

calculate *vb* En
De berechnen
Es calcular
Fr calculer
It calcolare
Pt calcular

calculateur analogique *(m)*
    Fr
De Analogrechner *(m)*
En analogue computer
Am analog computer
Es computadora analógica *(f)*
It calcolatore analogico *(m)*
Pt computador analógico *(m)*

calculateur digital *(m)* Fr
De Digitalrechner *(m)*
En digital computer
Es computadora numérica *(f)*
It elaboratore numerico *(m)*
Pt computador de dígitos *(m)*

calculation *n* En
De Berechnung *(f)*
Es cálculo *(m)*
Fr calcul *(m)*
It calculazione *(f)*
Pt cálculo *(m)*

calculator n En
De Rechenmaschine (f)
Es calculadora (f)
Fr machine à calculer (f)
It calcolatrice (f)
Pt máquina de calcular (f)

calculer vb Fr
De berechnen
En calculate
Es calcular
It calcolare
Pt calcular

cálculo (m) n Es, Pt
De Berechnung (f)
En calculation
Fr calcul (m)
It calculazione (f)

cálculo erróneo (m)
 Es
De Rechenfehler (m)
En miscalculation
Fr erreur de calcul (f)
It calcolo errato (m)
Pt erro de cálculo (m)

cálculo revisado (m)
 Es
De überarbeitete Schätzung
 (f)
En revised estimate
Fr devis rectifié (m)
It preventivo riveduto (m)
Pt estimativa revista (f)

cálculo suplementario (m)
 Es
De Nachschätzung (f)
En supplementary estimate
Fr devis supplémentaire (f)
It preventivo supplementare
 (m)
Pt estimativa suplementar (f)

cale (f) n Fr
De Laderaum (f)
En hold
Es bodega (f)
It stiva (f)
Pt porão (m)

calefacción central (f)
 Es
De Zentralheizung (f)
En central heating
Fr chauffage central (m)
It riscaldamento centrale (m)
Pt aquecimento central (m)

calendar n En
De Kalender (m)
Es calendario (m)
Fr calendrier (m)
It calendario (m)
Pt calendário (m)

calendario (m) n Es, It
De Kalender (m)
En calendar
Fr calendrier (m)
Pt calendário (m)

calendário (m) n Pt
De Kalender (m)
En calendar
Es calendario (m)
Fr calendrier (m)
It calendario (m)

calendar year En
De Kalenderjahr (n)
Es año civil (m)
Fr année civile (f)
It anno solare (m)
Pt ano civil (m)

calendrier (m) n Fr
De Kalender (m)
En calendar
Es calendario (m)
It calendario (m)
Pt calendário (m)

cale sèche (f) Fr
De Trockendock (n)
En dry dock
Es dique seco (m)
It bacino di carenaggio (m)
Pt doca-seca (f)

calibre padrão (m) Pt
De Normalmaß (n)
En standard gauge
Es calibre patrón (m)
Fr écartement normal (m)
It scartamento normale (m)

calibre patrón (m) Es
De Normalmaß (n)
En standard gauge
Fr écartement normal (m)
It scartamento normale (m)
Pt calibre padrão (m)

calidad (f) Es
De Qualität (f)
En quality
Fr qualité (f)

It qualità (f)
Pt qualidade (f)

calidad comerciable (f) Es
De marktgängige Qualität (f)
En merchantable quality
Fr qualité vendable (f)
It qualità commerciabile (f)
Pt qualidade comerciável (f)

**calidad del contenido
 desconocida** Es
De Qualität und Inhalt nicht
 bekannt
En quality and contents
 unknown
Fr qualité et contenu
 inconnus
It qualità e contenuto
 sconosciuti
Pt qualidade e conteúdo
 desconhecidos

calidad media razonable (f)
 Es
De gute Durchschnittsqualität
 (f)
En fair average quality (faq)
Fr qualité commerciale
 moyenne (f)
It bona qualità media (f)
Pt qualidade média razoável
 (f)

call (for funds) n En
De Kündigung (von Geldern)
 (f)
Es llamada (de fondos) (f)
Fr appel (de fonds) (m)
It richiesta (di fondi) (f)
Pt chamada (de fundos) (f)

call a strike En
De zum Streik auffordern
Es declararse en huelga
Fr ordonner une grève
It proclamare uno sciopero
Pt declarar greve

call off (a deal) En
De rückgängig machen
Es anular
Fr annuler
It annullare
Pt anular

call option En
De Kaufoption (f)
Es opción de compras (f)

Fr option d'achat *(f)*
It premio d'acquisto *(m)*
Pt opção de compra *(f)*

cámara de comercio *(f)* Es
De Handelskammer *(f)*
En chamber of commerce
Fr chambre de commerce *(f)*
It camera di commercio *(f)*
Pt câmara de comércio *(f)*

câmara de comércio *(f)* Pt
De Handelskammer *(f)*
En chamber of commerce
Es cámara de comercio *(f)*
Fr chambre de commerce *(f)*
It camera di commercio *(f)*

**cámara de compensacio-
nes** *(f)* Es
De Verrechnungsstelle *(f)*
En clearing house
Fr chambre de compensa-
tion *(f)*
It stanza di compensazione
(f)
Pt câmara de compensações
e rateio *(f)*

**câmara de compensações
e reteio** *(f)* Pt
De Verrechnungsstelle *(f)*
En clearing house
Es cámara de compensacio-
nes *(f)*
Fr chambre de compensa-
tion *(f)*
It stanza di compensazione
(f)

**Cámara Internacional de
Comercio** *(f)* Es
De Internationale Handels-
kammer *(f)*
En International Chamber of
Commerce
Fr Chambre de Commerce
Internationale *(f)*
It Camera di Commercio
Internazionale *(f)*
Pt Câmara Internacional do
Comércio *(f)*

**Câmara Internacional do
Comércio** *(f)* Pt
De Internationale Handels-
kammer *(f)*
En International Chamber of
Commerce

Es Cámara Internacional de
Comercio *(f)*
Fr Chambre de Commerce
Internationale *(f)*
It Camera di Commercio
Internazionale *(f)*

cambiale di favore *(f)* It
De Gefälligkeitswechsel *(m)*
En accommodation bill
Es pagaré de favor *(m)*
Fr billet de complaisance *(m)*
It letra de favor *(f)*

cambiale scontata *(f)* It
De Diskontwechsel *(m)*
En discounted bill
Es efecto descontado *(m)*
Fr effet escompté *(m)*
It letra descontada *(f)*

cambiale sull' estero *(f)* It
De Auslandswechsel *(m)*
En foreign bill
Es letra sobre el exterior *(f)*
Fr lettre de change sur
l'étranger *(f)*
It letra de país a país
(cambial) *(f)*

cambio *(m)* n Es, It
De Tausch *(m)*
En exchange
Fr échange *(m)*
Pt câmbio *(m)*

câmbio *(m)* n Pt
De Tausch; Wechselkurs *(m)*
En exchange; rate of
exchange
Es cambio; tipo de cambio
(m)
Fr échange; taux de change
(m)
It cambio; corso del cambio
(m)

cambio a termine *(m)* It
De Termindevisen *(f pl)*
En forward exchange
Es divisas a término *(f pl)*
Fr change à terme *(m)*
Pt divisas adiantada *(f pl)*

câmbio bloqueado *(m)* Pt
De blockierte Devisen *(f pl)*
En blocked exchange
Es devisas bloqueadas *(f pl)*

Fr devises bloquées *(f pl)*
It valute bloccate *(f pl)*

cambio fluttuante *(m)* It
De flexibler Wechselkurs *(m)*
En floating exchange rate
Es tipo de combio flotante *(m)*
Fr taux de change flottant *(m)*
Pt taxa de câmbio flutuante
(f)

camara di commercio *(f)* It
De Handelskammer *(f)*
En chamber of commerce
Es cámara de comercio *(f)*
Fr chambre de commerce *(f)*
Pt câmara de comércio *(f)*

**Camara di Commercio
Internazionale** *(f)* It
De Internationale Handels-
kammer *(f)*
En International Chamber of
Commerce
Es Cámara Internacional de
Commercio *(f)*
Fr Chambre de Commerce
Internationale *(f)*
Pt Câmara Internacional do
Comércio *(f)*

caminho de ferro *(m)* Pt
De Eisenbahn *(f)*
En railway
Es ferrocarril *(m)*
Fr chemin de fer *(m)*
It ferrovia *(f)*

camionnage *(m)* Fr
De Transport *(m)*
En haulage
Am trucking
Es transporte *(m)*
It transporto *(m)*
Pt tansporte *(m)*

campagna *(f)* n It
De Kampagne *(f)*
En campaign
Es campaña *(f)*
Fr campagne *(f)*
Pt campanha *(f)*

campagna pubblicitaria *(f)* It
De Werbefeldzug *(m)*
En advertising campaign; pu-
blicity campaign
Es campaña publicitaria *(f)*

Fr campagne de publicité *(f)*
Pt campanha publicitária *(f)*

campagne *(f) n* Fr
De Kampagne *(f)*
En campaign
Es campaña *(f)*
It campagna *(f)*
Pt campanha *(f)*

campagne de publicité *(f)* Fr
De Werbefeldzug *(m)*
En advertising campaign; publicity campaign
Es campaña publicitaria *(f)*
It campagna pubblicitaria *(f)*
Pt campanha publicitária *(f)*

campaign *n* En
De Kampagne *(f)*
Es campaña *(f)*
Fr campagne *(f)*
It campagna *(f)*
Pt campanha *(f)*

campaña *(f) n* Es
De Kampagne *(f)*
En campaign
Fr campagne *(f)*
It campagna *(f)*
Pt campanha *(f)*

campaña publicitaria *(f)* Es
De Werbefeldzug *(m)*
En advertising campaign; publicity campaign
Fr campagne de publicité *(f)*
It campagna pubblicitaria *(f)*
Pt campanha publicitária *(f)*

campanha *(f) n* Pt
De Kampagne *(f)*
En campaign
Es campaña *(f)*
Fr campagne *(f)*
It campagna *(f)*

campanha publicitária *(f)* Pt
De Werbefeldzug *(m)*
En advertising campaign; publicity campaign
Es campaña publicitaria *(f)*
Fr campagne de publicité *(f)*
It campagna pubblicitaria *(f)*

campione *(m) n* It
De Probe; Muster *(f n)*
En sample
Es muestra *(f)*

Fr échantillon *(m)*
Pt amostra *(f)*

campione a casaccio *(m)* It
De Stichprobe *(f)*
En random sample
Es muestra aleatoria *(f)*
Fr épreuve au hasard *(f)*
Pt amostra avulsa *(f)*

campione gratuito *(m)* It
De kostenlose Probe *(f)*
En free sample
Es muestra gratuita *(f)*
Fr échantillon gratuit *(f)*
Pt amostra grátis *(f)*

campione senza valore *(m)* It
De Muster ohne Wert *(n)*
En sample of no value
Es muestra sin valor *(f)*
Fr échantillon sans valeur *(m)*
Pt amostra sem valor *(f)*

canal *n* En, Es, Fr, Pt *(m)*
De Kanal *(m)*
It canale *(m)*

canale *(m) n* It
De Kanal *(m)*
En canal
Es canal *(m)*
Fr canal *(m)*
Pt canal *(m)*

canali d'informazione *(m pl)* It
De Werbeträger *(m pl)*
En media
Es medios de información *(m pl)*
Fr supports *(m pl)*
Pt meios de informação *(m pl)*

cancel *vb* En
De annullieren
Es cancelar
Fr annuler
It cancellare
Pt cancelar

cancel a cheque En
Am cancel a check
De einen Scheck rückgängig machen
Es anular un cheque
Fr annuler un chèque
It annullare un assegno
Pt cancelar um cheque

cancelación *(f) n* Es
De Annullierung *(f)*
En cancellation
Fr annulation *(f)*
It annullamento *(m)*
Pt cancelamento *(m)*

cancelamento *(m) n* Pt
De Annullierung *(f)*
En cancellation
Es cancelación *(m)*
Fr annulation *(f)*
It annullamento *(m)*

cancelar *vb* Es, Pt
De annullieren
En cancel
Fr annuler
It cancellare

cancelar uma dívida Pt
De eine Schuld begleichen
En discharge a debt
Es descargar una deuda
Fr acquitter une dette
It estinguere un debito

cancelar um cheque Pt
De einen Scheck rückgängig machen
En cancel a cheque
Am cancel a check
Es anular un cheque
Fr annuler un chèque
It annullare un assegno

cancelar um débito Pt
De eine Schuld erlassen
En write off a debt
Es cancelar una deuda
Fr amortir une créance
It cancellare un credito

cancelar una deuda Es
De eine Schuld erlassen
En write off a debt
Fr amortir une créance
It cancellare un credito
Es cancelar um débito

cancelar una pérdida Es
De einen Verlust abschreiben
En write off a loss
Fr amortir une perte
It cancellare una perdita
Pt anular um prejuízo

cancellare *vb* It
De annullieren; streichen
En cancel; delete

Es cancelar; tachar
Fr annuler; rayer
Pt cancelar; cortar

cancellare una perdita It
De einen Verlust abschreiben
En write off a loss
Es cancelar una pérdida
Fr amortir une perte
Pt anular um prejuízo

cancellare una credito It
De eine Schuld erlassen
En write off a debt
Es cancelar una deuda
Fr amortir une créance
Pt cancelar um débito

cancellation n En
De Annullierung (f)
Es cancelación (m)
Fr annulation (f)
It annullamento (m)
Pt cancelamento (m)

candidat (m) n Fr
De Bewerber (m)
En applicant
Es candidato (m)
It candidato (m)
Pt candidato (m)

candidato (m) n Es, It, Pt
De Bewerber (m)
En applicant
Fr candidat (m)

cantidad (f) n Es
De Menge (f)
En quantity
Fr quantité (f)
It quantità (f)
Pt quantidade (f)

cantiere (m) n It
De Schiffswerft (f)
En dockyard
Es astillero (m)
Fr chantier de construction de navires (m)
Pt estaleiro (m)

capacidad (f) n Es
De Fähigkeit; Inhalt (f m)
En capacity
Fr capacité (f)
It capacità (f)
Pt capacidade (f)

capacidad cúbica (f) Es
De Kubikinhalt (m)
En cubic capacity
Fr volume (m)
It volume (m)
Pt capacidade cúbica (f)

capacidade (f) n Pt
De Fähigkeit; Inhalt (f m)
En capacity
Es capacidad (f)
Fr capacité (f)
It capacità (m)

capacidade cúbica (f) Pt
De Kubikinhalt (m)
En cubic capacity
Es capacidad cúbica (f)
Fr volume (m)
It volume (m)

capacidade excessiva (f) Pt
De Überkapazität (f)
En overcapacity
Es exceso de capadidad (m)
Fr surcapacité (f)
It capacità in eccedenza (f)

capacità (f) n It
De Fähigkeit (f)
En capacity
Es capacidad (f)
Fr capacité (f)
Pt capacidade (f)

capacità creditizia (f) It
De Kreditfähigkeit (f)
En borrowing power
Es facultad de crédito (f)
Fr capacité à avoir du crédit (f)
Pt potencial de obtenção de crédito (m)

capacità in eccedenza (f) It
De Überkapazität (f)
En overcapacity
Es exceso de capacidad (m)
Fr surcapacité (f)
Pt capacidade excessiva (f)

capacité (f) n Fr
De Fähigkeit; Inhalt (f m)
En capacity
Es capacidad (f)
It capacità (f)
Pt capacidade (f)

capacité excédentaire (f) Fr
De übrige Ladefähigkeit (f)
En excess capacity
Es capacidad en exceso (f)
It capacità in eccesso (f)
Pt capacidade em excesso (f)

capacity n En
De Fähigkeit; Inhalt (f m)
Es capacidad (f)
Fr capacité (f)
It capacità (f)
Pt capacidade (f)

caparra (f) n It
De Anzahlung (f)
En deposit; first payment
Es desembolso inicial (m)
Fr arrhes (f pl)
Pt sinal (m)

capataz (m) n Es, Pt
De Vorarbeiter (m)
En foreman
Fr contremaître; chef d'équipe (m)
It capo operaio; capo squadra (m)

capataz jefe (m) Es
De Werkmeister (m)
En head foreman
Fr chef d'atelier (m)
It capo officina (m)
Pt encarregado-chefe (m)

capitaine (m) n Fr
De Kapitän (m)
En master of a ship
Es capitán de navio (m)
It capitano di nave (m)
Pt capitão de navio (m)

capitaine de port (m) Fr
De Hafenmeister (m)
En harbour-master
Es capitán de puerto (m)
It capitano di porto (m)
Pt capitão de porto (m)

capital n En, Es, Fr, Pt (m)
De Kapital (n)
It capitale (m)

capital account En
De Kapitalkonto (n)
Es cuenta de capital (f)
Fr compte capital (m)

It   conto capitale *(m)*
Pt   conta de capital *(f)*

capital a corto plazo *(m)* Es
De   kurzfristiges Kapital *(n)*
En   short-term capital
Fr   capitaux à court terme
      (m pl)
It   capitale a breve termine
      (m)
Pt   capital a curto prazo *(m)*

capital a curto prazo *(m)* Pt
De   kurzfristiges Kapital *(n)*
En   short-term capital
Es   capital a corto plazo *(m)*
Fr   capitaux à court terme
      (m pl)
It   capitale a breve termine
      (m)

capital a largo plazo *(m)* Es
De   langfristiges Kapital *(n)*
En   long-term capital
Fr   capitaux à long terme
      (m pl)
It   capitale consolidato a
      lunga scadenza *(m)*
Pt   capital a longo prazo *(m)*

capital allowances En
De   Steuerbegünstigung auf
      Anlagen *(f)*
Es   deducciones fiscales
      sobre inversiones *(f pl)*
Fr   déductions fiscales sur les
      investissements *(f pl)*
It   deduzioni fiscali sugli
      investimenti *(f pl)*
Pt   concessões sobre capital
      (f pl)

capital a longo prazo *(m)* Pt
De   langfristiges Kapital *(n)*
En   long-term capital
Es   capital a largo plazo *(m)*
Fr   capitaux à long terme
      (m pl)
It   capitale consolidato a
      lunga scadenza *(m)*

capital a préstamo *(m)* Es
De   Fremdkapital *(n)*
En   borrowed capital
Fr   capitaux empruntés *(m pl)*
It   capitale preso a prestito
      (m)
Pt   capital por empréstimo *(m)*

capital asset En
Am   fixed asset
De   Vermögensanlage *(f)*
Es   activo fijo *(m)*
Fr   actif immobilisé *(m)*
It   capitale fisso *(m)*
Pt   bens de capital *(m pl)*

capital autorisé *(m)* Fr
De   genehmigtes Kapital *(n)*
En   authorized capital
Es   capital autorizado *(m)*
It   capitale autorizzato *(m)*
Pt   capital autorizado *(m)*

capital autorizado *(m)* n
      Es, Pt
De   genehmigtes Kapital *(n)*
En   authorized capital
Fr   capital autorisé *(m)*
It   capitale autorizzato *(m)*

capital circulante *(m)* Es
De   Betriebskapital *(n)*
En   working capital
Fr   fonds de roulement *(m pl)*
It   capitale d'esercizio *(m)*
Pt   capital para movimentação
      (m)

capital de especulação *(m)*
      Pt
De   Spekulationskapital *(n)*
En   risk capital
Es   capital de especulación
      (m)
Fr   capitaux spéculatifs *(m pl)*
It   capitale di speculazione
      (m)

capital de especulación *(m)*
      Es
De   Spekulationskapital *(n)*
En   risk capital
Fr   capitaux spéculatifs *(m pl)*
It   capitale di speculazione
      (m)
Pt   capital de especulação *(m)*

capital de exploração *(m)* Pt
De   Betriebskapital *(n)*
En   trading capital
Es   capital de explotación *(m)*
Fr   fonds de roulement *(m)*
It   capitale d'esercizio *(m)*

capital de explotación *(m)* Es
De   Betriebskapital *(n)*
En   trading capital

Fr   fonds de roulement *(m)*
It   capitale d'esercizio *(m)*
Pt   capital de exploração *(m)*

capital de reserve *(m)* Es
De   nicht eingerufenes Kapital
      (n)
En   uncalled capital
Fr   capital non appelé *(m)*
It   capitale non richiamato
      (m)
Pt   capital irrealizado *(m)*

capital desembolsado *(m)* Es
De   eingezahltes Kapital *(n)*
En   paid-up capital
Fr   capital versé *(m)*
It   capitale versato *(m)*
Pt   capital realizado *(m)*

capitale *(m)* n It
De   Kapital *(n)*
En   capital
Es   capital *(m)*
Fr   capital *(m)*
Pt   capital *(m)*

capitale a breve termine *(m)*
      It
De   kurzfristiges Kapital *(n)*
En   short-term capital
Es   capital a corto plazo *(m)*
Fr   capitaux à court terme
      (m pl)
Pt   capital a curto prazo *(m)*

capitale autorizzato *(m)* It
De   genehmigtes Kapital *(n)*
En   authorized capital
Es   capital autorizado *(m)*
Fr   capital autorisé *(m)*
Pt   capital autorizado *(m)*

capitale azionario *(m)* It
De   Aktienkapital *(n)*
En   share capital
Am   stock capital
Es   capital en acciones *(m)*
Fr   capital social *(m)*
Pt   capital em acções *(m)*

**capitale consolidato a lunga
      scadenza** *(m)* It
De   langfristiges Kapital *(n)*
En   long-term capital
Es   capital a largo plazo *(m)*
Fr   capitaux à long terme
      (m pl)
Pt   capital a longo prazo *(m)*

capitale d'esercizio *(m)* It
De Betriebskapital *(n)*
En trading capital; working capital
Es capital de explotación; capital circulante *(m)*
Fr fonds de roulement *(m)*
Pt capital de exploração *(m)*

capitale di speculazione *(m)* It
De Spekulationskapital *(n)*
En risk capital
Es capital de especulación *(m)*
Fr capitaux spéculatifs *(m pl)*
Pt capital de especulação *(m)*

capitale emesso *(m)* It
De ausgegebenes Kapital *(n)*
En issued capital
Es capital emitido *(m)*
Fr capital versé *(m)*
Pt capital emitido *(m)*

capitale fisso *(m)* It
De feste Kapitalanlagen; Vermögensanlage *(f pl; f)*
En fixed capital; capital asset
Es capital fijo; activo fijo *(m)*
Fr capital fixe; actif immobilisé *(m)*
Pt capital fixado; bens de capital *(m; m pl)*

capital em acções *(m)* Pt
De Aktienkapital *(n)*
En share capital
Am stock capital
Es capital en acciones *(m)*
Fr capital social *(m)*
Pt capitale azionario *(m)*

capital emitido *(m)* Es, Pt
De ausgegebenes Kapital *(n)*
En issued capital
Fr capital versé *(m)*
It capitale emesso *(m)*

capital en acciones *(m)* Es
De Aktienkapital *(n)*
En share capital
Am stock capital
Fr capital social *(m)*
It capitale azionario *(m)*
Pt capital em acções *(m)*

capitale nominale *(m)* It
De Nennkapital *(m)*
En nominal capital

Es capital nominal *(m)*
Fr capital nominal *(m)*
Pt capital nominal *(m)*

capitale non emesso *(m)* It
De nicht ausgegebenes Kapital *(n)*
En unissued capital
Es capital no emitido *(m)*
Fr capitaux pas encore émis *(m pl)*
Pt capital não emitido *(m)*

capitale non richiamato *(m)* It
De nicht eingerufenes Kapital *(n)*
En uncalled capital
Es capital de reserva *(m)*
Fr capital non appelé *(m)*
Pt capital irrealizado *(m)*

capitale preso a prestito *(m)* It
De Fremdkapital *(n)*
En borrowed capital
Es capital a préstamo *(m)*
Fr capitaux empruntés *(m pl)*
Pt capital por empréstimo *(m)*

capitale sottoscritto *(m)* It
De gezeichnetes Kapital *(n)*
En subscribed capital
Es capital subscrito *(m)*
Fr capital souscrit *(m)*
Pt capital subscrito *(m)*

capitale versato *(m)* It
De eingezahltes Kapital *(n)*
En paid-up capital
Es capital desembolsado *(m)*
Fr capital versé *(m)*
Pt capital realizado *(m)*

capital expenditure En
De Kapitalauslagen *(f pl)*
Es inmovilizaciones *(f pl)*
Fr immobilisations *(f pl)*
It immobilizzazioni *(f pl)*
Pt despesas em termos de capital *(f pl)*

capital fijo *(m)* Es
De feste Kapitalanlagen *(f pl)*
En fixed capital
Fr capital fixe *(m)*
It capitale fisso *(m)*
Pt capital fixado *(m)*

capital fixado *(m)* Pt
De feste Kapitalanlagen *(f pl)*
En fixed capital
Es capital fijo *(m)*
Fr capital fixe *(m)*
It capitale fisso *(m)*

capital fixe *(m)* Fr
De feste Kapitalanlagen *(f pl)*
En fixed capital
Es capital fijo *(m)*
It capitale fisso *(m)*
Pt capital fixado *(m)*

capital gains En
De Kapitalgewinn *(n)*
Es beneficios sobre capital *(m pl)*
Fr gains en capital *(m pl)*
It plusvalore di capitale *(m pl)*
Pt lucros de capital *(m pl)*

capital gains tax En
De Kapitalertragsteuer *(f)*
Es impuesto sobre las ganancias de capital *(m)*
Fr impôt sur les plus-values en capital *(m)*
It imposta sul plusvalore di capitale *(f)*
Pt imposto sobre lucros de capital *(m)*

capital goods En
De Anlagegüter *(n pl)*
Es bienes de producción *(m pl)*
Fr biens d'équipement *(m pl)*
It beni strumentali *(m pl)*
Pt mercadorias de capital *(f pl)*

capital grants En
De Kapitalhilfe *(f)*
Es subvención de capital *(f)*
Fr subventions en capital *(f pl)*
It sovvenzioni di capitale *(f pl)*
Pt suvenções de capital *(f pl)*

capital-intensive *adj* En
De kapitalintensiv
Es intensivo de capital
Fr intensif de capital
It concentrato sul capitale
Pt intensivo em termos de capital

capital irrealizado *(m)* Pt
De nicht eingerufenes Kapital
   (n)
En uncalled capital
Es capital de reserva *(m)*
Fr capital non appelé *(m)*
It capitale non richiamato
   (m)

capitalisation *(f)* n Fr
De Kapitalisierung *(f)*
En capitalization
Es capitalización *(f)*
It capitalizzazione *(f)*
Pt capitalização *(f)*

capitaliser *vb* Fr
De kapitalisieren
En capitalize
Es capitalizar
It capitalizzare
Pt capitalizar

capitalism n En
De Kapitalismus *(m)*
Es capitalismo *(m)*
Fr capitalisme *(m)*
It capitalismo *(m)*
Pt capitalismo *(m)*

capitalisme *(m)* n Fr
De Kapitalismus *(m)*
En capitalism
Es capitalismo *(m)*
It capitalismo *(m)*
Pt capitalismo *(m)*

capitalismo *(m)* n Es, It, Pt
De Kapitalismus *(m)*
En capitalism
Fr capitalisme *(m)*

capitalista *(m)* n It, Pt
De Geldgeber *(m)*
En investor
Es inversionista *(m)*
Fr investisseur *(m)*

capitalização *(f)* n Pt
De Kapitalisierung *(f)*
En capitalization
Es capitalización *(f)*
Fr capitalisation *(f)*
It capitalizzazione *(f)*

capitalización *(f)* n Es
De Kapitalisierung *(f)*
En capitalization
Fr capitalisation *(f)*

It capitalizzazione *(f)*
Pt capitalização *(f)*

capitalizar *vb* Es, Pt
De kapitalisieren
En capitalize
Fr capitaliser
It capitalizzare

capitalization n En
De Kapitalisierung *(f)*
Es capitalización *(f)*
Fr capitalisation *(f)*
It capitalizzazione *(f)*
Pt capitalização *(f)*

capitalize *vb* En
De kapitalisieren
Es capitalizar
Fr capitaliser
It capitalizzare
Pt capitalizar

capitalized value En
De kapitalisierter Wert *(m)*
Es valor capitalizado *(m)*
Fr valeur capitalisée *(f)*
It valore capitalizzato *(m)*
Pt valor capitalizado *(m)*

capitalizzare *vb* It
De kapitalisieren
En capitalize
Es capitalizar
Fr capitaliser
Pt capitalizar

capitalizzazione *(f)* n It
De Kapitalisierung *(f)*
En capitalization
Es capitalización *(f)*
Fr capitalisation *(f)*
Pt capitalização *(f)*

capital loss En
De Kapitalverlust *(m)*
Es pérdida de capital *(f)*
Fr perte de capital *(f)*
It perdita di capitale *(f)*
Pt perdas de capital *(f pl)*

capital não emitido *(m)* Pt
De nicht ausgegebenes
   Kapital *(n)*
En unissued capital
Es capital no emitido *(m)*
Fr capitaux pas encore émis
   (m pl)
It capitale non emesso *(n)*

capital no emitido *(m)* Es
De nicht ausgegebenes
   Kapital *(n)*
En unissued capital
Fr capitaux pas encore émis
   (m pl)
It capitale non emesso *(m)*
Pt capital não emitido *(m)*

capital nominal *(m)* Es, Fr, Pt
De Nennkapital *(m)*
En nominal capital
It capitale nominale *(m)*

capital non appelé *(m)* Fr
De nicht eingerufenes Kapital
   (n)
En uncalled capital
Es capital de reserva *(m)*
It capitale non richiamato
   (m)
Pt capital irrealizado *(m)*

capital oisif *(m)* Fr
De totes Kapital *(n)*
En idle money
Es dinero sin invertir *(m)*
It denaro inattivo *(m)*
Pt dinheiro paralisado *(m)*

capital por empréstimo *(m)*
   Pt
De Fremdkapital *(n)*
En borrowed capital
Es capital a préstamo *(m)*
Fr capitaux empruntés *(m pl)*
It capitale preso a prestito
   (m)

capital realizado *(m)* Pt
De eingezahltes Kapital *(n)*
En paid-up capital
Es capital desembolsado *(m)*
Fr capital versé *(m)*
It capitale versato *(m)*

capital reserves En
De Kapitalreserve *(f)*
Es reserva de capital *(f)*
Fr réserve de capitaux *(f)*
It riserva di capitale *(f)*
Pt reservas de capital *(f pl)*

capital social *(m)* Fr
De Aktienkapital *(n)*
En share capital
Am stock capital
Es capital en acciones *(m)*

It capitale azionario *(m)*
Pt capital em acções *(m)*

capital souscrit *(m)* Fr
De gezeichnetes Kapital *(n)*
En subscribed capital
Es capital subscrito *(m)*
It capitale sottoscritto *(m)*
Pt capital subscrito *(m)*

capital subscrito *(m)* Es, Pt
De gezeichnetes Kapital *(n)*
En subscribed capital
Fr capital souscrit *(m)*
It capitale sottoscritto *(m)*

capital versé *(m)* Fr
De ausgegebenes Kapital;
   eingezahltes Kapital *(n)*
En issued capital; paid-up
   capital
Es capital emitido; capital
   desembolsado *(m)*
It capitale emesso; capitale
   versato *(m)*
Pt capital emitido; capital realizado *(m)*

capitán de navío *(m)* Es
De Kapitän *(m)*
En master of a ship
Fr capitaine *(m)*
It capitano di nave *(m)*
Pt capitão de navio *(m)*

capitán de puerto *(m)* Es
De Hafenmeister *(m)*
En harbour-master
Fr capitane de port *(m)*
It capitano di porto *(m)*
Pt capitão de porto *(m)*

capitano di nave *(m)* It
De Kapitän *(m)*
En master of a ship
Es capitán de navío *(m)*
Fr capitaine *(m)*
Pt capitão de navio *(m)*

capitano di porto *(m)* It
De Hafenmeister *(m)*
En harbour-master
Es capitán de puerto *(m)*
Fr capitaine de port *(m)*
Pt capitão de porto *(m)*

capitão de navio *(m)* Pt
De Kapitän *(m)*
En master of a ship

Es capitán de navío *(m)*
Fr capitaine *(m)*
It capitano di nave *(m)*

capitão de porto *(m)* Pt
De Hafenmeister *(m)*
En harbour-master
Es capitán de puerto *(m)*
Fr capitaine de port *(m)*
It capitano di porto *(m)*

capitaux à court terme *(m pl)*
   Fr
De kurzfristiges Kapital *(n)*
En short-term capital
Es capital a corto plazo *(m)*
It capitale a breve termine
   (m)
Pt capital a curto prazo *(m)*

capitaux à long terme *(m pl)*
   Fr
De langfristiges Kapital *(n)*
En long-term capital
Es capital a largo plazo *(m)*
It capitale consolidato a lun-
   ga scadenza *(m)*
Pt capital a longo prazo *(m)*

capitaux empruntés *(m pl)* Fr
De Fremdkapital *(n)*
En borrowed capital
Es capital a préstamo *(m)*
It capitale preso a prestito
   (m)
Pt capital por empréstimo *(m)*

capitaux pas encore émis
   (m pl) Fr
De nicht ausgegebenes Kapi-
   tal *(n)*
En unissued capital
Es capital no emitido *(m)*
It capitale non emesso *(m)*
Pt capital não emitido *(m)*

capitaux spéculatifs *(m pl)* Fr
De Spekulationskapital *(n)*
En risk capital
Es capital de especulación
   (m)
It capitale di speculazione
   (m)
Pt capital de especulação *(m)*

capo-famiglia *(m)* n It
De Hausherr *(m)*
En householder
Es jefe de familia *(m)*

Fr chef de famille *(m)*
Pt dono da casa *(m)*

capo officina *(m)* It
De Werkmeister *(m)*
En head foreman
Es capataz jefe *(m)*
Fr chef d'atelier *(m)*
Pt encarregado-chefe *(m)*

capo operaio *(m)* It
De Vorarbeiter *(m)*
En foreman
Es capataz *(m)*
Fr contremaître; chef d'équi-
   pe *(m)*
Pt encarregado; capataz *(m)*

capo reparto *(m)* It
De Abteilungsleiter *(m)*
En head of department
Es jefe de departamento *(m)*
Fr chef de service *(m)*
Pt chefe de departamento *(m)*

capo servizio acquisti *(m)* It
De Haupteinkäufer *(m)*
En head buyer
Es jefe del departamento de
   compras *(m)*
Fr chef du service de achats
   (m)
Pt chefe de compass *(m)*

capo ufficio *(m)* It
De Bürovorsteher
En office manager
Es jefe de oficina *(m)*
Fr chef de bureau *(m)*
Pt chefe de escritório *(m)*

car n En
De Auto; Wagen *(n m)*
Es coche *(m)*
Fr voiture; automobile *(f)*
It automobile; macchina *(f)*
Pt carro; automóvel *(m)*

caracteristica *(f)* n Es, Pt
De Merkmal *(n)*
En feature
Fr particularité *(f)*
It caratteristica *(f)*

caratteristica *(f)* n It
De Merkmal *(n)*
En feature
Es característica *(f)*

Fr particularité *(f)*
Pt característica *(f)*

carbón *(m) n* Es
De Kohle *(f)*
En coal
Fr houille; charbon *(f m)*
It carbone *(m)*
Pt carvão *(m)*

carbon copy En
De Durchschlag *(m)*
Es copia en papel carbón *(f)*
Fr copie au carbone *(f)*
It copia carbone *(f)*
Pt cópia a químico *(f)*

carbone *(m) n* It
De Kohle *(f)*
En coal
Es carbón *(m)*
Fr charbon *(m)*
Pt carvão *(m)*

carbonera *(f) n* Es
De Bunker *(m)*
En bunker
Fr soute *(f)*
It carbonile *(m)*
Pt carvoeira *(f)*

carbonile *(m) n* It
De Bunker *(m)*
En bunker
Es carbonera *(f)*
Fr soute *(f)*
Pt carvoeira *(f)*

carbon paper En
De Kohlepapier *(n)*
Es papel carbón *(m)*
Fr papier carbone *(m)*
It carta carbone *(f)*
Pt papel químico *(m)*

card *n* En
De Karte *(f)*
Es tarjeta *(f)*
Fr carte *(f)*
It scheda *(f)*
Pt cartão *(m)*

card index En
De Kartothek *(f)*
Es fichero *(m)*
Fr fichier *(m)*
It schedario *(m)*
Pt ficheiro *(m)*

card-index file En
De Kartei *(f)*
Es archivo de fichas *(m)*
Fr fichier *(m)*
It schedario *(m)*
Pt ficheiro com índice *(m)*

carga *(f) n* Es, Pt
De Ladung *(f)*
En cargo; loading
Fr cargaison; chargement *(f m)*
It carico; caricamento *(m)*

carga de convés *(f)* Pt
De Deckladung *(f)*
En deck cargo
Es carga en cubierta *(f)*
Fr cargaison de pont *(f)*
It carico in coperta *(m)*

cargador de muelle *(m)* Es
De Hafenarbeiter *(m)*
En docker
Am longshoreman
Fr docker *(m)*
It lavoratore del porto *(m)*
Pt trabalhador das docas *(m)*

carga en cubierta *(f)* Es
De Deckladung *(f)*
En deck cargo
Fr cargaison de pont *(f)*
It carico in coperta *(m)*
Pt carga de convés *(f)*

carga en granel *(f)* Es
De Schüttgut *(n)*
En bulk cargo
Fr cargaison en vrac *(f)*
It carico alla rinfusa *(m)*
Pt carga geral *(f)*

carga geral *(f)* Pt
De Schüttgut *(n)*
En bulk cargo
Es carga en granel *(f)*
Fr cargaison en vrac *(f)*
It carico alla rinfusa *(m)*

cargaison *(f) n* Fr
De Ladung *(f)*
En cargo
Es carga *(f)*
It carico *(m)*
Pt carga *(f)*

cargaison de pont *(f)* Fr
De Deckladung *(f)*
En deck cargo

Es carga en cubierta *(f)*
It carico in coperta *(m)*
Pt carga de convés *(f)*

cargaison en vrac *(f)* Fr
De Schüttgut *(n)*
En bulk cargo
Es carga en granel *(f)*
It carico alla rinfusa *(m)*
Pt carga geral *(f)*

cargo *n* En
De Ladung *(f)*
Es carga *(f)*
Fr cargaison; chargement *(f m)*
It carico *(m)*
Pt carga *(f)*

cargo *(m) n* Fr
De Frachtschiff *(n)*
En cargo boat
Es buque de carga *(m)*
It nave de carico *(f)*
Pt navio de carga *(m)*

cargo boat En
De Frachtschiff *(n)*
Es buque de carga *(m)*
Fr cargo *(m)*
It nave da carico *(f)*
Pt navio de carga *(m)*

cargos de salvamento *(m pl)* Es
De Bergegeld *(n)*
En salvage charges
Fr indemnité de sauvetage *(f)*
It spese de salvataggio *(f pl)*
Pt encargos de salvamento *(m pl)*

cargos imprevistos *(m pl)* Es
De Nebenkosten *(pl)*
En incidental charges
Fr charges annexes *(f pl)*
It spese accessorie *(f pl)*
Pt encargos ocasionais *(m pl)*

carico *(m) n* It
De Ladung *(f)*
En cargo; loading
Es carga *(f)*
Fr cargaison; chargement *(f m)*
Pt carga; carregamento *(f m)*

carico alla rinfusa *(m)* It
De Schüttgut *(n)*
En bulk cargo

Es carga en granel *(f)*
Fr cargaison en vrac *(f)*
Pt carga geral *(f)*

carico in coperta *(m)* It
De Deckladung *(f)*
En deck cargo
Es carga en cubierta *(f)*
Fr cargaison de pont *(f)*
Pt carga de convés *(f)*

carimbo *(m)* n Pt
De Stempel *(m)*
En (rubber) stamp
Es estampilla *(f)*
Fr tampon; timbre *(m)*
It stampiglia *(f)*

carimbo de datas *(m)* Pt
De Tagesstempel *(m)*
En date-stamp
Es sello de fecha *(m)*
Fr dateur *(m)*
It timbro a data *(m)*

carnet de chèques *(m)* Fr
De Scheckheft *(n)*
En cheque book
Am check book
Es libro de cheques *(m)*
It libretto assegni *(m)*
Pt livro de cheques *(m)*

carnet de compte *(m)* Fr
De Bankbuch; Sparbuch *(n)*
En passbook
Am bankbook
Es libreta de banco *(f)*
It libretto di conto *(m)*
Pt livrete de conta *(f)*

carnet de identidad *(m)* Es
De Personalausweis *(m)*
En identity card
Fr carte d'identité *(f)*
It carta d'identità *(f)*
Pt bilhete de identidade *(m)*

caro *adj* Es, It, Pt
De kostspielig; teuer
En expensive
Fr cher

carpeta *(f)* n Es
De Mappe *(f)*
En folder
Fr chemise *(f)*
It cartelle *(f)*
Pt pasta *(f)*

carregamento *(m)* n Pt
De Ladung *(f)*
En loading
Es carga *(f)*
Fr chargement *(m)*
It carico; caricamento *(m)*

carretta *(f)* n It
De Trampschiff *(n)*
En tramp steamer
Es vapor volandero *(m)*
Fr navire de tramping *(m)*
Pt vapor de serviço
    autónomo *(m)*

carriage forward En
Am F.O.B. shipping point
De Portonachnahme
Es a porte debido
Fr en port dû
It porto assegnato
Pt transporte a pagar

carriage free En
Am F.O.B. destination
De frachtfrei
Es franco de porte
Fr franco
It porto franco
Pt porte grátis

carriage paid En
Am freight charges paid
De franko
Es a porte pagado
Fr port payé
It franco di porto
Pt porte pago

carrier n En
Am conveyer
De Spediteur *(m)*
Es transportador *(m)*
Fr expéditeur *(m)*
It vettore *(m)*
Pt transportador *(m)*

carro *(m)* n Pt
De Auto; Wagen *(n m)*
En car
Es coche *(m)*
Fr voiture; automobile *(f)*
It automobile; macchina *(f)*

carrozza ferroviaria *(f)* It
De Eisenbahnwagen *(m)*
En railway carriage
Am railroad car
Es vagón de ferrocarril *(m)*

Fr wagon de chemin de fer
    (m)
Pt vagão de caminhos de ferro
    (m)

carry forward amount Am
En amount carried forward
De Übertrag *(m)*
Es suma y sigue *(f)*
Fr report à nouveau *(m)*
It ammontare da riportare
    (m)
Pt importância transportada
    (f)

carry out En
De durchführen
Es ejecutar
Fr exécuter
It eseguire
Pt executar

carta *(f)* n Es, Pt
De Brief *(m)*
En letter
Fr lettre *(f)*
It lettera *(f)*

carta assorbente *(f)* It
De Löschpapier *(n)*
En blotting paper
Es papel secante *(m)*
Fr papier buvard *(m)*
Pt papel mata-borrão *(m)*

carta carbone *(f)* It
De Kohlepapier *(n)*
En carbon paper
Es papel carbón *(m)*
Fr papier carbone *(m)*
Pt papel químico *(m)*

carta certificada *(f)* Es
De eingeschriebener Brief *(m)*
En registered letter
Fr lettre recommandée *(f)*
It lettera raccomandata *(f)*
Pt carta registada *(f)*

**carta comercial de primera
  orden** *(f)* Es
De erstklassiger Handels-
    wechsel *(m)*
En prime trade bill
Fr papier de haut commerce
    (m)
It carta commerciale di
    primo ordine *(f)*

Pt estatuto de comercialização de primeira ordem
(m)

**carta commerciale di primo
ordine** *(f)* It
De erstklassiger Handels-
wechsel *(m)*
En prime trade bill
Es carta comercial de primera
orden *(f)*
Fr papier de haut commerce
(m)
Pt estatuto de comercialização de primeira ordem
(m)

carta de crédito *(f)* Es, Pt
De Kreditbrief *(m)*
En letter of credit
Fr lettre de crédit *(f)*
It lettera di credito *(f)*

carta de crédito confirmada
(f) Es, Pt
De bestätigter Kreditbrief *(m)*
En confirmed letter of credit
Fr lettre de crédit confirmée
(f)
It lettera di credito
confermata *(f)*

carta de crédito irrevocable
(f) Es
De unwiderruflicher Kreditbrief *(m)*
En irrevocable letter of credit
Fr lettre de crédit irrévocable
(f)
It letter di credito
irrevocabile *(f)*
Pt carta de crédito
irrevogável *(f)*

**carta de crédito irrevocable
confirmada** *(f)* Es
De bestätigter unwiderruflicher Kreditbrief *(m)*
En confirmed irrevocable
letter of credit
Fr lettre de crédit irrévocable
confirmée *(f)*
It lettera di credito confermata e irrevocabile *(f)*
Pt carta de crédito irre-
vogável confirmada *(f)*

carta de crédito irrevogável
(f) Pt
De unwiderruflicher Kreditbrief *(m)*
En irrevocable letter of credit
Es carta de crédito irre-
vocable *(f)*
Fr lettre de crédit irrévocable
(f)
It lettera di credito irrevocabile *(f)*

**carta de crédito irrevogável
confirmada** *(f)* Pt
De bestätigter unwiderruflicher Kreditbrief *(m)*
En confirmed irrevocable
letter of credit
Es carta de crédito irre-
vocable confirmada *(f)*
Fr lettre de crédit irrévocable
confirmée *(f)*
It lettera di credito confermata e irrevocabile *(f)*

carta de hipoteca *(f)* Es, Pt
De Verpfändungsurkunde *(f)*
En letter of hypothecation
Fr lettre hypothécaire *(f)*
It atto ipotecario *(m)*

carta de indemnización *(f)* Es
De Ausfallbürgschaft *(f)*
En letter of indemnity
Fr cautionnement *(m)*
It lettera die garanzia *(f)*
Pt documento de garantia
(m)

carta de porte aéreo *(f)* Es
De Luftfrachtbrief *(m)*
En air waybill
Fr lettre de transport aérien *(f)*
It nota di spedizione aerea *(f)*
Pt guia de porte aéreo *(f)*

**carta de publicidad de
ventas** *(f)* Es
De Werbebrief *(m)*
En publicity letter; sales letter
Fr lettre de publicité ventes *(f)*
It lettera di pubblicità
vendite *(f)*
Pt carta de publicidade de
vendas *(f)*

carta de trabalho *(f)* Pt
De Arbeitserlaubnis *(n)*
En work permit

Es permiso de trabajo *(m)*
Fr permis de travail *(m)*
It permesso di lavoro *(m)*

carta di credito *(f)* It
De Kreditkarte *(f)*
En credit card
Es tarjeta de crédito *(f)*
Fr carte de crédit *(f)*
Pt cartão de crédito *(m)*

carta d'identità *(f)* It
De Personalausweis *(m)*
En identity card
Es carnet de identidad *(m)*
Fr carte d'identité *(f)*
Pt bilhete de identidade *(m)*

carta expressa *(f)* Pt
De Eilbrief *(m)*
En express letter
Am special delivery
Es carta urgente *(f)*
Fr lettre par exprès *(f)*
It lettera espresso *(f)*

carta millimetrata *(f)* It
De Millimeterpapier *(n)*
En graph paper
Es papel milimetrado *(m)*
Fr papier millimétré *(m)*
Pt papel milimetrado *(m)*

carta moneta *(f)* It
De Papiergeld *(n)*
En paper money
Es papel monetario *(m)*
Fr papier-monnaie *(m)*
Pt papel-moeda *(m)*

cartão *(m)* n Pt
De Karte *(f)*
En card
Es tarjeta *(f)*
Fr carte *(f)*
It scheda *(f)*

cartão de crédito *(m)* Pt
De Kreditkarte *(f)*
En credit card
Es tarjeta de crédito *(f)*
Fr carte de crédit *(f)*
It carta di credito *(f)*

carta por avião *(f)* Pt
De Luftpostbrief *(m)*
En air letter
Es carta por avión *(f)*
Fr aérogramme *(m)*
It lettera aerea *(f)*

carta por avión *(f)* Es
De Luftpostbrief *(m)*
En air letter
Fr aérogramme *(m)*
It lettera aerea *(f)*
Pt carta por avião *(f)*

carta registada *(f)* Pt
De eingeschriebener Brief *(m)*
En registered letter
Es carta certificada *(f)*
Fr lettre recommandée *(f)*
It lettera raccomandata *(f)*

carta urgente *(f)* Es
De Eilbrief *(m)*
En express letter
Am special delivery
Fr lettre par exprès *(f)*
It lettera espresso *(f)*
Pt carta expressa *(f)*

carte *(f)* n Fr
De Karte *(f)*
En card
Es tarjeta *(f)*
It scheda *(f)*
Pt cartão *(m)*

carte d'identité *(f)* Fr
De Personalausweis *(m)*
En identity card
Es carnet de identidad *(m)*
It carta d'identità *(f)*
Pt bilhete de identidade *(m)*

carte de chèque *(f)* Fr
De Scheckkarte *(f)*
En cheque card
Am bank credit card
Es tarjeta de cheque *(f)*
It scheda per assegni *(f)*
Pt cartão de validação de cheques *(m)*

carte de crédit *(f)* Fr
De Kreditkarte *(f)*
En credit card
Es tarjeta de crédito *(f)*
It carta di credito *(f)*
Pt cartão de crédito *(m)*

carte di bordo *(f pl)* It
De Schiffspapiere *(n pl)*
En ship's papers
Es documentación marítima *(f)*
Fr papiers de bord *(m pl)*
Pt documentação do navio *(f)*

carteira de investimentos *(m)* Pt
De Investitionsportefeuille *(n)*
En investment portfolio
Es cartera de inversiones *(f)*
Fr portefeuille d'investissements *(m)*
It portafoglio titoli *(m)*

cartel n En, Es, Fr, Pt *(m)*
De Kartell *(n)*
It cartello *(m)*

cartella *(f)* n It
De Mappe
En folder
Es carpeta *(f)*
Fr chemise *(f)*
Pt pasta *(f)*

cartello *(m)* n It
De Kartell *(n)*
En cartel
Es cartell *(m)*
Fr cartel *(m)*
Pt cartel *(m)*

carte perforée Fr
De Lochkarte *(f)*
En punched card
Es tarjeta perforada *(f)*
It scheda perforata *(f)*
Pt ficha perfurada *(f)*

cartera (ministerial) *(f)* n Es
De Portefeuille, Geschäftsbereich *(n m)*
En portfolio
Fr portefeuille *(f)*
It portafoglio *(m)*
Pt pasta *(f)*

cartera de inversiones *(f)* Es
De Investitionsportefeuille *(n)*
En investment portfolio
Fr portefeuille d'investissements *(m)*
It portafoglio titoli *(m)*
Pt carteira de investimentos *(m)*

carton n En, Fr *(m)*
De Karton *(m)*
Es cartón *(m)*
It cartone *(m)*
Pt caixa de cartão *(f)*

cartón *(m)* n Es
De Karton *(m)*
En carton
Fr carton *(m)*
It cartone *(m)*
Pt caixa de cartão *(f)*

cartone *(m)* n It
De Karton *(m)*
En carton
Es cartón *(m)*
Fr carton *(m)*
Pt caixa de cartão *(f)*

carvão *(m)* n Pt
De Kohle *(f)*
En coal
Es carbón *(m)*
Fr houille; charbon *(f m)*
It carbone

carvoeira *(f)* n Pt
De Bunker *(m)*
En bunker
Es carbonera *(f)*
Fr soute *(f)*
It carbonile *(m)*

casa *(f)* n Es, It, Pt
De Haus; Haushalt *(n m)*
En house; household
Fr maison; ménage *(f m)*

casa commerciale *(f)* It
De Firma *(f)*
En business; firm
Es casa de comercio *(f)*
Fr maison de commerce *(f)*
Pt casa de comércio *(f)*

casa da moeda *(f)* Pt
De Münze *(f)*
En mint
Es casa de la moneda *(f)*
Fr la Monnaie
It zecca *(f)*

casa de comercio *(f)* Es
De Firma *(f)*
En business; firm
Fr maison de commerce *(f)*
It casa commerciale *(f)*
Pt casa de comércio *(f)*

casa de comércio *(f)* Pt
De Firma *(f)*
En business; firm
Es casa de comercio *(f)*
Fr maison de commerce *(f)*
It casa commerciale *(f)*

casa de descuentos *(f)* Es
De Diskontbank *(f)*
En discount house
Fr maison d'escompte *(f)*
It banca di sconto *(f)*
Pt agência corretora de
descontos *(f)*

casa de la moneda *(f)* Es
De Münze *(f)*
En mint
Fr la Monnaie
It zecca *(f)*
Pt casa da moeda *(f)*

casa di vecchia fondazione
(f) It
De alteingeführtes Geschäft
(n)
En old-established business
Es casa sólida *(f)*
Fr maison solide *(f)*
Pt empresa de há muito
estabelecida *(f)*

casa editora *(f)* Pt
De Verlag *(m)*
En publishing house
Es casa editorial *(f)*
Fr maison d'édition *(f)*
It casa editrice *(f)*

casa editorial *(f)* Es
De Verlag *(m)*
En publishing house
Fr maison d'édition *(f)*
It casa editrice *(f)*
Pt casa editora *(f)*

casa editrice *(f)* It
De Verlag *(m)*
En publishing house
Es casa editorial *(f)*
Fr maison d'éditon *(f)*
Pt casa editora *(f)*

casa sólida *(f)* Es
De alteingeführtes Geschäft
(n)
En old-established business
Fr maison solide *(f)*
It casa di vecchia
fondazione *(f)*
Pt empresa de há muito
estabelecida *(f)*

case (legal) *(n)* En
De Rechtsfall *(m)*
Es causa *(f)*

Fr procès *(m)*
It causa *(f)*
Pt causa *(f)*

cash *(n)* En
De Bargeld *(n)*
Es dinero efectivo *(m)*
Fr espèces *(f pl)*
It denaro contante *(m)*
Pt dinheiro de contado *(m)*

cash *(vb)* En
De einkassieren
Es cobrar
Fr encaisser
It incassare
Pt cobrar

cash a cheque En
Am cash a check
De einen Scheck einlösen
Es cobrar un cheque
Fr toucher un chèque
It incassare un assegno
Pt cobrar um cheque

cash against documents
(c.a.d.) En
De bar gegen Versandpapiere
Es al contado contra docu-
mentos
Fr comptant contre docu-
ments
It contanti contro documenti
Pt em dinheiro contra
documentação

cash balance En
De Kassensaldo *(m)*
Es resto en efectivo *(m)*
Fr solde de caisse *(m)*
It residuo di cassa *(m)*
Pt saldo em dinheiro *(m)*

cash book En
De Kassenbuch *(n)*
Es libro de caja *(m)*
Fr livre de caisse *(m)*
It libro cassa *(m)*
Pt livro de caixa *(m)*

cash-box *(f)* En
De Geldkassette *(f)*
Es caja *(f)*
Fr caisse *(f)*
It cassetta *(f)*
Pt caixa *(f)*

cash deal En
De Bargeschäft *(n)*
Es trato al contado *(m)*
Fr transaction au comptant
(f)
It operazione a contanti *(f)*
Pt negócio em dinheiro *(m)*

cash-desk *(n)* En
De Kasse *(f)*
Es caja *(f)*
Fr caisse *(f)*
It cassa *(f)*
Pt caixa *(f)*

cash discount En
De Barrabatt *(m)*
Es descuento de caja *(m)*
Fr escompte de caisse *(m)*
It sconto per pagamento a
contanti *(m)*
Pt desconto de contado *(m)*

cash dispenser En
De Bargeldauszahlungs-
automat *(m)*
Es caja automática *(f)*
Fr distributeur d'argent
comptant *(m)*
It cassa automatica *(f)*
Pt caixa automática *(f)*

cash flow En
De Cash-flow *(m)*
Es flujo de caja *(m)*
Fr cash flow *(m)*
It flusso di cassa *(m)*
Pt movimento em dinheiro
(m)

cash forecast En
De Barggeldvoraussage
Es previsión de fondos *(f)*
Fr prévision comptant *(f)*
It previsione contanti *(f)*
Pt previsão de fundos
(em dinheiro) *(f)*

cashier *(n)* En
Am teller
De Kassierer *(m)*
Es cajero *(m)*
Fr caissier *(m)*
It cassiere *(m)*
Pt caixa *(m)*

cash in hand En
De Barbestand *(m)*
Es efectivo en caja *(m)*

Fr   espèces en caisse *(f pl)*
It   pronti contanti *(m pl)*
Pt   fondos à ordem *(m pl)*

cash on delivery (c.o.d.) En
De   Lieferung gegen Nach-
       nahme
Es   entrega contra reembolso
Fr   paiement à la livraison
It   pagamento alla consegna
Pt   entrega contra reembolso

cash reserve En
De   Kassenreserve *(f)*
Es   reserva en efectivo *(f)*
Fr   réserve en espèces *(f)*
It   riserva in contanti *(f)*
Pt   reserva em dinheiro *(f)*

cash sale En
De   Kassageschäft
Es   venta al conta *(f)*
Fr   vente au comptant *(f)*
It   vendita a contanti *(f)*
Pt   venda a dinheiro *(f)*

cash with order En
De   gegen Barzahlung
Es   pagadero con el pedido
Fr   payable à la commande
It   pagamento con l'ordine
Pt   pagemento no acto de
       requisição

casilla de equipaje *(f)* Es
De   Gepäckschließfach *(n)*
En   luggage locker
Fr   coffre de bagages *(m)*
It   cassetta bagaglio *(f)*
Pt   depósito de bagagem
       individualizado *(m)*

cassa *(f)* n It
De   Kasse *(f)*
En   cash-desk
Es   caja *(f)*
Fr   caisse *(f)*
Pt   caixa *(f)*

cassa automatica *(f)* It
De   Bargeldauszahlungs-
       automat *(m)*
En   cash dispenser
Es   caja automática *(f)*
Fr   distributeur d'argent
       comptant *(m)*
Pt   caixa automática *(f)*

cassa di compensazione *(f)*
       It
De   Ausgleichsfonds *(m)*
En   equalization fund
Es   fondo de compensación
       (m)
Fr   fonds de régularisation
       (m pl)
Pt   fundo de compensação *(m)*

cassa di risparmio *(f)* It
De   Sparkasse *(f)*
En   savings bank
Es   caja de ahorros *(f)*
Fr   caisse d'épargne *(f)*
Pt   caixa económica *(f)*

cassa di risparmio postale *(f)*
       It
De   Postsparkasse *(f)*
En   Post Office Savings Bank
Es   caja postal de ahorros *(f)*
Fr   caisse d'épargne postale
       (f)
Pt   caixa económica postal *(f)*

cassaforte *(f)* n It
De   Geldschrank *(m)*
En   safe
Es   caja fuerte *(f)*
Fr   coffre-fort *(m)*
Pt   cofre *(m)*

cassetta *(f)* n It
De   Geldkassette *(f)*
En   cash-box
Es   caja *(f)*
Fr   caisse *(f)*
Pt   caixa *(f)*

cassetta bagaglio *(f)* It
De   Gepäckschließfach *(n)*
En   luggage locker
Es   casilla de equipaje *(f)*
Fr   coffre de bagages *(m)*
Pt   depósito de bagagem
       individualizado *(m)*

cassetta postale *(f)* It
De   Briefkasten *(m)*
En   letter box
Am   mail-box
Es   buzón *(m)*
Fr   boîte aux lettres *(f)*
Pt   caixa postal *(f)*

cassiere *(m)* n It
De   Kassierer *(m)*
En   cashier

Am   teller
Es   cajero *(m)*
Fr   caissier *(m)*
Pt   caixa *(m)*

casting vote En
De   entscheidende Stimme *(f)*
Es   voto decisivo *(m)*
Fr   voix prépondérante *(f)*
It   voto decisivo *(m)*
Pt   voto decisivo *(m)*

cast iron En
De   Gußeisen *(n)*
Es   hierro colado *(m)*
Fr   fonte de fer *(f)*
It   ghisa *(f)*
Pt   ferro fundido *(m)*

catálogo *(m)* n Es, Pt
De   Katalog *(m)*
En   catalogue
Fr   catalogue *(m)*
It   catalogo *(m)*

catalogo *(m)* n It
De   Katalog *(m)*
En   catalogue
Es   catálogo *(m)*
Fr   catalogue *(m)*
Pt   catálogo *(m)*

catálogo comercial *(m)* Es,
       Pt
De   Preiskatalog *(m)*
En   trade catalogue
Fr   tarif-album *(m)*
It   catalogo commerciale *(m)*

catalogo commerciale *(m)* It
De   Preiskatalog *(m)*
En   trade catalogue
Es   catálogo comercial *(m)*
Fr   tarif-album *(m)*
Pt   catálogo comercial *(m)*

catalogue *(n)* En, Fr *(m)*
De   Katalog *(m)*
Es   catálogo *(m)*
It   catalogo *(m)*
Pt   catálogo *(m)*

catalogue price En
De   Listenpreis *(m)*
Es   precio de catálogo *(m)*
Fr   prix-catalogue *(m)*
It   prezzo di catalogo *(m)*
Pt   preço de catálogo *(m)*

catena di montaggio (f) It
De Montageband (n)
En assembly line
Es línea de montaje (f)
Fr chaîne de montage (f)
Pt cadeia de montagem (f)

cattivo pagatore (m) It
De schlechter Zahler (m)
En slow payer
Es deudor moroso (m)
Fr mauvais payeur (m)
Pt mau-pagador (m)

caução (f) n Pt
De Haftkaution (f)
En bail
Es fianza (f)
Fr caution (f)
It cauzione (f)

caucionado (m) n Pt
De Gewahrsaminhaber (m)
En bailee
Es depositario (m)
Fr dépositaire (m)
It depositario (m)

causa (f) n Es, It, Pt
De Rechtsfall (m)
En (legal) case
Fr procès (m)

caution (f) n Fr
De Haftkaution; Bürgschaft (f)
En bail; surety
Es fianza; fiador (f m)
It cauzione; garante (f m)
Pt caução; fiador (f m)

cautionnement (m) n Fr
De Bürge; Ausfallbürgschaft (m f)
En surety; letter of indemnity
Es fianza; carta de indemnización (f)
It cauzione; lettera di garanzia (f)
Pt fiança; documento de garantia (f m)

cauzione (f) n It
De Haftkaution; Bürge (f m)
En bail; surety
Es fianza (f)
Fr caution; cautionnement (f m)
Pt caução; fiança (f)

cavallo (m) n It
De Pferdestärke (PS) (f)
En horse-power (hp)
Es caballo de vapor (cv) (m)
Fr cheval-vapeur (ch-v) (m)
Pt cavalo-vapor (m)

cavalo-vapor (m) n Pt
De Pferdestärke (PS) (f)
En horse-power (hp)
Es caballo de vapor (cv) (m)
Fr cheval-vapeur (ch-v) (m)
It cavallo (m)

caza de rebajas (f) Es
De Jagd nach Sonderangeboten (f)
En bargain-hunting
Fr chasse aux soldes (f)
It caccia alle occasioni (f)
Pt caça aos saldos (f)

cédant (m) n Fr
De Überträger; Zedent (m)
En assignor; transferor
Es cesionista (m)
It cedente (m)
Pt cessionista (m)

cedente (m) n It
De Überträger; Zedent (m)
En assignor; transferor
Es cesionista (m)
Fr cédant (m)
Pt cessionista (m)

céder Fr
De aufgeben; überweisen
En give up; transfer
Es renuciar; transferir
It cedere; trasferire
Pt desistir; transferir

cedere It
De aufgeben
En give up
Es renunciar
Fr céder
Pt desistir

cedola (f) n It
De Kupon (m)
En coupon
Es cupón (m)
Fr coupon (m)
Pt cupão (m)

cedola di dividendo (f) It
De Gewinnanteilschein (m)
En dividend warrant

Es cupón de dividendos (m)
Fr dividende-warrant (m)
Pt cédula de dividendo (f)

cédula de dividendo (f) Pt
De Gewinnanteilschein (m)
En dividend warrant
Es cupón de dividendos (m)
Fr dividende-warrant (m)
It cedola di dividendo (f)

cédula hipotecaria (f) Es
De Grund- und Gebäudeobligation (f)
En property bond
Fr obligation foncière (f)
It obbligazione fondiaria (f)
Pt título de investimento imobiliário (m)

celebrar una reunión Es
De eine Versammlung abhalten
En hold a meeting
Fr tenir une assemblée
It tenera una riunione
Pt fazer uma reunião

censimento (m) n It
De Volkszählung (f)
En census
Es censo (m)
Fr recensement (m)
Pt censo (m)

censo (m) n Es, Pt
De Volkszählung (f)
En census
Fr recensement (m)
It censimento (m)

census (n) En
De Volkszählung (f)
Es censo (m)
Fr recensement (m)
It censimento (m)
Pt censo (m)

center (n) Am
En centre
De Mitte (f)
Es centro (m)
Fr centre (m)
It centro (m)
Pt centro (m)

central buying office En
De Einkaufszentrale (f)
Es oficina central de compras (f)

Fr centrale d'achats (f)
It ufficio centrale d'acquisti (m)
Pt escritório central de compras (m)

centrale d'achats (f) Fr
De Einkaufszentrale (f)
En central buying office
Es oficina central de compras (f)
It ufficio centrale d'acquisti (m)
Pt escritório central de compras (m)

centrale telefonica (f) It
De Fernsprechamt (n)
En telephone exchange
Es central telefónica (f)
Fr centrale téléphonique (m)
Pt central telefónica (f)

central heating En
De Zentralheizung (f)
Es calefacción central (f)
Fr chauffage central (m)
It riscaldamento centrale (m)
Pt aquecimento central (m)

centralisation (f) n Fr
De Zentralisierung (f)
En centralization
Es centralización (f)
It centralizzazione (f)
Pt centralização (f)

centralização (f) n Pt
De Zentralisierung (f)
En centralization
Es centralización (f)
Fr centralisation (f)
It centralizzazione (f)

centralización (f) n Es
De Zentralisierung (f)
En centralization
Fr centralisation (f)
It centralizzazione (f)
Pt centralização (f)

centralization (n) En
De Zentralisierung (f)
Es centralización (f)
Fr centralisation (f)
It centralizzazione (f)
Pt centralização (f)

centralizzazione (f) n It
De Zentralisierung (f)
En centralization
Es centralización (f)
Fr centralisation (f)
Pt centralização (f)

central telefónica (f) Es, Pt
De Fernsprechamt (n)
En telephone exchange
Fr centrale téléphonique (m)
It centrale telefonica (f)

centrale téléphonique (m) Fr
De Fernsprechamt (n)
En telephone exchange
Es central telefónica (f)
It centrale telefonica (f)
Pt central telefónica (f)

centre n En, Fr (m)
Am center
De Mitte (f)
Es centro (m)
It centro (m)
Pt centro (m)

centre commercial (m) Fr
De Geschäftszentrum (n)
En shopping centre
Es centro de negocios (m)
It zona degli acquisti (f)
Pt centro de comércio (m)

centro (m) n Es, It, Pt
De Mitte (f)
En centre
Am center
Fr centre (m)

centro de comércio (m) Pt
De Geschäftszentrum (n)
En shopping centre
Es centro de negocios (m)
Fr centre commercial (m)
It zona degli acquisti (f)

centro de negocios (m) Es
De Geschäftszentrum (n)
En shopping centre
Fr centre commercial (m)
It zona degli acquisti (f)
pt centro de comércio (m)

centro de serviços de emprego (m) Pt
De Arbeitsnachweisstelle (f)
En employment exchange
Am state employment agency

Es bolsa de trabajo (f)
Fr bureau de placement (m)
It ufficio di collocamento (m)

centro fabril (m) Pt
De Industriegebiet (n)
En endustrial estate
Am industrial park (m)
Es precinto industrial (m)
Fr domaine industriel (m)
It centro industriale (m)

centro industriale (m) It
De Industriegebiet (n)
En industrial estate
Am industrial park
Es precinto industrial (m)
Fr domaine industriel (m)
Pt centro fabril (m)

cerdidão de óbito (f) Pt
De Totenschein (m)
En death certificate
Es partida de defunción (f)
Fr extrait d'acte de décès (m)
It certificato di morte (m)

certidão de peso (f) Pt
De Wiegeschein (m)
En weight note
Es certificado de pesaja (m)
Fr note de poids (f)
It distinta pesi (f)

certificado (m) n Es, Pt
De Bescheinigung (f)
En certificate; warrant
Fr certificat (m)
It certificato (m)

certificado de acción (m) Es
De Aktie (f)
En ordinary share certificate
Am stock certificate
Fr certificat d'action (m)
It certificato azionario (m)
Pt título de acções ordinárias (m)

certificado de declaración de entrada (m) Es
De Eintrittsdeklarations-schein (m)
En jerque note
Fr certificat d'entrée auto-risée (m)
It certificato di dichiarazio-ne d'entrata (m)
Pt certificado de verificação alfandegária (m)

certificado de origem

certificado de origem *(m)* Pt
De Ursprungszeugnis *(n)*
En certificate of origin
Es certificado de origen *(m)*
Fr certificat d'origine *(m)*
It certificato d'origine *(m)*

certificado de origen *(m)* Es
De Ursprungszeugnis *(n)*
En certificate of origin
Fr certificat d'origine *(m)*
It certificato d'origine *(m)*
Pt certificado de origem *(m)*

certificado de pesaje *(m)* Es
De Wiegeschein *(m)*
En weight note
Fr note de poids *(f)*
It distinta pesi *(f)*
Pt certidão de peso *(f)*

certificado de seguro *(m)* Es,
Pt
De Versicherungsschein *(m)*
En insurance certificate
Fr certificat d'assurance *(m)*
It certificato di assicurazione
(m)

certificado de verificação
alfandegária *(m)* Pt
De Eintrittsdeklarations-
schein *(m)*
En jerque note
Es certificado de declaración
de entrada *(m)*
Fr certificat d'entrée auto-
risée *(m)*
It certificato di dichiarazione
d'entrata *(m)*

certificar *(vb)* Es, Pt
De bescheinigen
En certify
Fr certifier
It certificare

certificare *(vb)* It
De bescheinigen
En certify
Es certificar
Fr certifier
Pt certificar

certificat *(m)* n Fr
De Bescheinigung *(f)*
En certificate; warrant
Es certificado *(m)*
It certificato *(m)*
Pt certificado *(m)*

certificat d'actions *(m)* Fr
De Aktienzertifikat *(n)*
En share certificate
Am certificate of stock
Es título de acción *(m)*
It certificato azionario *(m)*
Pt título de acções *(m)*

certificat d'assurance *(m)* Fr
De Versicherungsschein *(m)*
En insurance certificate
Es certificado de seguro *(m)*
It certificato di assicurazione
(m)
Pt certificado de seguro *(m)*

certificat d'entrée autori-
sée *(m)* Fr
De Eintrittsdeklarations-
schein *(m)*
En jerque note
Es certificato de declaración
de entrada *(m)*
It certificato di dichiarazione
d'entrata *(m)*
Pt certificado de verficação
alfandegária *(m)*

certificat d'immatriculation
(d'un navire) *(m)* Fr
De Schiffsregister *(n)*
En ship register
Es registro del barco *(m)*
It atto di nazionalità *(m)*
Pt registo do naivo *(m)*

certificat d'origine *(m)* Fr
De Ursprungszeugnis *(n)*
En certificate of origin
Es certificado de origen *(m)*
It certificato d'origine *(m)*
Pt certificado de origem *(m)*

certificate *(n)* En
De Bescheinigung *(f)*
Es certificado *(m)*
Fr certificat *(m)*
It certificato *(m)*
Pt certificado *(m)*

certificate of insurance En
De Versicherungsurkunde *(f)*
Es certificado de seguro *(m)*
Fr certificat d'assurance *(m)*
It certificato di assicurazione
(m)
Pt certificado de seguro *(m)*

certificate of origin En
De Ursprungszeugnis *(n)*
Es certificado de origen *(m)*
Fr certificat d'origine *(m)*
It certificato d'órigine *(m)*
Pt certificado de origem *(m)*

certificate of stock Am
En share certificate
De Aktienzertifikat; Anteil-
schein *(n m)*
Es título de acción *(m)*
Fr certificat d'actions *(m)*
It certificato azionario *(m)*
Pt título de acções *(m)*

certificato *(m)* n It
De Bescheinigung *(f)*
En certificate; warrant
Es certificado *(m)*
Fr certificat *(m)*
Pt certificado *(m)*

certificato azionario *(m)* It
De Aktienzertifikat; Aktie *(n f)*
En share certificate
Am certificate of stock
Es título de acción *(m)*
Fr certificat d'actions *(m)*
Pt título de acções *(m)*

certificato di assicurazione
(m) It
De Versicherungsurkunde *(f)*
En insurance certificate
Es certificado de seguro *(m)*
Fr certificat d'assurance *(m)*
Pt certificado de seguro *(m)*

certificato di deposito *(m)* It
De Depositenschein *(m)*
En deposit receipt
Es recibo de depósito *(m)*
Fr récépissé de dépôt *(m)*
Pt recibo de depósito *(m)*

certificato di dichiarazione
d'entrata *(m)* It
De Eintrittsdeklarations-
schein *(m)*
En jerque note
Es certificado de declaración
de entrada *(m)*
Fr certificat d'entrée auto-
risée *(m)*
Pt certificado de verificação
alfandegária *(m)*

certificato di morte *(m)* It
De Totenschein *(m)*
En death certificate
Es partida de defunción *(f)*
Fr extrait d'acte de décès *(m)*
Pt certidão de óbito *(f)*

certificato d'origine *(m)* It
De Ursprungszeugnis *(n)*
En certificate of origin
Es certificado de origen *(m)*
Fr certificat d'origine *(m)*
Pt certificado de origem *(m)*

certified cheque En
Am certified check
De bestätigter Scheck *(m)*
Es cheque certificado *(m)*
Fr chèque certifié *(m)*
It assegno garantito *(m)*
Pt cheque certificado *(m)*

certified true copy En
De beglaubigte Anschrift *(f)*
Es copia auténtica *(f)*
Fr copie certifiée *(f)*
It copia conforme *(f)*
Pt cópia autenticada *(f)*

certifier *vb* Fr
De bescheinigen
En certify
Es certificar
It certificare
Pt certificar

certify *vb* En
De bescheinigen
Es certificar
Fr certifier
It certificare
Pt certificar

cesión *(f)* n Es
De Überweisung; Übertragung *(f)*
En transfer; assignment
Fr transfert; cession *(m f)*
It cessione *(f)*
Pt trespasse; consignação *(m f)*

cesionario *(m)* n Es
De Zessionar *(m)*
En assignee; transferee
Fr cessionnaire *(m)*
It assegnatario; cessionario *(m)*
Pt cessionário *(m)*

cesionista *(m)* n Es
De Überträger; Zedent *(m)*
En assignor; transferor
Fr cédant *(m)*
It cedente *(m)*
Pt cessionista *(m)*

cession *(f)* n Fr
De Übertragung *(f)*
En assignment
Es cesión *(f)*
It cessione *(f)*
Pt consignação *(f)*

cessionario *(m)* n It
De Zessionar *(m)*
En transferee
Es cesionario *(m)*
Fr cessionnaire *(m)*
Pt cessionário *(m)*

cessionário *(m)* n Pt
De Zessionar *(m)*
En transferee
Es cesionario *(m)*
Fr cessionnaire *(m)*
It cessionario *(m)*

cessione *(f)* n It
De Übertragung *(f)*
En assignment
Es cesión *(f)*
Fr cession *(f)*
Pt consignação *(f)*

cessione *(f)* n It
De Überweisung; Übertragung *(f)*
En transfer; assignment
Es cesión *(f)*
Fr transfert; cession *(m f)*
Pt trespasse; consignação *(m f)*

cessionista *(m)* n Pt
De Überträger
En assignor; transferor
Es cesionista *(m)*
Fr cédant *(m)*
It cedente *(m)*

cessionnaire *(m)* n Fr
De Zessionar *(m)*
En assignee; transferee
Es cesionario *(m)*
It assegnatario; cessionario *(m)*
Pt cessionário *(m)*

chaîne de montage *(f)* Fr
De Montageband *(n)*
En assembly line
Es línea de montaje *(f)*
It catene di montaggio *(f)*
Pt cadeia de montagem *(f)*

chain store En
De Kettengeschäft *(n)*
Es sucursal de cadena de almacenes *(f)*
Fr magasin à succursales multiples *(m)*
It negozio a catena *(m)*
Pt sucursal de cadeia de armazéns *(f)*

chairman n En
De Vorsitzende(r) *(m)*
Es presidente *(m)*
Fr président *(m)*
It presidente *(m)*
Pt presidente *(m)*

chamada (de fundos) *(f)* Pt
De Kündigung (von Geldern) *(f)*
En call (for funds)
Es llamada (de fonds) *(f)*
Fr appel (de fonds) *(m)*
It richiesta (di fondi) *(f)*

chamada inter-urbana (troncas) *(f)* Pt
De Ferngespräch *(n)*
En trunk call
Am long distance call
Es llamada interurbana *(f)*
Fr appel téléphonique interurbain *(m)*
It comunicazione interurbana *(f)*

chamada telefónica *(f)* Pt
De Anruf *(m)*
En telephone call
Es llamda telefónica *(f)*
Fr appel téléphonique *(m)*
It chiamata telefonica *(f)*

chamber of commerce En
De Handelskammer *(f)*
Es cámara de comercio *(f)*
Fr chambre de commerce *(f)*
It camera di commercio *(f)*
Pt câmara de comércio *(f)*

chambre de commerce *(f)* Fr
De Handelskammer *(f)*
En chamber of commerce

Es cámera de comercio *(f)*
It camera di commercio *(f)*
Pt câmara de comércio *(f)*

**Chambre de Commerce
Internationale** *(f)* Fr
De Internationale Handels-
kammer *(f)*
En International Chamber of
Commerce
Es Cámara Internacional de
Comercio *(f)*
It Camera di Commercio
Internazionale *(f)*
Pt Câmara Internacional do
Comércio *(f)*

chambre de compensation
(f) Fr
De Verrechnungsstelle *(f)*
En clearing house
Es cámara de compensacio-
nes *(f)*
It stanza di compensazione
(f)
Pt câmara de compensações
e rateio *(f)*

change à terme *(m)* Fr
De Termindevisen *(f pl)*
En forward exchange
Es divisas a término *(f pl)*
It cambio a termine *(m)*
Pt divisas adiantada *(f pl)*

**chantier de construction de
navires** *(m)* Fr
De Schiffswerft *(f)*
En dockyard
Es astillero *(m)*
It cantiere *(m)*
Pt estaleiro *(m)*

chapa de vidro *(f)* Pt
De Spiegelglas *(n)*
En plate glas
Es vidrio plano pulido *(m)*
Fr verre à glaces; glace de
vitrage *(m f)*
It cristallo *(m)*

chapado en oro Es
De vergoldet
En gold-plated
Fr plaqué d'or
It placcato in oro
Pt laminado a ouro

charbon *(m)* n Fr
De Kohle; Holzkohle *(f)*
En coal; charcoal
Es carbón; carbón de leña *(m)*
It carbone *(m)*
Pt carvão; carvão de lenha *(m)*

chargeable *adj* En
De anrechenbar
Es imputable; a cobrar
Fr imputable; imposable
It imputabile; imponibile
Pt a cobrar

charge account En
De Kundenkonto *(n)*
Es cuenta personal *(f)*
Fr compte personnel *(m)*
It conto personale *(m)*
Pt conto pessoal *(f)*

chargement *(m)* Fr
De Ladung *(f)*
En loading
Es carga *(f)*
It carico; caricamento *(m)*
Pt carregamento *(m)*

charges n pl En
De Kosten *(pl)*
Es costes *(m pl)*
Fr frais *(m pl)*
It spese *(f pl)*
Pt despeses *(f pl)*

charges annexes *(f pl)* Fr
De Nebenkosten *(pl)*
En incidental charges
Es cargos imprevitos *(m pl)*
It spese accessorie *(f pl)*
Pt enargos ocasionais *(m pl)*

charges forward En
De per Nachnahme
Es costes a reembolso
Fr frais à percevoir à la
livraison
It spese assegnate
Pt entrega contra reembolso

charges lourdes *(f pl)* Fr
De drückende Spesen *(f pl)*
En heavy charges
Es gastos fuertes *(m pl)*
It forti spese *(f pl)*
Pt encargos pesados *(m pl)*

chart n En
De Tabelle *(f)*
Es gráfico *(m)*

Fr graphique *(m)*
It grafico *(m)*
Pt tabela *(f)*

charterer n En
De Befrachter *(m)*
Es fletador *(m)*
Fr affréteur *(m)*
It noleggiatore *(m)*
Pt fretador *(m)*

chartering n En
De Befrachtung *(f)*
Es fletamento *(m)*
Fr affrètement *(m)*
It noleggio *(m)*
Pt fretamento *(m)*

chasse aux soldes *(f)* Fr
De Jagd nach Sonder-
angeboten *(f)*
En bargain-hunting
Es caza de rebajas *(f)*
It caccia alle occasioni *(f)*
Pt caça aos saldos *(f)*

chauffage central *(m)* Fr
De Zentralheizung *(f)*
En central heating
Es calefacción central *(f)*
It riscaldamento centrale *(m)*
Pt aquecimento central *(m)*

chave *(f)* n Pt
De Schlüssel *(m)*
En key
Es llave *(f)*
Fr clef *(f)*
It chiave *(f)*

cheap *adj* En
De billig
Es barato
Fr bon marché
It a buon mercato
Pt barato

cheaper *adj* En
De billiger
Es más barato
Fr meilleur marché
It meno caro
Pt mais barato

cheap money En
De billiges Geld *(n)*
Es dinero barato *(m)*
Fr argent bon marché *(m)*

It denaro a basso interesse
   (m)
Pt dinheiro barato *(m)*

cheat *vb* En
De betrügen
Es engañar
Fr tricher
It truffare
Pt enganar

check *n* Am
En cheque
De Scheck *(m)*
Es cheque *(m)*
Fr chèque *(m)*
It assegno *(m)*
Pt cheque *(m)*

check book Am
En cheque book
De Scheckheft *(n)*
Es libro de cheques *(m)*
Fr carnet de chèques;
   chèquier *(m)*
It libretto assegni *(m)*
Pt livro de cheques *(m)*

check digit En
De Kontrollziffer *(f)*
Es número de control *(m)*
Fr digit de contrôle *(m)*
It cifra di controllo *(f)*
Pt digito de controle *(m)*

checking account Am
En current account
De Kontokorrent *(n)*
Es cuenta corriente *(f)*
Fr compte courant *(m)*
It conto corrente *(m)*
Pt conta corrente *(f)*

check payable to bearer Am
En cheque payable to bearer
De Inhaberscheck *(m)*
Es cheque al portador *(m)*
Fr chèque payable au porteur
   (m)
It assegno al portatore *(m)*
Pt cheque ao portador *(m)*

chef comptable *(m)* Fr
De Oberbuchhalter *(m)*
En chief accountant
Es jefe de contabilidad *(m)*
It ragioniere capo *(m)*
Pt chefe contabilista *(m)*

chef d'atelier *(m)* Fr
De Werkmeister *(m)*
En head foreman
Es capataz jefe *(m)*
It capo officina *(m)*
Pt encarregado-chefe *(m)*

chef de bureau *(m)* Fr
De Bürovorsteher *(m)*
En office manager
Es jefe de oficina *(m)*
It capo ufficio *(m)*
Pt chefe de escritório *(m)*

chef de comptes client *(m)* Fr
De Kontaktgruppenleiter *(m)*
En account executive
Es ejecutivo de cuentea *(m)*
It direttore conto cliente *(m)*
Pt chefe de conta de cliente
   (m)

chef de famille *(m)* Fr
De Hausherr *(m)*
En householder
Es jefe de familia *(m)*
It capo-famiglia *(m)*
Pt dono da casa *(m)*

chef de service *(m)* Fr
De Abteilungsleiter *(m)*
En head of department
Es jefe de departamento *(m)*
It capo reparto *(m)*
Pt chefe de departamento *(m)*

chef du personnel *(m)* Fr
De Personalchef *(m)*
En personnel manager
Es jefe de personal *(m)*
It direttore del personale *(m)*
Pt chefe do pessoal *(m)*

chef du service des achats
   (m) Fr
De Haupteinkäufer *(m)*
En head buyer
Es jefe del departamento de
   compras *(m)*
It capo servizio acquisti *(m)*
Pt chefe de compras *(m)*

chef du service exportation
   (m) Fr
De Exportabteilungsleiter *(m)*
En export manager
Es jefe de exportación *(m)*
It direttore esportazione *(m)*
Pt gerente de exportações *(m)*

chefe contabilista *(m)* Pt
De Oberbuchhalter *(m)*
En chief accountant
Es jefe de contabilidad *(m)*
Fr chef comptable *(m)*
It ragioniere capo *(m)*

chefe de compras *(m)* Pt
De Haupteinkäufer *(m)*
En head buyer
Es jefe del departamento de
   compras *(m)*
Fr chef du service des achats
   (m)
It capo servizio acquisti *(m)*

chefe de conta de cliente *(m)*
   Pt
De Kontaktgruppenleiter *(m)*
En account executive
Es ejecutivo de cuenta *(m)*
Fr chef de comptes client *(m)*
It direttore conto cliente *(m)*

chefe de departamento *(m)*
   Pt
De Abteilungsleiter *(m)*
En head of department
Es jefe de departamento *(m)*
Fr chef de service *(m)*
It capo reparto *(m)*

chefe de escritório *(m)* Pt
De Bürovorsteher *(m)*
En office manager
Es jefe de oficina *(m)*
Fr chef de bureau *(m)*
It capo ufficio *(m)*

chefe de gerência *(m)* Pt
De Geschäftsführer *(m)*
En chief executive *(m)*
Es jefe ejecutivo *(m)*
Fr directeur général *(m)*
It direttore generale *(m)*

chefe de vendas *(m)* Pt
De Verkaufsleiter *(m)*
En sales manager
Es jefe de ventas *(m)*
Fr directeur commercial *(m)*
It direttore commerciale *(m)*

chefe do pessoal *(m)* Pt
De Personalchef *(m)*
En personnel manager
Es jefe de personal *(m)*
Fr chef du personnel *(m)*
It direttore del personale *(m)*

chegada *(f) n* Pt
De Ankunft *(f)*
En arrival
Es llegada *(f)*
Fr arrivée *(f)*
It arrivo *(m)*

cheio *adj* Pt
De voll
En full
Es lleno
Fr plein
It pieno

chemical engineering En
De Chemietechnik *(f)*
Es ingeniería química *(f)*
Fr génie chimique *(m)*
It ingegneria chimica *(f)*
Pt engenharia química *(f)*

Chemietechnik *(f) n* De
En chemical engineering
Es ingeniería química *(f)*
Fr génie chimique *(m)*
It ingegneria chimica *(f)*
Pt engenharia química *(f)*

chemin de fer *(m)* Fr
De Eisenbahn *(f)*
En railway
Es ferrocarril *(m)*
It ferrovia *(f)*
Pt caminho de ferro *(m)*

chemise *(f) n* Fr
De Mappe *(f)*
En folder
Es carpeta *(f)*
It cartella *(f)*
Pt pasta *(f)*

cheque *n* En, Es, Pt *(m)*
Am check
De Scheck *(m)*
Fr chèque *(m)*
It assegno *(m)*

chèque *(m) n* Fr
De Scheck *(m)*
En cheque
Am check
Es cheque *(m)*
It assegno *(m)*
Pt cheque *(m)*

cheque abierto *(m)* Es
De Inhaberscheck *(m)*
En open cheque

Fr chèque ouvert *(m)*
It assegno aperto *(m)*
Pt cheque em branco *(m)*

cheque a fecha retrasada
(m) Es
De nachdatierter Scheck *(m)*
En postdates cheque
Fr chèque postdaté *(m)*
It assegno postdatato *(m)*
Pt cheque post-datado *(m)*

cheque al portador *(m)* Es
De Inhaberscheck *(m)*
En cheque payable to bearer
Fr chèque payable au porteur
(m)
It assegno al portatore *(m)*
Pt cheque ao portador *(m)*

cheque ao portador *(m)*
Pt
De Inhaberscheck *(m)*
En cheque payable to bearer
Es cheque al portador *(m)*
Fr chèque payable au porteur
(m)
It assegno al portatore *(m)*

chèque barré *(m)* Fr
De Verrechnungsscheck *(m)*
En crossed cheque
Es cheque cruzado *(m)*
It assegno sbarrato *(m)*
Pt cheque cruzado *(m)*

cheque book En
Am check book
De Scheckheft *(n)*
Es libro de cheques *(m)*
Fr carnet de chèques:
chéquier *(m)*
It libretto assegni *(m)*
Pt livro de cheques *(m)*

cheque card En
Am bank credit card
De Scheckkarte *(f)*
Es tarjeta de cheque *(f)*
Fr carte de chèque *(f)*
It scheda per assegni *(f)*
Pt cartão de validação de
cheques *(m)*

cheque certificado *(m)* Es, Pt
De bestätigter Scheck *(m)*
En certified cheque
Fr chèque certifié *(m)*
It assegno garantito *(m)*

chèque certifié *(m)* Fr
De bestätigter Scheck *(m)*
En certified cheque
Es cheque certificado *(m)*
It assegno garantito *(m)*
Pt cheque certificado *(m)*

cheque cruzado *(m)* Es, Pt
De Verrechnungsscheck *(m)*
En crossed cheque *(f)*
Fr chèque barré *(m)*
It assegno sbarrato *(m)*

cheque de viajante *(m)* Pt
De Reisescheck *(m)*
En traveller's cheque
Es cheque de viajero *(m)*
Fr chèque de voyage *(m)*
It assegno turistico *(m)*

cheque de viajero *(m)* Es
De Reisescheck *(m)*
En traveller's cheque
Fr chèque de voyage *(m)*
It assegno turistico *(m)*
Pt cheque de viajante *(m)*

chèque de voyage *(m)* Fr
De Reisescheck *(m)*
En traveller's cheque
Es cheque de viajero *(m)*
It assegno turistico *(m)*
Pt cheque de viajante *(m)*

cheque em branco *(m)* Pt
De Blankoscheck *(m)*
En blank cheque; open
cheque
Es cheque en blanco; cheque
abierto *(m)*
Fr chèque en blanc; chèque
ouvert *(m)*
It assegno in bianco;
assegno aperto *(m)*

chèque en blanc *(m)* Fr
De Blankoscheck *(m)*
En blank cheque
Es cheque en blanco *(m)*
It assegno in bianco *(m)*
Pt cheque em branco *(m)*

cheque en blanco *(m)* Es
De Blankoscheck *(m)*
En blank cheque
Fr chèque en blanc *(m)*
It assegno in bianco *(m)*
Pt cheque em branco *(m)*

cheque falsificado *(m)* Es, Pt
De gefälschter Scheck *(m)*
En forged cheque
Fr faux chèque *(m)*
It assegno falsificato *(m)*

chèque ouvert *(m)* Fr
De Inhaberscheck *(m)*
En open cheque
Es cheque abierto *(m)*
It assegno aperto *(m)*
Pt cheque em branco *(m)*

chèque payable au porteur
        (m) Fr
De Inhaberscheck *(m)*
En cheque payable to bearer
Es cheque al portador *(m)*
It assegno al portatore *(m)*
Pt cheque ao portador *(m)*

cheque payable to bearer En
De Inhaberscheck *(m)*
Es cheque al portador *(m)*
Fr chèque payable au porteur
        (m)
It assegno al portatore *(m)*
Pt cheque ao portador *(m)*

cheque post-datado *(m)* Pt
De nachdatierter Scheck *(m)*
En postdated cheque
Es cheque a fecha retrasada
        (m)
Fr chèque postdaté *(m)*
It assegno postdatato *(m)*

chèque postdaté *(m)* Fr
De nachdatierter Scheck *(m)*
En postdated cheque
Es cheque a fecha retrasada
        (m)
It assegno postdatato *(m)*
Pt cheque post-datado *(m)*

cher *adj* Fr
De kostspielig; teuer
En expensive
Es caro
It caro
Pt caro

cheval-vapeur (ch-v) *(m)* Fr
De Pferdestärke (PS) *(f)*
En horse-power (hp)
Es caballo de vapor (cv) *(m)*
It cavallo *(m)*
Pt cavalo-vapor *(m)*

chiamata telefonica *(f)* It
De Anruf *(m)*
En telephone call
Es llamada telefónica *(f)*
Fr appel téléphonique *(m)*
Pt chamada telefónica *(f)*

chiatta *(f)* n It
De Lastkahn; Leichter *(m)*
En barge; lighter
Es barcaza; gabarra *(f)*
Fr péniche; allège *(f)*
Pt barcaça *(f)*

chiave *(f)* n It
De Schlussel *(m)*
En key
Es llave *(f)*
Fr clef *(f)*
Pt chave *(f)*

chief accountant En
De Oberbuchhalter *(m)*
Es jefe de contabilidad *(m)*
Fr chef comptable *(m)*
It ragioniere capo *(m)*
Pt chefe contabilista *(m)*

chief executive En
De Geschäftsführer *(m)*
Es jefe ejecutivo *(m)*
Fr directeur général *(m)*
It direttore generale *(m)*
Pt chefe de gerência *(m)*

chiffre *(m)* n Fr
De Zahl *(f)*
En figure
Es cifra *(f)*
It cifra *(f)*
Pt número *(m)*

chiffre d'affaires *(m)* Fr
De Umsatz *(m)*
En turnover
Es volumen de ventas *(m)*
It giro d'affari *(m)*
Pt movimento de dinheiro *(m)*

chômage *(m)* n Fr
De Arbeitslosigkeit *(f)*
En unemployment
Es desempleo *(m)*
It disoccupazione *(f)*
Pt desemprego *(m)*

chômage saisonnier *(m)* Fr
De jahreszeitlich bedingte
        Arbeitslosigkeit *(f)*

En seasonal unemployment
Es paro de temporada *(m)*
It disoccupazione stagio-
        nale *(f)*
Pt desemprego de estação *(m)*

cibernética *(f)* n Es, Pt
De Kybernetik *(f)*
En cybernetics
Fr cybernétique *(f)*
It cibernetica *(f)*

cibernetica *(f)* n It
De Kybernetik *(f)*
En cybernetics
Es cibernética *(f)*
Fr cybernétique *(f)*
Pt cibernética *(f)*

ciclo comercial *(m)* Pt
De Handelszyklus *(m)*
En trade cycle
Es ciclo del negocio *(m)*
Fr cycle de commerce *(m)*
It ciclo degli affari *(m)*

ciclo d'affari *(m)* It
De Konjunkturzyklus *(m)*
En business cycle
Es ciclo económico *(m)*
Fr cycle économique *(m)*
Pt ciclo económico *(m)*

ciclo degli affari *(m)* It
De Handelszyklus *(m)*
En trade cycle
Es ciclo del negocio *(m)*
Fr cycle de commerce *(m)*
Pt ciclo comercial *(m)*

ciclo del negocio *(m)* Es
De Handelszyklus *(m)*
En trade cycle
Fr cycle de commerce *(m)*
It ciclo degli affari *(m)*
Pt ciclo comercial *(m)*

ciclo económico *(m)* Es, Pt
De Konjunkturzyklus *(m)*
En business cycle
Fr cycle économique *(m)*
It ciclo d'affari *(m)*

ciência de vender *(f)* Pt
De Verkaufsgewandtheit *(f)*
En salesmanship
Es arte de vender *(m)*
Fr art de vendre *(m)*
It arte della vendita *(f)*

cierre *(m) n* Es
De Aussperrung *(f)*
En lock-out
Fr lock-out *(m)*
It serrata *(f)*
Pt lockout *(m)*

cifra *(f) n* Es, It
De Zahl *(f)*
En figure
Fr chiffre *(m)*
Pt número *(m)*

cifra de ventas *(f)* Es
De Umsatz *(m)*
En sales figure *(m)*
Fr chiffre d'affaires *(f)*
It cifra di vendite *(f)*
Pt número de vendas *(m)*

cifra di controllo *(f)* It
De Kontrollziffer *(f)*
En check digit
Es número de control *(m)*
Fr digit de contrôle *(m)*
Pt dígito de controle *(m)*

cifra di vendite *(f)* It
De Umsatz *(m)*
En sales figure
Es cifra de ventas *(f)*
Fr chiffre d'affaires *(f)*
Pt número de vendas *(m)*

ci-joint *adj* Fr
De beiliegend
En enclosed
Es adjunto
It accluso
Pt incluso

cilindrada *(f) n* Es, Pt
De Hubraum *(m)*
En cubic capacity
Fr cylindrée *(f)*
It cilindrata *(f)*

cilindrata *(f) n* It
De Hubraum *(m)*
En cubic capacity
Es cilindrada *(f)*
Fr cylindrée *(f)*
Pt cilindrada *(f)*

cinta magnética *(f)* Es
De Magnetband *(n)*
En magnetic tape
Fr bande magnétique *(f)*
It nastro magnetico *(m)*
Pt fita magnética *(f)*

circulação *(f) n* Pt
De Strom *(m)*
En flow
Es flujo *(m)*
Fr flux *(m)*
It flusso *(m)*

citação *(f) n* Pt
De Vorladung *(f)*
En writ
Es auto; orden *(m) f*
Fr assignation *(f)*
It citazione *(f)*

citazione *(f) n* It
De Vorladung *(f)*
En writ
Es auto; orden *(m) f*
Fr assignation *(f)*
Pt citação; ordem *(f) m*

civil engineering En
De Ingenieurbau *(m)*
Es ingeniería civil *(f)*
Fr génie civil *(m)*
It ingegneria civile *(f)*
Pt engenharia civil *(f)*

civil servant En
Am government employee
De Beamte(r) *(m)*
Es funcionario del gobierno
   (m)
Fr fonctionnaire *(m)*
It impiegato statale *(m)*
Pt funcionário público *(m)*

claim *n* En
De Anspruch *(m)*
Es reclamación *(f)*
Fr réclamation; créance *(f)*
It reclamo *(m)*
Pt demanda; requerimento
   (f m)

classer *vb* Fr
De aufreihen
En file
Es archivar
It archiviare
Pt arquivar

classeur *(m) n* Fr
De Aktenschrank *(m)*
En filing cabinet
Es fichero *(m)*
It schedario *(m)*
Pt móvel ficheiro *(m)*

classified advertisement En
De Kleinanzeige *(f)*
Es anuncio por palabras *(m)*
Fr petite annonce *(f)*
It piccola pubblicità *(f)*
Pt anúncios classificados
   (m pl)

clause *n* En, Fr *(f)*
De Klausel *(f)*
Es cláusula *(f)*
It clausola *(f)*
Pt cláusula *(f)*

clause de dédit *(f)* Fr
De Bußklausel *(f)*
En forfeit clause
Es cláusula de decomiso *(f)*
It clausola di penalità per
   inadempienza *(f)*
Pt cláusula de cedência *(f)*

clause de résiliation *(f)* Fr
De Rücktrittsklausel *(f)*
En escape clause
Es cláusula evasiva *(f)*
It clausola risolutiva *(f)*
Pt cláusula de evasão *(f)*

clause pénale *(f)* Fr
De Strafklausel *(f)*
En penalty clause
Es cláusula de multa *(f)*
It clausola penale *(f)*
Pt cláusula de penalidade *(f)*

clause résolutoire *(f)* Fr
De Rücktrittsklausel *(f)*
En determination clause
Es cláusula resolutiva *(f)*
It clausola risolutiva *(f)*
Pt cláusula de rescisão *(f)*

clausola *(f) n* It
De Klausel *(f)*
En clause
Es cláusula *(f)*
Fr clause *(f)*
Pt cláusula *(f)*

**clausola di penalità per
   inadempienza** *(f)* It
De Bußklausel *(f)*
En forfeit clause
Es cláusula de decomiso *(f)*
Fr clause de dédit *(f)*
Pt cláusula de cedência *(f)*

clausola penale *(f)* It
De Strafklausel *(f)*
En penalty clause

Es cláusula de multa *(f)*
Fr clause pénale *(f)*
Pt cláusula de penalidade *(f)*

clausola risolutiva *(f)* It
De Rücktrittsklausel *(f)*
En determination clause
Es cláusula resolutiva *(f)*
Fr clause résolutoire *(f)*
Pt cláusula de rescisão *(f)*

cláusula *(f)* n Es, Pt
De Klausel *(f)*
En clause
Fr clause *(f)*
It clausola *(f)*

cláusula de actualização de preços *(f)* Pt
De Gleitklausel *(f)*
En escalator clause
Es cláusula de revisión de precios *(f)*
Fr échelle mobile *(f)*
It scala mobile *(f)*

cláusula de cedência *(f)* Pt
De Bußklausel *(f)*
En forfeit clause
Es cláusula de decomiso *(f)*
Fr clause de dédit *(f)*
It clausola di penalità per inadempienza *(f)*

cláusula de decomiso *(f)* Es
De Bußklausel *(f)*
En forfeit clause
Fr clause de dédit *(f)*
It clausola di penalità per inadempienza *(f)*
Pt cláusula de cedência *(f)*

cláusula de evasão *(f)* Pt
De Rücktrittsklausel *(f)*
En escape clause
Es cláusula evasiva *(f)*
Fr clause de résiliation *(f)*
It clausola risolutiva *(f)*

cláusula de multa *(f)* Es
De Strafklausel *(f)*
En penalty clause
Fr clause pénale *(f)*
It clausola penale *(f)*
Pt cláusula de penalidade *(f)*

cláusula de penalidade *(f)* Pt
De Strafklausel *(f)*
En penalty clause
Es cláusula de multa *(f)*

Fr clause pénale *(f)*
It clausola penale *(f)*

cláusula de rescisão *(f)* Pt
De Rücktrittsklausel *(f)*
En determination clause
Es cláusula resolutiva *(f)*
Fr clause résolutoire *(f)*
It clausola risolutiva *(f)*

cláusula de revisión de precios *(f)* Es
De Gleitklausel *(f)*
En escalator clause
Fr échelle mobile *(f)*
It scala mobile *(f)*
Pt cláusula de actualização de preços *(f)*

cláusula evasiva *(f)* Es
De Rücktrittsklausel *(f)*
En escape clause
Fr clause de résiliation *(f)*
It clausola risolutiva *(f)*
Pt cláusula de evasão *(f)*

cláusula resolutiva *(f)* Es
De Rücktrittsklausel *(f)*
En determination clause
Fr clause résolutoire *(f)*
It clausola risolutiva *(f)*
Pt cláusula de rescisão *(f)*

clave *(f)* n Es
De Schlüssel *(m)*
En code
Fr clef *(f)*
It codice *(m)*
Pt código *(m)*

clean bill of lading En
De echtes Konnossement *(n)*
Es conocimiento de embarque sin objecciones *(m)*
Fr connaissement sans réserve *(m)*
It polizza di carico senza riserve *(m)*
Pt conhecimento sem embargos *(m)*

clearing-bank n En
De Girobank *(f)*
Es banco de compensación *(m)*
Fr banque de virement *(f)*
It banco associata alla stanza di compensazione *(f)*
Pt banco de compensação e rateio *(m)*

clearing house En
De Verrechnungsstelle *(f)*
Es cámara de compensaciones *(f)*
Fr chambre de compensation *(f)*
It stanza di compensazione *(f)*
Pt câmara de compensações e rateio *(f)*

clear through customs En
De verzollen
Es retirar de aduanas
Fr dédouaner
It sdoganare
Pt despachar na alfândega

clef *(f)* n Fr
De Schlüssel *(m)*
En key; code
Es llave; clave *(f)*
It chiave; codice *(f m)*
Pt chave; código *(f m)*

clerk n En
De Angestellte(r) *(m)*
Es oficinista *(m)*
Fr commis *(m)*
It impiegato *(m)*
Pt empregado de escritório *(m)*

client n En, Fr *(m)*
De Kunde *(m)*
Es cliente *(m)*
It cliente *(m)*
Pt cliente *(m)*

cliente *(m)* n Es, It, Pt
De Kunde *(m)*
En customer
Fr client *(m)*

clientela *(f)* n Es, It, Pt
De Kundschaft *(f)*
En custom; clientele
Fr clientèle *(f)*

clientèle *(f)* n Fr
De Kundschaft *(f)*
En custom; clientele
Es clientela *(f)*
It clientela *(f)*
Pt clientela *(f)*

climatisation *(f)* n Fr
De Klimatisierung *(f)*
En air-conditioning

Es acondicionamiento de aire
(m)
It condizionamento dell'aria
(m)
Pt condicionamento do ar (m)

closed market En
De gesperrter Markt (m)
Es mercado cerrado (m)
Fr marché fermé (m)
It mercato chiuso (m)
Pt mercado fechado (m)

closing date En
De Schlußtermin (m)
Es último día (m)
Fr dernier jour (m)
It ultima data (f)
Pt último dia (m)

closing price En
De Schlußnotierung (f)
Es precio de cierre (m)
Fr cours de clôture (m)
It prezzo di chiusura (m)
Pt último preço (m)

coal n En
De Kohle (f)
Es carbón (m)
Fr houille; carbon (f m)
It carbone (m)
Pt carvão (m)

coal field En
De Kohlenrevier (n)
Es yacimiento de carbón (m)
Fr bassin houiller (m)
It bacino carbonifero (m)
Pt jazigo de carvão (m)

coalición de vendedores (f)
Es
De Preisabsprache (f)
En price ring
Fr coalition de vendeurs (f)
It sindacato dei prezzi (m)
Pt convénio de preços (m)

coalition de vendeurs (f) Fr
De Preisabsprache (f)
En price ring
Es coalición de vendedores (f)
It sindacato dei prezzi (m)
Pt convénio de preços (m)

coaseguro (m) n Es
De Versicherung auf Gegenseitigkeit (f)

En mutual insurance
Fr assurance mutuelle (f)
It mutua assicurazione (f)
Pt seguro mútuo (m)

cobertura (f) n Es, Pt
De Deckung (f)
En cover
Fr couverture (f)
It copertura (f)

**cobertura de la póliza de
seguro** (f) Es
De Versicherungsdeckung (f)
Es insurance cover
Fr garantie d'assurance (f)
It copertura assicurativa (f)
Pt cobertura de seguro (f)

cobertura de seguro (f) Pt
De Versicherungsdeckung (f)
En insurance cover
Es cobertura de la póliza de
seguro (f)
Fr garantie d'assurance (f)
It copertura assicurativa (f)

cobertura flotante (f) Es
De offene Versicherung (f)
En open cover
Fr police à aliment (f)
It polizza flottante (f)
Pt cobertura ilimitada (f)

cobertura ilimitada (f) Pt
De offene Versicherung (f)
En open cover
Es cobertura flotante (f)
Fr police à aliment (f)
It polizza flottante (f)

cobertura provisional (f) Es
De temporäre Deckung (f)
En temporary cover
Fr couverture temporaire (m)
It copertura provvisoria (f)
Pt cobertura provisória (f)

cobertura provisória (f) Pt
De temporäre Deckung (f)
En temporary cover
Es cobertura provisional (f)
Fr couverture temporaire (m)
It copertura provvisoria (f)

cobertura total (f) Pt
De Vollwertdeckung (f)
En full cover
Es garantía total (f)

Fr garantie totale (f)
It garanzia totale (f)

cobrador (m) n Pt
De Inkassobeauftragte(r) (m)
En debt collector
Es agente recaudador (m)
Fr agent de recouvrement (m)
It agente di ricupero crediti
(m)

cobrador de impostos (m) Pt
De Steuereinnehmer (m)
En tax collector
Es recaudador de impuestos
(m)
Fr percepteur des impôts (m)
It esattore delle imposte (m)

cobrar vb Es, Pt
De einkassieren
En cash
Fr encaisser
It incassare

cobrar uma dívida Pt
De Schulden eintreiben
En collect a debt
Es recaudar una deuda
Fr recouvrer une créance
It incassare un credito

cobrar um cheque Pt
De einen Scheck einlösen
En cash a cheque
Es cobrar un cheque
Fr toucher un chèque
It incassare un assegno

cobrar un cheque Es
De einen Scheck einlösen
En cash a cheque
Fr toucher un chèque
It incassare un assegno
Pt cobrar um cheque

cobrir-se vb Pt
De sich decken
En hedge
Es cubrirse
Fr arbitrager
It coprirsi

coche (m) n Es
De Auto; Wagen (n m)
En car
Fr voiture; automobile (f)
It automobile; macchina (f)
Pt carro; automóvel (m)

code (legal) n En
De Ordnung (f)
Es código (m)
Fr code (m)
It codice (m)
Pt código (m)

code (telegraphic) (n) En
De Schlüssel (m)
Es clave (f)
Fr clef (f)
It codice (m)
Pt código (m)

code (m) n Fr
De Ordnung (f)
En code
Es código (m)
It codice (m)
Pt código (m)

codice (m) n It
De Ordnung; Schlüssel (f m)
En code
Es código; clave (m f)
Fr code; clef (m f)
Pt código (m)

codice postale (m) It
De Postleitzahl (f)
En postcode
Am zip code
Es designación postal (f)
Fr indicatif postal (m)
Pt designação postal (f)

código (m) n Es
De Ordnung; Schlüssel (f m)
En code
Fr code; clef (m f)
It codice (m)
Pt código (m)

coefficiente di sicurezza (m)
It
De Sicherheitskoeffizient (m)
En safety factor
Es factor se seguridad (m)
Fr facteur de sécurité (m)
Pt factor de segurança (m)

coerção (f) n Pt
De Zwang (m)
En duress
Es compulsión (f)
Fr contrainte (f)
It costrizione (f)

coffee n En
De Kaffee (m)
Es café (m)
Fr café (m)
It caffè (m)
Pt café (m)

coffre-fort (m) n Fr
De Geldschrank (m)
En safe
Es caja fuerte (f)
It cassaforte (f)
Pt cofre (m)

coffre de bagages (m) Fr
De Gepäckschließfach (n)
En luggage locker
Es casilla de equipaje (f)
It casetta bagaglio (f)
Pt depósito de bagagem
    individualizado (m)

coffre de nuit (m) Fr
De Nachttresor (m)
En night safe
Es caja de seguridad
   nocturna (f)
It deposito notturno (m)
Pt cofre nocturno (m)

cofre (m) n Pt
De Geldschrank (m)
En safe
Es caja fuerte (f)
Fr coffre-fort (m)
It cassaforte (f)

cofre nocturno (m) Pt
De Nachttresor (m)
En night safe
Es caja de seguridad
   nocturna (f)
Fr coffre de nuit (m)
It deposito notturno (m)

coin n En
De Münze (f)
Es moneda (f)
Fr pièce (de monnaie) (f)
It moneta (f)
Pt moeda (f)

colaborar vb Es, Pt
De mitarbeiten
En collaborate
Fr collaborer
It collaborare

colaggio (m) n It
De Leck (n)
En leakage
Es escape (m)
Fr fuite (f)
Pt escape; fuga (m f)

colheita (f) n Pt
De Ernte (f)
En harvest
Es cosecha (f)
Fr moisson; récolte (f)
It raccolto (m)

collaborare (vb) It
De mitarbeiten
En collaborate
Es colaborar
Fr collaborer
Pt colaborar

collaborate vb En
De mitarbeiten
En colaborar
Fr collaborer
It collaborare
Pt colaborar

collaborer vb Fr
De mitarbeiten
En collaborate
Es colaborar
It collaborare
Pt colaborar

collateral (security) n En
De Sicherheit (f)
Es garantía colateral (f)
Fr nantissement (m)
It garanzia collaterale (f)
Pt garantia colateral (f)

collect a debt En
De Schulden eintreiben
Es recaudar una deuda
Fr recouvrer une créance
It incassare un credito
Pt cobrar uma dívida

collection charges En
De Einzugskosten (pl)
Es gastos de cobranza (m pl)
Fr frais d'encaissement (m pl)
It spese di riscossione (f pl)
Pt gastos de cobrança (m pl)

collective bargaining En
De Tarifvertragsverhandlung
   (f)

Es contratación collectiva *(f)*
Fr négociations de conven-
  tions collectives *(f pl)*
It contrattazione collettiva *(f)*
Pt regateio colectivo *(m)*

colonna *(f)* n It
De Spalte *(f)*
En column
Es columna *(f)*
Fr colonne *(f)*
Pt coluna *(f)*

colonne *(f)* n Fr
De Spalte *(f)*
En column
Es columna *(f)*
It colonna *(f)*
Pt coluna *(f)*

col presente It
De hiermit
Es hereby
Es por esto
Fr par la présente
Pt pelo presente

column n En
De Spalte *(f)*
Es columna *(f)*
Fr colonne *(f)*
It colonna *(f)*
Pt coluna *(f)*

columna *(f)* n Es
De Spalte *(f)*
En column
Fr colonne *(f)*
It colonna *(f)*
Pt coluna *(f)*

coluna *(f)* n Pt
De Spalte *(f)*
En column
Es columna *(f)*
Fr colonne *(f)*
It colonna *(f)*

com avaria Pt
De havariert
En with average (WA)
Es con avería
Fr avarié
It con avaria

comboio de mercadorias *(m)*
  Pt
De Güterzug *(m)*
En goods train

Am freight train
Es tren de mercancías *(m)*
Fr train de marchandises *(m)*
It treno merci *(m)*

comboio rápido *(m)* Pt
De D-Zug; Schnellzug *(m)*
En express train
Es tren expreso *(m)*
Fr train express *(m)*
It direttissimo; rapido *(m)*

com dividendo Pt
De mit Dividende
En cum dividend
Es con dividendo
Fr droit attaché
It con dividendo

comercializável *adj* Pt
De marktfähig
En marketable
Es vendible
Fr vendable
It vendibile

comerciante *(m)* n Es, Pt
De Händler; Kaufmann *(m)*
En dealer; merchant
Fr négociant *(m)*
It negoziante; commerciante
  (m)

comerciante al por menor
  (m) Es
De Einzelhändler; Klein-
  händler *(m)*
En retailer
Fr commerçant au détail *(m)*
It commerciante al minuto
  (m)
Pt comerciante a retalho;
  retalhista *(m)*

comerciante a retalho *(m)* Pt
De Einzelhändler; Klein-
  händler *(m)*
En retailer
Es comerciante al por mento
  (m)
Fr commerçant au détail *(m)*
It commerciante al minuto
  (m)

comercio *(m)* n Es
De Handel *(m)*
En commerce; trade
Fr commerce *(m)*

It commercio *(m)*
Pt comércio *(m)*

comércio *(m)* n Pt
De Handel *(m)*
En commerce; trade
Es comercio *(m)*
Fr commerce *(m)*
It commercio *(m)*

comercio al por mayor *(m)*
  Es
De Großhandel *(m)*
En wholesale trade
Fr commerce en gros *(m)*
It commercio all'ingrosso
  (m)
Pt comércio por atacado *(m)*

comercio al por menor *(m)*
  Es
De Einzelhandel *(m)*
En retail trade
Fr commerce en détail *(m)*
It commercio al minuto *(m)*
Pt comércio a retalho *(m)*

comércio a retalho *(m)* Pt
De Einzelhandel *(m)*
En retail trade
Es comercio al por menor *(m)*
Fr commerce en détail *(m)*
It commercio al minuto *(m)*

comercio exterior *(m)* Es
De Außenhandel *(m)*
En foreign trade
Fr commerce extérieur *(m)*
It commercio estero *(m)*
Pt comércio externo *(m)*

comércio externo *(m)* Pt
De Außenhandel *(m)*
En foreign trade
Es comercio exterior *(m)*
Fr commerce extérieur *(m)*
It commercio estero *(m)*

comércio franco *(m)* Pt
De Freihandel *(m)*
En free trade
Es comercio libre *(m)*
Fr libre-échange *(m)*
It libero scambio *(m)*

comércio interior *(m)* Es
De Binnenhandel *(m)*
En home trade
Am domestic sales

Fr   commerce intérieur *(m)*
It   commercio interno *(m)*
Pt   comércio interno *(m)*

comércio interno *(m)* Pt
De   Binnenhandel *(m)*
En   home trade
Am   domestic sales
Es   comercio interior *(m)*
Fr   commerce intérieur *(m)*
It   commercio interno *(m)*

comercio libre *(m)* Es
De   Freihandel *(m)*
En   free trade
Fr   libre-échange *(m)*
It   libero scambio *(m)*
Pt   comércio franco *(m)*

comercio multilateral *(m)* Es
De   mehrseitiges Handeln *(n)*
En   multilateral trade
Fr   commerce multilatéral *(m)*
It   commercio multilaterale *(m)*
Pt   comércio multilateral *(m)*

comércio multilateral *(m)* Pt
De   mehrseitiges Handeln *(n)*
En   multilateral trade
Es   comercio multilateral *(m)*
Fr   commerce multilatéral *(m)*
It   commercio multilaterale *(m)*

comércio por atacado *(m)* Pt
De   Großhandel *(m)*
En   wholesale trade
Es   comercio al por mayor *(m)*
Fr   commerce en gros *(m)*
It   commercio all'ingrosso *(m)*

comestibles *(m pl)* n Es
De   Eßwaren *(f pl)*
En   foodstuffs
Fr   alimentation *(f)*
It   generi alimentari *(m pl)*
Pt   géneros alimentícios *(m pl)*

comisión *(f)* n Es
De   Provision *(f)*
En   commission
Fr   commission *(f)*
It   provvigione *(f)*
Pt   comissão *(f)*

Comisión Europea *(f)* Es
De   Europäische Kommission *(f)*
En   European Commission
Fr   Commission des Communautés Européennes *(f)*
It   Commissione Europea *(f)*
Pt   Comissão Europeia *(f)*

comisionista *(m)* n Es
De   Kommissionär *(m)*
En   commission agent
Fr   commissionnaire en marchandises *(m)*
It   commissionario *(m)*
Pt   comissionista *(m)*

comissão *(f)* n Pt
De   Provision *(f)*
En   commission
Es   comisión *(f)*
Fr   commission *(f)*
It   provvigione *(f)*

Comissão Europeia *(f)* Pt
De   Europäische Kommission *(f)*
En   European Commission
Es   Comisión Europea *(f)*
Fr   Commission des Communautés Européennes *(f)*
It   Commissione Europea *(f)*

comissário de bordo *(m)* Pt
De   Zahlmeister *(m)*
En   purser
Es   contador de navio *(m)*
Fr   commissaire de la marine *(m)*
It   commissario di bordo *(m)*

comissionista *(m)* n Pt
De   Kommissionär *(m)*
En   commission agent
Es   comisionista *(m)*
Fr   commissionnaire en marchandises *(m)*
It   commissionario *(m)*

comitato *(m)* n It
De   Kommission *(f)*
En   committee
Es   comité *(m)*
Fr   comité *(f)*
Pt   comité *(m)*

comité *(m)* n Es, Fr, Pt
De   Kommission; Ausschuß *(f m)*

En   committee
It   comitato *(m)*

comité consultatif *(m)* Fr
De   Beratungsausschuß *(m)*
En   advisory board
Es   consejo consultivo *(m)*
It   consiglio consultivo *(m)*
Pt   comité consultivo *(m)*

comité consultivo *(m)* Pt
De   Beratungsausschuß *(m)*
En   advisory board
Es   consejo consultivo *(m)*
Fr   comité consultatif *(m)*
It   consiglio consultivo *(m)*

commande *(f)* n Fr
De   Bestellung *(f)*
En   order
Es   pedido *(m)*
It   ordine *(m)*
Pt   encomenda *(f)*

commande d'exportation *(f)* Fr
De   Exportauftrag *(m)*
En   export order
Es   pedido de exportación *(m)*
It   ordine per esportazione *(m)*
Pt   encomenda de exportação *(f)*

commande par lettre *(f)* Fr
De   Auftrag durch die Post *(m)*
En   mail order
Es   pedido por correo *(m)*
It   ordine per corrispondenza *(f)*
Pt   venda pelo correio *(f)*

commanditaire *(m)* n Fr
De   stiller Gesellschafter *(m)*
En   sleeping partner
Am   silent partner
Es   socio comanditario *(m)*
It   socio accomandante *(m)*
Pt   sócio comanditário *(m)*

commerçant au détail *(f)* Fr
De   Einzelhändler; Kleinhändler *(m)*
En   retailer
Es   comerciante al por menor *(m)*
It   commerciante al minuto *(m)*
Pt   comerciante a retalho; retalhista *(m)*

commerce n En, Fr (m)
De Handel (m)
Es comercio (m)
It commercio (m)
Pt comércio (m)

commerce de tourisme (m)
Fr
De Reisegewerbe (n)
En tourist trade
Es industria del turismo (f)
It commercio turistico (m)
Pt indústria do turismo (f)

commerce en détail (m) Fr
De Einzelhandel (m)
En retail trade
Es comercio al por menor (m)
It commercio al minuto (m)
Pt comércio a retalho (m)

commerce en gros (m) Fr
De Großhandel (m)
En wholesale trade
Es comercio al por mayor (m)
It commercio all'ingrosso (m)
Pt comércio por atacado (m)

commerce extérieur (m) Fr
De Außenhandel (m)
En foreign trade
Es comercio exterior (m)
It commercio estero (m)
Pt comércio externo (m)

commerce intérieur (m) Fr
De Binnenhandel (m)
En home trade
Am domestic sales
Es comercio interior (m)
It commercio interno (m)
Pt comércio interno (m)

commerce multilatéral (m) Fr
De mehrseitiges Handeln (n)
En multilateral trade
Es comercio multilateral (m)
It commercio multilaterale (m)
Pt comércio multilateral (m)

commercial invoice En
De Geschäftsfaktur (f)
Es factura comercial (f)
Fr facture commerciale (f)
It fattura commerciale (f)
Pt factura comercial (f)

commercial traveller En
Am salesman
De Handelsvertreter; Geschäftsreisende(r) (m)
Es viajante de comercio (m)
Fr commis-voyageur (m)
It viaggiatore di commercio (m)
Pt caixeiro viajante (m)

commercial vehicle En
De Nutzfahrzeug (n)
Es vehículo comercial (m)
Fr véhicule commerciale (f)
It veicolo commerciale (m)
Pt veículo comercial (m)

commerciante (m) n It
De Kaufmann (m)
En merchant
Es comerciante (m)
Fr négociant (m)
Pt comerciante (m)

commerciante al minuto (m) It
De Einzelhändler; Kleinhändler (m)
En retailer
Es comerciante al por menor (m)
Fr commerçant au détail (m)
Pt comerciante a retalho; retalhista (m)

commercio (m) n It
De Handel (m)
En commerce; trade
Es comercio (m)
Fr commerce (m)
Pt comércio (m)

commercio all'ingrosso (m) It
De Großhandel (m)
En wholesale trade
Es comercio al por mayor (m)
Fr commerce en gros (m)
Pt comércio por atacado (m)

commercio al minuto (m) It
De Einzelhandel (m)
En retail trade
Es comercio al por menor (m)
Fr commerce en détail (m)
Pt comércio a retalho (m)

commercio estero (m) It
De Außenhandel (m)
En foreign trade

Es comercio exterior (m)
Fr commerce extérieur (m)
Pt comércio externo (m)

commercio interno (m) It
De Binnenhandel (m)
En home trade
Am domestic sales
Es comercio interior (m)
Fr commerce intérieur (m)
Pt comércio interno (m)

commercio multilaterale (m) It
De mehrseitiges Handeln (n)
En multilateral trade
Es comercio multilateral (m)
Fr commerce multilatéral (m)
Pt comércio multilateral (m)

commercio turistico (m) It
De Reisegewerbe (n)
En tourist trade
Es industria del turismo (f)
Fr commerce de tourisme (m)
Pt indústria do turismo (f)

commesso di spedizioniere (m) It
De Expedient (m)
En shipping clerk
Es dependiente de muelle (m)
Fr expéditionnaire (m)
Pt despachante (m)

commis (m) n Fr
De Angestellte(r); Assistent (m)
En clerk; assistant
Es oficinista; asistente (m)
It impiegato; assistente (m)
Pt empregado de escritório; assistente (m)

commis-comptable (m) n Fr
De Buchhalter (m)
En ledger clerk
Am bookkeeper
Es contable (m)
It contabile (m)
Pt empregado de contabilidade (m)

commis-voyageur (m) n Fr
De Geschäftsreisende(r) (m)
En (commercial) traveller
Es viajante (m)
It viaggiatore di commercio (m)
Pt viajante (m)

commissaire-priseur *(m) n*
Fr
De Versteigerer *(m)*
En auctioneer
Es subastador *(m)*
It venditore all'asta *(m)*
Pt leiloeiro *(m)*

commissaire de la marine
(m) Fr
De Zahlmeister *(m)*
En purser
Es contador de navio *(m)*
It commissario di bordo *(m)*
Pt comissário do bordo *(m)*

commissario di bordo *(m)* It
De Zahlmeister *(m)*
En purser
Es contador de navio *(m)*
Fr commissaire de la marine
(m)
Pt comissário de bordo *(m)*

commission *n* En, Fr *(f)*
De Provision *(f)*
Es comisión *(f)*
It provvigione *(f)*
Pt comissão *(f)*

commission agent En
De Kommissionär *(m)*
Es comisionista *(m)*
Fr commissionnaire en mar-
chandises *(m)*
It commissionario *(m)*
Pt comissionista *(m)*

commissionario *(m) n* It
De Kommissionär *(m)*
En commission agent
Es comisionista *(m)*
Fr commissionnaire en mar-
chandises *(m)*
Pt comissionista *(m)*

**Commission des Commu-
nautés Européennes** *(f)*
Fr
De Europäische Kommission
(f)
En European Commission
Es Comisión Europea *(f)*
It Commissione Europea *(f)*
Pt Comissão Europeia *(f)*

Commissione Europea *(f)* It
De Europäische Kommission
(f)
En European Commission

Es Comisión Europea *(f)*
Fr Commission des Commu-
nautés Européennes *(f)*
Pt Comissão Europeia *(f)*

**commissionaire en
marchandises** *(m)* Fr
De Kommissionär *(m)*
En commission agent
Es comisionista *(m)*
It commissionario *(m)*
Pt comissionista *(m)*

committee *(n)* En
De Kommission; Ausschuß
(f m)
Es comité *(m)*
Fr comité *(f)*
It comitato *(m)*
Pt comité *(m)*

commodity *(n)* En
De Gut; Ware *(n f)*
Es mercadería *(f)*
Fr marchandise; produit *(f m)*
It merce; prodotto *(f m)*
Pt mercadoria; produto *(f m)*

commodity broker En
De Makler für Verbrauchs-
güter *(m)*
Es corredor de mercaderías
(m)
Fr courtier en marchandises
(m)
It sensale di merci *(m)*
Pt corretor de mercadorias
(m)

commodity market En
De Rohstoffmarkt *(m)*
Es mercado de materias
primas *(m)*
Fr marché de matières
premières *(m)*
It mercato di materie prime
(m)
Pt mercado de matérias pri-
mas *(m)*

Common Agricultural Policy
En
De gemeinsame Agrarpolitik
(f)
Es política agrícola común *(f)*
Fr politique agricole
commune *(f)*
It politica agricola comune *(f)*
Pt política agrícola comum *(f)*

common carrier En
De Güterbeförderer *(m)*
Es empresa de transportes *(f)*
Fr voiturier public *(m)*
It vettore *(m)*
Pt empresa de transportes *(f)*

**Common Commercial
Policy** En
De gemeinsame Handelspoli-
tik *(f)*
Es política comercial común
(f)
Fr politique commerciale
commune *(f)*
It politica commerciale co-
mune *(f)*
Pt política comercial comum
(f)

common external tariff En
De gemeinsamer Außentarif
(m)
Es tarifa exterior común *(f)*
Fr tarif extérieur commun *(m)*
It tariffa estera comune *(f)*
Pt tarifa externa comum *(f)*

Common Fisheries Policy
En
De gemeinsame Fischereipo-
litik *(f)*
Es política común de la
pesca *(f)*
Fr politique commune de la
pêche *(f)*
It politica comune della
pesca *(f)*
Pt política comum da pesca
(f)

Common Market En
De Gemeinsamer Markt *(m)*
Es mercado común *(m)*
Fr marché commun *(m)*
It mercato comune *(m)*
Pt mercado comum *(m)*

communal *adj* Fr
De Kommunal-
En municipal
Es municipal
It municipale
Pt municipal

communauté *(f) n* Fr
De Gemeinschaft *(f)*
En community *(f)*
Es comunidad *(f)*

It comunità *(f)*
Pt comunidade *(f)*

Communauté Économique Européenne *(f)* Fr
De Europäische Wirtschafts-gemeinschaft *(f)*
En European Economic Community
Es Comunidad Económica Europea *(f)*
It Comunità Economica Europea *(f)*
Pt Comunidade Económica Europeia *(f)*

Communauté Européenne de l'Energie Atomique *(f)* Fr
De Europäische Atomge-meinschaft *(f)*
En European Atomic Energy Community
Es Comunidad Europea de Energía Atómica *(f)*
It Comunità Europea dell'Energia Atomica *(f)*
Pt Comunidade Europeia de Energia Atómica *(f)*

Communauté Européenne du Charbon et de l'Acier *(f)* Fr
De Europäische Gemein-schaft für Kohle und Stahl *(f)*
En European Coal and Steel Community
Es Comunidad Europea de Carbón y Acero *(f)*
It Comunità Europea del Carbone e Acciaio *(f)*
Pt Comunidade Europeia do Carvão e do Aço *(f)*

communication *(n)* En, Fr *(f)*
De Benachrichtigung *(f)*
Es comunicación *(f)*
It comunicazione *(f)*
Pt comunicação *(f)*

community *(n)* En
De Gemeinschaft *(f)*
Es comunidad *(f)*
Fr communauté *(f)*
It comunità *(f)*
Pt comunidade *(f)*

compagnia di assicurazione *(f)* It
De Versicherungsgesellschaft *(f)*
En insurance company
Es compañía de seguros *(f)*
Fr compagnie d'assurance *(f)*
Pt companhia de seguros *(f)*

compagnie aérienne *(f)* Fr
De Fluggesellschaft *(f)*
En air line
Es línea aérea *(f)*
It linea aerea *(f)*
Pt companhia de aviação *(f)*

compagnie d'assurance *(f)* Fr
De Versicherungsgesellschaft *(f)*
En insurance company
Es compañía de seguros *(f)*
It compagnia di assicura-zione *(f)*
Pt companhia de seguros *(f)*

compagnie de navigation *(f)* Fr
De Reederei *(f)*
En shipping line
Es compañía navièra *(f)*
It società di navigazione *(f)*
Pt companhia de navegação *(f)*

companhia *(f) n* Pt
De Gesellschaft *(f)*
En company
Es compañía; empresa *(f)*
Fr société; entreprise *(f)*
It società *(f)*

companhia arrendatária *(f)* Pt
De Leasinggesellschaft *(f)*
En leasing company
Es compañía arrendataria *(f)*
Fr société de leasing *(f)*
It società di leasing *(m)*

companhia controladora *(f)* Pt
De Gesellschaft mit Kontroll-befugnis *(f)*
En controlling company
Es compañía directriz *(f)*
Fr société directrice *(f)*
It società direttrice *(f)*

companhia cotizada *(f)* Pt
De Gesellschaft notiert an der Börse *(f)*
En quoted company
Es compañía cotizada en bolsa *(f)*
Fr société cotée à la Bourse *(f)*
It società quotata in borsa *(f)*

companhia de aviação *(f)* Pt
De Fluggesellschaft *(f)*
En air line
Es línea aérea *(f)*
Fr compagnie aérienne *(f)*
It linea aerea *(f)*

companhia de investimen-tos *(f)* Pt
De Investierungsgesellschaft *(f)*
En investment company
Es compañía inversionista *(f)*
Fr société de placement *(f)*
It società per investimenti *(f)*

companhia de navegação *(f)* Pt
De Reederei *(f)*
En shipping line
Es compañía navièra *(f)*
Fr compagnie de navigation *(f)*
It società di navigazione *(f)*

companhia de seguros *(f)* Pt
De Versicherungsgesellschaft *(f)*
En insurance company
Es compañía de seguros *(f)*
Fr compagnie d'assurance *(f)*
It compagnia di assicura-zione *(f)*

companhia proprietária *(f)* Pt
De Dachgesellschaft *(f)*
En holding company
Es compañía tenedora *(f)*
Fr société holding *(f)*
It società holding *(f)*

companhia subsidiária *(f)* Pt
De Tochtergesellschaft *(f)*
En subsidiary company
Es filial; empresa subsidiaria *(f)*
Fr filiale *(f)*
It filiale *(f)*

compañía *(f)* n Es
De Gesellschaft *(f)*
En company
Fr société; entreprise *(f)*
It società *(f)*
Pt companhia *(f)*

compañía afiliada *(f)* Es
De Schwestergesellschaft *(f)*
En affiliated company
Fr société sœur*(f)*
It società affiliata *(f)*
Pt companhia subsidiária *(f)*

compañía arrendataria *(f)* Es
De Leasinggesellschaft *(f)*
En leasing company
Fr société de leasing *(f)*
It società di leasing *(f)*
Pt companhia arrendatária *(f)*

compañía asociada *(f)* Es
De Schwestergesellschaft *(f)*
En sister company
Fr société sœur *(f)*
It società sorella *(f)*
Pt empresa gémea *(f)*

compañía cotizada en bolsa
　(f) Es
De Gesellschaft notiert an der
　Börse *(f)*
En quoted company
Fr société cotée à la Bourse
　(f)
It società quotata in borsa *(f)*
Pt companhia cotizada *(f)*

compañía de explotación *(f)*
　Es
De Erschließungsgesellschaft
　(f)
En development company
Fr société d'exploitation *(f)*
It società d'imprese *(f)*
Pt empresa de exploração *(f)*

compañía de seguros *(f)* Es
De Versicherungsgesellschaft
　(f)
En insurance company
Fr compagnie d'assurance *(f)*
It compagnia di assicura-
　zione *(f)*
Pt companhia de seguros *(f)*

compañía directriz *(f)* Es
De Gesellschaft mit Kontroll-
　befugnis *(f)*
En controlling company

Fr société directrice *(f)*
It società direttrice *(f)*
Pt companhia controladora
　(f)

compañía inversionista *(f)*
　Es
De Investierungsgesellschaft
　(f)
En investment company
Fr société de placement *(f)*
It società per investimenti *(f)*
Pt companhia de investimen-
　tos *(f)*

compañía matriz *(f)* Es
De Muttergesellschaft *(f)*
En parent company
Fr société mère *(f)*
It società madre *(f)*
Pt empresa matriz *(f)*

compañía navièra *(f)* Es
De Reederei *(f)*
En shipping line
Fr compagnie de navigation
　(f)
It società di navigazione *(f)*
Pt companhia de navegação
　(f)

**Compañía privada de
　responsabilidad limitada**
　(f) Es
De Gesellschaft mit be-
　schränkter Haftung
　(GmbH) *(f)*
En private limited company
Fr Société à responsabilité
　limitée (SARL) *(f)*
It Società a responsabilità
　limitata (Srl) *(f)*
Pt Sociedade por quotas de
　responsabilidade limitada
　(f)

compañía tenedora *(f)* Es
De Dachgesellschaft *(f)*
En holding company
Fr société holding *(f)*
It società holding *(f)*
Pt companhia proprietária *(f)*

company n En
De Gesellschaft *(f)*
Es compañía; empresa *(f)*
Fr société; entreprise *(f)*
It società *(f)*
Pt companhia *(f)*

compensação *(f)* n Pt
De Entschädigung *(f)*
En compensation
Es compensación *(f)*
Fr compensation *(f)*
It compenso *(m)*

compensación *(f)* Es
De Entschädigung *(f)*
En compensation
Fr compensation *(f)*
It compenso *(m)*
Pt compensação *(f)*

compensar *vb* Es, Pt
De vergüten
En compensate
Fr compenser
It compensare

compensare *vb* It
De vergüten
En compensate
Es compensar
Fr compenser
Pt compensar

compensate *vb* En
De vergüten
Es compensar
Fr compenser
It compensare
Pt compensar

compensation n En, Fr *(f)*
De Entschädigung *(f)*
Es compensación *(f)*
It compenso *(m)*
Pt compensação *(f)*

compenser *vb* Fr
De vergüten
En compensate
Es compensar
It compensare
Pt compensar

compenso *(m)* n It
De Entschädigung *(f)*
En compensation
Es compensación *(f)*
Fr compensation *(f)*
Pt compensação *(f)*

compenso per il rischio *(m)*
　It
De Gefahrenzulage *(f)*
En danger money
Es suma para riesgos *(f)*

Fr prime de risque *(f)*
Pt prémio de risco *(M)*

compete *vb* En
De Konkurrenz machen
Es competir
Fr concurrencer
It competere
Pt competir

competere *vb* It
De Konkurrenz machen
En compete
Es competir
Fr concurrencer
Pt competir

competição *(f) n* Pt
De Wettbewerb *(m)*
En competition
Es competición *(f)*
Fr concurrence *(f)*
It concorrenza *(f)*

competición *(f) n* Es
De Wettbewerb *(m)*
En competition
Fr concurrence *(f)*
It concorrenza *(f)*
Pt competição *(f)*

competidor *adj* Es
De wetteifernd
En competitive
Fr compétitif
It in concorrenza
Pt competitivo

competir *vb* Es,Pt
De Konkurrenz machen
En compete
Fr concurrencer
It competere

compétitif *adj* Fr
De wetteifernd
En competitive
Es competidor
It in concorrenza
Pt competitivo

competition *n* En
De Wettbewerb *(m)*
Es competición *(f)*
Fr concurrence *(f)*
It concorrenza *(f)*
Pt competição *(f)*

competitive *adj* En
De wetteifernd
Es competidor
Fr compétitif
It in concorrenza
Pt competitivo

competitivo *adj* Pt
De wetteifernd
En competitive
Es competidor
Fr compétitif
It in concorrenza

compilazione dell'inventario
(f) It
De Bestandsaufnahme *(f)*
En stocktaking
Es inventario; balance *(m)*
Fr levée d'inventaire *(f)*
Pt inventário de existências
(m)

complessivo *adj* It
De gesamt
En aggregate
Es total
Fr global
Pt total

completo *adj* Es
De umfassend
En comprehensive
Fr exhaustif; complet
It comprensivo
Pt compreensivo

**comportamento
precedente** *(m)* It
De Leistung in der Vergan-
genheit *(f)*
En past performance
Es operación anterior *(f)*
Fr comportement antérieur
(m)
Pt desempenho anterior *(m)*

comportement antérieur *(m)*
Fr
De Leistung in der Vergan-
genheit *(f)*
En past performance
Es operación anterior *(f)*
It comportamento prece-
dente *(m)*
Pt desempenho anterior *(m)*

compound interest En
De Zinseszinsen *(m pl)*
Es interés compuesto *(m)*
Fr intérêts composés *(m pl)*
It interesse composto *(m)*
Pt juro composto *(m)*

compra *(f) n* Es, It, Pt
De Einkauf; Anschaffung *(m f)*
En purchase
Fr achat *(m)*

compra a plazos *(f)* Es
De Ratenkauf *(m)*
En hire-purchase
Fr location-vente *(f)*
It vendita a rate *(f)*
Pt venda a prestações *(f)*

comprador *(m) n* Es, Pt
De Käufer *(m)*
En buyer
Fr acheteur *(m)*
It compratore *(m)*

compra espontánea *(f)* Es
De Impulskaufen *(n)*
En impulse buying
Fr achat sur léntrainement du
moment *(m)*
It compra sullo stimolo del
momento *(f)*
Pt compra impulsiva *(f)*

compra impulsiva *(f)* Pt
De Impulskaufen *(n)*
En impulse buying
Es compra espontánea *(f)*
Fr achat sur léntrainement du
moment *(m)*
It compra sullo stimolo del
momento *(f)*

comprar *vb* Es, Pt
De kaufen
En buy
Fr acheter
It comprare

comprare *vb* It
De kaufen
En buy
Es comprar
Fr acheter
Pt comprar

**compra sullo stimolo del
momento** *(f)* It
De Impulskaufen *(n)*
En impulse buying

Es compra espontánea *(f)*
Fr achat sur l'entrainement du moment *(m)*
Pt compra impulsiva *(f)*

compratore *(m)* n It
De Käufer *(m)*
En buyer
Es comprador *(m)*
Fr acheteur *(m)*
Pt comprador *(m)*

compreensivo *adj* Pt
De umfassend
En comprehensive
Es completo
Fr exhaustif; complet
It comprensivo

comprehensive *adj* En
De umfassend
Es completo
Fr exhaustif; complet
It comprensivo
Pt compreensivo

comprehensive insurance
En
De kombinierte Versicherung *(f)*
Es seguro combinado *(m)*
Fr assurance combinée *(f)*
It asiicurazione mista *(f)*
Pt seguro compreensivo *(m)*

comprensivo *adj* It
De umfassend
En comprehensive
Es completo
Fr exhaustif; complet
Pt compreensivo

compromesso d'avaria *(m)*
It
De Havarieschein *(m)*
En average bond
Es fianza de avería *(f)*
Fr compromis d'averie *(m)*
Pt fiança de avaria *(f)*

compromis d'avarie *(m)* Fr
De Havarieschein *(m)*
En average bond
Es fianza de avería *(f)*
It compromesso d'avaria *(m)*
Pt fiança de avaria *(f)*

comproprietà *(f)* It
De Miteigentum *(n)*
En joint ownership

Es copropiedad *(f)*
Fr copropiété *(f)*
Pt co-propriedade *(f)*

comptabilité *(f)* n Fr
De Buchhaltung *(f)*
En book-keeping; accountancy
Es contabilidad *(f)*
It contabilità *(f)*
Pt contabilidade *(f)*

comptable *(m)* n Fr
De Buchhalter *(m)*
En accountant
Es contador *(m)*
It contabile *(m)*
Pt contabilista *(m)*

comptable de prix de revient
(m) Fr
De Kalkulator *(m)*
En cost accountant
Es contable de costes *(m)*
It contabile dei costi di produzione *(m)*
Pt calculador de custos *(m)*

**comptant contre
documents** Fr
De bar gegen Versandpapiere
En cash against documents (c.a.d.)
Es al contado contra documentos
It contanti contro documenti
Pt em dinheiro contra documentação

compte (en banque) *(m)* n Fr
De Konto *(n)*
En account
Es cuenta *(f)*
It conto *(m)*
Pt conta *(f)*

compte (note) *(m)* n Fr
De Rechnung *(f)*
En bill; account
Es cuenta; nota *(f)*
It conto; nota *(m f)*
Pt conta; nota *(f)*

compte bloqué *(m)* Fr
De gesperrtes Konto *(n)*
En blocked account
Es cuenta bloqueada *(f)*
It conto bloccato *(m)*
Pt conta bloqueada *(f)*

compte capital *(m)* Fr
De Kapitalkonto *(n)*
En capital account
Es cuenta de capital *(f)*
It conto capitale *(M)*
Pt conta de capital *(f)*

compte commercial *(m)* Fr
De Handelskonto *(n)*
En trade account
Es cuenta comercial *(f)*
It conto commerciale *(m)*
Pt conta comercial *(f)*

compte contrepartie *(f)* Fr
De Gegenkonto *(n)*
En contra account
Es contracuenta *(f)*
It conto d'ordine *(m)*
Pt contra-conta *(f)*

compte courant *(m)* Fr
De Kontokorrent *(n)*
En current account
Am checking account
Es cuenta corriente *(f)*
It conto corrente *(m)*
Pt conta corrente *(f)*

compte d'affectation *(m)* Fr
De Rückstellungskonto *(m)*
En appropriation account
Es cuenta de apropiación *(f)*
It conto di stanziamento *(m)*
Pt conta de apropriação *(f)*

compte d'agio *(m)* Fr
De Agiokonto *(n)*
En agio account
Es cuenta de agio *(f)*
It conto d'aggio *(m)*
Pt conta de ágio *(f)*

compte d'avances *(m)* Fr
De Darlehenskonto *(n)*
En advance account
Es cuenta de anticipos *(f)*
It conto anticipo *(m)*
Pt conta de adiantamentos *(f)*

compte d'ordre *(m)* Fr
De Übergangskonto *(n)*
En suspense account
Es cuenta suspensa *(f)*
It conto sospeso *(m)*
Pt conta pendente *(f)*

compte de contrôle *(m)* Fr
De Kontrollkonto *(n)*
En control account
Es cuenta de control *(f)*
It conto di controllo *(m)*
Pt conta de controlo *(f)*

compte découvert *(m)* Fr
De Konto überzogen *(n)*
En account overdrawn
Es cuenta en descubierto *(f)*
It conto scoperto *(m)*
Pt conta a descoberto *(f)*

compte de dépôt *(m)* Fr
De Depositenkonto *(n)*
En deposit account
Am interest-bearing account
Es cuenta de ahorras *(f)*
It conto di deposito *(m)*
Pt conta de depósito *(f)*

compte de mise à terre *(m)* Fr
De Löschungskonto *(n)*
En landing account
Es cuenta de desembarque *(f)*
It conto di sbarco *(m)*
Pt conta de descargas *(f)*

compte de revenus et dépenses *(m)* Fr
De Ausgaben- und Ertrags-konto *(n)*
En income and expenditure account
Es cuenta de ingresos y gastos *(f)*
It conto proventi e spese *(m)*
Pt conta de receitas e despesas *(f)*

compte des prêts *(m)* Fr
De Anleihekonto *(n)*
En loan account
Es cuenta de préstamos *(f)*
It conto anticipazioni *(m)*
Pt conta de empréstimos *(f)*

compte des speculations à la baisse *(m)* Fr
De Baissekonto *(n)*
En bear account
Es cuenta de especulaciones a la baja *(f)*
It conto di speculazioni al ribasso *(m)*
Pt conta de especulações baixistas *(f)*

compte en banque *(m)* Fr
De Bankkonto *(n)*
En bank account
Es cuenta bancaria *(f)*
It conto in banca *(m)*
Pt conta bancária *(f)*

compte identifié par numéro *(m)* Fr
De numeriertes Konto *(n)*
En numbered account
Es cuenta identificada con número *(f)*
It conto identificato da numero *(m)*
Pt conta numerada *(f)*

compte impersonnel *(m)* Fr
De Firmenkonto *(n)*
En impersonal account
Es cuenta simulada *(f)*
It conto d'ordine *(m)*
Pt conta impessoal *(f)*

compte joint *(m)* Fr
De Gemeinschaftskonto *(n)*
En joint account
Es cuenta común *(f)*
It conto in comune *(m)*
Pt conta conjunta *(f)*

compte nominal *(m)* Fr
De Firmenkonto *(n)*
En nominal account
Es cuenta de resultado *(f)*
It conto d'ordine *(m)*
Pt conta nominal *(f)*

compte personnel *(m)* Fr
De Kundenkonto *(n)*
En charge account
Es cuenta personal *(f)*
It conto personale *(m)*
Pt conta pessoal *(f)*

compte profits et pertes *(m)* Fr
De Gewinn- und Verlustkonto *(n)*
En profit and loss account
Es cuenta de ganacias y pérdidas *(f)*
It conto profitti e perdite *(m)*
Pt conta de lucros e perdas *(f)*

compte rendu *(m)* Fr
De zur Begleichung vorgelegte Rechnung *(f)*
En account rendered

Es cuenta rendida *(f)*
It conto reso *(m)*
Pt conta remetida *(f)*

comptes à payer *(m pl)* Fr
De Kreditoren *(m pl)*
En accounts payable
Es cuentas a pagar *(f pl)*
It conti passivi *(m pl)*
Pt contas a pagar *(f pl)*

comptes à percevoir *(m pl)* Fr
De ausstehende Schulden *(m pl)*
En outstanding accounts
Es cuentas pendientes *(f pl)*
It conti aperti *(m pl)*
Pt contas por saldar *(f pl)*

comptes consolidés *(m pl)* Fr
De konsolidierter Kontenabschluß *(m)*
En consolidated accounts
Es cuentas consolidadas *(f pl)*
It conti consolidati *(m pl)*
Pt contas consolidadas *(f pl)*

compte transférable *(m)* Fr
De Auslandskonto *(n)*
En external account
Am foreign currency account
Es cuenta exterior *(f)*
It conto estero *(m)*
Pt conta externa *(f)*

comptroller *n* En
De Rechnungsprüfer *(m)*
Es interventor *(m)*
Fr vérificateur des comptes *(m)*
It controllore *(m)*
Pt controlador *m*

compulsión *(f)* *n* Es
De Zwang *(m)*
En duress
Fr contrainte *(f)*
It contrizione *(f)*
Pt coerção *(f)*

compulsory *adj* En
De verbindlich
Es obligatorio
Fr obligatoire
It obbligatorio
Pt obrigatório

compulsory purchase En
De Enteignung *(f)*
Es expropiación *(f)*

Fr expropriation *(f)*
It espropriazione *(f)*
Pt expropriação *(f)*

compulsory winding-up En
Am forced liquidation
De Zwangsliquidation *(f)*
Es liquidación forzosa *(f)*
Fr liquidation forcée *(f)*
It liquidazione forzata *(f)*
Pt liquidação forçada *(f)*

computador *(m) n* Pt
De Rechner; Computer *(m)*
En computer
Es computadora *(f)*
Fr ordinateur *(m)*
It elaboratore; calcolatore *(m)*

computadora *(f) n* Es
De Rechner; Computer *(m)*
En computer
Fr ordinateur *(m)*
It elaboratore; calcolatore *(m)*
Pt computador *(m)*

computadora analógica *(f)*
Es
De Analogrechner *(m)*
En analogue computer
Fr calculateur analogique *(m)*
It calcolatore analogico *(m)*
Pt computador analógico *(m)*

computador analógico *(m)*
Pt
De Analogrechner *(m)*
En analogue computer
Es computadora analógica *(f)*
Fr calculateur analogique *(m)*
It calcolatore analogico *(m)*

computadora numérica *(f)*
Es
De Digitalrechner *(m)*
En digital computer
Fr calculateur digital *(m)*
It elaboratore numerico *(m)*
Pt computador de dígitos *(m)*

computador de dígitos *(m)*
Pt
De Digitalrechner *(m)*
En digital computer
Es computadora numérica *(f)*
Fr calculateur digital *(m)*
It elaboratore numerico *(m)*

computer *n* En
De Rechner; Computer *(m)*
Es computadora *(f)*
Fr ordinateur *(m)*
It elaboratore; calcolatore *(m)*
Pt computador *(m)*

Computer *(m)* De
En computer
Es computadora *(f)*
Fr ordinateur *(m)*
It elaboratore; calcolatore *(m)*
Pt computador *(m)*

computer language En
De Rechnersprache *(f)*
Es lenguaje de computadoras *(m)*
Fr langage-machine *(m)*
It linguaggio macchina *(m)*
Pt linguagem de computador *(f)*

computer printout En
De Ausgabedruck *(m)*
Es impresión *(f)*
Fr sortie sur imprimante *(f)*
It stampato d'uscita dell'elaboratore *(m)*
Pt informe impresso pelo computador *(m)*

computer program En
De Computerprogramm *(n)*
Es programa de computadora *(m)*
Fr programme d'ordinateur *(m)*
It programma di elaboratore *(m)*
Pt programa de computador *(m)*

Computerprogramm *(n) n* De
En computer program
Es programa de computadora *(m)*
Fr programme d'ordinateur *(m)*
It programma di elaboratore *(m)*
Pt programa de computador *(m)*

com recurso Pt
De mit Rückgriff
En with recourse

Es con recurso
Fr avec droit de recours
It con ricorso

comune accordo *(m)* It
De gegenseitiges Einvernehmen *(n)*
En mutual agreement
Es acuerdo común *(m)*
Fr accord mutuel *(m)*
Pt acordo mútuo *(m)*

comunicação *(f) n* Pt
De Benachrichtigung *(f)*
En communication
Es comunicación *(f)*
Fr communication *(f)*
It comunicazione *(f)*

comunicación *(f) n* Es
De Benachrichtigung *(f)*
En communication
Fr communication *(f)*
It comunicazione *(f)*
Pt comunicação *(f)*

comunicazione *(f)* It
De Benachrichtigung *(f)*
En communication
Es comunicación *(f)*
Fr communication *(f)*
Pt comunicação *(f)*

comunicazione interurbana *(f)* It
De Ferngespräch *(n)*
En trunk call
Am long distance call
Es llamada interurbana *(f)*
Fr appel téléphonique interurbain *(m)*
Pt chamada inter-urbana (troncas) *(f)*

comunidad *(f) n* Es
De Gemeinschaft *(f)*
En community
Fr communauté *(f)*
It comunità *(f)*
Pt comunidade *(f)*

comunidade *(f)* Pt
De Gemeinschaft *(f)*
En community
Es comunidad *(f)*
Fr communauté *(f)*
It comunitá *(f)*

**Comunidad Económica
Europea** *(f)* Es
De Europäische Wirtschafts-
gemeinschaft *(f)*
En European Economic
Community
Fr Communauté Écono-
mique Européenne *(f)*
It Comunità Economica Eu-
ropea *(f)*
Pt Comunidade Económica
Europeia *(f)*

**Comunidade Económica
Europeia** *(f)* Pt
De Europäische Wirtschafts-
gemeinschaft *(f)*
En European Economic
Community
Es Comunidad Económica
Europea *(f)*
Fr Communauté Écono-
mique Européenne *(f)*
It Comunità Economica Eu-
ropea *(f)*

**Comunidade Europeia de
Energia Atómica** *(f)* Pt
De Europäische Atomge-
meinschaft *(f)*
En European Atomic Energy
Community
Es Comunidad Europea de
Energía Atómica *(f)*
Fr Communauté Européenne
de l'Énergie Atomique *(f)*
It Comunità Europea
dell'Energia Atomica *(f)*

**Comunidade Europeia do
Carvão e do Aço** *(f)* Pt
De Europäische Gemein-
schaft für Kohle und Stahl
(f)
En European Coal and Steel
Community
Es Comunidad Europea de
Carbón y Acero *(f)*
Fr Communauté Européenne
du Charbon et de l'Acier *(f)*
It Comunità Europea del
Carbone e Acciaio *(f)*

**Comunidad Europea de
Carbón y Acero** *(f)* Es
De Europäische Gemein-
schaft für Kohle und Stahl
(f)
En European Coal and Steel
Community

Fr Communauté Européenne
du Charbon et de l'Acier *(f)*
It Comunità Europea del
Carbone e Acciaio *(f)*
Pt Comunidade Europeia
do Carvão e do Aço *(f)*

**Comunidad Europea de
Energía Atómica** *(f)* Es
De Europäische Atomge-
meinschaft *(f)*
En European Atomic Energy
Community
Fr Communauté Éuropéenne
de l'Énergie Atomique *(f)*
It Comunità Europea
dell'Energia Atomica *(f)*
Pt Comunidade Europeia de
Energia Atómica *(f)*

comunità *(f) n* It
De Gemeinschaft *(f)*
En community
Es comunidad *(f)*
Fr communauté *(f)*
Pt comunidade *(f)*

**Comunità Economica
Europea** *(f)* It
De Europäische Wirtschafts-
gemeinschaft *(f)*
En European Economic
Community
Es Comunidad Económica
Europea *(f)*
Fr Communauté Écono-
mique Européenne *(f)*
Pt Comunidade Económica
Europeia *(f)*

**Comunità Europea del
Carbone e Acciaio** *(f)* It
De Europäische Gemein-
schaft für Kohle und Stahl
(f)
En European Coal and Steel
Community
Es Comunidad Europea de
Carbón y Acero *(f)*
Fr Communauté Européenne
du Charbon et de l'Acier *(f)*
Pt Comunidade Europeia do
Carvão e do Aço *(f)*

**Comunità Europea
dell'Energia Atomica** *(f)* It
De Europäische Atomge-
meinschaft *(f)*
En European Atomic Energy
Community

Es Comunidad Europea de
Energía Atómica *(f)*
Fr Communauté Européenne
de l'Énergie Atomique *(f)*
Pt Comunidade Europeia de
Energia Atómica *(f)*

con avaria It
De havariert
En with average (WA)
Es con avería
Fr avarié
Pt com avaria

con avería Es
De havariert
En with average (WA)
Fr avarié
It con avaria
Pt com avaria

conceder (um desconto) Pt
De gewähren (einen Rabatt)
En allow (a discount)
Es conceder (un descuento)
Fr consentir (une remise)
It concedere (uno sconto)

conceder (un descuento) Es
De gewähren (einen Rabatt)
En allow (a discount)
Fr consentir (une remise)
It concedere (uno sconto)
Pt conceder (um desconto)

conceder compensação Pt
De Schadenersatz zugeste-
hen
En award damages
Es conceder daños
Fr adjuger des dommages-
intérêts
It concedere i danni

conceder daños Es
De Schadenersatz zugeste-
hen
En award damages
Fr adjuger des dommages-
intérêts
It concedere i danni
Pt conceder compensação

concedere (uno sconto) It
De gewähren (einen Rabatt)
En allow (a discount)
Es conceder (un descuento)
Fr consentir (une remise)
Pt conceder (um desconto)

concedere i danni It
De Schadenersatz zugeste-
hen
En award damages
Es conceder daños
Fr adjuger des dommages-
intérêts
Pt conceder compensação

**concedere la libertà provvi-
soria su cauzione** It
De gegen Haftkaution freige-
ben
En grant bail
Es conceder fianza
Fr admettre une caution
Pt autorizar caução

conceder fianza Es
De gegen Haftkaution
freigeben
En grant bail
Fr admettre une caution
It concedere la libertà
provvisoria su cauzione
Pt autorizar caução

concentrato sul capitale It
De kapitalintensiv
En capital-intensive
Es intensivo de capital
Fr intensif de capital
Pt intensivo em termos de
capital

concepteur-rédacteur (m)
Fr
De Textverfasser (m)
En copywriter
Es redactor (m)
It redattore pubblicitario (m)
Pt redactor de publicidade
(m)

concesión (f) n Es
De Konzession (f)
En franchise; concession
Fr concession (f)
It concessione (f)
Pt concessão (f)

concesión (de una patente)
(f) Es
De Erteilung (eines Patentes)
(f)
En grant (of a patent)
Fr délivrance (d'un brevet) (f)

It concessione (di brevetto)
(f)
Pt concessão (de uma patente) (f)

concesión minera (f) Es
De Bergwerkskonzession (f)
En mineral concession
Fr concession minière (f)
It concessione mineraria (f)
Pt concessão mineira (f)

concesión recíproca (f) Es
De Geben und Nehmen (n)
En give and take
Fr concessions mutuelles (f
pl)
It concessione reciproca (f)
Pt concessão mútua (f)

concessão (f) n Pt
De Konzession f)
En franchise; concession
Es concesión (f)
Fr concession (f)
It concessione (f)

concessão (de uma patente)
(f) Pt
De Erteilung (eines Patentes)
(f)
En grant (of patent)
Es concesión (de una
patente) (f)
Fr délivrance (d'un brevet) (f)
It concessione (di brevetto)
(f)

concessão mineira (f) Pt
De Bergwerkskonzession (f)
En mineral concession
Es concesión minera (f)
Fr concession minière (f)
It concessione mineraria (f)

concessão mútua (f) Pt
De Geben und Nehmen (n)
En give and take
Es concesión recíproca (f)
Fr concessions mutuelles
(f pl)
It concessione reciproca (f)

concession n En, Fr (f)
De Konzession (f)
Es concesión (f)
It concessione (f)
Pt concessão (f)

concessione (f) n It
De Konzession (f)
En concession; franchise
Es concesión (f)
Fr concession (f)
Pt concessão (f)

concessione (di brevetto) (f)
It
De Erteilung (eines Patentes)
(f)
En grant (of a patent)
Es concesión (de una paten-
te) (f)
Fr délivrance (d'un brevet) (f)
Pt concessão (de uma paten-
te) (f)

concessione mineraria (f) It
De Bergwerkskonzession (f)
En mineral concession
Es concesión minera (f)
Fr concession minière (f)
Pt concessão mineira (f)

concessione reciproca (f) It
De Geben und Nehmen
En give and take
Es concesión recíproca (f)
Fr concessions mutuelles (f)
Pt concessão mútua (f)

concession minière (f) Fr
De Bergwerkskonzession (f)
En mineral concession
Es concesión minera (f)
It concessione mineraria (f)
Pt concessão mineira (f)

concessions mutuelles (f pl)
Fr
De Geben und Nehmen
En give and take
Es concesión recíproca (f)
It concessione reciproca (f)
Pt concessão mútua (f)

concessões sobre capital
(f pl) Pt
De Steuerbegünstigung auf
Anlagen (f)
En capital allowances
Es deducciones fiscales
sobre inversiones (f pl)
Fr déductions fiscales sur les
investissements (f pl)
It deduzioni fiscali sugli in-
vestimenti (f pl)

concezione difettosa *(f)* It
De schlechte Ausführung *(f)*
En faulty design
Es diseño defectuoso *(m)*
Fr construction fautive *(f)*
Pt desenho defeituoso *(m)*

concierge *(m) n* Fr
De Hausmeister *(m)*
En hall-porter
Es conserje *(m)*
It portiere *(m)*
Pt porteiro *(m)*

conciliação *(f) n* Pt
De Schlichtung *(f)*
En conciliation
Es conciliación *(f)*
Fr conciliation *(f)*
It conciliazione *(f)*

conciliación *(f) n* Es
De Schlichtung *(f)*
En conciliation
Fr conciliation *(f)*
It conciliazione *(f)*
Pt conciliação *(f)*

conciliation *n* En, Fr *(f)*
De Schlichtung *(f)*
Es conciliación *(f)*
It conciliazione *(f)*
Pt conciliação *(f)*

conciliazione *(f) n* It
De Schlichtung *(f)*
En conciliation
Es conciliación *(f)*
Fr conciliation *(f)*
Pt conciliação *(f)*

concordat *(m) n* Fr
De Vergleichsabkommen *(n)*
En deed of composition
Es concordato *(m)*
It atto di concordato *(m)*
Pt concordata (por escrito) *(f)*

concordata (por escrito) *(f)* Pt
De Vergleichsabkommen *(m)*
En deed of composition
Es concordato *(m)*
Fr concordat *(m)*
It atto di concordato *(m)*

concordato *(m)* Es
De Vergleichsabkommen *(n)*
En deed of composition
Fr concordat *(m)*

It atto di concordato *(m)*
Pt concordata (por escrito) *(f)*

concorrenza *(f) n* It
De Wettbewerb *(m)*
En competition
Es competición *(f)*
Fr concurrence *(f)*
Pt competição *(f)*

concurrence *(f) n* Fr
De Wettbewerb *(m)*
En competition
Es competición *(f)*
It concorrenza *(f)*
Pt competição *(f)*

concurrencer *vb* Fr
De Konkurrenz machen
En compete
Es competir
It competere
Pt competir

concurso de acreedores *(m)*
Es
De Gläubigerversammlung *(f)*
En meeting of creditors
Fr assemblée de créanciers
(f)
It convocazione dei creditori
(f)
Pt reunião de credores *(f)*

condição *(f) n* Pt
De Bedingung *(f)*
En condition
Es condición *(f)*
Fr condition *(f)*
It condizione *(f)*

condição prévia *(f)* Pt
De aufschiebende Bedingung
(f)
En condition precedent
Es previa condición *(f)*
Fr condition suspensive *(f)*
It condizione sospensiva *(f)*

condición *(f) n* Es
De Bedingung *(f)*
En condition
Fr condition *(f)*
It condizione *(f)*
Pt condição *(f)*

condicional *adj* Es, Pt
De bedingt
En conditional

Fr conditionnel
It condizionale

condicionamento do ar *(m)*
Pt
De Klimatisierung *(f)*
En air-conditioning
Es acondicionamiento de aire
(m)
Fr climatisation *(f)*
It condizionamento dell'aria
(m)

condiciones *(f pl) n* Es
De Bedingungen *(f pl)*
En terms
Fr conditions *(f pl)*
It condizioni *(f pl)*
Pt condições *(f pl)*

condiciones del mercado
(f pl) Es
De Marktumstände *(f pl)*
En state of the market
Fr état du marché *(m)*
It condizioni del mercato
(f pl)
Pt situação do mercado *(f)*

condiciones de pago *(f pl)* Es
De Zahlungsbedingungen
(f pl)
En payment terms
Fr conditions de paiement
(f pl)
It condizioni di pagamento
(f pl)
Pt condições de pagamento
(f pl)

condiciones de trabajo *(f pl)*
Es
De Arbeitsbedingungen *(f pl)*
En working conditions
Fr conditions de travail *(f pl)*
It condizioni di lavoro *(f pl)*
Pt condições de trabalho *(f pl)*

condiciones implícitas *(f pl)*
Es
De stillschweigende Bedin-
gungen *(f pl)*
En implied terms
Fr conditions implicites *(f pl)*
It condizioni implicite *(f pl)*
Pt condições implícitas *(f pl)*

condiciones normales *(f pl)*
Es
De Standardbedingungen
(f pl)
En standard conditions
Fr conditions courantes *(f pl)*
It condizioni normali *(f pl)*
Pt condições normais *(f pl)*

condições *(f pl)* Pt
De Bedingungen *(f pl)*
En terms
Es condiciones *(f pl)*
Fr conditions *(f pl)*
It condizioni *(f pl)*

condições de pagamento
(f pl) Pt
De Zahlungsbedingungen
(f pl)
En payment terms
Es condiciones de pago *(f pl)*
Fr conditions de paiement
(f pl)
It condizioni di pagamento
(f pl)

condições de trabalho *(f pl)*
Pt
De Arbeitsbedingungen *(f pl)*
En working conditions
Es condiciones de trabajo
(f pl)
Fr conditions de travail *(f pl)*
It condizioni di lavoro *(f pl)*

condições implícitas *(f pl)* Pt
De stillschweigende Bedin-
gungen *(f pl)*
En implied terms
Es condiciones implícitas
(f pl)
Fr conditions implicites *(t pl)*
It condizioni implicite *(f pl)*

condições normais *(f pl)* Pt
De Standardbedingungen *(f
pl)*
En standard conditions
Es condiciones normales *(f pl)*
Fr conditions courantes *(f pl)*
It condizioni normali *(f pl)*

condition *n* En, Fr *(f)*
De Bedingung *(f)*
Es condición *(f)*
It condizione *(f)*
Pt condição *(f)*

conditional *adj* En
De bedingt
Es condicional
Fr conditionnel
It condizionale
Pt condicional

conditionnel *adj* Fr
De bedingt
En conditional
Es condicional
It condizionale
Pt condicional

condition precedent En
De aufschiebende Bedingung
(f)
Es previa condición *(f)*
Fr condition suspensive *(f)*
It condizione sospensiva *(f)*
Pt condição prévia *(f)*

conditions *(f pl) n* Fr
De Bedingungen *(f pl)*
En terms
Es condiciones *(f pl)*
It condizioni *(f pl)*
Pt condiçãos *(f pl)*

conditions courantes *(f pl)* Fr
De Standardbedingungen
(f pl)
En standard conditions
Es condiciones normales *(f pl)*
It condizioni normali *(f pl)*
Pt condições normais *(f pl)*

conditions de paiement *(f pl)*
Fr
De Zahlungsbedingungen
(f pl)
En payment terms
Es condiciones de pago *(f pl)*
It condizioni di pagamento
(f pl)
Pt condiçãos de pagamento
(f pl)

conditions de travail *(f pl)* Fr
De Arbeitsbedingungen *(f pl)*
En working conditions
Es condiciones de trabajo
(f pl)
It condizioni di lavoro *(f pl)*
Pt condições de trabalho *(f pl)*

conditions implicites *(f pl)* Fr
De stillschweigende Bedin-
gungen *(f pl)*
En implied terms

Es condiciones implícitas
(f pl)
It condizioni implicite *(f pl)*
Pt condições implícitas *(f pl)*

condition suspensive *(f)* Fr
De aufschiebende Bedingung
(f)
En condition precedent
Es previa condición *(f)*
It condizione sospensiva *(f)*
Pt condição prévia *(f)*

con dividendo Es, It
De mit Dividende
En cum dividend
Fr droit attaché
Pt com dividendo

condizionale *adj* It
De bedingt
En conditional
Es condicional
Fr conditionnel
Pt condicional

condizionamento dell'aria
(m) It
De Klimatisierung *(f)*
En air-conditioning
Es acondicionamiento de aire
(m)
Fr climatisation *(f)*
Pt condicionamento do ar *(m)*

condizione *(f) n* It
De Bedingung
En condition
Es condición *(f)*
Fr condition *(f)*
Pt condição *(f)*

condizione sospensiva *(f)* It
De aufschiebende Bedingung
(f)
En condition precedent
Es previa condición *(f)*
Fr condition suspensive *(f)*
Pt condição prévia *(f)*

condizioni *(f pl) n* It
De Bedingungen *(f pl)*
En terms
Es condiciones *(f pl)*
Fr conditions *(f pl)*
Pt condições *(f pl)*

condizioni del mercato *(f pl)*
It
De Marktumstände *(m pl)*
En state of the market

Es condiciones del mercado
(f pl)
Fr état du marché *(m)*
Pt situação do mercado *(f)*

condizioni di lavoro *(f pl)* It
De Arbeitsbedingungen *(f pl)*
En working conditions
Es condiciones de trabajo
(f pl)
Fr conditions de travail *(f pl)*
Pt condições de trabalho *(f pl)*

condizioni di pagamento
(f pl) It
De Zahlungsbedingungen
(f pl)
En payment terms
Es condiciones de pago *(f pl)*
Fr conditions de paiement
(f pl)
Pt condições de pagamento
(f pl)

condizioni implicite *(f pl)* It
De stillschweigende Bedin-
gungen *(f pl)*
En implied terms
Es condiciones implícitas
(f pl)
Fr conditions implicites *(f pl)*
Pt condições implícitas *(f pl)*

condizioni normali *(f pl)* It
De Standardbedingungen
(f pl)
En standard conditions
Es condiciones normales *(f pl)*
Fr conditions courantes *(f pl)*
Pt condições normais *(f pl)*

condominio *(m)* n It
De Miteigentum *(n)*
En co-ownership
Es copropiedad *(f)*
Fr copropriété *(f)*
Pt co-propriedade *(f)*

condotta leale *(f)* It
De anständige Handlungs-
weise *(f)*
En fair play
Es juego limpio *(m)*
Fr traitement juste *(m)*
Pt jogo limpo *(f)*

con esto Es
De hiermit
En herewith

Fr ci-joint; sous ce pli
It qui unito; con la presente
Pt incluso; junto

conference n En
De Kongreß *(m)*
Es conferencia *(f)*
Fr conférence *(f)*
It conferenza *(f)*
Pt conferência *(f)*

conférence *(f)* n Fr
De Kongreß *(m)*
En conference
Es conferencia *(f)*
It conferenza *(f)*
Pt conferência *(f)*

conferencia *(f)* n Es
De Kongreß *(m)*
En conference
Fr conférence *(f)*
It conferenza *(f)*
Pt conferência *(f)*

conferência *(f)* n Pt
De Kongreß *(m)*
En conference
Es conferencia *(f)*
Fr conférence *(f)*
It conferenza *(f)*

conferenza *(f)* n It
De Kongreß *(m)*
En conference
Es conferencia *(f)*
Fr conférence *(f)*
Pt conferência *(f)*

conférer des pleins pouvoirs
Fr
De eine Vollmacht erteilen
En execute a power of
attorney
Es otorgar poder notarial
It conferire una procura
Pt dar execução a poderes de
procuração

conferire una procura It
De eine Vollmacht erteilen
En execute a power of attor-
ney
Es otorgar poder notarial
Fr conférer des pleins pou-
voirs
Pt dar execução a poderes de
procuração

conferma *(f)* n It
De Bestätigung *(f)*
En confirmation
Es confirmación *(f)*
Fr confirmation *(f)*
Pt confirmação *(f)*

confermar vb It
De bestätigen
En confirm
Es confirmar
Fr confirmer
Pt confirmar

confermare per iscritto It
De schriftlich bestätigen
En confirm in writing
Es confirmar por escrito
Fr confirmer par écrit
Pt confirmar por escrito

confiar vb Es, Pt
De anvertrauen
En entrust
Fr confier
It affidare

confidence trick En
Am confidence game
De Schwindlertrick *(m)*
Es timo *(m)*
Fr escroquerie *(f)*
It truffa all'americana *(f)*
Pt conto do vigário *(m)*

confier vb Fr
De anvertrauen
En entrust
Es confiar
It affidare
Pt confiar

confirm vb En
De bestätigen
Es confirmar
Fr confirmer
It confermare
Pt confirmar

confirmarção *(f)* n Pt
De Bestätigung *(f)*
En confirmation
Es confirmación *(f)*
Fr confirmation *(f)*
It conferma *(f)*

confirmación *(f)* n Es
De Bestätigung *(f)*
En confirmation

Fr confirmation *(f)*
It conferma *(f)*
Pt confirmação *(f)*

confirmar *vb* Es, Pt
De bestätigen
En confirm
Fr confirmer
It confermare

confirmar por escrito Es, Pt
De schriftlich bestätigen
En confirm in writing
Fr confirmer par écrit
It confermare per iscritto

confirmation *n* En, Fr *(f)*
De Bestätigung *(f)*
Es confirmación *(f)*
It conferma *(f)*
Pt confirmação *(f)*

**confirmed irrevocable
letter of credit** En
De bestätigter unwiderruflicher Kreditbrief *(m)*
Es carta de crédito irrevocable confirmada *(f)*
Fr lettre de crédit irrévocable
confirmée *(f)*
Pt carta de crédito irre-
vogável confirmada *(f)*

confirmed letter of credit En
De bestätigter Kreditbrief *(m)*
Es carta de crédito confirma-
da *(f)*
Fr iettre de crédit confirmée
(f)
It lettera di credito confer-
mata *(f)*
Pt carta de crédito confirma-
da *(f)*

confirmer *vb* Fr
De bestätigen
En confirm
Es confirmar
It confermare
Pt confirmar

confirmer par écrit Fr
De schriftlich bestätigen
En confirm in writing
Es confirmar por escrito
It confermare per iscritto
Pt confirmar por escrito

confirm in writing En
De schriftlich bestätigen
Es confirmar por escrito
Fr confirmer par écrit
It confermare per iscritto
Pt confirmar por escrito

conflict *n* En
De Konflikt *(m)*
Es conflicto *(m)*
Fr conflit *(m)*
It conflitto *(m)*
Pt conflito *(m)*

conflicto *(m) n* Es
De Konflikt *(m)*
En conflict
Fr conflit *(m)*
It conflitto *(m)*
Pt conflito *(m)*

conflict of interest En
De widerstreitende Interessen
(n pl)
Es pugna de intereses *(f)*
Fr opposition d'intérêts *(f)*
It conflitto d'interessi *(m)*
Pt conflito de interesses *(m)*

conflicto laboral *(m)* Es
De Arbeitskonflikt *(m)*
En industrial dispute
Fr conflit ouvrier *(m)*
It vertenza operaia *(f)*
Pt conflito de trabalho *(m)*

conflit *(m) n* Fr
De Konflikt *(m)*
En conflict
Es conflicto *(m)*
It conflitto *(m)*
Pt conflito *(m)*

conflit du travail *(m)* Fr
De Arbeitsstreitigkeit *(f)*
En trade dispute
Es conflicto laboral *(m)*
It vertenza di lavoro *(f)*
Pt conflito comercial *(m)*

conflito *(m) n* Pt
De Konflikt *(m)*
En conflict
Es conflicto *(m)*
Fr conflit *(m)*
It conflitto *(m)*

conflito comercial *(m)* Pt
De Arbeitsstreitigkeit *(f)*
En trade dispute

Es conflicto laboral *(m)*
Fr conflit du travail *(m)*
It vertenza di lavoro *(f)*

conflito de interesses *(m)* Pt
De widerstreitende Interessen
(n pl)
En conflict of interest
Es pugna de intereses *(f)*
Fr opposition d'intérêts *(f)*
It conflitto d'interessi *(m)*

conflito de trabalho *(m)* Pt
De Arbeitskonflikt *(m)*
En industrial dispute
Es conflicto laboral *(m)*
Fr conflit ouvrier *(m)*
It vertenza operaia *(f)*

conflit ouvrier *(m)* Fr
De Arbeitskonflikt *(m)*
En industrial dispute
Es conflicto laboral *(m)*
It vertenza operaia *(m)*
Pt conflito de trabalho *(m)*

conflitto *(m) n* It
De Konflikt *(m)*
En conflict
Es conflicto *(m)*
Fr conflit *(m)*
Pt conflito *(m)*

conflitto d'interessi *(m)* It
De widerstreitende Interessen
(n pl)
En conflict of interest
Es pugna de intereses *(f)*
Fr opposition d'intérêts *(f)*
Pt conflito de interesses *(m)*

conforme à Fr
De in Übereinstimmung mit
En in accordance with
Es en conformidad con
It in conformità con
Pt em conformidade com

congedare *vb* It
De entlassen
En dismiss
Am fire
Es despedir
Fr congédier
Pt despedir

congédiement *(m) n* Fr
De Entlassung *(f)*
En dismissal

Am firing
Es despido *(m)*
It licenziamento *(m)*
Pt despedimento *(m)*

congédier *vb* Fr
De entlassen
En dismiss
Am fire
Es despedir
It congedare
Pt despedir

congédier un employé Fr
De einen Arbeitnehmer ent-
   lassen
En discharge an employee
Am fire an employee
Es despedir a un empleado
It licenziare un impiegato
Pt despedir um empregado

congelação de salários *(f)* Pt
De Lohnstopp *(m)*
En wage-freeze
Es bloqueo de salarios *(m)*
Fr blocage des salaires *(m)*
It blocco dei salari *(m)*

congés payés *(m pl)* Fr
De bezahlter Urlaub *(m)*
En holidays with pay
Es vacaciones retribuidas
   (f pl)
It vacanze retribuite *(f pl)*
Pt férias pagas *(f pl)*

congettura *(f)* n It
De Mutmaßung *(f)*
En guess-work
Es conjetura *(f)*
Fr conjecture *(f)*
Pt conjectura *(f)*

conhecimento *(m)* n Pt
De Kenntnis *(f)*
En knowledge
Es conocimientos *(m pl)*
Fr connaissance *(f)*
It conoscenza *(f)*

conhecimento (de em-
   barque) *(m)* Pt
De Konnossement *(n)*
En bill of lading
Es conocimiento (de em-
   barque) *(m)*
Fr connaissement *(m)*
It polizza di carico *(f)*

**conhecimento com em-
   bargos** *(m)* Pt
De einschränkendes Konnossement *(n)*
En foul (dirty) bill of lading
Es conocinemiento de em-
   barque con objecciones
   (m)
Fr connaissement avec
   réserve *(m)*
It polizza di carico con riserve *(f)*

**conhecimento de carga
   embarcada** *(m)* Pt
De Hafenkonnossement *(n)*
En shipped bill of lading
Es conocimiento de embar-
   que a bordo *(m)*
Fr connaissement de mar-
   chandises à bord *(m)*
It polizza di carico con mer-
   ce a bordo *(f)*

**conhecimento sem
   embargos** *(m)* Pt
De echtes Konnossement *(n)*
En clean bill of lading
Es conocimiento de embar-
   que sin objecciones *(m)*
Fr connaissement sans
   réserve *(m)*
It polizza di carico senza
   riserve *(f)*

conjectura *(f)* n Pt
De Mutmaßung *(f)*
En guess-work
Es conjetura *(f)*
Fr conjecture *(f)*
It congettura *(f)*

conjecture *(m)* n Fr
De Mutmaßung *(f)*
En guess-work
Es conjetura *(f)*
It congettura *(f)*
Pt conjectura *(f)*

conjetura *(f)* n Es
De Mutmaßung *(f)*
En guess-work
Fr conjecture *(f)*
It congettura *(f)*
Pt conjetura *(f)*

**conjointement et solidaire-
   ment** Fr
De gesamtschuldnerisch
En jointly and severally

Es en conjunto y separada-
   mente
It solidalmente e individual-
   mente
Pt em conjunto e por vários

conjunto de rutinas *(m)* Es
De Programmausrüstung *(f)*
En (computer) software
Fr software *(m)*
It programmatura; software
   (fm)
Pt sistema lógico; software
   (m)

connaissance *(f)* n Fr
De Kenntnis *(f)*
En knowledge
Es conocimientos *(m pl)*
It conoscenza *(f)*
Pt conhecimento *(m)*

connaissement *(m)* Fr
De Konnossement *(n)*
En bill of lading
Es conocimiento (de em-
   barque *(m)*
It polizza di carico *(f)*
Pt comhecimento *(m)*

**connaissement avec
   réserve** *(m)* Fr
De einschränkendes Konnossement *(n)*
En foul (dirty) bill of lading
Es conocimiento de embar-
   que con objecciones *(m)*
It polizza di carico con
   riserve *(f)*
Pt conhecimento com
   embarque *(m)*

**connaissement de mar-
   chandises à bord** *(m)* Fr
De Hafenkonnossement *(n)*
En shipped bill of lading
Es conocimiento de embar-
   que a bordo *(m)*
It polizza di carico con
   merce a bordo *(f)*
Pt conhecimento de carga
   embarcada *(m)*

**connaissement sans
   réserve** *(m)* Fr
De echtes Konnossement *(n)*
En clean bill of lading
Es conocimiento de embar-
   que sin objecciones *(m)*

It polizza di carico senza
    riserve (f)
Pt conhecimento sem
    embargos (m)

**conocimiento (de em-
barque)** (m) Es
De Konnossement (n)
En bill of lading
Fr connaissement (m)
It polizza di carico (f)
Pt conhecimento (m)

**conocimiento de embarque
a bordo** (m) Es
De Hafenkonnossement (n)
En shipped bill of lading
Fr connaissement de mar-
    chandises á bord (m)
It polizza di carico con mer-
    ce a bordo (f)
Pt conhecimento de carga
    embarcada (m)

**conocimiento de embarque
con objecciones** (m) Es
De einschränkendes Konnos-
    sement (n)
En foul (dirty) bill of lading
Fr connaissement avec
    réserve (m)
It polizza di carico con riser-
    ve (f)
Pt conhecimento com em-
    bargos (m)

**conocimiento de embarque
sin objecciones** (m) Es
De echtes Konnossement (n)
En clean bill of lading
Fr connaissement sans
    réserve (m)
It polizza di carico senza ri-
    serve (f)
Pt conhecimento sem em-
    bargos (m)

conocimientos (m pl) n Es
De Kenntnis (f)
En knowledge
Fr connaissance (f)
It conoscenza (f)
Pt conhecimento (m)

conoscenza (f) n It
De Kenntnis (f)
En knowledge
Es conocimientos (m pl)
Fr connaissance (f)
Pt conhecimento (m)

con plico a parte It
De getrennt
En under separate cover
Es por separado
Fr sous pli séparé
Pt em separado

con recurso Es
De mit Rückgriff
En with recourse
Fr avec droit de recours
It con ricorso
Pt com recurso

con ricorso It
De mit Rückgriff
En with recourse
Es con recurso
Fr avec droit de recours
Pt com recurso

consegna (f) n It
De Lieferung; Versendung (f)
En delivery; consignment
Es entrega; consignación (f)
Fr livraison; envoi (f m)
Pt entrega; consignação (f)

consegna a termine (f) It
De Terminlieferung (f)
En forward delivery
Es entrega futura (f)
Fr livraison à terme (f)
Pt entrega futura (f)

consegna deficiente (f) It
De mangelhafte Lieferung (f)
En short delivery
Es entrega deficiente (f)
Fr livraison incomplète (f)
Pt entrega insuficiente (f)

consegna franco It
De portofreie Lieferung
En delivery free
Es libre entrega
Fr livré franco
Pt remessa gratuita

consegnare vb It
De konsignieren; übersenden
En consign
Es consignar
Fr consigner
Pt consignar

consegnatario (m) n It
De Empfänger (m)
En consignee

Es consignatario (m)
Fr destinataire (m)
Pt consignatário (m)

conseil (m) n Fr
De Rat; Berater (m)
En council; consultant
Es consejo; consultor (m)
It consiglio; consulente (m)
Pt conselho; consultor (m)

conseil d'administration (m)
    Fr
De Vorstand (m)
En board of directors
Es consejo de administración
    (m)
It consiglio d'amministra-
    zione (m)
Pt direcção (f)

conseil en bravets (m) Fr
De Patentanwalt (m)
En patent agent
Es agente de patentes (m)
It agente di brevetti (m)
Pt agente de patentes (m)

conseil en publicité (m) Fr
De Werbeberater (m)
En advertising consultant
Es consultor de publicidad
    (m)
It consulente di pubblicità
    (m)
Pt perito de publicidade (m)

consejo (m) n Es
De Rat (m)
En council
Fr conseil (m)
It consiglio (m)
Pt conselho (m)

consejo consultivo (m) Es
De Beratungsausschuß (m)
En advisory board
Fr comité consultatif (m)
It consiglio consultivo (m)
Pt comité consultivo (m)

consejo de administración
    (m) Es
De Vorstand (m)
En board of directors
Fr conseil d'administration
    (m)
It consiglio d'amministra-
    zione (m)
Pt direcção (f)

conselho *(m) n* Pt
De Rat *(m)*
En council
Es consejo *(m)*
Fr conseil *(m)*
Pt consiglio *(m)*

consentir (une remise) Fr
De gewähren (einen Rabatt)
En allow (a discount)
Es conceder (un descuento)
It concedere (uno sconto)
Pt conceder (um desconto)

consequential damages En
De immaterieller Schaden *(m)*
Es daños indirectos *(m pl)*
Fr dommages indirects *(m pl)*
It danni indiretti *(m pl)*
Pt danos decorrentes *(m pl)*

consequential loss En
De Folgeschaden *(m)*
Es pérdida indirecta *(f)*
Fr perte indirect *(f)*
It perdita indiretta *(f)*
Pt perda por consequência *(f)*

conserje *(m) n* Es
De Hausmeister *(m)*
En hall-porter
Fr concierge *(m)*
It portiere *(m)*
Pt porteiro *(m)*

consertar *vb* Pt
De reparieren
En repair
Es reparar; componer
Fr réparer; réfectionner
It riparare; rifare

conservative estimate En
De vorsichtige Schätzung *(f)*
Es presupuesto prudente *(m)*
Fr évaluation prudente *(f)*
It valutazione prudente *(f)*
Pt avaliação cautelosa *(f)*

consiglio *(m) n* It
De Rat *(m)*
En council
Es consejo *(m)*
Fr conseil *(m)*
Pt conselho *(m)*

consiglio consultivo *(m)* It
De Beratungsausschuß *(m)*
En advisory board

Es consejo consultivo *(m)*
Fr comité consultatif *(m)*
Pt comité consultivo *(m)*

consignação *(f) n* Pt
De Versendung; Übertragung *(f)*
En consignment; assignment
Es consignación; cesión *(f)*
Fr expédition; cession *(f)*
It consegna; cessione *(f)*

consignación *(f) n* Es
De Versendung *(f)*
En consignment
Fr envoi; expédition *(m f)*
It consegna; spedizione *(f)*
Pt consignação *(f)*

consignador *(m) n* Es, Pt
De Absender *(m)*
En consignor
Fr expéditeur *(m)*
It speditore *(m)*

consignar *vb* Es, Pt
De konsignieren, übersenden
En consign
Fr consigner
It consegnare

consignatario *(m) n* Es
De Empfänger *(m)*
En consignee
Fr destinataire *(m)*
It consegnatario *(m)*
Pt consignatário *(m)*

consignatário *(m) n* Pt
De Empfänger *(m)*
En consignee
Es consignatario *(m)*
Fr destinataire *(m)*
It consegnatario *(m)*

consignee *n* En
De Empfänger *(m)*
Es consignatario *(m)*
Fr destinataire *(m)*
It consegnatario *(m)*
Pt consignatário *(m)*

consigner *vb* Fr
De konsignieren; übersenden
En consign
Es consignar
It consegnare
Pt consignar

consignment *n* En
De Versendung *(f)*
Es consignación *(f)*
Fr envoi; expédition *(m f)*
It consegna; spedizione *(f)*
Pt consignação *(f)*

consignment note En
De Frachtbrief *(m)*
Es nota de consignación *(f)*
Fr lettre de voiture *(f)*
It nota di spedizione *(f)*
Pt gua de consignação *(f)*

consignor *n* En
De Absender *(m)*
Es consignador *(m)*
Fr expéditeur *(m)*
It speditore *(m)*
Pt consignante *(m)*

consolato *(m) n* It
De Konsulat *(n)*
En consulate
Es consulado *(m)*
Fr consulat *(m)*
Pt consulado *(m)*

console *(m) n* It
De Konsul *(m)*
En consul
Es cónsul *(m)*
Fr consul *(m)*
Pt cônsul *(m)*

consolidado *adj* Es, Pt
De konsolidiert
En consolidated
Fr consolidé
It consolidato

consolidare *vb* It
De fundieren
En fund
Es fundar; consolidar
Fr fonder; consolider
Pt dotar de fundos

consolidated *adj* En
De konsolidiert
Es consolidado
Fr consolidé
It consolidato
Pt consolidado

consolidated accounts En
De konsolidierter Kontenab-
 schluß *(m)*
Es cuentas consolidadas *(f pl)*

Fr comptes consolidés *(m pl)*
It conti consolidati *(m pl)*
Pt contas consolidadas *(f pl)*

consolidato *adj* It
De konsolidiert
En consolidated
Es consolidado
Fr consolidé
Pt consolidado

consolidé *adj* Fr
De konsolidiert
En consolidated
Es consolidado
It consolidato
Pt consolidado

consommateur *(m)* n Fr
De Verbraucher; Konsument
(m)
En consumer
Es consumidor *(m)*
It consumatore *(m)*
Pt consumidor *(m)*

consommation *(f)* n Fr
De Verbrauch *(m)*
En consumption
Es consumición *(f)*
It consumo *(m)*
Pt consumo *(m)*

consorcio *(m)* n Es
De Konsortium *(n)*
En consortium
Fr consortium *(m)*
It consorzio *(m)*
Pt consórcio *(m)*

consórcio *(m)* n Pt
De Konsortium *(n)*
En consortium
Es consorcio *(m)*
Fr consortium *(m)*
It consorzio *(m)*

consórcio de seguradores
(m) Pt
De Versicherungssyndikat *(n)*
En underwriting syndicate
(insurance)
Es sindicato de seguros *(m)*
Fr syndicat d'assureurs *(m)*
It sindacato di assicuratori
(m)

consórcio de subscritores
(m) Pt
De Emissionssyndikat *(n)*
En underwriting syndicate
(new issues)
Es grupo de suscriptores *(m)*
Fr syndicat de garantie *(m)*
It consorzio finanziario *(m)*

consortium n En, Fr *(m)*
De Konsortium *(n)*
Es consorcio *(m)*
It consorzio *(m)*
Pt consórcio *(m)*

consorzio *(m)* n It
De Konsortium *(n)*
En consortium
Es consorcio *(n)*
Fr consortium *(m)*
Pt consórcio *(m)*

consorzio finanziario *(m)* It
De Syndikat *(n)*
En syndicate
Es sindicato *(m)*
Fr syndicat *(m)*
Pt sindicato *(m)*

consorzio per investimenti
(m) It
De Investment-Trust *(m)*
En investment trust
Es fideicomiso de inversiones
(m)
Fr société fiduciaire de
placements *(f)*
Pt instituição de investimentos
(f)

constituer *vb* Fr
De bilden
En form; constitute
Es constituir
It costituire
Pt constituir

constituir *vb* Es, Pt
De bilden
En form; constitute
Fr constituer
It costituire

costituire *vb* It
De bilden
En form; constitute
Es constituir
Fr constituer
Pt constituir

construction électrique *(f)* Fr
De Elektrotechnik *(f)*
En electrical engineering
Es ingeniería eléctrica *(f)*
It elettrotecnica *(f)*
Pt engenharia electrotécnica
(f)

construction fautive *(f)* Fr
De schlechte Ausführung *(f)*
En faulty design
Es diseño defectuoso *(m)*
It concezione difettosa *(f)*
Pt desenho defeituoso *(m)*

construction mécanique *(f)*
Fr
De Maschinenbau *(m)*
En mechanical engineering
Es ingeniería mecánica *(f)*
It ingegneria meccanica *(f)*
Pt engenharia mecânica *(f)*

constructive total loss Fr
De angenommener Totalver-
lust *(m)*
Es pérdida total constructiva
(f)
Fr perte réputée totale *(f)*
It perdita presunta totale *(f)*
Pt perda total construtiva *(f)*

construtor de obras *(m)* Pt
De Bauunternehmer *(m)*
En building contractor
Es contratista de obras *(m)*
Fr entrepreneur de bâtiment
(m)
It impresa edile *(f)*

consul n En, Fr *(m)*
De Konsul *(m)*
Es cónsul *(m)*
It console *(m)*
Pt cônsul *(m)*

cónsul *(m)* n Es
De Konsul *(m)*
En consul
Fr consul *(m)*
It console *(m)*
Pt cônsul *(m)*

cônsul *(m)* n Pt
De Konsul *(m)*
En consul
Es cónsul *(m)*
Fr consul *(m)*
It console *(m)*

consulado *(m) n* Es, Pt
De Konsulat *(n)*
En consulate
Fr consulat *(m)*
It consolato *(m)*

consular invoice En
De Konsulatsfaktura *(f)*
Es factura consular *(f)*
Fr facture consulaire *(f)*
It fattura consolare *(f)*
Pt factura consular *(f)*

consulat *(m) n* Fr
De Konsulat *(n)*
En consulate
Es consulado *(m)*
It consolato *(m)*
Pt consulado *(m)*

consulate *n* En
De Konsulat *(n)*
Es consulado *(m)*
Fr consulat *(m)*
It consolato *(m)*
Pt consulado *(m)*

consulente *(m) n* It
De Berater *(m)*
En consultant
Es consultor *(m)*
Fr conseil *(m)*
Pt consultor *(m)*

consulente di direzione
aziendale *(m)* It
De Geschäftsführungsberater
(m)
En management consultant
Es asesor administrativo *(m)*
Fr ingénieur-conseil en or-
ganisation *(m)*
Pt perito de administração *(m)*

consulente di pubblicità *(m)*
It
De Werbeberater *(m)*
En advertising consultant
Es consultor de publicidad
(m)
Fr conseil en publicité *(m)*
Pt perito de publicidade *(m)*

consultant *n* En
De Berater *(m)*
Es consultor *(m)*
Fr conseil *(m)*
It consulente *(m)*
Pt consultor *(m)*

consultatif *adj* Fr
De Beratung
En advisory
Es consultivo
It consultivo
Pt consultivo

consultivo *adj* Es, It, Pt
De Beratungs-
En advisory
Fr consultatif

consultor *(m) n* Es, Pt
De Berater *(m)*
En consultant
Fr conseil *(m)*
It consulente *(m)*

consultor de publicidad *(m)*
Es
De Werbeberater *(m)*
En advertising consultant
Fr conseil en publicité *(m)*
It consulente di pubblicità
(m)
Pt perito de publicidade *(m)*

consumatore *(m) n* It
De Verbraucher, Konsument
(m)
En consumer
Es consumidor *(m)*
Fr consommateur *(m)*
Pt consumidor *(m)*

consumer *n* En
De Verbraucher; Konsument
(m)
Es consumidor *(m)*
Fr consommateur *(m)*
It consumatore *(m)*
Pt consumidor *(m)*

consumer durables En
De dauerhafte Konsumgüter
(n pl)
Es bienes de consumo duraderos *(m pl)*
Fr biens de consommation
durables *(m pl)*
It beni di consumo durabili
(m pl)
Pt artigos de consumo perduráveis *(m pl)*

consumer goods En
De Konsumgüter *(n pl)*
Es bienes de consumo *(m pl)*

Fr biens de consommation
(m pl)
It beni di consumo *(m pl)*
Pt bens de consumo *(m pl)*

consumer group En
De Abnehmerverein *(m)*
Es grupo de consumidores
(m)
Fr groupe consommateur *(m)*
It gruppo di consumatori *(m)*
Pt grupo de consumidores
(m)

consumer non-durables En
De nichtdauerhafte Konsumgüter *(n pl)*
Es bienes de consumo perecederos *(m pl)*
Fr biens de consommation
non-durables *(m pl)*
It beni di consumo non durevoli *(m pl)*
Pt bens de consumo não
duráveis *(m pl)*

consumición *(f) n* Es
De Verbrauch *(m)*
En consumption
Fr consommation *(f)*
It consumo *(m)*
Pt consumo *(m)*

consumidor *(m) n* Es, Pt
De Verbraucher; Konsument
(m)
En consumer
Fr consommateur *(m)*
It consumatore *(m)*

consumo *(m) n* It, Pt
De Verbrauch *(m)*
En consumption
Es consumición *(f)*
Fr consommation *(f)*

consumo naturale *(m)* It
De natürlicher Abgang *(m)*
En natural wastage
Es merma natural *(f)*
Fr déperdition naturelle *(f)*
Pt desperdício natural *(m)*

consumption *n* En
De Verbrauch *(m)*
Es consumición *(f)*
Fr consommation *(f)*
It consumo *(m)*
Pt consumo *(m)*

conta (bancária) *(f) n* Pt
De Konto *(n)*
En account
Es cuenta *(f)*
Fr compte *(m)*
It conto *(m)*

conta *(f) n* Pt
De Rechnung *(f)*
En bill; account
Es cuenta, nota *(f)*
Fr compte; note *(m f)*
It conto; nota *(m f)*

conta a descoberto *(f)* Pt
De Überziehung *(f)*
En overdraft
Es sobregiro; saldo deudor
    (m)
Fr découvert; solde débiteur
    (m)
It scoperto *(m)*

conta bancária *(f)* Pt
De Bankkonto *(n)*
En bank account
Es cuenta bancaria *(f)*
Fr compte en banque *(m)*
It conto in banca *(m)*

contabile *(m)* It
De Buchhalter *(m)*
En accountant
Es contador *(m)*
Fr comptable *(m)*
Pt contabilista *(m)*

**contabile dei costi di produ-
zione** *(m)* It
De Kalkulator *(m)*
En cost accountant
Es contable de costes *(m)*
Fr comptable de prix de
    revient *(m)*
Pt calculador de custos *(m)*

contabilidad *(f) n* Es
De Buchhaltung *(f)*
En accountancy; book-
    keeping
Fr comptabilité *(f)*
It contabilità *(f)*
Pt contabilidade *(f)*

contabilidade *(f) n* Pt
De Buchhaltung *(f)*
En accountancy; book-
    keeping
Es contabilidad *(f)*

Fr comptabilité *(f)*
It contabilità *(f)*

**contabilidad por partida
sencilla** *(f)* Es
De einfache Buchführung *(f)*
En single-entry book-keep-
    ing
Fr comptabilité en partie
    simple *(f)*
It contabilità in partita sem-
    plice *(f)*
Pt contabilização por lança-
    mento simples *(f)*

contabilista *(m) n* Pt
De Buchhalter *(m)*
En accountant
Es contador *(m)*
Fr comptable *(m)*
It contabile *(m)*

contabilità *(f) n* It
De Buchhaltung *(f)*
En accountancy; book-
    keeping
Es contabilidad *(f)*
Fr comptabilité *(f)*
Pt contabilidade *(f)*

**contabilità in partita
semplice** *(f)* It
De einfache Buchführung *(f)*
En single-entry book-keep-
    ing
Es contabilidad por partida
    sencilla *(f)*
Fr comptabilité en partie
    simple *(f)*
Pt contabilização por lança-
    mento simples *(f)*

**contabilização por lança-
mento simples** *(f)* Pt
De einfache Buchführung *(f)*
En single-entry book-keep-
    ing
Es contabilidad por partida
    sencila *(f)*
Fr comptabilité en partie
    simple *(f)*
It contabilità in partie sem-
    plice *(f)*

contable *(m)* Es
De Buchhalter *(m)*
En ledger clerk
Am book-keeper
Fr commis-comptable *(m)*

It contabile *(m)*
Pt empregado de contabili-
    dade *(m)*

contable de costes *(m)* Es
De Kalkulator *(m)*
En cost accountant
Fr comptable de prix de re-
    vient *(m)*
It contabile dei costi di pro-
    duzione *(m)*
Pt calculador de custos *(m)*

conta bloqueada *(f)* Pt
De gesperrtes Konto *(n)*
En blocked account
Es cuenta bloqueada *(f)*
Fr compte bloqué *(m)*
It conto bloccato *(m)*

conta comercial *(f)* Pt
De Handelskonto *(n)*
En trade account
Es cuenta comercial *(f)*
Fr compte commercial *(m)*
It conto commerciale *(m)*

conta conjunta *(f)* Pt
De Gemeinschaftskonto *(n)*
En joint account
Es cuenta común *(f)*
Fr compte joint *(m)*
It conto in comune *(m)*

conta corrente *(f)* Pt
De Kontokorrent *(n)*
En current account
Am checking account
Es cuenta corriente *(f)*
Fr compte courant *(m)*
It conto corrente *(m)*

conta de adiantamentos *(f)*
    Pt
De Darlehenskonto *(n)*
En advance account
Es cuenta de anticipos *(f)*
Fr compte d'avances *(m)*
It conto anticipo *(m)*

conta de ágio *(f)* Pt
De Agiokonto *(n)*
En agio account
Es cuenta de agio *(f)*
Fr compte d'agio *(m)*
It conto d'aggio *(m)*

conta de apropriação *(f)* Pt
De Rückstellungskonto *(n)*
En appropriation account
Es cuenta de apropiación *(f)*
Fr compte d'affectation *(m)*
It conto di stanziamento *(m)*

conta de capital *(f)* Pt
De Kapitalkonto *(n)*
En capital account
Es cuenta de capital *(f)*
Fr compte capital *(m)*
It conto capitale *(m)*

conta de compensação de transacções *(f)* Pt
De Währungsausgleichs-
fonds *(m)*
En exchange equalization
account
Es cuenta de compensación
de cambio *(f)*
Fr fonds de stabilisation des
changes *(m pl)*
It conto per la stabilizzazione dei cambi *(m)*

conta de controlo *(f)* Pt
De Kontrollkonto *(n)*
En control account
Es cuenta de control *(f)*
Fr compte de contrôle *(m)*
It conto di controllo *(m)*

conta de depósito *(f)* Pt
De Depositenkonto *(n)*
En deposit account
Am interest-bearing account
Es cuenta de ahorras *(f)*
Fr compte de dépôt *(m)*
It conto di deposito *(m)*

conta de descargas *(f)* Pt
De Löschungskonto *(n)*
En landing account
Es cuenta de desembarque *(f)*
Fr compte de mise à terre *(m)*
It conto de sbarco *(m)*

conta de empréstimos *(f)* Pt
De Anleihekonto *(n)*
En loan account
Es cuenta de préstamos *(f)*
Fr compte des prêts *(m*
It conto anticipazioni *(m)*

conta de especulações baixistas *(f)* Pt
De Baissekonto *(n)*
En bear account

Es cuenta de especulaciones
a la baja *(f)*
Fr compte des speculations
à la baisse *(m)*
It conto di speculazioni al
ribasso *(m)*

conta de lucros e perdas *(f)* Pt
De Gewinn- und Verlustkonto
(n)
En profit and loss account
Es cuenta de ganancias y
pérdidas *(f)*
Fr compte profits et pertes
(m)
It conto profetti e perdite *(m)*

conta de receitas e despesas *(f)* Pt
De Ausgaben- und Ertrags-
konto *(n)*
En income and expenditure
account
Es cuenta de ingresos y
gastos *(f)*
Fr compte de revenus et
dépenses *(m)*
It conto proventi e spese *(m)*

contador *(m)* n Es
De Buchhalter *(m)*
En accountant
Fr comptable *(m)*
It contabile *(m)*
Pt contabilista *(m)*

contador de navio *(m)* Es
De Zahlmeister *(m)*
En purser
Fr commissaire de la marine
(m)
It commissario di bordo *(m)*
Pt comissário de bordo *(m)*

contador habilitado *(m)* Es
De Wirtschaftsprüfer *(m)*
En qualified accountant
Fr expert comptable *(m)*
It ragioniere diplomato *(m)*
Pt guarda-livros diplomado
(m)

conta externa *(f)* Pt
De Auslandskonto *(n)*
En external account
Am foreign currency account
Es cuenta exterior *(f)*
Fr compte transférable *(m)*
It conto estero *(m)*

conta impessoal *(f)* Pt
De Firmenkonto *(n)*
En impersonal account
Es cuenta simulada *(f)*
Fr compte impersonnnel *(m)*
It conto d'ordine *(m)*

containerisation *(f)* n Fr
De Containerisation *(f)*
En containerization
Es contenedorización *(f)*
It containerization *(f)*
Pt containerização *(f)*

Containerisation *(f)* n De
En containerization
Es contenedorización *(f)*
Fr containerisation *(f)*
It containerization *(f)*
Pt containerização *(f)*

containerização *(f)* n Pt
De Containerisation *(f)*
En containerization
Es contenedorización *(f)*
Fr containerisation *(f)*
It containerization *(f)*

containerization n En, It *(f)*
De Containerisation *(f)*
Es contenedorización *(f)*
Fr containerisation *(f)*
Pt containerização *(f)*

Containerschiff *(n)* n De
En container ship
Es barco de contenedores
(m)
Fr navire porte-containers
(m)
It nave da contenitori *(f)*
Pt navio de contentores *(m)*

container ship En
De Containerschiff *(n)*
Es barco de contenedores
(m)
Fr navire porte-containers
(m)
It nave da contenitori *(f)*
Pt navio de contentores *(m)*

conta nominal *(f)* Pt
De Firmenkonto *(n)*
En nominal account
Es cuenta de resultado *(f)*
Fr compte nominal *(m)*
It conto d'ordine *(m)*

contanti contro documenti It
De bar gegen Versandpapiere
En cash against documents
(c a d)
Es al contado contra docu-
mentos
Fr comptant contre docu-
ments
Pt em dinheiro contra docu-
mentação

conta numerada (f) Pt
De numeriertes Konto (n)
En numbered account
Es cuenta identificada con
número (f)
Fr compte identifié par
numéro (m)
It conto identificato da nu-
mero (m)

conta pendente (f) Pt
De Übergangskonto (n)
En suspense account
Es cuenta suspensa (f)
Fr compte d'ordre (m)
It conto sospeso (m)

conta pessoal (f) Pt
De Kundenkonto (n)
En charge account
Es cuenta personal (f)
Fr compte personnel (m)
It conto personale (m)

conta remetida (f) Pt
De zur Begleichung vorge-
legte Rechnung (f)
En account rendered
Es cuenta rendida (f)
Fr compte rendu (m)
It conto reso (m)

contas anuais (f) Pt
De Jahresabschluß (m)
En annual accounts
Es balance anual (m)
Fr bilan annuel (m)
It bilancio annuale (m)

contas a pagar (f pl) Pt
De Kreditoren (m pl)
En accounts payable
Es cuentas a pagar (f pl)
Fr comptes à payer (m pl)
It conti passivi (m pl)

contas a receber (f pl) Pt
De Debitoren (m pl)
En accounts receivable
Es cuentas a recibir (f pl)
Fr créances (f pl)
It conti attivi (m pl)

contas consolidadas (f pl) Pt
De konsolidierter Kontenab-
schluß (m)
En consolidated accounts
Es cuentas consolidadas (f pl)
Fr comptes consolidés (m pl)
It conti consolidati (m pl)

contas fiscalizadas (f pl) Pt
De geprüfte Geschäftsbücher
(n pl)
En audited accounts
Es cuentas revisadas (f pl)
Fr comptes vérifiés et certi-
fiés (m pl)
It conti verificati e certificati
(m pl)

contas por saldar (f pl) Pt
De ausstehende Schulden
(m pl)
En outstanding accounts
Es cuentas pendientes (f pl)
Fr comptes à percevoir (m pl)
It conti aperti (m pl)

contenedorización (f) n Es
De Containerisation (f)
En containerization
Fr containerisation (f)
It containerization (f)
Pt containerização (f)

contenido (m) n Es
De Inhalt (m)
En contents
Fr contenu (m)
It contenuto (m)
Pt conteúdo (m)

contents (n pl) En
De Inhalt (m)
Es contenido (m)
Fr contenu (m)
It contenuto (m)
Pt conteúdo (m)

contenu (m) n Fr
De Inhalt (m)
En contents
Es contenido (m)
It contenuto (m)
Pt conteúdo (m)

contenuto (m) n It
De Inhalt (m)
En contents
Es contenido (m)
Fr contenu (m)
Pt conteúdo (m)

contestation (f) n Fr
De Streit (m)
En dispute
Es disputa (t)
It disputa (f)
Pt disputa (f)

**contestation syndicale des
compétences** (f) Fr
De Fähigkeitsstreitigkeit (f)
En demarcation dispute
Es disputa sobre demarca-
ción (f)
It disputa di competenza (f)
Pt disputa sobre demar-
cação (f)

conteúdo (m) n Pt
De Inhalt (m)
En contents
Es contenido (m)
Fr contenu (m)
It contenuto (m)

conti aperti (m pl) It
De ausstehende Schulden
(m pl)
En outstanding accounts
Es cuentas pendientes (f pl)
Fr comptes à percevoir (m pl)
Pt contas por saldar (f pl)

conti attivi (m pl) It
De Debitoren (m pl)
En accounts receivable
Es cuentas a recibir (f pl)
Fr créances (f pl)
Pt contas a receber (f pl)

conti consolidati (m pl) It
De konsolidierter Kontenab-
schluß (m)
En consolidated accounts
Es cuentas consolidadas (f pl)
Fr comptes consolidés (m pl)
It contas consolidadas (f pl)

contingence (f) n Fr
De Eventualität (f)
En contingency
Es contingencia (f)
It contingenza (f)
Pt contingência (f)

contingencia (f) n Es
De Eventualität (f)
En contingency
Fr contingence (f)
It contingenza (f)
Pt contingência (f)

contingência (f) n Pt
De Eventualität (f)
En contingency
Es contingencia (f)
Fr contingence (f)
It contingenza (f)

contingency (n) En
De Eventualität (f)
Es contingencia (f)
Fr contingence (f)
It contingenza (f)
Pt contingência (f)

contingency reserve En
De Rückstellung für Eventual-
   verbindlichkeiten (f)
Es reserva para imprevistos
   (f)
Fr réserve de prévoyance (f)
It riserva di previdenza (f)
Pt reserva para as con-
   tingências (f)

contingent d'importation
   (m) Fr
De Einfuhrkontingent (n)
En import quota
Es cupo de importación (m)
It contingente d'importazio-
   ne (m)
Pt quota de importação (f)

contingente d'importazione
   (m) It
De Einfuhrkontingent (n)
En import quota
Es cupo de importación (m)
Fr contingent d'importation
   (m)
Pt quota de importação (f)

contingent liability En
De Eventualverpflichtung (f)
Es responsabilidad contin-
   gente (f)
Fr obligation éventuelle (f)
It sopravvenienza passiva (f)
Pt responsabilidade contin-
   gente (f)

contingenza (f) n It
De Eventualität (f)
En contingency
Es contingencia (f)
Fr contingence (f)
Pt contingência (f)

conti passivi (m pl) It
De Kreditoren (m pl)
En accounts payable
Es cuentas a pagar (f pl)
Fr comptes à payer (m pl)
Pt contas a pagar (f pl)

conti verificati e certificati
   (m pl) It
De geprüfte Geschäftsbücher
   (n pl)
En audited accounts
Es cuentas revisadas (f pl)
Fr comptes vérifiés et certi-
   fiés (m pl)
Pt contas fiscalizadas (f pl)

conto (in banca) (m) n It
De Konto (n)
En account
Es cuenta (f)
Fr compte (m)
Pt conta (f)

conto (nota) (m) n It
De Rechnung (f)
En bill; account
Es cuenta; nota (f)
Fr compte; note (m f)
Pt conta (f)

conto anticipazioni (m) It
De Anleihekonto (n)
En loan account
Es cuenta de préstamos (f)
Fr compte de prêts (m)
Pt conta de empréstimos (f)

conto bloccato (m) It
De gesperrtes Konto (n)
En blocked account
Es cuenta bloqueada (f)
Fr compte bloqué (m)
Pt conta bloqueada (f)

conto capitale (m) It
De Kapitalkonto (n)
En capital account
Es cuenta de capital (f)
Fr compte capital (m)
Pt conta de capital (f)

conto commerciale (m) It
De Handelskonto (n)
En trade account
Es cuenta comercial (f)
Fr compte commercial (m)
Pt conta comercial (f)

conto corrente (m) It
De Kontokorrent (n)
En current account
Am checking account
Es cuenta corriente (f)
Fr compte courant (m)
Pt conta corrente (f)

conto d'aggio (m) It
De Agiokonto (n)
En agio account
Es cuenta de agio (f)
Fr compte d'agio (m)
Pt conta de ágio (f)

conto di controllo (m) It
De Kontrollkonto (n)
En control account
Es cuenta de control (f)
Fr compte de contrôle (m)
Pt conta de controlo (f)

conto di deposito (m) It
De Depositenkonto (n)
En deposit account
Am interest-bearing account
Es cuenta de ahorras (f)
Fr compte de dépôt (m)
Pt conta de depósito (f)

conto di sbarco (m) It
De Löschungskonto (n)
En landing account
Es cuenta de desembarque (f)
Fr compte de mise à terre (m)
Pt conta de descargas (f)

conto di speculazioni al
   ribasso (m) It
De Baissekonto (n)
En bear account
Es cuenta de especulaciones
   à la baja (f)
Fr compte des speculations
   à la baisse (m)
Pt conta de especulações bai-
   xistas (f)

conto di stanziamento (m) It
De Rückstellungskonto (n)
En appropriation account
Es cuenta de apropiación (f)

Fr compte d'affectation *(m)*
Pt conta de apropriaçâo *(f)*

conto do vigário *(m)* Pt
De Schwindlertrick
En confidence trick
Am confidence game
Es timo *(m)*
Fr escroquerie *(f)*
It truffa all'americana *(f)*

conto estero *(m)* It
De Auslandskonto *(n)*
En external account
Am foreign currency account
Es cuenta exterior *(f)*
Fr compte transférable *(m)*
Pt conta externa *(f)*

**conto identificato da
  numero** *(m)* It
De numeriertes Konto *(n)*
En numbered account
Es cuenta indentificada con
  número *(f)*
Fr compte identifié par
  numéro *(m)*
Pt conta numerada *(f)*

conto in banca *(m)* It
De Bankkonto *(n)*
En bank account
Es cuenta bancaria *(f)*
Fr compte en banque *(m)*
Pt conta bancária *(f)*

conto in commune *(m)* It
De Gemeinschaftskonto *(n)*
En joint account
Es cuenta común *(f)*
Fr compte joint *(m)*
Pt conta conjunta *(f)*

**conto per la stabilizzazione
  dei cambi** *(m)* It
De Währungsausgleichs-
  fonds *(m)*
En exchange equalization
  account
Es cuenta de compensación
  de cambio *(f)*
Fr fonds de stabilisation des
  changes *(m pl)*
Pt conta de compensaçâo de
  transacçôes *(f)*

conto personale *(m)* It
De Kundenkonto *(n)*
En charge account

Es cuenta personal *(f)*
Fr compte personnel *(m)*
Pt conta pessoal *(f)*

conto profitti e perdite *(m)* It
De Gewinn- und Verlustkonto
  (n)
En profit and loss account
Es cuenta de ganancias y
  pérdidas *(f)*
Fr compte profits et pertes
  (m)
Pt conta de lucros e perdas *(f)*

conto proventi e spese *(m)* It
De Ausgaben- und Ertragskonto *(n)*
En income and expenditure
  account
Es cuenta de ingresos y
  gastos *(f)*
Fr compte de revenus et
  dépenses *(m)*
Pt conta de receitas e despesas *(f)*

conto reso *(m)* It
De zur Begleichung vorge-
  legte Rechnung *(f)*
En account rendered
Es cuenta rendida *(f)*
Fr compte rendu *(m)*
Pt conta remetida *(f)*

conto scoperto *(m)* It
De Konto überzogen *(n)*
En account overdrawn
Es cuenta en descubierto *(f)*
Fr compte découvert *(m)*
Pt conta a descoberto *(f)*

conto sospeso *(m)* It
De Übergangskonto *(n)*
En suspense account
Es cuenta suspensa *(f)*
Fr compte d'ordre *(m)*
Pt conta pendente *(f)*

contra account En
De Gegenkonto *(n)*
Es contracuenta *(f)*
Fr compte contrepartie *(m)*
It conto d'ordine *(m)*
Pt contra-conta *(f)*

contraband En
De Schmuggelware *(f)*
Es contrabando *(m)*
Fr contrebande *(f)*

It contrabbando *(m)*
Pt contrabando *(m)*

contrabando *(m) n* Es, Pt
De Schmuggelware *(f)*
En contraband
Fr contrebande *(f)*
It contrabbando *(m)*

contrabbandare *vb* It
De schmuggeln
En smuggle
Es pasar de contrabando
Fr faire la contrabande
Pt passar por contrabando

contrabbando *(m) n* It
De Schmuggelware *(f)*
En contraband
Es contrabando *(m)*
Fr contrebande *(f)*
Pt contrabando *(m)*

contra-conta *(f)* Pt
De Gegenkonto *(n)*
En contra account
Es contracuenta *(f)*
Fr compte contrepartie *(m)*
It conto d'ordine *(m)*

contract *n* En
De Vertrag *(m)*
Es contrato *(m)*
Fr contrat *(m)*
It contratto *(m)*
Pt contrato *(m)*

contract note En
De Schlußschein *(m)*
Es nota de contrato *(f)*
Fr bordereau d'achat *(m)*
It nota di contratto *(f)*
Pt nota-contrato *(f)*

contractor En
De Unternehmer *(m)*
Es contratista *(m)*
Fr entrepreneur *(m)*
It impresario *(m)*
Pt contratador *(m)*

contract price En
De Vertragspreis *(m)*
Es precio contractual *(m)*
Fr prix contractuel *(m)*
It prezzo contrattuale *(m)*
Pt preço contratual *(m)*

contractual *adj* En, Es
De vertraglich
Fr contractuel
It contrattuale
Pt contratual

contractuel *adj* Fr
De vertraglich
En contractual
Es contractual
It contrattuale
Pt contratual

contracuenta *(f)* Es
De Gegenkonto *(n)*
En contra account
Fr compte contrepartie *(m)*
It conto d'ordine *(m)*
Pt contra-conta *(f)*

contraffare *vb* It
De fälschen
En forge
Es falsificar
Fr contrefaire
Pt falsificar

contrainte *(f)* n Fr
De Zwang *(m)*
En duress
Es compulsión *(f)*
It costrizione *(f)*
Pt coerção *(f)*

contrainte sur les salaires *(f)* Fr
De Lohnbeschränkung *(f)*
En wage restraint
Es restricción de salario *(f)*
It restrizioni sui salari *(f pl)*
Pt restrição de salários *(f)*

contrair empréstimo Pt
De entleihen
En borrow
Es pedir un préstamo
Fr emprunter
Pt prestare *(f)*

contract *(m)* n Fr
De Vertrag *(m)*
En contract
Es contrato *(m)*
It contratto *(m)*
Pt contrato *(m)*

contratación collectiva *(f)* Es
De Tarifvertragsverhandlung *(f)*
En collective bargaining
Fr négociations de conventions collectives *(f pl)*
It contrattazione collettiva *(f)*
Pt regateio colectivo *(m)*

contratador *(m)* n Pt
De Unternehmer *(m)*
En contractor
Es contratista *(m)*
Fr entrepreneur *(m)*
It impresario *(m)*

contrat à la grosse aventure *(m)* Fr
De Bodmereibrief *(m)*
En bottomry bond
Es contrato de préstamo a la gruesa *(m)*
It contratto di prestito a cambio marittimo *(m)*
Pt título de bodemeria *(m)*

contrat d'arrangement *(m)* Fr
De Vergleichsabkommen *(n)*
En deed of arrangement
Es acta de disposición *(f)*
It atto di accordo *(m)*
Pt escritura de acordo *(f)*

contrat de service *(m)* Fr
De Dienstvertrag *(m)*
En service agreement
Es contrato de servicio *(m)*
It accordo di servizio *(m)*
Pt contrato de serviço *(m)*

contrat de société *(m)* Fr
De Gesellschaftsvertrag *(m)*
En articles of association
Am articles of incorporation
Es artículos de asociación *(m pl)*
It statuto sociale *(m)*
Pt escritura de sociedade *(f)*

contrat en régie *(m)* Fr
De Kosten und Vertrag
En cost-plus contract
Es contrato al costo más beneficio *(m)*
It contratto in economia *(m)*
Pt contrato de custo e adicionais *(m)*

contratista *(m)* n Es
De Unternehmer *(m)*
En contractor
Fr entrepreneur *(m)*
It impresario *(m)*
Pt contratador *(m)*

contratista de obras *(m)* Es
De Bauunternehmer *(m)*
En building contractor
Fr entrepreneur de bâtiment *(m)*
It impresa edile *(f)*
Pt construtor de obras *(m)*

contratista de transportes *(m)* Es
De Transportunternehmer *(m)*
En haulage contractor
Am trucking company
Fr entrepreneur de camionage *(m)*
It imprenditore di transporti *(m)*
Pt empreiteiro de transportes *(m)*

contrato *(m)* n Es, Pt
De Vertrag *(m)*
En contract
Fr contrat *(m)*
It contratto *(m)*

contrato al costo más beneficio *(m)* Es
De Kosten und Vertrag
En cost-plus contract
Fr contrat en régie *(m)*
It contratto in economia *(m)*
Pt contrato de custo e adicionais *(m)*

contrato de préstamo a la gruesa *(m)* Es
De Bodmereibrief *(m)*
En bottomry bond
Fr contrat à la grosse aventure *(m)*
It contratto di prestito a cambio marittimo *(m)*
Pt título de bodemeria *(m)*

contrato de reserva *(m)* Es
De Notvereinbarung *(f)*
En stand-by agreement
Fr accord en réserve *(m)*
It accordo di riserva *(m)*
Pt acordo a postos *(m)*

contrato de servicio *(m)* Es
De Dienstvertrag *(m)*
En service agreement
Fr contrat de service *(m)*
It accordo di servizio *(m)*
Pt contrato de serviço *(m)*

contrato de serviço *(m)* Pt
De Dienstvertrag *(m)*
En service agreement
Es contrato de servicio *(m)*
Fr contrat de service *(m)*
It accordo di servizio *(m)*

contrato global *(m)* Es, Pt
De Globalgeschäft *(n)*
En package deal
Fr marché global *(m)*
It contratto globale *(m)*

contrattazione collettiva *(f)* It
De Tarifvertragsverhandlung
   (f)
En collective bargaining
Es contratación collectiva *(f)*
Fr négociations de conven-
   tions collectives *(f pl)*
Pt regateio colectivo *(m)*

contratto *(m)* n It
De Vertrag *(m)*
En contract
Es contrato *(m)*
Fr contrat *(m)*
Pt contrato *(m)*

**contratto di noleggio a
tempo** *(m)* It
De Zeitcharter *(f)*
En time charter
Es fletamento de tiempo *(m)*
Fr affrètement à temps *(m)*
Pt fretamento de tempo *(m)*

**contratto di prestito a cam-
bio marittimo** *(m)* It
De Bodmereibrief *(m)*
En bottomry bond
Es contrato de préstamo a la
   gruesa *(m)*
Fr contrat à la grosse aven-
   ture *(m)*
Pt título de bodemeria *(m)*

contratto de vendita *(m)* It
De Kaufvertrag *(m)*
En bill of sale
Es escritura de venta *(f)*

Fr acte de vente *(f)*
Pt escritura de venda *(f)*

contratto globale *(m)* It
De Globalgeschäft *(n)*
En package deal
Es contrato global *(m)*
Fr marché global *(m)*
Pt contrato global *(m)*

contratto in economia *(m)* It
De Kosten und Vertrag
En cost-plus contract
Es contrato al costo más be-
   neficio *(m)*
Fr contrat en régie *(m)*
Pt contrato de custo e adi-
   cionais *(m)*

contratto vincolante *(m)* It
De bindender Vertrag *(m)*
En binding agreement
Es obligación irrevocable *(f)*
Fr convention irrévocable *(f)*
Pt accordo irrevocável *(m)*

contrattuale *adj* It
De vertraglich
En contractual
Es contractual
Fr contractuel
Pt contratual

contratual *adj* Pt
De vertraglich
En contractual
Es contractual
Fr contractuel
It contrattuale

contrebande *(f)* n Fr
De Schmuggelware *(f)*
En contraband
Es contrabando *(m)*
It contrabbando *(m)*
Pt contrabando *(m)*

contrefaçon *(f)* n Fr
De Fälschung *(f)*
En forgery
Es falsificación *(f)*
It falsificazione *(f)*
Pt falsifição *(f)*

contrefaçon littéraire *(f)* Fr
De Urheberrechtsverletzung
   (f)
En infringement of copyright

Es infracción de los derechos
   de autor *(f)*
It infrazione dei diritti d'autore *(f)*
Pt infraccâo de direitos de
   autor *(f)*

contrefaire *vb* Fr
De fälschen
En forge
Es falsificar
It contraffare
Pt falsificar

contremaître *(m)* n Fr
De Vorarbeiter *(m)*
En foreman
Es capataz *(m)*
It capo operaio; capo squa-
   dra *(m)*
Pt encarregado; capataz *(m)*

contresigner *(vb)* Fr
De gegenzeichnen
En countersign
Es refrendar
It controfirmare
Pt validar por assinatura

contribuable *(m)* n Fr
De Steuerzahler *(m)*
En tax payer
Es contribuyente *(m)*
It contribuente fiscale *(m)*
Pt contribuinte *(m)*

contribución *(f)* n Es
De Beitrag *(m)*
En contribution
Fr contribution *(f)*
It contributo *(m)*
Pt contribuição *(f)*

contribuciones directas *(f pl)*
   Es
De direkte Steuern *(f pl)*
En direct taxation
Fr contributions directes *(f pl)*
It imposte dirette *(f pl)*
Pt tributação directa *(f)*

contribuciones indirectas
   (f pl) Es
De indirekte Steuern *(f pl)*
En indirect taxation
Fr contributions indirectes
   (f pl)
It imposte indirette *(f pl)*
Pt tributação indirecta *(f)*

contribución municipal *(f)* Es
De Gemeindesteuer *(f)*
En rates
Am realty tax
Fr taxes municipales *(f pl)*
It tassa comunale *(f)*
Pt contribuições *(f pl)*

contribuente fiscale *(m)* It
De Steuerzahler *(m)*
En tax payer
Es contribuyente *(m)*
Fr contribuable *(m)*
Pt contribuinte *(m)*

contribuer *(vb)* Fr
De beitragen
En contribute
Es contribuir
It contribuire
Pt contribuir

contribuição *(f)* n Pt
De Beitrag *(m)*
En contribution
Es contribución *(f)*
Fr contribution *(f)*
It contributo *(m)*

contribuição indirecta *(f)* Pt
De indirekte Steuern *(f pl)*
En indirect taxation
Es contribuciones indirectas *(f pl)*
Fr contributions indirectes *(f pl)*
It imposte indirette *(f pl)*

contribuições *(f pl)* Pt
De Gemeindesteuer *(f)*
En rates
Am realty tax
Es contribución municipal *(f)*
Fr taxes municipales *(f pl)*
It tassa comunale *(f)*

contribuinte *(m)* n Pt
De Steuerzahler *(m)*
En tax payer
Es contribuyente *(m)*
Fr contribuable *(m)*
It contribuente fiscale *(m)*

contribuir *vb* Es, Pt
De beitragen
En contribute
Fr contribuer
It contribuire

contribuire *vb* It
De beitragen
En contribute
Es contribuir
Fr contribuer
Pt contribuir

contribute *vb* En
De beitragen
Es contribuir
Fr contribuer
It contribuire
Pt contribuir

contribution n En, Fr *(f)*
De Beitrag *(m)*
Es contribución *(f)*
It contributo *(m)*
Pt contribução *(f)*

contributions directes *(f pl)*
Fr
De direkte Steuern *(f pl)*
En direct taxation
Es contribuciones directas *(f pl)*
It imposte dirette *(f pl)*
Pt tributação directa *(f)*

contributions indirectes *(f pl)*
Fr
De indirekte Steuern *(f pl)*
En indirect taxation
Es contribuciones indirectas *(f pl)*
It imposte indirette *(f pl)*
Pt tributação indirecta *(f)*

contributo *(m)* n It
De Beitrag *(m)*
En contribution
Es contribución *(f)*
Fr contribution *(f)*
Pt contribução *(f)*

contributory pension En
De Kassenpension *(f)*
Es retiro contributivo *(m)*
Fr retraite de régime à cotisa-
tions *(f)*
It pensione a contributi *(f)*
Pt reforma de contribução
prévia *(f)*

contribuyente *(m)* n Es
De Steuerzahler *(m)*
En tax payer
Fr contribuable *(m)*

It contribuente fiscale *(m)*
Pt contribuinte *(m)*

controfirmare *vb* It
De gegenzeichnen
En countersign
Es refrendar
Fr contresigner
Pt validar por assinatura

control n En, Es *(m)*
De Aufsicht *f)*
Fr contrôle *(m)*
It controllo *(m)*
Pt controlo *(m)*

control account En
De Kontrollkonto *(n)*
Es cuenta de control *(f)*
Fr compte de contrôle *(m)*
It conto di controllo *(m)*
Pt conta de controlo *(f)*

controlador *(m)* n Pt
De Kontrolleur; Rechnungs-
prüfer *(m)*
En controller; comptroller
Es interventor *(m)*
Fr contrôleur; vérificateur des
comptes *(m)*
It controllore *(m)*

control al azar *(m)* Es
De Stichprobe *f)*
En spot check
Fr contrôle par sondage *(m)*
It controllo saltuario *(m)*
Pt controlo de ocasião *(m)*

control de aduanas *(m)* Es
De zollamtliche Untersuchung
(f)
En customs examination
Fr visite douanière *(f)*
It visita doganale *(f)*
Pt verificação alfandegária *(f)*

control de alquileres *(m)* Es
De Mietzinskontrolle *(f)*
En rent control
Fr contrôle des loyers *(m)*
It blocco degli affitti *(m)*
Pt controlo de rendas *(m)*

control calidad *(m)* Es
De Qualitätskontrolle *(f)*
En quality control
Fr contrôle de qualité *(m)*

It   controllo di qualità *(m)*
Pt   controlo de qualidade *(m)*

control precios *(m)* Es
De   Preiskontrolle *(f)*
En   price control
Fr   contrôle des prix *(m)*
It   controllo sui prezzi *(m)*
Pt   controlo de preços *(m)*

control de producción *(m)* Es
De   Produktionskontrolle *(f)*
En   production control
Fr   contrôle de production *(m)*
It   cotrollo della produzione
      (m)
Pt   controlo da produção *(m)*

contrôle *(m) n* Fr
De   Aufsicht *(f)*
En   control
Es   control *(m)*
It   controllo *(m)*
Pt   controlo *(m)*

contrôle budgétaire *(m)* Fr
De   Haushaltskontrolle *(f)*
En   budgetary control
Es   control presupuestario *(m)*
It   controllo a bilancio
      preventivo *(m)*
Pt   controlo orçamental *(m)*

contrôle de production *(m)*
      Fr
De   Produktionskontrolle *(f)*
En   production control
Es   control de producción *(m)*
It   controllo della produzione
      (m)
Pt   controlo da produção *(m)*

contrôle de qualité *(m)* Fr
De   Qualitätskontrolle *(f)*
En   quality control
Es   control de calidad *(m)*
It   controllo di qualitá *(m)*
Pt   controlo de qualidade *(m)*

contrôle des changes *(m)* Fr
De   Devisenkontrolle *(f)*
En   exchange control
Am   currency control
Es   fiscalización de cambios
      (f)
It   controllo sui cambi *(m)*
Pt   controlo de câmbios *(m)*

contrôle des loyers *(m)* Fr
De   Mietzinskontrolle *(f)*
En   rent control
Es   control de alquileres *(m)*
It   blocco degli affitti *(m)*
Pt   controlo de rendas *(m)*

contrôle des prix *(m)* Fr
De   Preiskontrolle *(f)*
En   price control
Es   control de precios *(m)*
It   controllo sui prezzi *(m)*
Pt   controlo de preços *(m)*

contrôle des stocks *(m)* Fr
De   Lagerverwaltung *(f)*
En   stock control
Es   fiscalizatión de las
      existencias *(f)*
It   controllo delle scorte *(m)*
Pt   controlo de existências *(m)*

contrôle par sondage *(m)* Fr
De   Stichprobe *(f)*
En   spot check
Es   control al azar *(m)*
It   controllo saltuario *(m)*
Pt   controlo de ocasião *(m)*

contrôleur *(m)* Fr
De   Kontrolleur *(m)*
En   controller
Es   interventor *(m)*
It   controllore *(m)*
Pt   controlador *(m)*

controller *n* En
De   Kontrolleur *(m)*
Es   interventor *(m)*
Fr   contrôleur *(m)*
It   cotrollore *(m)*
Pt   controlador *(m)*

controlling company En
De   Gesellschaft mit
      Kontrollbefugnis *(f)*
Es   compañía directriz *(f)*
Fr   société directrice *(f)*
It   società direttrice *(f)*
Pt   companhia controladora
      (f)

controlling interest En
De   Mehrheitsbeteiligung *(f)*
Es   interés mayoritario *(m)*
Fr   participation donnant le
      contrôle *(f)*
It   interesse della parte
      maggioritaria *(m)*
Pt   interesse maioritário *(m)*

controllo *(m) n* It
De   Aufsicht *(f)*
En   control
Es   control *(m)*
Fr   contrôle *(m)*
Pt   controlo *(m)*

**controllo a bilancio
      preventivo** *(m)* It
De   Haushaltskontrolle *(f)*
En   budgetary control
Es   control presupuestario *(m)*
Fr   contrôle budgétaire *(m)*
Pt   controlo orçamental *(m)*

controllo della produzione
      (m) It
De   Produktionskontrolle *(f)*
En   production control
Es   control de producción *(m)*
Fr   contrôle de production *(m)*
Pt   controlo da produçâo *(m)*

controllo delle scorte *(m)* It
De   Lagerverwaltung *(f)*
En   stock control
Es   fiscalización de las
      existencias *(f)*
Fr   contrôle des stocks *(m)*
Pt   controlo de existências *(m)*

controllo di qualità *(m)* It
De   Qualitätskontrolle *(f)*
En   quality control
Es   control de calidad *(m)*
Fr   contrôle de qualité *(m)*
Pt   controlo de qualidade *(m)*

controllore *(m) n* It
De   Kontrolleur;
      Rechnungsprüfer *(m)*
En   controller; comptroller
Es   interventor *(m)*
Fr   contrôleur; vérificateur des
      comptes *(m)*
Pt   controlador *(m)*

controllo saltuario *(m)* It
De   Stichprobe *(f)*
En   spot check
Es   control al azar *(m)*
Fr   contrôle par sondage *(m)*
Pt   controlo de ocasião *(m)*

controllo sui cambi *(m)* It
De   Devisenkontrolle *(f)*
En   exchange control
Am   currency control

controlo de qualidade *(m)* Pt
De Qualitätskontrolle *(f)*
En quality control
Es control de calidad *(m)*
Fr contrôle de qualité *(m)*
It controllo di qualità *(m)*

Es fiscalización de cambios *(m)*
Fr contrôle des changes *(m)*
Pt controlo de câmbios *(m)*

controllo sui prezzi *(m)* It
De Preiskontrolle *(f)*
En price control
Es control de precios *(m)*
Fr contrôle des prix *(m)*
Pt controlo de preços *(m)*

controlo *(m)* n Pt
De Aufsicht *(f)*
En control
Es control *(m)*
Fr contrôle *(m)*
It controllo *(m)*

controlo da produção *(m)* Pt
De Produktionskontrolle *(f)*
En production control
Es control de producción *(m)*
Fr contrôle de production *(m)*
It controllo della produzione *(m)*

controlo de câmbios *(m)* Pt
De Devisenkontrolle *(f)*
En exchange control
Am currency control
Es fiscalización de cambios *(m)*
Fr contrôle des changes *(m)*
It controllo sui cambi *(m)*

controlo de existências *(m)* Pt
De Lagerverwaltung *(f)*
En stock control
Es fiscalización de las existencias *(f)*
Fr contrôle des stocks *(m)*
It controllo delle scorte *(m)*

controlo de ocasião *(m)* Pt
De Stichprobe *(f)*
En spot check
Es control al azar *(m)*
Fr contrôle par sondage *(m)*
It controllo saltuario *(m)*

controlo de preços *(m)* Pt
De Preiskontrolle *(f)*
En price control
Es control de precios *(m)*
Fr contrôle des prix *(m)*
It controllo sui prezzi *(m)*

controlo de rendas *(m)* Pt
De Mietzinskontrolle *(f)*
En rent control
Es control de alquileres *(m)*
Fr contrôle des loyers *(m)*
It blocco degli affitti *(m)*

controlo orçamental *(m)* Pt
De Haushaltskontrolle *(f)*
En budgetary control
Es control presupuestario *(m)*
Fr contrôle budgétaire *(m)*
It controllo a bilancio preventivo *(m)*

control presupuestario *(m)* Es
De Haushaltskontrolle *(f)*
En budgetary control
Fr contrôle budgétaire *(m)*
It controllo a bilancio preventivo *(m)*
Pt controlo orçamental *(m)*

controstallia *(f)* n It
De Überliegezeit *(f)*
En demurrage
Es sobreestadía *(f)*
Fr surestarie *(f)*
Pt sobreestadia *(f)*

convene vb En
De einberufen
Es convenir
Fr convoquer
It convocare
Pt convocar

convénio de preços *(m)* Pt
De Preisabsprache *(f)*
En price ring
Es coalición de vendedores *(f)*
Fr coalition de vendeurs *(f)*
It sindacato dei prezzi *(m)*

convenio restrictivo *(m)* Es
De eingeschränkte Bestimmung *(f)*
En restrictive covenant
Fr accord restrictif *(m)*
It accordo restrittivo *(m)*
Pt obrigação retritiva *(f)*

convenir *(vb)* Es
De einberufen
En convene
Fr convoquer
It convocare
Pt convocar

convention *(f)* n Fr
De Abkommen *(n)*
En agreement
Es acuerdo *(m)*
It accordo *(m)*
Pt acordo *(m)*

convention des salaires *(f)* Fr
De Lohnvereinbarung *(f)*
En wages agreement
Es acuerdo sobre salarios *(m)*
It accordo sui salari *(m)*
Pt acordo sobre salários *(m)*

convention irrévocable *(f)* Fr
De bindender Vertrag *(m)*
En binding agreement
Es obligación irrevocable *(f)*
It contratto vincolante *(m)*
Pt acordo irrevogável *(m)*

convention tacite *(f)* Fr
De stillschweigendes Übereinkommen *(n)*
En tacit agreement
Es acuerdo tácito *(m)*
It accordo tacito *(m)*
Pt acordo tácito *(m)*

convention verbale *(f)* Fr
De Kavaliersabkommen *(n)*
En gentleman's agreement
Es acuerdo sobre palabra *(m)*
It accordo sulla parola *(m)*
Pt pacto de honra *(m)*

convenzione *(f)* n It
De Abkommen *(n)*
En convenant
Es pacto *(m)*
Fr convention *(f)*
Pt pacto *(m)*

conversão *(f)* n Pt
De Konversion *(f)*
En conversion
Es conversión *(f)*
Fr conversion *(f)*
It conversione *(f)*

conversion n En, Fr (f)
De Konversion (f)
Es conversión (f)
It conversione (f)
Pt conversão (f)

conversión (f) Es
De Konversion (f)
En conversion
Fr conversion (f)
It conversione (f)
Pt conversão (f)

conversione (f) n It
De Konversion (f)
En conversion
Es conversión (f)
Fr conversion (f)
Pt conversão (f)

conversion factor En
De Umrechnungskoeffizient
(m)
Es factor de conversión (m)
Fr facteur de conversion (m)
It fattore di conversione (m)
Pt factor de conversão (m)

convert vb En
De konvertieren
Es convertir
Fr convertir
It convertire
Pt convertir

convertibile adj It
De konvertierbar
En convertible
Es convertible
Fr convertible
Pt convertível

convertible adj En, Es, Fr
De konvertierbar
It convertibile
Pt convertível

convertir vb Es, Fr, Pt
De konvertieren
En convert
It convertire

convertire vb It
De konvertieren
En convert
Es convertir
Fr convertir
Pt convertir

convertível adj Pt
De konvertierbar
En convertible
Es convertible
Fr convertible
It convertibile

convés (m) n Pt
De Deck (n)
En deck
Es cubierta (f)
Fr pont (m)
It coperta; ponte (f m)

conveyance of property En
De Übertragung von Vermö-
gen (f)
Es traspaso de propiedad (m)
Fr transmission de biens (f)
It transferimento di beni (m)
Pt trespasse de propriedade
(m)

conveyer n Am
En carrier
De Spediteur (m)
Es transportador (m)
Fr expéditeur (m)
It transportador (m)

convidar vb Pt
De einladen
En invite
Es invitar
Fr inviter
It invitare

convite (m) n Pt
De Einladung; Aufforderung
(f)
En invitation
Es invitación (m)
Fr invitation; appel (f m)
It invito (m)

convocar vb Pt
De einberufen
En convene
Es convenir
Fr convoquer
It convocare

convocare vb It
De einberufen
En convene
Es convenir
Fr convoquer
Pt convocar

convocazione dei creditori
(f) It
De Gläubigerversammlung (f)
En meeting of creditors
Es concurso de acreedores
(m)
Fr assemblée de créanciers
(f)
Pt reunião de credores (f)

convoquer vb Fr
De einberufen
En convene
Es convenir
It convocare
Pt convocar

cooperação (f) n Pt
De Zusammenarbeit
En cooperation
Es cooperación (f)
Fr coopération (f)
It cooperazione (f)

cooperación (f) n Es
De Zusammenarbeit
En cooperation
Fr coopération (f)
It cooperazione (f)
Pt cooperação (f)

cooperation En
De Zusammenarbeit
Es cooperación (f)
Fr coopération (f)
It cooperazione (f)
Pt cooperação (f)

coopération (f) n Fr
De Zusammenarbeit
En cooperation
Es cooperación (f)
It cooperazione (f)
Pt cooperação (f)

cooperativa (f) n Es, It, Pt
De Genossenschaft (f)
En cooperative
Fr société coopérative (f)

cooperative n En
De Genossenschaft (f)
Es cooperativa (f)
Fr société coopérative (f)
It cooperativa (f)
Pt cooperativa (f)

cooperazione *(f)* n It
De Zusammenarbeit
En cooperation
Es cooperación *(f)*
Fr coopération *(f)*
Pt cooperação *(f)*

co-opt *vb* En
De hinzuwählen
Es cooptar
Fr coopter
It cooptare
Pt cooptar

cooptar *vb* Es, Pt
De hinzuwählen
En co-opt
Fr coopter
It cooptare

cooptare *vb* It
De hinzuwählen
En co-opt
Es cooptar
Fr coopter
Pt cooptar

coopter *vb* Fr
De hinzuwählen
En co-opt
Es cooptar
It cooptare
Pt cooptar

coordenação *(f)* n Pt
De Gleichordnung *(f)*
En coordination
Es coordinación *(f)*
Fr coordination *(f)*
It coordinamento *(m)*

coordinación *(f)* n Es
De Gleichordnung *(f)*
En coordination
Fr coordination *(f)*
It coordinamento *(m)*
Pt coordenação *(f)*

coordinamento *(m)* n It
De Gleichordnung *(f)*
En coordination
Es coordinación *(f)*
Fr coordination *(f)*
Pt coordenação *(f)*

coordination n En, Fr *(f)*
De Gleichordnung *(f)*
Es coordinación *(f)*

It coordinamento *(m)*
Pt coordinação *(f)*

co-ownership n En
De Miteigentum *(f)*
Es copropiedad *(f)*
Fr copropriété *(f)*
It comproprietà *(f)*
Pt co-propiedade *(f)*

coperta *(f)* n It
De Deck *(n)*
En deck
Es cubierta *(f)*
Fr pont *(m)*
Pt convés *(m)*

copertura *(f)* n It
De Deckung *(f)*
En cover
Es cobertura *(f)*
Fr couverture *(f)*
Pt cobertura *(f)*

copertura assicurativa *(f)* It
De Versicherungsdeckung *(f)*
En insurance cover
Es cubertura de la póliza de
  seguro *(f)*
Fr garantie d'assurance *(f)*
Pt cobertura de segru *(f)*

copertura provvisoria *(f)* It
De temporäre Deckung *(f)*
En temporary cover
Es cubertura provisional *(f)*
Fr couverture temporaire *(m)*
Pt cobertura provisória *(f)*

copia *(f)* n Es, It
De Abschrift; Kopie *(f)*
En copy
Fr copie *(f)*
Pt cópia *(f)*

cópia *(f)* n Pt
De Abschrift; Kopie *(f)*
En copy
Es copia *(f)*
Fr copie *(f)*
It copia *(f)*

cópia a químico *(f)* Pt
De Durchschlag *(f)*
En carbon copy
Es copia en papel carbón *(f)*
Fr copie au carbone *(f)*
It copia carbona *(f)*

copia auténtica *(f)* Es
De beglaubigte Abschrift *(f)*
En certified true copy
Fr copie certifiée *(f)*
It copia conforme *(f)*
Pt cópia autenticada *(f)*

cópia autenticada *(f)* Pt
De beglaubigte Abschrift *(f)*
En certified true copy
Es cópia auténtica *(f)*
Fr copie certifiée *(f)*
It copia conforme *(f)*

copia carbone *(f)* It
De Durchschlag *(f)*
En carbon copy
Es copia en papel carbón *(f)*
Fr copie au carbone *(f)*
Pt cópia a químico *(f)*

copia conforme *(f)* It
De beglaubigte Abschrift *(f)*
En certified true copy
Es copia auténtica *(f)*
Fr copie certifiée *(f)*
Pt cópia autenticada *(f)*

copia en papel carbón *(f)* Es
De Durchschlag *(m)*
En carbon copy
Fr copie au carbone *(f)*
It copia carbone *(f)*
Pt cópia a químico *(f)*

copiar *(vb)* Es, Pt
De kopieren
En copy
Fr transcrire
It copiare

cópia rascunho *(f)* Pt
De Entwurf *(m)*
En rough copy
Am draft
Es borrador *(m)*
Fr brouillon *(m)*
Pt brutta copia *(f)*

copiare *(vb)* It
De kopieren
En copy
Es copiar
Fr transcrire
Pt copiar

copie *(f)* n Fr
De Abschrift; Kopie *(f)*
En copy

Es copia *(f)*
It copia *(f)*
Pt cópia *(f)*

copie au carbone *(f)* Fr
De Durchschlag *(m)*
En carbon copy
Es copia en papel carbón *(f)*
It copia carbone *(f)*
Pt cópia a químico *(f)*

copie certifiée *(f)* Fr
De beglaubigte Abschrift *(f)*
En certified true copy
Es copia auténtica *(f)*
It copia conforme *(f)*
Pt cópia autenticada *(f)*

copie publicitaire *(f)* Fr
De Werbetext *(m)*
En advertising copy
Es material publicitario *(m)*
It testo pubblicitario *(m)*
Pt texto de publicidade *(m)*

coprirsi *vb* It
De sich decken
En hedge
Es cubrirse
Fr arbitrager
Pt cobrir-se

copropiedad *(f)* n Es
De Miteigentum *(n)*
En joint ownership
Fr copropriété *(f)*
It comproprietá *(f)*
Pt co-propriedada *(f)*

co-propriedade *(f)* n Pt
De Miteigentum *(n)*
En joint ownership
Es copropiedad *(f)*
Fr copropriété *(f)*
It comproprietà *(f)*

copropiété *(f)* n Fr
De Miteigentum *(n)*
En joint ownership
Es copropiedad *(f)*
It comproprietà *(f)*
Pt co-propriedade *(f)*

copy *vb* En
De kopieren
Es copiar
Fr transcire
It copiare
Pt copiar

copy n En
De Abschrift, Kopie *(f)*
Es copia *(f)*
Fr copie *(f)*
It copia *(f)*
Pt cópia *(f)*

copyright n En
De Urheberrecht *(n)*
Es derechos de autor *(m pl)*
Fr droit d'auteur *(m)*
It diritto d'autore *(m)*
Pt direitos de autor *(m pl)*

copy typist En
Am transcriber
De Abschreibtypistin *(f)*
Es mecanógrafa *(f)*
Fr dactylo copiste *(f)*
It dattilografa *(f)*
Pt dactilógrafa *(f)*

copywriter n En
De Textverfasser *(m)*
Es redactor *(m)*
Fr concepteur-rédacteur *(m)*
It redattore pubblicitario *(m)*
Pt redactor de publicidade *(m)*

corner a market n En
De den Markt beherrschen
Es acaparar el mercado
Fr accaparer le marché
It accaparrare il mercato
Pt dominar o mercado

corporação *(f)* n Pt
De Körperschaft *(f)*
En corporation
Es corporación *(f)*
Fr corporation *(f)*
It corporazione *(f)*

Corporação Internacional de Finanças *(f)* Pt
De Internationale Finanzkorporation *(f)*
En International Finance Corporation
Es Corporación Internacional de Finanzas *(f)*
Fr Société Financière Internationale *(f)*
It Corporazione Finanziaria Internazionale *(f)*

corporación *(f)* n Es
De Körperschaft *(f)*
En corporation
Fr corporation *(f)*
It corporazione *(f)*
Pt corporação *(f)*

Corporación Internacional de Finanzas *(f)* Es
De Internationale Finanzkorporation *(f)*
En International Finance Corporation
Fr Société Financière Internationale *(f)*
It Corporazione Finanziaria Internationale *(f)*
Pt Corporação Internacional de Finanças *(f)*

corporate *adj* En
De körperschaftlich
Es corporativo
Fr corporatif
It corporativo
Pt corporativo

corporate officer Am
En executive director
De geschäftsführender Direktor *(m)*
Es director ejecutivo *(m)*
Fr administrateur dirigeant *(m)*
It amministratore dirigente *(m)*
Pt director administrativo *(m)*

corporatif *adj* Fr
De körperschaftlich
En corporate
Es corporativo
It corporativo
Pt corporativo

corporation n En, Fr *(f)*
De Körperschaft *(f)*
Es corporación *(f)*
It corporazione *(f)*
Pt corporação *(f)*

corporation tax En
De Körperschaftsteuer *(f)*
Es impuesto sobre renta de la sociedad *(m)*
Fr impôt sur le revenu des sociétés *(m)*

It imposta sui proventi delle
società *(f)*
Pt imposto sobre corporação
(m)

corporativo *adj* Es, It, Pt
De körperschaftlich
En corporate
Fr corporatif

corporazione *(f) n* It
De Körperschaft *(f)*
En corporation
Es corporación *(f)*
Fr corporation *(f)*
Pt corporação *(f)*

**Corporazione Finanziaria
Internazionale** *(f)* It
De Internationale
Finanzkorporation *(f)*
En International Finance
Corporation
Es Corporación Internacional
de Finanzas *(f)*
Fr Société Financière
Internationale *(f)*
Pt Corporação Internacional
de Finanças *(f)*

correcção *(f) n* Pt
De Berichtigung *(f)*
En correction
Es corrección *(f)*
Fr correction *(f)*
It correzione *(f)*

corrección *(f) n* Es
De Berichtigung *(f)*
En correction
Fr correction *(f)*
It correzione *(f)*
Pt correcção *(f)*

correct *vb* En
De korrigieren
Es corregir
Fr corriger
It correggere
Pt corrigir

correction *n* En, Fr *(f)*
De Berichtigung *(f)*
Es corrección *(f)*
It correzione *(f)*
Pt correccção *(f)*

corredor *(m) n* Es
De Makler *(m)*
En broker
Fr courtier *(m)*
It sensale *(m)*
Pt corretor *(m)*

corredor de bolsa *(m)* Es
De Börsenmakler *(m)*
En stockbroker
Fr courtier en bourse *(m)*
It agente di borsa *(m)*
Pt corretor da bolsa *(m)*

corredor de cambios *(m)* Es
De Wechselmakler *(m)*
En bill broker
Fr courtier de bons *(m)*
It agente de sconto *(m)*
Pt corretor de câmbios *(m)*

corredor de mercaderías *(m)*
Es
De Makler für Verbrauchsgü-
ter *(m)*
En commodity broker
Fr courtier en marchandises
(m)
It sensale die merci *(m)*
Pt corretor de mercadorias
(m)

**corredor de seguro
marítimo** *(m)* Es
De Seetransportversiche-
rungsmakler *(m)*
En marine insurance broker
Fr courtier d'assurances
maritimes *(m)*
It agente d'assicurazioni
marittime *(m)*
Pt corretor de seguros
marítimos *(m)*

corredor de seguros *(m)* Es
De Versicherungsmakler *(m)*
En insurance broker
Fr courtier d'assurance *(m)*
It mediatore di assicurazioni
(m)
Pt corretor de seguros *(m)*

corredor marítimo *(m)* Es
De Schiffsmakler *(m)*
En shipbroker
Fr courtier maritime *(m)*
It sensale marittimo *(m)*
Pt corretor marítimo *(m)*

correduría de fincas *(f)* Es
De Immobilienbüro *(n)*
En estate agency
Am real estate agency
Fr agence immobilière *(f)*
It agenzia immobiliare *(f)*
Pt agência de propriedades
(f)

correggere *vb* It
De korrigieren
En correct
Es corregir
Fr corriger
Pt corrigir

corregir *vb* Es
De korrigieren
En correct
Fr corriger
It correggere
Pt corrigir

correio *(m) n* Pt
De Post *(f)*
En mail
Es correo *(m)*
Fr poste *(f)*
It posta *(f)*

correio aéreo *(m)* Pt
De Luftpost *(f)*
En airmail
Es correo aéreo *(m)*
Fr poste aérienne *(f)*
It posta aerea *(f)*

corrente *adj* It, Pt
De laufend
En current
Es corriente
Fr courant; en cours

corrente continua *(f)* It
De Gleichstrom *(m)*
En direct current (d. c.)
Es corriente continua *(f)*
Fr courant continu *(m)*
Pt corrente contínua *(f)*

corrente contínua *(f)* Pt
De Gleichstrom *(m)*
En direct current (d. c.)
Es corriente continua *(f)*
Fr courant continu *(m)*
It corrente continua *(f)*

correo *(m)* n Es
De Post *(f)*
En mail
Fr poste *(f)*
It posta *(f)*
Pt correio *(m)*

correo aéreo *(m)* Es
De Luftpost *(f)*
En airmail
Fr poste aérienne *(f)*
It posta aerea *(f)*
Pt correio aéreo *(m)*

correspondance *(f)* n Fr
De Briefwechsel *(m)*
En correspondence
Es correspondencia *(f)*
It corrispondenza *(f)*
Pt correspondência *(f)*

correspondence n En
De Briefwechsel *(m)*
Es correspondencia *(f)*
Fr correspondance *(f)*
It corrispondenza *(f)*
Pt correspondência *(f)*

correspondencia *(f)* n Es
De Briefwechsel *(m)*
En correspondence
Fr correspondance *(f)*
It corrispondenza *(f)*
Pt correspondência *(f)*

correspondência *(f)* n Pt
De Briefwechsel *(m)*
En correspondence
Es correspondencia *(f)*
Fr correspondance *(f)*
It corrispondenza *(f)*

corretagem *(f)* n Pt
De Maklergebühr *(f)*
En brokerage
Es corretaje *(m)*
Fr courtage *(m)*
It senseria *(f)*

corretaje *(m)* n Es
De Maklergebühr *(f)*
En brokerage
Fr courtage *(m)*
It senseria *(f)*
Pt corretagem *(f)*

corretor *(m)* n Pt
De Makler *(m)*
En broker

Es corredor *(m)*
Fr courtier *(m)*
It sensale *(m)*

corretor da bolsa *(m)* Pt
De Börsenmakler *(m)*
En stockbroker
Es corredor de bolsa *(m)*
Fr courtier en bourse *(m)*
It agente di borsa *(m)*

corretor de câmbios *(m)* Pt
De Wechselmakler *(m)*
En bill broker
Es corredor de cambios *(m)*
Fr courtier de bons *(m)*
It agente di sconto *(m)*

corretor de mercadorias *(m)*
Pt
De Makler für Verbrauchsgü-
ter *(m)*
En commodity broker
Es corredor de mercaderías
(m)
Fr courtier en marchandises
(m)
It sensale di merci *(m)*

corretor de opções *(m)* Pt
De Terminmakler *(m)*
En option dealer
Es operador a prima *(m)*
Fr opérateur à prime *(m)*
It operatore in contratti a
premio *(m)*

corretor de seguros *(m)* Pt
De Versicherungsmakler *(m)*
En insurance broker
Es corredor de seguros *(m)*
Fr courtier d'assurance *(m)*
It mediatore di assicurazioni
(m)

corretor marítimo *(m)* Pt
De Schiffsmakler *(m)*
En shipbroker
Es corredor marítimo *(m)*
Fr courtier maritime *(m)*
It sensale marittimo *(m)*

correzione *(f)* n It
De Berichtigung *(f)*
En correction
Es corrección *(f)*
Fr correction *(f)*
Pt correcção *(f)*

corriente *adj* Es
De laufend
En current
Fr courant; en cours
It corrente
Pt corrente

corriente continua *(f)* Es
De Gleichstrom *(m)*
En direct current (d. c.)
Fr courant continu *(m)*
It corrente continua *(f)*
Pt corrente continua *(f)*

corriger *vb* Fr
De korrigieren
En correct
Es corregir
It correggere
Pt corrigir

corrigir *vb* Pt
De korrigieren
En correct
Es corregir
Fr corriger
It correggere

corrispondenza *(f)* n It
De Briefwechsel *(m)*
En correspondence
Es correspondencia *(f)*
Fr correspondance *(f)*
Pt correspondência *(f)*

corrompere *vb* It
De bestechen
En bribe
Es sobornar
Fr corrompre
Pt subornar

corrompre *vb* Fr
De bestechen
En bribe
Es sobornar
It corrompere
Pt subornar

corruption *(f)* n Fr
De Bestechung *(f)*
En bribery; corruption
Es soborno *(m)*
It corruzione *(f)*
Pt suborno *(m)*

corruzione *(f)* n It
De Bestechung *(f)*
En bribery; corruption

Es soborno *(m)*
Fr corruption *(f)*
Pt suborno *(m)*

corso del cambio *(m)* It
De Umrechnungskurs *(m)*
En rate of exchange
Es tipo de cambio *(m)*
Fr cours de change *(m)*
Pt taxa de câmbio *(f)*

cortar *vb* Pt
De streichen
En delete
Es tachar; anular
Fr rayer; effacer
It cancellare

corte arbitrale *(f)* It
De Schiedsgericht *(n)*
En court of arbitration
Es tribunal arbitral *(m)*
Fr cour d'arbitrage *(m)*
Pt tribunal de arbitragem *(m)*

corte d'appello *(f)* It
De Berufungsgericht *(n)*
En court of appeal
Es tribunal de apelación *(m)*
Fr cour d'appel *(m)*
Pt tribunal de apelação *(m)*

cosecha *(f)* n Es
De Ernte *(f)*
En harvest
Fr moisson; récolte *(f)*
It raccolto *(m)*
Pt colheita *(f)*

cost n En
De Kosten *(pl)*
Es coste *(m)*
Fr coût *(m)*
It costo *(m)*
Pt custo *(m)*

cost *vb* En
De kosten
Es costar
Fr coûter
It costare
Pt custear

cost accountant En
De Kalkulator *(m)*
Es contable de costes *(m)*
Fr comptable de prix de
   revient *(m)*

It contabile deo costi di
   produzione *(m)*
Pt calculador de custos *(m)*

costo marginale *(m)* It
De Randkosten *(pl)*
En marginal cost
Es coste marginal *(m)*
Fr coût marginal *(m)*
Pt custo marginal *(m)*

cost analysis En
De Kostenanalyse *(f)*
Es análisis de costes *(m)*
Fr analyse des coûts *(f)*
It analisi dei costi *(f)*
Pt análise de custo *(f)*

cost and freight (c.&f.) En
De Kosten und Fracht
Es coste y flete
Fr coût et fret
It costo e nolo
Pt custo e frete

costar *vb* Es
De kosten
En cost
Fr coûter
It costare
Pt custear

costare *vb* It
De kosten
En cost
Es costar
Fr coûter
Pt custear

cost benefit analysis En
De Gewinnanalyse *(f)*
Es análisis de costes y
   beneficios *(m)*
Fr analyse des coûts et
   rendements *(f)*
It analisi dei costi e benefici
   (f)
Pt análise de custo e
   benefício *(f)*

coste *(m)* n Es
De Kosten *(pl)*
En cost
Fr coût *(m)*
It costo *(m)*
Pt custo *(m)*

coste contable *(m)* Es
De Buchwert der Einkäufe *(m)*
En book cost
Fr prix de revient comptable
   (m)
It costo contabile *(m)*
Pt custo contabilizado *(m)*

coste de la mano de obra *(m)*
   Es
De Lohnkosten *(pl)*
En cost of labour
Fr coût de la main-d'œuvre *(m)*
It costo di mano d'opera *(m)*
Pt custo da mão de obra *(m)*

coste de repuesto *(m)* Es
De Wiederanschaffungsko-
   sten *(pl)*
En replacement cost
Fr coût de remplacement *(m)*
It costo di rimpiazzo *(m)*
Pt custo de substituição *(m)*

coste de venta *(m)* Es
De Verkaufskosten *(pl)*
En selling cost
Fr frais de vente *(m)*
It costo di vendita *(m)*
Pt custo de venda *(m)*

coste de vida *(m)* Es
De Lebenshaltungskosten *(pl)*
En cost of living
Fr coût de la vie *(m)*
It costo della vita *(m)*
Pt custo de vida *(m)*

coste de vida más alto *(m)* Es
De erhöhte Lebenshaltungs-
   kosten *(pl)*
En increased cost of living
Fr renchérissement du coût
   de la vie *(m)*
It aumentato costo della vita
   (m)
Pt custo de vida mais
   elevado *(m)*

coste directo *(m)* Es
De direkte Kosten *(pl)*
En direct cost
Fr prix direct de revient *(m)*
It costo diretto *(m)*
Pt custo directo *(m)*

cost-effectiveness *(n)* En
De Wirtschaftlichkeit *(f)*
Es efectividad de coste *(f)*

Fr coût et efficacité
It rendimento della spesa *(m)*
Pt eficiência relativa ao custo
(f)

coste marginal *(m)* Es
De Randkosten *(pl)*
En marginal cost
Fr coût marginal *(m)*
It costo marginale *(m)*
Pt custo marginal *(m)*

coste por unidad *(m)* Es
De Einheitskosten *(pl)*
En unit cost
Fr coût de l'unité *(m)*
It costo unitario *(m)*
Pt custo por unidade *(m)*

coste primitivo *(m)* Es
De Anschaffungskosten *(pl)*
En historic cost
Fr coût d'acquisition primitif
(m)
It costo primitivo *(m)*
Pt custo original *(m)*

coste promedio *(m)* Es
De Durchschnittskosten *(pl)*
En average cost
Fr coût moyen *(m)*
It costo medio *(m)*
Pt custo médio *(m)*

costes *(m pl)* Es
De Kosten *(pl)*
En charges
Fr frais *(m pl)*
It spese *(f pl)*
Pt despesas *(f pl)*

costes a reembolso Es
De per Nachnahme
En charges forward
Fr frais à percevoir à la
livraison
It spese assegnate
Pt entrega contra reembolso

coste, seguro, y flete Es
De Kosten, Versicherung,
Fracht
En cost, insurance, and
freight (c. i. f.)
Fr coût, assurance, fret
It costo, assicurazione, nolo
Pt custo, seguro, e frete

costes incrementados *(m pl)*
Es
De erhöhte Kosten *(pl)*
En increased costs
Fr accroissement des coûts
(m)
It costi aumentati *(m pl)*
Pt custos aumentatos *(m pl)*

costes indirectos *(m pl)* Es
De Gemeinkosten *(pl)*
En indirect costs
Fr frais indirects *(m pl)*
It costi indiretti *(m pl)*
Pt custos indirectos *(m pl)*

coste social *(m)* Es
De Sozialkosten *(pl)*
En social cost
Fr coût social *(m)*
It costo sociale *(m)*
Pt custo social *(m)*

costes operacionales *(m pl)*
Es
De Betriebsausgaben *(f pl)*
En operating costs
Fr frais d'exploitation *(m pl)*
It spese di gestione *(f pl)*
Pt custos de exercício *(m pl)*

coste unitario *(m)* Es
De Einheitskosten *(pl)*
En unit cost
Fr coût de l'unité *(m)*
It costo unitario *(m)*
Pt custo por unidade *(m)*

coste variable *(m)* Es
De variable Kosten *(pl)*
En variable cost
Fr coût variable *(m)*
It costo variabile *(m)*
Pt custo variável *(m)*

coste y flete Es
De Kosten und Fracht
En cost and freight (c. & f.)
Fr coût et fret
It costo e nolo
Pt custo e frete

costi aumentati *(m pl)* It
De erhöhte Kosten *(pl)*
En increased costs
Es costes incrementados
(m pl)
Fr accroissement des coûts
(m)
Pt custos aumentados *(m pl)*

costi indiretti *(m pl)* It
De Gemeinkosten *(pl)*
En indirect costs
Es costes inderectos *(m pl)*
Fr frais indirects *(m pl)*
Pt custos indirectos *(m pl)*

cost, insurance, and freight
(c. i. f.) En
De Kosten, Versicherung,
Fracht
Es coste, seguro, y flete
Fr coût, assurance, fret
It costo, assicurazione, nolo
Pt custo, seguro, e frete

costituzione (di una società)
(f) n It
De Eintragung (einer Gesell-
schaft) *(f)*
En incorporation
Es incorporación *(f)*
Fr incorporation *(f)*
Pt incorporação *(f)*

costo *(m n)* It
De Kosten *(pl)*
En cost
Es coste *(m)*
Fr coût *(m)*
Pt custo *(m)*

costo, assicurazione, nolo It
De Kosten, Versicherung,
Fracht
En cost, insurance, and
freight (c. i. f.)
Es coste, seguro, y flete
Fr coût, assurance, fret
Pt custo, seguro, e frete

costo contabile *(m)* It
De Buchwert der Einkäufe *(m)*
En book cost
Es coste contable *(m)*
Fr prix de revient comptable
(m)
Pt custo contabilizado *(m)*

costo della vita *(m)* It
De Lebenshaltungskosten *(pl)*
En cost of living
Es coste de vida *(m)*
Fr coût de la vie *(m)*
Pt custo de vida *(m)*

costo di mano d'opera *(m)* It
De Lohnkosten *(pl)*
En cost of labour

costo diretto (continued)
Es coste de la mano de obra
(m)
Fr coût de la main-d'œuvre (m)
Pt custo da mão de obra (m)

costo diretto (m) It
De direkte Kosten (pl)
En direct cost
Es coste directo (m)
Fr prix direct de revient (m)
Pt custo directo (m)

costo di rimpiazzo (m) It
De Wiederanschaffungskosten (pl)
En replacement cost
Es coste de repuesto (m)
Fr coût de remplacement (m)
Pt custo de substituição (m)

costo di vendita (m) It
De Verkaufskosten (pl)
En selling cost
Es coste de venta (m)
Fr frais de vente (m)
Pt custo de venda (m)

costo effettivo (m) It
De Gestehungskosten (pl)
En actual cost
Es precio verdadero (m)
Fr prix de revient effectif (m)
Pt custo verdadeiro (m)

costo e nolo It
De Kosten und Fracht
En cost and freight (c. & f.)
Es coste y flete
Fr coût et fret
Pt custo e frete

cost of labour En
De Lohnkosten (pl)
Es coste de la mano de obra
(m)
Fr coût de la main-d'œuvre (m)
It costo di mano d'opera (m)
Pt custo da mão de obra (m)

cost of living En
De Lebenshaltungskosten (pl)
Es coste de vida (m)
Fr coût de la vie (m)
It costo della vita (m)
Pt custo de vida (m)

costo medio (m) It
De Durchschnittskosten (pl)
En average cost

Es coste promedio (m)
Fr coût moyen (m)
Pt custo médio (m)

costo primitivo (m) It
De Anschaffungskosten (pl)
En historic cost
Es coste primitivo (m)
Fr coût d'acquisition primitif
(m)
Pt custo original (m)

costo sociale (m) It
De Sozialkosten (pl)
En social cost
Es coste social (m)
Fr coût social (m)
Pt custo social (m)

costo unitario (m) It
De Einheitskosten (pl)
En unit cost
Es coste unitario (m)
Fr coût de l'unité (m)
Pt custo por unidade (m)

costo variabile (m) It
De variable Kosten (pl)
En variable cost
Es coste variable (m)
Fr coût variable (m)
Pt custo variável (m)

cost-plus contract En
De Kosten und Vertrag
Es contrato al costo más
beneficio (m)
Fr contrat en régie (m)
It contratto in economia (m)
Pt contrato de custo e
adicionais (m)

cost price En
De Einstandspreis (m)
Es precio de coste (m)
Fr prix de revient (m)
It prezzo di costo (m)
Pt preço de custo (m)

costrizione (f) n It
De Zwang (m)
En duress
Es compulsión (f)
Fr contrainte (f)
Pt coerção (f)

cota (f) n Pt
De Quote; Beteiligung (f)
En quota

Es cuota (f)
Fr quote-part (f)
It quota (f)

cotação (f) n Pt
De Kostenanschlag (m)
En quotation
Es cotización (f)
Fr cotation (f)
It quotazione (f)

cotação da bolsa (f) Pt
De Börsenkurs (m)
En stock-exchange
quotation
Es curso de bolsa (m)
Fr cours de bourse (m)
It quotazione di borsa (f)

cotation (f) n Fr
De Kostenanschlag (m)
En quotation
Es cotización (f)
It quotazione (f)
Pt cotação (f)

coter vb Fr
De (den Preis) angeben
En quote
Es cotizar
It quotare
Pt cotizar

coter sans obligation Fr
De nicht fest anbieten
En quote not firm
Es cotizar sin compromiso
It quotare senza impegno
Pt cotizar sem fixação de valor

cotización (f) n Es
De Kostenanschlag (m)
En quotation
Fr cotation (f)
It quotazione (f)
Pt cotação (f)

cotizar (vb) Es, Pt
De (den Preis) angeben
En quote
Fr coter
It quotare

cotizar sem fixação de valor
Pt
De nicht fest anbieten
En quote not firm
Es cotizar sin compromiso

Fr coter sans obligation
It quotare senza impegno

cotizar sin compromiso Es
De nicht fest anbieten
En quote not firm
Fr coter sans obligation
It quotare senza impegno
Pt cotizar sem fixação de valor

counsel n En
De Anwalt (m)
Es abogado (m)
Fr avocat
It avvocato (m)
Pt advogado (m)

counterfeit adj En
De falsch; verfälscht
Es falso; falsicado
Fr faux; contrefait
It falso; contraffatto
Pt falsificado

counterfoil n En
Am stub
De Talon (m)
Es talón (m)
Fr talon (m)
It matrice (f)
Pt talão (m)

countersign vb En
De gegenzeichnen
Es refrendar
Fr contresigner
It controfirmare
Pt validar por assinatura

country n En
De Land (n)
Es país (m)
Fr pays (m)
It paese (m)
Pt país (m)

country of origin En
De Herkunftsland (n)
Es pais de origen (m)
Fr pays de provenance (m)
It paese di origine (m)
Pt país de origem (m)

coupon n En, Fr (m)
De Kupon (m)
Es cupón (m)
It cedola (f)
Pt cupão (m)

courant adj Fr
De laufend
En current
Es corriente
It corrente
Pt corrente

courant continu (m) Fr
De Gleichstrom (m)
En direct current (d. c.)
Es corriente continua (f)
It corrente continua (f)
Pt corrente continua (f)

courbe de la demande (f) Fr
De Nachfragekurve (f)
En demand curve
Es curva de relación
demanda (f)
It curva della domanda (f)
Pt curva de procura (f)

cour d'appel (m) Fr
De Berufungsgericht (n)
En court of appeal
Es tribunal de apelación (m)
It corte d'appello (f)
Pt tribunal de apelação (m)

cour d'arbitrage (m) Fr
De Schiedsgericht (n)
En court of arbitration
Es tribunal arbitral (m)
It corte arbitrale (f)
Pt tribunal de arbitragem (m)

cours à terme (m) Fr
De Terminnotierung (f)
En forward price
Es precio a término (m)
It prezzo per futura
consegna (m)
Pt preço adiantado (m)

cours de bourse (m) Fr
De Börsenkurs (m)
En stock-exchange
quotation
Es curso de bolsa (m)
It quotazione di borsa (f)
Pt cotação da bolsa (f)

cours de change (m) Fr
De Umrechnungskurs (m)
En rate of exchange
Es tipo de cambio (m)
It corso del cambio (m)
Pt taxa de câmbio (f)

cours de clôture (m) Fr
De Schlußnotierung (f)
En closing price
Es precio de cierre (m)
It prezzo di chiusura (m)
Pt último preço (m)

cours du marché (m) Fr
De Marktpreis (m)
En market price
Es precio de mercado (m)
It prezzo del mercato (m)
Pt preço de mercado (m)

cours moyen (m) Fr
De Mittelpreis; Mittelkurs (m)
En middle price
Es precio medio (m)
It prezzo medio (m)
Pt preço médio (m)

courtage (m) n Fr
De Maklergebühr (f)
En brokerage
Es corretaje (m)
It senseria (f)
Pt corretagem (f)

courtier (m) n Fr
De Makler (m)
En broker
Es corredor (m)
It sensale (m)
Pt corretor (m)

courtier d'assurance (m) Fr
De Versicherungsmakler (m)
En insurance broker
Es corredor de seguros (m)
It mediatore di assicurazioni
(m)
Pt corretor de seguros (m)

**courtier d'assurances
maritimes** (m) Fr
De Seetransportversiche-
rungsmakler (m)
En marine insurance broker
Es corredor de seguro marítimo (m)
It agente d'assicurazioni
marittime (m)
Pt corretor de seguros
marítimos (m)

courtier de bons (m) Fr
De Wechselmakler (m)
En bill broker
Es corredor de cambios (m)

It agente di sconto *(m)*
Pt corretor de câmbios *(m)*

courtier en bourse *(m)* Fr
De Börsenmakler *(m)*
En stockbroker
Es corredor de bolsa *(m)*
It agente di borsa *(m)*
Pt corretor da bolsa *(m)*

courtier en marchandises
(m) Fr
De Makler für Verbrauchsgü-
ter *(m)*
En commodity broker
Es corredor de mercaderías
(m)
It sensale di merci *(m)*
Pt corretor de mercadorias
(m)

courtier maritime *(m)* Fr
De Schiffsmakler *(m)*
En shipbroker
Es corredor marítimo *(m)*
It sensale marittimo *(m)*
Pt corretor marítimo *(m)*

court of appeal En
De Berufungsgericht *(n)*
Es tribunal de apelación *(m)*
Fr cour d'appel *(m)*
It corte d'appello *(f)*
Pt tribunal de apelação *(m)*

court of arbitration En
De Schiedsgericht *(n)*
Es tribunal arbitral *(m)*
Fr cour d'arbitrage *(m)*
It corte arbitrale *(f)*
Pt tribunal de arbitragem *(m)*

court of law En
De Gericht *(n)*
Es tribunal *(m)*
Fr tribunal *(m)*
It tribunale *(m)*
Pt tribunal *(m)*

coût *(m)* n Fr
De Kosten *(pl)*
En cost
Es coste *(m)*
It costo *(m)*
Pt custo *(m)*

coût, assurance, fret Fr
De Kosten, Versicherung,
Fracht

En cost, insurance, and
freight (c. i. f.)
Es coste, seguro, y flete
It costo, assicurazione, nolo
Pt custo, seguro, e frete

coût d'acquisition primitif
(m) Fr
De Anschaffungskosten *(pl)*
En historic cost
Es coste primitivo *(m)*
It costo primitivo *(m)*
Pt custo original *(m)*

coût de la main-d'œuvre *(m)*
Fr
De Lohnkosten *(pl)*
En cost of labour
Es coste de la mano de obra
(m)
It costo di mano d'opera *(m)*
Pt custo da mão de obra *(m)*

coût de la vie *(m)* Fr
De Lebenshaltungskosten *(pl)*
En cost of living
Es coste de vida *(m)*
It costo della vita *(m)*
Pt custo de vida *(m)*

coût de l'unité *(m)* Fr
De Einheitskosten *(pl)*
En unit cost
Es coste por unidad *(m)*
It costo unitario *(m)*
Pt custo por unidade *(m)*

coût de remplacement *(m)* Fr
De Wiederanschaffungs-
kosten *(pl)*
En replacement cost
Es coste de repuesto *(m)*
It costo di rimpiazzo *(m)*
Pt custo de substituição *(m)*

coûter vb Fr
De Kosten
En cost
Es costar
It costare
Pt custear

coût et efficacité Fr
De Wirtschaftlichkeit *(f)*
En cost-effectiveness
Es efectividad de coste *(f)*
It rendimento della spesa *(m)*
Pt eficiência relativa ao custo
(f)

coût et fret Fr
De Kosten und Fracht
En cost and freight (c. & f.)
Es coste y flete
It costo e nolo
Pt custo e frete

coût marginal *(m)* Fr
De Randkosten *(pl)*
En marginal cost
Es coste marginal *(m)*
It costo marginale *(m)*
Pt custo marginal *(m)*

coût moyen *(m)* Fr
De Durchschnittskosten *(pl)*
En average cost
Es coste promedio *(m)*
It costo medio *(m)*
Pt custo médio *(m)*

coût social *(m)* Fr
De Sozialkosten *(pl)*
En social cost
Es coste social *(m)*
It costo sociale *(m)*
Pt custo social *(m)*

coût variable *(m)* Fr
De variable Kosten *(pl)*
En variable cost
Es coste variable *(m)*
It costo variabile *(m)*
Pt custo variável *(m)*

couverture *(f)* n Fr
De Deckung *(f)*
En cover
Es cobertura *(f)*
It copertura *(f)*
Pt cobertura *(f)*

couverture temporaire *(m)* Fr
De temporäre Deckung *(f)*
En temporary cover
Es cobertura provisional *(f)*
It copertura provvisoria *(f)*
Pt cobertura provisória *(f)*

covenant n En
De Abkommen *(n)*
Es pacto *(m)*
Fr convention *(f)*
It convenzione *(f)*
Pt pacto *(m)*

cover n En
De Deckung *(f)*
Es cobertura *(f)*

Fr couverture *(f)*
It copertura *(f)*
Pt cobertura *(f)*

cover note En
De Deckungszusage *(f)*
Es aviso de seguro del riesgo *(m)*
Fr lettre de couverture *(f)*
It nota di copertura *(f)*
Pt nota de cobertura *(f)*

crane *n* En
De Kran *(m)*
Es grúa *(f)*
Fr grue *(f)*
It gru *(f)*
Pt grua *(f)*

créance *(f) n* Fr
De Schuld *(f)*
En debt
Es deuda *(f)*
It debito *(m)*
Pt dívida *(f)*

créance douteuse *(f)* Fr
De zweifelhafte Forderung *(f)*
En doubtful debt
Es deuda de pago dudoso *(f)*
It credito dubbio *(f)*
Pt dívida duvidosa *(f)*

créance irrécouvrable *(f)* Fr
De uneinbringliche Schuld *(f)*
En bad debt
Es deuda incobrable *(f)*
It credito inesigibile *(m)*
Pt divida incobrável *(f)*

créances *(f pl) n* Fr
De Debitoren *(m pl)*
En accounts receivable
Es cuentas a recibir *(f pl)*
It conti attivi *(m pl)*
Pt contas a receber *(f pl)*

créancier *(m) n* Fr
De Gläubiger *(m)*
En creditor
Es acreedor *(m)*
It creditore *(m)*
Pt credor *(m)*

créancier chirographaire *(m)* Fr
De nicht gesicherter Gläubiger *(m)*
En unsecured creditor

Es acreedor no garantizado *(m)*
It creditore non garantito *(m)*
Pt credor sem garantia *(m)*

créancier privilégié *(m)* Fr
De bevorrechtigter Gläubiger *(m)*
En preferential creditor
Es acreedor privilegiado *(m)*
It creditore privilegiato *(m)*
Pt credor preferencial *(m)*

crecimiento *(m) n* Es
De Entwicklung; Wachstum *(f n)*
En growth
Fr croissance; développe-ment *(f m)*
It crescita; sviluppo *(f m)*
Pt crescimento *(m)*

crecimiento económico *(m)* Es
De Wirtschaftswachstum *(m)*
En economic growth
Fr croissance économique *(f)*
It sviluppo economico *(m)*
Pt crescimento económico *(m)*

credit *n* En
De Kredit *(m)*
Es crédito *(m)*
Fr crédit *(m)*
It credito *(m)*
Pt crédito *(m)*

crédit *(m)* Fr
De Kredit *(m)*
En credit
Es crédito *(m)*
It credito *(m)*
Pt crédito *(m)*

crédit à découvert *(m)* Fr
De offener Kredit *(m)*
En open credit
Es crédito en descubierto *(m)*
It credito allo scoperto *(m)*
Pt crédito em aberto *(m)*

credit balance En
De Kreditsaldo *(m)*
Es saldo acreedor *(m)*
Fr solde créditeur *(m)*
It saldo creditore *(m)*
Pt saldo credor *(m)*

crédit bancaire *(m)* Fr
De Bankkredit *(m)*
En bank credit
Es crédito bancario *(m)*
It credito bancario *(m)*
Pt crédito bancário *(m)*

credit card En
De Kreditkarte *(f)*
Es tarjeta de crédito *(f)*
Fr carte de crédit *(f)*
It carta di credito *(f)*
Pt cartão de crédito *(m)*

crédit de construction *(m)* Fr
De Baukredit *(m)*
En building loan
Es crédito de construcción *(m)*
It prestito immobiliare *(m)*
Pt empréstimo para construção *(m)*

crédit documentaire *(m)* Fr
De Dokumenten-Akkreditiv *(n)*
En documentary credit
Es crédito documentario *(m)*
It credito documentario *(m)*
Pt crédito contra documentação *(m)*

créditeur *(m) n* Fr
De Gläubiger *(m)*
En creditor
Es acreedor *(m)*
It creditore *(m)*
Pt credor *(m)*

créditeurs divers *(m pl)* Fr
De Kreditoren *(m pl)*
En sundry creditors
Es acreedores varios *(m pl)*
It creditori diversi *(m pl)*
Pt créditors diversos *(m pl)*

crediti bloccati *(m pl)* It
De eingefrorene Kredite *(m pl)*
En frozen credits
Es créditos congelados *(m pl)*
Fr crédits bloqués *(m pl)*
Pt créditos congelados *(m pl)*

credit insurance En
De Kreditversicherung *(f)*
Es seguro crediticio *(m)*
Fr assurance crédit *(f)*
It assicurazione credito *(f)*
Pt seguro de crédito *(m)*

credit note En
De Gutschriftanzeige (f)
Es nota e crédito (f)
Fr avis de crédit (f)
It nota di credito (f)
Pt aviso de crédito (m)

crédito (m) n Es, Pt
De Kredit (m)
En credit
Fr crédit (m)
It credito (m)

credito (m) n It
De Kredit (m)
En credit
Es crédito (m)
It crédit (m)
Pt crédito (m)

credito allo scoperto (m) It
De offener Kredit (m)
En open credit
Es crédito en descubierto (m)
Fr crédit à découvert (m)
Pt crédito em aberto (m)

crédito bancario (m) Es
De Bankkredit (m)
En bank credit
Fr crédit bancaire (m)
It credito bancario (m)
Pt crédito bancário (m)

credito bancario (m) It
De Bankkredit (m)
En bank credit
Es crédito bancario (m)
Fr crédit bancaire (m)
Pt crédito bancário (m)

crédito bancário (m) Pt
De Bankkredit (m)
En bank credit
Es crédito bancario (m)
Fr crédit bancaire (m)
It credito bancario (m)

**crédito contra
documentação** (m) Pt
De Dokumenten-Akkreditiv (n)
En documentary credit
Es crédito documentario (m)
Fr crédit documentaire (m)
It credito documentario (m)

credito d'accettazione (m) It
De Akzeptkredit (m)
En acceptance credit
Es crédito de aceptación (m)
Fr crédit par acceptation (m)
Pt crédito de aceitação (m)

crédito de aceitação (m) Pt
De Akzeptkredit (m)
En acceptance credit
Es crédito de aceptación (m)
Fr crédit par acceptation (m)
It credito d'accettazione (m)

crédito de aceptación (m) Es
De Akzeptkredit (m)
En acceptance credit
Fr crédit par acceptation (m)
It credito d'accettazione (m)
Pt crédito de aceitação (m)

crédito de construcción (m) Es
De Baukredit (m)
En building loan
Fr crédit de construction (m)
It prestito immobiliare (m)
Pt empréstimo para construção (m)

crédito documentario (m) Es
De Dokumenten-Akkreditiv (n)
En documentary credit
Fr crédit documentaire (m)
It credito documentario (m)
Pt crédito contra documentação (m)

credito documentario (m) It
De Dokumenten-Akkreditiv (n)
En documentary credit
Es crédito documentario (m)
Fr crédit documentaire (m)
Pt crédito contra documentação (m)

credito dubbio (m) It
De zweifelhafte Forderung (f)
En doubtful debt
Es deuda de pago dudoso (f)
Fr créance douteuse (f)
Pt dívida duvidosa (f)

crédito em aberto (m) Pt
De offener Kredit (m)
En open credit
Es crédito en descubierto (m)

Fr crédit à découvert (m)
It credito allo scoperto (m)

crédito em branco (m) Pt
De offener Kredit (m)
En blank credit
Es crédito en blanco (m)
Fr crédit à découvert (m)
It credito in bianco (m)

crédito en blanco (m) Es
De offener Kredit (m)
En blank credit
Fr crédit à découvert (m)
It credito in bianco (m)
Pt crédito em branco (m)

crédito en descubierto (m) Es
De offener Kredit (m)
En open credit
Fr crédit à découvert (m)
It credito allo scoperto (m)
Pt crédito em aberto (m)

credito in bianco (m) It
De offener Kredit (m)
En blank credit
Es crédito en blanco (m)
Fr crédit à découvert (m)
Pt crédito em branco (m)

credito inesigibile (m) It
De uneinbringliche Schuld (f)
En bad debt
Es deuda incobrable (f)
Fr créance irrécouvrable (f)
Pt dívida incobrável (f)

crédito provisional (m) Es
De Vorschußkredit (m)
En bridging loan
Am bridge-over
Fr crédit provisoire (m)
It credito provvisorio (m)
Pt crédito provisório (m)

crédito provisório (m) Pt
De Vorschußkredit (m)
En bridging loan
Am bridge-over
Es crédito provisional (m)
Fr crédit provisoire (m)
It credito provvisorio (m)

credito provvisorio (m) It
De Vorschußkredit (m)
En bridging loan
Am bridge-over

Es crédito provisional *(m)*
Fr crédit provisoire *(m)*
Pt crédito provisório *(m)*

creditor *n* En
De Gläubiger *(m)*
Es acreedor *(m)*
Fr créancier; créditeur *(m)*
It creditore *(m)*
Pt credor *(m)*

creditore *(m)* n Pt
De Gläubiger *(m)*
En creditor
Es acreedor *(m)*
Fr créancier; créditeur *(m)*
Pt credor *(m)*

creditore non garantito *(m)* It
De nicht gesicherter
  Gläubiger *(m)*
En unsecured creditor
Es acreedor no garantizado
  (m)
Fr créancier chirographaire
  (m)
Pt credor sem garantia *(m)*

crédito renovável *(m)* Pt
De automatisch sich erneu-
  erndes Akkreditiv *(n)*
En revolving credit
Es crédito reponible *(m)*
Fr accréditif automatique-
  ment renouvelable *(m)*
It credito rotativo *(m)*

crédito reponible *(m)* Es
De automatisch sich erneu-
  erndes Akkreditiv *(n)*
En revolving credit
Fr accréditif automatique-
  ment renouvelable *(m)*
It credito rotativo *(m)*
Pt crédito renovável *(m)*

creditore privilegiato *(m)* It
De bevorrechtigter Gläubiger
  (m)
En preferential creditor
Es acreedor privilegiado *(m)*
Fr créancier privilégié *(m)*
Pt credor preferencial *(m)*

creditori diversi *(m pl)* It
De Kreditoren *(m pl)*
En sundry creditors
Es acreedores varios *(m pl)*
Fr créditeurs divers *(m pl)*
Pt créditos diversos *(m pl)*

credito rotativo *(m)* It
De automatisch sich erneu-
  erndes Akkreditiv *(n)*
En revolving credit
Es crédito reponible *(m)*
Fr accréditif automatique-
  ment renouvelable *(m)*
Pt crédito renovável *(m)*

créditos congelados *(m pl)*
  Es, Pt
De eingefrorene Kredite *(m pl)*
En frozen credits
Fr crédits bloqués *(m pl)*
It crediti bloccati *(m pl)*

créditos diversos *(m pl)* Pt
De Kreditoren *(m pl)*
En sundry creditors
Es acreedores varios *(m pl)*
Fr créditeurs divers *(m pl)*
It creditori diversi *(m pl)*

crédit par acceptation *(m)* Fr
De Akzeptkredit *(m)*
En acceptance credit
Es crédito de aceptación *(m)*
It credito d'accettazione *(m)*
Pt crédito de aceitação *(m)*

crédit provisoire *(m)* Fr
De Vorschußkredit *(m)*
En bridging loan
Am bridge-over
Es crédito provisional *(m)*
It credito provvisorio *(m)*
Pt crédito provisório *(m)*

credit rating En
De Kreditwürdigkeit *(f)*
Es límite de crédito *(m)*
Fr degré de solvabilité *(m)*
It stima del credito *(f)*
Pt nível de crédito *(m)*

crédits bloqués *(m pl)* Fr
De eingefrorene Kredite *(m pl)*
En frozen credits
Es creditos congelados *(m pl)*
It crediti bloccati *(m pl)*
Pt créditos congelados *(m pl)*

credit squeeze En
De Kreditklemme *(f)*
Es escasez de créditos *(f)*
Fr resserrement de crédit *(m)*
It restrizione di credito *(f)*
Pt restrição de crédito *(f)*

credor *(m)* n Pt
De Gläubiger *(m)*
En creditor
Es acreedor *(m)*
Fr créancier; créditeur *(m)*
It creditore *(m)*

credor sem garantia *(m)* Pt
De nicht gesicherter
  Gläubiger *(m)*
En unsecured creditor
Es acreedor no garantizado
  (m)
Fr créancier chirographaire
  (m)
It creditore non garantito *(m)*

crescimento *(m)* n Pt
De Entwicklung; Wachstum *(f
  n)*
En growth
Es crecimiento *(m)*
Fr croissance; développe-
  ment *(f m)*
It crescita; sviluppo *(f m)*

crescimento económico *(m)*
  Pt
De Wirtschaftswachstum *(m)*
En economic growth
Es crecimiento económico
  (m)
Fr croissance économique *(f)*
It sviluppo economico *(m)*

crescita *(f)* n It
De Entwicklung; Wachstum *(f
  n)*
En growth
Es crecimiento *(m)*
Fr croissance; développe-
  ment *(f m)*
Pt crescimento *(m)*

crew En
De Mannschaft *(f)*
Es tripulación *(f)*
Fr équipage *(m)*
It equipaggio *(m)*
Pt tripulação *(f)*

crise économique *(f)* Fr
De Wirtschaftskrise *(f)*
En depression
Es crisis económica *(f)*
It crisi *(f)*
Pt depressão *(f)*

crisi *(f)* n It
De Wirtschaftskrise *(f)*
En depression
Es crisis económica *(f)*
Fr crise économique *(f)*
Pt depressão *(f)*

crisis económica *(f)* Es
De Wirtschaftskrise *(f)*
En depression
Fr crise économique *(f)*
It crisi *(f)*
Pt depressão *(f)*

cristal deslustrado *(m)* Es
De Mattscheibe *(f)*
En ground glass
Fr verre dépoli *(m)*
It vetro smerigliato *(m)*
Pt vidro esmerilado *(m)*

cristal de ventana *(m)* Es
De Fensterglas *(n)*
En window glass
Fr verre à vitres *(m)*
It vetro da finestre *(m)*
Pt vidro de montra *(m)*

cristallo *(m)* n It
De Spiegelglas *(n)*
En plate glass
Es vidrio plano pulido *(m)*
Fr verre à glaces; glace de vitrage *(m f)*
Pt chapa de vidro *(f)*

critical path analysis (c.p.a.) En
De Netzplantechnik *(f)*
Es análisis de recorrido crítico *(m)*
Fr analyse du chemin critique *(m)*
It analisi della linea critica *(f)*
Pt análise de transcurso crítico *(f)*

croissance *(f)* n Fr
De Entwicklung; Wachstum *(f n)*
En growth
Es crecimiento *(m)*
It crescita; sviluppo *(f m)*
Pt crescimento *(m)*

croissance économique *(f)* Fr
De Wirtschaftswachstum *(m)*
En economic growth

Es crecimiento económico *(m)*
It sviluppo enonomico *(m)*
Pt crescimento económico *(m)*

crollo di banca *(m)* It
De Bankkrach *(m)*
En bank crash
Es quiebra de banco *(f)*
Fr krach d'une banque *(m)*
Pt falência bancária *(f)*

crossed cheque En
De Verrechnungsscheck *(m)*
Es cheque cruzado *(m)*
Fr chèque barré *(m)*
It assegno sbarrato *(m)*
Pt cheque cruzado *(m)*

cuadro de conexión *(m)* Es
De Schalttafel *(f)*
En switchboard
Fr tableau de distribution *(m)*
It quadro di comando *(m)*
Pt quadro de distribuição *(m)*

cuarentena *(f)* n Es
De Quarantäne *(f)*
En quarantine
Fr quarantaine *(f)*
It quarantena *(f)*
Pt quarentena *(f)*

cubicación de obra *(f)* Es
De Kostenvoranschlag *(m)*
En bill of quantities
Fr devis *(m)*
It preventivo *(m)*
Pt relação de quantidades *(f)*

cubic capacity (cargo, bunker, etc.) En
De Kubikinhalt *(m)*
Es capacidad cúbica *(f)*
Fr volume *(m)*
It volume *(m)*
Pt capacidade cúbica *(f)*

cubic capacity (engine) En
De Hubraum *(m)*
Es cilindrada *(f)*
Fr cylindrée *(f)*
It cilindrata *(f)*
Pt cilindrada *(f)*

cubierta *(f)* n Es
De Deck *(n)*
En deck

Fr pont *(m)*
It coperta; ponte *(f m)*
Pt convés *(m)*

cubrirse *vb* Es
De sich decken
En hedge
Fr arbitrager
It coprirsi
Pt cobrir-se

cuenta (bancaria) *(f)* n Es
De Konto *(n)*
En account
Fr compte *(m)*
It conto *(m)*
Pt conta *(f)*

cuenta (nota) *(f)* Es
De Rechnung *(f)*
En bill; account
Fr compte; note *(m f)*
It conto; nota *(m f)*
Pt conta *(f)*

cuenta bancaria *(f)* Es
De Bankkonto *(n)*
En bank account
Fr compte en banque *(m)*
It conto in banca *(m)*
Pt conta bancária *(f)*

cuenta bloqueada *(f)* Es
De gesperrtes Konto *(n)*
En blocked account
Fr compte bloqué *(m)*
It conto bloccato *(m)*
Pt conta bloqueada *(f)*

cuenta comercial *(f)* Es
De Handelskonto *(n)*
En trade account
Fr compte commercial *(m)*
It conto commerciale *(m)*
Pt conta comercial *(f)*

cuenta común *(f)* Es
De Gemeinschaftskonto *(n)*
En joint account
Fr compte joint *(m)*
It conto in comune *(m)*
Pt conta conjunta *(f)*

cuenta corriente *(f)* Es
De Kontokorrent *(n)*
En current account
Am checking account
Fr compte courant *(m)*

It   conto corrente *(m)*
Pt   conta corrente *(f)*

cuenta de agio *(f)* Es
De Agiokonto *(n)*
En agio account
Fr   compte d'agio *(m)*
It   conto d'aggio *(m)*
Pt   conta de ágio *(f)*

cuenta de ahorras *(f)* Es
De Depositenkonto *(n)*
En deposit account
Am interest-bearing account
Fr   compte do dépôt *(m)*
It   conto di deposito *(m)*
Pt   conta de depósito *(f)*

cuenta de anticipos *(f)* Es
De Darlehenskonto *(n)*
En advance account
Fr   compte d'avances *(m)*
It   conto anticipo *(m)*
Pt   conta de adiantamentos *(f)*

cuenta de apropiación *(f)* Es
De Rückstellungskonto *(n)*
En appropriation account
Fr   compte d'affectation *(m)*
It   conto di stanziamento *(m)*
Pt   conta de apropriação *(f)*

cuenta de capital *(f)* Es
De Kapitalkonto *(n)*
En capital account
Fr   compte capital *(m)*
It   conto capitale *(m)*
Pt   conta de capital *(f)*

cuenta de compensación de cambio *(f)* Es
De Währungsausgleichs-fonds *(m)*
En exchange equalization account
Fr   fonds de stabilisation des changes *(m pl)*
It   conto per la stabilizzazione dei cambi *(m)*
Pt   conta de compensação de transacções *(f)*

cuenta de control *(f)* Es
De Kontrollkonto *(n)*
En control account
Fr   compte de contrôle *(m)*
It   conto di controllo *(m)*
Pt   conta de controlo *(f)*

cuenta de desembarque *(f)* Es
De Löschungskonto *(n)*
En landing account
Fr   compte de mise à terre *(m)*
It   conto di sbarco *(m)*
Pt   conta de descargas *(f)*

cuenta de especulaciones a la baja *(f)* Es
De Baissekonto *(n)*
En bear account
Fr   compte des speculations à la baisse *(m)*
It   conto di speculazioni al ribasso *(m)*
Pt   conta de especulações baixistas *(f)*

cuenta de ingresos y gastos *(f)* Es
De Ausgaben- und Ertragskonto *(n)*
En income and expenditure account
Fr   compte de revenus et dépenses *(m)*
It   conto proventi e spese *(m)*
Pt   conta de receitas e despesas *(f)*

cuenta de préstamos *(f)* Es
De Anleihekonto *(n)*
En loan account
Fr   compte des prêts *(m)*
It   conto anticipazioni *(m)*
Pt   conto de empréstimos *(f)*

cuenta de resultado *(f)* Es
De Firmenkonto *(n)*
En nominal account
Fr   compte nominal *(m)*
It   conto d'ordine *(m)*
Pt   conto nominal *(f)*

cuenta en descubierto *(f)* Es
De Konto überzogen *(n)*
En account overdrawn
Fr   compte découvert *(m)*
It   conto scoperto *(m)*
Pt   conto a descoberto *(f)*

cuenta exterior *(f)* Es
De Auslandskonto *(n)*
En external account
Am foreign currency account
Fr   compte transférable *(m)*
It   conto estero *(m)*
Pt   conta externa *(f)*

cuenta identificada con número *(f)* Es
De numeriertes Konto *(n)*
En numbered account
Fr   compte identifié par numéro *(m)*
It   conto indentificato da numero *(m)*
Pt   conta numerada *(f)*

cuenta personal *(f)* Es
De Kundenkonto *(n)*
En charge account
Fr   compte personnel *(m)*
It   conto personale *(m)*
Pt   conta pessoal *(f)*

cuenta rendida *(f)* Es
De zur Begleichung vorgelegte Rechnung *(f)*
En account rendered
Fr   compte rendu *(m)*
It   conto reso *(m)*
Pt   conta remetida *(f)*

cuentas a papar *(f pl)* Es
De Kreditoren *(m pl)*
En account payable
Fr   comptes à payer *(m pl)*
It   conti passivi *(m pl)*
Pt   contas a pagar *(f pl)*

cuentas a recibir *(f pl)* Es
De Debitoren *(m pl)*
En accounts receivable
Fr   créances *(f pl)*
It   conti attivi *(m pl)*
Pt   contas a receber *(f pl)*

cuentas consolidadas *(f pl)* Es
De konsolidierter Kontenabschluß *(m)*
En consolidated accounts
Fr   comptes consolidés *(m pl)*
It   conti consolidati *(m pl)*
Pt   contas consolidadas *(f pl)*

cuenta simulada *(f)* Es
De Firmenkonto *(n)*
En impersonal account
Fr   compte impersonnel *(m)*
It   conto d'ordine *(m)*
Pt   conta impessoal *(f)*

cuentas pendientes *(f pl)* Es
De ausstehende Schulden *(m pl)*
En outstandig accounts

Fr comptes à percevoir *(m pl)*
It conti aperti *(m pl)*
Pt contas por saldar *(f pl)*

cuentas revisadas *(f pl)* Es
De geprüfte Geschäftsbücher
  (n pl)
En audited accounts
Fr comptes vérifiés et
  certifiés *(m pl)*
It conti verificati e certificati
  (m pl)
Pt contas fiscalizadas *(f pl)*

cuenta suspensa *(f)* Es
De Übergangskonto *(n)*
En suspense account
Fr compte d'ordre *(m)*
It conto sospeso *(m)*
Pt conta pendente *(f)*

cuestionario *(m)* n Es
De Fragebogen *(m)*
En questionnaire
Fr questionnaire *(m)*
It questionario *(m)*
Pt questionário *(m)*

cum dividend En
De mit Dividende
Es con dividendo
Fr droit attaché
It con dividendo
Pt com dividendo

cumplimiento *(m)* n Es
De Erfüllung *(f)*
En fulfilment
Fr accomplissement *(m)*
It adempimento *(m)*
Pt cumprimento *(m)*

cumplir *vb* Es
De erfüllen
En fulfil
Fr remplir
It adempiere
Pt cumprir

cumprimento *(m)* n Pt
De Erfüllung *(f)*
En fulfilment
Es cumplimiento *(m)*
Fr accomplissement *(m)*
It adempimento *(m)*

cumpimento final *(m)* Pt
De Rechnungsentlastung *(f)*
En final discharge

Es finiquito *(m)*
Fr quitus *(m)*
It quietanza finale *(f)*

cumprir *vb* Pt
De erfüllen
En fulfil
Es cumplir
Fr remplir
It adempiere

cumulatif *adj* Fr
De kumulativ
En cumulative
Es acumulativo
It cumulativo
Pt cumulativo

cumulative *adj* En
De kumulativ
Es acumulativo
Fr cumulatif
It cumulativo
Pt cumulativo

cumulativo *adj* It, Pt
De kumulativ
En cumulative
Es acumulativo
Fr cumulatif

cuota *(f)* n Es
De Quote; Beteiligung *(f)*
En quota
Fr quote-part *(f)*
It quota *(f)*
Pt cota; quota-parte *(f)*

cupão *(m)* n Pt
De Kupon *(m)*
En coupon
Es cupón *(m)*
Fr coupon *(m)*
It cedola *(f)*

cupe de importación *(m)* Es
De Einfuhrkontingent *(n)*
En import quota
Fr contingent d'importation
  (m)
It contingente d'importazio-
  ne *(m)*
Pt quota de importação *(f)*

cupón *(m)* n Es
De Kupon *(m)*
En coupon
Fr coupon *(m)*
It cedola *(f)*
Pt cupão *(m)*

cupón de dividendos *(m)* Es
De Gewinnanteilschein *(m)*
En dividend warrant
Fr dividende-warrant *(m)*
It cedola di dividendo *(f)*
Pt cédula de dividendo *(f)*

curador *(m)* n Pt
De Nachlaßverwalter *(m)*
En administrator (of an estate)
Es administrador *(m)*
Fr curateur *(m)*
It curatore *(m)*

curateur *(m)* n Fr
De Nachlaßverwalter *(m)*
En administrator (of an estate)
Es administrador *(m)*
It curatore *(m)*
Pt curador *(m)*

curatore *(m)* n It
De Konkursverwalter;
  Nachlaßverwalter *(m)*
En (official) receiver;
  administrator
Es sindico; administrador *(m)*
Fr syndic de faillite; curateur
  (m)
Pt síndico; curador *(m)*

currency n En
De Währung *(f)*
Es moneda *(f)*
Fr monnaie *(f)*
It valuta *(f)*
Pt moeda *(f)*

currency area En
De Währungsgebiet *(n)*
Es zona monetaria *(f)*
Fr zone monétaire *(f)*
It zona monetaria *(f)*
Pt zona monetária *(f)*

currency control Am
En exchange control
De Devisenkontrolle *(f)*
Es fiscalización de cambios
  (f)
Fr contrôle des changes *(m)*
It controllo sui cambi *(m)*
Pt controlo de câmbios *(m)*

current *adj* En
De laufend
Es corriente
Fr courant; en cours
It corrente
Pt corrente

current account En
Am checking account
De Kontokorrent (n)
Es cuenta corriente (f)
Fr compte courant (m)
It conto corrente (m)
Pt conta corrente (f)

current assets En
De Umlaufvermögen (n)
Es activo realizable (m)
Fr actif courant (m)
It attivo liquido (m)
Pt bens no activo actual
   (m pl)

current liabilities En
De laufende Verbindlichkeiten
   (f pl)
Es pasivo exigible (m)
Fr passif exigible (m)
It passività esigibili (f pl)
Pt passivo actual (m)

current year En
De laufendes Jahr (n)
Es año en curso (m)
Fr année en cours (f)
It anno in corso (m)
Pt ano corrente (m)

curso de bolsa (m) Es
De Börsenkurs (m)
En stock-exchange
   quotation
Fr cours de bourse (m)
It quotazione di borsa (f)
Pt cotação da bolsa (f)

curva della domanda (f) It
De Nachfragekurve (f)
En demand curve
Es curva de relación
   demanda (f)
Fr courbe de la demande (f)
Pt curva de procura (f)

curva de procura (f) Pt
De Nachfragekurve (f)
En demand curve
Es curva de relación
   demanda (f)
Fr courbe de la demande (f)
It curva della domanda (f)

curva de relación demanda
   (f) Es
De Nachfragekurve (f)
En demand curve

Fr courbe de la demande (f)
It curva della domanda (f)
Pt curva de procura (f)

custas de manejo (f pl) Pt
De Umschlagspesen (f)
En handling charges
Es gastos de manutención
   (m pl)
Fr frais de manutention (m pl)
It spese di gestione (f pl)

custas de registo (f pl) Pt
De Anmeldegebühr (f)
En registration fee
Es derechos de registro (m pl)
Fr droit d'enregistrement (m)
It tassa di registrazione (f)

custear vb Pt
De kosten
En cost
Es costar
Fr coûter
It costare

custo (m) n Pt
De Kosten (pl)
En cost
Es coste (m)
Fr coût (m)
It costo (m)

custo contabilizado (m) Pt
De Buchwert der Einkäufe (m)
En book cost
Es coste contable (m)
Fr prix de revient comptable
   (m)
It costo contabile (m)

custo da mão de obra (m) Pt
De Lohnkosten (pl)
En cost of labour
Es coste de la mano de obra
   (m)
Fr coût de la main-d'œuvre (m)
It costo di mano d'opera (m)

custo de substituição (m) Pt
De Wiederanschaffungs-
   kosten (pl)
En replacement cost
Es coste de repuesto (m)
Fr coût de remplacement (m)
It costo di rimpiazzo (m)

custo de venda (m) Pt
De Verkaufskosten (pl)
En selling cost
Es coste de venta (m)
Fr frais de vente (m)
It costo di vendita (m)

custo de vida (m) Pt
De Lebenshaltungskosten (pl)
En cost of living
Es coste de vida (m)
Fr coût de la vie (m)
It costo della vita (m)

custo de vida mais elevado
   (m) Pt
De erhöhte Lebenshaltungs-
   kosten (pl)
En increased cost of living
Es coste de vida más alto (m)
Fr renchérissement du coût
   de la vie (m)
It aumentato costo della vita
   (m)

custodia (f) Es, It
De sichere Verwahrung (f)
En safe custody
Fr bonne garde (f)
Pt custódia segura (f)

custódia segura (f) Pt
De sichere Verwahrung (f)
En safe custody
Es custodia (f)
Fr bonne garde (f)
It custodia (f)

custo directo (m) Pt
De direkte Kosten (pl)
En direct cost
Es coste directo (m)
Fr prix direct de revient (m)
It costo diretto (m)

custo e frete Pt
De Kosten und Fracht
En cost an freight (c. & f.)
Es coste y flete
Fr coût et fret
It costo e nolo

custom (clientele) n En
De Kundschaft (f)
Es clientela (f)
Fr clientèle (f)
It clientela (f)
Pt clientela (f)

custo marginal *(m)* Pt
De Randkosten *(pl)*
En marginal cost
Es coste marginal *(m)*
Fr coût marginal *(m)*
It costo marginale *(m)*

custo médio *(m)* Pt
De Durchschnittskosten *(pl)*
En average cost
Es coste promedio *(m)*
Fr coût moyen *(m)*
It costo medio *(m)*

customer *n* En
De Kunde *(m)*
Es cliente *(m)*
Fr client *(m)*
It cliente *(m)*
Pt cliente *(m)*

custom of the trade En
De Handelsgebrauch *(m)*
Es uso comercial *(m)*
Fr usage commercial *(m)*
It uso commerciale *(m)*
Pt uso comercial *(m)*

customs *pl n* En
De Zoll *(n)*
Es aduana *(f)*
Fr douane *(f)*
It dogana *(f)*
Pt alfândega *(f)*

customs barrier En
De Zollschranke *(f)*
Es barrera aduanera *(f)*
Fr barrière douanière *(f)*
It barriera doganale *(f)*
Pt barreira alfandegária *(f)*

customs clearance En
De Zollabfertigung *(f)*
Es paso de aduanas *(f)*
Fr dédouanement *(m)*
It sdoganamento *(m)*
Pt despacho alfandegário *(m)*

customs declaration En
De Zollerklärung *(f)*
Es declaración de aduana *(f)*
Fr déclaration en douane *(f)*
It dichiarazione doganale *(f)*
Pt declaração alfandegária *(f)*

customs duty En
De Zoll *(m)*
Es derechos de aduanas
      (m pl)

Fr droit de douane *(m)*
It diritto doganale *(m)*
Pt direitos alfandegários
      (m pl)

customs examination En
De zollamtliche Untersuchung
      (f)
Es control de aduanas *(m)*
Fr visite douanière *(f)*
It visita doganale *(f)*
Pt verificação alfandegária *(f)*

customs union En
De Zollunion *(f)*
Es unión aduanera *(f)*
Fr union douanière *(f)*
It unione doganale *(f)*
Pt união aduaneira *(f)*

custo original *(m)* Pt
De Anschaffungskosten *(pl)*
En historic cost
Es coste primitivo *(m)*
Fr coût d'acquisition primitif
      (m)
It costo primitivo *(m)*

custo por unidade *(m)* Pt
De Einheitskosten *(pl)*
En unit cost
Es coste por unidad *(m)*
Fr coût de l'unité *(m)*
It costo unitario *(m)*

custos aumentados *(m pl)* Pt
De erhöhte Kosten *(pl)*
En increased costs
Es costes incrementados
      (m pl)
Fr accroissement des coûts
      (m)
It costi aumentati *(m pl)*

custos de exercício *(m pl)* Pt
De Betriebsausgaben *(f pl)*
En operating costs
Es costes operacionales
      (m pl)
Fr frais d'exploitation *(m pl)*
It spese di gestione *(f pl)*

custo, seguro, e frete Pt
De Kosten, Versicherung,
      Fracht
En cost, insurance, and
      freight (c.i.f.)
Es coste, seguro, y flete

Fr coût, assurance, fret
It costo, assicurazione, nolo

custos indirectos *(m pl)* Pt
De Gemeinkosten *(pl)*
En indirect costs
Es costes indirectos *(m pl)*
Fr frais indirects *(m pl)*
It costi indiretti *(m pl)*

custo social *(m)* Pt
De Sozialkosten *(pl)*
En social cost
Es coste social *(m)*
Fr coût social *(m)*
It costo sociale *(m)*

custo variável *(m)* Pt
De variable Kosten *(pl)*
En variable cost
Es coste variable *(m)*
Fr coût variable *(m)*
It costo variabile *(m)*

custo verdadeiro *(m)* Pt
De Gestehungskosten *(pl)*
En actual cost
Es precio verdadero *(m)*
Fr prix de revient effectif *(m)*
It costo effettivo *(m)*

cybernetics *n* En
De Kybernetik *(f)*
Es cibernética *(f)*
Fr cybernétique *(f)*
It cibernetica *(f)*
Pt cibernética *(f)*

cybernétique *(f) n* Fr
De Kybernetik *(f)*
En cybernetics
Es cibernética *(f)*
It cibernetica *(f)*
Pt cibernética *(f)*

cycle de commerce *(m)* Fr
De Handelszyklus *(m)*
En trade cycle
Es ciclo del negocio *(m)*
It ciclo degli affari *(m)*
Pt ciclo comercial *(m)*

cycle économique *(m)* Fr
De Konjunkturzyklus *(m)*
En business cycle
Es ciclo económico *(m)*
It ciclo d'affari *(m)*
Pt ciclo económico *(m)*

cylindrée *(f)* Fr
De Hubraum *(m)*
En cubic capacity
Es cilindrada *(f)*
It cilindrata *(f)*
Pt cilindrada *(f)*

D

d'accord avec Fr
De im Einvernehmen mit
En in agreement with
Es de acuerdo con
It d'accordo con
Pt de acordo com

d'accordo con It
De im Einvernehmen mit
En in agreement with
Es de acuerdo con
Fr d'accord avec
Pt de acordo con

Dachgesellschaft *(f)* n
De
En holding company
Es compañía tenedora *(f)*
Fr société holding *(f)*
It società holding *(f)*
Pt companhia proprietária *(f)*

dactilógrafa *(f)* n Pt
De Abschreibtypistin *(f)*
En copy typist
Am transcriber
Es mecanógrafa *(f)*
Fr dactylo copiste *(f)*
It dattilografa *(f)*

dactylo copiste *(f)* Fr
De Abschreibtypistin *(f)*
En copy typist
Am transcriber
Es mecanógrafa *(f)*
It dattilografa *(f)*
Pt dactilógrafa *(f)*

dados *(m pl)* n Pt
De Daten *(n pl)*
En data
Es datos *(m pl)*
Fr données *(f pl)*
It dati *(m pl)*

damage n En
De Beschädigung; Schaden
   (f m)
Es daño *(m)*
Fr dommage; avarie *(m f)*
It danno *(m)*
Pt dano *(m)*

damaged goods En
De beschädigte Waren *(f pl)*
Es mercancías averiadas *(f pl)*
Fr marchandises avariées
   (f pl)
It merce avariata *(f)*
Pt mercadorias danificadas
   (f pl)

damage in transit En
De Beschädigung beim
   Transport *(f)*
Es daños en ruta *(m pl)*
Fr avaries de route *(f pl)*
It danno durante trasporto
   (m)
Pt danos em trânsito *(m pl)*

damages n pl En
De Schadenersatz *(m)*
Es daños *(m pl)*
Fr dommages-intérêts *(m pl)*
It danni *(m pl)*
Pt danos *(m pl)*

Dampfer *(m)* n De
En steamer
Es buque de vapor *(m)*
Fr bateau à vapeur *(m)*
It vapore *(m)*
Pt vapor *(m)*

danger money En
De Gefahrenzulage *(f)*
Es suma para riesgos *(f)*
Fr prime de risque *(f)*
It compenso per il rischio *(m)*
Pt prémio de risco *(m)*

dangerous goods En
De gefährliche Waren
   (f pl)
Es mercancías peligrosas
   (f pl)
Fr marchandises dangereu-
   ses *(f pl)*
It merce pericolosa *(f)*
Pt mercadorias perigosas
   (f pl)

danni *(m pl)* n It
De Schadenersatz *(m)*
En damages

Es daños *(m pl)*
Fr dommages-intérêts
   (m pl)
Pt danos *(m pl)*

danni indiretti *(m pl)* It
De immaterieller Schaden
   (m)
En consequential damages
Es daños indirectos *(m pl)*
Fr dommages indirects *(m pl)*
Pt danos decorrentes *(m pl)*

danni liquidati *(m pl)*
   It
De Konventionalstrafe *(t)*
En liquidated damages
Es daños liquidados *(m pl)*
Fr dommages-intérêts fixés
   en argent *(m pl)*
Pt danos liquidados
   (m pl)

danni nominali *(m pl)* It
De Ordnungsentschädigung
   (f)
En nominal damages
Es daños nominales *(m pl)*
Fr indemnité de principe *(f)*
Pt danos nominais *(m pl)*

danni particolari *(m pl)* It
De Ersatz immateriellen
   Schadens *(m)*
En special damages
Es daños especiales *(m pl)*
Fr dommages indirects *(m pl)*
Pt indemnização especial *(f)*

danno *(m)* n It
De Beschädigung; Schaden
   (m)
En damage; injury
Es daño *(m)*
Fr dommage; avarie *(m f)*
Pt dano; injúria *(m f)*

danno causato dall'acqua
   (m) It
De Wasserschaden *(m)*
En water damage
Es daño causado por el agua
   (m)
Fr dégâts des eaux *(m pl)*
Pt dano causado por água
   (m)

danno d'acqua di mare *(m)*
   It
De Seewasserschaden *(m)*
En sea-water damage

Es daño de agua de mar *(m)*
Fr dégâts d'eau de mer *(m pl)*
Pt dano causado por água
do mar *(m)*

danno d'acqua dolce *(m)* It
De Süßwasserschaden *(m)*
En fresh-water damage
Es daño de agua dulce *(m pl)*
Fr dégâts d'eau douce *(m)*
Pt dano causado por água
doce *(m)*

danno durante trasporto *(m)*
It
De Beschädigung beim
Transport *(f)*
En damage in transit
Es daños en ruta *(m pl)*
Fr avaries de route *(f pl)*
Pt danos em trânsito *(m pl)*

danno indiretto *(m)* It
De indirekter Schaden *(m)*
En consequential damage
Es daños indirectos *(m pl)*
Fr dommage indirect *(m)*
Pt dano por consequência
(m)

daño *(m)* n Es
De Beschädigung, Schaden
(f m)
En damage; injury
Fr dommage; avarie *(m f)*
It danno *(m)*
Pt dano; injúria *(m f)*

dano *(m)* n Pt
De Beschädigung, Schaden
(f m)
En damage; injury
Es daño *(m)*
Fr dommage; avarie *(m f)*
It danno *(m)*

dano causado por água *(m)*
Pt
De Wasserschaden *(m)*
En water damage
Es daño causado por el agua
(m)
Fr dégâts des eaux *(m pl)*
It danno causato dall'acqua
(m)

**dano causado por água
doce** *(m)* Pt
De Süßwasserschaden *(m)*
En fresh-water damage

Es daño de agua dulce *(m)*
Fr dégâts d'eau douce *(m pl)*
It danno d'acqua dolce *(m)*

**dano causado pro água do
mar** *(m)* Pt
De Seewasserschaden *(m)*
En sea-water damage
Es daño de agua de mar *(m)*
Fr dégâts d'eau de mer *(m pl)*
It danno d'acqua di mare *(m)*

daño causado por el agua
(m) Es
De Wasserschaden *(m)*
En water damage
Fr dégâts des eaux *(m pl)*
It danno causato dall'acqua
(m)
Pt dano causado por água
(m)

daño de agua de mar *(m)* Es
De Seewasserschaden *(m)*
En sea-water damage
Fr dégâts d'eau de mer *(m pl)*
It danno d'acqua di mare *(m)*
Pt dano causado pela água
do mar *(m)*

daño de agua dulce *(m)* Es
De Süßwasserschaden *(m)*
En fresh-water damage
Fr dégâts d'eau douce *(m pl)*
It danno d'acqua dolce *(m)*
Pt dano causado por água
doce *(m)*

dano por consequência *(m)*
Pt
De indirekter Schaden *(m)*
En consequential damage
Es daños indirectos *(m pl)*
Fr dommage indirect *(m)*
It dano indiretto *(m)*

daños *(m pl)* n Es
De Schadenersatz *(m)*
En damages
Fr dommages-intérêts *(m pl)*
It danni *(m pl)*
Pt danos *(m pl)*

danos *(m pl)* n Pt
De Schadenersatz *(m)*
En damages
Es daños *(m pl)*
Fr dommages-intérêts *(m pl)*
It danni *(m pl)*

danos decorrentes *(m pl)* Pt
De immaterieller Schaden *(m)*
En consequential damage
Es daños indirectos *(m pl)*
Fr dommages indirects *(m pl)*
It danni indiretti *(m pl)*

danos em trânsito *(m pl)* Pt
De Beschädigung beim
Transport *(f)*
En damage in transit
Es daños en ruta *(m pl)*
Fr avaries de route *(f pl)*
It danno durante trasporto
(m)

daños en ruta *(m pl)* Es
De Beschädigung beim
Transport *(f)*
En damage in transit
Fr avaries de route *(f pl)*
It danno durante trasporto
(m)
Pt danos em trânsito *(m pl)*

daños especiales *(m pl)* Es
De Ersatz immateriellen
Schadens *(m)*
En special damages
Fr dommages indirects *(m pl)*
It danni particolari *(m pl)*
Pt indemnização especial *(f)*

daños indirectos *(m pl)* Es
De immaterieller Schaden *(m)*
En consequential damages
Fr dommages indirects *(m pl)*
It danni indiretti *(m pl)*
Pt danos decorrentes *(m pl)*

daños liquidados *(m pl)* Es
De Konventionalstrafe *(f)*
En liquidated damages
Fr dommages-intérêts fixés
en argent *(m pl)*
It danni liquidati *(m pl)*
Pt danos liquidados *(m pl)*

danos liquidados *(m pl)* Pt
De Konventionalstrafe *(f)*
En liquidated damages
Es daños liquidados *(m pl)*
Fr dommages-intérêts fixés
en argent *(m pl)*
It danni liquidati *(m pl)*

danos nominais *(m pl)* Pt
De Ordnungsentschädigung
(f)
En nominal damages

Es daños nominales *(m pl)*
Fr indemnité de principe *(f)*
It danni nominali *(m pl)*

daños nominales *(m pl)* Es
De Ordnungsentschädigung *(f)*
En nominal damages
Fr indemnité de principe *(f)*
It danni nominali *(m pl)*
Pt danos nominais *(m pl)*

dare impulso a It
De fördern
En promote (a product)
Es promover
Fr promouvoir
Pt promover

dare una settimana di preavviso It
De einwöchig kündigen
En giva a week's notice
Es dar una semana de aviso
Fr donner ses huit jours
Pt dar um prazo de uma semana para despedimento

dar execução a um testamento Pt
De ein Testament vollstrecken
En execute a will
Es ejecutar un testamento
Fr exécuter un testament
It eseguire un testamento

dar execução a um título legal Pt
De eine Urkunde unterzeichnen
En execute a deed
Es firmar una escritura
Fr passer un acte
It perfezionare un atto

dar execução a poderes de procuração Pt
De eine Vollmacht erteilen
En execute a power of attorney
Es otorgar poder notarial
Fr conférer des pleins pouvoirs
It conferire una procura

Darlehenskonto *(n) n* De
En advance account
Es cuenta de anticipos *(f)*
Fr compte d'avances *(m)*

It conto anticipo *(m)*
Pt conta de adiantamentos *(f)*

darlehensweise De
En on loan
Es en préstamo
Fr sous forme de prêt
It in prestito
Pt por empréstimo

dar um prazo de uma semana (para despedimento) Pt
De einwöchig kündigen
En give a week's notice
Es dar una semana de aviso
Fr donner ses huit jours
It dare una settimana di preavviso

dar una semana de aviso Es
De einwöchig kündigen
En give a week's notice
Fr donner ses huit jours
It dare una settimana di preavviso
Pt dar um prazo de uma semana para despedimento

data *pl n* En
De Daten *(n pl)*
Es datos *(m pl)*
Fr données *(f pl)*
It dati *(m pl)*
Pt dados *(m pl)*

data *(f) n* It, Pt
De Datum *(n)*
En date
Es fecha *(f)*
Fr date *(f)*

data capture En
De Datenerfassung *(f)*
Es recogida de datos *(f)*
Fr saisie des données *(f)*
It raccolta dati *(f)*
Pt recolha de dados *(f)*

data de entrega *(f)* Pt
De Liefertermin *(m)*
En delivery date
Es fecha de entrega *(f)*
Fr date de livraison *(f)*
It data di consegna *(f)*

data de resgate *(f)* Pt
De Einlösungstag *(m)*
En redemption date
Es fecha de reembolso *(f)*

Fr date du remboursement *(f)*
It data di rimborso *(f)*

data de vencimento *(f)* Pt
De Fälligkeitstag *(m)*
En date of maturity; due date
Es fecha de vencimiento *(f)*
Fr date d'échéance *(f)*
It data di scadenza *(f)*

data di consegna *(f)* It
De Liefertermin *(m)*
En delivery date
Es fecha de entrega *(f)*
Fr date de livraison *(f)*
Pt data de entrega *(f)*

data di partenza *(f)* It
De Abgangstag *(m)*
En sailing date
Es día de salida *(m)*
Fr date de départ *(f)*
Pt dia de saída *(m)*

data di rimborso *(f)* It
De Einlösungstag *(m)*
En redemption date
Es fecha de reembolso *(f)*
Fr date du remboursement *(f)*
Pt data de resgate *(f)*

data di scadenza *(f)* It
De Fälligkeitstag *(m)*
En date of maturity; due date
Es fecha de vencimiento *(f)*
Fr date d'échéance *(f)*
Pt date de vencimento *(f)*

data processing En
De Datenverarbeitung *(f)*
Es tratamiento de datos *(m)*
Fr traitement d'informatique *(m)*
It elaborazione dei dati *(f)*
Pt processamento de dados *(m)*

date *n* En, Fr *(f)*
De Datum *(n)*
Es fecha *(f)*
It data *(f)*
Pt data *(f)*

date d'échéance *(f)* Fr
De Fälligkeitstag *(m)*
En date of maturity
Es fecha de vencimiento *(f)*
It data di scadenza *(f)*
Pt data de vencimento *(f)*

date de départ *(f)* Fr
De Abgangstag *(m)*
En sailing date
Es día de salida *(m)*
It data di partenza *(f)*
Pt dai de saída *(m)*

date de livraison *(f)* Fr
De Liefertermin *(m)*
En delivery date
Es fecha de entrega *(f)*
It data di consegna *(f)*
Pt data de entrega ou
    remessa *(f)*

date du remboursement *(f)*
    Fr
De Einlösungstag *(m)*
En redemption date
Es fecha de reembolso *(f)*
It data di rimborso *(f)*
Pt data de resgate *(f)*

date limite *(f)* Fr
De Verfallstermin *(m)*
En deadline
Es fecha tope *(f)*
It ultima data o ora possibile
    (f)
Pt data de vencimento *(f)*

Daten *(n pl)* n De
En data
Es datos *(m pl)*
Fr données *(f pl)*
It dati *(m pl)*
Pt dados *(m pl)*

Datenerfassung *(f)* n De
En data capture
Es recogida de datos *(f)*
Fr saisie des données *(f)*
It raccolta dati *(f)*
Pt recolha de dados *(f)*

Datenverarbeitung *(f)* n De
En data processing
Es tratamiento de datos *(m)*
Fr traitement d'informatique
    (m)
It elaborazione dei dati *(f)*
Pt processamento de dados
    (m)

date of maturity En
De Fälligkeitstag *(m)*
Es fecha de vencimiento *(f)*
Fr date d'échéance *(f)*

It data di scadenza *(f)*
Pt data de vencimento *(f)*

date-stamp n En
De Tagesstempel *(m)*
Es sello de fecha *(m)*
Fr dateur *(m)*
It timbro a data *(m)*
Pt carimbo de datas *(m)*

dateur *(m)* n Fr
De Tagesstempel *(m)*
En date-stamp
Es sello de fecha *(m)*
It timbro a data *(m)*
Pt carimbo de datas *(m)*

dati *(m pl)* n It
De Daten *(n pl)*
En data
Es datos *(m pl)*
Fr données *(f pl)*
Pt dados *(m pl)*

datore di lavoro *(m)* It
De Arbeitgeber *(m)*
En employer
Es patrono *(m)*
Fr employeur *(m)*
Pt patrão *(m)*

datos *(m pl)* n Es
De Daten *(n pl)*
En data
Fr données *(f pl)*
It dati *(m pl)*
Pt dados *(m pl)*

dattilografa *(f)* n It
De Abschreibtypistin *(f)*
En copy typist
Am transcriber
Es mecanógrafa *(f)*
Fr dactylo copiste *(f)*
Pt dactilógrafa *(f)*

dattiloscritto *(m)* n It
De Maschinenschrift *(f)*
En typescript
Es texto mecanografiado *(m)*
Fr manuscrit dactylographié
    (m)
Pt texto dactilografado *(m)*

Datum *(n)* n De
En date
Es fecha *(f)*
Fr date *(f)*
It data *(f)*
Pt data *(f)*

Dauer *(f)* n De
En duration
Es duración *(f)*
Fr durée *(f)*
It durata *(f)*
Pt duração *(f)*

dauerhafte Konsumgüter *(n*
    pl) De
En consumer durables
Es bienes de consumo
    duraderos *(m pl)*
Fr biens de consommation
    durables *(m pl)*
It beni de consumo durabili
    (m pl)
Pt artigos de consumo
    perduráveis *(m pl)*

Dauerschuldverschreibung
    (f) n De
En perpetual debenture
Es obligación a perpetuidad
    (f)
Fr obligation perpétuelle *(f)*
It obbligazione perpetua *(f)*
Pt obrigação perenidade *(f)*

da vendere o rimandare It
De Rücksendung, wenn
    unverkauft
En sale or return
Es venta o devolución
Fr vente avec faculté de
    retour
Pt ventda ou devolução

day n En
De Tag *(m)*
Es día *(m)*
Fr jour *(m)*
It giorno *(m)*
Pt dia *(m)*

day after tomorrow En
De übermorgen
Es pasado mañana
Fr après demain
It dopodomani
Pt depois de amanhã

day before yesterday En
De vorgestern
Es anteayer
Fr avant-hier
It avantieri
Pt anteontem

day-book n En
De Tagebuch (n)
Es diario (m)
Fr journal (m)
It giornale (m)
Pt diário (m)

day off En
De dienstfreier Tag (m)
Es día libre (m)
Fr jour de congé (m)
It giorno di riposo (m)
Pt dia de folga (m)

day-shift n En
De Tagschicht (f)
Es turno de día (m)
Fr équipe du jour (f)
It turno de giorno (m)
Pt turno de dia (m)

days of grace En
De Nachfrist (f)
Es días de gracia (f pl)
Fr délai supplémentaire (m)
It giorni di grazia (m pl)
Pt dias de tolerância (m pl)

day-to-day En
De täglich
Es día a día
Fr au jour le jour
It di giorno in giorno
Pt día a dia

dazio d'importazione (m) It
De Einfuhrzoll (m)
En import duty
Es decheros de importación (m pl)
Fr droits d'entrée (m pl)
Pt direitos de importação (m pl)

dazio pagato It
De verzollt
En duty-paid
Es derechos pagados
Fr acquitté
Pt direitos pagos

de acordo com Pt
De im Einvernehmen mit
En in agreement with
Es de acuerdo con
Fr d'accord avec
It d'accordo con

de acuerdo con Es
De im Einvernehmen mit
En in agreement with
Fr d'accord avec
It d'accordo con
Pt de acordo com

deadline n En
De Verfallstermin (m)
Es fecha tope (f)
Fr date limite (f)
It ultima data o ora possibile (f)
Pt data de vencimento (f)

deadweight n En
De Tragfähigkeit (f)
Es peso muerto (m)
Fr port en lourd (m)
It peso morto (m)
Pt peso morto (m)

deal n En
De Abschluß (m)
Es negocio (m)
Fr affaire (f)
It affare (f)
Pt negócio (m)

dealer n En
De Händler (m)
Es comerciante (m)
Fr négociant (m)
It negoziante; commerciante (m)
Pt negociante (m)

dear money En
De teures Geld (n)
Es dinero caro (m)
Fr agent cher (m)
It denaro ad alto interesse (m)
Pt dinheiro caro (m)

death n En
De Tod (m)
Es muerte (m)
Fr mort (f)
It morte (f)
Pt morte (f)

death certificate En
De Totenschein (m)
Es partida de defunción (f)
Fr extrait d'acte de décès (m)
It certificato di morte (m)
Pt certidão de óbito (f)

death duties En
Am estate taxes
De Erbschaftsteuern (f pl)
Es derechos sucesorios (m pl)
Fr droits de succession (m pl)
It diritti di successione (m pl)
Pt impostos de sucessão (m pl)

death rate En
De Sterblichkeitsziffer (f)
Es mortalidad (f)
Fr taux de mortalité (m)
It tasso di mortalità (m)
Pt taxa de mortalidade (f)

debenture n En
De Obligation; Schuldver-schreibung (f)
Es obligación (f)
Fr obligation (f)
It obbligazione (f)
Pt obrigação (f)

debenture holder En
De Obligationsinhaber (m)
Es obligacionista (m)
Fr porteur d'obligations; obligataire (m)
It obbligazionista (m)
Pt titular de obrigação (m)

Debet (n) n De
En debit
Es débito (m)
Fr doit; débit (m)
It debito; dare (m)
Pt débito (m)

debit n En
De Debet; Soll (n)
Es débito (m)
Fr doit; débit (m)
It debito; dare (m)
Pt débito (m)

débit (m) n Fr
De Debet; Soll (n)
En debit
Es débito (m)
It debito; dare (m)
Pt débito (m)

debit balance En
De Sollsaldo (m)
Es saldo en débito (m)
Fr solde débiteur (m)
It saldo debitore (m)
Pt saldo devedor (m)

débit direct *(m)* Fr
De direkte Belastung *(f)*
En direct debit
Es débito directo *(m)*
It debito diretto *(m)*
Pt débito directo *(m)*

débiteur *(m)* n Fr
De Schuldner *(m)*
En debtor
Es deudor *(m)*
It debitore *(m)*
Pt devedor *(m)*

debit note En
De Lastschrift *(f)*
Es nota de débito *(f)*
Fr avis de débit *(m)*
It nota di addebito *(f)*
Pt aviso de débito *(m)*

débito *(m)* n Es, Pt
De Debet; Soll *(n)*
En debit
Fr doit; débit *(m)*
It debito; dare *(m)*

debito *(m)* n It
De Debet; Schuld *(n f)*
En debit; debt
Es débito; deuda *(m f)*
Fr débit; créance *(m f)*
Pt débito; dívida *(m f)*

debito attivo *(m)* It
De Buchschuld *(f)*
En book debt
Es deuda contabilizada *(f)*
Fr dette comptable *(f)*
Pt débito contabilizado *(m)*

débito contabilizado *(m)* Pt
De Buchschuld *(f)*
En book debt
Es deuda contabilizada *(f)*
Fr dette comptable *(f)*
It debito attivo *(m)*

débito directo *(m)* Es, Pt
De direkte Belastung *(f)*
En direct debit
Fr débit direct *(m)*
It debito diretto *(m)*

debito diretto *(m)* It
De direkte Belastung *(f)*
En direct debit
Es débito directo *(m)*

Fr débit direct *(m)*
Pt débito directo *(m)*

debito pubblico *(m)* It
De Staatsschuld *(f)*
En national debt
Es deuda pública *(f)*
Fr dette publique *(f)*
Pt dívida pública *(f)*

debitore *(m)* n It
De Schuldner *(m)*
En debtor
Es deudor *(m)*
Fr débiteur *(m)*
Pt devedor *(m)*

Debitoren *(m pl)* n De
En accounts receivable
Es cuentas a recibir *(f pl)*
Fr créanes *(f pl)*
It conti attivi *(m pl)*
It contas a receber *(f pl)*

de boa fé Pt
De auf Treu und Glauben
En in good faith
Es de buena fé
Fr de bonne foi
It in buona fede

de bonne foi Fr
De auf Treu und Glauben
En in good faith
Es de buena fé
It in buona fede
Pt de boa fé

déboursement *(m)* n Fr
De Auszahlung *(f)*
En disbursement
Es desembolso *(m)*
It esborso *(m)*
Pt desembolso *(m)*

debt n En
De Schuld *(f)*
Es deuda *(f)*
Fr créance *(f)*
It debito *(m)*
Pt dívida *(f)*

debt collector En
De Inkassobeauftragte(r) *(m)*
Es agente recaudador *(m)*
Fr agent de recouvrement *(m)*
It agente di ricupero crediti *(m)*
Pt cobrador *(m)*

debtor n En
De Schuldner *(m)*
Es deudor *(m)*
Fr débiteur *(m)*
It debitore *(m)*
Pt devedor *(m)*

de buena fé Es
De auf Treu und Glauben
En in good faith
Fr de bonne foi
It in buona fede
Pt de boa fé

decadimento incorporato *(m)* It
De eingebautes Veralten *(n)*
En built-in obsolescene
Es decaimiento incorporado *(m)*
Fr désuétude incorporée *(f)*
Pt obsolência pré-incorporada *(f)*

decaimiento incorporado *(m)* Es
De eingebautes Veralten *(n)*
En built-in obsolescence
Fr désuétude incorporée *(f)*
It decadimento incorporato *(m)*
Pt obsolência pré-incorporada *(f)*

décentraliser *vb* Fr
De dezentralisieren
En decentralize
Es decentralizar
It decentralizzare
Pt descentralizar

decentralizar *vb* Es
De dezentralisieren
En decentralize
Fr décentraliser
It decentralizzare
Pt descentralizar

decentralize *vb* En
De dezentralisieren
Es decentralizar
Fr décentraliser
It decentralizzare
Pt descentralizar

decentralizzare *vb* It
De dezentralisieren
En decentralize
Es decentralizar

Fr décentraliser
Pt descentralizar

déchets *(m pl) n* Fr
De Abfallprodukt *(n)*
En waste products
Es desperdicios *(m pl)*
It produtto di rifiuto *(m)*
Pt desperdícios *(m pl)*

déchets toxiques *(m pl)* Fr
De giftiger Abfall *(m)*
En toxic waste
Es efluentes tóxicos *(m pl)*
It rifiuti tossici *(m pl)*
Pt despejos tóxicos *(m pl)*

decide *vb* En
De entscheiden
Es decidir
Fr décider
It decidere
Pt decidir

décider *vb* Fr
De entscheiden
En decide
Es decidir
It decidere
Pt decidir

decidere *vb* It
De entscheiden
En decide
Es dicidir
Fr décider
Pt decidir

decidir *vb* Es, Pt
De entscheiden
En decide
Fr décider
It decidere

decimal *adj* En, Es, Pt
De dezimal
Fr décimal
It decimale

décimal *adj* Fr
De dezimal
En decimal
Es decimal
It decimale
Pt decimal

decimale *adj* It
De dezimal
En decimal

Es decimal
Fr décimal
Pt decimal

decisão *(f) n* Pt
De Entscheidung *(f)*
En decision
Es decisión *(f)*
Fr décision *(f)*
It decisione *(f)*

decisão arbitragem *(f)* Pt
De Schiedsspruch *(m)*
En arbitration award
Es sentencia arbitral *(f)*
Fr sentence arbitrale *(f)*
It lodo arbitrale *(m)*

decision *n* En
De Entscheidung *(f)*
Es decisión *(f)*
Fr décision *(f)*
It decisione *(f)*
Pt decisão *(f)*

decisión *(f) n* Es
De Entscheidung *(f)*
En decision
Fr décision *(f)*
It decisione *(f)*
Pt decisão *(f)*

décision *(f) n* Fr
De Entscheidung *(f)*
En decision
Es decisión *(f)*
It decisione *(f)*
Pt decisão *(f)*

decisione *(f) n* It
De Entscheidung *(f)*
En decision
Es decisión *(f)*
Fr décision *(f)*
Pt decisaão *(f)*

decision theory En
De Entscheidungslehre *(f)*
Es teoría de la decisión *(f)*
Fr théorie de la décision *(f)*
It teoria della decisione *(f)*
Pt teoria de deciasão *(f)*

deck (of a ship) *n* En
De Deck *(n)*
Es cubierta *(f)*
Fr pont *(m)*
It coperta; ponte *(f m)*
Pt convés *(m)*

Deck *(n) n* De
En deck
Es cubierta *(f)*
Fr pont *(m)*
It coperta; ponte *(f m)*
Pt convés *(m)*

deck cargo En
De Deckladung *(f)*
Es carga en cubierta *(f)*
Fr cargaison de pont *(f)*
It carico in coperta *(m)*
Pt carga de convés *(f)*

Deckladung *(f) n* De
En deck cargo
Es carga en cubierta *(f)*
Fr cargaison de pont *(f)*
It carico in coperta *(m)*
Pt carga de convés *(f)*

Deckung *(f) n* De
En cover
Es cobertura *(f)*
Fr couverture *(f)*
It copertura *(f)*
Pt cobertura *(f)*

Deckungszusage *(f) n* De
En cover note
Es aviso de seguro del riesgo *(m)*
Fr lettre de couverture *(f)*
It nota di copertura *(f)*
Pt nota de cobertura *(f)*

declaração *(f) n* Pt
De Erklärung *(f)*
En declaration
Es declaración *(f)*
Fr déclaration *(f)*
It dichiarazione *(f)*

declaração alfandegária *(f)* Pt
De Zollerklärung *(f)*
En customs declaration
Es declaración de aduana *(f)*
Fr déclaration en douane *(f)*
It dichiarazione doganale *(f)*

declaração de expedição *(f)* Pt
En Absendungserklärung *(f)*
En declaration of shipment
Es declaración de expedición *(f)*
Fr déclaration d'expédition *(f)*
It dichiarazione d'imbarco *(f)*

declaração de propósito *(f)*
Pt
De Willenserklärung *(f)*
En declaration of intent
Es declaración de intención
    (f)
Fr déclaration d'intention *(f)*
It dichiarazione d'intenzione
    (f)

declaração fiscal *(f)* Pt
De Einkommensteuererklä-
    rung *(f)*
En income-tax return
Es declaración fiscal *(f)*
Fr déclaration de revenu *(f)*
It dichiarazione del reddito
    (f)

**declaração para efeitos de
    tributação** *(f)* Pt
De Steuererklärung *(f)*
En tax return
Es declaración de ingresos *(f)*
Fr déclaration de l'impôt *(f)*
It dichiarazione fiscale *(f)*

declaração sob juramento *(f)*
Pt
De beeidigte Erklärung *(f)*
En affidavit
Es declaratión jurada *(f)*
Fr déclaration sous serment
    (f)
It dichiarazione giurata *(f)*

declaración *(f)* n Es
De Erklärung *(f)*
En declaration
Fr déclaration *(f)*
It dichiarazione *(f)*
Pt declaração *(f)*

declaración de aduana *(f)* Es
De Zollerklärung *(f)*
En customs declaration
Fr déclaration en douane *(f)*
It dichiarazione doganale *(f)*
Pt declaração alfandegária *(f)*

declaración de expedición
    (f) Es
De Absendungserklärung *(f)*
En declaration of shipment
Fr déclaration d'expédition *(f)*
It dichiarazione d'im.barco *(f)*
Pt declaração de expedição *(f)*

declaración de ingresos *(f)*
Es
De Steuererklärung *(f)*
En tax return
Fr déclaration de l'impôt *(f)*
It dichiarazione fiscale *(f)*
Pt declaração para efeitos de
    tributação *(f)*

declaración de intención *(f)*
Es
De Willenserklärung *(f)*
En declaration of intent
Fr déclaration d'intention *(f)*
It dichiarazione d'intenzione
    (f)
Pt declaração de propósito *(f)*

declaración falso *(f)* Es
De Verdrehung *(f)*
En misrepresentation
Fr déclaration inexacte *(f)*
It dichiarazione falsa *(f)*
Pt deturpação *(f)*

declaración fiscal *(f)* Es
De Einkommensteuererklä-
    rung *(f)*
En income-tax return
Fr déclaration de revenu *(f)*
It dichiarazione del reddito
    (f)
Pt declaração fiscal *(f)*

declaración jurada *(f)* Es
De beeidigte Erklärung *(f)*
En affidavit
Fr déclaration sous serment
    (f)
It dichiarazione giurata *(f)*
Pt declaração sob juramento
    (f)

declarar vb Es, Pt
De erklären
En declare
Fr déclarer
It dichiarare

declarar greve Pt
De zum Streik auffordern
En call a strike
Es declararse en huelga
Fr ordonner une grève
It proclamare uno sciopero

declarar huelga Es
De streiken
En strike

Fr faire la grève
It scioperare
Pt fazer greve

declarase en huelga Es
De zum Streik auffordern
En call a strike
Fr ordonner une grève
It proclamare uno sciopero
Pt declarar greve

declaration n E
De Erklärung *(f)*
Es declaración *(f)*
Fr déclaration *(f)*
It dichiarazione *(f)*
Pt declaração *(f)*

déclaration *(f)* n Fr
De Erklärung *(f)*
En declaration
Es declaración *(f)*
It dichiarazione *(f)*
Pt declaração *(f)*

déclaration de l'impôt *(f)* Fr
De Steuererklärung *(f)*
En tax return
Es declaración de ingresos *(f)*
It dichiarazione fiscale *(f)*
Pt declaração para efeitos de
    tributação *(f)*

déclaration de revenu *(f)* Fr
De Einkommensteuererklä-
    rung *(f)*
En income-tax return
Es declaración fiscal *(f)*
It dichiarazione del reddito
    (f)
Pt declaração fiscal *(f)*

déclaration d'expédition *(f)*
    Fr
De Absendungserklärung *(f)*
En declaration of shipment
Es declaración de expedición
    (f)
It dichiarazione d'imbarco *(f)*
Pt declaração de expedição *(f)*

déclaration d'intention *(f)* Fr
De Willenserklärung *(f)*
En declaration of intent
Es declaracion de intención
    (f)
It dichiarazione d'intenzione
Pt declaração de propósito *(f)*

déclaration en douane *(f)* Fr
De Zollerklärung *(f)*
En customs declaration
Es declaración de aduana *(f)*
It dichiarazione doganale *(f)*
Pt declaração alfandegária *(f)*

déclaration inexacte *(f)* Fr
De Verdrehung *(f)*
En misrepresentation
Es declaración falsa *(f)*
It dichiarazione falsa *(f)*
Pt deturpação *(f)*

declaration of intent En
De Willenserklärung *(f)*
Es declaración de intención
(f)
Fr déclaration d'intention *(f)*
It dichiarazione d'intenzione
(f)
Pt declaração de propósito *(f)*

declaration of shipment En
De Absendungserklärung *(f)*
Es declaración de expedición
(f)
Fr déclaration d'expédition *(f)*
It dichiarazione d'imbarco *(f)*
Pt declaração de expedição *(f)*

déclaration sous sement *(f)*
Fr
De beeidigte Erklärung *(f)*
En affidavit
Es declaración jurada *(f)*
It dichiarazione giurata *(f)*
Pt declaração sob juramento
(f)

declare *vb* En
De erklären
Es declarar
Fr déclarer
It dichiarare
Pt declarar

declared value En
De angegebener Zollwert *(m)*
Es valor declarado *(m)*
Fr valeur déclarée *(f)*
It valore dichiarato *(m)*
Pt valor declarado *(m)*

déclarer *vb* Fr
De erklären
En declare
Es declarar
It dichiarare
Pt declarar

de classe superior Pt
De hochwertig
En top quality
Es de primera calidad
Fr de première qualité
It di qualità superiore

découvert *(m) n* Fr
De Überziehung *(f)*
En overdraft
Es sobregiro; saldo deudor
(m)
It scoperto *(m)*
Pt conta a descoberto *(f)*

decreciente *adj* Es
De abnehmend
Es diminishing
Fr décroissant
It decrescente
Pt decrescente

decrescente *adj* It, Pt
De abnehmend
En diminishing
Es decreciente
Fr décroissant

décroissant *adj* Fr
De abnehmend
En diminishing
Es decreciente
It decrescente
Pt decrescente

dédommager *vb* Fr
De entschädigen
En indemnify
Es indemnizar; resarcir
It indennizzare; risarcire
Pt indemnizar

dédouané Fr
De verzollt
En out of bond
Es despachado de aduanas
It sdoganato
Pt despachado da alfândega

dédouanement *(m) n* Fr
De Zollabfertigung *(f)*
En customs clearance
Es paso de aduanas *(f)*
It sdoganamento *(m)*
Pt despacho alfandegário *(m)*

dédouaner Fr
De verzollen
En clear through customs

Es retirar de aduanas
It sdoganare
Pt despachar na alfândega

dedução adiada *(f)* Pt
De nachträglicher
Umsatzbonus *(m)*
En deffered rebate
Es descuento diferido *(m)*
Fr rabais différé *(m)*
It sconto differito *(m)*

**deducciones fiscales sobre
inversiones** *(f pl)* Es
De Steuerbegünstigung auf
Anlagen *(f)*
En capital allowances
Fr déductions fiscales sur les
investissements *(f pl)*
It deduzioni fiscali sugli
investimenti *(f pl)*
Pt concessões sobre capital
(f pl)

deducibile da tassa It
De steuerabsetzbar
En tax deductible
Es deducible de impuestos
Fr déductible à l'impôt
Pt impostos a deduzir

deducible de impuestos Es
De steuerabsetzbar
En tax deductible
Fr déductible à l'impôt
It deducibile da tassa
Pt ilíquido de impostos

deducir *vb* Es
De abziehen
En deduct
Fr déduire
It dedurre
Pt deduzir

deduct *vb* En
De abziehen
Es deducir
Fr déduire
It dedurre
Pt deduzir

déductible à l'impôt Fr
De steuerabsetzbar
En tax deductible
Es deducible de impuestos
It deducibile da tassa
Pt ilíquido de impostos

déductions fiscales sur les investissements *(f pl)* Fr
De Steuerbegünstigung auf Anlagen *(f)*
En capital allowances
Es deducciones fiscales sobre inversiones *(f pl)*
It deduzioni fiscali sugli investimenti *(f pl)*
Pt concessões sobre capital *(f pl)*

déduire *vb* Fr
De abziehen
En deduct
Es deducir
It dedurre
Pt deduzir

dedurre *vb* It
De abziehen
En deduct
Es deducir
Fr déduire
Pt deduzir

deduzioni fiscali sugli investimenti *(f pl)* It
De Steuerbegünstigung auf Anlagen *(f)*
En capital allowances
Es deducciones fiscales sobre inversiones *(f pl)*
Fr déductions fiscales sur les investissements *(f pl)*
Pt concessões sobre capital *(f pl)*

deduzir *vb* Pt
De abziehen
En deduct
Es deducir
Fr déduire
It dedurre

deed (document) *n* En
De Urkunde *(f)*
Es título; escritura *(m f)*
Fr acte; titre *(m)*
It atto *(m)*
Pt título; escritura *(m f)*

deed of arrangement En
De Vergleichsabkommen *(n)*
Es acta de desposición *(f)*
Fr contrat d'arrangement *(m)*
It atto di accordo *(m)*
Pt ascritura de acordo *(f)*

deed of assignment En
De Abtretungsvertrag *(m)*
Es título des asignación *(m)*
Fr acte attributif *(m)*
It atto de cessione *(m)*
Pt título de consignação *(m)*

deed of composition En
De Vergleichsabkommen *(n)*
Es concordato *(m)*
Fr concordat *(m)*
It atto di concordato *(m)*
Pt concordata (por escrito) *(f)*

deed of covenant En
De Pakt *(m)*
Es pacto *(m)*
Fr pacte *(m)*
It patto *(m)*
Pt escritura de compromisso *(f)*

de fábrica Es
De ab Werk
En ex works
Fr prise usine
It franco fabbrica
Pt na fábrica

défaillance *(f)* *n* Fr
De Nichteinhaltung *(f)*
En default
Es falta *(f)*
It mancanza *(f)*
Pt falta *(f)*

defalcador *(m)* *n* Es
De Veruntreuer
En embezzler
Fr détourneur *(m)*
It malversatore *(m)*
Pt desfalcador *(m)*

defalcar *vb* Es
De unterschlagen
En embezzle
Fr détourner
It appropriarsi indebitamente
Pt desfalcar

defalco *(m)* *n* Es
De Unterschlagung *(f)*
En embezzlement
Fr détournement de fonds *(m)*
It appropriazione indebita *(f)*
Pt desfalque *(m)*

default *(n)* En
De Nichteinhaltung *(f)*
Es falta *(f)*
Fr défaillance; défaut *(f m)*
It mancanza *(f)*
Pt falta *(f)*

défaut *(m)* *n* Fr
De Nichteinhaltung; Mangel *(f m)*
En default; defect
Es falta; defecto *(f m)*
It mancanza; difetto *(f m)*
Pt falta; pefeito *(f m)*

défaut de paiement *(m)* Fr
De Nichtzahlung *(f)*
En faulure to pay
Es falta de pago *(f)*
It mancato pagamento *(m)*
Pt falta de pagamento *(f)*

defect *n* En
De Mangel *(m)*
Es defecto *(m)*
Fr défaut *(m)*
It difetto *(m)*
Pt defeito *(m)*

defecto *(m)* *n* Es
De Mangel *(m)*
En defect
Fr défaut *(m)*
It difetto *(m)*
Pt defeito *(m)*

defecto latente *(m)* Es
De versteckter Mangel *(m)*
En latent defect
Fr vice caché *(m)*
It difetto latente *(m)*
Pt defeito latente *(m)*

défectueux *adj* Fr
De fehlerhaft
En faulty
Es defectuoso
It difettoso
Pt defeituoso

defectuoso *adj* Es
De fehlerhaft
En faulty
Fr défectueux
It defittoso
Pt defeituoso

defeito *(m) n* Pt
De Mangel *(m)*
En defect
Es defecto *(m)*
Fr défaut *(m)*
It difetto *(m)*

defeito latente *(m)* Pt
De versteckter Mangel *(m)*
En latent defect
Es defecto latente *(m)*
Fr vice caché *(m)*
It difetto latente *(m)*

defeituoso *adj* Pt
De fehlerhaft
En faulty
Es defectuoso
Fr défectueux
It difettoso

defer *vb* En
De zurückstellen
Es aplazar
Fr différer; ajourner
It differire
Pt adiar

deferred annuity En
De Anwartschaft auf Leibrente *(f)*
Es anualidad aplazada *(f)*
Fr annuité différée *(f)*
It rendita vitalizia differita *(f)*
Pt anuidade diferida *(f)*

deferred liabilities En
De aufgeschobene Schulden *(f pl)*
Es pasivo transitorio *(m)*
Fr passif différé *(m)*
It passività differite *(f pl)*
Pt passivo adiado *(m)*

deferred payment En
De gestundete Zahlung *(f)*
Es pago aplazado *(m)*
Fr paiement différé
It pagamento differito *(m)*
Pt pagamento adiado *(m)*

deferred rebate En
De nachträglicher Umsatzbonus *(m)*
Es descuento diferido *(m)*
Fr rabais différé *(m)*
It sconto differito *(m)*
Pt dedução adiada *(f)*

deferred shares En
De Nachzugsaktien *(f pl)*
Es acciones aplazadas *(f pl)*
Fr actions différées *(f pl)*
It azioni postergate *(f pl)*
Pt acções diferidas *(f pl)*

deferred taxation En
De latente Steuerpflicht *(f)*
Es tasación diferida *(f)*
Fr imposition différée *(f)*
It tassazione differita *(f)*
Pt tributação diferida *(f)*

deficiencia *(f) n* Es
De Mangel; Fehlbetrag *(m)*
En deficiency
Fr manque; insuffisance *(m f)*
It ammanco; insufficienza *(m f)*
Pt deficiência; defeito *(f m)*

deficiência *(f) n* Pt
De Mangel; Fehlbetrag *(m)*
En deficiency
Es dificiencia *(f)*
Fr manque; insuffisance *(m f)*
It ammanco; insufficienza *(m f)*

deficiency *n* En
De Mangel; Fehlbetrag *(m)*
Es deficiencia *(f)*
Fr manque; insuffisance *(m f)*
It ammanco; insufficienza *(m f)*
Pt deficiência; defeito *(f m)*

deficit *n* En, It *(m)*
De Defizit *(n)*
Es déficit *(m)*
Fr déficit *(m)*
Pt déficit *(m)*

déficit *(m) n* Es, Fr, Pt
De Defizit *(n)*
En deficit
It deficit *(m)*

Defizit *(n) n* De
En deficit
Es déficit *(m)*
Fr déficit *(m)*
It deficit *(m)*
Pt déficit *(m)*

deflação *(f) n* Pt
De Deflation *(f)*
En deflation

Es deflación *(f)*
Fr déflation *(f)*
It deflazione *(f)*

deflación *(f) n* Es
De Deflation *(f)*
En deflation
Fr déflation *(f)*
It deflazione *(f)*
Pt deflação *(f)*

deflation *n* En
De Deflation *(f)*
Es deflación *(f)*
Fr déflation *(f)*
It deflazione *(f)*
Pt deflação *(f)*

déflation *(f) n* Fr
De Deflation *(f)*
En deflation
Es deflación *(f)*
It deflazione *(f)*
Pt deflação *(f)*

Deflation *(f) n* De
En deflation
Es deflación *(f)*
Fr déflation *(f)*
It deflazione *(f)*
Pt deflação *(f)*

deflazione *(f) n* It
De Deflation *(f)*
En deflation
Es deflación *(f)*
Fr déflation *(f)*
Pt deflação *(f)*

defunct company En
De erloschene Gesellschaft *(f)*
Es sociedad extinta *(f)*
Fr société liquidée *(f)*
It società estinta *(f)*
Pt empresa extinta *(f)*

dégâts d'eau de mer *(m pl)* Fr
De Seewasserschaden *(m)*
En sea-water damage
Es daño de agua de mar *(m)*
It danno d'acqua di mare *(m)*
Pt dano causado por água do mar *(m)*

dégâts d'eau douce *(m pl)* Fr
De Süßwasserschaden *(m)*
En fresh-water damage
Es daño de agua dulce *(m)*

It danno d'acqua dolce *(m)*
Pt dano causado por água
doce *(m)*

dégâts des eaux *(m pl)* Fr
De Wasserschaden *(m)*
En water damage
Es daño causado por el agua
(m)
It danno causato dall'acqua
(m)
Pt dano causado por água
(m)

degré de solvabilité *(m)* Fr
De Kreditwürdigkeit *(f)*
En credit rating
Es límite de crédito *(m)*
It stima del credito *(f)*
Pt nível de crédito *(m)*

dégrèvement *(m)* Fr
De Steuererleichterung *(f)*
En tax relief
Es desgravación *(f)*
It sgravio fiscale *(m)*
Pt insenção de imposto *(f)*

**dégrèvement de charges
fiscales doubles** *(m)* Fr
De Doppelbesteuerungser-
leichterung *(f)*
En double taxation relief
Es desgravación de tributación doble *(f)*
It sgravio per doppia
tassazione *(m)*
Pt isenção de tributação dupla
(f)

délai de paiement *(m)* Fr
De Verlängerung einer Zah-
lungsfrist *(f)*
En extension of payment time
Es prórroga de pago *(f)*
It proroga di pagamento *(f)*
Pt prorrogação de pagamento
(f)

délai supplémentaire *(m)* Fr
De Nachfrist *(f)*
En days of grace
Es días de gracia *(f pl)*
It giorni di grazia *(m pl)*
Pt dias de tolerância *(m pl)*

delay *n* En
De Verzug *(m)*
Es retraso *(m)*

Fr retard; délai *(m)*
It ritardo *(m)*
Pt atraso *(m)*

del credere agent En
De Delkrederevertreter *(m)*
Es agente del crédere *(m)*
Fr agent ducroire *(m)*
It agente con del credere *(m)*
Pt agente del credere *(m)*

delegação *(f)* n Pt
De Delegierung *(f)*
En delegation
Es delegación *(f)*
Fr délégation *(f)*
It delegazione *(f)*

delegación *(f)* n Es
De Delegierung *(f)*
En delegation
Fr délégation *(f)*
It delegazione *(f)*
Pt delegação *(f)*

delegado *(m)* n Es, Pt
De Delegierte(r) *(m)*
En delegate
Fr délégué *(m)*
It delegato *(m)*

delegate n En
De Delegierte(r) *(m)*
Es delegado *(m)*
Fr délégué *(m)*
It delegato *(m)*
Pt delegado *(m)*

delegation n En
De Delegierung *(f)*
Es delegación *(f)*
Fr délégation *(f)*
It delegazione *(f)*
Pt delegação *(f)*

délégation *(f)* n Fr
De Delegierung *(f)*
En delegation
Es delegación *(f)*
It delegazione *(f)*
Pt delegação *(f)*

delegato *(m)* n It
De Delegierte(r) *(m)*
En delegate
Es delegado *(m)*
Fr délégué *(m)*
Pt delegado *(m)*

delegazione *(f)* n It
De Delegierung *(f)*
En delegation
Es delegación *(f)*
Fr délégation *(f)*
Pt delegação *(f)*

Delegierte(r) *(m)* n De
En delegate
Es delegado *(m)*
Fr délégué *(m)*
It delegato *(m)*
Pt delegado *(m)*

Delegierung *(f)* n De
En delegation
Es delegación *(f)*
Fr délégation *(f)*
It delegazione *(f)*
Pt delegação *(f)*

délégué *(m)* n Fr
De Delegierte(r) *(m)*
En delegate
Es delegado *(m)*
It delegato *(m)*
Pt delegado *(m)*

delete *vb* En
De streichen
Es tachar; anular
Fr rayer; effacer
It cancellare
Pt cortar; riscar

deliberazione *(f)* n It
De Beschluß *(m)*
En resolution
Es resuloción *(f)*
Fr resolution *(f)*
Pt resolução; proposta *(f)*

delivered price En
De Lieferpreis *(m)*
Es precio incluida entrega *(m)*
Fr prix livraison inclus *(m)*
It prezzo incluso consegna
(m)
Pt preço incluindo portes *(m)*

delivery n En
De Lieferung *(f)*
Es entrega *(f)*
Fr livraison *(f)*
It consegna *(f)*
Pt entrega *(f)*

delivery date En
De Liefertermin *(m)*
Es fecha de entrega *(f)*

Fr date de livraison *(f)*
It data di consegna *(f)*
Pt data di entrega ou
  remessa *(f)*

delivery free En
De portofreie Lieferung
Es libre entrega
Fr livré franco
It consegna franco
Pt remessa gratuita

delivery note En
De Lieferschein *(m)*
Es aviso de entrega *(m)*
Fr bordereau de livraison *(m)*
It nota di consegna *(f)*
Pt guia de entrega *(f)*

délivrance (d'un brevet) *(f)* Fr
De Erteilung (eines Patentes)
  (f)
En grat (of a patent)
Es concesión (de una
  patente) *(f)*
It concessione (di brevetto)
  (f)
Pt concessão (de uma paten-
  te) *(f)*

Delkrederevertreter *(m) n* De
En del credere agent
Es agente del crédere *(m)*
Fr agent ducroire *(m)*
It agente con del credere *(m)*
Pt agente del credere *(m)*

demain *adv* Fr
De morgen
En tomorrow
Es mañana
It domani
Pt amanhã

demanda *(f) n* Pt
De Anspruch *(m)*
En claim
Es reclamación *(f)*
Fr réclamation; créance *(f)*
It reclamo *(m)*

demanda *(f) n* Es
De Nachfrage *(f)*
En inquiry
Fr demande *(f)*
It domanda *(f)*
Pt pergunta *(f)*

demanda de salário *(f)* Pt
De Lohnforderung *(f)*
En wage claim
Es reclamación de salario *(f)*
Fr revendication de salaire *(f)*
It rivendicazione salariale *(f)*

demand curve En
De Nachfragekurve *(f)*
Es curva de relación
  demanda *(f)*
Fr courbe de la demande *(f)*
It curva della domanda *(f)*
Pt curva de procura *(f)*

demande *(f) n* Fr
De Nachfrage; Antrag *(f m)*
En inquiry; application
Es demanda; solicitud *(f)*
It domanda *(f)*
Pt pergunta; requisação *(f)*

demandé Fr
De gefragt
En in demand
Es solicitado
It ricercato
Pt procurado

demarcation dispute En
De Fähigkeitsstreitigkeit *(f)*
Es disputa sobre demarca-
  ción *(f)*
Fr contestation syndicale des
  compétences *(f)*
It disputa di competenza *(f)*
Pt disputa sobre demarcação
  (f)

se démettre *vb* Fr
De zurücktreten
En resign
Es dimitir
It dimettersi
Pt demitir-se

demi-salaire *(m) n* Fr
De Halbsold *(m)*
En half-pay
Es medio salario *(m)*
It mezza paga *(f)*
Pt meio-salário *(m)*

demitir-se *vb* Pt
De zurücktreten
En resign
Es dimitir
Fr se démettre
It dimettersi

demonstrar *vb* Pt
De beweisen
En establish; prove
Es demostrar; probar
Fr démontrer
It dimostrare; provare

démontrer *vb* Fr
De beweisen
En establish; prove
Es demostrar; probar
It dimostrare; provare
Pt demonstrar; provar

demostrar *vb* Es
De beweisen
En establish; prove
Fr démontrer
It dimostrare; provare
Pt demonstrar; provar

demurrage *n* En
De Überliegezeit *(f)*
Es sobreestadía *(f)*
Fr surestarie *(f)*
It controstallia *(f)*
Pt sobreestadia *(f)*

denaro *(m) n* It
De Geld *(n)*
En money
Es dinero *(m)*
Fr argent *(m)*
Pt dinheiro *(m)*

denaro a basso interesse *(m)*
  It
De billiges Geld *(n)*
En cheap money
Es dinero barato *(m)*
Fr argent bon marché *(m)*
Pt dinheiro barato *(m)*

denaro a corso legale *(m)* It
De gesetzliches Zahlungsmit-
  tel *(n)*
En legal tender
Es moneda legal *(f)*
Fr monnaie légale *(f)*
Pt moeda legal *(f)*

denaro ad alto interesse *(m)*
  It
De teures Geld *(n)*
En dear money
Es dinero caro *(m)*
Fr argent cher *(m)*
Pt dinheiro caro *(m)*

denaro a vista *(m)* It
De Sichtgelder *(n pl)*
En money on call
Es dinero a la vista *(m)*
Fr argent à vue *(m)*
Pt dinheiro à ordem *(m)*

denaro contante *(m)* It
De Bargeld *(n)*
En cash
Es dinero efectivo *(m)*
Fr espèces; argent comptant *(f pl; m)*
Pt dinheiro de contado *(m)*

denaro inattivo *(m)* It
De totes Kapital *(n)*
En idle money
Es dinero sin invertir *(m)*
Fr capital oisif *(m)*
Pt dinheiro paralisado *(m)*

déni *(m) n* Fr
De Ablehnung *(f)*
En disclaimer
Es renuncia *(f)*
It rinunzia *(f)*
Pt descarte *(m)*

den Markt beherrschen De
En corner a market
Es acaparar el mercado
Fr accaparer le marché
It accaparrare il mercato
Pt dominar o mercado

denomination (of shares) *n* En
De Stückelung *(f)*
Es valor *(m)*
Fr valeur nominale *(f)*
It taglio *(m)*
Pt valor nominal *(m)*

denominazione commerciale *(f)* It
De Firmenname *(m)*
En trade name
Es razón social *(f)*
Fr raison sociale *(f)*
Pt razão comercial *(f)*

departamento *(m) n* Es, Pt
De Abteilung *(f)*
En department
Fr département *(m)*
It dipartimento *(m)*

departamento de contabilidade *(m)* Pt
De Buchhaltung *(f)*
En accounts department

Am accounting department
Es departamento de contabilidad *(m)*
Fr service de la comptabilité *(m)*
It ufficio contabilità *(m)*

departamento de vendas *(m)* Pt
De Verkaufsabteilung *(f)*
En sales department
Es departamento de ventas *(m)*
Fr service ventes *(m)*
It ufficio vendite *(m)*

departamento de ventas *(m)* Es
De Verkaufsabteilung *(f)*
En sales department
Fr service ventes *(m)*
It ufficio vendite *(m)*
Pt departamento de vendas *(m)*

département *(m) n* Fr
De Abteilung *(f)*
En department
Es departamento *(m)*
It dipartimento *(m)*
Pt departamento *(m)*

department *n* En
De Abteilung *(f)*
Es departamento *(m)*
Fr département *(m)*
It dipartimento *(m)*
Pt departamento *(m)*

department store En
De Warenhaus *(n)*
Es grandes almacenes *(m pl)*
Fr grand magasin *(m)*
It grande magazzino *(m)*
Pt armazém *(m)*

dependiente de muelle *(m)* Es
De Expedient *(m)*
En shipping clerk
Fr expéditionnaire *(m)*
It commesso di spedizioniere *(m)*
Pt despachante *(m)*

dépense déductible *(f)* Fr
De abziehbare Unkosten *(f pl)*
En allowable expense
Es gastos deducibles *(m pl)*

It spesa permessa *(f)*
Pt despesas deduzíveis *(f pl)*

dépenses de publicité *(f pl)* Fr
De Werbekosten *(pl)*
En adervertising expenditure
Es gastos publicitarios *(m pl)*
It spese di pubblicità *(f pl)*
Pt despesa com publicidade *(f)*

déperdition naturelle *(f)* Fr
De natürlicher Abgang *(m)*
En natural wastage
Es merma natural *(f)*
It consumo naturale *(m)*
Pt desperdício natural *(m)*

déplacement *(m) n* Fr
De Tonnengehalt *(m)*
En displacement
Es desplazamiento *(m)*
It dislocamento *(m)*
Pt deslocação *(f)*

depleting assets Am
En wasting assets
De kurzlebige Aktiva *(n pl)*
Es activo gastable *(m)*
Fr actifs défectibles *(m pl)*
It attività in esaurimento *(f pl)*
Pt bens em uso ou deterioração *(m pl)*

depois de amanhã Pt
De übermorgen
En day after tomorrow
Es pasado mañana
Fr après demain
It dopodomani

déport *(m) n* Fr
De Kursabschlag *(m)*
En backwardation
Es prima de aplazamiento *(f)*
It deporto *(m)*
Pt juro de mora *(m)*

deporto *(m) n* It
De Kursabschlag *(m)*
En backwardation
Es prima de aplazamiento *(f)*
Fr déport *(m)*
Pt juro de mora *(m)*

déposant *(m) n* Fr
De Einzahler *(m)*
En depositor

Es depositante *(m)*
It depositante *(m)*
Pt depositante *(m)*

déposer *vb* Fr
De einlegen
En file
Es interponer
It depositare
Pt registar

déposer (à la banque) Fr
De einlegen; einzahlen
En bank
Es depositar (en el banco)
It depositare (in una banca)
Pt depositar (no banco)

deposit (in bank) *n* En
De Depot *(n)*
Es depósito *(m)*
Fr dépôt *(m)*
It deposito *(m)*
Pt depósito *(m)*

deposit (first payment) *n* En
De Anzahlung *(f)*
Es desembolso inicial *(m)*
Fr arrhes *(f pl)*
It caparra *(f)*
Pt sinal *(m)*

deposit account En
Am interest-bearing account
De Depositenkonto *(n)*
Es cuenta de ahorras *(f)*
Fr compte de dépôt *(m)*
It conto di deposito *(m)*
Pt conta de depósito *(f)*

dépositaire *(m)* *n* Fr
De Verwahrer; Gewahrsam-
    inhaber *(m)*
En depository; bailee
Es depositario *(m)*
It depositario *(m)*
Pt depositário; caucionado
    (m)

depositante *(m)* *n* Es, It, Pt
De Einzahler *(m)*
En depositor
Fr déposant *(m)*

depositar (en el banco) Es
De einlegen; einzahlen
En bank
Fr déposer (à la banque)
It depositare (in una banca)
Pt depositar (no banco)

depositar (no banco) Pt
De einlegen; einzahlen
En bank
Es depositar (en el banco)
Fr déposer (à la banque)
It depositare (in una banca)

depositare *vb* It
De einlegen
En file
Es interponer
Fr déposer
Pt registar

depositare (in una banca) It
De einlegen; einzahlen
En bank
Es depositar (en el banco)
Fr déposer (à la banque)
Pt depositar (no banco)

depositario *(m)* *n* Es, It
De Verwahrer, Gewahrsamin-
    haber *(m)*
En depositary; bailee
Fr dépositaire *(m)*
Pt depositário; caucionado
    (m)

depositário *(m)* *n* Pt
De Verwahrer *(m)*
En depositary
Es depositario *(m)*
Fr dépositaire *(m)*
It depositario *(m)*

depositary *n* En
De Verwahrer *(m)*
Es depositario *(m)*
Fr dépositaire *(m)*
It depositario *(m)*
Pt depositário *(m)*

Depositeneinlage *(f)* *n* De
En fixed deposit
Es depósito a plazo fijo *(m)*
Fr dépôt à terme (fixe) *(m)*
It deposito a termine fisso
    (m)
Pt depósito a prazo *(m)*

Depositenkonto *(n)* *n* De
En deposit account
Am interest-bearing account
Es cuenta de ahorras *(f)*
Fr compte de dépôt *(m)*
It conto di deposito *(m)*
Pt conta de depósito *(f)*

Depositenschein *(m)* *n* De
En deposit receipt
Es recibo de depósito *(m)*
Fr récépissé de dépôt *(m)*
It certificato di deposito *(m)*
Pt receibo de depósito *(m)*

depósito *(m)* *n* Es, Pt
De Depot *(n)*
En deposit
Fr dépôt *(m)*
It deposito *(m)*

deposito *(m)* *n* It
De Depot *(n)*
En deposit
Es depósito *(m)*
Fr dépôt *(m)*
Pt depósito *(m)*

depósito a plazo fijo *(m)* Es
De Depositeneinlage *(f)*
En fixed deposit
Fr dépôt à terme (fixe) *(m)*
It deposito a termine fisso
    (m)
Pt depósito a prazo *(m)*

depósito a prazo *(m)* Pt
De Depositeneinlage *(f)*
En fixed deposit
Es depósito a plazo fijo *(m)*
Fr dépôt à terme (fixe) *(m)*
It deposito a termine fisso
    (m)

deposito a termine fisso *(m)*
    It
De Depositeneinlage *(f)*
En fixed deposit
Es depósito a plazo fijo *(m)*
Fr dépôt à terme (fixe) *(m)*
Pt depósito a prazo *(m)*

depósito bancario *(m)* Es
De Bankeinlage *(f)*
En bank deposit
Fr dépôt bancaire *(m)*
It deposito bancario *(m)*
Pt depósito bancário *(m)*

deposito bancario *(m)* It
De Bankeinlage *(f)*
En bank deposit
Es depósito bancario *(m)*
Fr dépôt bancaire *(m)*
Pt depósito bancário *(m)*

depósito bancário *(m)* Pt
De Bankeinlage *(f)*
En bank deposit
Es depósito bancario *(m)*
Fr dépôt bancaire *(m)*
It deposito bancario *(m)*

depósito em cofre forte *(m)*
Pt
De Verwahrung im Stahlfach
   (f)
En safe deposit
Es depósito en caja fuerte *(m)*
Fr dépôt en coffre-fort *(m)*
It servizio di cassette di
   sicurezza *(m)*

depósito en caja fuerte *(m)*
Es
De Verwahrung im Stahlfach
   (f)
En safe deposit
Fr dépôt en coffre-fort *(m)*
It servizio de cassette di
   sicurezza *(m)*
Pt depósito em cofre forte *(m)*

deposito notturno *(m)* It
De Nachttresor *(m)*
En night safe
Es caja de seguridad
   nocturna *(f)*
Fr coffre de nuit *(m)*
Pt cofre nocturno *(m)*

depositor *n* En
De Einzahler *(m)*
Es depositante *(m)*
Fr déposant *(m)*
It depositante *(m)*
Pt depositante *(m)*

depósitos bloquedos *(m pl)*
Es, Pt
De gesperrte Einlagen *(f pl)*
En blocked deposits
Fr dépôts bloqués *(m pl)*
It deposito con vincolo
   bloccato *(m)*

deposit receipt En
De Depositenschein *(m)*
Es recibo de depósito *(m)*
Fr récépissé de dépôt *(m)*
It certificato di deposito *(m)*
Pt recibo de depósito *(m)*

dépôt *(m)* *n* Fr
De Depot *(n)*
En deposit
Es depósito *(m)*
It deposito *(m)*
Pt depósito *(m)*

Depot *(n)* *n* De
En deposit
Es depósito *(m)*
Fr dépôt *(m)*
It deposito *(m)*
Pt depósito *(m)*

dépôt à terme (fixe) *(m)* Fr
De Depositeneinlage *(f)*
En fixed deposit
Es depósito a plazo fijo *(m)*
It deposito a termine fisso
   (m)
Pt depósito a prazo *(m)*

dépôt bancaire *(m)* Fr
De Bankeinlage *(f)*
En bank deposit
Es depósito bancario *(m)*
It deposito bancario *(m)*
Pt depósito bancário *(m)*

dépôt en coffre-fort *(m)* Fr
De Verwahrung im Stahlfach
   (f)
En safe deposit
Es depósito en caja fuerte *(m)*
It servizio de cassette di
   sicurezza *(m)*
Pt depósito em cofre forte *(m)*

dépôts bloqués *(m pl)* Fr
De gesperrte Einlagen *(f pl)*
En blocked deposits
Es depósitos bloquedos
   (m pl)
It deposito con vincolo
   bloccato *(m)*
Pt depósitos bloqueados
   (m pl)

depreciação *(f)* *n* Pt
De Entwertung;
   Abschreibung *(f)*
En depreciation
Es depreciación *(f)*
Fr dépréciation;
   amortissement *(f m)*
It ammortamento *(m)*

depreciação acelerada *(f)* Pt
De beschleunigte
   Abschreibung *(f)*
En accelerated depreciation
Es depreciación acelerada
   (m)
Fr amortissement accéléré
   (m)
It deprezzamento accelerato
   (m)

depreciación *(f)* *n* Es
De Entwertung;
   Abschreibung *(f)*
En depreciation
Fr dépréciation;
   amortissement *(f m)*
It ammortamento *(m)*
Pt depreciação; amortização *(f)*

depreciación acelerada *(f)*
Es
De beschleunigte
   Abschreibung *(f)*
En accelerated depreciation
Fr amortissement accéléré
   (m)
It deprezzamento accelerato
   (m)
Pt depreciação acelerada *(f)*

depreciar *vb* Es, Pt
De entwerten
En depreciate
Fr déprécier
It deprezzare

depreciate *vb* En
De entwerten
Es depreciar
Fr déprécier
It deprezzare
Pt depreciar

depreciation *n* En
De Entwertung;
   Abschreibung *(f)*
Es depreciación *(f)*
Fr dépréciation;
   amortissement *(f m)*
It ammortamento *(m)*
Pt depreciação; amortização *(f)*

dépréciation *(f)* *n* Fr
De Entwertung;
   Abschreibung *(f)*
En depreciation
Es depreciación *(f)*

It ammortamento *(m)*
Pt depreciação; amortização *(f)*

depreciation allowance En
De Abschreibung für
    Abnutzung (AfA) *(f)*
Es provisión para
    amortización *(f)*
Fr provision pour
    amortissement *(f)*
It quota di ammortamento *(f)*
Pt provisão para amortização
    (f)

dépréciation de la monnaie
    (f) Fr
De Geldabwertung *(f)*
En depreciation of money
Es desvalorización de la
    moneda *(f)*
It svalutazione della moneta
    (f)
Pt desvalorização da moeda *(f)*

depreciation of money En
De Geldabwertung *(f)*
Es desvalorización de la
    moneda *(f)*
Fr dépréciation de la
    monnaie *(f)*
It svalutazione della moneta
    (f)
Pt desvalorização da moeda *(f)*

déprécier *vb* Fr
De entwerten
En depreciate
Es depreciar
It deprezzare
Pt depreciar

de première qualité Fr
De hochwertig
En top quality
Es de primera calidad
It de qualità superiore
Pt de classe superior

depressão *(f)* *n* Pt
De Wirtschaftskrise *(f pl)*
En depression
Es crisis económica *(f)*
Fr crise économique *(f)*
It crisi *(f)*

depression *n* En
De Wirtschaftskrise *(f)*
Es crisis económica *(f)*
Fr crise économique *(f)*

It crisi *(f)*
Pt depressão *(f)*

deprezzamento accelerato
    (m) It
De beschleunigte
    Abschreibung *(f)*
En accelerated depreciation
Es depreciación acelerada *(f)*
Fr amortissement accéléré
    (m)
Pt depreciação acelerada *(f)*

deprezzare *vb* It
De entwerten
En depreciate
Es depreciar
Fr déprécier
Pt depreciar

de primera calidad Es
De hochwertig
En top quality
Fr de première qualité
It di qualità superiore
Pt de classe superior

de qualité inférieure Fr
De minderwertig
En low-grade
Es baja calidad
It di qualità inferiore
Pt baixo-nível

derecho de entrada *(m)* Es
De Eintrittgebühr *(f)*
En entrance fee
Fr droit d'entrée *(m)*
It tassa d'entrata *(f)*
Pt taxa de admissão *(f)*

derecho de retencíon *(m)* Es
De Pfandrecht *(n)*
En lien
Fr droit de retention *(m)*
It diritto di sequestro *(m)*
Pt dereito de retenção *(m)*

derechos *(m pl)* *n* Es
De Rechte; Gebühr *(n pl; f)*
En rights; duty
Fr droits; taxe *(m pl; f)*
It diritti; tassa *(m pl; f)*
Pt direitos; taxa *(m pl; f)*

derechos de aduanas *(m pl)*
    Es
De Zoll *(m)*
En customs duty

Fr droit de douane *(m)*
It diritto doganale *(m)*
Pt direitos alfandegários
    (m pl)

derechos de auto *(m pl)* Es
De Urheberrecht *(n)*
En copyright
Fr droit d'auteur *(m)*
It diritto d'autore *(m)*
Pt direitos de auto *(m pl)*

derechos de importación
    (m pl) Es
De Einfuhrzoll *(m)*
En import duty
Fr droits d'entrée *(m pl)*
It dazio d'importazione *(m)*
Pt direitos de importação
    (m pl)

derechos de muelle *(m pl)* Es
De Dockgebühr *(f)*
En dock dues
Fr droits de dock *(m pl)*
It diritti di dock *(m pl)*
Pt encargos de doca *(m pl)*

derechos de registro *(m pl)*
    Es
De Anmeldegebühr *(f)*
En registration fee
Fr droit d'enregistrement *(m)*
It tassa di registrazione *(f)*
Pt custas de registo *(f pl)*

derechos de sucesión *(m pl)*
    Es
De Nachlaßsteuer *(f)*
En estate duty
Am estate tax
Fr droits de succession *(m pl)*
It diritti di succession *(m pl)*
Pt dereitos de sucessão *(m pl)*

derechos mineros *(m pl)* Es
De Mineralgewinnungsrechte
    (n pl)
En mineral rights
Fr droits miniers *(m pl)*
It diritti minerari *(m pl)*
Pt direitos mineiros *(m pl)*

derechos pagados Es
De verzollt
En duty-paid
Fr acquitté
It dazio pagato
Pt direitos pagos

derechos portuarios *(m pl)*
Es
De Hafengebühren *(f pl)*
En port charges
Fr droits de port *(m pl)*
It diritti portuali *(m pl)*
Pt direitos portuários *(m pl)*

derechos preferenciales
(m pl) Es
De Vorzugssatz *(m)*
En preferential duty
Fr tarif de faveur *(m)*
It tariffa preferenziale *(f)*
Pt direito preferencial *(f)*

dernier jour *(m)* Fr
De Schlußtermin *(m)*
En closing date
Es último día *(m)*
It ultima data *(f)*
Pt último dia *(m)*

dernier versement *(m)* Fr
De letzte Rate *(f)*
En final instalment
Es último plazo *(m)*
It ultima rata *(f)*
Pt última prestação *(f)*

desacuerdo *(m)* n Es
De Abweichung *(f)*
En discrepancy
Fr écart *(m)*
It divergenza *(f)*
Pt discrepância *(f)*

desalojar um inquilino Pt
De einen Mieter entfernen
En evict a tenant
Es desalojar un inquilino
Fr expulser un locataire
It sfrattare un locatario

desalojar un inquilino Es
De einen Mieter entfernen
En evict a tenant
Fr expulser un locataire
It sfrattare un locatario
Pt desalojar um inquilino

desarmar *vb* Es, Pt
De auflegen
En lay up
Fr désarmer
It disarmare

désarmer *vb* Fr
De auflegen
En lay up
Es desarmar
It disarmare
Pt desarmar

descanso *(m)* n Es
De Freizeit *(f)*
En leisure
Fr loisir *(m)*
It svago *(m)*
Pt lazer *(m)*

descargar una deuda Es
De eine Schuld begleichen
En discharge a debt
Fr acquitter une dette
It estinguere un debito
Pt cancelar uma dívida

descarte *(m)* n Pt
De Ablehnung *(f)*
En disclaimer
Es renuncia *(f)*
Fr déni *(m)*
It rinunzia *(f)*

descentralizar *vb* Pt
De dezentralisieren
En decentralize
Es decentralizar
Fr décentraliser
It decentralizzare

desconto *(m)* n Pt
De Skonto; Nachlaß *(m)*
En discount; rebate
Es descuento; rebaja *(m f)*
Fr escompte; rabais *(m)*
It sconto; ribasso *(m)*

desconto à praça *(m)* Pt
De Händlerrabatt *(m)*
En trade discount
Es descuento comercial *(m)*
Fr rabais de demi-gros *(m)*
It sconto di rivendita *(m)*

desconto bancário *(m)* Pt
De Diskont *(m)*
En bank discount
Es descuento bancario *(m)*
Fr escompte en dehors *(m)*
It sconto di banca *(m)*

desconto de contado *(m)* Pt
De Barrabatt *(m)*
En cash discount

Es descouento de caja *(m)*
Fr escompte de caisse *(m)*
It sconto per pagamento a
    contanti *(m)*

desconto de exportação *(m)*
Pt
De Ausfuhrsonderrabatt *(m)*
En export rebate
Es descuento por
    exportación *(m)*
Fr remise sur les exports *(f)*
It sconto d'esportazione *(m)*

desconto por ausência de
reclamações *(m)* Pt
De Schadenfreiheitsrabatt *(m)*
En no-claims discount
Es bonificación por no-re-
    clamación *(f)*
Fr bonification pour non
    sinistre *(f)*
It sconto per assenza di
    sinistri *(m)*

descrição *(f)* n Pt
De Beschreibung *(f)*
En description
Es descripción *(f)*
Fr description *(f)*
It descrizione *(f)*

descrição da tarefa *(f)* Pt
De Arbeitsbeschreibung *(f)*
En job description
Es descripición del trabajo *(f)*
Fr description du travail *(f)*
It descrizione del lavoro *(f)*

descripción *(f)* n Es
De Beschreibung *(f)*
En description
Fr description *(f)*
It descrizione *(f)*
Pt descrição *(f)*

descripción del trabajo *(f)* Es
De Arbeitsbeschreibung *(f)*
En job description
Fr description du travail *(f)*
It descrizione del lavoro *(f)*
Pt descrição da tarefa *(f)*

description n En, Fr *(f)*
De Beschreibung *(f)*
Es descripción *(f)*
It descrizione *(f)*
Pt descrição *(f)*

description du travail *(f)* Fr
De Arbeitsbeschreibung *(f)*
En job description
Es descripición del trabajo *(f)*
It descrizione del lavoro *(f)*
Pt descrição da tarefa *(f)*

descrizione *(f)* n It
De Beschreibung *(f)*
En description
Es descripción *(f)*
Fr description *(f)*
Pt descrição *(f)*

descrizione del lavoro *(f)* It
De Arbeitsbeschreibung *(f)*
En job description
Es descripción del trabajo *(f)*
Fr description du travail *(f)*
Pt descrição da tarefa *(f)*

descuento *(m)* n Es
De Skonto *(m)*
En discount
Fr escompte *(m)*
It sconto; ribasso *(m)*
Pt desconto *(m)*

descuento bancario *(m)* Es
De Diskont *(m)*
En bank discount
Fr escompte en dehors *(m)*
It sconto di banca *(m)*
Pt desconto bancário *(m)*

descuento comercial *(m)* Es
De Händlerrabatt *(m)*
En trade discount
Fr rabais de demi-gros *(m)*
It sconto di rivendita *(m)*
Pt desconto à praça *(m)*

descuento de caja *(m)* Es
De Barrabatt *(m)*
En cash discount
Fr escompte de caisse *(m)*
It sconto per pagamento a
   contanti *(m)*
Pt desconto de contado *(m)*

descuento diferido *(m)* Es
De nachträglicher
   Umsatzbonus *(m)*
En deferred rebate
Fr rabais différé *(m)*
It sconto differito *(m)*
Pt dedução adiada *(f)*

descuento por exportación
   (m) Es
De Ausfuhrsonderrabatt *(m)*
En export rebate
Fr remise sur les exports *(f)*
It sconto d'esportazione *(m)*
Pt desconto de exportação
   (m)

de segunda mano Es
De aus zweiter Hand;
   Gebraucht-
En second-hand
Fr d'occasion
It di seconda mano
Pt de segunda mão

de segunda mão Pt
De aus zweiter Hand;
   Gebraucht-
Es second-hand
Es de segunda mano
Fr d'occasion
It di seconda mano

desembolso *(m)* n Es, Pt
De Ausgaben; Auszahlung
   (f pl; f)
En expenditure;
   disbursement
Fr frais; déboursement
   (m pl; m)
It spesa; esborso *(f m)*

desembolso inicial *(m)* Es
De Anzahlung *(f)*
En deposit; first payment
Fr arrhes *(f pl)*
It caparra *(f)*
Pt sinal *(m)*

desempenho *(m)* n Pt
De Erfüllung *(f)*
En performance
Es ejecución *(f)*
Fr exécution *(f)*
It esecuzione *(f)*

desempenho anterior *(m)* Pt
De Leistung in der
   Vergangenheit *(f)*
En past performance
Es operación anterior *(f)*
Fr comportement antérieur
   (m)
It comportamento
   precedente *(m)*

desempleo *(m)* n Es
De Arbeitslosigkeit *(f)*
En unemployment
Fr chômage *(m)*
It disoccupazione *(f)*
Pt desemprego *(m)*

desempregado *adj* Pt
De arbeitslos
En out of work
Es parado; sin trabajo
Fr en chômage
It disoccupato

desemprego *(m)* n Pt
De Arbeitslosigkeit *(f)*
En unemployment
Es desempleo *(m)*
Fr chômage *(m)*
It disoccupazione *(f)*

desemprego de estação *(m)*
   Pt
De jahreszeitlich bedingte
   Arbeitslosigkeit *(f)*
En seasonal unemployment
Es paro de temporada *(m)*
Fr chômage saisonnier *(m)*
It disoccupazione
   stagionale *(f)*

desenhador *(m)* n Pt
De Entwerfer *(m)*
En draughtsman
Es dibujante *(m)*
Fr dessinateur *(m)*
It disegnatore *(m)*

desenho *(m)* n Pt
De Zeichnung *(f)*
En design
Es diseño *(m)*
Fr dessein *(m)*
It disegno *(m)*

desfalcador *(m)* n Pt
De Veruntreuer *(m)*
En embezzler
Es defalcador *(m)*
Fr détourneur *(m)*
It malversatore *(m)*

desfalcar *vb* Pt
De unterschlagen
En embezzle
Es defalcar
Fr détourner
It appropriarsi
   indebitamente

desfalque (m) n Pt
De Unterschlagung (f)
En embezzlement
Es defalco (m)
Fr détournement de fonds
(m)
It appropriazione indebita (f)

desgaste (m) n Es, Pt
De natürliche Abnützung (f)
En wear and tear
Fr usure normale (f)
It logorio naturale (m)

desgravación (f) n Es
De Steuererleichterung (f)
En tax relief
Fr dégrèvement (m)
It sgravio fiscale (m)
Pt redução de imposto (f)

**desgravación de tributación
doble** (f) Es
De Doppelbesteuerungser-
leichterung (f)
En double taxation relief
Fr dégrèvement de charges
fiscales doubles (m)
It sgravio per doppia
tassazione (m)
Pt isenção de tributação dupla
(f)

deshipotecado Es
De von Hypothek befreit
En free from mortgage
Fr déshypothéqué
It libero d'ipoteca
Pt livre de hipoteca

deshonesto adj Es
De unehrlich
En dishonest
Fr malhonnête
It disonesto
Pt desonesto

déshypothéqué Fr
De von Hypothek befreit
En free from mortgage
Es deshipotecado
It libero d'ipoteca
Pt livre de hipoteca

design n En
De Zeichnung (f)
Es diseño (m)
Fr dessein (m)

It disegno (m)
Pt desenho (m)

designação postal (f) Pt
De Postleitzahl (f)
En postcode
Am zip code
Es designación postal (f)
Fr indicatif postal (m)
It codice postale (m)

designación postal (f) Es
De Postleitzahl (f)
En postcode
Am zip code
Fr indicatif postal (m)
It codice postale (m)
Pt designação postal (f)

designer n En
De Zeichner (m)
Es diseñador (m)
Fr dessinateur (m)
It disegnatore (m)
Pt desenhador (m)

desistir Pt
De aufgeben
En give up
Es renunciar
Fr céder
It cedere

desk n En
De Schreibtisch (m)
Es mesa (f)
Fr bureau (m)
It scrittoio (m)
Pt secretária (f)

deslocação (f) n Pt
De Tonnengehalt (m)
En displacement
Es desplazamiento (m)
Fr déplacement (m)
It dislocamento (m)

desonesto adj Pt
De unehrlich
En dishonest
Es deshonesto
Fr malhonnête
It disonesto

despachado da alfândega
Pt
De verzollt
En out of bond
Es despachado de aduanas

Fr dédouané
It sdoganato

despachado de aduanas Es
De verzollt
En out of bond
Fr dédouané
It sdoganato
Pt despachado da alfândega

despachante (m) Pt
De Expedient (m)
En shipping clerk
Es dependiente de muelle (m)
Fr expéditionnaire (m)
It commesso di
spedizioniere (m)

despachar na alfândega Pt
De verzollen
En clear through customs
Es retirar de aduanas
Fr dédouaner
It sdoganare

despacho (m) n Es
De Versand (m)
En despatch; dispatch
Fr envoi (m)
It spedizione; dispaccio (f m)
Pt despacho; remessa (m f)

despacho de aduana (m) Es
De Verzollung (f)
En customs clearance
Fr formalités douanières (f pl)
It sdoganamento (m)
Pt despacho de alfândega
(m)

despacho de alfândega (m)
Pt
De Verzollung (f)
En customs clearance
Es despacho de aduana (m)
Fr formalités douanières (f pl)
It sdoganamento (m)

despedimento (m) n Pt
De Entlassung (f)
En dismissal
Am firing
Es despido (m)
Fr congédiement (m)
It licenziamento (m)

despedir vb Es, Pt
De entlassen
En dismiss

Am fire
Fr congédier
It congedare

despejos tóxicos *(m pl)* Pt
De giftiger Abfall *(m)*
En toxic waste
Es efluentes tóxicos *(m pl)*
Fr déchets toxiques *(m pl)*
It rifiuti tossici *(m pl)*

desperdício natural *(m)* Pt
De natürlicher Abgang *(m)*
En natural wastage
Es merma natural *(f)*
Fr déperdition naturelle *(f)*
It consumo naturale *(m)*

desperdicios *(m pl)* n Es
De Abfallprodukt *(n)*
En waste products
Fr déchets *(m pl)*
It prodotto di rifiuto *(m)*
Pt desperdícios *(m pl)*

desperdícios *(m pl)* n Pt
De Abfallprodukt *(n)*
En waste products
Es desperdicios *(m pl)*
Fr déchets *(m pl)*
It prodotto di rifiuto *(m)*

despesa *(f)* n Pt
De Kosten *(pl)*
En expense
Es gasto *(m)*
Fr frais *(m pl)*
It spesa *(f)*

despesa com publicidade *(f)*
Pt
De Werbekosten *(pl)*
En advertising expenditure
Es gastos publicitarios *(m pl)*
Fr dépenses de publicité *(f pl)*
It spese di pubblicità *(f pl)*

despesas *(f pl)* n Pt
De Ausgaben; Kosten *(f pl)*
En expenditure; charges
Es desembolso; costes
 (m; m pl)
Fr frais *(m pl)*
It spesa; spese *(f; f pl)*

despesas deduzíveis *(f pl)* Pt
De abziehbare Unkosten *(f pl)*
En allowable expense
Es gastos deducibles *(m pl)*

Fr dépense déductible *(f)*
It spesa permessa *(f)*

**despesas de reprensenta-
 ção** *(f pl)* Pt
De Repräsentationskosten
 (pl)
En entertainment expenses
Es gastos de representación
 (m pl)
Fr frais de représentation
 (m pl)
It spese di rappresentanza
 (f pl)

despesas de viagem *(f pl)* Pt
De Reisekosten *(pl)*
En travelling expenses
Es dietas de viajes *(f pl)*
Fr frais de voyage *(m pl)*
It spese di viaggio *(f pl)*

despesas directas *(f pl)* Pt
De Einzelkosten *(pl)*
En direct expenses
Es gastos directos *(m pl)*
Fr frais directs *(m pl)*
It spese dirette *(f pl)*

despesas diversas *(f pl)* Pt
De verschiedene Ausgaben
 (f pl)
En sundry expenses
Es gastos varios *(m pl)*
Fr frais divers *(m pl)*
It spese varie *(f pl)*

despesas do exercício *(f pl)*
Pt
De Geschäftskosten *(pl)*
En business expenses
Es gastos de los negocios
 (m pl)
Fr frais commerciaux *(m pl)*
It spesa generali *(f pl)*

**despesas em termos de
 capital** *(f pl)* Pt
De Kapitalausgaben *(f pl)*
En capital expenditure
Es inmovilizaciones *(f pl)*
Fr immobilisations *(f pl)*
It immobilizzazioni *(f pl)*

despesass gerais *(f pl)* Pt
De allgemeine Unkosten *(pl)*
En general expenses
Es gastos generales *(m pl)*

Fr frais généraux *(m pl)*
It spese generali *(f pl)*

despesas ocasionais *(f pl)* Pt
De Nebenkosten *(f pl)*
En incidental expenses
Es gastos imprevistos *(m pl)*
Fr faux frais *(m pl)*
It spese impreviste *(f pl)*

despido *(m)* n Es
De Entlassung *(f)*
En dismissal
Am firing
Fr congédiement *(m)*
It licenziamento *(m)*
Pt despedimento *(m)*

desplazamiento *(m)* n Es
De Tonnengehalt *(m)*
En displacement
Fr déplacement *(m)*
It dislocamento *(m)*
Pt deslocação *(f)*

dessein *(m)* n Fr
De Zeichnung *(f)*
En design
Es diseño *(m)*
It disegno *(m)*
Pt desenho *(m)*

dessinateur *(m)* n Fr
De Entwerfer *(m)*
En draughtsman
Es dibujante *(m)*
It disegnatore *(m)*
Pt desenhador *(m)*

destilería *(f)* n Es
De Brennerei *(f)*
En distillery
Fr distillerie *(f)*
It distilleria *(f)*
Pt distilaria *(f)*

destinataire *(m)* n Fr
De Adressat; Empfänger *(m)*
En addressee consignee
Es destinatario;
 consignatario *(m)*
It destinatario;
 consegnatario *(m)*
Pt desinatário; conignatário
 (m)

destinatario *(m)* n Es, It
De Adressat *(m)*
En addressee

Fr destinataire *(m)*
Pt destinatário *(m)*

destinatário *(m) n* Pt
De Adressat *(m)*
En adressee
Es destinatario *(m)*
Fr destinataire *(m)*
It destinatario *(m)*

destination *n* En, Fr *(f)*
De Bestimmungsort *(m)*
Es destino *(m)*
It destinazione *(f)*
Pt destino *(m)*

destinazione *(f) n* It
De Bestimmungsort *(m)*
En destination
Es destino *(m)*
Fr destination *(f)*
Pt destino *(m)*

destino *(m) n* Es, Pt
De Bestimmungsort *(m)*
En destination
Fr destination *(f)*
It destinazione *(f)*

désuétude incorporée *(f)* Fr
De eingebautes Veralten *(n)*
En built-in obsolescence
Es decaimiento incorporado *(m)*
It decadimento incorporato *(m)*
Pt obsolência pré-incorporada *(f)*

desvalorização *(f) n* Pt
De Währungsabwertung *(f)*
En devaluation
Es devaluación *(f)*
Fr devaluation *(f)*
It svalutazione *(f)*

desvalorização da moeda *(f)* Pt
De Geldabwertung *(f)*
En depreciation of money
Es desvalorización de la moneda *(f)*
Fr dépréciation de la monnaie *(f)*
It svalutazione della moneta *(f)*

desvalorización de la moneda *(f)* Es
De Geldabwertung *(f)*
En depreciation of money
Fr dépréciation de la monnaie *(f)*
It svalutazione della moneta *(f)*
Pt desvalorização de moeda *(f)*

desviación normal *(f)* Es
De normale Abweichung *(f)*
En standard deviation
Fr déviation normale *(f)*
It deviazione normale *(f)*
Pt desvio normal *(m)*

desvio normal *(m)* Pt
De normale Abweichung *(f)*
En standard deviation
Es desiviación normal *(f)*
Fr déviation normale *(f)*
It deviazione normale *(f)*

détaillé *adj* Fr
De postenmäßig dargestellt
En itemized
Es detallado
It dettagliato
Pt pormenorizado

détails *(m pl) n* Fr
De Einzelheiten; Angaben *(f pl)*
En particulars
Es detalles *(m pl)*
It particolari *(m pl)*
Pt pormenores *(m pl)*

detallado *adj* Es
De postenmäßig dargestellt
En itemized
Fr détaillé
It dettagliato
Pt pormenorizado

detalles *(m pl)* Es
De Einzelheiten; Angaben *(f pl)*
En particulars
Fr détails *(m pl)*
It particolari *(m pl)*
Pt pormenores *(m pl)*

détenir des actions Fr
De beteiligt sein; Aktien besitzen
En hold shares
Es tener acciones

It tenere azioni
Pt reter acções

détenteur *(m) n* Fr
De Inhaber *(m)*
En holder
Es titular *(m)*
It titolare *(m)*
Pt titular *(m)*

détenteur de titres *(m)* Fr
De Aktieninhaber *(m)*
En stockholder
Es accionista *(m)*
It azionista *(m)*
Pt accionista *(m)*

detentore legittimo *(m)* It
De entgeltigter Besitzer *(m)*
En holder for value
Es tenedor legítimo *(m)*
Fr porteur à titre onéreux *(m)*
Pt proprietário legítimo *(m)*

determination clause En
De Rücktrittsklausel *(f)*
Es cláusula resulutiva *(f)*
Fr clause résolutoire *(f)*
It clausola risolutiva *(f)*
Pt cláusula de rescisão *(f)*

determination of a contract En
De Vertragsbeendigung *(f)*
Es rescisión de un contrato *(f)*
Fr résolution d'un contrat *(f)*
It risoluzione di un contratto *(f)*
Pt rescisão de contrato *(f)*

détournement de fonds *(m)* Fr
De Unterschlagung *(f)*
En embezzlement
Es defalco *(m)*
It appropriazione indebita *(f)*
Pt desfalque *(m)*

détourner *vb* Fr
De unterschlagen
En embezzle
Es defalcar
It appropriarsi indebitamente
Pt desfalcar

détourneur *(m) n* Fr
De Veruntreuer *(m)*
En embezzler

197

deviazione normale

Es defalcador *(m)*
It malversatore *(m)*
Pt desfalcador *(m)*

dettagliato *adj* It
De postenmäßig dargestellt
En itemized
Es detallado
Fr détaillé
Pt pormenorizado

dettare *vb* It
De diktieren
En dictate
Es dictar
Fr dlcter
Pt ditar

dettato *(m) n* It
De Diktat *(n)*
En dictation
Es dictado *(m)*
Fr dictée *(f)*
Pt ditado *(m)*

dette comptable *(f)* Fr
De Buchschuld *(f)*
En book debt
Es deuda contabilizada *(f)*
It debito attivo *(m)*
Pt débito contabilizado *(m)*

dette publique *(f)* Fr
De Staatsschuld *(f)*
En national debt
Es deuda pública *(f)*
It debito pubblico *(m)*
Pt dívida pública *(f)*

deturpação *(f) n* Pt
De Verdrehung *(f)*
En misrepresentation
Es declaración falsa *(f)*
Fr déclaration inexacte *(f)*
It dichiarazione falsa *(f)*

deuda *(f) n* Es
De Schuld *(f)*
En debt
Fr créance *(f)*
It debit *(m)*
Pt dívida *(f)*

deuda contabilizada *(f)* Es
De Buchschuld *(f)*
En book debt
Fr dette comptable *(f)*
It debito attivo *(m)*
Pt débito contabilizado *(m)*

deuda de pago dudoso *(f)* Es
De zweifelhafte Forderung *(f)*
En doubtful debt
Fr créance douteuse *(f)*
It credito dubbio *(m)*
Pt dívida duvidosa *(f)*

deuda incobrable *(f)* Es
De uneinbringliche Schuld *(f)*
En bad debt
Fr créance irrécouvrable *(f)*
It credito inesigibile *(m)*
Pt dívida incobrável *(f pl)*

deuda pública *(f)* Es
De Staatsschuld *(f)*
En national debt
Fr dette publique *(f)*
It debito pubblico *(m)*
Pt dívida pública *(f)*

deudor *(m) n* Es
De Schuldner *(m)*
En debtor
Fr débiteur *(m)*
It debitore *(m)*
Pt devedor *(m)*

deudor moroso *(m)* Es
De schlechter Zahler *(m)*
En slow payer
Fr mauvais payeur *(m)*
It cattivo pagatore *(m)*
Pt mau-pagador *(m)*

de valeur Fr
De wertvoll
En valuable
Es valioso
It di valore
Pt valioso

devaluación *(f) n* Es
De Währungsabwertung *(f)*
En devaluation
Fr dévaluation *(f)*
It svalutazione *(f)*
Pt desvalorização *(f)*

devaluation *n* En
De Währungsabwertung *(f)*
Es devaluación *(f)*
Fr dévaluation *(f)*
It svalutazione *(f)*
Pt desvalorização *(f)*

dévaluation *(f) n* Fr
De Währungsabwertung *(f)*
En devaluation

Es devaluación *(f)*
It svalutazione *(f)*
Pt desvalorização *(f)*

devedor *(m) n* Pt
De Schuldner *(m)*
En debtor
Es deudor *(m)*
Fr débiteur *(m)*
It debitore *(m)*

developing country En
De Entwicklungsland *(n)*
Es pais en desarrollo *(m)*
Fr pays en voie de développement *(m)*
It paese in via di sviluppo *(m)*
Pt país em desenvolvimento *(m)*

development (of property, etc.) *n* En
De Erschließung *(f)*
Es explotación *(f)*
Fr exploitation; lotissement *(f m)*
It valorizzazione *(f)*
Pt exploração *(f)*

development area En
De Ortsplanungsgebiet *(n)*
Es zona de desarrollo *(f)*
Fr zone de développement *(f)*
It zona di sviluppo *(f)*
Pt zona de desenvolvimento *(f)*

development company En
De Erschließungsgesellschaft *(f)*
Es compañía de explotación *(f)*
Fr société d'exploitation *(f)*
It società d'imprese *(f)*
Pt empresa de exploração *(f)*

déviation normale *(f)* Fr
De normale Abweichung *(f)*
En standard deviation
Es desviación normal *(f)*
It deviazione normale *(f)*
Pt deviso normal *(m)*

deviazione normale *(f)* It
De normale Abweichung *(f)*
En standard deviation
Es desviación normal *(f)*
Fr déviation normale *(f)*
Pt desvio normal *(m)*

devis *(m) n* Fr
De Kostenvoranschlag *(m)*
En estimate
Es presupuesto *(m)*
It preventivo *(m)*
Pt previsão *(f)*

devise *(f) n* Fr
De Devisen *(f pl)*
En foreign currency
Es divisas extranjeras *(f pl)*
It valuta estera *(f)*
Pt moeda estrangeira *(f)*

Devisen *(f pl) n* De
En foreign currency; foreign
exchange
Es divisas extranjeras *(f pl)*
Fr devise; devises *(f; f pl)*
It valuta estera *(f)*
Pt moeda estrangeira *(f)*

Devisenkontrolle *(f) n* De
En exchange control
Am currency control
Es fiscalización de cambios
(f)
Fr contrôle des changes *(m)*
It controllo sui cambi *(m)*
Pt controlo de câmbios *(m)*

Devisenkurs *(m) n* De
En foreign exchange rates
Es tasas de cambio exterior
(f pl)
Fr cours des changes *(m)*
It corso dei cambi *(m)*
Pt taxas de câmbio *(f pl)*

devises *(f pl) n* Fr
De Devisen *(f pl)*
En foreign exchange
Es divisas extranjeras *(f pl)*
It valuta estera *(f)*
Pt moeda estrangeira *(f)*

devises bloquées *(f pl)* Fr
De blockierte Devisen *(f pl)*
En blocked exchange
Es divisas bloquedas *(f pl)*
It valute bloccate *(f pl)*
Pt câmbio bloqueado *(m)*

devis rectifié *(m)* Fr
De überarbeitete Schätzung
(f)
En revised estimate
Es cálculo revisado *(m)*

It preventivo riveduto *(m)*
Pt estimativa revista *(f)*

devis supplémentaire *(m)* Fr
De Nachschätzung *(f)*
En supplementary estimate
Es cálculo suplementario *(m)*
It preventivo supplementare
(m)
Pt estimativa suplementar *(f)*

**devolver um cheque ao
sacado** Pt
De einen Scheck uneingelöst
lassen
En refer a cheque to drawer
Es rehusar pago de un
cheque
Fr refuser d'honorer un
chèque
It rifiutare di pagare un
assegno

dezentralisieren *vb* De
En decentralize
Es decentralizar
Fr décentraliser
It decentralizzare
Pt descentralizar

dezimal *adj* De
En decimal
Es decimal
Fr décimal
It decimale
Pt decimal

día *(m) n* Es
De Tag *(m)*
En day
Fr jour *(m)*
It giorno *(m)*
Pt dia *(m)*

dia *(m) n* Pt
De Tag *(m)*
En day
Es día *(m)*
Fr jour *(m)*
It giorno *(m)*

día a día Es
De täglich
En day-to-day
Fr au jour le jour
It di giorno in giorno
Pt dia a dia

dia a dia Pt
De täglich
En day-to-day
Es día a día
Fr au jour le jour
It di giorno in giorno

día de bolsa *(m)* Es
De Börsentag *(m)*
En (financial) market day
Fr jour de bourse *(m)*
It giorno di borsa *(m)*
Pt dia de bolsa *(m)*

dia de bolsa *(m)* Pt
De Börsentag *(m)*
En (financial) market day
Es día de bolsa *(m)*
Fr jour de bourse *(m)*
It giorno di borsa *(m)*

día de fiesta *(m)* Es
De gesetzlicher Feiertag *(m)*
En public holiday
Fr jour férié *(m)*
It giorno di festa *(m)*
Pt feriado *(m)*

dia de folga *(m)* Pt
De dienstfreier Tag *(m)*
En day off
Es día libre *(m)*
Fr jour de congé *(m)*
It giorno di riposo *(m)*

dia de liquidação *(m)* Pt
De Abrechnungstag *(m)*
En settlement day; account
day
Es día de liquidación *(m)*
Fr jour de règlement *(m)*
It giorno della liquidazione
(m)

día de liquidación *(m)* Es
De Abrechnungstag *(m)*
Es settlement day; account
day
Fr jour de règlement *(m)*
It giorno della liquidazione
(m)
Pt dia de liquidação *(m)*

día de mercado *(m)* Es
De Markttag *(m)*
En (local) market day
Fr jour de marché *(m)*
It giorno di mercato *(m)*
Pt dia de mercado *(m)*

dia de mercado *(m)* Pt
De Markttag *(m)*
En (local) market day
Es día de mercado *(m)*
Fr jour de marché *(m)*
It giorno di mercato *(m)*

día de pago *(m)* Es
De Zahltag *(m)*
En pay day
Fr jour de paiement *(m)*
It giorno di paga *(m)*
Pt dia de recebimento *(m)*

dia de recebimento *(m)* Pt
De Zahltag *(m)*
En pay day
Es día de pago *(m)*
Fr jour de paiement *(m)*
It giorno di paga *(m)*

dia de saída *(m)* Pt
De Abgangstag *(m)*
En sailing date
Es día de salida *(m)*
Fr date de départ *(f)*
It data di partenza *(f)*

día de salida *(m)* Es
De Abgangstag *(m)*
En sailing date
Fr date de départ *(f)*
It data di partenza *(f)*
Pt dia de saída *(m)*

dia de trabalho *(m)* Pt
De Arbeitstag *(m)*
En working day
Es día laborable *(m)*
Fr jour ouvrable *(m)*
It giornata lavorativa *(f)*

**dia de vencimento
trimestral** *(m)* Pt
De Quartalstag *(m)*
En quarter day
Es primer día del trimestre *(m)*
Fr jour du terme *(m)*
It giorno della pigione *(m)*

diagram *n* En
De graphische Darstellung *(f)*
Es diagrama *(m)*
Fr diagramme *(m)*
It diagramma *(m)*
Pt diagrama *(m)*

diagrama *(m) n* Es, Pt
De graphische Darstellung *(f)*
En diagram
Fr diagramme *(m)*
It diagramma *(m)*

diagrama de flujo *(m)* Es
De Flußdiagramm *(m)*
En flow chart
Fr ordinogramme *(m)*
It diagramma di flusso *(m)*
Pt gráfico de operação *(m)*

diagrama de bloque *(m)* Es
De Säulendiagramm *(m)*
En block diagram
Fr ordinogramme *(m)*
It schema a blocchi *(m)*
Pt organigrama *(m)*

diagramma *(m) n* It
De graphische Darstellung *(f)*
En diagram
Es diagrama *(m)*
Fr diagramme *(m)*
Pt diagrama *(m)*

diagramma di flusso *(m)* It
De Flußdiagramm *(m)*
En flow chart
Es diagrama de flujo *(m)*
Fr ordinogramme *(m)*
Pt gráfico de operação *(m)*

diagramme *(m) n* Fr
De graphische Darstellung *(f)*
En diagram
Es diagrama *(m)*
It diagramma *(m)*
Pt diagrama *(m)*

día laborable *(m)* Es
De Arbeitstag *(m)*
En working day
Fr jour ouvrable *(m)*
It giornata lavorativa *(f)*
Pt dia de trabalho *(m)*

día libre *(m)* Es
De dienstfreier Tag *(m)*
En day off
Fr jour de congé *(m)*
It giorno di riposo *(m)*
Pt dia de folga *(m)*

diario *(m) n* Es
De Tagebuch *(n)*
En day-book
Fr journal *(m)*

It giornale *(m)*
Pt diário *(m)*

diário *(m) n* Pt
De Tagebuch *(n)*
En journal; day-book
Es (libro) diario *(m)*
Fr journal *(m)*
It (libro) giornale *(m)*

diário de bordo *(m)* Pt
De Log *(n)*
En (ship's) log
Es diario de navegación *(m)*
Fr journal de navigation *(m)*
It solcometro *(m)*

diario de navegación *(m)* Es
De Log *(n)*
En (ship's) log
Fr journal de navigation *(m)*
It solcometro *(m)*
Pt diário de bordo *(m)*

días de gracia *(f pl)* Es
De Nachfrist *(f)*
En days of grace
Fr délai supplémentaire *(m)*
It giorni di grazia *(m pl)*
Pt dias de tolerância *(m pl)*

dias de tolerância *(m pl)* Pt
De Nachfrist *(f)*
En days of grace
Es días de gracia *(f pl)*
Fr délai supplémentaire *(m)*
It giorni di grazia *(m pl)*

dibujante *(m) n* Es
De Entwerfer *(m)*
En draughtsman
Fr dessinateur *(m)*
It disegnatore *(m)*
Pt desenhador *(m)*

dichiarare *vb* It
De erklären
En declare
Es declarar
Fr déclarer
Pt declarar

dichiarazione *(f) n* It
De Erklärung *(f)*
En declaration
Es declaración *(f)*
Fr déclaration *(f)*
Pt declaração *(f)*

dichiarazione del reddito (f)
It
De Einkommensteuer-
erklärung (f)
En income-tax return
Es declaración fiscal (f)
Fr déclaration de revenu (f)
Pt declaração fiscal (f)

dichiarazione d'imbarco (f) It
De Absendungserklärung (f)
En declaration of shipment
Es declaración de expedición
(f)
Fr déclaration d'expédition (f)
Pt declaração de expedição (f)

dichiarazione d'intenzione
(f) It
De Willenserklärung (f)
En declaration of intent
Es declaración de intención
(f)
Fr déclaration d'intention (f)
Pt declaração de propósito (f)

dichiarazione doganale (f) It
De Zollerklärung (f)
En customs declaration
Es declaración de aduana (f)
Fr déclaration en douane (f)
Pt declaração alfandegária (f)

dichiarazione falsa (f) It
De Verdrehung (f)
En misrepresentation
Es declaración falsa (f)
Fr déclaration inexacte (f)
Pt deturpação (f)

dichiarazione fiscale (f) It
De Steuererklärung (f)
En tax return
Es declaración de ingresos (f)
Fr déclaration de l'impôt (f)
Pt declaração para efeitos de
tributação (f)

dichiarazione giurata (f) It
De beeidigte Erklärung (f)
En affidavit
Es declaración jurada (f)
Fr déclaration sous serment
(f)
Pt declaração sob juramento
(f)

dictado (m) n Es
De Diktat (n)
En dictation
Fr dictée (f)
It dettato; dettatura (m f)
Pt ditado (m)

dictafone (m) Pt
De Diktaphon (n)
En dictating machine
Es dictáfono (m)
Fr machine à dictée (f)
It dittafono (m)

dictáfono (m) n Es
De Diktaphon (n)
En dictating machine
Fr machine à dictée (f)
It dittafono (m)
Pt dictafone (m)

dictaphone operator Am
En audio-typist
De Audiotypistin (f)
Es audio-mecanógrafa (f)
Fr dictaphoniste (f)
It dittafonista (f)
Pt audio-dactilógrafa (f)

dictaphoniste (f) n Fr
De Audiotypistin (f)
En audio-typist
Am dictaphone operator
Es audio-mecanógrafa (f)
It dittafonista (f)
Pt audio-dactilógrafa (f)

dictar vb Es
De diktieren
En dictate
Fr dicter
It dettare
Pt ditar

dictate vb En
De diktieren
Es dictar
Fr dicter
It dettare
Pt ditar

dictating machine En
De Diktaphon (n)
Es dictáfono (m)
Fr machine à dictée (f)
It dittafono (m)
Pt dictafone (m)

dictation n En
De Diktat (n)
Es dictado (m)
Fr dictée (f)
It dettato; dettatura (m f)
Pt ditado (m)

dictée (f) n Fr
De Diktat (n)
En dictation
Es dictado (m)
It dettato; dettatura (m f)
Pt ditado (m)

dicter vb Fr
De diktieren
En dictate
Es dictar
It dettare
Pt ditar

Diebstahl (m) n De
En theft
Es robo (m)
Fr vol (m)
It forto (m)
Pt furto (m)

dienstfreier Tag (m) De
En day off
Es día libre (m)
Fr jour de congé (m)
It giorno di riposo (m)
Pt dia de folga (m)

Dienstvertrag (m) n De
En service agreement
Es contrato de servicio (m)
Fr contrat de service (m)
It accordo di servizio (m)
Pt contrato de serviço (m)

dietas de viajes (f pl) Es
De Reisekosten (pl)
En travelling expenses
Fr frais de voyage (m pl)
It spese di viaggio (f pl)
Pt despesas de viagem (f pl)

diferença (f) n Pt
De Unterscheid (m)
En difference
Es diferencia (f)
Fr différence (f)
It differenza (f)

diferença de preço (f) Pt
De Preisunterschied (m)
En difference in price

Es diferencia de precio *(f)*
Fr écart de prix *(m)*
It differenza di prezzo *(f)*

diferencia *(f)* n Es
De Unterschied *(m)*
En difference
Fr différence *(f)*
It differenza *(f)*
Pt diferença *(f)*

diferencia de precio *(f)* Es
De Preisunterschied *(m)*
En difference in price
Fr écart de prix *(m)*
It differnza di prezzo *(f)*
Pt diferença de preço *(f)*

diferencial *(m)* n Es, Pt
De Differenz; Differential- *(f n)*
En differential
Fr différentiel *(m)*
It differenziale *(m)*

difetto *(m)* n It
De Mangel *(m)*
En defect
Es defecto *(m)*
Fr défaut *(m)*
Pt defeito *(m)*

difetto latente *(m)* It
De versteckter Mangel *(m)*
En latent defect
Es defecto latente *(m)*
Fr vice caché *(m)*
Pt defeito latente *(m)*

difettoso *adj* It
De fehlerhaft
En faulty
Es defectuoso
Fr défectueux
Pt defeituoso

difference n En
De Unterschied *(m)*
Es diferencia *(f)*
Fr différence *(f)*
It differenza *(f)*
Pt diferença *(f)*

différence *(f)* n Fr
De Unterschied *(m)*
En difference
Es diferencia *(f)*
It differenza *(f)*
Pt diferença *(f)*

difference in price En
De Preisunterschied *(m)*
Es diferencia de precio *(f)*
Fr écart de prix *(m)*
It differenza di prezzo *(f)*
Pt diferença de preço *(f)*

differential n En
De Differenz; Differential- *(f n)*
Es diferencial *(m)*
Fr différentiel *(m)*
It differenziale *(m)*
Pt diferencial *(m)*

différentiel *(m)* n Fr
De Differenz; Differential- *(t n)*
En differential
Es diferencial *(m)*
It differenziale *(m)*
Pt diferencial *(m)*

Differenz *(f)* n De
En differential
Es diferencial *(m)*
Fr différentiel *(m)*
It differenziale *(m)*
Pt diferencial *(m)*

differenza *(f)* n It
De Unterschied *(m)*
En difference
Es diferencia *(f)*
Fr différence *(f)*
Pt diferença *(f)*

differenza di prezzo *(f)* It
De Preisunterschied *(m)*
En difference in price
Es diferencia de precio *(f)*
Fr écart de prix *(m)*
Pt diferença de preço *(f)*

differenziale *(m)* n It
De Differenz; Differential- *(f n)*
En differential
Es diferencial *(m)*
Fr différentiel *(m)*
Pt diferencial *(m)*

différer *vb* Fr
De aufschieben; zurückstellen
En hold over; defer
Es aplazar; diferir
It differire
Pt diferir; adiar

differire *vb* It
De aufschieben; zurückstellen
En hold over; defer

Es aplazar; diferir
Fr différer; ajourner
Pt diferir; adiar

difficile *adj* Fr, It
De schwierig
En difficult
Es difícil
Pt difícil

difficoltà di vendita *(f)* It
De Kaufabneigung *(f)*
En sales resistance
Es dificultades de ventas *(f pl)*
Fr résistance à la vente *(f)*
Pt resistência contra vendas
(f)

difficult *adj* En
De schwierig
Es difícil
Fr difficile
It difficile
Pt difícil

difícil *adj* Es, Pt
De schwierig
En difficult
Fr difficile
It difficile

dificultades de ventas *(f pl)*
Es
De Kaufabneigung *(f)*
En sales resistance
Fr résistance à la vente *(f)*
It difficoltà di vendita *(f)*
Pt resistência contra vendas
(f)

di giorno in giorno It
De täglich
En day-to-day
Es día a día
Fr au jour le jour
Pt dia a dia

digital computer En
De Digitalrechner *(m)*
Es computadora numérica *(f)*
Fr calculateur digital *(m)*
It elaboratore numerico *(m)*
Pt computador de dígitos *(m)*

Digitalrechner *(m)* n De
En digital computer
Es computadora numérica *(f)*
Fr calculateur digital *(m)*
It elaboratore numerico *(m)*
Pt computador de dígitos *(m)*

digit de contrôle *(m)* Fr
De Kontrollziffer *(f)*
En check digit
Es número de control *(m)*
It cifra di controllo *(f)*
Pt dígito de controle *(m)*

dígito de controle *(m)* Pt
De Kontrollziffer *(f)*
En check digit
Es número de control *(m)*
Fr digit de contrôle *(m)*
It cifra di controllo *(f)*

digne de confiance Fr
De zuverlässig
En reliable
Es digno de confianza
It fidato; attendibile
Pt digno de confiança

digno de confiança Pt
De zuverlässig
En reliable
Es digno de confianza
Fr digne de confiance
It fidato; attendibile

digno de confianza Es
De zuverlässig
En reliable
Fr digne de confiance
It fidato; attendibile
Pt digno de confiança

digue *(m)* n Es
De Mole *(f)*
En jetty
Fr jetée; digue *(f)*
It molo *(m)*
Pt pontão; cais *(m)*

Diktaphon *(n)* n De
En dictating machine
Es dictáfono *(m)*
Fr machine à dictée *(f)*
It dittafono *(m)*
Pt dictafone *(m)*

Diktat *(n)* n De
En dictation
Es dictado *(m)*
Fr dictée *(f)*
It dettato; dettatura *(m f)*
Pt ditado *(m)*

diktieren *vb* De
En dictate
Es dictar

Fr dicter
It dettare
Pt ditar

dimettersi *vb* It
De zurücktreten
En resign
Es dimitir
Fr se démettre
Pt demitir-se

diminishing *adj* En
De abnehmend
Es decreciente
Fr décroissant
It decrescente
Pt decrescente

diminishing returns En
De abnehmender Ertrag *(m)*
Es rendimientos decrecientes
  (m pl)
Fr rendements décroissants
  (m pl)
It proventi decrescenti *(m pl)*
Pt rendimentos decrescentes
  (m pl)

diminuir *vb* Pt
De nachlassen
En fall off
Es disminuir
Fr ralentir
It diminuire

diminuire It
De nachlassen
En fall off
Es disminuir
Fr ralentir
Pt diminuir; decrescer

dimitir *vb* Es
De zurücktreten
En resign
Fr se démettre
It dimettersi
Pt demitir-se

dismostrare *vb* It
De beweisen
En establish; prove
Es demostrar; probar
Fr démontrer
Pt demonstrar; provar

dinero *(m)* n Es
De Geld *(n)*
En money

Fr argent *(m)*
It denharo *(m)*
Pt dinheiro *(m)*

dinero a la vista *(m)* Es
De Sichtgelder *(n pl)*
En money on call
Fr argent à vue *(m)*
It denharo a vista *(m)*
Pt dinheiro à ordem *(m)*

dinero barato *(m)* Es
De billiges Geld *(n)*
En cheap money
Fr argent bon marché *(m)*
It denharo a basso interesse
  (m)
Pt dinheiro barato *(m)*

dinero caro *(m)* Es
De teures Geld *(n)*
En dear money
Fr argent cher *(m)*
It denharo ad alto interesse
  (m)
Pt dinheiro caro *(m)*

dinero efectivo *(m)* Es
De Bargeld *(n)*
En cash
Fr espèces *(f pl)*
It denaro *(m)*
Pt dinheiro *(m)*

dinero sin invertir *(m)* Es
De totes Kapital *(n)*
En idle money
Fr capital oisif *(m)*
It denaro inattivo *(m)*
Pt dinheiro paralisado *(m)*

dinheiro *(m)* n Pt
De Geld *(n)*
En money
Es dinero *(m)*
Fr argent *(m)*
It denaro *(m)*

dinheiro à ordem *(m)* Pt
De Sichtgelder *(n pl)*
En money on call
Es dinero a la vista *(m)*
Fr argent à vue *(m)*
It denaro a vista *(m)*

dinheiro barato *(m)* Pt
De billiges Geld *(n)*
En cheap money
Es dinero barato *(m)*

Fr argent bon marché (m)
It deharo a basso interesse (m)

dinheiro caro (m) Pt
De teures Geld (n)
En dear money
Es dinero caro (m)
Fr argent cher (m)
It denaro ad alto interesse (m)

dinheiro de contado (m) Pt
De Bargeld (n)
En cash
Es dinero efectivo (m)
Fr espèces; argent comptant (f pl; m)
It denaro contante (m)

dinheiro paralisado (m) Pt
De totes Kapital (n)
En idle money
Es dinero sin invertir (m)
Fr capital oisif (m)
It denaro inattivo (m)

dipartimento (m) n It
De Abteilung (f)
En department
Es departamento (m)
Fr département (m)
Pt departamento (m)

Diplom (n) n De
En diploma
Es diploma (m)
Fr diplôme; brevet (m)
It diploma (m)
Pt diploma (m)

diploma (n) En; Es, It, Pt (m)
De Diplom (n)
Fr diplôme; brevet (m)

diplôme (m) n Fr
De Diplom (n)
En diploma
Es diploma (m)
It diploma (m)
Pt diploma (m)

di qualità inferiore It
De minderwertig
En low-grade
Es baja calidad
Fr de qualité inférieure
Pt baixo-nível

de qualità superiore It
De erstklassig
En high-grade
Es alta calidad
Fr de qualité supérieure
Pt alto-nível

dique de carenas (m) Es
De Trockendock (n)
En graving dock
Fr bassin de radoub (m)
It bacino di raddobbo (m)
Pt doca de querenas (f)

dique seco (m) Es
De Trockendock (n)
En dry dock
Fr cale sèche (f)
It bacino di carenaggio (m)
Pt doca-seca (f)

direcção (f) Pt
De Vorstand (m)
En management; board of directors
Es dirección; consejo de administración (f m)
Fr direction; conseil d'administration (f m)
It direzione; consiglio d'amministrazione (f m)

dirección (correo) (f) n Es
De Adresse (f)
En address
Fr adresse (f)
It indirizzo (m)
Pt endereço (m)

dirección (de una sociedad) (f) n Es
De Vorstand (m)
En management
Fr direction (f)
It direzione (f)
Pt gerência; direcção (f)

dirección superior (f) Es
De Direktion (f)
En top management
Fr haute direction (f)
It direzione superiore (f)
Pt gerência superior (f)

dirección telegráfica (f) Es
De Telegrammadresse (f)
En telegraphic address
Fr adresse télégraphique (f)

It indirizzo telegrafico (m)
Pt endereço telegráfico (m)

direct cost En
De direkte Kosten (pl)
Es coste directo (m)
Fr prix direct de revient (m)
It costo diretto (m)
Pt custo directo (m)

direct current (d. c.) En
De Gleichstrom (m)
Es corriente continua (f)
Fr courant continu (m)
It corrente continua (f)
Pt corrente contínua (f)

direct debit En
De direkte Belastung (f)
Es débito directo (m)
Fr débit direct (m)
It debito diretto (m)
Pt débito directo (m)

directeur (m) n Fr
De Geschäftsleiter; Direktor (m)
En manager; director
Es director (m)
It direttore (m)
Pt gerente; director (m)

directeur commercial (m) Fr
De Verkaufsleiter (m)
En sales manager
Es jefe de ventas (m)
It direttore commerciale (m)
Pt chefe de vendas (m)

directeur général (m) Fr
De Geschäftsführer (m)
En chief executive
Es jefe ejecutivo (m)
It direttore generale (m)
Pt chefe de gerência (m)

direct expenses En
De Einzelkosten (pl)
Es gastos directos (m pl)
Fr frais directs (m pl)
It spese dirette (f pl)
Pt despesas directas (f pl)

directions for use En
De Gebrauchsanweisung (f)
Es modo de empleo (m)
Fr mode d'emploi (f)
It istruzioni per l'uso (f pl)
Pt instruções para uso (f pl)

directiva (f) n Es
De Verordnung (f)
En directive
Fr directive (f)
It direttivo (m)
Pt ordem de serviço (f)

directive n En, Fr (f)
De Verordnung (f)
Es directiva (f)
It direttivo (m)
Pt ordem de serviço (f)

directivo (m) n Es
De Geschäftsleiter (m)
En executive
Fr dirigeant (m)
It dirigente (m)
Pt dirigente (m)

direct labour En
De produktive Arbeitskräfte
 (f pl)
Es jornales directos (m pl)
Fr travail en régie (m)
It lavoro in economia (m)
Pt trabalho directamente
 produtivo (m)

direct mail En
De Postversandwerbung (f)
Es progaganda directa por
 correo (f)
Fr publicité directe (f)
It pubblicità diretta (f)
Pt publicidade por correio ao
 domicílio (f)

director n En
De Verwaltungsrat; Direktor
 (m)
Es director (m)
Fr directeur; administrateur
 (m)
It direttore; amministratore
 (m)
Pt director (m)

director (m) n Es
De Direktor; Geschäftsleiter
 (m)
En director; manager
Fr directeur; administrateur
 (m)
It direttore; amministratore
 (m)
Pt director; gerente (m)

director (m) n Pt
De Direktor; Prinzipal (m)
En director; principal
Es director; principal (m)
Fr directeur; principal (m)
It direttore; principale (m)

director administrativo (m)
 Pt
De geschäftsführender
 Direktor (m)
En executive director
Am corporate officer
Es director ejecutivo (m)
Fr administrateur dirigeant
 (m)
It amministratore dirigente
 (m)

director de comercialização
 (m) Pt
De Absatzdirektor (m)
En marketing director
Es director mercantil (m)
Fr administrateur chef
 d'écoulement (m)
It direttore di mercato (m)

director ejecutivo (m) Es
De geschäftsführender
 Direktor (m)
En executive director
Am corporate officer
Fr administrateur dirigeant
 (m)
It amministratore dirigente
 (m)
Pt director administrativo (m)

director geral (m) Pt
De geschäftsleitender
 Direktor (m)
En managing director
Am president
Es director gerente (m)
Fr administrateur délégué (m)
It amministratore delegato
 (m)

director gerente (m) Es
De geschäftsleitender
 Direktor (m)
En managing director
Am president
Fr administrateur délégué (m)
It amministratore delegato
 (m)
Pt director geral (m)

director mercantil (m) Es
De Absatzdirektor (m)
En marketing director
Fr administrateur chef
 d'écoulement (m)
It direttore di mercato (m)
Pt director de comercialização
 (m)

directors' emoluments En
De Direktorenbezüge (m pl)
Es emolumentos de
 directores (m pl)
Fr émoluments des
 administrateurs (m pl)
It emolumenti degli ammini-
 stratori (m pl)
Pt emolumentos de
 directores (m pl)

directors' report En
De Vorstandsbericht (m)
Es informe de la
 administración (m)
Fr rapport des
 administrateurs (m)
It relazione degli amministra-
 tori (f)
Pt relatório de directores (m)

directory n En
De Adreßbuch (n)
Es guía (f)
Fr répertoire (m)
It guida (f)
Pt guia (m)

direct selling En
De Direktverkauf (m)
Es venta directa (f)
Fr vente directe (f)
It vendita diretta (f)
Pt venda directa ao
 consumidor (f)

direct taxation En
De direkte Steuern (f pl)
Es contribuciones directas
 (f pl)
Fr contributions directes (f pl)
It imposte dirette (f pl)
Pt tributação directa (f)

dereito de retenção (m) Pt
De Pfandrecht (n)
En lien
Es derecho de retencíon (m)
Fr droit de retention (m)
It diritto di sequestro (m)

direito preferencial *(m)* Pt
De   Vorzugssatz *(m)*
En   preferential duty
Es   derechos preferenciales
    (m pl)
Fr   tarif de faveur *(m)*
It   tariffa preferenziale *(f)*

direitos *(m pl)* Pt
De   Rechte; Gewinnanteil
    (n pl; m)
En   rights; royalty
Es   derechos *(m pl)*
Fr   droits; redevance *(m pl; f)*
It   diritti *(m pl)*

direitos alfandegários *(m pl)*
    Pt
De   Zoll *(m)*
En   customs duty
Es   derechos de aduanas
    (m pl)
Fr   droit de douane *(m)*
It   diritto doganale *(m)*

direitos de autor *(m pl)* Pt
De   Urheberrecht *(n)*
En   copyright
Es   derechos de autor *(m pl)*
Fr   droits d'auteur *(m pl)*
It   diritto d'autore *(m)*

direitos de importação *(m pl)*
    Pt
De   Einfuhrzoll *(m)*
En   import duty
Es   derechos de importación
    (m pl)
Fr   droits d'entrée *(m pl)*
It   dazio d'importazione *(m)*

direitos de sucessão *(m pl)* Pt
De   Nachlaßsteuer *(f)*
En   estate duty
Am   estate tax
Es   derechos de sucesión
    (m pl)
Fr   droits de succession *(m pl)*
It   diritti di successione *(m pl)*

direitos mineiros *(m pl)* Pt
De   Mineralgewinnungsrechte
    (n pl)
En   mineral rights
Es   derechos mineros *(m pl)*
Fr   droits miniers *(m pl)*
It   diritti minerari *(m pl)*

direitos pagos Pt
De   verzollt
En   duty-paid
Es   derechos pagados
Fr   acquitté
It   dazio pagato

direitos portuários *(m pl)* Pt
De   Hafengebühren *(f pl)*
En   port charges
Es   derechos portuarios *(m pl)*
Fr   droits de port *(m pl)*
It   diritti portuali *(m pl)*

direkte Belastung *(f)* De
En   direct debit
Es   débito directo *(m)*
Fr   débit direct *(m)*
It   debito diretto *(m)*
Pt   débito directo *(m)*

direkte Kosten *(pl)* De
En   direct cost
Es   coste directo *(m)*
Fr   prix direct de revient *(m)*
It   costo diretto *(m)*
Pt   custo directo *(m)*

direkte Steuern *(f pl)* De
En   direct taxation
Es   contribuciones directas
    (f pl)
Fr   contributions directes *(f pl)*
It   imposte dirette *(f pl)*
Pt   tributação directa *(f)*

Direktion *(f)* n De
En   top management
Es   dirección superior *(f)*
Fr   haute direction *(f)*
It   direzione superiore *(f)*
Pt   gerência superior *(f)*

Direktor *(m)* n De
En   director
Es   director *(m)*
Fr   directeur; administrateur
    (m)
It   direttore; amministratore
    (m)
Pt   director *(m)*

Direktorenbezüge *(m pl)* n De
En   directors' emoluments
Es   emolumentos de
    directores *(m pl)*
Fr   émoluments des
    administrateurs *(m pl)*

It   emolumenti degli
    amministratori *(m pl)*
Pt   emolumentos de
    directores *(m pl)*

Direktverkauf *(m)* n De
En   direct selling
Es   venta directa *(f)*
Fr   vente directe *(f)*
It   vendita diretta *(f)*
Pt   venda directa ao
    consumidor *(f)*

direttissimo *(m)* n It
De   D-Zug; Schnellzug *(m)*
En   express train
Es   tren expreso *(m)*
Fr   train express *(m)*
Pt   comboio rápido *(m)*

direttivo *(m)* n It
De   Verordnung *(f)*
En   directive
Es   directiva *(f)*
Fr   directive *(f)*
Pt   ordem de serviço *(f)*

direttore *(m)* n It
De   Geschäftsleiter *(m)*
En   manager
Es   director *(m)*
Fr   directeur *(m)*
Pt   gerente; director *(m)*

direttore commerciale *(m)* It
De   Verkaufsleiter *(m)*
En   sales manager
Es   jefe de ventas *(m)*
Fr   directeur commercial *(m)*
Pt   chefe de vendas *(m)*

direttore conto cliente *(m)* It
De   Kontaktgruppenleiter *(m)*
En   account executive
Es   ejecutive de cuenta *(m)*
Fr   chef de comptes client *(m)*
Pt   chefe de conta de cliente
    (m)

direttore del personale *(m)* It
De   Personalchef *(m)*
En   personnel manager
Es   jefe de personal *(m)*
Fr   chef du personnel *(m)*
Pt   chefe do pessoal *(m)*

direttore di mercato *(m)* It
De   Absatzdirektor *(m)*
En   marketing director

Es   director mercantil *(m)*
Fr   administrateur chef
     d'écoulement *(m)*
Pt   director de comercialização
     (m)

direttore esportazione *(m)* It
De   Exportabteilungsleiter *(m)*
En   export manager
Es   jefe de exportación *(m)*
Fr   chef du service
     exportation *(m)*
Pt   gerente de exportações *(m)*

direttore generale *(m)* It
De   Geschäftsführer *(m)*
En   chief executive
Es   jefe ejecutivo *(m)*
Fr   directeur général *(m)*
Pt   chefe de gerência *(m)*

direzione *(f)* n It
De   Vorstand *(m)*
En   management
Es   dirección *(f)*
Fr   administration *(f)*
Pt   gerência direcção *(f)*

direzione superiore *(f)* It
De   Direktion *(f)*
En   top management
Es   dirección superior *(f)*
Fr   haute direction *(f)*
Pt   gerência superior *(f)*

dirigeant *(m)* n Fr
De   Geschäftsleiter *(m)*
En   executive
Es   directivo *(m)*
It   dirigente *(m)*
Pt   dirigente *(m)*

dirigente *(m)* n It, Pt
De   Geschäftsleiter *(m)*
En   executive
Es   directivo *(m)*
Fr   dirigeant *(m)*

diritto di sequestro *(m)* It
De   Pfandrecht *(n)*
En   lien
Es   derecho de retencíon *(m)*
Fr   droit de retention *(m)*
Pt   direito de retenção *(m)*

diritti *(m pl)* n It
De   Rechte; Gewinnanteil, Ge-
     bühr *(n pl; m f)*
En   rights; royalties

Es   derechos *(m pl)*
Fr   droits; redevance *(m pl; f)*
Pt   direitos *(m pl)*

diritti di dock *(m pl)* It
De   Dockgebühr *(f)*
En   dock dues
Es   derechos de muelle *(m pl)*
Fr   droits de dock *(m pl)*
Pt   encargos de doca *(m pl)*

diritti di successione *(m pl)* It
De   Erbschaftsteuern *(f pl)*
En   death duties
Am   estate taxes
Es   derechos sucesorios *(m pl)*
Fr   droits de succession *(m pl)*
Pt   impostos de sucessão
     (m pl)

diritti minerari *(m pl)* It
De   Mineralgewinnungsrechte
     (m pl)
En   mineral rights
Es   derechos mineros *(m pl)*
Fr   droits miniers *(m pl)*
Pt   direitos mineiros *(m pl)*

diritti portuali *(m pl)* It
De   Hafengebühren *(f pl)*
En   port charges
Es   derechos portuarios *(m pl)*
Fr   droits de port *(m pl)*
Pt   direitos portuários *(m pl)*

diritto acquisito *(m)* It
De   festbegründetes Recht *(n)*
En   vested interest
Es   interés creado *(m)*
Fr   droit acquis *(m)*
Pt   interesse adquirido *(m)*

diritto d'autore *(m)* It
De   Urheberrecht *(n)*
En   copyright
Es   derechos de autor *(m pl)*
Fr   droits d'auteur *(m pl)*
Pt   direitos de autor *(m pl)*

diritto di sosta *(m)* It
De   Kaigeld *(n)*
En   wharfage
Es   muellaje *(m)*
Fr   quayage *(m)*
Pt   atracagem *(f)*

diritto doganale *(m)* It
De   Zoll *(m)*
En   customs duty

Es   derechos de aduanas
     (m pl)
Fr   droit de douane *(m)*
Pt   direitos alfandegários
     (m pl)

disagree *vb* En
De   nicht übereinstimmen
Es   no estar de acuerdo
Fr   être en désaccord
It   essere in disaccordo
Pt   discordar

disarmare *vb* It
De   auflegen
En   lay up
Es   desarmar
Fr   désarmer
Pt   desarmar

**disavanzo della bilancia
     commerciale** *(m)* It
De   Außenhandelsdefizit *(n)*
En   trade gap
Es   vacío comercial *(m)*
Fr   déficit du commerce
     extérieur *(m)*
Pt   vazio comercial *(m)*

disbursement n En
De   Auszahlung *(f)*
Es   desembolso *(m)*
Fr   déboursement *(m)*
It   esborso *(m)*
Pt   desembolso *(m)*

discharge a debt En
De   eine Schuld begleichen
Es   descargar una deuda
Fr   acquitter une dette
It   estinguere un debito
Pt   cancelar uma dívida

discharge an employee En
Am   fire an employee
De   einen Arbeitnehmer
     entlassen
Es   despedir a un empleado
Fr   congédier un employé
It   licenziare un impiegato
Pt   despedir um empregado

discharged bankrupt En
De   entlasteter Gemein-
     schuldner *(m)*
Es   fallido rehabilitado *(m)*
Fr   failli réhabilité *(m)*
It   fallito riabilitato *(m)*
Pt   falido reabilitado *(m)*

disclaimer *n* En
De Ablehnung *(f)*
Es renuncia *(f)*
Fr déni *(m)*
It rinunzia *(f)*
Pt descarte *(m)*

disclosure *n* En
De Offenlegung *(f)*
Es revelación *(f)*
Fr révélation; divulgation *(f)*
It rivelazione *(f)*
Pt revelação; divulgação *(f)*

discordar *vb* Pt
De nicht übereinstimmen
En disagree
Es no estar de acuerdo
Fr être en désaccord
It essere in disaccordo

discount *n* En
De Skonto *(m)*
Es descuento *(m)*
Fr escompte *(m)*
It sconto; ribasso *(m)*
Pt desconto *(m)*

discounted bill En
De Diskontwechsel *(m)*
Es efecto descontado *(m)*
Fr effet escompté *(m)*
It cambiale scontata *(f)*
Pt letra descontada *(f)*

discounted cash flow
(d.c.f.) En
De diskontierter Cash-flow
(m)
Es flujo de caja descontado
(m)
Fr flux monétaire actualisé
(m)
It flusso di cassa scontato
(m)
Pt movimento em dinheiro
descontado *(m)*

discount house En
De Diskontbank *(f)*
Es casa de descuentos *(f)*
Fr maison d'escompte *(f)*
It banca di sconto *(f)*
Pt agéncia corretora de
descontos *(f)*

discount market En
De Diskontmarkt *(m)*
Es mercado de descuentos
(m)

Fr marché de l'escompte *(m)*
It mercato di sconto *(m)*
Pt mercado de desconto *(m)*

discount rate En
De Diskontsatz *(m)*
Es tasa de descuento *(f)*
Fr taux d'escompte *(m)*
It tasso di sconto *(m)*
Pt taxa de desconto *(f)*

discrepância *(f)* *n* Pt
De Abweichung *(f)*
En discrepancy
Es desacuerdo *(m)*
Fr écart *(m)*
It divergenza *(f)*

discrepancy *n* En
De Abweichung *(f)*
Es desacuerdo *(m)*
Fr écart
It divergenza *(f)*
Pt discrepância *(f)*

discretionary trust En
De unumschränkte Treuhand
(f)
Es fideicomiso discrecional
(m)
Fr fidéicommis à
appréciation *(m)*
It fondo fiduciario
discrezionale *(m)*
Pt fundação discricionária *(f)*

discreto profitto *(m)* It
De angemessener Ertrag *(m)*
En fair return
Es beneficio rezonable *(m)*
Fr rendement équitable *(m)*
Pt rendimento justo *(m)*

discriminating tariff En
De diskriminierender Tarif *(m)*
Es tarifa diferencial *(f)*
Fr tarif discriminatoire *(m)*
It tariffa discriminante *(f)*
Pt tarifa descriminatória *(f)*

discriminatoire *adj* Fr
De unterschiedlich
En discriminatory
Es discriminatorio
It discriminatorio
Pt discriminatório

discriminatorio *adj* Es, It
De unterschiedlich
En discriminatory
Fr discriminatoire
Pt discriminatório

discriminatório *adj* Pt
De unterschiedlich
En discriminatory
Es discriminatorio
Fr discriminatoire
It discriminatorio

discriminatory *adj* En
De unterschiedlich
Es discriminatorio
Fr discriminatoire
It discriminatorio
Pt discriminatório

di seconda mano It
De aus zweiter Hand;
Gebraucht-
En second-hand
Es de segunda mano
Fr d'occasion
Pt de segunda mão

disegnatore *(m)* *n* It
De Zeichner; Entwerfer *(m)*
En designer; draughtsman
Es diseñador; dibujante *(m)*
Fr dessinateur *(m)*
Pt desenhador *(m)*

disegno *(m)* *n* It
De Zeichnung *(f)*
En design
Es diseño *(m)*
Fr dessein *(m)*
Pt desenho *(m)*

diseñador *(m)* *n* Es
De Zeichner *(m)*
En designer
Fr dessinateur *(m)*
It disegnatore *(m)*
Pt desenhador *(m)*

diseño *(m)* *n* Es
De Zeichnung *(f)*
En design
Fr dessein *(m)*
It disegno *(m)*
Pt desenho *(m)*

disette *(f)* *n* Fr
De Knappheit *(f)*
En short supply

Es escasez *(f)*
It scarsezza *(f)*
Pt escassez *(f)*

dishonest *adj* En
De unehrlich
Es deshonesto
Fr malhonnête
It disonesto
Pt desonesto

dishonour a bill En
De einen Wechsel nicht akzeptieren
Es protestar una letra
Fr ne pas honorer un effet
It non onorare un effetto
Pt protestar uma letra

disidente *adj* Es
De abweichend
En dissenting
Fr dissident
It dissidente
Pt dissidente

Diskont *(m) n* De
En bank discount
Es descuento bancario *(m)*
Fr escompte en dehors *(m)*
It sconto di banca *(m)*
Pt desconto bancário *(m)*

Diskontbank *(f) n* De
En discount bank
Es casa de descuentos *(f)*
Fr maison d'escompte *(f)*
It banca di sconto *(f)*
Pt agência corretora de descontos *(f)*

diskontierbare Wechsel *(m pl)* De
En bankable bills
Es efectos negociables *(m pl)*
Fr papier bancable *(m)*
It effetti scontabili *(m pl)*
Pt valores transaccionáveis pelo banco *(m pl)*

diskontierter Cash-flow *n* De
En discounted cash flow (d.c.f.)
Es flujo de descontado *(m)*
Fr flux monétaire actualisé *(m)*

It flusso di cassa scontato *(m)*
Pt movimento em dinheiro descontado *(m)*

diskontierte Wechsel *(m pl)* De
En bills discounted
Es efectos descontados *(m pl)*
Fr effets escomptés *(m pl)*
It effetti scontati *(m pl)*
Pt letras descontadas *(f pl)*

Diskontmarkt *(m) n* De
En discount market
Es mercado de descuentos *(m)*
Fr marché de l'escompte *(m)*
It mercato di sconto *(m)*
Pt mercado de desconto *(m)*

Diskontsatz *(m) n* De
En discount rate
Es tasa de descuento *(f)*
Fr taux d'escompte *(m)*
It tasso di sconto *(m)*
Pt taxa de desconto *(f)*

Diskontwechsel *(m) n* De
En discounted bill
Es efecto descontado *(m)*
Fr effect escompté *(m)*
It cambiale scontata *(f)*
Pt letra descontada *(f)*

diskriminierender Tarif *(m)* De
En discriminating tariff
Es tarifa diferencial *(f)*
Fr tarif discriminatoire *(m)*
It tariffa discriminante *(f)*
Pt tarifa discriminatória *(f)*

dislocamento *(m) n* It
De Tonnengehalt *(m)*
En displacement
Es desplazamiento *(m)*
Fr déplacement *(m)*
Pt deslocação *(f)*

dismiss *vb* En
Am fire
De entlassen
Es despedir
Fr congédier
It congedare
Pt despedir

dismissal *n* En
Am firing
De Entlassung *(f)*
Es despido *(m)*
Fr congédiement *(m)*
It licenziamento *(m)*
Pt despedimento *(m)*

disoccupato *adj* It
De arbeitslos
En out of work; unemployed
Es parado; sin trabajo
Fr en chômage
Pt desempregado

disoccupazione *(f) n* It
De Arbeitslosigkeit *(f)*
En unemployment
Es desempleo *(m)*
Fr chômage *(m)*
Pt desemprego *(m)*

disoccupazione stagionale *(f)* It
De jahreszeitlich bedingte Arbeitslosigkeit *(f)*
En seasonal unemployment
Es paro de temporada *(m)*
Fr chômage saisonnier *(m)*
Pt desemprego de estação *(m)*

desolución *(f) n* En
De Auflösung *(f)*
En dissolution
Fr dissolution *(f)*
It scioglimento *(m)*
Pt dissolução *(f)*

disonesto *adj* It
De unehrlich
En dishonest
Es deshonesto
Fr malhonnête
Pt desonesto

dispatch *vb* En
De absenden
Es expedir
Fr expédier
It spedire
Pt expedir

dispatch *n* En
De Versand *(m)*
Es despacho; expedición *(m f)*
Fr envoi *(m)*
It spedizione; dispaccio *(f m)*
Pt despacho; remessa *(m f)*

dispatch note En
De Versandschein *(m)*
Es aviso de expedición *(m)*
Fr bordereau d'expédition
(m)
It bollettino di spedizione *(m)*
Pt aviso de despacho *(m)*

displacement *n* En
De Tonnengehalt *(m)*
Es desplazamiento *(m)*
Fr déplacement *(m)*
It dislocamento *(m)*
Pt deslocação *(f)*

displacement-ton *n* En
De Verdrängungstonne *(f)*
Es tonelada de
desplazamiento *(f)*
Fr tonneau de déplacement
(m)
It tonnellata di dislocamento
(f)
Pt tonelada de deslocação *(f)*

display *n* En
De Schaustellung *(f)*
Es presentación *(f)*
Fr présentation *(f)*
It mostra *(f)*
Pt exposição *(f)*

display unit En
De Schaukasten *(m)*
Es presentación *(f)*
Fr présentoir *(m)*
It mostra *(f)*
Pt montra *(f)*

disponibile *adj* It
De verfügbar
En available
Es disponible
Fr disponible
Pt disponível

**disponibilidades de crédito
sem corbertura** *(f pl)* Pt
De Überziehungsdisposition
(f)
En overdraft facilities
Am overdraw facility
Es facilidades de descubierto
(f pl)
Fr facilités de caisse *(f pl)*
It facilitazione di scoperto *(f)*

disponibilità *(f) n* It
De flüssige Mittel *(n pl)*
En funds available
Es fondos disponibles *(m pl)*
Fr disponibilités *(f pl)*
Pt fundos disponíveis *(m pl)*

disponibilités *(f pl) n* Fr
De flüssige Mittel *(n pl)*
En funds available
Es fondos disponibles *(m pl)*
It fondi disponibili;
disponibilità *(m pl; f)*
Pt fundos disponíveis *(m pl)*

disponible *adj* Es, Pt
De verfügbar
En available
It disponibile
Pt disponível

disponível *adj* Pt
De verfügbar
En available
Es disponible
Fr disponible
It disponibile

disposable income En
De verfügbares Einkommen
(n)
Es renta disponible *(f)*
Fr revenu disponible *(m)*
It reddito disponibile *(m)*
Pt receita disponível *(f)*

disposable wrapping En
De wegwerfbare Verpackung
(f)
Es envoltura desechable *(f)*
Fr emballage perdu *(m)*
It imballaggio a perdere *(m)*
Pt embalagem a destruir *(f)*

disposal *n* En
De Verfügung *(f)*
Es disposición *(f)*
Fr disposition *(f)*
It disposizione *(f)*
Pt disposição *(f)*

disposição *(f) n* Pt
De Verfügung *(f)*
En disposal
Es disposición *(f)*
Fr disposition *(f)*
It disposizione *(f)*

disposición *(f) n* Es
De Verfügung *(f)*
En disposal
Fr disposition *(f)*
It disposizione *(f)*
Pt disposição *(f)*

disposition *(f) n* Fr
De Verfügung *(f)*
En disposal
Es disposición *(f)*
It disposizione *(f)*
Pt disposição *(f)*

disposizione *(f) n* It
De Verfügung *(t)*
En disposal
Es disposición *(f)*
Fr disposition *(f)*
Pt disposição *(f)*

disputa *(f) n* Es, It, Pt
De Streit *(m)*
En dispute
Fr contestation *(f)*

disputa di competenza *(f)* It
De Fähigkeitsstreitigkeit *(f)*
En demarcation dispute
Es disputa sobre
demarcación *(f)*
Fr contestation syndicale des
compétences *(f)*
Pt disputa sobre demarcação
(f)

disputa sobre demarcação
(f) Pt
De Fähigkeitsstreitigkeit *(f)*
En demarcation dispute
Es disputa sobre demarca-
ción *(f)*
Fr contestation syndicale des
compétences *(f)*
It disputa di competenza *(f)*

disputa sobre demarcación
(f) Es
De Fähigkeitsstreitigkeit *(f)*
En demarcation dispute
Fr contestation syndicale des
compétences *(f)*
It disputa di competenza *(f)*
Pt disputa sobre demarcação
(f)

dispute *n* En
De Streit *(m)*
Es disputa *(f)*

Fr contestation (f)
It disputa (f)
Pt disputa (f)

dissenting adj En
De abweichend
Es disedente
Fr dissident
It dissedente
Pt dissedente

dissident adj Fr
De abweichend
En dissenting
Es disidente
It dissidente
Pt dissidente

dissidente adj It, Pt
De abweichend
En dissenting
Es disidente
Fr dissident

dissolução (f) n Pt
De Auflösung (f)
En dissolution
Es disolución (f)
Fr dissolution (f)
It scioglimento (m)

dissolution n En, Fr (f)
De Auflösung (f)
Es desolución (f)
It scioglimento (m)
Pt dissolução (f)

distance n En, Fr (f)
De Entfernung (f)
Es distancia (f)
It distanza (f)
Pt distância (f)

distancia (f) n Es
De Entfernung (f)
En distance
Fr distance (f)
It distanza (f)
Pt distância (f)

distância (f) n Pt
De Entfernung (f)
En distance
Es distancia (f)
Fr distance (f)
It distanza (f)

distanza (f) n It
De Entfernung (f)
En distance
Es distancia (f)
Fr distance (f)
Pt distância (f)

distilaria (f) n Pt
De Brennerei (f)
En distillery
Es destilería (f)
Fr distillerie (f)
It distilleria (f)

distilleria (f) n It
De Brennerei (f)
En distillery
Es destilería (f)
Fr distillerie (f)
Pt distilaria (f)

distillerie (f) n Fr
De Brennerei (f)
En distillery
Es destilería (f)
It distilleria (f)
Pt distilaria (f)

distillery n En
De Brennerei (f)
Es destilería (f)
Fr distillerie (f)
It distilleria (f)
Pt distilaria (f)

distinta pesi (f) It
De Wiegeschein (m)
En weight note
Es certificado de pesaje (m)
Fr note de poids (f)
Pt certidão de peso (f)

distressed area En
De Notstandsgebiet (n)
Es región deprimida (f)
Fr région déprimée (f)
It area indigente (f)
Pt zona deprimida (f)

distressed goods En
De gepfändete Güter (n pl)
Es mercancías embargadas
(f pl)
Fr biens saisis (m pl)
It merce sequestrata (f)
Pt mercadorias embargadas
(f pl)

distribución (f) n Es
De Vertrieb; Verteilung (m f)
En distribution
Fr distribution (f)
It distribuzione (f)
Pt distribuição (f)

**distribución de las
frecuencias** (f) Es
De Häufigkeitsverteilung (f)
En frequency distribution
Fr distribution de fréquences
(f)
It distribuzione delle
frequenze (f)
Pt distribuição de frequência
(f)

distribuer vb Fr
De vertreiben; verteilen
En distribute
Es distribuir
It distribuire
Pt distribuir

distribuição (f) n Pt
De Vertrieb; Verteilung (m f)
En distribution (of goods)
Es distribución (f)
Fr distribution (f)
It distribuzione (f)

distribuição de frequência
(f) Pt
De Häufigkeitsverteilung (f)
En frequency distribution
Es distribución de las
frecuencias (f)
Fr distribution de fréquences
(f)
It distribuzione delle
frequenze (f)

distribuidor (m) n Es, Pt
De Verkaufsagent;
Konzessionär (m)
En distributor
Fr distributeur;
concessionnaire (m)
It distributore;
concessionario (m)

distribuir vb Es, Pt
De vertreiben; verteilen
En distribute
Fr distribuer
It distribuire

distribuire *vb* It
De vertreiben; verteilen
En distribute
Es distribuir
Fr distribuer
Pt distribuir

distribute (profits, dividends, etc.) *vb* En
De verteilen
Es repartir
Fr répartir
It ripartire
Pt repartir

distribute (goods) *vb* En
De vertreiben; verteilen
Es distribuir
Fr distribuer
It distribuire
Pt distribuir

distributeur *(m)* n Fr
De Verkaufsagent; Konzessionär *(m)*
En distributor
Es distribuidor; concesionario *(m)*
It distributore; concessionario *(m)*
Pt distribuidor; concessionário *(m)*

distributeur automatique *(m)* Fr
De Verkaufsautomat *(m)*
En vending machine
Es máquina expendedora *(f)*
It macchina venditrice automatica *(f)*
Pt máquina de vendas *(f)*

distributeur d'argent comptant *(m)* Fr
De Bargeldauszahlungsautomat *(m)*
En cash dispenser
Es caja automática *(f)*
It cassa automatica *(f)*
Pt caixa automática *(f)*

distribution n En, Fr *(f)*
De Verteilung; Vertrieb *(f m)*
Es reparto; distribución *(m f)*
It ripartizione; distribuzione *(f)*
Pt distribuição *(f)*

distribution de fréquences *(f)* Fr
De Häufigkeitsverteilung *(f)*
En frequency distribution
Es distribución de las frecuencias *(f)*
It distribuzione delle frequenze *(f)*
Pt distribuição de frequência *(f)*

distributor n En
De Verkaufsagent; Konzessionär *(m)*
Es distribuidor; concesionario *(m)*
Fr distributeur; concessionnaire *(m)*
It distributore; concessionario *(m)*
Pt distribuidor; concessionário *(m)*

distributore *(m)* n It
De Verkaufsagent; Konzessionär *(m)*
En distributor
Es distribuidor; concesionario *(m)*
Fr distributeur; concessionnaire *(m)*
Pt distribuidor; concessionário *(m)*

distribuzione *(f)* n It
De Vertrieb; Verteilung *(m f)*
En distribution
Es distribución *(f)*
Fr distribution *(f)*
Pt distribuição *(f)*

distribuzione delle frequenze *(f)* It
De Häufigkeitsverteilung *(f)*
En frequency distribution
Es distribución de las frecuencias *(f)*
Fr distribution de fréquences *(f)*
Pt distribuição de frequência *(f)*

ditado *(m)* n Pt
De Diktat *(n)*
En dictation
Es dictado *(m)*
Fr dictée *(f)*
It dettato; dettatura *(m f)*

ditar *vb* Pt
De diktieren
En dictate
Es dictar
Fr dicter
It dettare

ditta *(f)* n It
De Firma *(f)*
En firm; company
Es firma; casa *(f)*
Fr firme; maison *(f)*
Pt empresa; firma *(f)*

dittafonista *(f)* n It
De Audiotypistin *(f)*
En audio-typist
Am dictaphone-operator
Es audio-mecanógrafa *(f)*
Fr dictaphoniste *(f)*
Pt audio-dactilógrafa *(f)*

dittafono *(m)* n It
De Diktaphon *(n)*
En dictating machine
Es dictáfono *(m)*
Fr machine à dictée *(f)*
Pt dictafone *(m)*

di valore It
De wertvoll
En valuable
Es valioso
Fr de valeur
Pt valioso

divergenza *(f)* n It
De Abweichung *(f)*
En discrepancy
Es desacuerdo *(m)*
Fr écart *(m)*
Pt discrepância *(f)*

diversificação *(f)* n Pt
De Vervielfältigung der Produkte *(f)*
En diversification
Es diversificación *(f)*
Fr diversification *(f)*
It diversificazione *(f)*

diversificación *(f)* n Es
De Vervielfältigung der Produkte *(f)*
En diversification
Fr diversification *(f)*
It diversificazione *(f)*
Pt diversificação *(f)*

diversification *n* En, Fr *(f)*
De Vervielfältigung der
   Produkte *(f)*
Es diversificación *(f)*
It diversificazione *(f)*
Pt diversificação *(f)*

diversificazione *(f) n* It
De Vervielfältigung der
   Produkte *(f)*
En diversification
Es diversificación *(f)*
Fr diversification *(f)*
Pt diversificação *(f)*

dívida *(f) n* Pt
De Schuld *(f)*
En debt
Es deuda *(f)*
Fr créance *(f)*
It debito *(m)*

dívida duvidosa *(f)* Pt
De zweifelhafte Forderung *(f)*
En doubtful debt
Es deuda de pago dudoso *(f)*
Fr créance douteuse *(f)*
It credito dubbio *(m)*

dívida incobrável *(f)* Pt
De uneinbringliche Schuld *(f)*
En bad debt
Es deuda incobrable *(f)*
Fr créance irrécouvrable *(f)*
It credito inesigibile *(m)*

dívida pública *(f)* Pt
De Staatsschuld *(f)*
En national debt
Es deuda pública *(f)*
Fr dette publique *(f)*
It debito pubblico *(m)*

dividend *n* En
De Dividende *(f)*
Es dividendo *(m)*
Fr dividende *(m)*
It dividendo *(m)*
Pt dividendo *(m)*

dividende *(m) n* Fr
De Dividende *(f)*
En dividend
Es dividendo *(m)*
It dividendo *(m)*
Pt dividendo *(m)*

Dividende *(f) n* De
En dividend
Es dividendo *(m)*
Fr dividende *(m)*
It dividendo *(m)*
Pt dividendo *(m)*

dividende intérimaire *(m)* Fr
De vorläufige Dividende *(f)*
En intern dividend
Es dividendo provisional *(m)*
It acconto di dividendo *(m)*
Pt dividendo interino *(m)*

Dividendenstopp *(m) n* De
En dividend limitation
Es bloqueo de dividendos *(m)*
Fr blocage des dividendes
   (m)
It blocco dei dividendi *(m)*
Pt limitação de dividendos *(f)*

dividende semestrielle *(f)* Fr
De halbjährliche Dividende *(f)*
En half-yearly dividend
Es dividendo semestral *(m)*
It dividendo semestrale *(m)*
Pt dividendo semi-anual *(m)*

dividende-warrant *(m)* Fr
De Gewinnanteilschein *(m)*
En dividend warrant
Es cupón de dividendos *(m)*
It cedola di dividendo *(f)*
Pt cédula de dividendo *(f)*

dividend limitation En
De Dividendenstopp *(m)*
En bloqueo de dividendos *(m)*
Fr blocage des dividendes
   (m)
It blocco dei dividendi *(m)*
Pt limitação de dividendos *(f)*

dividendo *(m) n* En, It, Pt
De Dividende *(f)*
En dividend
Fr dividende *(m)*

dividendo excluído Pt
De ohne Dividende
En ex dividend
Es sin dividendo
Fr ex-dividende
It senza dividendo

dividendo final *(m)* Pt
De Schlußdividende *(f)*
En final dividend

Es saldo del dividendo *(m)*
Fr solde de dividende *(m)*
It saldo del dividendo *(m)*

dividendo interino *(m)* Pt
De vorläufige Dividende *(f)*
En intern dividend
Es dividendo provisional *(m)*
Fr dividende intérimaire *(m)*
It acconto di dividendo *(m)*

dividendo provisional *(m)* Es
De vorläufige Dividende *(f)*
En intern dividend
Fr dividende intérimaire *(m)*
It acconto di dividendo *(m)*
Pt dividendo interino *(m)*

dividendo semestral *(m)* Es
De halbjährliche Dividende *(f)*
En half-yearly dividend
Fr dividende semestrielle *(f)*
It dividendo semestrale *(m)*
Pt dividendo semi-anual *(m)*

dividendo semestrale *(m)* It
De halbjährliche Dividende *(f)*
En half-yearly dividend
Es dividendo semestral *(m)*
Fr dividende semestrielle *(f)*
Pt dividendo semi-anual *(m)*

dividendo semi-anual *(m)* Pt
De halbjährliche Dividende *(f)*
En half-yearly dividend
Es dividendo semestral *(m)*
Fr dividende semestrielle *(f)*
It dividendo semestrale *(m)*

dividend warrant En
De Gewinnanteilschein *(m)*
Es cupón de dividendos *(m)*
Fr dividende-warrant *(m)*
It cedola di dividendo *(f)*
Pt cédula de dividendo *(f)*

dividere *vb* It
De teilen
En share
Es repartir
Fr partager
Pt repartir

**dividere a metà la diffe-
   renza** It
De einen strittigen Preisunter-
   schied teilen
En split the difference
Es repartir la diferencia

Fr partager la différence
Pt dividir ao meio a diferença

dividir ao meio a diferença
Pt
De einen strittigen Preisunter-
schied teilen
En split the difference
Es repartir la diferencia
Fr partager la différence
It dividere a metà la
differenza

divieto d'importazione *(m)* It
De Einfuhrverbot *(n)*
En import ban
Es prohibición de
importación *(f)*
Fr prohibition d'entrée *(f)*
Pt proibição de importação *(f)*

divisão *(f)* n Pt
De Teilung *(f)*
En division
Es división *(f)*
Fr division *(f)*
It divisione *(f)*

divisão do trabalho *(f)* Pt
De Arbeitsteilung *(f)*
En division of labour
Es división del trabajo *(f)*
Fr division du travail *(f)*
It divisione del lavoro *(f)*

divisas adiantada *(f pl)* Pt
De Termindevisen *(f pl)*
En forward exchange
Es divisas a término *(f pl)*
Fr change à terme *(m)*
It cambio a termine *(m)*

divisas a término *(f pl)* Es
De Termindevisen *(f pl)*
En forward exchange
Fr change à terme *(m)*
It cambio a termine *(m)*
Pt divisas adiantada *(f pl)*

divisas bloqueadas *(f pl)* Es
De blockierte Devisen *(f pl)*
En blocked exchange
Fr devises bloquées *(f pl)*
It valute bloccate *(f pl)*
Pt câmbio bloqueado *(m)*

divisas extranjeras *(f pl)* Es
De Devisen *(f pl)*
En foreign currency

Fr devises *(f pl)*
It valuta estera *(f)*
Pt moeda estrangeira *(f)*

division n En, Fr *(f)*
De Teilung; Abteilung *(f)*
Es división; sección *(f)*
It divisione *(f)*
Pt divisão; secção *(f)*

división *(f)* n Es
De Teilung *(f)*
En division
Fr division *(f)*
It divisione *(f)*
Pt divisão *(f)*

división del trabajo *(f)* Es
De Arbeitsteilung *(f)*
En division of labour
Fr division du travail *(f)*
It divisione del lavoro *(f)*
Pt divisão do trabalho *(f)*

division du travail *(f)* Fr
De Arbeitsteilung *(f)*
En division of labour
Es división del trabajo *(f)*
It divisione del lavoro *(f)*
Pt divisão do trabalho *(f)*

divisione *(f)* n It
De Teilung; Abteilung *(f)*
En division
Es división; sección *(f)*
Fr division *(f)*
Pt divisão; secção *(f)*

divisione del lavoro *(f)* It
De Arbeitsteilung *(f)*
En division of labour
Es división del trabajo *(f)*
Fr division du travail *(f)*
Pt divisão do trabalho *(f)*

division of labour En
De Arbeitsteilung *(f)*
Es división del trabajo *(f)*
Fr division du travail *(f)*
It divisione del lavoro *(f)*
Pt divisão do trabalho *(f)*

doca *(f)* n Pt
De Dock *(n)*
En dock
Es muelle *(m)*
Fr dock; bassin *(m)*
It dock; bacino *(m)*

doca de querenas *(f)* Pt
De Trockendock *(n)*
En graving dock
Es dique de carenas *(m)*
Fr bassin de radoub *(m)*
It bacino di raddobbo *(m)*

doca-seca *(f)* n Pt
De Trockendock *(n)*
En dry dock
Es dique seco *(m)*
Fr cale sèche *(f)*
It bacino di caronaggio *(m)*

docas francas Pt
De frei Docklager
En delivered docks
Es franco en muelle
Fr franco dock
It franco dock

d'occasion Fr
De aus zweiter Hand;
Gebraucht-
En second-hand
Es se segunda mano
It di seconda mano
Pt de segunda mão

dock n En, Fr, It
De Dock *(n)*
Es muelle *(m)*
Pt doca *(f)*

Dock *(n)* n De
En dock
Es muelle *(m)*
Fr dock; bassin *(m)*
It dock; bacino *(m)*
Pt doca *(f)*

dock dues En
De Dockgebühr *(f)*
Es derechos de muelle *(m pl)*
Fr droits de dock *(m pl)*
It diritti di dock *(m pl)*
Pt encargos de doca *(m pl)*

Dockempfangsschein *(m)* n
De
En dock receipt
Es recibo de entrega en
muelle *(m)*
Fr quittance de dock *(f)*
It quietanza di darsena *(f)*
Pt recibo de doca *(m)*

docker n En, Fr (m)
Am longshoreman
De Hafenarbeiter (m)
Es cargador de muelle (m)
It lavoratore del porto (m)
Pt trabalhador das docas (m)

Dockgebühr (f) n De
En dock dues
Es derechos de muelle (m pl)
Fr droits de dock (m pl)
It diritti di dock (m pl)
Pt encargos de doca (m pl)

dock receipt En
De Dockempfangsschein (m)
Es recibo de entrega en
   muelle (m)
Fr quittance de dock (f)
It quietanza di darsena (f)
Pt recibo de doca (m)

dock strike En
De Hafenarbeiterstreik (m)
Es huelga de obreros de
   muelle (f)
Fr grève des dockers (f)
It sciopero portuale (m)
Pt greve na doca (f)

dockyard n En
De Schiffswerft (f)
Es astillero (m)
Fr chantier de construction
   de navires (m)
It cantiere (m)
Pt estaleiro (m)

document n En, Fr (m)
De Urkunde (f)
Es documento (m)
It documento (m)
Pt documento (m)

documentação do navio (f) Pt
De Schiffspapiere (n pl)
En ship's papers
Es documentación marítima
   (f)
Fr papiers de bord (m pl)
It carte di bordo (f pl)

documentación marítima (f)
   Es
De Schiffspapiere (n pl)
En ship's papers
Fr papiers de bord (m pl)
It carte di bordo (f pl)
Pt documentação do navio (f)

documentary bill En
De Dokumentenwechsel (m)
Es efecto documentario (m)
Fr traite documentaire (f)
It tratta documentaria (f)
Pt título documental (m)

documentary credit En
De Dokumenten-Akkreditiv
   (n)
Es crédito documentario (m)
Fr crédit documentaire (m)
It credito documentario (m)
Pt crédito contra
   documentação (m)

documentary evidence En
De Urkundenbeweis (m)
Es prueba documental (f)
Fr preuve écrite (f)
It prova scritta (f)
Pt prova documental (f)

**documenti contro
   accettazione** (m pl) It
De Dokumente gegen Akzept
   (n pl)
En documents against
   acceptance (d/a)
Es documentos contra
   acceptación (m pl)
Fr documents contre
   acceptation (m pl)
Pt documentos contra
   aceitação (m pl)

**documenti contra
   pagamento** (m pl) It
De Dokumente gegen
   Einlösung (n pl)
En documents against
   payment (d/p)
Es documentos contra pago
   (m pl)
Fr documents contre
   paiement (m pl)
Pt documentos contra
   pagamento (m pl)

documento (m) n Es, It, Pt
De Urkunde (f)
En document
Fr document (m)

documento de garantia (m)
   Pt
De Ausfallbürgschaft (f)
En letter of indemnity
Es carta de indemnización (f)

Fr cautionnement (m)
It lettere di garanzia (f)

document of title En
De Eigentumstitel (m)
Es título de propiedad (m)
Fr titre de propriété (m)
It titolo di proprietà (m)
pt título de progriedade (m)

**documentos contra
   acceptación** (m pl) Es
De Dokumente gegen Akzept
   (n pl)
En documents against
   acceptance (d/a)
Fr documents contre
   acceptation (m pl)
It documenti contro
   accettazione (m pl)
Pt documentos contra
   aceitação (m pl)

**documentos contra
   aceitação** (m pl) Pt
De Dokumente gegen Akzept
   (n pl)
En documents against
   acceptance (d/a)
Es documentos contra
   acceptación (m pl)
Fr documents contre
   acceptation (m pl)
It documenti contro
   accettazione (m pl)

**documentos contra
   pagamento** (m pl) Pt
De Dokumente gegen
   Einlösung (n pl)
En documents against
   payment (d/p)
Es documentos contra pago
   (m pl)
Fr documents contre
   paiement (m pl)
It documenti contro
   pagamento (m pl)

documentos contra pago
   (m pl) Es
De Dokumente gegen
   Einlösung (n pl)
En documents against
   payment (d/p)
Fr documents contre
   paiement (m pl)
It documenti contro
   pagamento (m pl)

Pt documentos contra
    pagamento (m pl)

**documents against
payment** (d/p) En
De Dokumente gegen
    Einlösung (n pl)
Es documentos contra pago
    (m pl)
Fr documents contre
    paiement (m pl)
It documenti contro
    pagamento (m pl)
Pt documentos contra
    pagamento (m pl)

**documents contre paie-
ment** (m pl) Fr
De Dokumente gegen
    Einlösung (n pl)
En documents against
    payment (d/p)
Es documentos contra pago
    (m pl)
It documenti contro
    pagamento (m pl)
Pt documentos contra
    pagamento (m pl)

dogana (f) n It
De Zoll (m)
En customs
Es aduana (f)
Fr douane (f)
Pt alfândega (f)

doit (m) n Fr
De Debet; Soll (n)
En debit
Es débito (m)
It debito; dare (m)
Pt débito (m)

Dokumente gegen Akzept
(n pl) De
En documents against
    acceptance (d/a)
Es documentos contra
    acceptación (m pl)
Fr documents contre
    acceptation (m pl)
It documenti contro
    accettazione (m pl)
Pt documentos contra
    aceitação (m pl)

**Dokumente gegen
Einlösung** (n pl) De
En documents against
    payment (d/p)

Es documentos contra pago
    (m pl)
Fr documents contre
    paiement (m pl)
It documenti contro
    pagamento (m pl)
Pt documentos contra
    pagamento (m pl)

Dokumenten-Akkreditiv (n)
    n De
En documentary credit
Es crédito documentario (m)
Fr crédit documentaire (m)
It credito documentario (m)
Pt crédito contra
    documentação (m)

Dokumentenwechsel (m) n
    De
En documentary bill
Es efecto documentario (m)
Fr traite documentaire (f)
It tratta documentaria (f)
Pt título documental (m)

dollars pétroliers (m pl) Fr
De Öldollar (m pl)
En petrodollars
Es petrodólares (m pl)
It petrodollari (m pl)
Pt petrodólares (m pl)

domaine industriel (m) Fr
De Industriegebiet (n)
En industrial estate
Am industrial park
Es precinto industrial (m)
It centro industriale (m)
Pt centro fabril (m)

domanda (f) n It
De Antrag; Nachfrage (m f)
En application; inquiry
Es solicitud; demanda (f)
Fr demande (f)
Pt requisição; pergunta (f)

domani adj It
De morgen
En tomorrow
Es mañana
Fr demain
Pt amanhã

domestic sales Am
En home trade
De Binnenhandel (m)
Es comercio interior (m)

Fr commerce intérieur (m)
It commercio interno (m)
Pt comércio interno (m)

dominar o mercado Pt
De den Markt beherrschen
En corner a market
Es acaparar el mercado
Fr accaparer le marché
It accaparrare il mercato

dommage (m) n Fr
De Beschädigung; Schaden
    (f m)
En damage; injury
Es daño (m)
It danno (m)
Pt dano; injúria (m f)

dommage indirect (m) Fr
De indirekter Schaden (m)
En consequential damage
Es daños indirectos (m pl)
It danno indiretto (m)
Pt dano por consequência
    (m)

dommages indirects (m pl) Fr
De immaterieller Schaden (m)
En consequential damages
Es daños indirectos (m pl)
It danni indiretti (m pl)
Pt danos decorrentes (m pl)

dommages indirects (m pl) Fr
De Ersatz immateriellen
    Schadens (m)
En special damages
Es daños especiales (m pl)
It danni particolari (m pl)
Pt indemnização especial (f)

dommages-intérêts (m pl) n
    Fr
De Schadenersatz (m)
En damages
Es daños (m pl)
It danni (m pl)
Pt danos (m pl)

**dommages-intérêts fixés
en argent** (m pl) Fr
De Konventionalstrafe (f)
En liquidated damages
Es daños liquidados (m pl)
It danni liquidati (m pl)
Pt danos liquidados (m pl)

don *(m)* n Fr
De Geschenk *(n)*
En gift
Es regalo *(m)*
It dono; donazione *(m f)*
Pt prenda; presente *(f m)*

dona de casa *(f)* Pt
De Hausfrau *(f)*
En housewife
Es ama de casa *(f)*
Fr ménagère *(f)*
It massaia *(f)*

donnée d'exécution *(f)* Fr
De Arbeitsaufgabe *(f)*
En job specification
Es especificación del trabajo
  (f)
It specifica del lavoro *(f)*
Pt especificação de obra *(f)*

données *(f pl)* n Fr
De Daten *(n pl)*
En data
Es datos *(m pl)*
It dati *(m pl)*
Pt dados *(m pl)*

donner de l'avancement à Fr
De befördern
En promote
Es ascender
It promuovere
Pt promover

donner des arrhes Fr
De hinterlegen
En pay a deposit
Es hacar un depósito
It versare un deposito
Pt pagar depósito

donner ses huit jours Fr
De einwöchig kündigen
En give a week's notice
Es dar una semana de aviso
It dare una settimana di
  preavviso
Pt dar um prazo de uma se-
  mana para despedimento

dono *(m)* n It
De Geschenk *(n)*
En gift
Es regalo *(m)*
Fr don; cadeau *(m)*
Pt prenda; presente *(f m)*

dono da casa *(m)* Pt
De Hausherr *(m)*
En householder
Es jefe de familia *(m)*
Fr chef de famille *(m)*
It capo-famiglia *(m)*

dono per corrompere *(m)* It
De Bestechungsgeld *(n)*
En bribe
Es soborno *(m)*
Fr pot-de-vin *(m)*
Pt suborno *(m)*

door-to-door selling En
De Haus-zu-Haus-Verkauf
  (m)
Es venta a domicilio *(f)*
Fr vente à domicile *(f)*
It vendita a domicilio *(f)*
Pt venda de porta-a-porta *(f)*

dopodomani *adv* It
De übermorgen
En day after tomorrow
Es pasado mañana
Fr après demain
Pt depois de amanhã

**Doppelbesteuerungs-
erleichterung** *(f)* n De
En double taxation relief
Es desgravación de tributación doble *(f)*
Fr dégrèvement de charges
  fiscales doubles *(m)*
It sgravio per doppia
  tassazione *(m)*
Pt isenção de tributação dupla
  (f)

doppelte Buchführung *(f)* De
En double entry book-
  keeping
Es partida doble *(f)*
Fr comptabilité en partie
  double *(f)*
It partita doppia *(f)*
Pt lançamento duplo *(m)*

dossier *(m)* n Fr
De Akte *(f)*
En file
Es archivo *(m)*
It archivio *(m)*
Pt ficheiro *(m)*

dotar *vb* Es, Pt
De ausstatten
En endow

Fr doter
It dotare

dotar de fundos Pt
De fundieren
En fund
Es fundar; consolidar
Fr fonder; consolider
It consolidare

dotare *vb* It
De ausstatten
En endow
Es dotar
Fr doter
Pt dotar

doter *vb* Fr
De ausstatten
En endow
Es dotar
It dotare
Pt dotar

douane *(f)* n Fr
De Zoll *(m)*
En customs
Es aduana *(f)*
It dogana *(f)*
Pt alfândega *(f)*

double *(m)* n Fr
De Duplikat *(n)*
En duplicate
Es duplicado *(m)*
It duplicato *(m)*
Pt duplicado *(m)*

double entry book-keeping
En
De doppelte Buchführung *(f)*
Es partida doble *(f)*
Fr comptabilité en partie
  double *(f)*
It partita doppia *(f)*
Pt lançamento duplo *(m)*

double option En, Fr *(f)*
De Stellagegeschäft *(n)*
Es opción doble *(f)*
It opzione doppia *(f)*
Pt opção dupla *(f)*

double taxation relief En
De Doppelbesteuerungser-
  leichterung *(f)*
Es desgravación de tributación doble *(f)*

Fr dégrèvement de charges
fiscales doubles *(m)*
It sgravio per doppia
tassazione *(m)*
Pt isenção de tributação dupla
(f)

doubtful debt En
De zweifelhafte Forderung *(f)*
Es deuda de pago dudoso *(f)*
Fr créance douteuse *(f)*
It credito dubbio *(m)*
Pt dívida duvidosa *(f)*

down-payment *n* En
De Sofortzahlung *(f)*
Es pago de entrada *(m)*
Fr acompte *(m)*
It acconto *(m)*
Pt pagamento inicial *(m)*

down time En
De Leerlaufzeit *(f)*
Es tiempo improductivo *(m)*
Fr temps d'arrêt *(m)*
It tempo improduttivo *(m)*
Pt tempo improdutivo *(m)*

draft (bank) *n* En
De Tratte *(f)*
Es letra *(f)*
Fr traite *(f)*
It tratta *(f)*
Pt letra *(f)*

draft (preliminary version) *n*
En
De Konzept *(n)*
Es borrador *(m)*
Fr projet *(m)*
It bozza *(f)*
Pt rascunho *(m)*

draft agreement En
De Entwurf eines
Übereinkommens *(m)*
Es proyecto de convenio *(m)*
Fr projet de convention *(m)*
It schema di contratto *(m)*
Pt projecto de acordo *(m)*

draft contract En
De Vertragsentwurf *(m)*
Es proyecto de contrato *(m)*
Fr projet de contrat *(m)*
It progetto di contratto *(m)*
Pt minuta de contrato *(f)*

draught (of a ship) *n* En
De Tiefgang *(m)*
Es calado *(m)*
Fr tirant d'eau *(m)*
It pescaggio *(m)*
Pt calado *(m)*

draughtsman *n* En
De Entwerfer *(m)*
Es dibujante *(m)*
Fr dessinateur *(m)*
It disegnatore *(m)*
Pt desenhador *(m)*

draw a cheque En
De einen Scheck ausstellen
Es extender un cheque
Fr tirer un chèque
It emettere un assegno
Pt passar um cheque

drawback (customs) *n* En
De Zollrückvergütung *(f)*
Es reembolso de derechos de
aduana *(m)*
Fr remboursement des droits
d'importation *(m)*
It rimborso d'esportazione
(m)
Pt reembolso de direitos
alfandegários *(m)*

drawee *n* En
De Bezogene(r) *(m)*
Es librado *(m)*
Fr tiré *(m)*
It trattario *(m)*
Pt sacado *(m)*

drawer *n* En
De Aussteller *(m)*
Es librador *(m)*
Fr tireur *(m)*
It traente *(m)*
Pt sacador *(m)*

drawing account En
De Girokonto *(n)*
Es cuenta corrienta *(f)*
Fr compte courant *(m)*
It conto corrente *(m)*
Pt conta corrente *(f)*

draw on reserves En
De die Reserven angreifen
Es sacar reservas
Fr prélever sur les réserves
It prelevare della riserve
Pt recorrer a reservas

draw up a contract En
De einen Vertrag formulieren
Es redactar un contrato
Fr rédiger un contrat
It redigere un contratto
Pt redigir um contrato

dresser un plan Fr
De planen
En schedule
Es programar
It programmare
Pt programar

Dritte(r) *(m) n* De
En third party
Es tercero *(m)*
Fr tiers *(m)*
It terzi *(m pl)*
Pt terceiros *(m pl)*

droit acquis *(m)* Fr
De festbegründetes Recht *(n)*
En vested interest
Es interés creado *(m)*
It diritto acquisito *(m)*
Pt interesse adquirido *(m)*

droit attaché Fr
De mit Dividende
En cum dividend
Es con dividendo
It con dividendo
Pt com dividendo

droits d'auteur *(m pl)* Fr
De Urheberrecht *(n)*
En copyright
Es derechos de autor *(m pl)*
It diritti d'autore *(m)*
Pt direitos de autor *(m pl)*

droit de douane *(m)* Fr
De Zoll *(m)*
En customs duty
Es derechos de aduanas
(m pl)
It diritti doganale *(m)*
Pt direitos alfandegários
(m pl)

droit d'enregistrement *(m)* Fr
De Anmeldegebühr *(f)*
En registration fee
Es derechos de registro *(m pl)*
It tassa di registrazione *(f)*
Pt custas de registo *(f pl)*

droit d'entrée *(m)* Fr
De Eintrittsgebühr *(f)*
En entrance fee
Es derecho de entrada *(m)*
It tassa d'entrata *(f)*
Pt taxa de admissão *(f)*

droit de retention *(m)* Fr
De Pfandrecht *(n)*
En lien
Es derecho de retención *(m)*
It diritti di sequestro *(m)*
Pt embargo; direito de
retenção *(m)*

droit de timbre *(m)* Fr
De Stempelgebühr *(f)*
En stamp duty
Es impuesto del timbre *(m)*
It tassa di bollo *(f)*
Pt imposto de selo *(m)*

droits *(m pl)* n Fr
De Rechte *(n pl)*
En rights
Es derechos *(m pl)*
It diritti *(m pl)*
Pt direitos *(m pl)*

droits d'entrée *(m pl)* Fr
De Einfuhrzoll *(m)*
En import duty
Es derechos de importación
(m pl)
It dazio d'importazione *(m)*
Pt direitos de importação *(m
pl)*

droits de dock *(m pl)* Fr
De Dockgebühr *(f)*
En dock dues
Es derechos de muelle *(m pl)*
It diritti di dock *(m pl)*
Pt encargos de doca *(m pl)*

droits de port *(m pl)* Fr
De Hafengebühren *(f pl)*
En port charges
Es derechos portuarios *(m pl)*
It diritti portuali *(m pl)*
Pt direitos protuários *(m pl)*

droits de succession *(m pl)*
Fr
De Nachlaßsteuer *(f)*
En estate duty
Am estate tax
Es derechos de sucesión
(m pl)

It diritti di successione *(m pl)*
Pt direitos de sucessão *(m pl)*

droits miniers *(m pl)* Fr
De Mineralgewinnungsrechte
(n pl)
En mineral rights
Es derechos mineros *(m pl)*
It diritti minerari *(m pl)*
Pt direitos mineiros *(m pl)*

droit sur la consommation
(m) Fr
De Verbrauchsabgabe *(f)*
En excise duty
Es impuesto de consumos
(m)
It imposta sul consumo *(f)*
Pt imposto indirecto *(m)*

drückende Spesen *(f pl)* De
En heavy charges
Es gastos fuertes *(m pl)*
Fr charges lourdes *(f pl)*
It forti spese *(f pl)*
Pt encargos pesados *(m pl)*

Druckmesser *(m)* n De
En pressure gauge
Es manómetro *(m)*
Fr manomètre; jauge de
pression *(m f)*
It manometro *(m)*
Pt manómetro *(m)*

dry dock En
De Trockendock *(n)*
Es dique seco *(m)*
Fr cale sèche *(f)*
It bacino di carenaggio *(m)*
Pt doca-seca *(f)*

Dubiosenreserve *(f)* n De
En bad debt reserve
Es reserva para deudas
incobrables *(f)*
Fr provision pour créances
douteues *(f)*
It riserva per crediti
inesigibili *(f)*
Pt reserva para dívidas
incobráveis *(f)*

due date En
De Fälligkeitstag *(m)*
Es fecha de vencimiento *(f)*
Fr date d'échéance *(f)*
It data di scadenza *(f)*
Pt data de vencimento *(f)*

due date Am
En settlement day
De Abrechnungstag *(m)*
Es día de liquidación *(m)*
Fr jour de règlement *(m)*
It giorno della liquidazione
(m)
Pt dia de liquidação *(m)*

dumping n En, Fr, It *(m)*
De Dumping *(n)*
Es inundación de mercancía
barata *(f)*
Pt saturação (de mercadorias
baratas); descarga *(f)*

Dumping *(n)* n De
En dumping
Es inundación de mercancía
barata *(f)*
Fr dumping *(m)*
It dumping *(m)*
Pt saturação (de mercadorias
baratas); descarga *(f)*

duplicado *(m)* n Es, Pt
De Duplikat *(n)*
En duplicate
Fr double; duplicata *(m)*
It duplicato *(m)*

duplicate n En
De Duplikat *(n)*
Es duplicado *(m)*
Fr double; duplicata *(m)*
It duplicato *(m)*
Pt duplicado *(m)*

duplicata *(m)* n Fr
De Duplikat *(n)*
En duplicate
Es duplicado *(m)*
It duplicato *(m)*
Pt duplicado *(m)*

duplicato *(m)* n It
De Duplikat *(n)*
En duplicate
Es duplicado *(m)*
Fr double; duplicata *(m)*
Pt duplicado *(m)*

Duplikat *(n)* n De
En duplicate
Es duplicado *(m)*
Fr double; duplicata *(m)*
It duplicato *(m)*
Pt duplicado *(m)*

durable goods En
De langlebige Güter *(n pl)*
Es mercancías no
     perecederas *(f pl)*
Fr biens durables *(m pl)*
It beni durevoli *(m pl)*
Pt mercadorias imperecíveis
     (f pl)

duração *(f) n* Pt
De Dauer *(f)*
En duration
Es duración *(f)*
Fr durée *(f)*
It durata *(f)*

duración *(f) n* Es
De Dauer *(f)*
En duration
Fr durée *(f)*
It durata *(f)*
Pt duração *(f)*

durata *(f) n* It
De Dauer *(f)*
En duration
Es duración *(f)*
Fr durée *(f)*
Pt duração *(f)*

duration *n* En
De Dauer *(f)*
Es duración *(f)*
Fr durée *(f)*
It durata *(f)*
Pt duração *(f)*

Durchfallquote *(f) n* De
En failure rate
Es proporción de fracasos *(f)*
Fr taux de défaillance *(m)*
It indice dei fallimenti *(m)*
Pt proporção de fracassos *(f)*

Durchführbarkeit *(f) n* De
En feasibility
Es practicabilidad *(f)*
Fr practicabilité *(f)*
It fattibilità *(f)*
Pt viabilidade *(f)*

Durchführbarkeitsanalyse
     (f) n De
En feasibility study
Es estudio de viabilidad *(m)*
Fr étude probatoire *(f)*
It studio delle possibilità *(m)*
Pt estudo de viabilidade *(m)*

durchführen De
En carry out
Es ejecutar
Fr exécuter
It eseguire
Pt executar

Durchschlag *(m) n* De
En carbon copy
Es copia en papal carbón *(f)*
Fr copie au carbone *(f)*
It copia carbone *(f)*
Pt cópia a químico *(f)*

Durchschnitt *(m) n* De
En average
Es promedio *(m)*
Fr moyenne *(f)*
It media *(f)*
Pt média *(f)*

Durchschnittskosten *(m pl) n*
     De
En average cost
Es coste promedio *(m)*
Fr coût moyen *(m)*
It costo medio *(m)*
Pt custo médio *(m)*

durée *(f) n* Fr
De Dauer *(f)*
En duration
Es duración *(n)*
It durata *(f)*
Pt duração *(f)*

durée du travail *(f) n* Fr
De Arbeitszeit *(f)*
En hours of work
Es jornada laboral *(f)*
It ore lavorative *(f pl)*
Pt horas de trabalho *(f pl)*

duress *n* En
De Zwang *(m)*
Es compulsión *(f)*
Fr contrainte *(f)*
It costrizione *(f)*
Pt coerção *(f)*

Düsenflugzeug *(n) n* De
En jet aircraft
Es avión jet *(m)*
Fr avion à réaction *(m)*
It aviogetto *(m)*
Pt avião jacto *(m)*

Düsenmotor *(m) n* De
En jet engine
Es motor de propulsión a
     chorro *(m)*
Fr réacteur *(m)*
It motore a reazione *(m)*
Pt motor a jacto *(m)*

dutiable *adj* En
De abgabenpflichtig
Es tasable
Fr taxable
It tassabile
Pt tributável

duty *n* En
De Gebühr *(f)*
Es derechos; impuesto *(m)*
Fr taxe; impôt *(f m)*
It tassa; imposta *(f)*
Pt taxa; imposto *(f m)*

duty-free *adj* En
De abgabenfrei
Es exento de impuestos
Fr exempt de douane
It esente da dazio
Pt isento de impostos

duty-free admission En
De zollfreie Einfuhr *(f)*
Es admisión libre de
     impuestos *(f)*
Fr admission en franchise *(f)*
It ammissione in franchigia
     doganale *(f)*
Pt admissão livre de impostos
     (f)

duty-paid *adj* En
De verzollt
Es derechos pagados
Fr acquitté
It dazio pagato
Pt direitos pagos

D-Zug *(m) n* De
En express train
Es tren expreso *(m)*
Fr train express *(m)*
It direttissimo; rapido *(m)*
Pt comboio rápido *(m)*

E

earn vb En
De verdienen
Es ganar
Fr gagner
It guadagnare
Pt ganhar

earned income En
De Arbeitseinkommen (n)
Es renta del trabajo (f)
Fr revenu du travail (m)
It reddito di lavoro (m)
Pt receita de trabalho (f)

earnings (wages) n pl En
De Lohn (m)
Es salario (m)
Fr salaire (m)
It guadagni (m pl)
Pt salário (m)

earnings per share En
De Gewinn pro Aktie (n)
Es beneficios por acción
(m pl)
Fr bénéfice par titre (m)
It profitti per azione (m pl)
Pt proventos pro acção (m pl)

eaux territoriales (f pl) Fr
De Hoheitsgewässer (n pl)
En territorial waters
Es aguas territoriales (f pl)
It acque territoriali (f pl)
Pt águas territoriais (f pl)

écart (m) n Fr
De Abweichung (f)
En discrepancy
Es desacuerdo (m)
It divergenza (f)
Pt discrepância (f)

écart de prix (m) Fr
De Preisunterschied (m)
En difference in price
Es diferencia de precio (f)
It differenza di prezzo (f)
Pt diferença de preço (f)

écartement normal (m) Fr
De Normalmaß; Normalspur-
weite (n f)
En standard gauge
Es calibre patrón (m)

It scartamento normale (m)
Pt calibre padrão (m)

eccedenza di peso (f) It
De Übergewicht (n)
En excess weight
Es peso excedente (m)
Fr excédent de poids (m)
Pt excesso de peso (m)

eccessivo adj It
De übermäßig
En excessive
Es excesivo
Fr excessif
Pt excessivo

eccesso (m) n It
De Überschuß (m)
Es surplus
Es excedente (m)
Fr surplus; excédent (m)
Pt excedente (m)

échange (m) n Fr
De Tausch (m)
En exchange
Es cambio (m)
It cambio (m)
Pt câmbio (m)

échantillon (m) n Fr
De Probe; Muster (f n)
En sample
Es muestra (f)
It campione (m)
Pt amostra (f)

échantillon gratuit (m) Fr
De kostenlose Probe (f)
En free sample
Es muestra gratuita (f)
It campione gratuito (m)
Pt amostra grátis (f)

échantillon sans valeur (m)
Fr
De Muster ohne Wert (n)
En sample on no value
Es muestra sin valor (f)
It campione senza valore (m)
Pt amostra sem valor (f)

echar al mar (carga) Es
De über Bord werfen
En jettison
Fr jeter à la mer
It fare gettito
Pt alijar

échéance (f) n Fr
De Fälligkeit (f)
En maturity
Es vencimiento (m)
It scadenza (f)
Pt vencimento (m)

échelle (f) n Fr
De Maßstab (m)
En scale
Es escala (f)
It scala (f)
Pt escala (f)

échelle mobile (f) Fr
De gleitende Skala (f)
En sliding scale
Es escala móvil (f)
It scala mobile (f)
Pt escala móvel (f)

échoir vb Fr
De fällig sein
En fall due
Es vencer
It scadere; essere pagabile
Pt vencer-se

échouer vb Fr
De versagen; durchfallen
En fail
Es fallar; faltar
It mancare; fallire
Pt falhar; faltar

echtes Konnossement (n) De
En clean bill of lading
Es conocimiento de embar-
que sin objecciones (m)
Fr connaissement sans
réserve (m)
It polizza di carico senza
riserve (f)
Pt conhecimento sem
embargos (m)

econometría (f) n Es
De Ökonometrie (f)
En econometrics
Fr économétrie (f)
It econometria (f)
Pt econometria (f)

econometria (f) n It, Pt
De Ökonometrie (f)
En econometrics n pl
Es econometría (f)
Fr économétrie (f)

econometrics *n* En
De Ökonometrie *(f)*
Es econometría *(f)*
Fr économétrie *(f)*
It econometria *(f)*
Pt econometria *(f)*

économétrie *(f) n* Fr
De Ökonometrie *(f)*
En econometrics
Es econometría *(f)*
It econometria *(f)*
Pt econometria *(f)*

economía *(f) n* Es
De Wirtschaft; Volkswirt-
   schaftslehre *(f)*
En (the) economy; economics
Fr économie; économie poli-
   tique *(f)*
It economia *(f)*
Pt economia *(f)*

economia *(f) n* It, Pt
De Wirtschaft; Volkswirt-
   schaftslehre *(f)*
En (the) economy; economics
Es economía *(f)*
Fr économie; économie poli-
   tique *(f)*

economía del mercado libre
   (f) Es
De freie Marktwirtschaft *(f)*
En free economy
Fr système économique du
   marché libre *(m)*
It economia di mercato
   libero *(f)*
Pt economia de mercado
   livre *(f)*

economia de mercado livre
   (f) Pt
De freie Marktwirtschaft *(f)*
En free economy
Es economía del mercado
   libre *(f)*
Fr système économique du
   marché libre *(m)*
It economia di mercato
   libero *(f)*

economia di mercato libero
   (f) It
De freie Marktwirtschaft *(f)*
En free economy
Es economía del mercado
   libre *(f)*

Fr système économique du
   marché libre *(m)*
Pt economia de mercado
   livre *(f)*

economia mista *(f)* It
De Gemischtwirtschaft *(f)*
En mixed economy
Es economía mixta *(f)*
Fr économie mixte *(f)*
Pt economia mixta *(f)*

economía mixta *(f)* Es
De Gemischtwirtschaft *(f)*
En mixed economy
Es économie mixte *(f)*
It economia mista *(f)*
Pt economia mixta *(f)*

economia mixta *(f)* Pt
De Gemischtwirtschaft *(f)*
En mixed economy
Es economía mixta *(f)*
Fr économie mixte *(f)*
It economia mista *(f)*

economia pianificata *(f)* It
De Planwirtschaft *(f)*
En planned economy
Es economía planificada *(f)*
Fr économie planifée *(f)*
Pt economia planeada *(f)*

economia planeada *(f)* Pt
De Planwirtschaft *(f)*
En planned economy
Es economía planificada *(f)*
Fr économie planifée *(f)*
It economia pianificata *(f)*

economía planificada *(f)* Es
De Planwirtschaft *(f)*
En planned economy
Fr économie planifée *(f)*
It economia pianificata *(f)*
Pt economia planeada *(f)*

economias de amplitude
   (f pl) Pt
De System der degressiven
   Kosten *(n)*
En economies of scale
Es economía en función de
   volumen *(f)*
Fr économies de grande
   échelle *(f pl)*
It economie in funzione della
   grandezza *(f pl)*

economic *adj* En
De wirtschaftlich
Es económico
Fr économique
It economico
Pt económico

economic growth En
De Wirtschaftswachstum *(m)*
Es crecimiento económico
   (m)
Fr croissance économique *(f)*
It sviluppo economico *(m)*
Pt crescimento económico
   (m)

económico *adj* Es, Pt
De wirtschaftlich
En economic
Fr économique
It economico

economico *adj* It
De wirtschaftlich
En economic
Es económico
Fr économique
Pt económico

economics *n* En
De Volkswirtschaftslehre *(f)*
Es economía *(f)*
Fr économie politique *(f)*
It economia *(f)*
Pt economia *(f)*

economic sanctions En
De wirtschaftliche Sanktionen
   (f pl)
Es sanciones económicas
   (f pl)
Fr sanctions économiques
   (f pl)
It sanzioni economiche *(f pl)*
Pt sanções económicas *(f pl)*

**économie; économie politi-
que** *(f) n* Fr
De Wirtschaft; Volkswirt-
   schaftslehre *(f)*
En (the) economy; economics
Es economía *(f)*
It economia *(f)*
Pt economia *(f)*

**economie in funzione della
grandezza** *(f pl)* It
De System der degressiven
   Kosten *(n)*

En economies of scale
Es economía en función de
volumen *(f)*
Fr économies de grande
échelle *(f pl)*
Pt economias de ammplitude
(f pl)

économie mixte *(f)* Fr
De Gemischtwirtschaft *(f)*
En mixed economy
Es economía mixta *(f)*
It economia mista *(f)*
Pt economia mixta *(f)*

économie planifiée *(f)* Fr
De Planwirtschaft *(f)*
En planned economy
Es economía planificada *(f)*
It economia pianificata *(f)*
Pt economia planeada *(f)*

**économies de grande
échelle** *(f pl)* Fr
De System der degressiven
Kosten *(n)*
En economies of scale
Es economía en función de
volumen *(f)*
It economie in funzione della
grandezza *(f pl)*
Pt economias de amplitude
(f pl)

economies of scale En
De System der degressiven
Kosten *(n)*
Es economía en función de
volumen *(f)*
Fr économies de grande
échelle *(f pl)*
It economie in funzione della
grandezza *(f pl)*
Pt economias de amplitude
(f pl)

économique *adj* Fr
De wirtschaftlich
En economic
Es económico
It economico
Pt económico

(the) economy *n* En
De Wirtschaft *(f)*
Es economía *(f)*
Fr économie *(f)*
It economia *(f)*
Pt economia *(f)*

écrire à la machine Fr
De auf der Schreibmaschine
schreiben
En type
Es escribir a máquina
It scrivere a macchina
Pt escrever à máquina

edifício de andares *(m)* Pt
De Wohnungsgebäude *(n)*
En block of flats
Am apartment house
Es bloque de pisos *(m)*
Fr immeuble *(m)*
It fabbricato di appartamenti
(m)

é favor enviar Pt
De bitte nachsenden
En please forward
Es se ruega hacer seguir
Fr prière de faire suivre
It far proseguire

efectividad de coste *(f)* Es
De Wirtschaftlichkeit *(f)*
En cost-effectiveness
Fr coût et efficacité
It rendimento della spesa *(m)*
Pt eficiência relativa ao custo
(f)

efectivo *adj* Es, Pt
De wirksam
En operative; effective
Fr actif; effectif
It attivo; operativo

efectivo en caja *(m)* Es
De Barbestand *(m)*
En cash in hand
Fr espèces en caisse *(f pl)*
It pronti contanti *(m pl)*
Pt fundos à ordem *(m pl)*

efecto descontado *(m)* Es
De Diskontwechsel *(m)*
En discounted bill
Fr effect escompté *(m)*
It cambiale scontata *(f)*
Pt letra descontada *(f)*

efecto documentario *(m)* Es
De Dokumentenwechsel *(m)*
En documentary bill
Fr traite documentaire *(f)*
It tratta documentaria *(f)*
Pt título documental *(m)*

efectos *(m pl)* *n* Es
De Effekten *(pl)*
En effects; securities
Fr effets *(m pl)*
It effetti *(m pl)*
Pt efeitos; títulos *(m pl)*

efectos a cobrar *(m pl)* Es
De fällige Wechsel *(m pl)*
En bills for collection
Fr effets en recouvrement
(m pl)
It effetti all'incasso *(m pl)*
Pt letras a descontar *(f pl)*

efectos a pagar *(m pl)* Es
De fällige Wechsel; Wechsel-
schulden *(m pl; f pl)*
En payables
Fr effets à payer *(m pl)*
It passività esigibili *(f)*
Pt contas a pagar *(f pl)*

efectos descontados *(m pl)*
Es
De diskontierte Wechsel *(m pl)*
En bills discounted
Fr effets escomptés *(m pl)*
It effetti scontati *(m pl)*
Pt letras descontadas *(f pl)*

efectos negociables *(m pl)*
Es
De diskontierbare Wechsel
(m pl)
En bankable bills
Fr papier bancable *(m)*
It effetti scontabili *(m pl)*
Pt valores transaccionáveis
pelo banco *(m pl)*

effectifs *(m)* *n* Fr
De Belegschaft *(f)*
En work force
Es masa obrera *(f)*
It massa lavoratrice *(f)*
Pt massa trabalhadora *(f)*

effectiveness *n* En
De Wirksamkeit *(f)*
Es eficacia *(f)*
Fr efficacité *(f)*
It efficacia *(f)*
Pt eficácia *(f)*

effects *pl* *n* En
De Effekten; Habe *(pl; f)*
Es efectos; bienes *(m pl)*
Fr effets; biens *(m pl)*

It   effetti; beni *(m pl)*
Pt   efeitos *(m pl)*

efeitos *(m pl) n* Pt
De Effekten; Habe *(pl; f)*
En effects
Es efectos; bienes *(m pl)*
Fr effets; biens *(m pl)*
It   effetti; beni *(m pl)*

Effekten *(m pl) n* De
En effects; securities
Es efectos *(m pl)*
Fr effets *(m pl)*
It   effetti *(m pl)*
Pt efeitos; títulos *(m pl)*

effet de commerce *(m)* Fr
De begebbares Wertpapier *(n)*
En negotiable instrument
Es título negociable *(m)*
It   titolo negoziabile *(m)*
Pt título negociável *(m)*

effet escompté *(m)* Fr
De Diskontwechsel *(m)*
En discounted bill
Es efecto descontado *(m)*
It   cambiale scontata *(f)*
Pt letra descontada *(f)*

effet exigible à vue *(m)* Fr
De Sichttratte *(f)*
En bill payable at sight
Es letra a la vista *(f)*
It   effetto pagabile a vista *(m)*
Pt letre à vista *(f)*

effets *(m pl) n* Fr
De Effekten *(pl)*
En effects; securities
Es efectos *(m pl)*
It   effetti *(m pl)*
Pt efeitos; títulos *(m pl)*

effets à payer *(m pl)* Fr
De Wechselschulden *(f pl)*
En bills payable
Es letras pagaderas *(f pl)*
It   effetti passivi *(m pl)*
Pt letras a pagar *(f pl)*

effets à recevoir *(m pl)* Fr
De Wechselforderungen *(f pl)*
En bills receivable
Es letras a cobrar *(f pl)*
It   effetti attivi *(m pl)*
Pt letras a cobrar *(f pl)*

effets en recouvrement
   (m pl) Fr
De fällige Wechsel *(m pl)*
En bills for collection
Es efectos a cobrar *(m pl)*
It   effetti all'incasso *(m pl)*
Pt letras a descontar *(f pl)*

effets escomptés *(m pl)* Fr
De diskontierte Wechsel *(m pl)*
En bills discounted
Es efectos descontados *(m pl)*
It   effetti scontati *(m pl)*
Pt letras descontadas *(f pl)*

effetti *(m pl) n* It
De Effekten *(pl)*
En effects; securities
Es efectos *(m pl)*
Fr effets *(m pl)*
Pt efeitos; títulos *(m pl)*

effetti all'incasso *(m pl)* It
De fällige Wechsel *(m pl)*
En bills for collection
Es efectos a cobrar *(m pl)*
Fr effets en recouvrement
   (m pl)
Pt letras a descontar *(f pl)*

effetti attivi *(m pl)* It
De Wechselforderungen *(f pl)*
En bills receivable
Es letras a cobrar *(f pl)*
Fr effets à recevoir *(m pl)*
Pt letras a cobrar *(f pl)*

effetti passivi *(m pl)* It
De Wechselschulden *(f pl)*
En bills payable
Es letras pagaderas *(f pl)*
Fr effets à payer *(m pl)*
Pt letras a pagar *(f pl)*

effetti scontabili *(m pl)* It
De diskontierbare Wechsel
   (m pl)
En bankable bills
Es efectos negociables *(m pl)*
Fr papier bancable *(m)*
Pt valores transaccionáveis
   pelo banco *(m pl)*

effetti scontati *(m pl)* It
De diskontierte Wechsel
   (m pl)
En bills discounted

Es efectos descontados
   (m pl)
Fr effets escomptés *(m pl)*
Pt letras descontadas *(f pl)*

effetto in bianco *(m)* It
De Blankowechsel *(m)*
En blank bill
Es letra en blanco *(f)*
Fr traite en blanc *(f)*
Pt letra em branco *(f)*

effetto pagabile a vista *(m)* It
De Sichttratte *(f)*
En bill payable at sight
Es letra a la vista *(f)*
Fr effet exigible à vue *(m)*
Pt letra à vista *(f)*

efficacia *(f) n* It
De Wirksamkeit *(f)*
En effectiveness
Es eficacia *(f)*
Fr efficacité *(f)*
Pt eficácia *(f)*

efficacité *(f) n* Fr
De Wirksamkeit; Leistungsfä-
   higkeit *(f)*
En effectiveness; efficiency
Es eficacia; eficiencia *(f)*
It   efficacia; efficienza *(f)*
Pt eficácia; eficiência *(f)*

efficiency *n* En
De Leistungsfähigkeit *(f)*
Es eficiencia *(f)*
Fr efficacité *(f)*
It   efficienza *(f)*
Pt eficiência *(f)*

efficienza *(f) n* It
De Leistungsfähigkeit *(f)*
En efficiency
Es eficiencia *(f)*
Fr efficacité *(f)*
Pt eficiência *(f)*

eficacia *(f) n* Es
De Wirksamkeit *(f)*
En effectiveness
Fr efficacité *(f)*
It   efficacia *(f)*
Pt eficácia *(f)*

eficácia *(f) n* Pt
De Wirksamkeit *(f)*
En effectiveness
Es eficacia *(f)*

Fr efficacité *(f)*
It efficacia *(f)*

eficiencia *(f) n* Es
De Leistungsfähigkeit *(f)*
En efficiency
Fr efficacité *(f)*
It efficienza *(f)*
Pt eficiência *(f)*

eficiência *(f) n* Pt
De Leistungsfähigkeit *(f)*
En efficiency
Es eficiencia *(f)*
Fr efficacité *(f)*
It efficienza *(f)*

eficiência relativa ao custo
(f) Pt
De Wirtschaftlichkeit *(f)*
En cost-effectiveness
Es efectividad de coste *(f)*
Fr coût et efficacité *(f)*
It rendimento della spesa *(m)*

efluentes tóxicos *(m pl)* Es
De giftiger Abfall *(m)*
En toxic waste
Fr déchets toxiques *(m pl)*
It rifiuti tossici *(m pl)*
Pt despejos tóxicos *(m pl)*

Ehre *(f) n* De
En honour
Es honor *(m)*
Fr honneur *(f)*
It onore *(m)*
Pt honra *(f)*

ehrenamtlich *adj* De
En honorary
Es honorario
Fr honoraire
It onorario
Pt honorário

ehrlich *adj* De
En honest
Es honesto
Fr honnête
It onesto
Pt honesto

Eigentum *(n) n* De
En property; ownership
Es propiedad *(f)*
Fr propriété *(f)*
It proprietà; beni *(f; m pl)*
Pt propriedade *(f)*

Eigentümer *(m) n* De
En owner
Es propietario; dueño *(m)*
Fr propriétaire *(m)*
It proprietario *(m)*
Pt proprietário; dono *(m)*

Eigentumstitel *(m) n* De
En title deed
Es título de propiedad *(m)*
Fr titre de propriété *(m)*
It titolo di proprietà *(m)*
Pt título de propriedade *(m)*

Eilbrief *(m) n* De
En express letter
Am special delivery
Es carta urgente *(f)*
Fr lettre par exprès *(f)*
It lettera espresso *(f)*
Pt carta expressa *(f)*

einberufen *vb* De
En convene
Es convenir
Fr convoquer
It convocare
Pt convocar

Einbruchsdiebstahl *(m) n* De
En burglary
Es robo *(m)*
Fr vol avec effraction *(m)*
It furto con scasso *(m)*
Pt roubo *(m)*

einfache Buchführung *(f)* De
En single-entry book-
keeping
Es contabilidad por partida
sencilla *(f)*
Fr comptabilité en partie
simple *(f)*
It contabilità in partita
simplice *(f)*
Pt contabilização por lançamento simples *(f)*

einfache Fahrkarte *(f)* De
En single fare
Am one way fare
Es pasaje de ida *(m)*
Fr billet d'aller *(m)*
It biglietto d'andata *(m)*
Pt passagem de ida *(f)*

einfache Zinsen *(m pl)* De
En simple interest
Es interés simple *(m)*

Fr intérêts simples *(m pl)*
It interesse semplice *(m)*
Pt juro simples *(m)*

Einfuhr *(f) n* De
En import
Es importación *(f)*
Fr importation *(f)*
It importazione *(f)*
Pt importação *(f)*

Einfuhrbeschränkungen
(f pl) n De
En import restrictions
Es restricciones de
importación *(f pl)*
Fr restrictions d'importation
(f pl)
It restrizioni delle
importazioni *(f pl)*
Pt restrições de importação *(f
pl)*

Einfuhrkontingent *(n) n* De
En import quota
Es cupo de importación *(m)*
Fr contingent d'importation
(m)
It contingente d'importa-
zione *(m)*
Pt quota de importação *(f)*

Einfuhrverbot *(n) n* De
En import ban
Es prohibición de
importación *(f)*
Fr prohibition d'entrée *(f)*
It divieto d'importazione *(m)*
Pt proibição de importação *(f)*

Einfuhrzoll *(m) n* De
En import duty
Es derechos de importación
(m pl)
Fr droits d'entrée *(m pl)*
It dazio d'importazione *(m)*
Pt direitos de importação
(m pl)

eingebautes Veralten *(n)* De
En built-in obsolescence
Es decaimiento incorporado
(m)
Fr désuétude incorporée *(f)*
It decadimento incorporato
(m)
Pt obsolência pré-incorpo-
rada *(f)*

eingefrorene Guthaben *(n pl)*
De
En frozen assets
Es activos congelados *(m pl)*
Fr fonds bloqués *(m pl)*
It   attivo congelato *(m)*
Pt bens do activo
    congelados *(m pl)*

eingefrorene Kredite *(m pl)*
De
En frozen credits
Es creditos congelados *(m pl)*
Fr crédits bloqués *(m pl)*
It   crediti bloccati *(m pl)*
Pt créditos congelados *(m pl)*

eingeschriebener Brief *(m)*
De
En registered letter
Es carta certificada *(f)*
Fr lettre recommandée *(f)*
It   lettera raccomandata *(f)*
Pt carta registada *(f)*

eingezahltes Kapital *(n)* De
En paid-up capital
Es capital desembolsado *(m)*
Fr capital versé *(m)*
It   capitale versato *(m)*
Pt capital realizado *(m)*

Eingliederung *(f)* n De
En integration
Es integración *(f)*
Fr intégration *(f)*
It   integrazione *(f)*
Pt integração *(f)*

Einheitskosten *(pl)* n De
En unit cost
Es coste por unidad *(m)*
Fr coût de l'unité *(m)*
It   costo unitario *(m)*
Pt custo por unidade *(m)*

Einheitssatz *(m)* n De
En flat rate
Es tarifa unificada *(f)*
Fr tarif uniforme *(m)*
It   tariffa uniforme *(f)*
Pt tarifa de base *(f)*

einkassieren *vb* De
En cash
Es cobrar
Fr encaisser
It   incassare
Pt cobrar

Einkauf *(m)* n De
En purchase
Es compra *(f)*
Fr achat *(m)*
It   compra *(f)*
Pt compra *(f)*

Einkäufe *(m pl)* n De
En purchases
Es adquisiciones *(f)*
Fr achats *(m pl)*
It   acquisti *(m pl)*
Pt aquisições *(f pl)*

Einkaufsbuch *(n)* n De
En bought ledger
Am purchase book
Es libro mayor de compras
    (m)
Fr grand-livre d'achats *(m)*
It   mastro acquisti *(m)*
Pt livro-mestre de compras
    (m)

Einkaufszentrale *(f)* n De
En central buying office
Es oficina central de compras
    (f)
Fr centrale d'achats *(f)*
It   ufficio centrale d'acquisti
    (m)
Pt escritório central de
    compras *(m)*

Einkommen *(n)* n De
En revenue; income
Es ingresos; rédito *(m pl; m)*
Fr revenu; rentes *(m; f pl)*
It   entrata; reddito *(f m)*
Pt rendimento; receita *(m f)*

Einkommensteuererklärung
    (f) n De
En income-tax return
Es declaración fiscal *(f)*
Fr déclaration de revenu *(f)*
It   dichiarazione del reddito
    (f)
Pt declaração fiscal *(f)*

Einkommensteuerjahr *(n)* n
    De
En income-tax year
Es año fiscal *(m)*
Fr exercice fiscal *(m)*
It   anno fiscale *(m)*
Pt ano fiscal *(m)*

einladen *vb* De
En invite
Es invitar
Fr inviter
It   invitare
Pt convidar

Einladung *(f)* n De
En invitation
Es invitación *(f)*
Fr invitation *(f)*
It   invito *(m)*
Pt convite *(m)*

einlegen; einzahlen (bei einer
    Bank) *vb* De
En bank
Es depositar (en el banco)
Fr déposer à la banque
It   depositare in una banca
Pt depositar (no banco)

einlegen (ein Patent) *vb* De
En file
Es interponer
Fr déposer
It   depositare
Pt registar

Einlösungsertrag *(m)* n De
En redemption yield
Es rédito de reembolso *(m)*
Fr rendement sur
    remboursement *(m)*
It   rendita di rimborso *(f)*
Pt rendimento de resgate *(m)*

Einlösungstag *(m)* n De
En redemption date
Es fecha de reembolso *(f)*
Fr date du remboursement *(f)*
It   data di rimborso *(f)*
Pt data de resgate *(f)*

Einrichtungen *(f pl)* n De
En facilities
Es facilidades *(f pl)*
Fr facilités *(f pl)*
It   facilitazione *(f)*
Pt facilidades *(f pl)*

einschätzen *vb* De
En estimate
Es estimar
Fr estimer
It   stimare
Pt avaliar

Einschiffung (f) n De
En embarcation
Es embarco (m)
Fr embarquement (m)
It imbarco (m)
Pt embarcação (f)

einschließlich adj De
En inclusive
Es incluido; inclusive
Fr inclus; compris
It incluso; compreso
Pt incluindo; incluso

einschränkende Bestimmung (f) De
En restrictive covenant
Es convenio restrictivo (m)
Fr accord restrictif (m)
It accordo restrittivo (m)
Pt obrigação restritiva (f)

einschränkendes Konnossement (n) De
En foul (dirty) bill of lading
Es conocimiento de embarque con objecciones (m)
Fr connaissement avec réserve (m)
It polizza di carico con riserve (f)
Pt conhecimento com embargos (m)

einsetzen vb De
En insert
Es insertar
Fr insérer
It inserire
Pt inserir

Einsichtnahme (f) n De
En inspection
Es inspección; examen (f)
Fr inspection; vérfication (f)
It ispezione (f)
Pt inspecção (f)

Einstandspreis (m) n De
En cost price
Es precio de coste (m)
Fr prix de revient (m)
It prezzo di costo (m)
Pt preço de custo (m)

einstweilig adj De
En temporary
Es temporal
Fr provisoire

It temporaneo
Pt temporário

einträglich adj De
En lucrative
Es lucrativo
Fr lucratif
It lucrativo
Pt lucrativo

Eintragung (f) n De
En entry
Es asiento (m)
Fr inscription (f)
It registrazione (f)
Pt lançamento (m)

Eintragung (einer Gesellschaft) (f) n De
En incorporation
Es incorporación (f)
Fr incorporation (f)
It costituzione (f)
Pt incorporação (f)

Eintritt (m) n De
En entry
Es entrada (f)
Fr entrée (f)
It entrata (f)
Pt admissão (f)

Eintritt frei De
En admission free
Es entrada gratuita
Fr entrée gratuite
It ingresso gratuito
Pt entrada grátis

Eintrittsdeklarationsschein (m) n De
En jerque note
Es certificado de declaración de entrada (m)
Fr certificat d'entrée autorisée (m)
It certificato di dichiarazione d'entrata (m)
Pt certificado de verificação alfandegária (m)

Eintrittsgebühr (f) n De
En entrance fee
Es derecho de entrada (m)
Fr droit d'entrée (m)
It tassa d'entrata (f)
Pt taxe de admissão (f)

Einwanderung (f) n De
En immigration
Es immigración (f)
Fr immigration (f)
It immigrazione (f)
Pt imigração (f)

einwöchig kündigen De
En give a week's notice
Es dar una semana de aviso
Fr donner ses huit jours
It dare una settimana di preavviso
Pt dar um prazo de uma semana para despedimento

Einzahler (m) n De
En depositor
Es depositante (m)
Fr déposant (m)
It depositante (m)
Pt depositante (m)

Einzelhandei (m) n De
En retail trade
Es comercio al por menor (m)
Fr commerce en détail (m)
It commercio al minuto (m)
Pt comércio a retalho (m)

Einzelhandelspreis (m) n De
En retail price
Es precio al por menor (m)
Fr prix de détail (m)
It prezzo al minuto (m)
Pt preço a retalho (m)

Einzelhändler (m) n De
En retailer
Es comerciante al por menor (m)
Fr commerçant au détail (m)
It commerciante al minuto (m)
Pt comerciante a retalho; retalhista (m)

Einzelheiten (f pl) n De
En particulars
Es detalles (m pl)
Fr détails (m pl)
It particolari (m pl)
Pt pormenores (m pl)

Einzelkosten (pl) n De
En direct expenses
Es gastos directos (m pl)
Fr frais directs (m pl)

It spese dirette *(f pl)*
Pt despesas directas *(f pl)*

Einzugskosten *(pl)* n De
En collection charges
Es gastos de cobranza *(m pl)*
Fr frais d'encaissement *(m pl)*
It spese di ricossione *(f pl)*
Pt gastos de cobrança *(m pl)*

Eisen *(n)* n De
En iron
Es hierro *(m)*
Fr fer *(m)*
It ferró *(m)*
Pt ferro *(m)*

Eisenbahn *(f)* n De
En railway
Es ferrocarril *(m)*
Fr chemin de fer *(m)*
It ferrovia *(f)*
Pt caminho de ferro *(m)*

Eisenbahnfahrplan *(m)* n De
En railway timetable
Es horario de trenes *(m)*
Fr indicateur des chemins de
   fer *(m)*
It orario ferroiario *(m)*
Pt horário de caminhos de
   ferro *(m)*

Eisenbahnwagen *(m)* n De
En railway carriage
Am railroad car
Es vagón de ferrocarril *(m)*
Fr wagon de chemin de fer
   (m)
It carrozza ferroiaria *(f)*
Pt vagão de caminhos de ferro
   (m)

Eisenerz *(n)* n De
En iron ore
Es mineral de hierro *(m)*
Fr minerai de fer *(m)*
It minerale di ferro *(m)*
Pt minério de ferro *(m)*

Eisenwaren *(f pl)* n De
En hardware; ironmongery
Es ferretería; quincallería *(f)*
Fr quincaillerie *(f)*
It ferramenta *(f)*
Pt ferragens *(f)*

ejecución *(d)* n Es
De Vollstreckung; Erfüllung *(f)*
En performance
Fr exécution *(f)*
It esecuzione *(f)*
Pt desempenho *(m)*

ejecutar *vb* Es
De vollstrecken; durchführen
En execute; carry out
Fr exécuter; réaliser
It eseguire; effettuare
Pt executar

ejecutar un testamento Es
De ein Testament vollstrecken
En execute a will
Fr exécuter un testament
It eseguire un testamento
Pt dar execução a um
   testamento

ejecutivo de cuenta *(m)* Es
De Kontaktgruppenleiter *(m)*
En account executive
Fr chef de comptes client *(m)*
It direttore conto cliente *(m)*
Pt chefe de conta de cliente
   (m)

ejercicio *(m)* n Es
De Abrechnungszeitraum *(m)*
En accounting period
Fr exercice *(f)*
It esercizio *(m)*
Pt exercício *(m)*

elaboratore *(m)* n It
De Rechner; Computer *(m)*
En computer
Es computadora *(f)*
Fr ordinateur *(m)*
Pt computador *(m)*

elaboratore numerico *(m)* It
De Digitalrechner *(m)*
En digital computer
Es computadora numérica *(f)*
Fr calculateur digital *(m)*
Pt computador de dígitos *(m)*

elaborazione dei dati *(f)* It
De Datenverarbeitung *(f)*
En data processing
Es tratamiento de datos *(m)*
Fr traitement d'informatique
   (m)
Pt processamento de dados
   (m)

elasticidad de precio *(f)* Es
De Preisdehnbarkeit *(f)*
En price elasticity
Fr élasticité-prix *(m)*
It elasticità di prezzo *(f)*
Pt flexibilidade de preços *(f)*

elasticità di prezzo *(f)* It
De Preisdehnbarkeit *(f)*
En price elasticity
Es elasticidad de precio *(f)*
Fr élasticité-prix *(m)*
Pt flexibilidade de preços *(f)*

élasticité-prix *(m)* n Fr
De Preisdehnbarkeit *(f)*
En price elasticity
Es elasticidad de precio *(f)*
It elasticità di prezzo *(f)*
Pt flexibilidade de preços *(f)*

electrical engineering En
De Elektrotechnik *(f)*
Es ingeniería eléctrica *(f)*
Fr construction électrique *(f)*
It elettrotecnica *(f)*
Pt engenharia electrotécnica
   (f)

electricidad *(f)* n Es
De Elektrizität *(f)*
En electricity
Fr électricité *(f)*
It elettricità *(f)*
Pt electricidade *(f)*

electricidade *(f)* n Pt
De Elektrizität *(f)*
En electricity
Es electricidad *(f)*
Fr électricité *(f)*
It elettricità *(f)*

électricité *(f)* n Fr
De Elektrizität *(f)*
En electricity
Es electricidad *(f)*
It elettricità *(f)*
Pt electricidade *(f)*

electricity n En
De Elektrizität *(f)*
Es electricidad *(f)*
Fr électricité *(f)*
It elettricità *(f)*
Pt electricidade *(f)*

electro-domésticos *(m pl) n*
Pt
De elektrische Haushaltsgüter
(n pl)
En household electrical
goods
Es aparatos eléctricos de
casa *(m pl)*
Fr électro-ménager *(m)*
It elettrodomestici *(m pl)*

électro-ménager *(m) n* Fr
De elektrische Haushaltsgüter
(n pl)
En household electrical
goods
Es aparatos eléctricos de
casa *(m pl)*
It elettrodomestici *(m pl)*
Pt electro-domésticos *(m pl)*

electronic *adj* En
De elektronisch
Es electrónico
Fr électronique
It elettronico
Pt electrónico

electrónica *(f)* Es, Pt
De Elektronik *(f)*
En electronics
Fr électronique *(f)*
It elettronica *(f)*

electrónico *adj* Es, Pt
De elektronisch
En electronic
Fr électronique
It elettronico

electronics *n* En
De Elektronik *(f)*
Es electrónica *(f)*
Fr électronique *(f)*
It elettronica *(f)*
Pt electrónica *(f)*

électronique *adj* Fr
De elektronisch
En electronic
Es electrónico
It elettronico
Pt electrónico

électronique *(f)* Fr
De Elektronik *(f)*
En electronics
Es electrónica *(f)*

It elettronica *(f)*
Pt electrónica *(f)*

elektrische Haushaltsgüter
(n pl) De
En household electrical
goods
Es aparatos eléctricos de
casa *(m pl)*
Fr électro-ménager *(m)*
It elettrodomestici *(m pl)*
Pt electro-domésticos *(m pl)*

Elektrizität *(f) n* De
En electricity
Es electricidad *(f)*
Fr électricité *(f)*
It elettricità *(f)*
Pt electricidade *(f)*

Elektronik *(f) n* De
En electronics
Es electrónica *(f)*
Fr électronique *(f)*
It elettronica *(f)*
Pt electrónica *(f)*

elektronisch *adj* De
En electric
Es electrónico
Fr électronique
It elettronico
Pt electrónico

Elektrotechnik *(f) n* De
En electrical engineering
Es ingeniería eléctrica *(f)*
Fr construction électrique *(f)*
It elettrotecnica *(f)*
Pt engenharia electrotécnica
(f)

elenco delle prenotazioni
(m) It
De Warteliste *(f)*
En waiting list
Es lista de espera *(f)*
Fr liste d'attente *(f)*
Pt lista de espera *(f)*

elenco telefonico *(m)* It
De Fernsprechbuch *(n)*
En telephone directory
Es guía de teléfonos *(f)*
Fr annuaire des téléphones
(m)
Pt lista telefónica *(f)*

elettricità *(f) n* It
De Elektrizität *(f)*
En electricity
Es electricidad *(f)*
Fr électricité *(f)*
Pt electricidade *(f)*

elettrodomestici *(m pl) n* It
De elektrische Haushaltsgüter
(n pl)
En household electrical
goods
Es aparatos eléctricos de
casa *(m pl)*
Fr électro-ménager *(m)*
Pt electro-domésticos *(m pl)*

elettronica *(f) n* It
De Elektronik *(f)*
En electronics
Es electrónica *(f)*
Fr électronique *(f)*
Pt electrónica *(f)*

elettronico *adj* It
De elektronisch
En electronic
Es electrónico
Fr électronique
Pt electrónico

elettrotecnica *(f)* It
De Elektrotechnik *(f)*
En electrical engineering
Es ingeniería eléctrica *(f)*
Fr construction électrique *(f)*
Pt engenharia electrotécnica
(f)

elevado *adj* Pt
De hoch
En high
Es alto; elevado
Fr haut; élevé
It alto; elevato

elevator *n* Am
En lift
De Aufzug *(m)*
Es ascensor *(m)*
Fr ascenseur *(m)*
It ascensore *(m)*
Pt ascensor *(m)*

em armazém Pt
De auf Lager
En at warehouse
Es en almacén

Fr   en dépôt
It   in deposito

embalagem *(f)* n Pt
De   Verpackung *(f)*
En   packing
Es   embalaje; envase *(m)*
Fr   emballage *(m)*
It   imballaggio *(m)*

embalegem a destruir *(f)* Pt
De   wegwerfbare Verpackung
     (f)
En   disposable wrapping
Es   envoltura desechable *(f)*
Fr   emballage perdu *(m)*
It   imballaggio a perdere *(m)*

embalaje *(m)* n Es
De   Verpackung *(f)*
En   packing
Fr   emballage *(m)*
It   imballaggio *(m)*
Pt   embalagem;
     empacotamento *(f m)*

emballage *(m)* n Fr
De   Verpackung *(f)*
En   packing
Es   embalaje; envase *(m)*
It   imballaggio *(m)*
Pt   embalagem;
     empacotamento *(f m)*

emballage perdu *(m)* Fr
De   wegwerfbare Verpackung
     (f)
En   disposable wrapping
Es   envoltura desechable *(f)*
It   imballaggio a perdere *(m)*
Pt   embalagem a destruir *(f)*

embarcação *(f)* n Pt
De   Einschiffung *(f)*
En   embarcation
Es   embarco *(m)*
Fr   embarquement *(m)*
It   imbarco *(m)*

embarcar *vb* Es, Pt
De   verschiffen;
     sich einschiffen
En   ship; embark
Fr   embarquer; s'embarquer
It   imbarcare

embarcation n En
De   Einschiffung *(f)*
Es   embarco *(m)*

Fr   embarquement *(m)*
It   imbarco *(m)*
Pt   embarcação *(f)*

embarco *(m)* n Es
De   Einschiffung *(f)*
En   embarcation
Fr   embarquement *(m)*
It   imbarco *(m)*
Pt   embarcação *(f)*

embark *vb* En
De   sich einschiffen
Es   embarcar
Fr   s'embarquer
It   imbarcare
Pt   embarcar

embarque *(m)* n Es, Pt
De   Verladung *(f)*
Es   shipment
Fr   embarquement *(m)*
It   imbarco *(m)*

embarquement *(m)* n Fr
De   Einschiffung; Verladung *(f)*
En   embarcation; shipment
Es   embarco; embarque *(m)*
It   imbarco *(m)*
Pt   embarcação; embarque
     (f m)

embarquer *vb* Fr
De   verschiffen
En   ship
Es   embarcar
It   imbarcare
Pt   embarcar

s'embarquer *vb* Fr
De   sich einschiffen
En   embark
Es   embarcar
It   imbarcare
Pt   embarcar

embezzle *vb* En
De   unterschlagen
Es   defalcar
Fr   détourner
It   appropriarsi
     indebitamente
Pt   desfalcar

embezzlement n En
De   Unterschlagung *(f)*
Es   defalco *(m)*
Fr   détournement de fonds
     (m)

It   appropriazione indebita *(f)*
Pt   desfalque *(m)*

embezzler n En
De   Veruntreuer *(m)*
Es   defalcador *(m)*
Fr   détourneur *(m)*
It   malversatore *(m)*
Pt   desfalcador *(m)*

em bom estado Pt
De   in gutem Zustand
En   in good repair
Es   en buen estado
Fr   en bon état
It   in buono stato

embotellamiento *(m)* n Es
De   Engpaß *(m)*
En   bottle-neck
Fr   goulot d'étranglement *(m)*
It   strozzatura *(f)*
Pt   engarrafamento *(m)*

emboltellamiento de tráfico
     (m) Es
De   Verkehrsstockung *(f)*
En   traffic jam
Fr   encombrement de
     circulation *(m)*
It   ingorgo stradale *(m)*
Pt   engarrafamento de tráfego
     (m)

**em caso de não
     cumprimento** Pt
De   bei Nichterfüllung
En   in case of default
Es   en caso de incumplimiento
Fr   en cas de défaillance
It   in caso di inadempienza

**em condições de
     navegação** Pt
De   seefest
En   seaworthy
Es   marinero
Fr   en état de navigabilité
It   atto a tenere il mare

em conformidade com Pt
De   in Übereinstimmung mit
En   in accordance with
Es   en conformidad con
Fr   conforme à
It   in conformità con

em conjunto e por vários Pt
De gesamtschuldnerisch
En jointly and severally
Es en conjunto y
   separadamente
Fr conjointement et soli-
   dairement
It solidalmente e individual-
   mente

em contrapartida Pt
De als Gegenrechnung
En per contra
Es en contrapartida
Fr en contrepartie; par contre
It in contropartita

**em dinheiro contra
documentação** Pt
De bar gegen Versandpapiere
En cash against documents
   (c.a.d.)
Es al contado contra
   documentos
Fr comptant contre
   documents
It contanti contro documenti

em duplicado Pt
De Duplikat- ; zweifach
En in duplicate
Es par duplicado
Fr en double
It in duplice copia

em espécie Pt
De in Waren
En in kind
Es en especie
Fr en nature
It in natura

emettere vb It
De ausgeben
En issue
Es emitir
Fr émettre
Pt emitir

emettere un assegno It
De einen Scheck ausstellen
En draw a cheque
Es extender un cheque
Fr tirer un chèque
Pt passar um cheque

émettre vb Fr
De ausgeben
En issue

Es emitir
It emettere
Pt emitir

émettre un emprunt Fr
De eine Anleihe begeben
En float a loan
Am raise a loan
Es emitir un empréstito
It lanciare un prestito
Pt lançar um empréstimo

émeutes et désordres Fr
De Aufruhr und innere
   Unruhen
En riot and civil commotion
Es revueltas y conmociones
   civiles
It rivolte e moti civili
Pt motins e perturbações civis

emisión de derechos (f) Es
De Sonderemission gegen
   Bezugsrechte (f)
En rights issue
Fr émission sous droit de
   souscription (f)
It emissione di diritti (f)
Pt emissão de direitos (f)

emisión fiduciaria (f) Es
De ungedecktes Geld (n)
En fiduciary issue
Fr émission fiduciaire (f)
It emissione fiduciaria (f)
Pt emissão fiduciária (f)

**emisión no totalmenta
subscrita** (f) Es
De nicht in voller Höhe ge-
   zeichnete Emission (f)
En undersubscribed issue
Fr émission non couverte (f)
It emissione non interamen-
   te sottoscritta (f)
Pt emissão não subscrita na
   totalidade (f)

emissão de direitos (f) Pt
De Sonderemission gegen
   Bezugsrechte (f)
En rights issue
Es emisión de derechos (f)
Fr émission sous droit de
   souscription (f)
It emissione di diritti (f)

emissão fiduciária (f) Pt
De ungedecktes Geld (n)
En fiduciary issue
Es emisión fiduciaria (f)
Fr émission fiduciaire (f)
It emissione fiduciaria (f)

**emissão não subscrita na
totalidade** (f) Pt
De nicht in voller Höhe ge-
   zeichnete Emission (f)
En undersubscribed issue
Es emisión no totalmente
   subscrita (f)
Fr émission non couverte (f)
It emissione non interamen-
   te sottoscritta (f)

emissão nova (f) Pt
De Ausgabe junger Aktien (f)
En new issue
Es nueva emisión (f)
Fr émission d'actions
   nouvelles (f)
It nuova emissione (f)

emissione fiduciaria (f) It
De ungedecktes Geld (n)
En fiduciary issue
Es emisión fiduciaria (f)
Fr émission fiduciaire (f)
Pt emissão fiduciária (f)

**emissione non interamente
sottoscritta** (f) It
De nicht in voller Höhe ge-
   zeichnete Emission (f)
En undersubscribed issue
Es emisión no totalmente
   subscrita (f)
Fr émission non couverte (f)
Pt emissão não subscrita na
   totalidade (f)

émission fiduciaire (f) Fr
De ungedecktes Geld (n)
En fiduciary issue
Es emisión fiduciaria (f)
It emissione fiduciária (f)
Pt emissão fiduciária (f)

émission non couverte (f) Fr
De nicht in voller Höhe ge-
   zeichnete Emission (f)
En undersubscribed issue
Es emisión no totalmente
   subscrita (f)

It emissione non
    interamente sottoscritta *(f)*
Pt emissão não subscrita na
    totalidade *(f)*

**émission sous droit de
souscription** *(f)* Fr
De Sonderemission gegen
    Bezugsrechte *(f)*
En rights issue
Es emisión de derechos *(f)*
It emissione di diritti *(f)*
Pt emissão de direitos *(f)*

Emissionssyndikat *(n)* n De
En underwriting syndicate
Es grupo de suscriptores *(m)*
Fr syndicat de garantie *(m)*
It consorzio finanziario *(m)*
Pt consórcio de subscritores
    (m)

emitir *vb* Es, Pt
De ausgeben
En issue
Fr émettre
It emettere

emitir un empréstito Es
De eine Anleihe begeben
En float a loan
Am raise a loan
Fr émettre un emprunt
It lanciare un prestito
Pt lançar um empréstimo

emmagasinage *(m)* n Fr
De Lagerung *(f)*
En storage
Es almacenamiento *(m)*
It magazzinaggio *(m)*
Pt armazenamento *(m)*

emmagasiner *(vb)* Fr
De lagern
En store
Es almacenar
It immagazzinare
Pt armazenar

emolument n En
De Bezüge *(m pl)*
Es emolumento *(m)*
Fr émoluments *(m pl)*
It emolumento *(m)*
Pt emolumento *(m)*

**emolumenti degli
amministratori** *(m pl)* It
De Direktorenbezüge *(m pl)*
En directors emoluments
Es emolumentos de
    directores *(m pl)*
Fr émoluments des
    administrateurs *(m pl)*
Pt emolumentos de
    directores *(m pl)*

emolumento *(m)* n Es, It, Pt
De Bezüge *(m pl)*
En emolument
Fr émoluments *(m pl)*

emolumentos de directores
(m pl) Es, Pt
De Direktorenbezüge *(m pl)*
En directors' emoluments
Fr émoluments des
    administrateurs *(m pl)*
It emolumenti degli
    amministratori *(m pl)*

émoluments *(m pl)* n Fr
De Bezüge *(m pl)*
En emolument
Es emolumento *(m)*
It emolumento *(m)*
Pt emolumento *(m)*

**émoluments des
administrateurs** *(m pl)* Fr
De Direktorenbezüge *(m pl)*
En directors' emoluments
Es emolumentos de
    directores *(m pl)*
It emolumenti degli
    amministratori *(m pl)*
Pt emolumentos de
    directores *(m pl)*

**empacotamento para
exportação** *(m)* Pt
De Exportverpackung *(f)*
En export packing
Es embalaje para exportación
    (m)
Fr emballage convenable à
    l'exportation *(m)*
It imballaggio per
    esportazione *(m)*

empêchement *(m)* n Fr
De Hinderung *(f)*
En hindrance
Es impedimento *(m)*

It impedimento *(m)*
Pt impedimento *(m)*

Empfang bestätigen De
En acknowledge receipt
Es acusar recibo
Fr accuser réception
It accusare ricevuta
Pt acusar e recepção

Empfänger *(m)* n De
En addressee; consignee
Es destinatario; consignata-
    rio *(m)*
Fr destinataire *(m)*
It destinatario;
    consegnatario *(m)*
Pt destinatário;
    consignatário *(m)*

Empfangsbestätigung *(f)* n
De
En acknowledgment of
    receipt
Es aviso de recepción *(m)*
Fr acusé de réception *(m)*
It avviso di recezione *(m)*
Pt aviso de recepção *(m)*

empfohlener Ladenpreis *(m)*
De
En recommended retail
    selling price
Es precio detallista
    recomendado *(m)*
Fr prix de détail racommandé
    (m)
It prezzo al minuto indicativo
    (m)
Pt preço de venda a retalho
    recomendado *(m)*

empleado *(m)* n Es
De Angestellte(r);
    Arbeitnehmer *(m)*
En employee
Fr employé *(m)*
It impiegato *(m)*
Pt empregado *(m)*

empleado a sueldo *(m)* Es
De Angestellte(r) *(m)*
En salaried employee
Fr appointé *(m)*
It stipendiato *(m)*
Pt assalariado *(m)*

emplear vb Es
De beschäftigen
En employ
Fr employer
It impiegare
Pt empregar

empleo (m) n Es
De Beschäftigung; Stellung (f)
En employment; job
Fr emploi (m)
It impiego (m)
Pt emprego (m)

emploi (m) n Fr
De Beschäftigung; Stellung (f)
En employment; job
Es empleo (m)
It impiego (m)
Pt emprego (m)

employ vb En
De beschäftigen
Es emplear
Fr employer
It impiegare
Pt empregar

employé (m) n Fr
De Angestellte(r);
   Arbeitnehmer (m)
En employee
Es empleado (m)
It impiegato (m)
Pt empregado (m)

employee n En
De Angestellte(r);
   Arbeitnehmer (m)
Es empleado (m)
Fr employé (m)
It impiegato (m)
Pt empregado (m)

employer vb Fr
De beschäftigen
En employ
Es emplear
It impiegare
Pt empregar

employer n En
De Arbeitgeber (m)
Es patrono (m)
Fr employeur (m)
It datore di lavoro (m)
Pt patrão (m)

employer's liability En
De Haftpflicht des
   Arbeitgebers (f)
Es responsabilidad del
   patrono (f)
Fr responsabilité patronale (f)
It responsabilità del datore
   di lavoro (f)
Pt responsabilidade do patrão
   (f)

employeur (m) n Fr
De Arbeitgeber (m)
En employer
Es patrono (m)
It datore di lavoro (m)
Pt patrão (m)

employment n En
De Beschäftigung (f)
Es empleo (m)
Fr emploi (m)
It impiego (m)
Pt emprego (m)

employment agency En
De Stellenvermittlungsbüro
Es agencia de colocaciones
   (f)
Fr agence de placement (f)
It agenzia di collocamento (f)
Pt agência de empregos (f)

employment exchange En
Am state employment agency
De Arbeitsnachweisstelle (f)
Es bolsa de trabajo (f)
Fr bureau de placement (m)
It ufficio di collocamento (m)
Pt centro de serviços de
   emprego (m)

employment tax En
De Lohnsummensteuer (f)
Es impuesto por empleado
   (m)
Fr taxe sur l'emploi (f)
It imposta sull'impiego (f)
Pt imposto sobre emprego
   (m)

empregado (m) n Pt
De Angestellte(r);
   Arbeitnehmer (m)
En employee
Es empleado (m)
Fr employé (m)
It empiegato (m)

**empregado de
contabilidade** (m) Pt
De Buchhalter (m)
En ledger clerk
Am bookkeeper
Es contable (m)
Fr commis-comptable (m)
It contabile (m)

empregado de escritório (m)
   Pt
De Angestellte(r) (m)
En clerk
Es oficinista (m)
Fr commis (m)
It impiegato (m)

**empregado por
conta-própria** (m) Pt
De selbständig Arbeitende(r)
   (m)
Es self-employed person
Es trabajador por cuenta
   propia (m)
Fr travailleur indépendant (m)
It lacoratore indipendente
   (m)

empregar vb Pt
De beschäftigen; anstellen
En employ; engage
Es emplear; apalabrar
Fr employer; engager
It impiegare; fissare

emprego (m) n Pt
De Beschäftigung; Stellung (f)
En employment; job
Es empleo (m)
Fr emploi (m)
It impiego (m)

empreiteiro de transportes
   (m) Pt
De Transportunternehmer (m)
En haulage contractor
Am trucking company
Es contratista de transportes
   (m)
Fr entrepreneur de
   camionnage (m)
It imprenditore di trasporti
   (m)

empresa (f) n Es, Pt
De Unternehmen; Firma (n f)
En enterprise; firm
Fr entreprise; firme (f)
It impresa; ditta (f)

empresa de exploração (f) Pt
De Erschließungsgesellschaft
   (f)
En development company
Es compañia de explotación
   (f)
Fr société d'exploitation (f)
It società d'imprese (f)

**empresa de há muito
estabelecida** (f) Pt
De alteingeführtes Geschäft
   (n)
En old-established business
Es casa sólida (f)
Fr maison solide (f)
It casa di vecchia
   fondazione (f)

empresa de transportes (f)
   Es, Pt
De Güterbeförderer (m)
En common carrier
Fr voiturier public (m)
It vettore (m)

**empresa de utilidade
pública** (f) Pt
De gemeinnütziges
   Unternehmen (n)
En untility company
Es empresa de servicios
   públicos (f)
Fr entreprise d'utilité
   publique (f)
It società di servizi pubblici
   (f)

empresa en común (f) Es
De Gemeinschaftsbetrieb (m)
En joint venture
Fr entreprise en participation
   (f)
It impresa in comparte-
   cipazione (f)
Pt iniciativa em comum (f)

empresa extinta (f) Pt
De erloschene Gesellschaft (f)
En defunct company
Es sociedad extinta (f)
Fr société liquidée (f)
It società estinta (f)

empresa financeira (f) Pt
De Finanzierungsgesellschaft
   (f)
En finance company

Es compañía de crédito
   comercial (f)
Fr société de financement (f)
It società finanziaria (f)

empresa gémea (f) Pt
De Schwestergesellschaft (f)
En sister company
Es compañía asociada (f)
Fr société sœur (f)
It società sorella (f)

empresa matriz (f) Pt
De Muttergesellschaft (f)
En parent company
Es compañía matriz (f)
Fr société mère (f)
It società madre (f)

empresa privada (f) Es, Pt
De Privatunternehmen (n)
En private enterprise
Fr entreprise privée (f)
It impresa privata (f)

empresario (m) n Es
De Unternehmer (m)
En entrepreneur
Fr entrepreneur (m)
It intraprenditore (m)
Pt empresário (m)

empresário (m) n Pt
De Unternehmer (m)
En entrepreneur
Es empresario (m)
Fr entrepreneur (m)
It intraprenditore (m)

emprestar vb Pt
De leihen
En lend
Es prestar
Fr prêter
It prestare

empréstimo (m) n Pt
De Anleihe (f)
En loan
Es empréstito (m)
Fr emprunt (m)
It prestito (m)

empréstimo bancário (m) Pt
De Bankdarlehen (n)
En bank loan
Es préstamo bancario (m)
Fr prêt bancaire (m)
It prestito bancario (m)

empréstimo do governo (m)
   Pt
De Staatsanleihe (f)
En government loan
Es empréstito público (m)
Fr emprunt public (m)
It prestito pubblico (m)

empréstimo externo (m) Pt
De Auslandsanleihe (f)
En external loan
Es préstamo exterior (m)
Fr emprunt extérieur (m)
It prestito esterno (m)

**empréstimo para constru-
ção** (m) Pt
De Baukredit (f)
En building loan
Es crédito de construcción
   (m)
Fr crédit de construction (m)
It prestito immobiliare (m)

empréstito (m) n Es
De Anleihe (f)
En loan
Fr emprunt (m)
It prestito (m)
Pt empréstimo (m)

empréstito público (m) Es
De Staatsanleihe (f)
En government loan
Fr emprunt public (m)
It prestito publicco (m)
Pt empréstimo do governo
   (m)

emprunt (m) n Fr
De Anleihe (f)
En loan
Es empréstito (m)
It prestito (m)
Pt empréstimo (m)

emprunter vb Fr
De entleihen
En borrow
Es pedir un préstamo
It prestare
Pt contrair empréstimo

emprunteur (m) n Fr
De Kreditnehmer (m)
En borrower
Es prestatario (m)
It accattatore (m)
Pt beneficiário de em-
   préstimo (m)

emprunt extérieur *(m)* Fr
De Auslandsanleihe *(f)*
En external loan
Es préstamo exterior *(m)*
It prestito esterno *(m)*
Pt empréstimo externo *(m)*

emprunt public *(m)* Fr
De Staatsanleihe *(f)*
En government loan
Es empréstito público *(m)*
It prestito pubblico *(m)*
Pt empréstimo do governo *(m)*

em reserva Pt
De vorrätig
En in stock
Es en almacén
Fr en magasin
It in magazzino

em separado (correio) Pt
De mit getrennter Post
En under separate cover
Es pro separado
Fr sous pli séparé
It con plico a parte

em trânsito Pt
De im Durchgangsverkehr
En in transit
Es en tránsito
Fr en transit
It in transito

en aduanas Es
De unter Zollverschluß
En in bond
Fr en entrepôt
It sotto vincolo doganale
Pt à ordem da alfândega

en almacén Es
De auf Lager
En at warehouse
Fr en dépôt
It in deposito
Pt em armazém

en almacén Es
De vorrätig
Es in stock
Fr en magasin
It in magazzino
Pt em reserva

en avant Fr
De Termin-
En forward
Es a término
It a termine
Pt adiante

en bon état Fr
De in gutern Zustand
En in good repair
Es en buen estado
It in buono stato
Pt em bom estado

en buen estado Es
De in gutem Zustand
En in good repair
Fr en bon état
It in buono stato
Pt em bom estado

encaisser *vb* Fr
De einkassieren
En cash
Es cobrar
It incassare
Pt cobrar

encarecer *vb* Es, Pt
De teurer werden; steigen
En advance in price
Fr renchérir
It aumentare di prezzo

encarecimento *(m) n* Pt
De Preiserhöhung *(f)*
En advance in price
Es encarecimiento *(m)*
Fr renchérissement *(m)*
It rialzo *(m)*

encarecimiento *(m) n* Es
De Preiserhöhung *(f)*
En advance in price
Fr renchérissement *(m)*
It rialzo *(m)*
Pt encarecimento *(m)*

encargos de armazenamento *(m pl)* Pt
De Lagergeld *(n)*
En storage charges
Es gastos de almacenaje *(m pl)*
Fr frais de magasinage *(m pl)*
It spese di magazzinaggio *(f pl)*

encargos de doca *(m pl)* Pt
De Dockgebühr *(f)*
En dock dues
Es derechos de muelle *(m pl)*
Fr droits de dock *(m pl)*
It diritti di dock *(m pl)*

encargos de salvamento *(m pl)* Pt
De Bergegeld *(n)*
En salvage charges
Es cargos de salvamento *(m pl)*
Fr indemnité de sauvetage *(f)*
It spese di salvataggio *(f pl)*

encargos ocasionais *(m pl)* Pt
De Nebenkosten *(pl)*
En incidental charges
Es cargos imprevistos *(m pl)*
Fr charges annexes *(f pl)*
It spese accessorie *(f pl)*

encargos pesados *(m pl)* Pt
De drückende Spesen *(f pl)*
En heavy charges
Es gastos fuertes *(m pl)*
Fr charges lourdes *(f pl)*
It forti spese *(f pl)*

encargo suplementar *(m)* Pt
De Zuschlagsgebühr *(f)*
En extra charge
Es suplemento *(m)*
Fr supplément *(m)*
It spesa supplementare *(f)*

encarregado *(m) n* Pt
De Vorarbeiter *(m)*
En foreman
Es capataz *(m)*
Fr contremaître; chef d'équipe *(m)*
It capo operaio; capo squadra *(m)*

encarregado-chefe *(m) n* Pt
De Werkmeister *(m)*
En head foreman
Es capataz jefe *(m)*
Fr chef d'atelier *(m)*
It capo officina *(m)*

en cas de défaillance Fr
De bei Nichterfüllung
En in case of default
En en caso de incumplimiento

It   in caso di inadempienza
Pt   em caso de não
     cumprimento

en caso de incumplimiento
     Es
De   bei Nichterfüllung
En   in case of default
Fr   en cas de défaillance
It   in caso di inadempienza
Pt   en caso de não
     cumprimento

enchérisseur *(m) n* Fr
De   Bietende(r) *(m)*
En   bidder
Es   ofertante *(m)*
It   offerente *(m)*
Pt   proponente *(m)*

en chômage Fr
De   arbeitslos
En   unemployed
Es   sin trabajo; parado
It   senza lavoro
Pt   desempregado

enclosed *adj* En
De   beiliegend
Es   adjunto
Fr   ci-joint; ci-inclus
It   accluso
Pt   incluso

enclosure *n* En
De   Beilage *(f)*
Es   anexo *(m)*
Fr   annexe *(f)*
It   allegato *(m)*
Pt   anexo *(m)*

encombrement de
     circulation *(m)* Fr
De   Verkehrsstockung *(f)*
En   traffic jam
Es   embotellamiento de
     tráfico *(m)*
It   ingorgo stradale *(m)*
Pt   engarrafamento de tráfego
     (m)

encomenda *(f) n* Pt
De   Bestellung; Auftrag *(f m)*
En   order
Es   pedido *(m)*
Fr   commande *(f)*
It   ordine *(m)*

encomenda (postal) *(f) n* Pt
De   Paket *(n)*
En   parcel
Es   paquete *(m)*
Fr   colis *(m)*
It   pacco *(m)*

encomenda de exportação
     (f) Pt
De   Exportauftrag *(m)*
En   export order
Es   pedido de exportación *(m)*
Fr   commande d'exportation
     (f)
It   ordine per esportazione
     (m)

encomendar *vb* Pt
De   bestellen
En   order
Es   hacer un pedido
Fr   commander
It   ordinare

en conformidad con Es
De   in Übereinstimmung mit
En   in accordance with
Fr   conforme à
It   in conformità con
Pt   em conformidade com

en conjunto y
     separadamente Es
De   gesamtschuldnerisch
En   jointly and severally
Fr   conjointement et
     solidairement
It   solidalmente e
     individualmente
Pt   em conjunto e por vários

en consignación Es
De   in Kommission
En   on consignment
Fr   en consignation
It   in conto deposito
Pt   à consignação

en consignation Fr
De   in Kommission
En   on consignment
Es   en consignación
It   in conto deposito
Pt   à consignação

en contrapartida Es
De   als Gegenrechnung
En   per contra
Fr   en contrepartie; par contre

It   in contropartita
Pt   em contrapartida

en contrepartie Fr
De   als Gegenrechnung
En   per contra
Es   en contrapartida
It   in contropartita
Pt   em contrapartida

encontro *(m) n* Pt
De   Verabredung *(f)*
En   appointment
Es   entrevista *(f)*
Fr   entrevue *(f)*
It   appuntamento *(m)*

encuesta *(f) n* Es
De   Untersuchung *(f)*
En   inquiry
Fr   enquête *(f)*
It   enchiesta *(f)*
Pt   inquérito *(m)*

end *n* En
De   Ende *(n)*
Es   fin *(m)*
Fr   fin *(m)*
It   fine *(f)*
Pt   fim *(m)*

Ende *(n) n* De
En   end
Es   fin *(m)*
Fr   fin *(m)*
It   fine *(f)*
Pt   fim *(m)*

en dépôt Fr
De   auf Lager
En   at warehouse
Es   en almacén
It   in deposito
Pt   em armazém

endereço *(m) n* Pt
De   Adresse *(f)*
En   address
Es   dirección *(f)*
Fr   adresse *(f)*
It   indirizzo *(m)*

endereço telegráfico *(m)* Pt
De   Telegrammadresse *(f)*
En   telegraphic address
Es   dirección telegráfica *(f)*
Fr   adresse télégraphique *(f)*
It   indirizzo telegrafico *(m)*

endeudado *adj* Es
De verschuldet
En indebted
Fr redevable; indetté
It indebitato
Pt endividado; em dívida

endgültig *adj* De
En final
Es final
Fr final
It finale
Pt final

endividado *adj* Pt
De verschuldet
En indebted
Es endeudado
Fr redevable; endetté
It indebitato

endorse (a bill) *vb* En
De indossieren
Es endosar
Fr endosser
It girare
Pt endossar

endorsement *n* En
De Indossament *(n)*
Es endoso *(m)*
Fr endossement; endos *(m)*
It girata *(f)*
Pt endosse *(m)*

endosar *vb* Es
De indossieren
En endorse
Fr endosser
It girare
Pt endossar

endoso *(m)* *n* Es
De Indossament *(n)*
En endorsement
Fr endossement; endos *(m)*
It girata *(f)*
Pt endosse *(m)*

endoso en blanco *(m)* Es
De Blankoindossament *(n)*
En blank endorsement
Fr endossement en blanc *(m)*
It girata in bianco *(f)*
Pt endosse em branco *(m)*

endoso restringido *(m)* Es
De Rektaindossement *(n)*
En restrictive endorsement

Fr endossement restrictif *(m)*
It girata restrittiva *(f)*
Pt endosse restritivo *(m)*

endossar *vb* Pt
De indossieren
En endorse
Es endosar
Fr endosser
It girare

endosse *(m)* *n* Pt
De Indossament *(n)*
En endorsement
Es endoso *(m)*
Fr endossement; endos *(m)*
it girata *(f)*

endosse em branco *(m)* Pt
De Blankoindossament *(n)*
En blank endorsement
Es endoso en blanco *(m)*
Fr endossement en blanc *(m)*
It girata in bianco *(f)*

endossement *(m)* *n* Fr
De Indossament *(n)*
En endorsement
Es endoso *(m)*
It girata *(f)*
Pt endosse *(m)*

endossement en blanc *(m)* Fr
De Blankoindossament *(n)*
En blank endorsement
Es endoso en blanco *(m)*
It girata in bianco *(f)*
Pt endosse em branco *(m)*

endossement restrictif *(m)*
  Fr
De Rektaindossement *(n)*
En restrictive endorsement
Es endoso restringido *(m)*
It girata restrittiva *(f)*
Pt endosse restritivo *(m)*

endosser *vb* Fr
De indossieren
En endorse
Es endosar
It girare
Pt endosser

endosse restrivito *(m)* Pt
De Rektaindossement *(n)*
En restrictive endorsement
Es endoso restringido *(m)*

Fr endossement restrictif *(m)*
It girata restrittiva *(f)*

en double Fr
De Duplikat-; zweifach
En in duplicate
Es par duplicado
It in duplice copia
Pt em duplicado

endow *vb* En
De ausstatten
Es dotar
Fr doter
It dotare
Pt dotar

endowment policy En
De Erlebensversicherung *(f)*
Es póliza dotal *(f)*
Fr assurance à terme fixe *(f)*
It assicurazione dotale *(f)*
Pt título de doação *(m)*

end-product *n* En
De Endprodukt *(n)*
Es producto final *(m)*
Fr produit final *(m)*
It prodotto finale *(m)*
Pt produto final *(m)*

Endprodukt *(n)* *n* De
En end-product
Es producto final *(m)*
Fr produit final *(m)*
It prodotto finale *(m)*
Pt produto final *(m)*

Endrechnung *(f)* *n* De
En final invoice
Es factura final *(f)*
Fr facture finale *(f)*
It fattura finale *(f)*
Pt factura final *(f)*

en el buque Es
De ab Schiff
En ex ship
Fr ex ship
It ex ship
Pt ex-navio

en el extranjero Es
De im Ausland
En abroad
Fr à l'étranger
It all'estero
Pt no estrangeiro

enemigo *(m)* *n* Es
De Feind *(m)*
En enemy
Fr ennemi *(m)*
It nemico *(m)*
Pt inimigo *(m)*

enemy *n* En
De Feind *(m)*
Es enemigo *(m)*
Fr ennemi *(m)*
It nemico *(m)*
Pt inimigo *(m)*

en entrepôt Fr
De unter Zollverschluß
En in bond
Es en aduanas
It sotto vincolo doganale
Pt à ordem da alfândega

en especie Es
De in Waren
En in kind
Fr en nature
It in natura
Pt em espécie

en état de navigabilité Fr
De seefest
En seaworthy
Es marinero
It atto a tenere il mare
Pt em condições de navega-
  ção

engage (staff) *vb* En
Am hire
De anstellen
Es apalabrar
Fr engager
It fissare
Pt empragar

engager *vb* Fr
De anstellen
En engage
Am hire
Es apalabrar
It fissare
Pt empregar

engañar *vb* Es
De betrügen
En cheat
Fr tricher
It truffare
Pt enganar

enganar *vb* Pt
De betrügen
En cheat
Es engañar
Fr tricher
It truffare

engarrafamento *(m)* *n* Pt
De Engpaß *(m)*
En bottle-neck
Es embotellamiento *(m)*
Fr goulot d'étranglement *(m)*
It strozzatura *(f)*

engarrafamento de tráfego
  (m) Pt
De Verkehrsstockung *(f)*
En traffic jam
Es embotellamiento de tráfico
  (m)
Fr encombrement de
  circulation *(m)*
It ingorgo stradale *(m)*

engenharia *(f)* *n* Pt
De Maschinenbau *(m)*
En engineering
Es ingeniería *(f)*
Fr génie *(m)*
It ingegneria *(f)*

engenharia civil *(f)* Pt
De Ingenieurbau *(m)*
En civil engineering
Es ingeniería civil *(f)*
Fr génie civil *(m)*
It ingegneria civile *(f)*

engenharia electrotécnica
  (f) Pt
De Elektrotechnik *(f)*
En electrical engineering
Es ingeniería eléctrica *(f)*
Fr construction électrique *(f)*
It elettrotecnica *(f)*

engenharia mecânica *(f)* Pt
De Maschinenbau *(m)*
En mechanical engineering
Es ingeniería mecánica *(f)*
Fr construction mécanique *(f)*
It ingegneria meccanica *(f)*

engenharia química *(f)* Pt
De Chemietechnik *(f)*
En chemical engineering
Es ingeniería química *(f)*
Fr génie chimique *(m)*
It ingegneria chimica *(f)*

engenheiro *(m)* *n* Pt
De Ingenieur *(m)*
En engineer
Es ingeniero *(m)*
Fr ingénieur *(m)*
It ingegnere *(m)*

engineer *n* En
De Ingenieur *(m)*
Es ingeniero *(m)*
Fr ingénieur *(m)*
It ingegnere *(m)*
Pt engenheiro *(m)*

engineering *n* En
De Maschinenbau *(m)*
Es ingeniería *(f)*
Fr génie *(m)*
It ingegneria *(f)*
Pt engenharia *(f)*

Engpaß *(m)* *n* De
En bottle-neck
Es embotellamiento *(m)*
Fr goulot d'étranglement *(m)*
It strozzatura *(f)*
Pt engarrafamento *(m)*

engranaje *(m)* *n* Es
De Getriebe *(n)*
En gearing
Fr engrenage *(m)*
It ingranaggio *(m)*
Pt engrenagem *(f)*

engrenage *(m)* *n* Fr
De Getriebe *(n)*
En gearing
Es engranaje *(m)*
It ingranaggio *(m)*
Pt engrenagem *(f)*

engrenagem *(f)* *n* Pt
De Getriebe *(n)*
En gearing
Es engranaje *(m)*
Fr engrenage *(m)*
It ingranaggio *(m)*

en magasin Fr
De vorrätig
En in stock
Es en almacén
It in magazzino
Pt em reserva

en muelle Es
De ab Kai
En ex quay

Fr à prendre sur quai
It sulla banchina
Pt ex-cais

en nature Fr
De in Waren
En in kind
Es en especie
It in natura
Pt em espécie

ennemi *(m) n* Fr
De Feind *(m)*
En enemy
Es enemigo *(m)*
It nemico *(m)*
Pt inimigo *(m)*

en port dû Fr
De Portonachnahme
En carriage forward
Am F.O.B. shipping point
Es a porte debido
It porto assegnato
Pt transporte a pagar

en préstamo Es
De darlehensweise
En on loan
Fr sous forme de prêt
It in prestito
Pt por empréstimo

enquête *(f) n* Fr
De Untersuchung *(f)*
En inquiry
Es encuesta *(f)*
It inchiesta *(f)*
Pt inquérito *(m)*

enquête sur les lieux *(f)* Fr
De Stellenüberblick *(m)*
En field study
Es estudio sobre el terreno
    (m)
It studio sul terreno *(m)*
Pt estudo de campo *(m)*

enregistrer *vb* Fr
De registrieren
En register
Es registrar
It registrare
Pt registar

ensaio *(m) n* Pt
De Probe *(f)*
En test; trial
Es ensayo; prueba *(m f)*

Fr essai; épreuve *(m f)*
It saggio; prova *(m f)*

ensayo *(m) n* Es
De Probe *(f)*
En test; trial
Fr essai; épreuve *(m f)*
It saggio; prova *(m f)*
Pt ensaio; prova *(m f)*

enseigne de convenance *(f)*
    Fr
De billige Flagge *(f)*
En flag of convenience
Es bandera de conveniencia
    (f)
It bandiera di conveninza *(f)*
Pt bandeira de conveniência
    (f)

enseignement supérieur *(m)*
    Fr
De Fortbildung *(f)*
En higher education
Es enseñanza superior *(f)*
It insegnamento superiore
    (m)
Pt instrução superior *(f)*

enseñanza superior *(f)* Es
De Fortbildung *(f)*
En higher education
Fr enseignement supérieur
    (m)
It insegnamento superiore
    (m)
Pt instrução superior *(f)*

en suspens Fr
De in der Schwebe
En in abeyance
Es en suspenso
It in sospeso
Pt pendente

en suspenso Es
De in der Schwebe
En in abeyance
Fr en suspens
It in sospeso
Pt pendente

Enteignung *(f) n* De
En expropriation
Es expropiación *(f)*
Fr expropriation *(f)*
It espropriazione *(f)*
Pt expropriação *(f)*

enterprise *n* En
De Unternehmen *(n)*
Es negocio *(m)*
Fr entreprise *(f)*
It impresa *(f)*
Pt empresa *(f)*

entertainment expenses En
De Repräsentationskosten
    (pl)
Es gastos de representación
    (m pl)
Fr frais de représentation
    (m pl)
It spese di rappresentanza
    (f pl)
Pt despesas de representação
    (f pl)

en-tête *(m) n* Fr
De Briefkopf *(m)*
En letterhead
Es membrete *(m)*
It intestazione *(f)*
Pt cabeçalho *(m)*

Entfernung *(f) n* De
En distance
Es distancia *(f)*
Fr distance *(f)*
It distanza *(f)*
Pt distância *(f)*

entgeltigter Besitzer *(m)* De
En holder for value
Es tenedor legítimo *(m)*
Fr porteur à titre onéreux *(m)*
It detentore legittimo *(m)*
Pt proprietário legítimo *(m)*

entlassen *vb* De
En dismiss
Am fire
Es despedir
Fr congédier
It congedare
Pt despedir

Entlassung *(f) n* De
En dismissal
Am firing
Es despido *(m)*
Fr congédiement *(m)*
It licenziamento *(m)*
Pt despedimento *(m)*

**entlasteter Gemeinschuld-
    ner** *(m)* De
En discharged bankrupt
Es fallido rehabilitado *(m)*

Fr failli réhabilité *(m)*
It fallito riabilitato *(m)*
Pt falido reabilitado *(m)*

entleihen *vb* De
En borrow
Es pedir un préstamo
Fr emprunter
It prestare
Pt contrair empréstimo

entrada *(f) n* Es
De Eintritt *(m)*
En entry; admission
Fr entrée *(t)*
It entrata *(f)*
Pt admissão *(f)*

entrada grátis *(f)* Pt
De Eintritt frei *(m)*
En admission free
Es entrada gratuita *(f)*
Fr entrée gratuite *(f)*
It ingresso gratuito *(m)*

entrada gratuita *(f)* Es
De Eintritt frei *(m)*
En admission free
Fr entrée gratuite *(f)*
It ingresso gratuito *(f)*
Pt entrada grátis *(f)*

entrance free En
De Eintrittsgebühr *(f)*
Es derecho de entrada *(m)*
Fr droit d'entrée *(m)*
It tassa d'entrata *(f)*
Pt taxa de admissão *(f)*

en transit Fr
De im Durchgangsverkehr
En in transit
Es en tránsito
It in transito
Pt em trânsito

en tránsito Es
De im Durchgangsverkehr
En in transit
Fr en transit
It in transito
Pt em trânsito

entrare in vigore It
De wirksam werden
En become operative
Es entrar en vigor
Fr entrer en vigueur
Pt entrar en vigor

entrar em vigor Pt
De wirksam werden
En become operative
Es entrar en vigor
Fr entrer en vigueur
It entrare in vigore

entrar en vigor Es
De wirksam werden
En become operative
Fr entrer en vigueur
It entrare in vigore
Pt entrar em vigor

entrata (ammissione) *(t) n* It
De Eintritt *(n)*
En entry; admission
Es entrada *(f)*
Fr entrée *(f)*
Pt admissão *(f)*

entrata (reddito) *(f) n* It
De Einkommen; Einkünfte *(n; f pl)*
En revenue
Es ingresos; rédito *(m pl; m)*
Fr revenu; rentes *(m; f pl)*
Pt rendimento *(m)*

entrata netta *(f)* It
De Nettoeinkommen *(f pl)*
En net revenue
Es ingresos netos *(m pl)*
Fr recettes nettes *(f pl)*
Pt receita líquida *(f)*

entredicho *(m) n* Es
De gerichtliche Verfügung *(f)*
En injunction
Fr injonction; arrêt de suspension *(f m)*
It ingiunzione *(f)*
Pt interdição *(f)*

entrée *(f) n* Fr
De Eintritt *(m)*
En entry; admission
Es entrada *(f)*
It entrata *(f)*
Pt admissão *(f)*

entrée gratuite *(f)* Fr
De Eintritt frei *(m)*
En admission free
Es entrada gratuita *(f)*
It ingresso gratuito *(m)*
Pt entrada grátis *(f)*

entrega *(f) n* Es, Pt
De Lieferung *(f)*
En delivery
Fr livraison *(f)*
It consegna *(f)*

entrega contra reembolso Es, Pt
De Lieferung gegen Nachnahme
En cash on delivery (c.o.d.)
Fr paiement à la livraison
It pagamento alla consegna

entrega deficiente *(f)* Es
De mangelhafte Lieferung *(f)*
En short delivery
Fr livraison incomplète *(f)*
It consegna deficiente *(f)*
Pt entrega insuficiente *(f)*

entrega futura *(f)* Es, Pt
De Terminlieferung *(f)*
En forward delivery
Fr livraison à terme *(f)*
It consegna a termine *(f)*

entrega imediata *(f)* Pt
De sofortige Lieferung *(f)*
En prompt delivery
Es entrega inmediata *(f)*
Fr livraison immédiate *(f)*
It pronta consegna *(f)*

entrega inmediata *(f)* Es
De sofortige Lieferung *(f)*
En prompt delivery
Fr livraison immédiate *(f)*
It pronta consegna *(f)*
Pt entrega imediata *(f)*

entrega insuficiente *(f)* Pt
De mangelhafte Lieferung *(f)*
En short delivery
Es entrega deficiente *(f)*
Fr livraison incomplète *(f)*
It consegna deficiente *(f)*

s'entremettre *vb* Fr
De vermitteln
En mediate
Es intermediar
It fare da intermediario
Pt intermediar

entrepôt *(m) n* Fr
De Warenlager *(n)*
En warehouse
Es almacén *(m)*

It magazzino *(m)*
Pt armazém *(m)*

entrepôt (en douane) *(m) n* Fr
De Lager unter Zollverschluß
(n)
En bonded warehouse
Es almacén de aduanas *(m)*
It magazzino doganale *(m)*
Pt armazém alfandegário *(m)*

entrepreneur *n* En
De Unternehmer *(m)*
Es empresario *(m)*
Fr entrepreneur *(m)*
It intraprenditore *(m)*
Pt empresário *(m)*

entrepreneur *(m) n* Fr
De Unternehmer *(m)*
En entrepreneur; contractor
Es empresario; contrastista
(m)
It intraprenditore; impresario
(m)
Pt empresário; contratador
(m)

entrepreneur de bâtiment
(m) Fr
De Bauunternehmer *(m)*
En building contractor
Es contratista de obras *(m)*
It impresa edile *(f)*
Pt construtor de obras *(m)*

**entrepreneur de
camionnage** *(m)* Fr
De Transportunternehmer *(m)*
En haulage contractor
Am trucking company
Es contratista de transportes
(m)
It imprenditore di trasporti
(m)
Pt empreiteiro de transportes
(m)

entreprise *(f) n* Fr
De Unternehmen *(n)*
En enterprise
Es negocio *(m)*
It impresa *(f)*
Pt empresa *(f)*

entreprise d'utilité publique
(f) Fr
De gemeinnütziges
Unternehmen *(n)*

En utility company
Es empresa de servicios
públicos *(f)*
It società di servizi pubblici
(f)
Pt empresa de utilidade
pública *(f)*

entreprise en participation
(f) Fr
De Gemeinschaftsbetrieb *(m)*
En joint venture
Es empresa en común *(f)*
It impresa in
compartecipazione *(f)*
Pt iniciativa em comun *(f)*

entreprise privée *(f)* Fr
De Privatunternehmen *(n)*
En private enterprise
Es empresa privada *(f)*
It impresa privata *(f)*
Pt empresa privada *(f)*

entrer en vigueur Fr
De wirksam werden
En become operative
Es entrar en vigor
It entrare in vigore
Pt entrar em vigor

entretien *(m) n* Fr
De Instandhaltung *(f)*
En maintenance
Es mantenimiento *(m)*
It manutenzione *(f)*
Pt manutenção *(f)*

entrevista *(f) n* Es, Pt
De Interview *(n)*
En interview
Fr interview; entrevue *(f)*
It intervista; abboccamento
(f m)

entrevistado *(m) n* Pt
De Befragte(r) *(m)*
En interviewee
Es persona entrevistada *(f)*
Fr personne interrogée *(f)*
It intervistato *(m)*

entrevistador *(m) n* Es, Pt
De Interviewer *(m)*
En interviewer
Fr intervieweur; enquêteur
(m)
It intervistatore *(m)*

entrevue *(f) n* Fr
De Verabredung; Interview *(n)*
En appointment; interview
Es entrevista *(f)*
It intervista *(f)*
Pt entrevista *(f)*

entrust *vb* En
De anvertrauen
Es confiar
Fr confier
It affidare
Pt confiar

entry (admission) *n* En
De Eintritt *(m)*
Es entrada *(f)*
Fr entrée *(f)*
It entrata *(f)*
Pt admissão *(f)*

entry (in book) *n* En
De Eintragung *(f)*
Es asiento *(m)*
Fr inscription *(f)*
It registrazione *(f)*
Pt lançamento *(m)*

entry-form *n* En
De Antragsformular *(n)*
Es solicitud de inscripción *(f)*
Fr feuille d'inscription *(f)*
It bolletta d'entrata *(f)*
Pt impresso de admissão *(m)*

entschädigen *vb* De
En indemnify
Es indemnizar; resarcir
Fr dédommager; indemniser
It indennizzare; risarcire
Pt indemnizar

Entschädigung *(f) n* De
En compensation; indemnity
Es compensación;
indemnización *(f)*
Fr compensation; indemnité
(f)
It compenso; indennità *(m)*
Pt compensação;
indemnização *(f)*

entscheiden *vb* De
En decide
Es decidir
Fr décider
It decidere
Pt decidir

entscheidende Stimme *(f)* De
En casting vote
Es voto decisivo *(m)*
Fr voix prépondérante *(f)*
It voto decisivo *(m)*
Pt voto decisivo *(m)*

Entscheidung *(f)* n De
En dicision
Es dicisión *(f)*
Fr décision *(f)*
It decisione *(f)*
Pt decisão *(f)*

Entscheidungslehre *(f)* De
En decision theory
Es teoría de la décisión *(f)*
Fr théorie de la décision *(f)*
It teoria della decisione *(f)*
Pt teoria de decisão *(f)*

Entwerfer *(m)* n De
En draughtsman
Es dibujante *(m)*
Fr dessinateur *(m)*
It disegnatore *(m)*
Pt desenhador *(m)*

entwerten vb De
En depreciate
Es depreciar
Fr déprécier
It deprezzare
Pt depreciar

Entwertung *(f)* n De
En depreciation
Es depreciación *(f)*
Fr dépréciation;
   amortissement *(f m)*
It ammortamento *(m)*
Pt depreciação; amortização *(f)*

Entwicklung *(f)* n De
En growth
Es crecimiento *(m)*
Fr croissance; développe-
   ment *(f m)*
It crescita; sviluppo *(f m)*
Pt crescimento *(m)*

Entwicklungsland *(n)* De
En developing country
Es pais en desarrollo *(m)*
Fr pays en voie de
   développement *(m)*
It paese in via di sviluppo *(m)*
Pt país em desenvolvimento
   (m)

Entwurf *(m)* n De
En plan
Es plan *(m)*
Fr projet *(m)*
It progetto *(m)*
Pt plano *(m)*

envelope n En, Pt *(m)*
De Umschlag *(m)*
Es sobre *(m)*
Fr enveloppe *(m)*
It busta *(f)*

**envelope de endereço
   exposto** *(m)* Pt
De Fensterbriefumschlag *(m)*
En window-envelope
Es sobre de ventanilla *(m)*
Fr enveloppe à fenêtre *(f)*
It busta con finestra *(f)*

enveloppe *(f)* n Fr
De Umschlag *(m)*
En envelope
Es sobre *(m)*
It busta *(f)*
Pt envelope *(m)*

enveloppe à fenêtre *(f)* Fr
De Fensterbriefumschlag *(m)*
En window-envelope
Es sobre de ventanilla *(m)*
It busta con finestra *(f)*
Pt envelope de endereço
   exposto *(m)*

en vigor Es
De in Kraft
En in force
Fr en vigueur
It in vigore
Pt vigente

en vigueur Fr
De in Kraft
En in force
Es en vigor
It in vigore
Pt vigente

**envío desde el punto de
   origen** *(m)* Es
De Versendung vom
   Ursprungsort *(f)*
En shipment from origin
Fr envoi du lieu de départ *(m)*
It spedizione dall'origine *(f)*
Pt carregamento desde a
   origem *(m)*

envoi *(m)* n Fr
De Versand; Versendung *(m f)*
En despatch; consignment
Es expedición; consignación
   (f)
It spedizione; consegna *(f)*
Pt remessa; consignação *(f)*

envoi du lieu de départ *(m)* Fr
De Versendung vom
   Ursprungsort *(f)*
En shipment from origin
Es envío desde el punto de
   origen *(m)*
It spedizione dall'origine *(f)*
Pt carregamento desde a
   origem *(m)*

envoltura desechable *(f)* Es
De wegwerfbare Verpackung
   (f)
En disposable wrapping
Fr emballage perdu *(m)*
It imballaggio a perdere *(m)*
Pt embalagem a destruir *(f)*

envoyer vb Fr
De expedieren; absenden
En send; forward
Es expedir; remitir
It spedire
Pt expedir; remeter

en vrac Fr
De in großer Menge;
   unverpackt
En in bulk
Es a granel
It alla rinfusa
Pt a granel

épargner vb Fr
De aufsparen
En save
Es ahorrar; economizar
It risparmiare; economizzare
Pt poupar; economizar

épreuve au hasard *(f)* Fr
De Stichprobe *(f)*
En random sample
Es muestra aleatoria *(f)*
It campione a casaccio *(m)*
Pt amostra avulsa *(f)*

equalization fund En
De Ausgleichsfonds *(m)*
Es fondo de compensación
   (m)

Fr fonds de régularisation *(m)*
It cassa di compensazione *(f)*
Pt fundo de compensação *(m)*

equilibrar uma conta Pt
De eine Rechnung ausgleichen
En balance an account
Es saldar una cuenta
Fr balancer un compte
It pareggiare un conto

equilibrar um orçamento Pt
De einen Haushaltsplan ins Gleichgewicht bringen
En balance a budget
Es balancear el presupuesto
Fr équilibrer un budget
It pareggiare un bilancio

équilibre *(m)* n Fr
De Gleichgewicht *(n)*
En equilibrium
Es equilibrio *(m)*
It equilibrio *(m)*
Pt equilíbrio *(m)*

équilibrer un budget Fr
De einen Haushaltsplan ins Gleichgewicht bringen
En balance a budget
Es balancear el presupuesto
It pareggiare un bilancio
Pt equilibrar um orçamento

equilibrio *(m)* n Es, It
De Gleichgewicht *(n)*
En equilibrium
Fr équilibre *(m)*
Pt equilíbrio *(m)*

equilíbrio *(m)* n Pt
De Gleichgewicht *(n)*
En equilibrium
Es equilibrio *(m)*
Fr équilibre *(m)*
It equilibrio *(m)*

equilibrium n En
De Gleichgewicht *(n)*
Es equilibrio *(m)*
Fr équilibre *(m)*
It equilibrio *(m)*
Pt equilíbrio *(m)*

équipage *(m)* n Fr
De Mannschaft *(f)*
En crew

Es tripulación *(f)*
It equipaggio *(m)*
Pt tripulação *(f)*

equipaggiamento *(m)* n It
De Ausrüstung *(f)*
En equipment
Es equipo *(m)*
Fr équipement *(m)*
Pt equipamento *(m)*

equipaggio *(m)* n It
De Mannschaft *(f)*
En crew
Es tripulación *(f)*
Fr équipage *(m)*
Pt tripulação *(f)*

equipaje de mano *(m)* Es
De Handgepäck *(n)*
En hand-luggage
Fr bagages à main *(m pl)*
It bagaglio a mano *(m)*
Pt bagagem de mão *(f)*

equipamento *(m)* n Pt
De Ausrüstung *(f)*
En equipment
Es equipo *(m)*
Fr équipement *(m)*
It equipaggiamento *(m)*

équipe *(f)* n Fr
De Schicht *(f)*
En shift
Es turno *(m)*
It turno *(m)*
Pt turno *(m)*

équipe de nuit *(f)* Fr
De Nachtschicht *(f)*
En night shift
Es turno de noche *(m)*
It turno di notte *(m)*
Pt turno da noite *(m)*

équipe du jour *(f)* Fr
De Tagschicht *(f)*
En day-shift
Es turno de día *(m)*
It turno di giorno *(m)*
Pt turno de dia *(m)*

équipement *(m)* n Fr
De Ausrüstung *(f)*
En equipment
Es equipo *(m)*
It equipaggiamento *(m)*
Pt equipamento *(m)*

equipment n En
De Ausrüstung *(f)*
Es equipo *(m)*
Fr équipement *(m)*
It equipaggiamento *(m)*
Pt equipamento *(m)*

equipo *(m)* n Es
De Ausrüstung *(f)*
En equipment
Fr équipement *(m)*
It equipaggiamento *(m)*
Pt equipamento *(m)*

equitable *adj* En
De billig
Es equitativo
Fr équitable
It equo
Pt equitativo

équitable *adj* Fr
De billig
En equitable
Es equitativo
It equo
Pt equitativo

equitativo *adj* Es, Pt
De billig
En equitable
Fr équitable
It equo

equo *adj* It
De billig
En equitable
Es equitativo
Fr équitable
Pt equitativo

Erbe *(m)* n De
En heir
Es heredero *(m)*
Fr héritier *(m)*
It erede *(m)*
Pt herdeiro *(m)*

Erbschaft *(f)* n De
En inheritance
Es herencia *(f)*
Fr succession *(f)*
It eredità *(f)*
Pt herança *(f)*

Erbschaftsteuern *(f pl)* n De
En death duties
Am estate taxes
Es derechos sucesorios *(m pl)*

Fr droits de succession *(m pl)*
It diritti di successione *(m pl)*
Pt impostos de sucessão
     (m pl)

Erdgas *(n) n* De
En natural gas
Es gas natural *(m)*
Fr gaz naturel *(m)*
It gas naturale *(m)*
Pt gás natural *(m)*

Erdgeschoß *(n) n* De
En ground floor
Es planta baja *(f)*
Fr rez-de-chaussée *(m)*
It pianterreno *(m)*
Pt rés-do-chão *(m)*

erede *(m) n* It
De Erbe
En heir
Es heredero *(m)*
Fr héritier *(m)*
Pt herdeiro *(m)*

eredità *(f) n* It
De Erbschaft *(f)*
En inheritance
Es herencia *(f)*
Fr succession *(f)*
Pt herança *(f)*

Erfindung *(f) n* De
En invention
Es invento; invención *(m f)*
Fr invention *(f)*
It invenzione *(f)*
Pt invenção *(f)*

Erfindungspatent *(n) n* De
En patent
Es patente *(f)*
Fr brevet d'invention *(m)*
It brevetto *(m)*
Pt patente *(f)*

erfüllen *vb* De
En fulfil
Es cumplir
Fr remplir
It adempiere
Pt cumprir

Erfüllung *(f) n* De
En fulfilment
Es cumplimiento *(m)*
Fr accomplissement *(m)*

It adempimento *(m)*
Pt cumprimento *(m)*

ergonomía *(f) n* Es
De Ergonomik *(f)*
En ergonomics
Fr ergonomie *(f)*
It ergonomica *(f)*
Pt ergonomia *(f)*

ergonomia *(f) n* Pt
De Ergonomik *(f)*
En ergonomics
Es ergonomía *(f)*
Fr ergonomie *(f)*
It ergonomica *(f)*

ergonomica *(f) n* It
De Ergonomik *(f)*
En ergonomics
Es ergonomía *(f)*
Fr ergonomie *(f)*
Pt ergonomia *(f)*

ergonomics *n* En
De Ergonomik *(f)*
Es ergonomía *(f)*
Fr ergonomie *(f)*
It ergonomica *(f)*
Pt ergonomia *(f)*

ergonomie *(f) n* Fr
De Ergonomik *(f)*
En ergonomics
Es ergonomía *(f)*
It ergonomica *(f)*
Pt ergonomia *(f)*

Ergonomik *(f) n* De
En ergonomics
Es ergonomía *(f)*
Fr ergonomie *(f)*
It ergonomica *(f)*
Pt ergonomia *(f)*

Erhebung *(f) n* De
En levy
Es impuesto *(m)*
Fr prélèvement *(m)*
It imposta *(f)*
Pt imposto *(m)*

erhöhte Kosten *(pl)* De
En increased costs
Es costes incrementados
     (m pl)
Fr accroissement des coûts
     (m)

It costi aumentati *(m pl)*
Pt custos aumentados *(m pl)*

Erhöhung (Preise) *(f) n* De
En advance in price
Es encarecimiento *(m)*
Fr renchérissement *(m)*
It rialzo *(m)*
Pt encarecimento *(m)*

erklären *vb* De
En declare
Es declarar
Fr déclarer
It dichiarare
Pt declarar

Erklärung *(f) n* De
En declaration
Es declaración *(f)*
Fr déclaration *(f)*
It dichiarazione *(f)*
Pt declaração *(f)*

Erlaubnis *(f) n* De
En permit; licence
Es permiso; licencia *(m f)*
Fr permis; licence *(m f)*
It permesso; licenza *(m f)*
Pt autorização; licença *(f)*

Erlebensversicherung *(f) n*
     De
En endowment policy
Es póliza dotal *(f)*
Fr assurance à terme fixe *(f)*
It assicurazione dotale *(f)*
Pt título de doação *(m)*

erloschene Gesellschaft *(f)*
     De
En defunct company
Es sociedad extinta *(f)*
Fr société liquidée *(f)*
It società estinta *(f)*
Pt empresa extinta *(f)*

ernennen *vb* De
En appoint
Es nombrar
Fr nommer
It nominare
Pt nomear

Ernte *(f) n* De
En harvest
Es cosecha *(f)*
Fr moisson; récolte *(f)*
It raccolto *(m)*
Pt colheita *(f)*

erreur *(f) n* Fr
De Fehler *(m)*
En error
Es error *(m)*
It errore *(m)*
Pt erro *(m)*

erreur de calcul *(f)* Fr
De Rechenfehler *(m)*
En miscalculation
Es cálculo erróneo *(m)*
It calcolo errato *(m)*
Pt erro de cálculo *(m)*

erro *(m) n* Pt
De Fehler *(m)*
En error
Es error *(m)*
Fr erreur *(f)*
It errore *(m)*

erro de cálculo *(m)* Pt
De Rechenfehler *(m)*
En miscalculation
Es cálculo erróneo *(m)*
Fr erreur de calcul *(f)*
It calcolo errato *(m)*

error *n* En, Es *(m)*
De Fehler *(m)*
Fr erreur *(f)*
It errore *(m)*
Pt erro *(m)*

errore *(m) n* It
De Fehler *(m)*
En error
Es error *(m)*
Fr erreur *(f)*
Pt erro *(m)*

Ersatz immateriellen Schadens *(m)* De
En special damages
Es daños especiales *(m pl)*
Fr dommages indirects *(m pl)*
It danni particolari *(m pl)*
Pt indemnização especial *(f)*

Erschließung *(f) n* De
En development
Es explotación *(f)*
Fr exploitation; lotissement *(f m)*
It valorizzazione *(f)*
Pt exploração *(f)*

Ersetzung *(f) n* De
En subrogation
Es subrogación *(f)*
Fr subrogation *(f)*
It surrogazione *(f)*
Pt sub-rogação *(f)*

erste Klasse *(f)* De
En first class
Es primera clase *(f)*
Fr première classe *(f)*
It prima classe *(f)*
Pt primeira classe *(f)*

erstklassig *adj* De
En first-class
Es de primera orden
Fr de première qualité
It di qualità superiore
Pt de primeira ordem

erstklassiger Handelswechsel *(m)* De
En prime trade bill
Es carta comercial de primera orden *(f)*
Fr papier de haut commerce *(m)*
It carta commerciale di primo ordine *(f)*
Pt estatuto de commercialização de primeira ordem *(m)*

Erteilung (eines Patentes) *(f)* De
En grant (of a patent)
Es concesión (de una patente) *(f)*
Fr délivrance (d'un brevet) *(f)*
It concessione (di brevetto) *(f)*
Pt concessão (de uma patente) *(f)*

Ertragsrate *(f) n* De
En rate of return
Es tipo de rédito *(m)*
Fr taux de rendement *(m)*
It tasso di reddito *(m)*
Pt taxa de rendimento *(f)*

Erwerb *(m) n* De
En acquisition
Es adquisición *(f)*
Fr acquisition *(f)*
It acquisizione *(f)*
Pt aquisição *(f)*

Erwerbsteuer *(f)* De
En purchase tax
Es impuesto sobre las compras *(m)*
Fr impôt sur les acquisitions *(m)*
It tassa sugli acquisti *(f)*
Pt imposto sobre aquisições *(m)*

Erzeuger *(m) n* De
En manufacturer
Es fabricante *(m)*
Fr fabricant *(m)*
It fabbricante *(m)*
Pt fabricante *(m)*

Erzeugnis *(f) n* De
En produce
Es producto *(m)*
Fr produit *(m)*
It prodotto *(m)*
Pt produto *(m)*

Erzeugung *(f) n* De
En production
Es producción *(f)*
Fr production *(f)*
It produzione *(f)*
Pt produção *(f)*

esame più attento *(m)* It
De Weiterüberlegung *(f)*
En further consideration
Es examen más detallado *(m)*
Fr examen plus attentif *(m)*
Pt consideração mais detalhada *(f)*

esaminare *vb* It
De untersuchen
En examine
Es examinar
Fr examiner
Pt examinar

esattore delle imposte *(m)* It
De Steuereinnehmer *(m)*
En tax collector
Es recaudador de impuestos *(m)*
Fr percepteur des impôts *(m)*
Pt cobrador de impostos *(m)*

esaurito *adj* It
De ausverkauft
En out of stock
Es stock agotado

Fr tout vendu
Pt esgotado

esborso *(m)* n It
De Auszahlung *(f)*
En disbursement
Es desembolso *(m)*
Fr déboursement *(m)*
Pt desembolso *(m)*

escala *(f)* n Es, Pt
De Maßstab *(m)*
En scale
Fr échelle *(f)*
It scala *(f)*

escala móvel *(f)* Pt
De gleitende Skala *(f)*
En sliding scale
Es escala móvil *(f)*
Fr échelle mobile *(f)*
It scala mobile *(f)*

escala móvil *(f)* Es
De gleitende Skala *(f)*
En sliding scale
Fr échelle mobile *(f)*
It scala mobile *(f)*
Pt escala móvel *(f)*

escalator clause En
De Gleitklausel *(f)*
Es cláusula de revisión de
   precios *(f)*
Fr échelle mobile *(f)*
It scala mobile *(f)*
Pt cláusula de actualização de
   preços *(f)*

escape *(m)* n Es, Pt
De Leck *(n)*
En leakage
Fr fuite *(f)*
It colaggio *(m)*

escape clause En
De Rücktrittsklausel *(f)*
Es cláusula evasiva *(f)*
Fr clause de résiliation *(f)*
It clausola risolutiva *(f)*
Pt cláusula de evasão *(f)*

escasez *(f)* n Es
De Knappheit *(f)*
En short supply
Fr disette *(f)*
It scarsezza *(f)*
Pt escassez *(f)*

escasez de créditos *(f)* Es
De Kreditklemme *(f)*
En credit squeeze
Fr resserrement de crédit *(m)*
It restrizione di credito *(f)*
Pt restrição de crédito *(f)*

escassez *(f)* n Pt
De Knappheit *(f)*
En short supply
Es escasez *(f)*
Fr disette *(f)*
It scarsezza *(f)*

escludere *vb* It
De ausschließen
En exclude
Es excluir
Fr exclure
Pt excluir

esclusione *(f)* n It
De Ausschluß *(m)*
En exclusion
Es exclusión *(f)*
Fr exclusion *(f)*
Pt exclusão *(f)*

escompte *(m)* n Fr
De Skonto *(m)*
En discount
Es descuento *(m)*
It sconto; ribasso *(m)*
Pt desconto *(m)*

escompte de caisse *(m)* Fr
De Barrabatt *(m)*
En cash discount
Es descuento de caja *(m)*
It sconto per pagamento a
   contanti *(m)*
Pt desconto de contado *(m)*

escompte en dehors *(m)* Fr
De Diskont *(m)*
En bank discount
Es descuento bancario *(m)*
It sconto di banca *(m)*
Pt desconto bancário *(m)*

esconderse *vb* Es
De sich heimlich
   davonmachen
En abscond
Fr s'enfuir; décamper
It nascondersi
Pt ausentar-se para parte
   incerta

escrever à máquina Pt
De auf der Schreibmaschine
   schreiben
En type
Es escribir a máquina
Fr écrire à la machine
It scrivere a macchina

escribir a máquina Es
De auf der Schreibmaschine
   schreiben
En type
Fr écrire à la machine
It scrivere a macchina
Pt escrever à máquina

escritório *(m)* n Pt
De Büro *(n)*
En office
Es oficina *(f)*
Fr bureau *(m)*
It ufficio *(m)*

escritório sem divisões *(m)*
   Pt
De Großraumbüro *(n)*
En open-plan office
Es oficina sin particiones *(f)*
Fr bureau sans cloisons *(m)*
It ufficio senza divisioni *(m)*

escritura de acordo *(f)* Pt
De Vergleichsabkommen *(n)*
En deed of arrangement
Es acta de disposición *(f)*
Fr contrat d'arrangement *(m)*
It atto di accordo *(m)*

escritura de sociedade *(f)* Pt
De Gesellschaftsvertrag *(m)*
En articles of association
Am articles of incorporation
Es artículos de asociación
   (m pl)
Fr contrat de société *(m)*
It statuto sociale *(m)*

escritura de transferencia *(f)*
   Es
De Übertragungsvertrag *(m)*
En transfer deed
Fr acte de cession *(m)*
It atto di trapasso *(m)*
Pt título de transferência *(m)*

escritura de venda *(f)* Pt
De Kaufvertrag *(m)*
En bill of sale

Es escritura de venta *(f)*
Fr acte de vente *(f)*
It contratto di vendita *(m)*

escritura de venta *(f)* Es
De Kaufvertrag *(m)*
En bill of sale
Fr acte de vente *(f)*
It contratto di vendita *(m)*
Pt escritura de venda *(f)*

esecutore *(m) n* It
De Vollstrecker *(m)*
En executor
Es albacea *(m)*
Fr exécuteur *(m)*
Pt executor *(m)*

esecuzione *(f) n* It
De Vollstreckung *(f)*
En execution
Es ejecución *(f)*
Fr exécution *(f)*
Pt desempenho *(m)*

eseguire *vb* It
De vollstrecken
En execute
Es ejecutar
Fr exécuter
Pt executar

eseguire un testamento It
De ein Testament vollstrecken
En execute a will
Es ejecutar un testamento
Fr exécuter un testament
Pt dar execução a um
   testamento

esente da dazio It
De abgabenfrei
En duty-free
Es exento de impuestos
Fr exempt de douane
Pt isento de impostos

esente da tassa It
De steuerfrei
En tax-free
Es exento de impuestos
Fr exempt d'impôts
Pt isento de impostos

esenzione *(f) n* It
De Befreiung *(f)*
En exemption
Es exención *(f)*

Fr exemption *(f)*
Pt isenção *(f)*

esercizio *(m) n* It
De Geschäftsjahr *(n)*
En financial year
Es ejercicio *(m)*
Fr exercice *(m)*
Pt ano financeiro *(m)*

esgotado *adj* Pt
De ausverkauft
En sold out
Es agotado
Fr tout vendu
It tutto venduto

esorbitante *adj* It
De unmäßig
En exorbitant
Es exorbitante
Fr exorbitant
Pt exorbitante

espèces *(f pl) n* Fr
De Bargeld *(n)*
En cash
Es dinero efectivo *(m)*
It denaro contante *(m)*
Pt dinheiro de contado *(m)*

espèces en caisse *(f pl)* Fr
De Barbestand *(m)*
En cash in hand
Es efectivo en caja *(m)*
It pronti contanti *(m pl)*
Pt fundos à ordem *(m pl)*

especialista *(m) n* Es, Pt
De Sachverständige(r) *(m)*
En specialist
Fr expert *(m)*
It specialista *(m)*

especificação de obra *(f)* Pt
De Arbeitsaufgabe *(f)*
En job specification
Es especificación del trabajo
   (f)
Fr donnée d'exécution *(f)*
It specifica del lavoro *(f)*

especificación del trabajo *(f)*
   Es
De Arbeitsaufgabe *(f)*
En job specification
Fr donnée d'exécution *(f)*
It specifica del lavoro *(f)*
Pt especificação de obra *(f)*

especular *vb* Es, Pt
De spekulieren
En speculate; job
Fr spéculer
It speculare

espere al aparato Es
De am Apparat bleiben
En hold the line
Fr ne quittez pas
It restare in linea
Pt aguarde

espionage industriel *(m)* Fr
De Wirtschaftsspionage *(f)*
En industrial espionage
Es espionaje industrial *(m)*
It spionaggio industriale *(m)*
Pt espionagem industrial *(f)*

espionagem industrial *(f)* Pt
De Wirtschaftsspionage *(f)*
En industrial espionage
Es espionaje industrial *(m)*
Fr espionage industriel *(m)*
It spionaggio industriale *(m)*

espionaje industrial *(m)* Es
De Wirtschaftsspionage *(f)*
En industrial espionage
Fr espionage industriel *(m)*
It spionaggio industriale *(m)*
Pt espionagem industrial *(f)*

espiral de inflación *(f)* Es
De Inflationsspirale *(f)*
En inflationary spiral
Fr spirale inflationniste *(f)*
It inflazione a spirale *(f)*
Pt espiral inflacionária *(f)*

espiral inflacionária *(f)* Pt
De Inflationsspirale *(f)*
En inflationary spiral
Es espiral de inflación *(f)*
Fr spirale inflationniste *(f)*
It inflazione a spirale *(f)*

esponenziale *adj* It
De Exponential-
En exponential
Es exponencial
Fr exponentiel
Pt exponencial

esportare *vb* It
De ausführen
En export
Es exportar

Fr exporter
Pt exportar

esportatore *(m)* n It
De Exporteur *(m)*
En exporter
Es exportador
Fr exportateur *(m)*
Pt exportador *(m)*

esportazioni invisibili *(f pl)* It
De unsichtbare Exporte *(m pl)*
En invisible exports
Es exportaciones invisibles
  (f pl)
Fr exportations invisibles
  (f pl)
Pt exportações invisíveis *(f pl)*

espositore *(m)* n It
De Aussteller *(m)*
En exhibitor
Es exhibidor *(m)*
Fr exposant *(m)*
Pt expositor *(m)*

esposizione *(f)* n It
De Ausstellung *(f)*
En exhibition
Es exposición *(f)*
Fr exposition *(f)*
Pt exposição *(f)*

espropriazione *(f)* n It
De Enteignung *(f)*
En expropriation
Es expropiación *(f)*
Fr expropriation *(f)*
Pt expropriação *(f)*

essai *(m)* n Fr
De Probe *(f)*
En test; trial
Es ensayo; prueba *(m f)*
It saggio; prova *(m f)*
Pt ensaio; prova *(m f)*

essai gratuit *(m)* Fr
De kostenlose Probe *(f)*
En free trial
Es prueba gratuita *(f)*
It prova gratuita *(f)*
Pt prova gratuita *(f)*

essentiel *adj* Fr
De wesentlich
En material
Es material

It materiale
Pt material

essere in disaccordo It
De nicht übereinstimmen
En disagree
Es no estar de acuerdo
Fr être en désaccord
Pt discordar

Eßwaren *(f pl)* n De
En foodstuffs
Es comestibles *(m pl)*
Fr alimentation *(f)*
It generi alimentari *(m pl)*
Pt géneros alimentícios *(m pl)*

estabelecer *vb* Pt
De gründen
En form; establish
Es establecer; formar
Fr former
It formare

establecer *vb* Es
De gründen
En form; establish
Fr former
It formare
Pt estabelecer

establish (a business, etc.) *vb*
  En
De einrichten
Es fundar; establecer
Fr fonder; établir
It fondare; istituire
Pt fundar; establelear

establish (proof, etc.) *vb* En
De beweisen
Es demostrar; probar
Fr démontrer
It dimostrare; provare
Pt demonstrar; provar

estação *(f)* n Pt
De Jahreszeit *(f)*
En season
Es estación *(f)*
Fr saison *(f)*
It stagione *(f)*

estação de correios *(f)* Pt
De Postamt *(n)*
En post office
Es oficina de correos *(f)*
Fr bureau de poste *(m)*
It ufficio postale *(m)*

estação terminal aérea *(f)* Pt
De Luftterminal *(n)*
En air terminal
Es terminal de aeropuerto *(f)*
Fr aérogare *(f)*
It aerostazione *(f)*

estación *(f)* n Es
De Jahreszeit *(f)*
En season
Fr saison *(f)*
It stagione *(f)*
Pt estação *(f)*

estadia *(f)* n Pt
De Liegezeit *(f)*
En lay days
Es estadía *(f)*
Fr staries *(f pl)*
It stallie *(f pl)*

estadía *(f)* n Es
De Liegezeit *(f)*
En lay days
Fr staries *(f pl)*
It stallie *(f)*
Pt estadia *(f)*

estadística *(f)* n Es
De Statistik *(f)*
En statistics
Fr statistique *(f)*
It statistica *(f)*
Pt estatística *(f)*

estafar *vb* Es
De schwindeln
En swindle
Fr filouter
It truffare
Pt enganar

estaleiro *(m)* n Pt
De Schiffswerft *(f)*
En dockyard
Es astillero *(m)*
Fr chantier de construction
  de navires *(m)*
It cantiere *(m)*

estampilla *(f)* n Es
De Stempel *(m)*
En (rubber) stamp
Fr tampon; timbre *(m)*
It stampiglia *(f)*
Pt carimbo *(m)*

estate (property) n En
De Vermögen (n)
Es finca (f)
Fr bien; propriété (m f)
It proprietà (f)
Pt bens; propriedade (m pl; f)

estate (after death) n En
De Nachlaß (m)
Es sucesión; herencia (f)
Fr succession (f)
It patrimonio; successione (m f)
Pt património; herança (m f)

estate agency En
Am real estate agency
De Immobilienbüro (n)
Es correduría de fincas (f)
Fr agence immobilière (f)
It agenzia immobiliare (f)
Pt agência de propriedades (f)

estate duty En
Am estate tax
De Nachlaßsteuer (f)
Es derechos de sucesión (m pl)
Fr droits de succession (m pl)
It diritti di successione (m pl)
Pt direitos de sucessão (m pl)

estatística (f) n Pt
De Statistik (f)
En statistics
Es estadística (f)
Fr statistique (f)
It statistica (f)

estatutario adj Es
De gesetzlich
En statutory
Fr statutaire
It statutario
Pt estatutário

estatutário adj Pt
De gesetzlich
En statutory
Es estatutario
Fr statutaire
It statutario

estatuto (m) n Es, Pt
De Gesetz (n)
En statute
Fr statut (m)
It statuto (m)

estatuto de associação (m) Pt
De Statuten (f pl)
En Memorandum and Articles of Association
Am articles of incorporation
Es estatutos; carta orgánica (m pl; f)
Fr statuts; acte constitutif (m pl; m)
It atto costitutivo e statuto sociale (m)

estatuto de comercializa- ção de primeira ordem (m) Pt
De erstklassiger Handelswechsel (m)
En prime trade bill
Es carta comercial de primera orden (f)
Fr papier de haut commerce (m)
It carta commerciale di primo ordine (f)

estatutos (m pl) Es
De Statuten (f pl)
En Memorandum and Articles of Association
Am articles of incorporation
Fr statuts; acte constitutif (m pl; m)
It atto costitutivo e statuto sociale (m)
Pt estatuto de associação (m)

estenodactilógrafa (f) n Pt
De Stenotypistin (f)
En shorthand typist
Es taquimecanógrafa (f)
Fr sténodactylographe (f)
It stenodattilografa (f)

estenografia (f) n Pt
De Kurzschrift (f)
En shorthand
Es taquigrafía (f)
Fr sténographie (f)
It stenografia (f)

esterlina verde (f) Es
De grünes Pfund (n)
En green pound
Fr livre sterling verte (f)
It sterlina verde (f)
Pt libra esterlina verde (f)

estiba (f) n Es
De Verstauung (f)
En stowage
Fr arrimage (m)
It stivaggio (m)
Pt estiva (f)

estibar vb Es
De verstauen
En stow
Fr arrimer
It stivare
Pt estivar

estimar vb Es
De einschätzen
En estimate
Fr estimer
It stimare
Pt avaliar

estimate vb En
De einschätzen
Es estimar
Fr estimer
It stimare
Pt avaliar

estimate n En
De Voranschlag (m)
Es presupuesto (m)
Fr devis (m)
It preventivo (m)
Pt previsão (f)

estimation approximative (f) Fr
De rohe Schätzung (f)
En rough estimate
Es presupuesto aproximado (m)
It valutazione approssimati- va (f)
Pt avaliação aproximada (f)

estimativa revista (f) Pt
De überarbeitete Schätzung (f)
En revised estimate
Es cálculo revisado (m)
Fr devis rectifié (m)
It preventivo riveduto (m)

estimativa suplementar (f) Pt
De Nachschätzung (f)
En supplementary estimate
Es cálculo suplementario (m)
Fr devis supplémentaire (f)
It preventivo supplementare (m)

estimer *vb* Fr
De einschätzen
En estimate
Es estimar
It stimare
Pt avaliar

estímulo *(m)* *n* Es
De Anreiz *(m)*
En incentive
Fr incitation; stimulant *(f m)*
It incentivo *(m)*
Pt incentivo *(m)*

estímulo de exportación *(m)*
Es
De Ausfuhranreiz *(m)*
En export incentive
Fr motif d'exportation *(m)*
It incentivo alla esportazione
(m)
Pt incentivo para a exportação
(m)

estinguere un debito It
De eine Schuld begleichen
En discharge a debt
Es descargar una deuda
Fr acquitter une dette
Pt cancelar uma dívida

estiva *(f)* *n* Pt
De Verstauung *(f)*
En stowage
Es estiba *(f)*
Fr arrimage *(m)*
It stivaggio *(m)*

estivar *vb* Pt
De verstauen
En stow
Es estibar
Fr arrimer
It stivare

estrangeiro *adj* Pt
De ausländisch; fremd
En foreign; alien
Es extranjero
Fr étranger
It straniero; estero

estrangeiro *(m)* *n* Pt
De Ausländer *(m)*
En foreigner
Es extranjero *(m)*
Fr étranger *(m)*
It straniero *(m)*

estrapolare *vb* It
De extrapolieren
En extrapolate
Es extrapolar
Fr extrapoler
Pt extrapolar

estratto conto *(m)* It
De Kontoauszug *(m)*
En statement of account
Es extracto de cuenta *(m)*
Fr relevé de compte *(m)*
Pt extracto de conta *(m)*

estudio del trabajo *(m)* Es
De Arbeitsstudie *(f)*
En work study
Fr étude du travail *(f)*
It studio di lavoro *(m)*
Pt estudo sobre trabalho *(m)*

**estudio de tiempo y
progreso** *(m)* Es
De Arbeitszeit- und
Ablaufstudie *(f)*
En time and motion study
Fr étude du temps et
mouvements *(f)*
It studio dei tempi e dei
movimenti *(m)*
Pt análise do tempo e
progresso *(f)*

estudio de viabilidad *(m)* Es
De Durchführbarkeitsanalyse
(f)
En feasibility study
Fr étude probatoire *(f)*
It studio delle possibilità *(m)*
Pt estudo de viabilidade *(m)*

estudio sobre el terreno *(m)*
Es
De Stellenüberblick *(m)*
En field study
Fr enquête sur les lieux *(f)*
It studio sul terreno *(m)*
Pt estudo de campo *(m)*

estudo de campo *(m)* Pt
De Stellenüberblick *(m)*
En field study
Es estudio sobre el terreno
(m)
Fr enquête sur les lieux *(f)*
It studio sul terreno *(m)*

estudo de viabilidade *(m)* Pt
De Durchführbarkeitsanalyse
(f)
En feasibility study
Es estudio de viabilidad *(m)*
Fr étude probatoire *(f)*
It studio delle possibilità *(m)*

estudo sobre trabalho *(m)* Pt
De Arbeitsstudie *(n)*
En work study
Es estudio del trabajo *(m)*
Fr étude du travail *(f)*
It studio di lavoro *(m)*

Etagenwohnung *(f)* *n* De
En flat
Am apartment
Es apartamento *(m)*
Fr appartement *(m)*
It appartamento *(m)*
Pt apartamento *(m)*

**Etagenwohnung mit
Bedienung** *(f)* De
En service flat
Es piso con servicio incluido
(m)
Fr appartement avec service
(m)
It appartamento con servizio
(m)
Pt andar com serviço
incluído *(m)*

étalage *(m)* *n* Fr
De Fensterauslage *(f)*
En window-display
Es exhibición en vitrina *(f)*
It mostra in vetrina *(f)*
Pt exposição de montra *(f)*

étalon or *(m)* *n* Fr
De Goldobligation *(f)*
En gold standard
Es patrón oro *(m)*
It base aurea *(f)*
Pt ouro-padrão *(m)*

état de finances *(m)* Fr
De Finanzausweis *(m)*
En financial statement
Es extracto financiero *(m)*
It relazione finanziaria *(f)*
Pt extracto financeiro *(m)*

état du marché *(m)* Fr
De Marktumstände *(m pl)*
En state of the market

Es condiciones del mercado
   (f pl)
It condizioni del mercato
   (f pl)
Pt situação do mercado *(f)*

etichetta *(f)* n It
De Etikett *(n)*
En label
Es etiqueta *(f)*
Fr étiquette *(f)*
Pt rótulo; etiqueta *(m f)*

Etikett *(n)* n De
En label
Es etiqueta *(f)*
Fr étiquette *(f)*
It etichetta *(f)*
Pt rótulo; etiqueta *(m f)*

etiqueta *(f)* n Es, Pt
De Etikett *(n)*
En label
Fr étiquette *(f)*
It etichetta *(f)*

étiquette *(f)* n Fr
De Etikett *(n)*
En label
Es etiqueta *(f)*
It etichetta *(f)*
Pt rótulo; etiqueta *(m f)*

étoffe *(f)* n Fr
De Stoff *(m)*
En material; cloth
Es tejido *(m)*
It stoffa; tessuto *(f m)*
Pt tecido *(m)*

étranger *adj* Fr
De ausländisch; fremd
En foreign; alien
Es extranjero
It straniero; estero
Pt estrangeiro

étranger *(m)* n Fr
De Ausländer *(m)*
En foreigner
Es extranjero *(m)*
It straniero *(m)*
Pt estrangeiro *(m)*

être en désaccord Fr
De nicht übereinstimmen
En disagree
Es no estar de acuerdo

It essere in disaccordo
Pt discordar

étude de motivation *(f)* Fr
De Motivforschung *(f)*
En motivational research
Es investigación de
   motivación *(f)*
It indagine sulle motivazioni
   (f)
Pt investigação sobre
   motivação *(f)*

étude du marché *(f)* Fr
De Marktforschung *(f)*
En market research
Es investigación del mercado
   (f)
It indagine di mercato *(f)*
Pt pesquisa de mercado *(f)*

**étude du temps et
mouvements** *(f)* Fr
De Arbeitszeit- und
   Ablaufstudie *(f)*
En time and motion study
Es estudio de tiempo y
   progreso *(m)*
It studio dei tempi e dei
   movimenti *(m)*
Pt análise do tempo e
   progresso *(f)*

étude du travail *(f)* Fr
De Arbeitsstudie *(f)*
En work study
Es estudio del trabajo *(m)*
It studio di lavoro *(m)*
Pt estudo sobre trabalho *(m)*

étude probatoire *(f)* Fr
De Durchführbarkeitsanalyse
   (f)
En feasibility study
Es estudio de viabilidad *(m)*
It studio delle possibilità *(m)*
Pt estudo de viabilidade *(m)*

**Europäische
Atomgemeinschaft** *(f)* De
En European Atomic Energy
   Community
Es Comunidad Europea de
   Energía Atómica *(f)*
Fr Communauté Européenne
   de l'Energie Atomique *(f)*

It Comunità Europea
   dell'Energia Atomica *(f)*
Pt Comunidade Europeia de
   Energia Atómica *(f)*

Europäischer Fonds *(m)* De
En European Fund
Es Fòndo Europeo *(m)*
Fr Fonds Européen *(m)*
It Fondo Europeo *(m)*
Pt Fundo Europeu *(m)*

**Europäische Gemeinschaft
für Kohle und Stahl** *(f)* De
En European Coal & Steel
   Community
Es Comunidad Europea de
   Carbón y Acero *(f)*
Fr Communauté Européenne
   du Charbon et de l'Acier *(f)*
It Comunità Europea del
   Carbone e Acciaio *(f)*
Pt Comunidade Europeia do
   Carvão e do Aço *(f)*

**Europäische
Investitionsbank** *(f)* De
En European Investment
   Bank
Es Banco Europeo de
   Inversiones *(m)*
Fr Banque Européenne
   d'Investissement *(f)*
It Banca Europea
   d'Investimenti *(f)*
Pt Banco Europeu de
   Investimentos *(m)*

Europäische Kommission *(f)*
De
En European Commission
Es Comisión Europea *(f)*
Fr Commission des Commu-
   nautés Européennes *(f)*
It Commissione Europea *(f)*
Pt Comissão Europeia *(f)*

**Europäisches Währungs-
abkommen (EWA)** *(n)* De
En European Monetary
   Agreement
Es Acuerdo Monetario
   Europeo (AME) *(m)*
Fr Accord Monétaire
   Européen (AME) *(m)*
It Accordo Monetario
   Europeo (AME) *(m)*
Pt Acordo Monetário
   Europeu (AME) *(m)*

**Europäische Wirtschafts-
gemeinschaft** (f) De
En European Economic
    Community
Es Comunidad Económica
    Europea (f)
Fr Communauté Économi-
    que Européenne (f)
It Comunità Economica
    Europea (f)
Pt Comunidade Económica
    Europeia (f)

**European Atomic Energy
Community** En
De Europäische Atomge-
    meinschaft (f)
Es Comunidad Europea de
    Energía Atómica (f)
Fr Communauté Européenne
    de l'Energie Atomique (f)
It Comunità Europea
    dell'Energia Atomica (f)
Pt Comunidade Europeia de
    Energia Atómica (f)

European Commission En
De Europäische Kommission
    (f)
Es Comisión Europea (f)
Fr Commission des Commu-
    nautés Européennes (f)
It Commissione Europea (f)
Pt Comissão Europeia (f)

**European Economic
Community** En
De Europäische Wirtschafts-
    gemeinschaft (f)
Es Comunidad Económica
    Europea (f)
Fr Communauté Économi-
    que Européenne (f)
It Comunità Economica
    Europea (f)
Pt Comunidade Económica
    Europeia (f)

European Free Trade Area
(EFTA) En
De Europäische
    Freihandelszone (f)
Es Zona Europea de
    Comercio Libre (f)
Fr Zone Européenne de Libre
    Échange (f)
It Zona Europea di Libero
    Scambio (f)
Pt Zona Europeia de
    Comércio Livre (f)

European Fund En
De Europäischer Fonds (m)
Es Fondo Europeo (m)
Fr Fonds Européen (m)
It Fondo Europeo (m)
Pt Fundo Europeu (m)

European Investment Bank
En
De Europäische
    Investitionsbank (f)
Es Banco Europeo de
    Inversiones (m)
Fr Banque Européenne
    d'Investissement (f)
It Banca Europea
    d'Investimenti (f)
Pt Banco Europeu de
    Investimentos (m)

**European Monetary
Agreement** En
De Europäisches Währungs-
    abkommen (EWA) (n)
Es Acuerdo Monetario
    Europeo (AME) (m)
Fr Accord Monétaire
    Européen (AME) (m)
It Accordo Monetario
    Europeo (AME) (m)
Pt Acordo Monetário
    Europeu (AME) (m)

evaluación (f) n Es
De Abschätzung (f)
En appraisal
Fr évaluation (f)
It valutazione (f)
Pt avaliação (f)

evaluar vb Es
De bewerten
En evaluate
Fr évaluer
It valutare
Pt avaliar

evaluar daños Es
De den Schadenersatzbetrag
    feststellen
En assess damages
Fr fixer des dommages-
    intérêts
It valutare i danni
Pt avaliar os danos

evaluate vb En
De bewerten
Es evaluar

Fr évaluer
It valutare
Pt avaliar

évaluation (f) n Fr
De Abschätzung;
    Wertbestimmung (f)
En appraisal; valuation
Es evaluación (f)
It valutazione (f)
Pt avaliação (f)

évaluation du coût des lots
(f) Fr
De Stapelkostenberechnung
    (f)
En batch costing
Es fijación de precio por lotes
    (f)
It valutazione del costo per
    partita (f)
Pt fixação do preço por lote (f)

évaluation du travail (f) Fr
De Arbeitsbewertung (f)
En job evaluation
Es valoración del trabajo (f)
It valutazione del lavoro (f)
Pt avaliação de tarefa (f)

évaluation prudente (f) Fr
De vorsichtige Schätzung (f)
En conservative estimate
Es presupuesto prudente (m)
It valutazione prudente (f)
Pt avaliação cautelosa (f)

évaluer vb Fr
De bewerten
En evaluate
Es evaluar
It valutare
Pt avaliar

**evasión de pago de
impuestos** (f) Es
De Steuerhinterziehung (f)
En evasion of tax
Fr fraude fiscale (f)
It evasione d'imposta (f)
Pt fuga a impostos (f)

evasione d'imposta (f) It
De Steuerhinterziehung (f)
En evasion of tax
Es evasión de pago de
    impuestos (f)
Fr fraude fiscale (f)
Pt fuga a impostos (f)

evasion of tax En
De Steuerhinterziehung *(f)*
Es evasión de pago de
   impuestos *(f)*
Fr fraude fiscale *(f)*
It evasione d'imposta *(f)*
Pt fuga a impostos *(f)*

Eventualität *(f) n* De
En contingency
Es contingencia *(f)*
Fr contingence *(f)*
It contingenza *(f)*
Pt contingência *(f)*

Eventualverpflichtung *(f)* De
En contingent liability
Es responsabilidad
   contingente *(f)*
Fr obligation éventuelle *(f)*
It sopravvenienza passiva *(f)*
Pt responsabilidade
   contingente *(f)*

evict a tenant En
De einen Mieter entfernen
Es desalojar un inquilino
Fr expulser un locataire
It sfrattare un locatario
Pt desalojar um inquilino

evidence *n* En
De Beweis *(m)*
Es evidencia *(f)*
Fr preuve *(f)*
It prova *(f)*
Pt prova *(f)*

evidencia *(f) n* Es
De Beweis *(m)*
En evidence
Fr preuve *(f)*
It prova *(f)*
Pt prova *(f)*

examen más detallado *(m)*
   Es
De Weiterüberlegung *(f)*
En further consideration
Fr examen plus attentif *(m)*
It esame più attento *(m)*
Pt consideração posterior
   mais detalhada *(f)*

examen médical *(m)* Fr
De ärztliche Untersuchung *(f)*
En medical examination
Es examen médico *(m)*

It visita medica *(f)*
Pt inspecção médica *(f)*

examen médico *(m)* Es
De ärztliche Untersuchung *(f)*
En medical examination
Fr examen médical *(m)*
It visita medica *(f)*
Pt inspecção médica *(f)*

examen plus attentif *(m)* Fr
De Weiterüberlegung *(f)*
En further consideration
Es examen más detallado *(m)*
It essame più attento *(m)*
Pt consideração posterior
   mais detalhada *(f)*

examinar *vb* Es, Pt
De untersuchen
En examine
Fr examiner
It esaminare

examine *vb* En
De untersuchen
Es examinar
Fr examiner
It esaminare
Pt examinar

examiner *vb* Fr
De untersuchen
En examine
Es examinar
It esaminare
Pt examinar

ex bond En
De verzollt
Es fuera de aduanas
Fr à l'acquitté
It sdoganato
Pt livre de alfândega

ex-cais Pt
De ab Kai
En ex quay
Fr en muelle
It à prendre sur quai
Pt sulla banchina

excédent de bagages *(m)* Fr
De Übergepäck *(n)*
En excess luggage
Es exceso de equipaje *(m)*
It bagaglio eccedente *(m)*
Pt excesso de bagagem *(m)*

excédent de poids *(m)* Fr
De Übergewicht *(n)*
En excess weight
Es peso excedente *(m)*
It eccedenza di peso *(f)*
Pt excesso de peso *(m)*

excedente *(m) n* Es, Pt
De Überschuß *(m)*
En surplus
Fr surplus; excédent *(m)*
It eccesso *(m)*

excesivo *adj* Es
De übermäßig
En excessive
Fr excessif
It eccessivo
Pt excessivo

exceso de capacidad *(m)* Es
De Überkapazität *(f)*
En overcapacity
Fr surcapacité *(f)*
It capacità in eccedenza *(f)*
Pt capacidade excessiva *(f)*

exceso de equipaje *(m)* Es
De Übergepäck *(n)*
En excess luggage
Fr excédent de bagages *(m)*
It bagaglio eccedente *(m)*
Pt excesso de bagagem *(m)*

exceso de peso *(m)* Es
De Übergewicht *(n)*
En overweight
Fr excédent de poids *(m)*
It soprappeso *(m)*
Pt peso excessivo *(m)*

exceso de producción *(m)* Es
De Überproduktion *(f)*
En overproduction
Fr surproduction *(f)*
It sovrapproduzione *(f)*
Pt produção excessiva *(f)*

excess (of weight, etc.) *n* En
De Überschuß *(m)*
Es exceso *(m)*
Fr excédent *(m)*
It soprappeso *(m)*
Pt excesso *(m)*

excess capacity En
De übrige Ladefähigkeit *(f)*
Es capacidad en exceso *(f)*
Fr capacité excédentaire *(f)*

It capacità in eccesso *(f)*
Pt capacidade em excesso *(f)*

excessif *adj* Fr
De übermäßig
En excessive
Es excesivo
It eccessivo
Pt excessivo

excessive *adj* En
De übermäßig
Es excesivo
Fr excessif
It eccessivo
Pt excessivo

excessivo *adj* Pt
De übermäßig
En excessive
Es excesivo
Fr excessif
It eccessivo

excess luggage En
De Übergepäck *(n)*
Es exceso de equipaje *(m)*
Fr excédent de bagages *(m)*
It bagaglio eccedente *(m)*
Pt excesso de bagagem *(m)*

excesso *(m)* n Pt
De Überschuß *(m)*
En excess
Es exceso *(m)*
Fr excédent *(m)*
It eccesso *(m)*

excesso de bagagem *(m)* Pt
De Übergepäck *(n)*
En excess luggage
Es exceso de equipaje *(m)*
Fr excédent de bagages *(m)*
It bagaglio eccedente *(m)*

excesso de peso *(m)* Pt
De Übergewicht *(n)*
En excess weight
Es peso excedente *(m)*
Fr excédent de poids *(m)*
It eccedenza di peso *(f)*

excess profits tax En
De Übergewinnsteuer *(f)*
Es impuesto sobre beneficios
    extraordinarios *(m pl)*
Fr impôts sur les
    superbénéfices *(m pl)*

It imposta sui soprapprofitti
    (f)
Pt imposto sobre lucros
    excessivos *(m)*

excess weight En
De Übergewicht *(n)*
Es peso excedente *(m)*
Fr excédent de poids *(m)*
It eccedenza di peso *(f)*
Pt excesso de peso *(m)*

exchange n En
De Tausch *(m)*
Es cambio *(m)*
Fr échange *(m)*
It cambio *(m)*
Pt câmbio *(m)*

exchange control En
Am currency control
De Devisenkontrolle *(f)*
Es fiscalización de cambios
    (f)
Fr contrôle des changes *(m)*
It controllo sui cambi *(m)*
Pt controlo de câmbios *(m)*

**exchange equalization
account** En
De Währungsausgleichs-
    fonds *(m)*
Es cuenta de compensación
    de cambio *(f)*
Fr fonds de stabilisation des
    changes *(m pl)*
It conto per la stabilizzazio-
    ne dei cambi *(m)*
Pt conta de compensação de
    transacções *(f)*

exchange rate En
De Wechselkurs *(m)*
Es tipo de cambio *(m)*
Fr taux de change *(m)*
It corso del cambio *(m)*
Pt câmbio *(m)*

exchequer n En
Am treasury
De Schatzamt *(n)*
Es hacienda *(f)*
Fr trésorerie *(f)*
It tesoro *(m)*
Pt tesouro *(m)*

exchequer bond (bill) En
Am treasury bond
De Schatzwechsel *(m)*

Es bono de tesorería *(m)*
Fr bon du trésor *(m)*
It buono del tesoro *(m)*
Pt título do tesouro *(m)*

excise n En
De indirekte Steuern *(f pl)*
Es contribuciones indirectas
    (f pl)
Fr contributions indirectes
    (f pl)
It imposte indirette *(f pl)*
Pt contribuição indirecta *(f)*

excise duty En
De Verbrauchsabgabe *(f)*
Es impuesto de consumos
    (m)
Fr droit sur la consommation
    (m)
It imposta sul consumo *(f)*
Pt imposto indirecto *(m)*

exclude vb En
De ausschließen
Es excluir
Fr exclure
It escludere
Pt excluir

excluding tax En
De außer Steuer
Es impuesto no incluido
Fr hors taxe (HT)
It tassa esclusa
Pt imposto excluídos

excluir vb Es, Pt
De ausschließen
En exclude
Fr exclure
It escludere

exclure vb Fr
De ausschließen
En exclude
Es excluir
It escludere
Pt excluir

exclusão *(f)* n Pt
De Ausschluß *(m)*
En exclusion
Es exclusión *(f)*
Fr exclusion *(f)*
Pt esclusione *(f)*

exclusion n En, Fr (f)
De Ausschluß (m)
Es exclusión (f)
It esclusione (f)
Pt exclusão (f)

exclusión (f) n Es
De Ausschluß (m)
En exclusion
Fr exclusion (f)
It esclusione (f)
Pt exclusão (f)

exclusive market En
De ausschließlicher Markt (m)
Es mercado exclusivo (m)
Fr marché exclusif (m)
It mercato esclusivo (m)
Pt mercado exclusivo (m)

ex coupon En
De ohne Coupon
Es sin cupón
Fr ex-coupon
It senza cedola
Pt talão excluído

ex-coupon Fr
De ohne Coupon
En ex coupon
Es sin cupón
It senza cedola
Pt talão excluído

ex dividend En
De ohne Dividende
Es sin dividendo
Fr ex-dividende
It senza dividendo
Pt dividendo excluído

ex-dividende Fr
De ohne Dividende
En ex dividend
Es sin dividendo
It senza dividendo
Pt dividendo excluído

ex-droits Fr
De ohne Bezugsrechte
En ex rights
Es sin privilegio
It senza diritti
Pt privilégios excluídos

execução judicial a uma hipoteca (f) Pt
De Zwangsvollstreckung (f)
En foreclosure

Es venta por juicio hipotecario (f)
Fr vente de l'immeuble hypothéqué (f)
It vendita per giudizio ipotecario (f)

executar vb Pt
De vollstrecken
En execute
Es ejecutar
Fr exécuter
It eseguire

execute vb En
De vollstrecken
Es ejecutar
Fr exécuter
It eseguire
Pt executar

execute a deed En
De eine Urkunde unterzeichnen
Es firmar una escritura
Fr passer un acte
It perfezionare un atto
Pt dar execução a um título legal

execute a power of attorney En
De eine Vollmacht erteilen
Es otorgar poder notarial
Fr conférer des pleins pouvoirs
It conferire una procura
Pt dar execução a poderes de procuração

execute a will En
De ein Testament vollstrecken
Es ejecutar un testamento
Fr exécuter un testament
It eseguire un testamento
Pt dar execução a um testamento

exécuter vb Fr
De vollstrecken
En execute
Es ejecutar
It eseguire
Pt executar

exécuter un testament Fr
De ein Testament vollstrecken
Es execute a will
Es ejecutar un testamento

It eseguire un testamento
Pt dar execução a um testamento

exécuteur (m) n Fr
De Vollstrecker (m)
En executor
Es albacea (m)
It esecutore (m)
Pt executor (m)

exécution (f) n Fr
De Vollstreckung (f)
En execution
Es ejecución (f)
It esecuzione (f)
Pt execução (f)

executive n En
De Geschäftsleiter (m)
Es directivo (m)
Fr dirigeant (m)
It dirigente (m)
Pt dirigente (m)

executive director En
Am corporate officer
De geschäftsführender Direktor (m)
Es director ejecutivo (m)
Fr administrateur dirigeant (m)
It amministratore dirigente (m)
Pt director administrativo (m)

executor n En, Pt (m)
De Vollstrecker (m)
Es albacea (m)
Fr exécuteur (m)
It esecutore (m)

executor da liquidação (m) Pt
De Masseverwalter; Sachwalter (m)
En liquidator
Es liquidador (m)
Fr liquidateur (m)
It liquidatore (m)

exempt de douane Fr
De abgabenfrei
En duty-free
Es exento de impuestos
It esente da dazio
Pt isento de impostos

exempt d'impôts Fr
De steuerfrei
En tax-free
Es exento de impuestos
It esente da tassa
Pt isento de impostos

exemption n En, Fr (f)
De Befreiung (f)
Es exención (f)
It esenzione (f)
Pt isenção (f)

exención (f) n Es
De Befreiung (t)
En exemption
Fr exemption (f)
It esenzione (f)
Pt isenção (f)

exento de impuestos Es
De steuerfrei
En tax-free
Fr exempt d'impôts
It esente da tassa
Pt isento de impostos

exercice (m) n Fr
De Abrechnungszeitraum;
    Geschäftsjahr (m n)
En accounting period; finan-
    cial year
Es ejercicio (m)
It esercizio (m)
Pt exercício (m)

exercice budgétaire (m) Fr
De Steuerjahr (n)
En fiscal year
Es año fiscal (m)
It anno fiscale (m)
Pt ano fiscal (m)

exercice fiscal (m) Fr
De Steuerjahr (n)
En tax year
Es año fiscal (m)
It anno fiscale (m)
Pt ano fiscal (m)

exercício (m) n Pt
De Abrechnungszeitraum (m)
En accounting period
Es ejercicio (m)
Fr exercice (m)
It esercizio (m)

exhaustif adj Fr
De umfassend
En comprehensive
Es completo
It comprensivo
Pt compreensivo

exhibidor (m) n Es
De Aussteller (m)
En exhibitor
Fr exposant (m)
It espositore (m)
Pt expositor (m)

exhibition n En
De Ausstellung (f)
Es exposición (f)
Fr exposition (f)
It esposizione (f)
Pt exposição (f)

exhibitor n En
De Aussteller (m)
Es exhibidor (m)
Fr exposant (m)
It espositore (m)
Pt expositor (m)

existencias (f pl) n Es
De Vorrat (m)
En stock
Fr stock; marchandises
    (m; f pl)
It stock; scorta (m f)
Pt existências (f pl)

existências (f pl) n Pt
De Vorrat (m)
En stock
Es stock; existencias (m; f pl)
Fr stock; marchandises
    (m; f pl)
It stock; scorta (m f)

ex-navio Pt
De ab Schiff
En ex ship
Es en el buque
Fr ex ship
It ex ship

exorbitant adj En, Fr
De unmäßig
Es exorbitante
It esorbitante
Pt exorbitante

exorbitante adj Es, Pt
De unmäßig
En exorbitant
Fr exorbitant
It esorbitante

expedição vb Pt
De absenden
En dispatch
Es expedir
Fr expédier
It spedire

Expedient (m) n De
En shipping clerk
Es dependiente de muelle (m)
Fr expéditionnaire (m)
It commesso di spedizio-
    niere (m)
Pt despachante (m)

expédier vb Fr
De absenden; expedieren
En dispatch; forward
Es expedir; remitir
It spedire
Pt expedir; remeter

expedieren vb De
En forward; dispatch
Es expedir; remitir
Fr envoyer; expédier
It spedire
Pt expedir; remeter

expedir vb Es, Pt
De expedieren; absenden
En forward; dispatch
Fr envoyer; expédier
It spedire

expéditeur (m) n Fr
De Spediteur; Absender (m)
En carrier; consignor
Es transportador; consigna-
    dor (m)
It vettore; speditore (m)
Pt transportador; con-
    signante (m)

expéditionnaire (m) n Fr
De Expedient (m)
En shipping clerk
Es dependiente de muelle (m)
It commesso di spedizio-
    niere (m)
Pt despachante (m)

expenditure n En
De Ausgaben (f pl)
Es desembolso (m)
Fr frais (m pl)
It spesa (f)
Pt despesas (f pl)

expense n En
De Kosten (pl)
Es gasto (m)
Fr frais (m pl)
It spesa (f)
Pt despesa (f)

expensive adj En
De teuer; kostspielig
Es caro
Fr cher
It caro
Pt caro

experiente (m) n Pt
De Sachkundige(r) (m)
En expert
Es experto (m)
Fr expert (m)
It competente (m)

expert n En. Fr (m)
De Sachkundige(r); Sachver-
    ständige(r) (m)
Es experto; especialista (m)
It esperto; perito (m)
Pt experiente; perito (m)

expert's report En
De Sachverständigengutach-
    ten (n)
Es informe del especialista
    (m)
Fr expertise (f)
It perizia (f)
Pt relatório do perito (m)

expert comptable (m) Fr
De Wirtschaftsprüfer (m)
En qualified accountant
Es contador habilitado (m)
It ragioniere diplomato (m)
Pt guarda-livros diplomado
    (m)

expertise (f) n Fr
De Sachverständigengutach-
    ten (n)
En expert's report
Es informe del especialista
    (m)

It perizia (f)
Pt relatório do perito (m)

experto (m) n Es
De Sachkundige(r) (m)
En expert
Fr expert (m)
It competente (m)
Pt experiente (m)

expiração (f) n Pt
De Ablauf (m)
En expiry
Es expiración (f)
Fr expiration (f)
It termine (m)

expiración (f) n Es
De Ablauf (m)
En expiry
Fr expiration (f)
It termine (m)
Pt expiração (f)

expiration (f) n Fr
De Ablauf (m)
En expiry
Es expiración (f)
It termine (m)
Pt expiração (f)

expiré adj Fr
De verfallen
En expired
Es vencido
It scaduto
Pt vencido

expired adj En
De verfallen
Es vencido
Fr expiré
It scaduto
Pt vencido

expiry n En
De Ablauf (m)
Es expiración (f)
Fr expiration (f)
It termine (m)
Pt expiração (f)

exploit vb En
De ausbeuten
Es explotar
Fr exploiter
It sfruttare
Pt explorar

exploitation (f) n Fr
De Erschließung (f)
En development
Es explotación (f)
It valorizzazione (f)
Pt exploração (f)

exploiter vb Fr
De ausbeuten
En exploit
Es explotar
It sfruttare
Pt explorar

exploração (f) n Pt
De Erschließung (f)
En development
Es explotación (f)
Fr exploitation; lotissement
    (f m)
It valorizzazione (f)

explorar vb Pt
De ausbeuten
En exploit
Es explotar
Fr exploiter
It sfruttare

explotación (f) n Es
De Erschließung (f)
En development
Fr exploitation; lotissement
    (f m)
It valorizzazione (f)
Pt exploração (f)

explotar vb Es
De ausbeuten
En exploit
Fr exploiter
It sfruttare
Pt explorar

exponencial adj Es, Pt
De Exponential-
En exponential
Fr exponentiel
It esponenziale

exponential adj En
De Exponential-
Es exponencial
Fr exponentiel
It esponenziale
Pt exponencial

Exponential- De
En exponential
Es exponencial
Fr exponentiel
It esponenziale
Pt exponencial

exponentiel adj Fr
De Exponential-
En exponential
Es exponencial
It esponenziale
Pt exponencial

export vb En
De ausführen
Es exportar
Fr exporter
It esportare
Pt exportar

Exportabteilungsleiter (m) n
De
En export manager
Es jefe de exportación (m)
Fr chef du service exporta-
    tion (m)
It direttore esportazione (m)
Pt gerente de exportações (m)

exportaciones invisibles
    (f pl) Es
De unsichtbare Exporte (m pl)
En invisible exports
Fr exportations invisibles (f
    pl)
It esportazioni invisibili (f pl)
Pt exportações invisíveis (f pl)

exportações invisíveis
    (f pl) Pt
De unsichtbare Exporte (m pl)
En invisible exports
Es exportaciones invisibles
    (f pl)
Fr exportations invisibles (f
    pl)
It esportazioni invisibili (f pl)

exportador (m) n Es, Pt
De Exporteur (m)
En exporter
Fr exportateur (m)
It esportatore (m)

exportar vb Es, Pt
De ausführen
En export

Fr exporter
It esportare

exportateur (m) n Fr
De Exporteur (m)
En exporter
Es exportador
It esportatore (m)
Pt exportador (m)

exportations invisibles (f pl)
    Fr
De unsichtbare Exporte (m pl)
En invisible exports
Es exportaciones invisibles
    (f pl)
It esportazioni invisibili (f pl)
Pt exportações invisíveis (f pl)

Exportauftrag (m) n De
En export order
Es pedido de exportación (m)
Fr commande d'exportation
    (f)
It ordine per esportazione
    (m)
Pt encomenda de exportação
    (f)

export bonus En
De Ausfuhrprämie (f)
Es subsidio a las exportacio-
    nes (m)
Fr prime à l'exportation (f)
It premio d'esportazione (m)
Pt subsídio de exportação (m)

exporter vb Fr
De ausführen
En export
Es exportar
It esportare
Pt exportar

exporter n En
De Exporteur (m)
Es exportador
Fr exportateur (m)
It esportatore (m)
Pt exportador (m)

Exporteur (m) n De
En exporter
Es exportador
Fr exportateur (m)
It esportatore (m)
Pt exportador (m)

export incentive En
De Ausfuhranreiz (m)
Es estímulo de exportación
    (m)
Fr motif d'exportation (m)
It incentivo alla esportazione
    (m)
Pt incentivo para a exportação
    (m)

export manager En
De Exportabteilungsleiter (m)
Es jefe de exportación (m)
Fr chef du service exporta-
    tion (m)
It direttore esportazione (m)
Pt gerente de exportações (m)

export order En
De Exportauftrag (m)
Es pedido de exportación (m)
Fr commande d'exportation
    (f)
It ordine per esportazione
    (m)
Pt encomenda de exportação
    (f)

export packing En
De Exportverpackung (f)
Es embalaje para exportación
    (m)
Fr emballage convenable à
    l'exportation (m)
It imballaggio per esporta-
    zione (m)
Pt empacotamento para
    exportação (m)

export permit En
De Ausfuhrgenehmigung (f)
Es permiso de exportación
    (m)
Fr autorisation d'exporter (f)
It permesso d'esportazione
    (m)
Pt licença de exportação (f)

export rebate En
De Ausfuhrsonderrabatt (m)
Es descuento por exporta-
    ción (m)
Fr remise sur les exports (f)
It sconto d'esportazione (m)
Pt desconto de exportação
    (m)

export sales En
De Ausfuhrverkäufe *(m pl)*
Es ventas de exportación *(f pl)*
Fr ventes d'exportation *(f pl)*
It vendite per esportazione *(f pl)*
Pt vendas de exportação *(f pl)*

Exportverpackung *(f) n* De
En export packing
Es embalaje para exportación *(m)*
Fr emballage convenable à l'exportation *(m)*
It imballaggio per esportazione *(m)*
Pt empacotamento para exportação *(m)*

exposant *(m) n* Fr
De Aussteller *(m)*
En exhibitor
Es exhibidor *(m)*
It espositore *(m)*
Pt expositor *(m)*

exposição *(f) n* Pt
De Ausstellung *(f)*
En exhibition
Es exposición *(f)*
Fr exposition *(f)*
It esposizione *(f)*

exposição de montra *(f)* Pt
De Fensterauslage *(f)*
En window-display
Es exhibición en vitrina *(f)*
Fr étalage *(m)*
It mostra in vetrina *(f)*

exposición *(f) n* Es
De Ausstellung *(f)*
En exhibition
Fr exposition *(f)*
It esposizione *(f)*
Pt exposição *(f)*

exposition *(f) n* Fr
De Ausstellung *(f)*
En exhibition
Es exposición *(f)*
It esposizione *(f)*
Pt exposição *(f)*

expositor *(m) n* Pt
De Aussteller *(m)*
En exhibitor
Es exhibidor *(m)*

Fr exposant *(m)*
It espositore *(m)*

express letter En
Am special delivery
De Eilbrief *(m)*
Es carta urgente *(f)*
Fr lettre per exprès *(f)*
It lettera espresso *(f)*
Pt carta expressa *(f)*

express train En
De D-Zug; Schnellzug *(m)*
Es tren expreso *(m)*
Fr train express *(m)*
It direttissimo; rapido *(m)*
Pt comboio rápido *(m)*

expropiación *(f)* Es
De Enteignung *(f)*
En expropriation
Fr expropriation *(f)*
It espropriazione *(f)*
Pt expropriação *(f)*

expropriação *(f) n* Pt
De Enteignung *(f)*
En expropriation
Es expropiación *(f)*
Fr expropriation *(f)*
It espropriazione *(f)*

expropriation *n* En
De Enteignung *(f)*
Es expropiación *(f)*
Fr expropriation *(f)*
It espropriazione *(f)*
Pt expropriação *(f)*

expropriation *(f) n* Fr
De Enteignung *(f)*
En expropriation
Es expropiación *(f)*
It espropriazione *(f)*
Pt expropriação *(f)*

expulser un locataire Fr
De einen Mieter entfernen
En evict a tenant
Es desalojar un inquilino
It sfrattare un lacatario
Pt desalojar um inquilino

ex quay En
De ab Kai
Es en muelle
Fr à prendre sur quai
It sulla banchina
Pt ex-cais

ex rights En
De ohne Bezugsrechte
Es sin privilegio
Fr ex-droits
It senza diritti
Pt privilégios excluídos

ex ship En, Fr, It
De ab Schiff
Es en el buque
Pt ex-navio

extender un cheque Es
De einen Scheck ausstellen
En draw a cheque
Fr tirer un chèque
It emettere un assegno
Pt passar um cheque

extension of credit En
De Verlängerung eines Kredites *(f)*
Es prórroga de crédito *(f)*
Fr prolongation d'un crédit *(f)*
It proroga di credito *(f)*
Pt prorrogação de crédito *(f)*

extension of payment time En
De Verlängerung einer Zahlungsfrist *(f)*
Es prórroga de pago *(f)*
Fr délai de paiement *(m)*
It proroga di pagamento *(f)*
Pt prorrogação de pagamento *(f)*

external account En
Am foreign currency account
De Auslandskonto *(n)*
Es cuenta exterior *(f)*
Fr compte transférable *(m)*
It conto estero *(m)*
Pt conta externa *(f)*

external loan En
De Auslandsanleihe *(f)*
Es préstamo exterior *(m)*
Fr emprunt extérieur *(m)*
It prestito esterno *(m)*
Pt empréstimo externo *(m)*

extra *adj* En, Es, It, Pt
De Sonder-
Fr supplémentaire

extra charge En
De Zuschlagsgebühr *(f)*
Es suplemento *(m)*

Fr supplément *(m)*
It spesa supplementare *(f)*
Pt encargo suplementar *(m)*

extracto de conta *(m)* Pt
De Kontoauszug *(m)*
En statement of account;
 bank statement
Es extracto de cuenta *(m)*
Fr relevé de compte *(m)*
It estratto conto *(m)*

extracto de cuenta *(m)* Es
De Kontoauszug *(m)*
En statement of account;
 bank statement
Fr relevé de compte *(m)*
It estratto conto *(m)*
Pt extracto de conta *(m)*

extracto financeiro *(m)* Pt
De Finanzausweis *(m)*
En financial statement
Es extracto financiero *(m)*
Fr état de finances *(m)*
It relazione finanziaria *(f)*

extracto financiero *(m)* Es
De Finanzausweis *(m)*
En financial statement
Fr état de finances *(m)*
It relazione finanziaria *(f)*
Pt extracto financeiro *(m)*

extrait d'acte de décès *(m)* Fr
De Totenschein *(m)*
En death certificate
Es partida de defunción *(f)*
It certificato di morte *(m)*
Pt certidão de óbito *(f)*

extranjero *adj* Es
De ausländisch; fremd
En foreign; alien
Fr étranger
It straniero; estero
Pt estrangeiro

extranjero *(m)* n Es
De Ausländer *(m)*
En foreigner
Fr étranger *(m)*
It straniero *(m)*
Pt estrangeiro *(m)*

**extraordinary general
 meeting** En
De außerordentliche Generalversammlung *(f)*

Es asamblea general extraordinaria *(f)*
Fr assemblée générale
 extraordninaire *(f)*
It assemblea generale
 straordinaria *(f)*
Pt assembleia geral extraordinária *(f)*

extraordinary resolution En
De Sonderentschluß *(m)*
Es resolución extraordinaria
 (f)
Fr résolution extraordinaire *(f)*
It deliberazione straordinaria
 (f)
Pt resolução extraordinária *(f)*

extrapolar *vb* Es, Pt
De extrapolieren
En extrapolate
Fr extrapoler
It estrapolare

extrapolate *vb* En
De extrapolieren
Es extrapolar
Fr extrapoler
It estrapolare
Pt extrapolar

extrapoler *vb* Fr
De extrapolieren
En extrapolate
Es extrapolar
It estrapolare
Pt extrapolar

extrapolieren *vb* De
En extrapolate
Es extrapolar
Fr extrapoler
It estrapolare
Pt extrapolar

ex warehouse En
De an Zollfreilager
Es puesto en almacén
Fr à prendre en entrepôt
It franco magazzino
Pt no armazém

ex works En
De ab Werk
Es de fábrica
Fr prise usine
It franco fabbrica
Pt na fábrica

F

f.a.s. Pt
De frei Schiffseite
En free alongside ship (fas)
Es franco al costado del
 buque
Fr franco le long du bord
It franco lungobordo

F.O.B. destination Am
En carriage free
De frachtfrei
Es franco de porte
Fr franco
It porto franco
Pt porte grátis

F.O.B. shipping point Am
En carriage forward
De Portonachnahme
Es a porte debido
Fr en port dû
It porto assegnato
Pt transporte a pagar

fabbrica *(f)* n It
De Fabrik *(f)*
En factory
Es fábrica *(f)*
Fr fabrique; usine *(f)*
Pt fábrica *(f)*

fabbricante *(m)* n It
De Erzeuger; Hersteller *(m)*
En manufacturer
Es fabricante *(m)*
Fr fabricant *(m)*
Pt fabricante *(m)*

fabbricato di appartamenti
 (m) It
De Wohnungsgebäude *(n)*
En block of flats
Am apartment house
Es bloque de pisos *(m)*
Fr immeuble *(m)*
Pt edifício de andares *(m)*

fabbricazione in massa *(f)* It
De Massenherstellung *(f)*
En mass production
Es producción en masa *(f)*
Fr production en masse *(f)*
Pt produção em massa *(f)*

fábrica (f) n Es, Pt
De Fabrik (f)
En factory
Fr fabrique; usine (f)
It fabbrica (f)

fabricant (m) n Fr
De Erzeuger; Hersteller (m)
En manufacturer
Es fabricante (m)
It fabbricante (m)
Pt fabricante (m)

fabricante (m) n Es, Pt
De Erzeuger; Hersteller (m)
En manufacturer
Fr fabricant (m)
It fabbricante (m)

Fabrik (f) n De
En factory
Es fábrica (f)
Fr fabrique; usine (f)
It fabbrica (f)
Pt fábrica (f)

fabrique (f) n Fr
De Fabrik (f)
En factory
Es fábrica (f)
It fabbrica (f)
Pt fábrica (f)

façade (f) n Fr
De Vorderfront (f)
En frontage
Es fachada (f)
It facciata (f)
Pt fachada (f)

facciata (f) n It
De Vorderfront (f)
En frontage
Es fachada (f)
Fr façade (f)
Pt fachada (f)

face value En
De Nennwert (m)
Es valor nominal (m)
Fr valeur nominale (f)
It valore nominale (m)
Pt valor nominal (m)

fachada (f) n Es, Pt
De Vorderfront (f)
En frontage
Fr façade (f)
It facciata (f)

facilidades (f pl) n Es, Pt
De Einrichtungen (f pl)
En facilities
Fr facilités (f pl)
It facilitazione (f)

facilidades de descubierto (f
pl) Es
De Überziehungsdisposition
(f)
En overdraft facilities
Am overdraw facility
Fr facilités de caisse (f pl)
It facilitazione di scoperto (f)
Pt disponibilidades de crédi-
to sem cobertura (f pl)

facilitazione (f) n It
De Einrichtungen (f pl)
En facilities
Es facilidades (f pl)
Fr facilités (f pl)
Pt facilidades (f pl)

facilitazione di scoperto (f) It
De Überziehungsdisposition
(f)
En overdraft facilities
Am overdraw facility
Es facilidades de descubierto
(f pl)
Fr facilités de caisse (f pl)
Pt disponibilidades de crédi-
to sem cobertura (f pl)

facilités (f pl) n Fr
De Einrichtungen (f pl)
En facilities
Es facilidades (f pl)
It facilitazione (f)
Pt facilidades (f pl)

facilités de caisse (f pl) Fr
De Überziehungsdisposition
(f)
En overdraft facilities
Am overdraw facility
Es facilidades de descubierto
(f pl)
It facilitazione di scoperto (f)
Pt disponibilidades de crédi-
to sem cobertura (f pl)

facilities n pl En
De Einrichtungen (f pl)
Es facilidades (f pl)
Fr facilités (f pl)
It facilitazione (f)
Pt facilidades (f pl)

fact n En
De Tatsache (f)
Es hecho (m)
Fr fait (m)
It fatto (m)
Pt facto (m)

facteur (m) n Fr
De Umstand (m)
En factor
Es factor (m)
It fattore (m)
Pt factor (m)

facteur de conversion (m) Fr
De Umrechnungskoeffizient
(m)
En conversion factor
Es factor de conversión (m)
It fattore di conversione (m)
Pt factor de conversão (m)

facteur de sécurité (m) Fr
De Sicherheitskoeffizient (m)
En safety factor
Es factor de seguridad (m)
It coefficiente di sicurezza
(m)
Pt factor de segurança (m)

facto (m) n Pt
De Tatsache (f)
En fact
Es hecho (m)
Fr fait (m)
It fatto (m)

factor n En; Es, Pt (m)
De Umstand (m)
Fr facteur (m)
It fattore (m)

factor de conversão (m) Pt
De Umrechnungskoeffizient
(m)
En conversion factor
Es factor de conversión (m)
Fr facteur de conversion (m)
It fattore di conversione (m)

factor de conversión (m) Es
De Umrechnungskoeffizient
(m)
En conversion factor
Fr facteur de conversion (m)
It fattore di conversione (m)
Pt factor de conversão (m)

factor de segurança *(m)* Pt
De Sicherheitskoeffizient *(m)*
En safety factor
Es factor de seguridad *(m)*
Fr facteur de sécurité *(m)*
It coefficiente di sicurezza
(m)

factor de seguridad *(m)* Es
De Sicherheitskoeffizient *(m)*
En safety factor
Fr facteur de sécurité *(m)*
It coefficiente di sicurezza
(m)
Pt factor de segurança *(m)*

factory *n* En
De Fabrik *(f)*
Es fábrica *(f)*
Fr fabrique; usine *(f)*
It fabbrica *(f)*
Pt fábrica *(f)*

factory inspector En
De Gewerbeaufsichtsbeam-
te(r) *(m)*
Es inspector de fábrica *(m)*
Fr inspecteur du travail *(m)*
It ispettore di fabbrica *(m)*
Pt inspector de fábrica *(m)*

factory worker En
De Gewerbearbeiter; Fabrik-
arbeiter *(m)*
Es obrero; operario *(m)*
Fr ouvrier *(m)*
It operaio *(m)*
Pt operário *(m)*

factura *(f)* *n* Es, Pt
De Faktura; Rechnung *(f)*
En invoice
Fr facture *(f)*
It fattura *(f)*

factura comercial *(f)* Es, Pt
De Geschäftsfaktur *(f)*
En commercial invoice
Fr facture commerciale *(f)*
It fattura commerciale *(f)*

factura consular *(f)* Es, Pt
De Konsulatsfaktura *(f)*
En consular invoice
Fr facture consulaire *(f)*
It fattura consolare *(f)*

factura final *(f)* Es, Pt
De Endrechnung *(f)*
En final invoice
Fr facture finale *(f)*
It fattura finale *(f)*

factura proforma *(f)* Es, Pt
De Proformarechnung *(f)*
En proforma invoice
Fr facture fictive *(f)*
It fattura proforma *(f)*

facturar *vb* Es, Pt
De fakturieren
En invoice
Fr facturer
It fatturare

facture *(f)* *n* Fr
De Faktura; Rechnung *(f)*
En invoice *(f)*
Es factura *(f)*
It fattura *(f)*
Pt factura *(f)*

facture commerciale *(f)* Fr
De Geschäftsfaktur *(f)*
En commercial invoice
Es factura comercial *(f)*
It fattura commerciale *(f)*
Pt factura comercial *(f)*

facture consulaire *(f)* Fr
De Konsulatsfaktura *(f)*
En consular invoice
Es factura consular *(f)*
It fattura consolare *(f)*
Pt factura consular *(f)*

facture fictive *(f)* Fr
De Proformarechnung *(f)*
En proforma invoice
Es factura proforma *(f)*
It fattura proforma *(f)*
Pt factura proforma *(f)*

facture finale *(f)* Fr
De Endrechnung *(f)*
En final invoice
Es factura final *(f)*
It fattura finale *(f)*
Pt factura final *(f)*

facturer *vb* Fr
De fakturieren
En invoice
Es facturar
It fatturare
Pt facturar

facultad de crédito *(f)* Es
De Kreditfähigkeit *(f)*
En borrowing power
Fr capacité à avoir du crédit
(f)
It capacità creditizia *(f)*
Pt potencial de obtenção de
crédito *(m)*

Fähigkeit *(f)* *n* De
En capacity
Es capacidad *(f)*
Fr capacité *(f)*
It capacità *(f)*
Pt capacidade *(f)*

Fähigkeitsstreitigkeit *(f)* *n* De
En demarcation dispute
Es disputa sobre demarca-
ción *(f)*
Fr contestation syndicale des
compétences *(f)*
It disputa di competenza *(f)*
Pt disputa sobre demarcação
(f)

Fährboot *(n)* *n* De
En ferry-boat
Es transbordador *(m)*
Fr bac *(m)*
It nave traghetto *(f)*
Pt barco de travessia *(m)*

Fahrgeld *(n)* *n* De
En fare
Es pasaje *(m)*
Fr prix du voyage *(m)*
It prezzo di viaggio *(m)*
Pt preço de passagem *(m)*

Fahrlässigkeit *(f)* *n* De
En negligence
Es negligencia *(f)*
Fr négligence *(f)*
It negligenza *(f)*
Pt negligência *(f)*

fail *vb* En
De versagen; durchfallen
Es fallar; faltar
Fr échouer; faillir
It mancare; fallire
Pt falhar; faltar

failli *(m)* *n* Fr
De Gemeinschuldner *(m)*
En bankrupt
Es quebrado *(m)*

It   fallito *(m)*
Pt falido *(m)*

failli non réhabilité *(m)* Fr
De noch nicht entlasteter
     Gemeinschuldner *(m)*
En undischarged bankrupt
Es fallido no rehabilitado *(m)*
It   fallíto non riabilitato *(m)*
Pt falido insolvente *(m)*

failli réhabilité *(m)* Fr
De entlasteter Gemein-
     schuldner *(m)*
En discharged bankrupt
Es fallido rehabilitado *(m)*
It   fallito riabilitato *(m)*
Pt falido reabilitado *(m)*

faillite *(f) n* Fr
De Konkurs; Zahlungsunfä-
     higkeit *(m f)*
En bankruptcy; insolvency
Es quiebra; insolvencia *(f)*
It   fallimento; insolvenza *(m f)*
Pt falência; insolvência *(f)*

failure (of a business) *n* En
Am bankruptcy
De Bankrott *(m)*
Es insolvencia *(f)*
Fr faillite *(f)*
It   fallimento *(m)*
Pt falência *(f)*

failure rate En
De Durchfallquote *(f)*
Es proporción de fracasos *(f)*
Fr taux de défaillance *(m)*
It   indice dei fallimenti *(m)*
Pt proporção de fracassos *(f)*

failure to pay En
De Nichtzahlung *(f)*
Es falta de pago *(f)*
Fr défaut de paiement *(m)*
It   mancato pagamento *(m)*
Pt falta de pagamento *(f)*

fair *n* En
De Messe *(f)*
Es feria *(f)*
Fr foire *(f)*
It   fiera *(f)*
Pt feira *(f)*

fair *adj* En
De recht und billig
Es razonable

Fr équitable
It   equo
Pt razoável

fair average quality (faq) En
De gute Durchschnittsqualität
     (f)
Es calidad media razonable *(f)*
Fr qualité commerciale
     moyenne *(f)*
It   buona qualità media *(f)*
Pt qualidade média razoável
     (f)

fair deal En
De anständige Abmachung *(f)*
Es trato equitativo *(m)*
Fr affaire équitable *(f)*
It   affare giusto *(m)*
Pt transacção razoável *(f)*

faire faillite Fr
De Konkurs anmelden
En go bankrupt
Es caer en quiebra
It   fallire
Pt falir

faire la contrebande Fr
De schmuggeln
En smuggle
Es pasar de contrabando
It   contrabbandare
Pt fazer contrabando

faire la grève Fr
De streiken
En strike
Es declarar huelga
It   scioperare
Pt fazer greve

faire une offre Fr
De eine Offerte machen
En make an offer
Es hacer una oferta
It   fare una offerta
Pt fazer uma oferta

faire protester (une lettre de
   change) Fr
De (einen Wechsel) protestie-
     ren
En protest (a bill)
Es protestar (una letra)
It   protestare (una cambiale)
Pt protestar (uma letra)

faire une contre-offre Fr
De ein Gegenangebot abge-
     ben
En make a counteroffer
Es hacer una contraoferta
It   fare una controfferta
Pt fazer uma contra-propo-
     sta

fair play En
De anständige Handlungs-
     weise *(f)*
Es juego limpio *(m)*
Fr traitement juste *(m)*
It   condotta leale *(f)*
Pt jogo limpio *(m)*

fair price En
De angemessener Preis *(m)*
Es precio razonable *(m)*
Fr prix raisonnable *(m)*
It   prezzo equo *(m)*
Pt preço razoável *(m)*

fair return En
De angemessener Ertrag *(m)*
Es beneficio razonable *(m)*
Fr rendement équitable *(m)*
It   discreto profitto *(m)*
Pt rendimento justo *(m)*

fair wear and tear En
De übliche Abnützung *(f)*
Es uso y desgaste razonable
     (m)
Fr usure normale *(f)*
It   usura normale *(f)*
Pt uso e desgaste razoável
     (m)

fait *(m) n* Fr
De Tatsache *(f)*
En fact
Es hecho *(m)*
It   fatto *(m)*
Pt facto *(m)*

fake *adj* En
De gefälscht
Es falso
Fr truqué
It   falso
Pt falsificado

Faktura *(f) n* De
En invoice
Es factura *(f)*
Fr facture *(f)*

It fattura *(f)*
Pt factura *(f)*

fakturieren *vb* De
En invoice
Es facturar
Fr facturer
It fatturare
Pt facturar

fakturierter Preis *(m)* De
En invoice price
Es precio facturado *(m)*
Fr prix facturé *(m)*
It prezzo di fattura *(m)*
Pt preço de factura *(m)*

falência *(f) n* Pt
De Konkurs; Bankrott *(m)*
En bankruptcy; failure
Es quiebra; bancarrota *(f)*
Fr faillite *(f)*
It fallimento; bancarotta *(m f)*

falência bancária *(f)* Pt
De Bankkrach *(m)*
En bank crash
Es quiebra de banco *(f)*
Fr krach d'une banque *(m)*
It crollo di banca *(m)*

falhar *vb* Pt
De versagen; durchfallen
En fail
Es fallar; faltar
Fr échouer; faillir
It mancare; fallire

falido *(m) n* Pt
De Gemeinschuldner *(m)*
En bankrupt
Es quebrado *(m)*
Fr failli *(m)*
It fallito *(m)*

falido insolvente *(m)* Pt
De noch nicht entlasteter
    Gemeinschuldner *(m)*
En undischarged bankrupt
Es fallido no rehabilitado *(m)*
Fr failli non réhabilité *(m)*
It fallito non riabilitato *(m)*

falido reabilitado *(m)* Pt
De entlasteter Gemein-
    schuldner *(m)*
En discharged bankrupt
Es fallido rehabilitado *(m)*

Fr failli réhabilité *(m)*
It fallito riabilitato *(m)*

falir *vb* Pt
De Konkurs anmelden
En go bankrupt
Es caer en quiebra
Fr faire faillite
It fallire

fall *n* En
De Sturz *(m)*
Es baja; caida *(f)*
Fr baisse; chute *(f)*
It caduta; ribasso *(f m)*
Pt baixa; rueda *(f)*

fall *vb* En
De stürzen
Es caer; bajar
Fr baisser; tomber
It cadere; ribassare
Pt cair; baixar

fallar *vb* Es
De versagen; durchfallen
En fail
Fr échouer; faillir
It mancare; fallire
Pt falhar; faltar

fall due En
De fällig sein
Es vencer
Fr échoir; venir à échéance
It scadere; essere pagabile
Pt vencer-se

fallido no rehabilitado *(m)* Es
De noch nicht entlasteter
    Gemeinschuldner *(m)*
En undischarged bankrupt
Fr failli non réhabilité *(m)*
It fallito non riabilitato *(m)*
Pt falido insolvente *(m)*

fallido rehabilitado *(m)* Es
De entlasteter Gemein-
    schuldner *(m)*
En discharged bankrupt
Fr failli réhabilité *(m)*
It fallito riabilitato *(m)*
Pt falido reabilitado *(m)*

fällige Wechsel *(m pl)* De
En bills for collection
Es efectos a cobrar *(m pl)*
Fr effets en recouvrement
    (m pl)

It effetti all'incasso *(m pl)*
Pt letras a descontar *(f pl)*

Fälligkeit *(f) n* De
En maturity
Es vencimiento *(m)*
Fr échéance *(f)*
It scadenza *(f)*
Pt vencimento *(m)*

Fälligkeitstag *(m) n* De
En date of maturity; due date
Es fecha de vencimiento *(f)*
Fr date d'échéance *(f)*
It data di scadenza *(f)*
Pt data de vencimento *(f)*

fällig sein De
En fall due
Es vencer
Fr échoir; venir à échéance
It scadere; essere pagabile
Pt vencer-se

fallimento *(m) n* It
De Konkurs *(m)*
En bankruptcy
Es quiebra *(f)*
Fr faillite *(f)*
Pt falência *(f)*

falling market En
De Markt mit Baissetendenz
    (m)
Es mercado en baja *(m)*
Fr marché orienté à la baisse
    (m)
It mercato in declino *(m)*
Pt mercado em decréscimo
    (m)

fallire *vb* It
De Konkurs anmelden
En go bankrupt
Es caer en quiebra
Fr faire faillite
Pt falir

fallito *(m) n* It
De Gemeinschuldner *(m)*
En bankrupt
Es quebrado *(m)*
Fr failli *(m)*
Pt falido *(m)*

fallito non riabilitato *(m)* It
De noch nicht entlasteter
    Gemeinschuldner *(m)*
En undischarged bankrupt

Es fallido no rehabilitado *(m)*
Fr failli non réhabilité *(m)*
Pt falido insolvente *(m)*

fallito riabilitato *(m)* It
De entlasteter Gemein-
schuldner *(m)*
En discharged bankrupt
Es fallido rehabilitado *(m)*
Fr failli réhabilité *(m)*
Pt falido reabilitado *(m)*

fall off En
De nachlassen
Es bajar de valor; disminuir
Fr ralentir; baisser de valeur
It diminuire
Pt diminuir; decrescer

falsch *adj* De
En false; counterfeit
Es falso; falsificado
Fr faux; contrefait
It falso; contraffatto
Pt falso; falsificado

fälschen *vb* De
En forge
Es falsificar
Fr contrefaire
It contraffare
Pt falsificar

Fälscher *(m)* *n* De
En forger
Es falsificador *(m)*
Fr faux-monnayeur; faus-
saire *(m)*
It falsificatore *(m)*
Pt falsificador *(m)*

Fälschung *(f)* *n* De
En forgery
Es falsificación *(f)*
Fr contrefaçon; faux *(f m)*
It falsificazione *(f)*
Pt falsificação *(f)*

false *adj* En
De falsch
Es falso
Fr faux
It falso
Pt falso

falsificação *(f)* *n* Pt
De Fälschung *(f)*
En forgery
Es falsificación *(f)*

Fr contrefaçon; faux *(f m)*
It falsificazione *(f)*

falsificación *(f)* *n* Es
De Fälschung *(f)*
En forgery
Fr contrefaçon; faux *(f m)*
It falsificazione *(f)*
Pt falsificação *(f)*

falsificado *adj* Pt
De falsch; verfälscht
En counterfeit
Es falso; falsificado
Fr faux; contrefait
It falso; contraffatto

falsificador *(m)* *n* Es, Pt
De Fälscher *(m)*
En forger
Fr faux-monnayeur; faus-
saire *(m)*
It falsificatore *(m)*

falsificar *vb* Es, Pt
De fälschen
En forge
Fr contrefaire
It contraffare

falsificatore *(m)* *n* It
De Fälscher *(m)*
En forger
Es falsificador *(m)*
Fr faux-monnayeur; faus-
saire *(m)*
Pt falsificador *(m)*

falsificazione *(f)* *n* It
De Fälschung *(f)*
En forgery
Es falsificación *(f)*
Fr contrefaçon; faux *(f m)*
Pt falsificação *(f)*

falso *adj* Es, It, Pt
De falsch; verfälscht
En false; counterfeit
Fr faux; contrefait

falta *(f)* *n* Es, Pt
De Nichteinhaltung *(f)*
En default
Fr défaillance; défaut *(f m)*
It mancanza *(f)*

falta de experiencia *(f)* Es
De Unerfahrenheit *(f)*
En inexperience

Fr manque de pratique *(m)*
It inesperienza *(f)*
Pt inexperiência *(f)*

falta de pagamento *(f)* Pt
De Nichtzahlung *(f)*
En failure to pay
Es falta de pago *(f)*
Fr défaut de paiement *(m)*
It mancato pagamento *(m)*

falta de pago *(f)* Es
De Nichtzahlung *(f)*
En failure to pay
Fr défaut de paiement *(m)*
It mancato pagamento *(m)*
Pt falta de pagamento *(f)*

fancy goods En
De Modeartikel *(m pl)*
Es artículos de fantasía *(m pl)*
Fr nouveautés *(f pl)*
It articoli fantasia *(m pl)*
Pt artigos de fantasia *(m pl)*

fare *n* En
De Fahrgeld *(n)*
Es pasaje *(m)*
Fr prix du voyage *(m)*
It prezzo di viaggio *(m)*
Pt preço de passagem *(m)*

fare da intermediario It
De vermitteln
En mediate
Es intermediar
Fr s'entremettre
Pt intermediar

fare gettito It
De über Bord werfen
En jettison
Es echar al mar
Fr jeter à la mer
Pt alijar

fare una controfferta It
De ein Gegenangebot abge-
ben
En make a counteroffer
Es hacer una contraoferta
Fr faire une contre-offre
Pt fazer uma contra-pro-
posta

fare una offerta It
De eine Offerte machen
En make an offer
Es hacer una oferta

Fr faire une offre
Pt fazer uma oferta

far proseguire It
De bitte nachsenden
En please forward
Es se ruega hacer seguir
Fr prière de faire suivre
Pt é favor enviar

Faß *(n) n* De
En barrel
Es barril *(m)*
Fr tonneau *(m)*
It botte *(f)*
Pt barril *(m)*

fattibilità *(f) n* It
De Durchführbarkeit *(f)*
En feasibility
Es practicabilidad *(f)*
Fr practicabilité *(f)*
Pt viabilidade *(f)*

fatto *(m) n* It
De Tatsache *(f)*
En fact
Es hecho *(m)*
Fr fait *(m)*
Pt facto *(m)*

fattore *(m) n* It
De Umstand *(m)*
En factor
Es factor *(m)*
Fr facteur *(m)*
Pt factor *(m)*

fattore di conversione *(m)* It
De Umrechnungskoeffizient
    (m)
En conversion factor
Es factor de conversión *(m)*
Fr facteur de conversion *(m)*
Pt factor de conversão *(m)*

fattura *(f) n* It
De Faktura; Rechnung *(f)*
En invoice
Es factura *(f)*
Fr facture *(f)*
Pt factura *(f)*

fattura commerciale *(f)* It
De Geschäftsfaktur *(f)*
En commercial invoice
Es factura comercial *(f)*
Fr facture commerciale *(f)*
Pt factura comercial *(f)*

fattura consolare *(f)* It
De Konsulatsfaktura *(f)*
En consular invoice
Es factura consular *(f)*
Fr facture consulaire *(f)*
Pt factura consular *(f)*

fattura finale *(f)* It
De Endrechnung *(f)*
En final invoice
Es factura final *(f)*
Fr facture finale *(f)*
Pt factura final *(f)*

fattura proforma *(f)* It
De Proformarechnung *(f)*
En proforma invoice
Es factura proforma *(f)*
Fr facture fictive *(f)*
Pt factura proforma *(f)*

fatturare *vb* It
De fakturieren
En invoice
Es facturar
Fr facturer
Pt facturar

faulty *adj* En
De fehlerhaft
Es defectuoso
Fr défectueux
It difettoso
Pt defeituoso

faux *adj* Fr
De falsch; verfälscht
En false; counterfeit
Es falso; falsificado
It falso; contraffatto
Pt falso; falsificado

faux-monnayeur *(m) n* Fr
De Fälscher *(m)*
En forger
Es falsificador *(m)*
It falsificatore *(m)*
Pt falsificador *(m)*

faux chèque *(m)* Fr
De gefälschter Scheck *(m)*
En forged cheque
Es cheque falsificado *(m)*
It assegno falsificato *(m)*
Pt cheque falsificado *(m)*

faux frais *(m pl)* Fr
De Nebenkosten *(pl)*
En incidental expenses

Es gastos imprevistos *(m pl)*
It spese impreviste *(f pl)*
Pt despesas ocasionais *(f pl)*

fazer a contabilidade Pt
De Konto führen
En keep the accounts
Es llevar la contabilidad
Fr tenir la comptabilité
It tenere la contabilità

fazer greve Pt
De streiken
En strike
Es declarar huelga
Fr faire la grève
It scioperare

fazer uma contra-proposta
    Pt
De ein Gegenangebot abge-
    ben
En make a counteroffer
Es hacer una contraoferta
Fr faire une contre-offre
It fare una controfferta

fazer uma oferta Pt
De eine Offerte machen
En make an offer
Es hacer una oferta
Fr faire une offre
It fare una offerta

fazer uma reunião Pt
De eine Versammlung
    abhalten
En hold a meeting
Es celebrar una reunión
Fr tenir une assemblée
It tenere una riunione

feasibility *n* En
De Durchführbarkeit *(f)*
Es practicabilidad *(f)*
Fr practicabilité *(f)*
It fattibilità *(f)*
Pt viabilidade *(f)*

feasibility study En
De Durchführbarkeitsanalyse
    (f)
Es estudio de viabilidad *(m)*
Fr étude probatoire *(f)*
It studio delle possibilità *(m)*
Pt estudo de viabilidade *(m)*

feature n En
De Merkmal (n)
Es característica (f)
Fr particularité (f)
It caratteristica (f)
Pt característica (f)

fecha (f) n Es
De Datum (n)
En date
Fr date (f)
It data (f)
Pt data (f)

fecha de entrega (f) Es
De Liefertermin (m)
En delivery date
Fr date de livraison (f)
It data di consegna (f)
Pt data de entrega (f)

fecha de reembolso (f) Es
De Einlösungstag (m)
En redemption date
Fr date du remboursement (f)
It data di rimborso (f)
Pt data de resgate (f)

fecha de vencimiento (f) Es
De Fälligkeitstag (m)
En date of maturity; due date
Fr date d'échéance (f)
It data di scadenza (f)
Pt data de vencimento (f)

fecha tope (f) Es
De Verfallstermin (m)
En deadline
Fr date limite (f)
It ultima data o ora possibile (f)
Pt data de vencimento (f)

fedeltà (f) n It
De Treue (f)
En fidelity
Es fidelidad (f)
Fr fidélité (f)
Pt fidelidade (f)

federal adj En, Es, Pt
De Bundes-
Fr fédéral
It federale

fédéral adj Fr
De Bundes-
En federal
Es federal

It federale
Pt federal

federale adj It
De Bundes-
En federal
Es federal
Fr fédéral
Pt federal

fee n En
De Gebühr (f)
Es honorario; derecho (m)
Fr redevance; honoraires (f; m pl)
It onorario; diritto (m)
Pt honorários (m pl)

feedback n En
De Rückkoppelung (f)
Es retroacción (f)
Fr rétroaction (f)
It retroazione (f)
Pt reacção (f)

Fehler (m) n De
En error
Es error (m)
Fr erreur (f)
It errore (m)
Pt erro (m)

fehlerhaft adj De
En faulty
Es defectuoso
Fr défectueux
It difettoso
Pt defeituoso

feilschen vb De
En haggle
Am bargain
Es regatear
Fr marchander; chipoter
It mercanteggiare; cavillare
Pt regatear

Feind (m) n De
En enemy
Es enemigo (m)
Fr ennemi (m)
It nemico (m)
Pt inimigo (m)

Feingehalt (Gold usw.) (m) n De
En fineness
Es ley (f)
Fr titre (m)

It finezza (f)
Pt purèza (f)

Feingehaltsstempel (m) n De
En hall-mark
Es punzón de garantía (m)
Fr poinçon de titre (m)
It punzonatura di garanzia (f)
Pt marca de garantia (f)

feira (f) n Pt
De Messe (f)
En fair
Es feria (f)
Fr foire (f)
It fiera (f)

feira comercial (f) Pt
De Handelsmesse (f)
En trade fair
Es feria de muestras (f)
Fr foire commerciale (f)
It fiera commerciale (f)

Fensterauslage (f) n De
En window-display
Es exhibición en vitrina (f)
Fr étalage (m)
It mostra in vetrina (f)
Pt exposição de montra (f)

Fensterbriefumschlag (m) n De
En window-envelope
Es sobre de ventanilla (m)
Fr enveloppe à fenêtre (f)
It busta con finestra (f)
Pt envelope de endereço exposto (m)

Fensterglas (n) n De
En window glass
Es cristal de ventana (m)
Fr verre à vitres (m)
It vetro da finestre (m)
Pt vidro de montra (m)

fer (m) n Fr
De Eisen (n)
En iron
Es hierro (m)
It ferro (m)
Pt ferro (m)

fer de fonte (m) Fr
De Gußeisen (n)
En cast iron
Es hierro colado (m)

It   ghisa (f)
Pt   ferro fundido (m)

fer en gueuse (m) Fr
De   Roheisen (n)
En   pig-iron
Es   hierro bruto (m)
It   pane di ghisa (m)
Pt   ferro em bruto (m)

feria (f) n Es
De   Messe (f)
En   fair
Fr   foire (f)
It   fiera (f)
Pt   teira (t)

feria de muestras (f) Es
De   Handelsmesse (f)
En   trade fair
Fr   foire commerciale (f)
It   fiera commerciale (f)
Pt   feira comercial (f)

feriado (m) n Pt
De   gesetzlicher Feiertag (m)
En   public holiday
Es   día de fiesta (m)
Fr   jour férié (m)
It   giorno di festa (m)

férias (f pl) n Pt
De   Ferien; Urlaub (pl; m)
En   vacation; holiday
Es   vacación (f)
Fr   vacances (f pl)
It   vacanza (f)

férias de verão (f pl) Pt
De   Sommerferien (pl)
En   summer holidays
Es   vacaciones de verano;
      veraneo (f pl; m)
Fr   vacances d'été (f pl)
It   vacanze estive (f pl)

férias pagas (f pl) Pt
De   bezahlter Urlaub (m)
En   holidays with pay
Es   vacaciones retribuidas
      (f pl)
Fr   congés payés (m pl)
It   vacanze retribuite (f pl)

Ferien (pl) n De
En   vacation; holiday
Es   vacación (f)
Fr   vacances (f pl)

It   vacanza (f)
Pt   férias (f pl)

fermacarte (m) n It
De   Büroklammer (f)
En   paper clip
Es   sujetapapeles (m)
Fr   attache-papiers (m)
Pt   grampo (m)

fermare un assegno It
De   einen Scheck sperren
En   stop a cheque
Es   suspender el pago de un
      cheque
Fr   bloquer un chèque
Pt   suspender o pagamento
      de um cheque

ferme adj Fr
De   fest
En   firm
Es   firme
It   fermo
Pt   firme

ferme et non révisable Fr
De   fest und unveränderlich
En   firm and not subject to
      alteration
Es   firme y no revisable
It   fermo e non modificabile
Pt   firme e irreversível

fermo adj It
De   fest
En   firm
Es   firme
Fr   ferme
Pt   firme

fermo e non modificabile It
De   fest und unveränderlich
En   firm and not subject to
      alteration
Es   firme y no revisable
Fr   ferme et non révisable
Pt   firme e irreversível

Ferngespräch (n) n De
En   trunk call
Am   long distance call
Es   llamada interurbana (f)
Fr   appel téléphonique
      interurbain (m)
It   comunicazione interurba-
      na (f)
Pt   chamada inter-urbana (f)

Fernschreiber (m) n De
En   Telex
Es   télex (m)
Fr   télex (m)
It   telex (m)
Pt   telex (m)

Fernsprechamt (n) n De
En   telephone exchange
Es   central telefónica (f)
Fr   central téléphonique (m)
It   centrale telefonica (f)
Pt   central telefónica (f)

Fernsprechbuch (n) n De
En   telephone directory
Es   guía de teléfonos (f)
Fr   annuaire des téléphones
      (m)
It   elenco telefonico (m)
Pt   lista telefónica (f)

Fernsprecher (m) n De
En   telephone
Es   teléfono (m)
Fr   téléphone (m)
It   telefono (m)
Pt   telefone (m)

ferragens (f pl) n Pt
De   Eisenwaren (f pl)
En   hardware; ironmongery
Es   ferretería; quincallería (f)
Fr   quincaillerie (f)
It   ferramenta (f)

ferramenta (f) n It
De   Eisenwaren (f pl)
En   hardware; ironmongery
Es   ferretería; quincallería (f)
Fr   quincaillerie (f)
Pt   ferragens (f pl)

ferretería (f) n Es
De   Eisenwaren (f pl)
En   hardware; ironmongery
Fr   quincaillerie (f)
It   ferramenta (f)
Pt   ferragens (f pl)

ferro (m) n It, Pt
De   Eisen (n)
En   iron
Es   hierro (m)
Fr   fer (m)

ferrocarril (m) n Es
De   Eisenbahn (f)
En   railway

Fr chemin de fer *(m)*
It ferrovia *(f)*
Pt caminho de ferro *(m)*

ferro em bruto *(m)* Pt
De Roheisen *(n)*
En pig-iron
Es hierro bruto *(m)*
Fr fer en gueuse *(m)*
It pane di ghisa *(m)*

ferro fundido *(m)* Pt
De Gußeisen *(n)*
En cast iron
Es hierro colado *(m)*
Fr fer de fonte *(m)*
It ghisa *(f)*

ferrovia *(f)* n It
De Eisenbahn *(f)*
En railway
Es ferrocarril *(m)*
Fr chemin de fer *(m)*
Pt caminho de ferro *(m)*

ferry-boat n En
De Fährboot *(n)*
Es transbordador *(m)*
Fr bac *(m)*
It nave traghetto *(f)*
Pt barco de travessia *(m)*

fest *adj* De
En firm; fixed
Es firme; fijo
Fr ferme; fixe
It fermo; fisso
Pt firme; fixado

festbegründetes Recht *(n)*
De
En vested interest
Es interés creado *(m)*
Fr droit acquis *(m)*
It diritto acquisito *(m)*
Pt interesse adquirido *(m)*

feste Kapitalanlagen *(f pl)* De
En fixed capital
Es capital fijo *(m)*
Fr capital fixe *(m)*
It capitale fisso *(m)*
Pt capital fixado *(m)*

feste Parität *(f)* De
En fixed parity
Es paridad fija *(f)*
Fr parité fixe *(f)*

It parità fissa *(f)*
Pt paridade fixa *(f)*

festes Angebot *(n)* De
En firm offer
Es oferta en firme *(f)*
Fr offre ferme *(f)*
It offerta ferma *(f)*
Pt oferta firme *(f)*

festività legali *(f)* It
De gesetzlicher Feiertag *(m)*
En public holiday
Am legal holiday
Es día de fiesta *(m)*
Fr jour férié *(m)*
Pt feriado *(m)*

fest und unveränderlich De
En firm and not subject to
 alteration
Es firme y no revisable
Fr ferme et non révisable
It fermo e non modificabile
Pt firme e irreversível

festverzinsliches
 Wertpapier *(n)* De
En fixed-interest security
Es obligación a interés fijo *(f)*
Fr valeur à revenu fixe *(f)*
It titolo a interesse fisso *(m)*
Pt obrigação de juro fixo *(f)*

Feuerversicherung *(f)* n De
En fire insurance
Es seguro de incendios *(m)*
Fr assurance incendie *(f)*
It assicurazione incendio *(f)*
Pt seguro de incêndio *(m)*

Feuerversicherungsschein
 (m) n De
En fire insurance policy
Es póliza de seguro de incen-
 dios *(f)*
Fr police incendie *(f)*
It polizza d'assicurazione in-
 cendio *(f)*
Pt apólice de seguro de in-
 cêndio *(f)*

feuille de paie *(f)* Fr
De Lohnbuch *(n)*
En payroll
Es nómina de pago *(f)*
It libro paga *(m)*
Pt folha de salários *(f)*

feuille d'inscription *(f)* Fr
De Antragsformular *(n)*
En entry-form
Es solicitud de inscripción *(f)*
It bolletta d'entrata *(f)*
Pt impresso de admissão *(m)*

fiador *(m)* n Es, Pt
De Bürgschaft; Bürge *(f m)*
En surety; guarantor
Fr caution; garant *(f m)*
It garante; avallante *(m)*

fiança *(f)* n Pt
De Bürge; Nebenbürgschaft
 (m f)
En surety; security
Es fianza *(f)*
Fr cautionnement; nantisse-
 ment *(m)*
It cauzione; pegno *(f m)*

fiança de avaria *(f)* Pt
De Havarieschein *(m)*
En average bond
Es fianza de avería *(f)*
Fr compromis d'avarie *(m)*
It compromesso d'avaria *(m)*

fianza *(f)* n Es
De Bürge; Nebenbürgschaft
 (m f)
En surety; security
Fr cautionnement; nantisse-
 ment *(m)*
It cauzione; pegno *(f m)*
Pt fiança *(f)*

fianza de avería *(f)* Es
De Havarieschein *(m)*
En average bond
Fr compromis d'avarie *(m)*
It compromesso d'avaria *(m)*
Pt fiança de avaria *(f)*

ficha *(f)* n Es, Pt
De Indexkarte *(f)*
En index card
Fr fiche *(f)*
It scheda *(f)*

ficha perfurada *(f)* Pt
De Lochkarte *(f)*
En punched card
Es tarjeta perforada *(f)*
Fr carte perforée *(f)*
It scheda perforata *(f)*

fiche *(f)* n Fr
De Indexkarte *(f)*
En index card
Es ficha *(f)*
It scheda *(f)*
Pt ficha *(f)*

ficheiro *(m)* n Pt
De Akte *(f)*
En file
Es archivo *(m)*
Fr dossier *(m)*
It archivio *(m)*

ficheiro com índice *(m)* Pt
De Kartei *(f)*
En card-index file
Es archivo de fichas *(m)*
Fr fichier *(m)*
It schedario *(m)*

fichero *(m)* n Es
De Kartothek; Aktenschrank
(f m)
En card index; filing cabinet
Fr fichier; classeur *(m)*
It schedario *(m)*
Pt ficheiro; móvel ficheiro *(m)*

fichier *(m)* n Fr
De Kartei *(f)*
En card-index file
Es archivo de fichas *(m)*
It schedario *(m)*
Pt ficheiro com índice *(m)*

ficticio *adj* Es
De unecht; Schein-
En fictitious
Fr fictif
It fittizio
Pt fictício

fictício *adj* Pt
De unecht; Schein-
En fictitious
Es ficticio
Fr fictif
It fittizio

fictif *adj* Fr
De unecht; Schein-
En fictitious
Es ficticio
It fittizio
Pt fictício

fictitious *adj* En
De unecht; Schein-
Es ficticio
Fr fictif
It fittizio
Pt fictício

fidato *adj* It
De zuverlässig
En reliable
Es digno de confianza
Fr digne de confiance
Pt digno de confiança

fidecommissario *(m)* n It
De Treuhänder *(m)*
En trustee
Es fideicomisario *(m)*
Fr fidéicommissaire *(m)*
Pt fiduciário *(m)*

fideicomisario *(m)* n Es
De Treuhänder *(m)*
En trustee
Fr fidéicommissaire *(m)*
It fidecommissario *(m)*
Pt fiduciário *(m)*

fideicomiso de inversiones
(m) Es
De Investment-Trust *(m)*
En investment trust
Fr société fiduciaire de
placements
It consorzio per investimenti
(m)
Pt instituição de investimentos
(f)

fideicomiso discrecional *(m)*
Es
De unumschränkte Treuhand
(f)
En discretionary trust
Fr fidéicommis à apprécia-
tion *(m)*
It fondo fiduciario discrezio-
nale *(m)*
Pt fundação discricionária *(f)*

fidéicommis à appréciation
(m) Fr
De unumschränkte Treuhand
(f)
En discretionary trust
Es fideicomiso discrecional
(m)

It fondo fiduciario discrezionale *(m)*
Pt fundação discricionária *(f)*

fidéicommissaire *(m)* n Fr
De Treuhänder *(m)*
En trustee
Es fideicomisario *(m)*
It fidecommissario *(m)*
Pt fiduciário *(m)*

fidelidad *(f)* n Es
De Treue *(f)*
En fidelity
Fr fidélité *(f)*
It fedeltà *(f)*
Pt fidelidade *(f)*

fidelidade *(f)* n Pt
De Treue *(f)*
En fidelity
Es fidelidad *(f)*
Fr fidélité *(f)*
It fedeltà *(f)*

fidélité *(f)* n Fr
De Treue *(f)*
En fidelity
Es fidelidad *(f)*
It fedeltà *(f)*
Pt fidelidade *(f)*

fidelity n En
De Treue *(f)*
Es fidelidad *(f)*
Fr fidélité *(f)*
It fedeltà *(f)*
Pt fidelidade *(f)*

fiduciaire *adj* Fr
De treuhänderisch
En fiduciary
Es fiduciario
It fiduciario
Pt fiduciário

fiduciario *adj* Es, It
De treuhänderisch
En fiduciary
Fr fiduciaire
Pt fiduciário

fiduciário *adj* Pt
De treuhänderisch
En fiduciary
Es fiduciario
Fr fiduciaire
It fiduciario

fiduciário *(m) n* Pt
De Treuhänder *(m)*
En trustee
Es fideicomisario *(m)*
Fr fidéicommissaire *(m)*
It fidecommissario *(m)*

fiduciary *adj* En
De treuhänderisch
Es fiduciario
Fr fiduciaire
It fiduciario
Pt fiduciário

fiduciary issue En
De ungedecktes Geld *(n)*
Es emisión fiduciaria *(f)*
Fr émission fiduciaire *(f)*
It emissione fiduciaria *(f)*
Pt emissão fiduciária *(f)*

field study En
De Stellenüberblick *(m)*
Es estudio sobre el terreno
(m)
Fr enquête sur les lieux *(f)*
It studio sul terreno *(m)*
Pt estudo de campo *(m)*

fiera *(f) n* It
De Messe *(f)*
En fair
Es feria *(f)*
Fr foire *(f)*
Pt feira *(f)*

fiera commerciale *(f)* It
De Handelsmesse *(f)*
En trade fair
Es feria de muestras *(f)*
Fr foire commerciale *(f)*
Pt feira comercial *(f)*

figure (number) *n* En
De Zahl *(f)*
Es cifra *(f)*
Fr chiffre *(m)*
It cifra *(f)*
Pt número *(m)*

fijación de precio por lotes
(f) Es
De Stapelkostenberechnung
(f)
En batch costing
Fr évaluation du coût des lots
(f)

It valutazione del costo per
partita *(f)*
Pt fixação do preço por lote *(f)*

fijo *adj* Es
De fest
En fixed
Fr fixe; fixé
It fisso; fissato
Pt fixado

file *n* En
De Akte *(f)*
Es archivo *(m)*
Fr dossier *(m)*
It archivio *(m)*
Pt ficheiro *(m)*

file (a patent) *vb* En
De einlegen
Es interponer
Fr déposer
It depositare
Pt registar

file (classify) *vb* En
De aufreihen
Es archivar
Fr classer
It archiviare
Pt arquivar

filial *(f) n* Pt
De Filiale; Zweigstelle *(f)*
En branch
Es sucursal *(f)*
Fr succursale; filiale *(f)*
It succursale; filiale *(f)*

filial *(f) n* Es
De Tochtergesellschaft *(f)*
En subsidiary company
Fr filiale *(f)*
It filiale *(f)*
Pt companhia subsidiária *(f)*

Filialbank *(f) n* De
En branch bank
Es sucursal del banco *(f)*
Fr banque succursale *(f)*
It banca succursale *(f)*
Pt filial de banco *(f)*

filial de banco *(f)* Pt
De Filialbank; Zweigbank *(f)*
En branch bank
Es sucursal del banco *(f)*
Fr banque succursale *(f)*
It banca succursale *(f)*

filiale *(f) n* Fr, It
De Tochtergesellschaft *(f)*
En subsidiary company
Es filial; empresa subsidiaria
(f)
Pt companhia subsidiária *(f)*

Filiale *(f) n* De
En branch
Es sucursal; filial *(f)*
Fr succursale; filiale *(f)*
It succursale; filiale *(f)*
Pt filial *(f)*

filing cabinet En
De Aktenschrank *(m)*
Es fichero *(m)*
Fr classeur *(m)*
It schedario *(m)*
Pt móvel ficheiro *(m)*

filouter *vb* Fr
De schwindeln
En swindle
Es estafar
It truffare
Pt enganar

fim *(m) n* Pt
De Ende *(n)*
En end
Es fin *(m)*
Fr fin *(f)*
It fine *(f)*

fin *n* Es *(m)*, Fr *(f)*
De Ende *(n)*
En end
It fine *(f)*
Pt fim *(m)*

final *adj* En, Es, Fr, Pt
De endgültig
It finale

final balance En
De Schlußbilanz *(f)*
Es saldo final *(m)*
Fr solde net *(m)*
It saldo finale *(m)*
Pt balanço final *(m)*

final discharge En
De Rechnungsentlastung *(f)*
Es finiquito *(m)*
Fr quitus *(m)*
It quietanza finale *(f)*
Pt cumprimento final *(m)*

final dividend En
De Schlußdividende *(f)*
Es saldo del dividendo *(m)*
Fr solde de dividende *(m)*
It saldo del dividendo *(m)*
Pt dividendo final *(m)*

finale *adj* It
De endgültig
En final
Es final
Fr final
Pt final

final instalment En
De letzte Rate *(f)*
Es último plazo *(m)*
Fr dernier versement *(m)*
It ultima rata *(f)*
Pt última prestação *(f)*

final invoice En
De Endrechnung *(f)*
Es factura final *(f)*
Fr facture finale *(f)*
It fattura finale *(f)*
Pt factura final *(f)*

finança *(f) n* Pt
De Finanz *(f)*
En finance
Es finanza *(f)*
Fr finance *(f)*
It finanza *(f)*

finance *vb* En
De finanzieren
Es financiar
Fr financer
It finanziare
Pt financiar

finance *n* En, Fr *(f)*
De Finanz *(f)*
Es finanza *(f)*
It finanza *(f)*
Pt finança *(f)*

finance company En
De Finanzierungsgesellschaft
   (f)
Es compañía de crédito co-
   mercial *(f)*
Fr société de financement *(f)*
It società finanziaria *(f)*
Pt empresa financeira *(f)*

financeiro *adj* Pt
De finanziell
En financial
Es financiero
Fr financier; fiscal
It finanziario

financer *vb* Fr
De finanzieren
En finance
Es financiar
It finanziare
Pt financiar

financial *adj* En
De finanziell
Es financiero
Fr financier; fiscal
It finanziario
Pt financeiro

financial statement En
De Finanzausweis *(m)*
Es extracto financiero *(m)*
Fr état de finances *(m)*
It relazione finanziaria *(f)*
Pt extracto financeiro *(m)*

financial year En
De Geschäftsjahr *(n)*
Es año económico *(m)*
Fr exercice *(m)*
It esercizio *(m)*
Pt ano financeiro *(m)*

financiar *vb* Es, Pt
De finanzieren
En finance
Fr financer
It finanziare

financier *adj* Fr
De finanziell
En financial
Es financiero
It finanziario
Pt financeiro

financiero *adj* Es
De finanziell
En financial
Fr financier; fiscal
It finanziario
Pt financeiro

Finanz *(f) n* De
En finance
Es finanza *(f)*
Fr finance *(f)*

It finanza *(f)*
Pt finança *(f)*

Finanz- De
En fiscal
Es fiscal
Fr fiscal; budgétaire
It fiscale
Pt fiscal

finanza *(f) n* Es, It
De Finanz *(f)*
En finance
Fr finance *(f)*
Pt finança *(f)*

Finanzausweis *(m) n* De
En financial statement
Es extracto financiero *(m)*
Fr état de finances *(m)*
It relazione finanziaria *(f)*
Pt extracto financeiro *(m)*

Finanzbank *(f) n* De
En investment bank
Es banco de inversiones *(m)*
Fr banque d'affaires *(f)*
It banca d'investimenti *(f)*
Pt banco de investimentos
   (m)

finanziare *vb* It
De finanzieren
En finance
Es financiar
Fr financer
Pt financiar

finanziario *adj* It
De finanziell
En financial
Es financiero
Fr financier; fiscal
Pt financeiro

finanziell *adj* De
En financial
Es financiero
Fr financier; fiscal
It finanziario
Pt financeiro

finanzieren *vb* De
En finance
Es financiar
Fr financer
It finanziare
Pt financiar

Finanzierungsgesellschaft
  (f) n De
En finance company
Es compañía de crédito co-
  mercial *(f)*
Fr société de financement *(f)*
It società finanziaria *(f)*
Pt empresa financeira *(f)*

finca *(f)* n Es
De Vermögen *(n)*
En estate; property
Fr bien; propriété *(m f)*
It proprietà *(f)*
Pt bens; propriedade *(m pl; f)*

fine *(f)* n It
De Ende *(n)*
En end
Es fin *(m)*
Fr fin *(f)*
Pt fim *(m)*

fine n En
De Geldstrafe *(f)*
Es sanción; multa *(f)*
Fr amende *(f)*
It multa *(f)*
Pt multa *(f)*

fineness (of gold, etc.) n En
De Feingehalt *(m)*
Es ley *(f)*
Fr titre *(m)*
It finezza *(f)*
Pt pureza *(f)*

finezza (d'oro, ecc.) *(f)* n It
De Feingehalt *(m)*
En fineness
Es ley *(f)*
Fr titre *(m)*
Pt pureza *(f)*

finiquito *(m)* n Es
De Rechnungsentlastung *(f)*
En final discharge
Fr quitus *(m)*
It quietanza finale *(f)*
Pt cumprimento final *(m)*

finta pelle *(f)* It
De Kunstleder *(n)*
En imitation leather
Es piel de imitación *(f)*
Fr simili-cuir *(m)*
Pt cabedal de imitação *(m)*

fire *vb* En
De entlassen
Es despedir
Fr congédier
It congedare
Pt despedir

fire n En
De Brand *(m)*
Es fuego; incendio *(m)*
Fr incendie *(f)*
It incendio *(m)*
Pt fogo; incêndio *(m)*

fire insurance En
De Feuerversicherung *(f)*
Es seguro de incendios *(m)*
Fr assurance incendie *(f)*
It assicurazione incendio *(f)*
Pt seguro de incêndio *(m)*

fire insurance policy En
De Feuerversicherungsschein
  (m)
Es póliza de seguro de incen-
  dios *(f)*
Fr police incendie *(f)*
It polizza d'assicurazione in-
  cendio *(f)*
Pt apólice de seguro de in-
  cêndio *(f)*

firing (dismissal) n En
De Entlassung *(f)*
Es despido *(m)*
Fr congédiement *(m)*
It licenziamento *(m)*
Pt despedimento *(m)*

firm *adj* En
De fest
Es firme
Fr ferme
It fermo
Pt firme

firm n En
Am company
De Firma *(f)*
Es firma; casa *(f)*
Fr firme; maison *(f)*
It ditta *(f)*
Pt empresa; firma *(f)*

firma *(f)* n Es, Pt
De Firma *(f)*
En firm
Fr firme; maison *(f)*
It ditta *(f)*

firma *(f)* n Es, It, Pt
De Unterschrift *(f)*
En signature
Fr signature *(f)*

Firma *(f)* n De
En firm; company
Es firma; casa *(f)*
Fr firme; maison *(f)*
It ditta *(f)*
Pt empresa; firma *(f)*

firma en blanco *(f)* Es
De Blankounterschrift *(f)*
En blank signature
Fr blanc-seing *(m)*
Pt assinatura em branco *(f)*

firma in bianco *(f)* It
De Blankounterschrift *(f)*
En blank signature
Es firma en blanco *(f)*
Fr blanc-seing *(m)*
Pt assinatura em branco *(f)*

**firm and not subject to
  alteration** En
De fest und unveränderlich
Es firme y no revisable
Fr ferme et non révisable
It fermo e non modificabile
Pt firme e irreversível

firmar una escritura Es
De eine Urkunde unterzeich-
  nen
En execute a deed
Fr passer un acte
It perfezionare un atto
Pt dar execução a um título
  legal

firme *adj* Es, Pt
De fest
En firm
Fr ferme
It fermo

firme *(f)* n Fr
De Firma *(f)*
En firm; company
Es firma; casa *(f)*
It ditta *(f)*
Pt empresa; firma *(f)*

firme e irreversível Pt
De fest und unveränderlich
En firm and not subject to
  alteration

Es firme y no revisable
Fr ferme et non révisable
It fermo e non modificabile

Firmenkonto *(n)* n De
En impersonal account
Es cuenta simulada *(f)*
Fr compte impersonnel *(m)*
It conto d'ordine *(m)*
Pt conta impessoal *(f)*

Firmenname *(m)* n De
En trade name
Es razón social *(f)*
Fr raison sociale *(f)*
It denominazione commer-
ciale *(f)*
Pt razão comercial *(f)*

firme y no revisable Es
De fest und unveränderlich
En firm and not subject to
alteration
Fr ferme et non révisable
It fermo e non modificabile
Pt firme e irreversível

firm offer En
De festes Angebot *(n)*
Es oferta en firme *(f)*
Fr offre ferme *(f)*
It offerta ferma *(f)*
Pt oferta firme *(f)*

first class En
De erste Klasse *(f)*
Es primera clase *(f)*
Fr première classe *(f)*
It prima classe *(f)*
Pt primeira classe *(f)*

first of exchange En
De Primawechsel *(m)*
Es primera de cambio *(f)*
Fr première de change *(f)*
It prima di cambio *(f)*
Pt primeira de câmbio *(f)*

fiscal *adj* En, Es, Fr, Pt
De Finanz-
It fiscale

fiscal de contas *(m)* Pt
De Bücherrevisor *(m)*
En auditor
Es revisor de conti *(m)*
Fr réviseur des comptes *(m)*
It sindaco *(m)*

fiscale *adj* It
De Finanz-
En fiscal
Es fiscal
Fr fiscal; budgétaire
Pt fiscal

**fiscalização contabilística
interna** *(f)* Pt
De interne Revision *(f)*
En internal audit
Es verificación contable in-
terna *(f)*
Fr vérification interne *(f)*
It verifica contabile interna *(f)*

fiscalização de contas *(f)* Pt
De Bücherrevision *(f)*
En audit
Es revisión de cuentas *(f)*
Fr vérification comptable *(f)*
It revisione dei conti *(f)*

fiscalización de cambios *(f)*
Es
De Devisenkontrolle *(f)*
En exchange control
Am currency control
Fr contrôle des changes *(m)*
It controllo sui cambi *(m)*
Pt controlo de câmbios *(m)*

**fiscalización de las
existencias** *(f)* Es
De Lagerverwaltung *(f)*
En stock control
Fr contrôle des stocks *(m)*
It controllo delle scorte *(m)*
Pt controlo de existências *(m)*

fiscalizar (as contas) *vb* Pt
De prüfen
En audit
Es revisar
Fr vérifier et certifier
It rivedere

fiscal year En
De Steuerjahr *(n)*
Es año fiscal *(m)*
Fr exercice budgétaire *(m)*
It anno fiscale *(m)*
Pt ano fiscal *(m)*

Fischerflotte *(f)* n De
En fishing fleet
Es flota pesquera *(f)*
Fr flottille de pêche *(f)*

It flotta peschereccia *(f)*
Pt frota de pesca *(f)*

fishing fleet En
De Fischerflotte *(f)*
Es flota pesquera *(f)*
Fr flottille de pêche *(f)*
It flotta peschereccia *(f)*
Pt frota de pesca *(f)*

fissare *vb* It
De anstellen
En engage
Am hire
Es apalabrar
Fr engager
Pt empregar

fissare un appuntamento It
De eine Verabredung treffen
En make an appointment
Es hacer una cita
Fr prendre un rendez-vous
Pt marcar um encontro

fisso *adj* It
De fest
En fixed
Es fijo
Fr fixe; fixé
Pt fixado

fita magnética *(f)* Pt
De Magnetband *(n)*
En magnetic tape
Es cinta magnética *(f)*
Fr bande magnétique *(f)*
It nastro magnetico *(m)*

fittizio *adj* It
De unecht; Schein-
En fictitious
Es ficticio
Fr fictif
Pt fictício

fixação do preço por lote *(f)*
Pt
De Stapelkostenberechnung
(f)
En batch costing
Es fijación de precio por lotes
(f)
Fr évaluation du coût des lots
(f)
It valutazione del costo per
partita *(f)*

fixado *adj* Pt
De fest
En fixed
Es fijo
Fr fixe; fixé
It fisso; fissato

fixe *adj* Fr
De fest
En fixed
Es fijo
It fisso; fissato
Pt fixado

fixed *adj* En
De fest
Es fijo
Fr fixe; fixé
It fisso; fissato
Pt fixado

fixed assets En
De Anlagevermögen *(n)*
Es activo fijo *(m)*
Fr immobilisations *(f pl)*
It immobilizzazioni; attivo
    fisso *(f pl; m)*
Pt bens fixos *(m pl)*

fixed capital En
De feste Kapitalanlagen *(f pl)*
Es capital fijo *(m)*
Fr capital fixe *(m)*
It capitale fisso *(m)*
Pt capital fixado *(m)*

fixed deposit En
De Depositeneinlage *(f)*
Es depósito a plazo fijo *(m)*
Fr dépôt à terme (fixe) *(m)*
It deposito a termine fisso
    (m)
Pt depósito a prazo *(m)*

fixed-interest security En
De festverzinsliches Wert-
    papier *(n)*
Es obligación a interés fijo *(f)*
Fr valeur à revenu fixe *(f)*
It titolo a interesse fisso *(m)*
Pt obrigação de juro fixo *(f)*

fixed parity En
De feste Parität *(f)*
Es paridad fija *(f)*
Fr parité fixe *(f)*
It parità fissa *(f)*
Pt paridade fixa *(f)*

fixer des dommages-
    intérêts Fr
De den Schadenersatzbetrag
    feststellen
En assess damages
Es evaluar daños
It valutare i danni
Pt avaliar os danos

flach *adj* De
En flat
Es llano; plano
Fr plat; uniforme
It piatto
Pt plano; liso

flag *n* En
De Flagge *(f)*
Es bandera *(f)*
Fr pavillon; drapeau *(m)*
It bandiera *(f)*
Pt bandeira *(f)*

Flagge *(f) n* De
En flag
Es bandera *(f)*
Fr pavillon; drapeau *(m)*
It bandiera *(f)*
Pt bandeira *(f)*

flag of convenience En
De billige Flagge *(f)*
Es bandera de conveniencia
    (f)
Fr enseigne de convenance
    (f)
It bandiera di convenienza *(f)*
Pt bandeira de conveniência
    (f)

flat *n* En
Am apartment
De Etagenwohnung *(f)*
Es apartamento *(m)*
Fr appartement *(m)*
It appartamento *(m)*
Pt apartamento *(m)*

flat *adj* En
De flach
Es llano; plano
Fr plat; uniforme
It piatto
Pt plano; liso

flat rate En
De Einheitssatz *(m)*
Es tarifa unificada *(f)*
Fr tarif uniforme *(m)*

It tariffa uniforme *(f)*
Pt tarifa de base *(f)*

flau *adj* De
En bearish
Es bajista
Fr orienté à la baisse
It ribassista
Pt baixista

fleet *n* En
De Flotte *(f)*
Es flota *(f)*
Fr flotte *(f)*
It flotta *(f)*
Pt frota *(f)*

flessibile *adj* It
De flexibel; anpassungsfähig
En flexible
Es flexible
Fr flexible
Pt flexível

fletador *(m) n* Es
De Befrachter *(m)*
En charterer
Fr affréteur *(m)*
It noleggiatore *(m)*
Pt fretador *(m)*

fletamento *(m) n* Es
De Befrachtung *(f)*
En chartering
Fr affrètement *(m)*
It noleggio *(m)*
Pt fretamento *(m)*

fletamento de tiempo *(m)* Es
De Zeitcharter *(f)*
En time charter
Fr affrètement à temps *(m)*
It contratto di noleggio a
    tempo *(m)*
Pt fretamento de tempo *(m)*

flete *(m) n* Es
De Fracht *(f)*
En freight
Fr fret *(m)*
It nolo *(m)*
Pt frete *(m)*

flete aéreo *(m)* Es
De Luftfracht *(f)*
En air freight
Fr fret aérien *(m)*
It trasporto aereo *(m)*
Pt frete aéreo *(m)*

flete pagado Es
De Fracht vorausbezahlt
En freight pre-paid
Fr fret payé d'avance
It nolo prepagato
Pt frete pago

flexibilidade de preços *(f)* Pt
De Preisdehnbarkeit *(f)*
En price-elasticity
Es elasticidad de precio *(f)*
Fr élasticité-prix *(m)*
It elasticità di prezzo *(f)*

flexibel *adj* De
En flexible
Es flexible
Fr flexible
It flessibile
Pt flexível

flexible *adj* En, Es, Fr
De flexibel; anpassungsfähig
It flessibile
Pt flexível

flexibler Wechselkurs *(m)* De
En floating exchange rate
Es tipo de cambio flotante *(m)*
Fr taux de change flottant *(m)*
It cambio fluttuante *(m)*
Pt taxa de câmbio flutuante
    (f)

flexível *adj* Pt
De flexibel; anpassungsfähig
En flexible
Es flexible
Fr flexible
It flessibile

flight *n* En
De Flug *(f)*
Es vuelo *(m)*
Fr vol *(m)*
It volo *(m)*
Pt voo *(m)*

float a company En
De eine Gesellschaft gründen
Es lanzar una compañía
Fr lancer une entreprise
It lanciare una società
Pt lançar uma empresa

float a loan En
Am raise a loan
De eine Anleihe begeben
Es emitir un empréstito

Fr émettre un emprunt
It lanciare un prestito
Pt lançar um empréstimo

floating crane En
De Pontonkran *(m)*
Es grúa flotante *(f)*
Fr ponton-grue *(m)*
It gru galleggiante *(f)*
Pt guindaste flutuante *(m)*

floating exchange rate En
De flexibler Wechselkurs *(m)*
Es tipo de cambio flotante *(m)*
Fr taux de change flottant *(m)*
It cambio fluttuante *(m)*
Pt taxa de câmbio flutuante
    (f)

floating policy En
De laufende Police *(f)*
Es póliza flotante *(f)*
Fr police flottante *(f)*
It polizza flottante *(f)*
Pt apólice flutuante *(f)*

floor space En
De Bodenfläche *(f)*
Es superficie de piso *(f)*
Fr surface de plancher *(f)*
It superficie di pavimento *(f)*
Pt área de chão *(f)*

flota *(f)* n Es
De Flotte *(f)*
En fleet
Fr flotte *(f)*
It flotta *(f)*
Pt frota *(f)*

flota mercanto *(f)* Es
De Handelsflotte *(f)*
En merchant fleet
Fr flotte marchande *(f)*
It flotta mercantile *(f)*
Pt frota mercante *(f)*

flota pesquera *(f)* Es
De Fischerflotte *(f)*
En fishing fleet
Fr flottille de pêche *(f)*
It flotta peschereccia *(f)*
Pt frota de pesca *(f)*

flott *adv* De
En afloat
Es a flote
Fr à flot

It flottante
Pt flutuante

flotta *(f)* n It
De Flotte *(f)*
En fleet
Es flota *(f)*
Fr flotte *(f)*
Pt frota *(f)*

flotta mercantile *(f)* It
De Handelsflotte *(f)*
En merchant fleet
Es flota mercanto *(f)*
Fr flotte marchande *(f)*
Pt frota mercante *(f)*

flottante *adv* It
De flott
En afloat
Es a flote
Fr à flot
Pt flutuante

flotta peschereccia *(f)* It
De Fischerflotte *(f)*
En fishing fleet
Es flota pesquera *(f)*
Fr flottille de pêche *(f)*
Pt frota de pesca *(f)*

flotte *(f)* n Fr
De Flotte *(f)*
En fleet
Es flota *(f)*
It flotta *(f)*
Pt frota *(f)*

Flotte *(f)* n De
En fleet
Es flota *(f)*
Fr flotte *(f)*
It flotta *(f)*
Pt frota *(f)*

flotte marohande *(f)* Fr
De Handelsflotte *(f)*
En merchant fleet
Es flota mercanto *(f)*
It flotta mercantile *(f)*
Pt frota mercante *(f)*

flottille de pêche *(f)* Fr
De Fischerflotte *(f)*
En fishing fleet
Es flota pesquera *(f)*
It flotta peschereccia *(f)*
Pt frota de pesca *(f)*

flow n En
De Strom (m)
Es flujo (m)
Fr flux (m)
It flusso (m)
Pt circulação; fluxo (f m)

flow chart En
De Flußdiagramm (m)
Es diagrama de flujo (m)
Fr ordinogramme (m)
It diagramma di flusso (m)
Pt gráfico de operação (m)

fluctuación (f) n Es
De Schwankung (f)
En fluctuation
Fr fluctuation (f)
It fluttuazione (f)
Pt flutuação (f)

fluctuaciones estacionales
(f pl) Es
De saisonbedingte Schwankungen (f pl)
En seasonal fluctuations
Fr variations saisonnières (f pl)
It fluttuazioni stagionali (f pl)
Pt flutuações de época (f pl)

fluctuando adj Es
De schwankend
En fluctuating
Fr fluctuant
It fluttuante
Pt flutuando

fluctuant adj Fr
De schwankend
En fluctuating
Es fluctuando
It fluttuante
Pt flutuando

fluctuar vb Es
De schwanken
En fluctuate
Fr fluctuer
It fluttuare
Pt flutuar

fluctuate vb En
De schwanken
Es fluctuar
Fr fluctuer
It fluttuare
Pt flutuar

fluctuating adj En
De schwankend
Es fluctuando
Fr fluctuant
It fluttuante
Pt flutuando

fluctuating rate En
De schwankender Kurs (m)
Es tipo oscilante (m)
Fr taux variable (m)
It tasso variabile (m)
Pt taxa variável (f)

fluctuation n En, Fr (f)
De Schwankung (f)
Es fluctuación (f)
It fluttuazione (f)
Pt flutuação (f)

fluctuations de personnel
(f pl) Fr
De Arbeitsplatzwechsel (m)
En labour turnover
Es movimiento de la mano de obra (m)
It movimento della mano d'opera (m)
Pt movimento de trabalhadores (m)

fluctuer vb Fr
De schwanken
En fluctuate
Es fluctuar
It fluttuare
Pt flutuar

Flug (f) n De
En flight
Es vuelo (m)
Fr vol (m)
It volo (m)
Pt voo (m)

Fluggesellschaft (f) n De
En air line
Es línea aérea (f)
Fr compagnie aérienne (f)
It linea aerea (f)
Pt companhia de aviação (f)

Flughafen (m) n De
En airport
Es aeropuerto (m)
Fr aéroport (m)
It aeroporto (m)
Pt aeroporto (m)

fluidez (f) n Es, Pt
De Flüssigkeit (f)
En fluidity
Fr fluidité (f)
It fluidità (f)

fluidità (f) n It
De Flüssigkeit (f)
En fluidity
Es fluidez (f)
Fr fluidité (f)
Pt fluidez (f)

fluidité (f) n Fr
De Flüssigkeit (f)
En fluidity
Es fluidez (f)
It fluidità (f)
Pt fluidez (f)

fluidity n En
De Flüssigkeit (f)
Es fluidez (f)
Fr fluidité (f)
It fluidità (f)
Pt fluidez (f)

flujo (m) n Es
De Strom (m)
En flow
Fr flux (m)
It flusso (m)
Pt circulação; fluxo (f m)

flujo de caja (m) Es
De Cash-flow (m)
En cash flow
Fr cash flow (m)
It flusso di cassa (m)
Pt movimento em dinheiro (m)

flujo de caja descontado (m)
Es
De diskontierter Cash-flow (m)
En discounted cash flow (d.c.f.)
Fr flux monétaire actualisé (m)
It flusso di cassa scontato (m)
Pt movimento em dinheiro descontado (m)

Flußdiagramm (m) n De
En flow chart
Es diagrama de flujo (m)
Fr ordinogramme (m)

It diagramma di flusso *(m)*
Pt gráfico de operação *(m)*

flüssige Aktiven *(n pl)* De
En liquid assets
Es activo líquido *(m)*
Fr actif liquide *(m)*
It disponibilità; attività liquida *(f)*
Pt bens de activo líquidos *(m pl)*

flüssige Mittel *(n pl)* De
En funds available
Es fondos disponibles *(m pl)*
Fr disponibilités *(f pl)*
It fondi disponibili *(m pl)*
Pt fundos disponíveis *(m pl)*

Flüssigkeit *(f)* n De
En fluidity
Es fluidez *(f)*
Fr fluidité *(f)*
It fluidità *(f)*
Pt fluidez *(f)*

flusso *(m)* n It
De Strom *(m)*
En flow
Es flujo *(m)*
Fr flux *(m)*
Pt circulação; fluxo *(f m)*

flusso di cassa *(m)* It
De Cash-flow *(m)*
En cash flow
Es flujo de caja *(m)*
Fr cash flow *(m)*
Pt movimento em dinheiro *(m)*

flusso di cassa scontato *(m)* It
De diskontierter Cash-flow *(m)*
En discounted cash flow (d.c.f.)
Es flujo de caja descontado *(m)*
Fr flux monétaire actualisé *(m)*
Pt movimento em dinheiro descontado *(m)*

fluttuante *adj* It
De schwankend
En fluctuating
Es fluctuando

Fr fluctuant
Pt flutuando

fluttuare *vb* It
De schwanken
En fluctuate
Es fluctuar
Fr fluctuer
Pt flutuar

fluttuazione *(f)* n It
De Schwankung *(f)*
En fluctuation
Es fluctuación *(f)*
Fr fluctuation *(f)*
Pt flutuação *(f)*

fluttuazioni stagionali *(f pl)* It
De saisonbedingte Schwankungen *(f pl)*
En seasonal fluctuations
Es fluctuaciones estacionales *(f pl)*
Fr variations saisonnières *(f pl)*
Pt flutuações de época *(f pl)*

flutuação *(f)* n Pt
De Schwankung *(f)*
En fluctuation
Es fluctuación *(f)*
Fr fluctuation *(f)*
It fluttuazione *(f)*

flutuações de época *(f pl)* Pt
De saisonbedingte Schwankungen *(f pl)*
En seasonal fluctuations
Es fluctuaciones estacionales *(f pl)*
Fr variations saisonnières *(f pl)*
It fluttuazioni stagionali *(f pl)*

flutuando *adj* Pt
De schwankend
En fluctuating
Es fluctuando
Fr fluctuant
It fluttuante

flutuante *adv* Pt
De flott
En afloat
Es a flote
Fr à flot
It flottante

flutuar *vb* Pt
De schwanken
En fluctuate
Es fluctuar
Fr fluctuer
It fluttuare

flux *(m)* n Fr
De Strom *(m)*
En flow
Es flujo *(m)*
It flusso *(m)*
Pt circulação; fluxo *(f m)*

flux monétaire actualisé *(m)* Fr
De diskontierter Cash-flow *(m)*
En discounted cash flow (d.c.f.)
Es flujo de caja descontado *(m)*
It flusso di cassa scontato *(m)*
Pt movimento em dinheiro descontado *(m)*

fluxo *(m)* n Pt
De Strom *(m)*
En flow
Es flujo *(m)*
Fr flux *(m)*
It flusso *(m)*

foglio d'ordinazione *(m)* It
De Bestellformular *(n)*
En order-form
Es solicitud de pedido *(f)*
Fr bulletin de commande *(m)*
Pt impresso de encomenda *(m)*

fogo *(m)* n Pt
De Brand *(m)*
En fire
Es fuego; incendio *(m)*
Fr incendie *(f)*
It incendio *(m)*

foire *(f)* n Fr
De Messe *(f)*
En fair
Es feria *(f)*
It fiera *(f)*
Pt feira *(f)*

foire commerciale *(f)* Fr
De Handelsmesse *(f)*
En trade fair

Es feria de muestras *(f)*
It fiera commerciale *(f)*
Pt feira comercial *(f)*

folder *n* En
De Mappe *(f)*
Es carpeta *(f)*
Fr chemise *(f)*
It cartella *(f)*
Pt pasta *(f)*

Folgeschaden *(m) n* De
En consequential loss
Es pérdida indirecta *(f)*
Fr perte indirect *(f)*
It perdita indiretta *(f)*
Pt perda por consequência *(f)*

folha de salários *(f)* Pt
De Lohnbuch *(n)*
En payroll
Es nómina de pago *(f)*
Fr feuille de paie *(f)*
It libro paga *(m)*

folheto publicitário *(m)* Pt
De Werbeschrift *(f)*
En advertising brochure
Es folleto publicitario *(m)*
Fr prospectus publicitaire *(m)*
It opuscolo pubblicitario *(m)*

folleto publicitario *(m)* Es
De Werbeschrift *(f)*
En advertising brochure
Fr prospectus publicitaire *(m)*
It opuscolo pubblicitario *(m)*
Pt folheto publicitário *(m)*

follow up En
De weiterverfolgen
Es perseguir
Fr poursuivre
It seguitare
Pt perseguir

fomento *(m) n* Pt
De Förderung *(f)*
En promotion
Es promoción *(f)*
Fr promotion *(f)*
It promozione *(f)*

fonction *(f) n* Fr
De Aufgabe *(f)*
En function
Es función *(f)*
It funzione *(f)*
Pt função *(f)*

fonctionnaire *(m) n* Fr
De Beamte(r) *(m)*
En civil servant
Am government employee
Es funcionario del gobierno *(m)*
It impiegato statale *(m)*
Pt funcionário público *(m)*

fonctionnel *adj* Fr
De sachlich; praktisch
En functional
Es funcional
It funzionale
Pt funcional

fonctionnel *(m) n* Fr
De persönlicher Assistent *(m)*
En personal assistant *(m)*
Am administrative assistant
Es asistente privado *(m)*
It assistente privato *(m)*
Pt secretário *(m)*

fondare *vb* It
De einrichten; gründen
En establish; found
Es fundar; establecer
Fr fonder; établir
Pt fundar; estabelecer

fondateur *(m) n* Fr
De Gründer *(m)*
En founder
Es fundador *(m)*
It fondatore *(m)*
Pt fundador *(m)*

fondatore *(m) n* It
De Gründer *(m)*
En founder
Es fundador *(m)*
Fr fondateur *(m)*
Pt fundador *(m)*

fonder (établir) *vb* Fr
De einrichten; gründen
En establish; found
Es fundar; establecer
It fondare; istituire
Pt fundar; estabelecer

fonder (une créance) *vb* Fr
De fundieren
En fund
Es fundar; consolidar
It consolidare
Pt dotar de fundos

fondersi *vb* It
De fusionieren
En amalgamate
Am merge
Es amalgamar
Fr fusionner
Pt amalgamar

fondi disponibili *(m pl)* It
De flüssige Mittel *(n pl)*
En funds available
Es fondos disponibles *(m pl)*
Fr disponibilités *(f pl)*
Pt fundos disponíveis *(m pl)*

fondo *(m) n* Es, It
De Fonds *(m)*
En fund
Fr fonds *(m)*
Pt fundos *(m pl)*

fondo circulante *(m)* Es
De Umlaufkapital *(n)*
En revolving fund
Fr fonds renouvelable *(m)*
It fondo rotativo *(m)*
Pt fundos renováveis *(m pl)*

fondo de amortización *(m)* Es
De Tilgungsfonds *(m)*
En sinking fund
Fr fonds d'amortissement *(m)*
It fondo di ammortamento *(m)*
Pt fundo de amortização *(m)*

fondo de compensación *(m)* Es
De Ausgleichsfonds *(m)*
En equalization fund
Fr fonds de régularisation *(m)*
It cassa di compensazione *(f)*
Pt fundo de compensação *(m)*

fondo de reserva *(m)* Es
De Reservefonds *(m)*
En reserve fund
Fr fonds de réserve *(m)*
It fondo di riserva *(m)*
Pt fundo de reserva *(m)*

fondo di ammortamento *(m)* It
De Tilgungsfonds *(m)*
En sinking fund
Es fondo de amortización *(m)*

Fr fonds d'amortissement *(m)*
Pt fundo de amortização *(m)*

fondo di riserva *(m)* It
De Reservefonds *(m)*
En reserve fund
Es fondo de reserva *(m)*
Fr fonds de réserve *(m)*
Pt fundo de reserva *(m)*

Fondo Europeo *(m)* Es, It
De Europäischer Fonds *(m)*
En European Fund
Fr Fonds Européen *(m)*
Pt Fundo Europou *(m)*

fondo fiduciario *(m)* Es, It
De Treuhandfonds *(m)*
En trust fund
Fr fonds fiduciaire *(m)*
Pt fundação fiduciária *(f)*

**fondo fiduciario discrezio-
nale** *(m)* It
De unumschränkte Treuhand
   (f)
En discretionary trust
Es fideicomiso discrecional
   (m)
Fr fidéicommis à apprécia-
   tion *(m)*
Pt fundação discricionária *(f)*

**Fondo Monetario Interna-
cional** *(m)* Es
De Internationaler Währungs-
   fonds (IWF)*(m)*
En International Monetary
   Fund (IMF)
Fr Fonds Monétaire Interna-
   tional (F.M.I.)*(m)*
It Fondo Monetario Inter-
   nazionale *(m)*
Pt Fundo Monetário Inter-
   nacional *(m)*

**Fondo Monetario Inter-
nazionale** *(m)* It
De Internationaler Währungs-
   fonds (IWF)*(m)*
En International Monetary
   Fund (IMF)
Es Fondo Monetario Inter-
   nacional *(m)*
Fr Fonds Monétaire Interna-
   tional (F.M.I.) *(m)*
Pt Fundo Monetário Inter-
   nacional *(m)*

fondo rotativo *(m)* It
De Umlaufkapital *(n)*
En revolving fund
Es fondo circulante *(m)*
Fr fonds renouvelable *(m)*
Pt fundos renováveis *(m pl)*

fondos disponibles *(m pl)* Es
De flüssige Mittel *(n pl)*
En funds available
Fr disponibilités *(f pl)*
It fondi disponibili *(m pl)*
Pt fundos disponíveis *(m pl)*

fonds *(m)* n Fr
De Fonds *(m)*
En fund
Es fondo *(m)*
It fondo *(m)*
Pt fundos *(m pl)*

Fonds *(m)* n De
En fund
Es fondo *(m)*
Fr fonds *(m)*
It fondo *(m)*
Pt fundos *(m pl)*

fonds bloqués *(m pl)* Fr
De eingefrorene Guthaben *(n
   pl)*
En frozen assets
Es activos congelados *(m pl)*
It attivo congelato *(m)*
Pt bens do activo congela-
   dos *(m pl)*

fonds d'amortissement *(m)*
   Fr
De Tilgungsfonds *(m)*
En sinking fund
Es fondo de amortización *(m)*
It fondo di ammortamento
   (m)
Pt fundo de amortização *(m)*

fonds de régularisation *(m)*
   Fr
De Ausgleichsfonds *(m)*
En equalization fund
Es fondo de compensación
   (m)
It cassa di compensazione
   (f)
Pt fundo de compensação *(m)*

fonds de réserve *(m)* Fr
De Reservefonds *(m)*
En reserve fund

Es fondo de reserva *(m)*
It fondo di riserva *(m)*
Pt fundo de reserva *(m)*

fonds de roulement *(m)* Fr
De Betriebskapital *(n)*
En trading capital
Es capital de explotación *(m)*
It capitale d'esercizio *(m)*
Pt capital de exploração *(m)*

**fonds de stabilisation des
   changes** *(m pl)* Fr
De Währungsausgleichs-
   fonds *(m)*
En exchange equalization
   account
Es cuenta de compensación
   de cambio *(f)*
It conto per la stabilizzazione dei cambi *(m)*
Pt conta de compensação de
   transacções *(f)*

Fonds Européen *(m)* Fr
De Europäischer Fonds *(m)*
En European Fund
Es Fondo Europeo *(m)*
It Fondo Europeo *(m)*
Pt Fundo Europeu *(m)*

fonds fiduciaire *(m)* Fr
De Treuhandfonds *(m)*
En trust fund
Es fondo fiduciario *(m)*
It fondo fiduciario *(m)*
Pt fundação fiduciária *(f)*

**Fonds Monétaire Interna-
   tional** (F.M.I.) *(m)* Fr
De Internationaler Währungs-
   fonds (IWF)*(m)*
En International Monetary
   Fund (IMF)
Es Fondo Monetario Inter-
   nacional *(m)*
It Fondo Monetario Inter-
   nazionale *(m)*
Pt Fundo Monetário Inter-
   nacional *(m)*

fonds renouvelable *(m)* Fr
De Umlaufkapital *(n)*
En revolving fund
Es fondo circulante *(m)*
It fondo rotativo *(m)*
Pt fundos renováveis *(m pl)*

foodstuffs (pl) n En
De Eßwaren (f pl)
Es comestibles (m pl)
Fr alimentation (f)
It generi alimentari (m pl)
Pt géneros alimentícios (m pl)

footnote n En
De Fußnote (f)
Es apostilla (f)
Fr apostille (f)
It postilla (f)
Pt nota de rcdapé (f)

força (f) n Pt
De Gewalt (f)
En force
Es fuerza (f)
Fr force (f)
It forza (f)

forçado adj Pt
De Zwangs-
En forced
Es forzado
Fr forcé
It forzato

forças armadas (f pl) Pt
De Streitkräfte (f pl)
En armed forces
Es fuerzas armadas (f pl)
Fr forces armées (f pl)
It forze armate (f pl)

forças de mercado (f pl) Pt
De Marktkräfte (f pl)
En market forces
Es fuerzas del mercado (f pl)
Fr forces du marché (f pl)
It forze di mercato (f pl)

force n En, Fr (f)
De Gewalt (f)
Es fuerza (f)
It forza (f)
Pt força (f)

forcé adj Fr
De Zwangs-
En forced
Es forzado
It forzato
Pt forçado

forced adj En
De Zwangs-
Es forzado
Fr forcé

It forzato
Pt forçado

forced liquidation Am
En compulsory winding-up
De Zwangsliquidation (f)
Es liquidación forzosa (f)
Fr liquidation forcée (f)
It liquidazione forzata (f)
Pt liquidação forçada (f)

forced sale En
De Zwangsverkauf (m)
Es venta forzosa (f)
Fr vente forcée (f)
It vendita forzosa (f)
Pt venda forçada (f)

forces armées (f pl) Fr
De Streitkräfte (f pl)
En armed forces
Es fuerzas armadas (f pl)
It forze armate (f pl)
Pt forças armadas (f pl)

forces du marché (f pl) Fr
De Marktkräfte (f pl)
En market forces
Es fuerzas del mercado (f pl)
It forze di mercato (f pl)
Pt forças de mercado (f pl)

fördern vb De
En promote
Es promover
Fr promouvoir
It dare impulso a
Pt promover

Forderung (f) n De
En claim; demand
Es reclamación (f)
Fr demande (f)
It domanda (f)
Pt reclamação (f)

Förderung (f) n De
En promotion
Es promoción (f)
Fr promotion (f)
It promozione (f)
Pt fomento (m)

forecast vb En
De vorhersehen
Es pronosticar
Fr prévoir
It pronosticare
Pt prognosticar

forecasting n En
De Voraussage (f)
Es pronóstico (m)
Fr prévision (f)
It previsione (f)
Pt previsão (f)

foreclosure n En
De Zwangsvollstreckung (f)
Es venta por juicio hipoteca-
rio (f)
Fr vente de l'immeuble
hypothéqué (f)
It vendita per giudizio ipote-
cario (f)
Pt execução judicial a uma
hipoteca (f)

foreign adj En
De ausländisch; fremd
Es extranjero
Fr étranger
It straniero; estero
Pt estrangeiro

foreign bill En
De Auslandswechsel (m)
Es letra sobre el exterior (f)
Fr lettre de change sur
l'étranger (f)
It cambiale sull'estero (f)
Pt letra de país a país (cam-
bial) (f)

foreign currency En
De Devisen (f pl)
Es divisas extranjeras (f pl)
Fr devises (f pl)
It valuta estera (f)
Pt moeda estrangeira (f)

foreign currency account
Am
En external account
De Auslandskonto (n)
Es cuenta exterior (f)
Fr compte transférable (m)
It conto estero (m)
Pt conta externa (f)

foreigner n En
De Ausländer (m)
Es extranjero m
Fr étranger (m)
It straniero (m)
Pt estrangeiro (m)

foreign exchange En
De Devisen *(f pl)*
Es divisas extranjeras *(f pl)*
Fr devises *(f pl)*
It valuta estera *(f)*
Pt moeda estrangeira *(f)*

foreign exchange rates En
De Devisenkurse *(m)*
Es tasas de cambio exterior
   (f pl)
Fr cours des changes *(m)*
It corso dei cambi *(m)*
Pt taxas de câmbio *(f pl)*

foreign labour En
De Fremdarbeiterschaft *(f)*
Es mano de obra extranjera *(f)*
Fr main-d'œuvre étrangère *(f)*
It mano d'opera straniera *(f)*
Pt mão-de-obra estrangeira
   (f)

foreign trade En
De Außenhandel *(m)*
Es comercio exterior *(m)*
Fr commerce extérieur *(m)*
It commercio estero *(m)*
Pt comércio externo *(m)*

foreman *n* En
De Vorarbeiter *(m)*
Es capataz *(m)*
Fr contremaître; chef
   d'équipe *(m)*
It capo operaio; capo squa-
   dra *(m)*
Pt encarregado; capataz *(m)*

forfeit clause En
De Bußklausel *(f)*
Es cláusula de decomiso *(f)*
Fr clause de dédit *(f)*
It clausola di penalità per
   inadempienza *(f)*
Pt cláusula de cedência *(f)*

forge *vb* En
De fälschen
Es falsificar
Fr contrefaire
It contraffare
Pt falsificar

forged cheque En
De gefälschter Scheck *(m)*
Es cheque falsificado *(m)*
Fr faux chèque *(m)*

It assegno falsificato *(m)*
Pt cheque falsificado *(m)*

forger *n* En
De Fälscher *(m)*
Es falsificador *(m)*
Fr faux-monnayeur; faus-
   saire *(m)*
It falsificatore *(m)*
Pt falsificador *(m)*

forgery *n* En
De Fälschung *(f)*
Es falsificación *(f)*
Fr contrefaçon; faux *(f m)*
It falsificazione *(f)*
Pt falsificação *(f)*

form (printed sheet) *n* En
De Formular *(n)*
Es formulario *(m)*
Fr formule *(f)*
It modulo *(m)*
Pt formulário *(m)*

form (shape) En
De Form *(f)*
Es forma *(f)*
Fr forme *(f)*
It forma *(f)*
Pt forma *(f)*

form (constitute) *vb* En
De bilden
Es constituir
Fr constituer
It costituire
Pt constituir

form (establish) *vb* En
De gründen
Es establecer; formar
Fr former
It formare
Pt estabelecer

Form *(f)* De
En form
Es forma *(f)*
Fr forme *(f)*
It forma *(f)*
Pt forma *(f)*

forma *(f)* Es, It, Pt
De Form *(f)*
En form
Fr forme *(f)*

formación profesional *(f)* Es
De Berufsausbildung *(f)*
En vocational training
Fr formation professionnelle
   (f)
It addestramento professio-
   nale *(m)*
Pt treino vocacional *(m)*

formal *adj* En, Es, Pt
De formell
Fr formel
It formale

formale *adj* It
De formell
En formal
Es formal
Fr formel
Pt formal

formalidad *(f)* *n* Es
De Formalität *(f)*
En formality
Fr formalité *(f)*
It formalità *(f)*
Pt formalidade *(f)*

formalidade *(f)* *n* Pt
De Formalität *(f)*
En formality
Es formalidad *(f)*
Fr formalité *(f)*
It formalità *(f)*

formalità *(f)* *n* It
De Formalität *(f)*
En formality
Es formalidad *(f)*
Fr formalité *(f)*
Pt formalidade *(f)*

Formalität *(f)* *n* De
En formality
Es formalidad *(f)*
Fr formalité *(f)*
It formalità *(f)*
Pt formalidade *(f)*

formalité *(f)* *n* Fr
De Formalität *(f)*
En formality
Es formalidad *(f)*
It formalità *(f)*
Pt formalidade *(f)*

formalités douanières
   (f pl) Fr
De Verzollung *(f)*
En customs clearance

Es despacho de aduana *(m)*
It sdoganamento *(m)*
Pt despacho de alfândega *(m)*

formality *n* En
De Formalität *(f)*
Es formalidad *(f)*
Fr formalité *(f)*
It formalità *(f)*
Pt formalidade *(f)*

formal notice En
De Inverzugsetzung *(f)*
Es aviso oficial *(m)*
Fr mise en demeure *(f)*
It intimazione *(f)*
Pt notificação formal *(f)*

formare *vb* It
De gründen
En form
Es establecer; formar
Fr former
Pt estabelecer

formation professionnelle *(f)* Fr
De Berufsausbildung *(f)*
En vocational training
Es formación profesional *(f)*
It addestramento professionale *(m)*
Pt treino vocacional *(m)*

forme *(f)* *n* Fr
De Form *(f)*
En form
Es forma *(f)*
It forma *(f)*
Pt forma *(f)*

formel *adj* Fr
De formell
En formal
Es formal
It formale
Pt formal

Formel *(f)* *n* De
En formula
Es fórmula *(f)*
Fr formule *(f)*
It formula *(f)*
Pt fórmula *(f)*

formell *adj* De
En formal
Es formal

Fr formel
It formale
Pt formal

former *vb* Fr
De gründen
En form
Es establecer; formar
It formare
Pt estabelecer

formlos (nicht formell) *adj* De
En informal
Es sin ceremonia
Fr sans formalités
It senza formalità
Pt sem formalidade

formula *n* En, It *(f)*
De Formel *(f)*
Es fórmula *(f)*
Fr formule *(f)*
Pt fórmula *(f)*

fórmula *(f)* *n* Es, Pt
De Formel *(f)*
En formula
Fr formule *(f)*
It formula *(f)*

formulaire *(m)* *n* Fr
De Vordruck *(m)*
En printed form
Es formulario; impreso *(m)*
It modulo stampato *(m)*
Pt impresso *(m)*

formulaire de demande *(m)* Fr
De Antragsformular *(n)*
En application form
Es formulario de solicitud *(m)*
It modulo di domanda *(m)*
Pt formulário de requisição *(m)*

formulaire en blanc *(m)* Fr
De Blankoformular *(n)*
En blank form
Es formulario en blanco *(m)*
It modulo in bianco *(m)*
Pt impresso em branco *(m)*

Formular *(n)* *n* De
En form
Es formulario *(m)*
Fr formule *(f)*
It modulo *(m)*
Pt formulário *(m)*

formulario *(m)* *n* Es
De Formular *(n)*
En form
Fr formule *(f)*
It modulo *(m)*
Pt formulário *(m)*

formulário *(m)* *n* Pt
De Formular *(n)*
En form
Es formulario *(m)*
Fr formule *(f)*
It modulo *(m)*

formulário de requisição *(m)* Pt
De Antragsformular *(n)*
En application form
Es formulario de solicitud *(m)*
Fr formulaire de demande *(m)*
It modulo di domanda *(m)*

formulario de solicitud *(m)* Es
De Antragsformular *(n)*
En application form
Fr formulaire de demande *(m)*
It modulo di domanda *(m)*
Pt formulário de requisição *(m)*

formulario en blanco *(m)* Es
De Blankoformular *(n)*
En blank form
Fr formulaire en blanc *(m)*
It modulo in bianco *(m)*
Pt impresso em branco *(m)*

formule *(f)* *n* Fr
De Formel *(f)*
En formula
Es fórmula *(f)*
It formula *(f)*
Pt fórmula *(f)*

formule (imprimée) *(f)* *n* Fr
De Formular *(n)*
En form
Es formulario *(m)*
It modulo *(m)*
Pt formulário *(m)*

fornecedor *(m)* *n* Pt
De Lieferant *(m)*
En supplier
Es proveedor *(m)*
Fr fournisseur *(m)*
It fornitore *(m)*

fornecer *vb* Pt
De beliefern
En supply
Es surtir
Fr fournir
It fornire

**fornecimentos em
existência** *(m pl)* Pt
De lieferfertiges Angebot *(n)*
En supplies on hand
Es provisiones existentes *(f
pl)*
Fr ressources existantes *(f pl)*
It forniture esistenti *(f pl)*

fornire *vb* It
De beliefern
En supply
Es surtir
Fr fournir
Pt fornecer

fornitore *(m) n* It
De Lieferant *(m)*
En supplier
Es proveedor *(m)*
Fr fournisseur *(m)*
Pt fornecedor *(m)*

forniture esistenti *(f pl)* It
De lieferfertiges Angebot *(n)*
En supplies on hand
Es provisiones existentes
(f pl)
Fr ressources existantes *(f pl)*
Pt fornecimentos em
existência *(m pl)*

Forschung *(f) n* De
En research
Es investigación *(f)*
Fr recherche *(f)*
It ricerca *(f)*
Pt investigação *(f)*

Fortbildung *(f) n* De
En higher education
Es enseñanza superior *(f)*
Fr enseignement supérieur
(m)
It insegnamento superiore
(m)
Pt instrução superior *(f)*

forte amende *(f)* Fr
De schwere Buße *(f)*
En heavy fine
Es sanción elevada *(f)*

It forte multa *(f)*
Pt multa pesada *(f)*

forte multa *(f)* It
De schwere Buße *(f)*
En heavy fine
Es sanción elevada *(f)*
Fr forte amende *(f)*
Pt multa pesada *(f)*

forte perdita *(f)* It
De schwere Verluste *(m pl)*
En heavy loss
Es fuerte pérdida; pérdida
sensible *(f)*
Fr lourde perte *(f)*
Pt perda avultada *(f)*

**Fortfall der Geschäfts-
grundlage** *(m)* De
En frustration
Es frustración *(f)*
Fr frustration *(f)*
It frustrazione *(f)*
Pt frustração *(f)*

forthcoming *adj* En
De bevorstehend
Es próximo
Fr prochain
It prossimo
Pt próximo

forti spese *(f pl)* It
De drückende Spesen *(f pl)*
En heavy charges
Es gastos fuertes *(m pl)*
Fr charges lourdes *(f pl)*
Pt encargos pesados *(m pl)*

forward *adj* En
De Termin-
Es a término
Fr en avant; à terme
It a termine
Pt adiante

forward *vb* En
De expedieren; absenden
Es expedir; remitir
Fr envoyer; expédier
It spedire
Pt expedir; remeter

forward dealings En
De Zeitgeschäfte *(n pl)*
Es negociaciones a término
(f pl)
Fr opérations à terme *(f pl)*

It operazioni a termine *(f pl)*
Pt transacções adiantadas
(f pl)

forward delivery En
De Terminlieferung *(f)*
Es entrega futura *(f)*
Fr livraison à terme *(f)*
It consegna a termine *(f)*
Pt entrega futura *(f)*

forward exchange En
De Termindevisen *(f pl)*
Es divisas a término *(f pl)*
Fr change à terme *(m)*
It cambio a termine *(m)*
Pt divisas adiantada *(f pl)*

forwarding agent En
De Spediteur *(m)*
Es agente expedidor *(m)*
Fr transitaire *(m)*
It spedizioniere *(m)*
Pt agente expedidor *(m)*

forward price En
De Terminnotierung *(f)*
Es precio a término *(m)*
Fr cours à terme *(m)*
It prezzo per futura conse-
gna *(m)*
Pt preço adiantado *(m)*

forza *(f) n* It
De Gewalt *(f)*
En force
Es fuerza *(f)*
Fr force *(f)*
Pt força *(f)*

forzado *adj* Es
De Zwangs-
En forced
Fr forcé
It forzato
Pt forçado

forzato *adj* It
De Zwangs-
En forced
Es forzado
Fr forcé
Pt forçado

forze armate *(f pl)* It
De Streitkräfte *(f pl)*
En armed forces
Es fuerzas armadas *(f pl)*
Fr forces armées *(f pl)*
Pt forças armadas *(f pl)*

forze di mercato *(f pl)* It
De Marktkräfte *(f pl)*
En market forces
Es fuerzas del mercado *(f pl)*
Fr forces du marché *(f pl)*
Pt forças de mercado *(f pl)*

forze di vendita *(f pl)* It
De Verkaufspersonal *(n)*
En sales force
Es personal de ventas *(m)*
Fr personnel de vente *(m)*
Pt pessoal de vendas *(m)*

foudre *(f) n* Fr
De Blitz *m*
En lightning
Es relámpago *(m)*
It fulmine *(m)*
Pt relâmpago *(m)*

foul (dirty) bill of lading En
De einschränkendes Konnos-
    sement *(n)*
Es conocimiento de embar-
    que con objecciones *(m)*
Fr connaissement avec
    réserve *(m)*
It polizza di carico con riser-
    ve *(f)*
Pt conhecimento com
    embargos *(m)*

found *vb* En
De gründen
Es fundar
Fr fonder
It fondare
Pt fundar

founder *n* En
De Gründer *(m)*
Es fundador *(m)*
Fr fondateur *(m)*
It fondatore *(m)*
Pt fundador *(m)*

founder member En
De Gründermitglied *(m)*
Es meimbro fundador *(m)*
Fr membre fondateur *(m)*
It socio fondatore *(m)*
Pt membro fundador *(m)*

founder's shares En
De Gründeraktien *(f pl)*
Es acciones del fundador
    (f pl)
Fr actions de fondateur *(f pl)*

It azioni del fondatore *(f pl)*
Pt acções de fundador *(f pl)*

fourgon *(m) n* Fr
De Packwagen *(m)*
En guard's van
Es furgón *(m)*
It bagagliaio *(m)*
Pt furgão *(m)*

fournir *vb* Fr
De beliefern
En supply
Es surtir
It fornire
Pt fornecer

fournisseur *(m) n* Fr
De Lieferant *(m)*
En supplier
Es proveedor *(m)*
It fornitore *(m)*
Pt fornecedor *(m)*

fracção *(f) n* Pt
De Bruchteil *(n)*
En fraction
Es fracción *(f)*
Fr fraction *(f)*
It frazione *(f)*

fracción *(f) n* Es
De Bruchteil *(n)*
En fraction
Fr fraction *(f)*
It frazione *(f)*
Pt fracção *(f)*

fraccionamiento de la carga
    (m) Es
De Löschen der Ladung *(n)*
En breaking bulk
Fr rupture de charge *(f)*
It inizio scarico *(m)*
Pt retalhar a carga

Fracht *(f) n* De
En freight
Es flete *(m)*
Fr fret *(m)*
It nolo *(f)*
Pt frete *(m)*

Frachtbrief *(m) n* De
En consignment note
Es nota de consignación *(f)*
Fr lettre de voiture *(f)*
It nota di spedizione *(f)*
Pt guia de transporte *(f)*

frachtfrei *adv* De
En carriage free
Am F.O.B. destination
Es franco de porte
Fr franco
It porto franco
Pt porte grátis

Frachtschiff *(n) n* De
En cargo boat
Es buque de carga *(m)*
Fr cargo *(m)*
It nave da carico *(f)*
Pt navio de carga *(m)*

Fracht vorausbezahlt De
En freight pre-paid
Es flete pagado
Fr fret payé d'avance
It nolo prepagato
Pt frete pago

fraction *n* En, Fr *(f)*
De Bruchteil *(n)*
Es fracción *(f)*
It frazione *(f)*
Pt fracção *(f)*

Fragebogen *(m) n* De
En questionnaire
Es cuestionario *(m)*
Fr questionnaire *(m)*
It questionario *(m)*
Pt questionário *(m)*

frágil *adj* Es, Pt
De zerbrechlich
En fragile
Fr fragile
It fragile

fragile *adj* En, Fr, It
De zerbrechlich
Es frágil
Pt frágil

frais *(m pl) n* Fr
De Kosten; Ausgaben *(pl; f pl)*
En charges; expenditure
Es costes; desembolso
    (m pl; m)
It spesa; spese *(f; f pl)*
Pt despesa; despesas *(f; f pl)*

**frais à percevoir à la livrai-
    son** Fr
De per Nachnahme
En charges forward
Es costes a reembolso

It   spese assegnate
Pt   entrega contra reembolso

frais bancaires *(m pl)* Fr
De   Bankspesen *(f pl)*
En   bank charges
Es   gastos de banco *(m pl)*
It   spese di banca *(f pl)*
Pt   taxas bancárias *(f pl)*

frais commerciaux *(m pl)* Fr
De   Geschäftskosten *(pl)*
En   business expenses
Es   gastos de los negocios
     (m pl)
It   spese generali *(f pl)*
Pt   despesas do exercício
     (f pl)

frais de magasinage *(m pl)* Fr
De   Lagergeld *(n)*
En   storage charges
Es   gastos de almacenaje
     (m pl)
It   spese di magazzinaggio
     (f pl)
Pt   encargos de armazena-
     mento *(m pl)*

frais de manutention *(m pl)* Fr
De   Umschlagspesen *(f)*
En   handling charges
Es   gastos de manutención
     (m pl)
It   spese di gestione *(f pl)*
Pt   custas de manejo *(f pl)*

frais d'encaissement *(m pl)*
     Fr
De   Einzugskosten *(pl)*
En   collection charges
Es   gastos de cobranza *(m pl)*
It   spese di riscossione *(f pl)*
Pt   gastos de cobrança *(m pl)*

frais de poste *(m pl)* Fr
De   Postspesen *(f pl)*
En   postage; postal charges
Es   gastos de correo *(m pl)*
It   spese postali *(f pl)*
Pt   despesas de franquia *(f pl)*

frais de représentation
     (m pl) Fr
De   Repräsentationskosten
     (pl)
En   entertainment expenses
Es   gastos de representación
     (m pl)

It   spese di rappresentanza
     (f pl)
Pt   despesas de representação
     (f pl)

frais de vente *(m)* Fr
De   Verkaufskosten *(pl)*
En   selling cost
Es   coste de venta *(m)*
It   costo di vendita *(m)*
Pt   custo de venda *(m)*

frais de voyage *(m pl)* Fr
De   Reisekosten *(pl)*
En   travelling expenses
Es   dietas de viajes *(f pl)*
It   spese di viaggio *(f pl)*
Pt   despesas de viagem *(f pl)*

frais d'exploitation *(m pl)* Fr
De   Betriebsausgaben *(f pl)*
En   operating costs
Es   costes operacionales
     (m pl)
It   spese di gestione *(f pl)*
Pt   custos de exercício *(m pl)*

frais directs *(m pl)* Fr
De   Einzelkosten *(pl)*
En   direct expenses
Es   gastos directos *(m pl)*
It   spese dirette *(f pl)*
Pt   despesas directas *(f pl)*

frais divers *(m pl)* Fr
De   verschiedene Ausgaben
     (f pl)
En   sundry expenses
Es   gastos varios *(m pl)*
It   spese varie *(f pl)*
Pt   despesas diversas *(f pl)*

frais généraux *(m pl)* Fr
De   allgemeine Unkosten;
     Generalunkosten *(pl)*
En   general expenses;
     overheads
Es   gastos generales *(m pl)*
It   spese generali *(f pl)*
Pt   despesas gerais *(f pl)*

frais indirects *(m pl)* Fr
De   Gemeinkosten *(pl)*
En   indirect costs
Es   costes indirectos *(m pl)*
It   costi indiretti *(m pl)*
Pt   custos indirectos *(m pl)*

franc d'avarie particulière
     Fr
De   frei von besonderer
     Havarie
En   free of particular average
     (fpa)
Es   franco de avería particular
It   franco di avaria particolare
Pt   franco de avaria particular

franc de toutes avaries Fr
De   ganz havariefrei
En   free of all averages
Es   franco de toda avería
It   franco d'ogni avaria
Pt   franco do todas as avarias

franchigia *(f)* n It
De   Franchise *(f)*
En   exemption
Es   franquicia *(f)*
Fr   franchise *(f)*
Pt   franquia *(f)*

franchise (concession) n En
De   Konzession *(f)*
Es   concesión *(f)*
Fr   concession *(f)*
It   concessione *(f)*
Pt   concessão *(f)*

franchise *(f)* n Fr
De   Franchise *(f)*
En   exemption
Es   franquicia *(f)*
It   franchigia *(f)*
Pt   franquia *(f)*

Franchise *(f)* n De
En   exemption
Es   franquicia *(f)*
Fr   franchise *(f)*
It   franchigia *(f)*
Pt   franquia *(f)*

franco *adv* Fr
De   frachtfrei
En   carriage free
Am   F.O.B. destination
Es   franco de porte
It   porto franco
Pt   porte grátis

franco à bord Fr
De   frei an Bord
En   free on board (fob)
Es   franco a bordo
It   franco a bordo
Pt   franco a bordo

franco a bordo Es, It, Pt
De frei an Bord
En free on board (fob)
Fr franco à bord

franco al costado del buque Es
De frei Schiffseite
En free alongside ship (fas)
Fr franco le long du bord
It franco lungobordo
Pt f.a.s.

franco banchina It
De frei Kai
En free on quay (foq)
Es franco sobre muelle
Fr franco quai
Pt franco sobre cais (foq)

francobollo *(m)* n It
De Briefmarke *(f)*
En postage stamp
Es sello de correos *(m)*
Fr timbre-poste *(m)*
Pt selo postal *(m)*

franco-comisión Es
De maklergebührenfrei
En free of commission
Fr franco courtage
It franco mediazione
Pt isento de comissão

franco courtage Fr
De maklergebührenfrei
En free of commission
Es franco-comisión
It franco mediazione
Pt isento de comissão

franco de avaria particular Pt
De frei von besonderer Havarie
En free of particular average (fpa)
Es franco de avería particular
Fr franc d'avarie particulière
It franco di avaria particolare

franco de avería particular Es
De frei von besonderer Havarie
En free of particular average (fpa)
Fr franc d'avarie particulière

It franco di avaria particolare
Pt franco de avaria particular

franco d'emballage Fr
De Verpackung inbegriffen
En including packing
Es franco embalaje
It imballaggio incluso
Pt incluindo embalagem

franco de porte Es
De portofrei; frachtfrei
En postage paid; carriage free
Fr port-payé; franco
It porto pagato; franco di porto
Pt porte pago; porte grátis

franco de toda avería Es
De ganz havariefrei
En free of all averages
Fr franc de toutes avaries
It franco d'ogni avaria
Pt franco de todas as avarias

franco de todas as avarias Pt
De ganz havariefrei
En free of all averages
Es franco de toda avería
Fr franc de toutes avaries
It franco d'ogni avaria

franco di avaria particolare It
De frei von besonderer Havarie
En free of particular average (fpa)
Es franco de avería particular
Fr franc d'avarie particulière
Pt franco de avaria particular

franco di porto It
De franko; portofrei
En carriage paid; carriage free
Am freight charges paid; F.O.B. destination
Es a porte pagado; franco de porte
Fr port-payé; franco
Pt porte pago; porte grátis

franco dock Fr, It
De frei Docklager
En delivered docks
Es franco en muelle
Pt docas francas

franco d'ogni avaria It
De ganz havariefrei
En free of all averages
Es franco de toda avería
Fr franc de toutes avaries
Pt franco de todas as avarias

franco embalaje Es
De Verpackung inbegriffen
En including packing
Fr franco d'emballage
It imballaggio incluso
Pt incluindo embalagem

franco en muelle Es
De frei Docklager
En delivered docks
Fr franco dock
It franco dock
Pt docas francas

franco fabbrica It
De ab Fabrik
En ex factory
Es de fábrica
Fr prise usine
Pt na fábrica

franco le long du bord Fr
De frei Schiffseite
En free alongside ship (fas)
Es franco al costado del buque
It franco lungobordo
Pt f.a.s.

franco lungobordo It
De frei Schiffseite
En free alongside ship (fas)
Es franco al costado del buque
Fr franco le long du bord
Pt f.a.s.

franco magazzino It
De an Zollfreilager
En ex warehouse
Es puesto en almacén
Fr à prendre en entrepôt
Pt no armazém

franco mediazione It
De maklergebührenfrei
En free of commission
Es franco-comisión
Fr franco courtage
Pt isento de comissão

franco quai Fr
De frei Kai
En free on quay (foq)
Es franco sobre muelle
It franco banchina
Pt franco sobre cais (foq)

franco sobre cais (foq) Pt
De frei Kai
En free on quay (foq)
Es franco sobre muelle
Fr franco quai
It franco banchina

franco sobre muelle Es
De frei Kai
En free on quay (foq)
Fr franco quai
It franco banchina
Pt franco sobre cais (foq)

franco sobre vagão Pt
De frei Waggon
En free on rail (for)
Es franco sobre vagón
Fr franco wagon
It franco vagone

franco sobre vagón Es
De frei Waggon
En free on rail (for)
Fr franco wagon
It franco vagone
Pt franco sobre vagão

franco vagone It
De frei Waggon
En free on rail (for)
Es franco sobre vagón
Fr franco wagon
Pt franco sobre vagão

franco wagon Fr
De frei Waggon
En free on rail (for)
Es franco sobre vagón
It franco vagone
Pt franco sobre vagão

Frankiermaschine (f) n De
En franking machine
Es máquina de franquear (f)
Fr machine à affranchir (f)
It affrancatrice postale (f)
Pt máquina de franquear (f)

franking machine En
De Frankiermaschine (f)
Es máquina de franquear (f)

Fr machine à affranchir (f)
It affrancatrice postale (f)
Pt máquina de franquear (f)

franko adv De
En carriage paid
Am freight charges paid
Es a porte pagado
Fr port-payé; franco
It franco di porto
Pt porte pago

franquia (f) n Pt
De Franchise (f)
En exemption
Es franquicia (f)
Fr franchise (f)
It franchigia (f)

franquicia (f) n Es
De Franchise (f)
En exemption
Fr franchise (f)
It franchigia (f)
Pt franquia (f)

fraud n En
De Betrug (m)
Es fraude (m)
Fr fraude (f)
It frode (f)
Pt fraude (f)

fraude n Es (m); Fr, Pt (f)
De Betrug (m)
En fraud
It frode (f)

fraude fiscale (f) Fr
De Steuerhinterziehung (f)
En evasion of tax
Es evasión de pago de
    impuestos (f)
It evasione d'Imposta (f)
Pt fuga a impostos (f)

fraudolento adj It
De betrügerisch
En fraudulent
Es fraudulento
Fr frauduleux
Pt fraudulento

fraudulent adj En
De betrügerisch
Es fraudulento
Fr frauduleux
It fraudolento
Pt fraudulento

fraudulento adj Es, Pt
De betrügerisch
En fraudulent
Fr frauduleux
It fraudolento

frauduleux adj Fr
De betrügerisch
En fraudulent
Es fraudulento
It fraudolento
Pt fraudulento

frazione (f) n It
De Bruchteil (n)
En fraction
Es fracción (f)
Fr fraction (f)
Pt fracção (f)

frecuencia (f) n Es
De Häufigkeit (f)
En frequency
Fr fréquence (f)
It frequenza (f)
Pt frequência (f)

free vb En
De befreien
Es liberar
Fr libérer; affranchir
It liberare
Pt libertar; livrar

free adj En
De frei; franko
Es libre; franco
Fr libre; franco
It libero; franco
Pt livre; franco

free alongside ship (fas) En
De frei Schiffseite
Es franco al costado del
    buque
Fr franco le long du bord
It franco lungobordo
Pt f.a.s.

free economy En
De freie Marktwirtschaft (f)
Es economía del mercado
    libre (f)
Fr système économique du
    marché libre (m)
It economia di mercato
    libero (f)
Pt economia de mercado
    livre (f)

free enterprise En
De freie Wirtschaft (f)
Es libre empresa (f)
Fr libre entreprise (f)
It libertà d'iniziativa (f)
Pt livre-empreendimento (m)

free from mortgage En
De von Hypothek befreit
Es deshipotecado
Fr déshypothéqué
It libero d'ipoteca
Pt livre de hipoteca

freehold n En
De uneingeschränkter
Grundbesitz (m)
Es propiedad absoluta (f)
Fr propriété foncière perpé-
tuelle (f)
It proprietà allodiale (f)
Pt propriedade absoluta (f)

freeholder n En
De uneingeschränkter Eigen-
tümer (m)
Es propietario absoluto (m)
Fr propriétaire foncier (m)
It proprietario allodiale (m)
Pt proprietário absoluto (m)

free of all averages En
De ganz havariefrei
Es franco de toda avería
Fr franc de toutes avaries
It franco d'ogni avaria
Pt franco de todas as avarias

free of commission En
De maklergebührenfrei
Es franco-comisión
Fr franco courtage
It franco mediazione
Pt isento de comissão

free of particular average
(fpa) En
De frei von besonderer
Havarie
Es franco de avería particular
Fr franc d'avarie particulière
It franco di avaria particolare
Pt franco de avaria particular

free on board (fob) En
De frei an Bord
Es franco a bordo
Fr franco à bord

It franco a bordo
Pt franco a bordo

free on quay (foq) En
De frei Kai
Es franco sobre muelle
Fr franco quai
It franco banchina
Pt franco sobre cais

free on rail (for) En
De frei Waggon
Es franco sobre vagón
Fr franco wagon
It franco vagone
Pt franco sobre vagão

free port En
De Freihafen (m)
Es puerto libre (m)
Fr port franc (m)
It porto franco (m)
Pt porto franco (m)

free sample En
De kostenlose Probe (f)
Es muestra gratuita (f)
Fr échantillon gratuit (m)
It campione gratuito (m)
Pt amostra grátis (f)

free ticket En
De Freikarte (f)
Es billete gratuito (m)
Fr billet de faveur (m)
It biglietto gratuito (m)
Pt bilhete gratuito (m)

free trade En
De Freihandel (m)
Es comercio libre (m)
Fr libre-échange (m)
It libero scambio (m)
Pt comércio franco (m)

free trial En
De kostenlose Probe (f)
Es prueba gratuita (f)
Fr essai gratuit (m)
It prova gratuita (f)
Pt prova gratuita (f)

frei adj De
En free
Es libre; franco
Fr libre; franco
It libero; franco
Pt livre; franco

frei an Bord De
En free on board (fob)
Es franco a bordo
Fr franco à bord
It franco a bordo
Pt franco a bordo

frei Docklager De
En delivered docks
Es franco en muelle
Fr franco dock
It franco dock
Pt docas francas

freie Marktwirtschaft (f) De
En free economy
Es economía del mercado
libre (f)
Fr système économique du
marché libre (m)
It economia di mercato
libero (f)
Pt economia de mercado
livre (f)

freier Markt (m) De
En open market
Es mercado libre (m)
Fr marché libre (m)
It mercato libero (m)
Pt mercado livre (m)

freie Wirtschaft (f) De
En free enterprise
Es libre empresa (f)
Fr libre entreprise (f)
It libertà d'iniziativa (f)
Pt livre-empreendimento (m)

freight n En
De Fracht (f)
Es flete (m)
Fr fret (m)
It nolo (m)
Pt frete (m)

freight charges paid En
De franko
Es a porte pagado
Fr port-payé
It franco di porto
Pt porte pago

freight pre-paid En
De Fracht vorausbezahlt
Es flete pagado
Fr fret payé d'avance
It nolo prepagato
Pt frete pago

freight ton En
De Handelstonne (f)
Es tonelada de flete (f)
Fr tonneau de fret (m)
It tonnellata di nolo (f)
Pt tonelada de frete (f)

freight train Am
En goods train
De Güterzug (m)
Es tren de mercancías (m)
Fr train de marchandises (m)
It treno merci (m)
Pt comboio de mercadorias
(m)

Freihafen (m) n De
En free port
Es puerto libre (m)
Fr port franc (m)
It porto franco (m)
Pt porto franco (m)

Freihandel (m) n De
En free trade
Es comercio libre (m)
Fr libre-échange (m)
It libero scambio (m)
Pt comércio franco (m)

frei Kai De
En free on quay (foq)
Es franco sobre muelle
Fr franco quai
It franco banchina
Pt franco sobre cais

Freikarte (f) n De
En free ticket
Es billete gratuito (m)
Fr billet de faveur (m)
It biglietto gratuito (m)
Pt bilhete gratuito (m)

frei Schiffseite De
En free alongside ship (fas)
Es franco al costado del
buque
Fr franco le long du bord
It franco lungobordo
Pt f.a.s.

frei von besonderer Havarie
De
En free of particular average
(fpa)
Es franco de avería particular
Fr franc d'avarie particulière

It franco di avaria particolare
Pt franco de avaria particular

frei Waggon De
En free on rail (for)
Es franco sobre vagón
Fr franco wagon
It franco vagone
Pt franco sobre vagão

freiwillig adj De
En voluntary
Es voluntario
Fr volontaire
It volontario
Pt voluntário

Freizeit (f) n De
En leisure
Es descanso (m)
Fr loisir (m)
It svago (m)
Pt lazer (m)

Fremdarbeiterschaft (f) n De
En foreign labour
Es mano de obra extranjera (f)
Fr main-d'œuvre étrangère (f)
It mano d'opera straniera (f)
Pt mão-de-obra estrangeira
(f)

Fremdkapital (n) n De
En borrowed capital
Es capital a préstamo (m)
Fr capitaux empruntés (m pl)
It capitale preso a prestito
(m)
Pt capital por empréstimo (m)

fréquence (f) n Fr
De Häufigkeit (f)
En frequency
Es frecuencia (f)
It frequenza (f)
Pt frequência (f)

frequência (f) n Pt
De Häufigkeit (f)
En frequency
Es frecuencia (f)
Fr fréquence (f)
It frequenza (f)

frequency n En
De Häufigkeit (f)
Es frecuencia (f)
Fr fréquence (f)

It frequenza (f)
Pt frequência (f)

frequency distribution En
De Häufigkeitsverteilung (f)
Es distribución de las fre-
cuencias (f)
Fr distribution de fréquences
(f)
It distribuzione delle fre-
quenze (f)
Pt distribuição de frequência
(f)

frequenza (f) n It
De Häufigkeit (f)
En frequency
Es frecuencia (f)
Fr fréquence (f)
Pt frequência (f)

fresh-water damage En
De Süßwasserschaden (m)
Es daño de agua dulce (m)
Fr dégâts d'eau douce (m pl)
It danno d'acqua dolce (m)
Pt dano causado por água
doce (m)

fret (m) n Fr
De Fracht (f)
En freight
Es flete (m)
It nolo (m)
Pt frete (m)

fretador (m) n Pt
De Befrachter (m)
En charterer
Es fletador (m)
Fr affréteur (m)
It noleggiatore (m)

fret aérien (m) Fr
De Luftfracht (f)
En air freight
Es flete aéreo (m)
It trasporto aereo (m)
Pt frete aéreo (m)

fretamento (m) n Pt
De Befrachtung (f)
En chartering
Es fletamento (m)
Fr affrètement (m)
It noleggio (m)

fretamento de tempo *(m)* Pt
De Zeitcharter *(f)*
En time charter
Es fletamento de tiempo *(m)*
Fr affrètement à temps *(m)*
It contratto di noleggio a
  tempo *(m)*

frete *(m) n* Pt
De Fracht *(f)*
En freight
Es flete *(m)*
Fr fret *(m)*
It nolo *(m)*

frete aéreo *(m)* Pt
De Luftfracht *(f)*
En air freight
Es flete aéreo *(m)*
Fr fret aérien *(m)*
It trasporto aereo *(m)*

frete pago Pt
De Fracht vorausbezahlt
En freight pre-paid
Es flete pagado
Fr fret payé d'avance
It nolo prepagato

fret payé d'avance Fr
De Fracht vorausbezahlt
En freight pre-paid
Es flete pagado
It nolo prepagato
Pt frete pago

Freundschaftsdienste *(m pl)*
De
En good office
Es buenos servicios *(m pl)*
Fr bons offices *(m pl)*
It buoni uffici *(m pl)*
Pt bons serviços *(m pl)*

friendly society En
Am lodge
De Versicherungsverein auf
  Gegenseitigkeit *(m)*
Es sociedad de socorro
  mutuo *(f)*
Fr société de secours mutuel
  (f)
It società di mutuo soccorso
  (f)
Pt mutualidade *(f)*

fringe benefits En
De Sozialleistungen *(f pl)*
Es beneficios suplementarios
  (m pl)

Fr avantages accessoires
  (m pl)
It vantaggi accessori *(m pl)*
Pt benefícios extras *(m pl)*

frode *(f) n* It
De Betrug *(m)*
En fraud
Es fraude *(m)*
Fr fraude *(f)*
Pt fraude *(f)*

frontage *n* En
De Vorderfront *(f)*
Es fachada *(f)*
Fr façade *(f)*
It facciata *(f)*
Pt fachada *(f)*

fronteira *(f) n* Pt
De Grenze *(f)*
En frontier
Es frontera *(f)*
Fr frontière *(f)*
It frontiera *(f)*

frontera *(f) n* Es
De Grenze *(f)*
En frontier
Fr frontière *(f)*
It frontiera *(f)*
Pt fronteira *(f)*

frontier *n* En
De Grenze *(f)*
Es frontera *(f)*
Fr frontière *(f)*
It frontiera *(f)*
Pt fronteira *(f)*

frontiera *(f) n* It
De Grenze *(f)*
En frontier
Es frontera *(f)*
Fr frontière *(f)*
Pt fronteira *(f)*

frontière *(f) n* Fr
De Grenze *(f)*
En frontier
Es frontera *(f)*
It frontiera *(f)*
Pt fronteira *(f)*

frota *(f) n* Pt
De Flotte *(f)*
En fleet
Es flota *(f)*

Fr flotte *(f)*
It flotta *(f)*

frota de pesca *(f)* Pt
De Fischerflotte *(f)*
En fishing fleet
Es flota pesquera *(f)*
Fr flottille de pêche *(f)*
It flotta peschereccia *(f)*

frota mercante *(f)* Pt
De Handelsflotte *(f)*
En merchant fleet
Es flota mercanto *(f)*
Fr flotte marchande *(f)*
It flotta mercantile *(f)*

frozen assets En
De eingefrorene Guthaben
  (n pl)
Es activos congelados *(m pl)*
Fr fonds bloqués *(m pl)*
It attivo congelato *(m)*
Pt bens do activo congela-
  dos *(m pl)*

frozen credits En
De eingefrorene Kredite *(m pl)*
Es creditos congelados *(m pl)*
Fr crédits bloqués *(m pl)*
It crediti bloccati *(m pl)*
Pt créditos congelados *(m pl)*

Fruchtwechsel *(m) n* De
En rotation of crops
Es rotación de cultivos *(f)*
Fr rotation des cultures *(f)*
It rotazione delle coltivazioni
  (f)
Pt rotação de culturas *(f)*

frustração *(f) n* Pt
De Fortfall der Geschäfts-
  grundlage *(m)*
En frustration
Es frustración *(f)*
Fr frustration *(f)*
It frustrazione *(f)*

frustración *(f) n* Es
De Fortfall der Geschäfts-
  grundlage *(m)*
En frustration
Fr frustration *(f)*
It frustrazione *(f)*
Pt frustração *(f)*

frustration n En, Fr (f)
De Fortfall der Geschäfts-
   grundlage (m)
Es frustración (f)
It frustrazione (f)
Pt frustração (f)

frustrazione (f) n It
De Fortfall der Geschäfts-
   grundlage (m)
En frustration
Es frustración (f)
Fr frustration (f)
Pt frustração (f)

fuego (m) n Es
De Brand (m)
En fire
Fr incendie (f)
It incendio (m)
Pt fogo; incêndio (m)

fuel-oil (m) Es
De Heizöl (n)
En fuel oil
Fr mazout (m)
It petrolio da ardere (m)
Pt petróleo combustível (m)

fuel oil n En
De Heizöl (n)
Es fuel-oil (m)
Fr mazout (m)
It petrolio da ardere (m)
Pt petróleo combustível (m)

fuera de aduanas Es
De verzollt
En ex bond
Fr à l'acquitté
It sdoganato
Pt livre de alfândega

fuerte pérdida (f) Es
De schwere Verluste (m pl)
En heavy loss
Fr lourde perte (f)
It forte perdita (f)
Pt perda avultada (f)

fuerza (f) n Es
De Gewalt (f)
En force
Fr force (f)
It forza (f)
Pt força (f)

fuerzas armadas (f pl) Es
De Streitkräfte (f pl)
En armed forces
Fr forces armées (f pl)
It forze armate (f pl)
Pt forças armadas (f pl)

fuerzas del mercado (f pl) Es
De Marktkräfte (f pl)
En market forces
Fr forces du marché (f pl)
It forze di mercato (f pl)
Pt forças de mercado (f pl)

fuga (m) n It
De Flug (f)
En flight
Es vuelo (m)
Fr vol (m)
Pt voo (m)

fuga a impostos (f) Pt
De Steuerhinterziehung (f)
En evasion of tax
Es evasión de pago de
   impuestos (f)
Fr fraude fiscale (f)
It evasione d'imposta (f)

führende Marke (f) De
En brand leader
Es marca directriz (f)
Fr marque de point (f)
It marca di punta (f)
Pt marca mais cotada (f)

fuite (f) n Fr
De Leck (n)
En leakage
Es escape (m)
It colaggio (m)
Pt escape; fuga (m f)

fulfil vb En
De erfüllen
Es cumplir
Fr remplir
It adempiere
Pt cumprir

fulfilment n En
De Erfüllung (f)
Es cumplimiento (m)
Fr accomplissement (m)
It adempimento (m)
Pt cumprimento (m)

full adj En
De voll
Es lleno
Fr plein
It pieno
Pt cheio

full cover En
De Vollwertdeckung (f)
Es garantía total (f)
Fr garantie totale (f)
It garanzia totale (f)
Pt cobertura total (f)

full employment En
De Vollbeschäftigung (f)
Es pleno empleo (m)
Fr plein emploi (m)
It piena occupazione (f)
Pt pleno emprego (m)

fully subscribed En
De vollgezeichnet
Es plenamente suscrito
Fr intégralement souscrit
It interamente sottoscritto
Pt totalmente subscrito

fulmine (m) n It
De Blitz (m)
En lightning
Es relámpago (m)
Fr foudre (f)
Pt relâmpago (m)

função (f) n Pt
De Aufgabe (f)
En function
Es función (f)
Fr fonction (f)
It funzione (f)

función (f) n Es
De Aufgabe (f)
En function
Fr fonction (f)
It funzione (f)
Pt função (f)

funcional adj Es, Pt
De sachlich
En functional
Fr fonctionnel
It funzionale

funcionario del gobierno (m)
   Es
De Beamte(r) (m)
En civil servant

Am government employee
Fr fonctionnaire *(m)*
It impiegato statale *(m)*
Pt funcionário público *(m)*

funcionário público *(m)* Pt
De Beamte(r) *(m)*
En civil servant
Am government employee
Es funcionario del gobierno *(m)*
Fr fonctionnaire *(m)*
It impiegato statale *(m)*

function *n* En
De Aufgabe *(f)*
Es función *(f)*
Fr fonction *(f)*
It funzione *(f)*
Pt função *(f)*

functional *adj* En
De sachlich
Es funcional
Fr fonctionnel
It funzionale
Pt funcional

fund *vb* En
De fundieren
Es fundar; consolidar
Fr fonder; consolider
It consolidare
Pt dotar de fundos

fund *n* En
De Fonds *(m)*
Es fondo *(m)*
Fr fonds *(m)*
It fondo *(m)*
Pt fundos *(m pl)*

fundação discricionária *(f)* Pt
De unumschränkte Treuhand *(f)*
En discretionary trust
Es fideicomiso discrecional *(m)*
Fr fidéicommis à appréciation *(m)*
It fondo fiduciario discrezionale *(m)*

fundação fiduciária *(f)* Pt
De Treuhandfonds *(m)*
En trust fond
Es fondo fiduciario *(m)*
Fr fonds fiduciaire *(m)*
It fondo fiduciario *(m)*

fundador *(m)* n Es, Pt
De Gründer *(m)*
En founder
Fr fondateur *(m)*
It fondatore *(m)*

fundar *vb* Es, Pt
De einrichten; gründen
En establish; found
Fr fonder; établir
It fondare; istituire

fundar (una deuda) *vb* Es
De fundieren
En fund
Fr fonder; consolider
It consolidare
Pt dotar de fundos

fundieren *vb* De
En fund
Es fundar; consolidar
Fr fonder; consolider
It consolidare
Pt dotar de fundos

fundo de amortização *(m)* Pt
De Tilgungsfonds *(m)*
En sinking fund
Es fondo de amortización *(m)*
Fr fonds d'amortissement *(m)*
It fondo di ammortamento *(m)*

fundo de compensação *(m)* Pt
De Ausgleichsfonds *(m)*
En equalization fund
Es fondo de compensación *(m)*
Fr fonds de régularisation *(m)*
It cassa di compensazione *(f)*

fundo de reserva *(m)* Pt
De Reservefonds *(m)*
En reserve fund
Es fondo de reserva *(m)*
Fr fonds de réserve *(m)*
It fondo di riserva *(m)*

Fundo Europeu *(m)* Pt
De Europäischer Fonds *(m)*
En European Fund
Es Fondo Europeo *(m)*
Fr Fonds Européen *(m)*
It Fondo Europeo *(m)*

Fundo Monetário Internacional *(m)* Pt
De Internationaler Währungsfonds (IWF)*(m)*
En International Monetary Fund (IMF)
Es Fondo Monetario Internacional *(m)*
Fr Fonds Monétaire International (F.M.I.)*(m)*
It Fondo Monetario Internazionale *(m)*

fundos *(m pl)* n Pt
De Fonds *(m)*
En fund
Es fondo *(m)*
Fr fonds *(m)*
It fondo *(m)*

fundos à ordem *(m pl)* Pt
De Barbestand *(m)*
En cash in hand
Es efectivo en caja *(m)*
Fr espèces en caisse *(f pl)*
It pronti contanti *(m pl)*

fundos disponíveis *(m pl)* Pt
De flüssige Mittel *(n pl)*
En funds available
Es fondos disponibles *(m pl)*
Fr disponibilités *(f pl)*
It fondi disponibili *(m pl)*

fundos renováveis *(m pl)* Pt
De Umlaufkapital *(n)*
En revolving fund
Es fondo circulante *(m)*
Fr fonds renouvelable *(m)*
It fondo rotativo *(m)*

funds available En
De flüssige Mittel *(n pl)*
Es fondos disponibles *(m pl)*
Fr disponibilités *(f pl)*
It fondi disponibili *(m pl)*
Pt fundos disponíveis *(m pl)*

funzionale *adj* It
De sachlich
En functional
Es funcional
Fr fonctionnel
Pt funcional

funzione *(f)* n It
De Aufgabe *(f)*
En function
Es función *(f)*

Fr fonction *(f)*
Pt função *(f)*

furgão *(m)* Pt
De Packwagen *(m)*
En guard's van
Es furgón *(m)*
Fr fourgon *(m)*
It bagagliaio *(m)*

furgón *(m)* Es
De Packwagen *(m)*
En guard's van
Fr fourgon *(m)*
It bagagliaio *(m)*
Pt furgão *(m)*

furnished flat En
Am furnished apartment
De möblierte Mietwohnung *(f)*
Es piso amueblado *(m)*
Fr appartement meublé *(m)*
It appartamento ammobilia-
    to *(m)*
Pt andar mobilado *(m)*

furniture *n* En
De Möbel *(n pl)*
Es muebles *(m pl)*
Fr meubles *(m pl)*
It mobilia *(f)*
Pt mobília *(f)*

further consideration En
De Weiterüberlegung *(f)*
Es examen más detallado *(m)*
Fr examen plus attentif *(m)*
It esame più attento *(m)*
Pt consideracão posterior
    mais detalhada *(f)*

further information En
De weitere Auskunft *(f)*
Es más detalles *(m pl)*
Fr renseignements complé-
    mentaires *(m pl)*
It ulteriori informazioni *(f pl)*
Pt informação adicional *(f)*

further particulars En
De nähere Umstände *(m pl)*
Es más detalles *(m pl)*
Fr plus amples renseigne-
    ments *(m pl)*
It ulteriori particolari *(m pl)*
Pt pormenores adicionais *(m
    pl)*

further reason En
De weitere Gründe *(m pl)*
Es rasones adicionales *(f pl)*
Fr raison supplémentaire *(f)*
It ulteriori motivi *(m pl)*
Pt razões adicionais *(f pl)*

furto *(m) n* It, Pt
De Diebstahl *(m)*
En theft
Es robo *(m)*
Fr vol *(m)*

furto con scasso *(m)* It
De Einbruchsdiebstahl *(m)*
En burglary
Es robo *(m)*
Fr vol avec effraction *(m)*
Pt roubo *(m)*

fusão *(f) n* Pt
De Verschmelzung *(f)*
En merger
Es fusión *(f)*
Fr fusion *(f)*
It fusione *(f)*

fusión *(f) n* Es
De Verschmelzung *(f)*
En merger
Fr fusion *(f)*
It fusione *(f)*
Pt fusão *(f)*

fusion *(f) n* Fr
De Verschmelzung *(f)*
En merger
Es fusión *(f)*
It fusione *(f)*
Pt fusão *(f)*

Fusion *(f) n* De
En amalgamation
Am merger
Es amalgamación *(f)*
Fr fusion *(f)*
It fusione *(f)*
Pt amalgamento *(m)*

fusione *(f) n* It
De Verschmelzung *(f)*
En merger
Es fusión *(f)*
Fr fusion *(f)*
Pt fusão *(f)*

fusionieren *vb* De
En amalgamate
Am merge

Es amalgamar
Fr fusionner
It fondersi
Pt amalgamar

fusionner *vb* Fr
De fusionieren
En amalgamate
Am merge
Es amalgamar
It fondersi
Pt amalgamar

Fußnote *(f) n* De
En footnote
Es apostilla *(f)*
Fr apostille *(f)*
It postilla *(f)*
Pt nota de rodapé *(f)*

futur *adj* Fr
De künftig
En future
Es futuro
It futuro; avvenire
Pt futuro

futura entrega *(f)* Es, Pt
De zukünftige Lieferung *(f)*
En future delivery
Fr livraison à terme *(f)*
It consegna a termine *(f)*

future *adj* En
De künftig
Es futuro
Fr futur
It futuro; avvenire
Pt futuro

future delivery En
De zukünftige Lieferung *(f)*
Es futura entrega *(f)*
Fr livraison à terme *(f)*
It consegna a termine *(f)*
Pt futura entrega *(f)*

futures market En
De Terminmarkt *(m)*
Es mercado de futuros *(m)*
Fr marché à terme *(m)*
It mercato a termine *(m)*
Pt mercado de futuros *(m)*

futuro *adj* Es, It, Pt
De künftig
En future
Fr futur

futuro proprietário *(m)* Pt
De gutgläubiger Besitzer *(m)*
En holder in due course
Es tenedor en buena fe *(m)*
Fr porteur de bonne foi *(m)*
It titolare in buona fede *(m)*

G

gagner *vb* Fr
De verdienen
En earn
Es ganar
It guadagnare
Pt ganhar

gain *n* En, Fr *(m)*
De Gewinn *(m)*
Es ganancia *(f)*
It guadagno *(m)*
Pt ganhos *(m pl)*

gains en capital *(m pl)* Fr
De Kapitalgewinn *(n)*
En capital gains
Es beneficios sobre capital
(m pl)
It plusvalore di capitale
(m pl)
Pt lucros de capital *(m pl)*

gamble *vb* En
De um Geld spielen; spekulie-
ren
Es jugar; especular
Fr jouer de l'argent; spéculer
It speculare; arrischiare
Pt jogar; especular

**gamble on the stock
exchange** En
De an der Börse spekulieren
Es jugar a la Bolsa
Fr jouer à la Bourse
It giocare in Borsa
Pt jogar na Bolsa

ganancia *(f)* n Es
De Gewinn *(m)*
En gain; profit
Fr gain; profit *(m)*
It guadagno; profitto *(m)*
Pt ganhos; lucro *(m pl; m)*

ganancia bruta *(f)* Es
De Bruttogewinn *(m)*
En gross profit
Fr bénéfice brut *(m)*
It utile lordo *(m)*
Pt lucro bruto *(m)*

ganancia neta *(f)* Es
De Reingewinn *(m)*
En net profit
Fr bénéfice net *(m)*
It utile netto *(m)*
Pt lucro liquido *(m)*

ganancia por realizar *(f)* Es
De imaginärer Gewinn *(m)*
En paper profit
Fr profit fictif *(m)*
It utile sulla carta *(m)*
Pt lucros no papel *(m pl)*

ganar *vb* Es
De verdienen
En earn
Fr gagner
It guadagnare
Pt ganhar

ganga *(f)* n Es
De Gelegenheitskauf *(m)*
En bargain
Fr occasion *(f)*
It occasione *(f)*
Pt pechincha *(f)*

ganhar *vb* Pt
De verdienen
En earn
Es ganar
Fr gagner
It guadagnare

ganhos *(m pl)* n Pt
De Gewinn *(m)*
En gain
Es ganancia *(f)*
Fr gain *(m)*
It guadagno *(m)*

ganz havariefrei De
En free of all averages
Es franco de toda avería
Fr franc de toutes avaries
It franco d'ogni avaria
Pt franco de todas as avarias

garage *n* En, Fr *(m)*
De Garage *(f)*
Es garaje *(m)*

It autorimessa *(f)*
Pt garagem *(f)*

Garage *(f)* n De
En garage
Es garaje *(m)*
Fr garage *(m)*
It autorimessa *(f)*
Pt garagem *(f)*

garagem *(f)* n Pt
De Garage *(f)*
En garage
Es garaje *(m)*
Fr garage *(m)*
It autorimessa *(f)*

garaje *(m)* n Es
De Garage *(f)*
En garage
Fr garage *(m)*
It autorimessa *(f)*
Pt garagem *(f)*

garant *(m)* n Fr
De Bürge *(m)*
En guarantor
Es garante; fiador *(m)*
It garante; avallante *(m)*
Pt fiador; avalizador *(m)*

garante *(m)* n Es, It
De Bürge *(m)*
En guarantor
Fr garant; avaliste *(m)*
Pt fiador; avalizador *(m)*

garantía *(f)* n Es
De Garantie *(f)*
En guarantee; warranty
Fr garantie *(f)*
It garanzia *(f)*
Pt garantia *(f)*

garantia *(f)* n Pt
De Garantie *(f)*
En guarantee; warranty
Es garantía *(f)*
Fr garantie *(f)*
It garanzia *(f)*

garantía bancaria *(f)* Es
De Bankgarantie *(f)*
En banker's indemnity
Am banker's guarantee
Fr garantie de banque *(f)*
It garanzia bancaria *(f)*
Pt garantia bancária *(f)*

garantia bancária *(f)* Pt
De Bankgarantie *(f)*
En banker's indemnity
Am banker's guarantee
Es garantía bancaria *(f)*
Fr garantie de banque *(f)*
It garanzia bancaria *(f)*

garantia colateral *(f)* Pt
De Sicherheit *(f)*
En collateral
Es garantía colateral *(f)*
Fr nantissement *(m)*
It garanzia collaterale *(f)*

garantía colateral *(f)* Es
De Sicherheit *(f)*
En collateral
Fr nantissement *(m)*
It garanzia collaterale *(f)*
Pt garantia colateral *(f)*

garantía total *(f)* Es
De Vollwertdeckung *(f)*
En full cover
Fr garantie totale *(f)*
It garanzia totale *(f)*
Pt cobertura total *(f)*

garantie *(f)* n Fr
De Garantie *(f)*
En guarantee; warranty
Es garantía *(f)*
It garanzia *(f)*
Pt garantia *(f)*

Garantie *(f)* n De
En guarantee; warranty
Es garantía *(f)*
Fr garantie *(f)*
It garanzia *(f)*
Pt garantia *(f)*

garantie d'assurance *(f)* Fr
De Versicherungsdeckung *(f)*
En insurance cover
Es cobertura de la póliza de
   seguro *(f)*
It copertura assicurativa *(f)*
Pt cobertura de seguro *(f)*

garantie de banque *(f)* Fr
De Bankgarantie *(f)*
En banker's indemnity
Am banker's guarantee
Es garantía bancaria *(f)*
It garanzia bancaria *(f)*
Pt garantia bancária *(f)*

garantie totale *(f)* Fr
De Vollwertdeckung *(f)*
En full cover
Es garantía total *(f)*
It garanzia totale *(f)*
Pt cobertura total *(f)*

garantir vb Fr, Pt
De Bürgschaft leisten;
   gewährleisten
En guarantee
Es garantizar; avalar
It garantire; avallare

garantire vb It
De Bürgschaft leisten;
   gewährleisten
En guarantee
Es garantizar; avalar
Fr garantir; avaliser
Pt garantir; assegurar

garantizar vb Es
De Bürgschaft leisten;
   gewährleisten
En guarantee
Fr garantir; avaliser
It garantire; avallare
Pt garantir; assegurar

garanzia *(f)* n It
De Garantie *(f)*
En guarantee; warranty
Es garantía *(f)*
Fr garantie *(f)*
Pt garantia *(f)*

garanzia bancaria *(f)* It
De Bankgarantie *(f)*
En banker's indemnity
Am banker's guarantee
Es garantía bancaria *(f)*
Fr garantie de banque *(f)*
Pt garantia bancária *(f)*

garanzia collaterale *(f)* It
De Sicherheit *(f)*
En collateral
Es garantía colateral *(f)*
Fr nantissement *(m)*
Pt garantia colateral *(f)*

garanzia totale *(f)* It
De Vollwertdeckung *(f)*
En full cover
Es garantía total *(f)*
Fr garantie totale *(f)*
Pt cobertura total *(f)*

garder en stock Fr
De vorrätig halten
En keep in stock
Es guardar en almacén
It tenere in magazzino
Pt reter em armazém

gardien de nuit *(m)* Fr
De Nachtwächter *(m)*
En nightwatchman
Es guarda de noche *(m)*
It guardiano notturno *(m)*
Pt guarda-nocturno *(m)*

gas n En; Es; It *(m)*
De Gas *(n)*
Fr gaz *(m)*
Pt gás *(m)*

gás *(m)* n Pt
De Gas *(n)*
En gas
Es gas *(m)*
Fr gaz *(m)*
It gas *(m)*

Gas *(n)* n De
En gas
Es gas *(m)*
Fr gaz *(m)*
It gas *(m)*
Pt gás *(m)*

gas de ciudad *(m)* Es
De Stadtgas *(n)*
En town gas
Fr gaz de ville *(m)*
It gas di carbon fossile *(m)*
Pt gás urbano *(m)*

gas di carbon fossile *(m)* It
De Stadtgas *(n)*
En town gas
Es gas de ciudad *(m)*
Fr gaz de ville *(m)*
Pt gás urbano *(m)*

gas natural *(m)* Es
De Erdgas *(n)*
En natural gas
Fr gaz naturel *(m)*
It gas naturale *(m)*
Pt gás natural *(m)*

gás natural *(m)* Pt
De Erdgas *(n)*
En natural gas
Es gas natural *(m)*
Fr gaz naturel *(m)*
It gas naturale *(m)*

gas naturale *(m)* It
De Erdgas *(n)*
En natural gas
Es gas natural *(m)*
Fr gaz naturel *(m)*
Pt gás natural *(m)*

gasto *(m) n* Es
De Kosten *(pl)*
En expense
Fr frais *(m pl)*
It spesa *(f)*
Pt despesa *(f)*

gastos de almacenaje *(m pl)*
Es
De Lagergeld *(n)*
En storage charges
Fr frais de magasinage *(m pl)*
It spese di magazzinaggio
(f pl)
Pt encargos de armazena-
mento *(m pl)*

gastos de banco *(m pl)* Es
De Bankspesen *(f pl)*
En bank charges
Fr frais bancaires *(m pl)*
It spese di banca *(f pl)*
Pt taxas bancárias *(f pl)*

gastos de cobrança *(m pl)* Pt
De Einzugskosten *(pl)*
En collection charges
Es gastos de cobranza *(m pl)*
Fr frais d'encaissement *(m pl)*
It spese di riscossione *(f pl)*

gastos de cobranza *(m pl)* Es
De Einzugskosten *(pl)*
En collection charges
Fr frais d'encaissement *(m pl)*
It spese di riscossione *(f pl)*
Pt gastos de cobrança *(m pl)*

gastos deducibles *(m pl)* Es
De abziehbare Unkosten *(pl)*
En allowable expense
Fr dépense déductible *(f)*
It spesa permessa *(f)*
Pt despesas deduzíveis *(f pl)*

gastos de los negocios *(m pl)*
Es
De Geschäftskosten *(pl)*
En business expenses
Fr frais commerciaux *(m pl)*
It spese generali *(f pl)*

Pt despesas do exercício
(f pl)

gastos de manutención
(m pl) Es
De Umschlagspesen *(f pl)*
En handling charges
Fr frais de manutention *(m pl)*
It spese di gestione *(f pl)*
Pt custas de manejo *(f pl)*

gastos de representación
(m pl) Es
De Repräsentationskosten
(pl)
En entertainment expenses
Fr frais de représentation
(m pl)
It spese di rappresentanza
(f pl)
Pt despesas de representação
(f pl)

gastos directos *(m pl)* Es
De Einzelkosten *(pl)*
En direct expenses
Fr frais directs *(m pl)*
It spese dirette *(f pl)*
Pt despesas directas *(f pl)*

gastos fuertes *(m pl)* Es
De drückende Spesen *(f pl)*
En heavy charges
Fr charges lourdes *(f pl)*
It forti spese *(f pl)*
Pt encargos pesados *(m pl)*

gastos generales *(m pl)* Es
De allgemeine Unkosten;
Generalunkosten *(pl)*
En general expenses; over-
heads
Fr frais généraux *(m pl)*
It spese generali *(f pl)*
Pt despesas gerais *(f pl)*

gastos imprevistos *(m pl)* Es
De Nebenkosten *(pl)*
En incidental expenses
Fr faux frais *(m pl)*
It spese impreviste *(f pl)*
Pt despesas ocasionais *(f pl)*

gastos publicitarios *(m pl)* Es
De Werbekosten *(pl)*
En advertising expenditure
Fr dépenses de publicité *(f pl)*
It spese di pubblicità *(f pl)*
Pt despesa com publicidade
(f)

gastos varios *(m pl)* Es
De verschiedene Ausgaben
(f pl)
En sundry expenses
Fr frais divers *(m pl)*
It spese varie *(f pl)*
Pt despesas diversas *(f pl)*

gás urbano *(m)* Pt
De Stadtgas *(n)*
En town gas
Es gas de ciudad *(m)*
Fr gaz de ville *(m)*
It gas di carbon fossile *(m)*

gaz *(m) n* Fr
De Gas *(n)*
En gas
Es gas *(m)*
It gas *(m)*
Pt gás *(m)*

gaz de ville *(m)* Fr
De Stadtgas *(n)*
En town gas
Es gas de ciudad *(m)*
It gas di carbon fossile *(m)*
Pt gás urbano *(m)*

gaz naturel *(m)* Fr
De Erdgas *(n)*
En natural gas
Es gas natural *(m)*
It gas naturale *(m)*
Pt gás natural *(m)*

gearing *n* En
De Getriebe *(n)*
Es engranaje *(m)*
Fr engrenage *(m)*
It ingranaggio *(m)*
Pt engrenagem *(f)*

Geben und Nehmen *(n)* De
En give and take
Es concesión recíproca *(f)*
Fr concessions mutuelles
(f pl)
It concessione reciproca *(f)*
Pt concessão mútua *(f)*

Gebrauchsanleitung *(f) n* De
En instructions for use
Es modo de empleo *(m)*
Fr mode d'emploi *(f)*
It istruzioni per l'uso *(f pl)*
Pt instruções para uso *(f pl)*

Gebühr *(f)* n De
En duty; tax
Es derechos; impuesto *(m)*
Fr taxe; impôt *(f m)*
It tassa; imposta *(f)*
Pt taxa; imposto *(f m)*

Gefahr *(f)* n De
En peril
Es peligro *(m)*
Fr péril *(m)*
It pericolo *(m)*
Pt perigo *(m)*

Gefahrenzulage *(f)* n De
En danger money
Es suma para riesgos *(f)*
Fr prime de risque *(f)*
It compenso per il rischio *(m)*
Pt prémio de risco *(m)*

gefährliche Waren *(f pl)* De
En dangerous goods
Es mercancías peligrosas
(f pl)
Fr marchandises dangereu-
ses *(f pl)*
It merce pericolosa *(f)*
Pt mercadorias perigosas
(f pl)

Gefälligkeitswechsel *(m)* n
De
En accommodation bill
Es pagaré de favor *(m)*
Fr billet de complaisance *(m)*
It cambiale di favora *(f)*
Pt letra de favor *(f)*

gefälscht *adj* De
En fake; forged
Es falso; falsificado
Fr faux; contrefait
It falso; falsificato
Pt falso; falsificado

gefälschter Scheck *(m)* De
En forged cheque
Es cheque falsificado *(m)*
Fr faux chèque *(m)*
It assegno falsificato *(m)*
Pt cheque falsificado *(m)*

gefragt *adj* De
En in demand
Es solicitado
Fr demandé
It ricercato
Pt procurado

**(ein) Gegenangebot
abgeben** De
En make a counteroffer
Es hacer una contraoferta
Fr faire une contre-offre
It fare una controfferta
Pt fazer uma contra-pro-
posta

gegen Barzahlung De
En cash with order
Es pagadero con el pedido
Fr payable à la commande
It pagamento con l'ordine
Pt pagamento no acto de re-
quisiçao

**gegen Haftkaution frei-
geben** De
En grant bail
Es conceder fianza
Fr admettre une caution
It concedere la libertà prov-
visoria su cauzione
Pt autorizar caução

Gegenkonto *(n)* n De
En contra account
Es contracuenta *(f)*
Fr compte contrepartie *(m)*
It conto d'ordine *(m)*
Pt contra-conta *(f)*

**gegenseitiges Einverneh-
men** *(n)* De
En mutual agreement
Es acuerdo común *(m)*
Fr accord mutuel *(m)*
It comune accordo *(m)*
Pt acordo mútuo *(m)*

gegenzeichnen *vb* De
En back; countersign
Es avalar; refrendar
Fr avaliser; contresigner
It avallare; controfirmare
Pt avalizar; validar por assi-
natura

Gegenzeichner *(m)* n De
En backer
Es avalista *(m)*
Fr avaliste *(m)*
It avallante *(m)*
Pt avalista *(m)*

Gehalt *(n)* n De
En salary
Es sueldo *(m)*

Fr traitement *(m)*
It stipendio *(m)*
Pt ordenado *(m)*

Geheimvertrag *(m)* n De
En secret agreement
Es acuerdo secreto *(m)*
Fr accord occulte *(m)*
It accordo segreto *(m)*
Pt acordo secreto *(m)*

Geld *(n)* n De
En money
Es dinero *(m)*
Fr argent *(m)*
It denaro *(m)*
Pt dinheiro *(m)*

Geldabwertung *(f)* n De
En depreciation of money
Es desvalorización de la mo-
neda *(f)*
Fr dépréciation de la mon-
naie *(f)*
It svalutazione della moneta
(f)
Pt desvalorização da moeda *(f)*

Geldgeber *(m)* n De
En investor
Es inversionista *(m)*
Fr investisseur *(m)*
It capitalista *(m)*
Pt capitalista *(m)*

Geldkassette *(f)* n De
En cash-box
Es caja *(f)*
Fr caisse *(f)*
It cassetta *(f)*
Pt caixa *(f)*

Geldmarkt *(m)* n De
En money market
Es mercado de dinero *(m)*
Fr marché monétaire *(m)*
It mercato di denaro *(m)*
Pt mercado monetário *(m)*

Geldschrank *(m)* n De
En safe
Es caja fuerte *(f)*
Fr coffre-fort *(m)*
It cassaforte *(f)*
Pt cofre *(m)*

Geldstrafe *(f)* n De
En fine
Es sanción; multa *(f)*

Fr amende (f)
It multa (f)
Pt multa (f)

Geldverleiher (m) n De
En moneylender
Es prestamista (m)
Fr prêteur d'argent (m)
It usuraio (m)
Pt prestamista (m)

Gelegenheitskauf (m) n De
En bargain
Es ganga (f)
Fr occasion (f)
It occasione (f)
Pt pechincha (f)

Gemeindesteuer (f) n De
En rates
Am realty tax
Es contribución municipal (f)
Fr taxes municipales (f pl)
It tassa comunale (f)
Pt contribuições (f pl)

Gemeinkosten (pl) n De
En indirect costs
Es costes indirectos (m pl)
Fr frais indirects (m pl)
It costi indiretti (m pl)
Pt custos indirectos (m pl)

gemeinnütziges Unternehmen (n) De
En utility company
Es empresa de servicios
públicos (f)
Fr entreprise d'utilité
publique (f)
It società di servizi pubblici
(f)
Pt empresa de utilidade
pública (f)

gemeinsame Agrarpolitik (f)
De
En Common Agricultural
Policy
Es política agricola común (f)
Fr politique agricole
commune (f)
It politica agricola comune (f)
Pt política agrícola comum (f)

gemeinsame Handelspolitik
(f) De
En Common Commercial
Policy

Es política comercial común
(f)
Fr politique commerciale
commune (f)
It politica commerciale
comune (f)
Pt política comercial comum
(f)

gemeinsamer Außentarif (m)
De
En common external tariff
Es tarifa exterior común (f)
Fr tarif extérieur commun (m)
It tariffa estera comune (f)
Pt tarifa externa comum (f)

gemeinsamer Markt (m) De
En Common Market
Es mercado común (m)
Fr marché commun (m)
It mercato comune (m)
Pt mercado comum (m)

Gemeinschaft (f) n De
En community
Es comunidad (f)
Fr communauté (f)
It comunità (f)
Pt comunidade (f)

Gemeinschaftsgründung
(f) n De
En joint venture
Es empresa en común (f)
Fr entreprise en participation
(f)
It impresa in compartecipa-
zione (f)
Pt iniciativa em comum (f)

Gemeinschaftskonto (n) n
De
En joint account
Es cuenta común (f)
Fr compte joint (m)
It conto in comune (m)
Pt conta conjunta (f)

Gemeinschuldner (m) n De
En bankrupt
Es quebrado (m)
Fr failli (m)
It fallito (m)
Pt falido (m)

Gemischtwirtschaft (f) n De
En mixed economy
Es economía mixta (f)

Fr économie mixte (f)
It economia mista (f)
Pt economia mixta (f)

genehmigtes Kapital (n) De
En authorized capital
Es capital autorizado (m)
Fr capital autorisé (m)
It capitale autorizzato (m)
Pt capital autorizado (m)

**General Agreement on Tar-
iffs and Trade** (GATT) En
De Allgemeines Zoll- und
Handelsabkommen (n)
Es Acuerdo General sobre
Tarifas Aduaneras y
Comercio (m)
Fr Accord Général sur les
Tarifs Douaniers et le
Commerce (m)
It Accordo Generale sulle
Tariffe Doganali e sul
Commercio (m)
Pt Acordo geral de Tarifas e
Comércio (m)

general average (G.A.) En
De große Havarie (f)
Es avería general (f)
Fr avaries communes (f pl)
It avaria generale (f)
Pt avaria grossa (f)

general expenses En
De allgemeine Unkosten (pl)
Es gastos generales (m pl)
Fr frais généraux (m pl)
It spese generali (f pl)
Pt despesas gerais (f pl)

general ledger En
De allgemeines Hauptbuch (n)
Es libro mayor general (m)
Fr journal général (m)
It libro mastro generale (m)
Pt livro-mestre geral (m)

general lien En
De allgemeines Pfandrecht (n)
Es privilegio general (m)
Fr privilège général (m)
It privilegio generale (m)
Pt privilégio geral (m)

general meeting En
De Hauptversammlung (f)
Es asamblea general (f)
Fr assemblée générale (f)

It   assemblea generale *(f)*
Pt   assembleia geral *(f)*

general public En
De   Öffentlichkeit *(f)*
Es   público en general *(m)*
Fr   grand public *(m)*
It   pubblico in genere *(m)*
Pt   público em geral *(m)*

Generalstreik *(m) n* De
En   general strike
Es   huelga general *(f)*
Fr   grève générale *(f)*
It   sciopero generale *(m)*
Pt   greve geral *(f)*

general strike En
De   Generalstreik *(m)*
Es   huelga general *(f)*
Fr   grève générale *(f)*
It   sciopero generale *(m)*
Pt   greve geral *(f)*

Generalunkosten *(pl) n* De
En   overhead costs
Es   gastos generales *(m pl)*
Fr   frais généraux *(m pl)*
It   spese generali *(f pl)*
Pt   despesas gerais *(f pl)*

generi alimentari *(m pl)* It
De   Eßwaren *(f pl)*
En   foodstuffs
Es   comestibles *(m pl)*
Fr   alimentation *(f)*
Pt   géneros alimentícios *(m pl)*

géneros alimentícios *(m pl)*
Pt
De   Eßwaren *(f pl)*
En   foodstuffs
Es   comestibles *(m pl)*
Fr   alimentation *(f)*
It   generi alimentari *(m pl)*

géneros de punto *(m pl)* Es
De   Strickwaren *(f pl)*
En   knitted goods
Fr   bonneterie *(f)*
It   maglieria *(f)*
Pt   artigos de malha de lã
      (m pl)

génie *(m) n* Fr
De   Maschinenbau *(m)*
En   engineering
Es   ingeniería *(f)*

It   ingegneria *(f)*
Pt   engenharia *(f)*

génie chimique *(m)* Fr
De   Chemietechnik *(f)*
En   chemical engineering
Es   ingeniería química *(f)*
It   ingegneria chimica *(f)*
Pt   engenharia química *(f)*

génie civil *(m)* Fr
De   Ingenieurbau *(m)*
En   civil engineering
Es   ingeniería civil *(f)*
It   ingegneria civile *(f)*
Pt   engenharia civil *(f)*

Genossenschaft *(f) n* De
En   cooperative
Es   cooperativa *(f)*
Fr   société coopérative *(f)*
It   cooperativa *(f)*
Pt   cooperativa *(f)*

gentleman's agreement En
De   Kavaliersabkommen *(n)*
Es   acuerdo sobre palabra *(m)*
Fr   convention verbale *(f)*
It   accordo sulla parola *(m)*
Pt   pacto de honra *(m)*

Gepäckschließfach *(n) n* De
En   luggage locker
Es   casilla de equipaje *(f)*
Fr   coffre de bagages *(m)*
It   cassetta bagaglio *(f)*
Pt   depósito de bagagem
      individualizado *(m)*

gepfändete Güter *(n pl)* De
En   distressed goods
Es   mercancías embargadas
      (f pl)
Fr   biens saisis *(m pl)*
It   merce sequestrata *(f)*
Pt   mercadorias embargadas
      (f pl)

geprüfte Geschäftsbücher
      (n pl) De
En   audited accounts
Es   cuentas revisadas *(f pl)*
Fr   comptes vérifiés et certi-
      fiés *(m pl)*
It   conti verificati e certificati
      (m pl)
Pt   contas fiscalizadas *(f pl)*

geral de contas-correntes
      (m) Pt
De   allgemeines Hauptbuch *(n)*
En   general ledger
Es   libro mayor general *(m)*
Fr   journal général *(m)*
It   libro mastro generale *(m)*

gérant d'affaires *(m)* Fr
De   Geschäftsführer *(m)*
En   business manager
Es   gerente de negocios *(m)*
It   direttore commerciale *(m)*
Pt   gerente de negócios *(m)*

gerechtfertigt *adj* De
En   justifiable
Es   justificable; legítimo
Fr   légitime
It   giustificabile; legittimo
Pt   justificável

Gerechtigkeit *(f) n* De
En   justice
Es   justicia *(f)*
Fr   justice *(f)*
It   giustizia *(f)*
Pt   justiça *(f)*

gerência *(f) n* Pt
De   Vorstand *(m)*
En   management
Es   dirección *(f)*
Fr   administration *(f)*
It   direzione; amministrazio-
      ne *(f)*

gerência superior *(f)* Pt
De   Direktion *(f)*
En   top management
Es   dirección superior *(f)*
Fr   haute direction *(f)*
It   direzione superiore *(f)*

gerenta de negocios *(m)* Es
De   Geschäftsführer *(m)*
En   business manager
Fr   gérant d'affaires *(m)*
It   direttore commerciale *(m)*
Pt   gerente de negócios *(m)*

gerente *(m) n* Pt
De   Geschäftsleiter *(m)*
En   manager
Es   director *(m)*
Fr   directeur *(m)*
It   direttore *(m)*

gerente de exportações *(m)*
Pt
De Exportabteilungsleiter *(m)*
En export manager
Es jefe de exportación *(m)*
Fr chef du service exportation *(m)*
It direttore esportazione *(m)*

gerente de negocios *(m)* Es
De Geschäftsführer *(m)*
En business manager
Fr gérant d'affaires
It direttore commerciale *(m)*
Pt gerente de negócios *(m)*

gerente de negócios *(m)* Pt
De Geschäftsführer *(m)*
En business manager
Es gerente de negocios *(m)*
Fr gérant d'affaires *(m)*
It direttore commerciale *(m)*

Gericht *(n)* n De
En court of law
Es tribunal *(m)*
Fr tribunal *(m)*
It tribunale *(m)*
Pt tribunal *(m)*

gerichtlich entscheiden De
En adjudicate
Es adjudicar
Fr juger
It aggiudicare
Pt adjudicar

gerichtliche Verfügung *(f)* De
En injunction
Es entredicho *(m)*
Fr injonction; ordonnance judiciaire *(f)*
It ingiunzione *(f)*
Pt interdição *(f)*

gerichtlich vorgehen gegen De
En institute proceedings against
Es iniciar un proceso contra
Fr intenter un procès à
It intentare un'azione legale contro
Pt instituir processo contra

gesamt *adj* De
En aggregate
Es total
Fr global

It complessivo
Pt total

gesamtschuldnerisch De
En jointly and severally
Es en conjunto y separadamente
Fr conjointement et solidairement
It solidalmente e individualmente
Pt em conjunto e por vários

Geschäft *(n)* n De
En business
Es negocios *(m pl)*
Fr affaires *(f pl)*
It affari *(m pl)*
Pt negócios *(m pl)*

Geschäftsbereich (eines Ministers) *(m)* n De
En portfolio
Es cartera *(f)*
Fr portefeuille *(f)*
It portafoglio *(m)*
Pt pasta *(f)*

Geschäftsbücher *(n pl)* n De
En books of account
Es libros de cuentas *(m pl)*
Fr livres comptables *(m pl)*
It libri contabili *(m pl)*
Pt livros de contabilidade *(m pl)*

Geschäftsfaktur *(f)* n De
En commercial invoice
Es factura comercial *(f)*
Fr facture commerciale *(f)*
It fattura commerciale *(f)*
Pt factura comercial *(f)*

Geschäftsführer *(m)* n De
En chief executive
Es jefe ejecutivo *(m)*
Fr directeur général *(m)*
It direttore generale *(m)*
Pt chefe de gerência *(m)*

Geschäftsführungsberater *(m)* n De
En management consultant
Es asesor administrativo *(m)*
Fr ingénieur-conseil en organisation *(m)*

It consulente di direzione aziendale *(m)*
Pt perito de administração *(m)*

Geschäftsjahr *(n)* n De
En financial year
Es año económico *(m)*
Fr exercice *(m)*
It esercizio *(m)*
Pt ano financeiro *(m)*

Geschäftskosten *(pl)* n De
En business expenses
Es gastos de los negocios *(m pl)*
Fr frais commerciaux *(m pl)*
It spese generali *(f pl)*
Pt despesas do exercício *(f pl)*

Geschäftsleiter *(m)* n De
En manager
Es director *(m)*
Fr directeur *(m)*
It direttore *(m)*
Pt gerente; director *(m)*

Geschäftsmann *(m)* n De
En businessman
Es hombre de negocios *(m)*
Fr homme d'affaires *(m)*
It uomo d'affari *(m)*
Pt homem de negócios *(m)*

Geschäftsreisende(r) *(m)* n De
En (commercial) traveller
Es viajante *(m)*
Fr commis-voyageur *(m)*
It viaggiatore di commercio *(m)*
Pt viajante *(m)*

Geschäftsstunden *(f pl)* n De
En office hours
Es horario de oficina *(m)*
Fr heures de bureau *(f pl)*
It orario d'ufficio *(m)*
Pt horário do escritório *(m)*

Geschäftswert *(m)* n De
En goodwill
Es valor de la clientela *(m)*
Fr bon vouloir *(m)*
It avviamento *(m)*
Pt boa vontade *(f)*

Geschäftszeit (f) n De
En business hours
Es horario de comercio (m)
Fr heures d'ouverture (f pl)
It orario d'apertura (m)
Pt horas de funcionamento
    (f pl)

Geschäftszentrum (n) n
De
En shopping centre
Es centro de negocios (m)
Fr centre commercial (m)
It zona degli acquisti (f)
Pt centro de comércio (m)

Geschenk (n) n De
En gift
Es regalo (m)
Fr don; cadeau (m)
It dono; donazione (m f)
Pt prenda; presente (f m)

(die) Geschworenen (pl) n De
En jury
Es jurado (m)
Fr jury (m)
It giuria (f)
Pt juri (m)

Gesellschaft (f) n De
En company
Es compañía; empresa (f)
Fr société; entreprise (f)
It società (f)
Pt companhia (f)

(eine) Gesellschaft gründen
De
En float a company
Es lanzar una compañía
Fr lancer une entreprise
It lanciare una società
Pt lançar uma empresa

**Gesellschaft mit
    beschränkter Haftung
    (GmbH)** (f) De
En private limited company
Es Compañía privada de re-
    sponsabilidad limi-
    tada (f)
Fr Société à responsabilité
    limitée (SARL) (f)
It Società a responsabilità
    limitata (Srl) (f)
Pt Sociedade por quotas de
    responsabilidade limitada
    (f)

**Gesellschaft mit Kontroll-
    befugnis** (f) De
En controlling company
Es compañía directriz (f)
Fr société directrice (f)
It società direttrice (f)
Pt companhia controladora
    (f)

**Gesellschaft notiert an der
    Börse** (f) De
En quoted company
Es compañía cotizada en
    bolsa (f)
Fr société cotée à la Bourse
    (f)
It società quotata in borsa (f)
Pt companhia cotizada (f)

Gesellschaftsvertrag (m) n
De
En articles of association
Am articles of incorporation
Es artículos de asociación
    (m pl)
Fr contrat de société (m)
It statuto sociale (m)
Pt escritura de sociedade (f)

Gesetz (n) n De
En statute
Es estatuto (m)
Fr statut (m)
It statuto (m)
Pt estatuto (m)

Gesetzgebung (f) n De
En legislation
Es legislación (f)
Fr législation (f)
It legislazione (f)
Pt legislação (f)

gesetzlich adj De
En statutory; lawful
Es estatutario; legitimo
Fr statutaire; légal
It statutario; legittimo
Pt estatutário; legítimo

gesetzlicher Feiertag (m) De
En public holiday
Es día de fiesta (m)
Fr jour férié (m)
It giorno di festa (m)
Pt feriado (m)

**gesicherte Schuldver-
    schreibung** (f) De
En secured debenture
Es obligación garantizada (f)
Fr obligation garantie (f)
It obbligazione garantita (f)
Pt obrigação com garantia (f)

gesperrte Einlagen (f pl) De
En blocked deposits
Es depósitos bloqueados
    (m pl)
Fr dépôts bloqués (m pl)
It deposito con vincolo
    bloccato (m)
Pt depósitos bloqueados
    (m pl)

gesperrter Markt (m) De
En closed market
Es mercado cerrado (m)
Fr marché fermé (m)
It mercato chiuso (m)
Pt mercado fechado (m)

gesperrtes Konto (n) De
En blocked account
Es cuenta bloqueada (f)
Fr compte bloqué (m)
It conto bloccato (m)
Pt conta bloqueada (f)

gestão (f) n Pt
De Verwaltung (f)
En administration
Es administración (f)
Fr gestion (f)
It gestione (f)

Gestehungskosten (m pl) n
De
En actual cost
Es precio verdadero (m)
Fr prix de revient effectif (m)
It costo effettivo (m)
Pt custo verdadeiro (m)

gestern adv De
En yesterday
Es ayer
Fr hier
It ieri
Pt ontem

gestion (f) n Fr
De Verwaltung (f)
En administration
Es administración (f)
It gestione (f)
Pt gestão (f)

gestione (f) n It
De Verwaltung (f)
En administration
Es administración (f)
Fr gestion (f)
Pt gestão (f)

gestundete Zahlung (f) De
En deferred payment
Es pago aplazado (m)
Fr paiement différé (m)
It pagamento differito (m)
Pt pagamento adiado (m)

Gesundheitsbrief (m) n De
En pratique
Es libre plática (f)
Fr libre pratique (f)
It libera pratica (f)
Pt livre prática (f)

Gesundheitsdienst (m) n De
En health service
Es servicio de sanidad (m)
Fr service de la santé (m)
It servizio sanitario (m)
Pt serviço de saúde (m)

Getriebe (n) n De
En gearing
Es engranaje (m)
Fr engrenage (m)
It ingranaggio (m)
Pt engrenagem (f)

gewähren (einen Rabatt) De
En allow (a discount)
Es conceder (un descuento)
Fr consentir (une remise)
It concedere (uno sconto)
Pt conceder (um desconto)

Gewahrsaminhaber (m) n De
En bailee
Es depositario (m)
Fr dépositaire (m)
It depositario (m)
Pt caucionado (m)

Gewalt (f) n De
En force
Es fuerza (f)
Fr force (f)
It forza (f)
Pt força (f)

Gewerbe (n) n De
En industry
Es industria (f)

Fr industrie (f)
It industria (f)
Pt indústria (f)

Gewerbe- De
En industrial
Es industrial
Fr industriel
It industriale
Pt industrial

Gewerbearbeiter (m) n De
En factory worker
Es obrero; operaio (m)
Fr ouvrier (m)
It operaio (m)
Pt operário (m)

**Gewerbeaufsichts-
beamte(r)** (m) n De
En factory inspector
Es inspector de fábrica (m)
Fr inspecteur du travail (m)
It ispettore di fabbrica (m)
Pt inspector de fábrica (m)

Gewerkschaft (f) n De
En trade union
Es sindicato (m)
Fr syndicat (m)
It sindacato (m)
Pt sindicato (m)

Gewicht (n) n De
En weight
Es peso (m)
Fr poids (m)
It peso (m)
Pt peso (m)

Gewinn (m) n De
En profit; gain
Es ganancia; beneficio (f m)
Fr bénéfice; profit (m)
It utile; profitto (m)
Pt lucro; benefício (m)

Gewinnanalyse (f) n De
En cost benefit analysis
Es análisis de costes y bene-
ficios (m)
Fr analyse des coûts et
rendements (f)
It analisi dei costi e benefici
(f)
Pt análise de custo e be-
nefício (f)

Gewinnanteilschein (m) n De
En dividend warrant
Es cupón de dividendos (m)
Fr dividende-warrant (m)
It cedola di dividendo (f)
Pt cédula de dividendo (f)

Gewinnausfall (m) n De
En loss of profits
Es lucro cesante (m)
Fr perte de bénéfices (f)
It perdita di utili (f)
Pt perda de lucros (f)

Gewinnbeteiligung (f) n De
En profit-sharing
Es participación en los bene-
ficios (f)
Fr participation aux béné-
fices (f)
It partecipazione agli utili (f)
Pt repartição dos lucros (f)

Gewinnler (m) n De
En profiteer
Es acaparador (m)
Fr profiteur (m)
It profittatore (m)
Pt especulador (m)

Gewinn pro Aktie (n) De
En earnings per share
Es beneficios por acción
(m pl)
Fr bénéfice par titre (m)
It profitti per azione (m pl)
Pt proventos por acção (m pl)

Gewinnrealisation (f) n De
En profit-taking
Es realización de utilidades (f)
Fr prise de bénéfices (f)
It realizzazione dell'utile (f)
Pt realização dos lucros (f)

Gewinn- und Verlustkonto
(n) De
En profit and loss account
Es cuenta de ganancias y
pérdidas (f)
Fr compte profits et pertes
(m)
It conto profitti e perdite (m)
Pt conta de lucros e perdas (f)

gewogener Durchschnitt (m)
De
En weighted average
Es media ponderada (f)

Fr moyenne pondérée (f)
It media ponderata (f)
Pt média ponderada (f)

gezeichnetes Kapital (n) De
En subscribed capital
Es capital subscrito (m)
Fr capital souscrit (m)
It capitale sottoscritto (m)
Pt capital subscrito (m)

ghisa (f) n It
De Gußeisen (n)
En cast iron
Es hierro colado (m)
Fr fer de fonte (m)
Pt ferro fundido (m)

giacimento petrolifero (m) It
De Ölfeld (n)
En oilfield
Es yacimiento de petróleo (m)
Fr gisement petrolifère (m)
Pt jazigo de petróleo (m)

gift n En
De Geschenk (n)
Es regalo (m)
Fr don; cadeau (m)
It dono; donazione (m f)
Pt prenda; presente (f m)

giftiger Abfall (m) De
En toxic waste
Es efluentes tóxicos (m pl)
Fr déchets toxiques (m pl)
It rifiuti tossici (m pl)
Pt despejos tóxicos (m pl)

gilt-edged securities En
De mündelsichere Wert-
papiere (n pl)
Es valores de toda confianza
(m pl)
Fr valeurs de tout repos (f pl)
It titoli di assoluta fiducia
(m pl)
Pt valores de toda confiança
(m pl)

giocare in Borsa It
De an der Börse spekulieren
En gamble on the stock
exchange
Es jugar a la Bolsa
Fr jouer à la Bourse
Pt jogar na Bolsa

giornale (m) n It
De Tagebuch (n)
En day-book
Es diario (m)
Fr journal (m)
Pt diário (m)

giornata lavorativa (f) It
De Arbeitstag (m)
En working day
Es día laborable (m)
Fr jour ouvrable (m)
Pt dia de trabalho (m)

giorni di grazia (m pl) It
De Nachfrist (f)
En days of grace
Es días de gracia (f pl)
Fr délai supplémentaire (m)
Pt dias de tolerância (m pl)

giorno (m) n It
De Tag (m)
En day
Es día (m)
Fr jour (m)
Pt dia (m)

giorno della pigione (m) It
De Quartalstag (m)
En quarter day
Es primer día del trimestre (m)
Fr jour du terme (m)
Pt dia de vencimento trimes-
tral (m)

giorno di borsa (m) It
De Börsentag (m)
En (financial) market day
Es día de bolsa (m)
Fr jour de bourse (m)
Pt dia de bolsa (m)

giorno di festa (m) It
De gesetzlicher Feiertag (m)
En public holiday
Es día de fiesta (m)
Fr jour férié (m)
Pt feriado (m)

giorno di liquidazione (m) It
De Abrechnungstag (m)
En account day
Am settlement date
Es día de liquidación (m)
Fr jour de liquidation (m)
Pt dia de liquidação (m)

giorno di mercato (m) It
De Markttag (m)
En (local) market day
Es día de mercado (m)
Fr jour de place (m)
Pt dia de mercado (m)

giorno di paga (m) It
De Zahltag; Abrechnungstag
(m)
En pay day
Es día de pago (m)
Fr jour de paiement (m)
Pt dia de recebimento (m)

giorno di riposo (m) It
De dienstfreier Tag (m)
En day off
Es día libre (m)
Fr jour de congé (m)
Pt dia de folga (m)

girare vb It
De indossieren
En endorse
Es endosar
Fr endosser
Pt endossar

girar en descubierto Es
De überziehen
En overdraw
Fr mettre a découvert
It trarre allo scoperto
Pt levantar a descoberto

girata (f) n It
De Indossament (n)
En endorsement
Es endoso (m)
Fr endossement; endos (m)
Pt endosse (m)

girata in bianco (f) It
De Blankoindossament (n)
En blank endorsement
Es endoso en blanco (m)
Fr endossement en blanc (m)
Pt endosse em branco (m)

girata restrittiva (f) It
De Rektaindossement (n)
En restrictive endorsement
Es endoso restringido (m)
Fr endossement restrictif (m)
Pt endosse restritivo (m)

giro bancario   304

giro bancario *(m)* Es
De Banktratte *(f)*
En banker's draft
Fr traite bancaire *(f)*
It tratta bancaria *(f)*
Pt letra de banco *(f)*

Girobank *(f)* n De
En clearing-bank
Es banco de compensación
 (m)
Fr banque de virement *(f)*
It banca associata alla stan-
 za di compensazione *(f)*
Pt banco de compensação e
 rateio *(m)*

giro d'affari *(m)* It
De Umsatz *(m)*
En turnover
Es volumen de ventas *(m)*
Fr chiffre d'affaires *(m)*
Pt movimento de dinheiro *(m)*

giro postal *(m)* Es
De Postanweisung *(f)*
En postal order
Fr mandat-poste *(m)*
It vaglia postale *(f)*
Pt vale postal *(m)*

giro telegráfico *(m)* Es
De Kabelauszahlung *(f)*
En telegraphic transfer
Fr virement télégraphique *(m)*
It rimessa telegrafica *(f)*
Pt transferência telegráfica *(f)*

gisement petrolifère *(m)* Fr
De Ölfeld *(n)*
En oilfield
Es yacimiento de petróleo *(m)*
It giacimento petrolifero *(m)*
Pt jazigo de petróleo *(m)*

giudicare *vb* It
De urteilen
En judge
Es juzgar
Fr juger
Pt julgar

giudice *(m)* n It
De Richter *(m)*
En judge
Es juez *(m)*
Fr juge *(m)*
Pt juiz *(m)*

giudizio *(m)* n It
De Urteil *(n)*
En judgment
Es juicio; adjudicación *(m f)*
Fr jugement; arrêt *(m)*
Pt julgamento *(m)*

giuria *(f)* n It
De die Geschworenen; Jury
 (pl; f)
En jury
Es jurado *(m)*
Fr jury *(m)*
Pt juri *(m)*

giurisdizione *(f)* n It
De Rechtsprechung;
 Gerichtsbarkeit *(f)*
En jurisdiction
Es jurisdicción *(f)*
Fr juridiction *(f)*
Pt jurisdição *(f)*

giustificabile *adj* It
De gerechtfertigt
En justifiable
Es justificable; legítimo
Fr légitime
Pt justificável

giustizia *(f)* n It
De Gerechtigkeit *(f)*
En justice
Es justicia *(f)*
Fr justice *(f)*
Pt justiça *(f)*

give and take En
De Geben und Nehmen *(n)*
Es concesión recíproca *(f)*
Fr concessions mutuelles
 (f pl)
It concessione reciproca *(f)*
Pt conessão mútua *(f)*

give a week's notice En
De einwöchig kündigen
Es dar una semana de aviso
Fr donner ses huit jours
It dare una settimana di
 preavviso
Pt dar um prazo de uma se-
 mana para despedimento

give up En
De aufgeben
Es renunciar
Fr céder

It cedere
Pt desistir

Glas *(n)* n De
En glass
Es vidrio *(m)*
Fr verre *(m)*
It vetro *(m)*
Pt vidro *(m)*

glass n En
De Glas *(n)*
Es vidrio *(m)*
Fr verre *(m)*
It vetro *(m)*
Pt vidro *(m)*

Gläubiger *(m)* n De
En creditor
Es acreedor *(m)*
Fr créancier; créditeur *(m)*
It creditore *(m)*
Pt credor *(m)*

Gläubigerversammlung *(f)* n
 De
En meeting of creditors
Es reunión de acreedores *(f)*
Fr assemblée de créanciers
 (f)
It assemblea dei creditori *(f)*
Pt assembleia de credores *(f)*

Gleichgewicht *(n)* n De
En equilibrium
Es equilibrio *(m)*
Fr équilibre *(m)*
It equilibrio *(m)*
Pt equilíbrio *(m)*

Gleichordnung *(f)* n De
En coordination
Es coordinación *(f)*
Fr coordination *(f)*
It coordinamento *(m)*
Pt coordenação *(f)*

Gleichstrom *(m)* n De
En direct current (d.c.)
Es corriente continua *(f)*
Fr courant continu *(m)*
It corrente continua *(f)*
Pt corrente contínua *(f)*

gleitende Skala *(f)* De
En sliding scale
Es escala móvil *(f)*
Fr échelle mobile *(f)*

It   scala mobile *(f)*
Pt   escala móvel *(f)*

Gleitklausel *(f)* n De
En   escalator clause
Es   cláusula de revisión de
     precios *(f)*
Fr   échelle mobile *(f)*
It   scala mobile *(f)*
Pt   cláusula de actualização de
     preços *(f)*

global *adj* En, Es, Fr, Pt
De   Global-
It   globale

Global- De
En   global
Es   global
Fr   global
It   globale
Pt   global

globale *adj* It
De   Global-
En   global
Es   global
Fr   global
Pt   global

Globalgeschäft *(n)* n De
En   package deal
Es   contrato global *(m)*
Fr   marché global *(m)*
It   contratto globale *(m)*
Pt   contrato global *(m)*

goal n En
De   Ziel *(n)*
Es   meta; objetivo *(f m)*
Fr   bout *(m)*
It   scopo; traguardo *(m)*
Pt   meta; objectivo *(f m)*

go bail for En
De   Haftkaution geben
Es   salir fiados por
Fr   se porter garant de
It   rendersi garante di
Pt   prestar caução a favor de

go bankrupt En
De   Konkurs anmelden
Es   caer en quiebra
Fr   faire faillite
It   fallire
Pt   falir

gobierno *(m)* n Es
De   Regierung *(f)*
En   government
Fr   gouvernement *(m)*
It   governo *(m)*
Pt   governo *(m)*

going concern En
De   gewinnbringendes Unter-
     nehmen *(n)*
Es   negocio en marcha *(m)*
Fr   affaire qui marche *(f)*
It   azienda in piena attività *(f)*
Pt   negócio que vinga *(m)*

gold n En
De   Gold *(n)*
Es   oro *(m)*
Fr   or *(m)*
It   oro *(m)*
Pt   ouro *(m)*

Gold *(n)* n De
En   gold
Es   oro *(m)*
Fr   or *(m)*
It   oro *(m)*
Pt   ouro *(m)*

gold fields En
De   Goldgrube *(f)*
Es   yacimiento aurífero *(m)*
Fr   régions aurifères *(f pl)*
It   terreni auriferi *(m pl)*
Pt   jazigos de ouro *(m pl)*

Goldgrube *(f)* n De
En   gold fields
Es   yacimiento aurífero *(m)*
Fr   régions aurifères *(f pl)*
It   terreni auriferi *(m pl)*
Pt   jazigos de ouro *(m pl)*

Goldobligation *(f)* n De
En   gold standard
Es   patrón oro *(m)*
Fr   étalon or *(m)*
It   base aurea *(f)*
Pt   ouro-padrão *(m)*

gold-plated *adj* En
De   vergoldet
Es   chapado en oro
Fr   plaqué d'or
It   placcato in oro
Pt   laminado a ouro

gold shares En
De   Aktien von Goldberg-
     werken *(f pl)*
Es   acciones auríferas *(f pl)*
Fr   valeurs aurifères *(f pl)*
It   azioni aurifere *(f pl)*
Pt   acções de ouro *(f pl)*

gold standard En
De   Goldobligation *(f)*
Es   patrón oro *(m)*
Fr   étalon or *(m)*
It   base aurea *(f)*
Pt   ouro-padrão *(m)*

good *adj* En
De   gut
Es   bueno
Fr   bon
It   buono
Pt   bom

good (for) *adj* En
De   gut (für)
Es   válido
Fr   valable
It   valido
Pt   válido

good offices En
De   Freundschaftsdienste *(m
     pl)*
Es   buenos servicios *(m pl)*
Fr   bons offices *(m pl)*
It   buoni uffici *(m pl)*
Pt   bons serviços *(m pl)*

goods *pl* n En
De   Güter *(n pl)*
Es   mercancías *(f pl)*
Fr   marchandises *(f pl)*
It   merce *(f)*
Pt   mercadorias *(f pl)*

goods on approval En
De   Probegüter *(n pl)*
Es   mercancías sujetas a
     aprobación *(f pl)*
Fr   marchandises à condition
     (f pl)
It   merce soggetta ad appro-
     vazione *(f)*
Pt   artigos sujeitos a apro-
     vação *(m pl)*

goods on consignment En
De   Kommissionsgüter *(n pl)*
Es   mercancías en consigna-
     ción *(f pl)*

Fr marchandises en consi-
    gnation *(f pl)*
It merce in conto deposito *(f)*
Pt artigos à consignação *(m pl)*

goods train En
Am freight train
De Güterzug *(m)*
Es tren de mercancías *(m)*
Fr train de marchandises *(m)*
It treno merci *(m)*
Pt comboio de mercadorias
    (m)

goodwill *n* En
De Geschäftswert *(m)*
Es valor de la clientela *(m)*
Fr bon vouloir *(m)*
It avviamento *(m)*
Pt boa vontade *(f)*

gorjeta *(f) n* Pt
De Trinkgeld *(n)*
En tip; gratuity
Es propina *(f)*
Fr pourboire *(m)*
It mancia *(f)*

go-slow strike En
Am slow down
De Bummelstreik *(m)*
Es huelga de producción
    lenta *(f)*
Fr grève perlée *(f)*
It sciopero a singhiozzo *(m)*
Pt greve de abrandamento
    do ritmo de produção *(f)*

goulot d'étranglement *(m)* Fr
De Engpaß *(m)*
En bottle-neck
Es embotellamiento *(m)*
It strozzatura *(f)*
Pt engarrafamento *(m)*

gouvernement *(m) n* Fr
De Regierung *(f)*
En government
Es gobierno *(m)*
It governo *(m)*
Pt governo *(m)*

government *n* En
De Regierung *(f)*
Es gobierno *(m)*
Fr gouvernement *(m)*
It governo *(m)*
Pt governo *(m)*

government bond En
De Staatsobligation *(f)*
Es obligación del Estado *(f)*
Fr obligation d'État *(f)*
It obbligazione dello Stato *(f)*
Pt obrigação do Tesouro *(f)*

government employee Am
En civil servant
De Beamte(r) *(m)*
Es funcionario del gobierno
    (m)
Fr fonctionnaire *(m)*
It impiegato statale *(m)*
Pt funcionário público *(m)*

government loan En
De Staatsanleihe *(f)*
Es empréstito público *(m)*
Fr emprunt public *(m)*
It prestito pubblico *(m)*
Pt empréstimo do governo
    (m)

government securities En
De Regierungsschuldver-
    schreibungen *(f pl)*
Es títulos públicos *(m pl)*
Fr titres d'État *(m pl)*
It titoli di Stato *(m pl)*
Pt títulos do Tesouro *(m pl)*

government subsidy En
De Staatszuschuß *(m)*
Es subvención del Estado *(f)*
Fr subvention de l'État *(f)*
It sovvenzione dello Stato *(f)*
Pt subvenções do Estado *(f pl)*

governo *(m) n* It, Pt
De Regierung *(f)*
En government
Es gobierno *(m)*
Fr gouvernement *(m)*

Grad *(m) n* De
En grade
Es grado *(m)*
Fr grade *(m)*
It grado *(m)*
Pt grau *(m)*

grade *n* En, Fr *(m)*
De Grad *(m)*
Es grado *(m)*
It grado *(m)*
Pt grau *(m)*

grado *(m) n* Es, It
De Grad *(m)*
En grade
Fr grade *(m)*
Pt grau *(m)*

gráfico *(m) n* Es, Pt
De Tabelle; graphische Dar-
    stellung *(f)*
En chart; graph
Fr graphique *(m)*
It grafico *(m)*

grafico *(m) n* It
De Tabelle; graphische Dar-
    stellung *(f)*
En chart; graph
Es gráfico *(m)*
Fr graphique *(m)*
Pt gráfico *(m)*

gráfico de operação *(m)* Pt
De Flußdiagramm *(m)*
En flow chart
Es diagrama de flujo *(m)*
Fr ordinogramme *(m)*
It diagramma di flusso *(m)*

grampo *(m) n* Pt
De Büroklammer *(f)*
En paper clip
Es sujetapapeles *(m)*
Fr attache-papiers *(m)*
It fermacarte *(m)*

grande magazzino *(m)* It
De Warenhaus; Kaufhaus *(n)*
En department store
Es grandes almacenes *(m pl)*
Fr grand magasin *(m)*
Pt armazém *(m)*

grandes almacenes *(m pl)* Es
De Warenhaus; Kaufhaus *(n)*
En department store
Fr grand magasin *(m)*
It grande magazzino *(m)*
Pt armazém *(m)*

grand livre *(m)* Fr
De Hauptbuch *(n)*
En ledger
Es libro mayor *(m)*
It libro mastro *(m)*
Pt livro-mestre *(m)*

grand livre d'achats *(m)* Fr
De Einkaufsbuch *(n)*
En bought ledger

Am purchase book
Es libro mayor de compras
  (m)
It mastro acquisti *(m)*
Pt livro-mestre de compras
  (m)

grand livre des ventes *(m)* Fr
De Verkaufskontenbuch *(n)*
En sales ledger
Es libro mayor de ventas *(m)*
It partitario delle vendite *(m)*
Pt livro-mestre de vendas
  (m)

grand magasin *(m)* Fr
De Warenhaus; Kaufhaus *(n)*
En department store
Es grandes almacenes *(m pl)*
It grande magazzino *(m)*
Pt armazém *(m)*

grand public *(m)* Fr
De Öffentlichkeit *(f)*
En general public
Es público en general *(m)*
It pubblico in genere *(m)*
Pt público em geral *(m)*

grant (of a patent) *n* En
De Erteilung (eines Patentes)
  (f)
Es concesión (de una
  patente) *(f)*
Fr délivrance (d'un brevet) *(f)*
It concessione (di brevetto)
  (f)
Pt concessão (de uma
  patente) *(f)*

grant *n* En
De Unterstützung *(f)*
Es subvención *(f)*
Fr subvention *(f)*
It sovvenzione *(f)*
Pt subvenção *(f)*

grant bail En
De gegen Haftkaution frei-
  geben
Es conceder fianza
Fr admettre une caution
It concedere la libertà prov-
  visoria su cauzione
Pt autorizar caução

graph *n* En
De graphische Darstellung *(f)*
Es gráfico *(m)*

Fr graphique *(m)*
It grafico *(m)*
Pt gráfico *(m)*

graphique *(m)* *n* Fr
De Tabelle; graphische Dar-
  stellung *(f)*
En chart; graph
Es gráfico *(m)*
It grafico *(m)*
Pt gráfico *(m)*

graphische Darstellung *(f)*
  De
En diagram; graph
Es diagrama; gráfico *(m)*
Fr diagramme; graphique *(m)*
It diagramma; grafico *(m)*
Pt diagrama; gráfico *(m)*

graph paper En
De Millimeterpapier *(n)*
Es papel milimetrado *(m)*
Fr papier millimétré *(m)*
It carta millimetrata *(f)*
Pt papel milimetrado *(m)*

gratifica *(f)* *n* It
De Gratifikation *(f)*
En gratuity
Es gratificación *(f)*
Fr gratification *(f)*
Pt gratificação *(f)*

gratificação *(f)* *n* Pt
De Gratifikation *(f)*
En gratuity
Es gratificación *(f)*
Fr gratification *(f)*
It gratifica *(f)*

gratificación *(f)* *n* Es
De Gratifikation *(f)*
En gratuity
Fr gratification *(f)*
It gratifica *(f)*
Pt gratificação *(f)*

gratification *(f)* *n* Fr
De Gratifikation *(f)*
En gratuity
Es gratificación *(f)*
It gratifica *(f)*
Pt gratificação *(f)*

gratificazione *(f)* *n* It
De Prämie *(f)*
En bonus
Es prima; gratificación *(f)*

Fr prime; gratification *(f)*
Pt bónus; gratificação *(m f)*

Gratifikation *(f)* *n* De
En gratuity
Es gratificación *(f)*
Fr gratification *(f)*
It gratifica *(f)*
Pt gratificação *(f)*

Gratisaktien *(f pl)* *n* De
En bonus shares
Am stock dividend
Es acciones dadas como
  primas *(f pl)*
Fr actions d'attribution *(f pl)*
It azioni di godimento *(f pl)*
Pt acções de prémio *(f pl)*

gratuity *n* En
De Gratifikation *(f)*
Es gratificación *(f)*
Fr gratification *(f)*
It gratifica *(f)*
Pt gratificação *(f)*

grau *(m)* *n* Pt
De Grad *(m)*
En grade
Es grado *(m)*
Fr grade *(m)*
It grado *(m)*

graving dock En
De Trockendock *(n)*
Es dique de carenas *(m)*
Fr bassin de radoub *(m)*
It bacino di raddobbo *(m)*
Pt doca de querenas *(f)*

green pound En
De grünes Pfund *(n)*
Es esterlina verde *(f)*
Fr livre sterling verte *(f)*
It sterlina verde *(f)*
Pt libra esterlina verde *(f)*

greifbare Aktien *(n pl)* De
En tangible assets
Es activo tangible *(m)*
Fr biens immobiliers *(m pl)*
It beni materiali *(m pl)*
Pt bens visíveis *(m pl)*

Grenze *(f)* *n* De
En limit; frontier
Es límite; frontera *(m f)*
Fr limite; frontière *(f)*
It limite; frontiera *(m f)*
Pt limite; fronteira *(m f)*

grève *(f)* n Fr
De Streik *(m)*
En strike
Es huelga *(f)*
It sciopero *(m)*
Pt greve *(f)*

greve *(f)* n Pt
De Streik *(m)*
En strike
Es huelga *(f)*
Fr grève *(f)*
It sciopero *(m)*

grève avec occupation des lieux *(f)* Fr
De Sitzstreik *(m)*
En sit-down strike
Es huelga de brazos caídos *(f)*
It sciopero bianco *(m)*
Pt greve de braços caídos *(f)*

greve de braços caídos *(f)* Pt
De Sitzstreik *(m)*
En sit-down strike
Es huelga de brazos caídos *(f)*
Fr grève avec occupation des lieux *(f)*
It sciopero bianco *(m)*

grève des dockers *(f)* Fr
De Hafenarbeiterstreik *(m)*
En dock strike
Es huelga de obreros de muelle *(f)*
It sciopero portuale *(m)*
Pt greve na doca *(f)*

grève générale *(f)* Fr
De Generalstreik *(m)*
En general strike
Es huelga general *(f)*
It sciopero generale *(m)*
Pt greve geral *(f)*

greve geral *(f)* Pt
De Generalstreik *(m)*
En general strike
Es huelga general *(f)*
Fr grève générale *(f)*
It sciopero generale *(m)*

greve na doca *(f)* Pt
De Hafenarbeiterstreik *(m)*
En dock strike
Es huelga de obreros de muelle *(f)*
Fr grève des dockers *(f)*
It sciopero portuale *(m)*

greve não oficializada *(f)* Pt
De unanerkannter Streik *(m)*
En unofficial strike
Es huelga no-oficial *(f)*
Fr grève non reconnue *(f)*
It sciopero non ufficiale *(m)*

grève non reconnue *(f)* Fr
De unanerkannter Streik *(m)*
En unofficial strike
Es huelga no-oficial *(f)*
It sciopero non ufficiale *(m)*
Pt greve não oficializada *(f)*

grève officielle *(f)* Fr
De anerkannter Streik *(m)*
En official strike
Es huelga oficial *(f)*
It sciopero ufficiale *(m)*
Pt greve oficial *(f)*

greve oficial *(f)* Pt
De anerkannter Streik *(m)*
En official strike
Es huelga oficial *(f)*
Fr grève officielle *(f)*
It sciopero ufficiale *(m)*

grève perlée *(f)* Fr
De Bummelstreik *(m)*
En go-slow strike
Am slow down
Es huelga de producción lenta *(f)*
It sciopero a singhiozzo *(m)*
Pt greve de abrandamento do ritmo de produção *(f)*

grève sauvage *(f)* Fr
De wilder Streik *(m)*
En wildcat strike
Es huelga espontánea *(f)*
It sciopero selvaggio *(m)*
Pt greve não oficializada *(f)*

grevista *(m)* n Pt
De Streikende(r) *(m)*
En striker
Es huelguista *(m)*
Fr gréviste *(m)*
It scioperante *(m)*

gréviste *(m)* n Fr
De Streikende(r) *(m)*
En striker
Es huelguista *(m)*
It scioperante *(m)*
Pt grevista *(m)*

grief *(m)* n Fr
De Beschwerde *(f)*
En grievance
Es agravio *(m)*
It lagnanza *(f)*
Pt agravo *(m)*

grievance n En
De Beschwerde *(f)*
Es agravio *(m)*
Fr grief *(m)*
It lagnanza *(f)*
Pt agravo *(m)*

gross *adj* En
De brutto
Es bruto
Fr brut; gros
It lordo
Pt bruto

gross amount En
De Bruttobetrag *(m)*
Es importe bruto *(m)*
Fr montant brut *(m)*
It importo lordo *(m)*
Pt importância total *(f)*

gross domestic product (GDP) En
De Bruttoinlandsprodukt *(n)*
Es producto interior bruto *(m)*
Fr produit intérieur brut *(m)*
It prodotto interno lordo *(m)*
Pt produto interno bruto *(m)*

große Havarie *(f)* De
En general average (G.A.)
Es avería general *(f)*
Fr avaries communes *(f pl)*
It avaria generale *(f)*
Pt avaria grossa *(f)*

Großhandel *(m)* n De
En wholesale trade
Es comercio al por mayor *(m)*
Fr commerce en gros *(m)*
It commercio all'ingrosso *(m)*
Pt comércio por atacado *(m)*

Großhändler *(m)* n De
En wholesaler
Es mayorista *(m)*
Fr grossiste *(m)*
It grossista *(m)*
Pt grossista *(m)*

gross income En
De Bruttoeinkommen (n)
Es ingreso bruto (m)
Fr rendement brut (m)
It reddito lordo (m)
Pt receita bruta (f)

gross interest En
De Bruttozins (m)
Es interés bruto (m)
Fr intérêts bruts (m pl)
It interesse lordo (m)
Pt juro bruto (m)

grossista (m) n It, Pt
De Großhändler; Grossist (m)
En wholesaler
Es mayorista (m)
Fr grossiste (m)

grossiste (m) n Fr
De Großhändler; Grossist (m)
En wholesaler
Es mayorista (m)
It grossista (m)
Pt grossista (m)

gross margin En
De Bruttoverdienstspanne (f)
Es márgen bruto (m)
Fr marge brute de bénéfices (f)
It margine lordo (m)
Pt margem bruta (f)

gross national product (GNP) En
De Bruttosozialprodukt (n)
Es producto nacional bruto (m)
Fr produit national brut (m)
It prodotto nazionale lordo (m)
Pt produto nacional bruto (m)

gross premium En
De Bruttoprämie (f)
Es prima bruta (f)
Fr prime brute (f)
It premio lordo (m)
Pt prémio bruto (m)

gross profit En
De Bruttogewinn (m)
Es ganancia bruta (f)
Fr bénéfice brut (m)
It utile lordo (m)
Pt lucro bruto (m)

Großraumbüro (n) n De
En open-plan office
Es oficina sin particiones (f)
Fr bureau sans cloisons (m)
It ufficio senza divisioni (m)
Pt escritório sem divisões (m)

gross register ton En
De Bruttoregistertonne (f)
Es tonelada de registro bruto (f)
Fr tonneau de jauge brute (m)
It tonnellaggio lordo di registro (m)
Pt tonelada de registo bruto (f)

gross ton En
De Bruttotonne (f)
Es tonelada bruta (f)
Fr tonne forte (f)
It tonnellata lorda (f)
Pt tonelada de peso bruto (f)

gross tonnage En
De Bruttotonnage (f)
Es tonelaje bruto (m)
Fr tonnage brut (m)
It tonnellaggio lordo (m)
Pt tonelagem de peso bruto (f)

gross weight En
De Bruttogewicht (n)
Es peso bruto (m)
Fr poids brut (m)
It peso lordo (m)
Pt peso bruto (m)

ground floor En
De Erdgeschoß (n)
Es planta baja (f)
Fr rez-de-chaussée (m)
It pianterreno (m)
Pt rés-do-chão (m)

ground glass En
De Mattscheibe (f)
Es cristal deslustrado (m)
Fr verre dépoli (m)
It vetro smerigliato (m)
Pt vidro esmerilado (m)

ground-landlord n En
De Grundbesitzer (m)
Es propietario del terreno (m)
Fr propriétaire foncier (m)
It proprietario del terreno (m)
Pt proprietário do terreno (m)

ground-rent n En
De Grundpacht (f)
Es renta del terreno (f)
Fr rente foncière (f)
It affitto di terreno (m)
Pt renda sobre o terreno (f)

Groupagedienst (m) n De
En groupage service
Es servicio de agrupación (m)
Fr service de groupage (m)
It trasporto a collettame (m)
Pt serviço de agrupamento (m)

groupage service En
De Groupagedienst (m)
Es servicio de agrupación (m)
Fr service de groupage (m)
It trasporto a collettame (m)
Pt serviço de agrupamento (m)

groupe consommateur (m) Fr
De Abnehmerverein (m)
En consumer group
Es grupo de consumidores (m)
It gruppo di consumatori (m)
Pt grupo de consumidores (m)

Groupe des Dix (m) Fr
De Zehnerklub (m)
En Group of Ten
Es Grupo de los Diez (m)
It Gruppo dei Dieci (m)
Pt Grupo dos Dez (m)

group insurance En
De Gruppenversicherung (f)
Es seguro de grupo (m)
Fr assurance de groupe (f)
It assicurazione di gruppo (f)
Pt seguro de grupo (m)

Group of Ten En
De Zehnerklub (m)
Es Grupo de los Diez (m)
Fr Groupe des Dix (m)
It Gruppo dei Dieci (m)
Pt Grupo dos Dez (m)

growth n En
De Entwicklung; Wachstum (f n)
Es crecimiento (m)
Fr croissance; développement (f m)
It crescita; sviluppo (f m)
Pt crescimento (m)

growth stocks En
De wachstumsorientierte
   Wertpapiere *(n pl)*
Es títulos de crecimiento
   (m pl)
Fr titres avec perspectives de
   croissance *(m pl)*
It titoli di sviluppo *(m pl)*
Pt acções de acréscimo de
   capital *(f pl)*

gru *(f) n* It
De Kran *(m)*
En crane
Es grúa *(f)*
Fr grue *(f)*
Pt grua *(f)*

grua *(f) n* Pt
De Kran *(m)*
En crane
Es grúa *(f)*
Fr grue *(f)*
It gru *(f)*

grúa *(f) n* Es
De Kran *(m)*
En crane
Fr grue *(f)*
It gru *(f)*
Pt grua *(f)*

grúa flotante *(f)*
   Es
De Pontonkran *(m)*
En floating crane
Fr ponton-grue *(m)*
It gru galleggiante *(f)*
Pt guindaste flutuante *(m)*

grue *(f) n* Fr
De Kran *(m)*
En crane
Es grúa *(f)*
It gru *(f)*
Pt grua *(f)*

gru galleggiante *(f)*
   It
De Pontonkran *(m)*
En floating crane
Es grúa flotante *(f)*
Fr ponton-grue *(m)*
Pt guindaste flutuante *(m)*

Grundbesitzer *(m) n*
   De
En ground-landlord
Es propietario del terreno *(m)*

Fr propriétaire foncier *(m)*
It proprietario del terreno *(m)*
Pt proprietário do terreno *(m)*

gründen *vb* De
En found; establish
Es fundar; establecer
Fr fonder; établir
It fondare; stabilire
Pt fundar; estabelecer

Gründer *(m) n* De
En founder
Es fundador *(m)*
Fr fondateur *(m)*
It fondatore *(m)*
Pt fundador *(m)*

Gründeraktien *(f pl) n* De
En founder's shares
Es. acciones del fundador
   (f pl)
Fr actions de fondateur *(f pl)*
It azioni del fondatore *(f pl)*
Pt acções de fundador *(f pl)*

Gründermitglied *(m) n* De
En founder member
Es miembro fundador *(m)*
Fr membre fondateur *(m)*
It socio fondatore *(m)*
Pt membro fundador *(m)*

Grundjahr *(n) n* De
En base year
Es año de base *(m)*
Fr année de base *(f)*
It anno di base *(m)*
Pt ano base *(m)*

Grundlohn *(m) n* De
En basic pay
Am base pay
Es salario-base *(m)*
Fr salaire de base *(f)*
It salario fondamentale *(m)*
Pt salário-base *(m)*

Grundpacht *(f) n* De
En ground-rent
Es renta del terreno *(f)*
Fr rente foncière *(f)*
It affitto di terreno *(m)*
Pt renda sobre o terreno *(f)*

Grundsteuer *(f) n* De
En property tax
Es impuesto sobre la propie-
   dad *(m)*

Fr impôt foncier *(m)*
It imposta fondiaria *(f)*
Pt imposto sobre proprieda-
   de *(m)*

grünes Pfund *(n)* De
En green pound
Es esterlina verde *(f)*
Fr livre sterling verte *(f)*
It sterlina verde *(f)*
Pt libra esterlina verde *(f)*

grupo de consumidores *(m)*
   Es, Pt
De Abnehmerverein *(m)*
En consumer group
Fr groupe consommateur *(m)*
It gruppo di consumatori *(m)*

Grupo de los Diez *(m)* Es
De Zehnerklub *(m)*
En Group of Ten
Fr Groupe des Dix *(m)*
It Gruppo dei Dieci *(m)*
Pt Grupo dos Dez *(m)*

grupo de suscriptores *(m)* Es
De Emissionssyndikat *(n)*
En underwriting syndicate
Fr syndicat de garantie *(m)*
It consorzio finanziario *(m)*
Pt consórcio de subscritores
   (m)

Grupo dos Dez *(m)* Pt
De Zehnerklub *(m)*
En Group of Ten
Es Grupo de los Diez *(m)*
Fr Groupe des Dix *(m)*
It Gruppo dei Dieci *(m)*

Gruppenversicherung *(f) n*
   De
En group insurance
Es seguro de grupo *(m)*
Fr assurance de groupe *(f)*
It assicurazione di gruppo *(f)*
Pt seguro de grupo *(m)*

Gruppo dei Dieci *(m)* It
De Zehnerklub *(m)*
En Group of Ten
Es Grupo de los Diez *(m)*
Fr Groupe des Dix *(m)*
Pt Grupo dos Dez *(m)*

gruppo di consumatori *(m)* It
De Abnehmerverein *(m)*
En consumer group

Es grupo de consumidores
    (m)
Fr groupe consommateur (m)
Pt grupo de consumidores
    (m)

guadagnare vb It
De verdienen
En earn
Es ganar
Fr gagner
Pt ganhar

guadagno (m) n It
De Gewinn (m)
En gain
Es ganancia (f)
Fr gain (m)
Pt ganhos (m pl)

guarantee vb En
De Bürgschaft leisten; ge-
    währleisten
Es garantizar; avalar
Fr garantir; avaliser
It garantire; avallare
Pt garantir; assegurar

guarantee n En
De Garantie (f)
Es garantía (f)
Fr garantie (f)
It garanzia (f)
Pt garantia (f)

guarantor n En
De Bürge (m)
Es garante; fiador (m)
Fr garant; avaliste (m)
It garante; avallante (m)
Pt fiador; avalizador (m)

guarda de noche (m) Es
De Nachtwächter (m)
En nightwatchman
Fr gardien de nuit (m)
It guardiano notturno (m)
Pt guarda-nocturno (m)

guarda-livros diplomado
    (m) Pt
De Wirtschaftsprüfer (m)
En qualified accountant
Es contador habilitado (m)
Fr expert comptable (m)
It ragioniere diplomato (m)

guarda-nocturno (m) Pt
De Nachtwächter (m)
En nightwatchman
Es guarda de noche (m)
Fr gardien de nuit (m)
It guardiano notturno (m)

guardar vb Pt, Es
De halten
En hold
Fr tenir; détenir
It tenere

guardar en almacén Es
De vorrätig halten
En keep in stock
Fr garder en stock
It tenere in magazzino
Pt reter em armazém

guardar in ficeicomiso Es
De zu treuen Händen halten
En hold in trust
Fr tenir par fidéicommis
It tenere in fidecommesso
Pt reter em custódia

guardian (of a minor, etc.) n
    En
De Vormund (m)
Es tutor (m)
Fr tuteur (m)
It tutore (m)
Pt tutor (m)

guardiano notturno (m) It
De Nachtwächter (m)
En nightwatchman
Es guarda de noche (m)
Fr gardien de nuit (m)
Pt guarda-nocturno (m)

guard's van En
De Packwagen (m)
Es furgón (m)
Fr fourgon (m)
It bagagliaio (m)
Pt furgão (m)

guerra (f) n Es, It, Pt
De Krieg (m)
En war
Fr guerre (f)

guerra dei prezzi (f) It
De Preiskrieg (m)
En price war
Es guerra de precios (f)

Fr guerre des prix (f)
Pt guerra de preços (f)

guerra de precios (f) Es
De Preiskrieg (m)
En price war
Fr guerre des prix (f)
It guerra dei prezzi (f)
Pt guerra de preços (f)

guerra de preços (f) Pt
De Preiskrieg (m)
En price war
Es guerra de precios (f)
Fr guerre des prix (f)
It guerra dei prezzi (t)

guerre (f) n Fr
De Krieg (m)
En war
Es guerra (f)
It guerra (f)
Pt guerra (f)

guerre des prix (f) Fr
De Preiskrieg (m)
En price war
Es guerra de precios (f)
It guerra dei prezzi (f)
Pt guerra de preços (f)

guess-work n En
De Mutmaßung (f)
Es conjetura (f)
Fr conjecture (f)
It congettura (f)
Pt conjectura (f)

guía (f) n Es
De Adreßbuch (n)
En directory
Fr répertoire (m)
It guida (f)
Pt guia (m)

guia (m) n Pt
De Adreßbuch (n)
En directory
Es guía (f)
Fr répertoire (m)
It guida (f)

guía comercial (f) Es
De Handelsadreßbuch (n)
En trade directory
Fr guide de commerce (m)
It guida commerciale (f)
Pt guia comercial (m)

guia comercial *(m)* Pt
De Handelsadreßbuch *(n)*
En trade directory
Es guía comercial *(f)*
Fr guide de commerce *(m)*
It guida commerciale *(f)*

guía de carga *(f)* Es
De Frachtbrief *(m)*
En waybill
Fr lettre de voiture *(f)*
It lettera di vettura *(f)*
Pt guia de marcha *(f)*

guia de consignação *(f)* Pt
De Frachtbrief *(m)*
En consignment note
Es nota de consignación *(f)*
Fr lettre de voiture *(f)*
It nota di spedizione *(f)*

guia de entrega *(f)* Pt
De Lieferschein *(m)*
En delivery note
Es aviso de entrega *(m)*
Fr bordereau de livraison *(m)*
It nota di consegna *(f)*

guia de marcha *(f)* Pt
De Frachtbrief *(m)*
En waybill
Es guía de carga *(f)*
Fr lettre de voiture *(f)*
It lettera di vettura *(f)*

guia de porte aéreo *(f)* Pt
De Luftfrachtbrief *(m)*
En air waybill
Es carta de porte aéreo *(f)*
Fr lettre de transport aérien *(f)*
It nota di spedizione aerea *(f)*

guia de remessa *(f)* Pt
De Anzeige *(f)*
En advice note
Es aviso *(m)*
Fr lettre d'avis *(f)*
It lettera d'avviso *(f)*

guía de teléfonos *(f)* Es
De Fernsprechbuch *(n)*
En telephone directory
Fr annuaire des téléphones *(m)*
It elenco telefonico *(m)*
Pt lista telefónica *(f)*

guida *(f)* n It
De Adreßbuch *(n)*
En directory
Es guía *(f)*
Fr répertoire *(m)*
Pt guia *(m)*

guida commerciale *(f)* It
De Handelsadreßbuch *(n)*
En trade directory
Es guía comercial *(f)*
Fr guide de commerce *(m)*
Pt guia comercial *(m)*

guide de commerce *(m)* Fr
De Handelsadreßbuch *(n)*
En trade directory
Es guía comercial *(f)*
It guida commerciale *(f)*
Pt guia comercial *(m)*

guindaste flutuante *(m)*
Pt
De Pontonkran *(m)*
En floating crane
Es grúa flotante *(f)*
Fr ponton-grue *(m)*
It gru galleggiante *(f)*

gültig *adj* De
En valid
Es válido
Fr valable
It valido
Pt válido

Gummistempel *(m)* n De
En rubber stamp
Es estampilla de goma *(f)*
Fr tampon *(m)*
It stampino di gomma *(m)*
Pt carimbo *(m)*

Gußeisen *(n)* n De
En cast iron
Es hierro colado *(m)*
Fr fer de fonte *(m)*
It ghisa *(f)*
Pt ferro fundido *(m)*

gut *adj* De
En good
Es bueno
Fr bon
It buono
Pt bom

Gut *(n)* n De
En commodity
Es mercadería *(f)*
Fr marchandise *(f)*

It merce *(f)*
Pt mercadoria *(f)*

gute Durchschnittsqualität
(f) De
En fair average quality (faq)
Es calidad media razonable *(f)*
Fr qualité commerciale
moyenne *(f)*
It buona qualità media *(f)*
Pt qualidade média razoável
(f)

Güter *(n pl)* n De
En goods
Es mercancías *(f pl)*
Fr marchandises *(f pl)*
It merce *(f)*
Pt mercadorias *(f pl)*

Güterbeförderer *(m)* n De
En common carrier
Es empresa de transportes *(f)*
Fr voiturier public *(m)*
It vettore *(m)*
Pt empresa de transportes *(f)*

Güterzug *(m)* n De
En goods train
Am freight train
Es tren de mercancías *(m)*
Fr train de marchandises *(m)*
It treno merci *(m)*
Pt comboio de mercadorias
(m)

gutgläubiger Besitzer *(m)* De
En holder in due course
Es tenedor en buena fe *(m)*
Fr porteur de bonne foi *(m)*
It titolare in buona fede *(m)*
Pt futuro proprietário *(m)*

Gutschriftanzeige *(f)* n De
En credit note
Es nota de crédito *(f)*
Fr avis de crédit *(m)*
It nota di credito *(f)*
Pt aviso de crédito *(m)*

H

hacer efectivo Es
De bewerkstelligen; ausfüh-
ren
En implement
Fr exécuter

It attuare; effettuare
Pt executar

hacer una cita Es
De eine Verabredung treffen
En make an appointment
Fr prendre un rendez-vous
It fissare un appuntamento
Pt marcar um encontro

hacer una contraoferta Es
De ein Gegenangebot
　abgeben
En make a counteroffer
Fr faire une contre-offre
It fare una controfferta
Pt fazer uma contra-pro-
　posta

hacer una oferta Es
De eine Offerte machen
En make an offer
Fr faire une offre
It fare una offerta
Pt fazer uma oferta

hacer un depósito Es
De hinterlegen
En pay a deposit
Fr donner des arrhes
It versare un deposito
Pt pagar depósito

hacer un pedido Es
De bestellen
En order
Fr passer une commande
It ordinare
Pt encomendar

hacienda *(f)* n Es
De Schatzamt *(n)*
En exchequer
Am treasury
Fr trésorerie *(f)*
It tesoro *(m)*
Pt tesouro *(m)*

Hafen *(m)* n De
En port; harbour
Es puerto *(m)*
Fr port *(m)*
It porto *(m)*
Pt porto *(m)*

Hafenanlagen *(f pl)* n De
En harbour installations
Es instalaciones portuarias
　(f pl)

Fr installations portuaires
　(f pl)
It impianti portuali *(m pl)*
Pt instalações portuárias *(f pl)*

Hafenarbeiter *(m)* n De
En docker
Am longshoreman
Es cargador de muelle *(m)*
Fr docker *(m)*
It lavoratore del porto *(m)*
Pt trabalhador das docas *(m)*

Hafenarbeiterstreik *(m)* n De
En dock strike
Es huelga de obreros de
　muelle *(f)*
Fr grève des dockers *(f)*
It sciopero portuale *(m)*
Pt greve na doca *(f)*

Hafengebühren *(f pl)* n De
En port charges
Es derechos portuarios *(m pl)*
Fr droits de port *(m pl)*
It diritti portuali *(m pl)*
Pt direitos portuários *(m pl)*

Hafenkonnossement *(n)* n De
En shipped bill of lading
Es conocimiento de embar-
　que a bordo *(m)*
Fr connaissement de mar-
　chandises à bord *(m)*
It polizza di carico con mer-
　ce a bordo *(f)*
Pt conhecimento de carga
　embarcada *(m)*

Hafenmeister *(m)* n De
En harbour-master
Es capitán de puerto *(m)*
Fr capitaine de port *(m)*
It capitano di porto *(m)*
Pt capitão de porto *(m)*

Haftkaution *(f)* n De
En bail
Es fianza *(f)*
Fr caution *(f)*
It cauzione *(f)*
Pt caução *(f)*

Haftkaution geben De
En go bail for
Es salir fiados por
Fr se porter garant de
It rendersi garante di
Pt prestar caução a favor de

Haftpflichtversicherung *(f)* n
　De
En third-party insurance
Es seguro contra responsabi-
　lidad civil *(m)*
Fr assurance responsabilité
　civile (RC) *(f)*
It assicurazione contro terzi
　(f)
Pt seguro contra terceiros *(m)*

haggle *vb* En
Am bargain
De feilschen
Es regatear
Fr marchander; chipoter
It mercanteggiare; cavillare
Pt regatear

halb *adj* De
En half
Es medio
Fr à moitié; demi
It mezzo
Pt meio

(zum) halben Preise De
En half price
Es a mitad de precio
Fr à moitié prix
It metà prezzo
Pt metade do preço

halbjährlich *adj* De
En half-yearly
Es semestral
Fr semestriel
It semestrale
Pt semestral

halbjährliche Dividende *(f)*
　De
En half-yearly dividend
Es dividendo semestral *(m)*
Fr dividende semestrielle *(f)*
It dividendo semestrale *(m)*
Pt dividendo semi-anual *(m)*

Halbsold *(m)* n De
En half-pay
Es medio-salario *(m)*
Fr demi-salaire *(m)*
It mezza paga *(f)*
Pt meio-salário *(m)*

half *adj* En
De halb
Es medio
Fr à moitié; demi

It mezzo
Pt meio

half-pay n En
De Halbsold (m)
Es medio salario (m)
Fr demi-salaire (m)
It mezza paga (f)
Pt meio-salário (m)

half price En
De zum halben Preise
Es a mitad de precio
Fr à moitié prix
It metà prezzo
Pt metade do preço

half-year n En
De Semester (n)
Es semestre (m)
Fr semestre (m)
It semestre (m)
Pt semestre (m)

half-yearly adj En
De halbjährlich
Es semestral
Fr semestriel
It semestrale
Pt semestral

half-yearly dividend En
De halbjährliche Dividende (f)
Es dividendo semestral (m)
Fr dividende semestrielle (f)
It dividendo semestrale (m)
Pt dividendo semi-anual (m)

hall-mark n En
De Feingehaltsstempel (m)
Es punzón de garantía (m)
Fr poinçon de titre (m)
It punzonatura di garanzia (f)
Pt marca de garantia (f)

hall-porter n En
De Hausmeister (m)
Es conserje (m)
Fr concierge (m)
It portiere (m)
Pt porteiro (m)

halten vb De
En hold
Es tener
Fr tenir; détenir
It tenere
Pt guardar; conservar

Hand- De
En manual
Es manual
Fr manuel
It manuale
Pt manual

handbook n En
De Handbuch (n)
Es manual (m)
Fr manuel (m)
It manuale (m)
Pt manual (m)

Handbuch (n) n De
En handbook
Es manual (m)
Fr manuel (m)
It manuale (m)
Pt manual (m)

Handel (m) n De
En commerce; trade
Es comercio (m)
Fr commerce (m)
It commercio (m)
Pt comércio (m)

Handels- De
En mercantile
Es mercantil
Fr mercantile
It mercantile
Pt mercantil

Handelsadreßbuch (n) n De
En trade directory
Es guía comercial (f)
Fr guide de commerce (m)
It guida commerciale (f)
Pt guia comercial (m)

Handelsakzept (n) n De
En trade acceptance
Es acceptación comercial (f)
Fr acceptation de commerce (f)
It accettazione commerciale (f)
Pt aceitação comercial (f)

Handelsbank (f) n De
En merchant bank
Es banco mercantil (m)
Fr banque commerciale (f)
It banca commerciale (f)
Pt banco comercial (m)

Handelsbeschränkung (f) n De
En restraint of trade
Es restricción del commercio (f)
Fr restriction au commerce (f)
It restrizione del commercio (f)
Pt restrição de comércio (f)

Handelsbevollmächtigte(r) (m) n De
En accredited agent
Es agente acreditado (m)
Fr agent accrédité (m)
It agente accreditato (m)
Pt agente acreditado (m)

Handelsbilanz (f) n De
En balance of trade
Es balanza comercial (f)
Fr balance commerciale (f)
It bilancia commerciale (f)
Pt balança comercial (f)

Handelsblock (m) n De
En trade bloc
Es bloque comercial (m)
Fr bloc commercial (m)
It unione commerciale (f)
Pt bloque comercial (m)

Handelsflotte (f) n De
En merchant fleet
Es flota mercanto (f)
Fr flotte marchande (f)
It flotta mercantile (f)
Pt frota mercante (f)

Handelsgebrauch (m) n De
En custom of the trade
Es uso comercial (m)
Fr usage commercial (m)
It uso commerciale (m)
Pt uso comercial (m)

Handelskammer (f) n De
En chamber of commerce
Es cámara de comercio (f)
Fr chambre de commerce (f)
It camera di commercio (f)
Pt câmara de comércio (f)

Handelskonto (n) n De
En trade account
Es cuenta comercial (f)
Fr compte commercial (m)
It conto commerciale (m)
Pt conta comercial (f)

Handelsmarke *(f)* n De
En brand
Es marca (de fábrica) *(f)*
Fr marque de fabrique *(f)*
It marca (di fabbrica) *(f)*
Pt marca de fábrica *(f)*

Handelsmesse *(f)* n De
En trade fair
Es feria de muestras *(f)*
Fr foire commerciale *(f)*
It fiera commerciale *(f)*
Pt feira commercial *(f)*

Handelspreis *(m)* n De
En trade price
Es precio al comerciante *(m)*
Fr prix marchand *(m)*
It prezzo al commerciante *(m)*
Pt preço para comerciantes *(m)*

Handelsschiff *(n)* n De
En merchant ship
Es barco mercante *(m)*
Fr navire marchand *(m)*
It nave mercantile *(f)*
Pt navio mercante *(m)*

Handelsschranke *(f)* n De
En trade barrier
Es barrera comercial *(f)*
Fr barrière commerciale *(f)*
It barriera commerciale *(f)*
Pt barreira comercial *(f)*

Handelstonne *(f)* n De
En freight ton
Es tonelada de flete *(f)*
Fr tonneau de fret *(m)*
It tonnellata di nolo *(f)*
Pt tonelada de frete *(f)*

Handelsvertreter *(m)* n De
En mercantile agent
Am sales agent
Es agente mercantil *(m)*
Fr agent de commerce *(m)*
It agente di commercio *(m)*
Pt agente comercial *(m)*

Handelszyklus *(m)* n De
En trade cycle
Es ciclo del negocio *(m)*
Fr cycle de commerce *(m)*
It ciclo degli affari *(m)*
Pt ciclo comercial *(m)*

Handgepäck *(n)* n De
En hand-luggage
Es equipaje de mano *(m)*
Fr bagages à main *(m pl)*
It bagaglio a mano *(m)*
Pt bagagem de mão *(f)*

hand in one's resignation En
De den Rücktritt einreichen
Es presentar la dimisión
Fr remettre sa démission
It rassegnare le dimissioni
Pt apresentar demissão

Händler *(m)* n De
En dealer
Es comerciante *(m)*
Fr négociant *(m)*
It negoziante; commerciante *(m)*
Pt negociante *(m)*

Händlerrabatt *(m)* n De
En trade discount
Es descuento comercial *(m)*
Fr rabais de demi-gros *(m)*
It sconto di rivendita *(m)*
Pt desconto à praça *(m)*

handle with care! En
De Vorsicht; zerbrechlich
Es frágil!
Fr fragile!
It fragile!
Pt frágil!

handling charges En
De Umschlagspesen *(f)*
Es gastos de manutención *(m pl)*
Fr frais de manutention *(m pl)*
It spese di gestione *(f pl)*
Pt custas de manejo *(f pl)*

hand-luggage n En
De Handgepäck *(n)*
Es equipaje de mano *(m)*
Fr bagages à main *(m pl)*
It bagaglio a mano *(m)*
Pt bagagem de mão *(f)*

harbour n En
De Hafen *(m)*
Es puerto *(m)*
Fr port *(m)*
It porto *(m)*
Pt porto *(m)*

harbour dues En
De Hafengebühren *(f pl)*
Es derechos de puerto *(m pl)*
Fr droits de port *(m pl)*
It diritti portuali *(m pl)*
Pt direitos portuários *(m pl)*

harbour installations En
De Hafenanlagen *(f pl)*
Es instalaciones portuarias *(f pl)*
Fr installations portuaires *(f pl)*
It impianti portuali *(m pl)*
Pt instalações portuárias *(f pl)*

harbour-master n En
De Hafenmeister *(m)*
Es capitán de puerto *(m)*
Fr capitaine de port *(m)*
It capitano di porto *(m)*
Pt capitão de porto *(m)*

hard currency En
De harte Währung *(f)*
Es moneda fuerta *(f)*
Fr monnaie forte *(f)*
It valuta forte *(f)*
Pt moeda forte *(f)*

hard sell En
De aufdringliches Verkaufen *(n)*
Es venta insistente *(f)*
Fr vente débrouillarde *(f)*
It vendita facendo sforzo *(f)*
Pt venda insistente *(f)*

hardware (ironmongery) n En
De Eisenwaren *(f pl)*
Es ferretería; quincallería *(f)*
Fr quincaillerie *(f)*
It ferramenta *(f)*
Pt ferragens *(f pl)*

hardware (computers) n En
De Maschinenausrüstung; Hardware *(f)*
Es mecánica de la máquina; hardware *(f m)*
Fr hardware *(m)*
It componenti di macchina calcolatore; hardware *(m pl; m)*
Pt sistema físico; hardware *(m)*

harte Währung *(f)* De
En hard currency
Es moneda fuerta *(f)*
Fr monnaie forte *(f)*
It valuta forte *(f)*
Pt moeda forte *(f)*

harvest *n* En
De Ernte *(f)*
Es cosecha *(f)*
Fr moisson; récolte *(f)*
It raccolto *(m)*
Pt colheita *(f)*

hasard *(m)* *n* Fr
De Wagnis *(n)*
En hazard
Es azar; riesgo *(m)*
It rischio *(m)*
Pt risco; azar *(m)*

hasarder *vb* Fr
De wagen
En hazard
Es arriesgar
It arrischiare
Pt arriscar

Häufigkeit *(f)* *n* De
En frequency
Es frecuencia *(f)*
Fr fréquence *(f)*
It frequenza *(f)*
Pt frequência *(f)*

Häufigkeitsverteilung *(f)* *n* De
En frequency distribution
Es distribución de las fre-
    cuencias *(f)*
Fr distribution de fréquences
    (f)
It distribuzione delle fre-
    quenze *(f)*
Pt distribuição de frequência
    (f)

haulage *n* En
Am trucking
De Transport *(m)*
Es transporte *(m)*
Fr camionnage; transport *(m)*
It trasporto *(m)*
Pt transporte *(m)*

haulage contractor En
Am trucking company
De Transportunternehmer *(m)*
Es contratista de transportes
    (m)

Fr entrepreneur de camion-
    nage *(m)*
It imprenditore di trasporti
    (m)
Pt empreiteiro de transportes
    (m)

Hauptbuch *(n)* *n* De
En ledger
Es libro mayor *(m)*
Fr grand livre *(m)*
It libro mastro *(m)*
Pt livro-mestre *(m)*

Hauptbüro *(n)* *n* De
En head office
Es oficina central *(f)*
Fr siège; bureau principal *(m)*
It sede; ufficio centrale *(f m)*
Pt sede; escritório central
    (f m)

Haupteinkäufer *(m)* *n* De
En head buyer
Es jefe del departamento de
    compras *(m)*
Fr chef du service des achats
    (m)
It capo servizio acquisti *(m)*
Pt chefe de compras *(m)*

Hauptverkehrszeit *(f)* *n* De
En rush hour
Es hora punta *(f)*
Fr heures d'affluence *(f pl)*
It ora di punta *(f)*
Pt hora de ponta *(f)*

Hauptversammlung *(f)* *n* De
En general meeting
Es asamblea general *(f)*
Fr assemblée générale *(f)*
It assemblea generale *(f)*
Pt assembleia geral *(f)*

Haus *(n)* *n* De
En house
Es casa *(f)*
Fr maison *(f)*
It casa *(f)*
Pt casa *(f)*

Hausfrau *(f)* *n* De
En housewife
Es ama de casa *(f)*
Fr ménagère *(f)*
It massaia *(f)*
Pt dona de casa *(f)*

Haushalt *(m)* *n* De
En household
Es hogar *(m)*
Fr ménage *(m)*
It famiglia *(f)*
Pt casa *(f)*

Haushaltskontrolle *(f)* *n* De
En budgetary control
Es control presupuestario *(m)*
Fr contrôle budgétaire *(m)*
It controllo a bilancio pre-
    ventivo *(m)*
Pt controlo orçamental *(m)*

Haushaltsplan *(m)* *n* De
En budget
Es presupuesto *(m)*
Fr budget *(m)*
It bilancio preventivo *(m)*
Pt orçamento *(m)*

**(einen) Haushaltsplan ins
    Gleichgewicht bringen**
    De
En balance a budget
Es balancear el presupuesto
Fr équilibrer un budget
It pareggiare un bilancio
Pt equilibrar um orçamento

Hausherr *(m)* *n* De
En householder
Es jefe de familia *(m)*
Fr chef de famille *(m)*
It capo-famiglia *(m)*
Pt dono da casa *(m)*

Hausmeister *(m)* *n* De
En hall-porter
Es conserje *(m)*
Fr concierge *(m)*
It portiere *(m)*
Pt porteiro *(m)*

hausse *(f)* *n* Fr
De Steigen; Zunahme *(n f)*
En increase; rise
Es incremento; aumento *(m)*
It incremento; crescita *(m f)*
Pt aumento; incremento *(m)*

Hausse *(f)* *n* De
En boom
Es bonanza *(f)*
Fr haute conjoncture *(f)*
It rialzo *(m)*
Pt bonança *(f)*

Haussemarkt *(m)* n De
En bull market
Es mercado alcista *(m)*
Fr marché orienté à la hausse *(m)*
It mercato tendente al rialzo *(m)*
Pt mercado de tendência altista *(m)*

Haussespekulant *(m)* n De
En bull
Es alcista *(m)*
Fr haussier *(m)*
It rialzista *(m)*
Pt altista *(m)*

haussier *(m)* n Fr
De Haussespekulant *(m)*
En bull
Es alcista *(m)*
It rialzista *(m)*
Pt altista *(m)*

haussier *adj* Fr
De steigend
En bullish
Es alcista
It rialzista
Pt altista

Haus-zu-Haus-Verkauf *(m)* n De
En door-to-door selling
Es venta a domicilio *(f)*
Fr vente à domicile *(f)*
It vendita a domicilio *(f)*
Pt venda de porta-a-porta *(f)*

haut *adj* Fr
De hoch
En high
Es alto; elevado
It alto; elevato
Pt elevado

haute conjoncture *(f)* Fr
De Hausse *(f)*
En boom
Es bonanza *(f)*
It rialzo *(m)*
Pt bonança *(f)*

haute direction *(f)* Fr
De Direktion *(f)*
En top management
Es dirección superior *(f)*
It direzione superiore *(f)*
Pt gerência superior *(f)*

hautes mers *(f pl)* Fr
De hohe See *(f)*
En high seas
Es altamar *(f)*
It alto mare *(m)*
Pt alto-mar *(m)*

Havarie *(f)* n De
En average
Es avería *(f)*
Fr avarie *(f)*
It avaria *(f)*
Pt avaria *(f)*

havariert *adj* De
En with average (WA)
Es con avería
Fr avarié
It con avaria
Pt com avaria

Havarieschein *(m)* n De
En average bond
Es fianza de avería *(f)*
Fr compromis d'avarie *(m)*
It compromesso d'avaria *(m)*
Pt fiança de avaria *(f)*

hazard *vb* En
De wagen
Es arriesgar
Fr hasarder
It arrischiare
Pt arriscar

hazard n En
De Wagnis *(n)*
Es azar; riesgo *(m)*
Fr hasard; risque *(m)*
It rischio *(m)*
Pt risco; azar *(m)*

head buyer En
De Haupteinkäufer *(m)*
Es jefe de departamento de compras *(m)*
Fr chef du service des achats *(m)*
It capo servizio acquisti *(m)*
Pt chefe de compras *(m)*

head foreman En
De Werkmeister *(m)*
Es capataz jefe *(m)*
Fr chef d'atelier *(m)*
It capo officina *(m)*
Pt encarregado-chefe *(m)*

head of department En
De Abteilungsleiter *(m)*
Es jefe de departamento *(m)*
Fr chef de service *(m)*
It capo reparto *(m)*
Pt chefe de departamento *(m)*

head office En
De Hauptbüro *(n)*
Es oficina central *(f)*
Fr siège; bureau principal *(m)*
It sede; ufficio centrale *(f m)*
Pt sede; escritório central *(f m)*

health insurance En
De Krankenversicherung *(f)*
Es seguro de enfermedad *(m)*
Fr assurance maladie *(f)*
It assicurazione malattia *(f)*
Pt seguro de doença *(m)*

health service En
De Gesundheitsdienst *(m)*
Es servicio de sanidad *(m)*
Fr service de la santé *(m)*
It servizio sanitario *(m)*
Pt serviço de saúde *(m)*

heavy *adj* En
De schwer
Es pesado; fuerte
Fr lourd; fort
It pesante; forte
Pt pesado

heavy charges En
De drückende Spesen *(f pl)*
Es gastos fuertes *(m pl)*
Fr charges lourdes *(f pl)*
It forti spese *(f pl)*
Pt encargos pesados *(m pl)*

heavy fine En
De schwere Buße *(f)*
Es sanción elevada *(f)*
Fr forte amende *(f)*
It forte multa *(f)*
Pt multa pesada *(f)*

heavy industry En
De Schwerindustrie *(f)*
Es industria pesada *(f)*
Fr industrie lourde *(f)*
It industria pesante *(f)*
Pt indústria pesada *(f)*

heavy loss En
De schwere Verluste *(m pl)*
Es fuerte pérdida; pérdida
  sensible *(f)*
Fr lourde perte *(f)*
It forte perdita *(f)*
Pt perda avultada *(f)*

hecho *(m) n* Es
De Tatsache *(f)*
En fact
Fr fait *(m)*
It fatto *(m)*
Pt facto *(m)*

hedge *vb* En
De sich decken
Es cubrirse
Fr arbitrager
It coprirsi
Pt cobrir-se

Heimathafen *(m) n* De
En port of registration
Es puerto de matrícula *(m)*
Fr port d'attache *(m)*
It porto d'immatricolazione
  (m)
Pt porto de matrícula *(m)*

heir *n* En
De Erbe *(m)*
Es heredero *(m)*
Fr héritier *(m)*
It erede *(m)*
Pt herdeiro *(m)*

Heizöl *(n) n* De
En fuel oil
Es fuel-oil *(m)*   .
Fr mazout *(m)*
It petrolio da ardere *(m)*
Pt petróleo combustível *(m)*

help *n* En
De Hilfe *(f)*
Es ayuda *(f)*
Fr secours *(m)*
It aiuto *(m)*
Pt ajuda *(f)*

herança *(f) n* Pt
De Erbschaft *(f)*
En inheritance
Es herencia *(f)*
Fr succession *(f)*
It eredità *(f)*

herdeiro *(m) n* Pt
De Erbe *(m)*
En heir
Es heredero *(m)*
Fr héritier *(m)*
It erede *(m)*

hereby *adv* En
De hiermit
Es por esto
Fr par la présente acte
It col presente; con questo
Pt pelo presente

heredero *(m) n* Es
De Erbe *(m)*
En heir
Fr héritier *(m)*
It erede *(m)*
Pt herdeiro *(m)*

herencia *(f) n* Es
De Erbschaft; Nachlaß *(f m)*
En inheritance; estate
Fr succession *(f)*
It eredità; successione *(f)*
Pt herança; património *(f m)*

herewith *adv* En
De hiermit
Es con esto; adjunto
Fr ci-joint; sous ce pli
It qui unito; con la presente
Pt incluso; junto

héritier *(m) n* Fr
De Erbe *(m)*
En heir
Es heredero *(m)*
It erede *(m)*
Pt herdeiro *(m)*

Herkunftsland *(n) n* De
En country of origin
Es pais de origen *(m)*
Fr pays de provenance *(m)*
It paese di origine *(m)*
Pt país de origem *(m)*

heure *(f) n* Fr
De Stunde *(f)*
En hour
Es hora *(f)*
It ora *(f)*
Pt hora *(f)*

heure du déjeuner *(f)* Fr
De Mittagspause *(f)*
En lunch-hour

Es hora del almuerzo *(f)*
It ora di colazione *(f)*
Pt hora do almoço *(f)*

heure légale *(f)* Fr
De Normalzeit *(f)*
En standard time
Es hora oficial *(f)*
It ora legale *(f)*
Pt hora normal *(f)*

heures d'affluence *(f pl)* Fr
De Hauptverkehrszeit *(f)*
En rush hour
Es hora punta *(f)*
It ora di punta *(f)*
Pt hora de ponta *(f)*

heures de bureau *(f pl)* Fr
De Geschäftsstunden *(f pl)*
En office hours
Es horario de oficina *(m)*
It orario d'ufficio *(m)*
Pt horário do escritório *(m)*

heures de pointe *(f pl)* Fr
De Verkehrsspitze *(f)*
En peak hours
Es horas punta *(f pl)*
It ore di punta *(f pl)*
Pt horas de ponta *(f pl)*

heures d'ouverture *(f pl)* Fr
De Geschäftszeit *(f)*
En business hours
Fr horario de comercio *(m)*
It orario d'apertura *(m)*
Pt horas de funcionamento
  (f pl)

heures-homme *(f pl) n* Fr
De Arbeitsstunde pro Mann *(f)*
En man-hours
Es horas-hombre *(f pl)*
It ore-uomo *(f pl)*
Pt horas-homem *(f pl)*

heures supplémentaires
  (f pl) Fr
De Überstunden *(f pl)*
En overtime
Es horas extraordinarias *(f pl)*
It lavoro straordinario *(m)*
Pt horas extraordinárias *(f pl)*

hidden reserve En
De stille Reserve *(f)*
Es reserva latente *(f)*

Fr réserve cachée *(f)*
It riserva occulta *(f)*
Pt reserva oculta *(f)*

hidden tax En
De versteckte Belastung *(f)*
Es impuesto latente *(m)*
Fr imposition latente *(f)*
It tassa invisibile *(f)*
Pt imposto ocultado *(m)*

hier *adv* Fr
De gestern
En yesterday
Es ayer
It ieri
Pt ontem

hiermit *adv* De
En hereby; herewith
Es por esto; con esto
Fr par la présente; ci-joint
It col presente; con questo
Pt pelo presente; incluso

hierro *(m)* *n* Es
De Eisen *(n)*
En iron
Fr fer *(m)*
It ferro *(m)*
Pt ferro *(m)*

hierro bruto *(m)* Es
De Roheisen *(n)*
En pig-iron
Fr fer en gueuse *(m)*
It pane di ghisa *(m)*
Pt ferro em bruto *(m)*

hierro colado *(m)* Es
De Gußeisen *(n)*
En cast iron
Fr fer de fonte *(m)*
It ghisa *(f)*
Pt ferro fundido *(m)*

high *adj* En
De hoch
Es alto; elevado
Fr haut; élevé
It alto; elevato
Pt elevado

higher education En
De Fortbildung *(f)*
Es enseñanza superior *(f)*
Fr enseignement supérieur *(m)*

It insegnamento superiore *(m)*
Pt instrução superior *(f)*

highest bidder En
De Meistbietende(r) *(m)*
Es ofertante más alto *(m)*
Fr plus offrant enchérisseur *(m)*
It miglior offerente *(m)*
Pt proponente mais elevado *(m)*

high-grade *adj* En
De erstklassig
Es alta calidad
Fr à haute teneur
It di qualità superiore
Pt alto-nível

high seas En
De hohe See *(f)*
Es altamar *(f)*
Fr hautes mers *(f pl)*
It alto mare *(m)*
Pt alto-mar *(m)*

Hilfe *(f)* *n* De
En help
Es ayuda *(f)*
Fr secours *(m)*
It aiuto *(m)*
Pt ajuda *(f)*

hinauslaufend auf De
En amounting to
Es ascendiendo a
Fr à concurrence de
It ammontante a
Pt no montante de

Hinderung *(f)* *n* De
En hindrance
Es impedimento *(m)*
Fr empêchement *(m)*
It impedimento *(m)*
Pt impedimento *(m)*

hindrance *n* En
De Hinderung *(f)*
Es impedimento *(m)*
Fr empêchement *(m)*
It impedimento *(m)*
Pt impedimento *(m)*

hinterlegen *vb* De
En deposit
Es depositar

Fr déposer
It depositare
Pt depositar

hinzufügen *vb* De
En add
Es añadir
Fr ajouter
It aggiungere
Pt adicionar

hinzuwählen *vb* De
En co-opt
Es cooptar
Fr coopter
It cooptare
Pt cooptar

hipoteca *(f)* *n* Es, Pt
De Hypothek *(f)*
En mortgage; hypothecation
Fr hypothèque; nantissement *(f m)*
It ipoteca *(f)*

hipotecar *vb* Es, Pt
De verpfänden
En hypothecate
Fr hypothéquer
It ipotecare

hipótese *(f)* *n* Pt
De Hypothese *(f)*
En hypothesis
Es hipótesis *(f)*
Fr hypothèse *(f)*
It ipotesi *(f)*

hipótesis *(f)* *n* Es
De Hypothese *(f)*
En hypothesis
Fr hypothèse *(f)*
It ipotesi *(f)*
Pt hipótese *(f)*

hire (personnel) *vb* En
De anstellen
Es apalabrar
Fr engager
It fissare
Pt empregar

hire *vb* En
De mieten
Es alquilar
Fr louer
It noleggiare; affittare
Pt alugar

hire-purchase n En
De Ratenkauf (m)
Es compra a plazos (f)
Fr location-vente; vente à
   tempérament (f)
It vendita a rate (f)
Pt venda a pretações (f)

hirer n En
De Mieter (m)
Es alquilador; arrendador (m)
Fr locataire (m)
It noleggiatore (m)
Pt alugador (m)

histogram n En
De Histogramm (n)
Es histograma (m)
Fr histogramme (m)
It istogramma (m)
Pt histograma (m)

histograma (m) n Es, Pt
De Histogramm (n)
En histogram
Fr histogramme (m)
It istogramma (m)

Histogramm (n) n De
En histogram
Es histograma (m)
Fr histogramme (m)
It istogramma (m)
Pt histograma (m)

histogramme (m) n Fr
De Histogramm (n)
En histogram
Es histograma (m)
It istogramma (m)
Pt histograma (m)

historic cost En
De Anschaffungskosten (pl)
Es coste primitivo (m)
Fr coût d'acquisition primitif
   (m)
It costo primitivo (m)
Pt custo original (m)

hoard n En
De Hortung (f)
Es atesoramiento (m)
Fr thésaurisation (f)
It ammasso (m)
Pt acumulação (f)

hoch adj De
En high
Es alto; elevado
Fr haut; élevé
It alto; elevato
Pt elevado

hochwertig adj De
En top quality
Es de primera calidad
Fr de première qualité
It di qualità superiore
Pt de classe superior

hogar (m) n Es
De Haushalt (m)
En household
Fr ménage (m)
It famiglia (f)
Pt casa (f)

Hoheitsgewässer (n pl) De
En territorial waters
Es aguas territoriales (f pl)
Fr eaux territoriales (f pl)
It acque territoriali (f pl)
Pt águas territoriais (f pl)

hohe See (f) De
En high seas
Es altamar (f)
Fr hautes mers (f pl)
It alto mare (m)
Pt alto-mar (m)

hold (of a ship) (n) En
De Laderaum (m)
Es bodega (f)
Fr cale (f)
It stiva (f)
Pt porão (m)

hold vb En
De halten
Es tener
Fr tenir; détenir
It tenere
Pt guardar; conservar

hold a meeting En
De eine Versammlung abhal-
   ten
Es celebrar una reunión
Fr tenir une assemblée
It tenere una riunione
Pt fazer uma reunião

holder n En
De Inhaber (m)
Es titular (m)
Fr détenteur (m)
It titolare (m)
Pt titular (m)

holder for value En
De entgeltigter Besitzer (m)
Es tenedor legítimo (m)
Fr porteur à titre onéreux (m)
It detentore legittimo (m)
Pt proprietário legítimo (m)

holder in due course En
De gutgläubiger Besitzer (m)
Es tenedor en buena fe (m)
Fr porteur de bonne foi (m)
It titolare in buona fede (m)
Pt proprietário de boa fé

holding company En
De Dachgesellschaft (f)
Es compañía tenedora (f)
Fr société holding (f)
It società holding (f)
Pt companhia proprietária (f)

hold in trust En
De zu treuen Händen halten
Es guardar in fideicomiso
Fr tenir par fidéicommis
It tenere in fidecommesso
Pt reter em custódia

hold over En
De aufschieben
Es aplazar; diferir
Fr différer
It differire
Pt diferir; adiar

hold shares En
De beteiligt sein; Aktien
   besitzen
Es tener acciones
Fr détenir des actions
It tenere azioni
Pt reter acções

hold the line! En
De am Apparat bleiben, bitte!
Es espere al aparato!
Fr ne quittez pas!
It restare in linea!
Pt aguarde!

holiday n En
Am vacation
De Ferien; Urlaub (pl; m)
Es vacaciones (f pl)
Fr vacances (f pl)
It vacanza (f)
Pt férias (f pl)

holidays with pay En
De bezahlter Urlaub (m)
Es vacaciones retribuidas
   (f pl)
Fr congés payés (m pl)
It vacanze retribuite (f pl)
Pt férias pagas (f pl)

hombre de negocios (m) Es
De Geschäftsmann (m)
En businessman
Fr homme d'affaires (m)
It uomo d'affari (m)
Pt homem de negócios (m)

homem de negócios (m) Pt
De Geschäftsmann (m)
En businessman
Es hombre de negocios (m)
Fr homme d'affaires (m)
It uomo d'affari (m)

home trade En
Am domestic sales
De Binnenhandel (m)
Es comercio interior (m)
Fr commerce intérieur (m)
It commercio interno (m)
Pt comércio interno (m)

homme d'affaires (m) Fr
De Geschäftsmann (m)
En businessman
Es hombre de negocios (m)
It uomo d'affari (m)
Pt homem de negócios (m)

**homologation d'un
   testament** (f) Fr
De Testamentseröffnung;
   Bestätigung (f)
En probate
Es validación de los testa-
   mentos (f)
It omologazione di testa-
   mento (f)
Pt validação testamentária (f)

honest adj En
De ehrlich
Es honesto

Fr honnête
It onesto
Pt honesto

honesto adj Es, Pt
De ehrlich
En honest
Fr honnête
It onesto

honnête adj Fr
De ehrlich
En honest
Es honesto
It onesto
Pt honesto

honneur (f) n Fr
De Ehre (f)
En honour
Es honor (m)
It onore (m)
Pt honra (f)

honor (m) n Es
De Ehre (f)
En honour
Fr honneur (f)
It onore (m)
Pt honra (f)

honoraire adj Fr
De ehrenamtlich
En honorary
Es honorario
It onorario
Pt honorário

honoraires (m pl) n Fr
De Vergütung; Honorar (f n)
En fee
Es honorario (m)
It onorario (m)
Pt honorários (m pl)

Honorar (n) n De
En fee
Es honorario (m)
Fr honoraires (m pl)
It onorario (m)
Pt honorários (m pl)

honorario (m) n Es
De Vergütung; Honorar (f n)
En fee
Fr honoraires (m pl)
It onorario (m)
Pt honorários (m pl)

honorario adj Es
De ehrenamtlich
En honorary
Fr honoraire
It onorario
Pt honorário

honorário adj Pt
De ehrenamtlich
En honorary
Es honorario
Fr honoraire
It onorario

honorários (m pl) n Pt
De Vergütung; Honorar (f n)
En fee
Es honorario (m)
Fr honoraires (m pl)
It onorario (m)

honorary adj En
De ehrenamtlich
Es honorario
Fr honoraire
It onorario
Pt honorário

honorer vb Fr
De honorieren
En honour
Es honrar
It onorare
Pt honrar

honorieren vb De
En honour
Es honrar
Fr honorer
It onorare
Pt honorificar

honorificar vb Es
De honorieren
En honour
Fr honorer
It onorare

honour vb En
De honorieren
Es honrar
Fr honorer
It onorare
Pt honorificar

honour n En
De Ehre (f)
Es honor (m)

Fr honneur *(f)*
It onore *(m)*
Pt honra *(f)*

honra *(f)* n Pt
De Ehre *(f)*
En honour
Es honor *(m)*
Fr honneur *(f)*
It onore *(m)*

honrar *vb* Es
De honorieren
En honour
Fr honorer
It onorare
Pt honorificar

hora *(f)* n Es, Pt
De Stunde *(f)*
En hour
Fr heure *(f)*
It ora *(f)*

hora del almuerzo *(f)* Es
De Mittagspause *(f)*
En lunch-hour
Fr heure du déjeuner *(f)*
It ora di colazione *(f)*
Pt hora do almoço *(f)*

hora de ponta *(f)* Pt
De Hauptverkehrszeit *(f)*
En rush hour
Es hora punta *(t)*
Fr heures d'affluence *(f pl)*
It ora di punta *(f)*

hora do almoço *(f)* Pt
De Mittagspause *(f)*
En lunch-hour
Es hora del almuerzo *(f)*
Fr heure du déjeuner *(f)*
It ora di colazione *(f)*

hora normal *(f)* Pt
De Normalzeit *(f)*
En standard time
Es hora oficial *(f)*
Fr heure légale *(f)*
It ora legale *(f)*

hora oficial *(f)* Es
De Normalzeit *(f)*
En standard time
Fr heure légale *(f)*
It ora legale *(f)*
Pt hora normal *(f)*

hora punta *(f)* Es
De Hauptverkehrszeit *(f)*
En rush hour
Fr heures d'affluence
It ora di punta *(f)*
Pt hora de ponta *(f)*

horário de caminhos de ferro *(m)* Pt
De Eisenbahnfahrplan *(m)*
En railway timetable
Es horario de trenes *(m)*
Fr indicateur des chemins de fer *(m)*
It orario ferroviario *(m)*

horario de comercio *(m)* Es
De Geschäftszeit *(f)*
En business hours
Fr heures d'ouverture *(f pl)*
It orario d'apertura *(m)*
Pt horas de funcionamento *(f pl)*

horario de oficina *(m)* Es
De Geschäftsstunden *(f pl)*
En office hours
Fr heures de bureau *(f pl)*
It orario d'ufficio *(m)*
Pt horário do escritório *(m)*

horario de trenes *(m)* Es
De Eisenbahnfahrplan *(m)*
En railway timetable
Fr indicateur des chemins de fer *(m)*
It orario ferroviario *(m)*
Pt horário de caminhos de ferro *(m)*

horário do escritório *(m)* Pt
De Geschäftsstunden *(f pl)*
En office hours
Es horario de oficina *(m)*
Fr heures de bureau *(f pl)*
It orario d'ufficio *(m)*

horas de funcionamento *(f pl)* Pt
De Geschäftszeit *(f)*
En business hours
Es horario de comercio *(m)*
Fr heures d'ouverture *(f pl)*
It orario d'apertura *(m)*

horas de ponta *(f pl)* Pt
De Verkehrsspitze *(f)*
En peak hours
Es horas punta *(f pl)*
Fr heures de pointe *(f pl)*
It ore di punta *(f pl)*

horas de trabalho *(f pl)* Pt
De Arbeitszeit *(f)*
En hours of work
Es jornada laboral *(f)*
Fr durée du travail *(f)*
It ore lavorative *(f pl)*

horas extraordinarias *(f pl)* Es
De Überstunden *(f pl)*
En overtime
Fr heures supplémentaires *(f pl)*
It lavoro straordinario *(m)*
Pt horas extraordinárias *(f pl)*

horas extraordinárias *(f pl)* Pt
De Überstunden *(f pl)*
En overtime
Es horas extraordinarias *(f pl)*
Fr heures supplémentaires *(f pl)*
It lavoro straordinario *(m)*

horas-hombre *(f pl)* Es
De Arbeitsstunde pro Mann *(f)*
En man-hours
Fr heures-homme *(f pl)*
It ore-uomo *(f pl)*
Pt horas-homem *(f pl)*

horas-homem *(f pl)* n Pt
De Arbeitsstunde pro Mann *(f)*
En man-hours
Es horas-hombre *(f pl)*
Fr heures-homme *(f pl)*
It ore-uomo *(f pl)*

horas punta *(f pl)* Es
De Verkehrsspitze *(f)*
En peak hours
Fr heures de pointe *(f pl)*
It ore di punta *(f pl)*
Pt horas de ponta *(f pl)*

horizontaler Zusammenschluß *(m)* De
En horizontal integration
Es integración horizontal *(f)*
Fr intégration horizontale *(f)*
It integrazione orizzontale *(f)*
Pt integração horizontal *(f)*

horizontal integration En
De horizontaler Zusammenschluß *(m)*
Es integración horizontal *(f)*
Fr intégration horizontale *(f)*
It integrazione orizzontale *(f)*
Pt integração horizontal *(f)*

horse-power (hp) n En
De Pferdestärke (PS) (f)
Es caballo de vapor (cv) (m)
Fr cheval-vapeur (ch-v) (m)
It cavallo (m)
Pt cavalo-vapor (m)

hors taxe (HT) Fr
De außer Steuer
En excluding tax
Es impuesto no incluido
It tassa esclusa
Pt impostos excluídos

Hortung (f) n De
En hoard
Es atesoramiento (m)
Fr thésaurisation (f)
It ammasso (m)
Pt acumulação (f)

hotel n En, Es, Pt (m)
De Hotel (n)
Fr hôtel (m)
It albergo (m)

hôtel (m) n Fr
De Hotel (n)
En hotel
Es hotel (m)
It albergo (m)
Pt hotel (m)

Hotel (n) n De
En hotel
Es hotel (m)
Fr hôtel (m)
It albergo (m)
Pt hotel (m)

houille (f) n Fr
De Kohle (f)
En coal
Es carbón (m)
It carbone (m)
Pt carvão (m)

hour n En
De Stunde (f)
Es hora (f)
Fr heure (f)
It ora (f)
Pt hora (f)

hours of work En
De Arbeitszeit (f)
Es jornada laboral (f)
Fr durée du travail (f)
It ore lavorative (f pl)
Pt horas de trabalho (f pl)

house n En
De Haus (n)
Es casa (f)
Fr maison (f)
It casa (f)
Pt casa (f)

household n En
De Haushalt (m)
Es hogar (m)
Fr ménage (m)
It famiglia (f)
Pt casa (f)

household electrical goods
En
De elektrische Haushaltsgüter
(n pl)
Es aparatos eléctricos de
casa (m pl)
Fr électro-ménager (m)
It elettrodomestici (m pl)
Pt electro-domésticos (m pl)

householder n En
De Hausherr (m)
Es jefe de familia (m)
Fr chef de famille (m)
It capo-famiglia (m)
Pt dono da casa (m)

household insurance En
De Wohnungsversicherung (f)
Es seguro de casa (m)
Fr assurance ménagère (f)
It assicurazione domestica
(f)
Pt seguro de casa (m)

housewife n En
De Hausfrau (f)
Es ama de casa (f)
Fr ménagère (f)
It massaia (f)
Pt dona de casa (f)

Hubraum (m) n De
En cubic capacity
Es cilindrada (f)
Fr cylindrée (f)
It cilindrata (f)
Pt cilindrada (f)

huelga (f) n Es
De Streik (m)
En strike
Fr grève (f)
It sciopero (m)
Pt greve (f)

huelga de brazos caídos (f)
Es
De Sitzstreik (m)
En sit-down strike
Fr grève avec occupation
des lieux (f)
It sciopero bianco (m)
Pt greve de braços caídos (f)

**huelga de obreros de
muelle** (f) Es
De Hafenarbeiterstreik (m)
En dock strike
Fr grève des dockers (f)
It sciopero portuale (m)
Pt greve na doca (f)

huelga de producción lenta
(f) Es
De Bummelstreik (m)
En go-slow strike
Am slow down
Fr grève perlée (f)
It sciopero a singhiozzo (m)
Pt greve de abrandamento
do ritmo de produção (f)

huelga espontánea (f) Es
De wilder Streik (m)
En wildcat strike
Fr grève sauvage (f)
It sciopero selvaggio (m)
Pt greve não oficializada (f)

huelga general (f) Es
De Generalstreik (m)
En general strike
Fr grève générale (f)
It sciopero generale (m)
Pt greve geral (f)

huelga no-oficial (f) Es
De unanerkannter Streik (m)
En unofficial strike
Fr grève non reconnue (f)
It sciopero non ufficiale (m)
Pt greve não oficializada (f)

huelga oficial (f) Es
De anerkannter Streik (m)
En official strike
Fr grève officielle (f)
It sciopero ufficiale (m)
Pt greve oficial (f)

huelguista (m) n Es
De Streikende(r) (m)
En striker

Fr gréviste *(m)*
It scioperante *(m)*
Pt grevista *(m)*

hull insurance En
De Kaskoversicherung *(f)*
Es seguro del casco *(m)*
Fr assurance sur le corps *(f)*
It assicurazione corpo *(m)*
Pt seguro do casco *(m)*

human relations En
De zwischenmenschliche
    Beziehungen *(f pl)*
Es relaciones humanas *(f pl)*
Fr relations humaines *(f pl)*
It relazioni umane *(f pl)*
Pt relações humanas *(f pl)*

Hundertsatz *(m) n* De
En percentage
Es porcentaje *(m)*
Fr pourcentage *(m)*
It percentuale *(f)*
Pt percentagem *(f)*

hypothecate *vb* En
De verpfänden
Es hipotecar
Fr hypothéquer
It ipotecare
Pt hipotecar

hypothecation *n* En
De Hypothek *(f)*
Es hipoteca *(f)*
Fr nantissement *(m)*
It ipoteca *(f)*
Pt hipoteca *(f)*

Hypothek *(f) n* De
En mortgage; hypothecation
Es hipoteca *(f)*
Fr hypothèque; nantisse-
    ment *(f m)*
It ipoteca *(f)*
Pt hipoteca *(f)*

hypothekarisch gesicherte
    Schuldverschreibung *(f)*
    De
En mortgage debenture
Es obligación hipotecaria *(f)*
Fr obligation hypothécaire *(f)*
It obbligazione ipotecaria *(f)*
Pt obrigação hipotecária *(f)*

hypothèque *(f) n* Fr
De Hypothek *(f)*
En mortgage
Es hipoteca *(f)*
It ipoteca *(f)*
Pt hipoteca *(f)*

hypothéquer *vb* Fr
De verpfänden
En hypothecate
Es hipotecar
It ipotecare
Pt hipotecar

hypothèse *(f) n* Fr
De Hypothese *(f)*
En hypothesis
Es hipótesis *(f)*
It ipotesi *(f)*
Pt hipótese *(f)*

Hypothese *(f) n* De
En hypothesis
Es hipótesis *(f)*
Fr hypothèse *(f)*
It ipotesi *(f)*
Pt hipótese *(f)*

hypothesis *n* En
De Hypothese *(f)*
Es hipótesis *(f)*
Fr hypothèse *(f)*
It ipotesi *(f)*
Pt hipótese *(f)*

I

I.O.U. (I owe you) En
De Schuldschein *(m)*
Es pagaré *(m)*
Fr reconnaissance de dette
    (f)
It pagherò *(m)*
Pt vale *(m)*

idea *n* En; Es, It *(f)*
De Idee *(f)*
Fr idée *(f)*
Pt idéia *(f)*

idée *(f) n* Fr
De Idee *(f)*
En idea
Es idea *(f)*
It idea *(f)*
Pt idéia *(f)*

Idee *(f) n* De
En idea
Es idea *(f)*
Fr idée *(f)*
It idea *(f)*
Pt idéia *(f)*

idéia *(f) n* Pt
De Idee *(f)*
En idea
Es idea *(f)*
Fr idée *(f)*
It idea *(f)*

identificar *vb* Es, Pt
De identifizieren
En identify
Fr identifier
It identificare

identificare *vb* It
De identifizieren
En identify
Es identificar
Fr identifier
Pt identificar

identifier *vb* Fr
De identifizieren
En identify
Es identificar
It identificare
Pt identificar

identifizieren *vb* De
En identify
Es identificar
Fr identifier *(f)*
It identificare *(m)*
Pt identificar *(f)*

identify *vb* En
De identifizieren
Es identificar
Fr identifier
It identificare
Pt identificar

identity card En
De Personalausweis *(m)*
Es carnet de identidad *(m)*
Fr carte d'identité *(f)*
It carta d'identità *(f)*
Pt bilhete de identidade *(m)*

idle capacity En
De ungenutzte Ladefähigkeit
    (f)

Es   potencial no utilizado *(m)*
Fr   potentiel non utilisé *(m)*
It   potenziale non utilizzato *(m)*
Pt   potencial não utilizado *(m)*

idle money En
De   totes Kapital *(n)*
Es   dinero sin invertir *(m)*
Fr   capital oisif *(m)*
It   denaro inattivo *(m)*
Pt   dinheiro paralisado *(m)*

idle time En
De   unproduktive Zeit *(f)*
Es   tiempo libre *(m)*
Fr   temps improductif *(m)*
It   tempo passivo *(m)*
Pt   tempo improdutivo *(m)*

ieri *(adv)* It
De   gestern
En   yesterday
Es   ayer
Fr   hier
Pt   ontem

ilegal *(adj)* Es, Pt
De   ungesetzlich
En   illegal
Fr   illégal
It   illegale

ilegible *(adj)* Es
De   unleserlich
En   illegible
Fr   illisible
It   illeggibile
Pt   ilegível

ilegível *(adj)* Pt
De   unleserlich
En   illegible
Es   ilegible
Fr   illisible
It   illeggibile

ilíquido de impostos Pt
De   steuerabsetzbar
En   tax-deductible
Es   deducible de impuestos
Fr   déductible à l'impôt
It   deducibile da tassa

illegal *(adj)* En
De   ungesetzlich
Es   ilegal

Fr   illégal
It   illegale
Pt   ilegal

illégal *(adj)* Fr
De   ungesetzlich
En   illegal
Es   ilegal
It   illegale
Pt   ilegal

illegale *(adj)* It
De   ungesetzlich
En   illegal
Es   ilegal
Fr   illégal
Pt   ilegal

illeggibile *(adj)* It
De   unleserlich
En   illegible
Es   ilegible
Fr   illisible
Pt   ilegível

illegible *(adj)* En
De   unleserlich
Es   ilegible
Fr   illisible
It   illeggibile
Pt   ilegível

illisible *(adj)* Fr
De   unleserlich
En   illegible
Es   ilegible
It   illeggibile
Pt   ilegível

imaginärer Gewinn *(m)* De
En   paper profit
Es   ganancia por realizar *(f)*
Fr   profit fictif *(m)*
It   utile sulla carta *(m)*
Pt   lucros no papel *(m pl)*

imaginärer Verlust *(m)* De
En   paper loss
Es   pérdida por realizar *(f)*
Fr   perte fictive *(f)*
It   perdita sulla carta *(f)*
Pt   perda no papel *(f)*

im Ausland De
En   abroad
Es   en el extranjero
Fr   à l'étranger
It   all'estero
Pt   no estrangeiro

imballaggio *(m)* n It
De   Verpackung *(f)*
En   packing
Es   embalaje; envase *(m)*
Fr   emballage *(m)*
Pt   embalagem;
     empacotamento *(f m)*

imballaggio a perdere *(m)* It
De   wegwerfbare Verpackung *(f)*
En   disposable wrapping
Es   envoltura desechable *(f)*
Fr   emballage perdu *(m)*
Pt   embalagem a destruir *(f)*

imballaggio incluso It
De   Verpackung inbegriffen
En   including packing
Es   franco embalaje
Fr   franco d'emballage
Pt   incluindo embalagem

imbarcare *(vb)* It
De   verschiffen;
     sich einschiffen
En   ship; embark
Es   embarcar
Fr   embarquer; s'embarquer
Pt   embarcar

imbarco *(m)* n It
De   Verladung; Einschiffung *(f)*
En   shipment; embarcation
Es   embarque; embarco *(m)*
Fr   embarquement *(m)*
Pt   embarque *(m)*

im Durchgangsverkehr De
En   in transit
Es   en tránsito
Fr   en transit
It   in transito
Pt   em trânsito

imediato *(m)* n Pt
De   Maat *(m)*
En   mate
Es   primer oficial *(m)*
Fr   second *(m)*
It   primo ufficiale *(m)*

im Einvernehmen mit De
En   in agreement with
Es   de acuerdo con
Fr   d'accord avec
It   d'accordo con
Pt   de acordo com

imigração *(f)* n Pt
De Einwanderung *(f)*
En immigration
Es inmigración *(f)*
Fr immigration *(f)*
It immigrazione *(f)*

imitação *(f)* n Pt
De Nachahmung *(f)*
En imitation
Es imitación *(f)*
Fr imitation *(f)*
It imitazione *(f)*

imitación *(f)* n Es
De Nachahmung *(f)*
En imitation
Fr imitation *(f)*
It imitazione *(f)*
Pt imitação *(f)*

imitation n En, Fr *(f)*
De Nachahmung *(f)*
Es imitación *(f)*
It imitazione *(f)*
Pt imitação *(f)*

imitation gold En
De Kunstgold *(n)*
Es oro de imitación *(m)*
Fr similor *(m)*
It similoro *(m)*
Pt ouro de imitação *(m)*

imitation leather En
De Kunstleder *(n)*
Es piel de imitación *(f)*
Fr simili-cuir *(m)*
It finta pelle *(f)*
Pt cabedal de imitação *(m)*

imitazione *(f)* n It
De Nachahmung *(f)*
En imitation
Es imitación *(f)*
Fr imitation *(f)*
Pt imitação *(f)*

immagazzinare vb It
De lagern
En store
Es almacenar
Fr emmagasiner
Pt armazenar

immaterieller Schaden *(m)*
De
En consequential damages
Es daños indirectos *(m pl)*

Fr dommages indirects *(m pl)*
It danni indiretti *(m pl)*
Pt danos decorrentes *(m pl)*

immeuble *(m)* n Fr
De Wohnungsgebäude *(n)*
En block of flats
Am apartment house
Es bloque de pisos *(m)*
It fabbricato di appartamenti *(m)*
Pt edifício de andares *(m)*

immigration n En, Fr *(f)*
De Einwanderung *(f)*
Es inmigración *(f)*
It immigrazione *(f)*
Pt imigração *(f)*

immigrazione *(f)* n It
De Einwanderung *(f)*
En immigration
Es inmigración *(f)*
Fr immigration *(f)*
Pt imigração *(f)*

Immobilienbüro *(n)* n De
En estate agency
Am real estate agency
Es correduría de fincas *(f)*
Fr agence immobilière *(f)*
It agenzia immobiliare *(f)*
Pt agência de propriedades *(f)*

immobilisations *(f pl)* n Fr
De Anlagevermögen *(n)*
En fixed assets
Es activo fijo *(m)*
It immobilizzazioni; attivo fisso *(f pl; m)*
Pt bens fixos *(m pl)*

immobilizzazioni *(f pl)* n It
De Anlagevermögen *(n)*
En fixed assets
Es activo fijo *(m)*
Fr immobilisations *(f pl)*
Pt bens fixos *(m pl)*

imparcial adj Es, Pt
De unparteiisch
En impartial
Fr impartial
It imparziale

impartial adj En, Fr
De unparteiisch
Es imparcial

It imparziale
Pt imparcial

imparziale adj It
De unparteiisch
En impartial
Es imparcial
Fr impartial
Pt imparcial

impedimento *(m)* n Es, It, Pt
De Hinderung *(f)*
En hindrance
Fr empêchement *(m)*

impersonal account En
De Firmenkonto *(n)*
Es cuenta simulada *(f)*
Fr compte impersonnel *(m)*
It conto d'ordine *(m)*
Pt conta impessoal *(f)*

impianti portuali *(m pl)* It
De Hafenanlagen *(f pl)*
En harbour installations
Es instalaciones portuarias *(f pl)*
Fr installations portuaires *(f pl)*
Pt instalações portuárias *(f pl)*

impianto *(m)* n It
De Anlage *(f)*
En plant; installation
Es planta; instalación *(f)*
Fr appareil; installation *(m f)*
Pt instalação *(f)*

impianto piloto *(m)* It
De Musteranlage *(f)*
En pilot plant
Es instalación piloto *(f)*
Fr installation pilote *(f)*
Pt instalação piloto *(f)*

impiegare vb It
De beschäftigen
En employ
Es emplear
Fr employer
Pt empregar

impiegato *(m)* n It
De Angestellte(r); Arbeitnehmer *(m)*
En employee; clerk
Es empleado; oficinista *(m)*
Fr employé; commis *(m)*
Pt empregado; empregado de escritório *(m)*

impiegato statale *(m)* It
De Beamte(r) *(m)*
En civil servant
Am government employee
Es funcionario del gobierno *(m)*
Fr fonctionnaire *(m)*
Pt funcionário público *(m)*

impiego *(m)* n It
De Beschäftigung; Stellung *(f)*
En employment; post
Es empleo *(m)*
Fr emploi *(m)*
Pt emprego *(m)*

implement *vb* En
De bewerkstelligen; ausführen
Es hacer efectivo; ejecutar
Fr exécuter
It attuare; effettuare
Pt executar

implicar *vb* Es
De andeuten
En imply
Fr impliquer
It implicare
Pt significar

implicare *vb* It
De andeuten
En imply
Es implicar
Fr impliquer
Pt significar

implicit *adj* En
De stillschweigend
Es implícito
Fr implicite
It implicito
Pt implícito

implicite *adj* Fr
De stillschweigend
En implicit
Es implícito
It implicito
Pt implícito

implícito *adj* Es, Pt
De stillschweigend
En implicit
Fr implicite
It implicito

implicito *adj* It
De stillschweigend
En implicit
Es implícito
Fr implicite
Pt implícito

implied terms En
De stillschweigende Bedingungen *(f pl)*
Es condiciones implícitas *(f pl)*
Fr conditions implicites *(f pl)*
It condizioni implicite *(f pl)*
Pt condições implícitas *(f pl)*

impliquer *vb* Fr
De andeuten
En imply
Es implicar
It implicare
Pt significar

imply *vb* En
De andeuten
Es implicar
Fr impliquer
It implicare
Pt significar

import *n* En
De Einfuhr *(f)*
Es importación *(f)*
Fr importation *(f)*
It importazione *(f)*
Pt importação *(f)*

importação *(f)* n Pt
De Einfuhr *(f)*
En import
Es importación *(f)*
Fr importation *(f)*
It importazione *(f)*

importación *(f)* n Es
De Einfuhr *(f)*
En import
Fr importation *(f)*
It importazione *(f)*
Pt importação *(f)*

importador *(m)* n Es, Pt
De Importeur *(m)*
En importer
Fr importateur *(m)*
It importatore *(m)*

importância líquida *(f)* Pt
De Nettobetrag *(m)*
En net amount
Es importe neto *(m)*
Fr montant net *(m)*
It importo netto *(m)*

importância total *(f)* Pt
De Bruttobetrag *(m)*
En gross amount
Es importe bruto *(m)*
Fr montant brut *(m)*
It importo lordo *(m)*

importância transportada *(f)* Pt
De Übertrag *(m)*
En amount carried forward
Am carry forward amount
Es suma y sigue *(f)*
Fr report à nouveau *(m)*
It ammontare da riportare *(m)*

importateur *(m)* n Fr
De Importeur *(m)*
En importer
Es importador *(m)*
It importatore *(m)*
Pt importador *(m)*

importation *n* En, Fr *(f)*
De Einfuhr *(f)*
Es importación *(f)*
It importazione *(f)*
Pt importação *(f)*

importatore *(m)* n It
De Importeur *(m)*
En importer
Es importador *(m)*
Fr importateur *(m)*
Pt importador *(m)*

importazione *(f)* n It
De Einfuhr *(f)*
En import
Es importación *(f)*
Fr importation *(f)*
Pt importação *(f)*

import ban En
De Einfuhrverbot *(n)*
Es prohibición de importación *(f)*
Fr prohibition d'entrée *(f)*
It divieto d'importazione *(m)*
Pt proibição de importação *(f)*

import duty En
De Einfuhrzoll *(m)*
Es derechos de importación
(m pl)
Fr droits d'entrée *(m pl)*
It dazio d'importazione *(m)*
Pt direitos de importação
(m pl)

importe bruto *(m)* Es
De Bruttobetrag *(m)*
En gross amount
Fr montant brut *(m)*
It importo lordo *(m)*
Pt importância total *(f)*

importe neto *(m)* Es
De Nettobetrag *(m)*
En net amount
Fr montant net *(m)*
It importo netto *(m)*
Pt importância líquida *(f)*

importer n En
De Importeur *(m)*
Es importador *(m)*
Fr importateur *(m)*
It importatore *(m)*
Pt importador *(m)*

Importeur *(m)* n De
En importer
Es importador *(m)*
Fr importateur *(m)*
It importatore *(m)*
Pt importador *(m)*

import licence En
De Importlizenz; Einfuhr-
erlaubnis *(f)*
Es permiso de importación
(m)
Fr licence d'importation *(f)*
It permesso d'importazione
(m)
Pt licença de importação *(f)*

Importlizenz *(f)* n De
En import licence
Es permiso de importación
(m)
Fr licence d'importation *(f)*
It permesso d'importazione
(m)
Pt licença de importação *(f)*

importo lordo *(m)* It
De Bruttobetrag *(m)*
En gross amount

Es importe bruto *(m)*
Fr montant brut *(m)*
Pt importância total *(f)*

importo netto *(m)* It
De Nettobetrag *(m)*
En net amount
Es importe neto *(m)*
Fr montant net *(m)*
Pt importância líquida *(f)*

importo nominale *(m)* It
De Nominalbetrag *(m)*
En nominal amount
Es suma nominal *(f)*
Fr montant nominal *(m)*
Pt quantia nominal *(f)*

import quota En
De Einfuhrkontingent *(n)*
Es cupo de importación *(m)*
Fr contingent d'importation
(m)
It contingente d'importa-
zione *(m)*
Pt quota de importação *(f)*

import restrictions En
De Einfuhrbeschränkungen
(f pl)
Es restricciones de importación *(f pl)*
Fr restrictions
d'importation *(f pl)*
It restrizioni delle importazioni *(f pl)*
Pt restrições de importação
(f pl)

imposible adj Es
De unmöglich
En impossible
Fr impossible
It impossibile
Pt impossível

imposition *(f)* n Fr
De Besteuerung *(f)*
En taxation
Es tributación *(f)*
It tassazione *(f)*
Pt tributação *(f)*

imposition différée *(f)* Fr
De latente Steuerpflicht *(f)*
En deferred taxation
Es tasación diferida *(f)*
It tassazione differita *(f)*
Pt tributação diferida *(f)*

imposition latente *(f)* Fr
De versteckte Belastung *(f)*
En hidden tax
Es impuesto latente *(m)*
It tassa invisibile *(f)*
Pt imposto ocultado *(m)*

impossibile adj It
De unmöglich
En impossible
Es imposible
Fr impossible
Pt impossível

impossible adj En, Fr
De unmöglich
Es imposible
It impossibile
Pt impossível

impossível adj Pt
De unmöglich
En impossible
Es imposible
Fr impossible
It impossibile

imposta *(f)* n It
De Steuer; Erhebung *(f)*
En tax; levy
Es impuesto *(m)*
Fr impôt; prélèvement *(m)*
Pt imposto *(m)*

imposta fondiaria *(f)* It
De Grundsteuer *(f)*
En property tax
Es impuesto sobre la propie-
dad *(m)*
Fr impôt foncier *(m)*
Pt imposto sobre proprie-
dade *(m)*

**imposta negativa sul
reddito** *(f)* It
De negative Einkommen-
steuer *(f)*
En negative income tax
Es impuesto negativo sobre
renta *(m)*
Fr impôt négatif sur le revenu
(m)
Pt imposto negativo sobre
receita *(m)*

**imposta sui proventi delle
società** *(f)* It
De Körperschaftsteuer *(f)*
En corporation tax

Es impuesto sobre renta de la sociedad *(m)*
Fr impôt sur le revenu des sociétés *(m)*
Pt imposto sobre corporação *(m)*

imposta sui soprapprofitti *(f)* It
De Übergewinnsteuer *(f)*
En excess profits tax
Es impuesto sobre beneficios extraordinarios *(m pl)*
Fr impôts sur les superbénéfices *(m pl)*
Pt imposto sobre lucros excessivos *(m)*

imposta sul consumo *(f)* It
De Verbrauchsabgabe *(f)*
En excise duty
Es impuesto de consumos *(m)*
Fr droit sur la consommation *(m)*
Pt imposto indirecto *(m)*

imposta sulle vendite *(f)* It
De Warenumsatzsteuer *(f)*
En sales tax
Es impuesto sobre la venta *(m)*
Fr taxe de vente *(f)*
Pt imposto sobre vendas *(m)*

imposta sull'impiego *(f)* It
De Lohnsummensteuer *(f)*
En employment tax
Es impuesto por empleado *(m)*
Fr taxe sur l'emploi *(f)*
Pt imposto sobre emprego *(m)*

imposta sul plusvalore di capitale *(f)* It
De Kapitalertragsteuer *(f)*
En capital gains tax
Es impuesto sobre las ganancias de capital *(m)*
Fr impôt sur les plus-values en capital *(m)*
Pt imposto sobre lucros de capital *(m)*

imposta sul reddito *(f)* It
De Einkommensteuer *(f)*
En income tax

Es impuesto sobre la renta *(m)*
Fr impôt sur le revenu *(m)*
Pt imposto de receitas *(m)*

imposta sul valore aggiunto (IVA) *(f)* It
De Mehrwertsteuer *(f)*
En value added tax (VAT)
Es impuesto sobre valor añadido *(m)*
Fr taxe sur la valeur ajoutée (TVA) *(f)*
Pt imposto sobre valor aduzido *(m)*

imposte dirette *(f pl)* It
De direkte Steuern *(f pl)*
En direct taxation
Es contribuciones directas *(f pl)*
Fr contributions directes *(f pl)*
Pt tributação directa *(f)*

imposte indirette *(f pl)* It
De indirekte Steuern *(f pl)*
En indirect taxation; excise
Es contribuciones indirectas *(f pl)*
Fr contributions indirectes *(f pl)*
Pt tributação indirecta *(f)*

imposto *(m) n* Pt
De Steuer; Erhebung *(f)*
En tax; levy
Es impuesto *(m)*
Fr impôt; prélèvement *(m)*
It imposta *(f)*

imposto de luxo *(m)* Pt
De Luxussteuer *(f)*
En luxury tax
Es impuesto de lujo *(m)*
Fr impôt de luxe *(m)*
It tassa sugli articoli di lusso *(f)*

imposto de receitas *(m)* Pt
De Einkommensteuer *(f)*
En income tax
Es impuesto sobre la renta *(m)*
Fr impôt sur le revenu *(m)*
It imposta sul reddito *(f)*

imposto de selo *(m)* Pt
De Stempelgebühr *(f)*
En stamp duty

Es impuesto del timbre *(m)*
Fr droit de timbre *(m)*
It tassa di bollo *(f)*

imposto indirecto *(m)* Pt
De Verbrauchsabgabe *(f)*
En excise duty
Es impuesto de consumos *(m)*
Fr droit sur la consommation *(m)*
It imposta sul consumo *(f)*

imposto negativo sobre receita *(m)* Pt
De negative Einkommensteuer *(f)*
En negative income tax
Es impuesto negativo sobre renta *(m)*
Fr impôt négatif sur le revenu *(m)*
It imposta negativa sul reddito *(f)*

imposto ocultado *(m)* Pt
De versteckte Belastung *(f)*
En hidden tax
Es impuesto latente *(m)*
Fr imposition latente *(f)*
It tassa invisibile *(f)*

impostos de sucessão *(m pl)* Pt
De Erbschaftsteuern *(f pl)*
En death duties
Am estate taxes
Es derechos sucesorios *(m pl)*
Fr droits de succession *(m pl)*
It diritti di successione *(m pl)*

impostos excluídos Pt
De außer Steuer
En excluding tax
Es impuesto no incluido
Fr hors taxe (HT)
It tassa esclusa

imposto sobre aquisições *(m)* Pt
De Erwerbsteuer *(f)*
En purchase tax
Es impuesto sobre las compras *(m)*
Fr impôt sur les acquisitions *(m)*
It tassa sugli acquisti *(f)*

imposto sobre corporação
(m) Pt
De Körperschaftsteuer *(f)*
En corporation tax
Es impuesto sobre renta de la
sociedad *(m)*
Fr impôt sur le revenu des
sociétés *(m)*
It imposta sui proventi delle
società *(f)*

imposto sobre emprego *(m)*
Pt
De Lohnsummensteuer *(f)*
En employment tax
Es impuesto por empleado
(m)
Fr taxe sur l'emploi *(f)*
It imposta sull'impiego *(f)*

**imposto sobre lucros de
capital** *(m)* Pt
De Kapitalertragsteuer *(f)*
En capital gains tax
Es impuesto sobre las ga-
nancias de capital *(m)*
Fr impôt sur les plus-values
en capital *(m)*
It imposta sul plusvalore di
capitale *(f)*

**imposto sobre lucros
excessivos** *(m)* Pt
De Übergewinnsteuer *(f)*
En excess profits tax
Es impuesto sobre beneficios
extraordinarios *(m pl)*
Fr impôts sur les superbéné-
fices *(m pl)*
It imposta sui soprapprofitti
(f)

imposto sobre propriedade
(m) Pt
De Grundsteuer *(f)*
En property tax
Es impuesto sobre la propie-
dad *(m)*
Fr impôt foncier *(m)*
It imposta fondiaria *(f)*

**imposto sobre valor
aduzido** *(m)* Pt
De Mehrwertsteuer *(f)*
En value added tax (VAT)
Es impuesto sobre valor aña-
dido *(m)*

Fr taxe sur la valeur ajoutée
(TVA) *(f)*
It imposta sul valore aggiun-
to (IVA) *(f)*

imposto sobre vendas *(m)* Pt
De Warenumsatzsteuer *(f)*
En sales tax
Es impuesto sobre la venta
(m)
Fr taxe de vente *(f)*
It imposta sulle vendite *(f)*

impôt *(m)* n Fr
De Steuer *(f)*
En tax
Es impuesto *(m)*
It imposta *(f)*
Pt imposto *(m)*

impôt de luxe *(m)* Fr
De Luxussteuer *(f)*
En luxury tax
Es impuesto de lujo *(m)*
It tassa sugli articoli di lusso
(f)
Pt imposto de luxo *(m)*

impôt foncier *(m)* Fr
De Grundsteuer *(f)*
En property tax
Es impuesto sobre la propie-
dad *(m)*
It imposta fondiaria *(f)*
Pt imposto sobre proprieda-
de *(m)*

impôt sur les acquisitions
(m) Fr
De Erwerbsteuer *(f)*
En purchase tax
Es impuesto sobre las com-
pras *(m)*
It tassa sugli acquisti *(f)*
Pt imposto sobre aquisições

impôt négatif sur le revenu
(m) Fr
De negative Einkommen-
steuer *(f)*
En negative income tax
Es impuesto negativo sobre
renta *(m)*
It imposta negativa sul reddito *(f)*
Pt imposto negativo sobre
receita *(m)*

impôt sur le revenu *(m)* Fr
De Einkommensteuer *(f)*
En income tax
Es impuesto sobre la renta
(m)
It imposta sul reddito *(f)*
Pt imposto de receitas *(m)*

**impôt sur le revenu des
sociétés** *(m)* Fr
De Körperschaftsteuer *(f)*
En corporation tax
Es impuesto sobre renta de la
sociedad *(m)*
It imposta sui proventi delle
società *(f)*
Pt imposto sobre corporação
(m)

**impôt sur les plus-values en
capital** *(m)* Fr
De Kapitalertragsteuer *(f)*
En capital gains tax
Es impuesto sobre las ga-
nancias de capital *(m)*
It imposta sul plusvalore di
capitale *(f)*
Pt imposto sobre lucros de
capital *(m)*

imprenditore di trasporti *(m)*
It
De Transportunternehmer *(m)*
En haulage contractor
Am trucking company
Es contratista de transportes
(m)
Fr entrepreneur de camion-
nage *(m)*
Pt empreiteiro de transportes
(m)

impresa *(f)* n It
De Unternehmen *(n)*
En enterprise
Es negocio *(m)*
Fr entreprise *(f)*
Pt empresa *(f)*

impresa edile *(f)* It
De Bauunternehmer *(m)*
En building contractor
Es contratista de obras *(m)*
Fr entrepreneur de bâtiment
(m)
Pt construtor de obras *(m)*

impresa privata *(f)* It
De   Privatunternehmen *(n)*
En   private enterprise
Es   empresa privada *(f)*
Fr   entreprise privée *(f)*
Pt   empresa privada *(f)*

impresario *(m)* n It
De   Unternehmer *(m)*
En   contractor
Es   contratista *(m)*
Fr   entrepreneur *(m)*
Pt   contratador *(m)*

impresión *(f)* n Es
De   Ausgabedruck *(m)*
En   computer printout
Fr   sortie sur imprimante *(f)*
It   stampato d'uscita
      dell'elaboratore *(m)*
Pt   informe impresso pelo
      computador *(m)*

impresso *(m)* n Pt
De   Vordruck *(m)*
En   printed form
Es   formulario; impreso *(m)*
Fr   formulaire *(m)*
It   modulo stampato *(m)*

impresso de admissão *(m)* Pt
De   Antragsformular *(n)*
En   entry-form
Es   solicitud de inscripción *(f)*
Fr   feuille d'inscription *(f)*
It   bolletta d'entrata *(f)*

impresso de encomenda *(m)*
    Pt
De   Bestellformular *(n)*
En   order-form
Es   solicitud de pedido *(f)*
Fr   bulletin de commande *(m)*
It   foglio d'ordinazione *(m)*

impresso em branco *(m)* Pt
De   Blankoformular *(n)*
En   blank form
Es   formulario en blanco *(m)*
Fr   formulaire en blanc *(m)*
It   modulo in bianco *(m)*

improductif *adj* Fr
De   unproduktiv
En   unproductive
Es   improductivo
It   improduttivo
Pt   improdutivo

improductivo *adj* Es
De   unproduktiv
En   unproductive
Fr   improductif
It   improduttivo
Pt   improdutivo

improdutivo *adj* Pt
De   unproduktiv
En   unproductive
Es   improductivo
Fr   improductif
It   improduttivo

improduttivo *adj* It
De   unproduktiv
En   unproductive
Es   improductivo
Fr   improductif
Pt   improdutivo

improvement n En
De   Verbesserung *(f)*
Es   mejora *(f)*
Fr   amélioration *(f)*
It   miglioramento *(m)*
Pt   melhoramento *(m)*

impuesto *(m)* n Es
De   Steuer; Erhebung *(f)*
En   tax; levy
Fr   impôt; prélèvement *(m)*
It   imposta *(f)*
Pt   imposto *(m)*

impuesto de consumos *(m)*
    Es
De   Verbrauchsabgabe *(f)*
En   excise duty
Fr   droit sur la consommation
      (m)
It   imposta sul consumo *(f)*
Pt   imposto indirecto *(m)*

impuesto del timbre *(m)* Es
De   Stempelgebühr *(f)*
En   stamp duty
Fr   droit de timbre *(m)*
It   tassa di bollo *(f)*
Pt   imposto de selo *(m)*

impuesto de lujo *(m)* Es
De   Luxussteuer *(f)*
En   luxury tax
Fr   impôt de luxe *(m)*
It   tassa sugli articoli di lusso
      (f)
Pt   imposto de luxo *(m)*

impuesto latente *(m)* Es
De   versteckte Belastung *(f)*
En   hidden tax
Fr   imposition latente *(f)*
It   tassa invisibile *(f)*
Pt   imposto ocultado *(m)*

impuesto no incluido Es
De   außer Steuer
En   excluding tax
Fr   hors taxe (HT)
It   tassa esclusa
Pt   impostos excluídos

impuesto por empleado *(m)*
    Es
De   Lohnsummensteuer *(f)*
En   employment tax
Fr   taxe sur l'emploi *(f)*
It   imposta sull'impiego *(f)*
Pt   imposto sobre emprego
      (m)

impuesto sobre beneficios
    extraordinarios *(m pl)* Es
De   Übergewinnsteuer *(f)*
En   excess profits tax
Fr   impôts sur les superbéné-
      fices *(m pl)*
It   imposta sui soprapprofitti
      (f)
Pt   imposto sobre lucros ex-
      cessivos *(m)*

impuesto sobre la propie-
    dad *(m)* Es
De   Grundsteuer *(f)*
En   property tax
Fr   impôt foncier *(m)*
It   imposta fondiaria *(f)*
Pt   imposto sobre proprieda-
      de *(m)*

impuesto sobre la renta *(m)*
    Es
De   Einkommensteuer *(f)*
En   income tax
Fr   impôt sur le revenu *(m)*
It   imposta sul reddito *(f)*
Pt   imposto de receitas *(m)*

impuesto sobre las
    compras *(m)* Es
De   Erwerbsteuer *(f)*
En   purchase tax
Fr   impôt sur les acquisitions
      (m)
It   tassa sugli acquisti *(f)*
Pt   imposto sobre aquisições
      (m)

**impuesto sobre las ganan-
cias de capital** *(m)* Es
De Kapitalertragsteuer *(f)*
En capital gains tax
Fr impôt sur les plus-values
    en capital *(m)*
It imposta sul plusvalore di
    capitale *(f)*
Pt imposto sobre lucros de
    capital *(m)*

impuesto sobre la venta *(m)*
    Es
De Warenumsatzsteuer *(f)*
En sales tax
Fr taxe de vente *(f)*
It imposta sulle vendite *(f)*
Pt imposto sobre vendas *(m)*

**impuesto sobre renta de la
sociedad** *(m)* Es
De Körperschaftsteuer *(f)*
En corporation tax
Fr impôt sur le revenu des
    sociétés *(m)*
It imposta sui proventi delle
    società *(f)*
Pt imposto sobre corporação
    (m)

**impuesto sobre valor
añadido** *(m)* Es
De Mehrwertsteuer *(f)*
En value added tax (VAT)
Fr taxe sur la valeur ajoutée
    (TVA) *(f)*
It imposta sul valore
    aggiunto (IVA) *(f)*
Pt imposto sobre valor
    aduzido *(m)*

impulse buyir.g En
De Impulskaufen *(n)*
Es compra espontánea *(f)*
Fr achat sur l'entraînement
    du moment *(m)*
It compra sullo stimolo del
    momento *(f)*
Pt compra impulsiva *(f)*

Impulskaufen *(n)* n De
En impulse buying
Es compra espontánea *(f)*
Fr achat sur l'entraînement
    du moment *(m)*
It compra sullo stimolo del
    momento *(f)*
Pt compra impulsiva *(f)*

imputabile *adj* It
De anrechenbar
En chargeable
Es imputable; a cobrar
Fr imputable; imposable
Pt a cobrar

imputable *adj* Es, Fr
De anrechenbar
En chargeable
It imputabile; imponibile
Pt a cobrar

im Wert steigen De
En appreciate (in value)
Es subir (en valor)
Fr apprécier
It aumentare (di valore)
Pt aumentar; subir

in abeyance En
De in der Schwebe;
    unentschlossen
Es en suspenso
Fr en suspens
It in sospeso
Pt pendente

in acconto It
De a conto; auf Abschlag
En on account
Es a cuenta
Fr à valoir
Pt por conta

in accordance with En
De in Übereinstimmung mit
Es en conformidad con
Fr conforme à
It in conformità con
Pt em conformidade com

inadempienza *(f)* n It
De Nichterfüllung *(f)*
En nonfulfilment
Es incumplimiento *(m)*
Fr non-exécution *(f)*
Pt não cumprimento *(m)*

in agreement with En
De im Einvernehmen mit
Es de acuerdo con
Fr d'accord avec
It d'accordo con
Pt de acordo com

**in Ausführung begriffene
Arbeit** *(f)* De
En work on hand
Es trabajo en curso *(m)*

Fr travail en cours *(m)*
It lavoro in corso *(m)*
Pt trabalho em mão *(m)*

inautorizado *adj* Es
De unbefugt
En unauthorized
Fr non autorisé
It non autorizzato
Pt não autorizado

in bond En
De unter Zollverschluß
Es en aduanas
Fr en entrepôt
It sotto vincolo doganale
Pt à ordem da alfândega

in bulk En
De in großer Menge
Es a granel
Fr en vrac
It alla rinfusa
Pt a granel

in buona fede It
De auf Treu und Glauben
En in good faith
Es de buena fé
Fr de bonne foi
Pt de boa fé

in buono stato It
De in gutem Zustand
En in good repair
Es en buen estado
Fr en bon état
Pt em bom estado

incapacité *(f)* n Fr
De Unfähigkeit *(f)*
En inefficiency
Es incompetencia *f*
It inefficienza *(f)*
Pt ineficiência *(f)*

in case of default En
De bei Nichterfüllung
Es en caso de incumplimiento
Fr en cas de défaillance
It in caso di inadempienza
Pt em caso de não
    cumprimento

in caso di inadempienza It
De bei Nichterfüllung
En in case of default
Es en caso de incumplimiento
Fr en cas de défaillance
Pt em caso de não
    cumprimento

incassare *vb* It
De einkassieren
En cash
Es cobrar
Fr encaisser
Pt cobrar

incassare un assegno It
De einen Scheck einlösen
En cash a cheque
Es cobrar un cheque
Fr toucher un chèque
Pt cobrar um cheque

incassare un credito It
De Schulden eintreiben
En collect a debt
Es recaudar una deuda
Fr recouvrer une créance
Pt cobrar uma dívida

incendie *(f)* n Fr
De Brand *(m)*
En fire
Es fuego; incendio *(m)*
It incendio *(m)*
Pt fogo; incêndio *(m)*

incendio *(m)* n It
De Brand *(m)*
En fire
Es fuego; incendio *(m)*
Fr incendie *(f)*
Pt fogo; incêndio *(m)*

incentive n En
De Anreiz *(m)*
Es estímulo; incentivo *(m)*
Fr incitation; stimulant *(f m)*
It incentivo *(m)*
Pt incentivo *(m)*

incentivo *(m)* n Es, It, Pt
De Anreiz *(m)*
En incentive
Fr incitation; stimulant *(f m)*

incentivo alla esportazione
(m) It
De Ausfuhranreiz *(m)*
En export incentive
Es estímulo de exportación
(m)
Fr motif d'exportation *(m)*
Pt incentivo para a exportação
(m)

incentivo de inversión *(m)* Es
De Investierungsanreiz *(m)*
En investment incentive
Fr stimulant de l'ínvestisse-
ment *(m)*
It incentivo d'investimento
(m)
Pt incentivo de investimento
(m)

incentivo de investimento
(m) Pt
De Investierungsanreiz *(m)*
En investment incentive
Es incentivo de inversión *(m)*
Fr stimulant de l'investisse-
ment *(m)*
It incentivo d'investimento
(m)

incentivo d'investimento *(m)*
It
De Investierungsanreiz *(m)*
En investment incentive
Es incentivo de inversión *(m)*
Fr stimulant de l'investisse-
ment *(m)*
Pt incentivo de investimento
(m)

incentivo para a exportação
(m) Pt
De Ausfuhranreiz *(m)*
En export incentive
Es estímulo de exportación
(m)
Fr motif d'exportation *(m)*
It incentivo alla esportazione
(m)

inch n En
De Zoll (Längenmaß) *(m)*
Es pulgada *(f)*
Fr pouce *(m)*
It pollice *(m)*
Pt polegada *(f)*

inchiesta *(f)* n It
De Untersuchung *(f)*
En investigation; inquiry
Es investigación; encuesta *(f)*
Fr investigation; enquête *(f)*
Pt investigação; inquérito *(f m)*

incidental charges En
De Nebenkosten *(pl)*
Es cargos imprevistos *(m pl)*

Fr charges annexes *(f pl)*
It spese accessorie *(f pl)*
Pt encargos ocasionais *(m pl)*

incidental expenses En
De Nebenkosten *(pl)*
Es gastos imprevistos *(m pl)*
Fr faux frais *(m pl)*
It spese impreviste *(f pl)*
Pt despesas ocasionais *(f pl)*

incitation *(f)* n Fr
De Anreiz *(m)*
En incentive
Es estímulo; incentivo *(m)*
It Incentivo *(m)*
Pt incentivo *(m)*

including packing En
De Verpackung inbegriffen
Es franco embalaje
Fr franco d'emballage
It imballaggio incluso
Pt incluindo embalagem

incluido *adj* Es
De einschließlich
En inclusive
Fr inclus; compris
It incluso; compreso
Pt incluindo; incluso

incluindo *adj* Pt
De einschließlich
En inclusive
Es incluido
Fr inclus; compris
It incluso; compreso

incluindo embalagem Pt
De Verpackung inbegriffen
En including packing
Es franco embalaje
Fr franco d'emballage
It imballaggio incluso

inclus *adj* Fr
De einschließlich
En inclusive
Es incluido; inclusive
It incluso; compreso
Pt incluindo; incluso

inclusive *adj* En
De einschließlich
Es incluido; inclusive
Fr inclus; compris
It incluso; compreso
Pt incluindo

incluso *adj* Pt
De beiliegend
En enclosed
Es adjunto
Fr ci-joint; ci-inclus
It accluso

incluso *adj* It
De einschließlich
En inclusive
Es incluido; inclusive
Fr inclus; compris
Pt incluindo

income *n* En
De Einkommen *(n)*
Es ingresos; renta *(m pl; f)*
Fr revenu *(m)*
It reddito *(m)*
Pt receita *(f)*

income and expenditure account En
De Ausgaben- und Ertragskonto *(n)*
Es cuenta de ingresos y gastos *(f)*
Fr compte de revenus et dépenses *(m)*
It conto proventi e spese *(m)*
Pt conta de receitas e despesas *(f)*

incomes policy En
De Lohnpolitik *(f)*
Es plan de renta *(m)*
Fr politique des salaires *(f)*
It politica dei redditi *(f)*
Pt programa salários *(m)*

income tax En
De Einkommensteuer *(f)*
Es impuesto sobre la renta *(m)*
Fr impôt sur le revenu *(m)*
It imposta sul reddito *(f)*
Pt imposto de receitas *(m)*

income-tax return En
De Einkommensteuer- erklärung *(f)*
Es declaración fiscal *(f)*
Fr déclaration de revenu *(f)*
It dichiarazione del reddito *(f)*
Pt declaração fiscal *(f)*

income-tax year En
De Einkommensteuerjahr *(n)*
Es año fiscal *(m)*
Fr exercice fiscal *(m)*
It anno fiscale *(m)*
Pt ano fiscal *(m)*

incompetencia *(f)* n Es
De Unfähigkeit *(f)*
En inefficiency
Fr incapacité *(f)*
It inefficienza *(f)*
Pt ineficiência *(f)*

incomplet *adj* Fr
De unvollständig
En incomplete
Es incompleto
It incompleto
Pt incompleto

incomplete *adj* En
De unvollständig
Es incompleto
Fr incomplet
It incompleto
Pt incompleto

incompleto *adj* Es, It, Pt
De unvollständig
En incomplete
Fr incomplet

in concorrenza It
De wetteifernd
En competitive
Es competidor
Fr compétitif
Pt competitivo

in conformità con It
De in Übereinstimmung mit
En in accordance with
Es en conformidad con
Fr conforme à
Pt em conformidade com

in conto deposito It
De in Kommission
En on consignment
Es en consignación
Fr en consignation
Pt à consignação

in contropartita It
De als Gegenrechnung
En per contra
Es en contrapartida
Fr en contrepartie; par contre
Pt em contrapartida

incorporação *(f)* n Pt
De Eintragung (einer Gesellschaft) *(f)*
En incorporation
Es incorporación *(f)*
Fr incorporation *(f)*
It costituzione *(f)*

incorporación *(f)* n Es
De Eintragung (einer Gesellschaft) *(f)*
En incorporation
Fr incorporation *(f)*
It costituzione *(f)*
Pt incorporação *(f)*

incorporation *n* En, Fr *(f)*
De Eintragung (einer Gesellschaft) *(f)*
Es incorporación *(f)*
It costituzione *(f)*
Pt incorporação *(f)*

increase *vb* En
De steigen; zunehmen
Es aumentar; alzar
Fr augmenter; hausser
It aumentare; crescere
Pt aumentar

increase *n* En
De Steigen; Zunahme *(n f)*
Es incremento; aumento *(m)*
Fr hausse; augmentation *(f)*
It incremento; crescita *(m f)*
Pt aumento; incremento *(m)*

increased cost of living En
De erhöhte Lebenshaltungs- kosten *(pl)*
Es coste de vida más alto *(m)*
Fr renchérissement du coût de la vie *(m)*
It aumentato costo della vita *(m)*
Pt custo de vida mais elevado *(m)* .

increased costs En
De erhöhte Kosten *(pl)*
Es costes incrementados *(m pl)*

Fr accroissement des coûts
(m)
It costi aumentati *(m pl)*
Pt custos aumentados *(m pl)*

increase of capital En
De Kapitalerhöhung *(f)*
Es aumento de capital *(m)*
Fr augmentation de capital *(f)*
It aumento di capitale *(m)*
Pt aumento de capital *(m)*

increment *n* En
De Wertzuwachs *(m)*
Es aumento; incremento *(m)*
Fr accroissement;
plus-value *(m f)*
It incremento *(m)*
Pt aumento; incremento *(m)*

incremento *(m) n* Es, It, Pt
De Steigen; Wertzuwachs
(n m)
En increase; increment
Fr hausse; accroissement
(f m)

incumplimiento *(m) n* Es
De Nichterfüllung *(f)*
En nonfulfilment
Fr non-exécution *(f)*
It inadempienza *(f)*
Pt não cumprimento *(m)*

**incumplimiento del
contrato** *(m)* Es
De Vertragsverletzung *(f)*
En breach of contract
Fr rupture de contrat *(f)*
It rottura di contratto *(f)*
Pt rotura de contrato *(f)*

indagine di mercato *(f)* It
De Marktforschung *(f)*
En market research
Es investigación del mercado
(f)
Fr étude du marché *(f)*
Pt pesquisa de mercado *(f)*

indagine sul funzionamento
(f) It
De Unternehmensforschung
(f)
En operational research (OR)
Es investigación operacional
(f)

Fr recherche opérationnelle
(f)
Pt investigação operacional *(f)*

indagine sulle motivazioni *(f)*
It
De Motivforschung *(f)*
En motivational research
Es investigación de motiva-
ción *(f)*
Fr étude de motivation *(f)*
Pt investigação sobre moti-
vação *(f)*

indebitato *adj* It
De verschuldet
En indebted
Es endeudado
Fr endetté
Pt endividado; em dívida

indepted *adj* En
De verschuldet
Es endeudado
Fr endetté
It indebitato
Pt endividado; em dívida

in demand En
De gefragt
Es solicitado
Fr demandé
It ricercato
Pt procurado

indemnify *vb* En
De entschädigen
Es indemnizar; resarcir
Fr dédommager; indemniser
It indennizzare; risarcire
Pt indemnizar

indemnité *(f) n* Fr
De Entschädigung *(f)*
En indemnity
Es indemnización *(F)*
It indennità; garanzia *(f)*
Pt indemnização *(f)*

indemnité d'assurance *(f)* Fr
De Versicherungsanspruch
(m)
En insurance claim
Es reclamación de seguro *(f)*
It sinistro; reclamo d'inden-
nizzo *(m)*
Pt reclamação de seguro *(f)*

indemnité de principe *(f)* Fr
De Ordnungsentschädigung
(f)
En nominal damages
Es daños nominales *(m pl)*
It danni nominali *(m pl)*
Pt danos nominais *(m pl)*

indemnité de sauvetage *(f)* Fr
De Bergegeld *(n)*
En salvage charges
Es cargos de salvamento *(m
pl)*
It spese di salvataggio *(f pl)*
Pt encargos de salvamento
(m pl)

indemnity *n* En
De Entschädigung *(f)*
Es indemnización *(f)*
Fr indemnité; garantie *(f)*
It indennità; garanzia *(f)*
Pt indemnização *(f)*

indemnização *(f) n* Pt
De Entschädigung *(f)*
En indemnity
Es indemnización *(f)*
Fr indemnité *(f)*
It indennità *(f)*

indemnização especial *(f)* Pt
De Ersatz immateriellen
Schadens *(m)*
En special damages
Es daños especiales *(m pl)*
Fr dommages indirects *(m pl)*
It danni particolari *(m pl)*

indemnización *(f) n* Es
De Entschädigung *(f)*
En indemnity
Fr indemnité; garantie *(f)*
It indennità; garanzia *(F)*
Pt garantia; caução *(f)*

indemnizar *vb* Es, Pt
De entschädigen
En indemnify
Fr dédommager; indemniser
It indennizzare; risarcire

indennità *(f) n* It
De Entschädigung *(f)*
En indemnity
Es indemnización *(f)*
Fr indemnité *(f)*
Pt indemnização *(f)*

indennità di disoccupazione
(f) It
De Arbeitslosenunterstützung
(f)
En unemployment benefit
Es subsidio de paro *(m)*
Fr secours de chômage *(m)*
Pt subsídio de desemprego
(m)

indennizzare *vb* It
De entschädigen
En indemnify
Es indemnizar; resarcir
Fr dédommager; indemniser
Pt indemnizar

indépendant *adj* Fr
De selbständig
En independent
Es independiente
It indipendente
Pt independente

independent *adj* En
De selbständig
Es independiente
Fr indépendant
It indipendente
Pt independente

independente *adj* Pt
De selbständig
En independent
Es independiente
Fr indépendant
It indipendente

independiente *adj* Es
De selbständig
En independent
Fr indépendant
It indipendente
Pt independente

in deposito It
De auf Lager
En at warehouse
Es en almacén
Fr en dépôt
Pt em armazém

in der Schwebe De
En in abeyance
Es in suspenso
Fr en suspens
It in sospeso
Pt pendente

index *n* En, Fr *(m)*
De Index *(m)*
Es índice *(m)*
It indice *(m)*
Pt índice *(m)*

Index *(m)* n, De
En index
Es índice *(m)*
Fr indice; index *(m)*
It indice *(m)*
Pt índice *(m)*

index card En
De Indexkarte *(f)*
Es ficha *(f)*
Fr fiche *(f)*
It scheda *(f)*
Pt ficha *(f)*

Indexkarte *(f)* n De
En index card
Es ficha *(f)*
Fr fiche *(f)*
It scheda *(f)*
Pt ficha *(f)*

**indicateur des chemins de
fer** *(m)* Fr
De Eisenbahnfahrplan *(m)*
En railway timetable
Es horario de trenes *(m)*
It orario ferroviario *(m)*
Pt horário de caminhos de
ferro *(m)*

indicatif postal *(m)* Fr
De Postleitzahl *(f)*
En postcode
Am zip code
Es designación postal *(f)*
It codice postale *(m)*
Pt designação postal *(f)*

índice *(m)* n Es, Pt
De Index *(m)*
En index
Fr indice; index *(m)*
It indice *(m)*

indice *(m)* n Fr, It
De Index *(m)*
En index
Es índice *(m)*
Pt índice *(m)*

índice das acções *(m)* Pt
De Aktienindex *(m)*
En share index

Es índice de las acciones *(m)*
Fr indice des actions *(m)*
It indice delle azioni *(m)*

indice dei fallimenti *(m)* It
De Durchfallquote *(f)*
En failure rate
Es proporción de fracasos *(f)*
Fr taux de défaillance *(m)*
Pt proporção de fracassos *(f)*

índice de las acciones *(m)* Es
De Aktienindex *(m)*
En share index
Fr indice des actions *(m)*
It indice delle azioni *(m)*
Pt índice das acções *(m)*

indice delle azioni *(m)* It
De Aktienindex *(m)*
En share index
Es índice de las acciones *(m)*
Fr indice des actions *(m)*
Pt índice das acções *(m)*

indice des actions *(m)* Fr
De Aktienindex *(m)*
En share index
Es índice de las acciones *(m)*
It indice delle azioni *(m)*
Pt índice das acções *(m)*

indipendente *adj* It
De selbständig
En independent
Es independiente
Fr indépendant
Pt independente

indirect costs En
De Gemeinkosten *(pl)*
Es costes indirectos *(m pl)*
Fr frais indirects *(m pl)*
It costi indiretti *(m pl)*
Pt custos indirectos *(m pl)*

indirect taxation En
De indirekte Steuern *(f pl)*
Es contribuciones indirectas
(f pl)
Fr contributions indirectes
(f pl)
It imposte indirette *(f pl)*
Pt tributação indirecta *(f)*

indirekter Schaden *(m)* De
En consequential damage
Es daños indirectos *(m pl)*
Fr dommage indirect *(m)*

It   danno indiretto *(m)*
Pt dano por consequência
     (m)

indirekte Steuern *(f pl)* De
En indirect taxation
Es contribuciones indirectas
     (f pl)
Fr   contributions indirectes
     (f pl)
It   imposte indirette *(f pl)*
Pt tributação indirecta *(f)*

indirizzo *(m) n* It
De Adresse *(f)*
En address
Es dirección *(f)*
Fr   adresse *(f)*
Pt endereço *(m)*

indirizzo telegrafico *(m)* It
De Telegrammadresse *(f)*
En telegraphic address
Es dirección telegráfica *(f)*
Fr   adresse télégraphique *(f)*
Pt endereço telegráfico *(m)*

indossament *(n) n* De
En endorsement
Es endoso *(m)*
Fr   endossement; endos *(m)*
It   girata *(f)*
Pt endosse *(m)*

indossieren *vb* De
En endorse
Es endosar
Fr   endosser
It   girare
Pt endossar

in duplicate En
De Duplikat-; zweifach
Es par duplicado
Fr   en double
It   in duplice copia
Pt em duplicado

in duplice copia It
De Duplikat-; zweifach
En in duplicate
Es par duplicado
Fr   en double
Pt em duplicado

industria *(f) n* Es, It
De Industrie; Gewerbe *(f n)*
En industry

Fr   industrie *(f)*
Pt indústria *(f)*

indústria *(f) n* Pt
De Industrie; Gewerbe *(f n)*
En industry
Es industria *(f)*
Fr   industrie *(f)*
It   industria *(f)*

indústria chave *(f)* Pt
De Schlüsselindustrie *(f)*
En key industry
Es industria clave *(f)*
Fr   industrie-clef *(f)*
It   industria chiave *(f)*

industria chiave *(f)* It
De Schlüsselindustrie *(f)*
En key industry
Es industria clave *(f)*
Fr   industrie-clef *(f)*
Pt indústria chave *(f)*

industria clave *(f)* Es
De Schlüsselindustrie *(f)*
En key industry
Fr   industrie-clef *(f)*
It   industria chiave *(f)*
Pt indústria chave *(f)*

industria del turismo *(f)* Es
De Reisegewerbe *(n)*
En tourist trade
Fr   commerce de tourisme *(m)*
It   commercio turistico *(m)*
Pt indústria do turismo *(f)*

indústria do turismo *(f)* Pt
De Reisegewerbe *(n)*
En tourist trade
Es industria del turismo *(f)*
Fr   commerce de tourisme *(m)*
It   commercio turistico *(m)*

industrial *(m) n* Es, Pt
De Industrielle(r) *(m)*
En industrialist
Fr   industriel *(m)*
It   industriale *(m)*

industrial *adj* En, Es, Pt
De industriell; Gewerbe-
Fr   industriel
It   industriale

industrial accident En
De Arbeitsunfall *(m)*
Es accidente de trabajo *(m)*

Fr   accident du travail *(m)*
It   infortunio sul lavoro *(m)*
Pt acidente de trabalho *(m)*

industrial dispute En
De Arbeitskonflikt *(m)*
Es conflicto laboral *(m)*
Fr   conflit ouvrier *(m)*
It   vertenza operaia *(f)*
Pt conflito de trabalho *(m)*

industriale *(m) n* It
De Industrielle(r) *(m)*
En industrialist
Es industrial *(m)*
Fr   industriel *(m)*
Pt industrial *(m)*

industriale *adj* It
De industriell; Gewerbe-
En industrial
Es industrial
Fr   industriel
Pt industrial

industrial espionage En
De Wirtschaftsspionage *(f)*
Es espionaje industrial *(m)*
Fr   espionage industriel *(m)*
It   spionaggio industriale *(m)*
Pt espionagem industrial *(f)*

industrial estate En
Am industrial park
De Industriegebiet *(n)*
Es precinto industrial *(m)*
Fr   domaine industriel *(m)*
It   centro industriale *(m)*
Pt centro fabril *(m)*

industrialist *n* En
De Industrielle(r) *(m)*
Es industrial *(m)*
Fr   industriel *(m)*
It   industriale *(m)*
Pt industrial *(m)*

industrial park Am
En industrial estate
De Industriegebiet *(n)*
Es precinto industrial *(m)*
Fr   domaine industriel *(m)*
It   centro industriale *(m)*
Pt centro fabril *(m)*

industrial psychology En
De Arbeitspsychologie *(f)*
Es psicología industrial *(f)*

Fr psychotechnique *(f)*
It psicologia industriale *(f)*
Pt psicologia industrial *(f)*

industrial relations En
De Arbeitsbeziehungen *(f pl)*
Es relaciones humanas industriales *(f pl)*
Fr relations humaines dans l'entreprise *(f pl)*
It relazioni nell'industria *(f pl)*
Pt relações industriais *(f pl)*

industria nacionalizada *(f)* Es
De verstaatlichte Industrie *(f)*
En nationalized industry
Fr industrie nationalisée *(f)*
It industria nazionalizzata *(f)*
Pt indústria nacionalizada *(f)*

indústria nacionalizada *(f)* Pt
De verstaatlichte Industrie *(f)*
En nationalized industry
Es industria nacionalizada *(f)*
Fr industrie nationalisée *(f)*
It industria nazionalizzata *(f)*

industria nazionalizzata *(f)* It
De verstaatlichte Industrie *(f)*
En nationalized industry
Es industria nacionalizada *(f)*
Fr industrie nationalisée *(f)*
Pt indústria nacionalizada *(f)*

industria pesada *(f)* Es
De Schwerindustrie *(f)*
En heavy industry
Fr industrie lourde *(f)*
It industria pesante *(f)*
Pt indústria pesada *(f)*

indústria pesada *(f)* Pt
De Schwerindustrie *(f)*
En heavy industry
Es industria pesada *(f)*
Fr industrie lourde *(f)*
It industria pesante *(f)*

industria pesante *(f)* It
De Schwerindustrie *(f)*
En heavy industry
Es industria pesada *(f)*
Fr industrie lourde *(f)*
Pt indústria pesada *(f)*

industrie *(f)* n Fr
De Industrie; Gewerbe *(f n)*
En industry

Es industria *(f)*
It industria *(f)*
Pt indústria *(f)*

Industrie *(f)* n De
En industry
Es industria *(f)*
Fr industrie *(f)*
It industria *(f)*
Pt indústria *(f)*

industrie-clef *(f)* n Fr
De Schlüsselindustrie *(f)*
En key industry
Es industria clave *(f)*
It industria chiave *(f)*
Pt indústria chave *(f)*

Industriegebiet *(n)* n De
En industrial estate
Am industrial park
Es precinto industrial *(m)*
Fr domaine industriel *(m)*
It centro industriale *(m)*
Pt centro fabril *(m)*

industriel *(m)* n Fr
De Industrielle(r) *(m)*
En industrialist
Es industrial *(m)*
It industriale *(m)*
Pt industrial *(m)*

industriel *adj* Fr
De industriell; Gewerbe-
En industrial
Es industrial
It industriale
Pt industrial

industriell *adj* De
En industrial
Es industrial
Fr industriel
It industriale
Pt industrial

Industrielle(r) *(m)* n De
En industrialist
Es industrial *(m)*
Fr industriel *(m)*
It industriale *(m)*
Pt industrial *(m)*

industrie lourde *(f)* Fr
De Schwerindustrie *(f)*
En heavy industry

Es industria pesada *(f)*
It industria pesante *(f)*
Pt indústria pesada *(f)*

industrie nationalisée *(f)* Fr
De verstaatlichte Industrie *(f)*
En nationalized industry
Es industria nacionalizada *(f)*
It industria nazionalizzata *(f)*
Pt indústria nacionalizada *(f)*

industry n En
De Industrie; Gewerbe *(f n)*
Es industria *(f)*
Fr industrie *(f)*
It industria *(f)*
Pt indústria *(f)*

inefficacité *(f)* n Fr
De Unfähigkeit *(f)*
En inefficiency
Es incompetencia *(f)*
It inefficienza *(f)*
Pt ineficiência *(f)*

inefficiency n En
De Unfähigkeit *(f)*
Es incompetencia *(f)*
Fr incapacité *(f)*
It inefficienza *(f)*
Pt ineficiência *(f)*

inefficienza *(f)* n It
De Unfähigkeit *(f)*
En inefficiency
Es incompetencia *(f)*
Fr incapacité *(f)*
Pt ineficiência *(f)*

ineficiência *(f)* n Pt
De Unfähigkeit *(f)*
En inefficiency
Es incompetencia *(f)*
Fr incapacité *(f)*
It inefficienza *(f)*

inesperienza *(f)* n It
De Unerfahrenheit *(f)*
En inexperience
Es falta de experiencia *(f)*
Fr manque de pratique *(m)*
Pt inexperiência *(f)*

inexperience n En
De Unerfahrenheit *(f)*
Es falta de experiencia *(f)*
Fr manque de pratique *(m)*
It inesperienza *(f)*
Pt inexperiência *(f)*

inexperiência *(f)* *n* Pt
De Unerfahrenheit *(f)*
En inexperience
Es falta de experiencia *(f)*
Fr manque de pratique *(m)*
It inesperienza *(f)*

infiltração no mercado *(f)* Pt
De Markteindringen *(n)*
En market penetration
Es penetración en el mercado
 (f)
Fr pénétration du marché *(f)*
It penetrazione nel mercato
 (f)

inflação *(f)* *n* Pt
De Inflation *(f)*
En inflation
Es inflación *(f)*
Fr inflation *(f)*
It inflazione *(f)*

inflación *(f)* *n* Es
De Inflation *(f)*
En inflation
Fr inflation *(f)*
It inflazione *(f)*
Pt inflação *(f)*

inflation *n* En, Fr *(f)*
De Inflation *(f)*
Es inflación *(f)*
It inflazione *(f)*
Pt inflação *(f)*

Inflation *(f)* *n* De
En inflation
Es inflación *(f)*
Fr inflation *(f)*
It inflazione *(f)*
Pt inflação *(f)*

inflationary spiral En
De Inflationsspirale *(f)*
Es espiral de inflación *(f)*
Fr spirale inflationniste *(f)*
It inflazione a spirale *(f)*
Pt espiral inflacionária *(f)*

Inflationsspirale *(f)* *n* De
En inflationary spiral
Es espiral de inflación *(f)*
Fr spirale inflationniste *(f)*
It inflazione a spirale *(f)*
Pt espiral inflacionária *(f)*

inflazione *(f)* *n* It
De Inflation *(f)*
En inflation
Es inflación *(f)*
Fr inflation *(f)*
Pt inflação *(f)*

inflazione a spirale *(f)* It
De Inflationsspirale *(f)*
En inflationary spiral
Es espiral de inflación *(f)*
Fr spirale inflationniste *(f)*
Pt espiral inflacionária *(f)*

in force En
De In Kraft
Es en vigor
Fr en vigueur
It in vigore
Pt vigente

inform *vb* En
De benachrichtigen
Es informar; avisar
Fr informer; renseigner
It informare
Pt informar

informação *(f)* *n* Pt
De Auskunft *(f)*
En information
Es información *(f)*
Fr information; renseigne-
 ment *(f m)*
It informazione *(f)*

informação adicional *(f)* Pt
De weitere Auskunft *(f)*
En further information
Es más detalles *(m pl)*
Fr renseignements complé-
 mentaires *(m pl)*
It ulteriori informazioni *(f pl)*

informação do mercado *(f)* Pt
De Marktbericht *(m)*
En market report
Es informe del mercado *(m)*
Fr revue du marché *(f)*
It relazione sul mercato *(f)*

información *(f)* *n* Es
De Auskunft *(f)*
En information
Fr information; renseigne-
 ment *(f m)*
It informazione *(f)*
Pt informação *(f)*

informal *adj* En
De formlos; nicht formell
Es sin ceremonia
Fr sans formalités
It senza formalità
Pt sem formalidade

informar *vb* Es, Pt
De benachrichtigen
En inform
Fr informer; renseigner
It informare

informare *vb* It
De benachrichtigen
En inform
Es informar; avisar
Fr informer; renseigner
Pt informar

information *n* En, Fr *(f)*
De Auskunft *(f)*
Es información *(f)*
It informazione *(f)*
Pt informação *(f)*

information retrieval En
De Informationswieder-
 gewinnung *(f)*
Es rebusca de información *(f)*
Fr récupération de données
 (f)
It ricupero d'informazioni *(m)*
Pt recuperação de informação
 (f)

**Informationswiedergewin-
 nung** *(f)* *n* De
En information retrieval
Es rebusca de información *(f)*
Fr récupération de données
 (f)
It ricupero d'informazioni *(m)*
Pt recuperação de informação
 (f)

informazione *(f)* *n* It
De Auskunft *(f)*
En information
Es información *(f)*
Fr information; renseigne-
 ment *(f m)*
Pt informação *(f)*

informe *(m)* *n* Es
De Bericht; Meldung *(m f)*
En report

Fr rapport; compte-rendu
(m)
It relazione; rapporto (f m)
Pt relatório (m)

informe de la administración (m) Es
De Vorstandsbericht (m)
En directors' report
Fr rapport des administrateurs (m)
It relazione degli amministratori (f)
Pt relatório de directores (m)

informe del especialista (m) Es
De Sachverständigengutachten (n)
En expert's report
Fr expertise (f)
It perizia (f)
Pt relatório do perito (m)

informe del mercado (m) Es
De Marktbericht (m)
En market report
Fr revue du marché (f)
It relazione sul mercato (f)
Pt informação do mercado (f)

informe de los interventores (m) Es
De Bericht des Abschlußprüfers (m)
En auditor's report
Fr rapport des vérificateurs des comptes (m)
It relazione dei sindaci (f)
Pt relatório do fiscal de contas (m)

informe impresso pelo computador (m) Pt
De Ausgabedruck (m)
En computer printout
Es impresión (f)
Fr sortie sur imprimante (f)
It stampato d'uscita dell'elaboratore (m)

informer vb Fr
De benachrichtigen
En inform
Es informar; avisar
It informare
Pt informar

infortunio sul lavoro (m) It
De Arbeitsunfall (m)
En industrial accident
Es accidente de trabajo (m)
Fr accident du traval (m)
Pt acidente de trabalho (m)

infracção (f) n Pt
De Verletzung; Verstoß (f m)
En infringement
Es infracción (f)
Fr infraction (f)
It infrazione (f)

infracción (f) n Es
De Verletzung; Verstoß (f m)
En infringement
Fr infraction (f)
It infrazione (f)
Pt infracção (f)

infracción de los derechos de autor (f) Es
De Urheberrechtsverletzung (f)
En infringement of copyright
Fr contrefaçon littéraire (f)
It infrazione dei diritti d'autore (f)
Pt infracção de direitos de autor (f)

infraction (f) n Fr
De Verletzung; Verstoß (f m)
En infringement
Es infracción (f)
It infrazione (f)
Pt infracção (f)

infrazione (f) n It
De Verletzung; Verstoß (f m)
En infringement
Es infracción (f)
Fr infraction (f)
Pt infracção (f)

infrazione dei diritti d'autore (f) It
De Urheberrechtsverletzung (f)
En infringement of copyright
Es infracción de los derechos de autor (f)
Fr contrefaçon littéraire (f)
Pt infracção de direitos de autor (f)

infringement n En
De Verletzung; Verstoß (f m)
Es infracción (f)

Fr infraction (f)
It infrazione (f)
Pt infracção (f)

infringement of copyright En
De Urheberrechtsverletzung (f)
Es infracción de los derechos de autor (f)
Fr contrefaçon littéraire (f)
It infrazione dei diritti d'autore (f)
Pt infracção de direitos de autor (f)

ingegnere (m) n It
De Ingenieur (m)
En engineer
Es ingeniero (m)
Fr ingénieur (m)
Pt engenheiro (m)

ingegneria (f) n It
De Maschinenbau (m)
En engineering
Es ingeniería (f)
Fr génie (m)
Pt engenharia (f)

ingegneria chimica (f) It
De Chemietechnik (f)
En chemical engineering
Es ingenieria química (f)
Fr génie chimique (f)
Pt engenharia química (f)

ingegneria civile (f) It
De Ingenieurbau (m)
En civil engineering
Es ingeniería civil (f)
Fr génie civil (m)
Pt engenharia civil (f)

ingegneria meccanica (f) It
De Maschinenbau (m)
En mechanical engineering
Es ingenieria mecánica (f)
Fr construction mécanique (f)
Pt engenharia mecânica (f)

ingenieria (f) n Es
De Maschinenbau (m)
En engineering
Fr génie (m)
It ingegneria (f)
Pt engenharia (f)

ingeniera civil (f) Es
De Ingenieurbau (m)
En civil engineering
Fr génie civil (m)

It   ingegneria civile *(f)*
Pt   engenharia civil *(f)*

ingeniería eléctrica *(f)* Es
De   Elektrotechnik *(f)*
En   electrical engineering
Fr   construction électrique *(f)*
It   elettrotecnica *(f)*
Pt   engenharia electrotécnica
       (f)

ingeniería mecánica *(f)* Es
De   Maschinenbau *(m)*
En   mechanical engineering
Fr   construction mécanique *(f)*
It   ingegneria meccanica *(f)*
Pt   engenharia mecânica *(f)*

ingeniería química *(f)* Es
De   Chemietechnik *(f)*
En   chemical engineering
Fr   génie chimique *(m)*
It   ingegneria chimica *(f)*
Pt   engenharia química *(f)*

ingeniero *(m)* n Es
De   Ingenieur *(m)*
En   engineer
Fr   ingénieur *(m)*
It   ingegnere *(m)*
Pt   engenheiro *(m)*

ingénieur *(m)* n Fr
De   Ingenieur *(m)*
En   engineer
Es   ingeniero *(m)*
It   ingegnere *(m)*
Pt   engenheiro *(m)*

Ingenieur *(m)* n De
En   engineer
Es   ingeniero *(m)*
Fr   ingénieur *(m)*
It   ingegnere *(m)*
Pt   engenheiro *(m)*

Ingenieurbau *(m)* n De
En   civil engineering
Es   ingeniería civil *(m)*
Fr   génie civil *(m)*
It   ingegneria civile *(f)*
Pt   engenharia civil *(f)*

**ingénieur-conseil en
    organisation** *(m)* Fr
De   Geschäftsführungsberater
       (m)
En   management consultant
Es   asesor administrativo *(m)*

It   consulente di direzione
       aziendale *(m)*
Pt   perito de administração *(m)*

ingiunzione *(f)* n It
De   gerichtliche Verfügung *(f)*
En   injunction
Es   entredicho *(m)*
Fr   injonction; arrêt de
       suspension *(f m)*
Pt   interdição *(f)*

in good faith En
De   auf Treu und Glauben
Es   de buena fé
Fr   de bonne foi
It   in buona fede
Pt   de boa fé

in good repair En
De   in gutem Zustand
Es   en buen estado
Fr   en bon état
It   in buono stato
Pt   em bom estado

ingorgo stradale *(m)* It
De   Verkehrsstockung *(f)*
En   traffic jam
Es   embotellamiento de tráfico
       (m)
Fr   encombrement de circula-
       tion *(m)*
Pt   engarrafamento de tráfego
       (m)

ingot n En
De   Barren *(m)*
Es   lingote *(m)*
Fr   lingot; barre *(m f)*
It   lingotto *(m)*
Pt   lingote *(m)*

ingranaggio *(m)* n It
De   Getriebe *(n)*
En   gearing
Es   engranaje *(m)*
Fr   engrenage *(m)*
Pt   engrenagem *(f)*

ingreso bruto *(m)* Es
De   Bruttoeinkommen *(n)*
En   gross income
Fr   rendement brut *(m)*
It   reddito lordo *(m)*
Pt   receita bruta *(f)*

ingreso neto *(f)* Es
De   Nettoeinkommen *(n)*
En   net income
Fr   revenu net *(m)*

It   reddito netto *(m)*
Pt   receita líquida *(f)*

ingresos *(m pl)* n Es
De   Einkommen; Einkünfte
       (n; f pl)
En   revenue; income
Fr   revenu; rentes *(m; f pl)*
It   entrata; reddito *(f m)*
Pt   rendimento; receita *(m f)*

ingresos netos *(m pl)* Es
De   Nettoeinnahmen *(f pl)*
En   net revenue
Fr   recettes nettes *(f pl)*
It   entrata netta *(f)*
Pt   receita líquida *(f)*

ingresos no imponibles
    (m pl) Es
De   steuerfreies Einkommen
       (n)
En   nontaxable income
Fr   revenu non imposable *(m)*
It   reddito non tassabile *(m)*
Pt   receita não tributável *(f)*

ingresso gratuito *(m)* It
De   Eintritt frei *(m)*
En   admission free
Es   entrada gratuita *(f)*
Fr   entrée gratuite *(f)*
Pt   entrada grátis *(f)*

in großer Menge De
En   in bulk
Es   a granel
Fr   en vrac
It   alla rinfusa
Pt   a granel

in gutem Zustand De
En   in good repair
Es   en buen estado
Fr   en bon état
It   in buono stato
Pt   em bom estado

Inhaber *(m)* n De
En   holder
Es   titular *(m)*
Fr   détenteur *(m)*
It   titolare *(m)*
Pt   titular *(m)*

Inhabereffekten *(n pl)* n De
En   bearer securities
Es   valores al portador *(m pl)*
Fr   valeurs au porteur *(f pl)*

It   valori al portatore *(m pl)*
Pt valores ao portador *(m pl)*

Inhaberobligation *(f) n* De
En bearer debenture
Es obligación al portador *(f)*
Fr obligation au porteur *(f)*
It   obbligazione al portatore *(f)*
Pt obrigação ao portador *(f)*

Inhaberscheck *(m) n* De
En cheque payable to bearer
Es cheque al portador *(m)*
Fr chèque payable au porteur *(m)*
It   assegno al portatore *(m)*
Pt cheque ao portador *(m)*

(an den) Inhaber zahlbar De
En payable to bearer
Es pagadero al portador
Fr payable au porteur
It   pagabile al portatore
Pt pagável ao portador

Inhalt *(m) n* De
En contents
Es contenido *(m)*
Fr contenu *(m)*
It   contenuto *(m)*
Pt conteúdo *(m)*

inheritance *n* En
De Erbschaft *(f)*
Es herencia *(f)*
Fr succession *(f)*
It   eredità *(f)*
Pt herança *(f)*

inicial *adj* Es, Pt
De Anfangs-
En initial
Fr initial; premier
It   iniziale

iniciar un proceso contra Es
De gerichtlich vorgehen gegen
En institute proceedings against
Fr intenter un procès à
It   intentare un'azione legale contro
Pt instituir processo contra

iniciativa em comum *(f)* Pt
De Gemeinschaftsbetrieb *(f)*
En joint venture
Es empresa en común *(f)*

Fr entreprise en participation *(f)*
It   impresa in compartecipazione *(f)*

inimigo *(m) n* Pt
De Feind *(m)*
En enemy
Es enemigo *(m)*
Fr ennemi *(m)*
It   nemico *(m)*

initial *vb* En
De paraphieren
Es rubricar; poner iniciales a
Fr parapher; viser
It   siglare
Pt rubricar

initial *adj* En, Fr
De Anfangs-
Es inicial; primario
It   iniziale
Pt inicial

iniziale *adj* It
De Anfangs-
En initial
Es inicial; primario
Fr initial; premier
Pt inicial

inizio scarico *(m)* It
De Löschen der Ladung *(n)*
En breaking bulk
Es fraccionamiento de la carga *(m)*
Fr rupture de charge *(f)*
Pt retalhar a carga

injonction *(f) n* Fr
De gerichtliche Verfügung *(f)*
En injunction
Es entredicho *(m)*
It   ingiunzione *(f)*
Pt interdição *(f)*

injunction *n* En
De gerichtliche Verfügung *(f)*
Es entredicho *(m)*
Fr injonction; arrêt de suspension *(f m)*
It   ingiunzione *(f)*
Pt interdição *(f)*

injured party En
De Verletzte(r) *(m)*
Es parte lesionada *(f)*
Fr partie lésée *(f)*
It   parte lesa *(f)*
Pt parte lesada *(f)*

injury *n* En
De Schaden *(m)*
Es daño *(m)*
Fr dommage; avarie *(m f)*
It   danno *(m)*
Pt dano; injúria *(m f)*

Inkassobeauftragte(r) *(m) n* De
En debt collector
Es agente recaudador *(m)*
Fr agent de recouvrement *(m)*
It   agente di ricupero crediti *(m)*
Pt cobrador *(m)*

in kind En
De in Waren
Es en especie
Fr en nature
It   in natura
Pt em espécie

in Kommission De
En on consignment
Es en consignación
Fr en consignation
It   in conto deposito
Pt á consignação

in Kraft De
En in force
Es en vigor
Fr en vigueur
It   in vigore
Pt vigente

in magazzino It
De vorrätig
En in stock
Es en almacén
Fr en magasin
Pt em reserva

inmigración *(f) n* Es
De Einwanderung *(f)*
En immigration
Fr immigration *(f)*
It   immigrazione *(f)*
Pt imigração *(f)*

inmovilizaciones *(f pl) n* Es
De Kapitalauslagen *(f pl)*
En capital expenditure
Fr immobilisations *(f pl)*
It   immobilizzazioni *(f pl)*
Pt despesas em termos de capital *(f pl)*

in natura It
De in Waren
En in kind
Es en especie
Fr en nature
Pt em espécie

innerlich adj De
En internal; intrinsic
Es interno; intrínseco
Fr interne; intrinsèque
It interno; intrinseco
Pt interno; intrínseco

innerlicher Wert (m) De
En intrinsic value
Es valor intrínseco (m)
Fr valeur intrinsèque (f)
It valore intrinseco (m)
Pt valor intrínseco (m)

innovación (f) n Es
De Neuerung (f)
En innovation
Fr innovation (f)
It innovazione (f)
Pt inovação (f)

innovation n En, Fr (f)
De Neuerung (f)
Es innovación (f)
It innovazione (f)
Pt inovação (f)

innovazione (f) n It
De Neuerung (f)
En innovation
Es innovación (f)
Fr innovation (f)
Pt inovação (f)

inovação (f) n Pt
De Neuerung (f)
En innovation
Es innovación (f)
Fr innovation (f)
It innovazione (f)

in piego a parte It
De mit getrennter Post
En under separate cover
Es por correo aparte
Fr sous pli séparé
Pt por correio separado

in prestito It
De darlehensweise
En on loan
Es en préstamo
Fr sous forme de prêt
Pt por empréstimo

inquérito (m) n Pt
De Untersuchung (f)
En inquiry
Es encuesta (f)
Fr enquête (f)
It inchiesta (f)

inquilino (m) n Es, Pt
De Mieter (m)
En tenant
Fr locataire (m)
It affittuario; locatario (m)

inquiry (for information, etc.) n
En
De Nachfrage (f)
Es demanda (f)
Fr demande (f)
It domanda (f)
Pt pergunta (f)

inquiry (legal) n En
De Untersuchung (f)
Es encuesta (f)
Fr enquête (f)
It inchiesta (f)
Pt inquérito (m)

inscription (f) n Fr
De Eintragung (f)
En entry
Es asiento (m)
It registrazione (f)
Pt lançamento (m)

insegnamento superiore (m)
It
De Fortbildung (f)
En higher education
Es enseñanza superior (f)
Fr enseignement supérieur
(m)
Pt instrução superior (f)

insérer vb Fr
De einsetzen; inserieren
En insert
Es insertar
It inserire
Pt inserir

inserir vb Pt
De einsetzen; inserieren
En insert
Es insertar
Fr insérer
It inserire

inserire vb It
De einsetzen; inserieren
En insert
Es insertar

Fr insérer
Pt inserir

insert vb En
De einsetzen; inserieren
Es insertar
Fr insérer
It inserire
Pt inserir

insertar vb Es
De einsetzen; inserieren
En insert
Fr insérer
It inserire
Pt inserir

inserzionista (m) n It
De Anzeiger (m)
En advertiser
Es anunciante (m)
Fr annonceur (m)
Pt anunciante (m)

insolvable adj Fr
De zahlungsunfähig
En insolvent
Es insolvente; quebrado
It insolvente
Pt insolvente

insolvencia (f) n Es
De Zahlungsunfähigkeit (f)
En insolvency
Fr faillite; déconfiture (f)
It insolvenza (f)
Pt insolvência (f)

insolvência (f) n Pt
De Zahlungsunfähigkeit (f)
En insolvency
Es insolvencia; quiebra (f)
Fr faillite; déconfiture (f)
It insolvenza (f)

insolvency n En
De Zahlungsunfähigkeit (f)
Es insolvencia; quiebra (f)
Fr faillite; déconfiture (f)
It insolvenza (f)
Pt insolvência (f)

insolvent adj En
De zahlungsunfähig
Es insolvente; quebrado
Fr insolvable
It insolvente
Pt insolvente

insolvente adj Es, It, Pt
De zahlungsunfähig
En insolvent
Fr insolvable

insolvenza (f) n It
De Zahlungsunfähigkeit (f)
En insolvency
Es insolvencia; quiebra (f)
Fr faillite; déconfiture (f)
Pt insolvência (f)

in sospeso It
De in der Schwebe; unent-
schlossen
En in abeyance
Es en suspenso
Fr en suspens
Pt pendente

inspecção (f) n Pt
De Einsichtnahme (f)
En inspection
Es inspección; examen (f m)
Fr inspection; vérification (f)
It ispezione (f)

inspecção médica (f) Pt
De ärztliche Untersuchung (f)
En medical examination
Es examen médico (m)
Fr examen médical (m)
It visita medica (f)

inspección (f) n Es
De Einsichtnahme (f)
En inspection
Fr inspection; vérification (f)
It ispezione (f)
Pt inspecção (f)

inspecteur (m) n Fr
De Aufsichtsbeamte(r) (m)
En inspector
Es inspector (m)
It ispettore (m)
Pt inspector (m)

inspecteur du travail (m) Fr
De Gewerbeaufsichtsbeam-
te(r) (m)
En factory inspector
Es inspector de fábrica (m)
It ispettore di fabbrica (m)
Pt inspector de fábrica (m)

inspection n En, Fr (f)
De Einsichtnahme (f)
Es inspección; examen (f m)
It ispezione (f)
Pt inspecção (f)

inspector n En, Es, Pt (m)
De Aufsichtsbeamte(r) (m)
Fr inspecteur; vérificateur (m)
It ispettore (m)

inspector de fábrica (m) Es,
Pt
De Gewerbeaufsichtsbeam-
te(r) (m)
En factory inspector
Fr inspecteur du travail (m)
It ispettore di fabbrica (m)

instalação (f) n Pt
De Anlage (f)
En installation
Es instalación (f)
Fr installation (f)
It impianto (m)

instalação fabril (f) Pt
De Anlage (f)
En plant
Es planta; instalación (f)
Fr appareil; installation (m f)
It impianto; macchinario (m)

instalação piloto (f) Pt
De Musteranlage (f)
En pilot plant
Es instalación piloto (f)
Fr installation pilote (f)
It impianto piloto (m)

instalación (f) n Es
De Anlage (f)
En installation
Fr installation (f)
It impianto; installazione
(m f)
Pt instalação (f)

instalaciones portuarias
(f pl) Es
De Hafenanlagen (f pl)
En harbour installations
Fr installations portuaires
(f pl)
It impianti portuali (m pl)
Pt instalações portuárias (f pl)

instalación piloto (f) Es
De Musteranlage (f)
En pilot plant
Fr installation pilote (f)
It impianto piloto (m)
Pt instalação piloto (f)

instalações portuárias (f pl)
Pt
De Hafenanlagen (f pl)
En harbour installations

Es instalaciones portuarias
(f pl)
Fr installations portuaires
(f pl)
It impianti portuali (m pl)

installation n En, Fr (f)
De Anlage (f)
Es instalación (f)
It impianto; installazione
(m f)
Pt instalação (f)

installation pilote (f) Fr
De Musteranlage (f)
En pilot plant
Es instalación piloto (f)
It impianto piloto (m)
Pt instalação piloto (f)

installations portuaires (f pl)
Fr
De Hafenanlagen (f pl)
En harbour installations
Es instalaciones portuarias
(f pl)
It impianti portuali (m pl)
Pt instalações portuárias (f pl)

instalment n En
De Rate (f)
Es plazo (m)
Fr acompte (m)
It rata (f)
Pt prestação (f)

instalment plan En
De Ratenverkauf (m)
Es pago a plazos (m)
Fr vente à tempérament (f)
It sistema di pagamento a
rate (f)
Pt plano de prestações (m)

Instandhaltung (f) n De
En maintenance
Es mantenimiento (m)
Fr entretien (m)
It manutenzione (f)
Pt manutenção (f)

instigar vb Es, Pt
De anstiften
En instigate
Fr provoquer
It provocare; istigare

instigate vb En
De anstiften
Es instigar; provocar
Fr provoquer

It   provocare; istigare
Pt   instigar

institución *(f) n* Es
De   Institut; Anstalt *(n f)*
En   institution
Fr   institut *(m)*
It   istituzione; istituto *(f m)*
Pt   instituição *(f)*

instituição *(f) n* Pt
De   Institut; Anstalt *(n f)*
En   institution
Es   institución; istituto *(f m)*
Fr   institut *(m)*
It   istituzione; istituto *(f m)*

**instituição de investimen-
tos** *(f)* Pt
De   Investment-Trust *(m)*
En   investment trust
Es   fideicomiso de inversiones
      (m)
Fr   société fiduciaire de
      placements *(f)*
It   consorzio per investimenti
      (m)

instituir processo contra Pt
De   gerichtlich vorgehen
      gegen
En   institute proceedings
      against
Es   iniciar un proceso contra
Fr   intenter un procès à
It   intentare un'azione legale
      contro

institut *(m) n* Fr
De   Institut; Anstalt *(n f)*
En   institution
Es   institución; istituto *(f m)*
It   istituzione; istituto *(f m)*
Pt   instituição *(f)*

Institut *(n) n* De
En   institution
Es   institución; istituto *(f m)*
Fr   institut *(m)*
It   istituzione; istituto *(f m)*
Pt   instituição *(f)*

**institute proceedings
against** En
De   gerichtlich vorgehen
      gegen
Es   iniciar un proceso contra
Fr   intenter un procès à
It   intentare un'azione legale
      contro
Pt   instituir processo contra

institution *n* En
De   Institut; Anstalt *(n f)*
Es   institución; instituto *(f m)*
Fr   institut *(m)*
It   istituzione; istituto *(f m)*
Pt   instituição *(f)*

in stock En
De   vorrätig
Es   en almacén
Fr   en magasin
It   in magazzino
Pt   em reserva

instrução *(f) n* Pt
De   Anleitung *(f)*
En   instruction
Es   instrucción *(f)*
Fr   instruction *(f)*
It   istruzione *(f)*

instrução superior *(f)* Pt
De   Fortbildung *(f)*
En   higher education
Es   enseñanza superior *(f)*
Fr   enseignement supérieur
      (m)
It   insegnamento superiore
      (m)

instrucción *(f) n* Es
De   Anleitung *(f)*
En   instruction
Fr   instruction *(f)*
It   istruzione *(f)*
Pt   instrução *(f)*

instruções para uso *(f pl)* Pt
De   Gebrauchsanweisung *(f)*
En   instructions for use
Es   modo de empleo *(m)*
Fr   mode d'emploi *(f)*
It   istruzioni per l'uso *(f pl)*

instruction *n* En, Fr *(f)*
De   Anleitung *(f)*
Es   instrucción *(f)*
It   istruzione *(f)*
Pt   instrução *(f)*

instructions for use En
De   Gebrauchsanleitung *(f)*
Es   modo de empleo *(m)*
Fr   mode d'emploi *(f)*
It   istruzioni per l'uso *(f pl)*
Pt   instruções para uso *(f pl)*

instrument *n* En, Fr *(m)*
De   Instrument *(n)*
Es   instrumento *(m)*
It   strumento *(m)*
Pt   instrumento *(m)*

Instrument *(n) n* De
En   instrument
Es   instrumento *(m)*
Fr   instrument *(m)*
It   strumento *(m)*
Pt   instrumento *(m)*

instrument d'analyse *(m)* Fr
De   Analysenwerkzeug *(n)*
En   analytical tool
Es   instrumento de análisis *(m)*
It   strumento d'analisi *(m)*
Pt   instrumento de análise *(m)*

instrumento *(m) n* Es, Pt
De   Instrument *(n)*
En   instrument
Fr   instrument *(m)*
It   strumento *(m)*

instrumento de análise *(m)*
Pt
De   Analysenwerkzeug *(n)*
En   analytical tool
Es   instrumento de análisis *(m)*
Fr   instrument d'analyse *(m)*
It   strumento d'analisi *(m)*

instrumento de análisis *(m)*
Es
De   Analysenwerkzeug *(n)*
En   analytical tool
Fr   instrument d'analyse *(m)*
It   strumento d'analisi *(m)*
Pt   instrumento de análise *(m)*

insurable *adj* En
De   versicherbar
Es   asegurable
Fr   assurable
It   assicurabile
Pt   susceptível de ser objecto
      de seguro

insurance *n* En
De   Versicherung *(f)*
Es   seguro *(m)*
Fr   assurance *(f)*
It   assicurazione *(f)*
Pt   seguro *(m)*

insurance agent En
De   Versicherungsvertreter *(m)*
Es   agente de seguros *(m)*
Fr   agent d'assurances *(m)*
It   agente d'assicurazioni *(f)*
Pt   agente de seguros *(m)*

insurance broker En
De Versicherungsmakler *(m)*
Es corredor de seguros *(m)*
Fr courtier d'assurance *(m)*
It mediatore di assicurazioni *(m)*
Pt corretor de seguros *(m)*

insurance certificate En
De Versicherungsschein *(m)*
Es certificado de seguro *(m)*
Fr certificat d'assurance *(m)*
It certificato di assicurazione *(m)*
Pt certificado de seguro *(m)*

insurance claim En
De Versicherungsanspruch *(m)*
Es reclamación de seguro *(f)*
Fr indemnité d'assurance *(f)*
It sinistro; reclamo d'indennizzo *(m)*
Pt reclamação de seguro *(f)*

insurance company En
De Versicherungsgesellschaft *(f)*
Es compañía de seguros *(f)*
Fr compagnie d'assurance *(f)*
It compagnia di assicurazione *(f)*
Pt companhia de seguros *(f)*

insurance cover En
De Versicherungsdeckung *(f)*
Es cobertura de la póliza de seguro *(f)*
Fr garantie d'assurance *(f)*
It copertura assicurativa *(f)*
Pt cobertura de seguro *(f)*

insurance policy En
De Versicherungspolice *(f)*
Es póliza de seguro *(f)*
Fr police d'assurance *(f)*
It polizza di assicurazione *(f)*
Pt apólice de seguros *(f)*

insurance premium En
De Versicherungsprämie *(f)*
Es prima de póliza de seguro *(f)*
Fr prime d'assurance *(f)*
It premio di assicurazione *(m)*
Pt prémio de seguro *(m)*

insure *vb* En
De versichern
Es asegurar
Fr assurer

It assicurare
Pt segurar

insured *n* En
De Versicherte(r) *(m)*
Es asegurado *(m)*
Fr assuré *(m)*
It assicurato *(m)*
Pt titular de seguro *(m)*

insurer *n* En
De Versicherer *(m)*
Es asegurador *(m)*
Fr assureur *(m)*
It assicuratore *(m)*
Pt segurador *(m)*

intangible assets En
De nicht greifbare Aktiven *(n pl)*
Es activo intangible *(m)*
Fr actif incorporel *(m)*
It beni incorporali *(m pl)*
Pt bens intocáveis *(m pl)*

integração *(f)* n Pt
De Eingliederung *(f)*
En integration
Es integración *(f)*
Fr intégration *(f)*
It integrazione *(f)*

integração horizontal *(f)* Pt
De horizontaler Zusammenschluß *(m)*
En horizontal integration
Es integración horizontal *(f)*
Fr intégration horizontale *(f)*
It integrazione orizzontale *(f)*

integração vertical *(f)* Pt
De vertikaler Zusammenschluß *(m)*
En vertical integration
Es integración vertical *(f)*
Fr integration verticale *(f)*
It integrazione verticale *(f)*

integración *(f)* n Es
De Eingliederung *(f)*
En integration
Fr intégration *(f)*
It integrazione *(f)*
Pt integração *(f)*

integración horizontal *(f)* Es
De horizontaler Zusammenschluß *(m)*
En horizontal integration
Fr intégration horizontale *(f)*
It integrazione orizzontale *(f)*
Pt integração horizontal *(f)*

integración vertical *(f)* Es
De vertikaler Zusammenschluß *(m)*
En vertical integration
Fr intégration verticale *(f)*
It integrazione verticale *(f)*
Pt integração vertical *(f)*

intégralement souscrit Fr
De vollgezeichnet
En fully subscribed
Es plenamente suscrito
It interamente sottoscritto
Pt totalmente subscrito

integration *n* En
De Eingliederung *(f)*
Es integración *(f)*
Fr intégration *(f)*
It integrazione *(f)*
Pt integração *(f)*

intégration *(f)* n Fr
De Eingliederung *(f)*
En integration
Es integración *(f)*
It integrazione *(f)*
Pt integração *(f)*

intégration horizontale *(f)* Fr
De horizontaler Zusammenschluß *(m)*
En horizontal integration
Es integración horizontal *(f)*
It integrazione orizzontale *(f)*
Pt integração horizontal *(f)*

intégration verticale *(f)* Fr
De vertikaler Zusammenschluß *(m)*
En vertical integration
Es integración vertical *(f)*
It integrazione verticale *(f)*
Pt integração vertical *(f)*

integrazione *(f)* n It
De Eingliederung *(f)*
En integration
Es integración *(f)*
Fr intégration *(f)*
Pt integração *(f)*

integrazione orizzontale *(f)* It
De horizontaler Zusammenschluß *(m)*
En horizontal integration
Es integración horizontal *(f)*
Fr intégration horizontale *(f)*
Pt integração horizontal *(f)*

integrazione verticale *(f)* It
De vertikaler Zusammen-
schluß *(m)*
En vertical integration
Es integración vertical *(f)*
Fr intégration verticale *(f)*
Pt integração vertical *(f)*

intensif de capital Fr
De kapitalintensiv
En capital-intensive
Es intensivo de capital
It concentrato sul capitale
Pt intensivo em termos de
capital

intensivo de capital Es
De kapitalintensiv
En capital-intensive
Fr intensif de capital
It concentrato sul capitale
Pt intensivo em termos de
capital

**intentare un'azione legale
contro** It
De gerichtlich vorgehen
gegen
En institute proceedings
against
Es iniciar un proceso contra
Fr intenter un procès à
Pt instituir processo contra

intenter un procès à Fr
De gerichtlich vorgehen
gegen
En institute proceedings
against
Es iniciar un proceso contra
It intentare un'azione legale
contro
Pt instituir processo contra

interamente sottoscritto It
De vollgezeichnet
En fully subscribed
Es plenamente suscrito
Fr intégralement souscrit
Pt totalmente subscrito

interés *(m)* n Es
De Zinsen *(m pl)*
En interest
Fr intérêt; prime *(m f)*
It interesse *(m)*
Pt juro *(m)*

interés acumulado *(m)* Es
De aufgelaufene Zinsen *(m pl)*
En accrued interest

Fr intérêts accumulés *(m pl)*
It interesse maturato *(m)*
Pt juro acumulado *(m)*

interés bruto *(m)* Es
De Bruttozins *(m)*
En gross interest
Fr intérêts bruts *(m pl)*
It interesse lordo *(m)*
Pt juro bruto *(m)*

interés compuesto *(m)* Es
De Zinseszinsen *(m pl)*
En compound interest
Fr intérêts composés *(m pl)*
It interesse composto *(m)*
Pt juro composto *(m)*

interés creado *(m)* Es
De festbegründetes Recht *(n)*
En vested interest
Fr droit acquis *(m)*
It diritto acquisito *(m)*
Pt interesse adquirido *(m)*

interés mayoritario *(m)* Es
De Mehrheitsbeteiligung *(f)*
En controlling interest
Fr participation donnant le
contrôle *(f)*
It interesse della parte mag-
gioritaria *(m)*
Pt interesse maioritário *(m)*

interesse *(m)* n It
De Zinsen *(m pl)*
En interest
Es interés *(m)*
Fr intérêt; prime *(m f)*
Pt juro *(m)*

interesse adquirido *(m)* Pt
De festbegründetes Recht *(n)*
En vested interest
Es interés creado *(m)*
Fr droit acquis *(m)*
It diritto acquisito *(m)*

interesse composto *(m)* It
De Zinseszinsen *(m pl)*
En compound interest
Es interés compuesto *(m)*
Fr intérêts composés *(m pl)*
Pt juro composto *(m)*

**interesse della parte mag-
gioritaria** *(m)* It
De Mehrheitsbeteiligung *(f)*
En controlling interest
Es interés mayoritario *(m)*

Fr participation donnant le
contrôle *(f)*
Pt interesse maioritário *(m)*

interesse lordo *(m)* It
De Bruttozins *(m)*
En gross interest
Es interés bruto *(m)*
Fr intérêts bruts *(m pl)*
Pt juro bruto *(m)*

interesse maioritário *(m)* Pt
De Mehrheitsbeteiligung *(f)*
En controlling interest
Es interés mayoritario *(m)*
Fr participation donnant le
contrôle *(f)*
It interesse della parte mag-
gioritaria *(m)*

interesse maturato *(m)* It
De aufgelaufene Zinsen *(m pl)*
En accrued interest
Es interés acumulado *(m)*
Fr intérêts accumulés *(m pl)*
Pt juro acumulado *(m)*

**interessenza a cambio
marittimo** *(f)* It
De Bodmereidarlehenszinsen
(m pl)
En bottomry interest
Es interés de préstamo a la
gruesa *(m)*
Fr profit maritime *(m)*
Pt juro de bodemeria *(m)*

interessenza di minoranza
(f) It
De Minoritätsbeteiligung *(f)*
En minority interest
Es participación de la minoría
(f)
Fr participation de la minorité
(f)
Pt interesse representado
pela minoria *(m)*

**interesse representado pela
minoria** *(m)* Pt
De Minoritätsbeteiligung *(f)*
En minority interest
Es participación de la minoría
(f)
Fr participation de la minorité
(f)
It interessenza di minoranza
(f)

interesse semplice *(m)* It
De einfache Zinsen *(m pl)*
En simple interest
Es interés simple *(m)*
Fr intérêts simples *(m pl)*
Pt juro simples *(m)*

interés simple *(m)* Es
De einfache Zinsen *(m pl)*
En simple interest
Fr intérêts simples *(m pl)*
It interesse semplice *(m)*
Pt juro simples *(m)*

interest *n* En
De Zinsen *(m pl)*
Es interés *(m)*
Fr intérêt; prime *(m f)*
It interesse *(m)*
Pt juro *(m)*

interest-bearing account
Am
En deposit account
De Depositenkonto *(n)*
Es cuenta de ahorras *(f)*
Fr compte de dépôt *(m)*
It conto di deposito *(m)*
Pt conta de depósito *(f)*

interest rates En
De Zinssätze *(m pl)*
Es tasas de interés *(f pl)*
Fr taux d'intérêt *(m pl)*
It tassi d'interesse *(m pl)*
Pt taxas de juro *(f pl)*

intérêt *(m) n* Fr
De Zinsen *(m pl)*
En interest
Es interés *(m)*
It interesse *(m)*
Pt juro *(m)*

intérêts accumulés *(m pl)* Fr
De aufgelaufene Zinsen *(m pl)*
En accrued interest
Es interés acumulado *(m)*
It interesse maturato *(m)*
Pt juro acumulado *(m)*

intérêts bruts *(m pl)* Fr
De Bruttozins *(m)*
En gross interest
Es interés bruto *(m)*
It interesse lordo *(m)*
Pt juro bruto *(m)*

intérêts composés *(m pl)* Fr
De Zinseszinsen *(m pl)*
En compound interest

Es interés compuesto *(m)*
It interesse composto *(m)*
Pt juro composto *(m)*

intérêts simples *(m pl)* Fr
De einfache Zinsen *(m pl)*
En simple interest
Es interés simple *(m)*
It interesse semplice *(m)*
Pt juro simples *(m)*

interim dividend En
De vorläufige Dividende *(f)*
Es dividendo provisional *(m)*
Fr dividende intérimaire *(m)*
It acconto di dividendo *(m)*
Pt dividendo interino *(m)*

interim financial statement
En
De Zwischenbilanz *(f)*
Es extracto financiero provi-
sional *(m)*
Fr bilan intérimaire *(m)*
It rendiconto finanziario
provvisorio *(m)*
Pt extracto financeiro interino
(m)

intermediação *(f) n* Pt
De Vermittlung *(f)*
En mediation
Es intermediación *(f)*
Fr médiation *(f)*
It mediazione *(f)*

intermediación *(f) n* Es
De Vermittlung *(f)*
En mediation
Fr médiation *(f)*
It mediazione *(f)*
Pt intermediação *(f)*

intermédiaire *(m) n* Fr
De Zwischenhändler *(m)*
En middle man
Es intermediario *(m)*
It intermediario *(m)*
Pt intermediário *(m)*

intermediar *vb* Es, Pt
De vermitteln
En mediate
Fr s'entremettre
It fare da intermediario

intermediario *(m) n* Es, It
De Zwischenhändler *(m)*
En middle man
Fr intermédiaire *(m)*
Pt intermediário *(m)*

intermediário *(m) n* Pt
De Zwischenhändler *(m)*
En middle man
Es intermediario *(m)*
Fr intermédiaire *(m)*
It intermediario *(m)*

internácional *adj* Es
De international
En international
Fr international
It internazionale
Pt internacional

internacional *adj* Pt
De international
En international
Es internácional
Fr international
It internazionale

internal *adj* En
De innerlich; inländisch
Es interno; interior
Fr interne; intérieur
It interno
Pt interno

internal audit En
De interne Revision *(f)*
Es verificación contable
interna *(f)*
Fr vérification interne *(f)*
It verifica contabile interna *(f)*
Pt fiscalização contabilística
interna *(f)*

international *adj* De, En, Fr
Es internácional
It internazionale
Pt internacional

**International Bank for
Reconstruction and
Development** En
De Internationale Bank für
Wiederaufbau und Wirt-
schaftsförderung *(f)*
Es Banco Internacional
para Reconstrucción y
Desarrollo *(m)*
Fr Banque Internationale
pour la Reconstruction et
le Développement *(f)*
It Banca Internazionale per
la Ricostruzione e lo Svi-
luppo *(f)*
Pt Banco Internacional de
Reconstrução e Desen-
volvimento *(m)*

International Chamber of Commerce En
De Internationale Handels-
      kammer (f)
Es Cámara Internacional de
      Comercio (f)
Fr Chambre de Commerce
      Internationale (f)
It   Camera di Commercio
      Internazionale (f)
Pt Câmara Internacional do
      Comércio (f)

**Internationale Arbeitsorga-
nisation (IAO)** (f) De
En International Labour
      Organization (ILO)
Es Organisación Laboral
      Internacional (f)
Fr Organisation Internatio-
      nale du Travail (O.I.T.) (f)
Pt Organização Internacional
      do Trabalho (f)

**Internationale Bank für
Wiederaufbau und Wirt-
schaftsförderung** (f) De
En International Bank for
      Reconstruction and
      Development
Es Banco Internacional
      para Reconstrucción y
      Desarrollo (m)
Fr Banque Internationale
      pour la Reconstruction et
      le Développement (f)
It   Banca Internazionale per
      la Ricostruzione e lo Svi-
      luppo (f)
Pt Banco Internacional de
      Reconstrução e Desenvol-
      vimento (m)

**Internationale Finanz-
korporation** (f) De
En International Finance Cor-
      poration
Es Corporación Internacional
      de Finanzas (f)
Fr Société Financière Inter-
      nationale (f)
It   Corporazione Finanziaria
      Internazionale (f)
Pt Corporação Internacional
      de Finanças (f)

**Internationale Handels-
kammer** (IWF) (f) De
En International Chamber of
      Commerce
Es Cámara Internacional de
      Comercio (f)

Fr Chambre de Commerce
      Internationale (F.N.I.) (f)
It   Camera di Commercio
      Internazionale (f)
Pt Câmara Internacional do
      Comércio (f)

**Internationaler Währungs-
fonds** (m) De
En International Monetary
      Fund (IMF)
Es Fondo Monetario Inter-
      nacional (m)
Fr Fonds Monétaire Inter-
      national (m)
It   Fondo Monetario Inter-
      nazionale (m)
Pt Fundo Monetário Inter-
      nacional (F.M.I.) (m)

**International Finance Cor-
poration** En
De Internationale Finanz-
      korporation (f)
Es Corporación Internacional
      de Finanzas (f)
Fr Société Financière Inter-
      nationale (f)
It   Corporazione Finanziaria
      Internazionale (f)
Pt Corporação Internacional
      de Finanças (f)

**International Labour
Organization** (ILO) En
De Internationale Arbeits-
      organisation (IAO) (f)
Es Organisación Laboral
      Internacional (f)
Fr Organisation Internatio-
      nale du Travail (O.I.T.) (f)
It   Organizzazione Interna-
      zionale del Lavoro (f)
Pt Organização Internacional
      do Trabalho (f)

**International Monetary
Fund** (IMF) En
De Internationaler Währungs-
      fonds (IWF) (m)
Es Fondo Monetario Inter-
      nacional (m)
Fr Fonds Monétaire Inter-
      national (F.M.I.) (m)
It   Fondo Monetario Inter-
      nazionale (m)
Pt Fundo Monetário Inter-
      nacional (F.M.I.) (m)

internazionale adj It
De international
En international
Es internácional
Fr international
Pt internacional

interne adj Fr
De innerlich; inländisch
En internal
Es interno; interior
It   interno
Pt interno

interne Revision (f) De
En internal audit
Es verificación contable in-
      terna (f)
Fr vérification interne (f)
It   verifica contabile interna (f)
Pt fiscalização contabilística
      interna (f)

interno adj Es, It, Pt
De innerlich; inländisch
En internal
Fr interne; intérieur

interpolação (f) n Pt
De Einschaltung (f)
En interpolation
Es interpolación (f)
Fr interpolation (f)
It   interpolazione (f)

interpolación (f) n Es
De Einschaltung (f)
En interpolation
Fr interpolation (f)
It   interpolazione (f)
Pt interpolação (f)

interpolation n En, Fr (f)
De Einschaltung (f)
Es interpolación (f)
It   interpolazione (f)
Pt interpolação (f)

interpolazione (f) n It
De Einschaltung (f)
En interpolation
Es interpolación (f)
Fr interpolation (f)
Pt interpolação (f)

interponer vb Es
De einlegen
En file; lodge
Fr déposer
It   depositare
Pt registar

interpretação (f) n Pt
De Auslegung (f)
En interpretation
Es interpretación (f)
Fr interprétation (f)
It interpretazione (f)

interpretación (f) n Es
De Auslegung (f)
En interpretation
Fr interprétation (f)
It interpretazione (f)
Pt interpretação (f)

interpretation n En
De Auslegung (f)
Es interpretación (f)
Fr interprétation (f)
It interpretazione (f)
Pt interpretação (f)

interprétation (f) n Fr
De Auslegung (f)
En interpretation
Es interpretación (f)
It interpretazione (f)
Pt interpretação (f)

interpretazione (f) n It
De Auslegung (f)
En interpretation
Es interpretación (f)
Fr interprétation (f)
Pt interpretação (f)

intervalle d'acceptation (f) Fr
De Akzeptfrist (f)
En acceptance interval
Es intervalo de aceptación
(m)
It intervallo dell'accettazione
(m)
Pt intervalo de aceitação (m)

intervallo dell'accettazione
(m) It
De Akzeptfrist (f)
En acceptance interval
Es intervalo de aceptación
(m)
Fr intervalle d'acceptation (f)
Pt intervalo de aceitação (m)

intervalo de aceitação (m) Pt
De Akzeptfrist (f)
En acceptance interval
Es intervalo de aceptación
(m)
Fr intervalle d'acceptation (f)
It intervallo dell'accettazione
(m)

intervalo de aceptación
(m) Es
De Akzeptfrist (f)
En acceptance interval
Fr intervalle d'acceptation (f)
It intervallo dell'accettazione
(m)
Pt intervalo de aceitação (m)

Intervention (bei Wechsel-
akzept) (f) De
En acceptance for honour
Es aceptación por interven-
ción (f)
Fr acceptation par interven-
tion (f)
It accettazione per interven-
to (f)
Pt aceitação por intervenção (f)

intervention price En
De Interventionspreis (m)
Es precio de intervención (m)
Fr prix d'intervention (m)
It prezzo d'intervento (m)
Pt preço de intervenção (m)

Interventionspreis (m) n De
En intervention price
Es precio de intervención (m)
Fr prix d'intervention (m)
It prezzo d'intervento (m)
Pt preço de intervenção (m)

interventor (m) n Es
De Rechnungsprüfer (m)
En comptroller
Fr vérificateur des comptes
(m)
It controllore (m)
Pt controlador (m)

interview n En, Fr (f)
De Interview (n)
Es entrevista (f)
It intervista; abboccamento
(f m)
Pt entrevista; encontro (f m)

Interview (n) n De
En interview
Es entrevista (f)
Fr interview; entrevue (f)
It intervista; abboccamento
(f m)
Pt entrevista; encontro (f m)

interviewee n En
De Befragte(r) (m)
Es persona entrevistada (f)
Fr personne interrogée (f)

It intervistato (m)
Pt entrevistador (m)

interviewer n En
De Interviewer (m)
Es entrevistador (m)
Fr intervieweur; enquêteur
(m)
It intervistatore (m)
Pt entrevistador (m)

Interviewer (m) n De
En interviewer
Es entrevistador (m)
Fr intervieweur; enquêteur
(m)
It intervistatore (m)
Pt entrevistador (m)

intervieweur (m) n Fr
De Interviewer (m)
En interviewer
Es entrevistador (m)
It intervistatore (m)
Pt entrevistador (m)

intervista (f) n It
De Interview (n)
En interview
Es entrevista (f)
Fr interview; entrevue (f)
Pt entrevista; encontro (f m)

intervistato (m) n It
De Befragte(r) (m)
En interviewee
Es persona entrevistada (f)
Fr personne interrogée (f)
Pt entrevistador (m)

intervistatore (m) n It
De Interviewer (m)
En interviewer
Es entrevistador (m)
Fr intervieweur; enquêteur
(m)
Pt entrevistador (m)

intestazione (f) n It
De Briefkopf (m)
En letterhead
Es membrete (m)
Fr en-tête (m)
Pt cabeçalho (m)

intimazione (f) n It
De Inverzugsetzung (f)
En formal notice
Es aviso oficial (m)
Fr mise en demeure (f)
Pt notificação formal (f)

in transit En
De im Durchgangsverkehr
Es en tránsito
Fr en transit
It in transito
Pt em trânsito

in transito It
De im Durchgangsverkehr
En in transit
Es en tránsito
Fr en transit
Pt em trânsito

intraprenditore (m) n It
De Unternehmer (m)
En entrepreneur
Es empresario (m)
Fr entrepreneur (m)
Pt empresário (m)

intrínseco adj Es, Pt
De innerlich; wahr
En intrinsic
Fr intrinsèque
It intrinseco

intrinsèque adj Fr
De innerlich; wahr
En intrinsic
Es intrínseco
It intrinseco
Pt intrínseco

intrinsic adj En
De innerlich; wahr
Es intrínseco
Fr intrinsèque
It intrinseco
Pt intrínseco

intrinseco adj It
De innerlich; wahr
En intrinsic
Es intrínseco
Fr intrinsèque
Pt intrínseco

intrinsic value En
De innerlicher Wert (m)
Es valor intrínseco (m)
Fr valeur intrinsèque (f)
It valore intrinseco (m)
Pt valor intrínseco (m)

in Übereinstimmung mit De
En in accordance with
Es en conformidad con
Fr conforme à
It in conformità con
Pt em conformidade com

**inundación de mercancía
barata** (f) Es
De Dumping (n)
En dumping
Fr dumping (m)
It dumping (m)
Pt saturação (de mercadorias
baratas); descarga (f)

invalid adj En
De ungültig
Es inválido
Fr invalide
It invalido
Pt inválido

invalide adj Fr
De ungültig
En invalid
Es inválido
It invalido
Pt inválido

inválido adj Es, Pt
De ungültig
En invalid
Fr invalide
It invalido

invalido adj It
De ungültig
En invalid
Es inválido
Fr invalide
Pt inválido

invenção (f) n Pt
De Erfindung (f)
En invention
Es invento; invención (m f)
Fr invention (f)
It invenzione (f)

inventaire (m) n Fr
De Inventar (n)
En inventory
Es inventario (m)
It inventario (m)
Pt inventário (m)

Inventar (n) n De
En inventory
Es inventario (m)
Fr inventaire (m)
It inventario (m)
Pt inventário (m)

inventario (m) n Es, It
De Inventar (n)
En inventory

Fr inventaire (m)
Pt inventário (m)

inventário (m) n Pt
De Inventar (n)
En inventory
Es inventario (m)
Fr inventaire (m)
It inventario (m)

invention n En, Fr (f)
De Erfindung (f)
Es invento; invención (m f)
It invenzione (f)
Pt Invenção (f)

invento (m) n Es
De Erfindung (f)
En invention
Fr invention (f)
It invenzione (f)
Pt invenção (f)

inventory n En
De Inventar (n)
Es inventario (m)
Fr inventaire (m)
It inventario (m)
Pt inventário (m)

invenzione (f) n It
De Erfindung (f)
En invention
Es invento; invención (m f)
Fr invention (f)
Pt invenção (f)

inversión (f) n Es
De Kapitalanlage; Investie-
rung (f)
En investment
Fr investissement; placement
(m)
It Investimento (m)
Pt investimento (m)

inversionista (m) n Es
De Geldgeber (m)
En investor
Fr investisseur (m)
It capitalista (m)
Pt capitalista (m)

invertir vb Es
De anlegen
En invest
Fr investir; placer
It investire
Pt investir

Inverzugsetzung *(f) n* De
En formal notice
Es aviso oficial *(m)*
Fr mise en demeure *(f)*
It intimazione *(f)*
Pt notificação formal *(f)*

invest *vb* En
De anlegen; investieren
Es invertir
Fr investir; placer
It investire
Pt investir

investieren *vb* De
En invest
Es invertir
Fr investir; placer
It investire
Pt investir

Investierung *(f) n* De
En investment
Es inversión *(f)*
Fr investissement *(m)*
It investimento *(m)*
Pt investimento *(m)*

Investierungsanreiz *(m) n* De
En investment incentive
Es incentivo de inversión *(m)*
Fr stimulant de l'investisse-
ment *(m)*
It incentivo d'investimento
(m)
Pt incentivo de investimento
(m)

Investierungsgesellschaft
(f) n De
En investment company
Es compañía inversionista *(f)*
Fr société de placement *(f)*
It società per investimenti *(f)*
Pt companhia de investimen-
tos *(f)*

investigação *(f) n* Pt
De Untersuchung; Forschung
(f)
En investigation; research
Es investigación *(f)*
Fr investigation; recherche *(f)*
It investigazione; ricerca *(f)*

**investigação e desenvolvi-
mento** Pt
De Zweckforschung; For-
schung und Entwicklung
(F & E) *(f)*
En research and development
(R & D)

Es investigación y desarrollo
Fr recherche industrielle *(f)*
It studi e sviluppi

investigação operacional *(f)*
Pt
De Unternehmensforschung
(f)
En operational research (OR)
Es investigación operacional
(f)
Fr recherche opérationnelle
(f)
It indagine sul funzionamen-
to *(f)*

investigación *(f) n* Es
De Untersuchung; Forschung
(f)
En investigation; research
Fr investigation; recherche *(f)*
It investigazione; ricerca *(f)*
Pt investigação; pesquisa *(f)*

investigación del mercado
(f) Es
De Marktforschung *(f)*
En market research
Fr étude du marché *(f)*
It indagine di mercato *(f)*
Pt pesquisa de mercado *(f)*

investigación de motivación
(f) Es
De Motivforschung *(f)*
En motivational research
Fr étude de motivation *(f)*
It indagine sulle motivazioni
(f)
Pt investigação sobre moti-
vação *(f)*

investigación operacional *(f)*
Es
De Unternehmensforschung
(f)
En operational research (OR)
Fr recherche opérationnelle
(f)
It indagine sul funzionamen-
to *(f)*
Pt investigação operacional *(f)*

investigación y desarrollo
Es
De Zweckforschung; For-
schung und
Entwicklung (F & E) *(f)*
En research and development
(R & D)
Fr recherche industrielle *(f)*

It studi e sviluppi
Pt investigação e desenvolvimento

investigation *n* En, Fr *(f)*
De Untersuchung *(f)*
Es investigación *(f)*
It inchiesta; investigazione
(f)
Pt investigação; pesquisa *(f)*

investimento *(m) n* It, Pt
De Kapitalanlage; Investie-
rung *(f)*
En investment
Es inversión *(f)*
Fr investissement; placement
(f)

investir *vb* Fr, Pt
De anlegen; investieren
En invest
Es invertir
It investire

investire *vb* It
De anlegen; investieren
En invest
Es invertir
Fr investir; placer
Pt investir

investissement *(m) n* Fr
De Kapitalanlage; Investie-
rung *(f)*
En investment
Es inversión *(f)*
It investimento *(m)*
Pt investimento *(m)*

investisseur *(m) n* Fr
De Geldgeber *(m)*
En investor
Es inversionista *(m)*
It capitalista *(m)*
Pt capitalista *(m)*

Investitionsanalyst *(m) n* De
En investment analyst
Es analizador de inversiones
(m)
Fr analyste d'investisse-
ments *(m)*
It analizzatore d'investimenti
(m)
Pt analisador de investimen-
tos *(m)*

Investitionsportefeuille *(n) n*
De
En investment portfolio
Es cartera de inversiones *(f)*

Fr portefeuille d'investissements (m)
It portafoglio titoli (m)
Pt carteira de investimentos
(f)

investment n En
De Kapitalanlage; Investie-
rung (f)
Es inversión (f)
Fr investissement; placement
(m)
It investimento (m)
Pt investimento (m)

investment analyst En
De Investitionsanalyst (m)
Es analizador de inversiones
(m)
Fr analyste d'investisse-
ments (m)
It analizzatore d'investimenti
(m)
Pt analisador de investimen-
tos (m)

investment bank En
De Finanzbank (f)
Es banco de inversiones (m)
Fr banque d'affaires (f)
It banca d'investimenti (f)
Pt banco de investimentos
(m)

investment company En
De Investierungsgesellschaft
(f)
Es compañía inversionista (f)
Fr société de placement (f)
It società per investimenti (f)
Pt companhia de investimen-
tos (f)

investment incentive En
De Investierungsanreiz (m)
Es incentivo de inversión (m)
Fr stimulant de l'investisse-
ment (m)
It incentivo d'investimento
(m)
Pt incentivo de investimento
(m)

investment income En
De Einkommen aus Kapital-
anlagen (n)
Es renta de inversiones (f)
Fr revenu de placements (m)
It reddito degli investimenti
(m)
Pt rendimento de capitais in-
vestidos (m)

investment portfolio En
De Investitionsportefeuille (n)
Es cartera de inversiones (f)
Fr portefeuille d'investisse-
ments (m)
It portafoglio titoli (m)
Pt carteira de investimentos
(f)

investment trust En
De Investment-Trust (m)
Es fideicomiso de inversiones
(m)
Fr société fiduciaire de
placements (f)
It consorzio per investimenti
(m)
Pt instituição de investimentos
(f)

Investment-Trust (m) n De
En investment trust
Es fideicomiso de inversiones
(m)
Fr société fiduciaire de
placements (f)
It consorzio per investimenti
(m)
Pt instituição de investimentos
(f)

investor n En
De Geldgeber (m)
Es inversionista (m)
Fr investisseur (m)
It capitalista (m)
Pt capitalista (m)

in vigore It
De in Kraft
En in force
Es en vigor
Fr en vigueur
Pt vigente

invisible exports En
De unsichtbare Exporte (m pl)
Es exportaciones invisibles
(f pl)
Fr exportations invisibles
(f pl)
It esportazioni invisibili (f pl)
Pt exportações invisíveis (f pl)

invitación (f) n Es
De Einladung; Aufforderung
(f)
En invitation
Fr invitation; appel (f m)
It invito (m)
Pt convite (m)

invitar vb Es
De einladen; auffordern
En invite
Fr inviter
It invitare
Pt convidar

invitare vb It
De einladen; auffordern
En invite
Es invitar
Fr inviter
Pt convidar

invitation n En, Fr (f)
De Einladung; Aufforderung
(f)
Es invitación (f)
It invito (m)
Pt convite (m)

invite vb En
De einladen; auffordern
Es invitar
Fr inviter
It invitare
Pt convidar

inviter vb Fr
De einladen; auffordern
En invite
Es invitar
It invitare
Pt convidar

invito (m) n It
De Einladung; Aufforderung
(f)
En invitation
Es invitación (f)
Fr invitation; appel (f m)
Pt convite (m)

invoice vb En
De fakturieren
Es facturar
Fr facturer
It fatturare
Pt facturar

invoice n En
De Faktura; Rechnung (f)
Es factura (f)
Fr facture (f)
It fattura (f)
Pt factura (f)

invoice price En
De fakturierter Preis (m)
Es precio facturado (m)
Fr prix facturé (m)

It prezzo di fattura *(m)*
Pt preço de factura *(m)*

in Waren De
En in kind
Es en especie
Fr en nature
It in natura
Pt em espécie

ipoteca *(f)* n It
De Hypothek *(f)*
En mortgage; hypothecation
Es hipoteca *(f)*
Fr hypothèque; nantisse-
ment *(f m)*
Pt hipoteca *(f)*

ipotecare *vb* It
De verpfänden
En hypothecate
Es hipotecar
Fr hypothéquer
Pt hipotecar

ipotesi *(f)* n It
De Hypothese *(f)*
En hypothesis
Es hipótesis *(f)*
Fr hypothèse *(f)*
Pt hipótese *(f)*

iron n En
De Eisen *(n)*
Es hierro *(m)*
Fr fer *(m)*
It ferro *(m)*
Pt ferro *(m)*

iron ore En
De Eisenerz *(n)*
Es mineral de hierro *(m)*
Fr minerai de fer *(m)*
It minerale di ferro *(m)*
Pt minério de ferro *(m)*

irrécouvrable *adj* Fr
De unersetzlich; uneinbring-
lich
En irrecoverable
Es irrecuperable
It irrecuperabile
Pt irrecuperável

irrecoverable *adj* En
De unersetzlich; uneinbring-
lich
Es irrecuperable
Fr irrécouvrable
It irrecuperabile
Pt irrecuperável

irrecuperabile *adj* It
De unersetzlich; uneinbring-
lich
En irrecoverable
Es irrecuperable
Fr irrécouvrable
Pt irrecuperável

irrecuperable *adj* Es
De unersetzlich; uneinbring-
lich
En irrecoverable
Fr irrécouvrable
It irrecuperabile
Pt irrecuperável

irrecuperável *adj* Pt
De unersetzlich
En irrecoverable
Es irrecuperable
Fr irrécouvrable
It irrecuperabile

irredeemable debenture En
De uneinlösbare Schuldver-
schreibung *(f)*
Es obligación no amortizable
(f)
Fr obligation irremboursable
(f)
It obbligazione irredimibile *(f)*
Pt obrigação não amortizável *(f)*

irrevocable letter of credit
En
De unwiderruflicher Kredit-
brief *(m)*
Es carta de crédito
irrevocable *(f)*
Fr lettre de crédit irrévocable
(f)
It lettera di credito
inevocabile *(f)*
Pt carta de crédito
irrevogável *(f)*

Irrtum vorbehalten De
En errors and omissions
excepted
Es salvo error u omisión
Fr sauf erreur ou omission
It salvo errori ed omissioni
Pt salvo erro e omissão

isenção *(f)* n Pt
De Befreiung *(f)*
En exemption
Es exención *(f)*
Fr exemption *(f)*
It esenzione *(f)*

isenção de imposto *(f)* Pt
De Steuererleichterung *(f)*
En tax relief
Es desgravación *(f)*
Fr dégrèvement *(m)*
It sgravio fiscale *(m)*

isenção de tributação dupla *(f)*
Pt
De Doppelbesteuerungs-
erleichterung *(f)*
En double taxation relief
Es desgravación de tributa-
ción doble *(f)*
Fr dégrèvement de charges
fiscales doubles *(m)*
It sgravio per doppia tassa-
zione *(m)*

isento de comissão Pt
De maklergebührenfrei
En free of commission
Es franco-comisión
Fr franco courtage
It franco mediazione

isento de impostos Pt
De abgabenfrei
En duty-free
Es exento de impuestos
Fr exempt de douane
It esente da dazio

isento de impostos Pt
De steuerfrei
En tax-free
Es exento de impuestos
Fr exempt d'impôts
It esente da tassa

ispettore *(m)* n It
De Aufsichtsbeamte(r) *(m)*
En inspector
Es inspector *(m)*
Fr inspecteur; vérificateur *(m)*
Pt inspector *(m)*

ispettore di fabbrica *(m)* It
De Gewerbeaufsichtsbeam-
te(r) *(m)*
En factory inspector
Es inspector de fábrica *(m)*
Fr inspecteur du travail *(m)*
Pt inspector de fábrica *(m)*

ispezione *(f)* n It
De Einsichtnahme *(f)*
En inspection
Es inspección; examen *(f m)*
Fr inspection; vérification *(f)*
Pt inspecção *(f)*

issue *vb* En
De ausgeben
Es emitir
Fr émettre
It emettere
Pt emitir

issued capital En
De ausgegebenes Kapital *(n)*
Es capital emitido *(m)*
Fr capital versé *(m)*
It capitale emesso *(m)*
Pt capital emitido *(m)*

issuing bank En
De Notenbank *(f)*
Es banco emisor *(m)*
Fr banque d'émission *(f)*
It banca di emissione *(f)*
Pt banco emissor *(m)*

istituzione *(f)* n It
De Institut; Anstalt *(n f)*
En institution
Es institución; instituto *(f m)*
Fr institut *(m)*
Pt instituição *(f)*

istogramma *(m)* n It
De Histogramm *(n)*
En histogram
Es histograma *(m)*
Fr histogramme *(m)*
Pt histograma *(m)*

istruzione *(f)* n It
De Anleitung *(f)*
En instruction
Es instrucción *(f)*
Fr instruction *(f)*
Pt instrução *(f)*

istruzioni per l'uso *(f pl)* It
De Gebrauchsanweisung *(f)*
En directions for use
Es modo de empleo *(m)*
Fr mode d'emploi *(f)*
Pt instruções para uso *(f pl)*

itemized *adj* En
De postenmäßig dargestellt
Es detallado
Fr détaillé
It dettagliato
Pt pormenorizado

Items of expenditure En
De Aufwendungsposten *(f pl)*
Es artículos de gasto *(m pl)*
Fr postes de dépense *(m pl)*

It articoli di spesa *(m pl)*
Pt itens de despesa *(m pl)*

itens de despesa *(m pl)* Pt
De Aufwendungsposten *(f pl)*
En items of expenditure
Es artículos de gasto *(m pl)*
Fr postes de dépense *(m pl)*
It articoli di spesa *(m pl)*

J

Jagd nach Sonderangeboten *(f)* De
En bargain-hunting
Es caza de rebajas *(f)*
Fr chasse aux soldes *(f)*
It caccia alle occasioni *(f)*
Pt caça aos saldos *(f)*

Jahresabschluß *(m)* n De
En annual accounts
Es balance anual *(m)*
Fr bilan annuel *(m)*
It bilancio annuale *(m)*
Pt balancete anual *(m)*

Jahresbericht *(m)* n De
En annual report
Es memoria anual *(f)*
Fr rapport annuel *(m)*
It relazione annuale *(f)*
Pt relatório anual *(m)*

Jahreshauptversammlung *(f)* De
En annual general meeting
Am stockholders' meeting
Es asamblea general anual *(f)*
Fr assemblée d'actionnaires annuelle *(f)*
It assemblea generale annuale *(f)*
Pt assembleia geral anual *(f)*

Jahreskurs *(m)* n De
En annual rate
Es tasa anual *(f)*
Fr taux annuel *(m)*
It tasso annuale *(m)*
Pt taxa anual *(f)*

Jahreszeit *(f)* n De
En season
Es estación *(f)*
Fr saison *(f)*

It stagione *(f)*
Pt estação *(f)*

jahreszeitlich bedingte Arbeitslosigkeit *(f)* De
En seasonal unemployment
Es paro de temporada *(m)*
Fr chômage saisonnier *(m)*
It disoccupazione stagionale *(f)*
Pt desemprego de estação *(m)*

jährlich *adj* De
En annual
Es anual
Fr annuel
It annuale
Pt anual

jazigo de carvão *(m)* Pt
De Kohlenrevier *(n)*
En coal field
Es yacimiento de carbón *(m)*
Fr bassin houiller *(m)*
It bacino carbonifero *(m)*

jazigo de petróleo *(m)* Pt
De Ölfeld *(n)*
En oilfield
Es yacimiento de petróleo *(m)*
Fr gisement petrolifère *(m)*
It giacimento petrolifero *(m)*

jazigos de ouro *(m pl)* Pt
De Goldgrube *(f)*
En gold fields
Es yacimiento aurífero *(m)*
Fr réglons aurifères *(f pl)*
It terreni auriferi *(m pl)*

jefe de contabilidad *(m)* Es
De Oberbuchhalter *(m)*
En chief accountant
Fr chef comptable *(m)*
It ragioniere capo *(m)*
Pt chefe contabilista *(m)*

jefe de departamento *(m)* Es
De Abteilungsleiter *(m)*
En head of department
Fr chef de service *(m)*
It capo reparto *(m)*
Pt chefe de departamento *(m)*

jefe de exportación *(m)* Es
De Exportabteilungsleiter *(m)*
En export manager
Fr chef du service exportation *(m)*
It direttore esportazione *(m)*
Pt gerente de exportações *(m)*

jefe de familia *(m)* Es
De Hausherr *(m)*
En householder
Fr chef de famille *(m)*
It capo-famiglia *(m)*
Pt dono da casa *(m)*

jefe del departamento de compras *(m)* Es
De Haupteinkäufer *(m)*
En head buyer
Fr chef du service des achats *(m)*
It capo servizio acquisti *(m)*
Pt chefe de compras *(m)*

jefe de oficina *(m)* Es
De Bürovorsteher *(m)*
En office manager
Fr chef de bureau *(m)*
It capo ufficio *(m)*
Pt chefe de escritório *(m)*

jefe de personal *(m)* Es
De Personalchef *(m)*
En personnel manager
Fr chef du personnel *(m)*
It direttore del personale *(m)*
Pt chefe do pessoal *(m)*

jefe de ventas *(m)* Es
De Verkaufsleiter *(m)*
En sales manager
Fr directeur commercial *(m)*
It direttore commerciale *(m)*
Pt chefe de vendas *(m)*

jefe ejecutivo *(m)* Es
De Geschäftsführer *(m)*
En chief executive
Fr directeur général *(m)*
It direttore generale *(m)*
Pt chefe de gerência *(m)*

jerque note En
De Eintrittsdeklarationsschein *(m)*
Es certificado de declaración de entrada *(m)*
Fr certificat d'entrée autorisée *(m)*
It certificato di dichiarazione d'entrata *(m)*
Pt certificado de verificação alfandegária *(m)*

jet aircraft En
De Düsenflugzeug *(n)*
Es avión jet *(m)*
Fr avion à réaction *(m)*

It aviogetto *(m)*
Pt avião a jacto *(m)*

jetée *(f) n* Fr
De Mole *(f)*
En jetty
Es digue *(m)*
It molo *(m)*
Pt pontão; cais *(m)*

jet engine En
De Düsenmotor *(m)*
Es motor de propulsión a chorro *(m)*
Fr réacteur *(m)*
It motore a reazione *(m)*
Pt motor a jacto *(m)*

jeter à la mer (la cargaison) Fr
De über Bord werfen
En jettison
Es echar al mar
It fare gettito
Pt alijar

jettison *vb* En
De über Bord werfen
Es echar al mar
Fr jeter à la mer
It fare gettito
Pt alijar

jetty *n* En
De Mole *(f)*
Es digue *(m)*
Fr jetée; digue *(f)*
It molo *(m)*
Pt pontão; cais *(m)*

job (post, situation, etc.) *n* En
De Stellung *(f)*
Es empleo *(m)*
Fr emploi *(m)*
It impiego *(m)*
Pt emprego *(m)*

job (occupation) *n* En
De Beruf *(m)*
Es trabajo *(m)*
Fr occupation *(f)*
It lavoro *(m)*
Pt ocupação *(f)*

job *vb* En
De spekulieren
Es especular
Fr spéculer
It speculare; trafficare
Pt especular

job costing En
De Kostenstellenrechnung *(f)*
Es evaluación del trabajo *(f)*
Fr évaluation du coût de tache *(f)*
It valutazione dei lavori durante la fabbricazione *(f)*
Pt cálculo do custo de obra *(m)*

job description En
De Arbeitsbeschreibung *(f)*
Es descripción del trabajo *(f)*
Fr description du travail *(f)*
It descrizione del lavoro *(f)*
Pt descrição da tarefa *(f)*

job evaluation En
De Arbeitsbewertung *(f)*
Es valoracion del trabajo *(f)*
Fr évaluation du travail *(f)*
It valutazione del lavoro *(f)*
Pt avaliação de tarefa *(f)*

job specification En
De Arbeitsaufgabe *(f)*
Es especificación del trabajo *(f)*
Fr donnée d'exécution *(f)*
It specifica del lavoro *(f)*
Pt especificação de obra *(f)*

jogar na Bolsa Pt
De an der Börse spekulieren
En gamble on the stock exchange
Es jugar a la Bolsa
Fr jouer à la Bourse
It giocare in Borsa

jogo limpo *(m)* Pt
De anständige Handlungsweise *(f)*
En fair play
Es juego limpio *(m)*
Fr traitement juste *(m)*
It condotta leale *(f)*

joint account En
De Gemeinschaftskonto *(n)*
Es cuenta común *(f)*
Fr compte joint *(m)*
It conto in comune *(m)*
Pt conta conjunta *(f)*

joint and several bond En
De Solidarobligation *(f)*
Es obligación solidaria e indivisa *(f)*
Fr obligation conjointe et solidaire *(f)*

It obbligazione solidale (f)
Pt título solidário de diversos (m)

jointly and severally En
De gesamtschuldnerisch
Es en conjunto y separada-mente
Fr conjointement et soli-dairement
It solidalmente e individual-mente
Pt em conjunto e por vários

joint ownership En
De Miteigentum (n)
Es copropiedad (f)
Fr copropriété (f)
It comproprietà (f)
Pt co-propriedade (f)

joint venture En
De Gemeinschaftsgründung (f)
Es empresa en común (f)
Fr entreprise en participation (f)
It impresa in compartecipa-zione (f)
Pt iniciativa em comun (f)

jornada laboral (f) Es
De Arbeitszeit (f)
En hours of work
Fr durée du travail (f)
It ore lavorative (f pl)
Pt horas de trabalho (f pl)

jouer à la Bourse Fr
De an der Börse spekulieren
En gamble on the stock ex-change
Es jugar a la Bolsa
It giocare in Borsa
Pt jogar na Bolsa

jour (m) n Fr
De Tag (m)
En day
Es día (m)
It giorno (m)
Pt dia (m)

jour de bourse (m) Fr
De Börsentag (m)
En (financial) market day
Es día de bolsa (m)
It giorno di borsa (m)
Pt dia de bolsa (m)

jour de congé (m) Fr
De dienstfreier Tag (m)
En day off
Es día libre (m)
It giorno di riposo (m)
Pt dia de folga (m)

jour de liquidation (m) Fr
De Abrechnungstag (m)
En account day
Am settlement date
Es día de liquidación (m)
It giorno di liquidazione (m)
Pt dia de liquidação (m)

jour de marché (m) Fr
De Markttag (m)
En (local) market day
Es día de mercado (m)
It giorno di mercato (m)
Pt dia de mercado (m)

jour de paiement (m) Fr
De Zahltag; Abrechnungstag (m)
En pay day
Es día de pago (m)
It giorno di paga (m)
Pt dia de recebimento (m)

jour de règlement (m) Fr
De Abrechnungstag (m)
En settlement day
Am due date
Es día de liquidación (m)
It giorno della liquidazione (m)
Pt dia de liquidação (m)

jour du terme (m) Fr
De Quartalstag (m)
En quarter day
Es primer día del trimestre (m)
It giorno della pigione (m)
Pt dia de vencimento trimes-tral (m)

jour férié (m) Fr
De gesetzlicher Feiertag (m)
En public holiday
Es día de fiesta (m)
It giorno di festa (m)
Pt feriado (m)

journal n En, Fr (m)
De Tagebuch (n)
Es diario (m)
It giornale (m)
Pt diário (m)

journal de navigation (m) Fr
De Log (n)
En (ship's) log
Es diario de navegación (m)
It solcometro (m)
Pt diário de bordo (m)

journal-entry n En
De Tagebuchposten (m)
Es asiento en el libro diario (m)
Fr article d'un livre journal (m)
It registrazione a giornale (f)
Pt anotação de diário (f)

journal général (m) Fr
De allgemeines Hauptbuch (n)
En general ledger
Es libro mayor general (m)
It libro mastro generale (m)
Pt livro-mestre geral (m)

jour ouvrable (m) Fr
De Arbeitstag (m)
En working day
Es día laborable (m)
It giornata lavorativa (f)
Pt dia de trabalho (m)

judge vb En
De urteilen
Es juzgar
Fr juger
It giudicare
Pt julgar

judge n En
De Richter (m)
Es juez (m)
Fr juge (m)
It giudice (m)
Pt juiz (m)

judgment n En
De Urteil (n)
Es juicio; adjudicación (m f)
Fr jugement; arrêt (m)
It giudizio (m)
Pt julgamento (m)

juego limpio (m) Es
De anständige Handlungs-weise (f)
En fair play
Fr traitement juste (m)
It condotta leale (f)
Pt jogo limpo (m)

juez *(m) n* Es
De Richter *(m)*
En judge
Fr juge *(m)*
It giudice *(m)*
Pt juiz *(m)*

juez árbitro *(m)* Es
De Schiedsobmann *(m)*
En umpire
Fr surarbitre *(m)*
It terzo arbitro *(m)*
Pt juiz árbitro *(m)*

jugar a la Bolsa Es
De an der Börse spekulieren
En gamble on the stock exchange
Fr jouer à la Bourse
It giocare in Borsa
Pt jogar na Bolsa

juge *(m) n* Fr
De Richter *(m)*
En judge
Es juez *(m)*
It giudice *(m)*
Pt juiz *(m)*

jugement *(m) n* Fr
De Urteil *(n)*
En judgment
Es juicio; adjudicación *(m f)*
It giudizio *(m)*
Pt julgamento *(m)*

juger *vb* Fr
De urteilen
En judge
Es juzgar
It giudicare
Pt julgar

juicio *(m) n* Es
De Urteil *(n)*
En judgment
Fr jugement; arrêt *(m)*
It giudizio *(m)*
Pt julgamento *(m)*

juiz *(m) n* Pt
De Richter *(m)*
En judge
Es juez *(m)*
Fr juge *(m)*
It giudice *(m)*

juiz árbitro *(m)* Pt
De Schiedsobmann *(m)*
En umpire
Es juez árbitro *(m)*
Fr surarbitre *(m)*
It terzo arbitro *(m)*

julgamento *(m) n* Pt
De Urteil *(n)*
En judgment
Es juicio; adjudicación *(m f)*
Fr jugement; arrêt *(m)*
It giudizio *(m)*

julgar *vb* Pt
De urteilen
En judge
Es juzgar
Fr juger
It giudicare

jüngerer Teilhaber *(m)* De
En junior partner
Es segundo asociado *(m)*
Fr associé en second *(m)*
It socio giovane *(m)*
Pt sócio júnior *(m)*

junior partner En
De jüngerer Teilhaber *(m)*
Es segundo asociado *(m)*
Fr associé en second *(m)*
It socio giovane *(m)*
Pt sócio júnior *(m)*

jurado *(m) n* Es
De die Geschworenen; Jury *(pl f)*
En jury
Fr jury *(m)*
It giuria *(f)*
Pt júri *(m)*

júri *(m) n* Pt
De die Geschworenen; Jury *(pl f)*
En jury
Es tribunal de jurados *(m)*
Fr jury *(m)*
It giuria *(f)*

juridiction *(f) n* Fr
De Rechtsprechung; Gerichtsbarkeit *(f)*
En jurisdiction
Es jurisdicción *(f)*
It giurisdizione *(f)*
Pt jurisdição *(f)*

jurisdição *(f) n* Pt
De Rechtsprechung; Gerichtsbarkeit *(f)*
En jurisdiction
Es jurisdicción *(f)*
Fr juridiction *(f)*
It giurisdizione *(f)*

jurisdicción *(f) n* Es
De Rechtsprechung; Gerichtsbarkeit *(f)*
En jurisdiction
Fr juridiction *(f)*
It giurisdizione *(f)*
Pt jurisdição *(f)*

jurisdiction *n* En
De Rechtsprechung; Gerichtsbarkeit *(f)*
Es jurisdicción *(f)*
Fr juridiction *(f)*
It giurisdizione *(f)*
Pt jurisdição *(f)*

juro *(m) n* Pt
De Zinsen *(m pl)*
En interest
Es interés *(m)*
Fr intérêt; prime *(m f)*
It interesse *(m)*

juro acumulado *(m)* Pt
De aufgelaufene Zinsen *(m pl)*
En accrued interest
Es interés acumulado *(m)*
Fr intérêts accumulés *(m pl)*
It interesse maturato *(m)*

juro composto *(m)* Pt
De Zinseszinsen *(m pl)*
En compound interest
Es interés compuesto *(m)*
Fr intérêts composés *(m pl)*
It interesse composto *(m)*

juro de bodemeria *(m)* Pt
De Bodmereidarlehenszinsen *(m pl)*
En bottomry interest
Es interés de préstamo a la gruesa *(m)*
Fr profit maritime *(m)*
It interessenza a cambio marittimo *(f)*

juro de mora *(m)* Pt
De Kursabschlag *(m)*
En backwardation

Es prima de aplazamiento *(f)*
Fr déport *(m)*
It deporto *(m)*

juro simples *(m)* Pt
De einfache Zinsen *(m pl)*
En simple interest
Es interés simple *(m)*
Fr intérêts simples *(m pl)*
It interesse semplice *(m)*

jury *n* En, Fr *(m)*
De die Geschworenen; Jury
   (pl; f)
Es jurado *(m)*
It giurla *(f)*
Pt júri *(m)*

justiça *(f)* n Pt
De Gerechtigkeit *(f)*
En justice
Es justicia *(f)*
Fr justice *(f)*
It giustizia *(f)*

justice *n* En, Fr *(f)*
De Gerechtigkeit *(f)*
Es justicia *(f)*
It giustizia *(f)*
Pt justiça *(f)*

justicia *(f)* n Es
De Gerechtigkeit *(f)*
En justice
Fr justice *(f)*
It giustizia *(f)*
Pt justiça *(f)*

justifiable *adj* En
De gerechtfertigt
Es justificable; legítimo
Fr légitime
It giustificabile; legittimo
Pt justificável

justificable *adj* Es
De gerechtfertigt
En justifiable
Fr légitime
It giustificabile; legittimo
Pt justificável

justificável *adj* Pt
De gerechtfertigt
En justifiable
Es justificable; legítimo
Fr légitime
It giustificabile; legittimo

juzgar *vb* Es
De urteilen
En judge
Fr juger
It giudicare
Pt julgar

K

Kabelauszahlung *(f)* n De
En telegraphic transfer
Es giro telegráfico *(m)*
Fr virement télégraphique *(m)*
It rimessa telegrafica *(f)*
Pt transferência telegráfica *(f)*

Kaffee *(m)* n De
En coffee
Es café *(m)*
Fr café *(m)*
It caffè *(m)*
Pt café *(m)*

Kai *(m)* n De
En quay; wharf
Es muelle *(m)*
Fr quai *(m)*
It banchina; scalo *(f m)*
Pt cais *(m)*

Kaigeld *(n)* n De
En wharfage
Es muellaje *(m)*
Fr quayage *(m)*
It diritto di sosta *(m)*
Pt atracagem *(f)*

Kalender *(m)* n De
En calendar
Es calendario *(m)*
Fr calendrier *(m)*
It calendario *(m)*
Pt calendário *(m)*

Kalenderjahr *(n)* n De
En calendar year
Es año civil *(m)*
Fr année civile *(f)*
It anno solare *(m)*
Pt ano civil *(m)*

Kalkulator *(m)* n De
En cost accountant
Es contable de costes *(m)*
Fr comptable de prix de revient *(m)*
It contabile dei costi di produzione *(m)*
Pt calculador de custos *(m)*

Kampagne *(f)* n De
En campaign
Es campaña *(f)*
Fr campagne *(f)*
It campagna *(f)*
Pt campanha *(f)*

Kanal *(m)* n De
En canal
Es canal *(m)*
Fr canal *(m)*
It canale *(m)*
Pt canal *(m)*

Kapital *(n)* n De
En capital; principal
Es capital; principal *(m)*
Fr capital; principal *(m)*
It capitale *(m)*
Pt capital *(m)*

Kapitalanlage *(f)* n De
En investment
Es inversión *(f)*
Fr investissement; placement
   (m)
It investimento *(m)*
Pt investimento *(m)*

Kapitalauslagen *(f pl)* n De
En capital expenditure
Es inmovilizaciones *(f pl)*
Fr immobilisations *(f pl)*
It immobilizzazioni *(f pl)*
Pt despesas em termos de
   capital *(f pl)*

Kapitaleinkommen *(n)* n De
En unearned income
Es rentas *(f pl)*
Fr rente *(f)*
It reddito di capitale *(m)*
Pt rendimento do capital *(m)*

Kapitalerhöhung *(f)* n De
En increase of capital
Es aumento de capital *(m)*
Fr augmentation de capital *(f)*
It aumento di capitale *(m)*
Pt aumento de capital *(m)*

Kapitalertrag *(m)* n De
En return on capital
Es beneficio sobre capital *(m)*
Fr rémunération du capital *(f)*
It reddito del capitale *(m)*
Pt juro sobre o capital *(m)*

Kapitalertragsteuer (f) n De
En capital gains tax
Es impuesto sobre las ga-
nancias de capital (m)
Fr impôt sur les plus-values
en capital (m)
It imposta sul plusvalore di
capitale (f)
Pt imposto sobre lucros de
capital (m)

Kapitalgewinn (n) n De
En capital gains
Es beneficios sobre capital
(m pl)
Fr gains en capital (m pl)
It plusvalore di capitale
(m pl)
Pt lucros de capital (m pl)

Kapitalherabsetzung (f) n De
En reduction of capital
Es reducción de capital (f)
Fr réduction de capital (f)
It riduzione del capitale (f)
Pt redução de capital (f)

Kapitalhilfe (f) n De
En capital grants
Es subvención de capital (f)
Fr subventions en capital
(f pl)
It sovvenzioni di capitale (f
pl)
Pt subvenções de capital (f pl)

kapitalintensiv adj De
En capital-intensive
Es intensivo de capital
Fr intensif de capital
It concentrato sul capitale
Pt intensivo em termos de
capital

kapitaliseren vb De
En capitalize
Es capitalizar
Fr capitaliser
It capitalizzare
Pt capitalizar

kapitalisierter Wert (m) De
En capitalized value
Es valor capitalizado (m)
Fr valeur capitalisée (f)
It valore capitalizzato (m)
Pt valor capitalizado (m)

Kapitalisierung (f) n De
En capitalization
Es capitalización (f)
Fr capitalisation (f)

It capitalizzazione (f)
Pt capitalização (f)

Kapitalismus (m) n De
En capitalism
Es capitalismo (m)
Fr capitalisme (m)
It capitalismo (m)
Pt capitalismo (m)

Kapitalkonto (n) n De
En capital account
Es cuenta de capital (f)
Fr compte capital (m)
It conto capitale (m)
Pt conta de capital (f)

Kapitalreserve (f) n De
En capital reserves
Es reserva de capital (f)
Fr réserve de capitaux (f)
It riserva di capitale (f)
Pt reservas de capital (f pl)

Kapitalverlust (m) n De
En capital loss
Es pérdida de capital (f)
Fr perte de capital (f)
It perdita di capitale (f)
Pt perdas de capital (f pl)

Kapitän (m) n De
En master of a ship
Es capitán de navio (m)
Fr capitaine (m)
It capitano di nave (m)
Pt capitão de navio (m)

Karte (f) n De
En card
Es tarjeta (f)
Fr carte (f)
It scheda (f)
Pt cartão (m)

Kartei (f) n De
En card-index file
Es archivo de fichas (m)
Fr fichier (m)
It schedario (m)
Pt ficheiro com índice (m)

Kartell (n) n De
En cartel
Es cartel (m)
Fr cartel (m)
It cartello (m)
Pt cartel (m)

Karton (m) n De
En carton
Es cartón (m)
Fr carton (m)
It cartone (m)
Pt caixa de cartão (f)

Kartothek (f) n De
En card index
Es fichero (m)
Fr fichier (m)
It schedario (m)
Pt ficheiro (m)

Kaskoversicherung (f) n De
En hull insurance
Es seguro del casco (m)
Fr assurance sur le corps (f)
It assicurazione corpo (m)
Pt seguro do casco (m)

Kassageschäft (n) n De
En cash sale
Es venta al conta (f)
Fr vente au comptant (f)
It vendita a contanti (f)
Pt venda a dinheiro (f)

Kasse (f) n De
En cash-desk
Es caja (f)
Fr caisse (f)
It cassa (f)
Pt caixa (f)

Kassenbuch (n) n De
En cash book
Es libro de caja (m)
Fr livre de caisse (m)
It libro cassa (m)
Pt livro de caixa (m)

Kassenpension (f) n De
En contributory pension
Es retiro contributivo (m)
Fr retraite de régime à cotisa-
tions (f)
It pensione a contributi (f)
Pt reforma de contribuição
prévia (f)

Kassenreserve (f) n De
En cash reserve
Es reserva en efectivo (f)
Fr réserve en espèces (f)
It riserva in contanti (f)
Pt reserva em dinheiro (f)

Kassensaldo (m) n De
En cash balance
Es resto en efectivo (m)
Fr solde de caisse (m)

It residuo di cassa *(m)*
Pt saldo em dinheiro *(m)*

Kassierer *(m) n* De
En cashier
Am teller
Es cajero *(m)*
Fr caissier *(m)*
It cassiere *(m)*
Pt caixa *(m)*

Katalog *(m) n* De
En catalogue
Es catálogo *(m)*
Fr catalogue *(m)*
It catalogo *(m)*
Pt catálogo *(m)*

Kauf *(m) n* De
En purchase
Es compra *(f)*
Fr achat *(m)*
It compra *(f)*
Pt compra *(f)*

Kaufabneigung *(f) n* De
En sales resistance
Es dificultades de ventas *(f pl)*
Fr résistance à la vente *(f)*
It difficoltà di vendita *(f)*
Pt resitência contra venda *(f)*

kaufen *vb* De
En buy
Es comprar
Fr acheter
It comprare
Pt comprar

Käufer *(m) n* De
En buyer
Es comprador *(m)*
Fr acheteur *(m)*
It compratore *(m)*
Pt comprador *(m)*

Kaufkraft *(f) n* De
En purchasing power
Es poder de compra *(m)*
Fr pouvoir d'achat *(m)*
It potere d'acquisto *(m)*
Pt poder de compra *(m)*

Kaufmann *(m) n* De
En merchant
Es comerciante *(m)*
Fr négociant *(m)*
It commerciante *(m)*
Pt comerciante *(m)*

Kaufoption *(f) n* De
En call option
Es opción de compras *(f)*
Fr option d'achat *(f)*
It premio d'acquisto *(m)*
Pt opção de compra *(f)*

Kaufpreis *(m) n* De
En purchase price
Es precio de compra *(m)*
Fr prix d'achat *(m)*
It prezzo d'acquisto *(m)*
Pt preço de compra *(m)*

Kaufvertrag *(m) n* De
En bill of sale
Es escritura de venta *(f)*
Fr acte de vente *(f)*
It contratto di vendita *(m)*
Pt escritura de venda *(f)*

Kavaliersabkommen *(n) n* De
En gentleman's agreement
Es acuerdo sobre palabra *(m)*
Fr convention verbale *(f)*
It accordo sulla parola *(m)*
Pt pacto de honra *(m)*

keep *vb* En
De behalten; unterhalten
Es tener; conservar
Fr tenir; maintenir
It tenere; mantenere
Pt manter; reter

keep in stock En
De vorrätig halten
Es guardar en almacén
Fr garder en stock
It tenere in magazzino
Pt reter em armazém

keep the accounts En
De Konto führen
Es llevar la contabilidad
Fr tenir la comptabilité
It tenere la contablilità
Pt fazer a contabilidade

Kenntnis *(f) n* De
En knowledge
Es conocimientos *(m pl)*
Fr connaissance *(f)*
It conoscenza *(f)*
Pt conhecimento *(m)*

Kettengeschäft *(n) n* De
En chain store
Es sucursal de cadena de almacenes *(f)*

Fr magasin à succursales multiples *(m)*
It negozio a catena *(m)*
Pt sucursal de cadeia de armazéns *(f)*

key (for locks, etc.) *n* En
De Schlüssel *(m)*
Es llave *(f)*
Fr clef *(f)*
It chiave *(f)*
Pt chave *(f)*

key (of typewriter, etc.) *n* En
De Taste *(f)*
Es tecla *(f)*
Fr touche *(f)*
It tasto *(m)*
Pt tecla *(f)*

key industry En
De Schlüsselindustrie *(f)*
Es industria clave *(f)*
Fr industrie-clef *(f)*
It industria-chiave *(f)*
Pt indústria chave *(f)*

key-punch *n* En
De manueller Locher *(m)*
Es perforación en clave *(f)*
Fr perforatrice à clavier *(f)*
It perforatore *(f)*
Pt perfurador *(m)*

Klausel *(f) n* De
En clause
Es cláusula *(f)*
Fr clause *(f)*
It clausola *(f)*
Pt cláusula *(f)*

Kleinanzeige *(f) n* De
En classified advertisement
Es anuncio por palabras *(m)*
Fr petite annonce *(f)*
It piccola pubblicità *(f)*
Pt anúncios classificados *(m pl)*

kleine Kasse *(f)* De
En petty cash
Es caja menor *(f)*
Fr petite caisse *(f)*
It piccola cassa *(f)*
Pt despesas de caixa *(f pl)*

Kleingeld *(n) n* De
En small change
Es moneda suelta *(f)*
Fr petite monnaie *(f)*
It spiccioli *(m pl)*
Pt troco miúdo *(m)*

Klimatisierung *(f)* n De
En air-conditioning
Es acondicionamiento de aire
(m)
Fr climatisation *(f)*
It condizionamento dell'aria
(m)
Pt condicionamento do ar *(m)*

Knappheit *(f)* n De
En short supply
Es escasez *(f)*
Fr disette *(f)*
It scarsezza *(f)*
Pt escassez *(f)*

knitted goods En
De Strickwaren *(f pl)*
Es géneros de punto *(m pl)*
Fr bonneterie *(f)*
It maglieria *(f)*
Pt artigos de malha de lã *(m pl)*

knot n En
De Knoten *(m)*
Es nudo *(m)*
Fr nœud *(m)*
It nodo *(m)*
Pt nó *(m)*

Knoten *(m)* n De
En knot
Es nudo *(m)*
Fr nœud *(m)*
It nodo *(m)*
Pt nó *(m)*

knowledge n En
De Kenntnis *(f)*
Es conocimientos *(m pl)*
Fr connaissance *(f)*
It conoscenza *(f)*
Pt conhecimento *(m)*

Kohle *(f)* n De
En coal
Es carbón *(m)*
Fr charbon; houille *(m f)*
It carbone *(m)*
Pt carvão *(m)*

Kohlenrevier *(n)* n De
En coal field
Es yacimiento de carbón *(m)*
Fr bassin houiller *(m)*
It bacino carbonifero *(m)*
Pt jazigo de carvão *(m)*

Kohlepapier *(n)* n De
En carbon paper
Es papel carbón *(m)*

Fr papier carbone *(m)*
It carta carbone *(f)*
Pt papel químico *(m)*

kombinierte Versicherung *(f)*
De
En comprehensive insurance
Es seguro combinado *(m)*
Fr assurance combinée *(f)*
It assicurazione mista *(f)*
Pt seguro compreensivo *(m)*

Kommanditgesellschaft *(f)* n
De
En limited partnership
Es sociedad en comandita *(f)*
Fr société en commandité *(f)*
It società in accomandita
semplice *(f)*
Pt sociedade em comandita
(f)

Kommission *(f)* n De
En committee
Es comité *(m)*
Fr comité *(f)*
It comitato *(m)*
Pt comité *(m)*

Kommissionär *(m)* n De
En commission agent
Es comisionista *(m)*
Fr commissionnaire en mar-
chandises *(m)*
It commissionario *(m)*
Pt comissionista *(m)*

Kommissionsgüter *(n pl)* n
De
En goods on consignment
Es mercancías en consigna-
ción *(f pl)*
Fr marchandises en consig-
nation *(f pl)*
It merce in conto deposito *(f)*
Pt artigos à consignação *(m pl)*

Kommunal- De
En municipal
Es municipal
Fr communal
It municipale
Pt municipal

Konflikt *(m)* n De
En conflict
Es conflicto *(m)*
Fr conflit *(m)*
It conflitto *(m)*
Pt conflito *(m)*

Kongreß *(m)* n De
En conference
Es conferencia *(f)*
Fr conférence *(f)*
It conferenza *(f)*
Pt conferência *(f)*

Konjunkturzyklus *(m)* n De
En business cycle
Es ciclo económico *(m)*
Fr cycle économique *(m)*
It ciclo d'affari *(m)*
Pt ciclo económico *(m)*

Konkurrenz machen De
En compete
Es competir
Fr concurrencer
It competere
Pt competir

Konkurs *(m)* n De
En bankruptcy
Es quiebra *(f)*
Fr faillite *(f)*
It fallimento *(m)*
Pt falência *(f)*

Konkurs anmelden De
En go bankrupt
Es caer en quiebra
Fr faire faillite
It fallire
Pt falir

Konkursverwalter *(m)* n De
En (official) receiver
Es síndico *(m)*
Fr syndic de faillite *(m)*
It curatore *(m)*
Pt síndico *(m)*

Konnossement *(n)* n De
En bill of lading
Es conocimiento (de em-
barque) *(m)*
Fr connaissement *(m)*
It polizza di carico *(f)*
Pt conhecimento (de em-
barque) *(m)*

konsignieren vb De
En consign
Es consignar
Fr consigner
It consegnare
Pt consignar

konsolidiert adj De
En consolidated
Es consolidado

Fr consolidé
It consolidato
Pt consolidado

konsolidierter Konten-abschluß *(m)* De
En consolidated accounts
Es cuentas consolidadas *(f pl)*
Fr comptes consolidés *(m pl)*
It conti consolidati *(m pl)*
Pt contas consolidadas *(f pl)*

Konsortium *(n)* n De
En consortium
Es consorcio *(m)*
Fr consortium *(m)*
It consorzio *(m)*
Pt consórcio *(m)*

Konsul *(m)* n De
En consul
Es cónsul *(m)*
Fr consul *(m)*
It console *(m)*
Pt cônsul *(m)*

Konsulat *(n)* n De
En consulate
Es consulado *(m)*
Fr consulat *(m)*
It consolato *(m)*
Pt consulado *(m)*

Konsulatsfaktura *(f)* n De
En consular invoice
Es factura consular *(f)*
Fr facture consulaire *(f)*
It fattura consolare *(f)*
Pt factura consular *(f)*

Konsumgüter *(n pl)* n De
En consumer goods
Es bienes de consumo *(m pl)*
Fr biens de consommation *(m pl)*
It beni di consumo *(m pl)*
Pt bens de consumo *(m pl)*

Kontaktgruppenleiter *(m)* n De
En account executive
Es ejecutivo de cuenta *(m)*
Fr chef de comptes client *(m)*
It direttore conto cliente *(m)*
Pt chefe de conta de cliente *(m)*

Konto *(n)* n De
En account
Es cuenta *(f)*

Fr compte *(m)*
It conto *(m)*
Pt conta *(f)*

Kontoauszug *(m)* n De
En statement of account
Es extracto de cuenta *(m)*
Fr relevé de compte *(m)*
It estratto conto *(m)*
Pt extracto de conta *(m)*

Kontobuch *(n)* n De
En account book
Es libro de cuentas *(m)*
Fr livre de comptes *(m)*
It libro di conti *(m)*
Pt livro de contas *(m)*

Konto führen De
En keep the accounts
Es llevar la contabilidad
Fr tenir la comptabilité
It tenere la contabilità
Pt fazer a contabilidade

Kontokorrent *(n)* n De
En current account
Am checking account
Es cuenta corriente *(f)*
Fr compte courant *(m)*
It conto corrente *(m)*
Pt conta corrente *(f)*

Konto überzogen De
En account overdrawn
Es cuenta en descubierto *(f)*
Fr compte découvert *(m)*
It conto scoperto *(m)*
Pt conta a descoberto *(f)*

Kontrolleur *(m)* n De
En controller
Es interventor *(m)*
Fr contrôleur *(m)*
It controllore *(m)*
Pt controlador *(m)*

Kontrollkonto *(n)* n De
En control account
Es cuenta de control *(f)*
Fr compte de contrôle *(m)*
It conto di controllo *(m)*
Pt conta de controlo *(f)*

Kontrollziffer *(f)* n De
En check digit
Es número de control *(m)*
Fr digit de contrôle *(m)*
It cifra di controllo *(f)*
Pt dígito de controle *(m)*

Konventionalstrafe *(f)* n De
En liquidated damages
Es daños liquidados *(m pl)*
Fr dommagnes-intérêts fixés en argent *(m pl)*
It danni liquidati *(m pl)*
Pt danos liquidados *(m pl)*

Konversion *(f)* n De
En conversion
Es conversión *(f)*
Fr conversion *(f)*
It conversione *(f)*
Pt conversão *(f)*

konvertierbar *adj* De
En convertible
Es convertible
Fr convertible
It convertible
Pt convertível

konvertieren *vb* De
En convert
Es convertir
Fr convertir
It convertire
Pt convertir

Konzept *(n)* n De
En draft
Es borrador *(m)*
Fr projet *(m)*
It bozza *(f)*
Pt rascunho *(m)*

Konzession *(f)* n De
En concession; franchise
Es concesión *(f)*
Fr concession *(f)*
It concessione *(f)*
Pt concessão *(f)*

kopieren *vb* De
En copy
Es copiar
Fr transcrire
It copiare
Pt copiar

Körperschaft *(f)* n De
En corporation
Es corporación *(f)*
Fr corporation *(f)*
It corporazione *(f)*
Pt corporação *(f)*

körperschaftlich *adj* De
En corporate
Es corporativo

Fr corporatif
It corporativo
Pt corporativo

Körperschaftsteuer *(f) n* De
En corporation tax
Es impuesto sobre renta de la sociedad *(m)*
Fr impôt sur le revenu des sociétés *(m)*
It imposta sui proventi delle società *(f)*
Pt imposto sobre corporação *(m)*

korrigieren *vb* De
En correct
Es corregir
Fr corriger
It correggere
Pt corrigir

kosten *vb* De
En cost
Es costar
Fr coûter
It costare
Pt custear

Kosten *(pl) n* De
En cost; charges
Es coste; gastos *(m; m pl)*
Fr coût; frais *(m; m pl)*
It costo; spese *(m; f pl)*
Pt custo; despesas *(m; f pl)*

Kostenanalyse *(f) n* De
En cost analysis
Es análisis de costes *(m)*
Fr analyse des coûts *(f)*
It analisi dei costi *(f)*
Pt análise de custo *(f)*

Kostenanschlag *(m) n* De
En quotation
Es cotización *(f)*
Fr cotation *(f)*
It quotazione *(f)*
Pt cotação *(f)*

Kostenvoranschlag *(m) n* De
En bill of quantities
Es cubicación de obra *(f)*
Fr devis *(m)*
It preventivo *(m)*
Pt relação de quantidades *(f)*

kostenlose Probe *(f)* De
En free sample
Es muestra gratuita *(f)*
Fr échantillon gratuit *(m)*

It campione gratuito *(m)*
Pt amostra grátis *(f)*

Kosten und Fracht De
En cost and freight *(c. & f.)*
Es coste y flete
Fr coût et fret
It costo e nolo
Pt custo e frete

Kosten und Vertrag De
En cost-plus contract
Es contrato al costo más beneficio *(m)*
Fr contrat en régie *(m)*
It contratto in economia *(m)*
Pt contrato de custo e adicionais *(m)*

kostspielig *adj* De
En expensive
Es caro
Fr cher
It caro
Pt caro

krach d'une banque *(m)* Fr
De Bankkrach *(m)*
En bank crash
Es quiebra de banco *(f)*
It crollo di banca *(m)*
Pt falência bancária *(f)*

Kran *(m) n* De
En crane
Es grúa *(f)*
Fr grue *(f)*
It gru *(f)*
Pt grua *(f)*

Krankenversicherung *(f) n* De
En health insurance
Es seguro de enfermedad *(m)*
Fr assurance maladie *(f)*
It assicurazione malattia *(f)*
Pt seguro de doença *(m)*

Kredit *(m) n* De
En credit
Es crédito *(m)*
Fr crédit *(m)*
It credito *(m)*
Pt crédito *(m)*

Kreditbank *(f) n* De
En lending bank
Es banco de préstamos *(m)*
Fr banque de prêts *(f)*
It banca di prestiti *(f)*
Pt banco de empréstimos *(m)*

Kreditbrief *(m) n* De
En letter of credit
Es carta de crédito *(f)*
Fr lettre de crédit *(f)*
It lettera di credito *(f)*
Pt carta de crédito *(f)*

Kreditfähigkeit *(f) n* De
En borrowing power
Es facultad de crédito *(f)*
Fr capacité à avoir du crédit *(f)*
It capacità creditizia *(f)*
Pt potencial de obtenção de crédito *(m)*

Kreditkarte *(f) n* De
En credit card
Es tarjeta de crédito *(f)*
Fr carte de crédit *(f)*
It carta di credito *(f)*
Pt cartão de crédito *(m)*

Kreditklemme *(f) n* De
En credit squeeze
Es escasez de créditos *(f)*
Fr resserrement de crédit *(m)*
It restrizione di credito *(f)*
Pt restrição de crédito *(f)*

Kreditnehmer *(m) n* De
En borrower
Es prestatario *(m)*
Fr emprunteur *(m)*
It accattatore *(m)*
Pt beneficiário de empréstimo *(m)*

Kreditoren *(m pl) n* De
En accounts payable
Es cuentas a pagar *(f pl)*
Fr comptes à payer *(m pl)*
It conti passivi *(m pl)*
Pt contas a pagar *(f pl)*

Kreditsaldo *(m) n* De
En credit balance
Es saldo acreedor *(m)*
Fr solde créditeur *(m)*
It saldo creditore *(m)*
Pt saldo credor *(m)*

Kreditversicherung *(f) n* De
En credit insurance
Es seguro crediticio *(m)*
Fr assurance crédit *(f)*
It assicurazione credito *(f)*
Pt seguro de crédito *(m)*

Kreditwürdigkeit *(f)* n De
En credit rating
Es límite de crédito *(m)*
Fr degré de solvabilité *(m)*
It stima del credito *(f)*
Pt nível de crédito *(m)*

Krieg *(m)* n De
En war
Es guerra *(f)*
Fr guerre *(f)*
It guerra *(f)*
Pt guerra *(f)*

Kriegsrisikoversicherung *(f)*
  n De
En war-risk insurance
Es seguro contra riesgo de
    guerra *(m)*
Fr assurance du risque de
    guerre *(f)*
It assicurazione contro i
    rischi di guerra *(f)*
Pt seguro contra risco de
    guerra *(m)*

Kubikinhalt *(m)* n De
En cubic capacity
Es capacidad cúbica *(f)*
Fr volume *(m)*
It volume *(m)*
Pt capacidade cúbica *(f)*

kumulativ *adj* De
En cumulative
Es acumulativo
Fr cumulatif
It cumulativo
Pt cumulativo

kumulative Vorzugsaktien
  (f pl) De
En cumulative preference
    shares
Es valores privilegiados cu-
    mulativos *(m pl)*
Fr actions de priorité cumula-
    tives *(f pl)*
It azioni preferenziali cumu-
    lative *(f pl)*
Pt acções preferenciais cumu-
    lativas *(f pl)*

kündbare Obligation *(f)* De
En redeemable bond
Es obligación reembolsable
    (f)
Fr obligation amortissable *(f)*
It obbligazione redimibile *(f)*
Pt obrigação reembolsável *(f)*

Kunde *(n)* n De
En customer
Es cliente *(m)*
Fr client *(m)*
It cliente *(m)*
Pt cliente *(m)*

Kundenkonto *(n)* n De
En charge account
Es cuenta personal *(f)*
Fr compte personnel *(m)*
It conto personale *(m)*
Pt conta pessoal *(f)*

kündigen (vorläufig) De
En lay off
Es despedir
Fr licencier
It licenziare
Pt despedir

Kündigung (von Geldern) *(f)*
  De
En call (for funds)
Es llamada (de fondos) *(f)*
Fr appel (de fonds) *(m)*
It richiesta (di fondi) *(f)*
Pt chamada (de fundos) *(f)*

Kundschaft *(f)* n De
En custom: clientele
Es clientela *(f)*
Fr clientèle *(f)*
It clientela *(f)*
Pt clientela *(f)*

künftig *adj* De
En future
Es futuro
Fr futur
It futuro: avvenire
Pt futuro

Kunstgold *(n)* n De
En imitation gold
Es oro de imitación *(m)*
Fr similor *(m)*
It similoro *(m)*
Pt ouro de imitação *(m)*

Kunstleder *(n)* n De
En imitation leather
Es piel de imitación *(f)*
Fr simili-cuir *(m)*
It finta pelle *(f)*
Pt cabedal de imitação *(m)*

Kupon *(m)* n De
En coupon
Es cupón *(m)*
Fr coupon *(m)*
It cedola *(f)*
Pt cupão *(m)*

Kursabschlag *(m)* n De
En backwardation
Es prima de aplazamiento *(f)*
Fr déport *(m)*
It deporto *(m)*
Pt juro de mora *(m)*

Kursvergleich *(m)* n De
En arbitrage
Es arbitraje *(m)*
Fr arbitrage *(m)*
It arbitraggio *(m)*
Pt arbitragem *(f)*

kurzfristig *adj* De
En short-term
Es a corto plazo
Fr à court terme
It a breve termine
Pt a curto prazo

kurzfristiges Kapital *(n)* De
En short-term capital
Es capital a corto plazo *(m)*
Fr capitaux à court terme
    (m pl)
It capitale a breve termine
    (m)
Pt capital a curto prazo *(m)*

kurzfristiges Wertpapier *(n)*
  De
En short-dated security
Es título a corto plazo *(m)*
Fr titre à court terme *(m)*
It titolo a breve scadenza *(m)*
Pt título a curto prazo *(m)*

kurzlebige Aktiva *(n pl)* De
En wasting assets
Am depleting assets
Es activo gastable *(m)*
Fr actifs défectibles *(m pl)*
It attività in esaurimento *(f pl)*
Pt bens em uso ou deterio-
    ração *(m pl)*

Kurzschrift *(f)* n De
En shorthand
Es taquigrafía *(f)*
Fr sténographie *(f)*
It stenografia *(f)*
Pt estenografia *(f)*

Küstenschiffahrt (f) n De
En cabotage
Es cabotaje (m)
Fr cabotage (m)
It cabotaggio (m)
Pt cabotagem (f)

Kybernetik (f) n De
En cybernetics
Es cibernética (f)
Fr cybernétique (f)
It cibernetica (f)
Pt cibernética (f)

L

label n En
De Etikett (n)
Es etiqueta (f)
Fr étiquette (f)
It etichetta (f)
Pt rótulo etiqueta (m f)

laboratoire de langues (m) Fr
De Sprachlabor (n)
En language laboratory
Es laboratorio de idiomas (m)
It laboratorio di linguaggio (m)
Pt laboratório de línguas (m)

laboratorio de idiomas (m) Es
De Sprachlabor (n)
En language laboratory
Fr laboratoire de langues (m)
It laboratorio di linguaggio (m)
Pt laboratório de línguas (m)

laboratório de línguas (m) Pt
De Sprachlabor (n)
En language laboratory
Es laboratorio de idiomas (m)
Fr laboratoire de langues (m)
It laboratorio di linguaggio (m)

laboratorio di linguaggio (m) It
De Sprachlabor (n)
En language laboratory
Es laboratorio de idiomas (m)
Fr laboratoire de langues (m)
Pt laboratório de línguas (m)

labour force En
De Arbeitskräfte (f pl)
Es mano de obra (f)
Fr main d'œuvre (m)
It mano d'opera (f)
Pt trabalhadores: mão de obra (m f)

labour market En
De Arbeitsmarkt (m)
Es mercado de mano de obra (m)
Fr marché du travail (m)
It mercato della mano d'opera (m)
Pt mercado de mão-de-obra (m)

labour relations En
De Arbeitsverhältnisse (n pl)
Es relaciones patrón-obero (f pl)
Fr rapports du travail (m pl)
It relazioni con la mano d'opera (f pl)
Pt relações de trabalho (f pl)

labour turnover En
De Arbeitsplatzwechsel (m)
Es movimiento de la mano de obra (m)
Fr fluctuations de personnel (f pl)
It movimento della mano d'opera (m)
Pt movimento de trabalhadores (m)

labour union En
De Gewerkschaft (f)
Es sindicato obrero (m)
Fr syndicat (m)
It sindacato operaio (m)
Pt sindicato (m)

Ladelinie (f) n De
En loadline
Es linea de carga (f)
Fr ligne de charge (f)
It linea di carico (f)
Pt linha limite de carga (f)

Laden (m) n De
En shop
Es tienda (f)
Fr magasin (m)
It bottega (f)
Pt loja (f)

Ladeplan (m) n De
En stowage plan
Es plan de estiba (m)
Fr plan d'làrrimage (m)
It plano di stivaggio (m)
Pt plano de estiva (m)

Laderaum (m) n De
En hold
Es bodega (f)
Fr cale (f)
It stiva (f)
Pt porão (m)

Ladung (f) n De
En cargo loading
Es carga (f)
Fr cargaison; chargement (f m)
It carico; caricamento (m)
Pt carga; carregamento (f m)

Ladungsverzeichnis (n) n De
En manifest
Es manifiesto (m)
Fr manifeste (m)
It manifesto (m)
Pt manifesto (m)

Lager (n) n De
En store
Es almacén (m)
Fr magasin (m)
It magazzino (m)
Pt armazém (m)

Lagergeld (n) n De
En storage charges
Es gastos de almacenaje (m pl)
Fr frais de magasinage (m pl)
It spese di magazzinaggio (f pl)
Pt encargos de armazenamento (m pl)

lagern vb De
En store
Es almacenar
Fr emmagasiner
It immagazzinare
Pt armazenar

Lagerschein (m) n De
En warrant
Es certificado (m)
Fr certificat (m)
It certificato (m)
Pt certificado (m)

Lagerung (f) n De
En storage
Es almacenamiento (m)
Fr emmagasinage (m)
It magazzinaggio (m)
Pt armazenamento (m)

Lager unter Zollverschluß
(n) De
En bonded warehouse
Es almacén de aduanas (m)
Fr entrepôt (m)
It magazzino doganale (m)
Pt armazém alfandegário (m)

Lagerverwaltung (f) n De
En stock control
Es fiscalización de las existencias (f)
Fr contrôle des stocks (m)
It controllo scorte (m)
Pt controlo de existências (m)

lagnanza (f) n It
De Beschwerde (f)
En grievance
Es agravio (m)
Fr grief (m)
Pt agravo (m)

laminado a ouro Pt
De vergoldet
En gold-plated
Es chapado en oro
Fr plaqué d'or
It placcato in oro

lançamento (m) n Pt
De Eintragung (f)
En entry
Es asiento (m)
Fr inscription (f)
It registrazione (f)

lançamento duplo (m) Pt
De doppelte Buchführung (f)
En double entry bookkeeping
Es partida doble (f)
Fr compatibilite en partie double (f)
It partita doppia (f)

lançar (um produto) vb Pt
De auf den Markt bringen
En launch
Es lanzar
Fr lancer sur le marché
It lanciare

lançar uma empresa Pt
De eine Gesellschaft gründen
En float a company
Es lanzar una compañía
Fr lancer une entreprise
It lanciare una società

lançar um empréstimo Pt
De eine Anleihe begeben
En float a loan
Am raise a loan
Es lanzar un empréstito
Fr émettre un emprunt
It lanciare un prestito

lancer sur le marché Fr
De auf den Markt bringen
En launch
Es lanzar
It lanciare
Pt lançar

lancer une entreprise Fr
De eine Gesellschaft gründen
En float a company
Es lanzar una compañía
It lanciare una società
Pt lançar uma empresa

lanciare (un prodotto) vb It
De auf den Markt bringen
En launch
Es lanzar
Fr lancer sur le marché
Pt lançar

lanciare una società It
De eine Gesellschaft gründen
En float a company
Es lanzar una compañía
Fr lancer une entreprise
Pt lançar uma empresa

lanciare un prestito It
De eine Anleihe begeben
En float a loan
Am raise a loan
Es emitir un empréstito
Fr émettre un emprunt
Pt lançar um empréstimo

Land (n) n De
En country
Es país (m)
Fr pays (m)
It paese (m)
Pt país (m)

land bank En
De Landbank (f)
Es banco agrícola (m)
Fr banque agricole (f)
It banca agricola (f)
Pt banco d'agricultura (m)

Landbank (f) n De
En land bank
Es banco agricola (m)
Fr banque agricole (f)
It banca agricola (f)
Pt banco d'agricultura (m)

landing account En
De Löschungskonto (n)
Es cuenta de desembarque (f)
Fr compte de mise à terre (m)
It conto di sbarco (m)
Pt conta de descargas (f)

landlord (of property) n En
De Vermieter (m)
Es propietario; arrendador (m)
Fr propriétaire (m)
It proprietario; locatore (m)
Pt proprietário; senhorio (m)

Landwirtschaft (f) n De
En agriculture
Es agricultura (f)
Fr agriculture (f)
It agricoltura (f)
Pt agricultura (f)

langage-machine (m) n Fr
De Maschinensprache (f)
En machine language
Es lenguaje de máquina (m)
It linguaggio di macchina (m)
Pt linguagem de máquina (f)

langfristig adj De
En long-term
Es a largo plazo
Fr à long terme
It a lunga scadenza
Pt a longo prazo

langfristiges Kapital (n) n De
En long-term capital
Es capital a largo plazo (m)
Fr capitaux à long terme (m pl)
It capitale consolidato a lunga scadenza (m)
Pt capital a longo prazo (m)

langlebige Güter *(n pl)* De
En durable goods
Es mercancías no perecede-
ras *(f pl)*
Fr biens durables *(m pl)*
It beni durevoli *(m pl)*
Pt mercadorias imperecíveis
(f pl)

language *n* En
De Sprache *(f)*
Es lingua; lenguaje *(f m)*
Fr langue *(f)*
It lingua; linguaggio *(f m)*
Pt língua *(f)*

language laboratory En
De Sprachlabor *(n)*
Es laboratorio de idiomas *(m)*
Fr laboratoire de langues *(m)*
It laboratorio di linguaggio
(m)
Pt laboratório de línguas *(m)*

langue *(f)* n Fr
De Sprache *(f)*
En language
Es lingua *(f)*
It lingua *(f)*
Pt língua *(f)*

lanzar (un producto) *vb* Es
De auf den Markt bringen
En launch
Fr lancer sur le marché
It lanciare
Pt lançar

lanzar una compañía Es
De eine Gesellschaft gründen
En float a company
Fr lancer une entreprise
It lanciare una società
Pt lançar uma empresa

last in, first out (LIFO) En
De LIFO
Es última entrada, primera sa-
lida
Fr LIFO
It ultimo a entrare, primo a
uscire
Pt último a entrar, pimeiro a
saír

Lastkahn *(m)* n De
En barge
Es barcaza *(f)*

Fr péniche *(f)*
It chiatta *(f)*
Pt barcaça *(f)*

lastre *(m)* n Es
De Ballast *(m)*
En ballast
Fr lest *(m)*
It zavorra *(f)*
Pt lastro *(m)*

lastro *(m)* n Pt
De Ballast *(m)*
En ballast
Es lastre *(m)*
Fr lest *(m)*
Fr zavorra *(f)*

Lastschrift *(f)* n De
En debit note
Es nota de débito *(f)*
Fr avis de débit *(f)*
It nota di addebito *(f)*
Pt aviso de débito *(m)*

**Lateinamerikanische
Freihandelszone** *(f)* De
En Latin American Free Trade
Association (LAFTA)
Es Asociación de Mercado
Libre de América Latina *(f)*
Fr Association Latine-
Américaine de Libre-
Échange *(f)*
It Associazione di Libero
Scambio dell'America La-
tina *(f)*
Pt Associação do Comércio
Livre da América Latina *(f)*

latent defect En
De versteckter Mangel *(m)*
Es defecto latente *(m)*
Fr vice caché *(m)*
It difetto latente *(m)*
Pt defeito latente *(m)*

latente Steuerpflicht *(f)* De
En deferred taxation
Es tasación diferida *(f)*
Fr imposition différée *(f)*
It tassazione differita *(f)*
Pt tributação diferida *(f)*

**Latin American Free Trade
Association** (LAFTA) En
De Lateinamerikanische Frei-
handelszone *(f)*

Es Asociación de Mercado
Libre de América Latina *(f)*
Fr Association Latine-
Américaine de Libre-
Échange *(f)*
It Associazione di Libero
Scambio dell'America La-
tina *(f)*
Pt Associação do Comércio
Livre da América Latina *(f)*

laufend *adj* De
En current
Es corriente
Fr courant; en cours
It corrente
Pt corrente

laufende Police *(f)* De
En floating policy
Es póliza flotante *(f)*
Fr police flottante *(f)*
It polizza flottante *(f)*
Pt apólice flutuante *(f)*

laufendes Jahr *(n)* De
En current year
Es año en curso *(m)*
Fr année en cours *(f)*
It anno in corso *(m)*
Pt ano corrente *(m)*

laufende Verbindlichkeiten
(f pl) De
En current liabilities
Es pasivo exigible *(m)*
Fr passif exigible *(m)*
It passività esigibili *(f pl)*
Pt passivo actual *(m)*

Laufzeit *(f)* n De
En tenor
Es tenor *(m)*
Fr teneur *(f)*
It tenore *(m)*
Pt prazo de circulação *(m)*

launch (a product) *vb* En
De auf den Markt bringen
Es lanzar
Fr lancer sur le marché
It lanciare
Pt lançar

lavoratore *(m)* n It
De Arbeiter *(m)*
En worker

Es trabajador *(m)*
Fr ouvrier *(m)*
Pt trabalhador *(m)*

lavoratore del porto *(m)* It
De Hafenarbeiter *(m)*
En docker
Am longshoreman
Es cargador de muelle *(m)*
Fr docker *(m)*
Pt trabalhador das docas *(m)*

lavoratore indipendente *(m)*
It
De selbständig Arbeitende(r)
(m)
En self-employed person
Es trabajador por cuenta
propia *(m)*
Fr travailleur indépendant *(m)*
Pt empregado por conta-
própria *(m)*

lavoro *(m)* n It
De Arbeit; Beruf *(f m)*
En work; occupation
Es trabajo *(m)*
Fr travail; occupation *(m f)*
Pt trabalho; ocupação *(m f)*

lavoro a cottimo *(m)* It
De Akkordarbeit *(f)*
En piecework
Es trabajo a destajo *(m)*
Fr travail à la tâche *(m)*
Pt trabalho por peça *(m)*

lavoro a turno *(m)* It
De Schichtarbeit *(f)*
En shiftwork
Es trabajo por torno *(m)*
Fr travail par équipes *(m)*
Pt trabalho por turno *(m)*

lavoro in corso *(m)* It
De Arbeit in der Ausführung *(f)*
En work in progress
Am work in process
Es trabajo en curso *(m)*
Fr travaux en cours *(m pl)*
Pt trabalho em curso *(m)*

lavoro in economia *(m)* It
De produktive Arbeitskräfte
(f pl)
En direct labour
Es jornales directos *(m pl)*
Fr travail en régie *(m)*
Pt trabalho directamente
produtivo *(m)*

lavoro notturno *(m)* It
De Nachtarbeit *(f)*
En nightwork
Es trabajo nocturno *(m)*
Fr travail de nuit *(m)*
Pt trabalho nocturno *(m)*

lavoro straordinario *(m)* It
De Überstunden *(f pl)*
En overtime
Es horas extraordinarias *(f pl)*
Fr heures supplémentaires
(f pl)
Pt horas extraordinárias *(f pl)*

law n En
De Recht *(n)*
Es ley
Fr loi *(f)*
It legge *(f)*
Pt lei *(f)*

lawful adj En
De gesetzlich; rechtlich
Es licito; legitimo
Fr licite; légal
It lecito; legittimo
Pt legítimo; legal

lay days En
De Liegezeit *(f)*
Es estadía *(f)*
Fr staries *(f pl)*
It stallie *(f)*
Pt estadia *(f)*

lay off En
De (vorläufig) kündigen
Es despedir
Fr licencier
It (temporaneamente) licen-
ziare
Pt despedir

lay up (a ship) vb En
De auflegen
Es desarmar
Fr désarmer
It disarmare
Pt desarmar

lazer *(m)* n Pt
De Freizeit *(f)*
En leisure
Es descanso *(m)*
Fr loisir *(m)*
It svago *(m)*

leakage n En
De Leck *(n)*
Es escape *(m)*
Fr fuite *(f)*
It colaggio *(m)*
Pt escape; fuga *(m f)*

lease n En
De Verpachtung *(f)*
Es alquiler *(m)*
Fr bail *(m)*
It affitto *(m)*
Pt aluguer; arrendamento *(m)*

leasehold n En
De Pachtung *(f)*
Es arrendamiento *(m)*
Fr tenure à bail *(f)*
It proprietà fondiaria in affit-
to *(f)*
Pt título de arrendamento *(m)*

leasing company En
De Leasinggesellschaft *(f)*
Es compañía arrendataria *(f)*
Fr société de leasing *(f)*
It società di leasing *(f)*
Pt companhia arrendatária *(f)*

Leasinggesellschaft *(f)* n De
En leasing company
Es compañía arrendataria *(f)*
Fr société de leasing *(f)*
It società di leasing *(f)*
Pt companhia arrendatária *(f)*

leather goods En
De Lederwaren *(f pl)*
Es marroquinería *(f)*
Fr maroquinerie *(f)*
It pelletterie *(f pl)*
Pt artigos de cabedal *(m pl)*

Lebenshaltung *(f)* n De
En standard of living
En nivel de vida *(m)*
Fr niveau de vie *(m)*
It tenore di vita *(m)*
Pt nível de vida *(m)*

Lebenshaltungskosten *(pl)* n
De
En cost of living
Es coste de vida *(m)*
Fr coût de la vie *(m)*
It costo della vita *(m)*
Pt custo de vida *(m)*

lebenslängliche Nutznießung *(f)* De
En life-interest
Es usufructo vitalicio *(m)*
Fr usufruit viager *(m)*
It usufrutto vitalizio *(m)*
Pt usufruto vitalíeis *(m)*

Lebensversicherung *(f)* n De
En life insurance
Es seguro de vida *(m)*
Fr assurance sur la vie *(f)*
It assicurazione sulla vita *(f)*
Pt seguro de vida *(m)*

lecito *adj* It
De gesetzlich
En lawful
Es licito
Fr licite
Pt legítimo

Leck *(n)* n De
En leakage
Es escape *(m)*
Fr fuite *(f)*
It colaggio *(m)*
Pt escape; fuga *(m f)*

Lederwaren *(f pl)* n De
En leather goods
Es marroquinería *(f)*
Fr maroquinerie *(f)*
It pelletterie *(f pl)*
Pt artigos de cabedal *(m pl)*

ledger n En
De Hauptbuch *(n)*
Es libro mayor *(m)*
Fr grand livre *(m)*
It libro mastro *(m)*
Pt livro-mestre *(m)*

ledger clerk En
Am bookkeeper
De Buchhalter *(m)*
Es contable *(m)*
Fr commis-comptable *(m)*
It contabile *(m)*
Pt empregado de contabilidade *(m)*

Leerlaufzeit *(f)* n De
En down time
Es tiempo improductivo *(m)*
Fr temps d'arrêt *(m)*
It tempo improduttivo *(m)*
Pt tempo improdutivo *(m)*

legal *adj* De, En, Es, Pt
Fr légal; judiciaire
It legale; giuridico

légal *adj* Fr
De rechtsgültig; legal
En legal
Es legal; juridico
It legale; giuridico
Pt legal

legal action En
De Prozeß; Klage *(m f)*
Es pleito *(m)*
Fr action juridique *(f)*
It processo *(m)*
Pt acção judicial *(f)*

legale *adj* It
De rechtsgültig; legal
En legal
Es legal; juridico
Fr légal; judiciaire
Pt legal

legal holiday Am
En Bank Holiday
De gesetzlicher Feiertag *(m)*
Es día de fiesta *(m)*
Fr jour férié *(m)*
It festività legali *(f)*
Pt feriado *(m)*

legal liability En
De Rechtshaftung *(f)*
Es responsabilidad legal *(f)*
Fr responsabilité légale *(f)*
It responsabilità legale *(f)*
Pt responsabilidade legal *(f)*

legal representative En
De Rechtsvertreter *(m)*
Es representante legal *(m)*
Fr représentant mandaté *(m)*
It mandatario *(m)*
Pt representante legal *(m)*

legal tender En
De gesetzliches Zahlungsmittel *(n)*
Es moneda legal *(f)*
Fr monnaie légale *(f)*
It denaro a corso legale *(m)*
Pt moeda legal *(f)*

legge *(f)* n It
De Recht *(n)*
En law

Es ley *(f)*
Fr loi *(f)*
Pt lei *(f)*

legislação *(f)* n Pt
De Gesetzgebung *(f)*
En legislation
Es legislación *(f)*
Fr législation *(f)*
It legislazione *(f)*

legislación *(f)* n Es
De Gesetzgebung *(f)*
En legislation
Fr législation *(f)*
It legislazione *(f)*
Pt legislação *(f)*

legislation n En
De Gesetzgebung *(f)*
Es legislación *(f)*
Fr législation *(f)*
It legislazione *(f)*
Pt legislação *(f)*

législation *(f)* n Fr
De Gesetzgebung *(f)*
En legislation
Es legislación *(f)*
It legislazione *(f)*
Pt legislação *(f)*

legislazione *(f)* n It
De Gesetzgebung *(f)*
En legislation
Es legislación *(f)*
Fr législation *(f)*
Pt legislação *(f)*

légitime *adj* Fr
De gerechtfertigt; gesetzlich
En justifiable; lawful
Es justificable; legítimo
It giustificabile; legittimo
Pt justificável; legítimo

legítimo *adj* Es
De gesetzlich; rechtlich
En lawful; legal
Fr licite; légal
It lecito; legittimo

legítimo *adj* Pt
De gesetzlich; rechtlich
En lawful; legal
Es legítimo
Fr licite; légal
It lecito; legittimo

Lehre (Lehrzeit) *(f)* n De
En apprenticeship
Am trainee period
Es aprendizaje *(m)*
Fr apprentissage *(m)*
It tirocinio *(m)*
Pt aprendizagem *(f)*

Lehrling *(m)* n De
En apprentice
Am trainee
Es aprendiz *(m)*
Fr apprenti *(m)*
It apprendista *(m)*
Pt aprendiz *(m)*

lei *(f)* n Pt
De Recht *(n)*
En law
Es ley *(f)*
Fr loi *(f)*
It legge *(f)*

Leichter *(m)* n De
En lighter
Es barcaza; gabarra *(f)*
Fr allège *(f)*
It chiatta *(f)*
Pt barcaça *(f)*

leihen *vb* De
En lend
Es prestar
Fr prêter
It prestare
Pt emprestar

leilão *(m)* n Pt
De Versteigerung *(f)*
En auction
Es subasta *(f)*
Fr vente aux enchères *(f)*
It asta *(f)*

leiloeiro *(m)* n Pt
De Versteigerer *(m)*
En auctioneer
Es subastador *(m)*
Fr commissaire-priseur *(m)*
It venditore all'asta *(m)*

Leistungsfähigkeit *(f)* n De
En efficiency
Es eficiencia *(f)*
Fr efficacité *(f)*
It efficienza *(f)*
Pt eficiência *(f)*

Leistungslohn *(m)* n De
En payment by results
Es pago por resultados *(m)*
Fr salaire au rendement *(m)*
It pagamento secondo i risultati *(m)*
Pt pagamento relativo aos resultados *(m)*

leisure n En
De Freizeit *(f)*
Es descanso *(m)*
Fr loisir *(m)*
It svago *(m)*
Pt lazer *(m)*

Leitung (Telefon) *(f)* n De
En (telephone) line
Es línea (telefónica) *(f)*
Fr ligne (téléphone) *(f)*
It linea (telefonica) *(f)*
Pt linha (telefónica) *(f)*

lend *vb* En
De leihen
Es prestar
Fr prêter
It prestare
Pt emprestar

lending bank En
De Kreditbank *(f)*
Es banco de préstamos *(m)*
Fr banque de prêts *(f)*
It banca di prestiti *(f)*
Pt banco de empréstimos *(m)*

lenguaje de máquina *(m)* Es
De Maschinensprache *(f)*
En machine language
Fr langage-machine *(m)*
It linguaggio di macchina *(m)*
Pt llnguagem de máquina *(f)*

lessee n En
De Mieter *(m)*
Es arrendatario *(m)*
Fr locataire *(m)*
It locatario *(m)*
Pt locatário; arrendatário *(m)*

lessor n En
De Vermieter *(m)*
Es arrendador *(m)*
Fr bailleur *(m)*
It locatore *(m)*
Pt senhorio; arrendador *(m)*

lest *(m)* n Fr
De Ballast *(m)*
En ballast
Es lastre *(m)*
It zavorra *(f)*
Pt lastro *(m)*

letra *(f)* n Es, Pt
De Tratte *(f)*
En draft
Fr traite *(f)*
It tratta *(f)*

letra a la vista *(f)* Es
De Sichttratte *(f)*
En sight draft
Fr traite à vue *(f)*
It tratta a vista *(f)*
Pt letra à vista *(f)*

letra à vista *(f)* Pt
De Sichttratte *(f)*
En sight draft
Es letra a la vista *(f)*
Fr traite à vue *(f)*
It tratta a vista *(f)*

letra de adjudicación *(f)* Es
De Verteilungsbrief *(m)*
En allotment letter
Fr avis d'attribution *(m)*
It lettera da ripartizione *(f)*
Pt aviso de aporcionamento *(m)*

letra de cambio *(f)* Es
De Wechsel; Tratte *(m f)*
En bill of exchange
Fr lettre de change *(f)*
It tratta cambiale *(f)*
Pt letra do câmbio *(f)*

letra de câmbio *(f)* Pt
De Wechsel; Tratte *(m f)*
En bill of exchange
Es letra de cambio *(f)*
Fr lettre de change *(f)*
It tratta cambiale *(f)*

letra de favor *(f)* Pt
De Gefälligkeitswechsel *(m)*
En accommodation bill
Es pagaré de favor *(m)*
Fr billet de complaisance *(m)*
It cambiale di favore *(f)*

letra de país a país (cambial)
(f) Pt
De Auslandswechsel *(m)*
En foreign bill
Es letra sobre el exterior *(f)*
Fr lettre de change sur
l'étranger *(f)*
It cambiale sull'estero *(f)*

letra descontada *(f)* Pt
De Diskontwechsel *(m)*
En discounted bill
Es efecto descontado *(m)*
Fr effet escompté *(m)*
It cambiale scontata *(f)*

letra em branco *(f)* Pt
De Blankowechsel *(m)*
En blank bill
Es letra en blanco *(f)*
Fr traite en blanc *(f)*
It effetto in bianco *(m)*

letra en blanco *(f)* Es
De Blankowechsel *(m)*
En blank bill
Fr traite en blanc *(f)*
It effetto in bianco *(m)*
Pt letra em branco *(f)*

letras a cobrar *(f pl)* Es, Pt
De Wechselforderungen *(f pl)*
En bills receivable
Fr effets à recevoir *(m pl)*
It effetti attivi *(m pl)*

letras a descontar *(f pl)* Pt
De fällige Wechsel *(m pl)*
En bills for collection
Es efectos a cobrar *(m pl)*
Fr effets en recouvrement
(m pl)
It effetti all'incasso *(m pl)*

letras a pagar *(f pl)* Pt
De Wechselschulden *(f pl)*
En bills payable
Es letras pagaderas *(f pl)*
Fr effets à payer *(m pl)*
It effetti passivi *(m pl)*

letras descontadas *(f pl)* Pt
De diskontierte Wechsel *(m pl)*
En bills discounted
Es efectos descontados
(m pl)
Fr effets escomptés *(m pl)*
It effetti scontati *(m pl)*

letra sobre el exterior *(f)* Es
De Auslandswechsel *(m)*
En foreign bill
Fr lettre de change sur
l'étranger *(f)*
It cambiale sull'estero *(f)*
Pt letra de país a país (cam-
bial) *(f)*

letras pagaderas *(f pl)* Es
De Wechselschulden *(f pl)*
En bills payable
Fr effets à payer *(m pl)*
It effetti passivi *(m pl)*
Pt letras a pagar *(f pl)*

letter *n* En
De Brief *(m)*
Es carta; letra *(f)*
Fr lettre *(f)*
It lettera *(f)*
Pt carta *(f)*

lettera *(f) n* It
De Brief *(m)*
En letter
Es carta; letra *(f)*
Fr lettre *(f)*
Pt carta *(f)*

lettera aerea *(f)* It
De Luftpostbrief *(m)*
En air letter
Es carta por avión *(f)*
Fr aérogramme *(m)*
Pt carta por avião *(f)*

lettera da ripartizione *(f)* It
De Verteilungsbrief *(m)*
En allotment letter
Es letra de adjudicación *(f)*
Fr avis d'attribution *(m)*
Pt aviso de aporcionamento
(m)

lettera d'avviso *(f)* It
De Anzeige *(f)*
En advice note
Es aviso *(m)*
Fr lettre d'avis *(f)*
Pt guia de remessa *(f)*

lettera di credito *(f)* It
De Kreditbrief *(m)*
En letter of credit
Es carta de crédito *(f)*
Fr lettre de crédit *(f)*
Pt carta de crédito *(f)*

**lettera di credito conferma-
ta e irrevocabile** *(f)* It
De bestätigter unwiderruflicher Kreditbrief *(m)*
En confirmed irrevocable letter of credit
Es carta de crédito irrevocable confirmada *(f)*
Fr lettre de crédit irrévocable
confirmée *(f)*
Pt carta de crédito irre-
vogável confirmada *(f)*

**lettera di credito
irrevocabile** *(f)* It
De unwiderruflicher Kreditbrief *(m)*
En irrevocable letter of credit
Es carta de crédito irrevocable *(f)*
Fr lettre de crédit irrévocable
(f)
Pt carta de crédito irre-
vogável *(f)*

lettera di garanzia *(f)* It
De Ausfallbürgschaft *(f)*
En letter of indemnity
Es carta de indemnización *(f)*
Fr cautionnement *(m)*
Pt documento de garantia
(m)

lettera di vettura *(f)* It
De Frachtbrief *(m)*
En waybill
Es guía de carga *(f)*
Fr lettre de voiture *(f)*
Pt guia de transporte *(f)*

lettera espresso *(f)* It
De Eilbrief *(m)*
En express letter
Am special delivery
Es carta urgente *(f)*
Fr lettre par exprès *(f)*
Pt carta expressa *(f)*

lettera raccomandata *(f)* It
De eingeschriebener Brief *(m)*
En registered letter
Es carta certificada *(f)*
Fr lettre recommandée *(f)*
Pt carta registada *(f)*

letter-box *n* En
Am mail-box
De Briefkasten *(m)*
Es buzón *(m)*

Fr boîte aux lettres (f)
It cassetta postale (f)
Pt caixa postal (f)

letterhead n En
De Briefkopf (m)
Es membrete (m)
Fr en-tête (m)
It intestazione (f)
Pt cabeçalho (m)

letter of credit En
De Kreditbrief (m)
Es carta de crédito (f)
Fr lettre de crédit (f)
It lettera di credito (f)
Pt carta de crédito (f)

letter of hypothecation En
De Verpfändungsurkunde (f)
Es carta de hipoteca (f)
Fr lettre hypothécaire (f)
It atto ipotecario (m)
Pt carta de hipoteca (f)

letter of indemnity En
De Ausfallbürgschaft (f)
Es carta de indemnización (f)
Fr cautionnement (m)
It lettera di garanzia (f)
Pt documento de garantia (m)

letters patent En
Am patent
De Patenturkunde (f)
Es patente de invención (f)
Fr brevet (m)
It brevetto (m)
Pt patente de invenção (f)

lettre (f) n Fr
De Brief (m)
En letter
Es carta; letra (f)
It lettera (f)
Pt carta (f)

lettre d'avis (f) Fr
De Anzeige (f)
En advice note
Es aviso (m)
It lettera d'avviso (f)
Pt guia de remessa (f)

lettre de change (f) Fr
De Wechsel; Tratte (m f)
En bill of exchange

Es letra de cambio (f)
It tratta cambiale (f)
Pt letra de câmbio (f)

lettre de change sur l'étranger (f) Fr
De Auslandswechsel (m)
En foreign bill
Es letra sobre el exterior (f)
It cambiale sull' estero (f)
Pt letra de país a país (cambial) (f)

lettre de couverture (f) Fr
De Deckungszusage (f)
En cover note
Es aviso de seguro del riesgo (m)
It nota di copertura (f)
Pt nota de cobertura (f)

lettre de crédit (f) Fr
De Kreditbrief (m)
En letter of credit
Es carta de crédito (f)
It lettera di credito (f)
Pt carta de crédito (f)

lettre de crédit confirmée (f) Fr
De bestätigter Kreditbrief (m)
En confirmed letter of credit
Es carta de crédito confirmada (f)
It lettera di credito confermata (f)
Pt carta de crédito confirmada (f)

lettre de crédit irrévocable (f) Fr
De unwiderruflicher Kreditbrief (m)
En irrevocable letter of credit
Es carta de crédito irrevocable (f)
It lettera di credito irrevocabile (f)
Pt carta de crédito irrevogável (f)

lettre de crédit irrévocable confirmée (f) Fr
De bestätigter unwiderruflicher Kreditbrief (m)
En confirmed irrevocable letter of credit
Es carta de crédito irrevocable confirmada (f)

It lettera di credito confermata e irrevocabile (f)
Pt carta de crédito irrevogável confirmada (f)

lettre de transport aérien (f) Fr
De Luftfrachtbrief (m)
En air waybill
Es carta de porte aéreo (f)
It nota di spedizione aerea (f)
Pt guia de porte aéreo (f)

lettre de voiture (f) Fr
De Frachtbrief (m)
En waybill
Es guía de carga (f)
It lettera di vettura (f)
Pt guia de transporte (f)

lettre hypothécaire (f) Fr
De Verpfändungsurkunde (f)
En letter of hypothecation
Es carta de hipoteca (f)
It atto ipotecario (m)
Pt carta de hipoteca (f)

lettre par exprès (f) Fr
De Eilbrief (m)
En express letter
Am special delivery
Es carta urgente (f)
It lettera espresso (f)
Pt carta expressa (f)

lettre recommandée (f) Fr
De eingeschriebener Brief (m)
En registered letter
Es carta certificada (f)
It lettera raccomandata (f)
Pt carta registada (f)

letzte Rate (f) De
En final instalment
Es último plazo (m)
Fr dernier versement (m)
It ultima rata (f)
Pt última prestação (f)

levantar a descoberto Pt
De überziehen
En overdraw
Es girar en descubierto
Fr mettre à découvert
It trarre allo scoperto

levée d'inventaire (f) Fr
De Bestandsaufnahme (f)
En stocktaking

Es inventario; balance *(m)*
It compilazione dell'inventario *(f)*
Pt inventário de existências *(m)*

levy *n* En
De Erhebung *(f)*
Es impuesto *(m)*
Fr prélèvement *(m)*
It imposta *(f)*
Pt imposto *(m)*

ley *(f)* *n* Es
De Recht *(n)*
En law
Fr loi *(f)*
It legge *(f)*
Pt lei *(f)*

liability *n* En
De Verpflichtung *(f)*
Es responsabilidad *(f)*
Fr responsabilité *(f)*
It responsabilità *(f)*
Pt responsabilidade *(f)*

liable for damages En
De schadenersatzpflichtig
Es responsable por daños
Fr passible de dommages-intérêts
It responsabile per i danni
Pt responsável por danos

libera pratica *(f)* It
De Gesundheitsbrief *(m)*
En pratique
Es libre plática *(f)*
Fr libre pratique *(f)*
Pt livre prática *(f)*

liberar *vb* Es
De befreien
En free
Fr libérer; affranchir
It liberare
Pt libertar; livrar

liberare *vb* It
De befreien
En free
Es liberar
Fr libérer; affranchir
Pt libertar; livrar

libération intégrale *(f)* Fr
De volle Zahlung *(f)*
En payment in full

Es pago en pleno *(m)*
It pagamento in pieno *(m)*
Pt pagamento completo *(m)*

libérer *vb* Fr
De befreien
En free
Es liberar
It liberare
Pt libertar; livrar

libero *adj* It
De frei
En free
Es libre
Fr libre
Pt livre

libero d'ipoteca It
De von Hypothek befreit
En free from mortgage
Es deshipotecado
Fr déshypothéqué
Pt livre de hipoteca

libero scambio *(m)* It
De Freihandel *(m)*
En free trade
Es comercio libre *(m)*
Fr libre-échange *(m)*
Pt comércio franco *(m)*

libertà d'iniziativa *(f)* It
De freie Wirtschaft *(f)*
En free enterprise
Es libre empresa *(f)*
Fr libre entreprise *(f)*
Pt livre-empreendimento *(m)*

libertar *vb* Pt
De befreien
En free
Es liberar
Fr libérer; affranchir
It liberare

librado *(m)* *n* Es
De Bezogene(r) *(m)*
En drawee
Fr tiré *(m)*
It trattario *(m)*
Pt sacado *(m)*

librador *(m)* *n* Es
De Aussteller *(m)*
En drawer
Fr tireur *(m)*
It traente *(m)*
Pt sacador *(m)*

libra esterlina *(f)* Es
De Pfund Sterling *(n)*
En pound sterling
Fr livre sterling *(f)*
It lira sterlina *(f)*
Pt libra esterlina *(f)*

libra esterlina *(f)* Pt
De Pfund Sterling *(n)*
En pound sterling
Es libra esterlina *(f)*
Fr livre sterling *(f)*
It lira sterlina *(f)*

libra esterlina verde *(f)* Pt
De grünes Pfund *(n)*
En green pound
Es esterlina verde *(f)*
Fr livre sterling verte *(f)*
It sterlina verde *(f)*

libre *adj* Es, Fr
De frei
En free
It libero
Pt livre

libre-échange *(m)* Fr
De Freihandel *(m)*
En free trade
Es comercio libre *(m)*
It libero scambio *(m)*
Pt comércio franco *(m)*

libre empresa *(f)* Es
De freie Wirtschaft *(f)*
En free enterprise
Fr libre entreprise *(f)*
It libertà d'iniziativa *(f)*
Pt livre-empreendimento *(m)*

libre entrega Es
De portofreie Lieferung
En delivery free
Fr livré franco
It consegna franco
Pt remessa gratuita

libre entreprise *(f)* Fr
De freie Wirtschaft *(f)*
En free enterprise
Es libre empresa *(f)*
It libertà d'iniziativa *(f)*
Pt livre-empreendimento *(m)*

libre plática *(f)* Es
De Gesundheitsbrief *(m)*
En pratique
Fr libre pratique *(f)*

It libera pratica (f)
Pt livre prática (f)

libre pratique (f) Fr
De Gesundheitsbrief (m)
En pratique
Es libre plática (f)
It libera pratica (f)
Pt livre prática (f)

libre service (m) Fr
De Selbstbedienung (f)
En self-service
Es auto-servicio (m)
It servirsi da sè (m)
Pt self-service (m)

libreta de banco (f) Es
De Bankbuch; Sparbuch (n)
En passbook
Am bankbook
Fr livret de compte (m)
It libretto di conto (m)
Pt livrete de conta (m)

libretto assegni (m) It
De Scheckheft (n)
En cheque book
Am check book
Es libro de cheques (m)
Fr carnet de chèques;
    chéquier (m)
Pt livro de cheques (m)

libretto di conto (m) It
De Bankbuch; Sparbuch (n)
En passbook
Am bankbook
Es libreta de banco (f)
Fr livret de compte (m)
Pt livrete de conta (m)

libri contabili (m pl) It
De Geschäftsbücher (n pl)
En books of account
Es libros de cuentas (m pl)
Fr livres comptables (m pl)
Pt livros de contabilidade
    (m pl)

libro cassa (m) It
De Kassenbuch (n)
En cash book
Es libro de caja (m)
Fr livre de caisse (m)
Pt livro de caixa (m)

libro de caja (m) Es
De Kassenbuch (n)
En cash book
Fr livre de caisse (m)
It libro cassa (m)
Pt livro de caixa (m)

libro de cheques (m) Es
De Scheckheft (n)
En cheque book
Am check book
Fr carnet de chèques;
    chéquier (m)
It libretto assegni (m)
Pt livro de cheques (m)

libro de consulta (m) Es
De Nachschlagewerk (n)
En reference book
Fr ouvrage de référence (m)
It libro di consultazione (m)
Pt livro de consulta (m)

libro de cuentas (m) Es
De Kontobuch (n)
En account book
Fr livre de comptes (m)
It libro di conti (m)
Pt livro de contas (m)

libro degli ordini (m) It
De Auftragsbuch (n)
En order book
Es libro de pedidos (m)
Fr livre de commandes (m)
Pt livro de encomendas (m)

libro de pedidos (m) Es
De Auftragswerk (n)
En order book
Fr livre de commandes (m)
It libro degli ordini (m)
Pt livro de encomendas (m)

libro diario (m) Es
De Tagebuch (n)
En journal
Fr journal (m)
It libro giornale (m)
Pt diário (m)

libro di consultazione (m) It
De Nachschlagewerk (n)
En reference book
Es libro de consulta (m)
Fr ouvrage de référence (m)
Pt livro de consulta (m)

libro di conti (m) It
De Kontobuch (n)
En account book
Es libro de cuentas (m)
Fr livre de comptes (m)
Pt livro de contas (m)

libro giornale (m) It
De Tagebuch (n)
En journal
Es libro diario (m)
Fr journal (m)
Pt diário (m)

libro mastro (m) It
De Hauptbuch (n)
En ledger
Es libre mayor (m)
Fr grand livre (m)
Pt livro-mestre (m)

libro mastro generale (m) It
De allgemeines Hauptbuch (n)
En general ledger
Es libro mayor general (m)
Fr journal général (m)
Pt livro-mestre geral (m)

libro mayor (m) Es
De Hauptbuch (n)
En ledger
Fr grand livre (m)
It libro mastro (m)
Pt livro-mestre (m)

libro mayor de compras (m)
    Es
De Einkaufsbuch (n)
En bought ledger
Am purchase book
Fr grand livre d'achats (m)
It mastro acquisti (m)
Pt livro de compras (m)

libro mayor de ventas (m) Es
De Verkaufskontenbuch (n)
En sales ledger
Fr grand livre des ventes (m)
It partitario delle vendite (m)
Pt livro de vendas (m)

libro mayor general (m) Es
De allgemeines Hauptbuch (n)
En general ledger
Fr journal général (m)
It libro mastro generale (m)
Pt livro-mestre geral (m)

libro paga (m) It
De Lohnbuch (n)
En payroll
Es nómina de pago (f)
Fr feuille de paie (f)
Pt folha de salários (f)

libros de cuentas (m pl)
Es
De Geschäftsbücher (n pl)
En books of account
Fr livres comptables (m pl)
It libri contabili (m pl)
Pt livros de contabilidade
(m pl)

licença (f) n Pt
De Erlaubnis (f)
En licence
Es licencia; permiso (f m)
Fr licence (f)
It licenza; permesso (f m)

licença de exportação (f)
Pt
De Ausfuhrgenehmigung (f)
En export permit
Es permiso de exportación
(m)
Fr autorisation d'exporter (f)
It permesso d'esportazione
(m)

licença de importação (f)
Pt
De Einfuhrerlaubnis (f)
En import licence
Es permiso de importación
(m)
Fr licence d'importation (f)
It permesso d'importazione
(m)

licence n En, Fr (f)
De Erlaubnis (f)
Es licencia; permiso (f m)
It licenza; permesso (f m)
Pt licença (f)

licence d'importation (f)
Fr
De Einfuhrerlaubnis (f)
En import licence
Es permiso de importación
(m)
It permesso d'importazione
(m)
Pt licença de importação (f)

licencia (f) n Es
De Erlaubnis (f)
En licence
Fr licence (f)
It licenza; permesso
(f m)
Pt licença (f)

licencier vb Fr
De kündigen
En dismiss; fire
Es despedir
It licenziare
Pt despedir

licenza (f) n It
De Erlaubnis (f)
En licence
Es licencia; permiso (f m)
Fr licence (f)
Pt licença (f)

licenziamento (m) n
It
De Entlassung (f)
En firing; dismissal
Es despido (m)
Fr congédiement (m)
Pt despedimento (m)

licenziare vb It
De entlassen
En dismiss; fire
Es despedir
Fr congédier; licencier
Pt despedir

licite adj Fr
De gesetzlich; rechtlich
En lawful; legal
Es licito; legitimo
It lecito; legittimo
Pt legítimo; legal

licito adj Es
De gesetzlich; rechtlich
En lawful; legal
Fr licite; légal
It lecito; legittimo
Pt legítimo; legal

Lieferant (m) n De
En supplier
Es proveedor (m)
Fr fournisseur (m)
It fornitore (m)
Pt fornecedor (m)

Lieferhafen (m) n De
En port of discharge
Es puerto de descarga (m)
Fr port de livraison (m)
It porto di scarico (m)
Pt porto de descarga (m)

liefern vb De
En deliver; supply
Es entregar; provecer
Fr livrer; fournir
It consegnare; fornire
Pt entregar; fornecer

Lieferpreis (m) n De
En delivered price
Es precio incluida entrega (m)
Fr prix livraison inclus (m)
It prezzo incluso consegna
(m)
Pt preço incluindo portes (m)

Lieferschein (m) n De
En delivery note
Es aviso de entrega (m)
Fr bordereau de livraison (m)
It nota di consegna (f)
Pt guia de entrega (f)

Liefertermin (m) n De
En delivery date
Es fecha de entrega (f)
Fr date de livraison (f)
It data di consegna (f)
Pt data de entrega (f)

Lieferung (f) n De
En delivery
Es entrega (f)
Fr livraison (f)
It consegna (f)
Pt entrega (f)

**Lieferung gegen
Nachnahme** De
En cash on delivery (c.o.d.)
Es entrega contra reembolso
Fr paiement à la livraison
It pagamento alla consegna
Pt entrega contra reembolso

Liegezeit (f) n De
En lay days
Es estadía (f)
Fr staries (f pl)
It stallie (f pl)
Pt estadia (f)

lien n En
De Pfandrecht (n)
Es derecho de retención (m)
Fr droit de retention (m)
It diritto di sequestro (m)
Pt direito de retenção (m)

life assurance En
Am life insurance
De Lebensversicherung (f)
Es seguro de vida (m)
Fr assurance sur la vie (f)
It assicurazione sulla vita (f)
Pt seguro de vida (m)

life-interest n En
De lebenslängliche Nutznie-
    ßung (f)
Es usufructo vitalicio (m)
Fr usufruit viager (m)
It usufrutto vitalizio (m)
Pt usufruto vitalício (m)

LIFO En, Fr, De
Es última entrada; primera sa-
    lida
It ultimo a entrare; primo a
    uscire
Pt último a entrar; primeiro a
    sair

lift (n) En
Am elevator
De Aufzug (m)
Es ascensor (m)
Fr ascenseur (m)
It ascensore (m)
Pt ascensor (m)

lighter n En
De Leichter (m)
Es barcaza; gabarra (f)
Fr allège (f)
It chiatta (f)
Pt barcaça (f)

lightning n En
De Blitz (m)
Es relámpago (m)
Fr foudre (f)
It fulmine (m)
Pt relâmpago (m)

ligne (de chemin de fer) (f) n Fr
De Linie; Eisenbahnlinie (f)
En (railway) line
Es línea (ferroviaria) (f)

It linea (ferroviaria) (f)
Pt linha (de caminho de ferro)
    (f)

ligne (de téléphone) (f) n Fr
De Leitung (Telefon) (f)
En (telephone) line
Es línea (telefónica) (f)
It linea (telefonica) (f)
Pt linha (telefónica) (f)

ligne de charge (f) Fr
De Ladelinie (f)
En loadline
Es línea de carga (f)
It linea di canoo (f)
Pt linha limite de carga (f)

limit n En
De Grenze (f)
Es límite (m)
Fr limite (f)
It limite (m)
Pt limite (m)

limitação de dividendos (f) Pt
De Dividendenstopp (m)
En dividend limitation
Es bloqueo de dividendos (m)
Fr blocage des dividendes
    (m)
It blocco dei dividendi (m)

limitado adj Es, Pt
De beschränkt
En limited
Fr limité
It limitato

limitato adj It
De beschränkt
En limited
Es limitado
Fr limité
Pt limitado

límite (m) n Es
De Grenze (f)
En limit
Fr limite (f)
It limite (m)
Pt limite (m)

limite n Fr (f); It, Pt (m)
De Grenze (f)
En limit
Es límite (m)

limité adj Fr
De beschränkt
En limited
Es limitado
It limitato
Pt limitado

limited adj En
De beschränkt
Es limitado
Fr limité
It limitato
Pt limitado

límite de crédito (m) Es
De Kreditwürdigkeit (f)
En credit rating
Fr degré de solvabilité (m)
It stima del credito (f)
Pt nível de crédito (m)

limited partnership En
De Kommanditgesellschaft (f)
Es sociedad en comandita (f)
Fr société en commandité (f)
It società in accomandita
    semplice (f)
Pt sociedade em comandita
    (f)

line (railway) n En
De Linie; Eisenbahnlinie (f)
Es línea (ferroviaria) (f)
Fr ligne (de chemin de fer) (f)
It linea (ferroviaria) (f)
Pt linha (de caminho de ferro)
    (f)

line (telephone) n En
De Leitung (Telefon) (f)
Es línea (telefónica) (f)
Fr ligne (de téléphone) (f)
It linea (telefonica) (f)
Pt linha (telefónica) (f)

linea (ferroviaria) (f) n Es
De Linie; Eisenbahnlinie (f)
En (railway) line
Fr ligne (de chemin de fer) (f)
It linea (ferroviaria) (f)
Pt linha (de caminho de ferro)
    (f)

linea (ferroviaria) (f) n It
De Linie; Eisenbahnlinie (f)
En (railway) line
Es línea (ferroviaria) (f)
Fr ligne (de chemin de fer) (f)
Pt linha (de caminho de ferro)
    (f)

linea (telefónica) *(f) n* Es
De Leitung (Telefon) *(f)*
En (telephone) line
Fr ligne (de téléphone) *(f)*
It linea (telefonica) *(f)*
Pt linha (telefónica) *(f)*

linea (telefonica) *(f) n* It
De Leitung (Telefon) *(f)*
En (telephone) line
Es línea (telefónica) *(f)*
Fr ligne (de téléphone) *(f)*
Pt linha (telefónica) *(f)*

linea aérea *(f)* Es
De Fluggesellschaft *(f)*
En air line
Fr compagnie aérienne *(f)*
It linea aerea *(f)*
Pt companhia de aviação *(f)*

linea aerea *(f)* It
De Fluggesellschaft *(f)*
En air line
Es línea aérea *(f)*
Fr compagnie aérienne *(f)*
Pt companhia de aviação *(f)*

línea de carga *(f)* Es
De Ladelinie *(f)*
En loadline
Fr ligne de charge *(f)*
It linea di carico
Pt linha limite de carga *(f)*

línea de montaje *(f)* Es
De Montageband *(n)*
En essembly line
Fr chaîne de montage *(f)*
It catena di montaggio *(f)*
Pt cadeia de montagem *(f)*

linea di carico *(f)* It
De Ladelinie *(f)*
En loadline
Es línea de carga *(f)*
Fr ligne de charge *(f)*
Pt linha limite de carga *(f)*

liner *n* En
De Linienschiff *(n)*
Es vapor de línea *(m)*
Fr paquebot *(m)*
It nave di linea *(f)*
Pt paquete *(m)*

lingot *(m) n* Fr
De Barren *(m)*
En ingot
Es lingote *(m)*
It lingotto *(m)*
Pt lingote *(m)*

lingote *(m) n* Es, Pt
De Barren *(m)*
En ingot
Fr lingot; barre *(m f)*
It lingotto *(m)*

lingotto *(m) n* It
De Barren *(m)*
En ingot
Es lingote *(m)*
Fr lingot; barre *(m f)*
Pt lingote *(m)*

lingua *(f) n* Es, It
De Sprache *(f)*
En language
Fr langue *(f)*
Pt língua *(f)*

língua *(f) n* Pt
De Sprache *(f)*
En language
Es lingua *(f)*
Fr langue *(f)*
It lingua *(f)*

linguagem de máquina *(f)* Pt
De Maschinensprache *(f)*
En machine language
Es lenguaje de máquina *(m)*
Fr langage-machine *(m)*
It linguaggio di macchina *(m)*

linguaggio di macchina *(m)* It
De Maschinensprache *(f)*
En machine language
Es lenguaje de máquina *(m)*
Fr langage-machine *(m)*
Pt linguagem de máquina *(f)*

linha (de caminho de ferro) *(f) n* Pt
De Linie; Eisenbahnlinie *(f)*
En (railway) line
Es línea (ferroviaria) *(f)*
Fr ligne (de chemin de fer) *(f)*
It linea (ferroviaria) *(f)*

linha (telefónica) *(f) n* Pt
De Leitung (Telefon) *(f)*
En line (telephone)
Es línea (telefónica) *(f)*
Fr ligne (de téléphone) *(f)*
It linea (telefonica) *(f)*

linha limite de carga *(f)* Pt
De Ladelinie *(f)*
En loadline
Es línea de carga *(f)*
Fr ligne de charge *(f)*
It linea di carico *(f)*

Linie (Eisenbahn) *(f) n* De
En (railway) line
Es línea (ferroviaria) *(f)*
Fr ligne (de chemin de fer) *(f)*
It linea (ferroviaria) *(f)*
Pt linha (de caminho de ferro) *(f)*

Linienschiff *(n) n* De
En liner
Es vapor de línea *(m)*
Fr paquebot *(m)*
It nave di linea *(f)*
Pt paquete *(m)*

liquidação *(f) n* Pt
De Liquidation; Auflösung *(f)*
En liquidation
Es liquidación *(f)*
Fr liquidation *(f)*
It liquidazione *(f)*

liquidação forçada *(f)* Pt
De Zwangsliquidation *(f)*
En compulsory winding-up
Am forced liquidation
Es liquidación forzosa *(f)*
Fr liquidation forcée *(f)*
It liquidazione forzata *(f)*

liquidación *(f) n* Es
De Liquidation; Auflösung *(f)*
En liquidation
Fr liquidation *(f)*
It liquidazione *(f)*
Pt liquidação *(f)*

liquidación forzosa *(f)* Es
De Zwangsliquidation *(f)*
En compulsory winding-up
Am forced liquidation
Fr liquidation forcée *(f)*
It liquidazione forzata *(f)*
Pt liquidação forçada *(f)*

liquidador *(m) n* Es
De Masseverwalter; Sachwalter *(m)*
En liquidator
Fr liquidateur *(m)*
It liquidatore *(m)*
Pt executor de liquidação *(m)*

liquidare una azienda It
De ein Unternehmen abwickeln
En wind up a business
Es liquidar un negocio
Fr liquider une entreprise
Pt liquidar um negócio

liquidar um negócio Pt
De ein Unternehmen abwickeln
En wind up a business
Es liquidar un negocio
Fr liquider une entreprise
It liquidare una azienda

liquidar un negocio Es
De ein Unternehmen abwickeln
En wind up a business
Fr liquider une entreprise
It liquidare una azienda
Pt liquidar um negócio

liquid assets En
De flüssige Aktiven *(n pl)*
Es activo líquido *(m)*
Fr actif liquide *(m)*
It disponibilità; attività liquida *(f)*
Pt bens de activo líquidos *(m pl)*

liquidated damages En
De Konventionalstrafe *(f)*
Es daños liquidados *(m pl)*
Fr dommages-intérêts fixés en argent *(m pl)*
It danni liquidati *(m pl)*
Pt danos liquidados *(m pl)*

liquidateur *(m) n* Fr
De Masseverwalter; Sachwalter *(m)*
En liquidator
Es liquidador *(m)*
It liquidatore *(m)*
Pt executor de liquidação *(m)*

liquidation *n* En
De Liquidation; Auflösung *(f)*
Es liquidación *(f)*
Fr liquidation *(f)*
It liquidazione *(f)*
Pt liquidação *(f)*

liquidation *(f) n* Fr
De Liquidation; Auflösung *(f)*
En liquidation
Es liquidación *(f)*
It liquidazione *(f)*
Pt liquidação *(f)*

Liquidation *(f) n* De
En liquidation
Es liquidación *(f)*
Fr liquidation *(f)*
It liquidazione *(f)*
Pt liquidação *(f)*

liquidation forcée *(f)* Fr
De Zwangsliquidation *(f)*
En compulsory winding-up
Am forced liquidation
Es liquidación forzosa *(f)*
It liquidazione forzata *(f)*
Pt liquidação forçada *(f)*

liquidator *n* En
De Masseverwalter; Sachwalter *(m)*
Es liquidador *(m)*
Fr liquidateur *(m)*
It liquidatore *(m)*
Pt executor de liquidação *(m)*

liquidatore *(m) n* It
De Masseverwalter; Sachwalter *(m)*
En liquidator
Es liquidador *(m)*
Fr liquidateur *(m)*
Pt executor de liquidação *(m)*

liquidazione *(f) n* It
De Liquidation; Auflösung *(f)*
En liquidation
Es liquidación *(f)*
Fr liquidation *(f)*
Pt liquidação *(f)*

liquidazione forzata *(f)* It
De Zwangsliquidation *(f)*
En compulsory winding-up
Am forced liquidation
Es liquidación forzosa *(f)*
Fr liquidation forcée *(f)*
Pt liquidação forçada *(f)*

liquider une entreprise Fr
De ein Unternehmen abwickeln
En wind up a business
Es liquidar un negocio
It liquidare una azienda
Pt liquidar um negócio

liquidez *(f) n* Es, Pt
De Liquidität *(f)*
En liquidity
Fr liquidité *(f)*
It liquidità *(f)*

liquidità *(f) n* It
De Liquidität *(f)*
En liquidity
Es liquidez *(f)*
Fr liquidité *(f)*
Pt liquidez *(f)*

Liquidität *(f) n* De
En liquidity
Es liquidez *(f)*
Fr liquidité *(f)*
It liquidità *(f)*
Pt liquidez *(f)*

liquidité *(f) n* Fr
De Liquidität *(f)*
En liquidity
Es liquidez *(f)*
It liquidità *(f)*
Pt liquidez *(f)*

liquidity *n* En
De Liquidität *(f)*
Es liquidez *(f)*
Fr liquidité *(f)*
It liquidità *(f)*
Pt liquidez *(f)*

líquido *adj* Pt
De Netto-; Rein-
En net
Es neto
Fr net
It netto

lira sterlina *(f)* It
De Pfund Sterling *(n)*
En pound sterling
Es libra esterlina *(f)*
Fr livre sterling *(f)*
Pt libra esterlina *(f)*

lista (f) n Es, It, Pt
De Liste; Tabelle (f)
En schedule; list
Fr liste; tableau (f m)

lista de espera (f) Es, Pt
De Warteliste (f)
En waiting list
Fr liste d'attente (f)
It elenco delle prenotazioni (m)

lista negra (f) Es, Pt
De schwarze Liste (f)
En black list
Fr liste noire (f)
It lista nera (f)

lista nera (f) It
De schwarze Liste (f)
En black list
Es lista negra (f)
Fr liste noire (f)
Pt lista negra (f)

lista telefónica (f) Pt
De Fernsprechbuch (n)
En telephone directory
Es guía de teléfonos (f)
Fr annuaire des télephones (m)
It elenco telefonico (m)

liste (f) n Fr
De Liste; Tabelle (f)
En list; schedule
Es lista; cuadro (f m)
It lista; tabella (f)
Pt lista; tabela (f)

Liste (f) n De
En list; schedule
Es lista; cuadro (f m)
Fr liste; tableau (f m)
It lista; tabella (f)
Pt lista; tabela (f)

liste d'attente (f) Fr
De Warteliste (f)
En waiting list
Es lista de espera (f)
It elenco delle prenotazioni (m)
Pt lista de espera (f)

Liste der Aktionäre (f) De
En share register
Es registro de las acciones (m)

Fr registre des actionnaires (m)
It registro delle azioni (m)
Pt registo de acções (m)

listed security En
De an der Börse notierte Wertpapiere (n pl)
Es valores cotizables (m pl)
Fr valeurs admises à la Bourse (f pl)
It titoli quotati in Borsa (m pl)
Pt valor de Bolsa com cotação oficial (m)

liste noire (f) Fr
De schwarze Liste (f)
En black list
Es lista negra (f)
It lista nera (f)
Pt lista negra (f)

Listenpreis (m) n De
En list price
Es precio de tarifa (m)
Fr prix courant (m)
It prezzo di listino (m)
Pt preço de tabela (m)

list price En
De Listenpreis (m)
Es precio de tarifa (m)
Fr prix courant (m)
It prezzo di listino (m)
Pt preço de tabela (m)

livello dei prezzi (m) It
De Preisebene (f)
En price level
Es nivel de precios (m)
Fr niveau des prix (m)
Pt nível de preços (m)

livraison (f) n Fr
De Lieferung (f)
En delivery
Es entrega (f)
It consegna (f)
Pt entrega (f)

livraison à terme (f) Fr
De Terminlieferung (f)
En forward delivery
Es entrega futura (f)
It consegna a termine (f)
Pt entrega futura (f)

livraison immédiate (f) Fr
De sofortige Lieferung (f)
En prompt delivery
Es entrega inmediata (f)
It pronta consegna (f)
Pt entrega imediata (f)

livraison incomplète (f) Fr
De mangelhafte Lieferung (f)
En short delivery
Es entrega deficiente (f)
It consegna deficiente (f)
Pt entrega insuficiente (f)

livre adj Pt
De frei
En free
Es libre
Fr libre
It libero

livre de alfândega Pt
De verzollt
En ex bond
Es fuera de aduanas
Fr à l'acquitté
It sdoganato

livre de caisse (m) Fr
De Kassenbuch (n)
En cash book
Es libro de caja (m)
It libro cassa (m)
Pt livro de caixa (m)

livre de commandes (m) Fr
De Auftragsbuch (n)
En order book
Es libro de pedidos (m)
It libro degli ordini (m)
Pt livro de encomendas (m)

livre de comptes (m) Fr
De Kontobuch (n)
En account book
Es libro de cuentas (m)
It libro di conti (m)
Pt livro de contas (m)

livre de hipoteca Pt
De von Hypothek befreit
En free from mortgage
Es deshipotecado
Fr déshypothéqué
It libero d'ipoteca

livre-empreendimento *(m)*
Pt
De freie Wirtschaft *(f)*
En free enterprise
Es libre empresa *(f)*
Fr libre entreprise *(f)*
It libertà d'iniziativa *(f)*

livré franco Fr
De portofreie Lieferung
En delivery free
Es libre entrega
It consegna franco
Pt remessa gratuita

livre prática *(f)* Pt
De Gesundheitsbrief *(m)*
En pratique
Es libre plática *(f)*
Fr libre pratique *(f)*
It libera pratica *(f)*

livres comptables *(m pl)* Fr
De Geschäftsbücher *(n pl)*
En books of account
Es libros de cuentas *(m pl)*
It libri contabili *(m pl)*
Pt livros de contabilidade
    (m pl)

livre sterling *(f)* Fr
De Pfund Sterling *(n)*
En pound sterling
Es libra esterlina *(f)*
It lira sterlina *(f)*
Pt libra esterlina *(f)*

livre sterling verte *(f)* Fr
De grünes Pfund *(n)*
En green pound
Es esterlina verde *(f)*
It sterlina verde *(f)*
Pt libra esterlina verde *(f)*

livret de compte *(m)* Fr
De Bankbuch; Sparbuch *(n)*
En passbook
Am bankbook
Es libreta de banco *(f)*
It libretto di conto *(m)*
Pt livrete de conta *(m)*

livrete de conta *(m)* Pt
De Bankbuch; Sparbuch *(n)*
En passbook
Am bankbook
Es libreta de banco *(f)*
Fr livret de compte *(m)*
It libretto di conto *(m)*

livro de caixa *(m)* Pt
De Kassenbuch *(n)*
En cash book
Es libro de caja *(m)*
Fr livre de caisse *(m)*
It libro cassa *(m)*

livro de cheques *(m)* Pt
De Scheckheft *(n)*
En cheque book
Am check book
Es libro de cheques *(m)*
Fr carnet de chèques;
    chéquier *(m)*
It libretto assegni *(m)*

livro de consulta *(m)* Pt
De Nachschlagewerk *(n)*
En reference book
Es libro de consulta *(m)*
Fr ouvrage de référence *(m)*
It libro di consultazione *(m)*

livro de contas *(m)* Pt
De Kontobuch *(n)*
En account book
Es libro de cuentas *(m)*
Fr livre de comptes *(m)*
It libro di conti *(m)*

livro de encomendas *(m)* Pt
De Auftragsbuch *(n)*
En order book
Es libro de pedidos *(m)*
Fr livre de commandes *(m)*
It libro degli ordini *(m)*

livro-mestre *(m)* Pt
De Hauptbuch *(n)*
En ledger
Es libro mayor *(m)*
Fr grand livre *(m)*
It libro mastro *(m)*

livro-mestre de compras
    (m) Pt
De Einkaufsbuch *(n)*
En bought ledger
Am purchase book
Es libro mayor de compras
    (m)
Fr grand livre d'achats *(m)*
It mastro acquisti *(m)*

livro-mestre de vendas *(m)*
Pt
De Verkaufskontenbuch *(n)*
En sales ledger

Es libro mayor de ventas *(m)*
Fr grand livre des ventes *(m)*
It partitario delle vendite *(m)*

livros de contabilidade *(m pl)*
Pt
De Geschäftsbücher *(n pl)*
En books of account
Es libros de cuentas *(m pl)*
Fr livres comptables *(m pl)*
It libri contabili *(m pl)*

llamada (de fondos) *(f)* n Es
De Kündigung (von Geldern)
    (f)
En call (for funds)
Fr appel (de fonds) *(m)*
It richiesta (di fondi) *(f)*
Pt chamada (de fundos) *(f)*

llamada interurbana *(f)* Es
De Ferngespräch *(n)*
En trunk call
Am long distance call
Fr appel téléphonique inter-
    urbain *(m)*
It comunicazione interurba-
    na *(f)*
Pt chamada inter-urbana
    (troncas) *(f)*

llamada telefónica *(f)* Es
De Anruf *(m)*
En telephone call
Fr appel téléphonique *(m)*
It chiamata telefonica *(f)*
Pt chamada telefónica *(f)*

llano *adj* Es
De flach
En flat
Fr plat; uniforme
It piatto
Pt plano; liso

llave *(f)* n Es
De Schlüssel *(m)*
En key
Fr clef *(f)*
It chiave *(f)*
Pt chave *(f)*

llegada *(f)* n Es
De Ankunft *(f)*
En arrival
Fr arrivée *(f)*
It arrivo *(m)*
Pt chegada *(f)*

lleno adj Es
De voll
En full
Fr plein
It pieno
Pt cheio

llevar la contabilidad Es
De Konto führen
En keep the account
Fr tenir la comptabilité
It tenere la contabilità
Pt fazer a contabilidade

loading n En
De Ladung (f)
Es carga (f)
Fr chargement (m)
It caricamento (m)
Pt carregamento (m)

loadline n En
De Ladelinie (f)
Es línea de carga (f)
Fr ligne de charge (f)
It linea di carico (f)
Pt linha limite de carga (f)

loan n En
De Anleihe (f)
Es empréstito (m)
Fr emprunt (m)
It prestito (m)
Pt empréstimo (m)

loan account En
De Anleihekonto (n)
Es cuenta de préstamos (f)
Fr compte des prêts (m)
It conto anticipazioni (m)
Pt conta de empréstimos (f)

loan stock En
De Anleihewerte (m pl)
Es títulos de préstamo (m pl)
Fr titres d'emprunt (m pl)
It titoli di prestito (m pl)
Pt títulos de empréstimo
(m pl)

locataire (m) n Fr
De Mieter (m)
En tenant; hirer; lessee
Es inquilino; alquilador; ar-
rendatario (m)
It affittuario; locatario; no-
leggiatore (m)
Pt inquilino; alugador; arren-
datário (m)

locatario (m) n It
De Mieter (m)
En lessee
Es arrendatario (m)
Fr locataire (m)
Pt locatário; arrendatário (m)

locatário (m) n Pt
De Mieter (m)
En lessee
Es arrendatario (m)
Fr locataire (m)
It locatario (m)

location-vente (f) n Fr
De Ratenkauf (m)
En hire-purchase
Es compra a plazos (f)
It vendita a rate (f)
Pt venda a prestações (f)

locatore (m) n It
De Vermieter (m)
En lessor
Es arrendador (m)
Fr bailleur (m)
Pt senhorio; arrendador (m)

Lochkarte (f) n De
En punched card
Es tarjeta perforada (f)
Fr carte perforée (f)
It scheda perforata (f)
Pt ficha perfurada (f)

lock-out n En, Fr (m)
De Aussperrung (f)
Es cierre (m)
It serrata (f)
Pt lockout (m)

lockout (m) n Pt
De Aussperrung (f)
En lock-out
Es cierre (m)
Fr lock-out (m)
It serrata (f)

lodge n Am
En friendly society
De Versicherungsverein auf
Gegenseitigkeit (m)
Es sociedad de socorro mu-
tuo (f)
Fr société de secours mutuel
(f)
It società di mutuo soccorso
(f)
Pt mutualidade (f)

lodo arbitrale (m) It
De Schiedsspruch (m)
En arbitration award
Es sentencia arbitral (f)
Fr sentence arbitrale (f)
Pt decisão de arbitragem (f)

log (ship's) n En
De Log (n)
Es diario de navegación (m)
Fr journal de navigation (m)
It solcometro (m)
Pt diário de bordo (m)

Log (n) n De
En log
Es diario de navegación (m)
Fr journal de navigation (m)
It solcometro (m)
Pt diário de bordo (m)

logic n En
De Logik (f)
Es lógica (f)
Fr logique (f)
It logica (f)
Pt lógica (f)

lógica (f) n Es, Pt
De Logik (f)
En logic
Fr logique (f)
It logica (f)

logica (f) n It
De Logik (f)
En logic
Es lógica (f)
Fr logique (f)
Pt lógica (f)

Logik (f) n De
En logic
Es lógica (f)
Fr logique (f)
It logica (f)
Pt lógica (f)

logique (f) n Fr
De Logik (f)
En logic
Es lógica (f)
It logica (f)
Pt lógica (f)

logística (f) n Es, Pt
De Logistik (f)
En logistics

Fr logistique (f)
It logistica (f)

logistica (f) n It
De Logistik (f)
En logistics
Es logística (f)
Fr logistique (f)
Pt logística (f)

logistics n En
De Logistik (f)
Es logística (f)
Fr logistique (f)
It logistica (t)
Pt logística (f)

Logistik (f) n De
En logistics
Es logística (f)
Fr logistique (f)
It logistica (f)
Pt logística (f)

logistique (f) n Fr
De Logistik (f)
En logistics
Es logística (f)
It logistica (f)
Pt logística (f)

logorio naturale (m) It
De natürliche Abnützung (f)
En wear and tear
Es desgaste natural (m)
Fr usure normale (f)
Pt desgaste (m)

Lohn (m) n De
En wage
Es salario (m)
Fr salaire (m)
It salario (m)
Pt salário (m)

Lohnbeschränkung (f) n De
En wage restraint
Es restricción de salario (f)
Fr contrainte sur les salaires (f)
It restrizioni sui salari (f pl)
Pt restrição de salários (f)

Lohnbuch (m) n De
En payroll
Es nómina de pago (f)
Fr feuille de paie (f)
It libro paga (m)
Pt folha de salários (f)

Lohnempfänger (m) n De
En wage earner
Es asalariado (m)
Fr salarié (m)
It salariato (m)
Pt assalariado (m)

Lohnforderung (f) n De
En wage claim
Es reclamación de salario (f)
Fr revendication de salaire (f)
It rivendicazione salariale (f)
Pt demanda de salário (f)

Lohnkosten (pl) n De
En cost of labour
Es coste de la mano de obra (m)
Fr coût de la main-d'œuvre (m)
It costo di mano d'opera (m)
Pt custo da mão de obra (m)

Lohnnachzahlung (f) n De
En back pay
Es pago atrasado (m)
Fr rappel de traitement (m)
It arretrati di paga (m pl)
Pt vencimento atrasado (m)

Lohnpolitik (f) n De
En incomes policy
Es plan de renta (m)
Fr politique des salaires (f)
It politica dei redditi (f)
Pt programa salários (m)

Lohnsatz (m) n De
En wage rate
Es tarifa de salarios (f)
Fr taux des salaires (m)
It tariffa salariale (f)
Pt base salarial (f)

Lohnstopp (m) n De
En wage-freeze
Es bloqueo de salarios (m)
Fr blocage des salaires (m)
It blocco dei salari (m)
Pt congelação de salários (f)

Lohnsummensteuer (f) n De
En employment tax
Es impuesto por empleado (m)
Fr taxe sur l'emploi (f)
It imposta sull'impiego (f)
Pt imposto sobre emprego (m)

Lohnvereinbarung (f) n De
En wages agreement
Es acuerdo sobre salarios (m)
Fr convention des salaires (f)
It accordo sui salari (m)
Pt acordo sobre salários (m)

loi (f) n Fr
De Recht (n)
En law
Es ley (f)
It legge (f)
Pt lei (f)

loisir (m) n Fr
De Freizeit (f)
En leisure
Es descanso (m)
It svago (m)
Pt lazer (m)

loja (f) n Pt
De Laden (m)
En shop
Es tienda (f)
Fr magasin (m)
It bottega (f)

long-dated adj En
De langfristig
Es a largo plazo
Fr à longue échéance
It a lunga scadenza
Pt a longo prazo

long distance call Am
En trunk call
De Ferngespräch (n)
Es llamada interurbana (f)
Fr appel téléphonique inter-urbain (m)
It comunicazione interurba-na (f)
Pt chamada inter-urbana (f)

longshoreman n Am
En docker
De Hafenarbeiter (m)
Es cargador de muelle (m)
Fr docker (m)
It lavoratore del porto (m)
Pt trabalhador das docas (m)

long-term adj En
De langfristig
Es a largo plazo
Fr à longue terme
It a lunga scadenza
Pt a longo prazo

long-term capital En
De langfristiges Kapital (n)
Es capital a largo plazo (m)
Fr capitaux à long terme
(m pl)
It capitale consolidato a lun-
ga scadenza (m)
Pt capital a longo prazo (m)

long ton En
De schwere Tonne (f)
Es tonelada inglesa (f)
Fr tonne forte (f)
It tonnellata inglese (f)
Pt tonelada inglesa (f)

lordo adj It
De brutto
En gross
Es bruto
Fr brut; gros
Pt bruto

Löschen der Ladung (n) De
En breaking bulk
Es fraccionamiento de la car-
ga (m)
Fr rupture de charge (f)
It inizio scarico (m)
Pt retalhar a carga

Löschpapier (n) n De
En blotting paper
Es papel secante (m)
Fr papier buvard (m)
It carta assorbente (f)
Pt papel mata-borrão (m)

Löschungskonto (n) n De
En landing account
Es cuenta de desembarque (f)
Fr compte de mise à terre (m)
It conto di sbarco (m)
Pt conta de descargas (f)

loss (n) En
De Verlust (m)
Es pérdida (f)
Fr perte (f)
It perdita (f)
Pt perda (f)

loss of profits En
De Gewinnausfall (m)
Es lucro cesante (m)
Fr perte de bénéfices (f)
It perdita di utili (f)
Pt perda de lucros (f)

lot (m) n Fr
De Stoß (m)
En batch
Es lote (m)
It lotto (m)
Pt lote (m)

lote (m) n Es, Pt
De Stoß (m)
En batch
Fr lot (m)
It lotto (m)

lote avulso (m) Pt
De Restpartie (f)
En odd lot
Es lote suelto (m)
Fr solde (m)
It partita spaiata (f)

lote suelto (m) Es
De Restpartie (f)
En odd lot
Fr solde (m)
It partita spaiata (f)
Pt lote avulso (m)

Lotse (m) n De
En (maritime) pilot
Es piloto (m)
Fr pilote (m)
It pilota (m)
Pt piloto (m)

lotto (m) n It
De Stoß (m)
En batch
Es lote (m)
Fr lot (m)
Pt lote (m)

louer vb Fr
De mieten; vermieten
En hire; rent
Es alquilar
It noleggiare; affittare
Pt alugar

lourd adj Fr
De schwer
En heavy
Es pesado
It pesante
Pt pesado

lourde perte (f) Fr
De schwere Verluste (m pl)
En heavy loss

Es fuerte pérdida; pérdida
sensible (f)
It forte perdita (f)
Pt perda avultada (f)

low-grade adj En
De minderwertig
Es baja calidad
Fr de qualité inférieure
It di qualità inferiore
Pt baixo-nível

loyer (m) n Fr
De Miete (f)
En rent
Es alquiler (m)
It pigione; affitto (f m)
Pt renda (f)

lucratif adj Fr
De einträglich; gewinnbrin-
gend
En lucrative
Es lucrativo
It lucrativo
Pt lucrativo

lucrative adj En
De einträglich; gewinnbrin-
gend
Es lucrativo
Fr lucratif
It lucrativo
Pt lucrativo

lucrativo adj Es, It, Pt
De einträglich; gewinnbrin-
gend
En lucrative
Fr lucratif

lucro (m) n Es, Pt
De Gewinn (m)
En profit
Fr bénéfice; profit (m)
It utile; profitto (m)

lucro bruto (m) Pt
De Bruttogewinn (m)
En gross profit
Es ganancia bruta (f)
Fr bénéfice brut (m)
It utile lordo (m)

lucro cesante (m) Es
De Gewinnausfall (m)
En loss of profits
Fr perte de bénéfices (f)
It perdita di utili (f)
Pt perda de lucros (f)

lucro líquido *(m)* Pt
De Reingewinn *(m)*
En net profit
Es ganancia neta *(f)*
Fr bénéfice net *(m)*
It utile netto *(m)*

lucros de capital *(m pl)* Pt
De Kapitalgewinn *(n)*
En capital gains
Es beneficios sobre capital *(m pl)*
Fr gains en capital *(m pl)*
It plusvalore di capitale *(m pl)*

lucros não distribuidos *(m pl)* Pt
De unverteilte Gewinne *(n pl)*
En undistributed profits
Es beneficios no distribuidos *(m pl)*
Fr bénéfices non répartis *(m pl)*
It profitti non distribuiti *(m pl)*

lucros no papel *(m pl)* Pt
De imaginärer Gewinn *(m)*
En paper profit
Es ganancia por realizar *(f)*
Fr profit fictif *(m)*
It utile sulla carta *(m)*

Luftfracht *(f)* n De
En air freight
Es flete aéreo *(m)*
Fr fret aérien *(m)*
It trasporto aereo *(m)*
Pt frete aéreo *(m)*

Luftfrachtbrief *(m)* n De
En air waybill
Es carta de porte aéreo *(f)*
Fr lettre de transport aérien *(f)*
It nota di spedizione aerea *(f)*
Pt guia de porte aéreo *(f)*

Luftpost *(f)* n De
En airmail
Es correo aéreo *(m)*
Fr poste aérienne *(f)*
It posta aerea *(f)*
Pt correio aéreo *(m)*

Luftpostbrief *(m)* n De
En air letter
Es carta por avión *(f)*

Fr aérogramme *(m)*
It lettera aerea *(f)*
Pt carta por avião *(f)*

Luftpostempfangs-bescheinigung *(f)* n De
En airmail receipt
Es recibo aeropostal *(m)*
Fr récépissé de poste aérienne *(m)*
It ricevimento per posta aerea *(m)*
Pt recibo de via aérea *(m)*

Luftterminal *(n)* n De
En air terminal
Es terminal de aeropuerto *(f)*
Fr aérogare *(f)*
It aerostazione *(f)*
Pt estação terminal aérea *(f)*

Lufttransport *(m)* n De
En air transport
Es transporte aéreo *(m)*
Fr transport aérien *(m)*
It trasporto aereo *(m)*
Pt transporte aéreo *(m)*

Luftverkehr *(m)* n De
En air traffic
Es tráfico aéreo *(m)*
Fr trafic aérien *(m)*
It traffico aereo *(m)*
Pt tráfego aéreo *(m)*

luggage locker En
De Gepäckschließfach *(n)*
Es casilla de equipaje *(f)*
Fr coffre de bagages *(m)*
It cassetta bagaglio *(f)*
Pt depósito de bagagem individualizado *(m)*

lump sum En
De Pauschalbetrag *(m)*
Es suma global *(f)*
Fr somme globale *(f)*
It somma globale *(f)*
Pt soma por inteiro *(f)*

lunch-hour n En
De Mittagspause *(f)*
Es hora del almuerzo *(f)*
Fr heure du déjeuner *(f)*
It ora di colazione *(f)*
Pt hora do almoço *(f)*

luxury goods En
De Luxuswaren *(f pl)*
Es artículos de lujo *(m pl)*
Fr articles de luxe *(m pl)*
It articoli di lusso *(m pl)*
Pt artigos de luxo *(m pl)*

luxury tax En
De Luxussteuer *(f)*
Es impuesto de lujo *(m)*
Fr impôt de luxe *(m)*
It tassa sugli articoli di lusso *(f)*
Pt imposto de luxo *(m)*

Luxussteuer *(f)* n De
En luxury tax
Es impuesto de lujo *(m)*
Fr impôt de luxe *(m)*
It tassa sugli articoli di lusso *(f)*
Pt imposto de luxo *(m)*

Luxuswaren *(f pl)* n De
En luxury goods
Es artículos de lujo *(m pl)*
Fr articles de luxe *(m pl)*
It articoli di lusso *(m pl)*
Pt artigos de luxo *(m pl)*

M

Maat *(m)* n De
En mate
Es primer oficial *(m)*
Fr second *(m)*
It primo ufficiale *(m)*
Pt imediato *(m)*

macchina *(f)* n It
De Maschine *(f)*
En machine
Es máquina *(f)*
Fr machine *(f)*
Pt máquina *(f)*

macchina da scrivere *(f)* It
De Schreibmaschine *(f)*
En typewriter
Es máquina de escribir *(f)*
Fr machine à écrire *(f)*
Pt máquina de escrever *(f)*

**macchina per stampare
indirizzi** (f) It
De Adressiermaschine (f)
En addressing machine
Es máquina de imprimir di-
recciones (f)
Fr machine à imprimer les
adresses (f)
Pt máquina de endereços (f)

macchinario (m) n It
De Maschinerie (f)
En machinery
Es maquinaría (f)
Fr machinerie (f)
Pt maquinaria (f)

**macchina venditrice
automatica** (f) It
De Verkaufsautomat (m)
En vending machine
Es máquina expendedora (f)
Fr distributeur automatique
(m)
Pt máquina de vendas (f)

machine n En, Fr (f)
De Maschine (f)
Es máquina (f)
It macchina (f)
Pt máquina (f)

machine à additionner (f) Fr
De Addiermaschine (f)
En adding machine
Es máquina de sumar (f)
It addizionatrice (f)
Pt máquina de somar (f)

machine à affranchir (f) Fr
De Frankiermaschine (f)
En franking machine
Es máquina de franquear (f)
It affrancatrice postale (f)
Pt máquina de franquear (f)

machine à calculer (f) Fr
De Rechenmaschine (f)
En calculator
Es calculadora (f)
It calcolatrice (f)
Pt máquina de calcular (f)

machine à dictée (f) Fr
De Diktaphon (n)
En dictating machine
Es dictáfono (m)
It dittafono (m)
Pt dictafone (m)

machine à écrire (f) Fr
De Schreibmaschine (f)
En typewriter
Es máquina de escribir (f)
It macchina da scrivere (f)
Pt máquina de escrever (f)

**machine à imprimer les
adresses** (f) Fr
De Adressiermaschine (f)
En addressing machine
Es máquina de imprimir di-
recciones (f)
It macchina per stampare
indirizzi (f)
Pt máquina de endereços (f)

machine down-time En
De Maschinenstillstandzeit (f)
Es tiempo improductivo de la
máquina (m)
Fr temps de panne machine
(m)
It tempo passivo di macchi-
na (m)
Pt tempo-morto da máquina
(m)

machine language En
De Maschinensprache (f)
Es lenguaje de máquina (m)
Fr langage-machine (m)
It linguaggio di macchina (m)
Pt linguagem da máquina (f)

machinerie n (f) Fr
De Maschinerie (f)
En machinery
Es maquinaría (f)
It macchinario (m)
Pt maquinaria (f)

machinery n En
De Maschinerie (f)
Es maquinaría (f)
Fr machinerie (f)
It macchinario (m)
Pt maquinaria (f)

magasin (m) n Fr
De Laden; Lager (m n)
En shop; store
Es tienda; almacén (f m)
It bottega; magazzino (f m)
Pt loja; armazém (f m)

**magasin à succursales
multiples** (m) Fr
De Kettengeschäft (n)

En chain store
Es sucursal de cadena de al-
macenes (f)
It negozio a catena (m)
Pt sucursal de cadeia de ar-
mazéns (f)

magazzino (m) n It
De Lager; Warenlager (n)
En store; warehouse
Es almacén (m)
Fr magasin; entrepôt (m)
Pt armazém (m)

magazzino doganale (m) It
De Lager unter Zollverschluß
(n)
En bonded warehouse
Es almacén de aduanas (m)
Fr entrepôt des douanes (m)
Pt armazém alfandegário (m)

magazzinaggio (m) n It
De Lagerung (f)
En storage
Es almacenamiento (m)
Fr emmagasinage (m)
Pt armazenamento (m)

maglieria (f) n It
De Strickwaren (f pl)
En knitted goods
Es géneros de punto (m pl)
Fr bonneterie (f)
Pt artigos de malha de lã (m pl)

Magnetband (n) n De
En magnetic tape
Es cinta magnética (f)
Fr bande magnétique (f)
It nastro magnetico (m)
Pt fita magnética (f)

magnetic tape En
De Magnetband (n)
Es cinta magnética (f)
Fr bande magnétique (f)
It nastro magnetico (m)
Pt fita magnética (f)

mail (n) En
De Post (f)
Es correo (m)
Fr poste (f)
It posta (f)
Pt correio (m)

management

mail-box n Am
En letter-box
De Briefkasten (m)
Es buzón (m)
Fr boîte aux lettres (f)
It cassetta postale (f)
Pt caixa postal (f)

mail order En
De Auftrag durch die Post (m)
Es pedido por correo (m)
Fr commande par lettre (f)
It ordine per corrispondenza (f)
Pt venda pelo correio (f)

mail transfer En
De Postüberweisung (f)
Es transferencia postal (f)
Fr virement postal (m)
It traferimento per posta (m)
Pt transferência postal (f)

main-d'œuvre (f) n Fr
De Arbeitskräfte; menschliche Arbeitskraft (f pl; f)
En manpower; labour force
Es mano de obra (f)
It mano d'opera (f)
Pt mão-de-obra (f)

main-d'œuvre étrangère (f) Fr
De Fremdarbeiterschaft (f)
En foreign labour
Es mano de obra extranjera (f)
It mano d'opera straniera (f)
Pt mão-de-obra estrangeira (f)

maintenance n En
De Instandhaltung (f)
Es mantenimiento (m)
Fr entretien (m)
It manutenzione (f)
Pt manutenção (f)

mais barato Pt
De billiger
En cheaper
Es más barato
Fr meilleur marché
It meno caro

maison (f) n Fr
De Haus (n)
En house
Es casa (f)
It casa (f)
Pt casa (f)

maison d'édition (f) Fr
De Verlag (m)
En publishing house
Es casa editorial (f)
It casa editrice (f)
Pt casa editora (f)

maison d'escompte (f) Fr
De Diskontbank (f)
En discount house
Es casa de descuentos (f)
It banca di sconto (f)
Pt agência corretora de descontos (f)

maison de commerce (f) Fr
De Firma (f)
En business; firm
Es casa de comercio (f)
It casa commerciale (f)
Pt casa de comércio (f)

maison solide (f) Fr
De alteingeführtes Geschäft (n)
En old-established business
Es casa sólida (f)
It casa di vecchia fondazione (f)
Pt empresa de há muito estabelecida (f)

majority holding En
De Mehrheitsbeteiligung (f)
Es tenencia de acciones por mayoría (f)
Fr participation majoritaire (f)
It partecipazione maggioritaria (f)
Pt propriedade em maioria (f)

make a counteroffer En
De ein Gegenangebot abgeben
Es hacer una contraoferta
Fr faire une contre-offre
It fare una controfferta
Pt fazer uma contra-proposta

make an appointment En
De eine Verabredung treffen
Es hacer una cita
Fr prendre un rendez-vous
It fissare un appuntamento
Pt marcar um encontro

make an offer En
De eine Offerte machen
Es hacer una oferta
Fr faire une offre
It fare una offerta
Pt fazer uma oferta

Makler (m) n De
En broker
Es corredor (m)
Fr courtier (m)
It sensale (m)
Pt corretor (m)

Makler für Verbrauchsgüter (m) De
En commodity broker
Es corredor de mercaderías (m)
Fr courtier en marchandises (m)
It sensale di merci (m)
Pt corretor de mercadorias (m)

Maklergebühr (f) n De
En brokerage
Es corretaje (m)
Fr courtage (m)
It senseria (f)
Pt corretagem (f)

maklergebührenfrei De
En free of commission
Es franco-comisión
Fr franco courtage
It franco mediazione
Pt isento de comissão

malhonnête adj Fr
De unehrlich
En dishonest
Fr deshonesto
It disonesto
Pt desonesto

malversatore (m) n It
De Veruntreuer (m)
En embezzler
Es defalcador (m)
Fr détourneur (m)
Pt desfalcador (m)

management n En
De Vorstand (m)
Es dirección (f)
Fr administration; gestion (f)

It direzione; amministrazione *(f)*
Pt gerência; direcção *(f)*

management consultant En
De Geschäftsführungsberater
(m)
Es asesor administrativo *(m)*
Fr ingénieur-conseil en or-
ganisation *(m)*
It consulente di direzione
aziendale *(m)*
Pt perito de administração *(m)*

manager *n* En
De Geschäftsleiter *(m)*
Es director *(m)*
Fr directeur *(m)*
It direttore *(m)*
Pt gerente; director *(m)*

managing director En
Am president
De geschäftsleitender Direk-
tor *(m)*
Es director gerente *(m)*
Fr administrateur délégué *(m)*
It amministratore delegato
(m)
Pt director geral *(m)*

mañana *adv* Es
De morgen
En tomorrow
Fr demain
It domani
Pt amanhã

mancanza *(f)* *n* It
De Nichteinhaltung *(f)*
En default
Es falta *(f)*
Fr défaillance; défaut *(f m)*
Pt falta *(f)*

mancare *vb* It
De versagen; durchfallen
En fail
Es fallar; faltar
Fr échouer; faillir
Pt falhar; faltar

mancata accettazione *(f)* It
De Nichtannahme *(f)*
En nonacceptance
Es rechazo *(m)*
Fr non-acceptation *(f)*
Pt não-aceitação *(f)*

mancato pagamento *(m)* It
De Nichtzahlung *(f)*
En failure to pay
Es falta de pago *(f)*
Fr défaut de paiement *(m)*
Pt falte de pagamento *(f)*

mancia *(f)* *n* It
De Trinkgeld *(n)*
En tip; gratuity
Es propina *(f)*
Fr pourboire *(m)*
Pt gorjeta *(f)*

mandant *(m)* *n* Fr
De Vollmachtgeber *(m)*
En principal
Es mandante *(m)*
It mandante *(m)*
Pt mandante *(m)*

mandante *(m)* *n* Es, It, Pt
De Vollmachtgeber *(m)*
En principal
Fr mandant *(m)*

mandante não divulgado *(m)*
Pt
De nicht bekanntgegebener
Auftraggeber *(m)*
En undisclosed principal
Es mandante no nombrado
(m)
Fr mandant non divulgé *(m)*
It mandante non nominato
(m)

mandante non nominato *(m)*
It
De nicht bekanntgegebener
Auftraggeber *(m)*
En undisclosed principal
Es mandante no nombrado
(m)
Fr mandant non divulgé *(m)*
Pt mandante não divulgado
(m)

mandante no nombrado *(m)*
Es
De nicht bekanntgegebener
Auftraggeber *(m)*
En undisclosed principal
Fr mandant non divulgé *(m)*
It mandante non nominato
(m)
Pt mandante não divulgado
(m)

mandant non divulgé *(m)* Fr
De nicht bekanntgegebener
Auftraggeber *(m)*
En undisclosed principal
Es mandante no nombrado
(m)
It mandante non nominato
(m)
Pt mandante não divulgado
(m)

mandat *(m)* *n* Fr
De Vollmacht; Vertretung *(f)*
En authority; agency
Es autoridad; mandato *(f m)*
It autorità; mandato *(f m)*
Pt autoridade; mandato *(f m)*

mandataire *(m)* *n* Fr
De Bevollmächtigte(r) *(m)*
En attorney
Es apoderado *(m)*
It mandatario *(m)*
Pt procurador *(m)*

mandatario *(m)* *n* It
De Bevollmächtigte(r) *(m)*
En attorney
Es apoderado *(m)*
Fr mandataire *(m)*
Pt procurador *(m)*

mandato *(m)* *n* Es, It, Pt
De Vertretung; Befugnis *(f)*
En legal agency; warrant
Fr mandat; ordonnance *(m f)*

mandat-poste *(m)* *n* Fr
De Postanweisung *(f)*
En postal order
Es giro postal *(m)*
It vaglia postale *(f)*
Pt vale postal *(m)*

Mangel *(m)* *n* De
En deficiency; defect
Es deficiencia; defecto *(f m)*
Fr manque; défaut *(m)*
It ammanco; difetto *(m)*
Pt deficiência; defeito *(f m)*

mangelhafte Lieferung *(f)* De
En short delivery
Es entrega deficiente *(f)*
Fr livraison incomplète *(f)*
It consegna deficiente *(f)*
Pt entrega insuficiente *(f)*

man-hours *n pl* En
De Arbeitsstunde pro Mann *(f)*
Es horas-hombre *(f pl)*
Fr heures-homme *(f pl)*
It ore-uomo *(f pl)*
Pt horas-homem *(f pl)*

manifest *n* En
De Ladungsverzeichnis *(n)*
Es manifiesto *(m)*
Fr manifeste *(m)*
It manifesto *(m)*
Pt manifesto *(m)*

manifeste *(m) n* Fr
De Ladungsverzeichnis *(n)*
En manifest
Es manifiesto *(m)*
It manifesto *(m)*
Pt manifesto *(m)*

manifesto *(m) n* It, Pt
De Ladungsverzeichnis *(n)*
En manifest
Es manifiesto *(m)*
Fr manifeste *(m)*

manifiesto *(m) n* Es
De Ladungsverzeichnis *(n)*
En manifest
Fr manifeste *(m)*
It manifesto *(m)*
Pt manifesto *(m)*

manipolazione *(f) n* It
De Schiebung *(f)*
En manipulation
Es manipulación *(f)*
Fr manipulation *(f)*
Pt manipulação *(f)*

manipulação *(f) n* Pt
De Schiebung *(f)*
En manipulation
Es manipulación *(f)*
Fr manipulation *(f)*
It manipulazione *(f)*

manipulación *(f) n* Es
De Schiebung *(f)*
En manipulation
Fr manipulation *(f)*
It manipulazione *(f)*
Pt manipulação *(f)*

manipulation *n* En, Fr *(f)*
De Schiebung *(f)*
Es manipulación *(f)*

It manipulazione *(f)*
Pt manipulação *(f)*

Mannschaft (eines Schiffes)
(f) n De
En crew
Es tripulación *(f)*
Fr équipage *(m)*
It equipaggio *(m)*
Pt tripulação *(f)*

mano de obra *(f)* Es
De Arbeitskräfte; menschliche
   Arbeitskraft *(f pl; f)*
En manpower; labour force
Fr main-d'œuvre *(f)*
It mano d'opera *(f)*
Pt mão-de-obra *(f)*

mano de obra extranjera *(f)*
   Es
De Fremdarbeiterschaft *(f)*
En foreign labour
Fr main-d'œuvre étrangère *(f)*
It mano d'opera straniera *(f)*
Pt mão-de-obra estrangeira
   (f)

mano d'opera *(f)* It
De Arbeitskräfte; menschliche
   Arbeitskraft *(f pl; f)*
En manpower; labour force
Es mano de obra *(f)*
Fr main-d'œuvre *(f)*
Pt mão-de-obra *(f)*

mano d'opera straniera *(f)* It
De Fremdarbeiterschaft *(f)*
En foreign labour
Es mano de obra extranjera *(f)*
Fr main-d'œuvre étrangère *(f)*
Pt mão-de-obra estrangeira
   (f)

manomètre *(m) n* Fr
De Druckmesser *(m)*
En pressure gauge
Es manómetro *(m)*
It manometro *(m)*
Pt manómetro *(m)*

manómetro *(m) n* Es, Pt
De Druckmesser *(m)*
En pressure gauge
Fr manomètre; jauge de
   pression *(m f)*
It manometro *(m)*

manometro *(m) n* It
De Druckmesser *(m)*
En pressure gauge
Es manómetro *(m)*
Fr manomètre; jauge de
   pression *(m f)*
Pt manómetro *(m)*

manpower *n* En
De Manneskraft *(f)*
Es mano de obra *(f)*
Fr main-d'œuvre *(f)*
It mano d'opera *(f)*
Pt mão-de-obra *(f)*

manquant *(m) n* Fr
De Abwesende(r) *(m)*
En absentee
Es ausente *(m)*
It assente *(m)*
Pt ausente *(m)*

manque *(m) n* Fr
De Mangel *(m)*
En deficiency
Es deficiencia *(f)*
It ammanco; insufficienza
   (m f)
Pt deficiência *(f)*

manque de pratique *(m)* Fr
De Unerfahrenheit *(f)*
En inexperience
Es falta de experiencia *(f)*
It inesperienza *(f)*
Pt inexperiência *(f)*

mantenimiento *(m) n* Es
De Instandhaltung *(f)*
En maintenance
Fr entretien *(m)*
It manutenzione *(f)*
Pt manutenção *(f)*

manter *vb* Pt
De behalten; unterhalten
En keep; maintain
Es tener; conservar
Fr tenir; maintenir
It tenere; mantenere

manual *n* En; Es, Pt *(m)*
De Handbuch *(n)*
Fr manuel *(m)*
It manuale *(m)*

manual *adj* En, Es, Pt
De Hand-
Fr manuel
It manuale

manuale *(m) n* It
De Handbuch *(n)*
En handbook
Es manual *(m)*
Fr manuel *(m)*
Pt manual *(m)*

manuale *adj* It
De Hand-
En manual
Es manual
Fr manuel
Pt manual

manuel *(m) n* Fr
De Handbuch *(n)*
En handbook
Es manual *(m)*
It manuale *(m)*
Pt manual *(m)*

manuel *adj* Fr
De Hand-
En manual
Es manual
It manuale
Pt manual

manueller Locher *(m)* De
En key-punch
Es perforación en clave *(f)*
Fr perforatrice à clavier *(f)*
It perforatore *(f)*
Pt perfurador *(m)*

manufacturer *n* En
De Erzeuger; Hersteller *(m)*
Es fabricante *(m)*
Fr fabricant *(m)*
It fabbricante *(m)*
Pt fabricante *(m)*

manuscrit dactylographié
(m) Fr
De Maschinenschrift *(f)*
En typescript
Es texto mecanografiado *(m)*
It dattiloscritto *(m)*
Pt texto dactilografado *(m)*

manutenção *(f) n* Pt
De Instandhaltung *(f)*
En maintenance
Es mantenimiento *(m)*
Fr entretien *(m)*
It manutenzione *(f)*

manutenzione *(f) n* It
De Instandhaltung *(f)*
En maintenance
Es mantenimiento *(m)*
Fr entretien *(m)*
Pt manutenção *(f)*

mão-de-obra *(f) n* Pt
De menschliche Arbeitskraft
(f)
En manpower
Es mano de obra *(f)*
Fr main-d'œuvre *(f)*
It mano d'opera *(f)*

mão-de-obra estrangeira *(f)*
Pt
De Fremdarbeiterschaft *(f)*
En foreign labour
Es mano de obra extranjera *(f)*
Fr main-d'œuvre étrangère *(f)*
It mano d'opera straniera *(f)*

Mappe *(f) n* De
En folder
Es carpeta *(f)*
Fr chemise *(f)*
It cartella *(f)*
Pt pasta *(f)*

máquina *(f) n* Es, Pt
De Maschine *(f)*
En machine
Fr machine *(f)*
It macchina *(f)*

máquina de calcular *(f)* Pt
De Rechenmaschine *(f)*
En calculator
Es calculadora *(f)*
Fr machine à calculer *(f)*
It calcolatrice *(f)*

máquina de endereços *(f)* Pt
De Adressiermaschine *(f)*
En addressing machine
Es máquina de imprimir di-
recciones *(f)*
Fr machine à imprimer les
adresses *(f)*
It macchina per stampare
indirizzi *(f)*

máquina de escrever *(f)* Pt
De Schreibmaschine *(f)*
En typewriter
Es máquina de escribir *(f)*
Fr machine à écrire *(f)*
It macchina da scrivere *(f)*

máquina de escribir *(f)* Es
De Schreibmaschine *(f)*
En typewriter
Fr machine à écrire *(f)*
It macchina da scrivere *(f)*
Pt máquina de escrever *(f)*

máquina de franquear *(f)* Es,
Pt
De Frankiermaschine *(f)*
En franking machine
Fr machine à affranchir *(f)*
It affrancatrice postale *(f)*

**máquina de imprimir
direcciones** *(f)* Es
De Adressiermaschine *(f)*
En addressing machine
Fr machine à imprimer les
adresses *(f)*
It macchina per stampare
indirizzi *(f)*
Pt máquina de endereços *(f)*

máquina de somar *(f)* Pt
De Addiermaschine *(f)*
En adding machine
Es máquina de sumar *(f)*
Fr machine à additionner *(f)*
It addizionatrice *(f)*

máquina de sumar *(f)* Es
De Addiermaschine *(f)*
En adding machine
Fr machine à additionner *(f)*
It addizionatrice *(f)*
Pt máquina de somar *(f)*

máquina de vendas *(f)* Pt
De Verkaufsautomat *(m)*
En vending machine
Es máquina expendedora *(f)*
Fr distributeur automatique
(m)
It macchina venditrice au-
tomatica *(f)*

máquina expendedora *(f)* Es
De Verkaufsautomat *(m)*
En vending machine
Fr distributeur automatique
(m)
It macchina venditrice au-
tomatica *(f)*
Pt máquina de vendas *(f)*

maquinaría *(f) n* Es
De Maschinerie *(f)*
En machinery

Fr machinerie (f)
It macchinario (m)
Pt maquinaria (f)

maquinaria (f) n Pt
De Maschinerie (f)
En machinery
Es maquinaría (f)
Fr machinerie (f)
It macchinario (m)

mar (m) n Es, Pt
De See (f)
En sea
Fr mer (f)
It mare (m)

marca (f) n Es, It, Pt
De Marke (f)
En brand
Fr marque (f)

marca de destino (f) Es
De Benennung des Bestim-
mungshafens (f)
En port mark
Fr marque de destination (f)
It marche di destinazione
(f pl)
Pt marca de porto (f)

marca de fábrica (f) Es
De Warenzeichen (n)
En trademark
Fr marque de fabrique (f)
It marchio di fabbrica (m)
Pt marca de fábrica (f)

marca de fábrica (f) Pt
De Warenzeichen (n)
En trademark
Es marca de fábrica (f)
Fr marque de fabrique (f)
It marchio di fabbrica (m)

marca de garantia (f) Pt
De Feingehaltsstempel (m)
En hall-mark
Es punzón de garantía (m)
Fr poinçon de titre (m)
It punzonatura di garanzia (f)

marca de porto (f) Pt
De Benennung des Bestim-
mungshafens (f)
En port mark
Es marca de destino (f)
Fr marque de destination (f)
It marche di destinazione
(f pl)

marca di punta (f) It
De führende Marke (f)
En brand leader
Es marca directriz (f)
Fr marque de point (f)
Pt marca mais cotada (f)

marca directriz (f) Es
De führende Marke (f)
En brand leader
Fr marque de point (f)
It marca di punta (f)
Pt marca mais cotada (f)

marca mais cotada (f) Pt
De führende Marke (f)
En brand leader
Es marca directriz (f)
Fr marque de point (f)
It marca di punta (f)

marcar um encontro Pt
De eine Verabredung treffen
En make an appointment
Es hacer una cita
Fr prendre un rendez-vous
It fissare un appuntamento

marchand de titres (m) Fr
De Börsenhändler (m)
En stockjobber
Es agiotista (m)
It aggiotatore (m)
Pt agiota (m)

marchander vb Fr
De feilschen
En haggle
Am bargain
Es regatear
It mercanteggiare; cavillare
Pt regatear

marchandise (f) n Fr
De Gut; Ware (n f)
En commodity; merchandise
Es mercadería; mercancía (f)
It merce; prodotto (f m)
Pt mercadoria; produto (f m)

marchandises (f pl) n Fr
De Güter (n pl)
En goods
Es mercancías (f pl)
It merce (f)
Pt mercadorias (f pl)

marchandises à condition
(f pl) Fr
De Probegüter (n pl)
En goods on approval
Es mercancías sujetas a
aprobación (f pl)
It merce soggetta ad appro-
vazione (f)
Pt artigos sujeitos a apro-
vação (m pl)

marchandises avariées (f pl)
Fr
De beschädigte Waren (f pl)
En damaged goods
Es mercancías averiadas (f pl)
It merce avariata (f)
Pt mercadorias danificadas
(f pl)

marchandises dangereuses
(f pl) Fr
De gefährliche Waren (f pl)
En dangerous goods
Es mercancías peligrosas
(f pl)
It merce pericolosa (f)
Pt mercadorias perigosas
(f pl)

marchandises de retour (f pl)
Fr
De Retourware (f)
En returned goods
Es mercancías devueltas (f pl)
It merce di ritorno (f pl)
Pt mercadorias devolvidas (f
pl)

marchandises disponibles
(f pl) Fr
De sofort lieferbare Waren
(f pl)
En spot goods
Es mercancías prontas (f pl)
It merce pronta (f)
Pt mercadorias prontas (f pl)

marchandises en douane
(f pl) Fr
De Waren unter Zollverschluß
(f pl)
En bonded goods
Es mercancías en aduana
(f pl)
It merci sotto vincolo doganale (f pl)
Pt mercadorias à ordem da
alfândega (f pl)

marchandises en magasin
(f pl) Fr
De Vorrat auf Lager *(m)*
En stock in hand
Es mercancías en almacén *(f pl)*
It merce in magazzino *(f)*
Pt mercadorias em existência *(f pl)*

marchandises périssables *(f pl)* Fr
De leicht verderbliche Waren *(f pl)*
En perishable goods
Es mercancías perecederas *(f pl)*
It merci deperibili *(f pl)*
Pt mercadorias perecíveis *(f pl)*

marché *(m)* n Fr
De Markt; Handel *(m)*
En market; deal
Es mercado; negocio *(m)*
It mercato; affare *(m)*
Pt mercado; negócio *(m)*

marché à terme *(m)* Fr
De Terminmarkt *(m)*
En futures market
Es mercado de futuros *(m)*
It mercato a termine *(m)*
Pt mercado de futuros *(m)*

marché commercial *(m)* Fr
De Warenmarkt *(m)*
En produce market
Es mercado de productos *(m)*
It mercato commerciale *(m)*
Pt mercado de produtos *(m)*

marché commun *(m)* Fr
De gemeinsamer Markt *(m)*
En Common Market
Es mercado común *(m)*
It mercato comune *(m)*
Pt mercado comum *(m)*

marché de l'escompte *(m)* Fr
De Diskontmarkt *(m)*
En discount market
Es mercado de descuentos *(m)*
It mercato di sconto *(m)*
Pt mercado de desconto *(m)*

marché de matières premières *(m)* Fr
De Rohstoffmarkt *(m)*
En commodity market
Es mercado de materias primas *(m)*
It mercato di materie prime *(m)*
Pt mercado de matérias primas *(m)*

marché des valeurs *(m)* Fr
De Aktienmarkt *(m)*
En share market
Am stock market
Es mercado de valores *(m)*
It mercato azionario *(m)*
Pt mercado de acções *(m)*

marche di destinazione *(f pl)* It
De Benennung des Bestimmungshafens *(f)*
En port mark
Es marca de destino *(f)*
Fr marque de destination *(f)*
Pt marca de porto *(f)*

marché du travail *(m)* Fr
De Arbeitsmarkt *(m)*
En labour market
Es mercado de mano de obra *(m)*
It mercato della mano d'opera *(m)*
Pt mercado de mão-de-obra *(m)*

marché exclusif *(m)* Fr
De ausschließlicher Markt *(m)*
En exclusive market
Es mercado exclusivo *(m)*
It mercato esclusivo *(m)*
Pt mercado exclusivo *(m)*

marché fermé *(m)* Fr
De gesperrter Markt *(m)*
En closed market
Es mercado cerrado *(m)*
It mercato chiuso *(m)*
Pt mercado fechado *(m)*

marché global *(m)* Fr
De Globalgeschäft *(n)*
En package deal
Es contrato global *(m)*
It contratto globale *(m)*
Pt contrato global *(m)*

marché libre *(m)* Fr
De freier Markt *(m)*
En open market
Es mercado libre *(m)*
It mercato libero *(m)*
Pt mercado livre *(m)*

marché monétaire *(m)* Fr
De Geldmarkt *(m)*
En money market
Es mercado de dinero *(m)*
It mercato di denaro *(m)*
Pt mercado monetário

marché noir *(m)* Fr
De schwarzer Markt *(m)*
En black market
Es mercado negro *(m)*
It mercato nero *(m)*
Pt mercado negro *(m)*

marché orienté à la baisse *(m)* Fr
De Baissemarkt *(m)*
En bear market; falling market
Es mercado bajista *(m)*
It mercato tendente al ribasso *(m)*
Pt mercado de tendência baixista *(m)*

marché orienté à la hausse *(m)* Fr
De Haussemarkt *(m)*
En bull market
Es mercado alcista *(m)*
It mercato tendente al rialzo *(m)*
Pt mercado de tendência altista *(m)*

marchio di fabbrica *(m)* It
De Warenzeichen *(n)*
En trademark
Es marca de fábrica *(f)*
Fr marque de fabrique *(f)*
Pt marca de fábrica *(f)*

mare *(m)* n It
De See *(f)*
En sea
Es mar *(m)*
Fr mer *(f)*
Pt mar *(m)*

marge *(f)* n Fr
De Spanne *(f)*
En margin

Es margen *(m)*
It margine *(m)*
Pt margem *(f)*

marge brute de bénéfices *(f)*
Fr
De Bruttoverdienstspanne *(f)*
En gross margin
Es márgen bruto *(m)*
It margine lordo *(m)*
Pt margem bruta *(f)*

margem *(f) n* Pt
De Spanne *(f)*
En margin
Es margen *(m)*
Fr marge *(f)*
It margine *(m)*

margem bruta *(f)* Pt
De Bruttoverdienstspanne *(f)*
En gross margin
Es márgen bruto *(m)*
Fr marge brute de bénéfices *(f)*
It margine lordo *(m)*

margem de lucro líquido *(f)* Pt
De Reingewinnspanne *(f)*
En net profit margin
Es margen de beneficio neto *(m)*
Fr marge nette de bénéfices *(f)*
It margine di utile netto *(m)*

margen *(m) n* Es
De Spanne *(f)*
En margin
Fr marge *(f)*
It margine *(m)*
Pt margem *(f)*

márgen bruto *(m)* Es
De Bruttoverdienstspanne *(f)*
En gross margin
Fr marge brute de bénéfices *(f)*
It margine lordo *(m)*
Pt margem bruta *(f)*

margen de beneficio neto *(m)* Es
De Reingewinnspanne *(m)*
En net profit margin

Fr marge nette de bénéfices *(f)*
It margine di utile netto *(m)*
Pt margem de lucro líquido *(f)*

marge nette de bénéfices *(f)*
Fr
De Reingewinnspanne *(f)*
En net profit margin
Es margen de beneficio neto *(m)*
It margine di utile netto *(m)*
Pt margem de lucro líquido *(f)*

margin *n* En
De Spanne *(f)*
Es margen *(m)*
Fr marge *(f)*
It margine *(m)*
Pt margem *(f)*

marginal analysis En
De Randanalyse *(f)*
Es análisis marginal *(m)*
Fr analyse marginale *(f)*
It analisi marginale *(f)*
Pt análise marginal *(f)*

marginal cost En
De Randkosten *(pl)*
Es coste marginal *(m)*
Fr coût marginal *(m)*
It costo marginale *(m)*
Pt custo marginal *(m)*

margine *(m) n* It
De Spanne *(f)*
En margin
Es margen *(m)*
Fr marge *(f)*
Pt margem *(f)*

margine di utile netto *(m)* It
De Reingewinnspanne *(m)*
En net profit margin
Es margen de beneficio neto *(m)*
Fr marge nette de bénéfices *(f)*
Pt margem de lucro líquido *(f)*

margine lordo *(m)* It
De Bruttoverdienstspanne *(m)*
En gross margin
Es márgen bruto *(m)*
Fr marge brute de bénéfices *(f)*
Pt margem bruta *(f)*

marine *adj* En
De See-
Es marítimo; marino
Fr maritime
It marino; marittimo
Pt marinho; marítimo

marine insurance broker En
De Seetransportversiche-
rungsmakler *(m)*
Es corredor de seguro
marítimo *(m)*
Fr courtier d'assurances maritimes *(m)*
It agente di assicurazioni
marittime *(m)*
Pt corretor de seguros
marítimos *(m)*

marinero *adj* Es
De seefest
En seaworthy
Fr en état de navigabilité
It atto a tenere il mare
Pt em condições de navegação

marinho *adj* Pt
De See-
En marine
Es marítimo; marino
Fr maritime
It marino; marittimo

marino *adj* Es, It
De See-
En marine
Fr maritime
Pt marinho; marítimo

maritime *adj* En, Fr
De See-
Es marítimo
It marittimo
Pt marítimo

marítimo *adj* Es, Pt
De See-
En maritime
Fr maritime
It marittimo

marittimo *adj* It
De See-
En maritime
Es marítimo
Fr maritime
Pt marítimo

Marke *(f)* n De
En brand
Es marca *(f)*
Fr marque *(f)*
It marca *(f)*
Pt marca *(f)*

Markenwaren *(f pl)* n De
En branded goods
Es artículos de marca *(m pl)*
Fr articles de marque *(m pl)*
It articoli di marca *(m pl)*
Pt artigos de marca *(m pl)*

market n En
De Markt *(m)*
Es mercado *(m)*
Fr marché *(m)*
It mercato *(m)*
Pt mercado *(m)*

marketable *adj* En
De marktfähig
Es vendible
Fr vendable
It vendibile
Pt comercializável

market day (local) En
De Markttag *(m)*
Es día de mercado *(m)*
Fr jour de marché *(m)*
It giorno di mercato *(m)*
Pt dia de mercado *(m)*

market day (financial) En
De Börsentag *(m)*
Es día de bolsa *(m)*
Fr jour de bourse *(m)*
It giorno di borsa *(m)*
Pt dia de bolsa *(m)*

market forces En
De Marktkräfte *(f pl)*
Es fuerzas del mercado *(f pl)*
Fr forces du marché *(f pl)*
It forze di mercato *(f pl)*
Pt forças de mercado *(f pl)*

marketing agreement En
De Absatzübereinkommen *(n)*
Es acuerdo mercantil *(m)*
Fr accord de commercialisa-
tion *(m)*
It accordo di mercato *(m)*
Pt acordo sobre comerciali-
zação *(m)*

marketing director En
De Absatzdirektor *(m)*
Es director mercantil *(m)*
Fr administrateur chef
d'écoulement *(m)*
It direttore di mercato *(m)*
Pt director de comercialização
(m)

market penetration En
De Markteindringen *(n)*
Es penetración en el mercado
(f)
Fr pénétration du marché *(f)*
It penetrazione nel mercato
(f)
Pt infiltração no mercado *(f)*

market price En
De Marktpreis *(m)*
Es precio de mercado *(m)*
Fr cours du marché *(m)*
It prezzo del mercato *(m)*
Pt preço de mercado *(m)*

market report En
De Marktbericht *(m)*
Es informe del mercado *(m)*
Fr revue du marché *(f)*
It relazione sul mercato *(f)*
Pt informação do mercado *(f)*

market research En
De Marktforschung *(f)*
Es investigación del mercado
(f)
Fr étude du marché *(f)*
It indagine di mercato *(f)*
Pt pesquisa de mercado *(f)*

market share En
De Marktanteil *(m)*
Es participación del mercado
(f)
Fr participation au marché *(f)*
It quota del mercato *(f)*
Pt quota-parte no mercado
(f)

market value En
De Marktwert *(m)*
Es valor de mercado *(m)*
Fr valeur marchande *(f)*
It valore di mercato *(m)*
Pt valor de mercado *(m)*

Markt *(m)* n De
En market
Es mercado *(m)*

Fr marché *(m)*
It mercato *(m)*
Pt mercado *(m)*

Marktanteil *(m)* n De
En market share
Es participación del mercado
(f)
Fr participation au marché *(f)*
It quota del mercato *(f)*
Pt quota-parte no mercado
(f)

Marktbericht *(m)* n De
En market report
Es informe del mercado *(m)*
Fr revue du marché *(f)*
It relazione sul mercato *(f)*
Pt informação do mercado *(f)*

Markteindringen *(n)* n De
En market penetration
Es penetración en el mercado
(f)
Fr pénétration du marché *(f)*
It penetrazione nel mercato
(f)
Pt infiltração no mercado *(f)*

marktfähig *adj* De
En marketable
Es vendible
Fr vendable
It vendibile
Pt comercializável

Marktforschung *(f)* n De
En market research
Es investigación del mercado
(f)
Fr étude du marché *(f)*
It indagine di mercato *(f)*
Pt pesquisa de mercado *(f)*

marktgängige Qualität *(f)* De
En merchantable quality
Es calidad comerciable *(f)*
Fr qualité vendable *(f)*
It qualità commerciabile *(f)*
Pt qualidade comerciável *(f)*

Marktkräfte *(f pl)* n De
En market forces
Es fuerzas del mercado *(f pl)*
Fr forces du marché *(f pl)*
It forze di mercato *(f pl)*
Pt forças de mercado *(f pl)*

Markt mit Baissetendenz *(m)*
De
En falling market
Es mercado en baja *(m)*
Fr marché orienté à la baisse
(m)
It mercato in declino *(m)*
Pt mercado em decréscimo
(m)

Marktpreis *(m) n* De
En market price
Es precio de mercado *(m)*
Fr cours du marché *(m)*
It prezzo del mercato *(m)*
Pt preço de mercado *(m)*

Markttag *(m) n* De
En market day
Es día de mercado *(m)*
Fr jour de marché *(m)*
It giorno di mercato *(m)*
Pt dia de mercado *(m)*

Marktumstände *(m pl) n* De
En state of the market
Es condiciones del mercado
(f pl)
Fr état du marché *(m)*
It condizioni del mercato
(f pl)
Pt situação do mercado *(f)*

Marktwert *(m) n* De
En market value
Es valor de mercado *(m)*
Fr valeur marchande *(f)*
It valore di mercato *(m)*
Pt valor de mercado *(m)*

maroquinerie *(f) n* Fr
De Lederwaren *(f pl)*
En leather goods
Es marroquinería *(f)*
It pelletterie *(f pl)*
Pt artigos de cabedal *(m pl)*

marque *(f) n* Fr
De Handelsmarke *(f)*
En brand
Es marca *(f)*
It marca *(f)*
Pt marca *(f)*

marque de destination *(f)* Fr
De Benennung des Bestim-
mungshafens *(f)*
En port mark
Es marca de destino *(f)*

It marche di destinazione
(f pl)
Pt marca de porto *(f)*

marque de fabrique *(f)* Fr
De Warenzeichen *(n)*
En trademark
Es marca de fábrica *(f)*
It marchio di fabbrica *(m)*
Pt marca de fábrica *(f)*

marque de point *(f)* Fr
De führende Marke *(f)*
En brand leader
Es marca directriz *(f)*
It marca di punta *(f)*
Pt marca mais cotada *(f)*

marroquinería *(f) n* Es
De Lederwaren *(f pl)*
En leather goods
Fr maroquinerie *(f)*
It pelletterie *(f pl)*
Pt artigos de cabedal *(m pl)*

masa obrera *(f)* Es
De Belegschaft *(f)*
En work force
Fr effectifs *(m pl)*
It massa lavoratrice *(f)*
Pt massa trabalhadora *(f)*

más barato Es
De billiger
En cheaper
Fr meilleur marché
It meno caro
Pt mais barato

Maschine *(f) n* De
En machine
Es máquina *(f)*
Fr machine *(f)*
It macchina *(f)*
Pt máquina *(f)*

Maschinenausrüstung *(f) n*
De
En computer hardware
Es mecánica de le máquina *(f)*
Fr hardware *(m)*
It componenti di macchina
calcolatore *(m pl)*
Pt sistema físico *(m)*

Maschinenbau *(m) n* De
En mechanical engineering
Es ingeniería mecánica *(f)*

Fr construction mécanique *(f)*
It ingegneria meccanica *(f)*
Pt engenharia mecânica *(f)*

Maschinenschrift *(f) n* De
En typescript
Es texto mecanografiado *(m)*
Fr manuscrit dactylographié
(m)
It dattiloscritto *(m)*
Pt texto dactilografado *(m)*

Maschinensprache *(f) n* De
En machine language
Es lenguaje de máquina *(m)*
Fr langage-machine *(m)*
It linguaggio di macchina *(m)*
Pt linguagem de máquina *(f)*

Maschinenstillstandzeit *(f) n*
De
En machine down-time
Es tiempo improductivo de la
máquina *(m)*
Fr temps de panne machine
(m)
It tempo passivo di macchi-
na *(m)*
Pt tempo-morto da máquina
(m)

Maschinerie *(f) n* De
En machinery
Es maquinaría *(f)*
Fr machinerie *(f)*
It macchinario *(m)*
Pt maquinaria *(f)*

más detalles *(m pl)* Es
De weitere Auskunft *(f)*
En further information
Fr renseignements complé-
mentaires *(m pl)*
It ulteriori informazioni *(f pl)*
Pt informação adicional *(f)*

más detalles *(m pl)* Es
De nähere Umstände *(m pl)*
En further particulars
Fr plus amples renseigne-
ments *(m pl)*
It ulteriori particolari *(m pl)*
Pt pormenores adicionais
(m pl)

Maß *(n) n* De
En measure
Es medida *(f)*

Fr mesure *(f)*
It misura *(f)*
Pt medida *(f)*

massaia *(f) n* It
De Hausfrau *(f)*
En housewife
Es ama de casa *(f)*
Fr ménagère *(f)*
Pt dona de casa *(f)*

massa lavoratrice *(f)* It
De Belegschaft *(f)*
En work force
Es masa obrera *(f)*
Fr effectifs *(m pl)*
Pt massa trabalhadora *(f)*

massa trabalhadora *(f)* Pt
De Belegschaft *(f)*
En work force
Es masa obrera *(f)*
Fr effectifs *(m pl)*
It massa lavoratrice *(f)*

Massenberechner *(m) n* De
En quantity surveyor
Es medidor de contidades de obra *(m)*
Fr métreur-vérificateur *(m)*
It perito misuratore *(m)*
Pt perito na avaliação de quantidades *(m)*

Massenfrachtführer *(m) n* De
En bulk carrier
Es transportador a grand *(m)*
Fr transporteur de marchandises en vrac *(m)*
It trasportatore di merce alla rinfusa *(m)*
Pt transportador de carga geral *(m)*

Massenherstellung *(f) n* De
En mass production
Es producción en masa *(f)*
Fr production en masse *(f)*
It fabbricazione in massa *(f)*
Pt produção em massa *(f)*

Masseverwalter *(m) n* De
En liquidator
Es liquidador *(m)*
Fr liquidateur *(m)*
It liquidatore *(m)*
Pt executor de liquidação *(m)*

massimo *adj* It
De maximal
En maximum
Es máximo
Fr maximum
Pt máximo

Maß oder Gewicht De
En weight or measurement
Es peso o cubicaje
Fr poids ou mesure
It peso o volume
Pt peso ou medida

mass production En
De Massenherstellung *(f)*
Es producción en masa *(f)*
Fr production en masse *(f)*
It fabbricazione in massa *(f)*
Pt produção em massa *(f)*

Maßstab *(m) n* De
En scale
Es escala *(f)*
Fr échelle *(f)*
It scala *(f)*
Pt escala *(f)*

master of a ship En
De Kapitän *(m)*
Es capitán de navío *(m)*
Fr capitaine *(m)*
It capitano di nave *(m)*
Pt capitão de navio *(m)*

mastro acquisti *(m)* It
De Einkaufsbuch *(n)*
En bought ledger
Am purchase book
Es libro mayor de compras *(m)*
Fr grand livre d'achats *(m)*
Pt livro-mestre de compras *(m)*

mate (of a ship) *n* En
De Maat *(m)*
Es primer oficial *(m)*
Fr second *(m)*
It primo ufficiale *(m)*
Pt imediato *(m)*

mate's receipt En
De Übernahmebescheinigung *(f)*
Es recibo de embarco *(m)*
Fr billet de bord *(m)*
It ricevuta d'imbarco *(f)*
Pt recibo de embarque *(m)*

materia *(f) n* Es, It
De Material *(n)*
En material
Fr matière *(f)*
Pt matéria *(f)*

matéria *(f) n* Pt
De Material *(n)*
En material
Es materia *(f)*
Fr matière *(f)*
It materia *(f)*

material (cloth) *n* En
De Stoff *(m)*
Es tejido *(m)*
Fr étoffe; tissu *(f m)*
It stoffa; tessuto *(f m)*
Pt tecido *(m)*

material (substance) *n* En
De Material *(n)*
Es materia *(f)*
Fr matière *(f)*
It materia *(f)*
Pt matéria *(f)*

material *adj* En, Es, Pt
De wesentlich
Fr essentiel
It materiale

Material *(n) n* De
En material
Es materia *(f)*
Fr matière *(f)*
It materia *(f)*
Pt matéria *(f)*

materiale *adj* It
De wesentlich
En material
Es material
Fr essentiel
Pt material

material publicitario *(m)* Es
De Werbetext *(m)*
En advertising copy
Fr copie publicitaire *(f)*
It testo pubblicitario *(m)*
Pt texto de publicidade *(m)*

materia prima *(f)* Es, It
De Rohstoff *(m)*
En raw material
Fr matière première *(f)*
Pt matéria prima *(f)*

matéria prima *(f)* Pt
De Rohstoff *(m)*
En raw material
Es materia prima *(f)*
Fr matière première *(f)*
It materia prima *(f)*

matière *(f)* n Fr
De Material *(n)*
En material (substance)
Es materia *(f)*
It materia *(f)*
Pt matéria *(f)*

matière première *(f)* Fr
De Rohstoff *(m)*
En raw material
Es materia prima *(f)*
It materia prima *(f)*
Pt matéria prima *(f)*

matrice *(f)* n It
De Talon *(m)*
En counterfoil
Am stub
Es talón *(m)*
Fr talon *(m)*
Pt talão *(m)*

Mattscheibe *(f)* n De
En ground glass
Es cristal deslustrado *(m)*
Fr verre dépoli *(m)*
It vetro smerigliato *(m)*
Pt vidro esmerilado *(m)*

maturazione *(f)* n It
De Auflaufen *(n)*
En accrual
Es acumulación *(f)*
Fr accumulation *(f)*
Pt acumulação *(f)*

maturity n En
De Fälligkeit *(f)*
Es vencimiento *(m)*
Fr échéance *(f)*
It scadenza *(f)*
Pt vencimento *(m)*

mau-pagador *(m)* n Pt
De schlechter Zahler *(m)*
En slow payer
Es deudor moroso *(m)*
Fr mauvais payeur *(m)*
It cattivo pagatore *(m)*

mauvais payeur *(m)* Fr
De schlechter Zahler *(m)*
En slow payer
Es deudor moroso *(m)*
It cattivo pagatore *(m)*
Pt mau-pagador *(m)*

maximal adj De
En maximum
Es máximo
Fr maximum
It massimo
Pt máximo

máximo adj Es, Pt
De maximal
En maximum
Fr maximum
It massimo

maximum adj En, Fr
De maximal
Es máximo
It massimo
Pt máximo

mayorista *(m)* n Es
De Großhändler; Grossist *(m)*
En wholesaler
Fr grossiste *(m)*
It grossista *(m)*
Pt vendedor por atacado *(m)*

mazout *(m)* n Fr
De Heizöl *(n)*
En fuel oil
Es fuel-oil *(m)*
It petrolio da ardere *(m)*
Pt petróleo combustível *(m)*

mean price En
De Mittelkurs *(m)*
Es precio medio *(m)*
Fr prix moyen *(m)*
It prezzo medio *(m)*
Pt preço médio *(m)*

measure n En
De Maß *(n)*
Es medida *(f)*
Fr mesure *(f)*
It misura *(f)*
Pt medida *(f)*

measure vb En
De messen
Es medir

Fr mesurer; mensurer
It misurare
Pt medir

measurement n En
De Messung *(f)*
Es medida; dimensión *(f)*
Fr mesurage *(f)*
It misura; dimensione *(f)*
Pt medida; dimensão *(f)*

mecánica de la máquina *(f)* Es
De Maschinenausrüstung *(f)*
En computer hardware
Fr hardware *(m)*
It componenti di macchina calcolatore *(m pl)*
Pt sistema físico *(m)*

mécanicien *(m)* n Fr
De Mechaniker *(m)*
En mechanic
Es mecánico *(m)*
It meccanico *(m)*
Pt mecânico *(m)*

mecánico *(m)* n Es
De Mechaniker *(m)*
En mechanic
Fr mécanicien *(m)*
It meccanico *(m)*
Pt mecânico *(m)*

mecânico *(m)* n Pt
De Mechaniker *(m)*
En mechanic
Es mecánico *(m)*
Fr mécanicien *(m)*
It meccanico *(m)*

mecanógrafa *(f)* n Es
De Abschreibtypistin *(f)*
En copy typist
Am transcriber
Fr dactylo copiste *(f)*
It dattilografa *(f)*
Pt dactilógrafa *(f)*

meccanico *(m)* n It
De Mechaniker *(m)*
En mechanic
Es mecánico *(m)*
Fr mécanicien *(m)*
Pt mecânico *(m)*

mechanic n En
De Mechaniker (m)
Es mecánico (m)
Fr mécanicien (m)
It meccanico (m)
Pt mecânico (m)

mechanical engineering En
De Maschinenbau (m)
Es ingeniería mecánica (f)
Fr construction mécanique (f)
It ingegneria meccanica (f)
Pt engenharia mecânica (f)

Mechaniker (m) n De
En mechanic
Es mecánico (m)
Fr mécanicien (m)
It meccanico (m)
Pt mecânico (m)

media (f) n It
De Durchschnitt (m)
En average
Es promedio (m)
Fr moyenne (f)
Pt média (f)

média (f) n Pt
De Durchschnitt (m)
En average
Es promedio (m)
Fr moyenne (f)
It media (f)

media n En
De Werbeträger (m pl)
Es medios de información
 (m pl)
Fr supports (m pl)
It canali d'informazione
 (m pl)
Pt meios de informação (m pl)

media aritmética (f) Es
De arithmetisches Mittel (n)
En arithmetic mean
Fr moyenne arithmétique (f)
It media aritmetica (f)
Pt média aritmética (f)

media aritmetica (f) It
De arithmetisches Mittel (n)
En arithmetic mean
Es media aritmética (f)
Fr moyenne arithmétique (f)
Pt média aritmética (f)

média aritmética (f) Pt
De arithmetisches Mittel (n)
En arithmetic mean
Es media aritmética (f)
Fr moyenne arithmétique (f)
It media aritmetica (f)

media ponderada (f) Es
De gewogener Durchschnitt
 (m)
En weighted average
Fr moyenne pondérée (f)
It media ponderata (f)
Pt média ponderada (f)

média ponderada (f) Pt
De gewogener Durchschnitt
 (m)
En weighted average
Es media ponderada (f)
Fr moyenne pondérée (f)
It media ponderata (f)

media ponderata (f) It
De gewogener Durchschnitt
 (m)
En weighted average
Es media ponderada (f)
Fr moyenne pondérée (f)
Pt média ponderada (f)

mediate vb En
De vermitteln
Es intermediar
Fr s'entremettre
It fare da intermediario
Pt intermediar

mediation n En
De Vermittlung (f)
Es intermediación (f)
Fr médiation (f)
It mediazione (f)
Pt intermediação (f)

médiation (f) Fr
De Vermittlung (f)
En mediation
Es intermediación (f)
It mediazione (f)
Pt intermediação (f)

mediatore di assicurazioni
 (m) It
De Versicherungsmakler (m)
En insurance broker
Es corredor de seguros (m)
Fr courtier d'assurance (m)
Pt corretor de seguros (m)

mediazione (f) n It
De Vermittlung (f)
En mediation
Es intermediación (f)
Fr médiation (f)
Pt intermediação (f)

medical examination En
De ärztliche Untersuchung (f)
Es examen médico (m)
Fr examen médical (m)
It visita medica (f)
Pt inspecção médica (f)

medida (f) n Es, Pt
De Maß, Messung (n f)
En measure; measurement
Fr mesure; mesurage (f m)
It misura (f)

**medidor de contidades de
 obra** (m) Es
De Massenberechner (m)
En quantity surveyor
Fr métreur-vérificateur (m)
It perito misuratore (m)
Pt perito na avaliação de
 quantidades (m)

medio adj Es
De halb
En half
Fr à moitié; demi
It mezzo
Pt meio

medio de publicidad (m) Es
De Werbemittel (n)
En advertising medium
Fr support publicitaire (m)
It mezzo pubblicitario (m)
Pt meio publicitário (m)

medio salario (m) Es
De Halbsold (m)
En half-pay
Fr demi-salaire (m)
It mezza paga (f)
Pt meio-salário (m)

medios de información (m pl)
 Es
De Werbeträger (m pl)
En media
Fr supports (m pl)
It canali d'informazione (m
 pl)
Pt meios de informação (m pl)

medir *vb* Es, Pt
De messen
En measure
Fr mesurer; mensurer
It misurare

meeting *n* En
De Versammlung *(f)*
Es reunión *(f)*
Fr réunion; assemblée *(f)*
It riunione; assemblea *(f)*
Pt reunião; assembleia *(f)*

meeting of creditors En
De Gläubigerversammlung *(f)*
Es concurso de acreedores *(m)*
Fr assemblée de créanciers *(f)*
It convocazione dei creditori *(f)*
Pt reunião de credores *(f)*

Mehrarbeit *(f)* *n* De
En overtime
Es horas extraordinarias *(f pl)*
Fr heures supplémentaires *(f pl)*
It lavoro stordinario *(m)*
Pt horas extraordinárias *(f)*

Mehrheitsbeteiligung *(f)* *n* De
En majority holding
Es tenencia de acciones por mayoría *(f)*
Fr participation majoritaire *(f)*
It partecipazione maggioritaria *(f)*
Pt propriedade em maioria *(f)*

mehrseitiges Handeln *n* De
En multilateral trade
Es comercio multilateral *(m)*
Fr commerce multilatéral *(m)*
It commercio multilateral *(m)*
Pt comércio multilaterial *(m)*

Mehrwert *(f)* *n* De
En added value
Es valor agregado *(m)*
Fr valeur ajoutée *(f)*
It valore aggiunto *(m)*
Pt valor adicionado *(m)*

Mehrwertsteuer *(f)* *n* De
En value added tax (VAT)
Es impuesto sobre valor aña-
dido *(m)*

Fr taxe sur la valeur ajoutée (TVA) *(f)*
It imposta sul valore aggiun-
to (IVA) *(f)*
Pt imposto sobre valor aduzido *(m)*

mellieur marché Fr
De billiger
En cheaper
Es más barato
It meno caro
Pt mais barato

Meinung *(f)* *n* De
En opinion
Es opinión *(f)*
Fr opinion *(f)*
It opinione *(f)*
Pt opinão *(f)*

meio *adj* Pt
De halb
En half
Es medio
Fr à moitié; demi
It mezzo

meio publicitário *(m)* Pt
De Werbemittel *(n)*
En advertising medium
Es medio de publicidad *(m)*
Fr support publicitaire *(m)*
It mezzo pubblicitario *(m)*

meio-salário *(m)* *n* Pt
De Halbsold *(m)*
En half-pay
Es medio salario *(m)*
Fr demi-salaire *(m)*
It mezza paga *(f)*

meios de informação *(m pl)* Pt
De Werbeträger *(m pl)*
En media
Es medios de información *(m pl)*
Fr supports *(m pl)*
It canali d'informazione *(m pl)*

Meistbietende(r) *(m)* *n* De
En highest bidder
Es ofertante más alto *(m)*
Fr plus offrant enchérisseur *(m)*
It miglior offerente *(m)*
Pt proponente mais elevado *(m)*

mejora *(f)* *n* Es
De Verbesserung *(f)*
En improvement
Fr amélioration *(f)*
It miglioramento *(f)*
Pt melhoramento *(m)*

melhoramento *(m)* *n* Pt
De Verbesserung *(f)*
En improvement
Es mejora *(f)*
Fr amélioration *(f)*
It miglioramento *(m)*

melhoria *(f)* *n* Pt
De Planungsgewinn *(m)*
En betterment
Es plusvalía *(f)*
Fr appréciation *(f)*
It plus-valore *(m)*

member *n* En
De Mitglied *(n)*
Es miembro; socio *(m)*
Fr membre *(m)*
It membro; socio *(m)*
Pt membro; sócio *(m)*

membre *(m)* *n* Fr
De Mitglied *(n)*
En member
Es miembro; socio *(m)*
It membro; socio *(m)*
Pt membro; sócio *(m)*

membre fondateur *(m)* Fr
De Gründermitglied *(m)*
En founder member
Es miembro fundador *(m)*
It socio fondatore *(m)*
Pt membro fundador *(m)*

membrete *(m)* *n* Es
De Briefkopf *(m)*
En letterhead
Fr en-tête *(m)*
It intestazione *(f)*
Pt cabeçalho *(m)*

membro *(m)* *n* It, Pt
De Mitglied *(n)*
En member
Es miembro; socio *(m)*
Fr membre *(m)*

membro fundador *(m)* Pt
De Gründermitglied *(m)*
En founder member

Es miembro fundador *(m)*
Fr membre fondateur *(m)*
It socio fondatore *(m)*

memorando *(m)* n Es, Pt
De Vermerk *(m)*
En memorandum
Fr note *(f)*
It promemoria *(f)*

memorandum n En
De Vermerk *(m)*
Es memorando; apunte *(m)*
Fr note *(f)*
It promemoria *(f)*
Pt memorando *(m)*

Memorandum and Articles of Association En
Am articles of incorporation
De Statuten *(f pl)*
Es estatutos; carta orgánica *(m pl; f)*
Fr statuts; acte constitutif *(m pl; m)*
It atto costitutivo e statuto sociale *(m)*
Pt estatuto de associação *(m)*

memoria anual *(f)* Es
De Jahresbericht *(m)*
En annual report
Fr rapport annuel *(m)*
It relazione annuale *(f)*
Pt relatório anual *(m)*

ménage *(m)* n Fr
De Haushalt *(m)*
En household
Es hogar *(m)*
It famiglia *(f)*
Pt casa *(f)*

ménagère *(f)* n Fr
De Hausfrau *(f)*
En housewife
Es ama de casa *(f)*
It massaia *(f)*
Pt dona de casa *(f)*

Menge *(f)* n De
En quantity
Es cantidad *(f)*
Fr quantité *(f)*
It quantità *(f)*
Pt quantidade *(f)*

meno caro It
De billiger
En cheaper
Es más barato
Fr meilleur marché
Pt mais barato

menschliche Arbeitskraft *(f)* n De
En manpower
Es mano de obra *(f)*
Fr main-d'œuvre *(f)*
It mano d'opera *(f)*
Pt mão-de-obra *(f)*

mensilità *(f)* n It
De Monatsrate *(f)*
En monthly instalment
Es mensualidad *(f)*
Fr mensualité *(f)*
Pt prestação mensal *(f)*

mensualidad *(f)* n Es
De Monatsrate *(f)*
En monthly instalment
Fr mensualité *(f)*
It mensilità *(f)*
Pt prestação mensal *(f)*

mensualité *(f)* n Fr
De Monatsrate *(f)*
En monthly instalment
Es mensualidad *(f)*
It mensilità *(f)*
Pt prestação mensal *(f)*

mer *(f)* n Fr
De See *(f)*
En sea
Es mar *(m)*
It mare *(m)*
Pt mar *(m)*

mercadería *(f)* n Es
De Gut; Ware *(n f)*
En commodity
Fr marchandise; produit *(f m)*
It merce; prodotto *(f m)*
Pt mercadoria; produto *(f m)*

mercado *(m)* n Es, Pt
De Markt *(m)*
En market
Fr marché *(m)*
It mercato *(m)*

mercado alcista *(m)* Es
De Haussemarkt *(m)*
En bull market

Fr marché orienté à la hausse *(m)*
It mercato tendente al rialzo *(m)*
Pt mercado de tendência altista *(m)*

mercado bajista *(m)* Es
De Baissemarkt *(m)*
En bear market
Fr marché orienté à la baisse *(m)*
It mercato tendente al ribasso *(m)*
Pt mercado de tendência baixista *(m)*

mercado cerrado *(m)* Es
De gesperrter Markt *(m)*
En closed market
Fr marché fermé *(m)*
It mercato chiuso *(m)*
Pt mercado fechado *(m)*

mercado comum *(m)* Pt
De gemeinsamer Markt *(m)*
En Common Market
Es mercado común *(m)*
Fr marché commun *(m)*
It mercato comune *(m)*

mercado común *(m)* Es
De gemeinsamer Markt *(m)*
En Common Market
Fr marché commun *(m)*
It mercato comune *(m)*
Pt mercado comum *(m)*

mercado de acções *(m)* Pt
De Aktienmarkt *(m)*
En share market
Am stock market
Es mercado de valores *(m)*
Fr marché des valeurs *(m)*
It mercato azionario *(m)*

mercado de desconto *(m)* Pt
De Diskontmarkt *(m)*
En discount market
Es mercado de descuentos *(m)*
Fr marché de l'escompte *(m)*
It mercato di sconto *(m)*

mercado de descuentos *(m)* Es
De Diskontmarkt *(m)*
En discount market

Fr marché de l'escompte *(m)*
It mercato di sconto *(m)*
Pt mercado de desconto

mercado de dinero *(m)* Es
De Geldmarkt *(m)*
En money market
Fr marché monétaire *(m)*
It mercato di denaro *(m)*
Pt mercado monetário *(m)*

mercado de futuros *(m)* Es,
Pt
De Terminmarkt *(m)*
En futures market
Fr marché à terme *(m)*
It mercato a termine *(m)*

mercado de mano de obra
(m) Es
De Arbeitsmarkt *(m)*
En labour market
Fr marché du travail *(m)*
It mercato della mano d'ope-
ra *(m)*
Pt mercado de mâo-de-
obra *(m)*

mercado de mâo-de-obra
(m) Pt
De Arbeitsmarkt *(m)*
En labour market
Es mercado de mano de obra
(m)
Fr marché du travail *(m)*
It mercato della mano d'ope-
ra *(m)*

**mercado de materias
primas** *(m)* Es
De Rohstoffmarkt *(m)*
En commodity market
Fr marché de matières pre-
mières *(m)*
It mercato di materie prime
(m)
Pt mercado de matérias pri-
mas *(m)*

**mercado de matérias
primas** *(m)* Pt
De Rohstoffmarkt *(m)*
En commodity market
Es mercado de materias pri-
mas *(m)*
Fr marché de matières pre-
mières *(m)*
It mercato di materie prime
(m)

mercado de productos *(m)*
Es
De Warenmarkt *(m)*
En produce market
Fr marché commercial *(m)*
It mercato commerciale *(m)*
Pt mercado de produtos *(m)*

mercado de produtos *(m)* Pt
De Warenmarkt *(m)*
En produce market
Es mercado de productos *(m)*
Fr marché commercial *(m)*
It mercato commerciale *(m)*

**mercado de tendência
altista** *(m)* Pt
De Haussemarkt *(m)*
En bull market
Es mercado alcista *(m)*
Fr marché orienté à la hausse
(m)
It mercato tendente al rialzo
(m)

mercado de valores *(m)* Es
De Aktienmarkt *(m)*
En share market
Am stock market
Fr marché des valeurs *(m)*
It mercato azionario *(m)*
Pt mercado de acções *(m)*

mercado em decréscimo *(m)*
Pt
De Markt mit Baissetendenz
(m)
En failing market
Es mercado en baja *(m)*
Fr marché orienté à la baisse
(m)
It mercato in declino *(m)*

mercado en baja *(m)* Es
De Markt mit Baissetendenz
(m)
En falling market
Fr marché orienté à la baisse
(m)
It mercato in declino *(m)*
Pt mercado em decréscimo
(m)

mercado exclusivo *(m)* Es, Pt
De ausschließlicher Markt *(m)*
En exclusive market
Fr marché exclusif *(m)*
It mercato esclusivo *(m)*

mercado fechado *(m)* Pt
De gesperrter Markt *(m)*
En closed market
Es mercado cerrado *(m)*
Fr marché fermé *(m)*
It mercato chiuso *(m)*

mercado libre *(m)* Es
De freier Markt *(m)*
En open market
Fr marché libre *(m)*
It mercato libero *(m)*
Pt mercado livre *(m)*

mercado livre *(m)* Pt
De freier Markt *(m)*
En open market
Es mercado libre *(m)*
Fr marché libre *(m)*
It mercato libero *(m)*

mercado monetário *(m)* Pt
De Geldmarkt *(m)*
En money market
Es mercado de dinero *(m)*
Fr marché monétaire *(m)*
It mercato di denaro *(m)*

mercado negro *(m)* Es, Pt
De schwarzer Markt *(m)*
En black market
Fr marché noir *(m)*
It mercato nero *(m)*

mercadoria *(f)* n Pt
De Gut; Ware *(n f)*
En commodity; merchandise
Es mercadería; producto *(f m)*
Fr marchandise; produit *(f m)*
It merce; prodotto *(f m)*

mercadorias *(f pl)* n Pt
De Güter *(n pl)*
En goods
Es mercancías *(f pl)*
Fr marchandises *(f pl)*
It merce *(f)*

**mercadorias à ordem da
alfândega** *(f pl)* Pt
De Waren unter Zollverschluß
(f pl)
En bonded goods
Es mercancías en aduana
(f pl)
Fr marchandises en douane
(f pl)
It merci sotto vincolo doganale *(f pl)*

mercadorias danificadas
(f pl) Pt
De beschädigte Waren *(f pl)*
En damaged goods
Es mercancías averiadas *(f pl)*
Fr marchandises avariées
   (f pl)
It merce avariata *(f)*

mercadorias de capital *(f pl)*
   Pt
De Anlagegüter *(n pl)*
En capital goods
Es bienes de producción
   (m pl)
Fr biens d'équipement *(m pl)*
It beni strumentali *(m pl)*

mercadorias devolvidas *(f pl)*
   Pt
De Retourwaren *(f)*
En returned goods
Es mercancías devueltas *(f pl)*
Fr marchandises de retour
   (f pl)
It merce di ritorno *(f pl)*

mercadorias embargadas
   (f pl) Pt
De gepfändete Güter *(n pl)*
En distressed goods
Es mercancías embargadas
   (f pl)
Fr biens saisis *(m pl)*
It merce sequestrata *(f)*

mercadorias em existência
   (f pl) Pt
De Vorrat auf Lager *(m)*
En stock in hand
Es mercancías en almacén
   (f pl)
Fr marchandises en magasin
   (f pl)
It merce in magazzino *(f)*

mercadorias imperecíveis
   (f pl) Pt
De langlebige Güter *(n pl)*
En durable goods
Es mercancías no perecede-
   ras *(f pl)*
Fr biens durables *(m pl)*
It beni durevoli *(m pl)*

mercadorias perecíveis *(f pl)*
   Pt
De leicht verderbliche Waren
   (f pl)
En perishable goods
Es mercancías perecederas
   (f pl)
Fr marchandises périssables
   (f pl)
It merci deperibili *(f pl)*

mercadorias perigosas *(f pl)*
   Pt
De gefährliche Waren *(f pl)*
En dangerous goods
Es mercancías peligrosas
   (f pl)
Fr marchandises dangereu-
   ses *(f pl)*
It merce pericolosa *(f)*

mercadorias prontas *(f pl)* Pt
De sofort lieferbare Waren
   (f pl)
En spot goods
Es mercancías prontas *(f pl)*
Fr marchandises disponibles
   (f pl)
It merce pronta *(f)*

mercancía *(f)* n Es
De Ware *(f)*
En merchandise
Fr marchandise *(f)*
It merce *(f)*
Pt mercadoria *(f)*

mercancías *(f pl)* n Es
De Güter *(n f)*
En goods
Fr marchandises *(f pl)*
It merce *(f)*
Pt mercadorias *(f pl)*

mercancías averiadas *(f pl)*
   Es
De beschädigte Waren *(f pl)*
En damaged goods
Fr marchandises avariées *(f
   pl)*
It merce avariata *(f)*
Pt mercadorias danificadas
   (f pl)

mercancías devueltas *(f pl)*
   Es
De Retourware *(f)*
En returned goods

Fr marchandises de retour
   (f pl)
It merce di ritorno *(f pl)*
Pt mercadorias devolvidas
   (f pl)

mercancías embargadas
   (f pl) Es
De gepfändete Güter *(n pl)*
En distressed goods
Fr biens saisis *(m pl)*
It merce sequestrata *(f)*
Pt mercadorias embargadas
   (f pl)

mercancías en aduana *(f pl)*
   Es
De Waren unter Zollverschluß
   (f pl)
En bonded goods
Fr marchandises en douane
   (f pl)
It merci sotto vincolo doga-
   nale *(f pl)*
Pt mercadorias à ordem da
   alfândega *(f pl)*

mercancías en almacén *(f pl)*
   Es
De Vorrat auf Lager *(m)*
En stock in hand
Fr marchandises en magasin
   (f pl)
It merce in magazzino *(f)*
Pt mercadorias em
   existência *(f pl)*

**mercancías en consigna-
   ción** *(f pl)* Es
De Kommissionsgüter *(n pl)*
En goods on consignment
Fr marchandises en con-
   signation *(f pl)*
It merce in conto deposito *(f)*
Pt artigos à consignação
   (m pl)

mercancías no perecederas
   (f pl) Es
De langlebige Güter *(n pl)*
En durable goods
Fr biens durables *(m pl)*
It beni durevoli *(m pl)*
Pt mercadorias imperecíveis
   (f pl)

mercancías peligrosas *(f pl)*
Es
De gefährliche Waren *(f pl)*
En dangerous goods
Fr marchandises dangereuses *(f pl)*
It merce pericolosa *(f)*
Pt mercadorias perigosas *(f pl)*

mercancías perecederas *(f pl)* Es
De leicht verderbliche Waren *(f pl)*
En perishable goods
Fr marchandises périssables *(f pl)*
It merci deperibili *(f pl)*
Pt mercadorias perecíveis *(f pl)*

mercancías prontas *(f pl)* Es
De sofort lieferbare Waren *(f pl)*
En spot goods
Fr marchandises disponibles *(f pl)*
It merce pronta *(f)*
Pt mercadorias prontas *(f pl)*

mercancías sujetas a aprobación *(f pl)* Es
De Probegüter *(n pl)*
En goods on approval
Fr marchandises à condition *(f pl)*
It merce soggetta ad approvazione *(f)*
Pt artigos sujeitos a aprovação *(m pl)*

mercanteggiare *(vb)* It
De feilschen
En haggle
Am bargain
Es regatear
Fr marchander; chipoter
Pt regatear

mercantil *(adj)* Es, Pt
De Handels-
En mercantile
Fr mercantile
It mercantile

mercantile *(adj)* En, Fr, It
De Handels-
Es mercantil
Pt mercantil

mercantile agent En
Am sales agent
De Handelsvertreter *(m)*
Es agente mercantil *(m)*
Fr agent de commerce *(m)*
It agente di commercio *(m)*
Pt agente comercial *(m)*

mercato *(m) n* It
De Markt *(m)*
En market
Es mercado *(m)*
Fr marché *(m)*
Pt mercado *(m)*

mercato a termine *(m)* It
De Terminmarkt *(m)*
En futures market
Es mercado de futuros *(m)*
Fr marché à terme *(m)*
Pt mercado de futuros *(m)*

mercato azionario *(m)* It
De Aktienmarkt *(m)*
En share market
Am stock market
Es mercado de valores *(m)*
Fr marché des valeurs *(m)*
Pt mercado de acções *(m)*

mercato chiuso *(m)* It
De gesperrter Markt *(m)*
En closed market
Es mercado cerrado *(m)*
Fr marché fermé *(m)*
Pt mercado fechado *(m)*

mercato commerciale *(m)* It
De Warenmarkt *(m)*
En produce market
Es mercado de productos *(m)*
Fr marché commercial *(m)*
Pt mercado de produtos *(m)*

mercato comune *(m)* It
De gemeinsamer Markt *(m)*
En Common Market
Es mercado común *(m)*
Fr marché commun *(m)*
Pt mercado comum *(m)*

mercato della mano d'opera *(m)* It
De Arbeitsmarkt *(m)*
En labour market
Es mercado de mano de obra *(m)*
Fr marché du travail *(m)*
Pt mercado de mão-de-obra *(m)*

mercato di denaro *(m)* It
De Geldmarkt *(m)*
En money market
Es mercado di dinero *(m)*
Fr marché monétaire *(m)*
Pt mercado monetário *(m)*

mercato di materie prime *(m)* It
De Rohstoffmarkt *(m)*
En commodity market
Es mercado de materias primas *(m)*
Fr marché de matières premières *(m)*
Pt mercado de matérias primas *(m)*

mercato di sconto *(m)* It
De Diskontmarkt *(m)*
En discount market
Es mercado de descuentos *(m)*
Fr marché de l'escompte *(m)*
Pt mercado de desconto *(m)*

mercato esclusivo *(m)* It
De ausschließlicher Markt *(m)*
En exclusive market
Es mercado exclusivo *(m)*
Fr marché exclusif *(m)*
Pt mercado exclusivo *(m)*

mercato in declino *(m)* It
De Markt mit Baissetendenz *(m)*
En falling market
Es mercado en baja *(m)*
Fr marché orienté à la baisse *(m)*
Pt mercado em decréscimo *(m)*

mercato libero *(m)* It
De freier Markt *(m)*
En open market
Es mercado libre *(m)*
Fr marché libre *(m)*
Pt mercado livre *(m)*

mercato nero *(m)* It
De schwarzer Markt *(m)*
En black market
Es mercado negro *(m)*
Fr marché noir *(m)*
Pt mercado negro *(m)*

mercato tendente al rialzo
(m) It
De Haussemarkt *(m)*
En bull market
Es mercado alcista *(m)*
Fr marché orienté à la hausse *(m)*
Pt mercado de tendência altista *(m)*

mercato tendente al ribasso
(m) It
De Baissemarkt *(m)*
En bear market
Es mercado bajista *(m)*
Fr marché orienté à la baisse *(m)*
Pt mercado de tendência baixista *(m)*

merce *(f) n* It
De Güter; Waren *(n pl; f pl)*
En goods; merchandise
Es mercancías *(f pl)*
Fr marchandises *(f pl)*
Pt mercadorias *(f pl)*

merce avariata *(f)* It
De beschädigte Waren *(f pl)*
En damaged goods
Es mercancías averiadas *(f pl)*
Fr marchandises avariées *(f pl)*
Pt mercadorias danificadas *(f pl)*

merce di ritorno *(f pl)* It
De Retourware *(f)*
En returned goods
Es mercancías devueltas *(f pl)*
Fr marchandises de retour *(f pl)*
Pt mercadorias devolvidas *(f pl)*

merce in conto deposito *(f)* It
De Kommissionsgüter *(n pl)*
En goods on consignment
Es mercancías en consignación *(f pl)*
Fr marchandises en consignation *(f pl)*
Pt artigos à consignação *(m pl)*

merce in magazzino *(f)* It
De Vorrat auf Lager *(m)*
En stock in hand
Es mercancías en almacén *(f pl)*
Fr marchandises en magasin *(f pl)*
Pt mercadorias em existência *(f pl)*

merce pericolosa *(f)* It
De gefährliche Waren *(f pl)*
En dangerous goods
Es mercancías peligosas *(f pl)*
Fr marchandises dangereuses *(f pl)*
Pt mercadorias perigosas *(f pl)*

merce pronta *(f)* It
De sofort lieferbare Waren *(f pl)*
En spot goods
Es mercancías prontas *(f pl)*
Fr marchandises disponibles *(f pl)*
Pt mercadorias prontas *(f pl)*

merce sequestrata *(f)* It
De gepfändete Güter *(n pl)*
En distressed goods
Es mercancías embargadas *(f pl)*
Fr biens saisis *(m pl)*
Pt mercadorias embargadas *(f pl)*

merce soggetta ad approvazione *(f)* It
De Probegüter *(n pl)*
En goods on approval
Es mercancías sujetas a aprobación *(f pl)*
Fr marchandises à condition *(f pl)*
Pt artigos sujeitos a aprovação *(m pl)*

merchandise *n* En
De Waren; Güter *(f pl; n pl)*
Es mercancías *(f pl)*
Fr marchandises *(f pl)*
It merce *(f)*
Pt mercadorias *(f pl)*

merchant En
De Kaufmann *(m)*
Es comerciante *(m)*
Fr négociant *(m)*
It commerciante *(m)*
Pt comerciante *(m)*

merchantable quality En
De marktgängige Qualität *(f)*
Es calidad comerciable *(f)*
Fr qualité vendable *(f)*
It qualità commerciabile *(f)*
Pt qualidade comerciável *(f)*

merchant bank En
De Handelsbank *(f)*
Es banco mercantil *(m)*
Fr banque commerciale *(f)*
It banca commerciale *(f)*
Pt banco comercial *(m)*

merchant fleet En
De Handelsflotte *(f)*
Es flota mercanto *(f)*
Fr flotte marchande *(f)*
It flotta mercantile *(f)*
Pt frota mercante *(f)*

merchant ship En
De Handelsschiff *(n)*
Es barco marcante *(m)*
Fr navire marchand *(m)*
It nave mercantile *(f)*
Pt navio mercante *(m)*

merci deperibili *(f pl)* It
De leicht verderbliche Waren *(f pl)*
En perishable goods
Es mercancías perecederas *(f pl)*
Fr marchandises périssables *(f pl)*
Pt mercadorias perecíveis *(f pl)*

merci sotto vincolo doganale *(f pl)* It
De Waren unter Zollverschluß *(f pl)*
En bonded goods
Es mercancías en aduana *(f pl)*
Fr marchandises en douane *(f pl)*
Pt mercadorias à ordem da alfândega *(f pl)*

merge *vb* En
De fusionieren
Es amalgamar

Fr fusionner
It fondersi
Pt amalgamar

merger n En
De Fusion (f)
Es fusión (f)
Fr fusion (f)
It fusione (f)
Pt fusão (f)

Merkmal (n) n De
En feature
Es característica (f)
Fr particularité (f)
It caratteristica (f)
Pt característica (f)

merma natural (f) Es
De natürlicher Abgang (m)
En natural wastage
Fr déperdition naturelle (f)
It consumo naturale (m)
Pt desperdício natural (m)

mesa (f) n Es
De Schreibtisch (m)
En desk
Fr bureau (m)
It scrittoio (m)
Pt secretária (f)

Messe (f) n De
En fair
Es feria (f)
Fr foire (f)
It fiera (f)
Pt feira (f)

messen vb De '
En measure
Es medir
Fr mesurer; mensurer
It misurare
Pt medir

Messung (f) n De
En measurement
Es medida (f)
Fr mesurage (m)
It misura (f)
Pt medida (f)

mesurage (m) n Fr
De Messung (f)
En measurement
Es medida (f)
It misura (f)
Pt medida (f)

mesure (f) n Fr
De Maß (n)
En measure
Es medida (f)
It misura (f)
Pt medida (f)

mesurer vb Fr
De messen
En measure
Es medir
It misurare
Pt medir

meta (f) n Es, Pt
De Ziel (n)
En goal
Fr bout (m)
It scopo (m)

metade do preço Pt
De zum halben Preis
En half price
Es a mitad de precio
Fr à moitié prix
It metà prezzo

metal no noble (m) Es
De unedles Metall (n)
En base metal
Fr métal vil (m)
It basso metallo (m)
Pt metal pobre (m)

metal pobre (m) Pt
De unedles Metall (n)
En base metal
Es metal no noble (m)
Fr métal vil (m)
It basso metallo (m)

metal vil (m) Fr
De unedles Metall (n)
En base metal
Es metal no noble (m)
It basso metallo (m)
Pt metal pobre (m)

metà prezzo It
De zum halben Preis
En half price
Es a mitad de precio
Fr à moitié prix
Pt metade do preço

métreur-vérificateur (m) n Fr
De Massenberechner (m)
En quantity surveyor

Es medidor de contidades de
obra (m)
It perito misuratore (m)
Pt perito na avaliação de
quantidades (m)

metrication En
De Einführung des metri-
schen Systems (f)
Es adopción del sistema
métrico (f)
Fr introduction du système
métrique (f)
It adozione del sistema metrico (f)
Pt adopção do sistema métrico (f)

metric system En
De metrisches System (n)
Es sistema métrico (m)
Fr système métrique (m)
It sistema metrico (m)
Pt sistema métrico (m)

metric ton (tonne) En
De metrische Tonne (f)
Es tonelada métrica (f)
Fr tonne métrique (f)
It tonnellata metrica (f)
Pt tonelada métrica (f)

metrisches System (n) De
En metric system
Es sistema métrico (m)
Fr système métrique (m)
It sistema metrico (m)
Pt sistema métrico (m)

meubles (m pl) n Fr
De Möbel (n pl)
En furniture
Es muebles (m pl)
It mobilia (f)
Pt mobília (f)

mezza paga (f) It
De Halbsold (m)
En half-pay
Es medio salario (m)
Fr demi-salaire (m)
Pt meio-salário (m)

mezzo (adj) It
De halb
En half
Es medio
Fr à moitié; demi
Pt meio

mezzo pubblicitario *(m)* It
De Werbemittel *(n)*
En advertising medium
Es medio de publicidad *(m)*
Fr support publicitaire *(m)*
Pt meio publicitário *(m)*

microficha *(f)* n Es, Pt
De Mikrofilmkarte *(f)*
En microfiche
Fr microfiche *(f)*
It microscheda *(f)*

microfiche n En, Fr *(f)*
De Mikrofilmkarte *(f)*
Es microficha
It microscheda *(f)*
Pt microficha *(f)*

microscheda *(f)* n It
De Mikrofilmkarte *(f)*
En microfiche
Es microficha *(f)*
Fr microfiche *(f)*
Pt microficha *(f)*

middle man En
De Mittelsperson; Zwischen-
händler *(m f)*
Es intermediario *(m)*
Fr intermédiaire *(m)*
It intermediario *(m)*
Pt intermediário *(m)*

middle price En
De Mittelpreis; Mittelkurs *(m)*
Es precio medio *(m)*
Fr cours moyen *(m)*
It prezzo medio *(m)*
Pt preço médio *(m)*

miembro *(m)* n Es
De Mitglied *(n)*
En member
Fr membre *(m)*
It membro; socio *(m)*
Pt membro; sócio *(m)*

miembro fundador *(m)* Es
De Gründermitglied *(m)*
En founder member
Fr membre fondateur *(m)*
It socio fondatore *(m)*
Pt membro fundador *(m)*

Miete *(f)* n De
En rent
Es alquiler *(m)*

Fr loyer *(m)*
It pigione; affitto *(f m)*
Pt renda *(f)*

mieten vb De
En hire; rent
Es alquilar
Fr louer
It noleggiare; affittare
Pt alugar

Mieter *(m)* n De
En hirer; tenant; lessee
Es alquilador; arrendatario;
inquilino *(m)*
Fr locataire *(m)*
It noleggiatore; locatario *(m)*
Pt alugador; locatário; inqui-
lino *(m)*

(einen) Mieter entfernen De
En evict a tenant
Es desalojar un inquilino
Fr expulser un locataire
It sfrattare un locatario
Pt desalojar um inquilino

Mietzinskontrolle *(f)* n De
En rent control
Es control de alquileres *(m)*
Fr contrôle des loyers *(m)*
It blocco degli affitti *(m)*
Pt controlo de rendas *(m)*

miglioramento *(m)* n It
De Verbesserung *(f)*
En improvement
Es mejora *(f)*
Fr amélioration *(f)*
Pt melhoramento *(m)*

miglior offerente *(m)* It
De Meistbietende(r) *(m)*
En highest bidder
Es ofertante más alto *(m)*
Fr plus offrant enchérisseur
(m)
Pt proponente mais elevado
(m)

Mikrofilmkarte *(f)* n De
En microfiche
Es microficha *(f)*
Fr microfiche *(f)*
It microscheda *(f)*
Pt microficha *(f)*

Millimeterpapier *(n)* n De
En graph paper
Es papel milimetrado *(m)*
Fr papier millimétré *(m)*
It carta millimetrata *(f)*
Pt papel milimetrado *(m)*

mina *(f)* n Es, Pt
De Bergwerk *(n)*
En mine
Fr mine *(f)*
It miniera *(f)*

minderwertig adj De
En low-grade
Es baja calidad
Fr de qualité inférieure
It di qualità inferiore
Pt baixo-nível

Mindestpreis *(m)* n De
En reserve price
Es precio mínimo fijado *(m)*
Fr prix minimal *(m)*
It prezzo minimo *(m)*
Pt preço de reserva *(m)*

mine n En, Fr *(f)*
De Bergwerk *(n)*
Es mina *(f)*
It miniera *(f)*
Pt mina *(f)*

minerai de fer *(m)* Fr
De Eisenerz *(n)*
En iron ore
Es mineral de hierro *(m)*
It minerale di ferro *(m)*
Pt minério de ferro *(m)*

mineral n En, Es, Pt
De Mineral *(n)*
Fr minéral *(m)*
It minerale *(m)*

minéral *(m)* n Fr
De Mineral *(n)*
En mineral
Es mineral *(m)*
It minerale *(m)*
Pt mineral *(m)*

Mineral *(n)* n De
En mineral
Es mineral *(m)*
Fr minéral *(m)*
It minerale *(m)*
Pt mineral *(m)*

mineral concession En
De Bergwerkskonzession (f)
Es concesión minera (f)
Fr concession minière (f)
It concessione mineraria (f)
Pt concessão mineira (f)

mineral de hierro (m) Es
De Eisenerz (n)
En iron ore
Fr minerai de fer (m)
It minerale di ferro (m)
Pt minério de ferro (m)

minerale (m) n It
De Mineral (n)
En mineral
Es mineral (m)
Fr minéral (m)
Pt mineral (m)

minerale di ferro (m) It
De Eisenerz (n)
En iron ore
Es mineral de hierro (m)
Fr mineral de fer (m)
Pt minério de ferro (m)

Mineralgewinnungsrechte
     (n pl) n De
En mineral rights
Es derechos mineros (m pl)
Fr droits miniers (m pl)
It diritti minerari (m pl)
Pt direitos mineiros (m pl)

mineral rigths En
De Mineralgewinnungsrechte
     (n pl)
Es derechos mineros (m pl)
Fr droits miniers (m pl)
It diritti minerari (m pl)
Pt direitos mineiros (m pl)

minério de ferro (m) Pt
De Eisenerz (n)
En iron ore
Es mineral de hierro (m)
Fr minerai de fer (m)
It minerale di ferro (m)

miniera (f) n It
De Bergwerk (n)
En mine
Es mina (f)
Fr mine (f)
Pt mina (f)

minimal adj De
En minimum
Es mínimo
Fr minimum
It minimo
Pt mínimo

mínimo adj Es, Pt
De minimal
En minimum
Fr minimum
It minimo

minimo adj It
De minimal
En mínimum
Es mínimum
Fr minimum
Pt mínimo

minimum adj En, Fr
De minimal
Es mínimo
It minimo
Pt mínimo

ministère (m) n Fr
De Ministerium (n)
En ministry
Es ministerio (m)
It ministero (m)
Pt ministério (m)

ministerio (m) n Es
De Ministerium (n)
En ministry
Fr ministère (m)
It ministero (m)
Pt ministério (m)

ministério (m) n Pt
De Ministerium (n)
En ministry
Es ministerio (m)
Fr ministère (m)
It ministero (m)

Ministerium (n) n De
En ministry
Es ministerio (m)
Fr ministère (m)
It ministero (m)
Pt ministério (m)

ministero (m) n It
De Ministerium (n)
En ministry

Es ministerio (m)
Fr ministère (m)
Pt ministério (m)

ministry n En
De Ministerium (n)
Es ministerio (m)
Fr ministère (m)
It ministero (m)
Pt ministério (m)

Minoritätsbeteiligung (f) n De
En minority interest
Es participación de la minoría
     (f)
Fr participation de la minorité
     (f)
It interessenza di minoranza
     (f)
Pt interesse representado pe-
     la minoria (m)

minority interest En
De Minoritätsbeteiligung (f)
Es participación de la minoría
     (f)
Fr participation de la minorité
     (f)
It interessenza di minoranza
     (f)
Pt interesse representado pe-
     la minoria (m)

mint (n) En
De Münze; Münzanstalt(f)
Es casa de la moneda (f)
Fr la Monnaie (f)
It zecca (f)
Pt casa da moeda (f)

minuta de contrato (f) Pt
De Vertragsentwurf (m)
En draft contract
Es proyecto de contrato (m)
Fr projet de contrat (m)
It progetto di contratto (m)

minutas de acta (f pl) Pt
De Protokoll (n)
En minutes
Es actas (f pl)
Fr procès-verbal (m)
It verbale (m)

minutes (of a meeting) n En
De Protokoll (n)
Es actas (f pl)
Fr procès-verbal (m)
It verbale (m)
Pt minutas de acta (f pl)

miscalculation n En
De Rechenfehler (m)
Es cálculo erróneo (m)
Fr erreur de calcul (f)
It calcolo errato (m)
Pt erro de cálculo (m)

mise en demeure (f) Fr
De Inverzugsetzung (f)
En formal notice
Es aviso oficial (m)
It intimazione (f)
Pt notificação formal (f)

misrepresentation n En
De Verdrehung (f)
Es declaración falsa (f)
Fr déclaration inexacte (f)
It dichiarazione falsa (f)
Pt deturpação (f)

misura (f) n It
De Maß; Messung (n f)
En measure; measurement
Es medida (f)
Fr mesure; mesurage (f m)
Pt medida (f)

misurare vb It
De messen
En measure
Es medir
Fr mesurer; mensurer
Pt medir

mitarbeiten vb De
En collaborate
Es colaborar
Fr collaborer
It collaborare
Pt colaborar

mit Dividende De
En cum dividend
Es con dividendo
Fr droit attaché
It con dividendo
Pt com dividendo

Miteigentum (n) n De
En co-ownership; joint
    ownership
Es copropiedad (f)
Fr copropriété (f)
It condomino; comproprietà
    (m f)
Pt co-propriedade (f)

mit getrennter Post De
En under separate cover
Es por correo aparte
Fr sous pli séparé
It in piego a parte
Pt por correio separado

Mitglied (n) n De
En member
Es miembro; socio (m)
Fr membre (m)
It membro; socio (m)
Pt membro; sócio (m)

mit Rückgriff De
En with recourse
Es con recurso
Fr avec droit de recours
It con ricorso
Pt com recurso

Mittagspause (f) n De
En lunch-hour
Es hora del almuerzo (f)
Fr heure du déjeuner (f)
It ora di colazione (f)
Pt hora do almoço (f)

Mitte (f) n De
En centre
Am center
Es centro (m)
Fr centre (m)
It centro (m)
Pt centro (m)

Mitteilung (f) n De
En notification
Es notificación (f)
Fr notification (f)
It notifica (f)
Pt notificação (f)

Mittelkurs (m) n De
En middle price
Es precio medio (m)
Fr cours moyen (m)
It prezzo medio (m)
Pt preço médio (m)

mixed economy En
De Gemischtwirtschaft (f)
Es economía mixta (f)
Fr économie mixte (f)
It economia mista (f)
Pt economia mixta (f)

Möbel (n pl) n De
En furniture
Es muebles (m pl)
Fr meubles (m pl)
It mobilia (f)
Pt mobília (f)

mobilia (f) n It
De Möbel (n pl)
En furniture
Es muebles (m pl)
Fr meubles (m pl)
Pt mobília (f)

mobília (f) n Pt
De Möbel (n pl)
En furniture
Es muebles (m pl)
Fr meubles (m pl)
It mobilia (f)

mobiliario (m) n Es
De bewegliche Güter (n pl)
En movable assets
Fr biens mobiliers (m pl)
It proprietà mobiliare (f)
Pt bens mobiliários (m pl)

mobilidade (f) n Pt
De Beweglichkeit (f)
En mobility
Es movilidad (f)
Fr mobilité (f)
It mobilità (f)

mobilità (f) n It
De Beweglichkeit (f)
En mobility
Es movilidad (f)
Fr mobilité (f)
Pt mobilidade (f)

mobilité (f) n Fr
De Beweglichkeit (f)
En mobility
Es movilidad (f)
It mobilità (f)
Pt mobilidade (f)

mobility n En
De Beweglichkeit (f)
Es movilidad (f)
Fr mobilité (f)
It mobilità (f)
Pt mobilidade (f)

möblierte Mietwohnung *(f)*
De
En furnished flat
Am furnished apartment
Es piso amueblado *(m)*
Fr appartement meublé *(m)*
It appartamento ammobilia-
   to *(m)*
Pt andar mobilado *(m)*

moção *(f)* n Pt
De Antrag *(m)*
En motion
Es moción *(f)*
Fr motion *(f)*
It mozione *(f)*

moción *(f)* n Es
De Antrag *(m)*
En motion
Fr motion *(f)*
It mozione *(f)*
Pt moção *(f)*

Modeartikel *(m pl)* n De
En fancy goods
Es artículos de fantasía *(m pl)*
Fr nouveautés *(f pl)*
It articoli fantasia *(m pl)*
Pt artigos de fantasia *(m pl)*

mode d'emploi *(m)* Fr
De Gebrauchsanweisung *(f)*
En directions for use
Es modo de empleo *(f)*
It istruzioni per l'uso *(f pl)*
Pt instruções para uso *(f pl)*

modificações *(f pl)* n Pt
De Umbau *(m)*
En alterations
Es reformas *(f pl)*
Fr travaux de transformation
   (m pl)
It modifiche *(f pl)*

modificações e renovações Pt
De Änderungen und Erneue-
   rungen
En alterations and renewals
Es reformas y renovaciones
Fr réfections et améliorations
It modifiche e rinnovamenti

modificações e reparações Pt
De Änderungen und Repara-
   turen
En alterations and repairs
Es reformas y reparaciones

Fr transformations et réparations
It modifiche e riparazioni

modifiche *(f pl)* n It
De Umbau *(m)*
En alterations
Es reformas *(f pl)*
Fr travaux de transformation
   (m pl)
Pt modificações *(f pl)*

modifiche e rinnovamenti It
De Änderungen und Erneue-
   rungen
En alterations and renewals
Es reformas y renovaciones
Fr réfections et améliorations
Pt modificações e renovações

modifiche e riparazioni It
De Änderungen und Repara-
   turen
En alterations and repairs
Es reformas y reparaciones
Fr transformations et répara-
   tions
Pt modificações e reparações

mode de empleo *(m)* Es
De Gebrauchsanweisung *(f)*
En directions for use
Fr mode d'emploi *(f)*
It istruzioni per l'uso *(f pl)*
Pt instruções para uso *(f pl)*

modulo *(m)* n It
De Formular *(n)*
En form
Es formulario *(m)*
Fr formule *(f)*
Pt formulário *(m)*

modulo di domanda *(m)* It
De Antragsformular *(n)*
En application form
Es formulario de solicitud *(m)*
Fr formulaire de demande *(m)*
Pt formulário de requisição *(m)*

modulo in bianco *(m)* It
De Blankoformular *(n)*
En blank form
Es formulario en blanco *(m)*
Fr formulaire en blanc *(m)*
Pt impresso em branco *(m)*

modulo stampato *(m)* It
De Vordruck *(m)*
En printed form
Es formulario; impreso *(m)*
Fr formulaire *(m)*
Pt impresso *(m)*

moeda *(f)* n Pt
De Währung; Münze *(f)*
En currency; coin
Es moneda *(f)*
Fr monnaie; pièce *(f)*
It valuta; moneta *(f)*

moeda de reserva *(f)* Pt
De Reservewährung *(f)*
En reserve currency
Es moneda de reserva *(f)*
Fr monnaie de réserve *(f)*
It valuta di riserva *(f)*

moeda estrangeira *(f)* Pt
De Devisen *(f pl)*
En foreign currency
Es divisas extranjeras *(f pl)*
Fr devises *(f pl)*
It valuta estera *(f)*

moeda forte *(f)* Pt
De harte Währung *(f)*
En hard currency
Es moneda fuerta *(f)*
Fr monnaie forte *(f)*
It valuta forte *(f)*

moeda fraca *(f)* Pt
De schwache Währung *(f)*
En soft currency
Es moneda débil *(f)*
Fr monnaie faible *(f)*
It valuta debole *(f)*

moeda legal *(f)* Pt
De gesetzliches Zahlungsmit-
   tel *(n)*
En legal tender
Es moneda legal *(f)*
Fr monnaie légale *(f)*
It denaro a corso legale *(m)*

möglich adj De
En possible; potential
Es posible; potencial
Fr possible; potentiel
It possibile; potenziale
Pt possível; potencial

moisson *(f) n* Fr
De Ernte *(f)*
En harvest
Es cosecha *(f)*
It raccolto *(m)*
Pt colheita *(f)*

Mole *(f) n* De
En jetty
Es digue *(m)*
Fr jetée; digue *(f)*
It molo *(m)*
Pt pontão; cais *(m)*

molo *(m) n* It
De Mole *(f)*
En jetty
Es digue *(m)*
Fr jetée; digue *(f)*
Pt pontão; cais *(m)*

moltiplicare *vb* It
De vervielfältigen
En multiply
Es multiplicar
Fr multiplier
Pt multiplicar

moltiplicatore *(m) n* It
De Vervielfältiger *(m)*
En multiplier
Es multiplicador *(m)*
Fr multiplicateur *(m)*
Pt multiplicador *(m)*

Monatsrate *(f) n* De
En monthly instalment
Es mensualidad *(f)*
Fr mensualité *(f)*
It mensilità *(f)*
Pt prestação mensal *(f)*

moneda *(f) n* Es
De Währung; Münze *(f)*
En currency; coin
Fr monnaie; pièce *(f)*
It valuta; moneta *(f)*
Pt moeda *(f)*

moneda débil *(f)* Es
De schwache Währung *(f)*
En soft currency
Fr monnaie faible *(f)*
It valuta debole *(f)*
Pt moeda fraca *(f)*

moneda de reserva *(f)* Es
De Reservewährung *(f)*
En reserve currency
Fr monnaie de réserve *(f)*
It valuta di riserva *(f)*
Pt moeda de reserva *(f)*

moneda fuerta *(f)* Es
De harte Währung *(f)*
En hard currency
Fr monnaie forte *(f)*
It valuta forte *(f)*
Pt moeda forte *(f)*

moneda legal *(f)* Es
De gesetzliches Zahlungsmittel *(n)*
En legal tender
Fr monnaie légale *(f)*
It denaro a corso legale *(m)*
Pt moeda legal *(f)*

moneda suelta *(f)* Es
De Kleingeld *(n)*
En small change
Fr petite monnaie *(f)*
It spiccioli *(m pl)*
Pt troco miúdo *(m)*

moneta *(f) n* It
De Münze *(f)*
En coin
Es moneda *(f)*
Fr pièce de monnaie *(f)*
Pt moeda *(f)*

monetary policy En
De Währungspolitik *(f)*
Es política monetaria *(f)*
Fr politique monétaire *(f)*
It politica monetaria *(f)*
Pt política monetária *(f)*

monetary reform En
De Währungsreform *(f)*
Es reforma monetaria *(f)*
Fr réforme monétaire *(f)*
It riforma monetaria *(f)*
Pt reforma monetária *(f)*

money *n* En
De Geld *(n)*
Es dinero *(m)*
Fr argent *(m)*
It denaro *(m)*
Pt dinheiro *(m)*

moneylender *n* En
De Geldverleiher *(m)*
Es prestamista *(m)*
Fr prêteur d'argent *(m)*
It usuraio *(m)*
Pt prestamista *(m)*

money market En
De Geldmarkt *(m)*
Es mercado de dinero *(m)*
Fr marché monétaire *(m)*
It mercato di denaro *(m)*
Pt mercado monetário *(m)*

money on call En
De Sichtgelder *(n pl)*
Es dinero a la vista *(m)*
Fr argent à vue *(m)*
It denaro a vista *(m)*
Pt dinheiro à ordem *(m)*

monnaie *(f) n* Fr
De Währung *(f)*
En currency
Es moneda *(f)*
It valuta *(f)*
Pt moeda *(f)*

(la) Monnaie *(f) n* Fr
De Münze *(f)*
En mint
Es casa de la moneda *(f)*
It zecca *(f)*
Pt casa da moeda *(f)*

monnaie de réserve *(f)* Fr
De Reservewährung *(f)*
En reserve currency
Es moneda de reserva *(f)*
It valuta di riserva *(f)*
Pt moeda de reserva *(f)*

monnaie faible *(f)* Fr
De schwache Währung *(f)*
En soft currency
Es moneda débil *(f)*
It valuta debole *(f)*
Pt moeda fraca *(f)*

monnaie forte *(f)* Fr
De harte Währung *(f)*
En hard currency
Es moneda fuerta *(f)*
It valuta forte *(f)*
Pt moeda forte *(f)*

monnaie légale (f) Fr
De gesetzliches Zahlungsmittel (n)
En legal tender
Es moneda legal (f)
It denaro a corso legale (m)
Pt moeda legal (f)

Monopol (n) n De
En monopoly
Es monopolio (m)
Fr monopole (m)
It monopolio (m)
Pt monopólio (m)

monopole (m) n Fr
De Monopol (n)
En monopoly
Es monopolio (m)
It monopolio (m)
Pt monopólio (m)

monopolio (m) n Es, It
De Monopol (n)
En monopoly
Fr monopole (m)
Pt monopólio (m)

monopólio (m) n Pt
De Monopol (n)
En monopoly
Es monopolio (m)
Fr monopole (m)
It monopolio (m)

monopoly n En
De Monopol (n)
Es monopolio (m)
Fr monopole (m)
It monopolio (m)
Pt monopólio (m)

Montageband (n) n De
En assembly line
Es línea de montaje (f)
Fr chaîne de montage (f)
It catena di montaggio (f)
Pt cadeia de montagem (f)

montant brut (m) Fr
De Bruttobetrag (m)
En gross amount
Es importe bruto (m)
It importo lordo (m)
Pt importância total (f)

montant net (m) Fr
De Nettobetrag (m)
En net amount

Es importe neto (m)
It importo netto (m)
Pt importância líquida (f)

montant nominal (m) Fr
De Nominalbetrag (m)
En nominal amount
Es suma nominal (f)
It importo nominale (m)
Pt quantia nominal (f)

monthly instalment En
De Monatsrate (f)
Es mensualidad (f)
Fr mensualité (f)
It mensilità (f)
Pt prestação mensal (f)

montra (f) n Pt
De Schaukasten (m)
En display unit
Es presentación (f)
Fr présentoir (m)
It mostra (f)

moratoire (m) n Fr
De Zahlungsaufschub (m)
En moratorium
Es moratorio (m)
It moratoria (f)
Pt moratória (f)

moratoria (f) n It
De Zahlungsaufschub (m)
En moratorium
Es moratorio (m)
Fr moratoire (m)
Pt moratória (f)

moratória (f) n Pt
De Zahlungsaufschub (m)
En moratorium
Es moratorio (m)
Fr moratoire (m)
It moratoria (f)

moratorio (m) n Es
De Zahlungsaufschub (m)
En moratorium
Fr moratoire (m)
It moratoria (f)
Pt moratória (f)

moratorium n En
De Zahlungsaufschub (m)
Es moratorio (m)
Fr moratoire (m)
It moratoria (f)
Pt moratória (f)

morgen adj De
En tomorrow
Es mañana
Fr demain
It domani
Pt amanhã

mort (f) n Fr
De Tod (m)
En death
Es muerte (m)
It morte (f)
Pt morte (f)

mortalidad (f) n Es
De Sterblichkeitsziffer (f)
En death rate
Fr taux de mortalité (m)
It tasso di mortalità (m)
Pt taxa de mortalidade (f)

morte (f) n It, Pt
De Tod (m)
En death
Es muerte (m)
Fr mort (f)

mortgage n En
De Hypothek (f)
Es hipoteca (f)
Fr hypothèque (f)
It ipoteca (f)
Pt hipoteca (f)

mortgage debenture En
De hypothekarisch gesicherte Schuldverschreibung (f)
Es obligación hipotecaria (f)
Fr obligation hypothécaire (f)
It obbligazione ipotecaria (f)
Pt obrigação hipotecária (f)

mostra (f) n It
De Schaustellung (f)
En display
Es presentación (f)
Fr présentation (f)
Pt exposição (f)

mostra in vetrina (f) It
De Fensterauslage (f)
En window-display
Es exhibición en vitrina (f)
Fr étalage (m)
Pt exposição de montra (f)

motif d'exportation *(m)* Fr
De Ausfuhranreiz *(m)*
En export incentive
Es estímulo de exportación *(m)*
It incentivo alla esportazione *(m)*
Pt incentivo para a exportação *(m)*

motins e perturbações civis Pt
De Aufruhr und innere Unruhen
En riot and civil commotion
Es revueltas y conmociones civiles
Fr émeutes et désordres
It rivolte e moti civili

motion *n* En, Fr *(f)*
De Antrag *(m)*
Es moción *(f)*
It mozione *(f)*
Pt moção *(f)*

motivational research En
De Motivforschung *(f)*
Es investigación de motivación *(f)*
Fr étude de motivation *(f)*
It indagine sulle motivazioni *(f)*
Pt investigação sobre motivação *(f)*

Motivforschung *(f)* *n* De
En motivational research
Es investigación de motivación *(f)*
Fr étude de motivation *(f)*
It indagine sulle motivazioni *(f)*
Pt investigação sobre motivação *(f)*

motor a jacto *(m)* Pt
De Düsenmotor *(m)*
En jet engine
Es motor de propulsión a chorro *(m)*
Fr réacteur *(m)*
It motore a reazione *(m)*

motor de propulsión a chorro *(m)* Es
De Düsenmotor *(m)*
En jet engine

Fr réacteur *(m)*
It motore a reazione *(m)*
Pt motor a jacto *(m)*

motore a reazione *(m)* It
De Düsenmotor *(m)*
En jet engine
Es motor de propulsión a chorro *(m)*
Fr réacteur *(m)*
Pt motor a jacto *(m)*

movable assets En
De bewegliche Güter *(n pl)*
Es mobiliario *(m)*
Fr biens mobiliers *(m pl)*
It proprietà mobiliare *(f)*
Pt bens mobiliários *(m pl)*

móvel ficheiro *(m)* Pt
De Aktenschrank *(m)*
En filing cabinet
Es fichero *(m)*
Fr classeur *(m)*
It schedario *(m)*

movilidad *(f)* *n* Es
De Beweglichkeit *(f)*
En mobility
Fr mobilité *(f)*
It mobilitá *(f)*
Pt mobilidade *(f)*

movimento de dinheiro *(m)* Pt
De Umsatz *(m)*
En turnover
Es volumen de ventas *(m)*
Fr chiffre d'affaires *(m)*
It giro d'affari *(m)*

movimento della mano d'opera *(m)* It
De Arbeitsplatzwechsel *(m)*
En labour turnover
Es movimiento de la mano de obra *(m)*
Fr fluctuations de personnel *(f pl)*
Pt movimento de trabalhadores *(m)*

movimento de trabalhadores *(m)* Pt
De Arbeitsplatzwechsel *(m)*
En labour turnover
Es movimiento de la mano de obra *(m)*

Fr fluctuations de personnel *(f pl)*
It movimento della mano d'opera *(m)*

movimento em dinheiro *(m)* Pt
De Cash-flow *(m)*
En cash flow
Es flujo de caja *(m)*
Fr cash flow *(m)*
It flusso di cassa *(m)*

movimiento de la mano de obra *(m)* Es
De Arbeitsplatzwechsel *(m)*
En labour turnover
Fr fluctuations de personnel *(f pl)*
It movimento della mano d'opera *(m)*
Pt movimento de trabalhadores *(m)*

moyenne *(f)* *n* Fr
De Durchschnitt *(m)*
En average
Es promedio *(m)*
It media *(f)*
Pt média *(f)*

moyenne arithmétique *(f)* Fr
De arithmetisches Mittel *(n)*
En arithmetic mean
Es media aritmética *(f)*
It media aritmetica *(f)*
Pt média aritmética *(f)*

moyenne pondérée *(f)* Fr
De gewogener Durchschnitt *(m)*
En weighted average
Es media ponderada *(f)*
It media ponderata *(f)*
Pt média ponderada *(f)*

mozione *(f)* *n* It
De Antrag *(m)*
En motion
Es moción *(f)*
Fr motion *(f)*
Pt moção *(f)*

muebles *(m pl)* *n* Es
De Möbel *(n pl)*
En furniture
Fr meubles *(m pl)*
It mobilia *(f)*
Pt mobília *(f)*

muellaje *(m)* n Es
De Kaigeld *(n)*
En wharfage
Fr quayage *(m)*
It diritto di sosta *(m)*
Pt atracagem *(f)*

muelle *(m)* n Es
De Kai; Dock *(m n)*
En quay; wharf; dock
Fr quai; dock *(m)*
It banchina; dock *(f m)*
Pt cais; doca *(m f)*

muerte *(m)* n Es
De Tod *(m)*
En death
Fr mort *(f)*
It morte *(f)*
Pt morte *(f)*

muestra *(f)* n Es
De Probe; Muster *(f n)*
En sample
Fr échantillon *(m)*
It campione *(m)*
Pt amostra *(f)*

muestra aleatoria *(f)* Es
De Stichprobe *(f)*
En random sample
Fr épreuve au hasard *(f)*
It campione a casaccio *(m)*
Pt amostra avulsa *(f)*

muestra gratuita *(f)* Es
De kostenlose Probe *(f)*
En free sample
Fr échantillon gratuit *(m)*
It campione gratuito *(m)*
Pt amostra grátis *(f)*

muestra sin valor *(f)* Es
De Muster ohne Wert *(n)*
En sample of no value
Fr échantillon sans valeur *(m)*
It campione senza valore *(m)*
Pt amostra sem valor *(f)*

multa *(f)* n Es, It, Pt
De Geldstrafe *(f)*
En fine
Fr amende *(f)*

multa pesada *(f)* Pt
De schwere Buße *(f)*
En heavy fine

Es sanción elevada *(f)*
Fr forte amende *(f)*
It forte multa *(f)*

multilateral trade En
De mehrseitiges Handeln *(n)*
Es comercio multilateral *(m)*
Fr commerce multilatéral *(m)*
It commercio multilaterale *(m)*
Pt comércio multilateral *(m)*

multiplicador *(m)* n Es, Pt
De Vervielfältiger *(m)*
En multiplier
Fr multiplicateur *(m)*
It moltiplicatore *(m)*

multiplicar *vb* Es, Pt
De vervielfältigen
En multiply
Fr multiplier
It moltiplicare

multiplicateur *(m)* n Fr
De Vervielfältiger *(m)*
En multiplier
Es multiplicador *(m)*
It moltiplicatore *(m)*
Pt multiplicador *(m)*

multiplier n En
De Vervielfältiger *(m)*
Es multiplicador *(m)*
Fr multiplicateur *(m)*
It moltiplicatore *(m)*
Pt multiplicador *(m)*

multiplier *vb* Fr
De vervielfältigen
En multiply
Es multiplicar
It moltiplicare
Pt multiplicar

multiply *vb* En
De vervielfältigen
Es multiplicar
Fr multiplier
It moltiplicare
Pt multiplicar

**mündelsichere Wert-
papiere** *(n pl)* De
En gilt-edged securities
Es valores de toda confianza *(m pl)*
Fr valeurs de tout repos *(f pl)*

It titoli di assoluta fiducia *(m pl)*
Pt valores de toda confiança *(m pl)*

municipal *adj* En, Es, Pt
De Kommunal-
Fr communal
It municipale

municipale *adj* It
De Kommunal-
En municipal
Es municipal
Fr communal
Pt municipal

Münze *(f)* n De
En coin
Es moneda *(f)*
Fr pièce de monnaie *(f)*
It moneta *(f)*
Pt moeda *(f)*

Münze (Münzanstalt) *(f)* n De
En mint
Es casa de la moneda *(f)*
Fr la Monnaie *(f)*
It zecca *(f)*
Pt casa da moeda *(f)*

Musteranlage *(f)* n De
En pilot plant
Es instalación piloto *(f)*
Fr installation pilote *(f)*
It impianto piloto *(m)*
Pt instalação piloto *(f)*

Muster ohne Wert n De
En sample of no value
Es muestra sin valor *(f)*
Fr échantillon sans valeur *(m)*
It campione senza valore *(m)*
Pt amostra sem valor *(f)*

Mutmaßung *(f)* n De
En guess-work
Es conjetura *(f)*
Fr conjecture *(f)*
It congettura *(f)*
Pt conjectura *(f)*

Muttergesellschaft *(f)* n De
En parent company
Es compañía matriz *(f)*
Fr société mère *(f)*
It società madre *(f)*
Pt empresa matriz *(f)*

mutua assicurazione *(f)* It
De Versicherung auf Gegen-
  seitigkeit *(f)*
En mutual insurance
Es coaseguro *(m)*
Fr assurance mutuelle *(f)*
Pt seguro mútuo *(m)*

mutual agreement En
De gegenseitiges Einvernehmen *(n)*
Es acuerdo común *(m)*
Fr accord mutuel *(m)*
It comune accordo *(m)*
Pt acordo mútuo *(m)*

mutualidade *(f)* n Pt
De Versicherungsverein auf
  Gegenseitigkeit *(m)*
En friendly society
Am lodge
Es sociedad de socorro mutuo *(f)*
Fr société de secours mutuel *(f)*
It società di mutuo soccorso *(f)*

mutual insurance En
De Versicherung auf Gegen-
  seitigkeit *(f)*
Es coaseguro *(m)*
Fr assurance mutuelle *(f)*
It mutua assicurazione *(f)*
Pt seguro mútuo *(m)*

N

Nachahmung *(f)* n De
En imitation
Es imitación *(f)*
Fr imitation *(f)*
It imitazione *(f)*
Pt imitação *(f)*

nachdatierter Scheck *(m)* De
En postdated cheque
Es cheque a fecha retrasada *(m)*
Fr chèque postdaté *(m)*
It assegno postdatato *(m)*
Pt cheque post-datado *(m)*

Nachfrage *(f)* n De
En demand; inquiry
Es demanda *(f)*
Fr demande *(f)*
It domanda *(f)*
Pt procura; pergunta *(f)*

Nachfragekurve *(f)* n De
En demand curve
Es curva de relación demanda *(f)*
Fr courbe de la demande *(f)*
It curva della domanda *(f)*
Pt curva de procura *(f)*

Nachfrist *(f)* n De
En days of grace
Es días de gracia *(f pl)*
Fr délai supplémentaire *(m)*
It giorni di grazia *(m pl)*
Pt dias de tolerância *(m pl)*

Nachlaß (Erbschaft) *(m)* n De
En estate
Es herencia *(f)*
Fr succession *(f)*
It patrimonio; successione *(m f)*
Pt património; herança *(m f)*

Nachlaß (Rabatt) *(m)* n De
En rebate
Es rebaja *(f)*
Fr rabais *(m)*
It ribasso; sconto *(m)*
Pt desconto *(m)*

nachlassen vb De
En fall off; decrease
Es bajar de valor; disminuir
Fr ralentir; baisser de valeur
It diminuire
Pt diminuir; decrescer

Nachlaßsteuer *(f)* n De
En estate duty; estate tax
Es derechos de sucesión *(m pl)*
Fr droits de succession *(m pl)*
It diritti di successione *(m pl)*
Pt direitos de sucessão *(m pl)*

Nachlaßverwalter *(m)* n De
En administrator
Es administrador *(m)*
Fr curateur *(m)*
It curatore *(m)*
Pt curador *(m)*

nachprüfen vb De
En verify
Es verificar
Fr vérifier
It verificare
Pt verificar

Nachrichtenbüro *(n)* n De
En news agency
Es agencia de prensa *(f)*
Fr agence de presse *(f)*
It agenzia d'informazioni *(f)*
Pt agência de notícias *(f)*

Nachschätzung *(f)* n De
En supplementary estimate
Es cálculo suplementario *(m)*
Fr devis supplémentaire *(m)*
It preventivo supplementare *(m)*
Pt estimativa suplementar *(f)*

Nachschlagewerk *(n)* n De
En reference book
Es libro de consulta *(m)*
Fr ouvrage de référence *(m)*
It libro di consultazione *(m)*
Pt livro de consulta *(m)*

Nachschrift *(f)* n De
En postscript (PS)
Es posdata *(f)*
Fr post-scriptum; postface *(m f)*
It poscritto (PS) *(m)*
Pt pós-escrito; post-scriptum (PS) *(m)*

Nachtarbeit *(f)* n De
En nightwork
Es trabajo nocturno *(m)*
Fr travail de nuit *(m)*
It lavoro notturno *(m)*
Pt trabalho nocturno *(m)*

Nachteil *(m)* n De
En prejudice
Es prejuicio; perjuicio *(m)*
Fr préjudice *(m)*
It pregiudizio *(m)*
Pt desvantagem; prejuízo *(f m)*

nachträglicher Umsatzbonus *(m)* De
En deferred rebate
Es descuento diferido *(m)*

Fr   rabais différé *(m)*
It   sconto differito *(m)*
Pt   dedução adiada *(f)*

Nachtschicht *(f)* n De
En   night shift
Es   turno de noche *(m)*
Fr   équipe de nuit *(m)*
It   turno di notte *(m)*
Pt   turno da noite *(m)*

Nachttresor *(m)* n De
En   night safe
Es   caja de seguridad noctur-
     na *(f)*
Fr   coffre de nuit *(m)*
It   deposito notturno *(m)*
Pt   cofre nocturno *(m)*

Nachtwächter *(m)* n De
En   nightwatchman
Es   guarda de noche *(m)*
Fr   gardien de nuit *(m)*
It   guardiano notturno *(m)*
Pt   guarda-nocturno *(m)*

Nachzugsaktien *(f pl)* n De
En   defered shares
Es   acciones aplazadas *(f pl)*
Fr   actions différées *(f pl)*
It   azioni postergate *(f pl)*
Pt   acções diferidas *(f pl)*

nacional *adj* Es, Pt
De   national
En   national
Fr   national
It   nazionale

nacionalidad *(f)* n Es
De   Staatsangehörigkeit *(f)*
En   nationality
Fr   nationalité *(f)*
It   nazionalità *(f)*
Pt   nacionalidade *(f)*

nacionalidade *(f)* n Pt
De   Staatsangehörigkeit *(f)*
En   nationality
Es   nacionalidad *(f)*
Fr   nationalité *(f)*
It   nazionalità *(f)*

nacionalização *(f)* n Pt
De   Verstaatlichung *(f)*
En   nationalization
Es   nacionalización *(f)*
Fr   nationalisation *(f)*
It   nazionalizzazione *(f)*

nacionalización *(f)* n Es
De   Verstaatlichung *(f)*
En   nationalization
Fr   nationalisation *(f)*
It   nazionalizzazione *(f)*
Pt   nacionalização *(f)*

nada lucrativo Es
De   unvorteilhaft
En   unprofitable
Fr   sans profit
It   poco proficuo
Pt   não lucrativo

na fábrica Pt
De   ab Fabrik
En   ex factory
Es   de fábrica
Fr   prise usine
It   franco fabbrica

nähere Umstände *(m pl)* De
En   further particulars
Es   más detalles *(m pl)*
Fr   plus amples renseigne-
     ments *(m pl)*
It   ulteriori particolari *(m pl)*
Pt   pormenores adicionais
     (m pl)

naked bond Am
En   unsecured debenture
De   ungesicherte Schuldver-
     schreibung *(f)*
Es   obligación no garantizada
     (f)
Fr   obligation sans garantie *(f)*
It   obbligazione non garantita
     (f)
Pt   obrigação sem garantia *(f)*

nantissement *(m)* n Fr
De   Nebenbürgschaft; Hypo-
     thek *(f)*
En   security; hypothecation
Es   fianza; hipoteca *(f)*
It   pegno; ipoteca *(m f)*
Pt   fiança; hipoteca *(f)*

não-aceitação *(f)* n Pt
De   Nichtannahme *(f)*
En   nonacceptance
Es   rechazo *(m)*
Fr   non-acceptation *(f)*
It   mancata accettazione *(f)*

não autorizado Pt
De   unbefugt
En   unauthorized

Es   inautorizado
Fr   non autorisé
It   non autorizzato

não-cumprimento *(m)* n Pt
De   Nichterfüllung *(f)*
En   nonfulfilment
Es   incumplimiento *(m)*
Fr   non-exécution *(f)*
It   inadempienza *(f)*

não lucrativo Pt
De   unvorteilhaft
En   unprofitable
Es   nada lucrativo
Fr   sans profit
It   poco proficuo

**não transaccionável por
terceiros** Pt
De   nicht übertragbar
En   not negotiable
Es   no negociable
Fr   non négociable
It   non negoziabile

nascondersi *vb* It
De   sich heimlich davonma-
     chen
En   abscond
Es   esconderse
Fr   s'enfuir; décamper
Pt   ausentar-se para parte in-
     certa

nastro magnetico *(m)* It
De   Magnetband *(n)*
En   magnetic tape
Es   cint magnética *(f)*
Fr   bande magnétique *(f)*
Pt   fita magnética *(f)*

national *adj* De, En, Fr
Es   nacional
It   nazionale
Pt   nacional

national debt En
De   Staatsschuld *(f)*
Es   deuda pública *(f)*
Fr   dette publique *(f)*
It   debito pubblico *(m)*
Pt   dívida pública *(f)*

Nationaleinkommen *(n)* n De
En   national income
Es   renta nacional *(f)*
Fr   revenu national *(m)*
It   reddito nazionale *(m)*
Pt   receita pública *(f)*

national income En
De Nationaleinkommen (n)
Es renta nacional (f)
Fr revenu national (m)
It reddito nazionale (m)
Pt receita pública (f)

national insurance En
Am social security
De staatliche Versicherung (f)
Es seguridad social (f)
Fr assurance d'état (f)
It assicurazione obbligatoria (f)
Pt seguro nacional (m)

nationalisation (f) n Fr
De Verstaatlichung (f)
En nationalization
Es nacionalización (f)
It nazionalizzazione (f)
Pt nacionalização (f)

nationalité (f) n Fr
De Staatsangehörigkeit (f)
En nationality
Es nacionalidad (f)
It nazionalità (f)
Pt nacionalidade (f)

nationality n En
De Staatsangehörigkeit (f)
Es nacionalidad (f)
Fr nationalité (f)
It nazionalità (f)
Pt nacionalidade (f)

nationalization n En
De Verstaatlichung (f)
Es nacionalización (f)
Fr nationalisation (f)
It nazionalizzazione (f)
Pt nacionalização (f)

nationalized industry En
De verstaatlichte Industrie (f)
Es industria nacionalizada (f)
Fr industrie nationalisée (f)
It industria nazionalizzata (f)
Pt indústria nacionalizada (f)

natural gas En
De Erdgas (n)
Es gas natural (m)
Fr gaz naturel (m)
It gas naturale (m)
Pt gás natural (m)

natural wastage En
De natürlicher Abgang (m)
Es merma natural (f)
Fr déperdition naturelle (f)
It consumo naturale (m)
Pt desperdício natural (m)

natürliche Abnützung (f) De
En wear and tear
Es desgaste natural (m)
Fr usure normale (f)
It logorio naturale (m)
Pt desgaste (m)

natürlicher Abgang (m) De
En natural wastage
Es merma natural (f)
Fr déperdition naturelle (f)
It consumo naturale (m)
Pt desperdício natural (m)

nautical adj En
De nautisch
Es náutico
Fr nautique
It nautico
Pt náutico

náutico adj Es, Pt
De nautisch
En nautical
Fr nautique
It nautico

nautico adj It
De nautisch
En nautical
Es náutico
Fr nautique
Pt náutico

nautique adj Fr
De nautisch
En nautical
Es náutico
It nautico
Pt náutico

nautisch adj De
En nautical
Es náutico
Fr nautique
It nautico
Pt náutico

nave (f) n It
De Schiff (n)
En ship

Es barco (m)
Fr navire (m)
Pt naivo (m)

nave da carico (f) It
De Frachtschiff (n)
En cargo boat
Es buque de carga (m)
Fr cargo (m)
Pt navio de carga (m)

nave da contenitori (f) It
De Containerschiff (n)
En container ship
Es barco de contenedores (m)
Fr navire porte-containers (m)
Pt navio de contentores (m)

nave di linea (f) It
De Linienschiff (n)
En liner
Es vapor de línea (m)
Fr paquebot (m)
Pt paquete (m)

navegable adj Es
De schiffbar
En navigable
Fr navigable
It navigabile
Pt navegável

navegação (f) n Pt
De Schiffahrt (f)
En navigation
Es navegación (f)
Fr navigation (f)
It navigazione (f)

navegación (f) n Es
De Schiffahrt (f)
En navigation
Fr navigation (f)
It navigazione (f)
Pt navegação (f)

navegável adj Pt
De schiffbar
En navigable
Es navegable
Fr navigable
It navigabile

nave mercantile (f) It
De Handelsschiff (n)
En merchant ship

Es barco mercante *(m)*
Fr navire marchand *(m)*
Pt navio mercante *(m)*

nave traghetto *(f)* It
De Fährboot *(n)*
En ferry-boat
Es transbordador *(m)*
Fr bac *(m)*
Pt barco de travessia *(m)*

navigabile *adj* It
De schiffbar
En navigable
Es navegable
Fr navigable
Pt navegável

navigable *adj* En, Fr
De schiffbar
Es navegable
It navigabile
Pt navegável

navigation *n* En, Fr *(f)*
De Schiffahrt *(f)*
Es navegación *(f)*
It navigazione *(f)*
Pt navegação *(f)*

navigazione *(f)* n It
De Schiffahrt *(f)*
En navigation
Es navegación *(f)*
Fr navigation *(f)*
Pt navegação *(f)*

navio *(m)* n Pt
De Schiff *(n)*
En ship
Es barco *(m)*
Fr navire *(m)*
It nave *(f)*

navio de carga *(m)* Pt
De Frachtschiff *(n)*
En cargo boat
Es buque de carga *(m)*
Fr cargo *(m)*
It nave da carico *(f)*

navio de contentores *(m)* Pt
De Containerschiff *(n)*
En container ship
Es barco de contenedores *(m)*
Fr navire porte-containers *(m)*
It nave da contenitori *(f)*

navio mercante *(m)* Pt
De Handelsschiff *(n)*
En merchant ship
Es barco mercante *(m)*
Fr navire marchand *(m)*
It nave mercantile *(f)*

navire *(m)* n Fr
De Schiff *(n)*
En ship
Es barco *(m)*
It nave *(f)*
Pt navio *(m)*

navire de tramping *(m)* Fr
De Trampschiff *(n)*
En tramp steamer
Es vapor volandero *(m)*
It carretta *(f)*
Pt vapor de serviço autónomo *(m)*

navire marchand *(m)* Fr
De Handelsschiff *(n)*
En merchant ship
Es barco mercante *(m)*
It nave mercantile *(f)*
Pt navio mercante *(m)*

navire porte-containers *(m)* Fr
De Containerschiff *(n)*
En container ship
Es barco de contenedores *(m)*
It nave da contenitori *(f)*
Pt navio de contentores *(m)*

nazionale *adj* It
De national
En nacional
Es nacional
Fr national
Pt nacional

nazionalità *(f)* n It
De Staatsangehörigkeit *(f)*
En nationality
Es nacionalidad *(f)*
Fr nationalité *(f)*
Pt nacionalidade *(f)*

nazionalizzazione *(f)* n It
De Verstaatlichung *(f)*
En nationalization
Es nacionalización *(f)*
Fr nationalisation *(f)*
Pt nacionalização *(f)*

Nebenbürgschaft *(f)* n De
En security
Es fianza *(f)*
Fr nantissement *(m)*
It pegno *(m)*
Pt fiança *(f)*

Nebenkosten *(pl)* n De
En incidental expenses
Es gastos imprevistos *(m pl)*
Fr faux frais *(m pl)*
It spese impreviste *(f pl)*
Pt despesas ocasionais *(f pl)*

Nebenprodukt *(n)* n De
En by-product
Es producto derivado *(m)*
Fr sous-produit *(m)*
It sottoprodotto *(m)*
Pt produto derivado *(m)*

negative balance Am
En adverse balance
De Passivsaldo *(m)*
Es saldo adverso *(m)*
Fr balance déficitaire *(f)*
It saldo passivo *(m)*
Pt saldo negativo *(m)*

negative Einkommensteuer *(f)* De
En negative income tax
Es impuesto negativo sobre renta *(m)*
Fr impôt négatif sur le revenu *(m)*
It imposta negativa sul reddito *(f)*
Pt imposto negativo sobre receita *(m)*

negative income tax En
De negative Einkommensteuer *(f)*
Es impuesto negativo sobre renta *(m)*
Fr impôt négatif sur le revenu *(m)*
It imposta negativa sul reddito *(f)*
Pt imposto negativo sobre receita *(m)*

negligence *n* En
De Fahrlässigkeit *(f)*
Es negligencia *(f)*
Fr négligence *(f)*
It negligenza *(f)*
Pt negligência *(f)*

négligence *(f)* n Fr
De Fahrlässigkeit *(f)*
En negligence
Es negligencia *(f)*
It negligenza *(f)*
Pt negligência *(f)*

negligencia *(f)* n Es
De Fahrlässigkeit *(f)*
En negligence
Fr négligence *(f)*
It negligenza *(f)*
Pt negligência *(f)*

negligência *(f)* n Pt
De Fahrlässigkeit *(f)*
En negligence
Es negligencia *(f)*
Fr négligence *(f)*
It negligenza *(f)*

negligenza *(f)* n It
De Fahrlässigkeit *(f)*
En negligence
Es negligencia *(f)*
Fr négligence *(f)*
Pt negligência *(f)*

negociable adj Es
De begebbar
En negotiable
Fr négociable
It negoziabile
Pt negociável

négociable adj Fr
De begebbar
En negotiable
Es negociable
It negoziabile
Pt negociável

negociação *(f)* n Pt
De Verhandlung *(f)*
En negotiation
Es negociación *(f)*
Fr négociation *(f)*
It trattativa *(f)*

negociación *(f)* n Es
De Verhandlung *(f)*
En negotiation
Fr négociation *(f)*
It trattativa *(f)*
Pt negociação *(f)*

negociaciones a término
(f pl) Es
De Zeitgeschäfte *(n pl)*
En forward dealings
Fr opérations à terme *(f pl)*
It operazioni a termine *(f pl)*
Pt transacções adiantadas
(f pl)

négociant *(m)* n Fr
De Händler; Kaufmann *(m)*
En dealer; merchant
Es comerciante *(m)*
It negoziante; commerciante
(m)
Pt negociante; comerciante
(m)

negociante *(m)* n Es, Pt
De Händler *(m)*
En dealer
Fr négociant *(m)*
It negoziante; commerciante
(m)

negociar vb Es, Pt
De verhandeln
En negotiate
Fr négocier
It negoziare

**négociations de conven-
tions collectives** *(f pl)* Fr
De Tarifvertragsverhandlung
(f)
En collective bargaining
Es contratación collectiva *(f)*
It contrattazione collettivo *(f)*
Pt regateio colectivo *(m)*

negociável adj Pt
De begebbar
En negotiable
Es negociable
Fr négociable
It negoziabile

négocier vb Fr
De verhandeln
En negotiate
Es negociar
It negoziare
Pt negociar

negocio *(m)* n Es
De Handel; Geschäft *(m n)*
En trade; deal

Fr affaires; affaire *(f pl; f)*
It negozio; affare *(m)*
Pt negócio *(m)*

negócio *(m)* n Pt
De Handel; Geschäft *(m n)*
En trade; deal
Es negocio *(m)*
Fr affaires; affaire *(f pl; f)*
It negozio; affare *(m)*

negócio em dinheiro *(m)* Pt
De Bargeschäft *(n)*
En cash deal
Es trato al contado *(m)*
Fr transaction au comptant
(f)
It operazione a contanti *(f)*

negocios *(m pl)* Es
De Geschäft *(n)*
En business
Fr affaires *(f pl)*
It affari *(m pl)*
Pt negócios *(m pl)*

negócios *(m pl)* n Pt
De Geschäft *(n)*
En business
Es negocios *(m pl)*
Fr affaires *(f pl)*
It affari *(m pl)*

negotiable adj En
De begebbar
Es negociable
Fr négociable
It negoziabile
Pt negociável

negotiable instrument En
De begebbares Wertpapier *(n)*
Es título negociable *(m)*
Fr effet de commerce *(m)*
It titolo negoziabile *(m)*
Pt título negociável *(m)*

negotiate vb En
De verhandeln
Es negociar
Fr négocier
It negoziare
Pt negociar

negotiation n En
De Verhandlung *(f)*
Es negociación *(f)*
Fr négociation *(f)*
It trattativa *(f)*
Pt negociação *(f)*

négociation *(f) n* Fr
De Verhandlung *(f)*
En negotiation
Es negociación *(f)*
It trattativa *(f)*
Pt negociação *(f)*

negoziabile *adj* It
De begebbar
En negotiable
Es negociable
Fr négociable
Pt negociável

negoziante *(m) n* It
De Händler *(m)*
En dealer
Es comerciante *(m)*
Fr négociant *(m)*
Pt negociante *(m)*

negoziare *vb* It
De verhandeln
En negotiate
Es negociar
Fr négocier
Pt negociar

negozio *(m) n* It
De Handel; Geschäft *(m n)*
En trade, business
Es negocio *(m)*
Fr affaires; affaire *(f pl; f)*
Pt negócio *(m)*

negozio a catena *(m)* It
De Kettengeschäft *(n)*
En chain store
Es sucursal de cadena de almacenes *(f)*
Fr magasin à succursales multiples *(m)*
Pt sucursal de cadeia de armazéns *(f)*

nemico *(m) n* It
De Feind *(m)*
En enemy
Es enemigo *(m)*
Fr ennemi *(m)*
Pt inimigo *(m)*

Nennkapital *(m) n* De
En nominal capital
Es capital nominal *(m)*
Fr capital nominal *(m)*
It capitale nominale *(m)*
Pt capital nominal *(m)*

Nennpreis *(m) n* De
En nominal price
Es precio nominal *(m)*
Fr prix nominal *(m)*
It prezzo nominale *(m)*
Pt preço nominal *(m)*

Nennwert *(m) n* De
En nominal value
Es valor nominal *(m)*
Fr valeur nominale *(f)*
It valore nominale *(m)*
Pt valor nominal *(m)*

ne pas honorer un effet Fr
De einen Wechsel nicht akzeptieren
En dishonour a bill
Es protestar una letra
It non onorare un effetto
Pt protestar uma letra

ne quittez pas! Fr
De am Apparat bleiben
En hold the line
Es espere al aparato
It restare in linea
Pt aguarde

net *adj* En, Fr
De Netto-, Rein-
Es neto
It netto
Pt líquido

net amount En
De Nettobetrag *(m)*
Es importe neto *(m)*
Fr montant net *(m)*
It importo netto *(m)*
Pt importância líquida *(f)*

net assets En
De Reinvermögen *(n)*
Es activo neto *(m)*
Fr actif net *(m)*
It attivo netto *(m)*
Pt bens líquidos *(m pl)*

net income En
De Nettoeinkommen *(n)*
Es ingreso neto *(f)*
Fr revenu net *(m)*
It reddito netto *(m)*
Pt receita líquida *(f)*

neto *adj* Es
De Netto-, Rein-
En net

Fr net
It netto
Pt líquido

net price En
De Nettopreis; Nettokurs *(m)*
Es precio neto *(m)*
Fr prix net *(m)*
It prezzo netto *(m)*
Pt preço líquido *(m)*

net proceeds En
De Reinerlös *(m)*
Es rédito neto *(m)*
Fr produit net *(m)*
It ricavo netto *(m)*
Pt proventos líquidos *(m pl)*

net profit En
De Reingewinn *(m)*
Es ganancia neta *(f)*
Fr bénéfice net *(m)*
It utile netto *(m)*
Pt lucro líquido *(m)*

net profit margin En
De Reingewinnspanne *(f)*
Es margen de beneficio neto *(m)*
Fr marge nette de bénéfices *(f)*
It margine di utile netto *(m)*
Pt margem de lucro líquido *(f)*

net revenue En
De Nettoeinnahmen *(f pl)*
Es ingresos netos *(m pl)*
Fr recettes nettes *(f pl)*
It entrata netta *(f)*
Pt receita líquida *(f)*

netto *adj* It
De Netto-, Rein-
En net
Es neto
Fr net
Pt líquido

Netto- De
En net
Es neto
Fr net
It netto
Pt líquido

Nettobetrag *(m) n* De
En net amount
Es importe neto *(m)*

Fr montant net *(m)*
It importo netto *(m)*
Pt importância líquida *(f)*

Nettoeinkommen *(n)* n De
En net income
Es ingreso neto *(f)*
Fr revenu net *(m)*
It reddito netto *(m)*
Pt receita líquida *(f)*

Nettoeinnahmen *(f pl)* n De
En net revenue
Es ingresos netos *(m pl)*
Fr recettes nettes *(f pl)*
It entrata netta *(f)*
Pt receita líquida *(f)*

Nettoertrag *(m)* n De
En net yield
Es rendimiento neto *(m)*
Fr rendement net *(m)*
It reddito netto *(m)*
Pt rendimento líquido *(m)*

Nettolohn *(m)* n De
En take-home pay
Es paga neta *(f)*
Fr salaire net *(m)*
It paga netta *(f)*
Pt salário líquido *(m)*

Nettopreis *(m)* n De
En net price
Es precio neto *(m)*
Fr prix net *(m)*
It prezzo netto *(m)*
Pt preço líquido *(m)*

net weight En
De Reingewicht *(n)*
Es peso neto *(m)*
Fr poids net *(m)*
It peso netto *(m)*
Pt peso líquido *(m)*

network n En
De Netz *(n)*
Es red *(f)*
Fr réseau *(m)*
It rete *(f)*
Pt rede *(f)*

net yield En
De Nettoertrag *(m)*
Es rendimiento neto *(m)*

Fr rendement net *(m)*
It reddito netto *(m)*
Pt rendimento líquido *(m)*

Netz *(n)* n De
En network
Es red *(f)*
Fr réseau *(m)*
It rete *(f)*
Pt rede *(f)*

Netzplantechnik *(f)* n De
En critical path analysis
  (c.p.a.)
Es análisis de recorrido críti-
  co *(m)*
Fr analyse du chemin critique
  (m)
It analisi della linea critica *(f)*
Pt análise de transcurso críti-
  co *(f)*

Neuerung *(f)* n De
En innovation
Es innovación *(f)*
Fr innovation *(f)*
It innovazione *(f)*
Pt inovação *(f)*

new issue En
De Ausgabe junger Aktien *(f)*
Es nueva emisión *(f)*
Fr émission d'actions nouvel-
  les *(f)*
It nuova emissione *(f)*
Pt emissão nova *(f)*

news agency En
De Nachrichtenbüro *(n)*
Es agencia de prensa *(f)*
Fr agence de presse *(f)*
It agenzia d'informazioni *(f)*
Pt agência de notícias *(f)*

Nichtannahme *(f)* n De
En nonacceptance
Es rechazo *(m)*
Fr non-acceptation *(f)*
It mancata accettazione *(f)*
Pt não-aceitação *(f)*

nicht ausgegebenes Kapital
  (n) De
En unissued capital
Es capital no emitido *(m)*
Fr capitaux pas encore émis
  (m pl)
It capitale non emesso *(m)*
Pt capital não emitido *(m)*

**nicht bekanntgegebener
  Auftraggeber** *(m)* De
En undisclosed principal
Es mandante no nombrado
  (m)
Fr mandant non divulgé *(m)*
It mandante non nominato
  (m)
Pt mandante não divulgado
  (m)

**nicht dauerhafte Ver-
  brauchsgüter** *(n pl)* De
En consumer non-durables
Es bienes de consumo perecederos *(m pl)*
Fr biens de consommation
  non-durables *(m pl)*
It beni di consumo non durevoli *(m pl)*
Pt bens de consumo não
  duráveis *(m pl)*

nicht eingerufenes Kapital
  (n) De
En uncalled capital
Es capital de reserva *(m)*
Fr capital non appelé *(m)*
It capitale non richiamato
  (m)
Pt capital irrealizado *(m)*

Nichteinhaltung *(f)* n De
En default
Es falta *(f)*
Fr défaillance; défaut *(f m)*
It mancanza *(f)*
Pt falta *(f)*

Nichterfüllung *(f)* n De
En nonfulfilment
Es incumplimiento *(m)*
Fr non-exécution *(f)*
It inadempienza *(f)*
Pt não cumprimento *(m)*

nicht fest anbieten De
En quote not firm
Es cotizar sin compromiso
Fr coter sans obligation
It quotare senza impegno
Pt cotizar sem fixação de valor

nicht gesicherter Gläubiger
  (m) De
En unsecured creditor
Es acreedor no garantizado
  (m)

Fr créancier chirographaire *(m)*
It creditore non garantito *(m)*
Pt credor sem garantia *(m)*

nicht greifbare Aktiven *(n pl)* De
En intangible assets
Es activo intangible *(m)*
Fr actif incorporel *(m)*
It beni incorporali *(m pl)*
Pt bens intocáveis *(m pl)*

nichtig *adj* De
En void
Es nulo
Fr nul
It nullo
Pt nulo

nicht notierte Werte *(m pl)* De
En unquoted securities
Es títulos no cotizados *(m pl)*
Fr valeurs non cotées *(f pl)*
It titoli non quotati *(m pl)*
Pt títulos não cotados *(m pl)*

**nicht rückzahlbare Schuld-
verschreibung** *(f)* De
En undated debenture
Es obligación sin fecha *(f)*
Fr obligation non amortissa-
ble *(f)*
It obbligazione senza data *(f)*
Pt obrigação sem data *(f)*

nicht übereinstimmen De
En disagree
Es no estar de acuerdo
Fr être en désaccord
It essere in disaccordo
Pt discordar

nicht übertragbar De
En not negotiable
Es no negociable
Fr non négociable
It non negoziabile
Pt não transaccionável por
terceiros

Nichtzahlung *(f)* *n* De
En failure to pay
Es falta de pago *(f)*
Fr défaut de paiement *(m)*
It mancato pagamento *(m)*
Pt falta de pagamento *(f)*

Nießbrauchnutzer *(m)* *n* De
En beneficial owner
Es usufructuario *(m)*
Fr usufruitier *(m)*
It usufruttuario *(m)*
Pt usufrutuário *(m)*

Nießbrauchsrecht *(n)* *n* De
En usufruct; beneficial
interest
Es usufructo *(m)*
Fr usufruit *(m)*
It usufrutto *(m)*
Pt usufruto *(m)*

night safe En
De Nachttresor *(m)*
Es caja de seguridad noctur-
na *(f)*
Fr coffre de nuit *(m)*
It deposito notturno *(m)*
Pt cofre nocturno *(m)*

night shift En
De Nachtschicht *(f)*
Es turno de noche *(m)*
Fr équipe de nuit *(m)*
It turno di notte *(m)*
Pt turno da noite *(m)*

nightwatchman *n* En
De Nachtwächter *(m)*
Es guarda de noche *(m)*
Fr gardien de nuit *(m)*
It guardiano notturno *(m)*
Pt guarda-nocturno *(m)*

nightwork *n* En
De Nachtarbeit *(f)*
Es trabajo nocturno *(m)*
Fr travail de nuit *(m)*
It lavoro notturno *(m)*
Pt trabalho nocturno *(m)*

nil balance En
Am zero balance
De Nullsaldo *(m)*
Es saldo nulo *(m)*
Fr solde nul *(m)*
It saldo nullo *(m)*
Pt saldo nulo *(m)*

niveau des prix *(m)* Fr
De Preisebene *(f)*
En price level
Es nivel de precios *(m)*
It livello dei prezzi *(m)*
Pt nível de preços *(m)*

niveau de vie *(m)* Fr
De Lebenshaltung *(f)*
En standard of living
Es nivel de vida *(m)*
It tenore di vita *(m)*
Pt nível de vida *(m)*

nível de crédito *(m)* Pt
De Kreditwürdigkeit *(f)*
En credit rating
Es límite de crédito *(m)*
Fr degré de solvabilité *(m)*
It stima del credito *(f)*

nível de precios *(m)* Es
De Preisebene *(f)*
En price level
Fr niveau des prix *(m)*
It livello dei prezzi *(m)*
Pt nível de preços *(m)*

nível de preços *(m)* Pt
De Preisebene *(f)*
En price level
Es nivel de precios *(m)*
Fr niveau des prix *(m)*
It livello dei prezzi *(m)*

nível de vida *(m)* Es
De Lebenshaltung *(f)*
En standard of living
Fr niveau de vie *(m)*
It tenore di vita *(m)*
Pt nível de vida *(m)*

nível de vida *(m)* Pt
De Lebenshaltung *(f)*
En standard of living
Es nivel de vida *(m)*
Fr niveau de vie *(m)*
It tenore di vita *(m)*

nó *(m)* *n* Pt
De Knoten *(m)*
En knot
Es nudo *(m)*
Fr nœud *(m)*
It nodo *(m)*

no armazém Pt
De an Zollfreilager
En ex warehouse
Es puesto en almacén
Fr à prendre en entrepôt
It franco magazzino

noch nicht entlasteter Gemeinschuldner *(m)* De
En undischarged bankrupt
Es fallido no rehabilitado *(m)*
Fr failli non réhabilité *(m)*
It fallito non riabilitato *(m)*
Pt falido insolvente *(m)*

no-claims discount (bonus) En
De Schadenfreiheitsrabatt *(m)*
Es bonificación por no-recla-
   mación *(f)*
Fr bonification pour non
   sinistre *(f)*
It sconto per assenza di
   sinistri *(m)*
Pt desconto por ausência de
   reclamações *(m)*

nodo *(m)* n It
De Knoten *(m)*
En knot
Es nudo *(m)*
Fr nœud *(m)*
Pt nó *(m)*

no estar de acuerdo Es
De nicht übereinstimmen
En disagree
Fr être en désaccord
It essere in disaccordo
Pt discordar

no estrangeiro Pt
De im Ausland
En abroad
Es en el extranjero
Fr à l'étranger
It all'estero

nœud *(m)* n Fr
De Knoten *(m)*
En knot
Es nudo *(m)*
It nodo *(m)*
Pt nó *(m)*

noleggiare vb It
De mieten
En hire
Es alquilar
Fr louer
Pt alugar

noleggiatore *(m)* n It
De Mieter; Befrachter *(m)*
En hirer; charterer
Es alquilador; fletador *(m)*

Fr locataire; affréteur *(m)*
Pt alugador; fretador *(m)*

noleggio *(m)* n It
De Befrachtung *(f)*
En chartering
Es fletamento *(m)*
Fr affrètement *(m)*
Pt fretamento *(m)*

nolo *(m)* n It
De Fracht *(f)*
En freight
Es flete *(m)*
Fr fret *(m)*
Pt frete *(m)*

nolo prepagato It
De Fracht vorausbezahlt
En freight pre-paid
Es flete pagado
Fr fret payé d'avance
Pt frete pago

nombrar vb Es
De ernennen
En appoint
Fr nommer
It nominare
Pt nomear

nombre comercial *(m)* Es
De Markenbezeichnung *(f)*
En brand name
Fr marque de fabrique *(f)*
It marca *(f)*
Pt marca *(f)*

nomeado *(m)* n Pt
De Benannte(r); Vorgeschla-
   gene(r) *(m)*
En nominee
Es nominatario *(m)*
Fr personne dénommée *(f)*
It persona nominata *(f)*

nomear adj Pt
De ernennen
En appoint
Es nombrar
Fr nommer
It nominare

Nomenclatura de Bruselas *(f)* Es
De Brüsseler Verzeichnis *(n)*
En Brussels Nomenclature
Fr Nomenclature de
   Bruxelles (N.D.B.) *(f)*

It Nomenclatura di Bruxelles
   (f)
Pt Nomenclatura de Bruxelas
   (f)

Nomenclatura de Bruxelas *(f)* Pt
De Brüsseler Verzeichnis *(n)*
En Brussels Nomenclature
Es Nomenclatura de Bruselas
   (f)
Fr Nomenclature de
   Bruxelles (N.D.B.) *(f)*
It Nomenclatura di Bruxelles
   (f)

Nomenclatura di Bruxelles *(f)* It
De Brüsseler Verzeichnis *(n)*
En Brussels Nomenclature
Es Nomenclatura de Bruselas
   (f)
Fr Nomenclature de
   Bruxelles (N.D.B.) *(f)*
Pt Nomenclatura de Bruxelas
   (f)

Nomenclature de Bruxelles **(N.D.B.)** *(f)* Fr
De Brüsseler Verzeichnis *(n)*
En Brussels Nomenclature
Es Nomenclatura de Bruselas
   (f)
It Nomenclatura di Bruxelles
   (f)
Pt Nomenclatura de Bruxelas
   (f)

nómina de pago *(f)* Es
De Lohnbuch *(n)*
En payroll
Fr feuille de paie *(f)*
It libro paga *(m)*
Pt folha de salários *(f)*

nominal adj En, Es, Fr, Pt
De nominell
It nominale

nominal account En
De Firmenkonto *(n)*
Es cuenta de resultado *(f)*
Fr compte nominal *(m)*
It conto d'ordine *(m)*
Pt conta nominal *(f)*

nominal amount En
De Nominalbetrag *(m)*
Es suma nominal *(f)*
Fr montant nominal *(m)*
It importo nominale *(m)*
Pt quantia nominal *(f)*

Nominalbetrag *(m) n* De
En nominal amount
Es suma nominal *(f)*
Fr montant nominal *(m)*
It importo nominale *(m)*
Pt quantia nominal *(f)*

nominal capital En
De Nennkapital *(n)*
Es capital nominal *(m)*
Fr capital nominal *(m)*
It capitale nominale *(m)*
Pt capital nominal *(m)*

nominal damages En
De Ordnungsentschädigung
 (f)
Es daños nominales *(m pl)*
Fr indemnité de principe *(f)*
It danni nominali *(m pl)*
Pt danos nominais *(m pl)*

nominale *adj* It
De nominell
En nominal
Es nominal
Fr nominal
Pt nominal

nominal price En
De Nennpreis *(m)*
Es precio nominal *(m)*
Fr prix nominal *(m)*
It prezzo nominale *(m)*
Pt preço nominal *(m)*

nominal value En
De Nennwert *(m)*
Es valor nominal *(m)*
Fr valeur nominale *(f)*
It valore nominale *(m)*
Pt valor nominal *(m)*

nominare *vb* It
De ernennen
En appoint
Es nombrar
Fr nommer
Pt nomear

nominatario *(m) n* Es
De Benannte(r); Vorgeschla-
 gene(r) *(m)*
En nominee
Fr personne dénommée *(f)*
It persona nominata *(f)*
Pt nomeado *(m)*

nominee *n* En
De Benannte(r); Vorgeschla-
 gene(r) *(m)*
Es nominatario *(m)*
Fr personne dénommée *(f)*
It persona nominata *(f)*
Pt nomeado *(m)*

nominell *adj* De
En nominal
Es nominal
Fr nominal
It nominale
Pt nominal

nommer *vb* Fr
De ernennen
En appoint
Es nombrar
It nominare
Pt nomear

no montante de Pt
De hinauslaufend auf
En amounting to
Es ascendiendo a
Fr à concurrence de
It ammontante a

nonacceptance *n* En
De Nichtannahme *(f)*
Es rechazo *(m)*
Fr non-acceptation *(f)*
It mancata accettazione *(f)*
Pt não-aceitação *(f)*

non-acceptation *(f) n* Fr
De Nichtannahme *(f)*
En nonacceptance
Es rechazo *(m)*
It mancata accettazione *(f)*
Pt não-aceitação *(f)*

non autorisé Fr
De unbefugt
En unauthorized
Es inautorizado
It non autorizzato
Pt não autorizado

non autorizzato It
De unbefugt
En unauthorized
Es inautorizado
Fr non autorisé
Pt não autorizado

noncontributory pension En
De Pension ohne Beitrags-
 pflicht *(f)*
Es pensión sin entregas del
 beneficiario *(f)*
Fr pension non-contribuable
 (f)
It pensione senza contributi
 (f)
Pt pensão sem contribuição
 prévia *(f)*

no negociable Es
De nicht übertragbar
En not negotiable
Fr non négociable
It non-negoziabile
Pt não transacionável por
 terceiros

non-exécution *(f) n* Fr
De Nichterfüllung *(f)*
En nonfulfilment
Es incumplimiento *(m)*
It inadempienza *(f)*
Pt não cumprimento *(m)*

nonfulfilment *n* En
De Nichterfüllung *(f)*
Es incumplimiento *(m)*
Fr non-exécution *(f)*
It inadempienza *(f)*
Pt não cumprimento *(m)*

non négociable Fr
De nicht übertragbar
En not negotiable
Es no negociable
It non negoziabile
Pt não transacionável por
 terceiros

non negoziabile It
De nicht übertragbar
En not negotiable
Es no negociable
Fr non négociable
Pt não transacionável por
 terceiros

non onorare un effetto It
De einen Wechsel nicht ak-
    zeptieren
En dishonour a bill
Es protestar una letra
Fr ne pas honorer un effet
Pt protestar uma letra

nonprofitmaking adj En
De ohne Gewinnabsicht
Es sin finos lucrativos
Fr sans but lucratif
It senza scopo di lucro
Pt sem fins lucrativos

nontaxable income En
De steuerfreies Einkommen
    (n)
Es ingresos no imponibles
    (m pl)
Fr revenu non imposable (m)
It reddito non tassabile (m)
Pt receita não tributável (f)

nonvoting shares En
De Aktien ohne Stimmrecht
    (f pl)
Es acciones sin derecho a
    voto (f pl)
Fr actions sans droit de vote
    (f pl)
It azioni senza diritto a voto
    (f pl)
Pt acções sem direito a voto
    (f pl)

norm n En
De Norm (f)
Es norma (f)
Fr norme (f)
It norma (f)
Pt norma (f)

Norm (f) n De
En norm
Es norma (f)
Fr norme (f)
It norma (f)
Pt norma (f)

norma (f) n Es, It, Pt
De Norm; Standard (f m)
En norm; standard
Fr norme; étalon (f m)

normale Abweichung (f) De
En standard deviation
Es desviación normal (f)

Fr déviation normale (f)
It deviazione normale (f)
Pt desvio normal (m)

Normalmaß (n) n De
En standard gauge
Es calibre patrón (m)
Fr écartement normal (m)
It scartamento normale (m)
Pt calibre padrão (m)

Normalzeit (f) n De
En standard time
Es hora oficial (f)
Fr heure légale (f)
It ora legale (f)
Pt hora normal (f)

norme (f) n Fr
De Standard; Norm (m f)
En standard; norm
Es norma; standard (f m)
It norma (f)
Pt padrão; norma (m f)

nota (f) n Es, It, Pt
De Rechnung (f)
En bill; account
Fr note; compte (f m)

nota-contrato (f) n Pt
De Schlußschein (m)
En contract note
Es nota de contrato (f)
Fr bordereau d'achat (m)
It nota di contratto (f)

nota de banco (f) Pt
De Banknote (f)
En banknote; bill
Es billete de banco (m)
Fr billet de banque (m)
It biglietto di banca (m)

nota de cobertura (f) Pt
De Deckungszusage (f)
En cover note
Es aviso de seguro del riesgo
    (m)
Fr lettre de couverture (f)
It nota di copertura (f)

nota de consignación (f) Es
De Frachtbrief (m)
En consignment note
Fr lettre de voiture (f)
It nota di spedizione (f)
Pt guia de consignação (f)

nota de contrato (f) Es
De Schlußschein (m)
En contract note
Fr bordereau d'achat (m)
It nota di contratto (f)
Pt nota-contrato (f)

nota de crédito (f) Es
De Gutschriftanzeige (f)
En credit note
Fr avis de crédit (m)
It nota di credito (f)
Pt aviso de crédito (m)

nota de débito (f) Es
De Lastschrift (f)
En debit note
Fr avis de débit (m)
It nota di addebito (f)
Pt aviso de débito (m)

nota de rodapé (f) Pt
De Fußnote (f)
En footnote
Es apostilla (f)
Fr apostille (f)
It postilla (f)

nota di addebito (f) It
De Lastschrift (f)
En debit note
Es nota de débito (f)
Fr avis de débit (m)
Pt aviso de débito (m)

nota di consegna (f) It
De Lieferschein (m)
En delivery note
Es aviso de entrega (m)
Fr bordereau de livraison (m)
Pt guia de entrega (f)

nota di contratto (f) It
De Schlußschein (m)
En contract note
Es nota de contrato (f)
Fr bordereau d'achat (m)
Pt nota-contrato (f)

nota di copertura (f) It
De Deckungszusage (f)
En cover note
Es aviso de seguro del riesgo
    (m)
Fr lettre de couverture (f)
Pt nota de cobertura (f)

nota di credito *(f)* It
De Gutschriftanzeige *(f)*
En credit note
Es nota de crédito *(f)*
Fr avis de crédit *(m)*
Pt aviso de crédito *(m)*

nota di spedizione *(f)* It
De Frachtbrief *(m)*
En consignment note
Es nota de consignación *(f)*
Fr lettre de voiture *(f)*
Pt guia de transporte *(f)*

nota di spedizione aerea *(f)* It
De Luftfrachtbrief *(m)*
En air waybill
Es carta de porte aéreo *(f)*
Fr lettre de transport aérien *(f)*
Pt guia de porte aéreo *(f)*

notaio pubblico *(m)* It
De Notar *(m)*
En notary public
Es notario público *(m)*
Fr notaire *(m)*
Pt notário público *(m)*

notaire *(m)* n Fr
De Notar *(m)*
En notary public
Es notario público *(m)*
It notaio pubblico *(m)*
Pt notário público *(m)*

Notar *(m)* n De
En notary public
Es notario público *(m)*
Fr notaire *(m)*
It notaio pubblico *(m)*
Pt notário público *(m)*

notario público *(m)* Es
De Notar *(m)*
En notary public
Fr notaire *(m)*
It notaio pubblico *(m)*
Pt notário público *(m)*

notário público *(m)* Pt
De Notar *(m)*
En notary public
Es notario público *(m)*
Fr notaire *(m)*
It notaio pubblico *(m)*

notary public En
De Notar *(m)*
Es notario público *(m)*

Fr notaire *(m)*
It notaio pubblico *(m)*
Pt notário público *(m)*

not binding Am
En without prejudice
De ohne Verbindlichkeit
Es sin prejuicio
Fr sous toutes réserves
It senza pregiudizio
Pt sem compromisso

note *(f)* n Fr
De Rechnung *(f)*
En bill; account
Es cuenta; nota *(f)*
It conto; nota *(m f)*
Pt conta; nota *(f)*

note de poids *(f)* Fr
De Wiegeschein *(m)*
En weight note
Es certificado de pesaje *(m)*
It distinta pesi *(f)*
Pt certidão de peso *(f)*

Notenbank *(f)* n De
En issuing bank
Es banco emisor *(m)*
Fr banque d'émission *(f)*
It banca di emissione *(f)*
Pt banco emissor *(m)*

notice n En
De Benachrichtigung *(f)*
Es aviso *(m)*
Fr avis; préavis *(m)*
It avviso; preavviso *(m)*
Pt aviso *(m)*

notifica *(f)* n It
De Mitteilung *(f)*
En notification
Es notificación *(f)*
Fr notification *(f)*
Pt notificação *(f)*

notificação *(f)* n Pt
De Mitteilung *(f)*
En notification
Es notificación *(f)*
Fr notification *(f)*
It notifica *(f)*

notificação formal *(f)* Pt
De Inverzugsetzung *(f)*
En formal notice

Es aviso oficial *(m)*
Fr mise en demeure *(f)*
It intimazione *(f)*

notificación *(f)* n Es
De Mitteilung *(f)*
En notification
Fr notification *(f)*
It notifica *(f)*
Pt notificação *(f)*

notification n En, Fr *(f)*
De Mitteilung *(f)*
Es notificación *(f)*
It notifica *(f)*
Pt notificação *(f)*

not negotiable En
De nicht übertragbar
Es no negociable
Fr non négociable
It non negoziabile
Pt não transaccionável por
terceiros

Notstandsgebiet *(n)* n De
En distressed area
Es región deprimida *(f)*
Fr région déprimée *(f)*
It area indigente *(f)*
Pt zona deprimida *(f)*

Notvereinbarung *(f)* n De
En stand-by agreement
Es contrato de reserva *(m)*
Fr accord en réserve *(m)*
It accordo di riserva *(m)*
Pt acordo a postos *(m)*

nouveautés *(f pl)* n Fr
De Modeartikel *(m pl)*
En fancy goods
Es artículos de fantasía *(m pl)*
It articoli fantasia *(m pl)*
Pt artigos de fantasia *(m pl)*

nudo *(m)* n Es
De Knoten *(m)*
En knot
Fr nœud *(m)*
It nodo *(m)*
Pt nó *(m)*

nueva emisión *(f)* Es
De Ausgabe junger Aktien *(f)*
En new issue
Fr émission d'actions nouvel-
les *(f)*
It nuova emissione *(f)*
Pt emissão nova *(f)*

nul *adj* Fr
De nichtig
En void
Es nulo
It nullo
Pt nulo

nul et non avenu Fr
De null und nichtig
En null and void
Es nulo y sin valor
It nullo e senza effetto
Pt nulo e sem valor

null and void En
De null und nichtig
Es nulo y sin valor
Fr nul et non avenu
It nullo e senza effetto
Pt nulo e sem valor

nullo *adj* It
De nichtig
En void
Es nulo
Fr nul
Pt nulo

nullo e senza effetto It
De null und nichtig
En null and void
Es nulo y sin valor
Fr nul et non avenu
Pt nulo e sem valor

Nullsaldo *(m)* *n* De
En nil balance
Am zero balance
Es saldo nulo *(m)*
Fr solde nul *(m)*
It saldo nullo *(m)*
Pt saldo nulo *(m)*

null und nichtig De
En null and void
Es nulo y sin valor
Fr nul et non avenu
It nullo e senza effetto
Pt nulo e sem valor

nulo *adj* Es, Pt
De nichtig
En void
Fr nul
It nullo

nulo e sem valor Pt
De null und nichtig
En null and void

Es nulo y sin valor
Fr nul et non avenu
It nullo e senza effetto

nulo y sin valor Es
De null und nichtig
En null and void
Fr nul et non avenu
It nullo e senza effetto
Pt nulo e sem valor

number *n* En
De Nummer; Anzahl *(f)*
Es número *(m)*
Fr numéro *(m)*
It numero *(m)*
Pt número *(m)*

numbered account En
De numeriertes Konto *(n)*
Es cuenta identificada con
    número *(f)*
Fr compte identifié par
    numéro *(m)*
It conto identificato da nu-
    mero *(m)*
Pt conta numerada *(f)*

numeriertes Konto *(n)* De
En numbered account
Es cuenta identificada con
    número *(f)*
Fr compte identifié par
    numéro *(m)*
It conto identificato da nu-
    mero *(m)*
Pt conta numerada *(f)*

número *(m)* *n* Es, Pt
De Nummer; Anzahl *(f)*
En number
Fr numéro *(m)*
It numero *(m)*

numéro *(m)* *n* Fr
De Nummer; Anzahl *(f)*
En number
Es número *(m)*
It numero *(m)*
Pt número *(m)*

numero *(m)* *n* It
De Nummer; Anzahl *(f)*
En number
Es número *(m)*
Fr numéro *(m)*
Pt número *(m)*

número de control *(m)* Es
De Kontrollziffer *(f)*
En check digit
Fr digit de contrôle *(m)*
It cifra di controllo *(f)*
Pt dígito de controle *(m)*

número de telefone *(m)* Pt
De Telefonnummer *(f)*
En telephone number
Es número de teléfono *(m)*
Fr numéro de téléphone *(m)*
It numero di telefono *(m)*

número de teléfono *(m)* Es
De Telefonnummer *(f)*
En telephone number
Fr numéro de téléphone *(m)*
It numero di telefono *(m)*
Pt número de telefone *(m)*

numéro de téléphone *(m)* Fr
De Telefonnummer *(f)*
En telephone number
Es número de teléfono *(m)*
It numero di telefono *(m)*
Pt número de telefone *(m)*

numero di telefono *(m)* It
De Telefonnummer *(f)*
En telephone number
Es número de teléfono *(m)*
Fr numéro de téléphone *(m)*
Pt número de telefone *(m)*

Nummer *(f)* *n* De
En number
Es número *(m)*
Fr numéro *(m)*
It numero *(m)*
Pt número *(m)*

nuova emissione *(f)* It
De Ausgabe junger Aktien *(f)*
En new issue
Es nueva emisión *(f)*
Fr émission d'actions nouvel-
    les *(f)*
Pt emissão nova *(f)*

Nutzfahrzeug *(n)* *n* De
En commercial vehicle
Es vehículo comercial *(m)*
Fr véhicule commerciale *(f)*
It veicolo commerciale *(m)*
Pt veículo comercial *(m)*

O

obbligatorio *adj* It
De verbindlich
En compulsory
Es obligatorio
Fr obligatoire
Pt obrigatório

obbligazione *(f)* n It
De Obligation; Schuldver-
   schreibung *(f)*
En debenture
Es obligación *(f)*
Fr obligation *(f)*
Pt obrigação *(f)*

obbligazione al portatore *(f)*
   It
De Inhaberobligation *(f)*
En bearer debenture
Es obligación al portador *(f)*
Fr obligation au porteur *(f)*
Pt obrigação ao portador *(f)*

obbligazione dello Stato *(f)* It
De Staatsobligation *(f)*
En government bond
Es obligación del Estado *(f)*
Fr obligation d'État *(f)*
Pt obrigação do Tesouro *(f)*

obbligazione fondiaria *(f)* It
De Grund- und Gebäude-
   obligation *(f)*
En property bond
Es cédula hipotecaria *(f)*
Fr obligation foncière *(f)*
Pt título de investimento
   imobiliário *(m)*

obbligazione garantita *(f)* It
De gesicherte Schuldver-
   schreibung *(f)*
En secured debenture
Es obligación garantizada *(f)*
Fr obligation garantie *(f)*
Pt obrigação com garantia *(f)*

obbligazione ipotecaria *(f)* It
De hypothekarisch gesicherte
   Schuldverschreibung *(f)*
En mortgage debenture
Es obligación hipotecaria *(f)*
Fr obligation hypothécaire *(f)*
Pt obrigação hipotecária *(f)*

obbligazione irredimibile *(f)*
   It
De uneinlösbare Schuldver-
   schreibung *(f)*
En irredeemable debenture
Es obligación no amortizable
   (f)
Fr obligation irremboursable
   (f)
Pt obrigação não amortizável *(f)*

obbligazione non garantita
   (f) It
De ungesicherte Schuldver-
   schreibung *(f)*
En unsecured debenture
Am naked bond
Es obligación no garantizada
   (f)
Fr obligation sans garantie *(f)*
Pt obrigação sem garantia *(f)*

obbligazione perpetua *(f)* It
De Dauerschuldverschrei-
   bung *(f)*
En perpetual debenture
Es obligación a perpetuidad
   (f)
Fr obligation perpétuelle *(f)*
Pt obrigação de perenidade *(f)*

obbligazione redimibile *(f)* It
De kündbare Obligation *(f)*
En redeemable bond
Es obligación reembolsable
   (f)
Fr obligation amortissable *(f)*
Pt obrigação reembolsável *(f)*

obbligazione senza data *(f)* It
De unbefristete Obligation *(f)*
En undated debenture
Es obligación sin fecha *(f)*
Fr obligation non amortissa-
   ble *(f)*
Pt obrigação sem data *(f)*

obbligazione solidale *(f)* It
De Solidarobligation *(f)*
En joint and several bond
Es obligación solidaria e indi-
   visa *(f)*
Fr obligation conjointe et so-
   lidaire *(f)*
Pt título solidário de diversos
   (m)

obbligazionista *(f)* n It
De Obligationsinhaber *(m)*
En debenture holder
Es obligacionista *(m)*
Fr porteur d'obligations;
   obligataire *(m)*
Pt titular de obrigação *(m)*

obenerwähnt *adj* De
En above-mentioned
Es susodicho
Fr susmentionné
It suddetto
Pt supracitado

Oberbuchhalter *(m)* n De
En chief accountant
Es jefe de contabilidad *(m)*
Fr chef comptable *(m)*
It ragioniere capo *(m)*
Pt chefe contabilista *(m)*

objectivo *(m)* n Pt
De Ziel *(n)*
En target
Es objetivo *(m)*
Fr but *(m)*
It bersaglio *(m)*

objetivo *(m)* n Es
De Ziel *(n)*
En target
Fr but *(m)*
It bersaglio *(m)*
Pt objectivo *(m)*

obligación *(f)* n Es
De Obligation; Schuldver-
   schreibung *(f)*
En debenture
Fr obligation *(f)*
It obbligazione *(f)*
Pt obrigação *(f)*

obligación a interés fijo *(f)* Es
De festverzinsliches Wertpa-
   pier *(n)*
En fixed-interest security
Fr valeur à revenu fixe *(f)*
It titolo a interesse fisso *(m)*
Pt obrigação de juro fixo *(f)*

obligación al portador *(f)* Es
De Inhaberobligation *(f)*
En bearer debenture
Fr obligation au porteur *(f)*
It obbligazione al portatore
   (f)
Pt obrigação ao portador *(f)*

obligación a perpetuidad *(f)*
Es
De Dauerschuldverschrei-
   bung *(f)*
En perpetual debenture
Fr obligation perpétuelle *(f)*
It obbligazione perpetua *(f)*
Pt obrigação de perenidade *(f)*

obligación del Estado *(f)* Es
De Staatsobligation *(f)*
En government bond
Fr obligation d'État *(f)*
It obbligazione dello Stato *(f)*
Pt obrigação do Tesouro *(f)*

obligación garantizada *(f)* Es
De gesicherte Schuldver-
   schreibung *(f)*
En secured debenture
Fr obligation garantie *(f)*
It obbligazione garantita *(f)*
Pt obrigação com garantia *(f)*

obligación hipotecaria *(f)* Es
De hypothekarisch gesicherte
   Schuldverschreibung *(f)*
En mortgage debenture
Fr obligation hypothécaire *(f)*
It obbligazione ipotecaria *(f)*
Pt obrigação hipotecária *(f)*

obligación irrevocable *(f)* Es
De bindender Vertrag *(m)*
En binding agreement
Fr convention irrévocable *(f)*
It contratto vincolante *(m)*
Pt acordo irrevogável *(m)*

obligacionista *(m)* n Es
De Obligationär *(m)*
En bondholder; debenture
   holder
Fr obligataire *(f)*
It obbligazionista *(m)*
Pt titular de obrigações *(m)*

obligación no amortizable *(f)*
Es
De uneinlösbare Schuldver-
   schreibung *(f)*
En irredeemable debenture
Fr obligation irremboursable
   (f)
It obbligazione irredimibile *(f)*
Pt obrigação não amortizável *(f)*

obligación no garantizada *(f)*
Es
De ungesicherte Schuldver-
   schreibung *(f)*
En unsecured debenture
Am naked bond
Fr obligation sans garantie *(f)*
It obbligazione non garantita
   (f)
Pt obrigação sem garantia *(f)*

obligación reembolsable *(f)*
Es
De kündbare Obligation *(f)*
En redeemable bond
Fr obligation amortissable *(f)*
It obbligazione redimibile *(f)*
Pt obrigação reembolsável *(f)*

**obligación sin fecha de
vencimiento** *(f)* Es
De Schuldverschreibung
   ohne Fälligkeitsdatum *(f)*
En undated debenture
Fr obligation sans date
   d'échéance *(f)*
It obbligazione senza data di
   scadenza *(f)*
Pt obrigação sem data de
   vencimento *(f)*

**obligación solidaria e
indivisa** *(f)* Es
De Solidarobligation *(f)*
En joint and several bond
Fr obligation conjointe et so-
   lidaire *(f)*
It obbligazione solidale *(f)*
Pt título solidário de diversos
   (m)

obligataire *(m)* n Fr
De Obligationär *(m)*
En bondholder
Es obligacionista *(m)*
It portatore di obbligazioni
   (m)
Pt titular de obrigações *(m)*

obligation *(f)* n Fr
De Obligation; Schuldver-
   schreibung *(f)*
En debenture; bond
Es obligación *(f)*
It obbligazione *(f)*
Pt obrigação *(f)*

Obligation *(f)* n De
En debenture; bond
Es obligación *(f)*
Fr obligation *(f)*
It obbligazione *(f)*
Pt obrigação *(f)*

obligation amortissable *(f)* Fr
De kündbare Obligation *(f)*
En redeemable bond
Es obligación reembolsable
   (f)
It obbligazione redimibile *(f)*
Pt obrigação reembolsável *(f)*

Obligationär *(m)* n De
En bondholder
Es obligacionista *(m)*
Fr obligataire *(m)*
It portatore di obbligazioni
   (m)
Pt titular de obrigações *(m)*

obligation au porteur *(f)* Fr
De Inhaberobligation *(f)*
En bearer debenture
Es obligación al portador *(f)*
It obbligazione al portatore
   (f)
Pt obrigação ao portador *(f)*

**obligation conjointe et
solidaire** *(f)* Fr
De Solidarobligation *(f)*
En joint and several bond
Es obligación solidaria e indi-
   visa *(f)*
It obbligazione solidale *(f)*
Pt título solidário de diversos
   (m)

obligation d'État *(f)* Fr
De Staatsobligation *(f)*
En government bond
Es obligación del Estado *(f)*
It obbligazione dello Stato *(f)*
Pt obrigação do Tesouro *(f)*

obligation éventuelle *(f)* Fr
De Eventualverpflichtung *(f)*
En contingent liability
Es responsabilidad contin-
   gente *(f)*
It sopravvenienza passiva *(f)*
Pt responsabilidade contin-
   gente *(f)*

obligation foncière *(f)* Fr
De Grund- und Gebäude-
　obligation *(f)*
En property bond
Es cédula hipotecaria *(f)*
It obbligazione fondiaria *(f)*
Pt título de investimento
　imobiliário *(m)*

obligation garantie *(f)* Fr
De gesicherte Schuldver-
　schreibung *(f)*
En secured debenture
Es obligación garantizada *(f)*
It obbligazione garantita *(f)*
Pt obrigação com garantia *(f)*

obligation hypothécaire *(f)* Fr
De hypothekarisch gesicherte
　Schuldverschreibung *(f)*
En mortgage debenture
Es obligación hipotecaria *(f)*
It obbligazione ipotecaria *(f)*
Pt obrigação hipotecária *(f)*

obligation irremboursable *(f)*
　Fr
De uneinlösbare Schuldver-
　schreibung *(f)*
En irredeemable debenture
Es obligación no amortizable
　(f)
It obbligazione irredimibile *(f)*
Pt obrigação não amortizável *(f)*

obligation perpétuelle *(f)* Fr
De Dauerschuldverschrei-
　bung *(f)*
En perpetual debenture
Es obligación a perpetuidad
　(f)
It obbligazione perpetua *(f)*
Pt obrigação de perenidade *(f)*

obligation sans date
　d'échéance *(f)* Fr
De Schuldverschreibung
　ohne Fälligkeitsdatum *(f)*
En undated bond
Es obligación sin fecha de
　vencimiento *(f)*
It obbligazione senza data di
　scadenza *(f)*
Pt obrigação sem data de
　vencimento *(f)*

obligation sans garantie *(f)*
　Fr
De ungesicherte Schuldver-
　schreibung *(f)*
En unsecured debenture
Am naked bond
Es obligación no garantizada
　(f)
It obbligazione non garantita
　(f)
Pt obrigação sem garantia *(f)*

Obligationsinhaber *(m) n* De
En debenture holder
Es obligacionista *(m)*
Fr porteur d'obligations;
　obligataire *(m)*
It obbligazionista *(f)*
Pt titular de obrigação *(m)*

obligatoire *adj* Fr
De verbindlich
En compulsory
Es obligatorio
It obbligatorio
Pt obrigatório

obligatorio *adj* Es
De verbindlich
En compulsory
Fr obligatoire
It obbligatorio
Pt obrigatório

obrero *(m) n* Es
De Arbeiter *(m)*
En worker; workman
Fr ouvrier *(m)*
It operaio *(m)*
Pt operário *(m)*

obrigação *(f) n* Pt
De Obligation; Schuldver-
　schreibung *(f)*
En debenture
Es obligación *(f)*
Fr obligation *(f)*
It obbligazione *(f)*

obrigação ao portador *(f)* Pt
De Inhaberobligation *(f)*
En bearer debenture
Es obligación al portador *(f)*
Fr obligation au porteur *(f)*
It obbligazione al portatore
　(f)

obrigação com garantia *(f)* Pt
De gesicherte Schuldver-
　schreibung *(f)*
En secured debenture
Es obligación garantizada *(f)*
Fr obligation garantie *(f)*
It obbligazione garantita *(f)*

obrigação de juro fixo *(f)* Pt
De festverzinsliches Wertpa-
　pier *(n)*
En fixed-interest security
Es obligación a interés fijo *(f)*
Fr valeur à revenu fixe *(f)*
It titolo a interesse fisso *(m)*

obrigação de perenidade *(f)*
　Pt
De Dauerschuldverschrei-
　bung *(f)*
En perpetual debenture
Es obligación a perpetuidad
　(f)
Fr obligation perpétuelle *(f)*
It obbligazione perpetua *(f)*

obrigação do Tesouro *(f)* Pt
De Staatsobligation *(f)*
En government bond
Es obligación del Estado *(f)*
Fr obligation d'État *(f)*
It obbligazione dello Stato *(f)*

obrigação hipotecária *(f)* Pt
De hypothekarisch gesicherte
　Schuldverschreibung *(f)*
En mortgage debenture
Es obligación hipotecaria *(f)*
Fr obligation hypothécaire *(f)*
It obbligazione ipotecaria *(f)*

obrigação não amortizável
　(f) Pt
De uneinlösbare Schuldver-
　schreibung *(f)*
En irredeemable debenture
Es obligación no amortizable
　(f)
Fr obligation irremboursable
　(f)
It obbligazione irredimibile *(f)*

obrigação reembolsável
　(f) Pt
De kündbare Obligation *(f)*
En redeemable bond
Es obligación reembolsable
　(f)
Fr obligation amortissable *(f)*
It obbligazione redimibile *(f)*

obrigação restritiva *(f)* Pt
De einschränkende Bestim-
   mung *(f)*
En restrictive covenant
Es convenio restrictivo *(m)*
Fr accord restrictif *(m)*
It accordo restrittivo *(m)*

**obrigação sem data de
   vencimento** *(f)* Pt
De Schuldverschreibung
   ohne Fälligkeitsdatum *(f)*
En undated debenture
Es obligación sin fecha de
   vencimiento *(f)*
Fr obligation sans date
   d'échéance *(f)*
It obbligazione senza data di
   scadenza *(f)*

obrigação sem garantia *(f)* Pt
De ungesicherte Schuldver-
   schreibung *(f)*
En unsecured debenture
Am naked bond
Es obligación no garantizada
   (f)
Fr obligation sans garantie *(f)*
It obbligazione non garantita
   (f)

obrigatório *adj* Pt
De verbindlich
En compulsory
Es obligatorio
Fr obligatoire
It obbligatorio

**obsolência pré-incor-
   porada** *(f)* Pt
De eingebautes Veralten *(n)*
En built-in obsolescence
Es decaimiento incorporado
   (m)
Fr désuétude incorporée *(f)*
It decadimento incorporato
   (m)

occasion *(f) n* Fr
De Gelegenheitskauf *(m)*
En bargain
Es ganga *(f)*
It occasione *(f)*
Pt pechincha *(f)*

occasione *(f) n* It
De Gelegenheitskauf *(m)*
En bargain

Es ganga *(f)*
Fr occasion *(f)*
Pt pechincha *(f)*

occupation *n* En
De Beschäftigung *(f)*
Es ocupación; empleo *(f m)*
Fr occupation; emploi *(f m)*
It occupazione; impiego
   (f m)
Pt ocupação *(f)*

occupation *(f) n* Fr
De Beschäftigung *(f)*
En occupation; job
Es ocupación; empleo *(f m)*
It occupazione; impiego
   (f m)
Pt ocupação *(f)*

occupational hazard En
De Berufsrisiko *(n)*
Es riesgo profesional *(m)*
Fr risque professionnel *(m)*
It rischio del lavoro *(m)*
Pt acidente próprio da pro-
   fissão *(m)*

occupazione *(f) n* It
De Beschäftigung *(f)*
En occupation; job
Es ocupación; empleo *(f m)*
Fr occupation; emploi *(f m)*
Pt ocupação *(f)*

ocupação *(f) n* Pt
De Beschäftigung *(f)*
En occupation; job
Es ocupación; empleo *(f m)*
Fr occupation; emploi *(f m)*
It occupazione; impiego
   (f m)

ocupación *(f) n* Es
De Beschäftigung *(f)*
En occupation; job
Fr occupation; emploi *(f m)*
It occupazione; impiego
   (f m)
Pt ocupação *(f)*

odd lot En
De Restpartie *(f)*
Es lote suelto *(m)*
Fr solde *(m)*
It partita spaiata *(f)*
Pt lote avulso *(m)*

oferecer *vb* Pt
De anbieten
En offer
Es ofrecer
Fr offrir
It offrire

oferta *(f) n* Es, Pt
De Angebot; Offerte *(n f)*
En bid; offer
Fr offre *(f)*
It offerta *(f)*

oferta a preço excepcional
   (f) Pt
De Sonderangebot *(n)*
En bargain offer
Es oferta de ocasión *(f)*
Fr offre exceptionelle *(f)*
It offerta di occasione *(f)*

oferta a prima *(f)* Es
De Verkauf mit Zugaben *(m)*
En premium offer
Fr offre à prime *(f)*
It offerta sopra la pari *(f)*
Pt oferta-prémio *(f)*

oferta de adquisición *(f)* Es
De Übernahmeangebot *(n)*
En take-over bid
Fr offre de rachat *(f)*
It offerta di acquisto *(f)*
Pt proposta de apropriação *(f)*

oferta de ocasión *(f)* Es
De Sonderangebot *(n)*
En bargain offer
Fr offre exceptionelle *(f)*
It offerta di occasione *(f)*
Pt oferta a preço excepcional
   (f)

oferta en firme *(f)* Es
De festes Angebot *(n)*
En firm offer
Fr offre ferme *(f)*
It offerta ferma *(f)*
Pt oferta firme *(f)*

oferta e procura Pt
De Angebot und Nachfrage
En supply and demand
Es oferta y demanda
Fr offre et demande
It offerta e domanda

oferta especial *(f)* Es, Pt
De Sonderangebot *(m)*
En special offer
Fr offre spéciale *(f)*
It offerta speciale *(f)*

oferta firme *(f)* Pt
De festes Angebot *(n)*
En firm offer
Es oferta en firme *(f)*
Fr offre ferme *(f)*
It offerta ferma *(f)*

ofertante *(m)* n Es
De Bietende(r) *(m)*
En bidder
Fr enchérisseur *(m)*
It offerente *(m)*
Pt proponente *(m)*

ofertante más alto *(m)* Es
De Meistbietende(r) *(m)*
En highest bidder
Fr plus offrant enchérisseur *(m)*
It miglior offerente *(m)*
Pt proponente mais elevado *(m)*

oferta-prémio *(f)* n Pt
De Verkauf mit Zugaben *(m)*
En premium offer
Es oferta a prima *(f)*
Fr offre à prime *(f)*
It offerta sopra la pari *(f)*

oferta y demanda Es
De Angebot und Nachfrage
En supply and demand
Fr offre et demande
It offerta e domanda
Pt oferta e procura

offene Handelsgesellschaft (OHG) *(f)* De
En partnership
Es sociedad regular colectiva (SRC) *(f)*
Fr société en nom collectif *(f)*
It società *(f)*
Pt sociedade em nome colectivo *(f)*

offene Position *(f)* De
En open position
Es posición descubierta *(f)*
Fr position ouverte *(f)*
It posizione aperta *(f)*
Pt posição em aberto *(f)*

offener Kredit *(m)* De
En open credit
Es crédito en descubierto *(m)*
Fr crédit à découvert *(m)*
It credito allo scoperto *(m)*
Pt crédito em aberto *(m)*

offene Versicherung *(f)* De
En open cover
Es cobertura flotante *(f)*
Fr police à aliment *(f)*
It polizza flottante *(f)*
Pt cobertura ilimitada *(f)*

Offenlegung *(f)* n De
En disclosure
Es revelación *(f)*
Fr révélation; divulgation *(f)*
It rivelazione *(f)*
Pt revelação; divulgação *(f)*

öffentlich adj De
En public
Es público
Fr public
It pubblico
Pt público

öffentliche Hand *(f)* De
En public sector
Es sector público *(m)*
Fr secteur public *(m)*
It settore statale *(m)*
Pt sector público *(m)*

Öffentlichkeit *(f)* n De
En (general) public
Es público *(m)*
Fr grand public *(m)*
It pubblico *(m)*
Pt público *(m)*

offer n En
De Offerte *(f)*
Es oferta *(f)*
Fr offre *(f)*
It offerta *(f)*
Pt oferta *(f)*

offer vb En
De anbieten
Es ofrecer
Fr offrir
It offrire
Pt oferecer

offerente *(m)* n It
De Bietende(r) *(m)*
En bidder

Es ofertante *(m)*
Fr enchérisseur *(m)*
Pt proponente *(m)*

offer for sale En
De zum Verkauf anbieten
Es ofrecer en venta
Fr offrir en vente
It offrire in vendita
Pt pôr à venda

offerta *(f)* n It
De Angebot; Offerte *(n f)*
En bid; offer
Es oferta *(f)*
Fr offre *(f)*
Pt oferta *(f)*

offerta di acquisto *(f)* It
De Übernahmeangebot *(n)*
En take-over bid
Es oferta de adquisición *(f)*
Fr offre de rachat *(f)*
Pt proposta de apropriação *(f)*

offerta di occasione *(f)* It
De Sonderangebot *(n)*
En bargain offer
Es oferta de ocasión *(f)*
Fr offre exceptionelle *(f)*
Pt oferta a preço excepcional *(f)*

offerta e domanda It
De Angebot und Nachfrage
En supply and demand
Es oferta y demanda
Fr offre et demande
Pt oferta e procura

offerta ferma *(f)* It
De festes Angebot *(n)*
En firm offer
Es oferta en firme *(f)*
Fr offre ferme *(f)*
Pt oferta firme *(f)*

offerta sopra la pari *(f)* It
De Verkauf mit Zugaben *(m)*
En premium offer
Es oferta a prima *(f)*
Fr offre à prime *(f)*
Pt oferta-prémio *(f)*

offerta speciale *(f)* It
De Sonderangebot *(m)*
En special offer
Es oferta especial *(f)*
Fr offre spéciale *(f)*
Pt oferta especial *(f)*

Offerte *(f)* n De
En offer
Es oferta *(f)*
Fr offre *(f)*
It offerta *(f)*
Pt oferta *(f)*

office n En
De Büro *(n)*
Es oficina *(f)*
Fr bureau *(m)*
It ufficio *(m)*
Pt escritório *(m)*

office hours En
De Geschäftsstunden *(f pl)*
Es horario de oficina *(m)*
Fr heures de bureau *(f pl)*
It orario d'ufficio *(m)*
Pt horário do escritório *(m)*

office manager En
De Bürovorsteher *(m)*
Es jefe de oficina *(m)*
Fr chef de bureau *(m)*
It capo ufficio *(m)*
Pt chefe de escritório *(m)*

official adj En
De amtlich
Es oficial
Fr officiel
It ufficiale
Pt oficial

official strike En
De anerkannter Streik *(m)*
Es huelga oficial *(f)*
Fr grève officielle *(f)*
It sciopero ufficiale *(m)*
Pt greve oficial *(f)*

officiel adj Fr
De amtlich
En official
Es oficial
It ufficiale
Pt oficial

offre *(f)* n Fr
De Angebot; Offerte *(n f)*
En bid; offer
Es oferta *(f)*
It offerta *(f)*
Pt oferta *(f)*

offre à prime *(f)* Fr
De Verkauf mit Zugaben *(m)*
En premium offer

Es oferta a prima *(f)*
It offerta sopra la pari *(f)*
Pt oferta-prémio *(f)*

offre de rachat *(f)* Fr
De Übernahmeangebot *(n)*
En take-over bid
Es oferta de adquisición *(f)*
It offerta di acquisto *(f)*
Pt proposta de apropriação *(f)*

offre et demande Fr
De Angebot und Nachfrage
En supply and demand
Es oferta y demanda
It offerta e domanda
Pt oferta e procura

offre exceptionelle *(f)* Fr
De Sonderangebot *(n)*
En bargain offer
Es oferta de ocasión *(f)*
It offerta di occasione *(f)*
Pt oferta a preço excepcional *(f)*

offre ferme *(f)* Fr
De festes Angebot *(n)*
En firm offer
Es oferta en firme *(f)*
It offerta ferma *(f)*
Pt oferta firme *(f)*

offre spéciale *(f)* Fr
De Sonderangebot *(m)*
En special offer
Es oferta especial *(f)*
It offerta speciale *(f)*
Pt oferta especial *(f)*

offrir vb Fr
De anbieten
En offer
Es ofrecer
It offrire
Pt oferecer

offrire vb It
De anbieten
En offer
Es ofrecer
Fr offrir
Pt oferecer

offrire in vendita It
De zum Verkauf anbieten
En offer for sale

Es ofrecer en venta
Fr offrir en vente
Pt pôr à venda

offrir en vente Fr
De zum Verkauf anbieten
En offer for sale
Es ofrecer en venta
It offrire in vendita
Pt pôr à venda

oficial adj Es, Pt
De amtlich
En official
Fr officiel
It ufficiale

oficina *(f)* n Es
De Büro *(n)*
En office
Fr bureau *(m)*
It ufficio *(m)*
Pt escritório *(m)*

oficina central *(f)* Es
De Hauptbüro *(f)*
En head office
Fr siège; bureau principal *(m)*
It sede; ufficio centrale *(f m)*
Pt sede; escritório central *(f m)*

oficina central de compras *(f)* Es
De Einkaufszentrale *(f)*
En central buying office
Fr centrale d'achats *(f)*
It ufficio centrale d'acquisti *(m)*
Pt escritório central de compras *(m)*

oficina de correos *(f)* Es
De Postamt *(n)*
En post office
Fr bureau de poste *(m)*
It ufficio postale *(m)*
Pt estação de correios *(f)*

oficinista *(m)* n Es
De Angestellte(r) *(m)*
En clerk
Fr commis *(m)*
It impiegato *(m)*
Pt empregado de escritório *(m)*

ofrecer *vb* Es
De anbieten
En offer
Fr offrir
It offrire
Pt oferecer

ofrecer en venta Es
De zum Verkauf anbieten
En offer for sale
Fr offrir en vente
It offrire in vendita
Pt pôr à venda

ohne Bezugsrechte De
En ex rights
Es sin privilegio
Fr ex-droits
It senza diritti
Pt privilégios excluídos

ohne Coupon De
En ex coupon
Es sin cupón
Fr ex coupon
It senza cedola
Pt talão excluído

ohne Dividende De
En ex dividend
Es sin dividendo
Fr ex-dividende
It senza dividendo
Pt dividendo excluído

ohne Gewinnabsicht De
En nonprofitmaking
Es sin finos lucrativos
Fr sans but lucratif
It senza scopo di lucro
Pt sem fins lucrativos

ohne Rückgriff De
En without recourse
Es sin recurso
Fr sans droit de recours
It senza ricorso
Pt sem recurso

ohne Verbindlichkeit De
En without prejudice
Am not binding
Es sin prejuicio
Fr sous toutes réserves
It senza pregiudizio
Pt sem compromisso

oilfield *n* En
De Ölfeld *(n)*
Es yacimiento de petróleo *(m)*
Fr gisement petrolifère *(m)*
It giacimento petrolifero *(m)*
Pt jazigo de petróleo *(m)*

Ökonometrik *(f)* *n* De
En econometrics
Es econometría *(f)*
Fr économétrie *(f)*
It econometria *(f)*
Pt econometria *(f)*

old-age ponsion En
De Altersversorgung; Rente *(f)*
Es retiro de vejez *(m)*
Fr pension de retraite *(f)*
It pensione per la vecchiaia *(f)*
Pt pensão *(f)*

old-established business En
De alteingeführtes Geschäft *(n)*
Es casa sólida *(f)*
Fr maison solide *(f)*
It casa di vecchia fondazione *(f)*
Pt empresa de há muito estabelecida *(f)*

Öldollar *(m)* *n* De
En petrodollar
Es petrodólar *(m)*
Fr dollar pétrolier *(m)*
It petrodollaro *(m)*
Pt petrodólar *(m)*

Ölfeld *(n)* *n* De
En oilfield
Es yacimiento de petróleo *(m)*
Fr gisement petrolifère *(m)*
It giacimento petrolifero *(m)*
Pt jazigo de petróleo *(m)*

Oligopol *(n)* *n* De
En oligopoly
Es oligopolio *(m)*
Fr oligopole *(m)*
It oligopolio *(m)*
Pt oligopólio *(m)*

oligopole *(m)* *n* Fr
De Oligopol *(n)*
En oligopoly

Es oligopolio *(m)*
It oligopolio *(m)*
Pt oligopólio *(m)*

oligopolioy *(m)* *n* Es, It
De Oligopol *(n)*
En oligopoly
Fr oligopole *(m)*
Pt oligopólio *(m)*

oligopólio *(m)* *n* Pt
De Oligopol *(n)*
En oligopoly
Es oligopolio *(m)*
Fr oligopole *(m)*
It oligopolio *(m)*

oligopoly *n* En
De Oligopol *(n)*
Es oligopolio *(m)*
Fr oligopole *(m)*
It oligopolio *(m)*
Pt oligopólio *(m)*

omisión *(f)* *n* Es
De Auslassung; Unterlassung *(f)*
En omission
Fr omission *(f)*
It omissione *(f)*
Pt omissão *(f)*

omissão *(f)* *n* Pt
De Auslassung; Unterlassung *(f)*
En omission
Es omisión *(f)*
Fr omission *(f)*
It omissione *(f)*

omission *n* En, Fr *(f)*
De Auslassung; Unterlassung *(f)*
Es omisión *(f)*
It omissione *(f)*
Pt omissão *(f)*

omissione *(f)* *n* It
De Auslassung; Unterlassung *(f)*
En omission
Es omisión *(f)*
Fr omission *(f)*
Pt omissão *(f)*

omologazione di testamento *(f)* It
De Testamentseröffnung; Be-
     stätigung *(f)*
En probate
Es validación de los testa-
     mentos *(f)*
Fr homologation d'un testa-
     ment *(f)*
Pt validação testamentária *(f)*

on account En
De a conto; auf Abschlag
Es a cuenta
Fr à valoir
It in acconto
Pt por conta

on condition En
De vorausgesetzt
Es a condición
Fr sous réserve
It a condizione
Pt sob condição de

on consignment En
De in Kommission
Es en consignación
Fr en consignation
It in conto deposito
Pt à consignação

on demand En
De auf Verlangen
Es a vista
Fr sur demande
It a vista
Pt à vista; sob demanda

onesto *adj* It
De ehrlich
En honest
Es honesto
Fr honnête
Pt honesto

one way fare Am
En single fare
De einfache Fahrkarte *(f)*
Es pasaje de ida *(m)*
Fr billet d'aller *(m)*
It biglietto d'andata *(m)*
Pt passagem de ida *(f)*

on hand En
De vorrätig
Es disponible

Fr disponible
It disponibile
Pt à mão; ao dispôr

on loan En
De darlehensweise
Es en préstamo
Fr sous forme de prét
It in prestito
Pt por empréstimo

onorare *vb* It
De honorieren
En honour
Es honrar
Fr honorer
Pt honorificar

onorario *(m)* *n* It
De Vergütung; Honorar *(f n)*
En fee
Es honorario *(m)*
Fr honoraires *(m pl)*
Pt honorários *(m pl)*

onorario *adj* It
De ehrenamtlich
En honorary
Es honorario
Fr honoraire
Pt honorário

onore *(m)* *n* It
De Ehre *(f)*
En honour
Es honor *(m)*
Fr honneur *(f)*
Pt honra *(f)*

ontem *adv* Pt
De gestern
En yesterday
Es ayer
Fr hier
It ieri

opção *(f)* *n* Pt
De Option *(f)*
En option
Es opción *(f)*
Fr option *(f)*
It opzione *(f)*

opção de compra *(f)* Pt
De Kaufoption *(f)*
En call option
Es opción de compras *(f)*
Fr option d'achat *(f)*
It premio d'acquisto *(m)*

opção de venda *(f)* Pt
De Verkaufsoption *(f)*
En put option
Es opción de venta *(f)*
Fr option à vendre *(f)*
It premio a vendere *(m)*

opção dupla *(f)* Pt
De Stellagegeschäft *(n)*
En double option
Es opción doble *(f)*
Fr double option *(f)*
It opzione doppia *(f)*

opción *(f)* *n* Es
De Option *(f)*
En option
Fr option *(f)*
It opzione *(f)*
Pt opção *(f)*

opción de compras *(f)* Es
De Kaufoption *(f)*
En call option
Fr option d'achat *(f)*
It premio d'acquisto *(m)*
Pt opção de compra *(f)*

opción de venta *(f)* Es
De Verkaufsoption *(f)*
En put option
Fr option à vendre *(f)*
It premio a vendere *(m)*
Pt opção de venda *(f)*

opción doble *(f)* Es
De Stellagegeschäft *(n)*
En double option
Fr double option *(f)*
It opzione doppia *(f)*
Pt opção dupla *(f)*

open cheque En
De Inhaberscheck *(m)*
Es cheque abierto *(m)*
Fr chèque ouvert *(m)*
It assegno aperto *(m)*
Pt cheque em branco *(m)*

open cover En
De offene Versicherung *(f)*
Es cobertura flotante *(f)*
Fr police à aliment *(f)*
It polizza flottante *(f)*
Pt cobertura ilimitada *(f)*

open credit En
De offener Kredit *(m)*
Es crédito en descubierto *(m)*

Fr crédit à découvert *(m)*
It credito allo scoperto *(m)*
Pt crédito em aberto *(m)*

open market En
De freier Markt *(m)*
Es mercado libre *(m)*
Fr marché libre *(m)*
It mercato libero *(m)*
Pt mercado livre *(m)*

open-plan office En
De Großraumbüro *(n)*
Es oficina sin particiones *(f)*
Fr bureau sans cloisons *(m)*
It ufficio senza divisioni *(m)*
Pt escritório sem divisões *(m)*

open position En
De offene Position *(f)*
Es posición descubierta *(f)*
Fr position ouverte *(f)*
It posizione aperta *(f)*
Pt posição em aberto *(f)*

operación anterior *(f)* Es
De Leistung in der Vergangenheit *(f)*
En past performance
Fr comportement antérieur *(m)*
It comportamento precedente *(m)*
Pt desempenho anterior *(m)*

operación (mercantil) *(f)* Es
De Transaktion; Abschluß *(f m)*
En transaction
Fr opération *(f)*
It operazione *(f)*
Pt transacção *(f)*

operador a prima *(m)* Es
De Terminmakler *(m)*
En option dealer
Fr opérateur à prime *(m)*
It operatore in contratti a premio *(m)*
Pt corretor de opções *(m)*

operaio *(m)* It
De Arbeiter *(m)*
En worker
Es obrero; operario *(m)*
Fr ouvrier *(m)*
Pt operário *(m)*

operário *(m)* Pt
De Arbeiter *(m)*
En worker
Es obrero; operario *(m)*
Fr ouvrier *(m)*
It operaio *(m)*

opérateur à prime *(m)* Fr
De Terminmakler *(m)*
En option dealer
Es operador a prima *(m)*
It operatore in contratti a premio *(m)*
Pt corretor de opções *(m)*

operating costs En
De Betriebsausgaben *(f pl)*
Es costes operacionales *(m pl)*
Fr frais d'exploitation *(m pl)*
It spese di gestione *(f pl)*
Pt custos de exercício *(m pl)*

opération (affaire) *(f)* n Fr
De Transaktion; Abschluß *(f m)*
En transaction
Es operación (mercantil) *(f)*
It operazione *(f)*
Pt transacção *(f)*

operational research (OR) En
De Unternehmensforschung *(f)*
Es investigación operacional *(f)*
Fr recherche opérationnelle *(f)*
It indagine sul funzionamento *(f)*
Pt investigação operacional *(f)*

opérations à terme *(f pl)* Fr
De Zeitgeschäfte *(n pl)*
En forward dealings
Es negociaciones a término *(f pl)*
It operazioni a termine *(f pl)*
Pt transacções adiantadas *(f pl)*

operative *adj* En
De wirksam
Es operativo; activo
Fr actif
It attivo; operativo
Pt efectivo; em vigor

operativo *adj* Es, It
De wirksam
En operative
Fr actif
Pt efectivo; em vigor

operatore in contratti a premio *(m)* It
De Terminmakler *(m)*
En option dealer
Es operador a prima *(m)*
Fr opérateur à prime *(m)*
Pt corretor de opções *(m)*

operazione *(f)* n It
De Transaktion; Abschluß *(f m)*
En transaction
Es operación (mercantil) *(f)*
Fr opération *(f)*
Pt transacção *(f)*

operazione a contanti *(f)* It
De Bargeschäft *(n)*
En cash deal
Es trato al contado *(m)*
Fr transaction au comptant *(f)*
Pt negócio em dinheiro *(m)*

operazioni a termine *(f pl)* It
De Zeitgeschäfte *(n pl)*
En forward dealings
Es negociaciones a término *(f pl)*
Fr opérations à terme *(f pl)*
Pt transacções adiantadas *(f pl)*

opinião *(f)* n Pt
De Meinung *(f)*
En opinion
Es opinión *(f)*
Fr opinion *(f)*
It opinione *(f)*

opinion n En, Fr *(f)*
De Meinung *(f)*
Es opinión *(f)*
It opinione *(f)*
Pt opinião *(f)*

opinión *(f)* n Es
De Meinung *(f)*
En opinion
Fr opinion *(f)*
It opinione *(f)*
Pt opinião *(f)*

opinione *(f)* n It
De Meinung *(f)*
En opinion
Es opinión *(f)*
Fr opinion *(f)*
Pt opinião *(f)*

opposition d'intérêts *(f)* Fr
De widerstreitende Interessen
 (n pl)
En conflict of interest
Es pugna de intereses *(f)*
It conflitto d'interessi *(m)*
Pt conflito de interesses *(m)*

option n En, Fr *(f)*
De Option *(f)*
Es opción *(f)*
It opzione *(f)*
Pt opção *(f)*

Option *(f)* n De
En option
Es opción *(f)*
Fr option *(f)*
It opzione *(f)*
Pt opção *(f)*

option à vendre *(f)* Fr
De Verkaufsoption *(f)*
En put option
Es opción de venta *(f)*
It premio a vendere *(m)*
Pt opção de venda *(f)*

option d'achat *(f)* Fr
De Kaufoption *(f)*
En call option
Es opción de compras *(f)*
It premio d'acquisto *(m)*
Pt opção de compra *(f)*

option dealer En
De Terminmakler *(m)*
Es operador a prima *(m)*
Fr opérateur à prime *(m)*
It operatore in contratti a
 premio *(m)*
Pt corretor de opções *(m)*

opuscolo pubblicitario *(m)* It
De Werbeschrift *(f)*
En advertising brochure
Es folleto publicitario *(m)*
Fr prospectus publicitaire *(m)*
Pt folheto publicitário *(m)*

opzione *(f)* n It
De Option *(f)*
En option
Es opción *(f)*
Fr option *(f)*
Pt opção *(f)*

opzione doppia *(f)* It
De Stellagegeschäft *(n)*
En double option
Es opción doble *(f)*
Fr double option *(f)*
Pt opção dupla *(f)*

or *(m)* n Fr
De Gold *(n)*
En gold
Es oro *(m)*
It oro *(m)*
Pt ouro *(m)*

ora *(f)* n It
De Stunde *(f)*
En hour
Es hora *(f)*
Fr heure *(f)*
Pt hora *(f)*

ora di colazione *(f)* It
De Mittagspause *(f)*
En lunch-hour
Es hora del almuerzo *(f)*
Fr heure du déjeuner *(f)*
Pt hora do almoço *(f)*

ora di punta *(f)* It
De Hauptverkehrszeit *(f)*
En rush hour
Es hora punta *(f)*
Fr heures d'affluence *(f)*
Pt hora de ponta *(f)*

ora legale *(f)* It
De Normalzeit *(f)*
En standard time
Es hora oficial *(f)*
Fr heure légale *(f)*
Pt hora normal *(f)*

orario d'apertura *(m)* It
De Geschäftszeit *(f)*
En business hours
Es horario de comercio *(m)*
Fr heures d'ouverture *(f pl)*
Pt horas de funcionamento
 (f pl)

orario d'ufficio *(m)* It
De Geschäftsstunden *(f pl)*
En office hours
Es horario de oficina *(m)*
Fr heures de bureau *(f pl)*
Pt horário do escritório *(m)*

orario ferroviario *(m)* It
De Eisenbahnfahrplan *(m)*
En railway timetable
Es horario de trenes *(m)*
Fr indicateur des chemins de
 fer *(m)*
Pt horário de caminhos de
 ferro *(m)*

orçamento *(m)* n Pt
De Haushaltsplan *(m)*
En budget
Es presupuesto *(m)*
Fr budget *(m)*
It bilancio preventivo *(m)*

ordem bancária *(f)* Pt
De Bankauftrag *(m)*
En banker's order
Es orden bancaria *(f)*
Fr ordre bancaire *(m)*
It ordine bancario *(m)*

ordem de serviço *(f)* Pt
De Verordnung *(f)*
En directive
Es directiva *(f)*
Fr directive *(f)*
It direttivo *(m)*

ordenado *(m)* n Pt
De Gehalt *(n)*
En salary
Es sueldo *(m)*
Fr traitement *(m)*
It stipendio *(m)*

orden bancaria *(f)* Es
De Bankauftrag *(m)*
En banker's order
Fr ordre bancaire *(m)*
It ordine bancario *(m)*
Pt ordem bancária *(f)*

orden del día *(m)* Es
De Tagesordnung *(f)*
En agenda
Fr ordre du jour *(m)*
It ordine del giorno *(m)*
Pt agenda *(f)*

**ordentliche General-
versammlung** *(f)* De
En ordinary general meeting
Am stockholders' meeting
Es asamblea general ordina-
ria *(f)*
Fr assemblée générale *(f)*
It assemblea generale ordi-
naria *(f)*
Pt assembleia geral ordinária
(f)

ordentliche Versammlung *(f)*
De
En statutory meeting
Es asamblea general *(f)*
Fr assemblée ordinaire *(f)*
It assemblea generale *(f)*
Pt assembleia estatutária *(f)*

order *n* En
De Bestellung *(f)*
Es pedido *(m)*
Fr commande *(f)*
It ordine *(m)*
Pt encomenda *(f)*

order *vb* En
De bestellen
Es hacer un pedido
Fr passer une commande
It ordinare
Pt encomendar

order book En
De Auftragsbuch *(n)*
Es libro de pedidos *(m)*
Fr livre de commandes *(m)*
It libro degli ordini *(m)*
Pt livro de encomendas *(m)*

order-form *n* En
De Bestellformular *(n)*
Es solicitud de pedido *(f)*
Fr bulletin de commande *(m)*
It foglio d'ordinazione *(m)*
Pt impresso de encomenda
(m)

ordinare *vb* It
De bestellen
En order
Es hacer un pedido
Fr passer une commande
Pt encomendar

ordinary general meeting En
De ordentliche Generalver-
sammlung *(f)*
Es asamblea general ordina-
ria *(f)*
Fr assemblée générale *(f)*
It assemblea generale ordi-
naria *(f)*
Pt assembleia geral ordinária
(f)

ordinary share En
De Stammaktie *(f)*
Es acción ordinaria *(f)*
Fr action ordinaire *(f)*
It azione ordinaria *(f)*
Pt acção ordinária *(f)*

ordinary share certificate
En
Am stock certificate
De Aktie *(f)*
Es certificado de acción *(m)*
Fr certificat d'action *(m)*
It certificato azionario *(m)*
Pt título de acções ordinárias
(m)

ordinateur *(m)* *n* Fr
De Rechner; Computer *(m)*
En computer
Es computadora *(f)*
It elaboratore; calcolatore
(m)
Pt computador *(m)*

ordine *(m)* *n* It
De Bestellung *(f)*
En order
Es pedido *(m)*
Fr commande *(f)*
Pt encomenda *(f)*

ordine bancario *(m)* It
De Bankauftrag *(m)*
En banker's order
Es orden bancaria *(f)*
Fr ordre bancaire *(m)*
Pt ordem bancária *(f)*

ordine del giorno *(m)* It
De Tagesordnung *(f)*
En agenda
Es orden del día *(m)*
Fr ordre du jour *(m)*
Pt agenda *(f)*

ordine per corrispondenza
(f) It
De Auftrag durch die Post *(m)*
En mail order
Es pedido por correo *(m)*
Fr commande par lettre *(f)*
Pt venda pelo correio *(f)*

ordine per esportazione *(m)*
It
De Exportauftrag *(m)*
En export order
Es pedido de exportación *(m)*
Fr commande d'exportation
(f)
Pt encomenda de exportação
(f)

ordinogramme *(m)* *n* Fr
De Flußdiagramm *(m)*
En flow chart
Es diagrama de flujo *(m)*
It diagramma di flusso *(m)*
Pt gráfico de operação *(m)*

Ordnung *(f)* *n* De
En (legal) code
Es código *(m)*
Fr code *(m)*
It codice *(m)*
Pt código *(m)*

Ordnungsentschädigung
(f) *n* De
En nominal damages
Es daños nominales *(m pl)*
Fr indemnité de principe *(f)*
It danni nominali *(m pl)*
Pt danos nominais *(m pl)*

ordonnance *(f)* *n* Fr
De Befugnis *(f)*
En warrant
Es mandato *(m)*
It mandato *(m)*
Pt mandato *(m)*

ordonner une grève Fr
De zum Streik auffordern
En call a strike
Es declararse en huelga
It proclamare uno sciopero
Pt declarar greve

ordre bancaire *(m)* Fr
De Bankauftrag *(m)*
En banker's order
Es orden bancaria *(f)*
It ordine bancario *(m)*
Pt ordem bancária *(f)*

ordre du jour *(m)* Fr
De Tagesordnung *(f)*
En agenda
Es orden del día *(m)*
It ordine del giorno *(m)*
Pt agenda *(f)*

ora di punta *(f pl)* It
De Verkehrsspitze *(f)*
En peak hours
Es horas punta *(f pl)*
Fr heures de pointe *(f pl)*
Pt horas de ponta *(f pl)*

ore lavorative *(f pl)* It
De Arbeitszeit *(f)*
En hours of work
Es jornada laboral *(f)*
Fr durée du travail *(f)*
Pt horas de trabalho *(f pl)*

ore-uomo *(f pl)* n It
De Arbeitsstunde pro Mann *(f)*
En man-hours
Es horas-hombre *(f pl)*
Fr heures-homme *(f pl)*
Pt horas-homem *(f pl)*

organigrama *(m)* Pt
De Säulendiagramm *(m)*
En block diagram
Es diagrama de bloque *(m)*
Fr ordinogramme *(m)*
It schema a blocchi *(m)*

organisation *(f)* n Fr
De Organisation *(f)*
En organization
Es organización *(f)*
It organizzazione *(f)*
Pt organização *(f)*

Organisation *(f)* n De
En organization
Es organización *(f)*
Fr organisation *(f)*
It organizzazione *(f)*
Pt organização *(f)*

**Organisation de Coopéra-
tion et de Développe-
ment Économiques**
(O.C.D.E.) *(f)* Fr
De Organisation für wirt-
schaftliche Zusammenar-
beit und Entwicklung
(O.E.C.D.) *(f)*

En Organization for Economic Cooperation and De-
velopment (OECD)
Es Organización para Cooperacion y Desarrollo Eco-
nomico *(f)*
It Organizzazione per la
Cooperazione e lo Svilup-
po Economico *(f)*
Pt Organização para a Cooperação e o Desenvolvimento
Económico *(f)*

**Organisation für wirtschaft-
liche Zusammenarbeit
und Entwicklung**
(O.E.C.D.) *(f)* De
En Organization for Economic Cooperation and De-
velopment (OECD)
Es Organización para Cooperacion y Desarrollo Eco-
nomico *(f)*
Fr Organisation de Coopération et de Développement
Economiques (O.C.D.E.)
(f)
It Organizzazione per la
Cooperazione e lo Svilup-
po Economico *(f)*
Pt Organização para a Cooperação e o Desenvolvimento
Económico *(f)*

**Organisation Internationale
du Travail** (O.I.T.) *(f)* Fr
De Internationale Arbeitsorganisation (IAO) *(f)*
En International Labour Organization (ILO)
Es Organización Laboral Internacional *(f)*
It Organizzazione Internazionale del Lavoro *(f)*
Pt Organização Internacional
do Trabalho *(f)*

**Organisation Mondiale de la
Santé** (OMS) Fr
De Weltgesundheitsorganisa-
tion (WHO) *(f)*
En World Health Organization
(WHO)
Es Organización Mundial de
la Salud (OMS) *(f)*
It Organizzazione Mundiale
della Sanità (OMS) *(f)*
Pt Organização Mondial da
Saúde (OMS) *(f)*

organização *(f)* n Pt
De Organisation *(f)*
En organization
Es organización *(f)*
Fr organisation *(f)*
It organizzazione *(f)*

**Organização Internacional
do Trabalho** *(f)* Pt
De Internationale Arbeitsor-
ganisation (IAO) *(f)*
En International Labour Or-
ganization (ILO)
Es Organización Laboral
Internacional (O.I.T.) *(f)*
Fr Organisation Internationa-
le du Travail *(f)*
It Organizzazione Interna-
zionale del Lavoro *(f)*

**Organização Mundial da
Saúde** (OMS) *(f)* Pt
De Weltgesundheitsorganisa-
tion (WHO) *(f)*
En World Health Organization
(WHO)
Es Organización Mundial de
la Salud (OMS) *(f)*
Fr Organisation Mondiale de
la Santé (OMS)
It Organizzazione Mondiale
della Sanità (OMS) *(f)*

**Organização para a Coope-
ração e o Desenvolvi-
mento Económico** *(f)* Pt
De Organisation für wirt-
schaftliche Zusammenar-
beit und Entwicklung
(O.E.C.D.) *(f)*
En Organization for Economic Cooperation and De-
velopment (OECD)
Es Organización para Cooperacion y Desarrollo Eco-
nomico *(f)*
Fr Organisation de Coopération et de Développement
Economiques (O.C.D.E.)
(f)
It Organizzazione per la
Cooperazione e lo Svilup-
po Economico *(f)*

organización *(f)* n Es
De Organisation *(f)*
En organization
Fr organisation *(f)*
It organizzazione *(f)*
Pt organização *(f)*

Organización Laboral Internacional *(f)* Es
De Internationale Arbeitsorganisation (IAO) *(f)*
En International Labour Organization (ILO)
Fr Organisation Internationale du Travail (O.I.T.) *(f)*
It Organizzazione Internazionale del Lavoro *(f)*
Pt Organização Internacional do Trabalho *(f)*

Organización Mundial de la Salud (OMS) *(f)* Es
De Weltgesundheitsorganisation (WHO) *(f)*
En World Health Organization (WHO)
Fr Organisation Mondiale de la Santé (OMS)
It Organizzazione Mondiale della Sanità (OMS) *(f)*
Pt Organização Mundial da Saúde (OMS) *(f)*

Organización para Cooperacion y Desarrollo Economico *(f)* Es
De Organisation für wirtschaftliche Zusammenarbeit und Entwicklung (O.E.C.D.) *(f)*
En Organization for Economic Cooperation and Development (OECD)
Fr Organisation de Coopération et de Développement Economiques (O.C.D.E.) *(f)*
It Organizzazione per la Cooperazione e lo Sviluppo Economico *(f)*
Pt Organização para a Cooperação e o Desenvolvimento Económico *(f)*

organization *n* En
De Organisation *(f)*
Es organización *(f)*
Fr organisation *(f)*
It organizzazione *(f)*
Pt organização *(f)*

Organization for Economic Cooperation and Development (OECD) En
De Organisation für wirtschaftliche Zusammenarbeit und Entwicklung (O.E.C.D.) *(f)*
Es Organización para Cooperacion y Desarrollo Economico *(f)*
Fr Organisation de Coopération et de Développement Economiques (O.C.D.E.) *(f)*
It Organizzazione per la Cooperazione e lo Sviluppo Economico *(f)*
Pt Organização para a Cooperação e o Desenvolvimento Económico *(f)*

organizzazione *(f) n* It
De Organisation *(f)*
En organization
Es organización *(f)*
Fr organisation *(f)*
Pt organização *(f)*

Organizzazione Internazionale del Lavoro *(f)* It
De Internationale Arbeitsorganisation (IAO) *(f)*
En International Labour Organization (ILO)
Es Organización Laboral Internacional *(f)*
Fr Organisation Internationale du Travail (O.I.T.) *(f)*
Pt Organização Internacional do Trabalho *(f)*

Organizzazione Mondiale della Sanità (OMS) *(f)* It
De Weltgesundheitsorganisation (WHO) *(f)*
En World Health Organization (WHO)
Es Organización Mundial de la Salud (OMS) *(f)*
Fr Organisation Mondiale de la Santé (OMS)
Pt Organização Mundial da Saúde (OMS) *(f)*

Organizzazione per la Cooperazione e lo Sviluppo Economico *(f)* It
De Organisation für wirtschaftliche Zusammenarbeit und Entwicklung (O.E.C.D.) *(f)*
En Organization for Economic Cooperation and Development (OECD)
Es Organización para Cooperacion y Desarrollo Economico *(f)*
Fr Organisation de Coopération et de Développement Economiques (O.C.D.E.) *(f)*
Pt Organização para a Cooperação e o Desenvolvimento Económico *(f)*

orienté à la baisse Fr
De flau
En bearish
Es bajista
It ribassista
Pt baixista

origem *(f) n* Pt
De Ursprung *(m)*
En origin
Es origen *(m)*
Fr origine *(f)*
It origine *(f)*

origen *(m) n* Es
De Ursprung *(m)*
En origin
Fr origine *(f)*
It origine *(f)*
Pt origem *(f)*

origin *n* En
De Ursprung *(m)*
Es origen *(m)*
Fr origine *(f)*
It origine *(f)*
Pt origem *(f)*

original *(m) n* Es, Fr, Pt
De Original *(n)*
En top copy
It originale *(m)*

Original *(n) n* De
En top copy
Es original *(m)*
Fr original *(m)*
It originale *(m)*
Pt original *(m)*

originale *(m)* n It
De Original *(n)*
En top copy
Es original *(m)*
Fr original *(m)*
Pt original *(m)*

origine *(f)* n Fr, It
De Ursprung *(m)*
En origin
Es origen *(m)*
Pt origem *(f)*

oro *(m)* n Es, It
De Gold *(n)*
En gold
Fr or *(m)*
Pt ouro *(m)*

oro de imitación *(m)* Es
De Kunstgold *(n)*
En imitation gold
Fr similor *(m)*
It similoro *(m)*
Pt ouro de imitação *(m)*

Ortsplanungsgebiet *(n)* n De
En development area
Es zona de desarrollo *(f)*
Fr zone de développement *(f)*
It zona di sviluppo *(f)*
Pt zona de desenvolvimento
    (f)

ostracismo *(m)* n It
De Boykott *(m)*
En blacking
Am boycott
Es boicoteo *(m)*
Fr boycottage *(m)*
Pt boicote *(m)*

otorgar poder notarial Es
De eine Vollmacht erteilen
En execute a power of attor-
    ney
Fr conférer des pleins pou-
    voirs
It conferire una procura
Pt dar execução a poderes de
    procuração

ouro *(m)* n Pt
De Gold *(n)*
En gold
Es oro *(m)*
Fr or *(m)*
It oro *(m)*

ouro de imitação *(m)* Pt
De Kunstgold *(n)*
En imitation gold
Es oro de imitación *(m)*
Fr similor *(m)*
It similoro *(m)*

ouro-padrão *(m)* n Pt
De Goldobligation *(f)*
En gold standard
Es patrón oro *(m)*
Fr étalon or *(m)*
It base aurea *(f)*

outer harbour En
De Außenhafen *(m)*
Es antepuerto *(m)*
Fr avant-port *(m)*
It avamporto *(m)*
Pt anteporto *(m)*

out of bond En
De verzollt
Es despachado de aduanas
Fr dédouané
It sdoganato
Pt despachado da alfândega

out of date En
De verfallen
Es vencido
Fr périmé
It scaduto
Pt vencido

out of stock En
De ausverkauft
Es stock agotado
Fr tout vendu
It esaurito
Pt esgotado

out of work En
De arbeitslos
Es parado; sin trabajo
Fr en chômage
It disoccupato
Pt desempregado

output n En
De Erzeugung *(f)*
Es rendimiento *(m)*
Fr rendement *(m)*
It produzione *(f)*
Pt rendimento; produção *(m f)*

outstanding accounts En
De ausstehende Schulden
    (m pl)
Es cuentas pendientes *(f pl)*
Fr comptes à percevoir *(m pl)*
It conti aperti *(m pl)*
Pt contas por saldar *(f pl)*

ouvrage de référence *(m)* Fr
De Nachschlagewerk *(n)*
En reference book
Es libro de consulta *(m)*
It libro di consultazione *(m)*
Pt livro de consulta *(m)*

ouvrier *(m)* n Fr
De Arbeiter *(m)*
En worker; workman
Es obrero; trabajador *(m)*
It operaio; lavoratore *(m)*
Pt operário; trabalhador *(m)*

overcapacity n En
De Überkapazität *(f)*
Es exceso de capacidad *(m)*
Fr surcapacité *(f)*
It capacità in eccedenza *(f)*
Pt capacidade excessiva *(f)*

overdraft n En
De Überziehung *(f)*
Es sobregiro; saldo deudor
    (m)
Fr découvert; solde débiteur
    (m)
It scoperto *(m)*
Pt conta a descoberto *(f)*

overdraft facilities En
Am overdraw facility
De Überziehungsdisposition
    (f)
Es facilidades de descubierto
    (f pl)
Fr facilités de caisse *(f pl)*
It facilitazione di scoperto *(f)*
Pt disponibilidades de crédi-
    to sem cobertura *(f pl)*

overdraw (an account) *vb* En
De überziehen
Es girar en descubierto
Fr mettre à découvert
It trarre allo scoperto
Pt levantar a descoberto

overdue *adj* En
De rückständig
Es vencido
Fr arriéré
It scaduto
Pt vencido

over-estimate *n* En
De Überschätzung *(f)*
Es presupuesto por exceso
   (m)
Fr surestimation *(f)*
It valutazione eccessiva *(f)*
Pt avaliação excessiva *(f)*

overheads *pl n* En
De Generalunkosten *(pl)*
Es gastos generales *(m pl)*
Fr frais généraux *(m pl)*
It spese generali *(f pl)*
Pt gastos gerais *(m pl)*

overproduction *n* En
De Überproduktion *(f)*
Es exceso de producción *(m)*
Fr surproduction *(f)*
It sovrapproduzione *(f)*
Pt produção excessiva *(f)*

overtime *n* En
De Überstunden *(f pl)*
Es horas extraordinarias *(f pl)*
Fr heures supplémentaires
   (f pl)
It lavoro straordinario *(m)*
Pt horas extraordinárias *(f pl)*

overweight *n* En
De Übergewicht *(n)*
Es exceso de peso *(m)*
Fr excédent *(m)*
It sovrappeso *(m)*
Pt peso excessivo *(m)*

owner *n* En
De Eigentümer *(m)*
Es propietario; dueño *(m)*
Fr propriétaire *(m)*
It proprietario *(m)*
Pt proprietário; dono *(m)*

ownership *n* En
De Eigentum *(n)*
Es propiedad *(f)*
Fr propriété *(f)*
It proprietà *(f)*
Pt propriedade *(f)*

P

pacco *(m) n* It
De Paket *(n)*
En parcel; package
Es paquete *(m)*
Fr paquet *(m)*
Pt pacote *(m)*

package *n* En
De Paket *(n)*
Es paquete *(m)*
Fr paquet *(m)*
It pacco; collo *(m)*
Pt pacote *(m)*

package deal En
De Globalgeschäft *(n)*
Es contrato global *(m)*
Fr maché global *(m)*
It contratto globale *(m)*
Pt contrato global *(m)*

packing *n* En
De Verpackung *(f)*
Es embalaje; envase *(m)*
Fr emballage *(m)*
It imballaggio *(m)*
Pt embalagem; empacota-
   mento *(f m)*

Packwagen *(m) n* De
En guard's van
Es furgón *(m)*
Fr fourgon *(m)*
It bagaliaio *(m)*
Pt furgão *(m)*

pacote *(m) n* Pt
De Paket *(n)*
En parcel; package
Es paquete *(m)*
Fr paquet *(m)*
It pacco; collo *(m)*

pacte *(m) n* Fr
De Pakt *(m)*
En deed of covenant
Es pacto *(m)*
It patto *(m)*
Pt pacto *(m)*

pacto *(m) n* Es, Pt
De Abkommen; Pakt *(m)*
En covenant; deed of cove-
   nant
Fr convention, pacte *(f m)*
It convenzione; patto *(f m)*

pacto de honra *(m)* Pt
De Kavaliersabkommen *(n)*
En gentleman's agreement
Es acuerdo sobre palabra *(m)*
Fr convention verbale *(f)*
It accordo sulla parola *(m)*

padrão *(m) n* Pt
De Standard; Norm *(m f)*
En standard
Es norma; standard *(f m)*
Fr norme; étalon *(f m)*
It norma *(f)*

padrone *(m) n* It
De Arbeitgeber; Chef *(m)*
En employer; principal
Es patrono; principal *(m)*
Fr patron; employeur *(m)*
Pt patrão; director *(m)*

paese *(m) n* It
De Land *(n)*
En country
Es país *(m)*
Fr pays *(m)*
Pt país *(m)*

paese di origine *(m)* It
De Herkunftsland *(n)*
En country of origin
Es país de origen *(m)*
Fr pays de provenance *(m)*
Pt país de origem *(m)*

paese in via di sviluppo *(m)* It
De Entwicklungsland *(n)*
En developing country
Es país en desarrollo *(m)*
Fr pays en voie de dévelop-
   pement *(m)*
Pt país em desenvolvimento
   (m)

paesi sottosviluppati *(m pl)* It
De unterentwickelte Länder
   (n pl)
En underdeveloped countries
Es países en desarrollo *(m pl)*
Fr pays sous-développés
   (m pl)
Pt países subdesenvolvidos
   (m pl)

pagabile *adj* It
De zahlbar
En payable
Es pagadero; pagable
Fr payable
Pt pagável

pagabile al portatore It
De an den Inhaber zahlbar
En payable to bearer
Es pagadero al portador
Fr payable au porteur
Pt pagável ao portador

pagabile a vista It
De zahlbar bei Sicht
En payable at sight
Es pagadero a la vista
Fr payable à vue
Pt pagável à vista

pagadero adj Es
De zahlbar
En payable
Fr payable
It pagabile
Pt pagável

pagadero a la vista Es
De zahlbar bei Sicht
En payable at sight
Fr payable à vue
It pagabile a vista
Pt pagável à vista

pagadero al portador Es
De an den Inhaber zahlbar
En payable to bearer
Fr payable au porteur
It pagabile al portatore
Pt pagável ao partador

pagadero a presentación Es
De zahlbar bei Vorlage
En payable on demand
Fr payable sur demande
It pagabile a vista
Pt pagável à vista

pagadero con el pedido Es
De gegen Barzahlung
En cash with order
Fr payable à la commande
It pagamento con l'ordine
Pt pagamento no acto de re-
  quisição

pagado por adelantado Es
De vorausbezahlt
En prepaid
Fr payé d'avance
It pagato in anticipo
Pt pago adiantadamente

pagamenti trimestrali (m pl)
  It
De vierteljährliche Zahlungen
  (f pl)
En quarterly payments
Es pagos trimestrales (m pl)
Fr paiements trimestriels
  (m pl)
Pt pagamentos trimestrais
  (m pl)

pagamento (m) n It, Pt
De Zahlung (f)
En payment
Es pago (m)
Fr paiement (m)

**pagamento a completa
  tacitazione** (m) It
De Zahlung zum vollen Aus-
  gleich (f)
En payment in full discharge
Es pago de liberación (m)
Fr paiement libératoire (m)
Pt pagamento contra exe-
  cução completa (m)

pagamento adiado (m) Pt
De gestundete Zahlung (f)
En deferred payment
Es pago aplazado (m)
Fr paiement différé (m)
It pagamento differito (m)

pagamento adiantado (m) Pt
De Vorauszahlung (f)
En prepayment; payment in
  advance
Es pago andelantado (m)
Fr paiement anticipé (m)
It pagamento anticipato (m)

pagamento alla consegna It
De Lieferung gegen Nach-
  nahme
En cash on delivery (c.o.d.)
Es entrega contra reembolso
Fr paiement à la livraison
Pt entrega contra reembolso

pagamento anticipato (m) It
De Vorauszahlung (f)
En prepayment; advance
  payment
Es pago andelantado (m)
Fr paiement anticipé (m)
Pt pagamento adiantado (m)

pagamento completo (m) Pt
De volle Zahlung (f)
En payment in full
Es pago en pleno (m)
Fr libération intégrale (f)
It pagamento in pieno (m)

pagamento con l'ordine It
De gegen Barzahlung
En cash with order
Es pagadero con el pedido
Fr payable à la commande
Pt pagamento no acto de re-
  quisição

**pagamento contra execução
  completa** (m) Pt
De Zahlung zum vollen Aus-
  gleich (f)
En payment in full discharge
Es pago de liberación (m)
Fr paiement libératoire (m)
It pagamento a completa ta-
  citazione (m)

pagamento differito (m) It
De gestundete Zahlung (f)
En deferred payment
Es pago aplazado (m)
Fr paiement différé (m)
Pt pagamento adiado (m)

pagamento in anticipo (m) It
De Vorauszahlung (f)
En payment in advance
Es pago por adelantado (m)
Fr paiement anticipé (m)
Pt pagamento adiantado (m)

pagamento in conto (m) It
De Anzahlung (f)
En payment on account
Es pago a cuenta (m)
Fr versement à compte (m)
Pt pagamento por conta (m)

pagamento inicial (m) Pt
De Sofortzahlung (f)
En down-payment
Es pago de entrada (m)
Fr acompte (m)
It acconto (m)

pagamento in pieno (m) It
De volle Zahlung (f)
En payment in full
Es pago en pleno (m)
Fr libération intégrale (f)
Pt pagamento completo (m)

pagamento no acto de requisição Pt
De gegen Barzahlung
En cash with order
Es pagadero con el pedido
Fr payable à la commande
It pagamento con l'ordine

pagamento parcial (m) Pt
De Ratenzahlung (f)
En part payment
Es pago parcial (m)
Fr paiement partiel (m)
It pagamento parziale (m)

pagamento parziale (m) It
De Ratenzahlung (f)
En part payment
Es pago parcial (m)
Fr paiement partiel (m)
Pt pagamento parcial (m)

pagamento por conta (m) Pt
De Anzahlung (f)
En payment on account
Es pago a cuenta (m)
Fr versement à compte (m)
It pagamento in conto (m)

pagamento relativo aos resultados (m) n Pt
De Leistungslohn (m)
En payment by results
Es pago por resultados (m)
Fr salaire au rendement (m)
It pagamento secondo i risultati (m)

pagamento sob protesto (m) Pt
De Zahlung unter Protest (f)
En payment under protest
Es pago sobre protesta (m)
Fr paiement sous protêt (m)
It pagamento sotto protesto (m)

pagamento sotto protesto (m) It
De Zahlung unter Protest (f)
En payment under protest
Es pago sobre protesta (m)
Fr paiement sous protêt (m)
Pt pagamento sob protesto (m)

pagamentos trimestrais (m pl) Pt
De vierteljährliche Zahlungen (f pl)
En quarterly payments
Es pagos trimestrales (m pl)
Fr paiements trimestriels (m pl)
It pagamenti trimestrali (m pl)

paga neta (f) Es
De Nettolohn (m)
En take-home pay
Fr salaire net (m)
It paga netta (f)
Pt salário líquido de descontos (m)

paga netta (f) It
De Nettolohn (m)
En take-home pay
Es paga neta (f)
Fr salaire net (m)
Pt salário líquido de descontos (m)

pagar vb Es, Pt
De zahlen
En pay
Fr payer
It pagare

pagar ao portador Pt
De zahlen bei Vorlage
En pay to bearer
Es páguese al portador
Fr payez au porteur
It pagare al portatore

pagar a plazos mensuales (semanales) Es
De monatlich (wöchentlich) in Raten zahlen
En pay by monthly (weekly) instalments
Fr payer par termes mensuels (hebdomadaires)
It pagare a rate mensili (settimanali)
Pt pagar a prestações mensais (semanais)

pagar a prestações mensais (semanais) Pt
De monatlich (wöchentlich) in Raten zahlen
En pay by monthly (weekly) instalments

Es pagar a plazos mensuales (semanales)
Fr payer par termes mensuels (hebdomadaires)
It pagare a rate mensili (settimanali)

pagar depósito Pt
De hinterlegen
En pay a deposit
Es hacer un depósito
Fr donner des arrhes
It versare un deposito

pagaré (m) n Es
De Schuldschein (m)
En promissory note; I.O.U.
Fr billet à ordre; reconnaissance de dette (m f)
It pagherò (m)
Pt promissória; vale (f m)

pagare vb It
De zahlen
En pay
Es pagar
Fr payer
Pt pagar

pagare al portatore It
De zahlen bei Vorlage
En pay to bearer
Es páguese al portador
Fr payez au porteur
Pt pagar ao portador

pagare a rate mensii (settimanali) It
De monatlich (wöchentlich) in Raten zahlen
En pay by monthly (weekly) instalments
Es pagar a plazos mensuales (semanales)
Fr payer par termes mensuels (hebdomadaires)
Pt pagar a prestações mensais (semanais)

pagaré de favor (m) Es
De Gefälligkeitswechsel (m)
En accommodation bill
Fr billet de complaisance (m)
It cambiale di favore (f)
Pt letra de favor (f)

pagato in anticipo It
De vorausbezahlt
En prepaid
Es pagado por adelantado
Fr payé d'avance
Pt pago adiantadamente

pagável adj Pt
De zahlbar
En payable
Es pagadero; pagable
Fr payable
It pagabile

pagável ao portador Pt
De an den Inhaber zahlbar
En payable to bearer
Es pagadero al portador
Fr payable au porteur
It pagabile al portatore

pagável à vista Pt
De zahlbar bei Sicht
En payable at sight
Es pagadero a la vista
Fr payable à vue
It pagabile a vista

pagherò (m) n It
De Schuldschein (m)
En promissory note; I.O.U.
Es pagaré (m)
Fr billet à ordre; reconnais-
sance de dette (m f)
Pt promissória; vale (f m)

pago (m) n Es
De Zahlung (f)
En payment
Fr versement (m)
It pagamento (m)
Pt pagamento (m)

pago a cuenta (m) Es
De Anzahlung (f)
En payment on account
Fr versement à compte (m)
It pagamento in conto (m)
Pt pagamento por conta (m)

pago adiantadamente Pt
De vorausbezahlt
En prepaid
Es pagado por adelantado
Fr payé d'avance
It pagato in anticipo

pago andelantado (m) Es
De Vorauszahlung (f)
En prepayment
Fr paiement anticipé (m)
It pagamento anticipato (m)
Pt pagamento adiantado (m)

pago aplazado (m) Es
De gestundete Zahlung (f)
En deferred payment
Fr paiement différé (m)
It pagamento differito (m)
Pt pagamento adiado (m)

pago a plazos (m) Es
De Ratenzahlung (f)
En payment by instalments
Fr paiement à temperament
(m)
It pagamento a rate (m)
Pt pagamento a prestações
(m)

pago atrasado (m) Es
De Lohnnachzahlung (f)
En back pay
Fr rappel de traitement (m)
It arretrati di paga (m pl)
Pt vencimento atrasado (m)

pago de entrada (m) Es
De Sofortzahlung (f)
En down-payment
Fr acompte (m)
It acconto (m)
Pt pagamento inicial (m)

pago de liberación (m) Es
De Zahlung zum vollen Aus-
gleich (f)
En payment in full discharge
Fr paiement libératoire (m)
It pagamento a completa ta-
citazione (m)
Pt pagamento contra exe-
cução completa (m)

pago en pleno (m) Es
De volle Zahlung (f)
En payment in full
Fr libération intégrale (f)
It pagamento in pieno (m)
Pt pagamento completo (m)

pago parcial (m) Es
De Ratenzahlung (f)
En part payment

Fr paiement partiel (m)
It pagamento parziale (m)
Pt pagamento parcial (m)

pago por adelantado (m) Es
De Vorauszahlung (f)
En payment in advance
Fr paiement anticipé (m)
It pagamento in anticipo (m)
Pt pagamento adiantado (m)

pago por resultados (m) Es
De Leistungslohn (m)
En payment by results
Fr salaire au rendement (m)
It pagamento secondo i ri-
sultati (m)
Pt pagamento relativo aos
resultados (m)

pago sobre protesta (m) Es
De Zahlung unter Protest (f)
En payment under protest
Fr paiement sous protêt (m)
It pagamento sotto protesto
(m)
Pt pagamento sob protesto
(m)

pagos trimestrales (m pl) Es
De vierteljährliche Zahlungen
(f pl)
En quarterly payments
Fr paiements trimestriels
(m pl)
It pagamenti trimestrali
(m pl)
Pt pagamentos trimestrais
(m pl)

páguese al portador Es
De zahlen bei Vorlage
En pay to bearer
Fr payez au porteur
It pagare al portatore
Pt pagar ao portador

paid-up capital En
De eingezahltes Kapital (n)
Es capital desembolsado (m)
Fr capital versé (m)
It capitale versato (m)
Pt capital realizado (m)

paid-up policy En
De beitragsfreie Police (f)
Es póliza liberada (f)

Fr assurance libérée *(f)*
It polizza interamente paga-
ta *(f)*
Pt apólice liquidada *(f)*

paiement à la livraison Fr
De Lieferung gegen Nach-
nahme
En cash on delivery (c.o.d.)
Es entrega contra reembolso
It pagamento alla consegna
Pt entrega contra reembolso

paiement anticipé *(m)* Fr
De Vorauszahlung *(f)*
En prepayment
Es pago andelantado *(m)*
It pagamento anticipato *(m)*
Pt pagamento adiantado *(m)*

paiement différé *(m)* Fr
De gestundete Zahlung *(f)*
En deferred payment
Es pago aplazado *(m)*
It pagamento differito *(m)*
Pt pagamento adiado *(m)*

paiement libératoire *(m)* Fr
De Zahlung zum vollen Aus-
gleich *(f)*
En payment in full discharge
Es pago de liberación *(m)*
It pagamento a completa ta-
citazione *(m)*
Pt pagamento contra exe-
cução completa *(m)*

paiement par anticipation
(m) Fr
De Vorauszahlung *(f)*
En advance payment
Es anticipo *(m)*
It pagamento anticipato *(m)*
Pt pagamento adiantado *(m)*

paiement partiel *(m)* Fr
De Ratenzahlung *(f)*
En part payment
Es pago parcial *(m)*
It pagamento parziale *(m)*
Pt pagamento parcial *(m)*

paiement sous protêt *(m)* Fr
De Zahlung unter Protest *(f)*
En payment under protest
Es pago sobre protesta *(m)*
It pagamento sotto protesto
(m)
Pt pagamento sob protesto
(m)

paiements trimestriels *(m pl)*
Fr
De vierteljährliche Zahlungen
(f pl)
En quarterly payments
Es pagos trimestrales *(m pl)*
It pagamenti trimestrali
(m pl)
Pt pagamentos trimestrais
(m pl)

país *(m) n* Es, Pt
De Land *(n)*
En country
Fr pays *(m)*
It paese *(m)*

país de origem *(m)* Pt
De Herkunftsland *(n)*
En country of origin
Es país de origen *(m)*
Fr pays de provenance *(m)*
It paese di origine *(m)*

país de origen *(m)* Es
De Herkunftsland *(n)*
En country of origin
Fr pays de provenance *(m)*
It paese di origine *(m)*
Pt país de origem *(m)*

país em desenvolvimento
(m) Pt
De Entwicklungsland *(n)*
En developing country
Es país en desarrollo *(m)*
Fr pays en voie de dévelop-
pement *(m)*
It paese in via di sviluppo *(m)*

país en desarrollo *(m)* Es
De Entwicklungsland *(n)*
En developing country
Fr pays en voie de dévelop-
pement *(m)*
It paese in via di sviluppo *(m)*
Pt país em desenvolvimento
(m)

países subdesenvolvidos
(m pl) Pt
De unterentwickelte Länder
(n pl)
En underdeveloped countries
Es países en desarrollo *(m pl)*
Fr pays sous-développés
(m pl)
It paesi sottosviluppati *(m pl)*

Paket *(n) n* De
En parcel; package
Es paquete *(m)*
Fr paquet *(m)*
It pacco; collo *(m)*
Pt pacote *(m)*

Paketpost *(f)* De
En parcel post
Es servicio de paquete postal
(m)
Fr service des colis postaux
(m)
It servizio dei pacchi postali
(m)
Pt serviço de encomendas
postais *(m)*

Pakt *(m) n* De
En deed of covenant
Es pacto *(m)*
Fr pacte *(m)*
It patto *(m)*
Pt pacto *(m)*

paleta *(f) n* Pt
De Palette *(f)*
En pallet
Es bandeja *(f)*
Fr palette *(f)*
It paletta *(f)*

palettisation *(f) n* Fr
De Palettieren *(n)*
En palletization
Es paletización *(f)*
It palettizzazione *(f)*
Pt paletização *(f)*

Palettieren *(n) n* De
En palletization
Es paletización *(f)*
Fr palettisation *(f)*
It palettizzazione *(f)*
Pt paletização *(f)*

paletização *(f) n* Pt
De Palettieren *(n)*
En palletization
Es paletización *(f)*
Fr palettisation *(f)*
It palettizzazione *(f)*

paletización *(f) n* Es
De Palettieren *(n)*
En palletization
Fr palettisation *(f)*
It palettizzazione *(f)*
Pt paletização *(f)*

paletta *(f)* n It
De Palette *(f)*
En pallet
Es bandeja *(f)*
Fr palette *(f)*
Pt paleta *(f)*

palette *(f)* n Fr
De Palette *(f)*
En pallet
Es bandeja *(f)*
It paletta *(f)*
Pt paleta *(f)*

Palette *(f)* n De
En pallet
Es bandeja *(f)*
Fr palette *(f)*
It paletta *(f)*
Pt paleta *(f)*

palettizzazione *(f)* n It
De Palettieren *(n)*
En palletization
Es paletización *(f)*
Fr palettisation *(f)*
Pt paletização *(f)*

pallet n En
De Palette *(f)*
Es bandeja *(f)*
Fr palette *(f)*
It paletta *(f)*
Pt paleta *(f)*

palletization n En
De Palettieren *(n)*
Es paletización *(f)*
Fr palettisation *(f)*
It palettizzazione *(f)*
Pt paletização *(f)*

pane di ghisa *(m)* It
De Roheisen *(n)*
En pig-iron
Es hierro bruto *(m)*
Fr fer en gueuse *(m)*
Pt ferro em bruto *(m)*

papel carbón *(m)* Es
De Kohlepapier *(n)*
En carbon paper
Fr papier carbone *(m)*
It carta carbone *(f)*
Pt papel químico *(m)*

papel mata-borrão *(m)* Pt
De Löschpapier *(n)*
En blotting paper
Fr papier buvard
Es papel secante *(m)*
It carta assorbente *(f)*

papel milimetrado *(m)* Es, Pt
De Millimeterpapier *(n)*
En graph paper
Fr papier millimétré *(m)*
It carta millimetrata *(f)*

papel-moeda *(m)* n Pt
De Papiergeld *(n)*
En paper money
Es papel monetario *(m)*
Fr papier-monnaie *(m)*
It carta moneta *(f)*

papel monetario *(m)* Es
De Papiergeld *(n)*
En paper money
Fr papier-monnaie *(m)*
It carta moneta *(f)*
Pt papel-moeda *(m)*

papel químico *(m)* Pt
De Kohlepapier *(n)*
En carbon paper
Es papel carbón *(m)*
Fr papier carbone *(m)*
It carta carbone *(f)*

papel secante *(m)* Es
De Löschpapier *(n)*
En blotting paper
Fr papier buvard *(m)*
It carta assorbente *(f)*
Pt papel mata-borrão *(m)*

paper clip En
De Büroklammer *(f)*
Es sujetapapeles *(m)*
Fr attache-papiers *(m)*
It fermacarte *(m)*
Pt grampo *(m)*

paper loss En
De imaginärer Verlust *(m)*
Es pérdida por realizar *(f)*
Fr perte fictive *(f)*
It perdita sulla carta *(f)*
Pt perda no papel *(f)*

paper money En
De Papiergeld *(n)*
Es papel monetario *(m)*

Fr papier-monnaie *(m)*
It carta moneta *(f)*
Pt papel-moeda *(m)*

paper profit En
De imaginärer Gewinn *(m)*
Es ganancia por realizar *(f)*
Fr profit fictif *(m)*
It utile sulla carta *(m)*
Pt lucros no papel *(m pl)*

papier bancable *(m)* Fr
De diskontierbare Wechsel *(m pl)*
En bankable bills
Es efectos negociables *(m pl)*
It effetti scontabili *(m pl)*
Pt valores transaccionáveis pelo banco *(m pl)*

papier buvard *(m)* Fr
De Löschpapier *(n)*
En blotting paper
Es papel secante *(m)*
It carta assorbente *(f)*
Pt papel mata-borrão *(m)*

papier carbone *(m)* Fr
De Kohlepapier *(n)*
En carbon paper
Es papel carbón *(m)*
It carta carbone *(f)*
Pt papel químico *(m)*

papier de haut commerce *(m)* Fr
De erstklassiger Handels-wechsel *(m)*
En prime trade bill
Es carta comercial de primera orden *(f)*
It carta commerciale di primo ordine *(f)*
Pt estatuto de comerciali-zação de primeira ordem *(m)*

Papiergeld *(n)* n De
En paper money
Es papel monetario *(m)*
Fr papier-monnaie *(m)*
It carta moneta *(f)*
Pt papel-moeda *(m)*

papier millimétré *(m)* Fr
De Millimeterpapier *(n)*
En graph paper
Es papel milimetrado *(m)*
It carta millimetrata *(f)*
Pt papel milimetrado *(m)*

papier-monnaie *(m)* *n* Fr
De Papiergeld *(n)*
En paper money
Es papel monetario *(m)*
It carta moneta *(f)*
Pt papel-moeda *(m)*

papiers de bord *(m pl)* Fr
De Schiffspapiere *(n pl)*
En ship's papers
Es documentación marítima
    (f)
It carte di bordo *(f pl)*
Pt documentação do navio *(f)*

paquebot *(m)* *n* Fr
De Linienschiff *(n)*
En liner
Es vapor de línea *(m)*
It nave di linea *(f)*
Pt paquete *(m)*

paquet *(m)* *n* Fr
De Paket *(n)*
En parcel; package
Es paquete *(m)*
It pacco; collo *(m)*
Pt pacote *(m)*

paquete *(m)* *n* Pt
De Linienschiff *(n)*
En liner
Es vapor de línea *(m)*
Fr paquebot *(m)*
It nave di linea *(f)*

paquete *(m)* *n* Es
De Paket *(n)*
En parcel; package
Fr paquet *(m)*
It pacco; collo *(m)*
Pt pacote *(m)*

parado Es
De arbeitslos
En out of work
Fr en chômage
It disoccupato
Pt desempregado

parapher *vb* Fr
De paraphieren
En initial
Es rubricar; poner iniciales a
It siglare
Pt rubricar

paraphieren *vb* De
En initial
Es rubricar; poner iniciales a
Fr parapher; viser
It siglare
Pt rubricar

par avion Fr
De per Luftpost
En by air
Es por avión
It per via aerea
Pt por avião

parcel (package) *n* En
De Paket *(n)*
Es paquete *(m)*
Fr paquet *(m)*
It pacco; collo *(m)*
Pt pacote *(m)*

parcel (of land) *n* En
Am plot
De Parzelle *(f)*
Es parcela *(f)*
Fr parcelle *(f)*
It pezzo; lotto *(m)*
Pt parcela *(f)*

parcela *(f)* *n* Es, Pt
De Parzelle *(f)*
En parcel (of land)
Am plot
Fr parcelle *(f)*
It pezzo; lotto *(m)*

parcelle *(f)* *n* Fr
De Parzelle *(f)*
En parcel (of land)
Am plot
Es parcela *(f)*
It pezzo; lotto *(m)*
Pt parcela *(f)*

parcel post En
De Paketpost *(f)*
Es servicio de paquete postal
    (m)
Fr service des colis postaux
    (m)
It servizio dei pacchi postali
    (m)
Pt serviço de encomendas
    postais *(m)*

par duplicado Es
De Duplikat-; zweifach
En in duplicate
Fr en double

It in duplice copia
Pt em duplicado

pareggiare un bilancio It
De einen Haushaltsplan ins
    Gleichgewicht bringen
En balance a budget
Es balancear el presupuesto
Fr équilibrer un budget
Pt equilibrar um orçamento

pareggiare un conto It
De eine Rechnung ausglei-
    chen
En balance an account
Es saldar una cuenta
Fr balancer un compte
Pt equilibrar uma conta

parent company En
De Muttergesellschaft *(f)*
Es compañía matriz *(f)*
Fr société mère *(f)*
It società madre *(f)*
Pt empresa matriz *(f)*

paridad *(f)* *n* Es
De Parität *(f)*
En parity
Fr parité *(f)*
It parità *(f)*
Pt paridade *(f)*

paridade *(f)* *n* Pt
De Parität *(f)*
En parity
Es paridad *(f)*
Fr parité *(f)*
It parità *(f)*

paridade fixa *(f)* Pt
De feste Parität *(f)*
En fixed parity
Es paridad fija *(f)*
Fr parité fixe *(f)*
It parità fissa *(f)*

paridad fija *(f)* Es
De feste Parität *(f)*
En fixed parity
Fr parité fixe *(f)*
It parità fissa *(f)*
Pt paridade fixa *(f)*

parità *(f)* *n* It
De Parität *(f)*
En parity
Es paridad *(f)*
Fr parité *(f)*
Pt paridade *(f)*

parità fissa *(f)* It
De feste Parität *(f)*
En fixed parity
Es paridad fija *(f)*
Fr parité fixe *(f)*
Pt paridade fixa *(f)*

Parität *(f)* n De
En parity
Es paridad *(f)*
Fr parité *(f)*
It parità *(f)*
Pt paridade *(f)*

parité *(f)* n Fr
De Parität *(f)*
En parity
Es paridad *(f)*
It parità *(f)*
Pt paridade *(f)*

parité fixe *(f)* Fr
De feste Parität *(f)*
En fixed parity
Es paridad fija *(f)*
It parità fissa *(f)*
Pt paridade fixa *(f)*

parity n En
De Parität *(f)*
Es paridad *(f)*
Fr parité *(f)*
It parità *(f)*
Pt paridade *(f)*

par la présente Fr
De hiermit
En hereby
Es por esto
It col presente; con questo
Pt pelo presente

paro de temporada *(m)* Es
De jahreszeitlich bedingte Ar-
    beitslosigkeit *(f)*
En seasonal unemployment
Fr chômage saisonnier *(m)*
It disoccupazione stagiona-
    le *(f)*
Pt desemprego de estação *(m)*

part *(f)* n Fr
De Teil *(m)*
En share
Es parte *(f)*
It parte *(f)*
Pt quota *(f)*

partager vb Fr
De teilen
En share
Es repartir
It dividere
Pt repartir

partager la différence Fr
De einen strittigen Preisunter-
    schied teilen
En split the difference
Es repartir la diferencia
It dividere a metà la
    differenza
Pt dividir ao meio a diferença

parte *(f)* n Es, It
De Teil *(m)*
En share
Fr part *(f)*
Pt quota *(f)*

partecipare vb It
De beteiligen
En participate
Es participar
Fr participer
Pt participar

partecipazione agli utili *(f)* It
De Gewinnbeteiligung *(f)*
En profit-sharing
Es participación en los bene-
    ficios *(f)*
Fr participation aux béné-
    fices *(f)*
Pt repartição dos lucros *(f)*

**partecipazione
    maggioritaria** *(f)* It
De Mehrheitsbeteiligung *(f)*
En majority holding
Es tenencia de acciones por
    mayoría *(f)*
Fr participation majoritaire *(f)*
Pt propriedade em maioria *(f)*

parte lesa *(f)* It
De Verletzte(r) *(m)*
En injured party
Es parte lesionada *(f)*
Fr partie lésée *(f)*
Pt parte lesada *(f)*

parte lesada *(f)* Pt
De Verletzte(r) *(m)*
En injured party
Es parte lesionada *(f)*
Fr partie léseé *(f)*
It parte lesa *(f)*

parte lesionada *(f)* Es
De Verletzte(r) *(m)*
En injured party
Fr partie lésée *(f)*
It parte lesa *(f)*
Pt parte lesada *(f)*

par tête Fr
De pro Kopf
En per capita
Es por cabeza
It a testa
Pt per capita

participación de la minoría
    (f) Es
De Minoritätsbeteiligung *(f)*
En minority interest
Fr participation de la minorité
    (f)
It interessenza di minoranza
    (f)
Pt interesse representado pe-
    la minoria *(m)*

participación del mercado
    (f) Es
De Marktanteil *(m)*
En market share
Fr participation au marché *(f)*
It quota del mercato *(f)*
Pt quota-parte no mercado
    (f)

**participación en los
    beneficios** *(f)* Es
De Gewinnbeteiligung *(f)*
En profit-sharing
Fr participation aux bénéfi-
    ces *(f)*
It partecipazione agli utili *(f)*
Pt repartição dos lucros *(f)*

participar vb Es, Pt
De beteiligen
En participate
Fr participer
It partecipare

participate vb En
De beteiligen
Es participar
Fr participer
It partecipare
Pt participar

participating policy Am
En with-profits policy
De Police mit Gewinnberech-
   tigung *(f)*
Es póliza con beneficios *(f)*
Fr police avec participation
   aux bénéfices *(f)*
It polizza con profitti *(f)*
Pt apólice com participação
   nos lucros *(f)*

participation au marché *(f)* Fr
De Marktanteil *(m)*
En market share
Es participación del mercado
   (f)
It quota del mercato *(f)*
Pt quota-parte no mercado
   (f)

participation aux bénéfices
   (f) Fr
De Gewinnbeteiligung *(f)*
En profit-sharing
Es participación en los bene-
   ficios *(f)*
It partecipazione agli utili *(f)*
Pt repartição dos lucros *(f)*

participation de la minorité
   (f) Fr
De Minoritätsbeteiligung *(f)*
En minority interest
Es participación de la minoría
   (f)
It interessenza di minoranza
   (f)
Pt interesse representado pe-
   la minoria *(m)*

**participation donnant le
   contrôle** *(f)* Fr
De Mehrheitsbeteiligung *(f)*
En controlling interest
Es interés mayoritario *(m)*
It interesse della parte mag-
   gioritaria *(m)*
Pt interesse maioritário *(m)*

participation majoritaire *(f)*
   Fr
De Mehrheitsbeteiligung *(f)*
En majority holding
Es tenencia de acciones por
   mayoría *(f)*
It partecipazione maggiori-
   taria *(f)*
Pt propriedade em maioria *(f)*

participer *vb* Fr
De beteiligen
En participate
Es participar
It partecipare
Pt participar

particolari *(m pl)* n It
De Einzelheiten; Angaben
   (f pl)
En particulars
Es detalles *(m pl)*
Fr détails *(m pl)*
Pt pormenores *(m pl)*

particular average En
De besondere Havarie *(f)*
Es avería particular *(f)*
Fr avarie particulière *(f)*
It avaria particolare *(f)*
Pt avaria particular *(f)*

particularité *(f)* n Fr
De Merkmal *(n)*
En feature
Es característica *(f)*
It caratteristica *(f)*
Pt característica *(f)*

particulars *pl* n En
De Einzelheiten; Angaben
   (f pl)
Es detalles *(m pl)*
Fr détails *(m pl)*
It particolari *(m pl)*
Pt pormenores *(m pl)*

partida de defunción *(f)* Es
De Totenschein *(m)*
En death certificate
Fr extrait d'acte de décès *(m)*
It certificato di morte *(m)*
Pt certidão de óbito *(f)*

partida doble *(f)* Es
De doppelte Buchführung *(f)*
En double entry book-
   keeping
Fr comptabilité en partie
   double *(f)*
It partita doppia *(f)*
Pt lançamento duplo *(m)*

partie lésée *(f)* Fr
De Verletzte(r) *(m)*
En injured party
Es parte lesionada *(f)*
It parte lesa *(f)*
Pt parte lesada *(f)*

partita doppia *(f)* It
De doppelte Buchführung *(f)*
En double entry book-
   keeping
Es partida doble *(f)*
Fr comptabilité en partie
   double *(f)*
Pt lançamento duplo *(m)*

partitario delle vendite *(m)* It
De Verkaufskontenbuch *(n)*
En sales ledger
Es libro mayor de ventas *(m)*
Fr grand livre des ventes *(m)*
Pt livro-mestre de vendas
   (m)

partita spaiata *(f)* It
De Restpartie *(f)*
En odd lot
Es lote suelto *(m)*
Fr solde *(m)*
Pt lote avulso *(m)*

partner n En
De Teilhaber *(m)*
Es socio *(m)*
Fr associé *(m)*
It socio *(m)*
Pt sócio *(m)*

partnership n En
De offene Handelsgesell-
   schaft (OHG) *(f)*
Es sociedad regular colectiva
   (SRC) *(f)*
Fr société en nom collectif *(f)*
It società *(f)*
Pt sociedade *(f)*

part payment En
De Ratenzahlung *(f)*
Es pago parcial *(m)*
Fr paiement partiel *(m)*
It pagamento parziale *(m)*
Pt pagamento parcial *(m)*

Parzelle *(f)* n De
En parcel (of land)
Am plot
Es parcela *(f)*
Fr parcelle *(f)*
It pezzo; lotto *(m)*
Pt parcela *(f)*

pasado mañana Es
De übermorgen
En day after tomorrow

Fr après demain
It dopodomani
Pt depois de amanhã

pasaje *(m)* n Es
De Fahrgeld *(n)*
En fare
Fr prix du voyage *(m)*
It prezzo di viaggio *(m)*
Pt preço de passagem *(m)*

pasaje de ida *(m)* Es
De einfache Fahrkarte *(f)*
En single fare
Am one way fare
Fr billet d'aller *(m)*
It biglietto d'andata *(m)*
Pt passagem de ida *(f)*

pasaje de ida y vuelta *(m)* Es
De Rückfahrkarte *(f)*
En return fare
Am roundtrip fare
Fr billet d'aller et retour *(m)*
It biglietto di andata e ritorno *(m)*
Pt passagem de ida e volta *(f)*

pasajero *(m)* n Es
De Reisende(r) *(m)*
En passenger
Fr passager *(m)*
It passeggero *(m)*
Pt passageiro *(m)*

pasar de contrabando Es
De schmuggeln
En smuggle
Fr faire la contrebande
It contrabbandare
Pt passar por contrabando

pasivo exigible *(m)* Es
De laufende Verbindlichkeiten *(f pl)*
En current liabilities
Fr passif exigible *(m)*
It passività esigibili *(f pl)*
Pt passivo actual *(m)*

pasivo transitorio *(m)* Es
De aufgeschobene Schulden *(f pl)*
En deferred liabilities
Fr passif différé *(m)*
It passività differite *(f pl)*
Pt passivo adiado *(m)*

paso de aduanas *(f)* Es
De Zollabfertigung *(f)*
En customs clearance
Fr dédouanement *(m)*
It sdoganamento *(m)*
Pt despacho alfandegário *(m)*

passageiro *(m)* n Pt
De Reisende(r) *(m)*
En passenger
Es pasajero *(m)*
Fr passager *(m)*
It passeggero *(m)*

passagem de ida *(f)* Pt
De einfache Fahrkarte *(f)*
En single fare
Am one way fare
Es pasaje de ida *(m)*
Fr billet d'aller *(m)*
It biglietto d'andata *(m)*

passagem de ida e volta *(f)* Pt
De Rückfahrkarte *(f)*
En return fare
Am roundtrip fare
Es pasaje de ida y vuelta *(m)*
Fr billet d'aller et retour *(m)*
It biglietto di andata e ritorno *(m)*

passager *(m)* n Fr
De Reisende(r) *(m)*
En passenger
Es pasajero *(m)*
It passeggero *(m)*
Pt passageiro *(m)*

passar por contrabando Pt
De schmuggeln
En smuggle
Es pasar de contrabando
Fr faire la contrebande
It contrabbandare

passar um cheque Pt
De einen Scheck ausstellen
En draw a cheque
Es extender un cheque
Fr tirer un chèque
It emettere un assegno

passbook n En
Am bankbook
De Bankbuch; Sparbuch *(n)*
Es libreta de banco *(f)*

Fr livret de compte *(m)*
It libretto di conto *(m)*
Pt livrete de conta *(m)*

passeggero *(m)* n It
De Reisende(r) *(m)*
En passenger
Es pasajero *(m)*
Fr passager *(m)*
Pt passageiro *(m)*

passenger n En
De Reisende(r) *(m)*
Es pasajero *(m)*
Fr passager *(m)*
It passeggero *(m)*
Pt passageiro *(m)*

passer un acte Fr
De eine Urkunde unterzeichnen
En execute a deed
Es firmar una escritura
It perfezionare un atto
Pt dar execução a um título legal

passer une commande Fr
De bestellen
En order
Es hacer un pedido
It ordinare
Pt encomendar

passif différé *(m)* Fr
De aufgeschobene Schulden *(f pl)*
En deferred liabilities
Es pasivo transitorio *(m)*
It passività differite *(f pl)*
Pt passivo adiado *(m)*

passif exigible *(m)* Fr
De laufende Verbindlichkeiten *(f pl)*
En current liabilities
Es pasivo exigible *(m)*
It passività esigibili *(f pl)*
Pt passivo actual *(m)*

passività differite *(f pl)* It
De aufgeschobene Schulden *(f pl)*
En deferred liabilities
Es pasivo transitorio *(m)*
Fr passif différé *(m)*
Pt passivo adiado *(m)*

passività esigibili (f pl) It
De laufende Verbindlichkeiten
(f pl)
En current liabilities
Es pasivo exigible (m)
Fr passif exigible (m)
Pt passivo actual (m)

passivo actual (m) Pt
De laufende Verbindlichkeiten
(f pl)
En current liabilities
Es pasivo exigible (m)
Fr passif exigible (m)
It passività esigibili (f pl)

passivo adiado (m) Pt
De aufgeschobene Schulden
(f pl)
En deferred liabilities
Es pasivo transitorio (m)
Fr passif différé (m)
It passività differite (f pl)

Passivsaldo (m) n De
En adverse balance
Am negative balance
Es saldo adverso (m)
Fr balance déficitaire (f)
It saldo passivo (m)
Pt saldo negativo (m)

pasta (ministerial) (f) n Pt
De Portefeuille; Geschäftsbe-
reich (n m)
En portfolio
Es cartera (f)
Fr portefeuille (f)
It portafoglio (m)

past performance En
De Leistung in der Vergan-
genheit (f)
Es operación anterior (f)
Fr comportement antérieur
(m)
It comportamento prece-
dente (m)
Pt desempenho anterior (m)

patent n En
De Erfindungspatent (n)
Es patente (f)
Fr brevet d'invention (m)
It brevetto (m)
Pt patente (f)

patent agent En
De Patentanwalt (m)
Es agente de patentes (m)
Fr conseil en brevets (m)
It agente di brevetti (m)
Pt agente de patentes (m)

Patentanwalt (m) n De
En patent agent
Es agente de patentes (m)
Fr conseil en brevets (m)
It agente di brevetti (m)
Pt agente de patentes (m)

patente (f) n Es, Pt
De Erfindungspatent (n)
En patent
Fr brevet d'invention (m)
It brevetto (m)

Patenturkunde (f) n De
En letters patent
Am patent
Es patente de invención (f)
Fr brevet (m)
It brevetto (m)
Pt patente de invenção (f)

patrão (m) n Pt
De Arbeitgeber; Chef (m)
En employer; principal
Es patrono; principal (m)
Fr employeur; patron (m)
It datore di lavoro; padrone
(m)

patrimonio (m) n It
De Nachlaß; Erbschaft (m f)
En estate
Es herencia (f)
Fr succession (f)
Pt património; herança (m f)

património (m) n Pt
De Nachlaß; Erbschaft (m f)
En estate
Es herencia (f)
Fr succession (f)
It patrimonio; successione
(m f)

patron (m) n Fr
De Arbeitgeber; Chef (m)
En employer; principal
Es patrono; principal (m)
It padrone; principale (m)
Pt patrão; director (m)

patrono (m) n Es
De Arbeitgeber; Chef (m)
En employer; principal
Fr employeur; patron (m)
It datore di lavoro; padrone
(m)
Pt patrão; director (m)

patrón oro (m) Es
De Goldobligation (f)
En gold standard
Fr étalon or (m)
It base aurea (f)
Pt ouro-padrão (m)

patto (m) n It
De Pakt (m)
En deed of covenant
Es pacto (m)
Fr pacte (m)
Pt pacto (m)

Pauschalbetrag (m) n De
En lump sum
Es suma global (f)
Fr somme globale (f)
It somma globale (f)
Pt soma por inteiro (f)

pavillon (drapeau) (m) n Fr
De Flagge (f)
En flag
Es bandera (f)
It bandiera (f)
Pt bandeira (f)

pawnbroker n En
De Pfandleiher (m)
Es prestamista (m)
Fr prêteur sur gage (m)
It prestatore su pegno (m)
Pt prestamista (m)

pay vb En
De zahlen
Es pagar
Fr payer
It pagare
Pt pagar

payable adj En, Fr
De zahlbar
Es pagadero; pagable
It pagabile
Pt pagável

payable à la commande Fr
De gegen Barzahlung
En cash with order
Es pagadero con el pedido
It pagamento con l'ordine
Pt pagamento no acto de re-
   quisição

payable at sight En
De zahlbar bei Sicht
Es pagadero a la vista
Fr payable à vue
It pagabile a vista
Pt pagável à vista

payable au porteur Fr
De an den Inhaber zahlbar
En payable to bearer
Es pagadero al portador
It pagabile al portatore
Pt pagável ao portador

payable à vue Fr
De zahlbar bei Sicht
En payable at sight
Es pagadero a la vista
It pagabile a vista
Pt pagável à vista

payable on demand En
De zahlbar bei Vorlage
Es pagadero a presentación
Fr payable sur demande
It pagabile a vista
Pt pagável à vista

payables pl n En
De fällige Wechsel; Wechsel-
   schulden (m pl; f pl)
Es efectos a pagar (m pl)
Fr effets à payer (m pl)
It passività esigibili (f)
Pt contas a pagar (f pl)

payable sur demande Fr
De zahlbar bei Vorlage
En payable on demand
Es pagadero a presentación
It pagabile a vista
Pt pagável à vista

payable to bearer En
De an den Inhaber zahlbar
Es pagadero al portador
Fr payable au porteur
It pagabile al portatore
Pt pagável ao portador

pay a deposit En
De hinterlegen
Es hacer un depósito
Fr donner des arrhes
It versare un deposito
Pt pagar depósito

**pay by monthly (weekly)
   instalments** En
De monatlich (wöchentlich) in
   Raten zahlen
Es pagar a plazos mensuales
   (semanales)
Fr payer par termes men-
   suels (hebdomadaires)
It pagare a rate mensili (set-
   timanali)
Pt pagar a prestações mensais
   (semanais)

pay day En
De Zahltag; Abrechnungstag
   (m)
Es día de pago (m)
Fr jour de paiement (m)
It giorno di paga (m)
Pt dia de recebimento (m)

payé d'avance Fr
De vorausbezahlt
En prepaid
Es pagado por adelantado
It pagato in anticipo
Pt pago adiantadamente

payee n En
De Zahlungsberechtigte(r) (m)
Es beneficiario (m)
Fr bénéficiaire (m)
It beneficiario (m)
Pt beneficiário de pagamento
   (m)

payer vb Fr
De zahlen
En pay
Es pagar
It pagare
Pt pagar

**payer par termes mensuels
   (hebdomadaires)** Fr
De monatlich (wöchentlich) in
   Raten zahlen
En pay by monthly (weekly)
   instalments
Es pagar a plazos mensuales
   (semanales)

It pagare a rate mensili (settimanali)
Pt pagar a prestações mensais
   (semanais)

payer une lettre de change
   Fr
De einen Wechsel einlösen
En retire a bill
Es recoger una letra
It ritirare un effetto
Pt recuperar uma letra

payez au porteur Fr
De zahlen bei Vorlage
En pay to bearer
Es páguese al portador
It pagare al portatore
Pt pagar ao portador

payment n En
De Zahlung (f)
Es pago (m)
Fr versement (m)
It pagamento (m)
Pt pagamento (m)

payment by results En
De Leistungslohn (m)
Es pago por resultados (m)
Fr salaire au rendement (m)
It pagamento secondo i ri-
   sultati (m)
Pt pagamento relativo aos
   resultados (m)

payment in advance En
De Vorauszahlung (f)
Es pago por adelantado (m)
Fr paiement anticipé (m)
It pagamento in anticipo (m)
Pt pagamento adiantato (m)

payment in full En
De volle Zahlung (f)
Es pago en pleno (m)
Fr libération intégrale (f)
It pagamento in pieno (m)
Pt pagamento completo (m)

payment in full discharge En
De Zahlung zum vollen Aus-
   gleich (f)
Es pago de liberación (m)
Fr paiement libératoire (m)
It pagamento a completa ta-
   citazione (m)
Pt pagamento contra exe-
   cução completa (m)

payment on account En
De Anzahlung (f)
Es pago a cuenta (m)
Fr versement à compte (m)
It pagamento in conto (m)
Pt pagamento por conta (m)

payment terms En
De Zahlungsbedingungen
(f pl)
Es condiciones de pago (f pl)
Fr conditions de paiement
(f pl)
It condizioni di pagamento
(f pl)
Pt condições de pagamento
(f pl)

payment under protest En
De Zahlung unter Protest (f)
Es pago sobre protesta (m)
Fr paiement sous protêt (m)
It pagamento sotto protesto
(m)
Pt pagamento sob protesto
(m)

payroll n En
De Lohnbuch (n)
Es nómina de pago (f)
Fr feuille de paie (f)
It libro paga (m)
Pt folha de salários (f)

pays (m) n Fr
De Land (n)
En country
Es país (m)
It paese (m)
Pt país (m)

pays de provenance (m) Fr
De Herkunftsland (n)
En country of origin
Es país de origen (m)
It paese di origine (m)
Pt país de origem (m)

**pays en voie de développe-
ment** (m) Fr
De Entwicklungsland (n)
En developing country
Es país en desarrollo (m)
It paese in via di sviluppo (m)
Pt país em desenvolvimento
(m)

pays sous-développés
(m pl) Fr
De unterentwickelte Länder
(n pl)
En underdeveloped countries
Es países en desarrollo (m pl)
It paesi sottosviluppati (m pl)
Pt países subdesenvolvidos
(m pl)

pay to bearer En
De zahlen bei Vorlage
Es páguese al portador
Fr payez au porteur
It pagare al portatore
Pt pagar ao portador

peak hours En
De Verkehrsspitze (f)
Es horas punta (f pl)
Fr heures de pointe (f pl)
It ore di punta (f pl)
Pt horas de ponta (f pl)

pechincha (f) n Pt
De Gelegenheitskauf (m)
En bargain
Es ganga (f)
Fr occasion (f)
It occasione (f)

pedido (m) n Es, Pt
De Bestellung; Anforderung (f)
En order; requisition
Fr commande; demande (f)
It ordine; requisizione (m f)

pedido de exportación (m)
Es
De Exportauftrag (m)
En export order
Fr commande d'exportation
(f)
It ordine per esportazione
(m)
Pt encomenda de exportação
(f)

pedido por correo (m) Es
De Auftrag durch die Post (m)
En mail order
Fr commande par lettre (f)
It ordine per corrispondenza
(f)
Pt venda pelo correio (f)

pedir un préstamo Es
De entleihen
En borrow

Fr emprunter
It prestare
Pt contrair empréstimo

pegno (m) n It
De Nebenbürgschaft (f)
En security; pledge
Es fianza (f)
Fr nantissement (m)
Pt fiança (f)

peligro (m) n Es
De Gefahr (f)
En peril
Fr péril (m)
It pericolo (m)
Pt perigo (m)

pelletterie (f pl) n It
De Lederwaren (f pl)
En leather goods
Es marroquinería (f)
Fr maroquinerie (f)
Pt artigos de cabedal (m pl)

pelo presente Pt
De hiermit
En hereby
Es por esto
Fr par la présente
It col presente; con questo

penalidade (f) n Pt
De Strafe (f)
En penalty
Es multa (f)
Fr pénalité (f)
It penalità (f)

penalità (f) n It
De Strafe (f)
En penalty
Es multa (f)
Fr pénalité (f)
Pt penalidade (f)

pénalité (f) n Fr
De Strafe (f)
En penalty
Es multa (f)
It penalità (f)
Pt penalidade (f)

penalty n En
De Strafe (f)
Es multa (f)
Fr pénalité (f)
It penalità (f)
Pt penalidade (f)

penalty clause En
De Strafklausel (f)
Es cláusula de multa (f)
Fr clause pénale (f)
It clausola penale (f)
Pt cláusula de penalidade (f)

pendant adj Fr
De schwebend
En pending
Es pendiente
It pendente
Pt pendente

pendente adj It, Pt
De schwebend
En pending
Es pendiente
Fr pendant

pendiente adj Es
De schwebend
En pending
Fr pendant
It pendente
Pt pendente

pending adj En
De schwebend
Es pendiente
Fr pendant
It pendente
Pt pendente

penetración en el mercado
(f) Es
De Markteindringen (n)
En market penetration
Fr pénétration du marché (f)
It penetrazione nel mercato
(f)
Pt infiltração no mercado (f)

pénétration du marché (f) Fr
De Markteindringen (n)
En market penetration
Es penetración en el mercado
(f)
It penetrazione nel mercato
(f)
Pt infiltração no mercado (f)

penetrazione nel mercato (f)
It
De Markteindringen (n)
En market penetration
Es penetración en el mercado
(f)

Fr pénétration du marché (f)
Pt infiltração no mercado (f)

péniche (f) n Fr
De Lastkahn (m)
En barge
Es barcaza (f)
It chiatta (f)
Pt barcaça (f)

pensão (f) n Pt
De Pension; Rente (f)
En pension
Es pensión (f)
Fr pension (f)
It pensione (f)

**pensão sem contribuição
prévia** (f) Pt
De Pension ohne Beitrags-
pflicht (f)
En noncontributory pension
Es pensión sin entregas del
beneficiario (f)
Fr pension non-contribuable
(f)
It pensione senza contributi
(f)

pension n En, Fr (f)
De Pension; Rente (f)
Es pensión (f)
It pensione (f)
Pt pensão (f)

pensión (f) n Es
De Pension; Rente (f)
En pension
Fr pension (f)
It pensione (f)
Pt pensão (f)

Pension (f) n De
En pension
Es pensión (f)
Fr pension (f)
It pensione (f)
Pt pensão (f)

pensionado (m) n Es
De Rentner (m)
En pensioner
Fr pensionnaire (m)
It pensionato (m)
Pt pensionista (m)

pensionato (m) n It
De Rentner (m)
En pensioner

Es pensionado; pensionista
(m)
Fr pensionnaire (m)
Pt pensionista (m)

pensione (f) n It
De Pension; Rente (f)
En pension
Es pensión (f)
Fr pension (f)
Pt pensão (f)

pensione a contributi (f) It
De Kassenpension (f)
En contributory pension
Es retiro contributivo (m)
Fr retraite de régime à cotisa-
tions (f)
Pt reforma de contribuição
prévia (f)

pensioner n En
De Rentner (m)
Es pensionado; pensionista
(m)
Fr pensionnaire (m)
It pensionato (m)
Pt pensionista (m)

pensione senza contributi (f)
It
De Pension ohne Beitrags-
pflicht (f)
En noncontributory pension
Es pensión sin entregas del
beneficiario (f)
Fr pension non-contribuable
(f)
Pt pensão sem contribuição
prévia (f)

pensionista (m) n Es, Pt
De Rentner (m)
En pensioner
Fr pensionnaire (m)
It pensionato (m)

pensionnaire (m) n Fr
De Rentner (m)
En pensioner
Es pensionado; pensionista
(m)
It pensionato (m)
Pt pensionista (m)

pension non-contribuable
(f) Fr
De Pension ohne Beitrags-
pflicht *(f)*
En noncontributory pension
Es pensión sin entregas del
beneficiario *(f)*
It pensione senza contributi
(f)
Pt pensão sem contribuição
prévia *(f)*

**pensión sin entregas del
beneficiario** *(f)* Es
De Pension ohne Beitrags-
pflicht *(f)*
En noncontributory pension
Fr pension non-contribuable
(f)
It pensione senza contributi
(f)
Pt pensão sem contribuição
prévia *(f)*

per capita En, Pt
De pro Kopf
Es por cabeza
Fr par tête
It a testa

per cent En
De Prozent
Es por ciento
Fr pour cent
It per cento
Pt por cento

percentage *n* En
De Prozentsatz *(m)*
Es porcentaje *(m)*
Fr pourcentage *(m)*
It percentuale *(f)*
Pt percentagem *(f)*

percentagem *(f) n* Pt
De Prozentsatz *(m)*
En percentage
Es porcentaje *(m)*
Fr pourcentage *(m)*
It percentuale *(f)*

per cento It
De Prozent
En per cent
Es por ciento
Fr pour cent
Pt por cento

percentuale *(f) n* It
De Prozentsatz *(m)*
En percentage
Es porcentaje *(m)*
Fr pourcentage *(m)*
Pt percentagem *(f)*

percepteur (des impôts) *(m)*
Fr
De Steuereinnehmer *(m)*
En tax collector
Es recaudador de impuestos
(m)
It esattore delle imposte *(m)*
Pt cobrador de impostos *(m)*

per contra En
De als Gegenrechnung
Es en contrapartida
Fr en contrepartie; par contre
It in contropartita
Pt em contrapartida

perda *(f) n* Pt
De Verlust *(m)*
En loss
Es pérdida *(f)*
Fr perte *(f)*
It perdita *(f)*

perda avultada *(f)* Pt
De schwere Verluste *(m pl)*
En heavy loss
Es fuerte pérdida; pérdida
sensible *(f)*
Fr lourde perte *(f)*
It forte perdita *(f)*

perda de capital *(f)* Pt
De Kapitalverlust *(m)*
En capital loss
Es pérdida de capital *(f)*
Fr perte de capital *(f)*
It perdita di capitale *(f)*

perda de lucros *(f)* Pt
De Gewinnausfall *(m)*
En loss of profits
Es lucro cesante *(m)*
Fr perte de bénéfices *(f)*
It perdita di utili *(f)*

perda em impostos *(f)* Pt
De Steuerverlust *(m)*
En tax loss
Es pérdida fiscal *(f)*
Fr perte fiscale *(f)*
It perdita a scopi fiscali *(f)*

perda no papel *(f)* Pt
De imaginärer Verlust *(m)*
En paper loss
Es pérdida por realizar *(f)*
Fr perte fictive *(f)*
It perdita sulla carta *(f)*

perda por consequência *(f)*
Pt
De Folgeschaden *(m)*
En consequential loss
Es pérdida indirecta *(f)*
Fr perte indirecte *(f)*
It perdita indiretta *(f)*

perda total construtiva *(f)* Pt
De angenommener Totalver-
lust *(m)*
En constructive total loss
Es pérdida total constructiva
(f)
Fr perte réputée totale *(f)*
It perdita presunta totale *(f)*

perda total efectiva *(f)* Pt
De wirklicher Totalverlust *(m)*
En actual total loss
Es pérdida total efectiva *(f)*
Fr perte totale effective *(f)*
It perdita totale assoluta *(f)*

pérdida *(f) n* Es
De Verlust *(m)*
En loss
Fr perte *(f)*
It perdita *(f)*
Pt perda *(f)*

pérdida de capital *(f)* Es
De Kapitalverlust *(m)*
En capital loss
Fr perte de capital *(f)*
It perdita di capitale *(f)*
Pt perda de capital *(f)*

pérdida fiscal *(f)* Es
De Steuerverlust *(m)*
En tax loss
Fr perte fiscale *(f)*
It perdita a scopi fiscali *(f)*
Pt perda em impostos *(f)*

pérdida indirecta *(f)* Es
De Folgeschaden *(m)*
En consequential loss
Fr perte indirecte *(f)*
It perdita indiretta *(f)*
Pt perda por consequência *(f)*

pérdida por realizar *(f)* Es
De imaginärer Verlust *(m)*
En paper loss
Fr perte fictive *(f)*
It perdita sulla carta *(f)*
Pt perda no papel *(f)*

pérdida total constructiva *(f)*
Es
De angenommener Totalver-
lust *(m)*
En constructive total loss
Fr perte réputée totale *(f)*
It perdita presunta totale *(f)*
Pt perda total construtiva *(f)*

pérdida total efectiva *(f)* Es
De wirklicher Totalverlust *(m)*
En actual total loss
Fr perte totale effective *(f)*
It perdita totale assoluta *(f)*
Pt perda total efetiva *(f)*

perdita *(f)* n It
De Verlust *(m)*
En loss
Es pérdida *(f)*
Fr perte *(f)*
Pt perda *(f)*

perdita a scopi fiscali *(f)* It
De Steuerverlust *(m)*
En tax loss
Es pérdida fiscal *(f)*
Fr perte fiscale *(f)*
Pt perda em impostos *(f)*

perdita di capitale *(f)* It
De Kapitalverlust *(m)*
En capital loss
Es pérdida de capital *(f)*
Fr perte de capital *(f)*
Pt perda de capital *(f)*

perdita di utili *(f)* It
De Gewinnausfall *(m)*
En loss of profits
Es lucro cesante *(m)*
Fr perte de bénéfices *(f)*
Pt perda de lucros *(f)*

perdita indiretta *(f)* It
De Folgeschaden *(m)*
En consequential loss
Es pérdida indirecta *(f)*
Fr perte indirect *(f)*
Pt perda por consequência *(f)*

perdita presunta totale *(f)* It
De angenommener Totalver-
lust *(m)*
En constructive total loss
Es pérdida total constructiva
(f)
Fr perte réputée totale *(f)*
Pt perda total construtiva *(f)*

perdita sulla carta *(f)* It
De imaginärer Verlust *(m)*
En paper loss
Es pérdida por realizar *(f)*
Fr perte fictive *(f)*
Pt perda no papel *(f)*

perdita totale assoluta *(f)* It
De wirklicher Totalverlust *(m)*
En actual total loss
Es pérdida total efectiva *(f)*
Fr perte totale effective *(f)*
Pt perda total efetiva *(f)*

perfezionare un atto It
De eine Urkunde unterzeich-
nen
En execute a deed
Es firmar una escritura
Fr passer un acte
Pt dar execução a um título le-
gal

perforación en clave *(f)* Es
De manueller Locher *(m)*
En key-punch
Fr perforatrice à clavier *(f)*
It perforatore *(f)*
Pt perfurador *(m)*

perforatore *(f)* It
De manueller Locher *(m)*
En key-punch
Es perforación en clave *(f)*
Fr perforatrice à clavier *(f)*
Pt perfurador *(m)*

perforatrice à clavier *(f)* Fr
De manueller Locher *(m)*
En key-punch
Es perforación en clave *(f)*
It perforatore *(f)*
Pt perfurador *(m)*

performance n En
De Erfüllung; Vollstreckung *(f)*
Es ejecución *(f)*
Fr exécution *(f)*
It esecuzione *(f)*
Pt desempenho *(m)*

perfurador *(m)* Pt
De manueller Locher *(m)*
En key-punch
Es perforación en clave *(f)*
Fr perforatrice à clavier *(f)*
It perforatore *(f)*

pergunta *(f)* n Pt
De Nachfrage *(f)*
En inquiry
Es demanda *(f)*
Fr demande *(f)*
It domanda *(f)*

pericolo *(m)* n It
De Gefahr *(f)*
En peril
Es peligro *(m)*
Fr péril *(m)*
Pt perigo *(m)*

perigo *(m)* n Pt
De Gefahr *(f)*
En peril
Es peligro *(m)*
Fr péril *(m)*
It pericolo *(m)*

peril n En
De Gefahr *(f)*
Es peligro *(m)*
Fr péril *(m)*
It pericolo *(m)*
Pt perigo *(m)*

péril *(m)* n Fr
De Gefahr *(f)*
En peril
Es peligro *(m)*
It pericolo *(m)*
Pt perigo *(m)*

périmé Fr
De verfallen
En out of date; expired
Es vencido
It scaduto
Pt vencido

perishable goods En
De leicht verderbliche Waren
(f pl)
Es mercancías perecederas
(f pl)
Fr marchandises périssables
(f pl)
It merci deperibili *(f pl)*
Pt mercadorias perecíveis
(f pl)

perito *(m) n* Es, It, Pt
De   Sachverständige(r);
    Fachmann *(m)*
En   expert; specialist
Fr   spécialiste; expert *(m)*

perito de administração *(m)*
    Pt
De   Geschäftsführungsberater
    (m)
En   management consultant
Es   asesor administrativo *(m)*
Fr   ingénieur-conseil en or-
    ganisation *(m)*
It   consulente di direzione
    aziendale *(m)*

perito de publicidade *(m)* Pt
De   Werbeberater *(m)*
En   advertising consultant
Es   consultor de publicidad
    (m)
Fr   conseil en publicité *(m)*
It   consulente di pubblicità
    (m)

perito misuratore *(m)* It
De   Massenberechner *(m)*
En   quantity surveyor
Es   medidor de contidades de
    obra *(m)*
Fr   métreur-vérificateur *(m)*
Pt   perito na avaliação de
    quantidades *(m)*

**perito na avaliação de
quantidades** *(m)* Pt
De   Massenberechner *(m)*
En   quantity surveyor
Es   medidor de contidades de
    obra *(m)*
Fr   métreur-vérificateur *(m)*
It   perito misuratore *(m)*

perizia *(f) n* It
De   Sachverständigengutach-
    ten *(n)*
En   expert's report
Es   informe del especialista
    (m)
Fr   expertise *(f)*
Pt   relatório do perito *(m)*

per Luftpost De
En   by air
Es   por avión
Fr   par avion
It   per via aerea
Pt   por avião

permesso *(m) n* It
De   Erlaubnis; Genehmigung
    (f)
En   permit
Es   permiso *(m)*
Fr   permis *(m)*
Pt   autorização *(f)*

permesso d'esportazione
    (m) It
De   Ausfuhrgenehmigung *(f)*
En   export permit
Es   permiso de exportación
    (m)
Fr   autorisation d'exporter *(f)*
Pt   licença de exportação *(f)*

permesso d'importazione
    (m) It
De   Einfuhrgenehmigung *(f)*
En   import licence
Es   permiso de importación
    (m)
Fr   licence d'importation *(f)*
Pt   licença de importação *(f)*

permesso di lavoro *(m)* It
De   Arbeitserlaubnis *(f)*
En   work permit
Es   permiso de trabajo *(m)*
Fr   permis de travail *(m)*
Pt   carta de trabalho *(f)*

permis *(m) n* Fr
De   Erlaubnis; Genehmigung
    (f)
En   permit
Es   permiso *(m)*
It   permesso *(m)*
Pt   autorização *(f)*

permis de travail *(m)* Fr
De   Arbeitserlaubnis *(f)*
En   work permit
Es   permiso de trabajo *(m)*
It   permesso di lavoro *(m)*
Pt   carta de trabalho *(f)*

permiso *(m) n* Es
De   Erlaubnis; Genehmigung
    (f)
En   permit
Fr   permis *(m)*
It   permesso *(m)*
Pt   autorização *(f)*

permiso de exportación *(m)*
    Es
De   Ausfuhrgenehmigung *(f)*
En   export permit
Fr   autorisation d'exporter *(f)*
It   permesso d'esportazione
    (m)
Pt   licença de exportação *(f)*

permiso de importación *(m)*
    Es
De   Einfuhrgenehmigung *(f)*
En   import licence
Fr   licence d'importation *(f)*
It   permesso d'importazione
    (m)
Pt   licença de importação *(f)*

permiso de trabajo *(m)* Es
De   Arbeitserlaubnis *(f)*
En   work permit
Fr   permis de travail *(m)*
It   permesso di lavoro *(m)*
Pt   carta de trabalho *(f)*

permit *n* En
De   Erlaubnis; Genehmigung
    (f)
Es   permiso *(m)*
Fr   permis *(m)*
It   permesso *(m)*
Pt   autorização *(f)*

per Nachnahme De
En   charges forward; cash on
    delivery
Es   entrega contra reembolso
Fr   frais à percevoir à la livrai-
    son
It   spese assegnate; paga-
    mento alla consegna
Pt   entrega contra reembolso

perpetual debenture En
De   Dauerschuldverschrei-
    bung *(f)*
Es   obligación a perpetuidad
    (f)
Fr   obligation perpétuelle *(f)*
It   obbligazione perpetua *(f)*
Pt   obrigação de perenidade *(f)*

perseguir *vb* Es, Pt
De   weiterverfolgen
En   follow up
Fr   poursuivre
It   seguitare

personal *(m)* *n* Es
De Personal *(n)*
En personnel
Fr personnel *(m)*
It personale *(m)*
Pt pessoal *(m)*

Personal *(n)* *n* De
En personnel
Es personal *(m)*
Fr personnel *(m)*
It personale *(m)*
Pt pessoal *(m)*

personal assistant (PA) En
Am administrative assistant
De persönlicher Assistent *(m)*
Es asistente privado *(m)*
Fr fonctionnel *(m)*
It assistente privato *(m)*
Pt secretário *(m)*

Personalausweis *(m)* *n* De
En identity card
Es carnet de identidad *(m)*
Fr carte d'identité *(f)*
It carta d'identità *(f)*
Pt bilhete de identidade *(m)*

Personalchef *(m)* *n* De
En personnel manager
Es jefe de personal *(m)*
Fr chef du personnel *(m)*
It direttore del personale *(m)*
Pt chefe do pessoal *(m)*

personal de ventas *(m)* Es
De Verkaufspersonal *(n)*
En sales force
Fr personnel de vente *(m)*
It forze di vendita *(f pl)*
Pt pessoal de vendas *(m)*

personale *(m)* *n* It
De Personal *(n)*
En personnel
Es personal *(m)*
Fr personnel *(m)*
Pt pessoal *(m)*

persönlicher Assistent *(m)*
De
En personal assistant (PA)
Am administrative assistant
Es asistente privado *(m)*
Fr fonctionnel *(m)*
It assistente privato *(m)*
Pt secretário *(m)*

personnel *n* En, Fr *(m)*
De Personal *(n)*
Es personal *(m)*
It personale *(m)*
Pt pessoal *(m)*

personnel de vente *(m)* Fr
De Verkaufspersonal *(n)*
En sales force
Es personal de ventas *(m)*
It forze di vendita *(f pl)*
Pt pessoal de vendas *(m)*

personnel manager En
De Personalchef *(m)*
Es jefe de personal *(m)*
Fr chef du personnel *(m)*
It direttore del personale *(m)*
Pt chefe do pessoal *(m)*

perte *(f)* *n* Fr
De Verlust *(m)*
En loss
Es pérdida *(f)*
It perdita *(f)*
Pt perda *(f)*

perte de bénéfices *(f)* Fr
De Gewinnausfall *(m)*
En loss of profits
Es lucro cesante *(m)*
It perdita di utili *(f)*
Pt perda de lucros *(f)*

perte de capital *(f)* Fr
De Kapitalverlust *(m)*
En capital loss
Es pérdida de capital *(f)*
It perdita di capitale *(f)*
Pt perda de capital *(f)*

perte fictive *(f)* Fr
De imaginärer Verlust *(m)*
En paper loss
Es pérdida por realizar *(f)*
It perdita sulla carta *(f)*
Pt perda no papel *(f)*

perte fiscale *(f)* Fr
De Steuerverlust *(m)*
En tax loss
Es pérdida fiscal *(f)*
It perdita a scopi fiscali *(f)*
Pt perda em impostos *(f)*

perte indirecte *(f)* Fr
De Folgeschaden *(m)*
En consequential loss

Es pérdida indirecta *(f)*
It perdita indiretta *(f)*
Pt perda por consequência *(f)*

perte réputée totale *(f)* Fr
De angenommener Totalverlust *(m)*
En constructive total loss
Es pérdida total constructiva *(f)*
It perdita presunta totale *(f)*
Pt perda total construtiva *(f)*

perte totale effective *(f)* Fr
De wirklicher Totalverlust *(m)*
En actual total loss
Es pérdida total efectiva *(f)*
It perdita totale assoluta *(f)*
Pt perda total efectiva *(f)*

per via aerea It
De per Luftpost
En by air
Es por avión
Fr par avion
Pt por avião

pesado *adj* Es, Pt
De schwer
En heavy
Fr lourd; fort
It pesante; forte

pesante *adj* It
De schwer
En heavy
Es pesado; fuerte
Fr lourd; fort
Pt pesado

pesar *vb* Es, Pt
De wiegen
En weigh
Fr peser
It pesare

pesare *vb* It
De wiegen
En weigh
Es pesar
Fr peser
Pt pesar

pescaggio *(m)* *n* It
De Tiefgang *(m)*
En draught
Es calado *(m)*
Fr tirant d'eau *(m)*
Pt calado *(m)*

peser *vb* Fr
De wiegen
En weigh
Es pesar
It pesare
Pt pesar

peso *(m) n* Es, It,
   Pt
De Gewicht *(n)*
En weigh
Fr poids *(m)*

peso bruto *(m)* Es, Pt
De Bruttogewicht *(n)*
En gross weight
Fr poids brut *(m)*
It peso lordo *(m)*

peso excedente *(m)* Es
De Übergewicht *(n)*
En excess weight
Fr excédent de poids *(m)*
It eccedenza di peso *(f)*
Pt excesso de peso *(m)*

peso líquido *(m)* Pt
De Reingewicht *(n)*
En net weight
Es peso neto *(m)*
Fr poids net *(m)*
It peso netto *(m)*

peso lordo *(m)* It
De Bruttogewicht *(n)*
En gross weight
Es peso bruto *(m)*
Fr poids brut *(m)*
Pt peso bruto *(m)*

peso morto *(m)* It,
   Pt
De Tragfähigkeit *(f)*
En deadweight
Es peso muerto *(m)*
Fr port en lourd *(m)*

peso muerto *(m)* Es
De Tragfähigkeit *(f)*
En deadweight
Fr port en lourd *(m)*
It peso morto *(m)*
Pt peso morto *(m)*

peso neto *(m)* Es
De Reingewicht *(n)*
En net weight

Fr poids net *(m)*
It peso netto *(m)*
Pt peso líquido *(m)*

peso netto *(m)* It
De Reingewicht *(n)*
En net weight
Es peso neto *(m)*
Fr poids net *(m)*
Pt peso líquido *(m)*

peso o cubicaje Es
De Maß oder Gewicht
En weight or measurement
Fr poids ou mesure
It peso o volume
Pt peso ou medida

peso ou medida Pt
De Maß oder Gewicht
En weight or measurement
Es peso o cubicaje
Fr poids ou mesure
It peso o volume

peso o volume It
De Maß oder Gewicht
En weight or measurement
Es peso o cubicaje
Fr poids ou mesure
Pt peso ou medida

pesquisa de mercado *(f)*
   Pt
De Marktforschung *(f)*
En market research
Es investigación del mercado
   (f)
Fr étude du marché *(f)*
It indagine di mercato *(f)*

pessoal *(m) n* Pt
De Personal *(n)*
En personnel
Es personal *(m)*
Fr personnel *(m)*
It personale *(m)*

pessoal de vendas *(m)*
   Pt
De Verkaufspersonal *(n)*
En sales force
Es personal de ventas *(m)*
Fr personnel de vente *(m)*
It forze di vendita *(f pl)*

petite annonce *(f)* Fr
De Kleinanzeige *(f)*
En classified advertisement
Es anuncio por palabras *(m)*
It piccola pubblicità *(f)*
Pt anúncios classificados *(m
   pl)*

petite caisse *(f)* Fr
De kleine Kasse *(f)*
En petty cash
Es caja menor *(f)*
It piccola cassa *(f)*
Pt despesas de caixa *(f pl)*

petite monnaie *(f)* Fr
De Kleingeld *(n)*
En small change
Es moneda suelta *(f)*
It spiccioli *(m pl)*
Pt troco miúdo *(m)*

petrodólares *(m pl) n*
   Es, Pt
De Öldollar *(m pl)*
En petrodollars
Fr dollars pétroliers *(m pl)*
It petrodollari *(m pl)*

petrodollari *(m pl) n* It
De Öldollar *(m pl)*
En petrodollars
Es petrodólares *(m pl)*
Fr dollars pétroliers *(m pl)*
Pt petrodólares *(m pl)*

petrodollars *pl n* En
De Öldollar *(m pl)*
Es petrodólares *(m pl)*
Fr dollars pétroliers *(m pl)*
It petrodollari *(m pl)*
Pt petrodólares *(m pl)*

petróleo combustível *(m)*
   Pt
De Heizöl *(n)*
En fuel oil
Es fuel-oil *(m)*
Fr mazout *(m)*
It petrolio da ardere *(m)*

petrolio da ardere *(m)*
   It
De Heizöl *(n)*
En fuel oil
Es fuel-oil *(m)*
Fr mazout *(m)*
Pt petróleo combustível *(m)*

petty cash En
De kleine Kasse (f)
Es caja menor (f)
Fr petite caisse (f)
It piccola cassa (f)
Pt despesas de caixa (f pl)

pezza d'appoggio (f) It
De Belegstück (n)
En voucher
Es pieza justificativa (f)
Fr pièce justificative; fiche (f)
Pt vale (m)

pezzo (m) n It
De Parzelle (f)
En parcel (of land)
Am plot
Es parcela (f)
Fr parcelle (f)
Pt parcela (f)

Pfandleiher (m) n De
En pawnbroker
Es prestamista (m)
Fr prêteur sur gage (m)
It prestatore su pegno (m)
Pt prestamista (m)

Pfandrecht (n) n De
En lien
Es derecho de retencíon (m)
Fr droit de retention (m)
It diritto di sequestro (m)
Pt direito de retenção (m)

Pferdestärke (PS) (f) n De
En horse-power (hp)
Es caballo de vapor (cv) (m)
Fr cheval-vapeur (ch-v) (m)
It cavallo (m)
Pt cavalo-vapor (m)

Pfund Sterling (n) De
En pound sterling
Es libra esterlina (f)
Fr livre sterling (f)
It lira sterlina (f)
Pt libra esterlina (f)

phantom operation Am
En bogus company
De Schwindelgesellschaft (f)
Es sociedad fantasma (f)
Fr société fantôme (f)
It società fasulla (f)
Pt sociedade fantasma (f)

piano di stivaggio (m) It
De Ladeplan (m)
En stowage plan
Es plan de estiba (m)
Fr plan d'arrimage (m)
Pt plano de estiva (m)

pianterreno (m) n It
De Erdgeschoß (n)
En ground floor
Es planta baja (f)
Fr rez-de-chaussée (m)
Pt rés-do-chão (m)

piatto adj It
De flach
En flat
Es llano; plano
Fr plat; uniforme
Pt plano; liso

picchetto (m) n It
De Posten (m)
En picket
Es piquete (m)
Fr piquet (m)
Pt piquete (m)

piccola cassa (f) It
De kleine Kasse (f)
En petty cash
Es caja menor (f)
Fr petite caisse (f)
Pt despesas de caixa (f pl)

piccola pubblicità (f) It
De Kleinanzeige (f)
En classified advertisement
Es anuncio por palabras (m)
Fr petite annonce (f)
Pt anúncios classificados (m pl)

picket n En
De Posten (m)
Es piquete (m)
Fr piquet (m)
It picchetto (m)
Pt piquete (m)

pièce (de monnaie) (f) Fr
De Münze (f)
En coin
Es moneda (f)
It moneta (f)
Pt moeda (f)

pièce justificative (f) Fr
De Belegstück (n)
En voucher
Es pieza justificativa (f)
It pezza d'appoggio (f)
Pt vale (m)

piecework n En
De Akkordarbeit (f)
Es trabajo a destajo (m)
Fr travail à la tâche (m)
It lavoro a cottimo (m)
Pt trabalho por peça (m)

piel de imitación (f) Es
De Kunstleder (n)
En imitation leather
Fr simili-cuir (m)
It finta pelle (f)
Pt cabedal de imitação (m)

piena occupazione (f) It
De Vollbeschäftigung (f)
En full employment
Es pleno empleo (m)
Fr plein emploi (m)
Pt pleno emprego (m)

pieno adj It
De voll
En full
Es lleno
Fr plein
Pt cheio

pier n Am
En quay
De Kai (m)
Es muelle (m)
Fr quai (m)
It banchina (f)
Pt cais (m)

pieza justificativa (f) Es
De Belegstück (n)
En voucher
Fr pièce justificative; fiche (f)
It pezza d'appoggio (f)
Pt vale (m)

pigione (f) n It
De Miete (f)
En rent
Es alquiler (m)
Fr loyer (m)
Pt renda (f)

pig-iron *n* En
De Roheisen *(n)*
Es hierro bruto *(m)*
Fr fer en gueuse *(m)*
It pane di ghisa *(m)*
Pt ferro em bruto *(m)*

pilot (sea) *n* En
De Lotse *(m)*
Es piloto *(m)*
Fr pilote *(m)*
It pilota *(m)*
Pt piloto *(m)*

pilota *(m) n* It
De Lotse *(m)*
En (sea) pilot
Es piloto *(m)*
Fr pilote *(m)*
Pt piloto *(m)*

pilote *(m) n* Fr
De Lotse *(m)*
En (sea) pilot
Es piloto *(m)*
It pilota *(m)*
Pt piloto *(m)*

piloto *(m) n* Es, Pt
De Lotse *(m)*
En (sea) pilot
Fr pilote *(m)*
It pilota *(m)*

pilot plant En
De Musteranlage *(f)*
Es instalación piloto *(f)*
Fr installation pilote *(f)*
It impianto piloto *(m)*
Pt instalação piloto *(f)*

piquet *(m) n* Fr
De Posten *(m)*
En picket
Es piquete *(m)*
It picchetto *(m)*
Pt piquete *(m)*

piquete *(m) n* Es, Pt
De Posten *(m)*
En picket
Fr piquet *(m)*
It picchetto *(m)*

piso amueblado *(m)* Es
De möblierte Mietwohnung *(f)*
En furnished flat
Am furnished apartment

Fr appartement meublé *(m)*
It appartamento ammobilia-
to *(m)*
Pt andar mobilado *(m)*

piso con servicio incluido
(m) Es
De Etagenwohnung mit Be-
dienung *(f)*
En service flat
Fr appartement avec service
(m)
It appartamento con servizio
(m)
Pt andar com serviço in-
cluído *(m)*

**piso independiente
completo** *(m)* Es
De Einfamilienwohnung *(f)*
En self-contained flat
Fr appartement indépendant
(m)
It appartamento indipenden-
te *(m)*
Pt andar independente *(m)*

placcato in oro It
De vergoldet
En gold-plated
Es chapado en oro
Fr plaqué d'or
Pt laminado a ouro

plan *n* En, Es, Fr *(m)*
De Plan *(m)*
It progetto; piano *(m)*
Pt plano *(m)*

Plan *(m) n* De
En plan
Es plan *(m)*
Fr projet; plan *(m)*
It progetto; piano *(m)*
Pt plano *(m)*

plan d'arrimage *(m)* Fr
De Ladeplan *(m)*
En stowage plan
Es plan de estiba *(m)*
It piano di stivaggio *(m)*
Pt plano de estiva *(m)*

plan de estiba *(m)* Es
De Ladeplan *(m)*
En stowage plan
Fr plan d'arrimage *(m)*
It piano di stivaggio *(m)*
Pt plano de estiva *(m)*

plan de propaganda *(m)* Es
De Werbeplan *(m)*
En advertising schedule
Fr programme des annonces
(m)
It programma delle inserzio-
ni *(m)*
Pt plano de campanha publi-
citária *(m)*

plan de renta *(m)* Es
De Lohnpolitik *(f)*
En incomes policy
Fr politique des salaires *(f)*
It politica dei redditi *(f)*
Pt programa salários *(m)*

planned economy En
De Planwirtschaft *(f)*
Es economía planificada *(f)*
Fr économie planifiée *(f)*
It economia pianificata *(f)*
Pt economia planeada *(f)*

plano *adj* Es, Pt
De flach
En flat
Fr plat; uniforme
It piatto

plano *(m) n* Pt
De Plan *(m)*
En plan
Es plan *(m)*
Fr plan; projet *(m)*
It piano; progetto *(m)*

**plano de campanha
publicitária** *(m)* Pt
De Werbeplan *(m)*
En advertising schedule
Es plan de propaganda *(m)*
Fr programme des annonces
(m)
It programma delle inserzio-
ni *(m)*

plano de estiva *(m)* Pt
De Ladeplan *(m)*
En stowage plan
Es plan de estiba *(m)*
Fr plan d'arrimage *(m)*
It piano di stivaggio *(m)*

plant (industrial) *n* En
De Anlage *(f)*
Es planta; instalación *(f)*
Fr appareil; installation *(m f)*

It   impianto; macchinario *(m)*
Pt   instalação fabril *(f)*

planta *(f)* n Es
De   Anlage *(f)*
En   plant
Fr   appareil; installation *(m f)*
It   impianto; macchinario *(m)*
Pt   instalação fabril *(f)*

planta baja *(f)* Es
De   Erdgeschoß *(n)*
En   ground floor
Fr   rez-de-chaussée *(m)*
It   pianterreno *(m)*
Pt   rés-do-chão *(m)*

Planungsgewinn *(m)* n De
En   betterment
Es   plusvalía *(f)*
Fr   appréciation *(f)*
It   plus-valore *(m)*
Pt   melhoria *(f)*

Planwirtschaft *(f)* n De
En   planned economy
Es   economía planificada *(f)*
Fr   économie planifiée *(f)*
It   economia pianificata *(f)*
Pt   economia planeada *(f)*

plaqué d'or Fr
De   vergoldet
En   gold-plated
Es   chapado en oro
It   placcato in oro
Pt   laminado a ouro

plat *adj* Fr
De   flach
En   flat
Es   llano; plano
It   piatto
Pt   plano; liso

plate glass En
De   Spiegelglas *(n)*
Es   vidrio plano pulido *(m)*
Fr   verre à glaces; glace de
        vitrage *(m f)*
It   cristallo *(m)*
Pt   chapa de vidro *(f)*

plazo *(m)* n Es
De   Rate *(f)*
En   instalment
Fr   acompte *(m)*
It   rata *(f)*
Pt   prestação *(f)*

please forward En
De   bitte nachsenden
Es   se ruega hacer seguir
Fr   prière de faire suivre
It   far proseguire
Pt   é favor enviar

plein *adj* Fr
De   voll
En   full
Es   lleno
It   pieno
Pt   cheio

plein emploi *(m)* Fr
De   Vollbeschäftigung *(f)*
En   full employment
Es   pleno empleo *(m)*
It   piena occupazione *(f)*
Pt   pleno emprego *(m)*

pleito *(m)* n Es
De   Prozeß; Klage *(m f)*
En   legal action; lawsuit
Fr   action juridique; procès
        (f m)
It   processo *(m)*
Pt   acção judicial *(f)*

plenamente suscrito Es
De   vollgezeichnet
En   fully subscribed
Fr   intégralement souscrit
It   interamente sottoscritto
Pt   totalmente subscrito

pleno empleo *(m)* Es
De   Vollbeschäftigung *(f)*
En   full employment
Fr   plein emploi *(m)*
It   piena occupazione *(f)*
Pt   pleno emprego *(m)*

pleno emprego *(m)* Pt
De   Vollbeschäftigung *(f)*
En   full employment
Es   pleno empleo *(m)*
Fr   plein emploi *(m)*
It   piena occupazione *(f)*

plot n Am
En   parcel (of land)
De   Parzelle *(f)*
Es   parcela *(f)*
Fr   parcelle *(f)*
It   pezzo; lotto *(m)*
Pt   parcela *(f)*

**plus amples renseigne-
    ments** *(m pl)* Fr
De   nähere Umstände *(m pl)*
En   further particulars
Es   más detalles *(m pl)*
It   ulteriori particolari *(m pl)*
Pt   pormenores adicionais
        (m pl)

plus offrant enchérisseur
        (m) Fr
De   Meistbietende(r) *(m)*
En   highest bidder
Es   ofertante más alto *(m)*
It   miglior offerente *(m)*
Pt   proponente mais elevado
        (m)

plusvalía *(f)* n Es
De   Planungsgewinn *(m)*
En   betterment
Fr   appréciation *(f)*
It   plus-valore *(m)*
Pt   melhoria *(f)*

plus-valore *(m)* n It
De   Planungsgewinn *(m)*
En   betterment
Es   plusvalía *(f)*
Fr   appréciation *(f)*
Pt   melhoria *(f)*

plusvalore di capitale *(m pl)* It
De   Kapitalgewinn *(n)*
En   capital gains
Es   beneficios sobre capital
        (m pl)
Fr   gains en capital *(m pl)*
Pt   lucros de capital *(m pl)*

población *(f)* n Es
De   Bevölkerung *(f)*
En   population
Fr   population *(f)*
It   popolazione *(f)*
Pt   população *(f)*

poco proficuo It
De   unvorteilhaft
En   unprofitable
Es   nada lucrativo
Fr   sans profit
Pt   não lucrativo

poder *(m)* n Es
De   Vollmacht *(f)*
En   power of attorney
Fr   pouvoirs; procuration *(m
        pl; f)*

It procura *(f)*
Pt poderes de procuração
(m pl)

poder de compra *(m)* Es, Pt
De Kaufkraft *(f)*
En purchasing power
Fr pouvoir d'achat *(m)*
It potere d'acquisto *(m)*

poder de negociación *(m)* Es
De Verhandlungsposition *(f)*
En bargaining power
Fr pouvoir de négociation *(m)*
It potere di contrattare *(m)*
Pt poder de regateio *(m)*

poder de regateio *(m)* Pt
De Verhandlungsposition *(f)*
En bargaining power
Es poder de negociación *(m)*
Fr pouvoir de négociation *(m)*
It potere di contrattare *(m)*

poderes de procuração
(m pl) Pt
De Vollmacht *(f)*
En power of attorney
Es poder *(m)*
Fr pouvoirs; procuration
(m pl; f)
It procura *(f)*

poder procuración *(m)* Es
De Stellvertretung *(f)*
En proxy
Fr procuration *(f)*
It procura *(f)*
Pt procuração *(f)*

poids *(m)* n Fr
De Gewicht *(n)*
En weight
Es peso *(m)*
It peso *(m)*
Pt peso *(m)*

poids brut *(m)* Fr
De Bruttogewicht *(n)*
En gross weight
Es peso bruto *(m)*
It peso lordo *(m)*
Pt peso bruto *(m)*

poids net *(m)* Fr
De Reingewicht *(n)*
En net weight

Es peso neto *(m)*
It peso netto *(m)*
Pt peso líquido *(m)*

poids ou mesure Fr
De Maß oder Gewicht
En weight or measurement
Es peso o cubicaje
It peso o volume
Pt peso ou medida

poinçon de titre *(m)* n Fr
De Feingehaltsstempel *(m)*
En hall-mark
Es punzón de garantía *(m)*
It punzonatura di garanzia *(f)*
Pt marca de garantia *(f)*

point de seuil *(m)* Fr
De Rentabilitätsgrenze *(f)*
En break-even point
Es punto de igualdad de in-
gresos y gastos *(m)*
It punto di pareggio *(m)*
Pt ponto de acerto *(m)*

Police (Versicherung) *(f)* n De
En policy
Es póliza *(f)*
Fr police *(f)*
It polizza *(f)*
Pt apólice *(f)*

police (d'assurance) *(f)* Fr
De Police *(f)*
En policy
Es póliza *(f)*
It polizza *(f)*
Pt apólice *(f)*

police à aliment *(f)* Fr
De offene Versicherung *(f)*
En open cover
Es cobertura flotante *(f)*
It polizza flottante *(f)*
Pt cobertura ilimitada *(f)*

**police avec participation
aux bénéfices** *(f)* Fr
De Police mit Gewinnberech-
tigung *(f)*
En with-profits policy
Am participating policy
Es póliza con beneficios *(f)*
It polizza con profitti *(f)*
Pt apólice com participação
nos lucros *(f)*

police d'assurance *(f)* Fr
De Versicherungspolice *(f)*
En insurance policy
Es póliza de seguro *(f)*
It polizza di assicurazione *(f)*
Pt apólice de seguros *(f)*

police flottante *(f)* Fr
De laufende Police *(f)*
En floating policy
Es póliza flotante *(f)*
It polizza flottante *(f)*
Pt apólice flutuante *(f)*

police incendie *(f)* Fr
De Feuerversicherungspolice
(f)
En fire insurance policy
Es póliza de seguro de incen-
dios *(f)*
It polizza d'assicurazione in-
cendio *(f)*
Pt apólice de seguro de in-
cêndio *(f)*

**Police mit Gewinnberechti-
gung** *(f)* De
En with-profits policy
Am participating policy
Es póliza con beneficios *(f)*
Fr police avec participation
aux bénéfices *(f)*
It polizza con profitti *(f)*
Pt apólice com participação
nos lucros *(f)*

policy (insurance) n En
De Police *(f)*
Es póliza *(f)*
Fr police *(f)*
It polizza *(f)*
Pt apólice *(f)*

policy (plan) n En
De Politik *(f)*
Es política *(f)*
Fr politique *(f)*
It politica *(f)*
Pt política *(f)*

política *(f)* n Es, Pt
De Politik *(f)*
En policy
Fr politique *(f)*
It politica *(f)*

politica *(f) n* It
De Politik *(f)*
En policy
Es política *(f)*
Fr politique *(f)*
Pt política *(f)*

política agrícola comum *(f)*
　 Pt
De gemeinsame Agrarpolitik
　 (f)
En Common Agricultural
　 Policy
Es política agricola común *(f)*
Fr politique agricole commu-
　 ne *(f)*
It politica agricola comune *(f)*

política agricola común *(f)*
　 Es
De gemeinsame Agrarpolitik
　 (f)
En Common Agricultural
　 Policy
Fr politique agricole commu-
　 ne *(f)*
It politica agricola comune *(f)*
Pt política agrícola comum *(f)*

politica agricola comune *(f)*
　 It
De gemeinsame Agrarpolitik
　 (f)
En Common Agricultural
　 Policy
Es política agricola común *(f)*
Fr politique agricole commu-
　 ne *(f)*
Pt política agrícola comum *(f)*

política comercial comum *(f)*
　 Pt
De gemeinsame Handelspoli-
　 tik *(f)*
En Common Commercial
　 Policy
Es política comercial común
　 (f)
Fr politique commerciale
　 commune *(f)*
It politica commerciale co-
　 mune *(f)*

política comercial común *(f)*
　 Es
De gemeinsame Handelspoli-
　 tik *(f)*
En Common Commercial
　 Policy

Fr politique commerciale
　 commune *(f)*
It politica commerciale co-
　 mune *(f)*
Pt política comercial comum
　 (f)

**politica commerciale
　 comune** *(f)* It
De gemeinsame Handelspoli-
　 tik *(f)*
En Common Commercial
　 Policy
Es política comercial común
　 (f)
Fr politique commerciale
　 commune *(f)*
Pt política comercial comum
　 (f)

política comum da pesca *(f)*
　 Pt
De gemeinsame Fischereipo-
　 litik *(f)*
En Common Fisheries Policy
Es política común de la pesca
　 (f)
Fr politique commune de la
　 pêche *(f)*
It politica comune della pes-
　 ca *(f)*

política común de la pesca
　 (f) Es
De gemeinsame Fischereipo-
　 litik *(f)*
En Common Fisheries Policy
Fr politique commune de la
　 pêche *(f)*
It politica comune della pes-
　 ca *(f)*
Pt política comum da pesca
　 (f)

politica comune della pesca
　 (f) It
De gemeinsame Fischereipo-
　 litik *(f)*
En Common Fisheries Policy
Es política común de la pesca
　 (f)
Fr politique commune de la
　 pêche *(f)*
Pt política comum da pesca
　 (f)

politica dei redditi *(f)* It
De Lohnpolitik *(f)*
En incomes policy

Es plan de renta *(m)*
Fr politique des salaires *(f)*
Pt programa salários *(m)*

política monetaria *(f)* Es
De Währungspolitik *(f)*
En monetary policy
Fr politique monétaire *(f)*
It politica monetaria *(f)*
Pt política monetária *(f)*

politica monetaria *(f)* It
De Währungspolitik *(f)*
En monetary policy
Es política monetaria *(f)*
Fr politique monétaire *(f)*
Pt política monetária *(f)*

política monetária *(f)* Pt
De Währungspolitik *(f)*
En monetary policy
Es política monetaria *(f)*
Fr politique monétaire *(f)*
It politica monetaria *(f)*

Politik *(f) n* De
En policy
Es política *(f)*
Fr politique *(f)*
It politica *(f)*
Pt política *(f)*

politique *(f) n* Fr
De Politik *(f)*
En policy
Es política *(f)*
It politica *(f)*
Pt política *(f)*

politique agricole commune
　 (f) Fr
De gemeinsame Agrarpolitik
　 (f)
En Common Agricultural
　 Policy
Es política agricola común *(f)*
It politica agricola comune *(f)*
Pt política agrícola comum *(f)*

**politique commerciale
　 commune** *(f)* Fr
De gemeinsame Handelspoli-
　 tik *(f)*
En Common Commercial
　 Policy
Es política comercial común
　 (f)
It politica commerciale co-
　 mune *(f)*
Pt política comercial comum
　 (f)

politique commune de la pêche *(f)* Fr
De gemeinsame Fischereipolitik *(f)*
En Common Fisheries Policy
Es política común de la pesca *(f)*
It politica comune della pesca *(f)*
Pt política comum da pesca *(f)*

politique des salaires *(f)* Fr
De Lohnpolitik *(f)*
En incomes policy
Es plan de renta *(m)*
It politica dei redditi *(f)*
Pt programa salários *(m)*

politique monétaire *(f)* Fr
De Währungspolitik *(f)*
En monetary policy
Es política monetaria *(f)*
It politica monetaria *(f)*
Pt política monetária *(f)*

póliza (de seguros) *(f)* Es
De Police *(f)*
En policy
Fr police *(f)*
It polizza *(f)*
Pt apólice *(f)*

póliza con beneficios *(f)* Es
De Police mit Gewinnberechtigung *(f)*
En with-profits policy
Am participating policy
Fr police avec participation aux bénéfices *(f)*
It polizza con profitti *(f)*
Pt apólice com participação nos lucros *(f)*

póliza de seguro *(f)* Es
De Versicherungspolice *(f)*
En insurance policy
Fr police d'assurance *(f)*
It polizza di assicurazione *(f)*
Pt apólice de seguros *(f)*

póliza de seguro de incendios *(f)* Es
De Feuerversicherungsschein *(m)*
En fire insurance policy
Fr police incendie *(f)*

It polizza d'assicurazione incendio *(f)*
Pt apólice de seguro de incêndio *(f)*

póliza de seguro sobre la vida *(f)* Es
De Versicherungspolice *(f)*
En life assurance policy
Fr police d'assurance *(f)*
It polizza d'assicurazione *(f)*
Pt apólice de seguro de vida *(f)*

póliza dotal *(f)* Es
De Erlebensversicherung *(f)*
En endowment policy
Fr assurance à terme fixe *(f)*
It assicurazione dotale *(f)*
Pt título de doação *(m)*

póliza flotante *(f)* Es
De laufende Police *(f)*
En floating policy
Fr police flottante *(f)*
It polizza flottante *(f)*
Pt apólice flutuante *(f)*

póliza liberada *(f)* Es
De beitragsfreie Police *(f)*
En paid-up policy
Fr assurance libérée *(f)*
It polizza interamente pagata *(f)*
Pt apólice liquidada *(f)*

polizza (di assicurazione) *(f)* It
De Police *(f)*
En policy
Es póliza *(f)*
Fr police *(f)*
Pt apólice *(f)*

polizza con profitti *(f)* It
De Police mit Gewinnberechtigung *(f)*
En with-profits policy
Am participating policy
Es póliza con beneficios *(f)*
Fr police avec participation aux bénéfices *(f)*
Pt apólice com participação nos lucros *(f)*

polizza di carico *(f)* It
De Konnossement *(n)*
En bill of lading
Es conocimiento (de embarque) *(m)*

Fr connaissement *(m)*
Pt conhecimento (de embarque) *(m)*

polizza di assicurazione *(f)* It
De Versicherungspolice *(f)*
En insurance policy
Es póliza de seguro *(f)*
Fr police d'assurance *(f)*
Pt apólice de seguros *(f)*

polizza di assicurazione incendio *(f)* It
De Feuerversicherungsschein *(m)*
En fire insurance policy
Es póliza de seguro de incendios *(f)*
Fr police incendie *(f)*
Pt apólice de seguro de incêndio *(f)*

polizza di carico con merce a bordo *(f)* It
De Hafenkonnossement *(n)*
En shipped bill of lading
Es conocimiento de embarque a bordo *(m)*
Fr connaissement de marchandises à bord *(m)*
Pt conhecimento de carga embarcada *(m)*

polizza di carico con riserve *(f)* It
De einschränkendes Konnossement *(n)*
En foul (dirty) bill of lading
Es conocimiento de embarque con objecciones *(m)*
Fr connaissement avec réserve *(m)*
Pt conhecimento com embargos *(m)*

polizza di carico senza riserve *(f)* It
De echtes Konnossement *(n)*
En clean bill of lading
Es conocimiento de embarque sin objecciones *(m)*
Fr connaissement sans réserve *(m)*
Pt conhecimento sem embargos *(m)*

polizza flottante *(f)* It
De laufende Police *(f)*
En floating policy
Es póliza flotante *(f)*
Fr police flottante *(f)*
Pt apólice flutuante *(f)*

polizza interamente pagata
(f) It
De beitragsfreie Police *(f)*
En paid-up policy
Es póliza liberada *(f)*
Fr assurance libérée *(f)*
Pt apólice liquidada *(f)*

pont *(m)* n Fr
De Deck *(n)*
En deck
Es cubierta *(f)*
It coperta; ponte *(f m)*
Pt convés *(m)*

pontão *(m)* n Pt
De Mole *(f)*
En jetty
Es digue *(m)*
Fr jetée; digue *(f)*
It molo *(:m)*

ponto de acerto *(m)* Pt
De Rentabilitätsgrenze *(f)*
En break-even point
Es punto de igualdad de in-
gresos y gastos *(m)*
Fr point de seuil *(m)*
It punto di pareggio *(m)*

ponton-grue *(m)* n Fr
De Pontonkran *(m)*
En floating crane
Es grúa flotante *(f)*
It gru galleggiante *(f)*
Pt guindaste flutuante *(m)*

Pontonkran *(m)* n De
En floating crane
Es grúa flotante *(f)*
Fr ponton-grue *(m)*
It gru galleggiante *(f)*
Pt guindaste flutuante *(m)*

popolazione *(f)* n It
De Bevölkerung *(f)*
En population
Es población *(f)*
Fr population *(f)*
Pt população *(f)*

população *(f)* n Pt
De Bevölkerung *(f)*
En population
Es población *(f)*
Fr population *(f)*
It popolazione *(f)*

population n En, Fr *(f)*
De Bevölkerung *(f)*
Es población *(f)*
It popolazione *(f)*
Pt população *(f)*

porão *(m)* n Pt
De Laderaum *(m)*
En (ship's) hold
Es bodega *(f)*
Fr cale *(f)*
It stiva *(f)*

pôr à venda Pt
De zum Verkauf anbieten
En offer for sale
Es ofrecer en venta
Fr offrir en vente
It offrire in vendita

por avião Pt
De per Luftpost
En by air
Es por avión
Fr par avion
It per via aerea

por avión Es
De per Luftpost
En by air
Fr par avion
It per via aerea
Pt por avião

por cabeza Es
De pro Kopf
En per capita
Fr par tête
It a testa
Pt per capita

porcentaje *(m)* n Es
De Prozentsatz *(m)*
En percentage
Fr pourcentage *(m)*
It percentuale *(f)*
Pt percentagem *(f)*

por cento Pt
De Prozent
En per cent

Es por ciento
Fr pour cent
It per cento

por ciento Es
De Prozent
En per cent
Fr pour cent
It per cento
Pt por cento

por conta Pt
De a conto; auf Abschlag
En on account
Es a cuenta
Fr à valoir
It in acconto

por correio separado Pt
De mit getrennter Post
En under separate cover
Es por correo aparte
Fr sous pli séparé
It in piego a parte

por correo aparte Es
De mit getrennter Post
En under separate cover
Fr sous pli séparé
It in piego a parte
Pt por correio separado

por empréstimo Pt
De darlehensweise
En on loan
Es en préstamo
Fr sous forme de prêt
It in prestito

por esto Es
De hiermit
En hereby
Fr par la présente
It col presente; con questo
Pt pelo presente

pormenores *(m pl)* Pt
De Einzelheiten; Angaben
(f pl)
En particulars
Es detalles *(m pl)*
Fr détails *(m pl)*
It particolari *(m pl)*

pormenores adicionais
(m pl) Pt
De nähere Umstände *(m pl)*
En further particulars

Es más detalles *(m pl)*
Fr plus amples renseigne-
   ments *(m pl)*
It ulteriori particolari *(m pl)*

pormenorizado *adj* Pt
De postenmäßig dargestellt
En itemized
Es detallado
Fr détaillé
It dettagliato

por separado Es
De getrennt
En under separate cover
Fr sous pli séparé
It con plico a parte
Pt em separado

port *n* En, Fr *(m)*
De Hafen *(m)*
Es puerto *(m)*
It porto *(m)*
Pt porto *(m)*

portafoglio (di un ministro)
   (m) n It
De Portefeuille; Geschäftsbe-
   reich *(n m)*
En portfolio
Es cartera *(f)*
Fr portefeuille *(f)*
Pt pasta *(f)*

portafoglio titoli *(m)* It
De Investitionsportefeuille *(n)*
En investment portfolio
Es cartera de inversiones *(f)*
Fr portefeuille d'investisse-
   ments *(m)*
Pt carteira de investimentos
   (f)

portatore di obbligazioni *(m)*
   It
De Obligationär *(m)*
En bondholder
Es obligacionista *(m)*
Fr obligataire *(m)*
Pt titular de obrigações *(m)*

port charges En
De Hafengebühren *(f pl)*
Es derechos portuarios *(m pl)*
Fr droits de port *(m pl)*
It diritti portuali *(m pl)*
Pt direitos portuários *(m pl)*

port d'attache *(m)* Fr
De Heimathafen *(m)*
En port of registration
Es puerto de matrícula *(m)*
It porto d'immatricolazione
   (m)
Pt porto de matrícula *(m)*

port d'escale *(m)* Fr
De Anlaufhafen *(m)*
En port of call
Es puerto de escala *(m)*
It porto di scalo *(m)*
Pt porto de escala *(m)*

port de destination *(m)* Fr
De Bestimmungshafen *(m)*
En port of destination
Es puerto de destino *(m)*
It porto di destinazione *(m)*
Pt porto de destino *(m)*

port de livraison *(m)* Fr
De Lieferhafen *(m)*
En port of discharge
Es puerto de descarga *(m)*
It porto di scarico *(m)*
Pt porto de descarga *(m)*

portefeuille (d'un ministre)
   (f) n Fr
De Portefeuille; Geschäftsbe-
   reich *(n m)*
En portfolio
Es cartera *(f)*
It portafoglio *(m)*
Pt pasta *(f)*

Portefeuille (eines Ministers)
   (n) n De
En portfolio
Es cartera *(f)*
Fr portefeuille *(f)*
It portafoglio *(m)*
Pt pasta *(f)*

portefeuille d'investisse-
   ments *(m)* Fr
De Investitionsportefeuille *(n)*
En investment portfolio
Es cartera de inversiones *(f)*
It portafoglio titoli *(m)*
Pt carteira de investimentos
   (f)

porte grátis Pt
De frachtfrei
En carriage free

Am F.O.B. destination
Es franco de porte
Fr franco
It porto franco

porteiro *(m) n* Pt
De Hausmeister *(m)*
En hall-porter
Es conserje *(m)*
Fr concierge *(m)*
It portiere *(m)*

port en lourd *(m)* Fr
De Tragfähigkeit *(f)*
En deadweight
Es peso muerto *(m)*
It peso morto *(m)*
Pt peso morto *(m)*

porte pago Pt
De franko
En carriage paid
Am freight charges paid
Es a porte pagado
Fr port payé
It franco di porto

portes pagos Pt
De portofrei
En postage paid
Es franco de porte
Fr port payé
It porto pagato

porteur à titre onéreux *(m)* Fr
De entgeltigter Besitzer *(m)*
En holder for value
Es tenedor legítimo *(m)*
It detentore legittimo *(m)*
Pt proprietário legítimo *(m)*

porteur d'obligations *(m)* Fr
De Obligationsinhaber *(m)*
En debenture holder
Es obligacionista *(m)*
It obbligazionista *(f)*
Pt titular de obrigação *(m)*

porteur de bonne fol *(m)* Fr
De gutgläubiger Besitzer *(m)*
En holder in due course
Es tenedor en buena fe *(m)*
It titolare in buona fede *(m)*
Pt proprietário de boa fé *(m)*

portfolio (of a minister) *n* En
De Portefeuille; Geschäftsbe-
    reich *(n m)*
Es cartera *(f)*
Fr portefeuille *(f)*
It portafoglio *(m)*
Pt pasta *(f)*

port franc *(m)* Fr
De Freihafen *(m)*
En free port
Es puerto libre *(m)*
It porto franco *(m)*
Pt porto franco *(m)*

portiere *(m)* *n* It
De Hausmeister *(m)*
En hall-porter
Es conserje *(m)*
Fr concierge *(m)*
Pt porteiro *(m)*

port mark En
De Benennung des Bestim-
    mungshafens *(f)*
Es marca de destino *(f)*
Fr marque de destination *(f)*
It marche di destinazione
    (f pl)
Pt marca de porto *(f)*

porto *(m)* *n* It, Pt
De Hafen *(m)*
En harbour; port
Es puerto *(m)*
Fr port *(m)*

porto assegnato It
De Portonachnahme
En carriage forward
Am F.O.B. shipping point
Es a porte debido
Fr en port dû
Pt transporte a pagar

porto de descarga *(m)* Pt
De Lieferhafen *(m)*
En port of discharge
Es puerto de descarga *(m)*
Fr port de livraison *(m)*
It porto di scarico *(m)*

porto de destino *(m)* Pt
De Bestimmungshafen *(m)*
En port of destination
Es puerto de destino *(m)*
Fr port de destination *(m)*
It porto di destinazione *(m)*

porto de escala *(m)* Pt
De Anlaufhafen *(m)*
En port of call
Es puerto de escala *(m)*
Fr port d'escale *(m)*
It porto di scalo *(m)*

porto de matrícula *(m)* Pt
De Heimathafen *(m)*
En port of registration
Es puerto de matrícula *(m)*
Fr port d'attache *(m)*
It porto d'immatricolazione
    (m)

porto di destinazione *(m)* It
De Bestimmungshafen *(m)*
En port of destination
Es puerto de destino *(m)*
Fr port de destination *(m)*
Pt porto de destino *(m)*

porto d'immatricolazione
    (m) It
De Heimathafen *(m)*
En port of registration
Es puerto de matrícula *(m)*
Fr port d'attache *(m)*
Pt porto de matrícula *(m)*

porto di scalo *(m)* It
De Anlaufhafen *(m)*
En port of call
Es puerto de escala *(m)*
Fr port d'escale *(m)*
Pt porto de escala *(m)*

porto di scarico *(m)* It
De Lieferhafen *(m)*
En port of discharge
Es puerto de descarga *(m)*
Fr port de livraison *(m)*
Pt porto de descarga *(m)*

port of call En
De Anlaufhafen *(m)*
Es puerto de escala *(m)*
Fr port d'escale *(m)*
It porto di scalo *(m)*
Pt porto de escala *(m)*

port of destination En
De Bestimmungshafen *(m)*
Es puerto de destino *(m)*
Fr port de destination *(m)*
It porto di destinazione *(m)*
Pt porto de destino *(m)*

port of discharge En
De Lieferhafen *(m)*
Es puerto de descarga *(m)*
Fr port de livraison *(m)*
It porto di scarico *(m)*
Pt porto de descarga *(m)*

porto franco It
De frachtfrei
En carriage free
Am F.O.B. destination
Es franco de porte
Fr franco
Pt porte grátis

porto franco *(m)* It, Pt
De Freihafen *(m)*
En free port
Es puerto libre *(m)*
Fr port franc *(m)*

port of registration En
De Heimathafen *(m)*
Es puerto de matrícula *(m)*
Fr port d'attache *(m)*
It porto d'immatricolazione
    (m)
Pt porto de matrícula *(m)*

portofrei De
En postage paid
Es franco de porte
Fr port payé
It porto pagato
Pt portes pagos

portofreie Lieferung De
En delivery free
Es libre entrega
Fr livré franco
It consegna franco
Pt remessa gratuita

Portonachnahme De
En carriage forward
Am F.O.B. shipping point
Es a porte debido
Fr en port dû
It porto assegnato
Pt transporte a pagar

porto pagato It
De portofrei
En postage paid
Es franco de porte
Fr port payé
Pt portes pagos

port payé Fr
De franko; portofrei
En carriage paid; postage paid
Es a porte pagado; franco de porte
It franco di porto; porto pagato
Pt porte pago

poscritto (PS) *(m)* It
De Nachschrift *(f)*
En postscript (PS)
Es posdata *(f)*
Fr post-scriptum; postface *(m f)*
Pt pós-escrito; post-scriptum (PS) *(m)*

posdata *(f)* n Es
De Nachschrift *(f)*
En postscript (PS)
Fr post-scriptum; postface *(m f)*
It poscritto (PS) *(m)*
Pt pós-escrito; post-scriptum (PS) *(m)*

pós-escrito *(m)* n Pt
De Nachschrift *(f)*
En postscript (PS)
Es posdata *(f)*
Fr post-scriptum; postface *(m f)*
It poscritto (PS) *(m)*

posição em aberto *(f)* Pt
De offene Position *(f)*
En open position
Es posición descubierta *(f)*
Fr position ouverte *(f)*
It posizione aperta *(f)*

posición descubierta *(f)* Es
De offene Position *(f)*
En open position
Fr position ouverte *(f)*
It posizione aperta *(f)*
Pt posição em aberto *(f)*

position ouverte *(f)* Fr
De offene Position *(f)*
En open position
Es posición descubierta *(f)*
It posizione aperta *(f)*
Pt posição em aberto *(f)*

posizione aperta *(f)* It
De offene Position *(f)*
En open position
Es posición descubierta *(f)*
Fr position ouverte *(f)*
Pt posição em aberto *(f)*

Post *(f)* n De
En mail
Es correo *(m)*
Fr poste *(f)*
It posta *(f)*
Pt correio *(m)*

posta *(f)* n It
De Post *(f)*
En mail
Es correo *(m)*
Fr poste *(f)*
Pt correio *(m)*

posta aerea *(f)* It
De Luftpost *(f)*
En airmail
Es correo aéreo *(m)*
Fr poste aérienne *(f)*
Pt correio aéreo *(m)*

postage n En
De Postgebühr *(f)*
Es tarifa postal; franqueo *(f m)*
Fr frais de poste *(m pl)*
It tariffa postale; affrancatura *(f)*
Pt tarifa postal *(f)*

postage paid En
De portofrei
Es franco de porte
Fr port payé
It porto pagato
Pt portes pagos

postage stamp En
De Briefmarke *(f)*
Es sello de correos *(m)*
Fr timbre-poste *(m)*
It francobollo *(m)*
Pt selo postal *(m)*

postal order En
De Postanweisung *(f)*
Es giro postal *(m)*
Fr mandat-poste *(m)*
It vaglia postale *(f)*
Pt vale postal *(m)*

Postamt *(n)* n De
En post office
Es oficina de correos *(f)*
Fr bureau de poste *(m)*
It ufficio postale *(m)*
Pt estação de correios *(f)*

Postanweisung *(f)* n De
En postal order
Es giro postal *(m)*
Fr mandat-poste *(m)*
It vaglia postale *(f)*
Pt vale postal *(m)*

postcode n En
Am zip code
De Postleitzahl *(f)*
Es designación postal *(f)*
Fr indicatif postal *(m)*
It codice postale *(m)*
Pt designação postal *(f)*

postdated cheque En
De nachdatierter Scheck *(m)*
Es cheque a fecha retrasada *(m)*
Fr chèque postdaté *(m)*
It assegno postdatato *(m)*
Pt cheque post-datado *(m)*

poste *(f)* n Fr
De Post *(f)*
En mail
Es correo *(m)*
It posta *(f)*
Pt correio *(m)*

poste aérienne *(f)* Fr
De Luftpost *(f)*
En airmail
Es correo aéreo *(m)*
It posta aerea *(f)*
Pt correio aéreo *(m)*

Posten *(m)* n De
En picket
Es piquete *(m)*
Fr piquet *(m)*
It picchetto *(m)*
Pt piquete *(m)*

postenmäßig dargestellt De
En itemized
Es detallado
Fr détaillé
It dettagliato
Pt pormenorizado

postes de dépense *(m pl)* Fr
De Aufwendungsposten *(f pl)*
En items of expenditure
Es artículos de gasto *(m pl)*
It articoli di spesa *(m pl)*
Pt itens de despesa *(m pl)*

postes rééquilibrants *(m pl)*
Fr
De Ausgleichsposten *(m pl)*
En balancing items
Es asientos saldados *(m pl)*
It voci di pareggio *(f pl)*
Pt valores de equilíbrio *(m pl)*

Postgebühr *(f)* n De
En postage
Es tarifa postal; franqueo *(f m)*
Fr frais de poste *(m pl)*
It tariffa postale; affrancatura *(f)*
Pt tarifa postal *(f)*

postilla *(f)* n It
De Fußnote *(f)*
En footnote
Es apostilla *(f)*
Fr apostille *(f)*
Pt nota de rodapé *(f)*

Postleitzahl *(f)* n De
En postcode
Am zip code
Es designación postal *(f)*
Fr indicatif postal *(m)*
It codice postale *(m)*
Pt designação postal *(f)*

post office En
De Postamt *(n)*
Es oficina de correos *(f)*
Fr bureau de poste *(m)*
It ufficio postale *(m)*
Pt estação de correios *(f)*

Post Office Savings Bank En
De Postsparkasse *(f)*
Es caja postal de ahorros *(f)*
Fr caisse d'épargne postale
(f)
It cassa di risparmio postale
(f)
Pt caixa económica postal *(f)*

postscript (PS) n En
De Nachschrift *(f)*
Es posdata *(f)*
Fr post-scriptum; postface
(m f)

It poscritto (PS) *(m)*
Pt pós-escrito; post-scriptum (PS) *(m)*

post-scriptum *(m)* n Fr
De Nachschrift *(f)*
En postscript (PS)
Es posdata *(f)*
It poscritto (PS) *(m)*
Pt pós-escrito; post-scriptum (PS) *(m)*

Postsparkasse *(f)* n De
En Post Office Savings Bank
Es caja postal de ahorros *(f)*
Fr caisse d'épargne postale
(f)
It cassa di risparmio postale
(f)
Pt caixa económica postal *(f)*

Postüberweisung *(f)* n De
En mail transfer
Es transferencia postal *(f)*
Fr virement postal *(m)*
It trasferimento per posta
(m)
Pt transferência postal *(f)*

Postversandwerbung *(f)* n
De
En direct mail
Es propaganda directa por
correo *(f)*
Fr publicité directe *(f)*
It pubblicità diretta *(f)*
Pt publicidade por correio ao
domicílio *(f)*

pot-de-vin *(m)* n Fr
De Bestechungsgeld *(n)*
En bribe
Es soborno *(m)*
It dono per corrompere *(m)*
Pt suborno *(m)*

potencial *adj* Es, Pt
De möglich; potentiell
En potential
Fr potentiel
It potenziale

potencial não utilizado *(m)* Pt
De ungenutzte Ladefähigkeit
(f)
En idle capacity
Es potencial no utilizado *(m)*
Fr potentiel non utilisé *(m)*
It potenziale non utilizzato
(m)

potencial no utilizado *(m)* Es
De ungenutzte Ladefähigkeit
(f)
En idle capacity
Fr potentiel non utilisé *(m)*
It potenziale non utilizzato
(m)
Pt potencial não utilizado *(m)*

potential *adj* En
De möglich; potentiell
Es potencial
Fr potentiel
It potenziale
Pt potencial

potentiel *adj* Fr
De möglich; potentiell
En potential
Es potencial
It potenziale
Pt potencial

potentiell *adj* De
En potential
Es potencial
Fr potentiel
It potenziale
Pt potencial

potentiel non utilisé *(m)* Fr
De ungenutzte Ladefähigkeit
(f)
En idle capacity
Es potencial no utilizado *(m)*
It potenziale non utilizzato
(m)
Pt potencial não utilizado *(m)*

potenziale *adj* It
De möglich; potentiell
En potential
Es potencial
Fr potentiel
Pt potencial

potenziale non utilizzato *(m)*
It
De ungenutzte Ladefähigkeit
(f)
En idle capacity
Es potencial no utilizado *(m)*
Fr potentiel non utilisé *(m)*
Pt potencial não utilizado *(m)*

potere d'acquisto *(m)* It
De Kaufkraft *(f)*
En purchasing power

Es poder de compra *(m)*
Fr pouvoir d'achat *(m)*
Pt poder de compra *(m)*

potere di contrattare *(m)* It
De Verhandlungsposition *(f)*
En bargaining power
Es poder de negociación *(m)*
Fr pouvoir de négociation *(m)*
Pt poder de regateio *(m)*

pound sterling En
De Pfund Sterling *(n)*
Es libra esterlina *(f)*
Fr livre sterling *(f)*
It lira sterlina *(f)*
Pt libra esterlina *(f)*

poupar *vb* Pt
De aufsparen
En save
Es ahorrar
Fr épargner
It risparmiare

pourboire *(m)* n Fr
De Trinkgeld *(n)*
En tip gratuity
Es propina *(f)*
It mancia *(f)*
Pt gorjeta *(f)*

pour cent Fr
De Prozent
En per cent
Es por ciento
It per cento
Pt por cento

pourcentage *(m)* n Fr
De Prozentsatz *(m)*
En percentage
Es porcentaje *(m)*
It percentuale *(f)*
Pt percentagem *(f)*

poursuivre *vb* Fr
De weiterverfolgen
En follow up
Es perseguir
It seguitare
Pt perseguir

pouvoir d'achat *(m)* Fr
De Kaufkraft *(f)*
En purchasing power
Es poder de compra *(m)*
It potere d'acquisto *(m)*
Pt poder de compra *(m)*

pouvoir de négociation *(m)*
Fr
De Verhandlungsposition *(f)*
En bargaining power
Es poder de negociación *(m)*
It potere di contrattare *(m)*
Pt poder de regateio *(m)*

pouvoirs *(m pl)* Fr
De Vollmacht *(f)*
En power of attorney
Es poder *(m)*
It procura *(f)*
Pt poderes de procuração
    (m pl)

power of attorney En
De Vollmacht *(f)*
Es poder *(m)*
Fr pouvoirs; procuration
    (m pl; f)
It procura *(f)*
Pt poderes de procuração
    (m pl)

practicabilidad *(f)* n Es
De Durchführbarkeit *(f)*
En feasibility
Fr practicabilité *(f)*
It fattibilità *(f)*
Pt viabilidade *(f)*

practicabilité *(f)* n Fr
De Durchführbarkeit *(f)*
En feasibility
Es practicabilidad *(f)*
It fattibilità *(f)*
Pt viabilidade *(f)*

práctica comercial desleal
    (f) Es
De unlautere Handelspraktik
    (f)
En unfair trade practice
Fr pratique de commerce
    déloyale *(f)*
It pratica commerciale sleale
    (f)
Pt prática comercial impró-
    pria *(f)*

Prämie *(f)* n De
En premium; bonus
Es prima; premio *(f m)*
Fr prime *(f)*
It premio *(m)*
Pt prémio *(m)*

prática comercial imprópria
    (f) Pt
De unlautere Handelspraktik
    (f)
En unfair trade practice
Es práctica comercial desleal
    (f)
Fr pratique de commerce
    déloyale *(f)*
It pratica commerciale sleale
    (f)

pratica commerciale sleale
    (f) It
De unlautere Handelspraktik
    (f)
En unfair trade practice
Es práctica comercial desleal
    (f)
Fr pratique de commerce
    déloyale *(f)*
Pt prática comercial impró-
    pria *(f)*

pratique n En
De Gesundheitsbrief *(m)*
Es libre plática *(f)*
Fr libre pratique *(f)*
It libera pratica *(f)*
Pt livre prática *(f)*

prazo de circulação *(m)* n Pt
De Laufzeit *(f)*
En tenor
Es tenor *(m)*
Fr teneur *(f)*
It tenore *(m)*

precinto industrial *(m)* Es
De Industriegebiet *(n)*
En industrial estate
Am industrial park
Fr domaine industriel *(m)*
It centro industriale *(m)*
Pt centro fabril *(m)*

precio *(m)* n Es
De Preis *(m)*
En price
Fr prix *(m)*
It prezzo *(m)*
Pt preço *(m)*

precio al comerciante *(m)* Es
De Handelspreis *(m)*
En trade price
Fr prix marchand *(m)*
It prezzo al commerciante
    (m)
Pt preço para comerciantes
    (m)

precio al por menor *(m)* Es
De Einzelhandelspreis *(m)*
En retail price
Fr prix de détail *(m)*
It prezzo al minuto *(m)*
Pt preço a retalho *(m)*

precio a término *(m)* Es
De Terminnotierung *(f)*
En forward price
Fr cours à terme *(m)*
It prezzo per futura conseg-na *(m)*
Pt preço adiantado *(m)*

precio contractual *(m)* Es
De Vertragspreis *(m)*
En contract price
Fr prix contractuel *(m)*
It prezzo contrattuale *(m)*
Pt preço contratual *(m)*

precio cotizado *(m)* Es
De angegebener Preis *(m)*
En quoted price
Fr prix coté *(m)*
It prezzo quotato *(m)*
Pt preço cotizado *(m)*

precio de catálogo *(m)* Es
De Listenpreis *(m)*
En catalogue price
Fr prix-catalogue *(m)*
It prezzo di catalogo *(m)*
Pt preço de catálogo *(m)*

precio de cierre *(m)* Es
De Schlußnotierung *(f)*
En closing price
Fr cours de clôture *(m)*
It prezzo di chiusura *(m)*
Pt último preço *(m)*

precio de compra *(m)* Es
De Kaufpreis *(m)*
En purchase price
Fr prix d'achat *(m)*
It prezzo d'acquisto *(m)*
Pt preço de compra *(m)*

precio de coste *(m)* Es
De Einstandspreis *(m)*
En cost price
Fr prix de revient *(m)*
It prezzo di costo *(m)*
Pt preço de custo *(m)*

precio de intervención *(m)* Es
De Interventionspreis *(m)*
En intervention price
Fr prix d'intervention *(m)*
It prezzo d'intervento *(m)*
Pt preço de intervenção *(m)*

precio de mercado *(m)* Es
De Marktpreis *(m)*
En market price
Fr cours du marché *(m)*
It prezzo del mercato *(m)*
Pt preço de mercado *(m)*

precio de ocasión *(m)* Es
De Spottpreis *(m)*
En bargain price
Fr prix de solde *(m)*
It prezzo d'occasione *(m)*
Pt preço excepcional *(m)*

precio de reventa *(m)* Es
De Wiederverkaufspreis *(m)*
En resale price
Fr prix de revente *(m)*
It prezzo di rivendita *(m)*
Pt preço de revenda *(m)*

precio detallista recomen-dado *(m)* Es
De empfohlener Ladenpreis *(m)*
En recommended retail sel-ling price
Fr prix de détail racommandé *(m)*
It prezzo al minuto indicativo *(m)*
Pt preço de venda a retalho recomendado *(m)*

precio de tarifa *(m)* Es
De Listenpreis *(m)*
En list price
Fr prix courant *(m)*
It prezzo di listino *(m)*
Pt preço de tabela *(m)*

precio de umbral *(m)* Es
De Schwellenpreis *(m)*
En threshold price
Fr prix de seuil *(m)*
It prezzo soglia *(m)*
Pt preço convencionado *(m)*

precio facturado *(m)* Es
De fakturierter Preis *(m)*
En invoice price
Fr prix facturé *(m)*
It prezzo di fattura *(m)*
Pt preço de factura *(m)*

precio incluida entrega *(m)* Es
De Lieferpreis *(m)*
En delivered price
Fr prix livraison inclus *(m)*
It prezzo incluso consegna *(m)*
Pt preço incluindo portes *(m)*

precio medio *(m)* Es
De Mittelkurs *(m)*
En mean price
Fr prix moyen *(m)*
It prezzo medio *(m)*
Pt preço médio *(m)*

precio mínimo fijado *(m)* Es
De Mindestpreis *(m)*
En reserve price
Fr prix minimal *(m)*
It prezzo minimo *(m)*
Pt preço de reserva *(m)*

precio neto *(m)* Es
De Nettopreis; Nettokurs *(m)*
En net price
Fr prix net *(m)*
It prezzo netto *(m)*
Pt preço líquido *(m)*

precio nominal *(m)* Es
De Nennpreis *(m)*
En nominal price
Fr prix nominal *(m)*
It prezzo nominale *(m)*
Pt preço nominal *(m)*

precio razonable *(m)* Es
De angemessener Preis *(m)*
En fair price
Fr prix raisonnable *(m)*
It prezzo equo *(m)*
Pt preço razoável *(m)*

precio verdadero *(m)* Es
De Gestehungskosten *(pl)*
En actual cost
Fr prix de revient effectif *(m)*
It costo effettivo *(m)*
Pt custo verdadeiro *(m)*

preço *(m) n* Pt
De Preis; Kurs *(m)*
En price
Es precio *(m)*
Fr prix *(m)*
It prezzo *(m)*

preço adiantado *(m)* Pt
De Terminnotierung *(f)*
En forward price
Es precio a término *(m)*
Fr cours à terme *(m)*
It prezzo per futura conseg-
na *(m)*

preço a retalho *(m)* Pt
De Einzelhandelspreis *(m)*
En retail price
Es precio al por menor *(m)*
Fr prix de détail *(m)*
It prezzo al minuto *(m)*

preço contratual *(m)* Pt
De Vertragspreis *(m)*
En contract price
Es precio contractual *(m)*
Fr prix contractuel *(m)*
It prezzo contrattuale *(m)*

preço convencionado *(m)* Pt
De Schwellenpreis *(m)*
En threshold price
Es precio de umbral *(m)*
Fr prix de seuil *(m)*
It prezzo soglia *(m)*

preço cotizado *(m)* Pt
De angegebener Preis *(m)*
En quoted price
Es precio cotizado *(m)*
Fr prix coté *(m)*
It prezzo quotato *(m)*

preço de catálogo *(m)* Pt
De Listenpreis *(m)*
En catalogue price
Es precio de catálogo *(m)*
Fr prix-catalogue *(m)*
It prezzo di catalogo *(m)*

preço de compra *(m)* Pt
De Kaufpreis *(m)*
En purchase price
Es precio de compra *(m)*
Fr prix d'achat *(m)*
It prezzo d'acquisto *(m)*

preço de custo *(m)* Pt
De Einstandspreis *(m)*
En cost price
Es precio de coste *(m)*
Fr prix de revient *(m)*
It prezzo di costo *(m)*

preço de factura *(m)* Pt
De fakturierter Preis *(m)*
En invoice price
Es precio facturado *(m)*
Fr prix facturé *(m)*
It prezzo di fattura *(m)*

preço de intervenção *(m)* Pt
De Interventionspreis *(m)*
En intervention price
Es precio de intervención *(m)*
Fr prix d'intervention *(m)*
It prezzo d'intervento *(m)*

preço de mercado *(m)* Pt
De Marktpreis *(m)*
En market price
Es precio de mercado *(m)*
Fr cours du marché *(m)*
It prezzo del mercato *(m)*

preço de passagem *(m)* Pt
De Fahrgeld *(n)*
En fare
Es pasaje *(m)*
Fr prix du voyage *(m)*
It prezzo di viaggio *(m)*

preço de reserva *(m)* Pt
De Mindestpreis *(m)*
En reserve price
Es precio mínimo fijado *(m)*
Fr prix minimal *(m)*
It prezzo minimo *(m)*

preço de revenda *(m)* Pt
De Wiederverkaufspreis *(m)*
En resale price
Es precio de reventa *(m)*
Fr prix de revente *(m)*
It prezzo di rivendita *(m)*

preço de tabela *(m)* Pt
De Listenpreis *(m)*
En list price
Es precio de tarifa *(m)*
Fr prix courant *(m)*
It prezzo di listino *(m)*

**preço de venda a retalho
recomendado** *(m)* Pt
De empfohlener Ladenpreis
(m)
En recommended retail selling price
Es precio detallista recomendado *(m)*
Fr prix de détail racommandé
(m)
It prezzo al minuto indicativo
(m)

preço excepcional *(m)* Pt
De Spottpreis *(m)*
En bargain price
Es precio de ocasión *(m)*
Fr prix de solde *(m)*
It prezzo d'occasione *(m)*

preço incluindo portes *(m)* Pt
De Lieferpreis *(m)*
En delivered price
Es precio incluida entrega *(m)*
Fr prix livraison inclus *(m)*
It prezzo incluso consegna
(m)

preço líquido *(m)* Pt
De Nettopreis; Nettokurs *(m)*
En net price
Es precio neto *(m)*
Fr prix net *(m)*
It prezzo netto *(m)*

preço médio *(m)* Pt
De Mittelkurs *(m)*
En mean price
Es precio medio *(m)*
Fr prix moyen *(m)*
It prezzo medio *(m)*

preço nominal *(m)* Pt
De Nennpreis *(m)*
En nominal price
Es precio nominal *(m)*
Fr prix nominal *(m)*
It prezzo nominale *(m)*

preço para comerciantes
(m) Pt
De Handelspreis *(m)*
En trade price
Es precio al comerciante *(m)*
Fr prix marchand *(m)*
It prezzo al commerciante
(m)

preço razoável *(m)* Pt
De angemessener Preis *(m)*
En fair price
Es precio razonable *(m)*
Fr prix raisonnable *(m)*
It prezzo equo *(m)*

prefabbricare *vb* It
De vorfabrizieren
En prefabricate
Es prefabricar
Fr préfabriquer
Pt pré-fabricar

prefabricar *vb* Es
De vorfabrizieren
En prefabricate
Fr préfabriquer
It prefabbricare
Pt pré-fabricar

pré-fabricar *vb* Pt
De vorfabrizieren
En prefabricate
Es prefabricar
Fr préfabriquer
It prefabbricare

prefabricate *vb* En
De vorfabrizieren
Es prefabricar
Fr préfabriquer
It prefabbricare
Pt pré-fabricar

préfabriquer *vb* Fr
De vorfabrizieren
En prefabricate
Es prefabricar
It prefabbricare
Pt pré-fabricar

preference share En
De Vorzugsaktie *(f)*
Es acción preferente *(f)*
Fr action privilégiée *(f)*
It azione privilegiata *(f)*
Pt acção preferencial *(f)*

preferential creditor En
De bevorrechtigter Gläubiger *(m)*
Es acreedor privilegiado *(m)*
Fr créancier privilégié *(m)*
It creditore privilegiato *(m)*
Pt credor preferencial *(m)*

preferential duty En
De Vorzugssatz *(m)*
Es derechos preferenciales *(m pl)*
Fr tarif de faveur *(m)*
It tariffa preferenziale *(f)*
Pt direito preferencial *(m)*

pregiudizio *(m)* *n* It
De Nachteil *(m)*
En prejudice
Es prejuicio; perjuicio *(m)*
Fr préjudice *(m)*
Pt prejuízo *(m)*

Preis *(m)* *n* De
En price
Es precio *(m)*
Fr prix *(m)*
It prezzo *(m)*
Pt preço *(m)*

Preisabsprache *(f)* *n* De
En price ring
Es coalición de vendedores *(f)*
Fr coalition de vendeurs *(f)*
It sindacato dei prezzi *(m)*
Pt convénio de preços *(m)*

Preisdehnbarkeit *(f)* *n* De
En price-elasticity
Es elasticidad de precio *(f)*
Fr élasticité-prix *(m)*
It elasticità di prezzo *(f)*
Pt flexibilidade de preços *(f)*

Preisebene *(f)* *n* De
En price level
Es nivel de precios *(m)*
Fr niveau des prix *(m)*
It livello dei prezzi *(m)*
Pt nível de preços *(m)*

Preiserhöhung *(f)* *n* De
En advance in price
Es encarecimiento *(m)*
Fr renchérissement *(m)*
It rialzo
Pt encarecimento *(m)*

Preisherabsetzung *(f)* *n* De
En price-cutting
Es reducción de precios *(f)*
Fr rabais des prix *(m)*
It riduzione dei prezzi *(f)*
Pt redução de preços *(f)*

Preiskatalog *(m)* *n* De
En trade catalogue
Es catálogo comercial *(m)*
Fr tarif-album *(m)*
It catalogo commerciale *(m)*
Pt catálogo comercial *(m)*

Preiskontrolle *(f)* *n* De
En price control
Es control de precios *(m)*
Fr contrôle des prix *(m)*
It controllo sui prezzi *(m)*
Pt controlo de preços *(m)*

Preiskrieg *(m)* *n* De
En price war
Es guerra de precios *(f)*
Fr guerre des prix *(f)*
It guerra dei prezzi *(f)*
Pt guerra de preços *(f)*

Preisunterschied *(m)* *n* De
En difference in price
Es diferencia de precio *(f)*
Fr écart de prix *(m)*
It differenza di prezzo *(f)*
Pt diferença de preço *(f)*

prejudice *n* En
De Nachteil *(m)*
Es prejuicio; perjuicio *(m)*
Fr préjudice *(m)*
It pregiudizio *(m)*
Pt prejuízo *(m)*

préjudice *(m)* *n* Fr
De Nachteil *(m)*
En prejudice
Es prejuicio; perjuicio *(m)*
It pregiudizio *(m)*
Pt prejuízo *(m)*

prejuicio *(m)* *n* Es
De Nachteil *(m)*
En prejudice
Fr préjudice *(m)*
It pregiudizio *(m)*
Pt prejuízo *(m)*

prejuízo *(m)* *n* Pt
De Nachteil *(m)*
En prejudice
Es prejuicio *(m)*
Fr préjudice *(m)*
It pregiudizio *(m)*

prelevare dalle riserve It
De die Reserven angreifen
En draw on reserves
Es sacar reservas
Fr prélever sur les réserves
Pt recorrer a reservas

prélèvement (m) n Fr
De Erhebung (f)
En levy
Es impuesto (m)
It imposta (f)
Pt imposto (m)

prélever sur les réserves Fr
De die Reserven angreifen
En draw on reserves
Es sacar reservas
It prelevare dalle riserve
Pt recorrer a reservas

préliminaire adj Fr
De vorläufig; einleitend
En preliminary
Es preliminar
It preliminare
Pt preliminar

preliminar adj Es, Pt
De vorläufig; einleitend
En preliminary
Fr préliminaire; préalable
It preliminare

preliminare adj It
De vorläufig; einleitend
En preliminary
Es preliminar
Fr préliminaire; préalable
Pt preliminar

preliminary adj En
De vorläufig; einleitend
Es preliminar
Fr préliminaire; préalable
It preliminare
Pt preliminar

première classe (f) Fr
De erste Klasse (f)
En first class
Es primera clase (f)
It prima classe (f)
Pt primeira classe (f)

première de change (f) Fr
De Primawechsel (m)
En first of exchange

Es primera de cambio (f)
It prima di cambio (f)
Pt primeira de câmbio (f)

premio (m) n It, Es
De Prämie (f)
En premium
Fr prime (f)
Pt prémio (m)

prémio (m) n Pt
De Prämie (f)
En premium
Es prima; premio (f m)
Fr prime (f)
It premio (m)

premio a vendere (m) It
De Verkaufsoption (f)
En put option
Es opción de venta (f)
Fr option à vendre (f)
Pt opção de venda (f)

prémio bruto (m) Pt
De Bruttoprämie (f)
En gross premium
Es prima bruta (f)
Fr prime brute (f)
It premio lordo (m)

premio d'acquisto (m) It
De Kaufoption (f)
En call option
Es opción de compras (f)
Fr option d'achat (f)
Pt opção de compra (f)

prémio de risco (m) Pt
De Gefahrenzulage (f)
En danger money
Es suma para riesgos (f)
Fr prime de risque (f)
It compenso per il rischio (m)

prémio de seguro (m) Pt
De Versicherungsprämie (f)
En insurance premium
Es prima de póliza de seguro (f)
Fr prime d'assurance (f)
It premio di assicurazione (m)

premio d'esportazione (m) It
De Ausfuhrprämie (f)
En export bonus

Es subsidio a las exportaciones (m)
Fr prime à l'exportation (f)
Pt subsídio de exportação (m)

premio di assicurazione (m) It
De Versicherungsprämie (f)
En insurance premium
Es prima de póliza de seguro (f)
Fr prime d'assurance (f)
Pt prémio de seguro (m)

premio lordo (m) It
De Bruttoprämie (f)
En gross premium
Es prima bruta (f)
Fr prime brute (f)
Pt prémio bruto (m)

premium n En
De Prämie (f)
Es prima; premio (f m)
Fr prime (f)
It premio (m)
Pt prémio (m)

premium offer En
De Verkauf mit Zugaben (m)
Es oferta a prima (f)
Fr offre à prime (f)
It offerta sopra la pari (f)
Pt oferta-prémio (f)

prenda (f) n Pt
De Geschenk (n)
En gift
Es regalo (m)
Fr don; cadeau (m)
It dono (m)

prendre un rendez-vous Fr
De eine Verabredung treffen
En make an appointment
Es hacer una cita
It fissare un appuntamento
Pt marcar um encontro

prepaid adj En
De vorausbezahlt
Es pagado por adelantado
Fr payé d'avance
It pagato in anticipo
Pt pago adiantadamente

preparação de montras *(f)* Pt
De Schaufensterdekoration *(f)*
En window-dressing
Es preparación de escapara-
tes *(f)*
Fr art de l'étalage *(m)*
It allestimento delle vetrine
(m)

**preparación de
escaparates** *(f)* Es
De Schaufensterdekoration *(f)*
En window-dressing
Fr art de l'étalage *(m)*
It allestimento delle vetrine
(m)
Pt preparação de montras *(f)*

prepayment *n* En
De Vorauszahlung *(f)*
Es pago andelantado *(m)*
Fr paiement anticipé *(m)*
It pagamento anticipato *(m)*
Pt pagamento adiantado *(m)*

**present a bill for
acceptance** En
De einen Wechsel vorlegen
Es presentar una letra para
aceptación
Fr présenter une traite à l'acceptation
It presentare una cambiale
per accettazione
Pt apresentar letra para aceite

**presentare una cambiale
per accettazione** It
De einen Wechsel vorlegen
En present a bill for acceptance
Es presentar una letra para
aceptación
Fr présenter une traite à l'acceptation
Pt apresentar letra para aceite

presentar la dimisión Es
De den Rücktritt einreichen
En hand in one's resignation
Fr remettre sa démission
It rassegnare le dimissioni
Pt apresentar demissão

**presentar una letra para
aceptatión** Es
De einen Wechsel vorlegen
En present a bill for acceptance
Fr présenter une traite à l'acceptation
It presentare una cambiale
per accettazione
Pt apresentar letra para aceite

**présenter une traite à
l'acceptation** Fr
De einen Wechsel vorlegen
En present a bill for acceptance
Es presentar una letra para
aceptación
It presentare una cambiale
per accettazione
Pt apresentar letra para aceite

présentoir *(m)* *n* Fr
De Schaukasten *(m)*
En display unit
Es presentación *(f)*
It mostra *(f)*
Pt montra *(f)*

président *(m)* *n* Fr
De Vorsitzende(r) *(m)*
En chairman
Es presidente *(m)*
It presidente *(m)*
Pt presidente *(m)*

presidente *(m)* *n* Es, It, Pt
De Vorsitzende(r) *(m)*
En chairman
Fr président *(m)*

pressure gauge En
De Druckmesser *(m)*
Es manómetro *(m)*
Fr manomètre; jauge de
pression *(m f)*
It manometro *(m)*
Pt manómetro *(m)*

prestação *(f)* *n* Pt
De Rate *(f)*
En instalment
Es plazo *(m)*
Fr acompte *(m)*
It rata *(f)*

prestação mensal *(f)* Pt
De Monatsrate *(f)*
En monthly instalment
Es mensualidad *(f)*
Fr mensualité *(f)*
It mensilità *(f)*

prestamista *(m)* *n* Es, Pt
De Geldverleiher; Pfandleiher
(m)
En moneylender; pawnbroker
Fr prêteur d'argent; prêteur
sur gage *(m)*
It usuraio; prestatore su
pegno *(m)*

préstamo bancario *(m)* Es
De Bankdarlehen *(n)*
En bank loan
Fr prêt bancaire *(m)*
It prestito bancario *(m)*
Pt empréstimo bancário *(m)*

préstamo exterior *(m)* Es
De Auslandsanleihe *(f)*
En external loan
Fr emprunt extérieur *(m)*
It prestito esterno *(m)*
Pt empréstimo externo *(m)*

prestar *vb* Es
De leihen
En lend
Fr prêter
It prestare
Pt emprestar

prestar caução a favor de Pt
De Haftkaution geben
En go bail for
Es salir fiados por
Fr se porter garant de
It rendersi garante di

prestare *vb* It
De leihen
En lend
Es prestar
Fr prêter
Pt emprestar

prestatario *(m)* *n* Es
De Kreditnehmer *(m)*
En borrower
Fr emprunteur *(m)*
It accattatore *(m)*
Pt beneficiário de emprésti-
mo *(m)*

prestatore su pegno *(m)* It
De Pfandleiher *(m)*
En pawnbroker
Es prestamista *(m)*
Fr prêteur sur gage *(m)*
Pt prestamista *(m)*

prestare *vb* It
De entleihen
En borrow
Es pedir un préstamo
Fr emprunter
Pt contrair empréstimo

prestito *(m) n* It
De Anleihe *(f)*
En loan
Es empréstito *(m)*
Fr emprunt *(m)*
Pt empréstimo *(m)*

prestito bancario *(m)* It
De Bankdarlehen *(n)*
En bank loan
Es préstamo bancario *(m)*
Fr prêt bancaire *(m)*
Pt empréstimo bancário *(m)*

prestito esterno *(m)* It
De Auslandsanleihe *(f)*
En external loan
Es préstamo exterior *(m)*
Fr emprunt extérieur *(m)*
Pt empréstimo externo *(m)*

prestito immobiliare *(m)* It
De Baukredit *(m)*
En building loan
Es crédito de construcción *(m)*
Fr crédit de construction *(m)*
Pt empréstimo para construção *(m)*

prestito pubblico *(m)* It
De Staatsanleihe *(f)*
En government loan
Es empréstito público *(m)*
Fr emprunt public *(m)*
Pt empréstimo do governo *(m)*

presupuesto *(m) n* Es
De Haushaltsplan; Voranschlag *(m)*
En budget; estimate
Fr budget; devis *(m)*

presupuesto aproximado *(m)* Es
De rohe Schätzung *(f)*
En rough estimate
Fr estimation approximative *(f)*
It valutazione approssimativa *(f)*
Pt avaliação aproximada *(f)*

presupuesto por defecto *(m)* Es
De Unterschätzung *(f)*
En under-estimate
Fr sous-estimation *(f)*
It sottovalutazione *(f)*
Pt avaliação insuficiente *(f)*

presupuesto por exceso *(m)* Es
De Überschätzung *(f)*
En over-estimate
Fr surestimation *(f)*
It valutazione eccessiva *(f)*
Pt avaliação excessiva *(f)*

presupuesto prudente *(m)* Es
De vorsichtige Schätzung *(f)*
En conservative estimate
Fr évaluation prudente *(f)*
It valutazione prudente *(f)*
Pt avaliação cautelosa *(f)*

prêt bancaire *(m)* Fr
De Bankdarlehen *(n)*
En bank loan
Es préstamo bancario *(m)*
It prestito bancario *(m)*
Pt empréstimo bancário *(m)*

prêter *vb* Fr
De leihen
En lend
Es prestar
It prestare
Pt emprestar

prêteur d'argent *(m)* Fr
De Geldverleiher *(m)*
En moneylender
Es prestamista *(m)*
It usuraio *(m)*
Pt prestamista *(m)*

prêteur sur gage *(m)* Fr
De Pfandleiher *(m)*
En pawnbroker
Es prestamista *(m)*
It prestatore su pegno *(m)*
Pt prestamista *(m)*

preuve *(f) n* Fr
De Beweis *(m)*
En evidence
Es evidencia *(f)*
It prova *(f)*
Pt prova *(f)*

preuve écrite *(f)* Fr
De Urkundenbeweis *(m)*
En documentary evidence
Es prueba documental *(f)*
It prova scritta *(f)*
Pt prova documental *(f)*

preventivo *(m) n* It
De Kostenvoranschlag *(m)*
En estimate
Es presupuesto *(m)*
Fr devis *(m)*
Pt previsão *(f)*

preventivo riveduto *(m)* It
De überarbeitete Schätzung *(f)*
En revised estimate
Es cálculo revisado *(m)*
Fr devis rectifié *(m)*
Pt estimativa revista *(f)*

preventivo supplementare *(m)* It
De Nachschätzung *(f)*
En supplementary estimate
Es cálculo suplementario *(m)*
Fr devis supplémentaire *(f)*
Pt estimativa suplementar *(f)*

previa condición *(f)* Es
De aufschiebende Bedingung *(f)*
En condition precedent
Fr condition suspensive *(f)*
It condizione sospensiva *(f)*
Pt condição prévia *(f)*

previsão *(f) n* Pt
De Voranschlag; Voraussage *(m f)*
En estimate; forecast
Es presupuesto; pronóstico *(m)*
Fr devis; prévision *(m f)*
It preventivo; previsione *(m f)*

It bilancio preventivo; preventivo *(m)*
Pt orçamento; previsão *(m f)*

previsão de fundos *(f)* Pt
De Bargeldvoraussage *(f)*
En cash forecast
Es previsión de fondos *(f)*
Fr prévision comptant *(f)*
It previsione contanti *(f)*

previsão de vendas *(f)* Pt
De Verkaufsvoraussage *(f)*
En sales forecast
Es pronóstico de ventas *(m)*
Fr prévision de ventes *(f)*
It previsione delle vendite *(f)*

prévision *(f)* n Fr
De Voraussage *(f)*
En forecasting
Es pronóstico *(m)*
It previsione *(f)*
Pt previsão *(f)*

prévision comptant *(f)* Fr
De Bargeldvoraussage *(f)*
En cash forecast
Es previsión de fondos *(f)*
It previsione contanti *(f)*
Pt previsão de fundos (em dinheiro) *(f)*

previsión de fondos *(f)* Es
De Bargeldvoraussage *(f)*
En cash forecast
Fr prévision comptant *(f)*
It previsione contanti *(f)*
Pt previsão de fundos *(f)*

prévision de ventes *(f)* Fr
De Verkaufsvoraussage *(f)*
En sales forecast
Es pronóstico de ventas *(m)*
It previsione delle vendite *(f)*
Pt previsão de vendas *(f)*

previsione *(f)* n It
De Voraussage *(f)*
En forecasting
Es pronóstico *(m)*
Fr prévision *(f)*
Pt previsão *(f)*

previsione contanti *(f)* It
De Bargeldvoraussage *(f)*
En cash forecast
Es previsión de fondos *(f)*
Fr prévision comptant *(f)*
Pt previsão de fundos *(f)*

previsione delle vendite *(f)* It
De Verkaufsvoraussage *(f)*
En sales forecast
Es pronóstico de ventas *(m)*
Fr prévision de ventes *(f)*
Pt previsão de vendas *(f)*

prévoir vb Fr
De vorhersehen
En forecast
Es pronosticar
It pronosticare
Pt prognosticar

prezzo *(m)* n It
De Preis; Kurs *(m)*
En price
Es precio *(m)*
Fr prix *(m)*
Pt preço *(m)*

prezzo al commerciante *(m)* It
De Handelspreis *(m)*
En trade price
Es precio al comerciante *(m)*
Fr prix marchand *(m)*
Pt preço para comerciantes *(m)*

prezzo al minuto *(m)* It
De Einzelhandelspreis *(m)*
En retail price
Es precio al por menor *(m)*
Fr prix de détail *(m)*
Pt preço a retalho *(m)*

prezzo al minuto indicativo *(m)* It
De empfohlener Ladenpreis *(m)*
En recommended retail selling price
Es precio detallista recomendado *(m)*
Fr prix de détail racommandé *(m)*
Pt preço de venda a retalho recomendado *(m)*

prezzo contrattuale *(m)* It
De Vertragspreis *(m)*
En contract price
Es precio contractual *(m)*
Fr prix contractuel *(m)*
Pt preço contratual *(m)*

prezzo d'acquisto *(m)* It
De Kaufpreis *(m)*
En purchase price
Es precio de compra *(m)*
Fr prix d'achat *(m)*
Pt preço de compra *(m)*

prezzo del mercato *(m)* It
De Marktpreis *(m)*
En market price
Es precio de mercado *(m)*
Fr cours du marché *(m)*
Pt preço de mercado *(m)*

prezzo di catalogo *(m)* It
De Listenpreis *(m)*
En catalogue price
Es precio de catálogo *(m)*
Fr prix-catalogue *(m)*
Pt preço de catálogo *(m)*

prezzo di chiusura *(m)* It
De Schlußnotierung *(f)*
En closing price
Es precio de cierre *(m)*
Fr cours de clôture *(m)*
Pt últímo preço *(m)*

prezzo di costo *(m)* It
De Einstandspreis *(m)*
En cost price
Es precio de coste *(m)*
Fr prix de revient *(m)*
Pt preço de custo *(m)*

prezzo di fattura *(m)* It
De fakturierter Preis *(m)*
En invoice price
Es precio facturado *(m)*
Fr prix facturé *(m)*
Pt preço de factura *(m)*

prezzo di listino *(m)* It
De Listenpreis *(m)*
En list price
Es precio de tarifa *(m)*
Fr prix courant *(m)*
Pt preço de tabela *(m)*

prezzo d'intervento *(m)* It
De Interventionspreis *(m)*
En intervention price
Es precio de intervención *(m)*
Fr prix d'intervention *(m)*
Pt preço de intervenção *(m)*

prezzo di rivendita *(m)* It
De Wiederverkaufspreis *(m)*
En resale price
Es precio de reventa *(m)*
Fr prix de revente *(m)*
Pt preço de revenda *(m)*

prezzo di viaggio *(m)* It
De Fahrgeld *(n)*
En fare
Es pasaje *(m)*
Fr prix du voyage *(m)*
Pt preço de passagem *(m)*

prezzo d'occasione *(m)* It
De Spottpreis *(m)*
En bargain price
Es precio de ocasión *(m)*
Fr prix de solde *(m)*
Pt preço excepcional *(m)*

prezzo equo *(m)* It
De angemessener Preis *(m)*
En fair price
Es precio razonable *(m)*
Fr prix raisonnable *(m)*
Pt preço razoável *(m)*

prezzo incluso consegna *(m)* It
De Lieferpreis *(m)*
En delivered price
Es precio incluida entrega *(m)*
Fr prix livraison inclus *(m)*
Pt preço incluindo portes *(m)*

prezzo medio *(m)* It
De Mittelkurs *(m)*
En mean price
Es precio medio *(m)*
Fr prix moyen *(m)*
Pt preço médio *(m)*

prezzo minimo *(m)* It
De Mindestpreis *(m)*
En reserve price
Es precio mínimo fijado *(m)*
Fr prix minimal *(m)*
Pt preço de reserva *(m)*

prezzo netto *(m)* It
De Nettopreis; Nettokurs *(m)*
En net price
Es precio neto *(m)*
Fr prix net *(m)*
Pt preço líquido *(m)*

prezzo nominale *(m)* It
De Nennpreis *(m)*
En nominal price
Es precio nominal *(m)*
Fr prix nominal *(m)*
Pt preço nominal *(m)*

prezzo per futura consegna *(m)* It
De Terminnotierung *(f)*
En forward price
Es precio a término *(m)*
Fr cours à terme *(m)*
Pt preço adiantado *(m)*

prezzo quotato *(m)* It
De angegebener Preis *(m)*
En quoted price
Es precio cotizado *(m)*
Fr prix coté *(m)*
Pt preço cotizado *(m)*

prezzo soglia *(m)* It
De Schwellenpreis *(m)*
En threshold price
Es precio de umbral *(m)*
Fr prix de seuil *(m)*
Pt preço convencionado *(m)*

price *n* En
De Preis; Kurs *(m)*
Es precio *(m)*
Fr prix *(m)*
It prezzo *(m)*
Pt preço *(m)*

price control En
De Preiskontrolle *(f)*
Es control de precios *(m)*
Fr contrôle des prix *(m)*
It controllo sui prezzi *(m)*
Pt controlo de preços *(m)*

price-cutting *n* En
De Preisherabsetzung *(f)*
Es reducción de precios *(f)*
Fr rabais des prix *(m)*
It riduzione dei prezzi *(f)*
Pt redução de preços *(f)*

price-earnings ratio (P/E) En
De Verhältnis des Aktienkurses zum Reingewinn *(n)*
Es proporción precio-ingresos *(f)*
Fr quotient cours-bénéfice *(m)*
It rapporto prezzo-utile *(m)*
Pt taxa custo-ganhos *(f)*

price-elasticity *n* En
De Preisdehnbarkeit *(f)*
Es elasticidad de precio *(f)*
Fr élasticité-prix *(m)*
It elasticità di prezzo *(f)*
Pt flexibilidade de preços *(f)*

price level En
De Preisebene *(f)*
Es nivel de precios *(m)*
Fr niveau des prix *(m)*
It livello dei prezzi *(m)*
Pt nível de preços *(m)*

price ring En
De Preisabsprache *(f)*
Es coalición de vendedores *(f)*
Fr coalition de vendeurs *(f)*
It sindacato dei prezzi *(m)*
Pt convénio de preços *(m)*

price war En
De Preiskrieg *(m)*
Es guerra de precios *(f)*
Fr guerre des prix *(f)*
It guerra dei prezzi *(f)*
Pt guerra de preços *(f)*

prière de faire suivre Fr
De bitte nachsenden
En please forward
Es se ruega hacer seguir
It far proseguire
Pt é favor enviar

prima *(f)* *n* Es
De Prämie *(f)*
En premium; bonus
Fr prime *(f)*
It premio *(m)*
Pt prémio *(m)*

prima bruta *(f)* Es
De Bruttoprämie *(f)*
En gross premium
Fr prime brute *(f)*
It premio lordo *(m)*
Pt prémio bruto *(m)*

prima classe *(f)* It
De erste Klasse *(f)*
En first class
Es primera clase *(f)*
Fr première classe *(f)*
Pt primeira classe *(f)*

prima de aplazamiento *(f)* Es
De Kursabschlag *(m)*
En backwardation
Fr déport *(m)*
It deporto *(m)*
Pt juro de mora *(m)*

prima de póliza de seguro *(f)*
Es
De Versicherungsprämie *(f)*
En insurance premium
Fr prime d'assurance *(f)*
It premio di assicurazione
(m)
Pt prémio de seguro *(m)*

prima di cambio *(f)* It
De Primawechsel *(m)*
En first of exchange
Es primera de cambio *(f)*
Fr première de change *(f)*
Pt primeira de câmbio *(f)*

Primawechsel *(m) n* De
En first of exchange
Es primera de cambio *(f)*
Fr première de change *(f)*
It prima di cambio *(f)*
Pt primeira de câmbio *(f)*

prime *(f) n* Fr
De Prämie *(f)*
En premium; bonus
Es prima; premio *(f m)*
It premio *(m)*
Pt prémio *(m)*

prime à l'exportation *(f)* Fr
De Ausfuhrprämie *(f)*
En export bonus
Es subsidio a las exportacio-
nes *(m)*
It premio d'esportazione *(m)*
Pt subsídio de exportação *(m)*

prime brute *(f)* Fr
De Bruttoprämie *(f)*
En gross premium
Es prima bruta *(f)*
It premio lordo *(m)*
Pt prémio bruto *(m)*

prime cost En
De Selbstkosten *(pl)*
Es precio de coste *(m)*
Fr prix de revient *(m)*
It prezzo di costo *(m)*
Pt preço de custo *(m)*

prime d'assurance *(f)* Fr
De Versicherungsprämie *(f)*
En insurance premium
Es prima de póliza de seguro
(f)
It premio di assicurazione
(m)
Pt prémio de seguro *(m)*

prime de risque *(f)* Fr
De Gefahrenzulage *(f)*
En danger money
Es suma para riesgos *(f)*
It compenso per il rischio *(m)*
Pt prémio de risco *(m)*

primeira classe *(f)* Pt
De erste Klasse *(f)*
En first class
Es primera clase *(f)*
Fr première classe *(f)*
It prima classe *(f)*

primeira de câmbio *(f)* Pt
De Primawechsel *(m)*
En first of exchange
Es primera de cambio *(f)*
Fr première de change *(f)*
It prima di cambio *(f)*

primera clase *(f)* Es
De erste Klasse *(f)*
En first class
Fr première classe *(f)*
It prima classe *(f)*
Pt primeira classe *(f)*

primera de cambio *(f)* Es
De Primawechsel *(m)*
En first of exchange
Fr première de change *(f)*
It prima di cambio *(f)*
Pt primeira de câmbio *(f)*

primer día del trimestre *(m)*
Es
De Quartalstag *(m)*
En quarter day
Fr jour du terme *(m)*
It giorno della pigione *(m)*
Pt dia de vencimento trime-
stral *(m)*

primer oficial *(m)* Es
De Maat *(m)*
En (ship's) mate
Fr second *(m)*
It primo ufficiale *(m)*
Pt imediato *(m)*

prime trade bill En
De erstklassiger Handels-
wechsel *(m)*
Es carta comercial de primera
orden *(f)*
Fr papier de haut commerce
(m)
It carta commerciale di primo ordine *(f)*
Pt estatuto de comercialização de primeira ordem
(m)

primo ufficiale *(m)* It
De Maat *(m)*
En (ship's) mate
Es primer oficial *(m)*
Fr second *(m)*
Pt imediato *(m)*

principal (head) *n* En
De Prinzipal; Direktor *(m)*
Es principal; jefe *(m)*
Fr patron; directeur *(m)*
It principale; direttore *(m)*
Pt director; reitor *(m)*

principal (capital) *n* En; Es, Fr
(m)
Am capital
De Kapital *(n)*
It capitale *(m)*
Pt capital *(m)*

principal (to a contract) *n* En
De Vollmachtgeber *(m)*
Es mandante *(m)*
Fr mandant *(m)*
It mandante *(m)*
Pt mandante *(m)*

principal (jefe) *(m) n* Es
De Prinzipal; Direktor *(m)*
En principal; head
Fr patron; directeur *(m)*
It principale; direttore *(m)*
Pt director; reitor *(m)*

principale *(m) n* It
De Prinzipal; Direktor *(m)*
En principal; head
Es principal; jefe *(m)*
Fr patron; directeur *(m)*
Pt director; reitor *(m)*

printed form En
De Vordruck *(m)*
Es formulario; impreso *(m)*
Fr formulaire *(m)*
It modulo stampato *(m)*
Pt impresso *(m)*

Prinzipal *(m) n* De
En principal; head
Es principal; jefe *(m)*
Fr patron; directeur *(m)*
It principale; direttore *(m)*
Pt director; reitor *(m)*

prioridad *(f) n* Es
De Vorrecht *(n)*
En priority
Fr priorité *(f)*
It priorità *(f)*
Pt prioridade *(f)*

prioridade *(f) n* Pt
De Vorrecht *(n)*
En priority
Es prioridad *(f)*
Fr priorité *(f)*
It priorità *(f)*

priorità *(f) n* It
De Vorrecht *(n)*
En priority
Es prioridad *(f)*
Fr priorité *(f)*
Pt prioridade *(f)*

priorité *(f) n* Fr
De Vorrecht *(n)*
En priority
Es prioridad *(f)*
It priorità *(f)*
Pt prioridade *(f)*

priority *n* En
De Vorrecht *(n)*
Es prioridad *(f)*
Fr priorité *(f)*
It priorità *(f)*
Pt prioridade *(f)*

prise de bénéfices *(f)* Fr
De Gewinnrealisation *(f)*
En profit-taking
Es realización de utilidades *(f)*
It realizzazione dell'utile *(f)*
Pt realização dos lucros *(f)*

prise usine Fr
De ab Werk
En ex works
Es de fábrica
It franco fabbrica
Pt na fábrica

Privatbank *(f) n* De
En private bank
Es banco privado *(m)*
Fr banque privée *(f)*
It banca privata *(f)*
Pt banco privado *(m)*

private bank En
De Privatbank *(f)*
Es banco privado *(m)*
Fr banque privée *(f)*
It banca privata *(f)*
Pt banco privado *(m)*

private enterprise En
De Privatunternehmen *(n)*
Es empresa privada *(f)*
Fr entreprise privée *(f)*
It impresa privata *(f)*
Pt empresa privada *(f)*

private limited company En
De Gesellschaft mit beschränkter Haftung (GmbH) *(f)*
Es Companía privada de responsabilidad limitada *(f)*
Fr Société à responsabilité limitée (SARL) *(f)*
It Società a responsabilità limitata (Srl) *(f)*
Pt Sociedade por quotas de responsabilidade limitada *(f)*

private sector En
De Privatwirtschaft *(f)*
Es sector privado *(m)*
Fr secteur privée *(m)*
It settore privato *(m)*
Pt sector privado *(m)*

Privatunternehmen *(n) n* De
En private enterprise
Es empresa privada *(f)*
Fr entreprise privée *(f)*
It impresa privata *(f)*
Pt empresa privada *(f)*

Privatwirtschaft *(f) n* De
En private sector
Es sector privado *(m)*

Fr secteur privée *(m)*
It settore privato *(m)*
Pt sector privado *(m)*

privilège général *(m)* Fr
De allgemeines Pfandrecht *(n)*
En general lien
Es privilegio general *(m)*
It privilegio generale *(m)*
Pt privilégio geral *(m)*

privilegio general *(m)* Es
De allgemeines Pfandrecht *(n)*
En general lien
Fr privilège général *(m)*
It privilegio generale *(m)*
Pt privilégio geral *(m)*

privilegio generale *(m)* It
De allgemeines Pfandrecht *(n)*
En general lien
Es privilegio general *(m)*
Fr privilège général *(m)*
Pt privilégio geral *(m)*

privilégio geral *(m)* Pt
De allgemeines Pfandrecht *(n)*
En general lien
Es privilegio general *(m)*
Fr privilège général *(m)*
It privilegio generale *(m)*

privilégios excluídos Pt
De ohne Bezugsrechte
En ex rights
Es sin privilegio
Fr ex-droits
It senza diritti

prix *(m) n* Fr
De Preis; Kurs *(m)*
En price
Es precio *(m)*
It prezzo *(m)*
Pt preço *(m)*

prix-catalogue *(m)* Fr
De Listenpreis *(m)*
En catalogue price
Es precio de catálogo *(m)*
It prezzo di catalogo *(m)*
Pt preço de catálogo *(m)*

prix contractuel *(m)* Fr
De Vertragspreis *(m)*
En contract price
Es precio contractual *(m)*
It prezzo contrattuale *(m)*
Pt preço contratual *(m)*

prix coté *(m)* Fr
De angegebener Preis *(m)*
En quoted price
Es precio cotizado *(m)*
It prezzo quotato *(m)*
Pt preço cotizado *(m)*

prix courant *(m)* Fr
De Listenpreis *(m)*
En list price
Es precio de tarifa *(m)*
It prezzo di listino *(m)*
Pt preço de tabela *(m)*

prix coûtant unitaire *(m)* Fr
De Einheitskosten *(f pl)*
En unit cost
Es coste unitario *(m)*
It costo unitario *(m)*
Pt custo por unidade *(m)*

prix d'achat *(m)* Fr
De Kaufpreis *(m)*
En purchase price
Es precio de compra *(m)*
It prezzo d'acquisto *(m)*
Pt preço de compra *(m)*

prix de détail *(m)* Fr
De Einzelhandelspreis *(m)*
En retail price
Es precio al por menor *(m)*
It prezzo al minuto *(m)*
Pt preço a retalho *(m)*

prix de détail racommandé
(m) Fr
De empfohlener Ladenpreis
(m)
En recommended retail selling price
Es precio detallista recomendado *(m)*
It prezzo al minuto indicativo
(m)
Pt preço de venda a retalho
recomendado *(m)*

prix de revente *(m)* Fr
De Wiederverkaufspreis *(m)*
En resale price
Es precio de reventa *(m)*
It prezzo di rivendita *(m)*
Pt preço de revenda *(m)*

prix de revient *(m)* Fr
De Einstandspreis *(m)*
En cost price
Es precio de coste *(m)*

It prezzo di costo *(m)*
Pt preço de custo *(m)*

prix de revient comptable
(m) Fr
De Buchwert der Einkäufe *(m)*
En book cost
Es coste contable *(m)*
It costo contabile *(m)*
Pt custo contabilizado *(m)*

prix de revient effectif *(m)* Fr
De Gestehungskosten *(pl)*
En actual cost
Es precio verdadero *(m)*
It costo effettivo *(m)*
Pt custo verdadeiro *(m)*

prix de seuil *(m)* Fr
De Schwellenpreis *(m)*
En threshold price
Es precio de umbral *(m)*
It prezzo soglia *(m)*
Pt preço convencionado *(m)*

prix de solde *(m)* Fr
De Spottpreis *(m)*
En bargain price
Es precio de ocasión *(m)*
It prezzo d'occasione *(m)*
Pt preço excepcional *(m)*

prix d'intervention *(m)* Fr
De Interventionspreis *(m)*
En intervention price
Es precio de intervención *(m)*
It prezzo d'intervento *(m)*
Pt preço de intervenção *(m)*

prix direct de revient *(m)* Fr
De direkte Kosten *(pl)*
En direct cost
Es coste directo *(m)*
It costo diretto *(m)*
Pt custo directo *(m)*

prix du voyage *(m)* Fr
De Fahrgeld *(n)*
En fare
Es pasaje *(m)*
It prezzo di viaggio *(m)*
Pt preço de passagem *(m)*

prix facturé *(m)* Fr
De fakturierter Preis *(m)*
En invoice price
Es precio facturado *(m)*
It prezzo di fattura *(m)*
Pt preço de factura *(m)*

prix livraison inclus *(m)* Fr
De Lieferpreis *(m)*
En delivered price
Es precio incluida entrega *(m)*
It prezzo incluso consegna
(m)
Pt preço incluindo portes *(m)*

prix marchand *(m)* Fr
De Handelspreis *(m)*
En trade price
Es precio al comerciante *(m)*
It prezzo al commerciante
(m)
Pt preço para comerciantes
(m)

prix minimal *(m)* Fr
De Mindestpreis *(m)*
En reserve price
Es precio mínimo fijado *(m)*
It prezzo minimo *(m)*
Pt preço de reserva *(m)*

prix moyen *(m)* Fr
De Mittelkurs *(m)*
En mean price
Es precio medio *(m)*
It prezzo medio *(m)*
Pt preço médio *(m)*

prix net *(m)* Fr
De Nettopreis; Nettokurs *(m)*
En net price
Es precio neto *(m)*
It prezzo netto *(m)*
Pt preço líquido *(m)*

prix nominal *(m)* Fr
De Nennpreis *(m)*
En nominal price
Es precio nominal *(m)*
It prezzo nominale *(m)*
Pt preço nominal *(m)*

prix raisonnable *(m)* Fr
De angemessener Preis *(m)*
En fair price
Es precio razonable *(m)*
It prezzo equo *(m)*
Pt preço razoável *(m)*

probabilidad *(f)* n Es
De Wahrscheinlichkeit *(f)*
En probability
Fr probabilité *(f)*
It probabilità *(f)*
Pt probabilidade *(f)*

probabilidade *(f)* n Pt
De Wahrscheinlichkeit *(f)*
En probability
Es probabilidad *(f)*
Fr probabilité *(f)*
It probabilità *(f)*

probabilità *(f)* n It
De Wahrscheinlichkeit *(f)*
En probability
Es probabilidad *(f)*
Fr probabilité *(f)*
Pt probabilidade *(f)*

probabilité *(f)* n Fr
De Wahrscheinlichkeit *(f)*
En probability
Es probabilidad *(f)*
It probabilità *(f)*
Pt probabilidade *(f)*

probability n En
De Wahrscheinlichkeit *(f)*
Es probabilidad *(f)*
Fr probabilité *(f)*
It probabilità *(f)*
Pt probabilidade *(f)*

probate n En
De Testamentseröffnung; Be-
stätigung *(f)*
Es validación de los testa-
mentos *(f)*
Fr homologation d'un testa-
ment *(f)*
It omologazione di testa-
mento *(f)*
Pt validação testamentária *(f)*

Probe *(f)* n De
En test; sample
Es ensayo; muestra *(m f)*
Fr épreuve; échantillon *(f m)*
It prova; campione *(f m)*
Pt prova; amostra *(f)*

Probebilanz *(f)* n De
En trial balance
Es balance de comprobación
de saldos *(m)*
Fr bilan de vérification *(m)*
It bilancio di verifica *(m)*
Pt balancete de verificação *(m)*

Probegüter *(n pl)* n De
En goods on approval
Es mercancías sujetas a
aprobación *(f pl)*

Fr marchandises à condition
(f pl)
It merce soggetta ad approvazione *(f)*
Pt artigos sujeitos a aprovação *(m pl)*

pro capite It
De pro Kopf
En per capita
Es por cabeza
Fr par tête
Pt per capita; por unidade

procedimento *(m)* n Pt
De Verfahren *(n)*
En procedure
Es procedimiento *(m)*
Fr procédure *(f)*
It procedura *(f)*

procedimiento *(m)* n Es
De Verfahren *(n)*
En procedure
Fr procédure *(f)*
It procedura *(f)*
Pt procedimento *(m)*

procedura *(f)* n It
De Verfahren *(n)*
En procedure
Es procedimiento *(m)*
Fr procédure *(f)*
Pt procedimento *(m)*

procedure n En
De Verfahren *(n)*
Es procedimiento *(m)*
Fr procédure *(f)*
It procedura *(f)*
Pt procedimento *(m)*

procédure *(f)* n Fr
De Verfahren *(n)*
En procedure
Es procedimiento *(m)*
It procedura *(f)*
Pt procedimento *(m)*

procès *(m)* n Fr
De Rechtsfall; Prozeß *(m)*
En lawsuit; trial
Es proceso; causa *(m f)*
It processo; causa *(m f)*
Pt processo; causa *(m f)*

proceso *(m)* n Es
De Rechtsfall; Prozeß *(m)*
En lawsuit; trial
Fr procès *(m)*
It processo; causa *(m f)*
Pt processo; causa *(m f)*

processamento de dados
(m) Pt
De Datenverarbeitung *(f)*
En data processing
Es tratamiento de datos *(m)*
Fr traitement d'informatique
(m)
It elaborazione dei dati *(f)*

processamento por danos
(m) Pt
De Schadenersatzklage *(f)*
En action for damages
Es acción por daños *(f)*
Fr action en dommages et
intérêts *(f)*
It processo per risarcimento
(m)

processo *(m)* It, Pt
De Rechtsfall; Prozeß *(m)*
En lawsuit; trial
Es proceso; causa *(m f)*
Fr procès *(m)*

processo per risarcimento
(m) It
De Schadenersatzklage *(f)*
En action for damages
Es acción por daños *(f)*
Fr action en dommages et
intérêts *(f)*
Pt processamento por danos
(m)

procès-verbal *(m)* n Fr
De Protokoll *(n)*
En minutes
Es actas *(f pl)*
It verbale *(m)*
Pt minutas de acta *(f pl)*

proclamare uno sciopero It
De zum Streik auffordern
En call a strike
Es declararse en huelga
Fr ordonner une grève
Pt declarar greve

procura *(f)* n It
De Vollmacht; Stellvertretung
(f)
En power of attorney; proxy
Es poder; procuración *(m f)*
Fr pouvoirs; procuration
(m pl; f)
Pt procuração *(f)*

procuração *(f)* n Pt
De Vollmacht; Stellvertretung
(f)
En power of attorney; proxy
Es poder; procuración *(m f)*
Fr pouvoirs; procuration
(m pl; f)
It procura *(f)*

procuración *(f)* n Es
De Vollmacht; Stellvertretung
(f)
En power of attorney; proxy
Fr pouvoirs; procuration
(m pl; f)
It procura *(f)*
Pt procuração *(f)*

procurado Pt
De gefragt
En in demand
Es solicitado
Fr demandé
It ricercato

procurador *(m)* n Es, Pt
De Bevollmächtigte(r); Stell-
vertreter *(m)*
En attorney; proxy
Fr mandataire *(m)*
It procuratore; mandatario
(m)

procuration *(f)* n Fr
De Vollmacht; Stellvertretung
(f)
En power of attorney; proxy
Es poder; procuración *(m f)*
It procura *(f)*
Pt procuração *(f)*

procuratore *(m)* n It
De Bevollmächtigte(r); Stell-
vertreter *(m)*
En attorney; proxy
Es procurador; apoderado
(m)
Fr mandataire *(m)*
Pt procurador *(m)*

prodotti di rifiuto *(m)* It
De Abfallprodukt *(n)*
En waste products
Es desperdicios *(m pl)*
Fr déchets *(m pl)*
Pt desperdícios *(m pl)*

prodotto *(m)* n It
De Produkt *(n)*
En product
Es producto *(m)*
Fr produit *(m)*
Pt produto *(m)*

prodotto finale *(m)* It
De Endprodukt *(n)*
En end-product
Es producto final *(m)*
Fr produit final *(m)*
Pt produto final *(m)*

prodotto interno lordo *(m)* It
De Bruttoinlandsprodukt *(n)*
En gross domestic product
(GDP)
Es producto interior bruto *(m)*
Fr produit intérieur brut *(m)*
Pt produto interno bruto *(m)*

prodotto nazionale lordo *(m)*
It
De Bruttosozialprodukt *(n)*
En gross national product
(GNP)
Es producto nacional bruto
(m)
Fr produit national brut *(m)*
Pt produto nacional bruto *(m)*

produção *(f)* n Pt
De Erzeugung *(f)*
En production
Es producción *(f)*
Fr production *(f)*
It produzione *(f)*

produção em massa *(f)* Pt
De Massenherstellung *(f)*
En mass production
Es producción en masa *(f)*
Fr production en masse *(f)*
It fabbricazione in massa *(f)*

produção excessiva *(f)* Pt
De Überproduktion *(f)*
En overproduction
Es exceso de producción *(m)*
Fr surproduction *(f)*
It sovrapproduzione *(f)*

producción *(f)* n Es
De Erzeugung *(f)*
En production
Fr production *(f)*
It produzione *(f)*
Pt produção *(f)*

producción en masa *(f)* Es
De Massenherstellung *(f)*
En mass production
Fr production en masse *(f)*
It fabbricazione in massa *(f)*
Pt produção em massa *(f)*

produce n En
De Erzeugnis *(f)*
Es productos *(m pl)*
Fr produit *(m)*
It prodotti *(m pl)*
Pt produtos *(m pl)*

produce market En
De Warenmarkt *(m)*
Es mercado de productos *(m)*
Fr marché commercial *(m)*
It mercato commerciale *(m)*
Pt mercado de produtos *(m)*

product n En
De Produkt *(n)*
Es producto *(m)*
Fr produit *(m)*
It prodotto *(m)*
Pt produto *(m)*

production n En, Fr *(f)*
De Erzeugung *(f)*
Es producción *(f)*
It produzione *(f)*
Pt produção *(f)*

production control En
De Produktionskontrolle *(f)*
Es control de producción *(m)*
Fr contrôle de production *(m)*
It controllo della produzione
(m)
Pt controlo da produção *(m)*

production en masse *(f)* Fr
De Massenherstellung *(f)*
En mass production
Es producción en masa *(f)*
It fabbricazione in massa *(f)*
Pt produção em massa *(f)*

productividad *(f) n* Es
De Produktivität *(f)*
En productivity
Fr productivité *(f)*
It produttività *(f)*
Pt produtividade *(f)*

productivité *(f) n* Fr
De Produktivität *(f)*
En productivity
Es productividad *(f)*
It produttività *(f)*
Pt produtividade *(f)*

productivity *n* En
De Produktivität *(f)*
Es productividad *(f)*
Fr productivité *(f)*
It produttività *(f)*
Pt produtividade *(f)*

producto *(m) n* Es
De Produkt *(n)*
En product
Fr produit *(m)*
It prodotto *(m)*
Pt produto *(m)*

producto derivado *(m)* Es
De Nebenprodukt *(n)*
En by-product
Fr sous-produit *(m)*
It sottoprodotto *(m)*
Pt produto derivado *(m)*

producto final *(m)* Es
De Endprodukt *(n)*
En end-product
Fr produit final *(m)*
It prodotto finale *(m)*
Pt produto final *(m)*

producto interior bruto *(m)*
     Es
De Bruttoinlandsprodukt *(n)*
En gross domestic product
     (GDP)
Fr produit intérieur brut *(m)*
It prodotto interno lordo *(m)*
Pt produto interno bruto *(m)*

producto nacional bruto *(m)*
     Es
De Bruttosozialprodukt *(n)*
En gross national product
     (GNP)
Fr produit national brut *(m)*

It prodotto nazionale lordo
     (m)
Pt produto nacional bruto *(m)*

produit *(m) n* Fr
De Produkt *(n)*
En product
Es producto *(m)*
It prodotto *(m)*
Pt produto *(m)*

produit final *(m)* Fr
De Endprodukt *(n)*
En end-product
Es producto final *(m)*
It prodotto finale *(m)*
Pt produto final *(m)*

produit intérieur brut *(m)* Fr
De Bruttoinlandsprodukt *(n)*
En gross domestic product
     (GDP)
Es producto interior bruto *(m)*
It prodotto interno lordo *(m)*
Pt produto interno bruto *(m)*

produit national brut *(m)* Fr
De Bruttosozialprodukt *(n)*
En gross national product
     (GNP)
Es producto nacional bruto
     (m)
It prodotto nazionale lordo
     (m)
Pt produto nacional bruto *(m)*

produit net *(m)* Fr
De Reinerlös *(m)*
En net proceeds
Es rédito neto *(m)*
It ricavo netto *(m)*
Pt proventos líquidos *(m pl)*

Produkt *(n) n* De
En product
Es producto *(m)*
Fr produit *(m)*
It prodotto *(m)*
Pt produto *(m)*

Produktionskontrolle *(f) n* De
En production control
Es control de producción *(m)*
Fr contrôle de production *(m)*
It controllo della produzione
     (m)
Pt controlo da produção *(m)*

produktive Arbeitskräfte
     (f pl) De
En direct labour
Es jornales directos *(m pl)*
Fr travail en régie *(m)*
It lavoro in economia *(m)*
Pt trabalho directamente
     produtivo *(m)*

Produktivität *(f) n* De
En productivity
Es productividad *(f)*
Fr productivité *(f)*
It produttività *(f)*
Pt produtividade *(f)*

produtividade *(f) n* Pt
De Produktivität *(f)*
En productivity
Es productividad *(f)*
Fr productivité *(f)*
It produttività *(f)*

produto *(m) n* Pt
De Produkt *(n)*
En product
Es producto *(m)*
Fr produit *(m)*
It prodotto *(m)*

produto derivado *(m)* Pt
De Nebenprodukt *(n)*
En by-product
Es producto derivado *(m)*
Fr sous-produit *(m)*
It sottoprodotto *(m)*

produto final *(m)* Pt
De Endprodukt *(n)*
En end-product
Es producto final *(m)*
Fr produit final *(m)*
It prodotto finale *(m)*

produto interno bruto *(m)* Pt
De Bruttoinlandsprodukt *(n)*
En gross domestic product
     (GDP)
Es producto interior bruto *(m)*
Fr produit intérieur brut *(m)*
It prodotto interno lordo *(m)*

produto nacional bruto *(m)*
     Pt
De Bruttosozialprodukt *(n)*
En gross national product
     (GNP)

Es producto nacional bruto
(m)
Fr produit national brut (m)
It prodotto nazionale lordo
(m)

produttività (f) n It
De Produktivität (f)
En productivity
Es productividad (f)
Fr productivité (f)
Pt produtividade (f)

produzione (f) n It
De Erzeugung (f)
En production; output
Es producción; rendimiento
(f m)
Fr production; rendement
(f m)
Pt produção; rendimento (f m)

profit n En, Fr (m)
De Gewinn, Profit (m)
Es ganancia; beneficio (f m)
It utile; profitto (m)
Pt lucro; benefício (m)

Profit (m) n De
En profit
Es ganancia; beneficio (f m)
Fr profit; bénéfice (m)
It utile; profitto (m)
Pt lucro; benefício (m)

profitability n En
De Rentabilität (f)
Es rentabilidad (f)
Fr rentabilité (f)
It redditività (f)
Pt rentabilidade (f)

profit and loss account En
De Gewinn- und Verlustkonto
(n)
Es cuenta de ganancias y
pérdidas (f)
Fr compte profits et pertes
(m)
It conto profitti e perdite (m)
Pt conta de lucros e perdas (f)

profiteer n En
De Gewinnler (m)
Es acaparador (m)
Fr profiteur (m)
It profittatore (m)
Pt especulador (m)

profiteur (m) n Fr
De Gewinnler (m)
En profiteer
Es acaparador (m)
It profittatore (m)
Pt especulador (m)

profit fictif (m) Fr
De imaginärer Gewinn (m)
En paper profit
Es ganancia por realizar (f)
It utile sulla carta (m)
Pt lucros no papel (m pl)

profit maritime (m) Fr
De Bodmereidarlehenszinsen
(m pl)
En bottomry interest
Es interés de préstamo a la
gruesa (m)
It interessenza a cambio ma-
rittimo (f)
Pt juro de bodemeria (m)

profit-sharing n En
De Gewinnbeteiligung (f)
Es participación en los bene-
ficios (f)
Fr participation aux béné-
fices (f)
It partecipazione agli utili (f)
Pt repartição dos lucros (f)

profit-taking n En
De Gewinnrealisation (f)
Es realización de utilidades (f)
Fr prise de bénéfices (f)
It realizzazione dell'utile (f)
Pt realização dos lucros (f)

profittatore (m) n It
De Gewinnler (m)
En profiteer
Es acaparador (m)
Fr profiteur (m)
Pt especulador (m)

profitti non distribuiti (m pl) It
De unverteilte Gewinne (n pl)
En undistributed profits
Es beneficios no distribuidos
(m pl)
Fr bénéfices non répartis
(m pl)
Pt lucros não distribuidos
(m pl)

profitti per azione (m pl) It
De Gewinn pro Aktie (n)
En earnings per share

Es beneficios por acción
(m pl)
Fr bénéfice par titre (m)
Pt proventos por acção (m pl)

profitto (m) n It
De Gewinn; Profit (m)
En profit
Es ganancia; beneficio (f m)
Fr bénéfice; profit (m)
Pt lucro; benefício (m)

proforma invoice En
De Proformarechnung (f)
Es factura proforma (f)
Fr facture fictive (f)
It fattura proforma (f)
Pt factura proforma (f)

Proformarechnung (f) n De
En proforma invoice
Es factura proforma (f)
Fr facture fictive (f)
It fattura proforma (f)
Pt factura proforma (f)

progetto (m) n It
De Entwurf; Plan (m)
En plan; project
Es plan; proyecto (m)
Fr projet; plan (m)
Pt plano; projecto (m)

progetto di contratto (m) It
De Vertragsentwurf (m)
En draft contract
Es proyecto de contrato (m)
Fr projet de contrat (m)
Pt minuta de contrato (f)

prognosticar vb Pt
De vorhersehen
En forecast
Es pronosticar
Fr prévoir
It pronosticare

program vb En
De programmieren
Es programar
Fr programmer
It programmare
Pt programar

programa de computador
(m) Pt
De Computerprogramm (n)
En computer program
Es programa de computado-
ra (m)

Fr programme d'ordinateur
(m)
It programma di elaboratore
(m)

programa de computadora
(m) Es
De Computerprogramm (n)
En computer program
Fr programme d'ordinateur
(m)
It programma di elaboratore
(m)
Pt programa de computador
(m)

programar vb Es, Pt
De programmieren
En program
Fr programmer
It programmare

programa salários (m) Pt
De Lohnpolitik (f)
En incomes policy
Es plan de renta (m)
Fr politique des salaires (f)
It politica dei redditi (f)

programma delle inserzioni
(m) It
De Werbeplan (m)
En advertising schedule
Es plan de propaganda (m)
Fr programme des annonces
(m)
Pt plano de campanha publi-
citária (m)

programma di elaboratore
(m) It
De Computerprogramm (n)
En computer program
Es programa de computado-
ra (m)
Fr programme d'ordinateur
(m)
Pt programa de computador
(m)

programmare vb It
De programmieren
En program
Es programar
Fr programmer
Pt programar

programmatura (f) n It
De Programmausrüstung (f)
En (computer) software

Es conjunto de rutinas; software (m)
Fr software (m)
Pt sistema lógico; software
(m)

Programmausrüstung (f) n
De
En (computer) software
Es conjunto de rutinas; soft-
ware (m)
Fr software (m)
It programmatura; software
(f m)
Pt sistema lógico; software
(m)

programme des annonces
(m) Fr
De Werbeplan (m)
En advertising schedule
Es plan de propaganda (m)
It programma delle inserzio-
ni (m)
Pt plano de campanha publi-
citária (m)

programme d'ordinateur (m)
Fr
De Computerprogramm (n)
En computer program
Es programa de computado-
ra (m)
It programma di elaboratore
(m)
Pt programa de computador
(m)

programmer vb Fr
De programmieren
En program
Es programar
It programmare
Pt programar

programmieren vb De
En program
Es programar
Fr programmer
It programmare
Pt programar

prohibición de importación
(f) Es
De Einfuhrverbot (n)
En import ban
Fr prohibition d'entrée (f)
It divieto d'importazione (m)
Pt proibição de importação (f)

prohibition d'entrée (f) Fr
De Einfuhrverbot (n)
En import ban
Es prohibición de importa-
ción (f)
It divieto d'importazione (m)
Pt proibição de importação (f)

proibição de importação (f)
Pt
De Einfuhrverbot (n)
En import ban
Es prohibición de importa-
ción (f)
Fr prohibition d'entrée (f)
It divieto d'importazione (m)

projecto de acordo (m) Pt
De Entwurf eines Überein-
kommens (m)
En draft agreement
Es proyecto de convenio (m)
Fr projet de convention (m)
It schema di contratto (m)

projet (m) n Fr
De Konzept; Plan (n m)
En draft; plan
Es borrador; plan (m)
It bozza; progetto (f m)
Pt rascunho; plano (m)

projet de contrat (m) Fr
De Vertragsentwurf (m)
En draft contract
Es proyecto de contrato (m)
It progetto di contratto (m)
Pt minuta de contrato (f)

projet de convention (m) Fr
De Entwurf eines Überein-
kommens (m)
En draft agreement
Es proyecto de convenio (m)
It schema di contratto (m)
Pt projecto de acordo (m)

pro Kopf De
En per capita
Es pro cabeza
Fr par tête
It a testa
Pt per capita

prolongation d'un crédit (f)
Fr
De Verlängerung eines Kredi-
tes (f)
En extension of credit
Es prórroga de crédito (f)
It proroga di credito (f)
Pt prorrogação de crédito (f)

promedio *(m)* n Es
De Durchschnitt *(m)*
En average
Fr moyenne *(f)*
It media *(f)*
Pt média *(f)*

promemoria *(f)* n It
De Vermerk *(m)*
En memorandum
Es memorando; apunte *(m)*
Fr note *(f)*
Pt memorando *(m)*

promissória *(f)* n Pt
De Schuldschein *(m)*
En promissory note
Es pagaré *(m)*
Fr billet à ordre *(m)*
It pagherò *(m)*

promissory note En
De Schuldschein *(m)*
Es pagaré *(m)*
Fr billet à ordre *(m)*
It pagherò *(m)*
Pt promissória *(f)*

promoção *(f)* n Pt
De Beförderung; Förderung *(f)*
En promotion; advancement
Es promoción; ascenso *(f m)*
Fr promotion; avancement *(f m)*
It promozione; avanzamento *(f m)*

promoção de vendas *(f)* Pt
De Werbung; Verkaufsförderung *(f)*
En sales promotion
Es promoción de ventas *(f)*
Fr promotion des ventes *(f)*
It sviluppo delle vendite *(m)*

promoción *(f)* n Es
De Beförderung; Förderung *(f)*
En promotion; advancement
Fr promotion; avancement *(f m)*
It promozione; avanzamento *(f m)*
Pt promoção; fomento *(f m)*

promoción de ventas *(f)* Es
De Werbung; Verkaufsförderung *(f)*
En sales promotion

Fr promotion des ventes *(f)*
It sviluppo delle vendite *(m)*
Pt promoção de vendas *(f)*

promote vb En
De fördern; befördern
Es promover; ascender
Fr promouvoir; donner de l'avancement à
It dare impulso a; promuovere
Pt promover

promotion n En, Fr *(f)*
De Beförderung; Förderung *(f)*
Es promoción; ascenso *(f m)*
It promozione; avanzamento *(f m)*
Pt promoção; fomento *(f m)*

promotion des ventes *(f)* Fr
De Werbung; Verkaufsförderung *(f)*
En sales promotion
Es promoción de ventas *(f)*
It sviluppo delle vendite *(m)*
Pt promoção de vendas *(f)*

promouvoir vb Fr
De befördern; fördern
En promote
Es promover; ascender
It promuovere; dare impulso a
Pt promover

promover vb Es, Pt
De befördern; fördern
En promote
Fr promouvoir; donner de l'avancement à
It promuovere; dare impulso a

promozione *(f)* n It
De Beförderung; Förderung *(f)*
En promotion
Es promoción; ascenso *(f m)*
Fr promotion; avancement *(f m)*
Pt promoção; fomento *(f m)*

prompt delivery En
De sofortige Lieferung *(f)*
Es entrega inmediata *(f)*
Fr livraison immédiate *(f)*
It pronta consegna *(f)*
Pt entrega imediata *(f)*

promuovere vb It
De befördern; fördern
En promote
Es promouvoir; donner de l'avancement à
Pt promover

pronosticar vb Es
De vorhersehen
En forecast
Fr prévoir
It pronosticare
Pt prognosticar

pronosticare vb It
De vorhersehen
En forecast
Es pronosticar
Fr prévoir
Pt prognosticar

pronóstico *(m)* n Es
De Voraussage *(f)*
En forecasting
Fr prévision *(f)*
It previsione *(f)*
Pt previsão *(f)*

pronóstico de ventas *(m)* Es
De Verkaufsvoraussage *(f)*
En sales forecast
Fr prévision de ventes *(f)*
It previsione delle vendite *(f)*
Pt previsão de vendas *(f)*

pronta consegna *(f)* It
De sofortige Lieferung *(f)*
En prompt delivery
Es entrega inmediata *(f)*
Fr livraison immédiate *(f)*
Pt entrega imediata *(f)*

pronti contanti *(m pl)* It
De Barbestand *(m)*
En cash in hand
Es efectivo en caja *(m)*
Fr espèces en caisse *(f pl)*
Pt fundos à ordem *(m pl)*

property bond En
De Grund- und Gebäudeobligation *(f)*
Es cédula hipotecaria *(f)*
Fr obligation foncière *(f)*
It obbligazione fondiaria *(f)*
Pt título de investimento imobiliário *(m)*

promuovere vb It
De befördern; fördern
En promote
Es promouvoir; donner de l'avancement à
Pt promover

property tax En
De Grundsteuer *(f)*
Es impuesto sobre la propie-
     dad *(m)*
Fr impôt foncier *(m)*
It imposta fondiaria *(f)*
Pt imposto sobre propieda-
     de *(m)*

propiedad *(f)* n Es
De Eigentum *(n)*
En ownership; property
Fr propriété *(f)*
It proprietà *(f)*
Pt propriedade *(f)*

propiedad estatal *(f)* Es
De Staatsbesitz *(m)*
En public ownership
Fr propriété publique *(f)*
It proprietà statale *(f)*
Pt propriedade pública *(f)*

propietario *(m)* n Es
De Eigentümer; Vermieter
     (m)
En owner; landlord
Fr propriétaire *(m)*
It proprietario; locatore *(m)*
Pt proprietário; senhorio *(m)*

propietario del terreno *(m)*
     Es
De Grundbesitzer *(m)*
En ground-landlord
Fr propriétaire foncier *(m)*
It proprietario del terreno *(m)*
Pt proprietário do terreno *(m)*

propina *(f)* n Es
De Trinkgeld *(n)*
En tip; gratuity
Fr pourboire *(m)*
It mancia *(f)*
Pt gorjeta *(f)*

proponente *(m)* n Pt
De Bietende(r) *(m)*
En bidder
Es ofertante *(m)*
Fr enchérisseur *(m)*
It offerente *(m)*

proponente mais elevado
     (m) Pt
De Meistbietende(r) *(m)*
En highest bidder

Es ofertante más alto *(m)*
Fr plus offrant enchérisseur
     (m)
It miglior offerente *(m)*

proporção *(f)* n Pt
De Verhältnis; Anteil *(n m)*
En proportion
Es proporción *(f)*
Fr proportion *(f)*
It proporzione *(f)*

proporção de fracassos *(f)*
     Pt
De Durchfallquote *(f)*
En failure rate
Es proporción de fracasos *(f)*
Fr taux de défaillance *(m)*
It indice dei fallimenti *(m)*

proporción *(f)* n Es
De Verhältnis; Anteil *(n m)*
En proportion
Fr proportion *(f)*
It proporzione *(f)*
Pt proporção *(f)*

proporcionalmente;
     a prorata Es
De anteilsmäßig; pro rata
En pro rata
Fr proportionnellement; au
     prorata
It proporzionalmente; pro ra-
     ta
Pt proporcionalmente; pro
     rata

proporcionalmente;
     pro rata Pt
De anteilsmäßig; pro rata
En pro rata
Fr proportionnellement; au
     prorata
Es proporcionalmente; a pro-
     rata
It proporzional-
     mente; pro rata

proporción de fracasos *(f)*
     Es
De Durchfallquote *(f)*
En failure rate
Fr taux de défaillance *(m)*
It indice dei fallimenti *(m)*
Pt proporção de fracassos *(f)*

proporción precio-ingresos
     (f) Es
De Verhältnis des Aktienkur-
     ses zum Reingewinn *(n)*
En price-earnings ratio
     (P/E)
Fr quotient cours-bénéfice
     (m)
It rapporto prezzo-utile
     (m)
Pt taxa custo-ganhos *(f)*

proportion n En, Fr *(f)*
De Verhältnis; Anteil *(n m)*
Es proporción *(f)*
It proporzione *(f)*
Pt proporção *(f)*

proportionnellement;
     au prorata Fr
De anteilsmäßig; pro rata
En pro rata
Es proporcionalmente; a pro-
     rata
It proporzionalemente; pro
     rata
Pt proporcionalmente; pro
     rata

proporzionalemente;
     pro rata It
De anteilsmäßig
En pro rata
Fr proportionnellement;
     au prorata
Es proporcionalmente; a pro-
     rata
Pt proporcionalmente; pro
     rata

proporzione *(f)* n It
De Verhältnis; Anteil *(n m)*
En proportion
Es proporción *(f)*
Fr proportion *(f)*
Pt proporção *(f)*

proposal n En
De Vorschlag *(m)*
Es propuesta *(f)*
Fr proposition *(f)*
It proposta *(f)*
Pt proposta *(f)*

proposition *(f)* n Fr
De Vorschlag *(m)*
En proposal
Es propuesta *(f)*
It proposta *(f)*
Pt proposta *(f)*

proposta *(f)* n It, Pt
De Vorschlag; Angebot *(m n)*
En proposal; offer
Es propuesta; oferta *(f)*
Fr proposition; offre *(f)*

proposta de apropriação *(f)*
Pt
De Übernahmeangebot *(n)*
En take-over bid
Es oferta de adquisición *(f)*
Fr offre de rachat *(f)*
It offerta di acquisto *(f)*

propriedade *(f)* n Pt
De Eigentum *(n)*
En property; ownership
Es propiedad *(f)*
Fr propriété *(f)*
It proprietà *(f)*

propriedade em maioria *(f)*
Pt
De Mehrheitsbeteiligung *(f)*
En majority holding
Es tenencia de acciones por
mayoría *(f)*
Fr participation majoritaire *(f)*
It partecipazione maggiori-
taria *(f)*

propriedade imobiliária *(f)* Pt
De unbewegliches Vermögen;
Immobilien *(n; f pl)*
En real estate
Es bienes inmuebles *(m pl)*
Fr biens immeubles *(m pl)*
It beni immobili *(m pl)*

propriedade pública *(f)* Pt
De Staatsbesitz *(m)*
En public ownership
Es propiedad estatal *(f)*
Fr propriété publique *(f)*
It proprietà statale *(f)*

proprietà *(f)* n It
De Eigentum *(n)*
En property; ownership
Es propiedad *(f)*
Fr propriété *(f)*
Pt propriedade *(f)*

propriétaire *(m)* n Fr
De Eigentümer; Vermieter *(m)*
En owner; landlord
Es propietario; arrendador
(m)
It proprietario; locatore *(m)*
Pt proprietário; senhorio *(m)*

propriétaire foncier *(m)* Fr
De Grundbesitzer *(m)*
En ground-landlord
Es propietario del terreno *(m)*
It proprietario del terreno *(m)*
Pt proprietário do terreno *(m)*

proprietà mobiliare *(f)* It
De bewegliche Güter *(n pl)*
En movable assets
Es mobiliario *(m)*
Fr biens mobiliers *(m pl)*
Pt bens mobiliários *(m pl)*

proprietario *(m)* n It
De Eigentümer; Vermieter *(m)*
En owner; landlord
Es propietario; arrendador
(m)
Fr propriétaire *(m)*
Pt proprietário; senhorio *(m)*

proprietário *(m)* n Pt
De Eigentümer; Vermieter *(m)*
En owner; landlord
Es propietario; arrendador
(m)
Fr propriétaire *(m)*
It proprietario; locatore *(m)*

proprietário de boa fé *(m)*
De gutgläubiger Besitzer *(m)*
En holder in due course
Es tenedor en buena fe *(m)*
Fr porteur de bonne fol *(m)*
It titolare in buona fede *(m)*

proprietario del terreno *(m)* It
De Grundbesitzer *(m)*
En ground-landlord
Es propietario del terreno *(m)*
Fr propriétaire foncier *(m)*
Pt proprietário do terreno *(m)*

proprietário do terreno *(m)*
Pt
De Grundbesitzer *(m)*
En ground-landlord
Es propietario del terreno *(m)*
Fr propiétaire foncier *(m)*
It proprietario del terreno *(m)*

proprietário legítimo *(m)* Pt
De entgeltigter Besitzer *(m)*
En holder for value
Es tenedor legítimo *(m)*
Fr porteur à titre onéreux *(m)*
It detentore legittimo *(m)*

proprietà statale *(f)* It
De Staatsbesitz *(m)*
En public ownership
Es propiedad estatal *(f)*
Fr propriété publique *(f)*
Pt propriedade pública *(f)*

propriété *(f)* n Fr
De Eigentum *(n)*
En property; ownership
Es propiedad *(f)*
It proprietà *(f)*
Pt propriedade *(f)*

propriété publique *(f)* Fr
De Staatsbesitz *(m)*
En public ownership
Es propiedad estatal *(f)*
It proprietà statale *(f)*
Pt propriedade pública *(f)*

propuesta *(f)* n Es
De Vorschlag *(m)*
En proposal
Fr proposition *(f)*
It proposta *(f)*
Pt proposta *(f)*

pro rata En
De anteilsmäßig; pro rata
Es proporcionalmente; a pro-
rata
Fr proportionnellement; au
prorata
It proporzionalmente; pro ra-
ta
Pt proporcionalemente; pro
rata

proroga di credito *(f)* It
De Verlängerung eines Kredi-
tes *(f)*
En extension of credit
Es prórroga de crédito *(f)*
Fr prolongation d'un crédit *(f)*
Pt prorrogação de crédito *(f)*

proroga di pagamento *(f)* It
De Verlängerung einer Zah-
lungsfrist *(f)*
En extension of payment time
Es prórroga de pago *(f)*
Fr delai de paiement *(m)*
Pt prorrogação de pagamento
(f)

prorrogação de crédito *(f)* Pt
De Verlängerung eines Kredi-
     tes *(f)*
En extension of credit
Es prórroga de crédito *(f)*
Fr prolongation d'un crédit *(f)*
It proroga di credito *(f)*

prorrogação de pagamento
     (f) Pt
De Verlängerung einer Zah-
     lungsfrist *(f)*
En extension of payment time
Es prórroga de pago *(f)*
Fr délai de paiement *(m)*
It proroga di pagamento *(f)*

prórroga de crédito *(f)* Es
De Verlängerung eines Kredi-
     tes *(f)*
En extension of credit
Fr prolongation d'un crédit *(f)*
It proroga di credito *(f)*
Pt prorrogação de crédito *(f)*

prórroga de pago *(f)* Es
De Verlängerungszeitraum
     (m)
En extension of payment time
Fr délai de paiement *(m)*
It proroga di pagamento *(f)*
Pt prorrogação de pagamento
     (f)

prospecto *(m)* n Es, Pt
De Prospekt *(m)*
En prospectus
Fr prospectus *(m)*
It prospetto; programma *(m)*

prospectus n En, Fr *(m)*
De Prospekt *(m)*
Es prospecto *(m)*
It prospetto; programma *(m)*
Pt prospecto *(m)*

prospectus publicitaire *(m)*
     Fr
De Werbeschrift *(f)*
En advertising brochure
Es folleto publicitario *(m)*
It opuscolo pubblicitario *(m)*
Pt folheto publicitário *(m)*

Prospekt *(m)* n De
En prospectus
Es prospecto *(m)*

Fr prospectus *(m)*
It prospetto; programma *(m)*
Pt prospecto *(m)*

prospetto *(m)* n It
De Prospekt *(m)*
En prospectus
Es prospecto *(m)*
Fr prospectus *(m)*
Pt prospecto *(m)*

protest n En
De Protest *(m)*
Es protesta *(f)*
Fr protêt *(m)*
It protesto *(m)*
Pt protesto *(m)*

protest (a bill) vb En
De protestieren
Es protestar
Fr faire protester
It protestare
Pt protestar

Protest *(m)* n De
En protest
Es protesta *(f)*
Fr protêt *(m)*
It protesto *(m)*
Pt protesto *(m)*

protesta *(f)* n Es
De Protest *(m)*
En protest
Fr protêt *(m)*
It protesto *(m)*
Pt protesto *(m)*

protestar (uma letra) Pt
De protestieren
En protest
Es protestar
Fr faire protester
It protestare

protestar (una letra) Es
De protestieren
En protest
Fr faire protester
It protestare
Pt protestar

protestare (una cambiale) It
De protestieren
En protest
Es protestar
Fr faire protester
Pt protestar

protestieren (einen Wechsel)
     De
En protest
Es protestar
Fr faire protester
It protestare
Pt protestar

protesto *(m)* n It, Pt
De Protest *(m)*
En protest
Es protesta *(f)*
Fr protêt *(m)*

protêt *(m)* n Fr
De Protect *(m)*
En protest
Es protesta *(f)*
It protesto *(m)*
Pt protesto *(m)*

Protokoll *(n)* n De
En minutes
Es actas *(f pl)*
Fr procès-verbal *(m)*
It verbale *(m)*
Pt minutas de acta *(f pl)*

prototipo *(m)* n Es, It
De Prototyp *(m)*
En prototype
Fr prototype *(m)*
Pt protótipo *(m)*

protótipo *(m)* n Pt
De Prototyp *(m)*
En prototype
Es prototipo *(m)*
Fr prototype *(m)*
It prototipo *(m)*

Prototyp *(m)* n De
En prototype
Es prototipo *(m)*
Fr prototype *(m)*
It prototipo *(m)*
Pt protótipo *(m)*

prototype n En, Fr *(m)*
De Prototyp *(m)*
Es prototipo *(m)*
It prototipo *(m)*
Pt protótipo *(m)*

prova *(f)* n It, Pt
De Probe; Beweis *(f m)*
En test; evidence
Es prueba; evidencia *(f)*
Fr épreuve; preuve *(f)*

prova documental *(f)* Pt
De Urkundenbeweis *(m)*
En documentary evidence
Es prueba documental *(f)*
Fr preuve écrite *(f)*
It prova scritta *(f)*

prova gratuita *(f)* It, Pt
De kostenlose Probe *(f)*
En free trial
Es prueba gratuita *(f)*
Fr essai gratuit *(m)*

prova scritta *(f)* It
De Urkundenbeweis *(m)*
En documentary evidence
Es prueba documental *(f)*
Fr preuve écrite *(f)*
Pt prova documental *(f)*

proveedor *(m)* n Es
De Lieferant *(m)*
En supplier
Fr fournisseur *(m)*
It fornitore *(m)*
Pt fornecedor *(m)*

proventi decrescenti *(m pl)* It
De abnehmender Ertrag *(m)*
En diminishing returns
Es rendimientos decrecientes *(m pl)*
Fr rendements décroissants *(m pl)*
Pt rendimentos decrescentes *(m pl)*

proventos líquidos *(m pl)* Pt
De Reinerlös *(m)*
En net proceeds
Es rédito neto *(m)*
Fr produit net *(m)*
It ricavo netto *(m)*

proventos por acção *(m pl)* Pt
De Gewinn pro Aktie *(n)*
En earnings per share
Es beneficios por acción *(m pl)*
Fr bénéfice par titre *(m)*
It profitti per azione *(m pl)*

provisão *(f)* n Pt
De Rabatt *(m)*
En allowance
Es bonificación *(f)*
Fr rabais *(m)*
It abbuono *(m)*

provisão para amortização *(f)* Pt
De Abschreibung für Abnut-
zung (AfA) *(f)*
En depreciation allowance
Es provisión para amortiza-
ción *(f)*
Fr provision pour amortisse-
ment *(f)*
It quota di ammortamento *(f)*

Provision *(f)* n De
En commission
Es comisión *(f)*
Fr commission *(f)*
It provvisione *(f)*
Pt comissão *(f)*

provisiones existentes *(f pl)* Es
De lieferfertiges Angebot *(n)*
En supplies on hand
Fr ressources existantes *(f pl)*
It forniture esistenti *(f pl)*
Pt fornecimentos em
existência *(m pl)*

provisión para amortización *(f)* Es
De Abschreibung für Abnut-
zung (AfA) *(f)*
En depreciation allowance
Fr provision pour amortisse-
ment *(f)*
It quota di ammortamento *(f)*
Pt provisão para amortização *(f)*

**provision pour amortisse-
ment** *(f)* Fr
De Abschreibung für Abnut-
zung (AfA) *(f)*
En depreciation allowance
Es provisión para amortiza-
ción *(f)*
It quota di ammortamento *(f)*
Pt provisão para amortização *(f)*

**provision pour créances
douteuses** *(f)* Fr
De Dubiosenreserve *(f)*
En bad debt reserve
Es reserva para deudas inco-
brables *(f)*
It riserva per crediti inesigi-
bili *(f)*
Pt reserva para dívidas in-
cobráveis *(f)*

provisoire *adj* Fr
De einstweilig
En temporary
Es temporal
It temporaneo
Pt temporário

provocare *vb* It
De anstiften
En instigate
Es instigar; provocar
Fr provoquer
Pt instigar

provoquer *vb* Fr
De anstiften
En instigate
Es instigar; provocar
It provocare; istigare
Pt instigar

provvisione *(f)* n It
De Provision *(f)*
En commission
Es comisión *(f)*
Fr commission *(f)*
Pt comissão *(f)*

proxy (power) n En
De Stellvertretung *(f)*
Es procuración *(f)*
Fr procuration *(f)*
It procura *(f)*
Pt procuração *(f)*

proxy (person) n En
De Stellvertreter *(m)*
Es apoderado *(m)*
Fr mandataire *(m)*
It procuratore *(m)*
Pt procurador *(m)*

proyecto de contrato *(m)* Es
De Vertragsentwurf *(m)*
En draft contract
Fr projet de contrat *(m)*
It progetto di contratto *(m)*
Pt minuta de contrato *(f)*

proyecto de convenio *(m)* Es
De Entwurf eines Überein-
kommens *(m)*
En draft agreement
Fr projet de convention *(f)*
It schema di contratto *(m)*
Pt projecto de acordo *(m)*

Prozent De
En per cent
Es por ciento
Fr pour cent
It per cento
Pt por cento

Prozentsatz *(m)* n De
En percentage
Es porcentaje *(m)*
Fr pourcentage *(m)*
It percentuale *(f)*
Pt percentagem *(f)*

Prozeß *(m)* n De
En lawsuit; trial
Es proceso; causa *(m f)*
Fr procès *(m)*
It processo; causa *(m f)*
Pt processo; causa *(m f)*

prueba *(f)* n Es
De Probe; Beweis *(f m)*
En test; evidence
Fr épreuve; preuve *(f)*
It prova *(f)*
Pt prova *(f)*

prueba documental *(f)* Es
De Urkundenbeweis *(m)*
En documentary evidence
Fr preuve écrite *(f)*
It prova scritta *(f)*
Pt prova documental *(f)*

prueba gratuita *(f)* Es
De kostenlose Probe *(f)*
En free trial
Fr essai gratuit *(m)*
It prova gratuita *(f)*
Pt prova gratuita *(f)*

prüfen *vb* De
En examine; audit
Es verificar; revisar
Fr examiner; vérifier et certi-
fier
It verificare; rivedere
Pt verificar; fiscalizar

psicología industrial *(f)* Es
De Arbeitspsychologie *(f)*
En industrial psychology
Fr psychotechnique *(f)*
It psicologia industriale *(f)*
Pt psicologia industrial *(f)*

psicologia industrial *(f)* Pt
De Arbeitspsychologie *(f)*
En industrial psychology
Es psicología industrial *(f)*
Fr psychotechnique *(f)*
It psicologia industriale *(f)*

psicologia industriale *(f)* It
De Arbeitspsychologie *(f)*
En industrial psychology
Es psicología industrial *(f)*
Fr psychotechnique *(f)*
Pt psicologia industrial *(f)*

psychotechnique *(f)* n Fr
De Arbeitspsychologie *(f)*
En industrial psychology
Es psicología industrial *(f)*
It psicologia industriale *(f)*
Pt psicologia industrial *(f)*

pubbliche relazioni *(f pl)* It
De Public Relations *(n pl)*
En public relations (PR)
Es relaciones públicas *(f pl)*
Fr relations publiques *(f pl)*
Pt relações públicas *(f pl)*

pubblicità *(f)* n It
De Reklame; Werbung *(f)*
En advertising; publicity
Es publicidad *(f)*
Fr publicité *(f)*
Pt publicidade *(f)*

pubblicità diretta *(f)* It
De Postversandwerbung *(f)*
En direct mail
Es propaganda directa por
correo *(f)*
Fr publicité directe *(f)*
Pt publicidade por correio ao
domicílio *(f)*

pubblico *adj* It
De öffentlich
En public
Es público
Fr public
Pt público

pubblico *(m)* n It
De Öffentlichkeit *(f)*
En (general) public
Es público *(m)*
Fr public *(m)*
Pt público *(m)*

public *adj* En, Fr
De öffentlich
Es público
It pubblico
Pt público

public n En, Fr *(m)*
De Öffentlichkeit *(f)*
Es público *(m)*
It pubblico *(m)*
Pt público *(m)*

public holiday En
De gesetzlicher Feiertag *(m)*
Es día de fiesta *(m)*
Fr jour férié *(m)*
It giorno di festa *(m)*
Pt feriado *(m)*

publicidad *(f)* n Es
De Reklame; Werbung *(f)*
En advertising; publicity
Fr publicité *(f)*
It pubblicità *(f)*
Pt publicidade *(f)*

publicidade *(f)* n Pt
De Reklame; Werbung *(f)*
En advertising; publicity
Es publicidad *(f)*
Fr publicité *(f)*
It pubblicità *(f)*

**publicidade por correio ao
domicílio** *(f)* Pt
De Postversandwerbung *(f)*
En direct mail
Es propaganda directa por
correo *(f)*
Fr publicité directe *(f)*
It pubblicità diretta *(f)*

publicité *(f)* n Fr
De Reklame; Werbung *(f)*
En advertising; publicity
Es publicidad *(f)*
It pubblicità *(f)*
Pt publicidade *(f)*

publicité directe *(f)* Fr
De Postversandwerbung *(f)*
En direct mail
Es propaganda directa por
correo *(f)*
It pubblicità diretta *(f)*
Pt publicidade por correio ao
domicílio *(f)*

publicity n En
De Werbung (f)
Es publicidad (f)
Fr publicité (f)
It pubblicità (f)
Pt publicidade (f)

publicity campaign En
De Werbefeldzug (m)
Es campaña publicitaria (f)
Fr campagne de publicité (f)
It campagna pubblicitaria (f)
Pt campanha publicitária (f)

public limited company En
De Aktiengesellschaft (AG) (f)
Es Sociedad anónima (SA) (f)
Fr Société anonyme (SA) (f)
It Società anonima (SA) (f)
Pt Sociedade Anónima (SA)
　(f)

público adj Es, Pt
De öffentlich
En public
Fr public
It pubblico

público (m) n Es, Pt
De Öffentlichkeit (f)
En (general) public
Fr public (m)
It pubblico (m)

public ownership En
De Staatsbesitz (m)
Es propiedad estatal (f)
Fr propriété publique (f)
It proprietà statale (f)
Pt propriedade pública (f)

public relations (PR) En
De Public Relations (n pl)
Es relaciones públicas (f pl)
Fr relations publiques (f pl)
It pubbliche relazioni (f pl)
Pt relações públicas (f pl)

Public Relations (n pl) n De
En public relations (PR)
Es relaciones públicas (f pl)
Fr relations publiques (f pl)
It pubbliche relazioni (f pl)
Pt relações públicas (f pl)

public sector En
De öffentliche Hand (f)
Es sector público (m)
Fr secteur public (m)

It settore statale (m)
Pt sector público (m)

publishing house En
De Verlag (m)
Es casa editorial (f)
Fr maison d'édition (f)
It casa editrice (f)
Pt casa editora (f)

puerto (m) n Es
De Hafen (m)
En port; harbour
Fr port (m)
It porto (m)
Pt porto (m)

puerto de descarga (m) Es
De Lieferhafen (m)
En port of discharge
Fr port de livraison (m)
It porto di scarico (m)
Pt porto de descarga (m)

puerto de destino (m) Es
De Bestimmungshafen (m)
En port of destination
Fr port de destination (m)
It porto di destinazione (m)
Pt porto de destino (m)

puerto de escala (m) Es
De Anlaufhafen (m)
En port of call
Fr port d'escale (m)
It porto di scalo (m)
Pt porto de escala (m)

puerto de matrícula (m) Es
De Heimathafen (m)
En port of registration
Fr port d'attache (m)
It porto d'immatricolazione
　(m)
Pt porto de matrícula (m)

puerto libre (m) Es
De Freihafen (m)
En free port
Fr port franc (m)
It porto franco (m)
Pt porto franco (m)

puesto en almacén Es
De an Zollfreilager
En ex warehouse
Fr à prendre en entrepôt
It franco magazzino
Pt no armazém

pugna de intereses (f) Es
De widerstreitende Interessen
　(n pl)
En conflict of interest
Fr opposition d'intérêts (f)
It conflitto d'interessi (m)
Pt conflito de interesses (m)

punched card En
De Lochkarte (f)
Es tarjeta perforada (f)
Fr carte perforée (f)
It scheda perforata (f)
Pt ficha perfurada (f)

**punto de igualdad de
　ingresos y gastos** (m) Es
De Rentabilitätsgrenze (f)
En break-even point
Fr point de seuil (m)
It punto di pareggio (m)
Pt ponto de acerto (m)

punto di pareggio (m) It
De Rentabilitätsgrenze (f)
En break-even point
Es punto de igualdad de in-
　gresos y gastos (m)
Fr point de seuil (m)
Pt ponto de acerto (m)

punzonatura di garanzia (f) It
De Feingehaltsstempel (m)
En hall-mark
Es punzón de garantía (m)
Fr poinçon de titre (m)
Pt marca de garantia (f)

punzón de garantía (m) Es
De Feingehaltsstempel (m)
En hall-mark
Fr poinçon de titre (m)
It punzonatura di garanzia (f)
Pt marca de garantia (f)

purchase n En
De Kauf; Anschaffung (m f)
Es compra (f)
Fr achat (m)
It compra (f)
Pt compra (f)

purchase book Am
En bought ledger
De Einkaufsbuch (n)
Es libro mayor de compras
　(m)

Fr grand livre d'achats *(m)*
It mastro acquisti *(m)*
Pt livro-mestre de compras
(m)

purchase price En
De Kaufpreis *(m)*
Es precio de compra *(m)*
Fr prix d'achat *(m)*
It prezzo d'acquisto *(m)*
Pt preço de compra *(m)*

purchases (in balance sheet)
(pl) n En
De Einkäufe *(m pl)*
Es adquisiciones *(f pl)*
Fr achats *(m pl)*
It acquisti *(m pl)*
Pt aquisições *(f pl)*

purchase tax En
De Erwerbssteuer *(f)*
Es impuesto sobre las com-
pras *(m)*
Fr impôt sur les acquisitions
(m)
It tassa sugli acquisti *(f)*
Pt imposto sobre aquisições
(m)

purchasing power En
De Kaufkraft *(f)*
Es poder de compra *(m)*
Fr pouvoir d'achat *(m)*
It potere d'acquisto *(m)*
Pt poder de compra *(m)*

purser *n* En
De Zahlmeister *(m)*
Es contador de navio *(m)*
Fr commissaire de la marine
(m)
It commissario di bordo *(m)*
Pt comissário de bordo *(m)*

put option En
De Verkaufsoption *(f)*
Es opción de venta *(f)*
Fr option à vendre *(f)*
It premio a vendere *(m)*
Pt opção de venda *(f)*

pyramid selling En
De Schneeball-Verkauf *(m)*
Es venta en pirámide *(f)*
Fr vente en pyramide *(f)*
It vendita a piramide *(f)*
Pt vendas em pirâmide *(f pl)*

Q

quadro de distribuição *(m)* Pt
De Schalttafel *(f)*
En switchboard
Es cuadro de conexión *(m)*
Fr tableau de distribution *(m)*
It quadro di comando *(m)*

quadro di comando *(m)* It
De Schalttafel *(f)*
En switchboard
Es cuadro de conexión *(m)*
Fr tableau de distribution *(m)*
Pt quadro de distribuição *(m)*

qual *(m) n* Fr
De Kai *(m)*
En quay; wharf
Es muelle *(m)*
It scalo *(m)*
Pt cais *(m)*

qualidade *(f) n* Pt
De Qualität *(f)*
En quality
Es calidad *(f)*
Fr qualité *(f)*
It qualità *(f)*

qualidade comerciável *(f)* Pt
De marktgängige Qualität *(f)*
En merchantable quality
Es calidad comerciable *(f)*
Fr qualité vendable *(f)*
It qualità commerciabile *(f)*

**qualidade e conteúdo
desconhecidos** Pt
De Qualität und Inhalt nicht
bekannt
En quality and contents unknown
Es calidad del contenido
desconocida
Fr qualité et contenu inconnus
It qualità e contenuto sconosciuti

qualidade média razoável *(f)*
Pt
De gute Durchschnittsqualität
(f)
En fair average quality (faq)
Es calidad media razonable *(f)*

Fr qualité commerciale
moyenne *(f)*
It buona qualità media *(f)*

qualifica *(f) n* It
De Qualifikation *(f)*
En qualification
Es requisito *(m)*
Fr qualification; capacité *(f)*
Pt qualificação *(f)*

qualificação *(f) n* Pt
De Qualifikation *(f)*
En qualification
Es requisito *(m)*
Fr qualification; capacité *(f)*
It qualifica; requisito *(f m)*

qualification *n* En, Fr *(f)*
De Qualifikation *(f)*
Es requisito *(m)*
It qualifica; requisito *(f m)*
Pt qualificação *(f)*

qualified acceptance En
De Annahme unter Vorbehalt
(f)
Es aceptación condicionada
(f)
Fr acceptation conditionnelle
(f)
It accettazione con riserva *(f)*
Pt aceitação com reservas *(f)*

qualified accountant En
De Wirtschaftsprüfer *(m)*
Es contador habilitado *(m)*
Fr expert comptable *(m)*
It ragioniere diplomato *(m)*
Pt guarda-livros diplomado
(m)

Qualifikation *(f) n* De
En qualification
Es requisito *(m)*
Fr qualification; capacité *(f)*
It qualifica; requisito *(f m)*
Pt qualificação *(f)*

qualità *(f) n* It
De Qualität *(f)*
En quality
Es calidad *(f)*
Fr qualité *(f)*
Pt qualidade *(f)*

qualità commerciabile *(f)* It
De marktgängige Qualität *(f)*
En merchantable quality
Es calidad comerciable *(f)*
Fr qualité vendable *(f)*
Pt qualidade comerciável *(f)*

qualità e contenuto sconosciuti It
De Qualität und Inhalt nicht bekannt
En quality and contents unknown
Es calidad del contenido desconocida
Fr qualité et contenu inconnus
Pt qualidade e conteúdo desconhecidos

Qualität *(f)* n De
En quality
Es calidad *(f)*
Fr qualité *(f)*
It qualità *(f)*
Pt qualidade *(f)*

Qualitätskontrolle *(f)* n De
En quality control
Es control de calidad *(m)*
Fr contrôle de qualité *(m)*
It controllo di qualità *(m)*
Pt controlo de qualidade *(m)*

Qualität und Inhalt nicht bekannt De
En quality and contents unknown
Es calidad del contenido desconocida
Fr qualité et contenu inconnus
It qualità e contenuto sconosciuti
Pt qualidade e conteúdo desconhecidos

qualité *(f)* n Fr
De Qualität *(f)*
En quality
Es calidad *(f)*
It qualità *(f)*
Pt qualidade *(f)*

qualité commerciale moyenne *(f)* Fr
De gute Durchschnittsqualität *(f)*
En fair average quality (faq)
Es calidad media razonable *(f)*
It buona qualità media *(f)*
Pt qualidade média razoável *(f)*

qualité et contenu inconnus Fr
De Qualität und Inhalt nicht bekannt
En quality and contents unknown
Es calidad del contenido desconocida
It qualità e contenuto sconosciuti
Pt qualidade e conteúdo desconhecidos

qualité vendable *(f)* Fr
De marktgängige Qualität *(f)*
En merchantable quality
Es calidad comerciable *(f)*
It qualità commerciable *(f)*
Pt qualidade comerciável *(f)*

quality n En
De Qualität *(f)*
Es calidad *(f)*
Fr qualité *(f)*
It qualità *(f)*
Pt qualidade *(f)*

quality and contents unknown En
De Qualität und Inhalt nicht bekannt
Es calidad del contenido desconocida
Fr qualité et contenu inconnus
It qualità e contenuto sconosciuti
Pt qualidade e conteúdo desconhecidos

quality control En
De Qualitätskontrolle *(f)*
Es control de calidad *(m)*
Fr contrôle de qualité *(m)*
It controllo di qualità *(m)*
Pt controlo de qualidade *(m)*

quantia *(f)* n Pt
De Betrag *(m)*
En amount
Es suma *(f)*
Fr somme *(f)*
It ammontare *(m)*

quantia nominal *(f)* Pt
De Nominalbetrag *(m)*
En nominal amount
Es suma nominal *(f)*
Fr montant nominal *(m)*
It importo nominale *(m)*

quantidade *(f)* n Pt
De Menge *(f)*
En quantity
Es cantidad *(f)*
Fr quantité *(f)*
It quantità *(f)*

quantità *(f)* n It
De Menge *(f)*
En quantity
Es cantidad *(f)*
Fr quantité *(f)*
Pt quantidade *(f)*

quantité *(f)* n Fr
De Menge *(f)*
En quantity
Es cantidad *(f)*
It quantità *(f)*
Pt quantidade *(f)*

quantity n En
De Menge *(f)*
Es cantidad *(f)*
Fr quantité *(f)*
It quantità *(f)*
Pt quantidade *(f)*

quantity surveyor En
De Massenberechner *(m)*
Es medidor de contidades de obra *(m)*
Fr métreur-vérificateur *(m)*
It perito misuratore *(m)*
Pt perito na avaliação de quantidades *(m)*

quarantaine *(f)* n Fr
De Quarantäne *(f)*
En quarantine
Es cuarentena *(f)*
It quarantena *(f)*
Pt quarentena *(f)*

Quarantäne *(f)* n De
En quarantine
Es cuarentena *(f)*
Fr quarantaine *(f)*
It quarantena *(f)*
Pt quarentena *(f)*

quarantena *(f)* n It
De Quarantäne *(f)*
En quarantine
Es cuarentena *(f)*
Fr quarantaine *(f)*
Pt quarentena *(f)*

quarantine n En
De Quarantäne *(f)*
Es cuarentena *(f)*
Fr quarantaine *(f)*
It quarantena *(f)*
Pt quarentena *(f)*

quarentena *(f)* n Pt
De Quarantäne *(f)*
En quarantine
Es cuarentena *(f)*
Fr quarantaine *(f)*
It quarantena *(f)*

Quartalstag *(m)* n De
En quarter day
Es primer día del trimestre *(m)*
Fr jour du terme *(m)*
It giorno della pigione *(m)*
Pt dia de vencimento trimestral *(m)*

quarter day En
De Quartalstag *(m)*
Es primer día del trimestre *(m)*
Fr jour du terme *(m)*
It giorno della pigione *(m)*
Pt dia de vencimento trimestral *(m)*

quarterly *adj* En
De vierteljährlich
Es trimestral
Fr trimestriel
It trimestrale
Pt trimestral

quarterly payments En
De vierteljährliche Zahlungen *(f pl)*
Es pagos trimestrales *(m pl)*
Fr paiements trimestriels *(m pl)*

It pagamenti trimestrali *(m pl)*
Pt pagamentos trimestrais *(m pl)*

quay n En
Am pier
De Kai *(m)*
Es muelle *(m)*
Fr quai *(m)*
It banchina *(f)*
Pt cais *(m)*

quayage *(m)* n Fr
De Kaigeld *(n)*
En wharfage
Es muellaje *(m)*
It diritto di sosta *(m)*
Pt atracagem *(f)*

quebrado *(m)* n Es
De Gemeinschuldner *(m)*
En bankrupt
Fr failli *(m)*
It fallito *(m)*
Pt falido *(m)*

questionario *(m)* n It
De Fragebogen *(m)*
En questionnaire
Es cuestionario *(m)*
Fr questionnaire *(m)*
Pt questionário *(m)*

questionário *(m)* n Pt
De Fragebogen *(m)*
En questionnaire
Es cuestionario *(m)*
Fr questionnaire *(m)*
It questionario *(m)*

questionnaire n En, Fr *(m)*
De Fragebogen *(m)*
Es cuestionario *(m)*
It questionario *(m)*
Pt questionário *(m)*

quiebra *(f)* n Es
De Konkurs *(m)*
En bankruptcy
Fr faillite *(f)*
It fallimento *(m)*
Pt falência *(f)*

quiebra de banco *(f)* Es
De Bankkrach *(m)*
En bank crash

Fr krach d'une banque *(m)*
It crollo di banca *(m)*
Pt falência bancária *(f)*

quietanza *(f)* n It
De Quittung *(f)*
En receipt; acquittance
Es recibo; satisfacción *(m f)*
Fr quittance *(f)*
Pt recibo; quitação *(m f)*

quietanza di darsena *(f)* It
De Dockempfangsschein *(m)*
En dock receipt
Es recibo de entrega en muelle *(m)*
Fr quittance de dock *(f)*
Pt recibo de doca *(m)*

quietanza finale *(f)* It
De Rechnungsentlastung *(f)*
En final discharge
Es finiquito *(m)*
Fr quitus *(m)*
Pt cumprimento final *(m)*

quincaillerie *(f)* n Fr
De Eisenwaren *(f pl)*
En hardware; ironmongery
Es ferretería; quincallería *(f)*
It ferramenta *(f)*
Pt ferragens *(f pl)*

quitação *(f)* n Pt
De Quittung *(f)*
En acquittance; discharge
Es finiquito *(m)*
Fr quittance *(f)*
It quietanza *(f)*

quittance n En, Fr *(f)*
De Quittung *(f)*
Es recibo *(m)*
It quietanza *(f)*
Pt recibo; quitação *(m f)*

quittance de dock *(f)* Fr
De Dockempfangsschein *(m)*
En dock receipt
Es recibo de entrega en muelle *(m)*
It quietanza di darsena *(f)*
Pt recibo de doca *(m)*

Quittung *(f)* n De
En receipt; acquittance
Es recibo; finiquito *(m)*
Fr quittance; acquit *(f m)*
It quietanza *(f)*
Pt recibo; quitação *(m f)*

quitus *(m)* n Fr
De Rechnungsentlastung *(f)*
En final discharge
Es finiquito *(m)*
It quietanza finale *(f)*
Pt cumprimento final *(m)*

quorum n En; Fr, It *(m)*
De beschlußfähige Anzahl *(f)*
Es quórum *(m)*
Pt quórum *(m)*

quórum *(m)* n Es, Pt
De beschlußfähige Anzahl *(f)*
En quorum
Fr quorum *(m)*
It quorum *(m)*

quota n En; It, Pt *(f)*
De Quote; Anteil *(f m)*
Es cuota *(f)*
Fr quote-part *(f)*

quota de importação *(f)* Pt
De Einfuhrkontingent *(n)*
En import quota
Es cupo de importación *(m)*
Fr contingent d'importation
(m)
It contingente d'importazio-
ne *(m)*

quota del mercato *(f)* It
De Marktanteil *(m)*
En market share
Es participación del mercado
(f)
Fr participation au marché *(f)*
Pt quota-parte no mercado
(f)

quota di ammortamento *(f)* It
De Abschreibung für Abnut-
zung *(f)*
En depreciation allowance
Es provisión por deprecia-
ción *(f)*
Fr provision pour amortisse-
ment *(f)*
Pt provisão para amortização
(f)

quota-parte *(f)* n Pt
De Quote; Anteil *(f m)*
En quota; share
Es cuota; parte *(f)*
Fr quote-part *(f)*
It quota; parte *(f)*

quota-parte no mercado *(f)*
Pt
De Marktanteil *(m)*
En market share
Es participación del mercado
(f)
Fr participation au marché *(f)*
It quota del mercato *(f)*

quotare vb It
De (den Preis) angeben
En quote
Es cotizar
Fr coter
Pt cotizar

quotare senza impegno It
De nicht fest anbieten
En quote not firm
Es cotizar sin compromiso
Fr coter sans obligation
Pt cotizar sem fixação de valor

quotation n En
De Kostenanschlag *(m)*
Es cotización *(f)*
Fr cotation *(f)*
It quotazione *(f)*
Pt cotação *(f)*

quotazione di borsa *(f)* It
De Börsenkurs *(m)*
En stock-exchange quota-
tion
Es curso de bolsa *(m)*
Fr cours de bourse *(m)*
Pt cotação da bolsa *(f)*

quotazione *(f)* n It
De Kostenanschlag *(m)*
En quotation
Es cotización *(f)*
Fr cotation *(f)*
Pt cotação *(f)*

quote vb En
De (den Preis) angeben
Es cotizar
Fr coter
It quotare
Pt cotizar

Quote *(f)* n De
En quota
Es cuota *(f)*
Fr quote-part *(f)*
It quota *(f)*
Pt cota; quota-parte *(f)*

quoted company En
De Gesellschaft notiert an der
Börse *(f)*
Es compañía cotizada en
bolsa *(f)*
Fr société cotée à la Bourse
(f)
It società quotata in borsa *(f)*
Pt companhia cotizada *(f)*

quoted price En
De angegebener Preis *(m)*
Es precio cotizado *(m)*
Fr prix coté *(m)*
It prezzo quotato *(m)*
Pt preço cotizado *(m)*

quote not firm En
De nicht fest anbieten
Es cotizar sin compromiso
Fr coter sans obligation
It quotare senza impegno
Pt cotizar sem fixação de valor

quote-part *(f)* n Fr
De Quote; Anteil *(f m)*
En quota; share
Es cuota; parte *(f)*
It quota; parte *(f)*
Pt cota; quota-parte *(f)*

quotient cours-bénéfice *(m)*
Fr
De Verhältnis des Aktienkur-
ses zum Reingewinn *(n)*
En price-earnings ratio (P/E)
Es proporción precio-ingre-
sos *(f)*
It rapporto prezzo-utile *(m)*
Pt taxa custo-ganhos *(f)*

R

rabais *(m)* n Fr
De Nachlaß; Rabatt *(m)*
En rebate; allowance
Es rebaja; bonificación *(f)*
It ribasso; abbuono *(m)*
Pt desconto; provisão *(m f)*

rabais de demi-gros *(m)* Fr
De Händlerrabatt *(m)*
En trade discount
Es descuento comercial *(m)*
It sconto di rivendita *(m)*
Pt desconto à praça *(m)*

rabais des prix *(m)* Fr
De Preisherabsetzung *(f)*
En price-cutting
Es reducción de precios *(f)*
It riduzione dei prezzi *(f)*
Pt redução de preços *(f)*

rabais différé *(m)* Fr
De nachträglicher Umsatzbo-
nus *(m)*
En deferred rebate
Es descuento diferido *(m)*
It sconto differito *(m)*
Pt dedução adiada *(f)*

Rabatt *(m) n* De
En rebate; allowance
Es rebaja; bonificación *(f)*
Fr rabais *(m)*
It ribasso; abbuono *(m)*
Pt desconto; provisão *(m f)*

ração *(f) n* Pt
De Ration *(f)*
En ration
Es ración *(f)*
Fr ration *(f)*
It razione *(f)*

raccolta dati *(f)* It
De Datenerfassung *(f)*
En data capture
Es recogida de datos *(f)*
Fr saisie des données *(f)*
Pt recolha de dados *(f)*

raccolto *(m) n* It
De Ernte *(f)*
En harvest
Es cosecha *(f)*
Fr moisson; récolte *(f)*
Pt colheita *(f)*

ración *(f) n* Es
De Ration *(f)*
En ration
Fr ration *(f)*
It razione *(f)*
Pt ração *(f)*

racionalização *(f) n* Pt
De Rationalisierung *(f)*
En rationalization
Es racionalización *(f)*
Fr rationalisation *(f)*
It razionalizzazione *(f)*

racionalización *(f) n* Es
De Rationalisierung *(f)*
En rationalization
Fr rationalisation *(f)*
It razionalizzazione *(f)*
Pt racionalização *(f)*

ragioniere capo *(m)* It
De Oberbuchhalter *(m)*
En chief accountant
Es jefe de contabilidad *(m)*
Fr chef comptable *(m)*
Pt chefe contabilista *(m)*

ragioniere diplomato *(m)* It
De Wirtschaftsprüfer *(m)*
En qualified accountant
Es contador habilitado *(m)*
Fr expert comptable *(m)*
Pt guarda-livros diplomado
(m)

railway *n* En
De Eisenbahn *(f)*
Es ferrocarril *(m)*
Fr chemin de fer *(m)*
It ferrovia *(f)*
Pt caminho de ferro *(m)*

railway carriage En
Am railroad car
De Eisenbahnwagen *(m)*
Es vagón de ferrocarril *(m)*
Fr wagon de chemin de fer
(m)
It carrozza ferroviaria *(f)*
Pt vagão de caminhos de ferro
(m)

railway receipt En
De Bahnfrachtbrief *(m)*
Es recibo ferroviario *(m)*
Fr bulletin de chargement *(m)*
It ricevuta ferroviaria *(f)*
Pt recibo ferroviário *(m)*

railway timetable En
De Eisenbahnfahrplan *(m)*
Es horario de trenes *(m)*
Fr indicateur des chemins de
fer *(m)*
It orario ferroviario *(m)*
Pt horário de caminhos de
ferro *(m)*

raise a loan Am
En float a loan
De eine Anleihe begeben

Es emitir un empréstito
Fr émettre un emprunt
It lanciare un prestito
Pt lançar um empréstimo

raison sociale *(f)* Fr
De Firmenname *(m)*
En trade name
Es razón social *(f)*
It denominazione commer-
ciale *(f)*
Pt razão comercial *(f)*

raisons supplémentaires
(f pl) Fr
De weitere Gründe *(m pl)*
En further reasons
Es rasones adicionales *(f pl)*
It ulteriori motivi *(m pl)*
Pt razões adicionais *(f pl)*

Randanalyse *(f) n* De
En marginal analysis
Es análisis marginal *(m)*
Fr analyse marginale *(f)*
It analisi marginale *(f)*
Pt análise marginal *(f)*

Randkosten *(pl) n* De
En marginal cost
Es coste marginal *(m)*
Fr coût marginal *(m)*
It costo marginale *(m)*
Pt custo marginal *(m)*

random sample En
De Stichprobe *(f)*
Es muestra aleatoria *(f)*
Fr épreuve au hasard *(f)*
It campione a casaccio *(m)*
Pt amostra avulsa *(f)*

ranimer l'économie Fr
De die Wirtschaft neu beleben
En reflate the economy
Es reanimar la economía
It ravvivare l'economia
Pt reflacionar a economia

rappel de traitement *(m)* Fr
De Lohnnachzahlung *(f)*
En back pay
Es pago atrasado *(m)*
It arretrati di paga *(m pl)*
Pt vencimento atrasado *(m)*

rapport *(m) n* Fr
De Bericht; Verhältnis *(m n)*
En report; relation
Es informe; relación *(m f)*
It relazione; rapporto *(f m)*
Pt relatório; razão *(m f)*

rapport annuel *(m)* Fr
De Jahresbericht *(m)*
En annual report
Es memoria anual *(f)*
It relazione annuale *(f)*
Pt relatório anual *(m)*

rapport des administra-
teurs *(m)* Fr
De Vorstandsbericht *(m)*
En directors'report
Es informe de la administra-
ción *(m)*
It relazione degli amministra-
tori *(f)*
Pt relatório de directores *(m)*

rapport des vérificateurs
des comptes *(m)* Fr
De Bericht des Abschlußprü-
fers *(m)*
En auditor's report
Es informe de los intervento-
res *(m)*
It relazione dei sindaci *(f)*
Pt relatório do fiscal de con-
tas *(m)*

rapporto *(m) n* It
De Verhältnis *(n)*
En ratio
Es razón; relación *(f)*
Fr rapport *(m)*
Pt razão *(f)*

rapporto prezzo-utile *(m)* It
De Verhältnis des Aktienkur-
ses zum Reingewinn *(n)*
En price-earnings ratio (P/E)
Es proporción precio-ingre-
sos *(f)*
Fr quotient cours-bénéfice
(m)
Pt taxa custo-ganhos *(f)*

rapports du travail *(m pl)* Fr
De Arbeitsverhältnisse *(n pl)*
En labour relations
Es relaciones patrón-obrero
(f pl)
It relazioni con la mano
d'opera *(f pl)*
Pt relações de trabalho *(f pl)*

rappresentante *(m) n* It
De Vertreter *(m)*
En representative
Es representante *(m)*
Fr représentant *(m)*
Pt representante *(m)*

rappresentante esclusivo
(m) It
De Alleinvertreter *(m)*
En sole agent
Es agente exclusivo *(m)*
Fr agent exclusif *(m)*
Pt agente exclusivo *(m)*

rappresentare *vb* It
De vertreten
En represent
Es representar
Fr représenter
Pt representar

rascunho *(m) n* Pt
De Konzept *(n)*
En draft
Es borrador *(m)*
Fr projet *(m)*
It bozza *(f)*

rasones adicionales *(f pl)* Es
De weitere Gründe *(m pl)*
En further reasons
Fr raisons supplémentaires
(f pl)
It ulteriori motivi *(m pl)*
Pt razões adicionais *(f pl)*

rassegnare le dimissioni It
De den Rücktritt einreichen
En hand in one's resignation
Es presentar la dimisión
Fr remettre sa démission
Pt apresentar demissão

rate *(f) n* It
De Rate *(f)*
En instalment
Es plazo *(m)*
Fr acompte *(m)*
Pt prestação *(f)*

rate *n* En
De Satz; Kurs *(m)*
Es tasa; tipo *(f m)*
Fr taux; cours *(m)*
It tasso; tariffa *(m f)*
Pt taxa *(f)*

Rate *(f) n* De
En instalment
Es plazo *(m)*
Fr acompte *(m)*
It rata *(f)*
Pt prestação *(f)*

Ratenkauf *(m) n* De
En hire-purchase
Es compra a plazos *(f)*
Fr location-vente; vente à
tempérament *(f)*
It vendita a rate *(f)*
Pt venda a prestações *(f)*

Ratenzahlung *(f) n* De
En part payment
Es pago parcial *(m)*
Fr paiement partiel *(m)*
It pagamento parziale *(m)*
Pt pagamento parcial *(m)*

rate of exchange En
De Umrechnungskurs *(m)*
Es tipo de cambio *(m)*
Fr cours de change *(m)*
It corso del cambio *(m)*
Pt taxa de câmbio *(f)*

rate of interest En
De Zinsfuß *(m)*
Es tipo de interés *(m)*
Fr taux d'intérêt *(m)*
It tasso d'interesse *(m)*
Pt taxa de juro *(f)*

rate of return En
De Ertragsrate *(f)*
Es tipo de rédito *(m)*
Fr taux de rendement *(m)*
It tasso di reddito *(m)*
Pt taxa de rendimento *(f)*

rates *pl n* En
Am realty tax
De Gemeindesteuer *(f)*
Es contribución municipal *(f)*
Fr taxes municipales *(f pl)*
It tassa comunale *(f)*
Pt contribuições municipais
(f pl)

ratifica *(f) n* It
De Ratifizierung *(f)*
En ratification
Es ratificación *(f)*
Fr ratification *(f)*
Pt ratificação *(f)*

ratificação *(f)* n Pt
De Ratifizierung *(f)*
En ratification
Es ratificación *(f)*
Fr ratification *(f)*
It ratifica *(f)*

ratificación *(f)* n Es
De Ratifizierung *(f)*
En ratification
Fr ratification *(f)*
It ratifica *(f)*
Pt ratificação *(f)*

ratificar *vb* Es, Pt
De ratifizieren
En ratify
Fr ratifier
It ratificare

ratificare *vb* It
De ratifizieren
En ratify
Es ratificar
Fr ratifier
Pt ratificar

ratification n En, Fr *(f)*
De Ratifizierung *(f)*
Es ratificación *(f)*
It ratifica *(f)*
Pt ratificação *(f)*

ratifier *vb* Fr
De ratifizieren
En ratify
Es ratificar
It ratificare
Pt ratificar

ratifizieren *vb* De
En ratify
Es ratificar
Fr ratifier
It ratificare
Pt ratificar

Ratifizierung *(f)* n De
En ratification
Es ratificación *(f)*
Fr ratification *(f)*
It ratifica *(f)*
Pt ratificação *(f)*

ratify *vb* En
De ratifizieren
Es ratificar
Fr ratifier
It ratificare
Pt ratificar

ratio n En
De Verhältnis *(n)*
Es razón; relación *(f)*
Fr rapport *(m)*
It rapporto *(m)*
Pt razão *(f)*

ration n En, Fr *(f)*
De Ration *(f)*
Es ración *(f)*
It razione *(f)*
Pt ração *(f)*

Ration *(f)* n De
En ration
Es ración *(f)*
Fr ration *(f)*
It razione *(f)*
Pt ração *(f)*

rationalisation *(f)* n Fr
De Rationalisierung *(f)*
En rationalization
Es racionalización *(f)*
It razionalizzazione *(f)*
Pt racionalização *(f)*

Rationalisierung *(f)* n De
En rationalization
Es racionalización *(f)*
Fr rationalisation *(f)*
It razionalizzazione *(f)*
Pt racionalização *(f)*

rationalization n En
De Rationalisierung *(f)*
Es racionalización *(f)*
Fr rationalisation *(f)*
It razionalizzazione *(f)*
Pt racionalização *(f)*

ravvivare l'economia It
De die Wirtschaft neu beleben
En reflate the economy
Es reanimar la economía
Fr ranimer l'économie
Pt reflacionar a economia

raw material En
De Rohstoff *(m)*
Es materia prima *(f)*
Fr matière première *(f)*
It materia prima *(f)*
Pt matéria prima *(f)*

rayer *vb* Fr
De streichen
En delete
Es tachar; anular

It cancellare
Pt cortar; riscar

razão *(f)* n Pt
De Grund; Verhältnis *(m n)*
En reason; ratio
Es razón; relación *(f)*
Fr raison; rapport *(f m)*
It ragione; rapporto *(f m)*

razão comercial *(f)* Pt
De Firmenname *(m)*
En trade name
Es razón social *(f)*
Fr raison sociale *(f)*
It denominazione commer-
     ciale *(f)*

razionalizzazione *(f)* n It
De Rationalisierung *(f)*
En rationalization
Es racionalización *(f)*
Fr rationalisation *(f)*
Pt racionalização *(f)*

razione *(f)* n It
De Ration *(f)*
En ration
Es ración *(f)*
Fr ration *(f)*
Pt ração *(f)*

razões adicionais *(f pl)* Pt
De weitere Gründe *(m pl)*
En further reasons
Es rasones adicionales *(f pl)*
Fr raisons supplémentaires
     (f pl)
It ulteriori motivi *(m pl)*

razón *(f)* n Es
De Verhältnis *(n)*
En ratio
Fr proportion *(f)*
It rapporto *(m)*
Pt razão *(f)*

razón social *(f)* Es
De Firmenname *(m)*
En trade name
Fr raison sociale *(f)*
It denominazione commer-
     ciale *(f)*
Pt razão comercial *(f)*

reabrir discussões Pt
De Verhandlungen wieder-
     aufnehmen
En re-open discussions
Es reabrir la discusión

Fr rouvrir la discussion
It riaprire la discussione

reabrir la discusión Es
De Verhandlungen wieder-
    aufnehmen
En re-open discussions
Fr rouvrir la discussion
It riaprire la discussione
Pt reabrir discussões

réacteur *(m)* n Fr
De Düsenmotor *(m)*
En jet engine
Es motor de propulsión a
    chorro *(m)*
It motore a reazione *(m)*
Pt motor a jacto *(m)*

real estate En
De unbewegliches Vermögen;
    Immobilien *(n; f pl)*
Es bienes inmuebles *(m pl)*
Fr biens immeubles *(m pl)*
It beni immobili *(m pl)*
Pt propriedade imobiliária *(f)*

real estate agency Am
En estate agency
De Immobilienbüro *(n)*
Es correduría de fincas *(f)*
Fr agence immobilière *(f)*
It agenzia immobiliare *(f)*
Pt agência de propriedades
    (f)

realização dos lucros *(f)* Pt
De Gewinnrealisation *(f)*
En profit-taking
Es realización de utilidades *(f)*
Fr prise de bénéfices *(f)*
It realizzazione dell'utile *(f)*

realización de utilidades *(f)*
    Es
De Gewinnrealisation *(f)*
En profit-taking
Fr prise de bénéfices *(f)*
It realizzazione dell'utile *(f)*
Pt realização dos lucros *(f)*

realizzazione dell'utile *(f)* It
De Gewinnrealisation *(f)*
En profit-taking
Es realización de utilidades *(f)*
Fr prise de bénéfices *(f)*
Pt realização dos lucros *(f)*

realty tax Am
En rates
De Gemeindesteuer *(f)*
Es contribución municipal *(f)*
Fr taxes municipales *(f pl)*
It tassa comunale *(f)*
Pt contribuições municipais
    (f pl)

reanimar la economía Es
De die Wirtschaft neu beleben
En reflate the economy
Fr ranimer l'économie
It ravvivare economia
Pt reflacionar a economia

reaseguro *(m)* n Es
De Rückversicherung *(f)*
En reinsurance
Fr réassurance *(f)*
It riassicurazione *(f)*
Pt re-seguro *(m)*

réassurance *(f)* n Fr
De Rückversicherung *(f)*
En reinsurance
Es reaseguro *(m)*
It riassicurazione *(f)*
Pt re-seguro *(m)*

rebaja *(f)* n Es
De Nachlaß; Rabatt *(m)*
En rebate
Fr rabais *(m)*
It ribasso; sconto *(m)*
Pt desconto *(m)*

rebate n En
De Nachlaß; Rabatt *(m)*
Es rebaja *(f)*
Fr rabais *(m)*
It ribasso; sconto *(m)*
Pt desconto *(m)*

rebocador *(m)* n Pt
De Schleppdampfer *(m)*
En tug-boat
Es remolcador *(m)*
Fr remorqueur *(m)*
It rimorchiatore *(m)*

rebusca de información *(f)*
    Es
De Informationswiederge-
    winnung *(f)*
En information retrieval

Fr récupération de données
    (f)
It ricupero d'informazioni *(m)*
Pt recuperação de informação
    (f)

recaudador de impuestos
    (m) Es
De Steuereinnehmer *(m)*
En tax collector
Fr percepteur des impôts *(m)*
It esattore delle imposte *(m)*
Pt cobrador de impostos *(m)*

recaudar vb Es
De einkassieren
En collect
Fr encaisser
It incassare
Pt cobrar

recaudar una deuda Es
De Schulden eintreiben
En collect a debt
Fr recouvrer une créance
It incassare un credito
Pt cobrar uma dívida

**recebido para
    carregamento** Pt
De zur Absendung empfan-
    gen
En received for shipment
Es recibido para envío
Fr reçu pour envoi
It ricevuto per caricazione

receipt n En
De Quittung *(f)*
Es recibo *(m)*
Fr quittance; acquit *(f m)*
It ricevuta *(f)*
Pt recibo *(m)*

receita *(f)* n Pt
De Einkommen *(n)*
En income
Es ingresos; renta *(m pl; f)*
Fr revenu *(m)*
It reddito *(m)*

receita bruta *(f)* Pt
De Bruttoeinkommen *(n)*
En gross income
Es ingreso bruto *(m)*
Fr rendement brut *(m)*
It reddito lordo *(m)*

receita de trabalho (f) Pt
De Arbeitseinkommen (n)
En earned income
Es renta del trabajo (f)
Fr revenu du travail (m)
It reddito di lavoro (m)

receita disponível (f) Pt
De verfügbares Einkommen
(n)
En disponable income
Es renta disponible (f)
Fr revenu disponible (m)
It reddito disponibile (m)

receita líquida (f) Pt
De Nettoeinkommen (n)
En net income
Es ingreso neto (f)
Fr revenu net (m)
It reddito netto (m)

receita não tributável (f) Pt
De steuerfreies Einkommen
(n)
En nontaxable income
Es renta no imponible (f)
Fr revenu non imposable (m)
It reddito non tassabile (m)

receita pública (f) Pt
De Nationaleinkommen (n)
En national income
Es renta nacional (f)
Fr revenu national (m)
It reddito nazionale (m)

receita tributável (f) Pt
De steuerpflichtiges Einkom-
men (n)
En taxable income
Es renta imponible (f)
Fr revenu imposable (m)
It reddito tassabile (m)

received for shipment En
De zur Absendung empfan-
gen
Es recibido para envío
Fr reçu pour envoi
It ricevuto per caricazione
Pt recebido para carrega-
mento

receiver (in bankruptcy) n En
De Konkursverwalter (m)
Es sindico (m)

Fr syndic de faillite (m)
It curatore (m)
Pt síndico (m)

recensement (m) n Fr
De Volkszählung (f)
En census
Es censo (m)
It censimento (m)
Pt censo (m)

récépissé de dépôt (m) Fr
De Depositenschein (m)
En deposit receipt
Es recibo de depósito (m)
It certificato di deposito (m)
Pt recibo de depósito (m)

**récépissé de poste
aérienne** (m) Fr
De Luftpostempfangsbe-
scheinigung (f)
En airmail receipt
Es recibo aeropostal (m)
It ricevimento per posta ae-
rea (m)
Pt recibo de via aérea (m)

recesión (f) n Es
De Rezession (f)
En recession
Fr récession (f)
It recessione (f)
Pt recessão (f)

recessão (f) n Pt
De Rezession (f)
En recession
Es recesión (f)
Fr récession (f)
It recessione (f)

recession n En
De Rezession (f)
Es recesión (f)
Fr récession (f)
It recessione (f)
Pt recessão (f)

récession (f) n Fr
De Rezession (f)
En recession
Es recesión (f)
It recessione (f)
Pt recessão (f)

recessione (f) n It
De Rezession (f)
En recession
Es recesión (f)
Fr récession (f)
Pt recessão (f)

recettes nettes (f pl) Fr
De Nettoeinnahmen (f pl)
En net revenue
Es ingresos netos (m pl)
It entrata netta (f)
Pt receita líquida (f)

rechazar una reclamación
Es
De einen Ersatzanspruch
nicht anerkennen
En repudiate a claim
Fr renier un sinistre
It respingere un reclamo
Pt repudiar uma reclamação

rechazo (m) n Es
De Nichtannahme; Ablehnung
(f)
En nonacceptance; rejection
Fr non-acceptation; refus (f
m)
It mancata accettazione; ri-
fiuto (f m)
Pt não-aceitação; rejeicão (f)

Rechenfehler (m) n De
En miscalculation
Es cálculo erróneo (m)
Fr erreur de calcul (f)
It calcolo errato (m)
Pt erro de cálculo (m)

Rechenmaschine (f) n De
En calculator
Es calculadora (f)
Fr machine à calculer (f)
It calcolatrice (f)
Pt máquina de calcular (f)

recherche (f) n Fr
De Forschung (f)
En research
Es investigación (f)
It ricerca (f)
Pt investigação (f)

recherche industrielle (f) Fr
De Zweckforschung; For-
schung und Entwick-
lung (F&E) (f)
En research and development
(R & D)
Es investigación y desarrollo
It studi e sviluppi
Pt investigação e desenvolvi-
mento

recherche opérationnelle (f)
Fr
De Unternehmensforschung
(f)
En operational research (OR)
Es investigación operacional
(f)
It indagine sul funzionamen-
to (f)
Pt investigação operacional (f)

Rechner (m) n De
En computer
Es computadora (f)
Fr ordinateur (m)
It elaboratore; calcolatore
(m)
Pt computador (m)

Rechnersprache (f) n De
En computer language
Es lenguaje de computadoras
(m)
Fr langage-machine (m)
It linguaggio macchina (m)
Pt linguagem de computador
(f)

Rechnung (f) n De
En bill; account
Es cuenta; nota (f)
Fr compte; note (m f)
It conto; nota (m f)
Pt conta (f)

Rechnungsentlastung (f) n
De
En final discharge
Es finiquito (m)
Fr quitus (m)
It quietanza finale (f)
Pt cumprimento final (m)

Rechnungsprüfer (m) n De
En comptroller
Es interventor (m)

Fr vérificateur des comptes
(m)
It controllore (m)
Pt controlador (m)

Recht (n) n De
En law; right
Es ley; derecho (f m)
Fr loi; droit (f m)
It legge; diritto (f m)
Pt lei; direito (f m)

Rechtsfall (m) n De
En (legal) case
Es causa (f)
Fr procès (m)
It causa (f)
Pt causa (f)

rechtsgültig adj De
En legal
Es legal
Fr légal
It legale
Pt legal

Rechtshaftung (f) n De
En legal liability
Es responsabilidad legal (f)
Fr responsabilité légale (f)
It responsabilità legale (f)
Pt responsabilidade legal (f)

Rechtsprechung (f) n De
En jurisdiction
Es jurisdicción (f)
Fr juridiction (f)
It giurisdizione (f)
Pt jurisdição (f)

Rechtsvertreter (m) n De
En legal representative
Es representante legal (m)
Fr représentant mandaté (m)
It mandatario (m)
Pt representante legal (m)

recht und billig De
En fair
Es razonable
Fr équitable
It equo
Pt razoável

recibido para envío Es
De zur Absendung empfan-
gen
En received for shipment
Fr reçu pour envoi

It ricevuto per caricazione
Pt recebido para carrega-
mento

recibo (m) n Es, Pt
De Quittung (f)
En receipt
Fr quittance; acquit (f m)
It ricevuta (f)

recibo aeropostal (m) Es
De Luftpostempfangsbe-
scheinigung (f)
En airmail receipt
Fr récépissé de poste
aérienne (m)
It ricevimento per posta ae-
rea (m)
Pt recibo de via aérea (m)

recibo de depósito (m) Es, Pt
De Depositenschein (m)
En deposit receipt
Fr récépissé de dépôt (m)
It certificato di desposito (m)

recibo de doca (m) Pt
De Dockempfangsschein (m)
En dock receipt
Es recibo de entrega en muel-
le (m)
Fr quittance de dock (f)
It quietanza di darsena (f)

recibo de embarco (m) Es
De Übernahmebescheinigung
(f)
En mate's receipt
Fr billet de bord (m)
It ricevuta d'imbarco (f)
Pt recibo de embarque (m)

recibo de embarque (m) Pt
De Übernahmebescheinigung
(f)
En mate's receipt
Es recibo de embarco (m)
Fr billet de bord (m)
It ricevuta d'imbarco (f)

recibo de entrega en muelle
(m) Es
De Dockempfangsschein (m)
En dock receipt
Fr quittance de dock (f)
It quietanza di darsena (f)
Pt recibo de doca (m)

recibo de via aérea (m) Pt
De Luftpostempfangsbe-
scheinigung (f)
En airmail receipt
Es recibo aeropostal (m)
Fr récépissé de poste
aérienne (m)
It ricevimento per posta ae-
rea (m)

recibo ferroviario (m) Es
De Bahnfrachtbrief (m)
En railway receipt
Fr bulletin de chargement (m)
It ricevuta ferroviaria (f)
Pt recibo ferroviário (m)

recibo ferroviário (m) Pt
De Bahnfrachtbrief (m)
En railway receipt
Es recibo ferroviario (m)
Fr bulletin de chargement (m)
It ricevuta ferroviaria (f)

reclamação (f) n Pt
De Anspruch (m)
En claim
Es reclamación (f)
Fr réclamation (f)
It reclamo (m)

reclamação de seguro (f) Pt
De Versicherungsanspruch
(m)
En insurance claim
Es reclamación de seguro (f)
Fr indemnité d'assurance (f)
It sinistro; reclamo d'inden-
nizzo (m)

reclamación (f) n Es
De Anspruch (m)
En claim
Fr réclamation (f)
It reclamo (m)
Pt reclamação (f)

reclamación de salario (f) Es
De Lohnforderung (f)
En wage claim
Fr revendication de salaire (f)
It rivendicazione salariale (f)
Pt demanda de salário (f)

reclamación de seguro (f) Es
De Versicherungsanspruch
(m)
En insurance claim
Fr indemnité d'assurance (f)

It sinistro; reclamo d'indennizzo (m)
Pt reclamação de seguro (f)

réclamation (f) n Fr
De Anspruch (m)
En claim
Es reclamación (f)
It reclamo (m)
Pt reclamação (f)

reclamo (m) n It
De Anspruch (m)
En claim
Es reclamación (f)
Fr réclamation; créance (f)
Pt reclamação (f)

recoger una letra Es
De einen Wechsel einlösen
En retire a bill
Fr payer une lettre de change
It ritirare un effetto
Pt recuperar una letra

recogida de datos (f) Es
De Datenerfassung (f)
En data capture
Fr saisie des données (f)
It raccolta dati (f)
Pt recolha de dados (f)

recolha de dados (f) Pt
De Datenerfassung (f)
En data capture
Es recogida de datos (f)
Fr saisie des données (f)
It raccolta dati (f)

recolte (f) n Fr
De Ernte (f)
En harvest
Es cosecha (f)
It raccolto (m)
Pt colheita (f)

**recommended retail selling
price** En
De empfohlener Ladenpreis
(m)
Es precio detallista recomendado (m)
Fr prix de détail racommandé
(m)
It prezzo al minuto indicativo
(m)
Pt preço de venda a retalho
recomendado (m)

reconnaissance de dette (f)
Fr
De Schuldschein (m)
En I.O.U. (I owe you)
Es pagaré (m)
It pagherò (m)
Pt vale (m)

reconstrução (f) n Pt
De Wiederaufbau (m)
En reconstruction
Es reconstrucción (f)
Fr reconstruction (f)
It ricostruzione (f)

reconstrucción (f) n Es
De Wiederaufbau (m)
En reconstruction
Fr reconstruction (f)
It ricostruzione (f)
Pt reconstrução (f)

reconstruction n En, Fr (f)
De Wiederaufbau (m)
Es reconstrucción (f)
It ricostruzione (f)
Pt reconstrução (f)

recorrer a reservas Pt
De die Reserven angreifen
En draw on reserves
Es sacar reservas
Fr prélever sur les réserves
It prelevare dalle riserve

recouvrer une créance Fr
De Schulden eintreiben
En collect a debt
Es recaudar una deuda
It incassare un credito
Pt cobrar uma dívida

recuperação de informação (f)
Pt
De Informationswiedergе-
winnung (f)
En information retrieval
Es rebusca de información (f)
Fr récupération de données
(f)
It ricupero d'informazioni (m)

recuperar uma letra Pt
De einen Wechsel einlösen
En retire a bill
Es recoger una letra
Fr payer une lettre de change
It ritirare un effetto

récupération de données (f)
Fr
De Informationswiedergewinnung (f)
En information retrieval
Es rebusca de información (f)
It ricupero d'informazioni (m)
Pt recuperação de informação (f)

reçu pour envoi Fr
De zur Absendung empfangen
En received for shipment
Es recibido para envío
It ricevuto per caricazione
Pt recebido para carregamento

red (f) n Es
De Netz (n)
En network
Fr réseau (m)
It rete (f)
Pt rede (f)

redactar un contrato Es
De einen Vertrag formulieren
En draw up a contract
Fr rédiger un contrat
It redigere un contratto
Pt redigir um contrato

redditività (f) n It
De Rentabilität (f)
En profitability
Es rentabilidad (f)
Fr rentabilité (f)
Pt rentabilidade (f)

reddito (m) n It
De Einkommen; Rendite (n f)
En income; yield
Es ingresos; rédito (m pl; m)
Fr revenu (m)
Pt receita; rédito (f m)

reddito degli investimenti (m) It
De Einkommen aus Kapitalanlagen (n)
En investment income
Es renta de inversiones (f)
Fr revenu de placements (m)
Pt rendimento de capitais investidos (m)

reddito del capitale (m) It
De Kapitalertrag (m)
En return on capital; unearned income
Es beneficio sobre capital (m)
Fr rémunération du capital (f)
Pt juro sobre o capital (m)

reddito di lavoro (m) It
De Arbeitseinkommen (n)
En earned income
Es renta del trabajo (f)
Fr revenu du travail (m)
Pt receita de trabalho (f)

reddito disponibile (m) It
De verfügbares Einkommen (n)
En disposable income
Es renta disponible (f)
Fr revenu disponible (m)
Pt receita disponível (f)

reddito lordo (m) It
De Bruttoeinkommen (n)
En gross income
Es ingreso bruto (m)
Fr rendement brut (m)
Pt receita bruta (f)

reddito nazionale (m) It
De Nationaleinkommen (n)
En national income
Es renta nacional (f)
Fr revenu national (m)
Pt receita pública (f)

reddito netto (m) It
De Nettoeinkommen (n)
En net income
Es ingreso neto (f)
Fr revenu net (m)
Pt receita líquida (f)

reddito non tassabile (m) It
De steuerfreies Einkommen (n)
En nontaxable income
Es ingresos no imponibles (m pl)
Fr revenu non imposable (m)
Pt receita não tributável (f)

reddito tassabile (m) It
De steuerpflichtiges Einkommen (n)
En taxable income

Es renta imponible (f)
Fr revenu imposable (m)
Pt receita tributável (f)

rede (f) n Pt
De Netz (n)
En network
Es red (f)
Fr réseau (m)
It rete (f)

redeem vb En
De tilgen; gutmachen
Es redimir; rescatar
Fr rembourser; dégager
It redimere; rimborsare
Pt remir; resgatar

redeemable bond En
De kündbare Obligation (f)
Es obligación reembolsable (f)
Fr obligation amortissable (f)
It obbligazione redimibile (f)
Pt obrigação reembolsável (f)

redemption n En
De Tilgung; Amortisation (f)
Es amortización (f)
Fr amortissement; remboursement (m)
It ammortamento (m)
Pt amortização (f)

redemption date En
De Einlösungstag (m)
Es fecha de reembolso (f)
Fr date du remboursement (f)
It data di rimborso (f)
Pt data de resgate (f)

redemption yield En
De Einlösungsertrag (m)
Es rédito de reembolso (m)
Fr rendement sur remboursement (m)
It rendita di rimborso (f)
Pt rendimento de resgate (m)

redevable adj Fr
De verbunden
En indebted
Es endeudado
It indebitato
Pt endividado

507

redevance *(f)* n Fr
De Tantieme; Miete *(f)*
En royalty; rental
Es derechos; alquiler *(m pl; m)*
It diritti; affitto *(m pl; m)*
Pt direitos; renda *(m pl; f)*

redigere un contratto It
De einen Vertrag formulieren
En draw up a contract
Es redactar un contrato
Fr rédiger un contrat
Pt redigir um contrato

rédiger un contrat Fr
De einen Vertrag formulieren
En draw up a contract
Es redactar un contrato
It redigere un contratto
Pt redigir um contrato

redigir um contrato Pt
De einen Vertrag formulieren
En draw up a contract
Es redactar un contrato
Fr rédiger un contrat
It redigere un contratto

redimere *vb* It
De tilgen; gutmachen
En redeem
Es redimir; rescatar
Fr rembourser; dégager
Pt remir; resgatar

redimir *vb* Es, Pt
De tilgen; gutmachen
En redeem
Fr rembourser; dégager
It redimere; rimborsare

rédito *(m)* n Es, Pt
De Rendite *(f)*
En yield; return
Fr revenu *(m)*
It reddito *(m)*

rédito de reembolso *(m)* Es
De Einlösungsertrag *(m)*
En redemption yield
Fr rendement sur rembour-
 sement *(m)*
It rendita di rimborso *(f)*
Pt rendimento de resgate *(m)*

rédito neto *(m)* Es
De Reinerlös *(m)*
En net proceeds

Fr produit net *(m)*
It ricavo netto *(m)*
Pt proventos líquidos *(m pl)*

redução de capital *(f)* Pt
De Kapitalherabsetzung *(f)*
En reduction of capital
Es reducción de capital *(f)*
Fr réduction de capital *(f)*
It riduzione del capitale *(f)*

redução de preços *(f)* Pt
De Preisherabsetzung *(f)*
En price-cutting
Es reducción de precios *(f)*
Fr rabais des prix *(m)*
It riduzione dei prezzi *(f)*

reducción de capital *(f)* Es
De Kapitalherabsetzung *(f)*
En reduction of capital
Fr réduction de capital *(f)*
It riduzione del capitale *(f)*
Pt redução de capital *(f)*

reducción de precios *(f)* Es
De Preisherabsetzung *(f)*
En price-cutting
Fr rabais des prix *(m)*
It riduzione dei prezzi *(f)*
Pt redução de preços *(f)*

réduction de capital *(f)* Fr
De Kapitalherabsetzung *(f)*
En reduction of capital
Es reducción de capital *(f)*
It riduzione del capitale *(f)*
Pt redução de capital *(f)*

reduction of capital En
De Kapitalherabsetzung *(f)*
Es reducción de capital *(f)*
Fr réduction de capital *(f)*
It riduzione del capitale *(f)*
Pt redução de capital *(f)*

Reederei *(f)* n De
En shipping line
Es compañia navièra *(f)*
Fr compagnie de navigation
 (f)
It società di navigazione *(f)*
Pt companhia de navegação
 (f)

reembolso *(m)* n Es, Pt
De Rückerstattung *(f)*
En refund
Fr remboursement *(m)*
It rimborso *(m)*

**reembolso de derechos de
 aduana** *(m)* Es
De Zollrückvergütung *(f)*
En (customs) drawback
Fr remboursement des droits
 d'importation *(m)*
It rimborso d'esportazione
 (m)
Pt reembolso de direitos al-
 fandegários *(m)*

**reembolso de direitos
 alfandegários** *(m)* Pt
De Zollrückvergütung *(f)*
En (customs) drawback
Es reembolso de derechos de
 aduana *(m)*
Fr remboursement des droits
 d'importation *(m)*
It rimborso d'esportazione
 (m)

re-export *vb* En
De wiederausführen
Es reexportar
Fr réexporter
It riesportare
Pt reexportar

reexportação *(f)* n Pt
De Wiederausfuhr *(f)*
En re-exportation
Es reexportación *(f)*
Fr réexportation *(f)*
It riesporto *(m)*

reexportación *(f)* n Es
De Wiederausfuhr *(f)*
En re-exportation
Fr réexportation *(f)*
It riesporto *(m)*
Pt reexportação *(f)*

reexportar *vb* Es, Pt
De wiederausführen
En re-export
Fr réexporter
It riesportare

re-exportation n En
De Wiederausfuhr *(f)*
Es reexportación *(f)*
Fr réexportation *(f)*
It riesporto *(m)*
Pt reexportação *(f)*

réexportation (f) n Fr
De Wiederausfuhr (f)
En re-exportation
Es reexportación (f)
It riesporto (m)
Pt reexportação (f)

réexporter vb Fr
De wiederausführen
En re-export
Es reexportar
It riesportare
Pt reexportar

réfections et améliorations
  Fr
De Änderungen und Erneue-
  rungen
En alterations and renewals
Es reformas y renovaciones
It modifiche e rinnovamenti
Pt modificações e renovações

refer a cheque to drawer En
Am refer a check to drawer
De einen Scheck uneingelöst
  lassen
Es rehusar pago de un che-
  que
Fr refuser d'honorer un
  chèque
It rifutare di pagare un as-
  segno
Pt devolver um cheque ao
  sacado

reference n En
De Referenz (f)
Es referencia (f)
Fr référence (f)
It referenza (f)
Pt referência (f)

référence (f) n Fr
De Referenz (f)
En reference
Es referencia (f)
It referenza (f)
Pt referência (f)

reference book En
De Nachschlagewerk (n)
Es libro de consulta (m)
Fr ouvrage de référence (m)
It libro di consultazione (m)
Pt livro de consulta (m)

référence commerciale (f) Fr
De Kreditauskunft (f)
En trade reference
Es referencia comercial (f)
It referenze commerciali (f pl)
Pt referência comercial (f)

référence de banquier (f) Fr
De Bankzeugnis (n)
En banker's reference
Es referencia bancaria (f)
It referenza bancaria (f)
Pt referência bancária (f)

referencia (f) n Es
De Referenz (f)
En reference
Fr référence (f)
It referenza (f)
Pt referência (f)

referência (f) n Pt
De Referenz (f)
En reference
Es referencia (f)
Fr référence (f)
It referenza (f)

referencia bancaria (f) Es
De Bankzeugnis (n)
En banker's reference
Fr référence de banquier (f)
It referenza bancaria (f)
Pt referência bancária (f)

referência bancária (f) Pt
De Bankzeugnis (n)
En banker's reference
Es referencia bancaria (f)
Fr référence de banquier (f)
It referenza bancaria (f)

referencia comercial (f) Es
De Kreditauskunft (f)
En trade reference
Fr référence commerciale (f)
It referenze commerciali (f pl)
Pt referência comercial (f)

referência comercial (f) Pt
De Kreditauskunft (f)
En trade reference
Es referencia comercial (f)
Fr référence commerciale (f)
It referenze commerciali (f pl)

Referenz (f) n De
En reference
Es referencia (f)
Fr référence (f)
It referenza (f)
Pt referência (f)

referenza (f) n It
De Referenz (f)
En reference
Es referencia (f)
Fr référence (f)
Pt referência (f)

referenza bancaria (f) It
De Bankzeugnis (n)
En banker's reference
Es referencia bancaria (f)
Fr référence de banquier (f)
Pt referência bancária (f)

referenze commerciali (f pl)
  It
De Kreditauskunft (f)
En trade reference
Es referencia comercial (f)
Fr référence commerciale (f)
Pt referência comercial (f)

reflacionar a economia Pt
De die Wirtschaft neu beleben
En reflate the economy
Es reanimar la economía
Fr ranimer l'économie
It ravvivare l'economia

reflate the economy En
De die Wirtschaft neu beleben
Es reanimar la economía
Fr ranimer l'économie
It ravvivare l'economia
Pt reflacionar a economia

reforma de contribuição
  prévia (f) Pt
De Kassenpension (f)
En contributory pension
Es retiro contributivo (m)
Fr retraite de régime à cotisa-
  tions (f)
It pensione a contributi (f)

reforma monetaria (f) Es
De Währungsreform (f)
En monetary reform

Fr réforme monétaire *(f)*
It riforma monetaria *(f)*
Pt reforma monetária *(f)*

reforma monetária *(f)* Pt
De Währungsreform *(f)*
En monetary reform
Es reforma monetaria *(f)*
Fr réforme monétaire *(f)*
It riforma monetaria *(f)*

reformas *(f pl)* Es
De Umbau *(m)*
En alterations
Fr travaux de transformation
    (m pl)
It modifiche *(f pl)*
Pt mocificações *(f pl)*

reformas y renovaciones Es
De Änderungen und Erneue-
    rungen
En alterations and renewals
Fr réfections et améliorations
It modifiche e rinnovamenti
Pt modificações e renovações

reformas y reparaciones Es
De Änderungen und Repara-
    turen
En alterations and repairs
Fr transformations et repara-
    tions
It modifiche e riparazioni
Pt modificações e reparações

réforme monétaire *(f)* Fr
De Währungsreform *(f)*
En monetary reform
Es reforma monetaria *(f)*
It riforma monetaria *(f)*
Pt reforma monetária *(f)*

refrendar *vb* Es
De gegenzeichnen
En countersign
Fr contresigner
It controfirmare
Pt validar por assinatura

refuge fiscal *(m)* Fr
De Steuerparadies *(n)*
En tax haven
Es refugio fiscal *(m)*
It rifugio fiscale *(m)*
Pt refúgio fiscal *(m)*

refugio fiscal *(m)* Es
De Steuerparadies *(n)*
En tax haven
Fr refuge fiscal *(m)*
It rifugio fiscale *(m)*
Pt refúgio fiscal *(m)*

refúgio fiscal *(m)* Pt
De Steuerparadies *(n)*
En tax haven
Es refugio fiscal *(m)*
Fr refuge fiscal *(m)*
It rifugio fiscale *(m)*

refund *n* En
De Rückerstattung *(f)*
Es reembolso *(m)*
Fr remboursement *(m)*
It rimborso *(m)*
Pt reembolso *(m)*

refus *(m)* *n* Fr
De Ablehnung *(f)*
En rejection
Es rechazo *(m)*
It rifiuto *(m)*
Pt rejeição *(f)*

**refuser d'honorer un
chèque** Fr
De einen Scheck uneingelöst
    lassen
En refer a cheque to drawer
Es rehusar pago de un che-
    que
It rifutare di pagare un as-
    segno
Pt devolver um cheque ao
    sacado

regalo *(m)* *n* Es
De Geschenk *(n)*
En gift
Fr don; cadeau *(m)*
It dono; donazione *(m f)*
Pt prenda; presente *(f m)*

regatear *vb* Es, Pt
De feilschen
En haggle
Am bargain
Fr marchander; chipoter
It mercanteggiare; cavillare

regatelo colectivo *(m)* Pt
De Tarifvertragsverhandlung
    (f)
En collective bargaining

Es contratación collectiva *(f)*
Fr négociations de conven-
    tions collectives *(f pl)*
It contrattazione collettiva *(f)*

Regierung *(f)* *n* De
En government
Es gobierno *(m)*
Fr gouvernement *(m)*
It governo *(m)*
Pt governo *(m)*

**Regierungsschuldver-
schreibungen** *(f pl)* *n* De
En Government securities
Es títulos públicos *(m pl)*
Fr titres d'Etat *(m pl)*
It titoli di Stato *(m pl)*
Pt títulos do Tesouro *(m pl)*

région déprimée *(f)* Fr
De Notstandsgebiet *(n)*
En distressed area
Es región deprimida *(f)*
It area indigente *(f)*
Pt zona deprimida *(f)*

región deprimida *(f)* Es
De Notstandsgebiet *(n)*
En distressed area
Fr région déprimée *(f)*
It area indigente *(f)*
Pt zona deprimida *(f)*

régions aurifères *(f pl)* Fr
De Goldgrube *(f)*
En gold fields
Es yacimiento aurífero *(m)*
It terreni auriferi *(m pl)*
Pt jazigos de ouro *(m pl)*

registar *vb* Pt
De registrieren; einlegen
En register; file
Es registrar; interponer
Fr enregistrer; déposer
It registrare; depositare

register *vb* En
De registrieren
Es registrar
Fr enregistrer
It registrare
Pt registar

registered letter En
De eingeschriebener Brief *(m)*
Es carta certificada *(f)*
Fr lettre recommandée *(f)*
It lettera raccomandata *(f)*
Pt carta registada *(f)*

registo de acções *(m)* Pt
De Liste der Aktionäre *(f)*
En share register
Es registro de las acciones *(m)*
Fr registre des actionnaires *(m)*
It registro delle azioni *(m)*

registo do navio *(m)* Pt
De Schiffsregister *(n)*
En ship's register
Es registro del barco *(m)*
Fr certificat d'immatriculation *(m)*
It atto di nazionalità *(m)*

registrar *vb* Es
De registrieren
En register
Fr enregistrer
It registrare
Pt registar

registrare *vb* It
De registrieren
En register
Es registrar
Fr enregistrer
Pt registar

registration fee En
De Anmeldegebühr *(f)*
Es derechos de registro *(m pl)*
Fr droit d'enregistrement *(m)*
It tassa di registrazione *(f)*
Pt custas de registo *(f pl)*

registrazione *(f)* n It
De Eintragung *(f)*
En entry
Es asiento *(m)*
Fr inscription *(f)*
Pt lançamento *(m)*

registrazione a giornale *(f)* It
De Tagebuchsposten *(m)*
En journal-entry
Es asiento en el libro diario *(m)*
Fr article d'un livre journal *(m)*
Pt anotação de diário *(f)*

registre des actionnaires *(m)*
Fr
De Liste der Aktionäre *(f)*
En share register
Es registro de las acciones *(m)*
It registro delle azioni *(m)*
Pt registo de acções *(m)*

registrieren *vb* De
En register
Es registrar
Fr enregistrer
It registrare
Pt registar

registro de las acciones *(m)*
Es
De Liste der Aktionäre *(f)*
En share register
Fr registre des actionnaires *(m)*
It registro delle azioni *(m)*
Pt registo de acções *(m)*

registro del barco *(m)* Es
De Schiffsregister *(n)*
En ship's register
Fr certificat d'immatriculation *(m)*
It atto di nazionalità *(m)*
Pt registo do navio *(m)*

registro delle azioni *(m)* It
De Liste der Aktionäre *(f)*
En share register
Es registro de las acciones *(m)*
Fr registre des actionnaires *(m)*
Pt registo de acções *(m)*

reglamento *(m)* n Es
De Verordnung *(f)*
En regulation
Fr règlement *(m)*
It regolamento *(m)*
Pt regulação *(f)*

règlement *(m)* n Fr
De Verordnung; Abrechnung *(f)*
En regulation; settlement
Es reglamento; ajuste *(m)*
It regolamento; quietanza *(m f)*
Pt ajuste; regulação *(m f)*

regolamento *(m)* n It
De Verordnung; Ausgleich *(f m)*
En regulation; settlement
Es reglamento; satisfacción *(m f)*
Fr règlement *(m)*
Pt regulação; satisfação *(f)*

regulação *(f)* n Pt
De Verordnung; Ausgleich *(f m)*
En regulation; settlement
Es reglamento; satisfacción *(m f)*
Fr règlement *(m)*
It regolamento *(m)*

rehusar pago un cheque Es
De einen Scheck uneingelöst lassen
En refer a cheque to drawer
Fr refuser d'honorer un chèque
It rifutare di pagare un assegno
Pt devolver um cheque ao sacado

Reinerlös *(m)* n De
En net proceeds
Es rédito neto *(m)*
Fr produit net *(m)*
It ricavo netto *(m)*
Pt proventos líquidos *(m pl)*

Reingewicht *(n)* n De
En net weight
Es peso neto *(m)*
Fr poids net *(m)*
It peso netto *(m)*
Pt peso líquido *(m)*

Reingewinn *(m)* n De
En net profit
Es ganancia neta *(f)*
Fr bénéfice net *(m)*
It utile netto *(m)*
Pt lucro líquido *(m)*

Reingewinnspanne *(f)* n De
En net profit margin
Es margen de beneficio neto *(m)*
Fr marge nette de bénéfices *(f)*
It margine di utile netto *(m)*
Pt margem de lucro líquido *(f)*

reinsurance *n* En
De Rückversicherung *(f)*
Es reaseguro *(m)*
Fr réassurance *(f)*
It riassicurazione *(f)*
Pt re-seguro *(m)*

Reinvermögen *(n) n* De
En net assets
Es activo neto *(m)*
Fr actif net *(m)*
It attivo netto *(m)*
Pt bens líquidos *(m pl)*

Reisebüro *(n) n* De
En travel agency
Es agencia de viajes *(f)*
Fr agence de voyages *(f)*
It agenzia di viaggi *(f)*
Pt agente de viagens *(m)*

Reisegewerbe *(n) n* De
En tourist trade
Es industria del turismo *(f)*
Fr commerce de tourisme *(m)*
It commercio turistico *(m)*
Pt indústria do turismo *(f)*

Reisekosten *(pl) n* De
En travelling expenses
Es dietas de viajes *(f pl)*
Fr frais de voyage *(m pl)*
It spese di viaggio *(f pl)*
Pt despesas de viagem *(f pl)*

Reisende(r) *(m) n* De
En passenger
Es pasajero *(m)*
Fr passager *(m)*
It passeggero *(m)*
Pt passageiro *(m)*

Reisescheck *(m) n* De
En traveller's cheque
Es cheque de viajero *(m)*
Fr chèque de voyage *(m)*
It assegno turistico *(m)*
Pt cheque de viajante *(m)*

rejection *n* En
De Ablehnung *(f)*
Es rechazo *(m)*
Fr refus *(m)*
It rifiuto *(m)*
Pt rejeição *(f)*

rejeição *(f) n* Pt
De Ablehnung *(f)*
En rejection

Es rechazo *(m)*
Fr refus *(m)*
It rifiuto *(m)*

Reklame *(f) n* De
En advertising
Es publicidad *(f)*
Fr publicité *(f)*
It pubblicità *(f)*
Pt publicidade *(f)*

Rektaindossement *(n) n* De
En restrictive endorsement
Es endoso restringido *(m)*
Fr endossement restrictif *(m)*
It girata restrittiva *(f)*
Pt endosse restritivo *(m)*

relação de quantidades *(f) Pt*
De Kostenvoranschlag *(m)*
En bill of quantities
Es cubicación de obra *(f)*
Fr devis *(m)*
It preventivo *(m)*

relaciones humanas *(f pl)* Es
De zwischenmenschliche Be-
     ziehungen *(f pl)*.
En human relations
Fr relations humaines *(f pl)*
It relazioni umane *(f pl)*
Pt relações humanas *(f pl)*

**relaciones humanas
industriales** *(f pl)* Es
De Arbeitsbeziehungen *(f pl)*
En industrial relations
Fr relations humaines dans
     l'entreprise *(f pl)*
It relazioni nell'industria *(f pl)*
Pt relações industriais *(f pl)*

relaciones patrón-obrero
     (f pl) Es
De Arbeitsverhältnisse *(n pl)*
En labour relations
Fr rapports du travail *(m pl)*
It relazioni con la mano
     d'opera *(f pl)*
Pt relações de trabalho *(f pl)*

relaciones públicas *(f pl)* Es
De Public Relations *(n pl)*
En public relations (PR)
Fr relations publiques *(f pl)*
It pubbliche relazioni *(f pl)*
Pt relações públicas *(f pl)*

relações de trabalho *(f pl)* Pt
De Arbeitsverhältnisse *(n pl)*
En labour relations
Es relaciones patrón-obrero
     (f pl)
Fr rapports du travail *(m pl)*
It relazioni con la mano
     d'opera *(f pl)*

relações humanas *(f pl)* Pt
De zwischenmenschliche Be-
     ziehungen *(f pl)*
En human relations
Es relaciones humanas *(f pl)*
Fr relations humaines *(f pl)*
It relazioni umane *(f pl)*

relações industriais *(f pl)* Pt
De Arbeitsbeziehungen *(f pl)*
En industrial relations
Es relaciones humanas indu-
     striales *(f pl)*
Fr relations humaines dans
     l'entreprise *(f pl)*
It relazioni nell'industria *(f pl)*

relações públicas *(f pl)* Pt
De Public Relations *(n pl)*
En public relations (PR)
Es relaciones públicas *(f pl)*
Fr relations publiques *(f pl)*
It pubbliche relazioni *(f pl)*

relámpago *(m) n* Es
De Blitz *(m)*
En lightning
Fr foudre *(f)*
It fulmine *(m)*
Pt relâmpago *(m)*

relâmpago *(m) n* Pt
De Blitz *(m)*
En lightning
Es relámpago *(m)*
Fr foudre *(f)*
It fulmine *(m)*

relations humaines *(f pl)* Fr
De zwischenmenschliche Be-
     ziehungen *(f pl)*
En human relations
Es relaciones humanas *(f pl)*
It relazioni umane *(f pl)*
Pt relações humanas *(f pl)*

**relations humaines dans
l'entreprise** *(f pl)* Fr
De Arbeitsbeziehungen *(f pl)*
En industrial relations

Es relaciones humanas industriales *(f pl)*
It relazioni nell'industria *(f pl)*
Pt relações industriais *(f pl)*

relations publiques *(f pl)* Fr
De Public Relations *(n pl)*
En public relations (PR)
Es relaciones públicas *(f pl)*
It pubbliche relazioni *(f pl)*
Pt relações públicas *(f pl)*

relatório *(m) n* Pt
De Bericht *(m)*
En report
Es informe *(m)*
Fr rapport *(m)*
It relazione *(m)*

relatório anual *(m)* Pt
De Jahresbericht *(m)*
En annual report
Es memoria anual *(f)*
Fr rapport annuel *(m)*
It relazione annuale *(f)*

relatório de directores *(m)* Pt
De Vorstandsbericht *(m)*
En directors' report
Es informe de la administración *(m)*
Fr rapport des administrateurs *(m)*
It relazione degli amministratori *(f)*

relatório do fiscal de contas *(m)* Pt
De Bericht des Abschlußprüfers *(m)*
En auditor's report
Es informe de los interventores *(m)*
Fr rapport des vérificateurs des comptes *(m)*
It relazione dei sindaci *(f)*

relatório do perito *(m)* Pt
De Sachverständigengutachten *(n)*
En expert's report
Es informe del especialista *(m)*
Fr expertise *(f)*
It perizia *(f)*

relazione *(f) n* It
De Bericht *(m)*
En report

Es informe *(m)*
Fr rapport *(m)*
Pt relatório *(m)*

relazione annuale *(f)* It
De Jahresbericht *(m)*
En annual report
Es memoria anual *(f)*
Fr rapport annuel *(m)*
Pt relatório anual *(m)*

relazione degli amministratori *(f)* It
De Vorstandsbericht *(m)*
En directors' report
Es informe de la administración *(m)*
Fr rapport des administrateurs *(m)*
Pt relatório de directores *(m)*

relazione dei sindaci *(f)* It
De Bericht des Abschlußprüfers *(m)*
En auditor's report
Es informe de los interventores *(m)*
Fr rapport des vérificateurs des comptes *(m)*
Pt relatório do fiscal de contas *(m)*

relazione finanziaria *(f)* It
De Finanzausweis *(m)*
En financial statement
Es extracto financiero *(m)*
Fr état de finances *(m)*
Pt extracto financeiro *(m)*

relazione sul mercato *(f)* It
De Marktbericht *(m)*
En market report
Es informe del mercado *(m)*
Fr revue du marché *(f)*
Pt informação do mercado *(f)*

relazioni con la mano d'opera *(f pl)* It
De Arbeitsverhältnisse *(n pl)*
En labour relations
Es relaciones patrón-obrero *(f pl)*
Fr rapports du travail *(m pl)*
Pt relações de trabalho *(f pl)*

relazioni nell'industria *(f pl)* It
De Arbeitsbeziehungen *(f pl)*
En industrial relations

Es relaciones humanas industriales *(f pl)*
Fr relations humaines dans l'entreprise *(f pl)*
Pt relações industriais *(f pl)*

relazioni umane *(f pl)* It
De zwischenmenschliche Beziehungen *(f pl)*
En human relations
Es relaciones humanas *(f pl)*
Fr relations humaines *(f pl)*
Pt relações humanas *(f pl)*

relevé de compte *(m)* Fr
De Kontoauszug *(m)*
En statement of account
Es extracto de cuenta *(m)*
It estratto conto *(m)*
Pt extracto de conta *(m)*

reliable *adj* En
De zuverlässig
Es digno de confianza
Fr digne de confiance
It fidato; attendibile
Pt digno de confiança

remboursement *(m) n* Fr
De Rückerstattung *(f)*
En refund
Es reembolso *(m)*
It rimborso *(m)*
Pt reembolso *(m)*

remboursement des droits d'importation *(m)* Fr
De Zollrückvergütung *(f)*
En (customs) drawback
Es reembolso de derechos de aduana *(m)*
It rimborso d'esportazione *(m)*
Pt reembolso de direitos alfandegários *(m)*

rembourser *vb* Fr
De tilgen; zurückzahlen
En redeem; reimburse
Es redimir; reembolsar
It redimere; rimborsare
Pt remir; reembolsar

remessa gratuita Pt
De portofreie Lieferung
En delivery free
Es libre entrega
Fr livré franco
It consegna franco

remettre sa démission Fr
De den Rücktritt einreichen
En hand in one's resignation
Es presentar la dimisión
It rassegnare le dimissioni
Pt apresentar demissão

remir vb Pt
De tilgen; gutmachen
En redeem
Es redimir
Fr rembourser; dégager
It redimere; rimborsare

remise sur les exports (f) Fr
De Ausfuhrsonderrabatt (m)
En export rebate
Es descuento por exporta-
ción (m)
It sconto d'esportazione (m)
Pt desconto de exportação
(m)

remolcador (m) n Es
De Schleppdampfer (m)
En tug-boat
Fr remorqueur (m)
It rimorchiatore (m)
Pt rebocador (m)

remorqueur (m) n Fr
De Schleppdampfer (m)
En tug-boat
Es remolcador (m)
It rimorchiatore (m)
Pt rebocador (m)

remplir vb Fr
De erfüllen
En fulfil
Es cumplir
It adempiere
Pt cumprir

remuneração (f) n Pt
De Vergütung (f)
En remuneration
Es remuneración (f)
Fr rémunération (f)
It rimunerazione (f)

remuneración (f) n Es
De Vergütung (f)
En remuneration
Fr rémunération (f)
It rimunerazione (f)
Pt remuneração (f)

remuneration n En
De Vergütung (f)
Es remuneración (f)
Fr rémunération (f)
It rimunerazione (f)
Pt remuneração (f)

rémunération (f) n Fr
De Vergütung (f)
En remuneration
Es remuneración (f)
It rimunerazione (f)
Pt remuneração (f)

rémunération du capital (f) Fr
De Kapitalertrag (m)
En return on capital
Es beneficio sobre capital (m)
It reddito del capitale (m)
Pt juro sobre o capital (m)

renchérir vb Fr
De teurer werden; steigen
En advance in price
Es encarecer
It aumentare di prezzo
Pt encarecer

renchérissement (m) n Fr
De Preiserhöhung (f)
En advance in price
Es encarecimiento (m)
It rialzo (m)
Pt encarecimento (m)

**renchérissement du coût de
la vie** (m) Fr
De erhöhte Lebenshaltungs-
kosten (pl)
En increased cost of living
Es coste de vida más alto (m)
It aumentato costo della vita
(m)
Pt custo de vida mais eleva-
do (m)

renda (f) n Pt
De Miete (f)
En rent
Es alquiler (m)
Fr loyer (m)
It pigione; affitto (f m)

renda sobre o terreno (f) Pt
De Grundpacht (f)
En ground-rent
Es renta del terreno (f)
Fr rente foncière (f)
It affitto di terreno (m)

rendement (m) n Fr
De Erzeugung; Rendite (f)
En output; yield
Es rendimiento; rédito (m)
It produzione; reddito (f m)
Pt rendimento; rédito (m)

rendement brut (m) Fr
De Bruttoeinkommen (n)
En gross income
Es ingreso bruto (m)
It reddito lordo (m)
Pt receita bruta (f)

rendement équitable (m) Fr
De angemessener Ertrag (m)
En fair return
Es beneficio razonable (m)
It discreto profitto (m)
Pt rendimento justo (m)

rendement net (m) Fr
De Nettoertrag (m)
En net yield
Es rendimiento neto (m)
It reddito netto (m)
Pt rendimento líquido (m)

rendements décroissants
(m pl) Fr
De abnehmender Ertrag (m)
En diminishing returns
Es rendimientos decrecientes
(m pl)
It proventi decrescenti (m pl)
Pt rendimentos decrescentes
(m pl)

**rendement sur rembourse-
ment** (m) Fr
De Einlösungsertrag (m)
En redemption yield
Es rédito de reembolso (m)
It rendita di rimborso (f)
Pt rendimento de resgate (m)

rendersi garante di It
De Haftkaution geben
En go bail for
Es salir fiados por
Fr se porter garant de
Pt prestar caução a favor de

**rendiconto finanziario
provvisorio** (m) It
De Zwischenbilanz (f)
En interim financial statement

Es extracto financiero provisional *(m)*
Fr bilan intérimaire *(m)*
Pt extracto financeiro interino *(m)*

rendimento *(m) n* Pt
De Erzeugung; Rendite *(f)*
En output; yield
Es rendimiento; rédito *(m)*
Fr rendement *(m)*
It produzione; reddito *(m)*

rendimento de capitais investidos *(m)* Pt
De Einkommen aus Kapitalanlagen *(n)*
En investment income
Es renta de inversiones *(f)*
Fr revenu de placements *(m)*
It reddito degli investimenti *(m)*

rendimento della spesa *(m)* It
De Wirtschaftlichkeit *(f)*
En cost-effectiveness
Es efectividad de coste *(f)*
Fr coût et efficacité
Pt eficiência relativa ao custo *(f)*

rendimento de resgate *(m)* Pt
De Einlösungsertrag *(m)*
En redemption yield
Es rédito de reembolso *(m)*
Fr rendement sur remboursement *(m)*
It rendita di rimborso *(f)*

rendimento do capital *(m)* Pt
De Kapitaleinkommen *(n)*
En unearned income
Es rentas *(f pl)*
Fr rente *(f)*
It reddito di capitale *(m)*

rendimento justo *(m)* Pt
De angemessener Ertrag *(m)*
En fair return
Es beneficio razonable *(m)*
Fr rendement équitable *(m)*
It discreto profitto *(m)*

rendimento líquido *(m)* Pt
De Nettoertrag *(m)*
En net yield

Es rendimiento neto *(m)*
Fr rendement net *(m)*
It reddito netto *(m)*

rendimentos decrescentes *(m pl)* Pt
De abnehmender Ertrag *(m)*
En diminishing returns
Es rendimientos decrecientes *(m pl)*
Fr rendements décroissants *(m pl)*
It proventi decrescenti *(m pl)*

rendimiento *(m) n* Es
De Erzeugung; Rendite *(f)*
En output; yield
Fr rendement *(m)*
It produzione; reddito *(m)*
Pt rendimento; rédito *(m)*

rendimiento neto *(m)* Es
De Nettoertrag *(m)*
En net yield
Fr rendement net *(m)*
It reddito netto *(m)*
Pt rendimento líquido *(m)*

rendimientos decrecientes *(m pl)* Es
De abnehmender Ertrag *(m)*
En diminishing returns
Fr rendements décroissants *(m pl)*
It proventi decrescenti *(m pl)*
Pt rendimentos decrescentes *(m pl)*

rendita di rimborso *(f)* It
De Einlösungsertrag *(m)*
En redemption yield
Es rédito de reembolso *(m)*
Fr rendement sur remboursement *(m)*
Pt rendimento de resgate *(m)*

rendita vitalizia differita *(f)* It
De Anwartschaft auf Leibrente *(f)*
En deferred annuity
Es anualidad aplazada *(f)*
Fr annuité différée *(f)*
Pt anuidade diferida *(f)*

Rendite *(f) n* De
En yield
Es rédito *(m)*
Fr revenu; rendement *(m)*

It reddito *(m)*
Pt rédito *(m)*

renier un sinistre Fr
De einen Ersatzanspruch nicht anerkennen
En repudiate a claim
Es rechazar una reclamación
It respingere un reclamo
Pt repudiar uma reclamação

renoncer à *vb* Fr
De verzichten auf
En renounce
Es renunciar
It rinunziare
Pt renunciar

renonciation *(f) n* Fr
De Verzicht *(m)*
En renunciation
Es renuncia *(f)*
It rinunzia *(f)*
Pt renúncia *(f)*

renounce *vb* En
De verzichten auf
Es renunciar
Fr renoncer à
It rinunziare
Pt renunciar

renseignements complémentaires *(m pl)* Fr
De weitere Auskunft *(f)*
En further information
Es más detalles *(m pl)*
It ulteriori informazioni *(f pl)*
Pt informação adicional *(f)*

rent *n* En
De Miete *(f)*
Es alquiler *(m)*
Fr loyer *(m)*
It pigione; affitto *(m)*
Pt renda *(f)*

rent *vb* En
De vermieten
Es alquilar
Fr louer; affermer
It affittare; appigionare
Pt alugar

rentabilidad *(f) n* Es
De Rentabilität *(f)*
En profitability
Fr rentabilité *(f)*
It redditività *(f)*
Pt rentabilidade *(f)*

rentabilidade (f) n Pt
De Rentabilität (f)
En profitability
Es rentabilidad (f)
Fr rentabilité (f)
It redditività (f)

Rentabilität (f) n De
En profitability
Es rentabilidad (f)
Fr rentabilité (f)
It redditività (f)
Pt rentabilidade (f)

Rentabilitätsgrenze (f) n De
En break-even point
Es punto de igualdad de in-
    gresos y gastos (m)
Fr point de seuil (m)
It punto di pareggio (m)
Pt ponto de acerto (m)

rentabilité (f) n Fr
De Rentabilität (f)
En profitability
Es rentabilidad (f)
It redditività (f)
Pt rentabilidade (f)

renta de inversiones (f) Es
De Einkommen aus Kapitalan-
    lagen (n)
En investment income
Fr revenu de placements (m)
It reddito degli investimenti
    (m)
Pt rendimento de capitais in-
    vestidos (m)

renta del terreno (f) Es
De Grundpacht (f)
En ground-rent
Fr rente foncière (f)
It affitto di terreno (m)
Pt renda sobre o terreno (f)

renta del trabajo (f) Es
De Arbeitseinkommen (n)
En earned income
Fr revenu du travail (m)
It reddito di lavoro (m)
Pt receita de trabalho (f)

renta disponible (f) Es
De verfügbares Einkommen
    (n)
En disposable income
Fr revenu disponible (m)
It reddito disponibile (m)
Pt receita disponível (f)

renta imponible (f) Es
De steuerpflichtiges Einkom-
    men (n)
En taxable income
Fr revenu imposable (m)
It reddito tassabile (m)
Pt receita tributável (f)

renta nacional (f) Es
De Nationaleinkommen (n)
En national income
Fr revenu national (m)
It reddito nazionale (m)
Pt receita pública (f)

rentas (f pl) Es
De Kapitaleinkommen (n)
En unearned income
Fr rente (f)
It reddito di capitale (m)
Pt rendimento do capital (m)

rent control En
De Mietzinskontrolle (f)
Es control de alquileres (m)
Fr contrôle des loyers (m)
It blocco degli affitti (m)
Pt controlo de rendas (m)

Rente (f) n De
En pension
Es pensión (f)
Fr pension (f)
It pensione (f)
Pt pensão (f)

rente foncière (f) Fr
De Grundpacht (f)
En ground-rent
Es renta del terreno (f)
It affitto di terreno (m)
Pt renda sobre o terreno (f)

rentes (f pl) n Fr
De Kapitaleinkommen (n)
En unearned income
Es rentas (f pl)
It reddito di capitale (m)
Pt rendimento do capital (m)

Rentner (m) n De
En pensioner
Es pensionado (m)
Fr pensionnaire (m)
It pensionato (m)
Pt pensionista (m)

renuncia (f) n Es
De Verzicht (m)
En renunciation
Fr renonciation (f)
It rinunzia (f)
Pt renúncia (f)

renúncia (f) n Pt
De Verzicht (m)
En renunciation
Es renuncia (f)
Fr renonciation (f)
It rinunzia (f)

renunciar vb Es, Pt
De aufgeben; verzichten auf
En give up; renounce
Fr céder; renoncer à
It cedere; rinunziare

renunciation n En
De Verzicht (m)
Es renuncia (f)
Fr renonciation (f)
It rinunzia (f)
Pt renúncia (f)

re-open discussions En
De Verhandlungen wieder-
    aufnehmen
Es reabrir la discusión
Fr rouvrir la discussion
It riaprire la discussione
Pt reabrir discussões

repair n En
De Reparatur (f)
Es reparación (f)
Fr réparation (f)
It riparazione (f)
Pt reparação (f)

repair vb En
De reparieren
Es reparar; componer
Fr réparer; réfectionner
It riparare; rifare
Pt consertar; reparar

reparação (f) n Pt
De Reparatur (f)
En repair
Es reparación (f)
Fr réparation (f)
It riparazione (f)

reparación *(f)* n Es
De Reparatur *(f)*
En repair
Fr réparation *(f)*
It riparazione *(f)*
Pt reparação *(f)*

reparar *vb* Es, Pt
De reparieren
En repair
Fr réparer; réfectionner
It riparare; rifare

réparation *(f)* n Fr
De Reparatur *(f)*
En repair
Es reparación *(f)*
It riparazione *(f)*
Pt reparação *(f)*

Reparatur *(f)* n De
En repair
Es reparación *(f)*
Fr réparation *(f)*
It riparazione *(f)*
Pt reparação *(f)*

réparer *vb* Fr
De reparieren
En repair
Es reparar; componer
It riparare; rifare
Pt consertar; reparar

reparieren *vb* De
En repair
Es reparar; componer
Fr réparer; réfectionner
It riparare; rifare
Pt consertar; reparar

repartição dos lucros *(f)* Pt
De Gewinnbeteiligung *(f)*
En profit-sharing
Es participación en los beneficios *(f)*
Fr participation aux bénéfices *(f)*
It partecipazione agli utili *(f)*

repartir *vb* Es, Pt
De verteilen; zuteilen
En distribute; apportion
Fr répartir
It ripartire

répartir *vb* Fr
De verteilen; zuteilen
En distribute; apportion

Es repartir
It ripartire
Pt repartir

reparto *(m)* n Es
De Verteilung *(f)*
En distribution
Fr distribution *(f)*
It ripartizione *(f)*
Pt distribuição *(f)*

répertoire *(m)* n Fr
De Adreßbuch *(n)*
En directory
Es guía *(f)*
It guida *(f)*
Pt guia *(m)*

replacement cost En
De Wiederanschaffungskosten *(pl)*
Es coste de repuesto *(m)*
Fr coût de remplacement *(m)*
It costo di rimpiazzo *(m)*
Pt custo de substituição *(m)*

reply paid En
Am post paid
De Rückantwort bezahlt
Es respuesta pagada
Fr réponse payée
It risposta pagata
Pt resposta paga

réponse *(f)* n Fr
De Antwort *(f)*
En answer
Es respuesta *(f)*
It risposta *(f)*
Pt resposta *(f)*

réponse payée Fr
De Rückantwort bezahlt
En reply paid
Am post paid
Es respuesta pagada
It risposta pagata
Pt resposta paga

report n En
De Bericht; Meldung *(m f)*
Es informe; reportaje *(m)*
Fr rapport; compte-rendu *(m)*
It relazione; rapporto *(f m)*
Pt relatório *(m)*

report à nouveau *(m)* Fr
De Saldovortrag *(m)*
En balance carried forward
Es saldo de entrada *(m)*
It saldo da riportare *(m)*
Pt saldo transportado *(m)*

Repräsentationskosten *(pl)* n De
En entertainment expenses
Es gastos de representación *(m pl)*
Fr frais de représentation *(m pl)*
It spese di rappresentanza *(f pl)*
Pt despesas de representação *(f pl)*

represent *vb* En
De vertreten
Es representar
Fr représenter
It rappresentare
Pt representar

représentant *(m)* n Fr
De Vertreter *(m)*
En representative
Es representante *(m)*
It rappresentante *(m)*
Pt representante *(m)*

representante *(m)* n Es, Pt
De Vertreter *(m)*
En representative
Fr représentant *(m)*
It rappresentante *(m)*

representante legal *(m)* Es, Pt
De Rechtsvertreter *(m)*
En legal representative
Fr représentant mandaté *(m)*
It mandatario *(m)*

représentant mandaté *(m)* Fr
De Rechtsvertreter *(m)*
En legal representative
Es representante legal *(m)*
It mandatario *(m)*
Pt representante legal *(m)*

representar *vb* Es, Pt
De vertreten
En represent
Fr représenter
It rappresentare

representative n En
De Vertreter (m)
Es representante (m)
Fr représentant (m)
It rappresentante (m)
Pt representante (m)

représenter vb Fr
De vertreten
En represent
Es representar
It rappresentare
Pt representar

repudiar uma reclamação Pt
De einen Ersatzanspruch
nicht anerkennen
En repudiate a claim
Es rechazar una reclamación
Fr renier un sinistre
It respingere un reclamo

repudiate a claim En
De einen Ersatzanspruch
nicht anerkennen
Es rechazar una reclamación
Fr renier un sinistre
It respingere un reclamo
Pt repudiar uma reclamação

request vb En
De verlangen
Es requisar
Fr réquisitionner
It requisire
Pt requisitar

requisar vb Es
De verlangen
En request
Fr réquisitionner
It requisire
Pt requisitar

requisição (f) n Pt
De Antrag (m)
En application
Es solicitud (f)
Fr demande (f)
It domanda (f)

requisire vb It
De verlangen
En request
Es requisar
Fr réquisitionner
Pt requisitar

requisitar vb Pt
De verlangen
En request
Es requisar
Fr réquisitionner
It requisire

requisition n En
De Anforderung (f)
Es pedido; solicitud (m f)
Fr demande (f)
It richiesta; requisizione (f)
Pt pedido (m)

réquisitionner vb Fr
De verlangen
En request
Es requisar
It requisire
Pt requisitar

requisito (m) n Es
De Qualifikation (f)
En qualification
Fr qualification; capacité (f)
It qualifica; requisito (f m)
Pt qualificação (f)

resale price En
De Wiederverkaufspreis (m)
Es precio de reventa (m)
Fr prix de revente (m)
It prezzo di rivendita (m)
Pt preço de revenda (m)

rescisão de contrato (f) Pt
De Vertragsbeendigung (f)
En determination of a con-
tract
Es rescisión de un contrato (f)
Fr résolution d'un contrat (f)
It risoluzione di un contratto
(f)

rescisión de un contrato (f)
Es
De Vertragsbeendigung (f)
En determination of a con-
tract
Fr résolution d'un contrat (f)
It risoluzione di un contratto
(f)
Pt rescisão de contrato (f)

rés-do-chão (m) Pt
De Erdgeschoß (n)
En ground floor

Es planta baja (f)
Fr rez-de-chaussée (m)
It pianterreno (m)

research n En
De Forschung (f)
Es investigación (f)
Fr recherche (f)
It ricerca (f)
Pt investigação (f)

research and development
(R & D) En
De Zweckforschung; For-
schung und Entwicklung
(F & E) (f)
Es investigación y desarrollo
Fr recherche industrielle (f)
It studi e sviluppi
Pt investigação e desenvolvi-
mento

réseau (m) n Fr
De Netz (n)
En network
Es red (f)
It rete (f)
Pt rede (f)

re-seguro (m) n Pt
De Rückversicherung (f)
En reinsurance
Es reaseguro (m)
Fr réassurance (f)
It riassicurazione (f)

reserva de capital (f) Es
De Kapitalreserve (f)
En capital reserves
Fr réserve de capitaux (f)
It riserva di capitale (f)
Pt reservas de capital (f pl)

reserva em dinheiro (f) Pt
De Kassenreserve (f)
En cash reserve
Es reserva en efectivo (f)
Fr réserve en espèces (f)
It riserva in contanti (f)

reserva en efectivo (f) Es
De Kassenreserve (f)
En cash reserve
Fr réserve en espèces (f)
It riserva in contanti (f)
Pt reserva em dinheiro (f)

reserva latente *(f)* Es
De stille Reserve *(f)*
En hidden reserve
Fr réserve cachée ;*(f)*
It riserva occulta *(f)*
Pt reserva oculta *(f)*

reserva oculta *(f)* Pt
De stille Reserve *(f)*
En hidden reserve
Es reserva latente *(f)*
Fr réserve cachée *(f)*
It riserva occulta *(f)*

**reserva para deudas
incobrables** *(f)* Es
De Dubiosenreserve *(f)*
En bad debt reserve
Fr provision pour créances
douteuses *(f)*
It riserva per crediti inesigibi-
li *(f)*
Pt reserva para dívidas in-
cobráveis *(f)*

**reserva para dívidas
incobráveis** *(f)* Pt
De Dubiosenreserve *(f)*
En bad debt reserve
Es reserva para deudas inco-
brables *(f)*
Fr provision pour créances
douteuses *(f)*
It riserva per crediti inesigibi-
li *(f)*

reserva para imprevistos *(f)*
Es
De Rückstellung für Eventual-
verbindlichkeiten *(f)*
En contingency reserve
Fr réserve de prévoyance *(f)*
It riserva di previdenza *(f)*
Pt reserva para as con-
tingências *(f)*

reservar *vb* Es, Pt
De vorbehalten
En reserve
Fr réserver
It riservare

reservas de capital *(f pl)* Pt
De Kapitalreserve *(f)*
En capital reserves
Es reserva de capital *(f)*
Fr réserve de capitaux *(f)*
It riserva di capitale *(f)*

reserve *vb* En
De vorbehalten
Es reservar
Fr réserver
It riservare
Pt reservar

réserve cachée *(f)* Fr
De stille Reserve *(f)*
En hidden reserve
Es reserva latente *(f)*
It riserva occulta *(f)*
Pt reserva oculta *(f)*

reserve currency En
De Reservewährung *(f)*
Es moneda de reserva *(f)*
Fr monnaie de réserve *(f)*
It valuta di riserva *(f)*
Pt moeda de reserva *(f)*

réserve de capitaux *(f)* Fr
De Kapitalreserve *(f)*
En capital reserves
Es reserva de capital *(f)*
It riserva di capitale *(f)*
Pt reservas de capital *(f pl)*

réserve de prévoyance *(f)* Fr
De Rückstellung für Eventual-
verbindlichkeiten *(f)*
En contingency reserve
Es reserva para imprevistos
(f)
It riserva di previdenza *(f)*
Pt reserva para as con-
tingências *(f)*

réserve en espèces *(f)* Fr
De Kassenreserve *(f)*
En cash reserve
Es reserva en efectivo *(f)*
It riserva in contanti *(f)*
Pt reserva em dinheiro *(f)*

Reservefonds *(m)* n De
En reserve fund
Es fondo de reserva *(m)*
Fr fonds de réserve *(m)*
It fondo di riserva *(m)*
Pt fundo de reserva *(m)*

reserve fund En
De Reservefonds *(m)*
Es fondo de reserva *(m)*
Fr fonds de réserve *(m)*
It fondo di riserva *(m)*
Pt fundo de reserva *(m)*

(die) Reserven angreifen De
En draw on reserves
Es sacar reservas
Fr prélever sur les réserves
It prelevare dalle riserve
Pt recorrer a reservas

reserve price En
De Mindestpreis *(m)*
Es precio mínimo fijado *(m)*
Fr prix minimal *(f)*
It prezzo minimo *(m)*
Pt preço de reserva *(m)*

réserver *vb* Fr
De vorbehalten
En reserve
Es reservar
It riservare
Pt reservar

Reservewährung *(f)* n De
En reserve currency
Es moneda de reserva *(f)*
Fr monnaie de réserve *(f)*
It valuta di riserva *(f)*
Pt moeda de reserva *(f)*

residuo di cassa *(m)* It
De Kassensaldo *(m)*
En cash balance
Es resto en efectivo *(m)*
Fr solde de caisse *(m)*
Pt saldo em dinheiro *(m)*

resign *vb* En
De zurücktreten
Es dimitir
Fr se démettre
It dimettersi
Pt demitir-se

résistance à la vente *(f)* Fr
De Kaufabneigung *(f)*
En sales resistance
Es dificultades de ventas *(f pl)*
It difficoltà di vendita *(f)*
Pt resistência contra vendas
(f)

resistência contra vendas *(f)*
Pt
De Kaufabneigung *(f)*
En sales resistance
Es dificultades de ventas *(f pl)*
Fr résistance à la vente *(f)*
It difficoltà di vendita *(f)*

resolução (f) n Pt
De Beschluß (m)
En resolution
Es resolución (f)
Fr résolution (f)
It deliberazione (f)

resolução extraordinária
(f) Pt
De Sonderentschluß (m)
En extraordinary resolution
Es resolución extraordinaria
(f)
Fr résolution extraordinaire (f)
It deliberazione straordinaria
(f)

resolución (f) n Es
De Beschluß (m)
En resolution
Fr résolution (f)
It deliberazione (f)
Pt resolução (f)

resolución extraordinaria (f)
Es
De Sonderentschluß (m)
En extraordinary resolution
Fr résolution extraordinaire (f)
It deliberazione straordinaria
(f)
Pt resolução extraordinária (f)

resolution n En (f)
De Beschluß (m)
Es resolución (f)
Fr résolution (f)
It deliberazione (f)
Pt resolução (f)

résolution n Fr (f)
De Beschluß (m)
En resolution (f)
Es resolución (f)
It deliberazione (f)
Pt resolução (f)

résolution d'un contrat (f) Fr
De Vertragsbeendigung (f)
En determination of a con-
tract
Es rescisión de un contrato (f)
It risoluzione di un contratto
(f)
Pt rescisão de contrato (f)

résolution extraordinaire (f)
Fr
De Sonderentschluß (m)
En extraordinary resolution
Es resolución extraordinaria
(f)
It deliberazione straordinaria
(f)
Pt resolução extraordinária (f)

respingere un reclamo It
De einen Ersatzanspruch
nicht anerkennen
En repudiate a claim
Es rechazar una reclamación
Fr renier un sinistre
Pt repudiar uma reclamação

responsabile per i danni It
De schadenersatzpflichtig
En liable for damages
Es responsable por daños
Fr passible de dommages-
intérêts
Pt responsável por danos

responsabilidad (f) n Es
De Verantwortlichkeit (f)
En responsibility; liability
Fr responsabilité (f)
It responsabilità (f)
Pt responsabilidade (f)

responsabilidad del patrono
(f) Es
De Haftpflicht des Arbeitge-
bers (f)
En employer's liability
Fr responsabilité patronale (f)
It responsabilità del datore
di lavoro (f)
Pt responsabilidade do patrão
(f)

responsabilidade (f) n Pt
De Verantwortlichkeit (f)
En responsibility; liability
Es responsabilidad (f)
Fr responsabilité (f)
It responsabilità (f)

**responsabilidade
contingente** (f) Pt
De Eventualverpflichtung (f)
En contingent liability
Es responsabilidad contin-
gente (f)
Fr obligation éventuelle (f)
It sopravvenienza passiva (f)

responsabilidade do patrão
(f) Pt
De Haftpflicht des Arbeitge-
bers (f)
En employer's liability
Es responsabilidad del patro-
no (f)
Fr responsabilité patronale (f)
It responsabilità del datore
di lavoro (f)

responsabilidade legal (f) Pt
De Rechtshaftung (f)
En legal liability
Es responsabilidad legal (f)
Fr responsabilité légale (f)
It responsabilità legale (f)

responsabilidad legal (f) Es
De Rechtshaftung (f)
En legal liability
Fr responsabilité légale (f)
It responsabilità legale (f)
Pt responsabilidade legal (f)

responsabilità (f) n It
De Verantwortlichkeit (f)
En responsibility; liability
Es responsabilidad (f)
Fr responsabilité (f)
Pt responsabilidade (f)

**responsabilità del datore di
lavoro** (f) It
De Haftpflicht des Arbeitge-
bers (f)
En employer's liability
Es responsabilidad del patro-
no (f)
Fr responsabilité patronale (f)
Pt responsabilidade do patrão
(f)

responsabilità legale (f) It
De Rechtshaftung (f)
En legal liability
Es responsabilidad legal (f)
Fr responsabilité légale (f)
Pt responsabilidade legal (f)

responsabilité (f) n Fr
De Verantwortlichkeit (f)
En responsibility; liability
Es responsabilidad (f)
It responsabilità (f)
Pt responsabilidade (f)

responsabilité légale *(f)* Fr
De Rechtshaftung *(f)*
En legal liability
Es responsabilidad legal *(f)*
It responsabilità legale *(f)*
Pt responsabilidade legal *(f)*

responsabilité patronale *(f)*
Fr
De Haftpflicht des Arbeitge-
bers *(f)*
En employer's liability
Es responsabilidad del patro-
no *(f)*
It responsabilità del datore
di lavoro *(f)*
Pt responsabilidade do patrão
(f)

responsable por daños Es
De schadenersatzpflichtig
En liable for damages
Fr passible de dommages-
intérêts
It responsabile per i danni
Pt responsável por danos

responsável por danos Pt
De schadenersatzpflichtig
En liable for damages
Es responsable por daños
Fr passible de dommages-
intérêts
It responsabile per i danni

responsibility *n* En
De Verantwortlichkeit *(f)*
Es responsabilidad *(f)*
Fr responsabilité *(f)*
It responsabilità *(f)*
Pt responsabilidade *(f)*

resposta *(f) n* Pt
De Antwort *(f)*
En answer
Es respuesta *(f)*
Fr réponse *(f)*
It risposta *(f)*

resposta paga Pt
De Rückantwort bezahlt
En reply paid
Am post paid
Es respuesta pagada
Fr réponse payée
It risposta pagata

respuesta *(f) n* Es
De Antwort *(f)*
En answer
Fr réponse *(f)*
It risposta *(f)*
Pt resposta *(f)*

respuesta pagada Es
De Rückantwort bezahlt
En reply paid
Am post paid
Fr réponse payée
It risposta pagata
Pt resposta paga

resserrement de crédit *(m)*
Fr
De Kreditklemme *(f)*
En credit squeeze
Es escasez de créditos *(f)*
It restrizione di credito *(f)*
Pt restrição de crédito *(f)*

ressources existantes *(f pl)*
Fr
De lieferfertiges Angebot *(n)*
En supplies on hand
Es provisiones existentes
(f pl)
It forniture esistenti *(f pl)*
Pt fornecimentos em
existência *(m pl)*

restare in linea It
De am Apparat bleiben
En hold the line
Es espere al aparato
Fr ne quittez pas
Pt aguarde

resto en efectivo *(m)* Es
De Kassensaldo *(m)*
En cash balance
Fr solde de caisse *(m)*
It residuo di cassa *(m)*
Pt saldo em dinheiro *(m)*

Restpartie *(f) n* De
En odd lot
Es lote suelto *(m)*
Fr solde *(m)*
It partita spaiata *(f)*
Pt lote avulso *(m)*

restraint of trade En
De Handelsbeschränkung *(f)*
Es restricción del commercio
(f)

Fr restriction au commerce *(f)*
It restrizione del commercio
(f)
Pt restrição de comércio *(f)*

restrição de comércio *(f)* Pt
De Handelsbeschränkung *(f)*
En restraint of trade
Es restricción del commercio
(f)
Fr restriction au commerce *(f)*
It restrizione del commercio
(f)

restrição de crédito *(f)* Pt
De Kreditklemme *(f)*
En credit squeeze
Es escasez de créditos *(f)*
Fr resserrement de crédit *(m)*
It restrizione di credito *(f)*

restrição de salários *(f)* Pt
De Lohnbeschränkung *(f)*
En wage restraint
Es restricción de salario *(f)*
Fr contrainte sur les salaires
(f)
It restrizioni sui salari *(f pl)*

restricción del commercio
(f) Es
De Handelsbeschränkung *(f)*
En restraint of trade
Fr restriction au commerce *(f)*
It restrizione del commercio
(f)
Pt restrição de comércio *(f)*

restricción de salario *(f)* Es
De Lohnbeschränkung *(f)*
En wage restraint
Fr contrainte sur les salaires
(f)
It restrizioni sui salari *(f pl)*
Pt restrição de salários *(f)*

**restricciones de importa-
ción** *(f pl)* Es
De Einfuhrbeschränkungen
(f pl)
En import restrictions
Fr restrictions d'importation
(f pl)
It restrizioni delle importazioni *(f pl)*
Pt restrições de importação
(f pl)

restrições de importação
(f pl) Pt
De Einfuhrbeschränkungen
(f pl)
En import restrictions
Es restricciones de importación *(f pl)*
Fr restrictions d'importation
(f pl)
It restrizioni delle importazioni *(f pl)*

restriction au commerce *(f)*
Fr
De Handelsbeschränkung *(f)*
En restraint of trade
Es restricción del commercio
(f)
It restrizione del commercio
(f)
Pt restrição de comércio *(f)*

restrictions d'importation
(f pl) Fr
De Einfuhrbeschränkungen
(f pl)
En import restrictions
Es restricciones de importación *(f pl)*
It restrizioni delle importazioni *(f pl)*
Pt restrições de importação
(f pl)

restrictive covenant En
De einschränkende Bestim-
mung *(f)*
Es convenio restrictivo *(m)*
Fr accord restrictif *(m)*
It accordo restrittivo *(m)*
Pt obrigação restritiva *(f)*

restrictive endorsement En
De Rektaindossement *(n)*
Es endoso restringido *(m)*
Fr endossement restrictif *(m)*
It girata restrittiva *(f)*
Pt endosse restritivo *(m)*

restrizione del commercio
(f) It
De Handelsbeschränkung *(f)*
En restraint of trade
Es restricción del commercio
(f)
Fr restriction au commerce *(f)*
Pt restrição de comércio *(f)*

restrizione di credito *(f)* It
De Kreditklemme *(f)*
En credit squeeze
Es escasez de créditos *(f)*
Fr resserrement de crédit *(m)*
Pt restrição de crédito *(f)*

**restrizioni delle
importazioni** *(f pl)* It
De Einfuhrbeschränkungen
(f pl)
En import restrictions
Es restricciones de importación *(f pl)*
Fr restrictions d'importation
(f pl)
Pt restrições de importação
(f pl)

restrizioni sui salari *(f pl)* It
De Lohnbeschränkung *(f)*
En wage restraint
Es restricción de salario *(f)*
Fr contrainte sur les salaires
(f)
Pt restrição de salários *(f)*

résumé *(m)* n Fr
De Abriß *(m)*
En abstract; summary
Es resumen *(m)*
It riassunto *(m)*
Pt resumo *(m)*

resumen *(m)* n Es
De Abriß *(m)*
En abstract; summary
Fr résumé *(m)*
It riassunto *(m)*
Pt resumo *(m)*

resumo *(m)* n Pt
De Abriß *(m)*
En abstract; summary
Es resumen *(m)*
Fr résumé *(m)*
It riassunto *(m)*

retailer n En
De Einzelhändler; Kleinhänd-
ler *(m)*
Es comerciante al por menor
(m)
Fr commerçant au détail *(m)*
It commerciante al minuto
(m)
Pt comerciante a retalho; re-
talhista *(m)*

retail price En
De Einzelhandelspreis *(m)*
Es precio al por menor *(m)*
Fr prix de détail *(m)*
It prezzo al minuto *(m)*
Pt preço a retalho *(m)*

retail trade En
De Einzelhandel *(m)*
Es comercio al por menor *(m)*
Fr commerce en détail *(m)*
It commercio al minuto *(m)*
Pt comércio a retalho *(m)*

retalhar a carga Pt
De Löschen der Ladung *(n)*
En breaking bulk
Es fraccionamiento de la car-
ga *(m)*
Fr rupture de charge *(f)*
It inizio scarico *(m)*

retard *(m)* n Fr
De Verzug *(m)*
En delay
Es retraso *(m)*
It ritardo *(m)*
Pt atraso *(m)*

rete *(f)* n It
De Netz *(n)*
En network
Es red *(f)*
Fr réseau *(m)*
Pt rede *(f)*

reter acções Pt
De beteiligt sein; Aktien besit-
zen
En hold shares
Es tener acciones
Fr détenir des actions
It tenere azioni

reter em armazém Pt
De vorrätig halten
En keep in stock
Es guardar en almacén
Fr garder en stock
It tenere in magazzino

reter em custódia Pt
De zu treuen Händen halten
En hold in trust
Es guardar in fideicomiso
Fr tenir par fidéicommis
It tenere in fidecommesso

retirar de aduanas Es
De verzollen
En clear through customs
Fr dédouaner
It sdoganare
Pt despachar na alfândega

retire a bill En
De einen Wechsel einlösen
Es recoger una letra
Fr payer une lettre de change
It ritirare un effetto
Pt recuperar uma letra

retirement n En
De Rücktritt; Pensionierung
(m f)
Es retiro (m)
Fr retraite (f)
It ritiro (m)
Pt aposentação (f)

retiro (m) n Es
De Rücktritt; Rente (m f)
En retirement; pension
Fr retraite; pension (f)
It ritiro; pensione (m f)
Pt aposentação; pensão (f)

retiro contributivo (m) Es
De Kassenpension (f)
En contributory pension
Fr retraite de régime à cotisa-
tions (f)
It pensione a contributi (f)
Pt reforma de contribuição
prévia (f)

retiro de vejez (m) Es
De Altersversorgung; Rente (f)
En old-age pension
Fr retraite pour la vieillesse (f)
It pensione per la vecchiaia
(f)
Pt pensão (f)

Retourware (f) n De
En returned goods
Es mercancías devueltas (f pl)
Fr marchandises de retour
(f pl)
It merce di ritorno (f pl)
Pt mercadorias devolvidas
(f pl)

retraite (f) n Fr
De Rücktritt; Rente (m f)
En retirement; pension
Es retiro (m)

It ritiro; pensione (m f)
Pt aposentação; pensão (f)

**retraite de régime à
cotisations** (f) Fr
De Kassenpension (f)
En contributory pension
Es retiro contributivo (m)
It pensione a contributi (f)
Pt reforma de contribuição
prévia (f)

retraite pour la vieillesse (f)
Fr
De Altersversorgung (f)
En old-age pension
Es retiro de vejez (m)
It pensione per la vecchiaia
(f)
Pt pensão (f)

retraso (m) n Es
De Verzug (m)
En delay
Fr retard; délai (m)
It ritardo (m)
Pt atraso (m)

rétroactif adj Fr
De rückwirkend
En retroactive
Es retroactivo
It retroattivo
Pt retroactivo

retroactive adj En
De rückwirkend
Es retroactivo
Fr rétroactif
It retroattivo
Pt retroactivo

retroactivo adj Es, Pt
De rückwirkend
En retroactive
Fr rétroactif
It retroattivo

retroattivo adj It
De rückwirkend
En retroactive
Es retroactivo
Fr rétroactif
Pt retroactivo

retten vb De
En save
Es salvar
Fr sauver
It salvare
Pt salvar

returned goods En
De Retourware (f)
Es mercancías devueltas (f pl)
Fr marchandises de retour
(f pl)
It merce di ritorno (f pl)
Pt mercadorias devolvidas
(f pl)

return fare En
Am roundtrip fare
De Rückfahrkarte (f)
Es pasaje de ida y vuelta (m)
Fr billet d'aller et retour (m)
It biglietto di andata e ritorno
(m)
Pt passagem de ida e volta (f)

return on capital En
De Kapitalertrag (m)
Es beneficio sobre capital (m)
Fr rémunération du capital (f)
It reddito del capitale (m)
Pt juro sobre o capital (m)

reunião (f) n Pt
De Versammlung (f)
En meeting
Es reunión (f)
Fr réunion; assemblée (f)
It riunione; assemblea (f)

reunião da administração
(f) Pt
De Vorstandssitzung (f)
En board meeting
Es reunión del consejo de
administración (f)
Fr réunion du conseil d'ad-
ministration (f)
It riunione del consiglio
d'amministrazione (f)

reunião de credores (f) Pt
De Gläubigerversammlung (f)
En meeting of creditors
Es concurso de acreedores
(m)
Fr assemblée de créanciers
(f)
It convocazione dei creditori
(f)

reunión (f) n Es
De Versammlung (f)
En meeting
Fr réunion; assemblée (f)
It riunione; assemblea (f)
Pt reunião; assembleia (f)

réunion (f) n Fr
De Versammlung (f)
En meeting
Es reunión (f)
It riunione; assemblea (f)
Pt reunião; assembleia (f)

reunión de acreedores (f) Es
De Gläubigerversammlung (f)
En meeting of creditors
Fr assemblée de créanciers (f)
It assemblea dei creditori (f)
Pt assembleia de credores (f)

reunión del consejo de administración (f) Es
De Vorstandssitzung (f)
En board meeting
Fr réunion du conseil d'administration (f)
It riunione del consiglio d'amministrazione (f)
Pt reunião da administração (f)

réunion de conseil d'administration (f) Fr
De Vorstandssitzung (f)
En board meeting
Es reunión del consejo de administración (f)
It riunione del consiglio d'amministrazione (f)
Pt reunião da administração (f)

revalorisation (f) n Fr
De Aufwertung (f)
En revaluation
Es revalorización (f)
It rivalutazione (f)
Pt revalorização (f)

revalorização (f) n Pt
De Aufwertung (f)
En revaluation
Es revalorización (f)
Fr revalorisation (f)
It rivalutazione (f)

revalorización (f) n Es
De Aufwertung (f)
En revaluation

Fr revalorisation (f)
It rivalutazione (f)
Pt revalorização (f)

revaluation n En
De Aufwertung (f)
Es revalorización (f)
Fr revalorisation (f)
It rivalutazione (f)
Pt revalorização (f)

revelação (f) n Pt
De Offenlegung (f)
En disclosure
Es revelación (f)
Fr révélation; divulgation (f)
It rivelazione (f)

revelación (f) n Es
De Offenlegung (f)
En disclosure
Fr révélation; divulgation (f)
It rivelazione (f)
Pt revelação; divulgação (f)

révélation (f) n Fr
De Offenlegung (f)
En disclosure
Es revelación (f)
It rivelazione (f)
Pt revelação; divulgação (f)

revendication de salaire (f) Fr
De Lohnforderung (f)
En wage claim
Es reclamación de salario (f)
It rivendicazione salariale (f)
Pt demanda de salário (f)

revenu (m) n Fr
De Einkommen; Einkünfte (n; f pl)
En income; revenue
Es ingresos; rédito (m pl; m)
It entrata; reddito (f m)
Pt receita; rendimento (f)

revenu de placements (m) Fr
De Einkommen aus Kapitalanlagen (n)
En investment income
Es renta de inversiones (f)
It reddito degli investimenti (m)
Pt rendimento de capitais investidos (m)

revenu disponible (m) Fr
De verfügbares Einkommen (n)
En disposable income
Es renta disponible (f)
It reddito disponibile (m)
Pt receita disponível (f)

revenu du travail (m) Fr
De Arbeitseinkommen (n)
En earned income
Es renta del trabajo (f)
It reddito di lavoro (m)
Pt receita de trabalho (f)

revenue n En
De Einkommen; Einkünfte (n; f pl)
Es ingresos; rédito (m pl; m)
Fr revenu; rentes (m; f pl)
It entrata; reddito (f m)
Pt rendimento (m)

revenu imposable (m) Fr
De steuerpflichtiges Einkommen (n)
En taxable income
Es renta imponible (f)
It reddito tassabile (m)
Pt receita tributável (f)

revenu national (m) Fr
De Nationaleinkommen (n)
En national income
Es renta nacional (f)
It reddito nazionale (m)
Pt receita pública (f)

revenu net (m) Fr
De Nettoeinkommen (n)
En net income
Es ingreso neto (f)
It reddito netto (m)
Pt receita líquida (f)

revenu non imposable (m) Fr
De steuerfreies Einkommen (n)
En nontaxable income
Es ingresos no imponibles (m pl)
It reddito non tassabile (m)
Pt receita não tributável (f)

revisar (cuentas) vb Es
De prüfen
En audit
Fr vérifier et certifier
It rivedere
Pt fiscalizar

revised estimate En
De überarbeitete Schätzung
(f)
Es cálculo revisado (m)
Fr devis rectifié (m)
It preventivo riveduto (m)
Pt estimativa revista (f)

réviseur des comptes (m) Fr
De Bücherrevisor (m)
En auditor
Es revisor de conti (m)
It sindaco (m)
Pt fiscal de contas (m)

revisión de cuentas (f) Es
De Bücherrevision (f)
En audit
Fr vérification comptable (f)
It revisione del conti (f)
Pt fiscalização de contas (f)

revisione del conti (f) It
De Bücherrevision (f)
En audit
Es revisión de cuentas (f)
Fr vérification comptable (f)
Pt fiscalização de contas (f)

revisor de conti (m) Es
De Bücherrevisor (m)
En auditor
Fr réviseur des comptes (m)
It sindaco (m)
Pt fiscal de contas (m)

revoca (f) n It
De Widerruf (m)
En revocation
Es revocación (f)
Fr révocation (f)
Pt revogação (f)

revocación (f) n Es
De Widerruf (m)
En revocation
Fr révocation (f)
It revoca (f)
Pt revogação (f)

revocar vb Es
De widerrufen
En revoke
Fr révoquer
It revocare
Pt revogar

revocare vb It
De widerrufen
En revoke
Es revocar
Fr révoquer
Pt revogar

revocation n En
De Widerruf (m)
Es revocación (f)
Fr révocation (f)
It revoca (f)
Pt revogação (f)

révocation (f) n Fr
De Widerruf (m)
En revocation
Es revocación (f)
It revoca (f)
Pt revogação (f)

revogação (f) n Pt
De Widerruf (m)
En revocation
Es revocación (f)
Fr révocation (f)
It revoca (f)

revogar vb Pt
De widerrufen
En revoke
Es revocar
Fr révoquer
It revocare

revoke vb En
De widerrufen
Es revocar
Fr révoquer
It revocare
Pt revogar

revolving credit En
De automatisch sich erneu-
erndes Akkreditiv (n)
Es crédito reponible (m)
Fr accréditif automatique-
ment renouvelable (m)
It credito rotativo (m)
Pt crédito renovável (m)

revolving fund En
De Umlaufkapital (n)
Es fondo circulante (m)
Fr fonds renouvelable (m)
It fondo rotativo (m)
Pt fundos renováveis (m pl)

révoquer vb Fr
De widerrufen
En revoke
Es revocar
It revocare
Pt revogar

revue du marché (f) Fr
De Marktbericht (m)
En market report
Es informe del mercado (m)
It relazione sul mercato (f)
Pt informação do mercado (f)

**revueltas y conmociones
civiles** Es
De Aufruhr und innere Unru-
hen
En riot and civil commotion
Fr émeutes et désordres
It rivolte e moti civili
Pt motins e perturbações civis

rez-de-chaussée (m) Fr
De Erdgeschoß (n)
En ground floor
Es planta baja (f)
It pianterreno (m)
Pt rés-do-chão (m)

Rezession (f) n De
En recession
Es recesión (f)
Fr récession (f)
It recessione (f)
Pt recessão (f)

rialzista (m) n It
De Haussespekulant (m)
En bull
Es alcista (m)
Fr haussier (m)
Pt altista (m)

rialzista adj It
De steigend
En bullish
Es alcista
Fr haussier
Pt altista

rialzo (m) n It
De Hausse (f)
En boom
Es bonanza (f)
Fr haute conjoncture (f)
Pt bonança (f)

rialzo (di prezzo) *(m) n* It
De Preiserhöhung *(f)*
En advance in price
Es encarecimiento *(m)*
Fr renchérissement *(m)*
Pt encarecimento *(m)*

riaprire la discussione It
De Verhandlungen wieder-
    aufnehmen
En re-open discussions
Es reabrir la discusión
Fr rouvrir la discussion
Pt reabrir discussões

riassicurazione *(f) n* It
De Rückversicherung *(f)*
En reinsurance
Es reaseguro *(m)*
Fr réassurance *(f)*
Pt re-seguro *(m)*

riassunto *(m) n* It
De Abriß *(m)*
En abstract; summary
Es resumen *(m)*
Fr résumé *(m)*
Pt resumo *(m)*

ribassista *(m) n* It
De Baissespekulant; Baissier
    (m)
En bear
Es bajista *(m)*
Fr baissier *(m)*
Pt baixista *(m)*

ribassista *adj* It
De flau
En bearish
Es bajista
Fr orienté à la baisse
Pt baixista

ribasso *(m) n* It
De Nachlaß; Rabatt *(m)*
En rebate
Es rebaja *(f)*
Fr rabais *(m)*
Pt desconto *(m)*

ricavo netto *(m)* It
De Reinerlös *(m)*
En net proceeds
Es rédito neto *(m)*
Fr produit net *(m)*
Pt proventos líquidos *(m pl)*

ricchezza *(f) n* It
De Wohlstand *(m)*
En wealth
Es riqueza *(f)*
Fr richesse *(f)*
Pt riqueza *(f)*

ricerca *(f) n* It
De Forschung *(f)*
En research
Es investigación *(f)*
Fr recherche *(f)*
Pt investigação *(f)*

ricercato It
De gefragt
En in demand
Es solicitado
Fr demandé
Pt procurado

ricevimento per posta aerea
    (m) It
De Luftpostempfangsbe-
    scheinigung *(f)*
En airmail receipt
Es recibo aeropostal *(m)*
Fr récépissé de poste
    aérienne *(m)*
Pt recibo de via aérea *(m)*

ricevuta *(f) n* It
De Quittung *(f)*
En receipt
Es recibo *(m)*
Fr quittance; acquit *(f m)*
Pt recibo *(m)*

ricevuta d'imbarco *(f)* It
De Übernahmebescheinigung
    (f)
En mate's receipt
Es recibo de embarco *(m)*
Fr billet de bord *(m)*
Pt recibo de embarque *(m)*

ricevuta ferroviaria *(f)* It
De Bahnfrachtbrief *(m)*
En railway receipt
Es recibo ferroviario *(m)*
Fr bulletin de chargement *(m)*
Pt recibo ferroviário *(m)*

ricevuto per caricazione It
De zur Absendung empfan-
    gen
En received for shipment

Es recibido para envío
Fr reçu pour envoi
Pt recebido para carrega-
    mento

richesse *(f) n* Fr
De Wohlstand *(m)*
En wealth
Es riqueza *(f)*
It ricchezza *(f)*
Pt riqueza *(f)*

richiesta *(f) n* It
De Anforderung *(f)*
En requisition
Es pedido; solicitud *(m f)*
Fr demande *(f)*
Pt pedido *(m)*

richiesta (di fondi) *(f)* It
De Kündigung (von Geldern)
    (f)
En call (for funds)
Es llamada (de fondos) *(f)*
Fr appel (de fonds) *(m)*
Pt chamada (de fundos) *(f)*

Richter *(m) n* De
En judge
Es juez *(m)*
Fr juge *(m)*
It giudice *(m)*
Pt juiz *(m)*

ricostruzione *(f) n* It
De Wiederaufbau *(m)*
En reconstruction
Es reconstrucción *(f)*
Fr reconstruction *(f)*
Pt reconstrução *(f)*

ricupero d'informazioni *(m)* It
De Informationswiederge-
    winnung *(f)*
En information retrieval
Es rebusca de información *(f)*
Fr récupération de données
    (f)
Pt recuperação de informação
    (f)

riduzione dei prezzi *(f)* It
De Preisherabsetzung *(f)*
En price-cutting
Es reducción de precios *(f)*
Fr rabais des prix *(m)*
Pt redução de preços *(f)*

riduzione del capitale *(f)* It
De Kapitalherabsetzung *(f)*
En reduction of capital
Es reducción de capital *(f)*
Fr réduction de capital *(f)*
Pt redução de capital *(f)*

riesgo *(m)* n Es
De Risiko *(n)*
En risk
Fr risque *(m)*
It rischio *(m)*
Pt risco *(m)*

riesgo profesional *(m)* Es
De Berufsrisiko *(n)*
En occupational hazard
Fr risque professionnel *(m)*
It rischio del lavoro *(m)*
Pt acidente próprio da pro-
fissão *(m)*

riesportare *vb* It
De wiederausführen
En re-export
Es reexportar
Fr réexporter
Pt reexportar

riesporto *(m)* n It
De Wiederausfuhr *(f)*
En re-exportation
Es reexportación *(f)*
Fr réexportation *(f)*
Pt reexportação *(f)*

rifiuti tossici *(m pl)* It
De giftiger Abfall *(m)*
En toxic waste
Es efluentes tóxicos *(m pl)*
Fr déchets toxiques *(m pl)*
Pt despejos tóxicos *(m pl)*

rifiuto *(m)* n It
De Ablehnung *(f)*
En rejection
Es rechazo *(m)*
Fr refus *(m)*
Pt rejeição *(f)*

riforma monetaria *(f)* It
De Währungsreform *(f)*
En monetary reform
Es reforma monetaria *(f)*
Fr réforme monétaire *(f)*
Pt reforma monetária *(f)*

rifugio fiscale *(m)* It
De Steuerparadies *(n)*
En tax haven
Es refugio fiscal *(m)*
Fr refuge fiscal *(m)*
Pt refúgio fiscal *(m)*

rights *pl* n En
De Rechte *(n pl)*
Es derechos *(m pl)*
Fr droits *(m pl)*
It diritti *(m pl)*
Pt direitos *(m pl)*

rights issue En
De Sonderemission gegen
Bezugsrechte *(f)*
Es emisión de derechos *(f)*
Fr émission sous droit de
souscription *(f)*
It emissione di diritti *(f)*
Pt emissão de direitos *(f)*

rimborso *(m)* n It
De Rückerstattung *(f)*
En refund
Es reembolso *(m)*
Fr remboursement *(m)*
Pt reembolso *(m)*

rimborso d'esportazione *(m)*
It
De Zollrückvergütung *(f)*
En (customs) drawback
Es reembolso de derechos de
aduana *(m)*
Fr remboursement des droits
d'importation *(m)*
Pt reembolso de direitos al-
fandegários *(m)*

rimessa telegrafica *(f)* It
De Kabelauszahlung *(f)*
En telegraphic transfer
Es giro telegráfico *(m)*
Fr virement télégraphique *(m)*
Pt transferência telegráfica *(f)*

rimorchiatore *(m)* n It
De Schleppdampfer *(m)*
En tug-boat
Es remolcador *(m)*
Fr remorqueur *(m)*
Pt rebocador *(m)*

rimunerazione *(f)* n It
De Vergütung *(f)*
En remuneration
Es remuneración *(f)*
Fr rémunération *(f)*
Pt remuneração *(f)*

rinunzia *(f)* n It
De Verzicht *(m)*
En renunciation
Es renuncia *(f)*
Fr renonciation *(f)*
Pt renúncia *(f)*

rinunziare *vb* It
De verzichten auf
En renounce
Es renunciar
Fr renoncer à
Pt renunciar

riot and civil commotion En
De Aufruhr und innere Unru-
hen
Es revueltas y conmociones
civiles
Fr émeutes et désordres
It rivolte e moti civili
Pt motins e perturbações civis

riparare *vb* It
De reparieren
En repair
Es reparar; componer
Fr reparer; réfectionner
Pt consertar; reparar

riparazione *(f)* n It
De Reparatur *(f)*
En repair
Es reparación *(f)*
Fr réparation *(f)*
Pt reparação *(f)*

ripartire *vb* It
De verteilen; zuteilen
En distribute; apportion
Es repartir
Fr répartir
Pt repartir

ripartizione *(f)* n It
De Verteilung *(f)*
En distribution; allotment
Es reparto; adjudicación *(f)*
Fr distribution; attribution *(f)*
Pt distribuição; aporciona-
mento *(f m)*

**ripartizione della
 tassazione** *(f)* It
De Steuerveranlagung *(f)*
En tax base
Es base contributiva *(f)*
Fr assiette de l'impôt *(f)*
Pt base de imposto *(f)*

riqueza *(f)* n Es, Pt
De Wohlstand *(m)*
En wealth
Fr richesse *(f)*
It ricchezza *(f)*

riscaldamento centrale *(m)* It
De Zentralheizung *(f)*
En central heating
Es calefacción central *(f)*
Fr chauffage central *(m)*
Pt aquecimento central *(m)*

rischio *(m)* n It
De Wagnis; Risiko *(n)*
En hazard; risk
Es azar; riesgo *(m)*
Fr hasard; risque *(m)*
Pt risco; azar *(m)*

rischio del lavoro *(m)* It
De Berufsrisiko *(n)*
En occupational hazard
Es riesgo profesional *(m)*
Fr risque professionnel *(m)*
Pt acidente próprio da pro-
 fissão *(m)*

risco *(m)* n Pt
De Wagnis; Risiko *(n)*
En hazard; risk
Es azar; riesgo *(m)*
Fr hasard; risque *(m)*
It rischio *(m)*

riserva di capitale *(f)* It
De Kapitalreserve *(f)*
En capital reserves
Es reserva de capital *(f)*
Fr réserve de capitaux *(f)*
Pt reservas de capital *(f pl)*

riserva di previdenza *(f)* It
De Rückstellung für Eventual-
 verbindlichkeiten *(f)*
En contingency reserve
Es reserva para imprevistos
 (f)
Fr réserve de prévoyance *(f)*
Pt reserva para as con-
 tingências *(f)*

riserva in contanti *(f)* It
De Kassenreserve *(f)*
En cash reserve
Es reserva en efectivo *(f)*
Fr réserve en espèces *(f)*
Pt reserva em dinheiro *(f)*

riserva occulta *(f)* It
De stille Reserve *(f)*
En hidden reserve
Es reserva latente *(f)*
Fr réserve cachée *(f)*
Pt reserva oculta *(f)*

riserva per crediti inesigibili
 (f) It
De Dubiosenreserve *(f)*
En bad debt reserve
Es reserva para deudas inco-
 brables *(f)*
Fr provision pour créances
 douteuses *(f)*
Pt reserva para dívidas in-
 cobráveis *(f)*

riservare *vb* It
De vorbehalten
En reserve
Es reservar
Fr réserver
Pt reservar

Risiko *(n)* n De
En risk
Es riesgo *(m)*
Fr risque *(m)*
It rischio *(m)*
Pt risco *(m)*

risk n En
De Risiko *(n)*
Es riesgo *(m)*
Fr risque *(m)*
It rischio *(m)*
Pt risco *(m)*

risk capital En
De Spekulationskapital *(n)*
Es capital de especulación
 (m)
Fr capitaux spéculatifs *(m pl)*
It capitale di speculazione
 (m)
Pt capital de especulação *(m)*

risoluzione di un contratto *(f)*
 It
De Vertragsbeendigung *(f)*
En determination of a con-
 tract
Es rescisión de un contrato *(f)*
Fr résolution d'un contrat *(f)*
Pt rescisão de contrato *(f)*

risparmiare *vb* It
De aufsparen
En save
Es ahorrar
Fr épargner
Pt poupar

risposta *(f)* n It
De Antwort *(f)*
En answer
Es respuesta *(f)*
Fr réponse *(f)*
Pt resposta *(f)*

risposta pagata It
De Rückantwort bezahlt
En reply paid
Am post paid
Es respuesta pagada
Fr réponse payée
Pt resposta paga

risque *(m)* n Fr
De Risiko *(n)*
En risk
Es riesgo *(m)*
It rischio *(m)*
Pt risco *(m)*

risque professionnel *(m)* Fr
De Berufsrisiko *(n)*
En occupational hazard
Es riesgo profesional *(m)*
It rischio del lavoro *(m)*
Pt acidente próprio da pro-
 fissão *(m)*

ritardo *(m)* n It
De Verzug *(m)*
En delay
Es retraso *(m)*
Fr retard; délai *(m)*
Pt atraso *(m)*

ritirare un effetto It
De einen Wechsel einlösen
En retire a bill
Es recoger una letra
Fr payer une lettre de change
Pt recuperar uma letra

ritiro *(m) n* It
De Rücktritt; Pensionierung
(m f)
En retirement
Es retiro *(m)*
Fr retraite *(f)*
Pt aposentação *(f)*

riunione *(f) n* It
De Versammlung *(f)*
En meeting
Es reunión *(f)*
Fr réunion; assemblée *(f)*
Pt reunião; assembleia *(f)*

**riunione del consiglio
d'amministrazione** *(f)* It
De Vorstandssitzung *(f)*
En board meeting
Es reunión del consejo de
administración *(f)*
Fr réunion de conseil d'admi-
nistration *(f)*
Pt reunião da administração *(f)*

rival *n* En; Es, Fr, Pt *(m)*
De Rivale *(m)*
It rivale *(m)*

rivale *(m) n* It
De Rivale *(m)*
En rival
Es rival *(m)*
Fr rival *(m)*
Pt rival *(m)*

Rivale *(m) n* De
En rival
Es rival *(m)*
Fr rival *(m)*
It rivale *(m)*
Pt rival *(m)*

rivalutazione *(f) n* It
De Aufwertung *(f)*
En revaluation
Es revalorización *(f)*
Fr revalorisation *(f)*
Pt revalorização *(f)*

rivedere (i conti) *vb* It
De prüfen
En audit
Es revisar
Fr vérifier et certifier
Pt fiscalizar as contas

rivelazione *(f) n* It
De Offenlegung *(f)*
En disclosure
Es revelación *(f)*
Fr révélation; divulgation *(f)*
Pt revelação; divulgação *(f)*

rivendicazione salariale *(f)* It
De Lohnforderung *(f)*
En wage claim
Es reclamación de salario *(f)*
Fr revendication de salaire *(f)*
Pt demanda de salário *(f)*

rivolte e moti civili It
De Aufruhr und innere Unru-
hen
En riot and civil commotion
Es revueltas y conmociones
civiles
Fr émeutes et désordres
Pt motins e perturbações civis

robo *(m) n* Es
De Diebstahl *(m)*
En theft
Fr vol *(m)*
It furto *(m)*
Pt furto *(m)*

Roheisen *(n) n* De
En pig-iron
Es hierro bruto *(m)*
Fr fer en gueuse *(m)*
It pane di ghisa *(m)*
Pt ferro em bruto *(m)*

rohe Schätzung *(f)* De
En rough estimate
Es presupuesto aproximado
(m)
Fr estimation approximative
(f)
It valutazione approssimati-
va *(f)*
Pt avaliação aproximada *(f)*

Rohstoff *(m) n* De
En raw material
Es materia prima *(f)*
Fr matière première *(f)*
It materia prima *(f)*
Pt matéria prima *(f)*

Rohstoffmarkt *(m) n* De
En commodity market
Es mercado de materias pri-
mas *(m)*

Fr marché de matières premières *(m)*
It mercato di materie prime
(m)
Pt mercado de matérias primas *(m)*

rotação de culturas *(f)* Pt
De Fruchtwechsel *(m)*
En rotation of crops
Es rotación de cultivos *(f)*
Fr rotation des cultures *(f)*
It rotazione delle coltivazioni
(f)

rotación de cultivos *(f)* Es
De Fruchtwechsel *(m)*
En rotation of crops
Fr rotation des cultures *(f)*
It rotazione delle coltivazioni
(f)
Pt rotação de culturas *(f)*

rotation des cultures *(f)* Fr
De Fruchtwechsel *(m)*
En rotation of crops
Es rotación de cultivos *(f)*
It rotazione delle coltivazioni
(f)
Pt rotação de culturas *(f)*

rotation of crops En
De Fruchtwechsel *(m)*
Es rotación de cultivos *(f)*
Fr rotation des cultures *(f)*
It rotazione delle coltivazioni
(f)
Pt rotação de culturas *(f)*

rottura di contratto *(f)* It
De Vertragsverletzung *(f)*
En breach of contract
Es incumplimiento del contra-
to *(m)*
Fr rupture de contrat *(f)*
Pt rotura de contrato *(f)*

rótulo *(m) n* Pt
De Etikett *(n)*
En label
Es etiqueta *(f)*
Fr étiquette *(f)*
It etichetta *(f)*

rotura de contrato *(f)* Pt
De Vertragsverletzung *(f)*
En breach of contract

Es incumplimiento del contra-
to *(m)*
Fr rupture de contrat *(f)*
It rottura di contratto *(f)*

rough estimate En
De rohe Schätzung *(f)*
Es presupuesto aproximado
(m)
Fr estimation approximative
(f)
It valutazione approssimati-
va *(f)*
Pt avaliação aproximada *(f)*

roundtrip fare Am
En return fare
De Rückfahrkarte *(f)*
Es pasaje de ida y vuelta *(m)*
Fr billet d'aller et retour *(m)*
It biglietto di andata e ritorno
(m)
Pt passagem de ida e volta *(f)*

rouvrir la discussion Fr
De Verhandlungen wieder-
aufnehmen
En re-open discussions
Es reabrir la discusión
It riaprire la discussione
Pt reabrir discussões

royalty *n* En
De Tantieme; Gewinnanteil
(f m)
Es derechos *(m pl)*
Fr redevance; droits *(f; m pl)*
It diritti *(m pl)*
Pt direitos *(m pl)*

rubber stamp En
De Gummistempel *(m)*
Es estampilla de goma *(f)*
Fr tampon *(m)*
It stampino di gomma *(m)*
Pt carimbo *(m)*

rubricar *vb* Es, Pt
De paraphieren
En initial
Fr parapher; viser
It siglare

Rückantwort bezahlt De
En reply paid
Am post paid
Es respuesta pagada

Fr réponse payée
It risposta pagata
Pt resposta paga

Rückerstattung *(f) n* De
En refund
Es reembolso *(m)*
Fr remboursement *(m)*
It rimborso *(m)*
Pt reembolso *(m)*

Rückfahrkarte *(f) n* De
En return fare
Am roundtrip fare
Es pasaje de ida y vuelta *(m)*
Fr billet d'aller et retour *(m)*
It biglietto di andata e ritorno
(m)
Pt passagem de ida e volta *(f)*

rückgängig machen (ein Ge-
schäft) De
En call off (a deal)
Es anular (un negocio)
Fr annuler (un marché)
It annullare (un affare)
Pt anular (uma transação)

Rückkaufswert *(m) n* De
En surrender value
Es valor de rescate *(m)*
Fr valeur di rachat *(f)*
It valore di riscatto *(m)*
Pt valor de resgate *(m)*

**Rücksendung wenn
unverkauft** De
En sale or return
Es venta o devolución
Fr vente avec faculté de re-
tour
It da vendere o rimandare
Pt venda ou devolução

Rückstand *(m) n* De
En arrears
Es atrasos *(m pl)*
Fr arrérages *(m pl)*
It arretrati *(m pl)*
Pt atrasos *(m pl)*

rückständig *adj* De
En overdue
Es vencido
Fr arriéré
It scaduto
Pt vencido

**Rückstellung für Eventual-
verbindlichkeiten** *(f)* De
En contingency reserve
Es reserva para imprevistos
(f)
Fr réserve de prévoyance *(f)*
It riserva di previdenza *(f)*
Pt reserva para as con-
tingências *(f)*

Rückstellungskonto *(n) n* De
En appropriation account
Es cuenta de apropiación *(f)*
Fr compte d'affectation *(m)*
It conto di stanziamento *(m)*
Pt conta de apropriação *(f)*

Rücktritt *(m) n* De
En retirement
Es retiro *(m)*
Fr retraite *(f)*
It ritiro *(m)*
Pt aposentação *(f)*

(den) Rücktritt einreichen
De
En hand in one's resignation
Es presentar la dimisión
Fr remettre sa démission
It rassegnare le dimissioni
Pt apresentar demissão

Rücktrittsklausel *(f) n* De
En determination clause
Es cláusula resolutiva *(f)*
Fr clause résolutoire *(f)*
It clausola risolutiva *(f)*
Pt cláusula de rescisão *(f)*

Rückversicherung *(f) n* De
En reinsurance
Es reaseguro *(m)*
Fr réassurance *(f)*
It riassicurazione *(f)*
Pt re-seguro *(m)*

rückwirkend *adj* De
En retroactive
Es retroactivo
Fr rétroactif
It retroattivo
Pt retroactivo

Ruhegeld *(n) n* De
En pension
Es pensión *(f)*
Fr pension *(f)*
It pensione *(f)*
Pt pensão *(f)*

rupture de charge *(f)* Fr
De Löschen der Ladung *(n)*
En breaking bulk
Es fraccionamiento de la carga *(m)*
It inizio scarico *(m)*
Pt retalhar a carga

rupture de contrat *(f)* Fr
De Vertragsverletzung *(f)*
En breach of contract
Es incumplimiento del contrato *(m)*
It rottura di contratto *(f)*
Pt rotura de contrato *(f)*

rupture de garantie *(f)* Fr
De Verletzung der Gewährleistungspflicht *(f)*
En breach of warranty
Es incumplimiento de la garantía *(m)*
It violazione di garanzia *(f)*
Pt violação de garantia *(f)*

rush hour En
De Hauptverkehrszeit *(f)*
Es hora punta *(f)*
Fr heures d'affluence *(f)*
It ora di punta *(f)*
Pt hora de ponta *(f)*

S

sacado *(m)* n Pt
De Bezogene(r) *(m)*
En drawee
Es librado *(m)*
Fr tiré *(m)*
It trattario *(m)*

sacador *(m)* n Pt
De Aussteller *(m)*
En drawer
Es librador *(m)*
Fr tireur *(m)*
It traente *(m)*

sacar reservas Es
De die Reserven angreifen
En draw on reserves
Fr prélever sur les réserves
It prelevare dalle riserve
Pt recorrer a reservas

Sachkundige(r) *(m)* n De
En expert
Es experto *(m)*
Fr expert *(m)*
It competente *(m)*
Pt experiente *(m)*

Sachverständigen-gutachten *(n)* n De
En expert's report
Es informe del especialista *(m)*
Fr expertise *(f)*
It perizia *(f)*
Pt relatório do perito *(m)*

Sachverständige(r) *(m)* n De
En expert; specialist
Es especialista *(m)*
Fr spécialiste; expert *(m)*
It perito; specialista *(m)*
Pt perito; especialista *(m)*

safe n En
De Geldschrank *(m)*
Es caja fuerte *(f)*
Fr coffre-fort *(m)*
It cassaforte *(f)*
Pt cofre *(m)*

safe custody En
De sichere Verwahrung *(f)*
Es custodia *(f)*
Fr bonne garde *(f)*
It custodia *(f)*
Pt custódia segura *(f)*

safe deposit En
De Verwahrung in Stahlfach *(f)*
Es depósito en caja fuerte *(m)*
Fr dépôt en coffre-fort *(m)*
It servizio di cassette di sicurezza *(m)*
Pt depósito em cofre forte *(m)*

safety factor En
De Sicherheitskoeffizient *(m)*
Es factor de seguridad *(m)*
Fr facteur de sécurité *(m)*
It coefficiente di sicurezza *(m)*
Pt factor de segurança *(m)*

saggio *(m)* n It
De Probe *(f)*
En assay; test
Es ensayo; prueba *(m f)*
Fr essai; épreuve *(m f)*
Pt ensaio; prova *(m f)*

sailing date En
De Abgangstag *(m)*
Es día de salida *(m)*
Fr date de départ *(f)*
It data di partenza *(f)*
Pt dia de saída *(m)*

saisie des données *(f)* Fr
De Datenerfassung *(f)*
En data capture
Es recogida de datos *(f)*
It raccolta dati *(f)*
Pt recolha de dados *(f)*

saison *(f)* n Fr
De Jahreszeit *(f)*
En season
Es estación *(f)*
It stagione *(f)*
Pt estação *(f)*

salaire *(m)* n Fr
De Lohn *(m)*
En wages; earnings
Es salario *(m)*
It guadagni *(m pl)*
Pt salário *(m)*

salaire au rendement *(m)* Fr
De Leistungslohn *(m)*
En payment by results
Es pago por resultados *(m)*
It pagamento secondo i risultati *(m)*
Pt pagamento relativo aos resultados *(m)*

salaire de base *(f)* Fr
De Grundlohn *(m)*
En basic pay
Am base pay
Es salario-base *(m)*
It salario fondamentale *(m)*
Pt salário-base *(m)*

salaire net *(m)* Fr
De Nettolohn *(m)*
En take-home pay
Es paga neta *(f)*
It paga netta *(f)*
Pt salário líquido *(m)*

salariato *(m)* n It
De Lohnempfänger *(m)*
En wage earner
Es asalariado *(m)*
Fr salarié *(m)*
Pt assalariado *(m)*

salarié *(m)* n Fr
De Lohnempfänger *(m)*
En wage earner
Es asalariado *(m)*
It salariato *(m)*
Pt assalariado *(m)*

salaried employee En
De Angestellte(r) *(m)*
Es empleado a sueldo *(m)*
Fr appointé *(m)*
It stipendiato *(m)*
Pt assalariado *(m)*

salario *(m)* n Es
De Lohn *(m)*
En wages; earnings
Fr salaire *(m)*
It guadagni *(m pl)*
Pt salário *(m)*

salário *(m)* n Pt
De Lohn *(m)*
En wages; earnings
Es salario *(m)*
Fr salaire *(m)*
It guadagni *(m pl)*

salario-base *(m)* n Es
De Grundlohn *(m)*
En basic pay
Am base pay
Fr salaire de base *(f)*
It salario fondamentale *(m)*
Pt salário-base *(m)*

salário-base *(m)* n Pt
De Grundlohn *(m)*
En basic pay
Am base pay
Es salario-base *(m)*
Fr salaire de base *(f)*
It salario fondamentale *(m)*

salario fondamentale *(m)* It
De Grundlohn *(m)*
En basic pay
Am base pay
Es salario-base *(m)*
Fr salaire de base *(f)*
Pt salário-base *(m)*

salário líquido *(m)* Pt
De Nettolohn *(m)*
En take-home pay
Es paga neta *(f)*
Fr salaire net *(m)*
It paga netta *(f)*

salary n En
De Gehalt *(n)*
Es sueldo *(m)*
Fr traitement *(m)*
It stipendio *(m)*
Pt ordenado *(m)*

saldar una cuenta Es
De eine Rechnung ausgleichen
En balance an account
Fr balancer un compte
It pareggiare un conto
Pt equilibrar uma conta

saldo *(m)* n Es, It, Pt
De Saldo *(m)*
En balance
Fr solde *(m)*

Saldo *(m)* n De
En balance
Es saldo *(m)*
Fr solde *(m)*
It saldo *(m)*
Pt saldo *(m)*

saldo acreedor *(m)* Es
De Kreditsaldo *(m)*
En credit balance
Fr solde créditeur *(m)*
It saldo creditore *(m)*
Pt saldo credor *(m)*

saldo activo *(m)* Es
De Aktivsaldo *(m)*
En active balance
Fr balance excédentaire *(f)*
It saldo attivo *(m)*
Pt saldo positivo *(m)*

saldo adverso *(m)* Es
De Passivsaldo *(m)*
En adverse balance
Am negative balance
Fr balance déficitaire *(f)*
It saldo passivo *(m)*
Pt saldo negativo *(m)*

saldo attivo *(m)* It
De Aktivsaldo *(m)*
En active balance
Es saldo activo *(m)*
Fr balance excédentaire *(f)*
Pt saldo positivo *(m)*

saldo creditore *(m)* It
De Kreditsaldo *(m)*
En credit balance

Es saldo acreedor *(m)*
Fr solde créditeur *(m)*
Pt saldo credor *(m)*

saldo credor *(m)* Pt
De Kreditsaldo *(m)*
En credit balance
Es saldo acreedor *(m)*
Fr solde créditeur *(m)*
It saldo creditore *(m)*

saldo de riportare *(m)* It
De Saldovortrag *(m)*
En balance carried forward
Es saldo de entrada *(m)*
Fr roport à nouveau *(m)*
Pt saldo transportado *(m)*

saldo de banco *(m)* Es
De Bankguthaben *(n)*
En bank balance
Fr solde en banque *(m)*
It saldo in banca *(m)*
Pt saldo no banco *(m)*

saldo debitore *(m)* It
De Sollsaldo *(m)*
En debit balance
Es saldo en débito *(m)*
Fr solde débiteur *(m)*
Pt saldo devedor *(m)*

saldo de entrada *(m)* Es
De Saldovortrag *(m)*
En balance carried forward
Fr report à nouveau *(m)*
It saldo da riportare *(m)*
Pt saldo transportado *(m)*

saldo del dividendo *(m)* Es, It
De Schlußdividende *(f)*
En final dividend
Fr solde de dividende *(m)*
Pt dividendo final *(m)*

saldo devedor *(m)* Pt
De Sollsaldo *(m)*
En debit balance
Es saldo en débito *(m)*
Fr solde débiteur *(m)*
It saldo debitore *(m)*

saldo dovuto *(m)* It
De Ausgleichssaldo *(m)*
En balance due
Es balance vencido *(m)*
Fr solde dû *(m)*
Pt saldo em dívida *(m)*

saldo em dinheiro *(m)* Pt
De Kassensaldo *(m)*
En cash balance
Es resto en efectivo *(m)*
Fr solde de caisse *(m)*
It residuo di cassa *(m)*

saldo em dívida *(m)* Pt
De Ausgleichssaldo *(m)*
En balance due
Es balance vencido *(m)*
Fr solde dû *(m)*
It saldo dovuto *(m)*

saldo em poder *(m)* Pt
De verfügbarer Saldo *(m)*
En balance in hand
Es sobrante *(m)*
Fr solde en caisse *(m)*
It saldo in cassa *(m)*

saldo en débito *(m)* Es
De Sollsaldo *(m)*
En debit balance
Fr solde débiteur *(m)*
It saldo debitore *(m)*
Pt saldo devedor *(m)*

saldo final *(m)* Es
De Schlußbilanz *(f)*
En final balance
Fr solde net *(m)*
It saldo finale *(m)*
Pt balanço final *(m)*

saldo finale *(m)* It
De Schlußbilanz *(f)*
En final balance
Es saldo final *(m)*
Fr solde net *(m)*
Pt balanço final *(m)*

saldo in banca *(m)* It
De Bankguthaben *(n)*
En bank balance
Es saldo de banco *(m)*
Fr solde en banque *(m)*
Pt saldo no banco *(m)*

saldo in cassa *(m)* It
De verfügbarer Saldo *(m)*
En balance in hand
Es sobrante *(m)*
Fr solde en caisse *(m)*
Pt saldo em poder *(m)*

saldo negativo *(m)* Pt
De Passivsaldo *(m)*
En adverse balance

Am negative balance
Es saldo adverso *(m)*
Fr balance déficitaire *(f)*
It saldo passivo *(m)*

saldo no banco *(m)* Pt
De Bankguthaben *(n)*
En bank balance
Es saldo de banco *(m)*
Fr solde en banque *(m)*
It saldo in banca *(m)*

saldo nullo *(m)* It
De Nullsaldo *(m)*
En nil balance
Am zero balance
Es saldo nulo *(m)*
Fr solde nul *(m)*
Pt saldo nulo *(m)*

saldo nulo *(m)* Es, Pt
De Nullsaldo *(m)*
En nil balance
Am zero balance
Fr solde nul *(m)*
It saldo nullo *(m)*

saldo passivo *(m)* It
De Passivsaldo *(m)*
En adverse balance
Am negative balance
Es saldo adverso *(m)*
Fr balance déficitaire *(f)*
Pt saldo negativo *(m)*

saldo positivo *(m)* Pt
De Kreditsaldo *(m)*
En credit balance
Es saldo activo *(m)*
Fr solde créditeur *(m)*
It saldo a credito *(m)*

saldo transportado *(m)* Pt
De Saldovortrag *(m)*
En balance carried forward
Es saldo de entrada *(m)*
Fr report à nouveau *(m)*
It saldo da riportare *(m)*

Saldovortrag *(m) n* De
En balance carried forward
Es saldo de entrada *(m)*
Fr report à nouveau *(m)*
It saldo da riportare *(m)*
Pt saldo transportado *(m)*

sale *n* En
De Verkauf *(m)*
Es venta *(f)*
Fr vente *(f)*
It vendita *(f)*
Pt venda *(f)*

sale by auction En
De Versteigerung *(f)*
Es venta a subasta *(f)*
Fr vente aux enchères *(f)*
It vendita all'asta *(f)*
Pt venda em leilão *(f)*

sale or return En
De Rücksendung wenn un-
    verkauft
Es venta o devolución
Fr vente avec faculté de re-
    tour
It da vendere o rimandare
Pt venda ou devolução

sales agent Am
En mercantile agent
De Handelsvertreter *(m)*
Es agente mercantil *(m)*
Fr agent de commerce *(m)*
It agente di commercio *(m)*
Pt agente comercial *(m)*

sales analysis En
De Verkaufsanalyse *(f)*
Es análisis de ventas *(m)*
Fr analyse des ventes *(f)*
It analisi delle vendite *(f)*
Pt análise de vendas *(f)*

sales department En
De Verkaufsabteilung *(f)*
Es departamento de ventas
    (m)
Fr service ventes *(m)*
It ufficio vendite *(m)*
Pt departamento de vendas
    (m)

sales figure En
De Umsatz *(m)*
Es cifra de ventas *(f)*
Fr chiffre d'affaires *(f)*
It cifra di vendite *(f)*
Pt número de vendas *(m)*

sales force En
De Verkaufspersonal *(n)*
Es personal de ventas *(m)*
Fr personnel de vente *(m)*
It forze di vendita *(f pl)*
Pt pessoal de vendas *(m)*

sales forecast En
De Verkaufsvoraussage *(f)*
Es pronóstico de ventas *(m)*
Fr prévision de ventes *(f)*
It previsione delle vendite *(f)*
Pt previsão de vendas *(f)*

sales ledger En
De Verkaufskontenbuch *(n)*
Es libro mayor de ventas *(m)*
Fr grand livre des ventes *(m)*
It partitario delle vendite *(m)*
Pt livro-mestre de vendas *(m)*

sales (publicity) letter En
De Werbebrief *(m)*
Es carta de publicidad de ventas *(f)*
Fr lettre de publicité ventes *(f)*
It lettera di pubblicità vendite *(f)*
Pt carta de publicidade de vendas *(f)*

salesman *n* En
De Verkäufer; Handelsvertreter *(m)*
Es vendedor; viajante de comercio *(m)*
Fr vendeur; commis-voyageur *(m)*
It venditore; commesso *(m)*
Pt vendedor; caixeiro *(m)*

sales manager En
De Verkaufsleiter *(m)*
Es jefe de ventas *(m)*
Fr directeur commercial *(m)*
It direttore commerciale *(m)*
Pt chefe de vendas *(m)*

salesmanship *n* En
De Verkaufsgewandtheit *(f)*
Es arte de vender *(m)*
Fr art de vendre *(m)*
It arte della vendita *(f)*
Pt ciência de vender *(f)*

sales promotion En
De Werbung; Verkaufsförderung *(f)*
Es promoción de ventas *(f)*
Fr promotion des ventes *(f)*
It sviluppo delle vendite *(m)*
Pt promoção de vendas *(f)*

sales resistance En
De Kaufabneigung *(f)*
Es dificultades de ventas *(f pl)*
Fr résistance à la vente *(f)*
It difficoltà di vendita *(f)*
Pt resistência contra vendas *(f)*

sales tax En
De Warenumsatzsteuer *(f)*
Es impuesto sobre la venta *(m)*
Fr taxe de vente *(f)*
It imposta sulle vendite *(f)*
Pt imposto sobre vendas *(m)*

salir fiados por Es
De Haftkaution geben
En go bail for
Fr se porter garant de
It rendersi garante di
Pt prestar caução a favor de

salvage *n* En
De Bergung *(f)*
Es salvamento *(m)*
Fr sauvetage *(m)*
It salvataggio *(m)*
Pt salvamento *(m)*

salvage charges En
De Bergegeld *(n)*
Es cargos de salvamento *(m pl)*
Fr indemnité de sauvetage *(f)*
It spese di salvataggio *(f pl)*
Pt encargos de salvamento *(m pl)*

salvamento *(m) n* Es, Pt
De Bergung *(f)*
En salvage
Fr sauvetage *(m)*
It salvataggio *(m)*

salvar *vb* Es, Pt
De retten
En save
Fr sauver
It salvare

salvare *vb* It
De retten
En save
Es salvar
Fr sauver
Pt salvar

salvataggio *(m) n* It
De Bergung *(f)*
En salvage
Es salvamento *(m)*
Fr sauvetage *(m)*
Pt salvamento *(m)*

salvo erro e omissão Pt
De Irrtum vorbehalten
En errors and omissions excepted (e & oe)
Es salvo error u omisión
Fr sauf erreur ou omission
It salvo errori ed omissioni

salvo errori ed omissioni It
De Irrtum vorbehalten
En errors and omissions excepted (e & oe)
Es salvo error u omisión
Fr sauf erreur ou omission
Pt salvo erro e omissão

salvo error u omisión Es
De Irrtum vorbehalten
En errors and omissions excepted (e & oe)
Fr sauf erreur ou omission
It salvo errori ed omissioni
Pt salvo erro e omissão

sample *n* En
De Probe; Muster *(f n)*
Es muestra *(f)*
Fr échantillon *(m)*
It campione *(m)*
Pt amostra *(f)*

sample of no value En
De Muster ohne Wert *(n)*
Es muestra sin valor *(f)*
Fr échantillon sans valeur *(m)*
It campione senza valore *(m)*
Pt amostra sem valor *(f)*

sanción *(f) n* Es
De Geldstrafe *(f)*
En fine
Fr amende *(f)*
It multa *(f)*
Pt multa *(f)*

sanción elevada *(f)* Es
De schwere Buße *(f)*
En heavy fine
Fr forte amende *(f)*
It forte multa *(f)*
Pt multa pesada *(f)*

sanciones económicas *(f pl)*
Es
De wirtschaftliche Sanktionen
 (f pl)
En economic sanctions
Fr sanctions économiques
 (f pl)
It sanzioni economiche *(f pl)*
Pt sanções económicas *(f pl)*

sanções económicas *(f pl)* Pt
De wirtschaftliche Sanktionen
 (f pl)
En economic sanctions
Es sanciones económicas
 (f pl)
Fr sanctions économiques
 (f pl)
It sanzioni economiche *(f pl)*

sanctions économiques *(f pl)*
Fr
De wirtschaftliche Sanktionen
 (f pl)
En economic sanctions
Es sanciones económicas
 (f pl)
It sanzioni economiche *(f pl)*
Pt sanções económicas *(f pl)*

sans but lucratif Fr
De ohne Gewinnabsicht
En nonprofitmaking
Es sin finos lucrativos
It senza scopo di lucro
Pt sem fins lucrativos

sans droit de recours Fr
De ohne Rückgriff
En without recourse
Es sin recurso
It senza ricorso
Pt sem recurso

sans formalités Fr
De formlos
En informal
Es sin ceremonia
It senza formalità
Pt sem formalidade

sans profit Fr
De unvorteilhaft
En unprofitable
Es nada lucrativo
It poco proficuo
Pt não lucrativo

sanzioni economiche *(f pl)* It
De wirtschaftliche Sanktionen
 (f pl)
En economic sanctions
Es sanciones económicas
 (f pl)
Fr sanctions économiques
 (f pl)
Pt sanções económicas *(f pl)*

satisfação *(f)* n Pt
De Zufriedenstellung; Aus-
 gleich *(f m)*
En satisfaction; settlement
Es satisfacción *(f)*
Fr satisfaction; règlement
 (f m)
It soddisfazione; regolamen-
 to *(f m)*

satisfacción *(f)* n Es
De Zufriedenstellung; Aus-
 gleich *(f m)*
En satisfaction; settlement
Fr satisfaction; règlement
 (f m)
It soddisfazione; regolamen-
 to *(f m)*
Pt satisfação *(f)*

satisfaction n En, Fr *(f)*
De Zufriedenstellung; Beglei-
 chung *(f)*
Es satisfacción *(f)*
It soddisfazione *(f)*
Pt satisfação *(f)*

saturação (de mercadorias ba-
 ratas) *(f)* n Pt
De Dumping *(n)*
En dumping
Es inundación de mercancía
 barata *(f)*
Fr dumping *(m)*
It dumping *(m)*

Satz *(m)* n De
En rate
Es tasa; tipo *(f m)*
Fr taux; cours *(m)*
It tasso; tariffa *(m f)*
Pt taxa *(f)*

sauf erreur ou omission Fr
De Irrtum vorbehalten
En errors and omissions ex-
 cepted (e & oe)

Es salvo error u omisión
It salvo errori ed omissioni
Pt salvo erro e omissão

Säulendiagramm *(m)* n De
En block diagram
Es diagrama de bloque *(m)*
Fr ordinogramme *(m)*
It schema a blocchi *(m)*
Pt organigrama *(m)*

sauver *vb* Fr
De retten
En save
Es salvar
It salvare
Pt salvar

sauvetage *(m)* n Fr
De Bergung *(f)*
En salvage
Es salvamento *(m)*
It salvataggio *(m)*
Pt salvamento *(m)*

save (appearances; situation,
 etc.) *vb* En
De retten
Es salvar
Fr sauver
It salvare
Pt salvar

save (money) *vb* En
De aufsparen
Es ahorrar; economizar
Fr épargner; économiser
It risparmiare; economizzare
Pt poupar; economizar

savings bank En
De Sparkasse *(f)*
Es caja de ahorros *(f)*
Fr caisse d'épargne *(f)*
It cassa di risparmio *(f)*
Pt caixa económica *(f)*

scadenza *(f)* n It
De Fälligkeit *(f)*
En maturity
Es vencimiento *(m)*
Fr échéance *(f)*
Pt vencimento *(m)*

scadere *vb* It
De fällig sein
En fall due
Es vencer
Fr échoir; venir à échéance
Pt vencer-se

scaduto *adj* It
De verfallen; rückständig
En expired; out of date; overdue
Es vencido
Fr expiré; perimé; arriéré
Pt vencido

scala *(f)* n It
De Skala; Maßstab *(f m)*
En scale
Es escala *(f)*
Fr échelle *(f)*
Pt escala *(f)*

scala mobile *(f)* It
De gleitende Skala *(f)*
En sliding scale
Es escala móvil *(f)*
Fr échelle mobile *(f)*
Pt escala móvel *(f)*

scale (fees, charges, etc.) n En
De Tarif *(m)*
Es tarifa *(f)*
Fr barème *(m)*
It tariffa *(f)*
Pt tarifa *(f)*

scale (of a map, etc.) n En
De Maßstab *(m)*
Es escala *(f)*
Fr échelle *(f)*
It scala *(f)*
Pt escala *(f)*

scales (weighing) pl n En
De Waage *(f)*
Es balanza *(f)*
Fr balance *(f)*
It bilancia *(f)*
Pt balança *(f)*

scalo *(m)* n It
De Kai *(m)*
En wharf
Es muelle *(m)*
Fr quai *(m)*
Pt cais *(m)*

scarsezza *(f)* n It
De Knappheit *(f)*
En short supply
Es escasez *(f)*
Fr disette *(f)*
Pt escassez *(f)*

scartamento normale *(m)* It
De Normalmaß; Normalspurweite *(n)*
En standard gauge
Es calibre patrón *(m)*
Fr écartement normal *(m)*
Pt calibre padrão *(m)*

sceau *(m)* n Fr
De Siegel *(n)*
En seal
Es sello *(m)*
It sigillo *(m)*
Pt selo *(m)*

Schaden *(m)* n De
En damage; injury
Es daño *(m)*
Fr dommage; avarie *(m f)*
It danno *(m)*
Pt dano *(m)*

Schadenersatz *(m)* n De
En damages
Es daños *(m pl)*
Fr dommages-intérêts *(m pl)*
It danni *(m pl)*
Pt danos *(m pl)*

(den) Schadenersatzbetrag feststellen De
En assess damages
Es evaluar daños
Fr fixer des dommages- intérêts
It valutare i danni
Pt avaliar os danos

Schadenersatzklage *(f)* n De
En action for damages
Es acción por daños *(f)*
Fr action en dommages et intérêts *(f)*
It processo per risarcimento *(m)*
Pt processamento por danos *(m)*

schadenersatzpflichtig *adj* De
En liable for damages
Es responsable por daños
Fr passible de dommagesintérêts
It responsabile per i danni
Pt responsável por danos

Schadenersatz zugestehen De
En award damages
Es conceder daños
Fr adjuger des dommagesintérêts
It concedere i danni
Pt conceder compensação

Schadenfreiheitsrabatt *(m)* De
En no-claims discount (bonus)
Es bonificación por no- reclamación *(f)*
Fr bonification pour non sinistre *(f)*
It sconto per assenza di sinistri *(m)*
Pt desconto por ausência de reclamações *(m)*

Schalttafel *(f)* n De
En switchboard
Es cuadro de conexión *(m)*
Fr tableau de distribution *(m)*
It quadro di comando *(m)*
Pt quadro de distribuição *(m)*

Schatzamt *(n)* n De
En exchequer
Am treasury
Es hacienda *(f)*
Fr trésorerie *(f)*
It tesoro *(m)*
Pt tesouro *(m)*

Schätzer *(m)* n De
En assessor
Es asesor *(m)*
Fr appréciateur *(m)*
It agente delle imposte *(m)*
Pt avaliador *(m)*

Schatzwechsel *(m)* n De
En exchequer bond
Am treasury bond
Es bono de tesorería *(m)*
Fr bon du trésor *(m)*
It buono del tesoro *(m)*
Pt título do tesouro *(m)*

Schaufensterdekoration *(f)* n De
En window-dressing
Es preparación de escaparates *(f)*

Fr art de l'étalage *(m)*
It allestimento delle vetrine
(m)
Pt preparação de montras *(f)*

Schaukasten *(m)* n De
En display unit
Es presentación *(f)*
Fr présentoir *(m)*
It mostra *(f)*
Pt montra *(f)*

Schaustellung *(f)* n De
En display
Es presentación *(f)*
Fr présentation *(f)*
It mostra *(f)*
Pt exposição *(f)*

Scheck *(m)* n De
En cheque
Am check
Es cheque *(m)*
Fr chèque *(m)*
It assegno *(m)*
Pt cheque *(m)*

(einen) Scheck ausstellen
De
En draw a cheque
Es extender un cheque
Fr tirer un chèque
It emettere un assegno
Pt passar um cheque

(einen) Scheck einlösen De
En cash a cheque
Es cobrar un cheque
Fr toucher un chèque
It incassare un assegno
Pt cobrar um cheque

Scheckheft *(n)* n De
En cheque book
An check book
Es libro de cheques *(m)*
Fr carnet de chèques;
chéquier *(m)*
It libretto assegni *(m)*
Pt livro de cheques *(m)*

Scheckkarte *(f)* n De
En cheque card
Am bank credit card
Es tarjeta de cheque *(f)*
Fr carte de chèque *(f)*
It scheda per assegni *(f)*
Pt cartão de validação de che-
ques *(m)*

Scheckkonto *(n)* n De
En drawing account
Es cuenta corrienta *(f)*
Fr compte courant *(m)*
It conto corrente *(m)*
Pt conta corrente *(f)*

**(einen) Scheck rückgängig
machen** De
En cancel a cheque
Es anular un cheque
Fr annuler un chèque
It annullare un assegno
Pt cancelar um cheque

(einen) Scheck sperren De
En stop a cheque
Es suspender el pago de un
cheque
Fr bloquer un chèque
It fermare un assegno
Pt suspender o pagamento
de um cheque

scheda *(f)* n It
De Karte; Indexkarte *(f)*
En card; index card
Es tarjeta; ficha *(f)*
Fr carte; fiche *(f)*
Pt cartão; ficha *(m f)*

scheda per assegni *(f)* It
De Scheckkarte *(f)*
En cheque card
Am bank credit card
Es tarjeta de cheque *(f)*
Fr carte de chèque *(f)*
Pt cartão de validação de che-
ques *(m)*

scheda perforata *(f)* It
De Lochkarte *(f)*
En punched card
Es tarjeta perforada *(f)*
Fr carte perforée
Pt ficha perfurada *(f)*

schedario *(m)* n It
De Kartothek; Aktenschrank
(f m)
En card index; filing cabinet
Es fichero *(m)*
Fr fichier; classeur *(m)*
Pt ficheiro *(m)*

schedule n En
De Plan; Programm *(m n)*
Es plano; programa *(m)*
Fr plan; programme *(m)*
It piano; programma *(m)*
Pt plano; programa *(m)*

schedule vb En
De planen; programmieren
Es programar
Fr programmer; planifier
It programmare
Pt programar

schema a blocchi *(m)* It
De Säulendiagramm *(m)*
En block diagram
Es diagrama de bloque *(m)*
Fr ordinogramme *(m)*
Pt organigrama *(m)*

schema di contratto *(m)* It
De Entwurf eines Überein-
kommens *(m)*
En draft agreement
Es proyecto de convenio *(m)*
Fr projet de convention *(m)*
Pt projecto de acordo *(m)*

Schicht *(f)* n De
En shift
Es turno *(m)*
Fr équipe *(f)*
It turno *(m)*
Pt turno *(m)*

Schiedsgericht *(n)* n De
En court of arbitration
Es tribunal arbitral *(m)*
Fr cour d'arbitrage *(m)*
It corte arbitrale *(f)*
Pt tribunal de arbitragem *(m)*

Schiedsgerichtsverfahren
(n) n De
En arbitration
Es arbitramento *(m)*
Fr arbitrage *(m)*
It arbitrato *(m)*
Pt arbitragem *(f)*

Schiedsobmann *(m)* n De
En umpire
Es juez árbitro *(m)*
Fr surarbitre *(m)*
It terzo arbitro *(m)*
Pt juiz árbitro *(m)*

Schiedsrichter *(m)* n De
En arbitrator
Es arbitrador *(m)*
Fr arbitre *(m)*
It arbitro *(m)*
Pt árbitro *(m)*

Schiedsspruch *(m)* n De
En arbitration award
Es sentencia arbitral *(f)*
Fr sentence arbitrale *(f)*
It lodo arbitrale *(m)*
Pt decisão de arbitragem *(f)*

Schiff *(n)* n De
En ship
Es barco *(m)*
Fr navire *(m)*
It nave *(f)*
Pt navio *(m)*

Schiffahrt *(f)* n De
En navigation
Es navegación *(f)*
Fr navigation *(f)*
It navigazione *(f)*
Pt navegação *(f)*

schiffbar *adj* De
En navigable
Es navegable
Fr navigable
It navigabile
Pt navegável

Schiffsmakler *(m)* n De
En shipbroker
Es corredor marítimo *(m)*
Fr courtier maritime *(m)*
It sensale marittimo *(m)*
Pt corretor marítimo *(m)*

Schiffspapiere *(n pl)* n De
En ship's papers
Es documentación marítima *(f)*
Fr papiers de bord *(m pl)*
It carte di bordo *(f pl)*
Pt documentação do navio *(f)*

Schiffsregister *(n)* n De
En ship's register
Es registro del barco *(m)*
Fr certificat d'immatriculation *(m)*
It atto di nazionalità *(m)*
Pt registo do navio *(m)*

Schiffswerft *(f)* n De
En dockyard
Es astillero *(m)*
Fr chantier de construction de navires *(m)*
It cantiere *(m)*
Pt estaleiro *(m)*

schlechter Zahler *(m)* De
En slow payer
Es deudor moroso *(m)*
Fr mauvais payeur *(m)*
It cattivo pagatore *(m)*
Pt mau-pagador *(m)*

Schleppdampfer *(m)* n De
En tug-boat
Es remolcador *(m)*
Fr remorqueur *(m)*
It rimorchiatore *(m)*
Pt rebocador *(m)*

Schlichtung *(f)* n De
En conciliation
Es conciliación *(f)*
Fr conciliation *(f)*
It conciliazione *(f)*
Pt conciliação *(f)*

Schlußbilanz *(f)* n De
En final balance
Es saldo final *(m)*
Fr solde net *(m)*
It saldo finale *(m)*
Pt balanço final *(m)*

Schlußschein *(m)* n De
En contract note
Es nota de contrato *(f)*
Fr bordereau d'achat *(m)*
It nota di contratto *(f)*
Pt nota-contrato *(f)*

Schlußdividende *(f)* n De
En final dividend
Es saldo del dividendo *(m)*
Fr solde de dividende *(m)*
It saldo del dividendo *(m)*
Pt dividendo final *(m)*

Schlüssel *(m)* n De
En key; code
Es llave; clave *(f)*
Fr clef *(f)*
It chiave; codice *(f m)*
Pt chave; código *(f m)*

Schlüsselindustrie *(f)* n De
En key industry
Es industria clave *(f)*
Fr industrie-clef *(f)*
It industria chiave *(f)*
Pt indústria chave *(f)*

Schlußnotierung *(f)* n De
En closing price
Es precio de cierre *(m)*
Fr cours de clôture *(m)*
It prezzo di chiusura *(m)*
Pt último preço *(m)*

Schlußtermin *(m)* n De
En closing date
Es último día *(m)*
Fr dernier jour *(m)*
It ultima data *(f)*
Pt último dia *(m)*

schmuggeln *vb* De
En smuggle
Es pasar de contrabando
Fr faire la contrebande
It contrabbandare
Pt passar por contrabando

Schmuggelware *(f)* n De
En contraband
Es contrabando *(m)*
Fr contrebande *(f)*
It contrabbando *(m)*
Pt contrabando *(m)*

Schneeballverkauf *(m)* De
En pyramid selling
Es venta en pirámide *(f)*
Fr vente en pyramide *(f)*
It vendita a piramide *(f)*
Pt vendas em pirâmide *(f pl)*

Schreibmaschine *(f)* n De
En typewriter
Es máquina de escribir *(f)*
Fr machine à écrire *(f)*
It macchina da scrivere *(f)*
Pt máquina de escrever *(f)*

(auf der) Schreibmaschine schreiben De
En type
Es escribir a máquina
Fr écrire à la machine
It scrivere a macchina
Pt escrever à máquina

Schreibtisch *(m)* n De
En desk
Es mesa *(f)*
Fr bureau *(m)*
It scrittoio *(m)*
Pt secretária *(f)*

schriftlich bestätigen De
En confirm in writing
Es confirmar por escrito
Fr confirmer par écrit
It confermare per iscritto
Pt confirmar por escrito

Schuld *(f)* n De
En debt
Es deuda *(f)*
Fr créance *(f)*
It debito *(m)*
Pt dívida *(f)*

(eine) Schuld begleichen De
En discharge a debt
Es descargar una deuda
Fr acquitter une dette
It estinguere un debito
Pt cancelar uma dívida

(eine) Schuld eintreiben De
En collect a debt
Es recaudar una deuda
Fr recouvrer une créance
It incassare un credito
Pt cobrar uma dívida

(eine) Schuld erlassen De
En write off a debt
Es cancelar una deuda
Fr amortir une créance
It cancellare un credito
Pt cancelar uma dívida

Schuldner *(m)* n De
En debtor
Es deudor *(m)*
Fr débiteur *(m)*
It debitore *(m)*
Pt devedor *(m)*

Schuldschein *(m)* n De
En promissory note; I.O.U.
Es pagaré *(m)*
Fr billet à ordre; reconnais-
    sance de dette *(m f)*
It pagherò *(m)*
Pt promissória; vale *(f m)*

**Schuldverschreibung ohne
    Fälligkeitsdatum** *(f)* De
En undated debenture
Es obligación sin fecha *(f)*
Fr obligation perpétuelle *(f)*
It obbligazione perpetua *(f)*
Pt obrigação sem data *(f)*

Schüttgut *(n)* n De
En bulk cargo
Es carga en granel *(f)*
Fr cargaison en vrac *(f)*
It carico alla rinfusa *(m)*
Pt carga geral *(f)*

schwache Währung *(f)* De
En soft currency
Es moneda débil *(f)*
Fr monnaie faible *(f)*
It valuta debole *(f)*
Pt moeda fraca *(f)*

schwanken *vb* De
En fluctuate
Es fluctuar
Fr fluctuer
It fluttuare
Pt flutuar

schwankend *adj* De
En fluctuating
Es fluctuando
Fr fluctuant
It fluttuante
Pt flutuando

schwankender Kurs *(m)* De
En fluctuating rate
Es tipo oscilante *(m)*
Fr taux variable *(m)*
It tasso variabile *(m)*
Pt taxa variável *(f)*

Schwankung *(f)* n De
En fluctuation
Es fluctuación *(f)*
Fr fluctuation *(f)*
It fluttuazione *(f)*
Pt flutuação *(f)*

schwarze Börse *(f)* De
En (securities) black market
Es bolsa negra *(f)*
Fr bourse noire *(f)*
It borsa nera *(f)*
Pt bolsa negra *(f)*

schwarze Liste *(f)* De
En black list
Es lista negra *(f)*
Fr liste noire *(f)*
It lista nera *(f)*
Pt lista negra *(f)*

schwarzer Markt *(m)* De
En black market
Es mercado negro *(m)*
Fr marché noir *(m)*
It mercato nero *(m)*
Pt mercado negro *(m)*

schwebend *adj* De
En pending
Es pendiente
Fr pendant
It pendente
Pt pendente

Schwellenpreis *(m)* n De
En threshold price
Es precio de umbral *(m)*
Fr prix de seuil *(m)*
It prezzo soglia *(m)*
Pt preço convencionado *(m)*

schwer *adj* De
En heavy
Es pesado; fuerte
Fr lourd; fort
It pesante; forte
Pt pesado

schwere Buße *(f)* De
En heavy fine
Es sanción elevada *(f)*
Fr forte amende *(f)*
It forte multa *(f)*
Pt multa pesada *(f)*

schwerer Verlust *(m)* De
En heavy loss
Es fuerte pérdida; pérdida
    sensible *(f)*
Fr lourde perte *(f)*
It forte perdita *(f)*
Pt perda avultada *(f)*

schwere Tonne *(f)* De
En long ton
Es tonelada inglesa *(f)*
Fr tonne forte *(f)*
It tonnellata inglese *(f)*
Pt tonelada inglesa *(f)*

Schwerindustrie *(f)* *n* De
En heavy industry
Es industria pesada *(f)*
Fr industrie lourde *(f)*
It industria pesante *(f)*
Pt indústria pesada *(f)*

Schwestergesellschaft *(f)* *n*
De
En sister company
Es compañía asociada *(f)*
Fr société sœur *(f)*
It società sorella *(f)*
Pt empresa gémea *(f)*

schwierig *adj* De
En difficult
Es difícil
Fr difficile
It difficile
Pt difícil

Schwindelgesellschaft *(f)* *n*
De
En bogus company
Am phantom operation
Es sociedad fantasma *(f)*
Fr société fantôme *(f)*
It società fasulla *(f)*
Pt sociedade fantasma *(f)*

schwindeln *vb* De
En swindle
Es estafar
Fr filouter
It truffare
Pt enganar

Schwindlertrick *(m)* *n* De
En confidence trick
Am confidence game
Es timo *(m)*
Fr escroquerie *(f)*
It truffa all'americana *(f)*
Pt conto do vigário *(m)*

scioglimento *(m)* *n* It
De Auflösung *(f)*
En dissolution
Es disolución *(f)*
Fr dissolution *(f)*
Pt dissolução *(f)*

scioperante *(m)* *n* It
De Streikende(r) *(m)*
En striker
Es huelguista *(m)*
Fr gréviste *(m)*
Pt grevista *(m)*

scioperare *vb* It
De streiken
En strike
Es declarer huelga
Fr faire la grève
Pt fazer greve

sciopero *(m)* *n* It
De Streik *(m)*
En strike
Es huelga *(f)*
Fr grève *(f)*
Pt greve *(f)*

sciopero a singhiozzo *(m)* It
De Bummelstreik *(m)*
En go-slow strike
Am slow down
Es huelga de producción lenta *(f)*
Fr grève perlée *(f)*
Pt greve de abrandamento de ritmo de produção *(f)*

sciopero bianco *(m)* It
De Sitzstreik *(m)*
En sit-down strike
Es huelga de brazos caídos *(f)*
Fr grève avec occupation des lieux *(f)*
Pt greve de braços caídos *(f)*

sciopero generale *(m)* It
De Generalstreik *(m)*
En general strike
Es huelga general *(f)*
Fr grève générale *(f)*
Pt greve geral *(f)*

sciopero non ufficiale *(m)* It
De unanerkannter Streik *(m)*
En unofficial strike
Es huelga no-oficial *(f)*
Fr grève non reconnue *(f)*
Pt greve não oficializada *(f)*

sciopero portuale *(m)* It
De Hafenarbeiterstreik *(m)*
En dock strike
Es huelga de obreros de muelle *(f)*
Fr grève des dockers *(f)*
Pt greve na doca *(f)*

sciopero selvaggio *(m)* It
De wilder Streik *(m)*
En wildcat strike

Es huelga espontánea *(f)*
Fr grève sauvage *(f)*
Pt greve não oficializada *(f)*

sciopero ufficiale *(m)* It
De anerkannter Streik *(m)*
En official strike
Es huelga oficial *(f)*
Fr grève officielle *(f)*
Pt greve oficial *(f)*

sconto *(m)* *n* It
De Skonto *(m)*
En discount
Es descuento *(m)*
Fr escompte *(m)*
Pt desconto *(m)*

sconto d'esportazione *(m)* It
De Ausfuhrsonderrabatt *(m)*
En export rebate
Es descuento por exportación *(m)*
Fr remise sur les exports *(f)*
Pt desconto de exportação *(m)*

sconto di banca *(m)* It
De Diskont *(m)*
En bank discount
Es descuento bancario *(m)*
Fr escompte en dehors *(m)*
Pt desconto bancário *(m)*

sconto differito *(m)* It
De nachträglicher Umsatzbonus *(m)*
En deferred rebate
Es descuento diferido *(m)*
Fr rabais différé *(m)*
Pt dedução adiada *(f)*

sconto di rivendita *(m)* It
De Händlerrabatt *(m)*
En trade discount
Es descuento comercial *(m)*
Fr rabais de demi-gros *(m)*
Pt desconto à praça *(m)*

sconto per assenza di sinistri *(m)* It
De Schadenfreiheitsrabatt *(m)*
En no-claims discount or bonus
Es bonificación por no-reclamación *(f)*
Fr bonification pour non sinistre *(f)*
Pt desconto por ausência de reclamações *(m)*

sconto per pagamento a contanti *(m)* It
De Barrabatt *(m)*
En cash discount
Es descuento de caja *(m)*
Fr escompte de caisse *(m)*
Pt desconto de contado *(m)*

scoperto *(m) n* It
De Überziehung *(f)*
En overdraft
Es sobregiro; saldo deudor *(m)*
Fr découvert; solde débiteur *(m)*
Pt conta a descoberto *(f)*

scopo *(m) n* It
De Ziel *(n)*
En goal
Es meta; objetivo *(f m)*
Fr bout *(m)*
Pt meta; objectivo *(f m)*

scopo dell'assemblea *(m)* It
De Tagesordnung *(f)*
En business before the meeting
Am agenda
Es orden del día *(f)*
Fr ordre du jour *(m)*
Pt agenda da reunião *(f)*

scorta *(f) n* It
De Vorrat *(m)*
En stock
Es stock; existencias *(m; f pl)*
Fr stock; marchandises *(m; f pl)*
Pt existências *(f pl)*

scorte di equilibrio *(f pl)* It
De Buffer-stocks *(m pl)*
En buffer stocks
Es existencias de regularización *(f pl)*
Fr stocks de régularisation *(m pl)*
Pt existências de regularização *(f pl)*

scrittoio *(m) n* It
De Schreibtisch *(m)*
En desk
Es mesa *(f)*
Fr bureau *(m)*
Pt secretária *(f)*

scrivere a macchina It
De auf der Schreibmaschine schreiben
En type
Es escribir a máquina
Fr écrire à la machine
Pt escrever à máquina

sdoganamento *(m) n* It
De Zollabfertigung *(f)*
En customs clearance
Es paso de aduanas *(f)*
Fr dédouanement *(m)*
Pt despacho alfandegário *(m)*

sdoganare *vb* It
De verzollen
En clear through customs
Es retirar de aduanas
Fr dédouaner
Pt despachar na alfândega

sdoganato *adj* It
De verzollt
En ex bond; out of bond
Es fuera de aduanas; despachado de aduanas
Fr à l'acquitté; dédouané
Pt livre de alfândega; despachado da alfândega

sea *n* En
De See *(f)*
Es mar *(m)*
Fr mer *(f)*
It mare *(m)*
Pt mar *(m)*

seal *n* En
De Siegel *(n)*
Es sello *(m)*
Fr sceau *(m)*
It sigillo *(m)*
Pt selo *(m)*

season *n* En
De Jahreszeit *(f)*
Es estación *(f)*
Fr saison *(f)*
It stagione *(f)*
Pt estação *(f)*

seasonal fluctuations En
De saisonbedingte Schwankungen *(f pl)*
Es fluctuaciones estacionales *(f pl)*

Fr variations saisonnières *(f pl)*
It fluttuazioni stagionali *(f pl)*
Pt flutuações de época *(f pl)*

seasonal unemployment En
De jahreszeitlich bedingte Arbeitslosigkeit *(f)*
Es paro de temporada *(m)*
Fr chômage saisonnier *(m)*
It disoccupazione stagionale *(f)*
Pt desemprego de estação *(m)*

sea-water damage En
De Seewasserschaden *(m)*
Es daño de agua de mar *(m)*
Fr dégâts d'eau de mer *(m pl)*
It danno d'acqua di mare *(m)*
Pt dano causado pela água do mar *(m)*

seaworthy *adj* En
De seefest
Es marinero
Fr en état de navigabilité
It atto a tenere il mare
Pt em condições de navegação

secção *(f) n* Pt
De Abteilung *(f)*
En division
Es sección *(f)*
Fr division *(f)*
It divisione *(f)*

sección *(f) n* Es
De Abteilung *(f)*
En division
Fr division *(f)*
It divisione *(f)*
Pt secção *(f)*

second *(m) n* Fr
De Maat *(m)*
En (ship's) mate
Es primer oficial *(m)*
It primo ufficiale *(m)*
Pt imediato *(m)*

seconda di cambio *(f)* It
De Sekundawechsel *(m)*
En second of exchange
Es segunda de cambio *(f)*
Fr seconde de change *(f)*
Pt segunda de câmbio *(f)*

seconde de change *(f)* Fr
De Sekundawechsel *(m)*
En second of exchange
Es segunda de cambio *(f)*
It seconda di cambio *(f)*
Pt segunda de câmbio *(f)*

second-hand *adj* En
De aus zweiter Hand; Gebraucht-
Es de segunda mano
Fr d'occasion
It di seconda mano
Pt de segunda mão

second of exchange En
De Sekundawechsel *(m)*
Es segunda de cambio *(f)*
Fr seconde de change *(f)*
It seconda di cambio *(f)*
Pt segunda de câmbio *(f)*

secours *(m)* n Fr
De Hilfe *(f)*
En help
Es ayuda *(f)*
It aiuto *(m)*
Pt ajuda *(f)*

secours de chômage *(m)* Fr
De Arbeitslosenunterstützung *(f)*
En unemployment benefit
Es subsidio de paro *(m)*
It indennità di disoccupazione *(f)*
Pt subsídio de desemprego *(m)*

secret agreement En
De Geheimvertrag *(m)*
Es acuerdo secreto *(m)*
Fr accord occulte *(m)*
It accordo segreto *(m)*
Pt acordo secreto *(m)*

secrétaire *(m/f)* n Fr
De Sekretär; Sekretärin *(m f)*
En (male or female) secretary
Es secretario; secretaria *(m f)*
It segretario; segretaria *(m f)*
Pt secretário; secretária *(m f)*

secretaria *(f)* n Es
De Sekretärin *(f)*
En (female) secretary
Fr secrétaire *(f)*
It segretaria *(f)*
Pt secretária *(f)*

secretária *(f)* n Pt
De Sekretärin; Schreibtisch *(f m)*
En (female) secretary; desk
Es secretaria; mesa *(f)*
Fr secrétaire; bureau *(f m)*
It segretaria; scrittoio *(f m)*

secretario *(m)* n Es
De Sekretär *(m)*
En (male) secretary
Fr secrétaire *(m)*
It segretario *(m)*
Pt secretário *(m)*

secretário *(m)* n Pt
De Sekretär *(m)*
En (male) secretary
Es secretario *(m)*
Fr secrétaire *(m)*
It segretario *(m)*

secretary n En
De Sekretär; Sekretärin *(m f)*
Es secretario; secretaria *(m f)*
Fr secrétaire *(m/f)*
It segretario; segretaria *(m f)*
Pt secretário; secretária *(m f)*

secret industriel *(m)* Fr
De Betriebsgeheimnis *(n)*
En trade secret
Es secreto comercial *(m)*
It segreto commerciale *(m)*
Pt segredo comercial *(m)*

secreto comercial *(m)* Es
De Betriebsgeheimnis *(n)*
En trade secret
Fr secret industriel *(m)*
It segreto commerciale *(m)*
Pt segredo comercial *(m)*

secteur privé *(m)* Fr
De Privatwirtschaft *(f)*
En private sector
Es sector privado *(m)*
It settore privato *(m)*
Pt sector privado *(m)*

secteur public *(m)* Fr
De öffentliche Hand *(f)*
En public sector
Es sector público *(m)*
It settore statale *(m)*
Pt sector público *(m)*

sector privado *(m)* Es, Pt
De Privatwirtschaft *(f)*
En private sector
Fr secteur privé *(m)*
It settore privato *(m)*

sector público *(m)* Es, Pt
De öffentliche Hand *(f)*
En public sector
Fr secteur public *(m)*
It settore statale *(m)*

secured debenture En
De gesicherte Schuldverschreibung *(f)*
Es obligación garantizada *(f)*
Fr obligation garantie *(f)*
It obbligazione garantita *(f)*
Pt obrigação com garantia *(f)*

sécurité *(f)* n Fr
De Sicherheit *(f)*
En security; safety
Es seguridad *(f)*
It sicurezza *(f)*
Pt segurança *(f)*

sécurité sociale *(f)* Fr
De Sozialversicherung *(f)*
En social security
Es seguridad social *(f)*
It sicurezza sociale *(f)*
Pt segurança social *(f)*

securities *(pl)* n En
De Effekten *(m pl)*
Es títulos; valores *(m pl)*
Fr titres; valeurs *(m pl; f pl)*
It titoli; valori *(m pl)*
Pt títulos; valores *(m pl)*

security (on loan, etc.) n En
De Nebenbürgschaft *(f)*
Es fianza *(f)*
Fr nantissement *(m)*
It pegno *(m)*
Pt fiança *(f)*

security (protection) n En
De Sicherheit *(f)*
Es seguridad *(f)*
Fr sécurité *(f)*
It sicurezza *(f)*
Pt segurança *(f)*

sede *(f)* n It, Pt
De Hauptbüro *(n)*
En head office
Es oficina central *(f)*
Fr siège; bureau principal *(m)*

See *(f)* n De
En sea
Es mar *(m)*
Fr mer *(f)*
It mare *(m)*
Pt mar *(m)*

See- De
En marine; maritime
Es marítimo; marino
Fr maritime
It marino; marittimo
Pt marinho; marítimo

seefest *adj* De
En seaworthy
Es marinero
Fr en état de navigabilité
It atto a tenere il mare
Pt em condições de navega-
    ção

Seereise *(f)* n De
En voyage
Es viaje *(m)*
Fr voyage *(m)*
It viaggio *(m)*
Pt viagem *(f)*

Seewasserschaden *(m)* n De
En sea-water damage
Es daño de agua de mar *(m)*
Fr dégâts d'eau de mer *(m pl)*
It danno d'acqua di mare *(m)*
Pt dano causado pela água
    do mar *(m)*

segredo comercial *(m)* Pt
De Betriebsgeheimnis *(n)*
En trade secret
Es secreto comercial *(m)*
Fr secret industriel *(m)*
It segreto commerciale *(m)*

segretaria *(f)* n It
De Sekretärin *(f)*
En (female) secretary
Es secretaria *(f)*
Fr secrétaire *(f)*
Pt secretária *(f)*

segretario *(m)* n It
De Sekretär *(m)*
En (male) secretary
Es secretario *(m)*
Fr secrétaire *(m)*
Pt secretário *(m)*

segreto commerciale *(m)* It
De Betriebsgeheimnis *(n)*
En trade secret
Es secreto comercial *(m)*
Fr secret industriel *(m)*
Pt segredo comercial *(m)*

seguitare *vb* It
De weiterverfolgen
En follow up
Es perseguir
Fr poursuivre
Pt perseguir

segunda de cambio *(f)* Es
De Sekundawechsel *(m)*
En second of exchange
Fr seconde de change *(f)*
It seconda di cambio *(f)*
Pt segunda de câmbio *(f)*

segunda de câmbio *(f)* Pt
De Sekundawechsel *(m)*
En second of exchange
Es segunda de cambio *(f)*
Fr seconde de change *(f)*
It seconda di cambio *(f)*

segundo asociado *(m)* Es
De jüngerer Teilhaber *(m)*
En junior partner
Fr associé en second *(m)*
It socio giovane *(m)*
Pt sócio júnior *(m)*

segurador *(m)* n Pt
De Versicherer *(m)*
En insurer
Es asegurador *(m)*
Fr assureur *(m)*
It assicuratore *(m)*

segurança *(f)* n Pt
De Sicherheit *(f)*
En security; safety
Es seguridad *(f)*
Fr sécurité *(f)*
It sicurezza *(f)*

segurança social *(f)* Pt
De Sozialversicherung *(f)*
En social security
Es seguridad social *(f)*
Fr sécurité sociale *(f)*
It sicurezza sociale *(f)*

segurar *vb* Pt
De versichern
En insure
Es asegurar
Fr assurer
It assicurare

seguridad *(f)* n Es
De Sicherheit *(f)*
En security; safety
Fr sécurité *(f)*
It sicurezza *(f)*
Pt segurança *(f)*

seguridad social *(f)* Es
De Sozialversicherung *(f)*
En social security
Fr sécurité sociale *(f)*
It sicurezza sociale *(f)*
Pt segurança social *(f)*

seguro *(m)* n Es, Pt
De Versicherung *(f)*
En insurance; assurance
Fr assurance *(f)*
It assicurazione *(f)*

seguro combinado *(m)* Es
De kombinierte Versicherung
    (f)
En comprehensive insurance
Fr assurance combinée *(f)*
It assicurazione mista *(f)*
Pt seguro compreensivo *(m)*

seguro compreensivo *(m)* Pt
De kombinierte Versicherung
    (f)
En comprehensive insurance
Es seguro combinado *(m)*
Fr assurance combinée *(f)*
It assicurazione mista *(f)*

**seguro contra responsabili-
dad civil** *(m)* Es
De Haftpflichtversicherung *(f)*
En third-party insurance
Fr assurance responsabilité
    civile (RC) *(f)*
It assicurazione contro terzi
    (f)
Pt seguro contra terceiros *(m)*

**seguro contra riesgo de
guerra** *(m)* Es
De Kriegsrisikoversicherung
    (f)
En war-risk insurance

Fr assurance du risque de
   guerre *(f)*
It assicurazione contro i
   rischi di guerra *(f)*
Pt seguro contra risco de
   guerra *(m)*

**seguro contra risco de
guerra** *(m)* Pt
De Kriegsrisikoversicherung
   (f)
En war-risk insurance
Es seguro contra riesgo de
   guerra *(m)*
Fr assurance du risque de
   guerre *(f)*
It assicurazione contro i
   rischi di guerra *(f)*

seguro contra terceiros *(m)*
   Pt
De Haftpflichtversicherung *(f)*
En third-party insurance
Es seguro contra responsabi-
   lidad civil *(m)*
Fr assurance responsabilité
   civile (RC) *(f)*
It assicurazione contro terzi
   (f)

seguro crediticio *(m)* Es
De Kreditversicherung *(f)*
En credit insurance
Fr assurance crédit *(f)*
It assicurazione credito *(f)*
Pt seguro de crédito *(m)*

seguro de casa *(m)* Es, Pt
De Wohnungsversicherung *(f)*
En household insurance
Fr assurance ménagère *(f)*
It assicurazione domestica
   (f)

seguro de crédito *(m)* Pt
De Kreditversicherung *(f)*
En credit insurance
Es seguro crediticio *(m)*
Fr assurance crédit *(f)*
It assicurazione credito *(f)*

seguro de doença *(m)* Pt
De Krankenversicherung *(f)*
En health insurance
Es seguro de enfermedad *(m)*
Fr assurance maladie *(f)*
It assicurazione malattia *(f)*

seguro de enfermedad *(m)*
   Es
De Krankenversicherung *(f)*
En health insurance
Fr assurance maladie *(f)*
It assicurazione malattia *(f)*
Pt seguro de doença *(m)*

seguro de grupo *(m)* Es, Pt
De Gruppenversicherung *(f)*
En group insurance
Fr assurance de groupe *(f)*
It assicurazione di gruppo *(f)*

seguro de incêndio *(m)* Pt
De Feuerversicherung *(f)*
En fire insurance
Es seguro de incendios *(m)*
Fr assurance incendie *(f)*
It assicurazione incendio *(f)*

seguro de incendios *(m)* Es
De Feuerversicherung *(f)*
En fire insurance
Fr assurance incendie *(f)*
It assicurazione incendio *(f)*
Pt seguro de incêndio *(m)*

seguro del casco *(m)* Es
De Kaskoversicherung *(f)*
En hull insurance
Fr assurance sur le corps *(f)*
It assicurazione corpo *(m)*
Pt seguro do casco *(m)*

seguro de vida *(m)* Es, Pt
De Lebensversicherung *(f)*
En life assurance
Am life insurance
Fr assurance sur la vie *(f)*
It assicurazione sulla vita *(f)*

seguro do casco *(m)* Pt
De Kaskoversicherung *(f)*
En hull insurance
Es seguro del casco *(m)*
Fr assurance sur le corps *(f)*
It assicurazione corpo *(m)*

seguro mútuo *(m)* Pt
De Versicherung auf Gegen-
   seitigkeit *(f)*
En mutual insurance
Es coaseguro *(m)*
Fr assurance mutuelle *(f)*
It mutua assicurazione *(f)*

seguro social *(m)* Pt
De Sozialversicherung *(f)*
En social security
Es seguridad social *(f)*
Fr sécurité sociale *(f)*
It sicurezza sociale *(f)*

Sekretär *(m)* n De
En (male) secretary
Es secretario *(m)*
Fr secrétaire *(m)*
It segretario *(m)*
Pt secretário *(m)*

Sekretärin *(f)* n De
En (female) secretary
Es secretaria *(f)*
Fr secrétaire *(f)*
It segretaria *(f)*
Pt secretária *(f)*

Sekundawechsel *(m)* n De
En second of exchange
Es segunda de cambio *(f)*
Fr seconde de change *(f)*
It seconda di cambio *(f)*
Pt segunda de câmbio *(f)*

selbständig *adj* De
En independent
Es independiente
Fr indépendant
It indipendente
Pt independente

Selbstbedienung *(f)* n De
En self-service
Es auto-servicio *(m)*
Fr libre service *(m)*
It servirsi da sè *(m)*
Pt self-service *(m)*

Selbstkosten *(pl)* n De
En prime cost
Es precio de coste *(m)*
Fr prix de revient *(m)*
It prezzo di costo *(m)*
Pt preço de custo *(m)*

self-contained flat En
De Einfamilienwohnung *(f)*
Es piso independiente com-
   pleto *(m)*
Fr appartement indépendant
   (m)
It appartamento indipenden-
   te *(m)*
Pt andar independente *(m)*

self-employed person En
De selbständig Arbeitende(r)
 (m)
Es trabajador por cuenta
 propia *(m)*
Fr travailleur indépendant *(m)*
It lavoratore indipendente
 (m)
Pt empregado por conta-
 própria *(m)*

self-service *n* En, Pt *(m)*
De Selbstbedienung *(f)*
Es auto-servicio *(m)*
Fr libre service *(m)*
It servirsi da sè *(m)*

sell *vb* En
De verkaufen
Es vender
Fr vendre
It vendere
Pt vender

selling cost En
De Verkaufskosten *(pl)*
Es coste de venta *(m)*
Fr frais de vente *(m)*
It costo di vendita *(m)*
Pt custo de venda *(m)*

sello *(m) n* Es
De Stempel; Siegel *(m)*
En stamp; seal
Fr tampon; sceau *(m)*
It bollo; sigillo *(m)*
Pt selo; carimbo *(m)*

sello de correos *(m)* Es
De Briefmarke *(f)*
En postage stamp
Fr timbre-poste *(m)*
It francobollo *(m)*
Pt selo postal *(m)*

sello de fecha *(m)* Es
De Tagesstempel *(m)*
En date-stamp
Fr dateur *(m)*
It timbro a data *(m)*
Pt carimbo de datas *(m)*

selo *(m) n* Pt
De Marke; Siegel *(f m)*
En stamp; seal
Es sello *(m)*
Fr timbre; sceau *(m)*
It bollo; sigillo *(m)*

selo postal *(m)* Pt
De Briefmarke *(f)*
En postage stamp
Es sello de correos *(m)*
Fr timbre-poste *(m)*
It francobollo *(m)*

Semester *(n) n* De
En half-year
Es semestre *(m)*
Fr semestre *(m)*
It semestre *(m)*
Pt semestre *(m)*

semestral *adj* Es, Pt
De halbjährlich
En half-yearly
Fr semestriel
It semestrale

semestrale *adj* It
De halbjährlich
En half-yearly
Es semestral
Fr semestriel
Pt semestral

semestre *(m) n* Es, Fr, It, Pt
De Semester *(n)*
En half-year

semestriel *adj* Fr
De halbjährlich
En half-yearly
Es semestral
It semestrale
Pt semestral

sem fins lucrativos Pt
De ohne Gewinnabsicht
En nonprofitmaking
Es sin finos lucrativos
Fr sans but lucratif
It senza scopo di lucro

sem formalidade Pt
De formlos
En informal
Es sin ceremonia
Fr sans formalités
It senza formalità

semidiestro *adj* Es
De angelernt
En semi-skilled
Fr semi-qualifié
It semiprovetto
Pt semiespecializado

semiespecializado *adj* Pt
De angelernt
En semi-skilled
Es semidiestro
Fr semi-qualifié
It semiprovetto

semiprovetto *adj* It
De angelernt
En semi-skilled
Es semidiestro
Fr semi-qualifié
Pt semiespecializado

semi-qualifié *adj* Fr
De angelernt
En semi-skilled
Es semidiestro
It semiprovetto
Pt semiespecializado

semi-skilled *adj* En
De angelernt
Es semidiestro
Fr semi-qualifié
It semiprovetto
Pt semiespecializado

sem prejuízo Pt
De ohne Verbindlichkeit
En without prejudice
Am not binding
Es sin prejuicio
Fr sous toutes réserves
It senza pregiudizio

sem recurso Pt
De ohne Rückgriff
En without recourse
Es sin recurso
Fr sans droit de recours
It senza ricorso

senhorio *(m) n* Pt
De Eigentümer; Vermieter *(m)*
En landlord; lessor
Es propietario; arrendador
 (m)
Fr propriétaire; bailleur *(m)*
It proprietario; locatore *(m)*

sensale *(m) n* It
De Makler *(m)*
En broker
Es corredor *(m)*
Fr courtier *(m)*
Pt corretor *(m)*

sensale di merci *(m)* It
De Makler für Verbrauchsgüter *(m)*
En commodity broker
Es corredor de mercaderías *(m)*
Fr courtier en marchandises *(m)*
Pt corretor de mercadorias *(m)*

sensale marittimo *(m)* It
De Schiffsmakler *(m)*
En shipbroker
Es corredor marítimo *(m)*
Fr courtier maritime *(m)*
Pt corretor marítimo *(m)*

senseria *(f)* n It
De Maklergebühr *(f)*
En brokerage
Es corretaje *(m)*
Fr courtage *(m)*
Pt corretagem *(f)*

sentence arbitrale *(f)* Fr
De Schiedsspruch *(m)*
En arbitration award
Es sentencia arbitral *(f)*
It lodo arbitrale *(m)*
Pt decisão de arbitragem *(f)*

sentencia arbitral *(f)* Es
De Schiedsspruch *(m)*
En arbitration award
Fr sentence arbitrale *(f)*
It lodo arbitrale *(m)*
Pt decisão de arbitragem *(f)*

senza cedola It
De ohne Coupon
En ex coupon
Es sin cupón
Fr ex coupon
Pt talão excluído

senza diritti It
De ohne Bezugsrechte
En ex rights
Es sin privilegio
Fr ex-droits
Pt privilégios excluídos

senza dividendo It
De ohne Dividende
En ex dividend
Es sin dividendo
Fr ex-dividende
Pt dividendo excluído

senza formalità It
De formlos
En informal
Es sin ceremonia
Fr sans formalités
Pt sem formalidade

senza lavoro It
De arbeitslos
En out of a job
Es sin trabajo; parado
Fr en chômage
Pt desempregado

senza pregiudizio It
De ohne Verbindlichkeit
En without prejudice
Am not binding
Es sin prejuicio
Fr sous toutes réserves
Pt sem prejuízo

senza ricorso It
De ohne Rückgriff
En without recourse
Es sin recurso
Fr sans droit de recours
Pt sem recurso

senza scopo di lucro It
De ohne Gewinnabsicht
En nonprofitmaking
Es sin finos lucrativos
Fr sans but lucratif
Pt sem fins lucrativos

se porter garant de Fr
De Haftkaution geben
En go bail for
Es salir fiados por
It rendersi garante di
Pt prestar caução a favor de

serrata *(f)* n It
De Aussperrung *(f)*
En lock-out
Es cierre *(m)*
Fr lock-out *(m)*
Pt lockout *(m)*

se ruega hacer seguir Es
De bitte nachsenden
En please forward
Fr prière de faire suivre
It far proseguire
Pt é favor enviar

service agreement En
De Dienstvertrag *(m)*
Es contrato de servicio *(m)*
Fr contrat de service *(m)*
It accordo di servizio *(m)*
Pt contrato de serviço *(m)*

service de groupage *(m)* Fr
De Groupagedienst *(m)*
En groupage service
Es servicio de agrupación *(m)*
It trasporto a collettame *(m)*
Pt serviço de agrupamento *(m)*

service de la comptabilité *(m)* Fr
De Buchhaltung *(f)*
En accounts department
Am accounting department
Es departamento de contabilidad *(m)*
It ufficio contabilità *(m)*
Pt departamento de contabilidade *(m)*

service de la santé *(m)* Fr
De Gesundheitsdienst *(m)*
En health service
Es servicio de sanidad *(m)*
It servizio sanitario *(m)*
Pt serviço de saúde *(m)*

service des colis postaux *(m)* Fr
De Paketpost *(f)*
En parcel post
Es servicio de paquete postal *(m)*
It servizio dei pacchi postali *(m)*
Pt serviço de encomendas postais *(m)*

service flat En
De Etagenwohnung mit Bedienung *(f)*
Es piso con servicio incluido *(m)*
Fr appartement avec service *(m)*
It appartamento con servizio *(m)*
Pt andar com serviço incluído *(m)*

service ventes *(m)* Fr
De Verkaufsabteilung *(f)*
En sales department
Es departamento de ventas *(m)*
It ufficio vendite *(m)*
Pt departamento de vendas *(m)*

servicio de agrupación *(m)* Es
De Groupagedienst *(m)*
En groupage service
Fr service de groupage *(m)*
It trasporto a collettame *(m)*
Pt serviço de agrupamento *(m)*

servicio de paquete postal *(m)* Es
De Paketpost *(f)*
En parcel post
Fr service des colis postaux *(m)*
It servizio dei pacchi postali *(m)*
Pt serviço de encomendas postais *(m)*

servicio de sanidad *(m)* Es
De Gesundheitsdienst *(m)*
En health service
Fr service de la santé *(m)*
It servizio sanitario *(m)*
Pt serviço de saúde *(m)*

serviço de agrupamento *(m)* Pt
De Groupagedienst *(m)*
En groupage service
Es servicio de agrupación *(m)*
Fr service de groupage *(m)*
It trasporto a collettame *(m)*

serviço de encomendas postais *(m)* Pt
De Paketpost *(f)*
En parcel post
Es servicio de paquete postal *(m)*
Fr service des colis postaux *(m)*
It servizio dei pacchi postali *(m)*

serviço de saúde *(m)* Pt
De Gesundheitsdienst *(m)*
En health service

Es servicio de sanidad *(m)*
Fr service de la santé *(m)*
It servizio sanitario *(m)*

servirsi da sè *(m)* It
De Selbstbedienung *(f)*
En self-service
Es auto-servicio *(m)*
Fr libre service *(m)*
Pt self-service *(m)*

servizio dei pacchi postali *(m)* It
De Paketpost *(f)*
En parcel post
Es servicio de paquete postal *(m)*
Fr service des colis postaux *(m)*
Pt serviço de encomendas postais *(m)*

servizio di cassette di sicurezza *(m)* It
De Verwahrung in Stahlfach *(f)*
En safe deposit
Es depósito en caja fuerte *(m)*
Fr dépôt en coffre-fort *(m)*
Pt depósito em cofre forte *(m)*

servizio sanitario *(m)* It
De Gesundheitsdienst *(m)*
En health service
Es servicio de sanidad *(m)*
Fr service de la santé *(m)*
Pt serviço de saúde *(m)*

settlement (of claim) *n* En
De Ausgleich *(m)*
Es satisfacción *(f)*
Fr règlement *(m)*
It regolamento *(m)*
Pt satisfação *(f)*

settlement (of accounts) *n* En
De Abrechnung *(f)*
Es ajuste *(m)*
Fr règlement *(m)*
It quietanza *(f)*
Pt ajuste *(m)*

settlement (agreement) *n* En
De Vereinbarung *(f)*
Es acuerdo *(m)*
Fr accord *(m)*
It accordo *(m)*
Pt acordo *(m)*

settlement day En
Am due date
De Abrechnungstag *(m)*
Es día de liquidación *(m)*
Fr jour de règlement *(m)*
It giorno della liquidazione *(m)*
Pt dia de liquidação *(m)*

settore privato *(m)* It
De Privatwirtschaft *(f)*
En private sector
Es sector privado *(m)*
Fr secteur privé *(m)*
Pt sector privado *(m)*

settore statale *(m)* It
De öffentliche Hand *(f)*
En public sector
Es sector público *(m)*
Fr secteur public *(m)*
Pt sector público *(m)*

severance pay En
De Abfindungssumme (bei Entlassung) *(f)*
Es indemnización de despido *(f)*
Fr indemnité de licenciement *(f)*
It sussidio per rottura del rapporto d'impiego *(m)*
Pt indemnização por despedimento *(f)*

sfrattare un locatario It
De einen Mieter entfernen
En evict a tenant
Es desalojar un inquilino
Fr expulser un locataire
Pt desalojar um inquilino

sfruttare *vb* It
De ausbeuten
En exploit
Es explotar
Fr exploiter
Pt explorar

sgravio fiscale *(m)* It
De Steuererleichterung *(f)*
En tax relief
Es desgravación *(f)*
Fr dégrèvement *(m)*
Pt isenção de imposto *(f)*

share *vb* En
De teilen
Es participar; repartir
Fr partager
It dividere; partecipare
Pt participar; repartir

share (in a private company) *n*
En
De Teil *(m)*
Es parte *(f)*
Fr part *(f)*
It parte *(f)*
Pt quota *(f)*

share (in a public company) *n*
En
De Aktie *(f)*
Es acción *(f)*
Fr action *(f)*
It azione *(f)*
Pt acção *(f)*

share capital En
Am stock capital
De Aktienkapital *(n)*
Es capital en acciones *(m)*
Fr capital social *(m)*
It capitale azionario *(m)*
Pt capital em acções *(m)*

share certificate En
Am certificate of stock
De Aktienzertifikat *(n)*
Es título de acción *(m)*
Fr certificat d'actions *(m)*
It certificato azionario *(m)*
Pt título de acções *(m)*

shareholder *n* En
Am stockholder
De Aktionär *(m)*
Es accionista *(m)*
Fr actionnaire *(m)*
It azionista *(m)*
Pt accionista *(m)*

share index En
De Aktienindex *(m)*
Es índice de las acciones *(m)*
Fr indice des actions *(m)*
It indice delle azioni *(m)*
Pt índice das acções *(m)*

share market En
Am stock market
De Aktienmarkt *(m)*
Es mercado de valores *(m)*

Fr marché des valeurs *(m)*
It mercato azionario *(m)*
Pt mercado de acções *(m)*

share register En
De Liste der Aktionäre *(f)*
Es registro de las acciones
(m)
Fr registre des actionnaires
(m)
It registro delle azioni *(m)*
Pt registo de acções *(m)*

shift (working) *n* En
De Schicht *(f)*
Es turno *(m)*
Fr équipe *(f)*
It turno *(m)*
Pt turno *(m)*

shiftwork *n* En
De Schichtarbeit *(f)*
Es trabajo por torno *(m)*
Fr travail par équipes *(m)*
It lavoro a turno *(m)*
Pt trabalho por turno *(m)*

ship *n* En
De Schiff *(n)*
Es barco *(m)*
Fr navire *(m)*
It nave *(f)*
Pt navio *(m)*

ship *vb* En
De verschiffen
Es embarcar
Fr embarquer
It imbarcare
Pt embarcar

shipbroker *n* En
De Schiffsmakler *(m)*
Es corredor marítimo *(m)*
Fr courtier maritime *(m)*
It sensale marittimo *(m)*
Pt corretor marítimo *(m)*

shipment *n* En
De Verladung *(f)*
Es embarque *(m)*
Fr embarquement *(m)*
It imbarco *(m)*
Pt embarque *(m)*

shipment from origin En
De Versendung vom Ur-
sprungsort *(f)*
Es envío desde el punto de
origen *(m)*
Fr envoi du lieu de départ *(m)*
It spedizione dall'origine *(f)*
Pt carregamento desde a
origem *(m)*

shipped bill of lading En
De Hafenkonnossement *(n)*
Es conocimiento de embar-
que a bordo *(m)*
Fr connaissement de mar-
chandises à bord *(m)*
It polizza di carico con mer-
ce a bordo *(f)*
Pt conhecimento de carga
embarcada *(m)*

shipping clerk En
De Expedient *(m)*
Es dependiente de muelle *(m)*
Fr expéditionnaire *(m)*
It commesso di spedizionie-
re *(m)*
Pt despachante *(m)*

shipping line En
De Reederei *(f)*
Es compañia navièra *(f)*
Fr compagnie de navigation
(f)
It società di navigazione *(f)*
Pt companhia de navegação
(f)

ship's papers En
De Schiffspapiere *(n pl)*
Es documentación marítima
(f)
Fr papiers de bord *(m pl)*
It carte di bordo *(f pl)*
Pt documentação do navio *(f)*

ship's register En
De Schiffsregister *(n)*
Es registro del barco *(m)*
Fr certificat d'immatriculation
(m)
It atto di nazionalità *(m)*
Pt registo do navio *(m)*

shop *n* En
De Laden *(m)*
Es tienda *(f)*
Fr magasin *(m)*
It bottega *(f)*
Pt loja *(f)*

shopping centre En
De Geschäftszentrum (n)
Es centro de negocios (m)
Fr centre commercial (m)
It zona degli acquisti (f)
Pt centro de comércio (m)

short-dated adj En
De kurzfristig
Es a corto plazo
Fr à courte échéance
It a breve scadenza
Pt a curto prazo

short-dated security En
De kurzfristiges Wertpapier (n)
Es título a corto plazo (m)
Fr titre à court terme (m)
It titolo a breve scadenza (m)
Pt título a curto prazo (m)

short delivery En
De mangelhafte Lieferung (f)
Es entrega deficiente (f)
Fr livraison incomplète (f)
It consegna deficiente (f)
Pt entrega insuficiente (f)

shorthand n En
De Kurzschrift (f)
Es taquigrafía (f)
Fr sténographie (f)
It stenografia (f)
Pt estenografia (f)

shorthand typist En
De Stenotypistin (f)
Es taquimecanógrafa (f)
Fr sténodactylographe (f)
It stenodattilografa (f)
Pt estenodactilógrafa (f)

short supply En
De Knappheit (f)
Es escasez (f)
Fr disette (f)
It scarsezza (f)
Pt escassez (f)

short-term adj En
De kurzfristig
Es a corto plazo
Fr à court terme
It a breve termine
Pt a curto prazo

short-term capital En
De kurzfristiges Kapital (n)
Es capital a corto plazo (m)
Fr capitaux à court terme (m pl)
It capitale a breve termine (m)
Pt capital a curto prazo (m)

sich decken De
En hedge
Es cubrirse
Fr arbitrager
It coprirsi
Pt cobrir-se

sich einschiffen De
En embark
Es embarcar
Fr s'embarquer
It imbarcare
Pt embarcar

sichere Verwahrung (f) De
En safe custody
Es custodia (f)
Fr bonne garde (f)
It custodia (f)
Pt custódia segura (f)

Sicherheit (f) n De
En security
Es seguridad (f)
Fr sécurité (f)
It sicurezza (f)
Pt segurança (f)

Sicherheitskoeffizient (m) n De
En safety factor
Es factor de seguridad (m)
Fr facteur de sécurité (m)
It coefficiente di sicurezza (m)
Pt factor de segurança (m)

Sichtgelder (n pl) n De
En money on call
Es dinero a la vista (m)
Fr argent à vue (m)
It denaro a vista (m)
Pt dinheiro à ordem (m)

Sichttratte (f) n De
En sight draft
Es letra a la vista (f)
Fr traite à vue (f)
It tratta a vista (f)
Pt letra à vista (f)

sicurezza (f) n It
De Sicherheit (f)
En security; safety
Es seguridad (f)
Fr sécurité (f)
Pt segurança (f)

sicurezza sociale (f) It
De Sozialversicherung (f)
En social security
Es seguridad social (f)
Fr sécurité sociale (f)
Pt segurança social (f)

siège (m) n Fr
De Hauptbüro (n)
En head office
Es oficina central (f)
It sede; ufficio centrale (f m)
Pt sede; escritório central (f m)

Siegel (n) n De
En seal
Es sello (m)
Fr sceau (m)
It sigillo (m)
Pt selo (m)

sight draft En
De Sichttratte (f)
Es letra a la vista (f)
Fr traite à vue (f)
It tratta a vista (f)
Pt letra à vista (f)

sigillo (m) n It
De Siegel (n)
En seal
Es sello (m)
Fr sceau (m)
Pt selo (m)

siglare vb It
De paraphieren
En initial
Es rubricar; poner iniciales a
Fr parapher; viser
Pt rubricar

signature n En, Fr (f)
De Unterschrift (f)
Es firma (f)
It firma (f)
Pt assinatura (f)

silent partner Am
En sleeping partner
De stiller Gesellschafter (m)

Es socio comanditario *(m)*
Fr commanditaire *(m)*
It socio accomandante *(m)*
Pt sócio comanditário *(m)*

símbolo *(m) n* Es, Pt
De Symbol *(n)*
En symbol
Fr symbole *(m)*
It símbolo *(m)*

simili-cuir *(m) n* Fr
De Kunstleder *(n)*
En imitation leather
Es piel de imitación *(f)*
It finta pelle *(f)*
Pt cabedal de imitação *(m)*

similor *(m) n* Fr
De Kunstgold *(n)*
En imitation gold
Es oro de imitación *(m)*
It similoro *(m)*
Pt ouro de imitação *(m)*

similoro *(m) n* It
De Kunstgold *(n)*
En imitation gold
Es oro de imitación *(m)*
Fr similor *(m)*
Pt ouro de imitação *(m)*

simple interest En
De einfache Zinsen *(m pl)*
Es interés simple *(m)*
Fr intérêts simples *(m pl)*
It interesse semplice *(m)*
Pt juro simples *(m)*

simulação *(f) n* Pt
De Simulation *(f)*
En simulation
Es simulación *(f)*
Fr simulation *(f)*
It simulazione *(f)*

simulación *(f) n* Es
De Simulation *(f)*
En simulation
Fr simulation *(f)*
It simulazione *(f)*
Pt simulação *(f)*

simulation *n* En, Fr *(f)*
De Simulation *(f)*
Es simulación *(f)*
It simulazione *(f)*
Pt simulação *(f)*

Simulation *(f) n* De
En simulation
Es simulación *(f)*
Fr simulation *(f)*
It simulazione *(f)*
Pt simulação *(f)*

simulazione *(f) n* It
De Simulation *(f)*
En simulation
Es simulación *(f)*
Fr simulation *(f)*
Pt simulação *(f)*

sinal (depósito) *(m) n* Pt
De Anzahlung *(f)*
En deposit
Es desembolso inicial *(m)*
Fr arrhes *(f pl)*
It caparra *(f)*

sin ceremonia Es
De formlos
En informal
Fr sans formalités
It senza formalità
Pt sem formalidade

sin cupón Es
De ohne Coupon
En ex coupon
Fr ex coupon
It senza cedola
Pt talão excluído

sindacato *(m) n* It
De Gewerkschaft *(f)*
En trade union
Es sindicato *(m)*
Fr syndicat *(m)*
Pt sindicato *(m)*

sindacato dei prezzi *(m)* It
De Preisabsprache *(f)*
En price ring
Es coalición de vendedores *(f)*
Fr coalition de vendeurs *(f)*
Pt convénio de preços *(m)*

sindacato di assicuratori *(m)* It
De Versicherungssyndikat *(n)*
En underwriting syndicate (insurance)
Es sindicato de seguros *(m)*
Fr syndicat d'assureurs *(m)*
Pt consórcio de seguradores *(m)*

sindaco *(m) n* It
De Bücherrevisor *(m)*
En auditor
Es revisor de conti *(m)*
Fr réviseur des comptes *(m)*
Pt fiscal de contas *(m)*

sindicato *(m) n* Es, Pt
De Gewerkschaft; Syndikat *(f n)*
En trade union; syndicate
Fr syndicat *(m)*
It sindicato; consorzio finanziaro *(m)*

sindicato de seguros *(m)* Es
De Versicherungssyndikat *(n)*
En underwriting syndicate
Fr syndicat d'assureurs *(m)*
It sindicato di assicuratori *(m)*
Pt consórcio de seguradores *(m)*

sindico *(m) n* Es
De Konkursverwalter *(m)*
En (official) receiver
Fr syndic de faillite *(m)*
It curatore *(m)*
Pt síndico *(m)*

síndico *(m) n* Pt
De Konkursverwalter *(m)*
En (official) receiver
Es sindico *(m)*
Fr syndic de faillite *(m)*
It curatore *(m)*

sin fines lucrativos Es
De ohne Gewinnabsicht
En nonprofitmaking
Fr sans but lucratif
It senza scopo di lucro
Pt sem fins lucrativos

single-entry book-keeping En
De einfache Buchführung *(f)*
Es contabilidad por partida sencilla *(f)*
Fr comptabilité en partie simple *(f)*
It contabilità in partita semplice *(f)*
Pt contabilização por lançamento simples *(f)*

single fare En
Am one way fare
De einfache Fahrkarte *(f)*
Es pasaje de ida *(m)*
Fr billet d'aller *(m)*
It biglietto d'andata *(m)*
Pt passagem de ida *(f)*

sinking fund En
De Tilgungsfonds *(m)*
Es fondo de amortización *(m)*
Fr fonds d'amortissement *(m)*
It fondo di ammortamento *(m)*
Pt fundo de amortização *(m)*

sin prejuicio Es
De ohne Verbindlichkeit
En without prejudice
Am not binding
Fr sous toutes réserves
It senza pregiudizio
Pt sem prejuízo

sin privilegio Es
De ohne Bezugsrechte
En ex rights
Fr ex-droits
It senza diritti
Pt privilégios excluídos

sin recurso Es
De ohne Rückgriff
En without recourse
Fr sans droit de recours
It senza ricorso
Pt sem recurso

sin trabajo Es
De arbeitslos
En out of a job
Fr en chômage
It senza lavoro
Pt desempregado

sistema *(m) n* Es, It, Pt
De System *(n)*
En system
Fr système *(m)*

sistema físico *(m)* Pt
De Maschinenausrüstung *(f)*
En (computer) hardware
Es mecánica de la máquina *(f)*
Fr hardware *(m)*
It componenti di macchina calcolatore *(m pl)*

sistema lógico *(m)* Pt
De Programmausrüstung *(f)*
En (computer) software
Es conjunto de rutinas; software *(m)*
Fr software *(m)*
It programmatura; software *(f m)*

sistema métrico *(m)* Es, Pt
De metrisches System *(n)*
En metric system
Fr système métrique *(m)*
It sistema metrico *(m)*

sistema metrico *(m)* It
De metrisches System *(n)*
En metric system
Es sistema métrico *(m)*
Fr système métrique *(m)*
Pt sistema métrico *(m)*

sister company En
De Schwestergesellschaft *(f)*
Es compañía asociada *(f)*
Fr société sœur *(f)*
It società sorella *(f)*
Pt empresa gémea *(f)*

sit-down strike En
De Sitzstreik *(m)*
Es huelga de brazos caídos *(f)*
Fr grève avec occupation des lieux *(f)*
It sciopero bianco *(m)*
Pt greve de braços caídos *(f)*

situação de regatear *(f)* Pt
De Verhandlungslage *(f)*
En bargaining position
Es situación de negociar *(f)*
Fr situation permettant de négocier *(f)*
It situazione permettente di trattare *(f)*

situação do mercado *(f)* Pt
De Marktumstände *(m pl)*
En state of the market
Es condiciones del mercado *(f pl)*
Fr état du marché *(m)*
It condizioni del mercato *(f pl)*

situación de negociar *(f)* Es
De Verhandlungslage *(f)*
En bargaining position

Fr situation permettant de négocier *(f)*
It situazione permettente di trattare *(f)*
Pt situação de regatear *(f)*

situation permettant de négocier *(f)* Fr
De Verhandlungslage *(f)*
En bargaining position
Es situación de negociar *(f)*
It situazione permettente di trattare *(f)*
Pt situação de regatear *(f)*

situazione permettente di trattare *(f)* It
De Verhandlungslage *(f)*
En bargaining position
Es situación de negociar *(f)*
Fr situation permettant de négocier *(f)*
Pt situação de regatear *(f)*

Sitzstreik *(m) n* De
En sit-down strike
Es huelga de brazos caídos *(f)*
Fr grève avec occupation des lieux *(f)*
It sciopero bianco *(m)*
Pt greve de braços caídos *(f)*

Skonto *(m) n* De
En discount
Es descuento *(m)*
Fr escompte *(m)*
It sconto; ribasso *(m)*
Pt desconto *(m)*

sleeping partner En
Am silent partner
De stiller Gesellschafter *(m)*
Es socio comanditario *(m)*
Fr commanditaire *(m)*
It socio accomandante *(m)*
Pt sócio comanditário *(m)*

sliding scale En
De gleitende Skala *(f)*
Es escala móvil *(f)*
Fr échelle mobile *(f)*
It scala mobile *(f)*
Pt escala móvel *(f)*

slow down Am
En go-slow strike
De Bummelstreik *(m)*
Es huelga de producción lenta *(f)*

Fr   grève perlée *(f)*
It   sciopero a singhiozzo *(m)*
Pt   greve de abrandamento
     do ritmo de produção *(f)*

slow payer En
De   schlechter Zahler *(m)*
Es   deudor moroso *(m)*
Fr   mauvais payeur *(m)*
It   cattivo pagatore *(m)*
Pt   mau-pagador *(m)*

small change En
De   Kleingeld *(n)*
Es   moneda suelta *(f)*
Fr   petite monnaie *(f)*
It   spiccioli *(m pl)*
Pt   troco miúdo *(m)*

smuggle *vb* En
De   schmuggeln
Es   pasar de contrabando
Fr   faire la contrebande
It   contrabbandare
Pt   passar por contrabando

sob condição Pt
De   vorausgesetzt
En   on condition
Es   a condición
Fr   sous réserve
It   a condizione

sobornar *vb* Es
De   bestechen
En   bribe
Fr   corrompre
It   corrompere
Pt   subornar

soborno *(m)* n Es
De   Bestechung; Beste-
     chungsgeld *(f n)*
En   bribery; bribe
Fr   corruption; pot-de-vin
     (f m)
It   corruzione; dono per cor-
     rompere *(f m)*
Pt   suborno *(m)*

sobrante *(m)* n Es
De   verfügbarer Saldo *(m)*
En   balance in hand
Fr   solde en caisse *(m)*
It   saldo in cassa *(m)*
Pt   saldo em poder *(m)*

sobre *(m)* n Es
De   Umschlag *(m)*
En   envelope
Fr   enveloppe *(f)*
It   busta *(f)*
Pt   envelope *(m)*

sobre de ventanilla *(m)* Es
De   Fensterbriefumschlag *(m)*
En   window-envelope
Fr   enveloppe à fenêtre *(f)*
It   busta con finestra *(f)*
Pt   envelope de endereço ex-
     posto *(m)*

sobreestadia *(f)* n Pt
De   Überliegezeit *(f)*
En   demurrage
Es   sobreestadía *(f)*
Fr   surestarie *(f)*
It   controstallia *(f)*

sobreestadía *(f)* n Es
De   Überliegezeit *(f)*
En   demurrage
Fr   surestarie *(f)*
It   controstallia *(f)*
Pt   sobreestadia *(f)*

sobregiro *(m)* n Es
De   Überziehung *(f)*
En   overdraft
Fr   découvert; solde débiteur
     (m)
It   scoperto *(m)*
Pt   conta a descoberto *(f)*

sobre partida Es
De   in Konsignation
En   on consignment
Fr   en consignation
It   in conto deposito
Pt   à consignação

sobretasa *(f)* n Es
De   Steuerzuschlag *(m)*
En   surtax
Fr   surtaxe *(f)*
It   soprattassa *(f)*
Pt   sobretaxa *(f)*

sobretaxa *(f)* n Pt
De   Steuerzuschlag *(m)*
En   surtax
Es   sobretasa *(f)*
Fr   surtaxe *(f)*
It   soprattassa *(f)*

social cost En
De   Sozialkosten *(f pl)*
Es   coste social *(m)*
Fr   coût social *(m)*
It   costo sociale *(m)*
Pt   custo social *(m)*

social security En
De   Sozialversicherung *(f)*
Es   seguridad social *(f)*
Fr   sécurité sociale *(f)*
It   sicurezza sociale *(f)*
Pt   segurança social *(f)*

Sociedad anónima (SA) *(f)* Es
De   Aktiengesellschaft (AG) *(f)*
En   public limited company
Fr   Société anonyme (SA) *(f)*
It   Società anonima (SA) *(f)*
Pt   Sociedade Anónima (SA)
     (f)

sociedad de socorro mutuo
     (f) Es
De   Versicherungsverein auf
     Gegenseitigkeit *(m)*
En   friendly society
Am   lodge
Fr   société de secours mutuel
     (f)
It   società di mutuo soccorso
     (f)
Pt   mutualidade *(f)*

sociedade *(f)* n Pt
De   Gesellschaft *(t)*
En   company
Es   sociedad *(f)*
Fr   société *(f)*
It   società *(f)*

Sociedade Anónima (SA) *(f)*
     Pt
De   Aktiengesellschaft (AG) *(f)*
En   limited liability company
Es   Sociedad anónima (SA) *(f)*
Fr   Société anonyme (SA) *(f)*
It   Società anonima (SA) *(f)*

sociedade em comandita *(f)*
     Pt
De   Kommanditgesellschaft *(f)*
En   limited partnership
Es   sociedad en comandita *(f)*
Fr   société en commandité *(f)*
It   società in accomandita
     semplice *(f)*

sociedade em nome colectivo *(f)* Pt
De offene Handelsgesell-
    schaft (OHG) *(f)*
En partnership
Es sociedad regular colectiva
    (SRC) *(f)*
Fr société en nom collectif *(f)*
It società *(f)*

sociedade fantasma *(f)* Pt
De Schwindelgesellschaft *(f)*
En bogus company
Am phantom operation
Es sociedad fantasma *(f)*
Fr société fantôme *(f)*
It società fasulla *(f)*

sociedad en comandita *(f)* Es
De Kommanditgesellschaft *(f)*
En limited partnership
Fr société en commandité *(f)*
It società in accomandita
    semplice *(f)*
Pt sociedade em comandita
    (f)

**Sociedade por quotas de
    responsabilidade
    limitada** *(f)* Pt
De Gesellschaft mit be-
    schränkter Haftung
    (GmbH) *(f)*
En private limited company
Es Companía privada de res-
    ponsabilidad limitada *(f)*
Fr Société à responsabilité
    limitée (SARL) *(f)*
It Società a responsabilità
    limitata (Srl) *(f)*

sociedad extinta *(f)* Es
De erloschene Gesellschaft *(f)*
En defunct company
Fr société liquidée *(f)*
It società estinta *(f)*
Pt empresa extinta *(f)*

sociedad fantasma *(f)* Es
De Schwindelgesellschaft *(f)*
En bogus company
Am phantom operation
Fr société fantôme *(f)*
It società fasulla *(f)*
Pt sociedade fantasma *(f)*

**sociedad regular colectiva
    (SRC)** *(f)* n Es
De Gesellschaft; offene Han-
    delsgesellschaft (OHG) *(f)*
En company; partnership
Fr société; société en nom
    collectif *(f)*
It società *(f)*
Pt sociedade; sociedade em
    nome colectivo *(f)*

società *(f)* n It
De Gesellschaft *(f)*
En company; partnership
Es compañía; sociedad regu-
    lar colectiva (SRC) *(f)*
Fr société; entreprise *(f)*
Pt sociedade; companhia *(f)*

società affiliata *(f)* It
De Schwestergesellschaft *(f)*
En affiliated company
Es compañía afiliada *(f)*
Fr société sœur *(f)*
Pt companhia subsidiária *(f)*

Società anonima (SA) *(f)* It
De Aktiengesellschaft (AG) *(f)*
En public limited company
Es Sociedad anónima (SA) *(f)*
Fr Société anonyme (SA) *(f)*
Pt Sociedade anónima (SA)
    (f)

**Società a responsabilità
    limitata (Srl)** *(f)* It
De Gesellschaft mit be-
    schränkter Haftung
    (GmbH) *(f)*
En private limited company
Es Companía privada de res-
    ponsabilidad limitada *(f)*
Fr Société à responsabilité
    limitée (SARL) *(f)*
Pt Sociedade por quotas de
    responsabilidade limitada
    (f)

società d'imprese *(f)* It
De Erschließungsgesellschaft
    (f)
En development company
Es compañía de explotación
    (f)
Fr société d'exploitation *(f)*
Pt empresa de exploração *(f)*

società di leasing *(f)* It
De Leasinggesellschaft *(f)*
En leasing company
Es compañía arrendataria *(f)*
Fr société de leasing *(f)*
Pt companhia arrendatária *(f)*

società di mutuo soccorso
    (f) It
De Versicherungsverein auf
    Gegenseitigkeit *(m)*
En friendly society
Am lodge
Es sociedad de socorro mu-
    tuo *(f)*
Fr société de secours mutuel
    (f)
Pt mutualidade *(f)*

società di navigazione *(f)* It
De Reederei *(f)*
En shipping line
Es compañía navièra *(f)*
Fr compagnie de navigation
    (f)
Pt companhia de navegação
    (f)

società direttrice *(f)* It
De Gesellschaft mit Kontroll-
    befugnis *(f)*
En controlling company
Es compañía directriz *(f)*
Fr société directrice *(f)*
Pt companhia controladora
    (f)

società di servizi pubblici *(f)*
    It
De gemeinnütziges Unter-
    nehmen *(n)*
En utility company
Es empresa de servicios
    publicos *(f)*
Fr entreprise d'utilité
    publique *(f)*
Pt empresa de utilidade
    publica *(f)*

società estinta *(f)* It
De erloschene Gesellschaft *(f)*
En defunct company
Es sociedad extinta *(f)*
Fr société liquidée *(f)*
Pt empresa extinta *(f)*

società fasulla *(f)* It
De Schwindelgesellschaft *(f)*
En bogus company
Am phantom operation
Es sociedad fantasma *(f)*
Fr société fantôme *(f)*
Pt sociedade fantasma *(f)*

società fiduciaria *(f)* It
De Treuhandgesellschaft *(f)*
En trust company
Es banco fideicomisario *(m)*
Fr société fiduciaire *(f)*
Pt empresa de investimentos *(f)*

società finanziaria *(f)* It
De Finanzierungsgesellschaft *(f)*
En finance company
Es compañía de crédito comercial *(f)*
Fr société de financement *(f)*
Pt empresa financeira *(f)*

società holding *(f)* It
De Dachgesellschaft *(f)*
En holding company
Es compañía tenedora *(f)*
Fr société holding *(f)*
Pt companhia proprietária *(f)*

società in accomandita semplice *(f)* It
De Kommanditgesellschaft *(f)*
En limited partnership
Es sociedad en comandita *(f)*
Fr société en commandité *(f)*
Pt sociedade em comandita *(f)*

società in nome collettivo *(f)* It
De offene Handelsgesellschaft *(f)*
En partnership
Es sociedad *(f)*
Fr société en nom collectif *(f)*
Pt sociedade em nome colectivo *(f)*

società madre *(f)* It
De Muttergesellschaft *(f)*
En parent company
Es compañía matriz *(f)*
Fr société mère *(f)*
Pt empresa matriz *(f)*

società per investimenti *(f)* It
De Investierungsgesellschaft *(f)*
En investment company
Es compañía inversionista *(f)*
Fr société de placement *(f)*
Pt companhia de investimentos *(f)*

società quotata in borsa *(f)* It
De Gesellschaft notiert an der Börse *(f)*
En quoted company
Es compañía cotizada en bolsa *(f)*
Fr société cotée à la Bourse *(f)*
Pt companhia cotizada *(f)*

società sorella *(f)* It
De Schwestergesellschaft *(f)*
En sister company
Es compañía asociada *(f)*
Fr société sœur *(f)*
Pt empresa gémea *(f)*

société *(f)* n Fr
De Gesellschaft *(f)*
En company
Es compañía; sociedad *(f)*
It società *(f)*
Pt sociedade, companhia *(f)*

Société anonyme (SA) *(f)* Fr
De Aktiengesellschaft (AG) *(f)*
En public limited company
Es Sociedad anónima (SA) *(f)*
It Società anonima (SA) *(f)*
Pt Sociedade Anónima (SA) *(f)*

Société à responsabilité limitée (SARL) *(f)* Fr
De Gesellschaft mit beschränkter Haftung (GmbH) *(f)*
En private limited company
Es Companía privada *(f)*
It Società a responsabilità limitata (Srl) *(f)*
Pt Sociedade por quotas de responsabilidade *(f)*

société coopérative *(f)* Fr
De Genossenschaft *(f)*
En cooperative
Es cooperativa *(f)*
It cooperativa *(f)*
Pt cooperativa *(f)*

société cotée à la Bourse *(f)* Fr
De Gesellschaft notiert an der Börse *(f)*
En quoted company
Es compañía cotizada en bolsa *(f)*
It società quotata in borsa *(f)*
Pt companhia cotizada *(f)*

société de financement *(f)* Fr
De Finanzierungsgesellschaft *(f)*
En finance company
Es compañía de crédito comercial *(f)*
It società finanziaria *(f)*
Pt empresa financeira *(f)*

société de leasing *(f)* Fr
De Leasinggesellschaft *(f)*
En leasing company
Es compañía arrendataria *(f)*
It società di leasing *(f)*
Pt companhia arrendatária *(f)*

société de placement *(f)* Fr
De Investierungsgesellschaft *(f)*
En investment company
Es compañía inversionista *(f)*
It società per investimenti *(f)*
Pt companhia de investimentos *(f)*

société de secours mutuel *(f)* Fr
De Versicherungsverein auf Gegenseitigkeit *(m)*
En friendly society
Am lodge
Es sociedad de socorro mutuo *(f)*
It società di mutuo soccorso *(f)*
Pt mutualidade *(f)*

société d' exploitation *(f)* Fr
De Erschließungsgesellschaft *(f)*
En development company
Es compañía de explotación *(f)*
It società d' imprese *(f)*
Pt empresa de exploração *(f)*

société directrice (f) Fr
De Gesellschaft mit Kontroll-
befugnis (f)
En controlling company
Es compañía directriz (f)
It società direttrice (f)
Pt companhia controladora
(f)

société en commandité (f) Fr
De Kommanditgesellschaft (f)
En limited partnership
Es sociedad en comandita (f)
It società in accomandita
semplice (f)
Pt sociedade em comandita
(f)

société en nom collectif (f) Fr
De offene Handelsgesell-
schaft (OHG) (f)
En partnership
Es sociedad regular colectiva
(SRC) (f)
It società in nome collettivo
(f)
Pt sociedade em nome colec-
tivo (f)

société fantôme (f) Fr
De Schwindelgesellschaft (f)
En bogus company
Am phantom operation
Es sociedad fantasma (f)
It società fasulla (f)
Pt sociedade fantasma (f)

société fiduciaire (f) Fr
De Treuhandgesellschaft (f)
En trust company
Es banco fideicomisario (m)
It società fiduciaria (f)
Pt empresa de investimentos
(f)

**société fiduciaire de
placements** (f) Fr
De Investment-Trust (m)
En investment trust
Es fideicomiso de inversiones
(m)
It consorzio per investimenti
(m)
Pt instituição de investimentos
(f)

**société Financière
Internationale** (f) Fr
De Internationale Finanzkor-
poration (f)
En International Finance Cor-
poration
Es Corporación International
de Finanzas (f)
It Corporazione Finanziaria
Internationale (f)
Pt Corporação International
de Finanças (f)

société holding (f) Fr
De Dachgesellschaft (f)
En holding company
Es compañía tenedora (f)
It società holding (f)
Pt companhia proprietária (f)

société liquidée (f) Fr
De erloschene Gesellschaft (f)
En defunct company
Es sociedad extinta (f)
It società estinta (f)
Pt empresa extinta (f)

société mère (f) Fr
De Muttergesellschaft (f)
En parent company
Es compañía matriz (f)
It società madre (f)
Pt empresa matritz (f)

société sœur (f) Fr
De Schwestergesellschaft (f)
En sister company
Es compañía asociada (f)
It società sorella (f)
Pt empresa gémea (f)

socio (m) n Es, It
De Teilhaber, Mitglied (m)
En partner; member
Fr associé; membre (m)
Pt sócio (m)

sócio (m) n Pt
De Teilhaber; Mitglied (m)
En partner; member
Es socio (m)
Fr associé; membre (m)
It socio (m)

socio accomandante (m) It
De stiller Gesellschafter (m)
En sleeping partner
Am silent partner

Es socio comanditario (m)
Fr commanditaire (m)
Fr sócio comanditário (m)

socio activo (m) Es
De aktiver Teilhaber (m)
En active partner
Fr associé en nom (m)
It socio attivo (m)
Pt sócio activo (m)

sócio activo (m) Pt
De aktiver Teilhaber (m)
En active partner
Es socio activo (m)
Fr associé en nom (m)
It socio attivo (m)

socio attivo (m) It
De aktiver Teilhaber (m)
En active partner
Es socio activo (m)
Fr associé en nom (m)
Pt sócio activo (m)

socio comanditario (m) Es
De stiller Gesellschafter (m)
En sleeping partner
Am silent partner
Fr commanditaire (m)
It socio accommandante (m)
Pt sócio comanditário (m)

sócio comanditário (m) Pt
De stiller Gesellschafter (m)
En sleeping partner
Am silent partner
Es socio comanditario (m)
Fr commanditaire (m)
It socio accommandante (m)

socio fondatore (m) It
De Gründermitglied (m)
En founder member
Es miembro fundador (m)
Fr membre fondateur (m)
Pt membro fundador (m)

socio giovane (m) It
De jüngerer Teilhaber (m)
En junior partner
Es segundo asociado (m)
Fr associé en second (m)
Pt sócio júnior (m)

sócio júnior (m) Pt
De jüngerer Teilhaber (m)
En junior partner

Es segundo asociado *(m)*
Fr associé en second *(m)*
It socio giovane *(m)*

soddisfazione *(f)* n It
De Zufriedenstellung; Beglei-
    chung *(f)*
En satisfaction
Es satisfacción *(f)*
Fr satisfaction *(f)*
Pt satisfação *(f)*

sofortige Lieferung *(f)* De
En prompt delivery
Es entrega inmediata *(f)*
Fr livraison immédiate *(f)*
It pronto consegna *(f)*
Pt entrega imediata *(f)*

sofort lieferbare Waren *(f pl)*
    De
En spot goods
Es mercancías prontas *(f pl)*
Fr marchandises disponibles
    (f pl)
It merce pronta *(f)*
Pt mercadorias prontas *(f pl)*

Sofortzahlung *(f)* n De
En down-payment
Es pago de entrada *(m)*
Fr acompte *(m)*
It acconto *(m)*
Pt pagamento inicial *(m)*

soft currency En
De schwache Währung *(f)*
Es moneda débil *(f)*
Fr monnaie faible *(f)*
It valuta debole *(f)*
Pt moeda fraca *(f)*

soft sell En
De unaufdringliches Verkau-
    fen *(n)*
Es venta sencilla *(f)*
Fr vente par des moyens
    discrets *(f)*
It vendere senza forzare *(m)*
Pt venda subtil *(f)*

software (computer) n En
De Programmausrüstung;
    Software *(f)*
Es conjunto de rutinas; soft-
    ware *(m)*
Fr software *(m)*

It programmatura; software
    (f m)
Pt sistema lógico; software
    (m)

solares *(m pl)* n Es
De Bauland *(n)*
En building land
Fr terrain à bâtir *(m)*
It terreno edile *(m)*
Pt terreno para construção *(m)*

solcometro *(m)* n It
De Log *(n)*
En (ship's) log
Es diario de navegación *(m)*
Fr journal de navigation *(m)*
Pt diário de bordo *(m)*

solde *(m)* n Fr
De Saldo; Restpartie *(m f)*
En balance; odd lot
Es saldo; lote suelto *(m)*
It saldo; partita spaiata *(m f)*
Pt saldo; lote avulso *(m)*

solde à reporter *(m)* Fr
De Übertrag *(m)*
En balance carried forward
Es balance a cuenta nueva
    (m)
It bilancio riportato *(m)*
Pt saldo transportado *(m)*

solde créditeur *(m)* Fr
De Kreditsaldo *(m)*
En credit balance
Es saldo acreedor *(m)*
It saldo creditore *(m)*
Pt saldo credor *(m)*

solde débiteur *(m)* Fr
De Sollsaldo *(m)*
En debit balance
Es saldo en débito *(m)*
It saldo debitore *(m)*
Pt saldo devedor *(m)*

solde de caisse *(m)* Fr
De Kassensaldo *(m)*
En cash balance
Es resto en efectivo *(m)*
It residuo di cassa *(m)*
Pt saldo em dinheiro *(m)*

solde de dividende *(m)* Fr
De Schlußdividende *(f)*
En final dividend

Es saldo del dividendo *(m)*
It saldo del dividendo *(m)*
Pt dividendo final *(m)*

solde dû *(m)* Fr
De Ausgleichssaldo *(m)*
En balance due
Es balance vencido *(m)*
It saldo dovuto *(m)*
Pt saldo em divida *(m)*

solde en banque *(m)* Fr
De Bankguthaben *(n)*
En bank balance
Es saldo de banco *(m)*
It saldo in banca *(m)*
Pt saldo no banco *(m)*

solde en caisse *(m)* Fr
De verfügbarer Saldo *(m)*
En balance in hand
Es sobrante *(m)*
It saldo in cassa *(m)*
Pt saldo em poder *(m)*

solde net *(m)* Fr
De Schlußbilanz *(f)*
En final balance
Es saldo final *(m)*
It saldo finale *(m)*
Pt balanço final *(m)*

solde nul *(m)* Fr
De Nullsaldo *(m)*
En nil balance
Am zero balance
Es saldo nulo *(m)*
It saldo nullo *(m)*
Pt saldo nulo *(m)*

sold out En
De ausverkauft
Es agotado
Fr tout vendu
It tutto venduto
Pt esgotado

sole agent En
De Alleinvertreter *(m)*
Es agente exclusivo *(m)*
Fr agent exclusif *(m)*
It rappresentante esclusivo
    (m)
Pt agente exclusivo *(m)*

solicitado *adj* Es
De gefragt
En in demand

Fr demandé
It ricercato
Pt procurado

solicitud (f) n Es
De Antrag (m)
En application
Fr demande (f)
It domanda (f)
Pt requisição (f)

solicitud de inscripción (f) Es
De Antragsformular (n)
En entry-form
Fr feuille d'inscription (f)
It bolletta d'entrata (f)
Pt impresso de admissão (m)

solicitud de pedido (f) Es
De Bestellformular (n)
En order-form
Fr bulletin de commande (m)
It foglio d'ordinazione (m)
Pt impresso de encomenda
   (m)

**solidalmente e individual-
   mente** It
De gesamtschuldnerisch
En jointly and severally
Es en conjunto y separada-
   mente
Fr conjointement et solidai-
   rement
Pt em conjunto e por vários

Solidarobligation (f) n De
En joint and several bond
Es obligación solidaria e indi-
   visa (f)
Fr obligation conjointe et so-
   lidaire (f)
It obbligazione solidale (f)
Pt título solidário de diversos
   (m)

Sollsaldo (m) n De
En debit balance
Es saldo en débito (m)
Fr solde débiteur (m)
It saldo debitore (m)
Pt saldo devedor (m)

solvable adj Fr
De zahlungsfähig
En solvent
Es solvente
It solvibile
Pt solvente

solvent adj En
De zahlungsfähig
Es solvente
Fr solvable
It solvibile
Pt solvente

solvente adj Es, Pt
De zahlungsfähig
En solvent
Fr solvable
It solvibile

solvibile adj It
De zahlungsfähig
En solvent
Es solvente
Fr solvable
Pt solvente

soma (f) n Pt
De Summe (f)
En sum; amount
Es suma (f)
Fr somme (f)
It somma (f)

soma por inteiro (f) Pt
De Pauschalbetrag (m)
En lump sum
Es suma global (f)
Fr somme globale (f)
It somma globale (f)

somar vb Pt
De addieren
En add up
Es sumar
Fr totaliser; additioner
It sommare

somma (f) n It
De Summe
En sum; amount
Es suma
Fr somme (f)
Pt soma (f)

somma globale (f) It
De Pauschalbetrag (m)
En lump sum
Es suma global (f)
Fr somme globale (f)
Pt soma por inteiro (f)

sommare vb It
De addieren
En add up

Es sumar
Fr totaliser; additioner
Pt somar

somme (f) n Fr
De Betrag; Summe (f)
En amount; sum
Es suma (f)
It ammontare (m)
Pt quantia (f)

somme globale (f) Fr
De Pauschalbetrag (m)
En lump sum
Es suma global (f)
It somma globale (f)
Pt soma por inteiro (f)

Sommerferien (pl f) n De
En summer holidays
Es vacaciones de verano;
   veraneo (f pl; m)
Fr vacances d'été (f pl)
It vacanze estive (f pl)
Pt férias de verão (f pl)

Sonderangebot (m) n De
En special offer
Es oferta especial (f)
Fr offre spéciale (f)
It offerta speciale (f)
Pt oferta especial (f)

**Sonderemission gegen
   Bezugsrechte** (f) De
En rights issue
Es emisión de derechos (f)
Fr émission sous droit de
   souscription (f)
It emissione di diritti (f)
Pt emissão de direitos (f)

Sonderentschluß (f) n De
En extraordinary resolution
Es resolución extraordinaria
   (f)
Fr résolution extraordinaire (f)
It deliberazione straordinaria
   (f)
Pt resolução extraordinária (f)

sopra la pari It
De über pari
En above par
Es a premio
Fr au-dessus du pair
Pt a prémio

soprappeso *(m)* n It
De Übergewicht *(n)*
En excess weight
Es peso excedente *(m)*
Fr excédent de poids *(m)*
Pt excesso de peso *(m)*

soprattassa *(f)* n It
De Steuerzuschlag *(n)*
En surtax
Es sobretasa *(f)*
Fr surtaxe *(f)*
Pt sobretaxa *(f)*

sopravvenienza passiva *(f)* It
Do Eventualverpflichtung *(f)*
En contingent liability
Es responsabilidad contin-
gente *(f)*
Fr obligation éventuelle *(f)*
Pt responsabilidade contin-
gente *(f)*

sortie sur imprimante *(f)* Fr
De Ausgabedruck *(m)*
En computer printout
Es impresión *(f)*
It stampato d'uscita dell'
elaboratore *(m)*
Pt informe impresso pelo
computador *(m)*

sottoprodotto *(m)* n It
De Nebenprodukt *(n)*
En by-product
Es producto derivado *(m)*
Fr sous-produit *(m)*
Pt produto derivado *(m)*

sottoscrizione *(f)* n It
De Zeichnung *(f)*
En subscription *(f)*
Es suscripción *(f)*
Fr souscription *(f)*
Pt subscrição *(f)*

sottovalutazione *(f)* n It
De Unterschätzung *(f)*
En under-estimate
Es presupuesto por defecto
(m)
Fr sous-estimation *(f)*
Pt avaliação insuficiente *(f)*

sotto vincolo doganale It
De unter Zollverschluß
En in bond

Es en aduanas
Fr en entrepôt
Pt à ordem da alfândega

sottrazione *(f)* n It
De Subtraktion *(f)*
En subtraction
Es substracción *(f)*
Fr soustraction*(f)*
Pt subtracção

soumission *(f)* n Fr
De Angebot *(n)*
En bid; tender
Es oferta *(f)*
It offerta *(f)*
Pt proposta *(t)*

sous-agent *(m)* n Fr
De Untervertreter *(m)*
En sub-agent
Es sub-agente *(m)*
It sub-agente *(m)*
Pt subagente *(m)*

souscription *(f)* n Fr
De Zeichnung *(f)*
En subscription
Es suscripción *(f)*
It sottoscrizione *(f)*
Pt subscrição *(f)*

sous-directeur *(m)* n Fr
De Unterdirektor *(m)*
En assistant manager
Es sub-director *(f)*
It vice-direttore *(m)*
Pt subdirector *(m)*

sous-estimation *(f)* n Fr
De Unterschätzung *(f)*
En under-estimate
Es presupuesto por defecto
(m)
It sottovalutazione *(f)*
Pt avaliação insuficiente *(f)*

sous forme de prêt Fr
De darlehensweise
En on loan
Es en préstamo
It in prestito
Pt por empréstimo

sous-location *(f)* n Fr
De Untervermietung *(f)*
En sub-letting
Es sub-alquiter *(m)*
It subaffitto *(m)*
Pt subaluguer *(m)*

sous pli séparé Fr
De mit getrennter Post
En under separate cover
Es por correo aparte
It in piego a parte
Pt por correio separado

sous-produit *(m)* n Fr
De Nebenprodukt *(n)*
En by-product
Es producto derivado *(m)*
It sottoprodotto *(m)*
Pt produto derivado *(m)*

sous réserve Fr
De vorausgesetzt
En on condition
Es a condición
It a condizione
Pt sob condição de

sous toutes réserves Fr
De ohne Verbindlichkeit
En without prejudice
Am not binding
Es sin prejuicio
It senza pregiudizio
Pt sem compromisso

soustraction *(f)* n) Fr
De Subtraktion *(f)*
En subtraction
Es substracción *(f)*
It sottrazione *(f)*
Pt subtracção *(f)*

soute *(f)* n Fr
De Bunker *(m)*
En bunker
Es carbonera *(f)*
It carbonile *(m)*
Pt carvoeira *(f)*

sovrapproduzione *(f)* n It
De Überproduktion *(f)*
En overproduction
Es exceso de producción *(m)*
Fr surproduction *(f)*
Pt produção excessiva *(f)*

sovvenzione dello Stato *(f)* It
De Staatszuschuß *(m)*
En government subsidy
Es subvención del Estado *(f)*
Fr subvention de l'État *(f)*
Pt subvenções do Estado
(f pl)

sovvenzenzioni di capitale
(f pl) It
De Kapitalhilfe *(f)*
En capital grants
Es subvención de capital *(f)*
Fr subventions en capital *(f pl)*
Pt subvenções de capital *(f pl)*

Sozialkosten *(pl)* n De
En social cost
Es coste social *(m)*
Fr coût social *(m)*
It costo sociale *(m)*
Pt custo social *(m)*

Sozialleistungen *(f pl)* n De
En fringe benefits
Es beneficios suplementarios *(m pl)*
Fr avantages accessoires *(m pl)*
It vantaggi accessori *(m pl)*
Pt benefícios extras *(m pl)*

Sozialversicherung *(f)* n De
En social security
Es seguridad social *(f)*
Fr sécurité sociale *(f)*
It sicurezza sociale *(f)*
Pt segurança social *(f)*

Spalte *(f)* n De
En column
Es columna *(f)*
Fr colonne *(f)*
It colonna *(f)*
Pt coluna *(f)*

Spanne *(f)* n De
En margin
Es margen *(m)*
Fr marge *(f)*
It margine *(m)*
Pt margem *(f)*

Sparkasse *(f)* n De
En savings bank
Es caja de ahorros *(f)*
Fr caisse d'épargne *(f)*
It cassa di risparmio *(f)*
Pt caixa económica *(f)*

special damages En
De Ersatz immateriellen Schadens *(m)*
Es daños especiales *(m pl)*

Fr dommages indirects *(m pl)*
It danni particolari *(m pl)*
Pt indemnização especial *(f)*

special delivery Am
En express letter
De Eilbrief *(m)*
Es carta urgente *(f)*
Fr lettre par exprès *(f)*
It lettera espresso *(f)*
Pt carta expressa *(f)*

specialist n En
De Sachverständige(r) *(m)*
Es especialista *(m)*
Fr spécialiste; expert *(m)*
It specialista *(m)*
Pt especialista *(m)*

specialista *(m)* n It
De Sachverständige(r) *(m)*
En specialist
Es especialista *(m)*
Fr spécialiste; expert *(m)*
Pt especialista *(m)*

spécialiste *(m)* n Fr
De Sachverständige(r) *(m)*
En specialist; expert
Es especialista *(m)*
It specialista *(m)*
Pt especialista *(m)*

special offer En
De Sonderangebot *(m)*
Es oferta especial *(f)*
Fr offre spéciale *(f)*
It offerta speciale *(f)*
Pt oferta especial *(f)*

specifica del lavoro *(f)* It
De Arbeitsaufgabe *(f)*
En job specification
Es especificación del trabajo *(f)*
Fr donnée d'exécution *(f)*
Pt especificação de obra *(f)*

speculare vb It
De spekulieren
En speculate; job
Es especular
Fr spéculer
Pt especular

speculate vb En
De spekulieren
Es especular

Fr spéculer
It speculare
Pt especular

spéculer vb Fr
De spekulieren
En speculate; job
Es especular
It speculare
Pt especular

spedieren vb De
En dispatch; forward
Es expedir
Fr expédier
It spedire
Pt expedir

spedire vb It
De expedieren; absenden
En forward; dispatch
Es expedir; remitir
Fr envoyer; expédier
Pt expedir; remeter

Spediteur *(m)* n De
En forwarding agent; carrier
Es agente expedidor; transportador *(m)*
Fr transitaire; expéditeur *(m)*
It spedizioniere; vettore *(m)*
Pt agente expedidor; transportador *(m)*

speditore *(m)* n It
De Absender *(m)*
En consignor
Es consignador *(m)*
Fr expéditeur *(m)*
Pt consignante *(m)*

spedizione *(f)* n It
De Versand; Spedition *(m f)*
En shipment; dispatch
Es despacho; expedición *(m f)*
Fr envoi; expédition *(m f)*
Pt despacho; expedição *(m f)*

spedizione dall'origine *(f)* It
De Versendung vom Ursprungsort *(f)*
En shipment from origin
Es envío desde el punto de origen *(m)*
Fr envoi du lieu de départ *(m)*
Pt carregamento desde a origem *(m)*

spedizioniere *(m)* n It
De Spediteur *(m)*
En forwarding agent
Es agente expedidor *(m)*
Fr transitaire *(m)*
Pt agente expedidor *(m)*

Spekulationskapital *(n)* n De
En risk capital
Es capital de especulación *(m)*
Fr capitaux spéculatifs *(m pl)*
It capitale di speculazione *(m)*
Pt capital de especulação *(m)*

spekulieren *vb* De
En speculate; job
Es especular
Fr spéculer
It speculare
Pt especular

spekulieren (an der Börse) De
En gamble on the stock exchange
Es jugar a la bolsa
Fr jouer à la bourse
It giocare in borsa
Pt jogar na bolsa

spesa *(f)* n It
De Ausgaben; Kosten *(f pl)*
En expenditure; expense
Es desembolso; gasto *(m)*
Fr frais *(m pl)*
Pt despesas *(f pl)*

spesa permessa *(f)* It
De abziehbare Unkosten *(f pl)*
En allowable expense
Es gastos deducibles *(m pl)*
Fr dépense déductible *(f)*
Pt despesas deduziveis *(f pl)*

spesa supplementare *(f)* It
De Zuschlagsgebühr *(f)*
En extra charge
Es suplemento *(m)*
Fr supplément *(m)*
Pt encargó suplementar *(m)*

spese accessorie *(f pl)* It
De Nebenkosten *(f pl)*
En incidental charges
Es cargos imprevistos *(m pl)*
Fr charges annexes *(f pl)*
Pt encargos ocasionais *(m pl)*

spese assegnate It
De per Nachnahme
En charges forward
Es costes a reembolso
Fr frais à percevoir à la livraison
Pt entrega contra reembolso

spese di banca *(f pl)* It
De Bankspesen *(f pl)*
En bank charges
Es gastos de banco *(m pl)*
Fr frais bancaires *(m pl)*
Pt taxas bancárias *(f pl)*

spese di gestione *(f pl)* It
De Betriebsausgaben *(f pl)*
En operating costs
Es costes operacionales *(m pl)*
Fr frais d'exploitation *(m pl)*
Pt custos de exercicio *(m pl)*

spese di magazzinaggio *(f pl)* It
De Lagergeld *(n)*
En storage charges
Es gastos de almacenaje *(m pl)*
Fr frais de magasinage *(m pl)*
Pt encargos de armazenamento *(m pl)*

spese di pubblicità *(f pl)* It
De Werbekosten *(f pl)*
En advertising expenditure
Es gastos publicitarios *(m pl)*
Fr dépenses de publicité *(f pl)*
Pt despesa com publicidade *(f)*

spese di rappresentanza *(f pl)* It
De Repräsentationskosten *(f pl)*
En entertainment expenses
Es gastos de representación *(m pl)*
Fr frais de représentation *(m pl)*
Pt despesas de representação *(f pl)*

spese dirette *(f pl)* It
De Einzelkosten *(f pl)*
En direct expenses
Es gastos directos *(m pl)*
Fr frais directs *(m pl)*
Pt despesas directas *(f pl)*

spese di riscossione *(f pl)* It
De Einzugskosten *(f pl)*
En collection charges
Es gastos de cobranza *(m pl)*
Fr frais d'encaissement *(m pl)*
Pt gastos de cobrança *(m pl)*

spese di salvataggio *(f pl)* It
De Bergegeld *(n)*
En salvage charges
Es cargos de salvamento *(m pl)*
Fr indemnité de sauvetage *(f)*
Pt encargos de salvamento *(m pl)*

spese di viaggio *(f pl)* It
De Reisekosten *(f pl)*
En travelling expenses
Es dietas de viajes *(f pl)*
Fr frais de voyage *(m pl)*
Pt despesas de viagem *(f pl)*

spese generali *(f pl)* It
De allgemeine Unkosten; Generalunkosten *(f pl)*
En general expenses; overheads
Es gastos generales *(m pl)*
Fr frais généraux *(m pl)*
Pt despesas gérais *(f pl)*

spese impreviste *(f pl)* It
De Nebenkosten *(f pl)*
En incidental expenses
Es gastos imprevistos *(m pl)*
Fr faux frais *(m pl)*
Pt despesas ocasionais *(f pl)*

spese varie *(f pl)* It
De verschiedene Ausgaben *(f pl)*
En sundry expenses
Es gastos varios *(m pl)*
Fr frais divers *(m pl)*
Pt despesas diversas *(f pl)*

spiccioli *(m pl)* It
De Kleingeld *(n)*
En small change
Es moneda suelta *(f)*
Fr petite monnaie *(f)*
Pt troco miúdo *(m)*

Spiegelglas *(n)* n De
En plate glass
Es vidrio plano pulido *(m)*

Fr verre à glaces; glace de vi-
trage (m f)
It cristallo (m)
Pt chapa de vidro (f)

spionaggio industriale (m) It
De Wirtschaftsspionage (f)
En industrial espionage
Es espionaje industrial (m)
Fr espionage industriel (m)
Pt espionagem industrial (f)

spirale inflationniste (f) Fr
De Inflationsspirale (f)
En inflationary spiral
Es espiral de inflación (f)
It inflazione a spirale (f)
Pt espiral inflacionária (f)

split the difference En
De einen strittigen Preisunter-
schied teilen
Es repartir la diferencia
Fr partager la différence
It dividere a metà la differen-
za
Pt dividir ao meio a diferença

spot check En
De Stichprobe (f)
Es control al azar (m)
Fr contrôle par sondage (m)
It controllo saltuario (m)
Pt controlo de ocasião (m)

spot goods En
De sofort lieferbare Waren
(f pl)
Es mercancías prontas (f pl)
Fr marchandises disponibles
(f pl)
It merce pronta (f)
Pt mercadorias prontas (f pl)

Spottpreis (m) n De
En bargain price
Es precio de ocasión (m)
Fr prix de solde (m)
It prezzo d'occasione (m)
Pt preço excepcional (m)

Sprache (f) n De
En language
Es lingua (f)
Fr langue (f)
It lingua (f)
Pt língua (f)

Sprachlabor (n) n De
En language laboratory
Es laboratorio de idiomas (m)
Fr laboratoire de langues (m)
It laboratorio di linguaggio
(m)
Pt laboratório de línguas (m)

Staatsangehörigkeit (f) n De
En nationality
Es nacionalidad (f)
Fr nationalité (f)
It nazionalità (f)
Pt nacionalidade (f)

Staatsanleihe (f) n De
En government loan
Es empréstito público (m)
Fr emprunt public (m)
It prestito pubblico (m)
Pt empréstimo do governo
(m)

Staatsbesitz (m) n De
En public ownership
Es propiedad estatal (f)
Fr propriété publique (f)
It proprietà statale (f)
Pt propriedade pública (f)

Staatsobligation (f) n De
En government bond
Es obligación del Estado (f)
Fr obligation d'État (f)
It obbligazione dello Stato (f)
Pt obrigação do Tesouro (f)

Staatsschuld (f) n De
En national debt
Es deuda pública (f)
Fr dette publique (f)
It debito pubblico (m)
Pt divida pública (f)

Staatsverwaltung (f) n De
En administration; govern-
ment
Es gobierno; ministerio (m)
Fr gouvernement (m)
It governo (m)
Pt governo; administração (m)

Staatszuschuß (m) n De
En government subsidy
Es subvención del Estado (f)
Fr subvention de l'État (f)
It sovvenzione dello Stato (f)
Pt subvenções do Estado (f pl)

Stadtgas (n) n De
En town gas
Es gas de ciudad (m)
Fr gaz de ville (m)
It gas di carbon fossile (m)
Pt gás urbano (m)

staff (personnel) n En
De Personal (n)
Es personal (m)
Fr personnel (m)
It personale (m)
Pt pessoal (m)

stagione (f) n It
De Jahreszeit (f)
En season
Es estación (f)
Fr saison (f)
Pt estação(f)

stallie (f pl) n It
De Liegezeit (f)
En lay days
Es estadía (f)
Fr staries (f pl)
Pt estadia (f)

Stammaktie (f) n De
En ordinary share
Es acción ordinaria (f)
Fr action ordinaire (f)
It azione ordinaria (f)
Pt acção ordinária (f)

stamp n En
De Marke; Stempel (f m)
Es sello; estampilla (m f)
Fr timbre; tampon (m)
It francobollo; stampiglia
(m f)
Pt selo; carimbo (m)

**stampato d'uscita dell'ela-
boratore** (m) It
De Ausgabedruck (m)
En computer printout
Es impresión (f)
Fr sortie sur imprimante (f)
Pt informe impresso pelo
computador (m)

stamp duty En
De Stempelgebühr (f)
Es impuesto del timbre (m)
Fr droit de timbre (m)
It tassa di bollo (f)
Pt imposto de selo (m)

stampiglia (f) n It
De Stempel (m)
En stamp
Es estampilla (f)
Fr tampon; timbre (m)
Pt carimbo (m)

standard n En
De Standard; Norm (m f)
Es norma; standard (f m)
Fr norme; étalon (f m)
It norma (f)
Pt padrão; norma (m f)

Standard (m) n De
En standard
Es norma; standard (f m)
Fr norme; étalon (f m)
It norma (f)
Pt padrão; norma (m f)

Standardbedingungen
(f pl) n De
En standard conditions
Es condiciones normales (f pl)
Fr conditions courantes (f pl)
It condizioni normali (f pl)
Pt condições normais (f pl)

standard conditions En
De Standardbedingungen
(f pl)
Es condiciones normales (f pl)
Fr conditions courantes (f pl)
It condizioni normali (f pl)
Pt condições normais (f pl)

standard deviation En
De normale Abweichung (f)
Es desviación normal (f)
Fr déviation normale (f)
It deviazione normale (f)
Pt desvio normal (m)

standard gauge En
De Normalmaß; Normalspur-
weite (n f)
Es calibre patron (m)
Fr écartement normal (m)
It scartamento normale (m)
Pt calibre padrão (m)

standard of living En
De Lebenshaltung (f)
Es nivel de vida (m)
Fr niveau de vie (m)
It tenore di vita (m)
Pt nível de vida (m)

standard time En
De Normalzeit (f)
Es hora oficial (f)
Fr heure légale (f)
It ora legale (f)
Pt hora normal (f)

stand-by agreement En
De Notvereinbarung (f)
Es contrato de reserva (m)
Fr accord en réserve (m)
It accordo di riserva (m)
Pt acordo a postos (m)

stanza di compensazione (f)
It
De Verrechnungsstelle (f)
En clearing house
Es cámara de compensacio-
nes (f)
Fr chambre de compensa-
tion (f)
Pt câmara de compensações
e rateio (f)

stanziamento (m) n It
De Zuführung (f)
En appropriation
Es apropiación (f)
Fr affectation (f)
Pt apropriação(f)

Stapelkostenberechnung
(f) n De
En batch costing
Es fijación de precio por lotes
(f)
Fr évaluation du coût des lots
(f)
It valutazione del costo per
partita (f)
Pt fixação do preço por lote (f)

staries (f pl) n Fr
De Liegezeit (f)
En lay days
Es estadía (f)
It stallie (f pl)
Pt estadia (f)

state employment agency
Am
En employment exchange
De Arbeitsnachweisstelle (f)
Es bolsa de trabajo (f)
Fr bureau de placement (m)
It ufficio di collocamento (m)
Pt centro de serviços de em-
prego (m)

statement of account En
De Kontoauszug (m)
Es extracto de cuenta (m)
Fr relevé de compte (m)
It estratto conto (m)
Pt extracto de conta (m)

state of the market En
De Marktumstände (m pl)
Es condiciones del mercado
(f pl)
Fr état du marché (m)
It condizioni del mercato (f
pl)
Pt situação do mercado (f)

statistica (f) n It
De Statistik (f)
En statistics
Es estadística (f)
Fr statistique (f)
Pt estatística (f)

statistics n En
De Statistik (f)
Es estadística (f)
Fr statistique (f)
It statistica (f)
Pt estatística (f)

Statistik (f) n De
En statistics
Es estadística (f)
Fr statistique (f)
It statistica (f)
Pt estatística (f)

statistique (f) n Fr
De Statistik (f)
En statistics
Es estadística (f)
It statistica (f)
Pt estatística (f)

statutario adj It
De gesetzlich
En statutory
Es estatutario
Fr statutaire
Pt estatutário

statut (m) n Fr
De Gesetz (n)
En statute
Es estatuto (m)
It statuto (m)
Pt estatuto (m)

statutaire adj Fr
De gesetzlich
En statutory
Es estatutario
It statutario
Pt estatutário

statute n En
De Gesetz (n)
Es estatuto (m)
Fr statut (m)
It statuto (m)
Pt estatuto (m)

Statuten (f pl) n De
En Memorandum and Articles
 of Association
Am articles of incorporation
Es estatutos; carta orgánica
 (m pl; f)
Fr statuts; acte constitutif
 (m pl; m)
It atto costitutivo e statuto
 sociale (m)
Pt estatuto de associação (m)

statuto (m) n It
De Gesetz (n)
En statute
Es estatuto (m)
Fr statut (m)
Pt estatuto (m)

statutory adj En
De gesetzlich
Es estatutario
Fr statutaire
It statutario
Pt estatutário

statutory meeting En
De ordentliche Versammlung
 (f)
Es asamblea general (f)
Fr assemblée ordinaire (f)
It assemblea generale (f)
Pt assembleia estatutária (f)

statuto sociale (m) It
De Gesellschaftsvertrag (m)
En articles of association
Am articles of incorporation
Es artículos de asociación
 (m pl)
Fr contrat de société (m)
Pt escritura de sociedade (f)

statuts (m pl) n Fr
De Statuten (f pl)
En Memorandum and Articles
 of Association
Am articles of incorporation
Es estatutos; carta orgánica
 (m pl; f)
It atto costitutivo e statuto
 sociale (m)
Pt estatuto de associação (m)

steamer n En
De Dampfer (m)
Es buque de vapor (m)
Fr bateau à vapeur (m)
It vapore (m)
Pt vapor (m)

steigen vb De
En increase
Es aumentar; alzar
Fr augmenter; hausser
It aumentare; crescere
Pt aumentar

Steigen (n) n De
En increase; rise
Es incremento; aumento (m)
Fr hausse; augmentation (f)
It incremento; crescita (m f)
Pt aumento; incremento (m)

steigend adj De
En bullish
Es alcista
Fr haussier
It rialzista
Pt altista

Stellagegeschäft (n) n De
En double option
Es opción doble (f)
Fr double option (f)
It opzione doppia (f)
Pt opção dupla (f)

Stellenüberblick (m) n De
En field study
Es estudio sobre el terreno
 (m)
Fr enquête sur les lieux (f)
It studio sul terreno (m)
Pt estudo de campo (m)

Stellenvermittlungsbüro
 (n) n De
En employment agency
Es agencia de colocaciones
 (f)

Fr agence de placement (f)
It agenzia di colocamento (f)
Pt agência de empregos (f)

Stellung (f) n De
En job; post
Es empleo (m)
Fr emploi (m)
It impiego (m)
Pt emprego (m)

**stellvertretende(r)
 Vorsitzende(r)** (m) De
En vice-chairman
Es vice-presidente (m)
Fr vice-président (m)
It vicepresidente (m)
Pt vice-presidente (m)

Stellvertreter (m) n De
En proxy
Es apoderado (m)
Fr mandataire (m)
It procuratore (m)
Pt procurador (m)

Stellvertretung (f) n De
En proxy
Es poder procuratión (m)
Fr procuration (f)
It procura (f)
Pt procuração (f)

Stempel (m) n De
En stamp
Es sello; estampilla (m f)
Fr tampon (m)
It stampo (m)
Pt carimbo (m)

Stempelgebühr (f) n De
En stamp duty
Es impuesto del timbre (m)
Fr droit de timbre (m)
It tassa di bollo (f)
Pt imposto de selo (m)

sténodactylographe (f) n Fr
De Stenotypistin (f)
En shorthand typist
Es taquimecanógrafa (f)
It stenodattilografa (f)
Pt estenodactilógrafa (f)

stenodattilografa (f) n It
De Stenotypistin (f)
En shorthand typist
Es taquimecanógrafa (f)
Fr sténodactylographe (f)
Pt estenodactilógrafa (f)

stenografia *(f)* n It
De Kurzschrift *(f)*
En shorthand
Es taquigrafía *(f)*
Fr sténographie *(f)*
Pt estenografia *(f)*

sténographie *(f)* n Fr
De Kurzschrift *(f)*
En shorthand
Es taquigrafía *(f)*
It stenografia *(f)*
Pt estenografia *(f)*

Stenotypistin *(f)* n De
En shorthand typist
Es taquimecanógrafa *(f)*
Fr sténodactylographe *(f)*
It stenodattilografa *(f)*
Pt estenodactilógrafa *(f)*

Sterblichkeitsziffer *(f)* n De
En death rate
Es mortalidad *(f)*
Fr taux de mortalité *(m)*
It tasso di mortalità *(m)*
Pt taxa de mortalidade *(f)*

sterlina verde *(f)* It
De grünes Pfund *(n)*
En green pound
Es esterlina verde *(f)*
Fr livre sterling verte *(f)*
Pt libra esterlina verde *(f)*

sterling area En
De Sterlinggebiet *(n)*
Es zona de la esterlina *(f)*
Fr zone sterling *(f)*
It zona della sterlina *(f)*
Pt zona esterlina *(f)*

Sterlinggebiet *(n)* n De
En sterling area
Es zona de la esterlina *(f)*
Fr zone sterling *(f)*
It zona della sterlina *(f)*
Pt zona esterlina *(f)*

Steuer *(f)* n De
En tax
Es impuesto *(m)*
Fr impôt *(m)*
It imposta *(f)*
Pt imposto *(m)*

steuerabsetzbar *adj* De
En tax deductible
Es deducible de impuestos

Fr déductible à l'impôt
It deducibile da tassa
Pt ilíquido de impostos

**Steuerbegünstigung auf
   Anlagen** *(f)* De
En capital allowances
Es deducciones fiscales so-
    bre inversiones *(f pl)*
Fr déductions fiscales sur les
    investissements *(f pl)*
It deduzioni fiscali sugli in-
    vestimenti *(f pl)*
Pt concessões sobre capital
    (f pl)

Steuereinnehmer *(m)* n De
En tax collector
Es recaudador de impuestos
    (m)
Fr percepteur des impôts *(m)*
It esattore delle imposte *(f)*
Pt cobrador de impostos *(m)*

Steuererklärung *(f)* n De
En tax return
Es declaración de ingresos *(f)*
Fr déclaration de l'impôt *(f)*
It dichiarazione fiscale *(f)*
Pt declaração para efeitos de
    tributação *(f)*

Steuererleichterung *(f)* n De
En tax relief
Es desgravación *(f)*
Fr dégrèvement *(m)*
It sgravio fiscale *(m)*
Pt isenção de imposto *(f)*

steuerfrei *adj* De
En tax-free
Es exento de impuestos
Fr exempt d'impôts
It esente da tassa
Pt isento de impostos

steuerfreies Einkommen *(n)*
   De
En nontaxable income
Es ingresos no imponibles
    (m pl)
Fr revenu non imposable *(m)*
It reddito non tassabile *(f)*
Pt receita não tributável *(f)*

Steuerhinterziehung *(f)* n De
En evasion of tax
Es evasión de pago de im-
    puestos *(f)*

Fr fraude fiscale *(f)*
It evasione d'imposta *(f)*
Pt fuga a impostos *(f)*

Steuerjahr *(n)* n De
En tax year
Es año fiscal *(m)*
Fr exercice fiscal *(m)*
It anno fiscale *(m)*
Pt ano fiscal *(m)*

Steuerparadies *(n)* n De
En tax haven
Es refugio fiscal *(m)*
Fr refuge fiscal *(m)*
It rifugio fiscale *(m)*
Pt refúgio fiscal *(m)*

Steuerveranlagung *(f)* n De
En tax base
Es base contributiva *(f)*
Fr assiette de l'impôt *(f)*
It ripartizione della tassazio-
    ne *(f)*
Pt base de imposto *(f)*

Steuerverlust *(m)* n De
En tax loss
Es pérdida fiscal *(f)*
Fr perte fiscale *(f)*
It perdita a scopi fiscali *(f)*
Pt perda em impostos *(f)*

Steuerzahler *(m)* n De
En tax payer
Es contribuyente *(m)*
Fr contribuable *(m)*
It contribuente fiscale *(m)*
Pt contribuinte *(m)*

Steuerzuschlag *(m)* n De
En surtax
Es sobretasa *(f)*
Fr surtaxe *(f)*
It soprattassa *(f)*
Pt sobretaxa *(f)*

Stichprobe *(f)* n De
En spot check
Es control al azar *(m)*
Fr contrôle par sondage *(m)*
It controllo saltuario *(m)*
Pt controlo de ocasião *(m)*

stille Reserve *(f)* De
En hidden reserve
Es reserva latente *(f)*
Fr réserve cachée *(f)*
It riserva occulta *(f)*
Pt reserva oculta *(f)*

stiller Gesellschafter *(m)* De
En sleeping partner
Am silent partner
Es socio comanditario *(m)*
Fr commanditaire *(m)*
It socio accomandante *(m)*
Pt sócio comanditário *(m)*

stillschweigend *adj* De
En implicit
Es implícito
Fr implicite
It implicito
Pt implícito

**stillschweigende
Bedingungen** *(f pl)* De
En implied terms
Es condiciones implícitas
(f pl)
Fr conditions implicites *(f pl)*
It condizioni implicite *(f pl)*
Pt condições implícitas *(f pl)*

**stillschweigendes
Übereinkommen** *(n)* De
En tacit agreement
Es acuerdo tácito *(m)*
Fr convention tacite *(f)*
It accordo tacito *(m)*
Pt acordo tácito *(m)*

stima del credito *(f)* It
De Kreditwürdigkeit *(f)*
En credit rating
Es límite de crédito *(m)*
Fr degré de solvabilité *(m)*
Pt nível de crédito *(m)*

stimare *vb* It
De einschätzen
En estimate
Es estimar
Fr estimer
Pt avaliar

stimmberechtigte Aktien
(f pl) De
En voting shares
Es acciones con derecho de
voto *(f pl)*
Fr actions avec droit de vote
(f pl)
It azioni con diritto di voto
(f pl)
Pt acções com direito a voto
(f pl)

stimmen *vb* De
En vote
Es votar
Fr voter
It votare
Pt votar

**stimulant de l'investisse-
ment** *(m)* Fr
De Investierungsanreiz *(m)*
En investment incentive
Es incentivo de inversión *(m)*
It incentivo d'investimento
(m)
Pt incentivo de investimento
(m)

stipendiato *(m) n* It
De Angestellte(r) *(m)*
En salaried employee
Es empleado a sueldo *(m)*
Fr appointé *(m)*
Pt assalariado *(m)*

stipendio *(m) n* It
De Gehalt *(n)*
En salary
Es sueldo *(m)*
Fr traitement *(m)*
Pt ordenado *(m)*

stiva *(f) n* It
De Laderaum *(m)*
En (ship's) hold
Es bodega *(f)*
Fr cale *(f)*
Pt porão *(m)*

stivaggio *(m) n* It
De Verstauung *(f)*
En stowage
Es estiba *(f)*
Fr arrimage *(m)*
Pt estiva *(f)*

stivare *vb* It
De verstauen
En stow
Es estibar
Fr arrimer
Pt estivar

stock (securities) *n* En
De Wertpapiere *(n pl)*
Es títulos; valores *(m pl)*
Fr titres; valeurs *(m pl; f pl)*
It titoli; valori *(m pl)*
Pt títulos; valores *(m pl)*

stock (of goods) *n* En
De Vorrat *(m)*
Es stock; existencias *(m; f pl)*
Fr stock; marchandises
(m; f pl)
It stock; scorta *(m f)*
Pt existências *(f pl)*

stock *(m) n* Es, Fr, It
De Vorrat *(m)*
En stock
Pt existências *(f pl)*

stock agotado Es
De ausverkauft
En out of stock
Fr tout vendu
It esaurito
Pt esgotado

stockbroker *n* En
De Börsenmakler *(m)*
Es corredor de bolsa *(m)*
Fr courtier en bourse *(m)*
It agente di borsa *(m)*
Pt corretor da bolsa *(m)*

stock capital Am
En share capital
De Aktienkapital *(n)*
Es capital en acciones *(m)*
Fr capital social *(m)*
It capitale azionario *(m)*
Pt capital em acções *(m)*

stock certificate Am
En ordinary share certificate
De Aktie *(f)*
Es certificado de acción *(m)*
Fr certificat d'action *(m)*
It certificato azionario *(m)*
Pt título de acções ordinárias
(m)

stock control En
De Lagerverwaltung *(f)*
Es fiscalización de las exi-
stencias *(f)*
Fr contrôle des stocks *(m)*
It controllo delle scorte *(m)*
Pt controlo de existências *(m)*

stock dividend Am
En bonus shares
De Gratisaktien *(f pl)*
Es acciones dadas como
primas *(f pl)*
Fr actions d'attribution *(f pl)*
It azioni di godimento *(f pl)*
Pt acções de prémio *(f pl)*

stocker *vb* Fr
De Vorratslager anlegen
En stockpile
Es acumular existencias
It ammassare
Pt acumular existências

stock exchange En
De Börse *(f)*
Es bolsa *(f)*
Fr bourse *(f)*
It borsa *(f)*
Pt bolsa *(f)*

stock-exchange quotation
En
De Börsenkurs *(m)*
Es curso de bolsa *(m)*
Fr cours de bourse *(m)*
It quotazione di borsa *(f)*
Pt cotação da bolsa *(f)*

stockholder *n* En
De Aktionär *(m)*
Es accionista *(m)*
Fr actionnaire *(m)*
It azionista *(m)*
Pt accionista *(m)*

stock in hand En
De Vorrat auf Lager *(m)*
Es mercancías en almacén
(f pl)
Fr marchandises en magasin
(f pl)
It merce in magazzino *(f)*
Pt mercadorias em
existência *(f pl)*

stockjobber *n* En
De Börsenhändler *(m)*
Es agiotista *(m)*
Fr marchand de titres *(m)*
It aggiotatore *(m)*
Pt agiota *(m)*

stock market Am
En share market
De Aktienmarkt *(m)*
Es mercado de valores *(m)*
Fr marché des valeurs *(m)*
It mercato azionario *(m)*
Pt mercado de acções *(m)*

stockpile *vb* En
De Vorratslager anlegen
Es acumular existencias

Fr stocker
It ammassare
Pt acumular existências

stocks de régularisation
(m pl) Fr
De buffer-stocks *(m pl)*
En buffer stocks
Es existencias de regulariza-
ción *(f pl)*
It scorte di equilibrio *(f pl)*
Pt existências de regulari-
zação *(f pl)*

stocktaking *n* En
De Bestandsaufnahme *(f)*
Es inventario; balance *(m)*
Fr levée d'inventaire *(f)*
It compilazione dell'inventa-
rio *(f)*
Pt inventário de existências
(m)

Stoff *(m) n* De
En material; cloth
Es tejido *(m)*
Fr étoffe; tissu *(f m)*
It stoffa; tessuto *(f m)*
Pt tecido *(m)*

stoffa *(f) n* It
De Stoff *(m)*
En material; cloth
Es tejido *(m)*
Fr étoffe; tissu *(f m)*
Pt tecido *(m)*

stop a cheque En
Am stop a check
De einen Scheck sperren
Es suspender el pago de un
cheque
Fr bloquer un chèque
It fermare un assegno
Pt suspender o pagamento
de um cheque

stop-gap *n* En
De Überbrückung *(f)*
Es recurso provisional *(m)*
Fr bouche-trou *(f)*
It provvedimento tempora-
neo *(m)*
Pt tapa-burocos *(m)*

storage *n* En
De Lagerung *(f)*
Es almacenamiento *(m)*

Fr emmagasinage *(m)*
It magazzinaggio *(m)*
Pt armazenamento *(m)*

storage charges En
De Lagergeld *(n)*
Es gastos de almacenaje
(m pl)
Fr frais de magasinage *(m pl)*
It spese di magazzinaggio *(f)*
Pt encargos de armazena-
mento *(m pl)*

store *vb* En
De lagern
Es almacenar
Fr emmagasiner
It immagazzinare
Pt armazenar

store *n* En
De Lager *(n)*
Es almacén *(m)*
Fr magasin *(m)*
It magazzino *(m)*
Pt armazém *(m)*

storm *n* En
De Sturm *(m)*
Es tormenta *(f)*
Fr tempête *(f)*
It tempesta *(f)*
Pt temporal *(m)*

Stoß *(m) n* De
En batch
Es lote *(m)*
Fr lot *(m)*
It lotto *(m)*
Pt lote *(m)*

stow *vb* En
De verstauen
Es estibar
Fr arrimer
It stivare
Pt estivar

stowage *n* En
De Verstauung *(f)*
Es estiba *(f)*
Fr arrimage *(m)*
It stivaggio *(m)*
Pt estiva *(f)*

stowage plan En
De Ladeplan *(m)*
Es plan de estiba *(m)*

Fr plan d'arrimage *(m)*
It piano di stivaggio *(m)*
Pt plano de estiva *(m)*

Strafe *(f) n* De
En penalty
Es multa *(f)*
Fr pénalité *(f)*
It penalità *(f)*
Pt penalidade *(f)*

Strafklausel *(f) n* De
En penalty clause
Es cláusula de multa *(f)*
Fr clause pénale *(f)*
It clausola penale *(f)*
Pt cláusula de penalidade *(f)*

straniero *adj* It
De ausländisch; fremd
En foreign; alien
Es extranjero
Fr étranger
Pt estrangeiro

straniero *(m) n* It
De Ausländer *(m)*
En foreigner
Es extranjero *(m)*
Fr étranger *(m)*
Pt estrangeiro *(m)*

streichen *vb* De
En delete
Es tachar; anular
Fr rayer; effacer
It cancellare
Pt cortar; riscar

Streik *(m) n* De
En strike
Es huelga *(f)*
Fr grève *(f)*
It sciopero *(m)*
Pt greve *(f)*

(zum) Streik auffordern De
En call a strike
Es declararse en huelga
Fr ordonner une grève
It proclamare uno sciopero
Pt declarar greve

streiken *vb* De
En strike
Es declarar huelga

Fr faire la grève
It scioperare
Pt fazer greve

Streikende(r) *(m) n* De
En striker
Es huelguista *(m)*
Fr gréviste *(m)*
It scioperante *(m)*
Pt grevista *(m)*

Streit *(m) n* De
En dispute
Es disputa *(f)*
Fr contestation *(f)*
It disputa *(f)*
Pt disputa *(f)*

Streitkräfte *(f pl) n* De
En armed forces
Es fuerzas armadas *(f pl)*
Fr forces armées *(f pl)*
It forze armate *(f pl)*
Pt forças armadas *(f pl)*

Strickwaren *(f pl) n* De
En knitted goods
Es géneros de punto *(m pl)*
Fr bonneterie *(f)*
It maglieria *(f)*
Pt artigos de malha de lã *(m pl)*

strike *n* En
De Streik *(m)*
Es huelga *(f)*
Fr grève *(f)*
It sciopero *(m)*
Pt greve *(f)*

strike *vb* En
De streiken
Es declarar huelga
Fr faire la grève
It scioperare
Pt fazer greve

striker *n* En
De Streikende(r) *(m)*
Es huelguista *(m)*
Fr gréviste *(m)*
It scioperante *(m)*
Pt grevista *(m)*

Strom *(m) n* De
En flow
Es flujo *(m)*
Fr flux *(m)*
It flusso *(m)*
Pt circulação *(f)*

strozzatura *(f) n* It
De Engpaß *(m)*
En bottle-neck
Es embotellamiento *(m)*
Fr goulot d'étranglement *(m)*
Pt engarrafamento *(m)*

strumento *(m) n* It
De Instrument *(n)*
En instrument
Es instrumento *(m)*
Fr instrument *(m)*
Pt instrumento *(m)*

strumento d'analisi *(m)* It
De Analysenwerkzeug *(n)*
En analytical tool
Es instrumento de análisis *(m)*
Fr instrument d'analyse *(m)*
Pt instrumento de análise *(m)*

stub *n* Am
En counterfoil
De Talon *(m)*
Es talón *(m)*
Fr talon *(m)*
It matrice *(f)*
Pt talão *(m)*

Stückelung *(f) n* De
En denomination
Es valor *(m)*
Fr valeur nominale *(f)*
It taglio *(m)*
Pt valor nominal *(m)*

studi e sviluppi It
De Zweckforschung; Forschung und Entwicklung (F & E) *(f)*
En research and development (R & D)
Es investigación y desarrollo
Fr recherche industrielle *(f)*
Pt investigação e desenvolvimento

studio dei tempi e dei movimenti *(m)* It
De Arbeitszeit- und Ablaufstudie *(f)*
En time and motion study
Es estudio de tiempo y progreso *(m)*
Fr étude du temps et mouvements *(f)*
Pt análise do tempo e progresso *(f)*

studio delle possibilità *(m)* It
De Durchführbarkeitsanalyse
(f)
En feasibility study
Es estudio de viabilidad *(m)*
Fr étude probatoire *(f)*
Pt estudo de viabilidade *(m)*

studio di lavoro *(m)* It
De Arbeitsstudie *(f)*
En work study
Es estudio del trabajo *(m)*
Fr étude du travail *(f)*
Pt estudo sobre trabalho *(m)*

studio sul terreno *(m)* It
De Stellenüberblick *(m)*
En field study
Es estudio sobre el terreno
(m)
Fr enquête sur les lieux *(f)*
Pt estudo de campo *(m)*

Stunde *(f)* n De
En hour
Es hora *(f)*
Fr heure *(f)*
It ora *(f)*
Pt hora *(f)*

Sturm *(m)* n De
En storm
Es tormenta *(f)*
Fr tempête *(f)*
It tempesta *(f)*
Pt temporal *(m)*

Sturz *(m)* n De
En fall; drop
Es baja; caida *(f)*
Fr baisse; chute *(f)*
It caduta; ribasso *(f; m)*
Pt baixa; queda *(f)*

stürzen *vb* De
En fall; drop
Es caer; bajar
Fr baisser; tomber
It cadere; ribassare
Pt cair; baixar

subaffitto *(m)* n It
De Untervermietung *(f)*
En sub-letting
Es sub-alquiler *(m)*
Fr sous-location *(m)*
Pt subaluguer *(m)*

sub-agent n En
De Untervertreter *(m)*
Es sub-agente *(m)*
Fr sous-agent *(m)*
It sub-agente *(m)*
Pt subagente *(m)*

subagente *(m)* n Pt
De Untervertreter *(m)*
En sub-agent
Es sub-agente *(m)*
Fr sous-agent *(m)*
It sub-agente *(m)*

sub-agente *(m)* n Es, It
De Untervertreter *(m)*
En sub-agent
Fr sous-agent *(m)*
Pt subagente *(m)*

sub-alquiler *(m)* n Es
De Untervermietung *(f)*
En sub-letting
Fr sous-location *(m)*
It subaffitto *(m)*
Pt subaluguer *(m)*

subalterne *(m)* n Fr
De Untergebene(r) *(m)*
En subordinate
Es subalterno *(m)*
It subalterno *(m)*
Pt subordinado *(m)*

subalterno *(m)* n Es, It
De Untergebene(r) *(m)*
En subordinate
Fr subalterne *(m)*
Pt subordinado *(m)*

subaluguer *(m)* n Pt
De Untervermietung *(f)*
En sub-letting
Es sub-alquiler *(m)*
Fr sous-location *(m)*
It subaffitto *(m)*

subasta *(f)* n Es
De Versteigerung *(f)*
En auction
Fr vente aux enchères *(f)*
It asta *(f)*
Pt leilão *(m)*

subastador *(m)* n Es
De Versteigerer *(m)*
En auctioneer

Fr commissaire-priseur *(m)*
It venditore all'asta *(m)*
Pt leiloeiro *(m)*

subdirector *(m)* n Pt
De Unterdirektor *(m)*
En assistant manager
Es sub-director *(m)*
Fr sous-directeur *(m)*
It vice-direttore *(m)*

sub-director *(m)* n Es
De Unterdirektor *(m)*
En assistant manager
Fr sous-directeur *(m)*
It vice-direttore *(m)*
Pt subdirector *(m)*

subida (en valor) *(f)* n Es
De Wertsteigerung *(f)*
En appreciation
Fr appréciation *(f)*
It aumento *(m)*
Pt aumento *(m)*

subir (en valor) *vb* Es
De im Wert steigen
En appreciate
Fr apprécier
It aumentare
Pt aumentar

sub-letting n En
De Untervermietung *(f)*
Es sub-alquiler *(m)*
Fr sous-location *(m)*
It subaffitto *(m)*
Pt subaluguer *(m)*

subordinado *(m)* n Pt
De Untergebene(r) *(m)*
En subordinate
Es subalterno *(m)*
Fr subalterne *(m)*
It subalterno *(m)*

subordinate n En
De Untergebene(r) *(m)*
Es subalterno *(m)*
Fr subalterne *(m)*
It subalterno *(m)*
Pt subordinado *(m)*

subornar *vb* Pt
De bestechen
En bribe
Es sobornar
Fr corrompre
It corrompere

suborno *(m) n* Pt
De Bestechung; Beste-
  chungsgeld *(f n)*
En bribery; bribe
Es soborno *(m)*
Fr corruption; pot-de-vin
  (f m)
It corruzione; dono per cor-
  rompere *(f m)*

sub-rogação *(f) n* Pt
De Ersetzung *(f)*
En subrogation
Es subrogación *(f)*
Fr subrogation *(f)*
It surrogazione *(f)*

subrogación *(f) n* Es
De Ersetzung *(f)*
En subrogation
Fr subrogation *(f)*
It surrogazione *(f)*
Pt sub-rogação *(f)*

subrogation *n* En, Fr *(f)*
De Ersetzung *(f)*
Es subrogación *(f)*
It surrogazione *(f)*
Pt sub-rogação *(f)*

subscribed capital En
De gezeichnetes Kapital *(n)*
Es capital subscrito *(m)*
Fr capital souscrit *(m)*
It capitale sottoscritto *(m)*
Pt capital subscrito *(m)*

subscrição *(f) n* Pt
De Zeichnung *(f)*
En subscription
Es suscripción *(f)*
Fr souscription *(f)*
It sottoscrizione *(f)*

subscription (to shares, etc.)
  n En
De Zeichnung *(f)*
Es suscripción *(f)*
Fr souscription *(f)*
It sottoscrizione *(f)*
Pt subscrição *(f)*

subscription (to a journal,
  etc.) *n* En
De Abonnement *(n)*
Es abono *(m)*
Fr abonnement *(m)*
It abbonamento *(m)*
Pt assinatura *(f)*

subsidiary company En
De Tochtergesellschaft *(f)*
Es filial; empresa subsidiaría
  (f)
Fr filiale *(f)*
It filiale *(f)*
Pt companhia subsidiária *(f)*

subsidio *(m) n* Es
De Subvention *(f)*
En subsidy
Fr subvention *(f)*
It sussidio *(m)*
Pt subsídio *(m)*

subsídio *(m) n* Pt
De Subvention *(f)*
En subsidy
Es subsidio *(m)*
Fr subvention *(f)*
It sussidio *(m)*

**subsidio a las exportacio-
  nes** *(m)* Es
De Ausfuhrprämie *(f)*
En export bonus
Fr prime à l'exportation *(f)*
It premio d'esportazione *(m)*
Pt subsídio de exportação *(m)*

subsídio de desemprego *(m)*
  Pt
De Arbeitslosenunterstützung
  (f)
En unemployment benefit
Es subsidio de paro *(m)*
Fr secours de chômage *(m)*
It indennità di disoccupa-
  zione *(f)*

subsídio de exportação *(m)*
  Pt
De Ausfuhrprämie *(f)*
En export bonus
Es subsidio a las exportacio-
  nes *(m)*
Fr prime à l'exportation *(f)*
It premio d'esportazione *(m)*

subsidio de paro *(m)* Es
De Arbeitslosenunterstützung
  (f)
En unemployment benefit
Fr secours de chômage *(m)*
It indennità di disoccupa-
  zione *(f)*
Pt subsídio de desemprego
  (m)

subsidy *n* En
De Subvention *(f)*
Es subsidio *(m)*
Fr subvention *(f)*
It sussidio *(m)*
Pt subsídio *(m)*

substracción *(f) n* Es
De Subtraktion *(f)*
En subtraction
Fr soustraction *(f)*
It sottrazione *(f)*
Pt subtracção *(f)*

subtracção *(f) n* Pt
De Subtraktion *(f)*
En subtraction
Es substracción *(f)*
Fr soustraction *(f)*
It sottrazione *(f)*

subtraction *n* En
De Subtraktion *(f)*
Es substracción *(f)*
Fr soustraction *(f)*
It sottrazione *(f)*
Pt subtracção *(f)*

Subtraktion *(f) n* De
En subtraction
Es substracción *(f)*
Fr soustraction *(f)*
It sottrazione *(f)*
Pt subtracção *(f)*

subvenção *(f) n* Pt
De Unterstützung; Subven-
  tion *(f)*
En grant; subsidy
Es subvención *(f)*
Fr subvention *(f)*
It sovvenzione *(f)*

subvención de capital *(f)* Es
De Kapitalhilfe *(f)*
En capital grants
Fr subventions en capital
  (f pl)
It sovvenzioni di capitale
  (f pl)
Pt subvenções de capital *(f pl)*

subvención del Estado *(f)* Es
De Staatszuschuß *(m)*
En government subsidy
Fr subvention de l'État *(f)*
It sovvenzione dello Stato *(f)*
Pt subvenções do Estado *(f pl)*

subvenções de capital *(f pl)*
Pt
De Kapitalhilfe *(f)*
En capital grants
Es subvención de capital *(f pl)*
Fr subventions en capital
　　(f pl)
It sovvenzioni di capitale *(f)*

subvenções do Estado *(f pl)*
Pt
De Staatszuschuß *(m)*
En government subsidy
Es subvención del Estado *(f)*
Fr subvention de l'État *(f)*
It sovvenzione dello Stato *(f)*

subvention *(f)* n Fr
De Subvention *(f)*
En subsidy
Es subsidio *(m)*
It sussidio *(m)*
Pt subsídio *(m)*

Subvention *(f)* n De
En subsidy
Es subsidio *(m)*
Fr subvention *(f)*
It sussidio *(m)*
Pt subsídio *(m)*

subvention de l'État *(f)* Fr
De Staatszuschuß *(m)*
En government subsidy
Es subvención del Estado *(f)*
It sovvenzione dello Stato *(f)*
Pt subvenções do Estado *(f pl)*

subventions en capital *(f pl)*
Fr
De Kapitalhilfe *(f)*
En capital grants
Es subvención de capital *(f)*
It sovvenzioni di capitale
　　(f pl)
Pt subvenções de capital *(f pl)*

succession *(f)* n Fr
De Erbschaft; Nachlaß *(f m)*
En inheritance; estate
Es sucesión *(f)*
It successione *(f)*
Pt sucessão *(f)*

successione *(f)* n It
De Erbschaft; Nachlaß *(f m)*
En inheritance; estate

Es sucesión *(f)*
Fr succession *(f)*
Pt sucessão *(f)*

succursale *(f)* n Fr, It
De Filiale; Zweigstelle *(f)*
En branch; branch office
Es sucursal; filial *(f)*
Pt sucursal; filial *(f)*

sucesión *(f)* n Es
De Erbschaft; Nachlaß *(f m)*
En estate; inheritance
Fr succession *(f)*
It successione *(f)*
Pt sucessão *(f)*

sucessão *(f)* n Pt
De Erbschaft; Nachlaß *(f m)*
En estate; inheritance
Es sucesión *(f)*
Fr succession *(f)*
It successione *(f)*

sucursal *(f)* n Es, Pt
De Filiale; Zweigstelle *(f)*
En branch; branch office
Fr succursale; filiale *(f)*
It succursale; filiale *(f)*

**sucursal de cadena de
　　almacenes** *(f)* Es
De Kettengeschäft *(n)*
En chain store
Fr magasin à succursales
　　multiples *(m)*
It negozio a catena *(m)*
Pt sucursal de cadeia de ar-
　　mazéns *(f)*

sucursal del banco *(f)* Es
De Filialbank; Zweigbank *(f)*
En branch bank
Fr banque succursale *(f)*
It banca succursale *(f)*
Pt filial de banco *(f)*

suddetto *adj* It
De obenerwähnt
En above-mentioned
Es susodicho
Fr susmentionné
Pt supracitado

sueldo *(m)* n Es
De Gehalt *(n)*
En salary

Fr traitement *(m)*
It stipendio *(m)*
Pt ordenado *(m)*

sujetapapeles *(m)* n Es
De Büroklammer *(f)*
En paper clip
Fr attache-papiers *(m)*
It fermacarte *(m)*
Pt grampo *(m)*

sulla banchina It
De ab Kai
En ex quay
Es en muelle
Fr à prendre sur quai
Pt ex-cais

suma *(f)* n Es
De Summe *(f)*
En sum
Fr somme *(f)*
It somma *(f)*
Pt soma *(f)*

suma global *(f)* Es
De Pauschalbetrag *(m)*
En lump sum
Fr somme globale *(f)*
It somma globale *(f)*
Pt soma por inteiro *(f)*

suma nominal *(f)* Es
De Nominalbetrag *(m)*
En nominal amount
Fr montant nominal *(m)*
It importo nominale *(m)*
Pt quantia nominal *(f)*

suma para riesgos *(f)* Es
De Gefahrenzulage *(f)*
En danger money
Fr prime de risque *(f)*
It compenso per il rischio *(m)*
Pt prémio de risco *(m)*

sumar *vb* Es
De addieren
Es add up
Fr totaliser; additioner
It sommare
Pt somar

suma y sigue *(f)* Es
De Übertrag *(m)*
En amount carried forward
Am carry forward amount

Fr report à nouveau *(m)*
It ammontare da riportare *(m)*
Pt importância transportada *(f)*

Summe *(f) n* De
En sum; amount
Es suma *(f)*
Fr somme *(f)*
It somma *(f)*
Pt soma *(f)*

summer holidays En
De Sommerferien *(f pl)*
Es vacaciones de verano; veraneo *(f pl; m)*
Fr vacances d'été *(f pl)*
It vacanze estive *(f pl)*
Pt férias de verão *(f pl)*

sundry creditors En
De Kreditoren *(m pl)*
Es acreedores varios *(m pl)*
Fr créditeurs divers *(m pl)*
It creditori diversi *(m pl)*
Pt créditos diversos *(m pl)*

sundry expenses En
De verschiedene Ausgaben *(f pl)*
Es gastos varios *(m pl)*
Fr frais divers *(m pl)*
It spese varie *(f pl)*
Pt despesas diversas *(f pl)*

superficie de piso *(f)* Es
De Bodenfläche *(f)*
En floor space
Fr surface de plancher *(f)*
It superficie di pavimento *(f)*
Pt área de chão *(f)*

superficie di pavimento *(f)* It
De Bodenfläche *(f)*
En floor space
Es superficie de piso *(f)*
Fr surface de plancher *(f)*
Pt área de chão *(f)*

supermarché *(m) n* Fr
De Supermarkt *(m)*
En supermarket
Es supermercado *(m)*
It supermercato *(m)*
Pt supermercado *(m)*

supermarket *n* En
De Supermarkt *(m)*
Es supermercado *(m)*
Fr supermarché *(m)*
It supermercato *(m)*
Pt supermercado *(m)*

Supermarkt *(m) n* De
En supermarket
Es supermercado *(m)*
Fr supermarché *(m)*
It supermercato *(m)*
Pt supermercado *(m)*

supermercado *(m) n* Es, Pt
De Supermarkt *(m)*
En supermarket
Fr supermarché *(m)*
It supermercato *(m)*

supermercato *(m) n* It
De Supermarkt *(m)*
En supermarket
Es supermercado *(m)*
Fr supermarché *(m)*
Pt supermercado *(m)*

supervisor *n* En, Es, Pt *(m)*
De Aufseher *(m)*
Fr surveillant *(m)*
It supervisore *(m)*

supervisore *(m) n* It
De Aufseher *(m)*
En supervisor
Es supervisor *(m)*
Fr surveillant *(m)*
Pt supervisor *(m)*

suplemento *(m) n* Es
De Zuschlagsgebühr *(f)*
En extra charge
Fr supplément *(m)*
It spesa supplementare *(f)*
Pt encargo suplementar *(m)*

supplément *(m) n* Fr
De Zuschlagsgebühr *(f)*
En extra charge
Es suplemento *(m)*
It spesa supplementare *(f)*
Pt encargo suplementar *(m)*

supplementary estimate En
De Nachschätzung *(f)*
Es cálculo suplementario *(m)*
Fr devis supplémentaire *(f)*
It preventivo supplementare *(m)*
Pt estimativa suplementar *(f)*

supplier *n* En
De Lieferant *(m)*
Es proveedor *(m)*
Fr fournisseur *(m)*
It fornitore *(m)*
Pt fornecedor *(m)*

supplies on hand En
De lieferfertiges Angebot *(n)*
Es provisiones existentes *(f pl)*
Fr ressources existantes *(f pl)*
It forniture esistenti *(f pl)*
Pt fornecimentos em existência *(m pl)*

supply *vb* En
De beliefern
Es surtir
Fr fournir
It fornire
Pt fornecer

supply and demand En
De Angebot und Nachfrage
Es oferta y demanda
Fr offre et demande
It offerta e domanda
Pt oferta e procura

support publicitaire *(m)* Fr
De Werbemittel *(n)*
En advertising medium
Es medio de publicidad *(m)*
It mezzo pubblicitario *(m)*
Pt meio publicitário *(m)*

supports *(m pl) n* Fr
De Werbeträger *(m pl)*
En media
Es medios de información *(m pl)*
It canali d'informazione *(m pl)*
Pt meios de informação *(m pl)*

supracitado *adj* Pt
De obenerwähnt
En above-mentioned
Es susodicho
Fr susmentionné
It suddetto

surarbitre *(m) n* Fr
De Schiedsobmann *(m)*
En umpire
Es juez árbitro *(m)*
It terzo arbitro *(m)*
Pt juiz árbitro *(m)*

surcapacité (f) n Fr
De Überkapazität (f)
En overcapacity
Es exceso de capacidad (m)
It capacità in eccedenza (f)
Pt capacidade excessiva (f)

sur demande Fr
De auf Verlangen
En on demand
Es a vista
It a vista
Pt à vista; sob demanda

surestarie (f) n Fr
De Überliegezeit (f)
En demurrage
Es sobreestadía (f)
It controstallia (f)
Pt sobreestradia (f)

surestimation (f) n Fr
De Überschätzung (f)
En over-estimate
Es presupuesto por exceso (m)
It valutazione eccessiva (f)
Pt avaliação excessiva (f)

surety (money) n En
De Bürgschaft (f)
Es fianza (f)
Fr cautionnement (m)
It cauzione (f)
Pt fiança (f)

surety (for a person) n En
De Bürge (m)
Es fiador (m)
Fr caution (f)
It garante (m)
Pt fiador (m)

surface de plancher (f) Fr
De Bodenfläche (f)
En floor space
Es superficie de piso (f)
It superficie di pavimento (f)
Pt área de chão (f)

surplus n En, Fr (m)
De Überschuß (m)
Es excedente (m)
It eccesso (m)
Pt excedente (m)

surproduction (f) n Fr
De Überproduktion (f)
En overproduction
Es exceso de producción (m)
It sovrapproduzione (f)
Pt produção excessiva (f)

surrender value En
De Rückkaufswert (m)
Es valor de rescate (m)
Fr valeur de rachat (f)
It valore di riscatto (m)
Pt valor de resgate (m)

surrogazione (f) n It
De Ersetzung (f)
En subrogation
Es subrogación (f)
Fr subrogation (f)
Pt sub-rogação (f)

surtax n En
De Steuerzuschlag (m)
Es sobretasa (f)
Fr surtaxe (f)
It soprattassa (f)
Pt sobretaxa (f)

surtaxe (f) n Fr
De Steuerzuschlag (m)
En surtax
Es sobretasa (f)
It soprattassa (f)
Pt sobretaxa (f)

surtir vb Es
De beliefern
En supply
Fr fournir
It fornire
Pt fornecer

surveillant (m) n Fr
De Aufseher (m)
En supervisor
Es supervisor (m)
It supervisore (m)
Pt supervisor (m)

suscripción (f) n Es
De Zeichnung (f)
En subscription
Fr souscription (f)
It sottoscrizione (f)
Pt subscrição (f)

susmentionné adj Fr
De obenerwähnt
En above-mentioned
Es susodicho
It suddetto
Pt supracitado

susodicho adj Es
De obenerwähnt
En above-mentioned
Fr susmentionné
It suddetto
Pt supracitado

suspender el pago de un cheque Es
De einen Scheck sperren
En stop a cheque
Fr bloquer un chèque
It fermare un assegno
Pt suspender o pagamento de um cheque

suspender o pagamento de um cheque Pt
De einen Scheck sperren
En stop a cheque
Es suspender el pago de un cheque
Fr bloquer un chèque
It fermare un assegno

suspense account En
De Übergangskonto (n)
Es cuenta suspensa (f)
Fr compte d'ordre (m)
It conto sospeso (m)
Pt conta pendente (f)

sussidio (m) n It
De Subvention (f)
En subsidy
Es subsidio (m)
Fr subvention (f)
Pt subsídio (m)

Süßwasserschaden (m) n De
En fresh-water damage
Es daño de agua dulce (m)
Fr dégâts d'eau douce (m pl)
It danno d'acqua dolce (m)
Pt dano causado por água doce (m)

svago (m) n It
De Freizeit (f)
En leisure
Es descanso (m)
Fr loisir (m)
Pt lazer (m)

svalutazione *(f)* n It
De Währungsabwertung
 (f)
En devaluation
Es devaluación *(f)*
Fr dévaluation *(f)*
Pt desvalorização *(f)*

sviluppo delle vendite *(m)*
 It
De Werbung; Verkaufsförde-
 rung *(f)*
En sales promotion
Es promoción de ventas *(f)*
Fr promotion des ventes *(f)*
Pt promoção de vendas *(f)*

sviluppo economico *(m)*
 It
De Wirtschaftswachstum *(m)*
En economic growth
Es crecimiento económico
 (m)
Fr croissance économique
 (f)
Pt crescimento económico
 (m)

swindle *vb* En
De schwindeln
Es estafar
Fr filouter
It truffare
Pt enganar

switchboard *n* En
De Schalttafel *(f)*
Es cuadro de conexión *(m)*
Fr tableau de distribution *(m)*
It quadro di comando *(m)*
Pt quadro de distribuição *(m)*

symbol *n* En
De Symbol *(n)*
Es símbolo *(m)*
Fr symbole *(m)*
It simbolo *(m)*
Pt símbolo *(m)*

Symbol *(n)* n De
En symbol
Es símbolo *(m)*
Fr symbole *(m)*
It simbolo *(m)*
Pt símbolo *(m)*

symbole *(m)* n Fr
De Symbol *(n)*
En symbol
Es símbolo *(m)*
It simbolo *(m)*
Pt símbolo *(m)*

syndicat *(m)* n Fr
De Syndikat; Gewerkschaft
 (n f)
En syndicate; trade union
Es sindicato *(m)*
It sindicato *(m)*
Pt sindicato *(m)*

syndicat d'assureurs *(m)*
 Fr
De Versicherungssyndikat *(n)*
En underwriting syndicate
 (insurance)
Es sindicato de seguros *(m)*
It sindicato di assicuratori
 (m)
Pt consórcio de seguradores
 (m)

syndicat de garantie *(m)*
 Fr
De Emissionssyndikat *(n)*
En underwriting syndicate
 (new issues)
Es grupo de suscriptores *(m)*
It consorzio finanziario *(m)*
Pt consórcio de subscritores
 (m)

syndicate *n* En
De Syndikat *(n)*
Es sindicato *(m)*
Fr syndicat *(m)*
It consorzio finanziario *(m)*
Pt sindicato *(m)*

syndic de faillite *(m)* Fr
De Konkursverwalter *(m)*
En (official) receiver
Es sindico *(m)*
It curatore *(m)*
Pt síndico *(m)*

Syndikat *(n)* n De
En syndicate
Es sindicato *(m)*
Fr syndicat *(m)*
It sindicato *(m)*
Pt sindicato *(m)*

system *n* En
De System *(n)*
Es sistema *(m)*
Fr système *(m)*
It sistema *(m)*
Pt sistema *(m)*

System *(n)* n De
En system
Es sistema *(m)*
Fr système *(m)*
It sistema *(m)*
Pt sistema *(m)*

Systemanalyse *(f)* n
 De
En systems analysis
Es análisis de sistemas *(m)*
Fr analyse de systèmes *(f)*
It analisi di sistemi *(f)*
Pt análise de sistemas *(f)*

système *(m)* n Fr
De System *(n)*
En system
Es sistema *(m)*
It sistema *(m)*
Pt sistema *(m)*

**système économique du
 marché libre** *(m)* Fr
De freie Marktwirtschaft *(f)*
En free economy
Es economía del mercado
 libre *(f)*
It economia de mercato
 libero *(f)*
Pt economia de mercado
 livre *(f)*

système métrique *(m)* Fr
De metrisches System *(n)*
En metric system
Es sistema métrico *(m)*
It sistema metrico *(m)*
Pt sistema métrico *(m)*

systems analysis En
De Systemanalyse *(f)*
Es análisis de sistemas *(m)*
Fr analyse de systèmes *(f)*
It analisi di sistemi *(f)*
Pt análise de sistemas *(f)*

T

tableau de distribution *(m)* Fr
De Schalttafel *(f)*
En switchboard
Es cuadro de conexión *(m)*
It quadro di comando *(m)*
Pt quadro de distribuição *(m)*

tachar *vb* Es
De streichen
En delete
Fr rayer; effacer
It cancellare
Pt cortar; riscar

tacit agreement En
De stillschweigendes Über-
    einkommen *(n)*
Es acuerdo tácito *(m)*
Fr convention tacite *(f)*
It accordo tacito *(m)*
Pt acordo tácito *(m)*

Tag *(m)* n De
En day
Es día *(m)*
Fr jour *(m)*
It giorno *(m)*
Pt dia *(m)*

Tagebuch *(n)* n De
En journal; day-book
Es libro diario *(m)*
Fr journal *(m)*
It libro giornale *(m)*
Pt diário *(m)*

Tagebuchsposten *(m)* n De
En journal-entry
Es asiento en el libro diario
    (m)
Fr article d'un livre journal *(m)*
It registrazione a giornale *(f)*
Pt anotação de diáro *(f)*

Tagesordnung *(f)* n De
En agenda
Es orden del día *(m)*
Fr ordre du jour *(m)*
It ordine del giorno *(m)*
Pt agenda *(f)*

Tagesstempel *(m)* n De
En date-stamp
Es sello de fecha *(m)*
Fr dateur *(m)*
It timbro a data *(m)*
Pt carimbo de datas *(m)*

täglich *adj* De
En daily
Es cotidiano
Fr cotidien
It quotidiano
Pt diário

taglio *(m)* n It
De Stückelung *(f)*
En denomination
Es valor *(m)*
Fr valeur nominale *(f)*
Pt valor nominal *(m)*

Tagschicht *(f)* n De
En day-shift
Es turno de día *(m)*
Fr équipe du jour *(f)*
It turno di giorno *(m)*
Pt turno de dia *(m)*

take-home pay En
De Nettolohn *(m)*
Es paga neta *(f)*
Fr salaire net *(f)*
It paga netta *(f)*
Pt salário líquido *(m)*

take-over bid En
De Übernahmeangebot *(n)*
Es oferta de adquisición *(f)*
Fr offre de rachat *(f)*
It offerta di acquisto *(f)*
Pt proposta de apropriação *(f)*

talão *(m)* n Pt
De Talon *(m)*
En counterfoil
Am stub
Es talón *(m)*
Fr talon *(m)*
It matrice *(f)*

talão excluído Pt
De ohne Coupon
En ex coupon
Es sin cupón
Fr ex coupon
It senza cedola

talón *(m)* n Es
De Talon *(m)*
En counterfoil
Am stub
Fr talon *(m)*
It matrice *(f)*
Pt talão *(m)*

talon *(m)* n Fr
De Talon *(m)*
En counterfoil
Am stub
Es talón *(m)*
It matrice *(f)*
Pt talão *(m)*

Talon *(m)* n De
En counterfoil
Am stub
Es talón *(m)*
Fr talon *(m)*
It matrice *(f)*
Pt talão *(m)*

tampon *(m)* n Fr
De Stempel *(m)*
En stamp
Es estampilla *(f)*
It stampiglia *(f)*
Pt carimbo *(m)*

tangible assets En
De greifbare Aktiven *(n pl)*
Es activo tangible *(m)*
Fr biens immobiliers *(m pl)*
It beni materiali *(m pl)*
Pt bens visíveis *(m pl)*

Tantieme *(f)* n De
En royalty
Es derechos *(m pl)*
Fr redevance; droits *(f; m pl)*
It diritti *(m pl)*
Pt direitos *(m pl)*

tapa-buracos *(m)* n Pt
De Überbrückung *(f)*
En stop-gap
Es recurso provisional *(m)*
Fr bouche-trou *(m)*
It provvedimento tempora-
    neo *(m)*

taquigrafía *(f)* n Es
De Kurzschrift *(f)*
En shorthand
Fr sténographie *(f)*
It stenografia *(f)*
Pt estenografia *(f)*

taquimecanógrafa *(f)* n Es
De Stenotypistin *(f)*
En shorthand typist
Fr sténodactylographe *(f)*
It stenodattilografa *(f)*
Pt estenodactilógrafa *(f)*

tara *(f) n* Es, It, Pt
De Tara *(f)*
En tare
Fr tare *(f)*

Tara *(f) n* De
En tare
Es tara *(f)*
Fr tare *(f)*
It tara *(f)*
Pt tara *(f)*

tare *n* En, Fr *(f)*
De Tara *(f)*
Es tara *(f)*
It tara *(f)*
Pt tara *(f)*

target *n* En
De Ziel *(n)*
Es objetivo *(m)*
Fr but *(m)*
It bersaglio *(m)*
Pt objectivo *(m)*

tarif *(m) n* Fr
De Tarif *(m)*
En tariff
Es tarifa *(f)*
It tariffa *(f)*
Pt tarifa *(f)*

Tarif *(m) n* De
En tariff
Es tarifa *(f)*
Fr tarif *(m)*
It tariffa *(f)*
Pt tarifa *(f)*

tarifa *(f) n* Es, Pt
De Tarif *(m)*
En tariff
Fr tarif *(m)*
It tariffa *(f)*

tarifa de salarios *(f)* Es
De Lohnsatz *(m)*
En wage rate
Fr taux des salaires *(m)*
It tariffa salariale *(f)*
Pt base salarial *(f)*

tarifa diferencial *(f)* Es
De diskriminierender Tarif *(m)*
En discriminating tariff
Fr tarif discriminatoire *(m)*
It tariffa discriminante *(f)*
Pt tarifa discriminatória *(f)*

tarifa discriminatória *(f)* Pt
De diskriminierender Tarif *(m)*
En discriminating tariff

Es tarifa diferencial *(f)*
Fr tarif discriminatoire *(m)*
It tariffa discriminante *(f)*

tarifa exterior común *(f)* Es
De gemeinsamer Außentarif
    (m)
En common external tariff
Fr tarif extérieur commun *(m)*
It tariffa estera comune *(f)*
Pt tarifa externa comum *(f)*

tarifa externa comum *(f)* Pt
De gemeinsamer Außentarif
    (m)
En common external tariff
Es tarifa exterior común *(f)*
Fr tarif extérieur commun *(m)*
It tariffa estera comune *(f)*

tarif-album *(m) n* Fr
De Preiskatalog *(m)*
En trade catalogue
Es catálogo comercial *(m)*
It catalogo commerciale *(m)*
Pt catálogo comercial *(m)*

tarifa para anuncios *(f)* Es
De Werbetarif *(m)*
En advertising rates
Fr tarifs de publicité *(m pl)*
It tariffa delle inserzioni *(f)*
Pt taxas de publicidade *(f pl)*

tarifa postal *(f)* Es, Pt
De Postgebühr *(f)*
En postage
Fr frais de poste *(m pl)*
It tariffa postale *(f)*

tarifa unificada *(f)* Es
De Einheitssatz *(m)*
En flat rate
Fr tarif uniforme *(m)*
It tariffa uniforme *(f)*
Pt tarifa de base *(f)*

tarif de faveur *(m)* Fr
De Vorzugssatz *(m)*
En preferential duty
Es derechos preferenciales
    (m pl)
It tariffa preferenziale *(f)*
Pt direito preferencial *(m)*

tarif discriminatoire *(m)* Fr
De diskriminierender Tarif *(m)*
En discriminating tariff
Es tarifa diferencial *(f)*
It tariffa discriminante *(f)*
Pt tarifa discriminatória *(f)*

tarif extérieur commun *(m)*
    Fr
De gemeinsamer Außentarif
    (m)
En common external tariff
Es tarifa exterior común *(f)*
It tariffa estera comune *(f)*
Pt tarifa externa comum *(f)*

tariff *n* En
De Tarif *(m)*
Es tarifa *(f)*
Fr tarif *(m)*
It tariffa *(f)*
Pt tarifa *(f)*

tariffa *(f) n* It
De Tarif *(m)*
En tariff
Es tarifa *(f)*
Fr tarif *(m)*
Pt tarifa *(f)*

tariffa delle inserzioni *(f)* It
De Werbetarif *(m)*
En advertising rates
Es tarifa para anuncios *(f)*
Fr tarifs de publicité *(m pl)*
Pt taxas de publicidade *(f pl)*

tariffa discriminante *(f)* It
De diskriminierender Tarif *(m)*
En discriminating tariff
Es tarifa diferencial *(f)*
Fr tarif discriminatoire *(m)*
Pt tarifa discriminatória *(f)*

tariffa estera comune *(f)* It
De gemeinsamer Außentarif
    (m)
En common external tariff
Es tarifa exterior común *(f)*
Fr tarif extérieur commun *(m)*
Pt tarifa externa comum *(f)*

tariff agreement En
De Zollabkommen *(n)*
Es acuerdo tarifario *(m)*
Fr accord tarifaire *(m)*
It accordo tariffario *(m)*
Pt acordo de tarifas *(m)*

tariffa postale *(f)* It
De Postgebühr *(f)*
En postage
Es tarifa postal *(f)*
Fr frais de poste *(m pl)*
Pt tarifa postal *(f)*

tariffa preferenziale *(f)* It
De Vorzugssatz *(m)*
En preferential duty
Es derechos preferenciales
    (m pl)
Fr tarif de faveur *(m)*
Pt direito preferencial *(m)*

tariffa salariale *(f)* It
De Lohnsatz *(m)*
En wage rate
Es tarifa de salarios *(f)*
Fr taux des salaires *(m)*
Pt base salarial *(f)*

tariffa uniforme *(f)* It
De Einheitssatz *(m)*
En flat rate
Es tarifa unificada *(f)*
Fr tarif uniforme *(m)*
Pt tarifa de base *(f)*

tarifs de publicité *(m pl)* Fr
De Werbetarif *(m)*
En advertising rates
Es tarifa para anuncios *(f)*
It tariffa delle inserzioni *(f)*
Pt taxas de publicidade *(f pl)*

tarif uniforme *(m)* Fr
De Einheitssatz *(m)*
En flat rate
Es tarifa unificada *(f)*
It tariffa uniforme *(f)*
Pt tarifa de base *(f)*

Tarifvertragsverhandlung
    (f) n De
En collective bargaining
Es contratación collectiva *(f)*
Fr négociations de conven-
    tions collectives *(f pl)*
It contrattazione collettiva *(f)*
Pt regateio colectivo *(m)*

tarjeta *(f)* n Es
De Karte *(f)*
En card
Fr carte *(f)*
It scheda *(f)*
Pt cartão *(m)*

tarjeta de cheque *(f)* Es
De Scheckkarte *(f)*
En cheque card
Am bank credit card
Fr carte de chèque *(f)*
It scheda per assegni *(f)*
Pt cartão de validação de che-
    ques *(m)*

tarjeta de crédito *(f)* Es
De Kreditkarte *(f)*
En credit card
Fr carte de crédit *(f)*
It carta di credito *(f)*
Pt cartão de crédito *(m)*

tarjeta perforada *(f)* Es
De Lochkarte *(f)*
En punched card
Fr carte perforée *(f)*
It scheda perforata *(f)*
Pt ficha perfurada *(f)*

tasa *(f)* n Es
De Satz; Kurs *(m)*
En rate
Fr taux; cours *(m)*
It tasso; tariffa *(m f)*
Pt taxa *(f)*

tasa anual *(f)* Es
De Jahreskurs *(m)*
En annual rate
Fr taux annuel *(m)*
It tasso annuale *(m)*
Pt taxa anual *(f)*

tasable *adj* Es
De abgabenpflichtig
En dutiable
Fr taxable
It tassabile
Pt tributável

tasación diferida *(f)* Es
De latente Steuerpflicht *(f)*
En deferred taxation
Fr imposition différée *(f)*
It tassazione differita *(f)*
Pt tributação diferida *(f)*

tasa de descuento *(f)* Es
De Diskontsatz *(m)*
En discount rate
Fr taux d'escompte *(m)*
It tasso di sconto *(m)*
Pt taxa de desconto *(f)*

tasas de cambio exterior
    (f pl) Es
De Devisenkurs *(m)*
En foreign exchange rates
Fr cours des changes *(m)*
It corso dei cambi *(m)*
Pt taxas de câmbio *(f pl)*

tasas de interés *(f pl)* Es
De Zinssätze *(m pl)*
En interest rates
Fr taux d'intérêt *(m pl)*
It tassi d'interesse *(m pl)*
Pt taxas de juro *(f pl)*

tassa *(f)* n It
De Gebühr; Abgabe *(f)*
En duty; tax
Es derechos; impuesto *(m)*
Fr taxe; impôt *(f m)*
Pt taxa; imposto *(f m)*

tassabile *adj* It
De abgabenpflichtig
En dutiable
Es tasable
Fr taxable
Pt tributável

tassa comunale *(f)* It
De Gemeindesteuer *(f)*
En rates
Am realty tax
Es contribución municipal *(f)*
Fr taxes municipales *(f pl)*
Pt contribuições municipais
    (f pl)

tassa d'entrata *(f)* It
De Eintrittsgebühr *(f)*
En entrance fee
Es derecho de entrada *(m)*
Fr droit d'entrée *(m)*
Pt taxa de admissão *(f)*

tassa di bollo *(f)* It
De Stempelgebühr *(f)*
En stamp duty
Es impuesto del timbre *(m)*
Fr droit de timbre *(m)*
Pt imposto de selo *(m)*

tassa di registrazione *(f)* It
De Anmeldegebühr *(f)*
En registration fee
Es derechos de registro *(m pl)*
Fr droit d'enregistrement *(m)*
Pt custas de registo *(f pl)*

tassa esclusa It
De außer Steuer
En excluding tax
Es impuesto no incluido
Fr hors tax (HT)
Pt impostos excluídos

tassa invisibile *(f)* It
De versteckte Belastung *(f)*
En hidden taxe
Es impuesto latente *(m)*
Fr imposition latente *(f)*
Pt imposto ocultado *(m)*

tassa sugli articoli di lusso *(f)*
It
De Luxussteuer *(f)*
En luxury tax
Es impuesto de lujo *(m)*
Fr impôt de luxe *(m)*
Pt imposto de luxo *(m)*

tassazione *(f)* n It
De Besteuerung *(f)*
En taxation
Es tributación *(f)*
Fr imposition *(f)*
Pt tributação *(f)*

tassazione differita *(f)* It
De latente Steuerpflicht *(f)*
En deferred taxation
Es tasación diferida *(f)*
Fr imposition différée *(f)*
Pt tributação diferida *(f)*

tassì *(m)* n It
De Taxi *(n)*
En taxi
Es taxi *(m)*
Fr taxi *(m)*
Pt taxi *(m)*

tasso *(m)* n It
De Satz; Kurs *(m)*
En rate
Es tasa; tipo *(f m)*
Fr taux; cours *(m)*
Pt taxa *(f)*

tasso annuale *(m)* It
De Jahreskurs *(m)*
En annual rate
Es tasa anual *(f)*
Fr taux annuel *(m)*
Pt taxa anual *(f)*

tasso d'interesse *(m)* It
De Zinsfuß *(m)*
En rate of interest
Es tipo de interés *(m)*
Fr taux d'intérêt *(m)*
Pt taxa de juro *(f)*

tasso di mortalità *(m)* It
De Sterblichkeitsziffer *(f)*
En death rate
Es mortalidad *(f)*
Fr taux de mortalité *(m)*
Pt taxa de mortalidade *(f)*

tasso di reddito *(m)* It
De Ertragsrate *(f)*
En rate of return
Es tipo de rédito *(m)*
Fr taux de rendement *(m)*
Pt taxa de rendimento *(f)*

tasso di sconto *(m)* It
De Diskontsatz *(m)*
En discount rate
Es tasa de descuento *(f)*
Fr taux d'escompte *(m)*
Pt taxa de desconto *(f)*

tassa sugli acquisti *(f)* It
De Erwerbssteuer
En purchase tax
Es impuesto sobre las compras *(m)*
Fr impôt sur les acquisitions *(m)*
Pt imposto sobre aquisições *(m)*

tasso variabile *(m)* It
De schwankender Kurs *(m)*
En fluctuating rate
Es tipo oscilante *(m)*
Fr taux variable *(m)*
Pt taxa variável *(f)*

Taste (Schreibmaschine) *(f)* n
De
En key
Es tecla *(f)*
Fr touche *(f)*
It tasto *(m)*
Pt tecla *(f)*

tasto (di macchina da
scrivere) *(m)* n It
De Taste *(f)*
En key
Es tecla *(f)*
Fr touche *(f)*
Pt tecla *(f)*

Tatsache *(f)* n De
En fact
Es hecho *(m)*
Fr fait *(m)*
It fatto *(m)*
Pt facto *(m)*

Tausch *(m)* n De
En exchange
Es cambio *(m)*
Fr échange *(m)*
It cambio *(m)*
Pt câmbio *(m)*

Tauschhandel treiben De
En barter
Es trocar
Fr troquer
It barattare
Pt trocar

taux *(m)* n Fr
De Satz; Kurs *(m)*
En rate
Es tasa; tipo *(f m)*
It tasso; tariffa *(m f)*
Pt taxa *(f)*

taux annuel *(m)* Fr
De Jahreskurs *(m)*
En annual rate
Es tasa anual *(f)*
It tasso annuale *(m)*
Pt taxa anual *(f)*

taux de change *(m)* Fr
De Wechselkurs *(m)*
En exchange rate
Es tipo de cambio *(m)*
It corso del cambio *(m)*
Pt taxa de câmbio *(f)*

taux de change flottant *(m)*
Fr
De flexibler Wechselkurs *(m)*
En floating exchange rate
Es tipo de cambio flotante *(m)*
It cambio fluttuante *(m)*
Pt taxa de câmbio flutuante
(f)

taux de défaillance *(m)* Fr
De Durchfallquote *(f)*
En failure rate
Es proporción de fracasos *(f)*
It indice dei fallimenti *(m)*
Pt proporção de fracassos *(f)*

taux d'escompte *(m)* Fr
De Diskontsatz *(m)*
En discount rate
Es tasa de descuento *(f)*
It tasso di sconto
Pt taxa de desconto *(f)*

taux de mortalité *(m)* Fr
De Sterblichkeitsziffer *(f)*
En death rate
Es mortalidad *(f)*
It tasso di mortalità *(m)*
Pt taxa de mortalidade *(f)*

taux de rendement *(m)* Fr
De Ertragsrate *(f)*
En rate of return
Es tipo de rédito *(m)*
It tasso di reddito *(m)*
Pt taxa de rendimento *(f)*

taux des salaires *(m)* Fr
De Lohnsatz *(m)*
En wage rate
Es tarifa de salarios *(f)*
It tariffa salariale *(f)*
Pt base salarial *(f)*

taux d'intérêt *(m)* Fr
De Zinsfuß *(m)*
En interest rate
Es tipo de interés *(m)*
It tasso d'interesse *(m)*
Pt taxa de juro *(f)*

taux variable *(m)* Fr
De schwankender Kurs *(m)*
En fluctuating rate
Es tipo oscilante *(m)*
It tasso variabile *(m)*
Pt taxa variável *(f)*

tax *n* En
De Steuer *(f)*
Es impuesto *(m)*
Fr impôt *(m)*
It imposta *(f)*
Pt imposto *(m)*

taxa *(f) n* Pt
De Satz; Gebühr *(m f)*
En rate; duty
Es tasa; impuesto *(f m)*
Fr taux; impôt *(m)*
It tasso; imposta *(m f)*

taxa anual *(f)* Pt
De Jahreskurs *(m)*
En annual rate
Es tasa anual *(f)*
Fr taux annuel *(m)*
It tasso annuale *(m)*

taxable *adj* Fr
De abgabenpflichtig
En dutiable

Es tasable
It tassabile
Pt tributável

taxable income En
De steuerpflichtiges Einkommen *(n)*
Es renta imponible *(f)*
Fr revenu imposable *(m)*
It reddito tassabile *(m)*
Pt receita tributável *(f)*

taxa custo-ganhos *(f)* Pt
De Verhältnis des Aktienkurses zum Reingewinn *(n)*
En price-earnings ratio (P/E)
Es proporción precio-ingresos *(f)*
Fr quotient cours-bénéfice *(m)*
It rapporto prezzo-utile *(m)*

taxa de admissão *(f)* Pt
De Eintrittsgebühr *(f)*
En entrance fee
Es derecho de entrada *(m)*
Fr droit d'entrée *(m)*
It tassa d'entrata *(f)*

taxa de câmbio *(f)* Pt
De Wechselkurs *(m)*
En exchange rate
Es tipo de cambio *(m)*
Fr taux de change *(m)*
It corso del cambio *(m)*

taxa de câmbio flutuante *(f)* Pt
De flexibler Wechselkurs *(m)*
En floating exchange rate
Es tipo de cambio flotante *(m)*
Fr taux de change flottant *(m)*
It cambio fluttuante *(m)*

taxa de desconto *(f)* Pt
De Diskontsatz *(m)*
En discount rate
Es tasa de descuento *(f)*
Fr taux d'escompte *(m)*
It tasso di sconto *(m)*

taxa de juro *(f)* Pt
De Zinsfuß *(m)*
En rate of interest
Es tipo de interés *(m)*
Fr taux d'intérêt *(m)*
It tasso d'interesse *(m)*

taxa de mortalidade *(f)* Pt
De Sterblichkeitsziffer *(f)*
En death rate
Es mortalidad *(f)*
Fr taux de mortalité *(m)*
It tasso di mortalità *(m)*

taxa de rendimento *(f)* Pt
De Ertragsrate *(f)*
En rate of return
Es tipo de rédito *(m)*
Fr taux de rendement *(m)*
It tasso di reddito *(m)*

taxas bancárias *(f pl)* Pt
De Bankspesen *(f pl)*
En bank charges
Es gastos de banco *(m pl)*
Fr frais bancaires *(m pl)*
It spese di banca *(f pl)*

taxas de publicidade *(f pl)* Pt
De Werbetarif *(m)*
En advertising rates
Es tarifa para anuncios *(f)*
Fr tarifs de publicité *(m pl)*
It tariffa delle inserzioni *(f)*

taxation *n* En
De Besteuerung *(f)*
Es tributación *(f)*
Fr imposition *(f)*
It tassazione *(f)*
Pt tributação *(f)*

taxa variável *(f)* Pt
De schwankender Kurs *(m)*
En fluctuating rate
Es tipo oscilante *(m)*
Fr taux variable *(m)*
It tasso variabile *(m)*

tax base En
De Steuerveranlagung *(f)*
Es base contributiva *(f)*
Fr assiette de l'impôt *(f)*
It ripartizione della tassazione *(f)*
Pt base de imposto *(f)*

tax collector En
De Steuereinnehmer *(m)*
Es recaudador de impuestos *(m)*
Fr percepteur des impôts *(m)*
It esattore delle imposte *(m)*
Pt cobrador de impostos *(m)*

tax-deductible *adj* En
De steuerabsetzbar
Es deducible de impuestos
Fr déductible à l'impôt
It deducibile da tassa
Pt ilíquido de impostos

taxe *(f)* n Fr
De Gebühr; Abgabe *(f)*
En duty; tax
Es derechos; impuesto *(m)*
It tassa; imposta *(f)*
Pt taxa; imposto *(f m)*

taxe de vente *(f)* Fr
De Warenumsatzsteuer *(f)*
En sales tax
Es impuesto sobre la venta
    (m)
It imposta sulle vendite *(f)*
Pt imposto sobre vendas *(m)*

taxes municipales *(f pl)* Fr
De Gemeindesteuer *(f)*
En rates
Am realty tax
Es contribución municipal *(f)*
It tassa comunale *(f)*
Pt contribuições municipais
    (f pl)

**taxe sur la valeur ajoutée
(TVA)** *(f)* Fr
De Mehrwertsteuer *(f)*
En value added tax (VAT)
Es impuesto sobre valor aña-
    dido *(m)*
It imposta sul valore aggiun-
    to (IVA) *(f)*
Pt imposto sobre valor adu-
    zido *(m)*

taxe sur l'emploi *(f)* Fr
De Lohnsummensteuer *(f)*
En employment tax
Es impuesto por empleado
    (m)
It imposta sull'impiego *(f)*
Pt imposto sobre emprego
    (m)

tax-free *adj* En
De steuerfrei
Es exento de impuestos
Fr exempt d'impôts
It esente da tassa
Pt isento de impostos

tax haven En
De Steuerparadies *(n)*
Es refugio fiscal *(m)*
Fr refuge fiscal *(m)*
It rifugio fiscale *(m)*
Pt refúgio fiscal *(m)*

taxi *n* En; Es, Fr, Pt *(m)*
De Taxi *(n)*
It tassi *(m)*

Taxi *(n)* n De
En taxi
Es taxi *(m)*
Fr taxi *(m)*
It tassi *(m)*
Pt taxi *(m)*

tax loss En
De Steuerverlust *(m)*
Es pérdida fiscal *(f)*
Fr perte fiscale *(f)*
It perdita a scopi fiscali *(f)*
Pt perda em impostos *(f)*

tax payer En
De Steuerzahler *(m)*
Es contribuyente *(m)*
Fr contribuable *(m)*
It contribuente fiscale *(m)*
Pt contribuinte *(m)*

tax relief En
De Steuererleichterung *(f)*
Es desgravación *(f)*
Fr dégrèvement *(m)*
It sgravio fiscale *(m)*
Pt isenção de imposto *(f)*

tax return En
De Steuererklärung *(f)*
Es declaración de ingresos *(f)*
Fr déclaration de l'impôt *(f)*
It dichiarazione fiscale *(f)*
Pt declaração para efeitos de
    tributação *(f)*

tax year En
De Steuerjahr *(n)*
Es año fiscal *(m)*
Fr exercice fiscal *(m)*
It anno fiscale *(m)*
Pt ano fiscal *(m)*

Technik *(f)* n De
En technique
Es técnica *(f)*
Fr technique *(f)*
It tecnica *(f)*
Pt técnica *(f)*

technique *n* En, Fr *(f)*
De Technik *(f)*
Es técnica *(f)*
It tecnica *(f)*
Pt técnica *(f)*

technologie *(f)* n Fr
De Technologie *(f)*
En technology
Es tecnología *(f)*
It tecnologia *(f)*
Pt tecnologia *(f)*

Technologie *(f)* n De
En technology
Es tecnología *(f)*
Fr technologie *(f)*
It tecnologia *(f)*
Pt tecnologia *(f)*

technology *n* En
De Technologie *(f)*
Es tecnología *(f)*
Fr technologie *(f)*
It tecnologia *(f)*
Pt tecnologia *(f)*

tecido *(m)* n Pt
De Stoff *(m)*
En material; cloth
Es tejido *(m)*
Fr étoffe; tissu *(f m)*
It stoffa; tessuto *(f m)*

técnica *(f)* n Es, Pt
De Technik *(f)*
En technique
Fr technique *(f)*
It tecnica *(f)*

tecnica *(f)* n It
De Technik *(f)*
En technique
Es técnica *(f)*
Fr technique *(f)*
Pt técnica *(f)*

tecnología *(f)* n Es
De Technologie *(f)*
En technology
Fr technologie *(f)*
It tecnologia *(f)*
Pt tecnologia *(f)*

tecnologia *(f)* n It, Pt
De Technologie *(f)*
En technology
Es tecnología *(f)*
Fr technologie *(f)*

Teil *(m) n* De
En share
Es parte *(f)*
Fr part *(f)*
It parte *(f)*
Pt quota *(f)*

teilen *vb* De
En share
Es repartir
Fr partager
It dividere
Pt repartir

Teilhaber *(m) n* De
En partner
Es socio *(m)*
Fr associé *(m)*
It socio *(m)*
Pt sócio *(m)*

Teilung *(f) n* De
En division
Es división *(f)*
Fr division *(f)*
It divisione *(f)*
Pt divisão *(f)*

tejido *(m) n* Es
De Stoff *(m)*
En material; cloth
Fr étoffe; tissu *(f m)*
It stoffa; tessuto *(f m)*
Pt tecido *(m)*

Telefon *(n) n* De
En telephone
Es teléfono*(m)*
Fr téléphone *(m)*
It telefono *(m)*
Pt telefone *(m)*

telefone *(m) n* Pt
De Fernsprecher; Telefon *(m n)*
En telephone
Es teléfono *(m)*
Fr téléphone *(m)*
It telefono *(m)*

Telefonist *(m) n* De
En telephone operator
Es telefonista *(m/f)*
Fr téléphoniste *(m/f)*
It telefonista *(m/f)*
Pt telefonista *(m/f)*

telefonista *(m/f)* Es, It, Pt
De Telelonist; Telefonistin *(m f)*
En telephone operator
Fr téléphoniste *(m/f)*

Telefonistin *(f) n* De
En (female) telephone operator
Es telefonista *(f)*
Fr téléphoniste *(f)*
It telefonista *(f)*
Pt telefonista *(f)*

Telefonnummer *(f) n* De
En telephone number
Es número de teléfono *(m)*
Fr numéro de téléphone *(m)*
It numero di telefono *(m)*
Pt número de telefone *(m)*

teléfono *(m) n* Es
De Fernsprecher; Telefon *(m n)*
En telephone
Fr téléphone *(m)*
It telefono *(m)*
Pt telefone *(m)*

telefono *(m) n* It
De Fernsprecher; Telefon *(m n)*
En telephone
Es teléfono *(m)*
Fr téléphone *(m)*
Pt telefone *(m)*

telégrafar *vb* Es
De telegrafieren
En telegraph
Fr télégraphier
It telegrafare
Pt telegrafar

telegrafar *vb* Pt
De telegrafieren
En telegraph
Es telégrafar
Fr télégraphier
It telegrafare

telegrafare *vb* It
De telegrafieren
En telegraph
Es telégrafar
Fr télégraphier
Pt telegrafar

telegrafieren *vb* De
En telegraph
Es telégrafar
Fr télégraphier
It telegrafare
Pt telegrafar

telegram *n* En
De Telegramm *(n)*
Es telegrama *(m)*
Fr télégramme *(m)*
It telegramma *(m)*
Pt telegrama *(m)*

telegrama *(m) n* Es, Pt
De Telegramm *(n)*
En telegram
Fr télégramme *(m)*
It telegramma *(m)*

Telegramm *(n) n* De
En telegram
Es telegrama *(m)*
Fr télégramme *(m)*
It telegramma *(m)*
Pt telegrama *(m)*

telegramma *(m) n* It
De Telegramm *(n)*
En telegram
Es telegrama *(m)*
Fr télégramme *(m)*
Pt telegrama *(m)*

Telegrammadresse *(f) n* De
En telegraphic address
Es dirección telegráfica *(f)*
Fr adresse télégraphique *(f)*
It indirizzo telegrafico *(m)*
Pt endereço telegráfico *(m)*

télégramme *(m) n* Fr
De Telegramm *(n)*
En telegram
Es telegrama *(m)*
It telegramma *(m)*
Pt telegrama *(m)*

telegraph *vb* En
De telegrafieren
Es telégrafar
Fr télégraphier
It telegrafare
Pt telegrafar

telegraphic address En
De Telegrammadresse *(f)*
Es dirección telegráfica *(f)*

Fr adresse télégraphique *(f)*
It indirizzo telegrafico *(m)*
Pt endereço telegráfico *(m)*

telegraphic transfer En
De Kabelauszahlung *(f)*
Es giro telegráfico *(m)*
Fr virement télégraphique *(m)*
It rimessa telegrafica *(f)*
Pt transferência telegráfica *(f)*

télégraphier *vb* Fr
De telegrafieren
En telegraph
Es telégrafar
It telegrafare
Pt telegrafar

telephone *n* En
De Fernsprecher; Telefon
   (m n)
Es teléfono *(m)*
Fr téléphone *(m)*
It telefono *(m)*
Pt telefone *(m)*

téléphone *(m) n* Fr
De Fernsprecher; Telefon
   (m n)
En telephone
Es teléfono *(m)*
It telefono *(m)*
Pt telefone *(m)*

telephone call En
De Anruf *(m)*
Es llamada telefónica *(f)*
Fr appel téléphonique *(m)*
It chiamata telefonica *(f)*
Pt chamada telefónica *(f)*

telephone directory En
De Fernsprechbuch *(n)*
Es guía de teléfonos *(f)*
Fr annuaire des téléphones
   (m)
It elenco telefonico *(m)*
Pt lista telefónica *(f)*

telephone exchange En
De Fernsprechamt *(n)*
Es central telefónica *(f)*
Fr central téléphonique *(m)*
It centrale telefonica *(f)*
Pt central telefónica *(f)*

telephone number En
De Telefonnummer *(f)*
Es número de teléfono *(m)*

Fr numéro de téléphone *(m)*
It numero di telefono *(m)*
Pt número de telefone *(m)*

telephone operator En
De Telefonist; Telefonistin
   (m f)
Es telefonista *(m/f)*
Fr téléphoniste *(m/f)*
It telefonista *(m/f)*
Pt telefonista *(m/f)*

téléphoniste *(m/f) n* Fr
De Telefonist; Telefonistin
   (m/f)
En telephone operator
Es telefonista *(m/f)*
It telefonista *(m/f)*
Pt telefonista *(m/f)*

telex *n* En, It, Pt *(m)*
De Fernschreiber *(m)*
Es télex *(m)*
Fr télex *(m)*

télex *(m) n* Es, Fr
De Fernschreiber *(m)*
En Telex
It telex *(m)*
Pt telex *(m)*

teller *n* Am
En cashier
De Kassierer *(m)*
Es cajero *(m)*
Fr caissier *(m)*
It cassiere *(m)*
Pt caixa *(m)*

témoin *(m) n* Fr
De Zeuge *(m)*
En witness
Es testigo *(m)*
It testimone *(m)*
Pt testemunha *(f)*

tempesta *(f) n* It
De Sturm *(m)*
En storm
Es tormenta *(f)*
Fr tempête *(f)*
Pt temporal *(m)*

tempête *(f) n* Fr
De Sturm *(m)*
En storm
Es tormenta *(f)*
It tempesta *(f)*
Pt temporal *(m)*

tempo improdutivo *(m)* Pt
De Leerlaufzeit *(f)*
En down time
Es tiempo improductivo *(m)*
Fr temps d'arrêt *(m)*
It tempo passivo *(m)*

tempo-morto da máquina
   (m) Pt
De Maschinenstillstandzeit *(f)*
En machine down-time
Es tiempo improductivo de la
   máquina *(m)*
Fr temps de panne machine
   (m)
It tempo passivo di macchi-
   na *(m)*

tempo passivo *(m)* It
De Leerlaufzeit *(f)*
En down time
Es tiempo improductivo *(m)*
Fr temps d'arrêt *(m)*
Pt tempo improdutivo *(m)*

tempo passivo di macchina
   (m) It
De Maschinenstillstandzeit *(f)*
En machine down-time
Es tiempo improductivo de la
   máquina *(m)*
Fr temps de panne machine
   (m)
Pt tempo-morto da máquina
   (m)

temporal *(m) n* Pt
De Sturm *(m)*
En storm
Es tormenta *(f)*
Fr tempête *(f)*
It tempesta *(f)*

temporal *adj* Es
De einstweilig
En temporary
Fr provisoire
It temporaneo
Pt temporário

temporaneo *adj* It
De einstweilig
En temporary
Es temporal
Fr provisoire
Pt temporário

temporäre Deckung *(f)* De
En temporary cover
Es cobertura provisional *(f)*
Fr couverture temporaire *(m)*
It copertura provisoria *(f)*
Pt cobertura provisória *(f)*

temporário *adj* Pt
De einstweilig
En temporary
Es temporal
Fr provisoire
It temporaneo

temporary *adj* En
De einstweilig
Es temporal
Fr provisoire
It temporaneo
Pt temporário

temporary cover En
De temporäre Deckung *(f)*
Es cobertura provisional *(f)*
Fr couverture provisoire *(f)*
It copertura provvisoria *(f)*
Pt cobertura provisória *(f)*

temps d'arrêt *(m)* Fr
De Leerlaufzeit *(f)*
En down time
Es tiempo improductivo *(m)*
It tempo improduttivo *(m)*
Pt tempo improdutivo *(m)*

temps de panne machine *(m)*
Fr
De Maschinenstillstandzeit *(f)*
En machine down-time
Es tiempo improductivo de la
máquina *(m)*
It tempo passivo di macchi-
na *(m)*
Pt tempo-morto da máquina
(m)

tenant *n* En
De Mieter *(m)*
Es inquilino *(m)*
Fr locataire *(m)*
It affittuario; locatario *(m)*
Pt inquilino *(m)*

tender *n* En
De Angebot *(n)*
Es oferta *(f)*
Fr soumission *(f)*
It offerta *(f)*
Pt proposta *(f)*

tenedor en buena fe *(m)* Es
De gutgläubiger Besitzer *(m)*
En holder in due course
Fr porteur de bonne foi *(m)*
It titolare in buona fede *(m)*
Pt futuro proprietário *(m)*

tenedor legítimo *(m)* Es
De entgeltigter Besitzer *(m)*
En holder for value
Fr porteur à titre onéreux *(m)*
It detentore legittimo *(m)*
Pt proprietário legítimo *(m)*

**tenencia de acciones por
mayoría** *(f)* Es
De Mehrheitsbeteiligung *(f)*
En majority holding
Fr participation majoritaire *(f)*
It partecipazione maggiori-
taria *(f)*
Pt propriedade em maioria *(f)*

tener *vb* Es
De halten
En hold
Fr tenir; détenir
It tenere
Pt reter

tener acciones Es
De beteiligt sein; Aktien besit-
zen
En hold shares
Fr détenir des actions
It tenere azioni
Pt reter acções

tenere *vb* It
De halten
En hold
Es tener
Fr tenir; détenir
Pt reter

tenere azioni It
De beteiligt sein; Aktien besit-
zen
En hold shares
Es tener acciones
Fr détenir des actions
Pt reter acções

tenere in fidecommesso It
De zu treuen Händen halten
En hold in trust
Es guardar in fideicomiso
Fr tenir par fidéicommis
Pt reter em custódia

tenere in magazzino It
De vorrätig halten
En keep in stock
Es guardar en almacén
Fr garder en stock
Pt reter em armazém

tenere la contabilità It
De Konto führen
En keep the accounts
Es llevar la contabilidad
Fr tenir la comptabilité
Pt fazer a contabilidade

tenere una riunione It
De eine Versammlung abhal-
ten
En hold a meeting
Es celebrar una reunión
Fr tenir une assemblée
Pt fazer uma reunião

teneur *(f)* *n* Fr
De Laufzeit *(f)*
En tenor
Es tenor *(m)*
It tenore *(m)*
Pt prazo de circulação *(m)*

tenir *vb* Fr
De halten
En hold
Es tener
It tenere
Pt reter

tenir la comptabilité Fr
De Konto führen
En keep the accounts
Es llevar la contabilidad
It tenere la contabilità
Pt fazer a contabilidade

tenir par fidéicommis Fr
De zu treuen Händen halten
En hold in trust
Es guardar in fideicomiso
It tenere in fidecommesso
Pt reter em custódia

tenir une assemblée Fr
De eine Versammlung abhal-
ten
En hold a meeting
Es celebrar una reunión
It tenere una riunione
Pt fazer uma reunião

tenor n En; Es (m)
De Laufzeit (f)
Fr teneur (f)
It tenore (m)
Pt prazo de circulação (m)

tenore (m) n It
De Laufzeit (f)
En tenor
Es tenor (m)
Fr teneur (f)
Pt prazo de circulação (m)

tenore di vita (m) It
De Lebenshaltung (f)
En standard of living
Es nivel de vida (m)
Fr niveau de vie (m)
Pt nível de vida (m)

teoria de decisão (f) Pt
De Entscheidungslehre (f)
En decision theory
Es teoría de la decisión (f)
Fr théorie de la décision (f)
It teoria della decisione (f)

teoría de la decisión (f) Es
De Entscheidungslehre (f)
En decision theory
Fr théorie de la décision (f)
It teoria della decisione (f)
Pt teoria de decisão (f)

teoria della decisione (f) It
De Entscheidungslehre (f)
En decision theory
Es teoría de la decisión (f)
Fr théorie de la décision (f)
Pt teoria de decisão (f)

terceiros (m pl) n Pt
De Dritte(r) (m)
En third party
Es tercero (m)
Fr tiers (m)
It terzi (m pl)

tercero (m) n Es
De Dritte(r) (m)
En third party
Fr tiers (m)
It terzi (m pl)
Pt terceiros (m pl)

Termin- De
En forward
Es a término

Fr en avant; à terme
It a termine
Pt adiante

terminal de aeropuerto (f) Es
De Luftterminal (n)
En air terminal
Fr aérogare (f)
It aerostazione (f)
Pt estação terminal aérea (f)

Termindevisen (f pl) n De
En forward exchange
Es divisas a término (f pl)
Fr change à terme (m)
It cambio a termine (m)
Pt divisas adiantada (f pl)

termine (m) n It
De Ablauf (m)
En expiry
Es expiración (f)
Fr expiration (f)
Pt expiração (f)

Terminlieferung (f) n De
En forward delivery
Es entrega futura (f)
Fr livraison à terme (f)
It consegna a termine (f)
Pt entrega futura (f)

Terminmakler (m) n De
En option dealer
Es operador a prima (m)
Fr opérateur à prime (m)
It operatore in contratti a premio (m)
Pt corretor de opções (m)

Terminmarkt (m) n De
En futures market
Es mercado de futuros (m)
Fr marché à terme (m)
It mercato a termine (m)
Pt mercado de futuros (m)

Terminnotierung (f) n De
En forward price
Es precio a término (m)
Fr cours à terme (m)
It prezzo per futura conseg-
na (m)
Pt preço adiantado (m)

terms pl n En
De Bedingungen (f pl)
Es condiciones (f pl)

Fr conditions (f pl)
It condizioni (f pl)
Pt condições (f pl)

terrain à bâtir (m) Fr
De Bauland (n)
En building land
Es solares (m pl)
It terreno edile (m)
Pt terreno para construção (m)

terreni auriferi (m pl) It
De Goldgrube (f)
En gold fields
Es yacimiento aurífero (m)
Fr régions aurifères (f pl)
Pt jazigos de ouro (m pl)

terreno edile (m) It
De Bauland (n)
En building land
Es solares (m pl)
Fr terrain à bâtir (m)
Pt terreno para construção (m)

terreno para construção (m)
Pt
De Bauland (n)
En building land
Es solares (m pl)
Fr terrain à bâtir (m)
It terreno edile (m)

territorial waters En
De Hoheitsgewässer (n pl)
Es aguas territoriales (f pl)
Fr eaux territoriales (f pl)
It acque territoriali (f pl)
Pt águas territoriais (f pl)

terzi (m pl) n It
De Dritte(r) (m)
En third party
Es tercero (m)
Fr tiers (m)
Pt terceiros (m pl)

terzo arbitro (m) It
De Schiedsobmann (m)
En umpire
Es juez árbitro (m)
Fr surarbitre (m)
Pt juiz árbitro (m)

tesoro (m) n It
De Schatzamt (n)
En exchequer
Am treasury

Es hacienda *(f)*
Fr trésorerie *(f)*
Pt tesouro *(m)*

tesouro *(m) n* Pt
De Schatzamt *(n)*
En exchequer
Am treasury
Es hacienda *(f)*
Fr trésorerie *(f)*
It tesoro *(m)*

tessile *(m) n* It
De Webware *(f)*
En textile
Es textil *(m)*
Fr textile *(m)*
Pt textil *(m)*

Testamentseröffnung *(f) n*
De
En probate
Es validación de los testa-
mentos *(f)*
Fr homologation d'un testa-
ment *(f)*
It omologazione di testa-
mento *(f)*
Pt validação testamentária *(f)*

testemunha *(f) n* Pt
De Zeuge *(m)*
En witness
Es testigo *(m)*
Fr témoin *(m)*
It testimone *(m)*

testigo *(m) n* Es
De Zeuge *(m)*
En witness
Fr témoin *(m)*
It testimone *(m)*
Pt testemunha *(f)*

testimone *(m) n* It
De Zeuge *(m)*
En witness
Es testigo *(m)*
Fr témoin *(m)*
Pt testemunha *(f)*

testo pubblicitario *(m)* It
De Werbetext *(m)*
En advertising copy
Es material publicitario *(m)*
Fr copie publicitaire *(f)*
Pt texto de publicidade *(m)*

teuer *adj* De
En expensive
Es caro
Fr cher
It caro
Pt caro

teurer werden *vb* De
En advance in price; go up
Es encarecer
Fr renchérir
It aumentare di prezzo
Pt encarecer

teures Geld *(n)* De
En dear money
Es dinero caro *(m)*
Fr argent cher *(m)*
It denaro ad alto interesse
(m)
Pt dinheiro caro *(m)*

textil *(m) n* Es, Pt
De Webware *(f)*
En textile
Fr textile *(m)*
Pt tessile *(m)*

textile *n* En, Fr *(m)*
De Webware *(f)*
Es textil *(m)*
It tessile *(m)*
Pt textil *(m)*

texto dactilografado *(m)* Pt
De Maschinenschrift *(f)*
En typescript
Es texto mecanografiado *(m)*
Fr manuscrit dactylographié
(m)
It dattiloscritto *(m)*

texto de publicidade *(m)* Pt
De Werbetext *(m)*
En advertising copy
Es material publicitario *(m)*
Fr copie publicitaire *(f)*
It testo pubblicitario *(m)*

texto mecanografiado *(m)* Es
De Maschinenschrift *(f)*
En typescript
Fr manuscrit dactylographié
(m)
It dattiloscritto *(m)*
Pt texto dactilografado *(m)*

Textverfasser *(m) n* De
En copywriter
Es redactor publicitario *(m)*
Fr concepteur-rédacteur *(m)*
It redattore pubblicitario *(m)*
Pt redactor de publicidade
(m)

theft *n* En
De Diebstahl *(m)*
Es robo *(m)*
Fr vol *(m)*
It furto *(m)*
Pt furto *(m)*

théorie de la décision *(f)* Fr
De Entscheidungslehre *(f)*
En decision theory
Es teoría de la decisión *(f)*
It teoria della decisione *(f)*
Pt teoria de decisão *(f)*

thésaurisation *(f) n* Fr
De Hortung *(f)*
En hoard
Es atesoramiento *(m)*
It ammasso *(m)*
Pt acumulação *(f)*

third party En
De Dritte(r) *(m)*
Es tercero *(m)*
Fr tiers *(m)*
It terzi *(m pl)*
Pt terceiros *(m pl)*

third-party insurance En
De Haftpflichtversicherung *(f)*
Es seguro contra responsabi-
lidad civil *(m)*
Fr assurance responsabilité
civile (RC) *(f)*
It assicurazione contro terzi
(f)
Pt seguro contra terceiros *(m)*

threshold price En
De Schwellenpreis *(m)*
Es precio de umbral *(m)*
Fr prix de seuil *(m)*
It prezzo soglia *(m)*
Pt preço convencionado *(m)*

Tiefgang *(m) n* De
En draught (of a ship)
Es calado *(m)*
Fr tirant d'eau *(m)*
It pescaggio *(m)*
Pt calado *(m)*

tiempo improductivo *(m)* Es
De Leerlaufzeit *(f)*
En down time
Fr temps d'arrêt *(m)*
It tempo passivo *(m)*
Pt tempo improdutivo *(m)*

tiempo improductivo de la máquina *(m)* Es
De Maschinenstillstandzeit *(f)*
En machine down-time
Fr temps de panne machine *(m)*
It tempo passivo di macchina *(m)*
Pt tempo-morto da máquina *(m)*

tienda *(f)* n Es
De Laden *(m)*
En shop
Fr magasin *(m)*
It bottega *(f)*
Pt loja *(f)*

tiers *(m)* n Fr
De Dritte(r) *(m)*
En third party
Es tercero *(m)*
It terzi *(m pl)*
Pt terceiros *(m pl)*

tilgen *vb* De
En redeem
Es redimir
Fr rembourser; dégager
It redimere; rimborsare
Pt remir; resgatar

Tilgung *(f)* n De
En redemption
Es amortización *(f)*
Fr amortissement *(f)*
Fr ammortamento *(m)*
Pt amortização *(f)*

Tilgungsfonds *(m)* n De
En sinking fund
Es fondo de amortización *(m)*
Fr fonds d'amortissement *(f)*
It fondo di ammortamento *(m)*
Pt fundo de amortização *(m)*

timbre *(m)* n Fr
De Stempel; Marke *(m f)*
En stamp

Es sello *(m)*
It timbro; francobollo *(m)*
Pt selo; carimbo *(m)*

timbre-poste *(m)* n Fr
De Briefmarke *(f)*
En postage stamp
Es sello de correos *(m)*
It francobollo *(m)*
Pt selo postal *(m)*

timbro a data *(m)* It
De Tagesstempel *(m)*
En date-stamp
Es sello de fecha *(m)*
Fr dateur *(m)*
Pt carimbo de datas *(m)*

time and motion study En
De Arbeitszeit- und Ablaufstudie *(f)*
Es estudio de tiempo y progreso *(m)*
Fr étude du temps et mouvements *(f)*
It studio dei tempi e dei movimenti *(m)*
Pt análise do tempo e progresso *(f)*

time charter En
De Zeitcharter *(f)*
Es fletamento de tiempo *(m)*
Fr affrètement à temps *(m)*
It contratto di noleggio a tempo *(m)*
Pt fretamento de tempo *(m)*

timo *(m)* n Es
De Schwindlertrick *(m)*
En confidence trick
Am confidence game
Fr vol à l'américaine *(m)*
It truffa all'americana *(f)*
Pt conto do vigário *(m)*

tip n En
De Trinkgeld *(n)*
Es propina *(f)*
Fr pourboire *(m)*
It mancia *(f)*
Pt gorjeta *(f)*

tipo de cambio *(m)* Es
De Wechselkurs *(m)*
En exchange rate
Fr taux de change *(m)*
It corso del cambio *(m)*
Pt taxa de câmbio *(f)*

tipo de cambio flotante *(m)* Es
De flexibler Wechselkurs *(m)*
En floating exchange rate
Fr taux de change flottant *(m)*
It cambio fluttuante *(m)*
Pt taxa de câmbio flutuante *(f)*

tipo de interés *(m)* Es
De Zinsfuß *(m)*
En rate of interest
Fr taux d'intérêt *(m)*
It tasso d'interesse *(m)*
Pt taxa de juro *(f)*

tipo de rédito *(m)* Es
De Ertragsrate *(f)*
En rate of return
Fr taux de rendement *(m)*
It tasso di reddito *(m)*
Pt taxa de rendimento *(f)*

tipo oscilante *(m)* Es
De schwankender Kurs *(m)*
En fluctuating rate
Fr taux variable *(m)*
It tasso variabile *(m)*
Pt taxa variável *(f)*

tirant d'eau *(m)* Fr
De Tiefgang *(m)*
En (ship's) draught
Es calado *(m)*
It pescaggio *(m)*
Pt calado *(m)*

tiré *(m)* n Fr
De Bezogene(r) *(m)*
En drawee
Es librado *(m)*
It trattario *(m)*
Pt sacado *(m)*

tirer un chèque Fr
De einen Scheck ausstellen
En draw a cheque
Es extender un cheque
It emettere un assegno
Pt passar um cheque

tireur *(m)* n Fr
De Aussteller *(m)*
En drawer
Es librador *(m)*
It traente *(m)*
Pt sacador *(m)*

tirocinio (m) n It
De Lehre (f)
En apprenticeship
Am trainee period
Es aprendizaje (m)
Fr apprentissage (m)
Pt aprendizagem (f)

title (legal) n En
De Anspruch; Titel (m)
Es título (m)
Fr titre; droit (m)
It titolo; diritto (m)
Pt título (m)

title deed En
De Eigentumstitel (m)
Es título de propiedad (m)
Fr titre de propriété (m)
It titolo di proprietà (m)
Pt título de propriedade (m)

titolare (m) n It
De Inhaber (m)
En holder
Es titular (m)
Fr détenteur (m)
Pt titular (m)

titolare in buona fede (m) It
De gutgläubiger Besitzer (m)
En holder in due course
Es tenedor en buena fe (m)
Fr porteur de bonne foi (m)
Pt futuro proprietário (m)

titoli (m pl) n It
De Wertpapiere; Effekten
(n pl; m pl)
En stock; securities
Es títulos; valores (m pl)
Fr titres; valeurs (m pl; f pl)
Pt títulos; valores (m pl)

titoli di assoluta fiducia (m pl)
It
De mündelsichere Wertpapie-
re (n pl)
En gilt-edged securities
Es valores de toda confianza
(m pl)
Fr valeurs de tout repos (f pl)
Pt valores de toda confiança
(m pl)

titoli di prestito (m pl) It
De Anleihewerte (m pl)
En loan stock

Es títulos de préstamo (m pl)
Fr titres d'emprunt (m pl)
Pt títulos de empréstimo
(m pl)

titoli di Stato (m pl) It
De Regierungsschuldver-
schreibungen (f pl)
En Government securities
Es títulos públicos (m pl)
Fr titres d'État (m pl)
Pt títulos do Tesouro (m pl)

titoli non quotati (m pl) It
De nicht notierte Werte (m pl)
En unquoted securities
Es títulos no cotizados (m pl)
Fr valeurs non cotées (f pl)
Pt títulos não cotados (m pl)

titoli quotati (in borsa) (m pl)
It
De an der Börse notierte
Wertpapiere (n pl)
En listed security
Es valores cotizables (m pl)
Fr valeurs admises à la Bour-
se (f pl)
Pt valor de Bolsa com cotação
oficial (m)

titolo (m) n It
De Titel; Wertpapier (m n)
En (legal) title; security
Es título (m)
Fr titre (m)
Pt título (m)

titolo a breve scadenza (m) It
De kurzfristiges Wertpapier
(n)
En short-dated security
Es título a corto plazo (m)
Fr titre à court terme (m)
Pt título a curto prazo (m)

titolo a interesse fisso (m) It
De festverzinsliches Wertpa-
pier (n)
En fixed-interest security
Es obligación a interés fijo (f)
Fr valeur à revenu fixe (f)
Pt obrigação de juro fixo (f)

titolo al portatore (m) It
De Inhaberobligation (f)
En bearer bond

Es título al portador (m)
Fr bon au porteur (m)
Pt título ao portador (m)

titolo di proprietà (m) It
De Eigentumstitel (m)
En title deed
Es título de propiedad (m)
Fr titre de propriété (m)
Pt título de propriedade (m)

titolo negoziabile (m) It
De begebbares Wertpapier (n)
En negotiable instrument
Es título negociable (m)
Fr effet de commerce (m)
Pt título negociável (m)

titre (m) n Fr
De Titel; Wertpapier (m n)
En (legal) title; security
Es título (m)
It titolo (m)
Pt título (m)

titre à court terme (m) Fr
De kurzfristiges Wertpapier
(n)
En short-dated security
Es título a corto plazo (m)
It titolo a breve scadenza (m)
Pt título a curto prazo (m)

titre de propriété (m) Fr
De Eigentumstitel (m)
En title deed
Es título de propiedad (m)
It titolo di proprietà (m)
Pt título de propriedade (m)

titres (m pl) n Fr
De Wertpapiere; Effekten
(n pl; m pl)
En stock; securities
Es títulos; valores (m pl)
It titoli; valori (m pl)
Pt títulos; valores (m pl)

**titres avec perspectives de
croissance** (m pl) Fr
De wachstumorientierte
Wertpapiere (n pl)
En growth stocks
Es títulos de crecimiento
(m pl)
It titoli di sviluppo (m pl)
Pt acções de acrésámo de ca-
pital (f pl)

titres d'emprunt *(m pl)* Fr
De Anleihewerte *(m pl)*
En loan stock
Es títulos de préstamo *(m pl)*
It titoli di prestito *(m pl)*
Pt títulos de empréstimo *(m pl)*

titres d'État *(m pl)* Fr
De Regierungsschuldver-
schreibungen *(f pl)*
En Government securities
Es títulos públicos *(m pl)*
It titoli di Stato *(m pl)*
Pt títulos do Tesouro *(m pl)*

titular *(m)* n Es, Pt
De Inhaber *(m)*
En holder
Fr détenteur *(m)*
It titolare *(m)*

titular de obrigação *(m)* Pt
De Obligationsinhaber *(m)*
En debenture holder; bond-
holder
Es obligacionista *(m)*
Fr porteur d'obligations;
obligataire *(m)*
It obbligazionista *(f)*

titular de seguro *(m)* Pt
De Versicherte(r) *(m)*
En insured
Es asegurado *(m)*
Fr assuré *(m)*
It assicurato *(m)*

título *(m)* n Es, Pt
De Titel; Wertpapier; Urkunde
(m n f)
En (legal) title; stock; deed
Fr titre; droit; acte *(m)*
It titolo; diritto; atto *(m)*

título a corto plazo *(m)* Es
De kurzfristiges Wertpapier
(n)
En short-dated security
Fr titre à court terme *(m)*
It titolo a breve scadenza *(m)*
Pt título a curto prazo *(m)*

título a curto prazo *(m)* Pt
De kurzfristiges Wertpapier
(n)
En short-dated security

Es título a corto plazo *(m)*
Fr titre à court terme *(m)*
It titolo a breve scadenza *(m)*

título al portador *(m)* Es
De Inhaberobligation *(f)*
En bearer bond
Fr bon au porteur *(m)*
It titolo al portatore *(m)*
Pt título ao portador *(m)*

título ao portador *(m)* Pt
De Inhaberobligation *(f)*
En bearer bond
Es título al portador *(m)*
Fr bon au porteur *(m)*
It titolo al portatore *(m)*

título de acción *(m)* Es
De Aktienzertifikat *(n)*
En share certificate
Am certificate of stock
Fr certificat d'actions *(m)*
It certificato azionario *(m)*
Pt título de acções *(m)*

título de acções *(m)* Pt
De Aktienzertifikat *(n)*
En share certificate
Am certificate of stock
Es título de acción *(m)*
Fr certificat d'actions *(m)*
It certificato azionario *(m)*

título de asignación *(m)* Es
De Abtretungsvertrag *(m)*
En deed of assignment
Fr acte attributif *(m)*
It atto di cessione *(m)*
Pt título de consignação *(m)*

título de bodemeria *(m)* Pt
De Bodmereibrief *(m)*
En bottomry bond
Es contrato de préstamo a la
gruesa *(m)*
Fr contrat à la grosse aven-
ture *(m)*
It contratto di prestito a
cambio marittimo *(m)*

título de consignação *(m)* Pt
De Abtretungsvertrag *(m)*
En deed of assignment
Es título de asignación *(m)*
Fr acte attributif *(m)*
It atto di cessione *(m)*

título de doação *(m)* Pt
De Erlebensversicherung *(f)*
En endowment policy
Es póliza dotal *(f)*
Fr assurance à terme fixe *(f)*
It assicurazione dotale *(f)*

**título de investimento
imobiliário** *(m)* Pt
De Grund- und Gebäude-
obligation *(f)*
En property bond
Es cédula hipotecaria *(f)*
Fr obligation foncière *(f)*
It obbligazione fondiaria *(f)*

título de propiedad *(m)* Es
De Eigentumstitel *(m)*
En title deed
Fr titre de propriété *(m)*
It titolo di proprietà *(m)*
Pt título de propriedade *(m)*

título de propriedade *(m)* Pt
De Eigentumstitel *(m)*
En titel deed
Es título de propiedad *(m)*
Fr titre de propriété *(m)*
It titolo di proprietà *(m)*

título de transferência *(m)* Pt
De Übertragungsvertrag *(m)*
En transfer deed
Es escritura de transferencia
(f)
Fr acte de cession *(m)*
It atto di trapasso *(f)*

título documental *(m)* Pt
De Dokumentenwechsel *(m)*
En documentary bill
Es efecto documentario *(m)*
Fr traite documentaire *(f)*
It tratta documentaria *(f)*

título de tesouro *(m)* Pt
De Schatzwechsel *(m)*
En exchequer bond
Am treasury bond
Es bono de tesorería *(m)*
Fr bon du trésor *(m)*
It buono del tesoro *(m)*

título negociable *(m)* Es
De begebbares Wertpapier *(n)*
En negotiable instrument
Fr effet de commerce *(m)*
It titolo negoziabile *(m)*
Pt título negociável *(m)*

título negociável *(m)* Pt
De begebbares Wertpapier *(n)*
En negotiable instrument
Es título negociable *(m)*
Fr effet de commerce *(m)*
It titolo negoziabile *(m)*

títulos *(m pl)* n Es, Pt
De Wertpapiere; Effekten
   (n pl; m pl)
En stocks; securities
Fr titres; valeurs *(m pl; f pl)*
It titoli; valori *(m pl)*

títulos de crecimiento *(m pl)*
   Es
De wachsturnorientierte
   Wertpapiere *(n pl)*
En growth stocks
Fr titres avec perspectives de
   croissance *(m pl)*
It titoli di sviluppo *(m pl)*
Pt acções de acréscimo de
   capital *(f pl)*

títulos de empréstimo *(m pl)*
   Pt
De Anleihewerte *(m pl)*
En loan stock
Es títulos de préstamo *(m pl)*
Fr titres d'emprunt *(m pl)*
It titoli di prestito *(m pl)*

títulos de préstamo *(m pl)* Es
De Anleihewerte *(m pl)*
En loan stock
Fr titres d'emprunt *(m pl)*
It titoli di prestito *(m pl)*
Pt títulos de empréstimo
   (m pl)

títulos do Tesouro *(m pl)* Pt
De Regierungsschuldver-
   schreibungen *(f pl)*
En Government securities
Es títulos públicos *(m pl)*
Fr titres d'État *(m pl)*
It titoli di Stato *(m pl)*

títulos não cotados *(m pl)* Pt
De nicht notierte Werte *(m pl)*
En unquoted securities
Es títulos no cotizados *(m pl)*
Fr valeurs non cotées *(f pl)*
It titoli non quotati *(m pl)*

títulos no cotizados *(m pl)* Es
De nicht notierte Werte *(m pl)*
En unquoted securities

Fr valeurs non cotées *(f pl)*
It titoli non quotati *(m pl)*
Pt títulos não cotados *(m pl)*

título solidário de diversos
   (m) Pt
De Solidarobligation *(f)*
En joint and several bond
Es obligación solidaria e indi-
   visa *(f)*
Fr obligation conjointe et so-
   lidaire *(f)*
It obbligazione solidale *(f)*

títulos públicos *(m pl)* Es
Do Regierungsschuldver-
   schreibungen *(f pl)*
En Government securities
Fr titres d'État *(m pl)*
It titoli di Stato *(m pl)*
Pt títulos do Tesouro *(m pl)*

Tochtergesellschaft *(f)* n De
En subsidiary company
Es filial; empresa subsidiaría
   (f)
Fr filiale *(f)*
It filiale *(f)*
Pt companhia subsidiária *(f)*

Tod *(m)* n De
En death
Es muerte *(m)*
Fr mort *(f)*
It morte *(f)*
Pt morte *(f)*

todos los riesgos *(m pl)* Es
De alle Gefahren *(f pl)*
En all risks
Fr tous risques *(m pl)*
It tutti i rischi *(m pl)*
Pt todos os riscos *(m pl)*

todos os riscos *(m pl)* Pt
De alle Gefahren *(f pl)*
En all risks
Es todos los riesgos *(m pl)*
Fr tous risques *(m pl)*
It tutti i rischi *(m pl)*

tomorrow *adv* En
De morgen
Es mañana
Fr demain
It domani
Pt amanhã

tonelada *(f)* n Es, Pt
De Tonne *(f)*
En tonne
Fr tonne *(f)*
It tonnellata *(f)*

tonelada bruta *(f)* Es
De Bruttotonne *(f)*
En gross ton
Fr tonne forte *(f)*
It tonnellata lorda *(f)*
Pt tonelada de peso bruto *(f)*

tonelada de deslocação *(f)*
   Pt
De Verdrängungstonne *(f)*
En displacement-ton
Es tonelada de desplaza-
   miento *(f)*
Fr tonneau de déplacement
   (m)
It tonnellata di dislocamento
   (f)

**tonelada de desplaza-
   miento** *(f)* Es
De Verdrängungstonne *(f)*
En displacement-ton
Fr tonneau de déplacement
   (m)
It tonnellata di dislocamento
   (f)
Pt tonelada de deslocação *(f)*

tonelada de flete *(f)* Es
D. Handelstonne *(f)*
En freight ton
Fr tonneau de fret *(m)*
It tonnellata di nolo *(f)*
Pt tonelada de frete *(f)*

tonelada de frete *(f)* Pt
De Handelstonne *(f)*
En freight ton
Es tonelada de flete *(f)*
Fr tonneau de fret *(m)*
It tonnellata di nolo *(f)*

tonelada de peso bruto *(f)* Pt
De Bruttotonne *(f)*
En gross ton
Es tonelada bruta *(f)*
Fr. tonne forte *(f)*
It tonnellata lorda *(f)*

tonelada de registo bruto *(f)*
   Pt
De Bruttoregistertonne *(f)*
En gross register ton

Es tonelada de registro bruto
    (f)
Fr tonneau de jauge brute *(m)*
It tonnellaggio lordo di regi-
    stro *(m)*

tonelada de registro bruto *(f)*
    Es
De Bruttoregistertonne *(f)*
En gross register ton
Fr tonneau de jauge brute *(m)*
It tonnellaggio lordo di regi-
    stro *(m)*
Pt tonelada de registo bruto
    (f)

tonelada inglesa *(f)* Es, Pt
De schwere Tonne *(f)*
En long ton
Fr tonne forte *(f)*
It tonnellata inglese *(f)*

tonelagem *(f)* n Pt
De Tonnengehalt *(m)*
En tonnage
Es tonelaja *(m)*
Fr tonnage *(m)*
It tonnellaggio *(m)*

tonelagem de peso bruto *(f)*
    Pt
De Bruttotonnage *(f)*
En gross tonnage
Es tonelaje bruto *(m)*
Fr tonnage brut *(m)*
It tonnellaggio lordo *(m)*

tonelaje *(m)* n Es
De Tonnengehalt *(m)*
En tonnage
Fr tonnage *(m)*
It tonnellaggio *(m)*
Pt tonelagem *(f)*

tonelaje bruto *(m)* Es
De Bruttotonnage *(f)*
En gross tonnage
Fr tonnage brut *(m)*
It tonnellaggio lordo *(m)*
Pt tonelagem de peso bruto
    (f)

tonnage n En, Fr *(m)*
De Tonnengehalt *(m)*
Es tonelaje *(m)*
It tonnellaggio *(m)*
Pt tonelagem *(f)*

tonnage brut *(m)* Fr
De Bruttotonnage *(f)*
En gross tonnage
Es tonelaje bruto *(m)*
It tonnellaggio lordo *(m)*
Pt tonelagem de peso bruto
    (f)

tonne n En, Fr *(f)*
De Tonne *(f)*
Es tonelada *(f)*
It tonnellata *(f)*
Pt tonelada *(f)*

Tonne *(f)* n De
En tonne
Es tonelada *(f)*
Fr tonne *(f)*
It tonnellata *(f)*
Pt tonelada *(f)*

tonneau *(m)* n Fr
De Faß *(n)*
En barrel
Es barril *(m)*
It botte *(f)*
Pt barril *(m)*

tonneau de déplacement *(m)*
    Fr
De Verdrängungstonne *(f)*
En displacement-ton
Es tonelada de desplaza-
    miento *(f)*
It tonnellata di dislocamento
    (f)
Pt tonelada de deslocação *(f)*

tonneau de fret *(m)* Fr
De Handelstonne *(f)*
En freight ton
Es tonelada de flete *(f)*
It tonnellata di nolo *(f)*
Pt tonelada de frete *(f)*

tonneau de jauge brute *(m)*
    Fr
De Bruttoregistertonne *(f)*
En gross register ton
Es tonelada de registro bruto
    (f)
It tonnellaggio lordo di regi-
    stro *(m)*
Pt tonelada de registo bruto
    (f)

tonne forte *(f)* Fr
De Bruttotonne *(f)*
En gross ton

Es tonelada bruta *(f)*
It tonnellata lorda *(f)*
Pt tonelada de peso bruto *(f)*

tonnellaggio *(m)* n It
De Tonnengehalt *(m)*
En tonnage
Es tonelaje *(m)*
Fr tonnage *(m)*
Pt tonelagem *(f)*

tonnellaggio lordo *(m)* It
De Bruttotonnage *(f)*
En gross tonnage
Es tonelaje bruto *(m)*
Fr tonnage brut *(m)*
Pt tonelagem de peso bruto
    (f)

**tonnellaggio lordo di
    registro** *(m)* It
De Bruttoregistertonne *(f)*
En gross register ton
Es tonelada de registro bruto
    (f)
Fr tonneau de jauge brute *(m)*
Pt tonelada de registo bruto
    (f)

tonnellata *(f)* n It
De Tonne *(f)*
En tonne
Es tonelada *(f)*
Fr tonne *(f)*
Pt tonelada *(f)*

tonnellata di dislocamento
    (f) It
De Verdrängungstonne *(f)*
En displacement-ton
Es tonelada de desplaza-
    miento *(f)*
Fr tonneau de déplacement
    (m)
Pt tonelada de deslacação *(f)*

tonnellata di nolo *(f)* It
De Handelstonne *(f)*
En freight ton
Es tonelada de flete *(f)*
Fr tonneau de fret *(m)*
Pt tonelada de frete *(f)*

tonnellata inglese *(f)* It
De schwere Tonne *(f)*
En long ton
Es tonelada inglesa *(f)*
Fr tonne forte *(f)*
Pt tonelada inglesa *(f)*

tonnellata lorda *(f)* It
De Bruttotonne *(f)*
En gross ton
Es tonelada bruta *(f)*
Fr tonne forte *(f)*
Pt tonelada de peso bruto *(f)*

Tonnengehalt *(m) n* De
En tonnage
Es tonelaje *(m)*
Fr tonnage *(m)*
It tonnellaggio *(m)*
Pt tonelagem *(f)*

top copy En
De Original *(n)*
Es original *(m)*
Fr original *(m)*
It originale *(m)*
Pt original *(m)*

top management En
De Direktion *(f)*
Es dirección superior *(f)*
Fr haute direction *(f)*
It direzione superiore *(f)*
Pt gerência superior *(f)*

top quality En
De hochwertig
Es de primera calidad
Fr de première qualité
It di qualità superiore
Pt de classe superior

tormenta *(f) n* Es
De Sturm *(m)*
En storm
Fr tempête *(f)*
It tempesta *(f)*
Pt temporal *(m)*

tort *n* En
De unerlaubte Handlung *(f)*
Es agravio *(m)*
Fr acte défendu *(m)*
It torto *(m)*
Pt agravo *(m)*

torto *(m) n* It
De unerlaubte Handlung *(f)*
En tort
Es agravio *(m)*
Fr acte défendu *(m)*
Pt agravo *(m)*

totaliser *vb* Fr
De addieren
En add up

Es sumar
It sommare
Pt somar

totalmente pago Pt
De voll bezahlt
En fully paid up
Es completamente pagado
Fr entièrement versé
It interamente pagato

totalmente subscrito Pt
De vollgezeichnet
En fully subscribed
Es plenamente suscrito
Fr intégralement souscrit
It interamente sottoscritto

Totenschein *(m) n* De
En death certificate
Es partida de defunción *(f)*
Fr extrait d'acte de décès *(m)*
It certificato di morte *(m)*
Pt certidão de óbito *(f)*

totes Kapital *(n)* De
En idle money
Es dinero sin invertir *(m)*
Fr capital oisif *(m)*
It denaro inattivo *(m)*
Pt dinheiro paralisado *(m)*

touche (de machine à
écrire) *(f) n* Fr
De Taste *(f)*
En key
Es tecla *(f)*
It tasto *(m)*
Pt tecla *(f)*

toucher un chèque Fr
De einen Scheck einlösen
En cash a cheque
Am cash a check
Es cobrar un cheque
It incassare un assegno
Pt cobrar um cheque

tourist trade En
De Reisegewerbe *(n)*
Es industria del turismo *(f)*
Fr commerce de tourisme *(m)*
It commercio turistico *(m)*
Pt indústria do turismo *(f)*

tous risques *(m pl)* Fr
De alle Gefahren *(f pl)*
En all risks

Es todos los riesgos *(m pl)*
It tutti i rischi *(m pl)*
Pt todos os riscos *(m pl)*

tout vendu Fr
De ausverkauft
En sold out
Es agatado
It tutto venduto
Pt esgotado

to whom it may concern En
De an alle, die es angeht
Es an quien concierna
Fr à qui de droit
It a tutti gli interessati
Pt a quem disser respeito

town gas En
De Stadtgas *(n)*
Es gas de ciudad *(m)*
Fr gaz de ville *(m)*
It gas di carbon fossile *(m)*
Pt gás urbano *(m)*

toxic waste En
De giftiger Abfall *(m)*
Es efluentes tóxicos *(m pl)*
Fr déchets toxiques *(m pl)*
It rifiuti tossici *(m pl)*
Pt despejos tóxicos *(m pl)*

trabajador *(m) n* Es
De Arbeiter *(m)*
En worker
Fr ouvrier *(m)*
It lavoratore *(m)*
Pt trabalhador *(m)*

**trabajador por cuenta
propia** *(m)* Es
De selbständig Arbeitende(r)
(m)
En self-employed person
Fr travailleur indépendant *(m)*
It lavoratore indipendente
(m)
Pt empregado por conta-
própria *(m)*

trabajo *(m) n* Es
De Arbeit; Beruf *(f m)*
En work; job
Fr travail; emploi *(m)*
It lavoro *(m)*
Pt trabalho *(m)*

trabajo a destajo *(m)* Es
De Akkordarbeit *(f)*
En piecework
Fr travail à la tâche *(m)*
It lavoro a cottimo *(m)*
Pt trabalho por peça *(m)*

trabajo en curso *(m)* Es
De Arbeit in der Ausführung *(f)*
En work-in-progress
Am work in process
Fr travaux en cours *(m pl)*
It lavoro in corso *(m)*
Pt trabalho em curso *(m)*

trabajo nocturno *(m)* Es
De Nachtarbeit *(f)*
En nightwork
Fr travail de nuit *(m)*
It lavoro notturno *(m)*
Pt trabalho nocturno *(m)*

trabajo por torno *(m)* Es
De Schichtarbeit *(f)*
En shiftwork
Fr travail par équipes *(m)*
It lavoro a turno *(m)*
Pt trabalho por turno *(m)*

trabalhador *(m)* n Pt
De Arbeiter *(m)*
En worker
Es trabajador *(m)*
Fr ouvrier *(m)*
It lavoratore *(m)*

trabalhador das docas *(m)* Pt
De Hafenarbeiter *(m)*
En docker
Am longshoreman
Es cargador de muelle *(m)*
Fr docker *(m)*
It lavoratore del porto *(m)*

trabalho *(m)* n Pt
De Arbeit *(f)*
En work
Es trabajo *(m)*
Fr travail *(m)*
It lavoro *(m)*

trabalho directamente produtivo *(m)* Pt
De produktive Arbeitskräfte *(f pl)*
En direct labour
Es jornales directos *(m pl)*
Fr travail en régie *(m)*
It lavoro in economia *(m)*

trabalho em curso *(m)* Pt
De Arbeit in der Ausführung *(f)*
En work-in-progress
Am work in process
Es trabajo en curso *(m)*
Fr travaux en cours *(m pl)*
It lavoro in corso *(m)*

trabalho por peca *(m)* Pt
De Akkordarbeit *(f)*
En piecework
Es trabajo a destajo *(m)*
Fr travail à la tâche *(m)*
It lavoro a cottimo *(m)*

trabalho nocturno *(m)* Pt
De Nachtarbeit *(f)*
En nightwork
Es trabajo nocturno *(m)*
Fr travail de nuit *(m)*
It lavoro notturno *(m)*

trabalho pour turno *(m)* Pt
De Schichtarbeit *(f)*
En shiftwork
Es trabajo por torno *(m)*
Fr travail par équipes *(m)*
It lavoro a turno *(m)*

trade n En
De Handel *(m)*
Es comercio *(m)*
Fr commerce *(m)*
It commercio *(m)*
Pt comércio *(m)*

trade acceptance En
De Handelsakzept *(n)*
Es acceptación comercial *(f)*
Fr acceptation de commerce *(f)*
It accettazione commerciale *(f)*
Pt aceitação comercial *(f)*

trade account En
De Handelskonto *(n)*
Es cuenta comercial *(f)*
Fr compte commercial *(m)*
It conto commerciale *(m)*
Pt conta comercial *(f)*

trade association En
De Unternehmensverband *(m)*
Es asociación comercial *(f)*
Fr association profession-nelle *(f)*
It associazione commerciale *(f)*
Pt associação comercial *(f)*

trade balance En
De Handelsbilanz *(f)*
Es balanza comercial *(f)*
Fr balance commerciale *(f)*
It bilancia commerciale *(f)*
Pt balança commerciale *(f)*

trade barrier En
De Handelsschranke *(f)*
Es barrera comercial *(f)*
Fr barrière commerciale *(f)*
It barriera commerciale *(f)*
Pt barreira comercial *(f)*

trade block En
De Handelsblock *(m)*
Es bloque comercial *(m)*
Fr bloc commercial *(m)*
It unione commerciale *(f)*
Pt bloque comercial *(m)*

trade catalogue En
De Preiskatalog *(m)*
Es catálogo comercial *(m)*
Fr tarif-album *(m)*
It catalogo commerciale *(m)*
Pt catálogo comercial *(m)*

trade cycle En
De Handelszyklus *(m)*
Es ciclo del negocio *(m)*
Fr cycle de commerce *(m)*
It ciclo degli affari *(m)*
Pt ciclo comercial *(m)*

trade directory En
De Handelsadreßbuch *(n)*
Es guía comercial *(f)*
Fr guide de commerce *(m)*
It guida commerciale *(f)*
Pt guia comercial *(m)*

trade discount En
De Händlerrabatt *(m)*
Es descuento comercial *(m)*
Fr rabais de demi-gros *(m)*
It sconto di rivendita *(m)*
Pt desconto à praça *(m)*

trade dispute En
De Arbeitsstreitigkeit *(f)*
Es conflicto laboral *(m)*
Fr conflit du travail *(m)*
It vertenza di lavoro *(f)*
Pt conflito comercial *(m)*

trade fair En
De Handelsmesse *(f)*
Es feria de muestras *(f)*
Fr foire commerciale *(f)*
It fiera commerciale *(f)*
Pt feira comercial *(f)*

trade gap En
De Außenhandelsdefizit *(n)*
Es vacío comercial *(m)*
Fr déficit du commerce exté-
rieur *(m)*
It disavanzo della bilancia
commerciale *(m)*
Pt vazio comercial *(m)*

trademark *n* En
De Warenzeichen *(n)*
Es marca de fábrica *(f)*
Fr marque de fabrique *(f)*
It marchio di fabbrica *(m)*
Pt marca de fábrica *(f)*

trade name En
De Firmenname *(m)*
Es razón social *(f)*
Fr raison sociale *(f)*
It denominazione commer-
ciale *(f)*
Pt razão comercial *(f)*

trade price En
De Handelspreis *(m)*
Es precio al comerciante *(m)*
Fr prix marchand *(m)*
It prezzo al commerciante
(m)
Pt preço para comerciantes
(m)

trade reference En
De Kreditauskunft *(f)*
Es referencia comercial *(f)*
Fr référence commerciale *(f)*
It referenze commerciali *(f pl)*
Pt referência comercial *(f)*

trade secret En
De Betriebsgeheimnis *(n)*
Es secreto comercial *(m)*
Fr secret industriel *(m)*
It segreto commerciale *(m)*
Pt segredo comercial *(m)*

trade union En
De Gewerkschaft *(f)*
Es sindicato *(m)*

Fr syndicat ouvrier *(m)*
It sindacato *(m)*
Pt sindicato *(m)*

trading capital En
De Betriebskapital *(n)*
Es capital de explotación *(m)*
Fr fonds de roulement *(m)*
It capitale d'esercizio *(m)*
Pt capital de exploração *(m)*

traente *(m) n* It
De Aussteller *(m)*
En drawer
Es librador *(m)*
Fr tireur *(m)*
Pt sacador *(m)*

tráfego aéreo *(m)* Pt
De Luftverkehr *(m)*
En air traffic
Es tráfico aéreo *(m)*
Fr trafic aérien *(m)*
It traffico aereo *(m)*

traffic jam En
De Verkehrsstockung *(f)*
Es embotellamiento de tráfico
(m)
Fr encombrement de circula-
tion *(m)*
It ingorgo stradale *(m)*
Pt engarrafamento de tráfego
(m)

traffico aereo *(m)* It
De Luftverkehr *(m)*
En air traffic
Es tráfico aéreo *(m)*
Fr trafic aérien *(m)*
Pt tráfego aéreo *(m)*

trafic aérien *(m)* Fr
De Luftverkehr *(m)*
En air traffic
Es tráfico aéreo *(m)*
It traffico aereo *(m)*
Pt tráfego aéreo *(m)*

tráfic aéreo *(m)* Es
De Luftverkehr *(m)*
En air traffic
Fr trafic aérien *(m)*
It traffico aereo *(m)*
Pt tréfego aéreo *(m)*

Tragfähigkeit *(f) n* De
En deadweight
Es peso muerto *(m)*
Fr port en lourd *(m)*
It peso morto *(m)*
Pt peso morto *(m)*

train de marchandises *(m)* Fr
De Güterzug *(m)*
En goods train
Am freight train
Es tren de mercancías *(m)*
It treno merci *(m)*
Pt comboio de mercadorias
(m)

train express *(m)* Fr
De D-Zug; Schnellzug *(m)*
En express train
Es tren expreso *(m)*
It direttissimo; rapido *(m)*
Pt comboio rápido *(m)*

traite *(f) n* Fr
De Tratte *(f)*
En draft
Es letra *(f)*
It tratta *(f)*
Pt letra *(f)*

traite à vue *(f)* Fr
De Sichttratte *(f)*
En sight draft
Es letra a la vista *(f)*
It tratta a vista *(f)*
Pt letra à vista *(f)*

traite bancaire *(f)* Fr
De Banktratte *(f)*
En banker's draft
Es giro bancario *(m)*
It tratta bancaria *(f)*
Pt letra de banco *(f)*

traite documentaire *(f)* Fr
De Dokumentenwechsel *(m)*
En documentary bill
Es efecto documentario *(m)*
It tratta documentaria *(f)*
Pt título documental *(m)*

traite en blanc *(f)* Fr
De Blankowechsel *(m)*
En blank bill
Es letra en blanco *(f)*
It effetto in bianco *(m)*
Pt letra em branco *(f)*

traitement *(m) n* Fr
De Gehalt *(n)*
En salary
Es sueldo *(m)*
It stipendio *(m)*
Pt ordenado *(m)*

traitement d'informatique
(m) Fr
De Datenverarbeitung *(f)*
En data processing
Es tratamiento de datos *(m)*
It elaborazione dei dati *(f)*
Pt processamento de dados
(m)

traitement juste *(m)* Fr
De anständige Handlungs-
weise *(f)*
En fair play
Es juego limpio *(m)*
It condotta leale *(f)*
Pt jogo limpo *(m)*

Trampschiff *(n) n* De
En tramp steamer
Es vapor volandero *(m)*
Fr navire de tramping *(m)*
It carretta *(f)*
Pt vapor de serviço autóno-
mo *(m)*

tramp steamer En
De Trampschiff *(n)*
Es vapor volandero *(m)*
Fr navire de tramping *(m)*
It carretta *(f)*
Pt vapor de serviço autóno-
mo *(m)*

transacção *(f) n* Pt
De Transaktion *(f)*
En transaction
Es transacción *(f)*
Fr transaction *(f)*
It transazione *(f)*

transacção razoável *(f)* Pt
De anständige Abmachung *(f)*
En fair deal
Es trato equitativo *(m)*
Fr affaire équitable *(f)*
It affare giusto *(m)*

transacción *(f) n* Es
De Transaktion *(f)*
En transaction

Fr transaction *(f)*
It transazione *(f)*
Pt transacção *(f)*

transacções adiantadas *(f pl)*
Pt
De Zeitgeschäfte *(n pl)*
En forward dealings
Es negociaciones a término *(f
pl)*
Fr opérations à terme *(f pl)*
It operazioni a termine *(f pl)*

transaction *n* En, Fr *(f)*
De Transaktion *(f)*
Es transacción *(f)*
It transazione *(f)*
Pt transacção *(f)*

transaction au comptant *(f)*
Fr
De Bargeschäft *(n)*
En cash deal
Es trato al contado *(m)*
It operazione a contanti *(f)*
Pt negócio em dinheiro *(m)*

Transaktion *(f) n* De
En transaction
Es transacción *(f)*
Fr transaction *(f)*
It transazione *(f)*
Pt transacção *(f)*

transatlántico *(m) n* Es
De Linienschiff *(n)*
En liner
Fr paquebot *(m)*
It nave di linea *(f)*
Pt paquete *(m)*

transazione *(f) n* It
De Transaktion *(f)*
En transaction
Es transacción *(f)*
Fr transaction *(f)*
Pt transacção *(f)*

transbordador *(m) n* Es
De Fährboot *(n)*
En ferry-boat
Fr bac *(m)*
It nave traghetto *(f)*
Pt barco de travessia *(m)*

transbordement *(m) n* Fr
De Umladung *(f)*
En transhipment

Es transbordo *(m)*
It trasbordo *(m)*
Pt transbordo *(m)*

transbordo *(m) n* Es, Pt
De Umladung *(f)*
En transhipment
Fr transbordement *(m)*
It trasbordo *(m)*

transcriber *n* Am
En copy typist
De Typistin *(f)*
Es mecanógrafa *(f)*
Fr dactylo copiste *(f)*
It dattilografa *(f)*
Pt dactilógrafa *(f)*

transcrire *vb* Fr
De kopieren
En copy
Es copiar
It copiare
Pt copiar

transfer (of ownership) *n* En
De Überweisung *(f)*
Es cesión *(f)*
Fr transfert; cession *(m f)*
It cessione *(f)*
Pt trespasse *(m)*

transfer (property, etc.) *vb* En
De überweisen
Es transferir
Fr céder; transférer
It trasferire
Pt transferir

transfer deed En
De Übertragungsvertrag *(m)*
Es escritura de transferencia
(f)
Fr acte de cession *(m)*
It atto di trapasso *(m)*
Pt título de transferência *(m)*

transferee *n* En
De Zessionar *(m)*
Es cesionario *(m)*
Fr cessionnaire *(m)*
It cessionario *(m)*
Pt cessionário *(m)*

transferencia bancaria *(f)* Es
De Banküberweisung *(f)*
En bank transfer
Fr virement bancaire *(m)*
It trasferimento bancario *(m)*
Pt transferência bancária *(f)*

transferência bancária (f) Pt
De Banküberweisung (f)
En bank transfer
Es transferencia bancaria (f)
Fr virement bancaire (m)
It trasferimento bancario (m)

transferencia postal (f) Es
De Postüberweisung (f)
En mail transfer
Fr virement postal (m)
It trasferimento per posta (m)
Pt transferência postal (f)

transferência postal (f) Pt
De Postüberweisung (f)
En mail transfer
Es transferencia postal (f)
Fr virement postal (m)
It trasferimento per posta (m)

transferência telegráfica (f) Pt
De Kabelauszahlung (f)
En telegraphic transfer
Es giro telegráfico (m)
Fr virement télégraphique (m)
It rimessa telegrafica (f)

transférer vb Fr
De überweisen
En transfer
Es transferir
It trasferire
Pt transferir

transferir vb Es, Pt
De überweisen
En transfer
Fr céder; transférer
It trasferire

transferor n En
De Zedent (m)
Es cesionista (m)
Fr cédant (m)
It cedente (m)
Pt cessionista (m)

transfert (f) n Fr
De Überweisung (f)
En transfer
Es cesión (f)
It cessione (f)
Pt trespasse (m)

transformations et réparations Fr
De Änderungen und Reparaturen
En alterations and repairs
Es reformas y reparaciones
It modifiche e riparazioni
Pt modificações e reparações

transhipment n En
De Umladung (f)
Es transbordo (m)
Fr transbordement (m)
It trasbordo (m)
Pt transbordo (m)

transitaire (m) n Fr
De Spediteur (m)
En forwarding agent
Es agente expedidor (m)
It spedizioniere (m)
Pt agente expedidor (m)

transmission de biens (f) Fr
De Übertragung von Vermögen (f)
En conveyance of property
Es traspaso de propiedad (m)
It trasferimento di beni (m)
Pt trespasse de propriedade (m)

transport n En, Fr (m)
De Beförderung; Transport (f m)
Es transporte (m)
It trasporto (m)
Pt transporte (m)

Transport (m) n De
En transport
Es transporte (m)
Fr transport (m)
It trasporto (m)
Pt transporte (m)

transportador (m) n Es, Pt
De Spediteur (m)
En carrier
Am conveyer
Fr expéditeur (m)
It vettore (m)

transportador a grand (m) Es
De Massenfrachtführer (m)
En bulk carrier

Fr transporteur de marchandises en vrac (m)
It transportatore di merce alla rinfusa (m)
Pt transportador de carga geral (m)

transportador de carga geral (m) Pt
De Massenfrachtführer (m)
En bulk carrier
Es transportador a grand (m)
Fr transporteur de marchandises en vrac (m)
It trasportatore di merce alla rinfusa (m)

transport aérien (m) Fr
De Lufttransport (m)
En air transport
Es transporte aéreo (m)
It trasporto aereo (m)
Pt transporte aéreo (m)

transporte (m) n Es, Pt
De Beförderung; Transport (f m)
En transport
Fr transport (m)
It trasporto (m)

transporte aéreo (m) Es, Pt
De Lufttransport (m)
En air transport
Fr transport aérien (m)
It trasporto aereo (m)

transporte a pagar (pelo destinatário) Pt
De Portonachnahme
En carriage forward
Am F.O.B. shipping point
Es a porte debido
Fr en port dû
It porto assegnato

transporteur de marchandises en vrac (m) Fr
De Massenfrachtführer (m)
En bulk carrier
Es transportador a grand (m)
It trasportatore di merce alla rinfusa (m)
Pt transportador de carga geral (m)

Transportunternehmer *(m)* n
De
En haulage contractor
Am trucking company
Es contratista de transportes
(m)
Fr entrepreneur de camion-
nage *(m)*
It imprenditore di trasporti
(m)
Pt empreiteiro de transportes
(m)

trarre allo scoperto It
De überziehen
En overdraw
Es girar en descubierto
Fr mettre à découvert
Pt levantar a descoberto

trasbordo *(m)* n It
De Umladung *(f)*
En transhipment
Es transbordo *(m)*
Fr transbordement *(m)*
Pt transbordo *(m)*

trasferimento bancario *(m)* It
De Banküberweisung *(f)*
En bank transfer
Es transferencia bancaria *(f)*
Fr virement bancaire *(m)*
Pt transferência bancária *(f)*

trasferimento di beni *(m)* It
De Übertragung von Vermö-
gen *(f)*
En conveyance of property
Es traspaso de propiedad *(m)*
Fr transmission de biens *(f)*
Pt trespasse de propriedade
(m)

trasferimento per posta *(m)*
It
De Postüberweisung *(f)*
En mail transfer
Es transferencia postal *(f)*
Fr virement postal *(m)*
Pt transferência postal *(f)*

trasferire *vb* It
De überweisen
En transfer
Es transferir
Fr transférer
Pt transferir

traspaso de propiedad *(m)*
Es
De Übertragung von Vermö-
gen *(f)*
En conveyance of property
Fr transmission de biens *(f)*
It trasferimento di beni *(m)*
Pt trespasse de propriedade
(m)

**trasportatore di merce alla
rinfusa** *(m)* It
De Massenfrachtführer *(m)*
En bulk carrier
Es transportador a grand *(m)*
Fr transporteur de marchan-
dises en vrac *(m)*
Pt transportador de carga
geral *(m)*

trasporto *(m)* n It
De Beförderung; Transport
(f m)
En transport
Es transporte *(m)*
Fr transport *(m)*
Pt transporte *(m)*

trasporto a collettame *(m)* It
De Groupagedienst *(m)*
En groupage service
Es servicio de agrupación *(m)*
Fr service de groupage *(m)*
Pt serviço de agrupamento
(m)

trasporto aereo *(m)* It
De Lufttransport *(m)*
En air transport
Es transporte aéreo *(m)*
Fr transport aérien *(m)*
Pt transporte aéreo *(m)*

tratamiento de datos *(m)* Es
De Datenverarbeitung *(f)*
En data processing
Fr traitement d'informatique
(m)
It elaborazione dei dati *(f)*
Pt processamento de dados
(m)

trato al contado *(m)* Es
De Bargeschäft *(n)*
En cash deal
Fr transaction au comptant
(f)
It operazione a contanti *(f)*
Pt negócio em dinheiro *(m)*

trato equitativo *(m)* Es
De anständige Abmachung *(f)*
En fair deal
Fr affaire équitable *(f)*
It affare giusto *(m)*
Pt transacção razoável *(f)*

tratta *(f)* n It
De Tratte *(f)*
En draft
Es letra *(f)*
Fr traite *(f)*
Pt letra *(f)*

tratta a vista *(f)* It
De Sichttratte *(f)*
En sight draft
Es letra a la vista *(f)*
Fr traite à vue *(f)*
Pt letra à vista *(f)*

tratta bancaria *(f)* It
De Banktratte *(f)*
En banker's draft
Es giro bancario *(m)*
Fr traite bancaire *(f)*
Pt letra de banco *(f)*

tratta cambiale *(f)* It
De Wechsel; Tratte *(m f)*
En bill of exchange
Es letra de cambio *(f)*
Fr lettre de change *(f)*
Pt letra de câmbio *(f)*

tratta documentaria *(f)* It
De Dokumentenwechsel *(m)*
En documentary bill
Es efecto documentario *(m)*
Fr traite documentaire *(f)*
Pt título documental *(m)*

trattario *(m)* n It
De Bezogene(r) *(m)*
En drawee
Es librado *(m)*
Fr tiré *(m)*
Pt sacado *(m)*

trattativa *(f)* n It
De Verhandlung *(f)*
En negotiation
Es negociación *(f)*
Fr négociation *(f)*
Pt negociação *(f)*

Tratte (f) n De
En draft
Es letra (f)
Fr traite (f)
It tratta (f)
Pt letra (f)

travail (m) n Fr
De Arbeit (f)
En work
Es trabajo (m)
It lavoro (m)
Pt trabalho (m)

travail à la tâche (m) Fr
De Akkordarbeit (f)
En piecework
Es trabajo a destajo (m)
It lavoro a cottimo (m)
Pt trabalho por peça (m)

travail de nuit (m) Fr
De Nachtarbeit (f)
En nightwork
Es trabajo nocturno (m)
It lavoro notturno (m)
Pt trabalho nocturno (m)

travail en régie (m) Fr
De produktive Arbeitskräfte
   (f pl)
En direct labour
Es jornales directos (m pl)
It lavoro in economia (m)
Pt trabalho directamente
   produtivo (m)

travailleur indépendant (m)
   Fr
De selbständig Arbeitende(r)
   (m)
En self-employed person
Es trabajador por cuenta
   propia (m)
It lavoratore indipendente
   (m)
Pt empregado por conta-
   própria (m)

travail par équipes (m) Fr
De Schichtarbeit (f)
En shiftwork
Es trabajo por torno (m)
It lavoro a turno (m)
Pt trabalho por turno (m)

travaux de transformation
   (m pl) Fr
De Umbau (m)
En alterations
Es reformas (f pl)
It modifiche (f pl)
Pt modificações (f pl)

travaux en cours (m pl) Fr
De Arbeit in der Ausführung (f)
En work-in-progress
Am work in process
Es trabajo en curso (m)
It lavoro in corso (m)
Pt trabalho em curso (m)

travel agent En
De Reisebüro (n)
Es agencia de viajes (f)
Fr agence de voyages (f)
It agenzia di viaggi (f)
Pt agente de viagens (m)

traveller's cheque En
Am traveler's check
De Reisescheck (m)
Es cheque de viajero (m)
Fr chèque de voyage (m)
It assegno turistico (m)
Pt cheque de viajante (m)

travelling expenses En
De Reisekosten (f pl)
Es dietas de viajes (f pl)
Fr frais de voyage (m pl)
It spese di viaggio (f pl)
Pt despesas de viagem (f pl)

treasury n Am
En exchequer
De Schatzamt (n)
Es hacienda (f)
Fr trésorerie (f)
It tesoro (m)
Pt tesouro (m)

treasury bond Am
En exchequer bond
De Schatzwechsel (m)
Es bono de tesorería (m)
Fr bon du trésor (m)
It buono del tesoro (m)
Pt título do tesouro (m)

treino vocacional (m) Pt
De Berufsausbildung (f)
En vocational training
Es formación profesional (f)

Fr formation professionnelle
   (f)
It addestramento professio-
   nale (m)

tren de mercancías (m) Es
De Güterzug (m)
En goods train
Am freight train
Fr train de marchandises (m)
It treno merci (m)
Pt comboio de mercadorias
   (m)

tren expreso (m) Es
De D-Zug; Schnellzug (m)
En express train
Fr train express (m)
It direttissimo; rapido (m)
Pt comboio rápido (m)

treno merci (m) It
De Güterzug (m)
En goods train
Am freight train
Es tren de mercancías (m)
Fr train de marchandises (m)
Pt comboio de mercadorias
   (m)

trésorerie (f) n Fr
De Schatzamt (n)
En exchequer
Am tresury
Es hacienda (f)
It tesoro (m)
Pt tesouro (m)

trespasse de propriedade
   (m) Pt
De Übertragung von Vermö-
   gen (f)
En conveyance of property
Es traspaso de propiedad (m)
Fr transmission de biens (f)
It trasferimento di beni (m)

Treue (f) n De
En fidelity
Es fidelidad (f)
Fr fidélité (f)
It fedeltà (f)
Pt fidelidade (f)

(zu) treuen Händen halten
   De
En hold in trust
Es guardar in fideicomiso

Fr tenir par fidéicommis
It tenere in fidecommesso
Pt guardar

Treuhänder *(m)* n De
En trustee
Es fideicomisario *(m)*
Fr fidéicommissaire *(m)*
It fidecommissario *(m)*
Pt fiduciário *(m)*

treuhänderisch *adj* De
En fiduciary
Es fiduciario
Fr fiduciaire
It fiduciario
Pt fiduciário

Treuhandfonds *(m)* n De
En trust fund
Es fondo fiduciario *(m)*
Fr fonds fiduciaire *(m)*
It fondo fiduciario *(m)*
Pt fundação fiduciária *(f)*

Treuhandgesellschaft *(f)* n
De
En trust company
Es banco fideicomisario *(m)*
Fr société fiduciaire *(f)*
It società fiduciaria *(f)*
Pt empresa de investimentos
(f)

trial balance En
De Probebilanz *(f)*
Es balance de comprobación
de saldos *(m)*
Fr bilan de vérification *(m)*
It bilancio di verifica *(m)*
Pt balancete de verificação *(m)*

tribunal *(m)* n Es, Fr, Pt
De Gericht *(n)*
En court (of law)
It tribunale *(m)*

tribunal arbitral *(m)* Es
De Schiedsgericht *(n)*
En court of arbitration
Fr cour d'arbitrage *(m)*
It tribunale arbitrale *(m)*
Pt tribunal de arbitragem *(m)*

tribunal de apelação *(m)* Pt
De Berufungsgericht *(n)*
En court of appeal

Es tribunal de apelación *(m)*
Fr cour d'appel *(m)*
It corte d'appello *(f)*

tribunal de apelación *(m)* Es
De Berufungsgericht *(n)*
En court of appeal
Fr cour d'appel *(m)*
It corte d'appello *(f)*
Pt tribunal de apelação *(m)*

tribunal de arbitragem *(m)* Pt
De Schiedsgericht *(n)*
En court of arbitration
Es tribunal arbitral *(m)*
Fr cour d'arbitrage *(m)*
It tribunale arbitrale *(f)*

tribunale *(m)* n It
De Gericht *(n)*
En court (of law)
Es tribunal *(m)*
Fr tribunal *(m)*
Pt tribunal *(m)*

tribunale arbitrale *(m)* It
De Schiedsgericht *(n)*
En court of arbitration
Es tribunal arbitral *(m)*
Fr cour d'arbitrage *(m)*
Pt tribunal de arbitragem *(m)*

tributação *(f)* n Pt
De Besteuerung *(f)*
En taxation
Es tributación *(f)*
Fr imposition *(f)*
It tassazione *(f)*

tributação diferida *(f)* Pt
De latente Steuerpflicht *(f)*
En deferred taxation
Es tasación diferida *(f)*
Fr imposition différée *(f)*
It tassazione differita *(f)*

tributação directa *(m)* Pt
De direkte Steuern *(f pl)*
En direct taxation
Es contribuciones directas
(f pl)
Fr contributions directes *(f pl)*
It imposte dirette *(f pl)*

tributação indirecta *(m)* Pt
De indirekte Steuern *(f pl)*
En indirect taxation
Es contribuciones indirectas
(f pl)

Fr contributions indirectes
(f pl)
It imposte *(f pl)*

tributación *(f)* n Es
De Besteuerung *(f)*
En taxation
Fr imposition *(f)*
It tassazione *(f)*
Pt tributação *(f)*

tributável *adj* Pt
De abgabenpflichtig
En dutiable
Es tasable
Fr taxable
It tassabile

tricher *vb* Fr
De betrügen
En cheat
Es engañar
It truffare
Pt enganar

trimestral *adj* Es, Pt
De vierteljährlich
En quarterly
Fr trimestriel
It trimestrale

trimestrale *adj* It
De vierteljährlich
En quarterly
Es trimestral
Fr trimestriel
Pt trimestral

trimestriel *adj* Fr
De vierteljährlich
En quarterly
Es trimestral
It trimestrale
Pt trimestral

Trinkgeld *(n)* n De
En tip
Es propina *(f)*
Fr pourboire *(m)*
It mancia *(f)*
Pt gorjeta *(f)*

tripulação *(f)* n Pt
De Mannschaft *(f)*
En crew
Es tripulación *(f)*
Fr équipage *(m)*
It equipaggio *(m)*

tripulación *(f)* n Es
De Mannschaft *(f)*
En crew
Fr équipage *(m)*
It equipaggio *(m)*
Pt tripulação *(f)*

trocar *vb* Es, Pt
De Tauschhandel treiben
En barter
Fr troquer
It barattare

Trockendock *(n)* n De
En dry dock
Es dique seco *(m)*
Fr cale sèche *(f)*
It bacino di carenaggio *(m)*
Pt doca-seca *(f)*

troco miúdo *(m)* Pt
De Kleingeld *(n)*
En small change
Es moneda suelta *(f)*
Fr petite monnaie *(f)*
It spiccioli *(m pl)*

troquer *vb* Fr
De Tauschhandel treiben
En barter
Es trocar
It barattare
Pt trocar

trucking n Am
En haulage
De Transport *(m)*
Es transporte *(m)*
Fr camionnage; transport *(m)*
It trasporto *(m)*
Pt transporte *(m)*

trucking company Am
En haulage contractor
De Transportunternehmer *(m)*
Es contratista de transportes *(m)*
Fr entrepreneur de camion-
    nage *(m)*
It imprenditore di trasporti *(m)*
Pt empreiteiro de transportes *(m)*

truffa all'americana *(f)* It
De Schwindlertrick *(m)*
En confidence trick
Am confidence game

Es timo *(m)*
Fr vol à l'américaine *(m)*
Pt conto do vigário *(m)*

truffare *vb* It
De betrügen
En cheat
Es engañar
Fr tricher
Pt enganar

trunk call En
Am long distance call
De Ferngespräch *(n)*
Es llamada interurbana *(f)*
Fr appel téléphonique inter-
    urbain *(m)*
It comunicazione interurba-
    na *(f)*
Pt chamada inter-urbana *(f)*

truqué *adj* Fr
De gefälscht
En fake
Es falso
It falso
Pt falsificado

trust company En
De Treuhandgesellschaft *(f)*
Es banco fideicomisario *(m)*
Fr société fiduciaire *(f)*
It società fiduciaria *(f)*
Pt empresa de investimentos *(f)*

trustee n En
De Treuhänder *(m)*
Es fideicomisario *(m)*
Fr fidéicommissaire *(m)*
It fidecommissario *(m)*
Pt fiduciário *(m)*

trust fund En
De Treuhandfonds *(m)*
Es fondo fiduciario *(m)*
Fr fonds fiduciaire *(m)*
It fondo fiduciario *(m)*
Pt fundação fiduciária *(f)*

tug-boat n En
De Schleppdampfer *(m)*
Es remolcador *(m)*
Fr remorqueur *(m)*
It rimorchiatore *(m)*
Pt rebocador *(m)*

turno *(m)* n Es, It, Pt
De Schicht *(f)*
En shift
Fr équipe *(f)*

turno da noite *(m)* Pt
De Nachtschicht *(f)*
En night shift
Es turno de noche *(m)*
Fr équipe de nuit *(m)*
It turno di notte *(m)*

turno de día *(m)* Es
De Tagschicht *(f)*
En day shift
Fr équipe du jour *(f)*
It turno di giorno *(m)*
Pt turno de dia *(m)*

turno de dia *(m)* Pt
De Tagschicht *(f)*
En day shift
Es turno de día *(m)*
Fr équipe du jour *(f)*
It turno di giorno *(m)*

turno de noche *(m)* Es
De Nachtschicht *(f)*
En night shift
Fr équipe de nuit *(m)*
It turno di notte *(m)*
Pt turno da noite *(m)*

turno di giorno *(m)* It
De Tagschicht *(f)*
En day shift
Es turno de día *(m)*
Fr équipe de jour *(f)*
Pt turno de dia *(m)*

turno di notte *(m)* It
De Nachtschicht *(f)*
En night shift
Es turno de noche *(m)*
Fr équipe de nuit *(m)*
Pt turno da noite *(m)*

turnover n En
De Umsatz *(m)*
Es volumen de ventas *(m)*
Fr chiffre d'affaires *(m)*
It giro d'affari *(m)*
Pt movimento de dinheiro *(m)*

tuteur (d'un mineur) *(m)* n Fr
De Vormund *(m)*
En guardian
Es tutor *(m)*
It tutore *(m)*
Pt tutor *(m)*

tutor *(m)* *n* Es, Pt
De Vormund *(m)*
En guardian
Fr tuteur *(m)*
It tutore *(m)*

tutore *(m)* *n* It
De Vormund *(m)*
En guardian
Es tutor *(m)*
Fr tuteur *(m)*
Pt tutor *(m)*

tutti i rischi *(m pl)* It
De alle Gefahren *(f pl)*
En all risks
Es todos los riesgos *(m pl)*
Fr tous risques *(m pl)*
Pt todos os riscos *(m pl)*

tutto venduto It
De ausverkauft
En sold out
Es agotado
Fr tout vendu
Pt esgotado

type *vb* En
De auf der Schreibmaschine schreiben
Es escribir a máquina
Fr écrire à la machine
It scrivere a macchina
Pt escrever à máquina

typescript *n* En
De Maschinenschrift *(f)*
Es texto mecanografiado *(m)*
Fr manuscrit dactylographié *(m)*
It dattiloscritto *(m)*
Pt texto dactilografado *(m)*

typewriter *n* En
De Schreibmaschine *(f)*
Es máquina de escribir *(f)*
Fr machien à écrire *(f)*
It macchina da scrivere *(f)*
Pt máquina de escrever *(f)*

U

überarbeitete Schätzung *(f)* De
En revised estimate
Es cálculo revisado *(m)*

Fr devis rectifié *(m)*
It preventivo riveduto *(m)*
Pt estimativa revista *(f)*

über Bord werfen De
En jettison
Es echar al mar
Fr jeter à la mer
It fare gettito
Pt alijar

Überbrückung *(f)* *n* De
En stop-gap
Es recurso provisional *(m)*
Fr bouche-trou *(m)*
It provvedimento temporaneo *(m)*
Pt tapa-buracos *(m)*

Übergangskonto *(n)* *n* De
En suspense account
Es cuenta suspensa *(f)*
Fr compte d'ordre *(m)*
It conto sospeso *(m)*
Pt conta pendente *(f)*

Übergepäck *(n)* *n* De
En excess luggage (baggage)
Es exceso de equipaje *(m)*
Fr excédent de bagages *(m)*
It bagaglio eccedente *(m)*
Pt excesso de bagagem *(m)*

Übergewicht *(n)* *n* De
En excess weight
Es peso excedente *(m)*
Fr excédent de poids *(m)*
It eccedenza di peso *(f)*
Pt excesso de peso *(m)*

Übergewicht *(n)* *n* De
En overweight
Es exceso de peso *(m)*
Fr excédent *(m)*
It sovrappeso *(m)*
Pt peso excessivo *(m)*

Übergewinnsteuer *(f)* *n* De
En excess profits tax
Es impuesto sobre beneficios extraordinarios *(m pl)*
Fr impôts sur les superbénéfices *(m pl)*
It imposta sui soprapprofitti *(f)*
Pt imposto sobre lucros excessivos *(m)*

Überkapazität *(f)* *n* De
En overcapacity
Es exceso de capacidad *(m)*
Fr surcapacité *(f)*
It capacità in eccedenza *(f)*
Pt capacidade excessiva *(f)*

Überliegezeit *(f)* *n* De
En demurrage
Es sobreestadía *(f)*
Fr surestarie *(f)*
It controstallia *(f)*
Pt sobreestadia *(f)*

übermäßig *adj* De
En excessive
Es excesivo
Fr excessif
It eccessivo
Pt excessivo

übermorgen *adv* De
En day after tomorrow
Es pasado mañana
Fr après demain
It dopodomani
Pt depois de amanhã

Übernahmeangebot *(n)* *n* De
En take-over bid
Es oferta de adquisición *(f)*
Fr offre de rachat *(f)*
It offerta di acquisto *(f)*
Pt proposta de apropriação *(f)*

Übernahmebescheinigung *(f)* *n* De
En mate's receipt
Es recibo de embarco *(m)*
Fr billet de bord *(m)*
It ricevuta d'imbarco *(f)*
Pt recibo de embarque *(m)*

über pari De
En above par
Es a premio
Fr au-dessus du pair
It sopra la pari
Pt a prémio

Überproduktion *(f)* *n* De
En overproduction
Es exceso de producción *(m)*
Fr surproduction *(f)*
It sovrapproduzione *(f)*
Pt produção excessiva *(f)*

Überschätzung *(f) n* De
En over-estimate
Es presupuesto por exceso
(m)
Fr surestimation *(f)*
It valutazione eccessiva *(f)*
Pt avaliação excessiva *(f)*

Überschuß *(m) n* De
En surplus; excess
Es excedente; exceso *(m)*
Fr surplus; excédent *(m)*
It eccesso; soprappeso *(m)*
Pt excédente; excesso *(m)*

Überstunden *(f pl) n* De
En overtime
Es horas extraordinarias
(f pl)
Fr heures supplémentaires
It lavoro straordinario *(m)*
Pt horas extraordinárias *(f pl)*

Übertrag *(m) n* De
En balance brougth down
Am balance carried forward
Es balance a cuenta nueva
(m)
Fr solde à reporter *(m)*
It bilancio riportato *(m)*
Pt saldo transportado *(m)*

Überträger (von Vermögen)
(m) n De
En assignor
Es cesionista *(m)*
Fr cédant *(m)*
It cedente *(m)*
Pt cessionista *(m)*

Übertragung *(f) n* De
En assignment; conveyance
of property
Es cesión; traspaso de propiedad *(f m)*
Fr cession; transmission de
biens *(f)*
It cessione; trasferimento di
beni *(f m)*
Pt consignação; trespasse de
propriedade *(f m)*

Übertragungsvertrag *(m) n*
De
En transfer deed
Es escritura de transferencia
(f)

Fr acte de cession *(m)*
It atto di trapasso *(m)*
Pt título de transferência *(m)*

überweisen *vb* De
En transfer
Es transferir
Fr transférer
It trasferire
Pt transferir

Überweisung *(f) n* De
En transfer
Es cesión *(f)*
Fr transfert; cession *(m f)*
It cessione *(f)*
Pt trespasse *(m)*

überziehen *vb* De
En overdraw
Es girar en descubierto
Fr mettre à découvert
It trarre allo scoperto
Pt levantar a descoberto

Überziehung *(f) n* De
En overdraft
Es sobregiro; saldo deudor
(m)
Fr découvert; solde débiteur
(m)
It scoperto *(m)*
Pt conta a descoberto *(f)*

Überziehungsdisposition
(f) n De
En overdraft facilities
Am overdraw facility
Es facilidades de descubierto
(f pl)
Fr facilités de caisse *(f pl)*
It facilitazione di scoperto *(f)*
Pt disponibilidades de crédi-
to sem cobertura *(f pl)*

übliche Abnützung *(f)* De
En fair wear and tear
Es uso y desgaste razonable
(m)
Fr usure normale *(f)*
It usura normale *(f)*
Pt uso e desgaste razoável
(m)

ufficiale *adj* It
De amtlich
En official
Es oficial
Fr officiel
Pt oficial

ufficio *(m) n* It
De Büro *(n)*
En office
Es oficina *(f)*
Fr bureau *(m)*
Pt escritório *(m)*

ufficio centrale d'acquisti
(m) It
De Einkaufszentrale *(f)*
En central buying office
Es oficina central de compras
(f)
Fr centrale d'achats *(f)*
Pt escritório central de com-
pras *(m)*

ufficio contabilità *(m)* It
De Buchhaltung *(f)*
En accounts department
Am accounting department
Es departamento de contabi-
lidad *(m)*
Fr service de la comptabilité
(m)
Pt departamento de contabi-
lidade *(m)*

ufficio di collocamento *(m)* It
De Arbeitsnachweisstelle *(f)*
En employment exchange
Am state employment agency
Es bolsa de trabajo *(f)*
Fr bureau de placement *(m)*
Pt centro de serviços de em-
prego *(m)*

ufficio postale *(m)* It
De Postamt *(m)*
En post office
Es oficina de correos *(f)*
Fr bureau de poste *(m)*
Pt estação de correios *(f)*

ufficio senza divisioni *(m)* It
De Großraumbüro *(n)*
En open-plan office
Es oficina sin particiones *(f)*
Fr bureau sans cloisons *(m)*
Pt escritório sem divisões *(m)*

ufficio vendite *(m)* It
De Verkaufsabteilung *(f)*
En sales department
Es departamento de ventas
(m)
Fr service ventes *(m)*
Pt departamento de vendas
(m)

ulteriori informazioni *(f pl)* It
De weitere Auskunft *(f)*
En further information
Es más detalles *(m pl)*
Fr renseignements complé-
   mentaires *(m pl)*
Pt informação adicional *(f)*

ulteriori motivi *(m pl)* It
De weitere Gründe *(m)*
En further reasons
Es rasones adicionales *(f pl)*
Fr raisons supplémentaires
   (f pl)
Pt razões adicionais *(f pl)*

ulteriori particolari *(m pl)* It
De nähere Umstände *(m pl)*
En further particulars
Es más detalles *(m pl)*
Fr plus amples renseigne-
   ments *(m pl)*
Pt pormenores adicionais
   (m pl)

ultima data *(f)* It
De Schlußtermin *(m)*
En closing date
Es último día *(m)*
Fr dernier jour *(m)*
Pt último dia *(m)*

**última entrada primera
   salida** Es
De LIFO
En last in, first out (LIFO)
Fr LIFO
It ultimo a entrare, primo a
   uscire
Pt último a entrar, primeiro a
   saír

última prestação *(f)* Pt
De letzte Rate *(f)*
En final instalment
Es último plazo *(m)*
Fr dernier versement *(m)*
It ultima rata *(f)*

ultima rata *(f)* It
De letzte Rate *(f)*
En final instalment
Es último plazo *(m)*
Fr dernier versement *(m)*
Pt última prestação *(f)*

**último a entrar, primeiro a
   saír** Pt
De LIFO
En last in, first out (LIFO)
Es última entrada, primera sa-
   lida
Fr LIFO
It ultimo a entrare; primo a
   uscire

**última a entrare, primo a
   uscire** It
De LIFO
En last in, first out (LIFO)
Es última entrada, primera sa-
   lida
Fr LIFO
Pt último a entrar, primeiro a
   saír

último día *(m)* Es
De Schlußtermin *(m)*
En closing date
Fr dernier jour *(m)*
It ultima data *(f)*
Pt último dia *(m)*

último dia *(m)* Pt
De Schlußtermin *(m)*
En closing date
Es último día *(m)*
Fr dernier jour *(m)*
It ultima data *(f)*

último plazo *(m)* Es
De letzte Rate *(f)*
En final instalment
Fr dernier versement *(m)*
It ultima rata *(f)*
Pt última prestação *(f)*

último preco *(m)* Pt
De Schlußnotierung *(f)*
En closing price
Es precio de cierre *(m)*
Fr cours de clôture *(m)*
It prezzo di chiusura *(m)*

Umbau *(m)* n De
En alterations
Es reformas *(f pl)*
Fr travaux de transformation
   (m pl)
It modifiche *(f pl)*
Pt modificações *(f pl)*

umfassend *adj* De
En comprehensive
Es completo
Fr exhaustif; complet
It comprensivo
Pt compreensivo

Umladung *(f)* n De
En transhipment
Es transbordo *(m)*
Fr transbordement *(m)*
It trasbordo *(m)*
Pt transbordo *(m)*

Umlaufkapital *(n)* n De
En revolving fund
Es fondo circulante *(m)*
Fr fonds renouvelable *(m)*
It fondo rotativo *(m)*
Pt fundos renováveis *(m pl)*

Umlaufvermögen *(n)* n De
En current assets
Es activo realizable *(m)*
Fr actif courant *(m)*
It attivo liquido *(m)*
Pt bens no activo actual *(m
   pl)*

umpire n En
De Schiedsobmann *(m)*
Es juez árbitro *(m)*
Fr surarbitre *(m)*
It terzo arbitro *(m)*
Pt juiz árbitro *(m)*

Umrechnungskoeffizient
   (m) n De
En conversion factor
Es factor de conversión *(m)*
Fr facteur de conversion *(m)*
It fattore di conversione *(m)*
Pt factor de conversão *(m)*

Umrechnungskurs *(m)* n De
En rate of exchange
Es tipo de cambio *(m)*
Fr cours de change *(m)*
It corso del cambio *(m)*
Pt taxa de câmbio *(f)*

Umsatz *(m)* n De
En turnover
Es volumen de ventas *(m)*
Fr chiffre d'affaires *(m)*
It giro d'affari *(m)*
Pt movimento de dinheiro *(m)*

Umschlag (m) n De
En envelope
Es sobre (m)
Fr enveloppe (f)
It busta (f)
Pt envelope (m)

Umschlagspesen (f) n De
En handling charges
Es gastos de manutención
(m pl)
Fr frais de manutention (m pl)
It spese di gestione (f pl)
Pt custos de manejo (f pl)

Umstand (m) n De
En factor
Es factor (m)
Fr facteur (m)
It fattore (m)
Pt factor (m)

unanerkannter Streik (m) De
En unofficial strike
Es huelga no-oficial (f)
Fr grève non reconnue (f)
It sciopero non ufficiale (m)
Pt greve não oficializada (f)

unaufdringliches Verkaufen
(n) De
En soft sell
Es venta sencilla (f)
Fr vente par des moyens
discrets (f)
It vendere senza forzare
Pt venda subtil (f)

unauthorized adj En
De unbefugt
Es inautorizado
Fr non autorisé
It non autorizzato
Pt não autorizado

unbefristete Obligation (f) De
En undated bond
Es obligación sin fecha de
vencimiento (f)
Fr obligation sans date
d'échéance (f)
It obbligazione senza data di
scadenza (f)
Pt obrigação sem data de
vencimento (f)

unbefugt adj De
En unauthorized
Es inautorizado

Fr non autorisé
It non autorizzato
Pt não autorizado

unbewegliches Vermögen
(n) De
En real estate
Es bienes inmuebles (m pl)
Fr biens immeubles (m pl)
It beni immobili (m pl)
Pt propriedade imobiliária (f)

uncalled capital En
De nicht eingerufenes Kapital
(n)
Es capital de reserva (m)
Fr capital non appelé (m)
It capitale non richiamato
(m)
Pt capital irrealizado (m)

undated bond En
De unbefristete Obligation (f)
Es obligación sin fecha de
vencimiento (f)
Fr obligation sans date
d'échéance (f)
It obbligazione senza data di
scadenza (f)
Pt obrigação sem data de
vencimento (f)

undated debenture En
De Schuldverschreibung
ohne Fälligkeitsdatum (f)
Es obligación sin fecha (f)
Fr obligation perpétuelle (f)
It obbligazione perpetua (f)
Pt obrigação sem data (f)

under-estimate n En
De Unterschätzung (f)
Es presupuesto por defecto
(m)
Fr sous-estimation (f)
It sottovalutazione (f)
Pt avaliação insuficiente (f)

underdeveloped countries
En
De unterentwickelte Länder
(n pl)
Es países en desarrollo (m pl)
Fr pays sous-développés
(m pl)
It paesi sottosviluppati (m pl)
Pt países subdesenvolvidos
(m pl)

under separate cover En
De mit getrennter Post
Es por correo aparte
Fr sous pli séparé
It in piego a parte
Pt por correio separado

undersubscribed issue n En
De nicht in voller Höhe ge-
zeichnete Emission (f)
Es emisión no totalmente
subscrita (f)
Fr émission non couverte (f)
It emissione non interamen-
te sottoscritta (f)
Pt emissão não subscrita na to-
talidade (f)

underwriter n En
De Versicherer (m)
Es asegurador (m)
Fr assureur (m)
It assicuratore (m)
Pt segurador (m)

underwriting syndicate
(insurance) En
De Versicherungssyndikat (n)
Es sindicato de seguros (m)
Fr syndicat d'assureurs (m)
It sindacato di assicuratori
(m)
Pt consórcio de seguradores
(m)

underwriting syndicate
(new issues) En
De Emissionssyndikat (n)
Es grupo de suscriptores (m)
Fr syndicat de garantie (m)
It consorzio finanziario (m)
Pt consórcio de subscritores
(m)

undischarged bankrupt En
De noch nicht entlasteter
Gemeinschuldner (m)
Es fallido no rehabilitado (m)
Fr failli non réhabilité (m)
It fallito non riabilitato (m)
Pt falido insolvente (m)

undisclosed principal En
De nicht bekanntgegebener
Auftraggeber (m)
Es mandante no nombrado
(m)

Fr   mandant non divulgé *(m)*
It   mandante non nominato
    (m)
Pt   mandante não divulgado
    (m)

undistributed profits En
De   unverteilte Gewinne *(n pl)*
Es   beneficios no distribuidos
    (m pl)
Fr   bénéfices non répartis
    (m pl)
It   profitti non distribuite
    (m pl)
Pt   lucros não distribuidos
    (m pl)

unearned income En
De   Kapitaleinkommen *(n)*
Es   rentas *(f pl)*
Fr   rente *(f)*
It   reddito di capitale *(m)*
Pt   rendimento do capital *(m)*

unedles Metall *(n)* De
En   base metal
Es   metal no noble *(m)*
Fr   métal vil *(m)*
It   basso metallo *(m)*
Pt   metal pobre *(m)*

unehrlich *adj* De
En   dishonest
Es   deshonesto
Fr   malhonnête
It   disonesto
Pt   desonesto

uneinbringliche Schuld *(f)* De
En   bad debt
Es   deuda incobrable *(f)*
Fr   créance irrécouvrable *(f)*
It   credito inesigibile *(m)*
Pt   dívida incobrável *(f)*

uneinlösbare Schuldver-
    schreibung *(f)* De
De   irredeemable debenture
Es   obligación no amortizable
    (f)
Fr   obligation irremboursable
    (f)
It   obbligazione irredimibile *(f)*
Pt   obrigação não amortizável *(f)*

unemployment *n* En
De   Arbeitslosigkeit *(f)*
Es   desempleo *(m)*
Fr   chômage *(m)*
It   disoccupazione *(f)*
Pt   desemprego *(m)*

unemployment benefit En
De   Arbeitslosenunterstützung
    (f)
Es   subsidio de paro *(m)*
Fr   secours de chômage *(m)*
It   indennità di disoccupa-
    zione *(f)*
Pt   subsídio de desemprego
    (m)

Unerfahrenheit *(f)* *n* De
En   inexperience
Es   falta de experiencia *(f)*
Fr   manque de pratique *(m)*
It   inesperienza *(f)*
Pt   inexperiência *(f)*

unerlaubte Abwesenheit *(f)*
    De
En   absenteeism
Es   ausentismo *(m)*
Fr   absentéisme *(m)*
It   assenteismo *(m)*
Pt   absentismo *(m)*

unerlaubte Handlung *(f)* De
En   tort
Es   agravio *(m)*
Fr   acte défendu *(m)*
It   torto *(m)*
Pt   agravo *(m)*

unersetzlich (Verlust usw.) *adj*
    De
En   irrecoverable
Es   irrecuperable
Fr   irrécouvrable
It   irrecuperabile
Pt   irrecuperável

Unfähigkeit *(f)* *n* De
En   inability; inefficiency
Es   incapacidad; incompeten-
    cia *(f)*
Fr   incapacité; inefficacité *(f)*
It   incapacità; inefficienza *(f)*
Pt   incapacidade; ineficiência
    (f)

unfair trade practice En
De   unlautere Handelspraktik
    (f)
Es   práctica comercial desleal
    (f)
Fr   pratique de commerce
    déloyale *(f)*
It   pratica commerciale sleale
    (f)
Pt   prática comercial impró-
    pria *(f)*

ungebildet *adj* De
En   uneducated; illiterate
Es   ignorante; analfabeto
Fr   ignorant; illettré
It   incolto; analfabeta
Pt   inculto; analfabeto

ungedecktes Geld *(n)* De
En   fiduciary issue
Es   emisión fiduciaria *(f)*
Fr   émission fiduciaire *(f)*
It   emissione fiduciaria *(f)*
Pt   emissão fiduciária *(f)*

ungenutzte Ladefähigkeit *(f)*
    De
En   idle capacity
Es   potencial no utilizado *(m)*
Fr   potentiel non utilisé *(m)*
It   potenziale non utilizzato
    (m)
Pt   potencial não utilizado *(m)*

ungesetzlich *adj* De
En   illegal
Es   ilegal
Fr   illégal
It   illegale
Pt   ilegal

ungesicherte Schuldver-
    schreibung *(f)* De
En   unsecured debenture
Am   naked bond
Es   obligación no garantizada
    (f)
Fr   obligation sans garantie *(f)*
It   obbligazione non garantita
    (f)
Pt   obrigação sem garantia *(f)*

ungültig *adj* De
En   invalid
Es   inválido
Fr   invalide
It   invalido
Pt   inválido

união aduaneira *(f)* Pt
De   Zollunion *(f)*
En   customs union
Es   unión aduanera *(f)*
Fr   union douanière *(f)*
It   unione doganale *(f)*

unidad de visualización *(f)* Es
De   Bildschirmeinheit *(f)*
En   visual-display unit (vdu)
Fr   unité de visualisation *(f)*

It unità di visualizzazione *(f)*
Pt móvel-montra de exposição de visuais *(f)*

unión aduanera *(f)* Es
De Zollunion *(f)*
En customs union
Fr union douanière *(f)*
It unione doganale *(f)*
Pt união aduaneira *(f)*

union douanière *(f)* Fr
De Zollunion *(f)*
En customs union
Es unión aduanera *(f)*
It unione doganale *(f)*
Pt união aduaneira *(f)*

unione commerciale *(f)* It
De Handelsblock *(m)*
En trade bloc
Es bloque comercial *(m)*
Fr bloc commercial *(m)*
Pt bloque comercial *(m)*

unione doganale *(f)* It
De Zollunion *(f)*
En customs union
Es unión aduanera *(f)*
Fr union douanière *(f)*
Pt união aduaneira *(f)*

unissued capital De
De nicht ausgegebenes Kapital *(n)*
Es capital no emitido *(m)*
Fr capitaux pas encore émis *(m pl)*
It capitale non emesso *(m)*
Pt capital não emitido *(m)*

unità di visualizzazione *(f)* It
De Bildschirmeinheit *(f)*
En visual-display unit (vdu)
Es unidad de visualización *(f)*
Fr unité de visualisation *(f)*
Pt móvel-montra de exposição de visuais *(f)*

unit cost En
De Einheitskosten *(pl)*
Es coste por unidad *(m)*
Fr coût de l'unité *(m)*
It costo unitario *(m)*
Pt custo por unidade *(m)*

unité de visualisation *(f)* Fr
De Bildschirmeinheit *(f)*
En visual-display unit (vdu)

Es unidad de visualización *(f)*
It unità di visualizzazione *(f)*
Pt móvel-montra de exposição de visuais *(f)*

unlautere Handelspraktik *(f)*
De
En unfair trade practice
Es práctica comercial desleal *(f)*
Fr pratique de commerce déloyale *(f)*
It pratica commerciale sleale *(f)*
Pt prática comercial imprópria *(f)*

unleserlich *adj* De
En illegible
Es ilegible
Fr illisible
It illeggibile
Pt ilegível

unmäßig *adj* De
En exorbitant
Es exorbitante
Fr exorbitant
It esorbitante
Pt exorbitante

unmöglich *adj* De
En impossible
Es imposible
Fr impossible
It impossibile
Pt impossível

unofficial strike En
De unanerkannter Streik *(m)*
Es huelga no-oficial *(f)*
Fr grève non reconnue *(f)*
It sciopero non ufficiale *(m)*
Pt greve não oficializada *(f)*

unparteiisch *adj* De
En impartial
Es imparcial
Fr impartial
It imparziale
Pt imparcial

unproductive *adj* En
De unproduktiv
Es improductivo
Fr improductif
It improduttivo
Pt improdutivo

unproduktiv *adj* De
En unproductive
Es improductivo
Fr improductif
It improduttivo
Pt improdutivo

unproduktive Zeit *(f)* De
En idle time
Es tiempo libre *(m)*
Fr temps improductif *(m)*
It tempo passivo *(m)*
Pt tempo improdutivo *(m)*

unprofitable *adj* En
De unvorteilhaft
Es nada lucrativo
Fr sans profit
It poco proficuo
Pt não lucrativo

unquoted securities En
De nicht notierte Werte *(m pl)*
Es títulos no cotizados *(m pl)*
Fr valeurs non cotées *(f pl)*
It titoli non quotati *(m pl)*
Pt títulos não cotados *(m pl)*

unsecured creditor En
De nicht gesicherter Gläubiger *(m)*
Es acreedor no garantizado *(m)*
Fr créancier chirographaire *(m)*
It creditore non garantito *(m)*
Pt credor sem garantia *(m)*

unsecured debenture En
Am naked bond
De ungesicherte Schuldverschreibung *(f)*
Es obligación no garantizada *(f)*
Fr obligation sans garantie *(f)*
It obbligazione non garantita *(f)*
Pt obrigação sem garantia *(f)*

unsichtbare Exporte *(m pl)*
De
En invisible exports
Es exportations invisibles *(f pl)*
Fr exportaciones invisibles *(f pl)*
It exportazioni invisibili *(f pl)*
Pt exportações invisíeis *(f pl)*

Unterdirektor *(m)* De
En assistant manager
Es sub-director *(m)*
Fr sous-directeur *(m)*
It vice-direttore *(m)*
Pt subdirector *(m)*

unterentwickelte Länder
(n pl) De
En underdeveloped countries
Es países en desarrollo *(m pl)*
Fr pays sous-développés
(m pl)
It paesi sottosviluppati *(m pl)*
Pt países subdesenvolvidos
(m pl)

Untergebene(r) *(m) n* De
En subordinate
Es subalterno *(m)*
Fr subalterne *(m)*
It subalterno *(m)*
Pt subordinado *(m)*

Unternehmen *(n) n* De
En enterprise
Es negocio *(m)*
Fr entreprise *(f)*
It impresa *(f)*
Pt empresa *(f)*

Unternehmensforschung
(f) n De
En operational research (OR)
Es investigación operacional
(f)
Fr recherche opérationnelle
(f)
It indagine sul funzionamen-
to *(f)*
Pt investigação operacional *(f)*

Unternehmer *(m) n* De
En contractor; entrepreneur
Es contratista; empresario
(m)
Fr entrepreneur *(m)*
It impresario; intraprenditore
(m)
Pt contratador; empresário
(m)

Unternehmerverband *(m) n*
De
En trade association
Es asociación comercial *(f)*
Fr association profession-
nelle *(f)*

It associazione commerciale
(f)
Pt associação comercial *(f)*

Unterschätzung *(f) n* De
En under-estimate
Es presupuesto por defecto
(m)
Fr sous-estimation *(f)*
It sottovalutazione *(f)*
Pt avaliação insuficiente *(f)*

Unterschied *(m) n* De
En difference
Es diferencia *(f)*
Fr différence *(f)*
It differenza *(f)*
Pt diferença *(f)*

unterschiedlich (Behandlung
usw.) *adj* De
En discriminatory
Es discriminatorio
Fr discriminatoire
It discriminatorio
Pt discriminatório

unterschlagen *vb* De
En embezzle
Es defalcar
Fr détourner
It appropriarsi indebitamen-
te
Pt desfalcar

Unterschlagung *(f) n* De
En embezzlement
Es defalco *(m)*
Fr détournement de fonds
(m)
It appropriazione indebita *(f)*
Pt desfalque *(m)*

Unterschrift *(f) n* De
En signature
Es firma *(f)*
Fr signature *(f)*
It firma *(f)*
Pt assinatura *(f)*

Unterstützung (geldlich) *(f) n*
De
En grant; subsidy
Es subvención *(f)*
Fr subvention *(f)*
It sovvenzione *(f)*
Pt subvenção *(f)*

untersuchen *vb* De
En examine
Es examinar
Fr examiner
It esaminare
Pt examinar

Untersuchung *(f) n* De
En investigation; legal inquiry
Es investigación; encuesta *(f)*
Fr investigation; enquête *(f)*
It inchiesta; investigazione
(f)
Pt investigação; inquérito *(f m)*

Untervermietung *(f) n* De
En sub-letting
Es sub-alquiler *(m)*
Fr sous-location *(m)*
It subaffitto *(m)*
Pt subaluguer *(m)*

Untervertreter *(m) n* De
En sub-agent
Es sub-agente *(m)*
Fr sous-agent *(m)*
It sub-agente *(m)*
Pt subagente *(m)*

unter Zollverschluß De
En in bond
Es en aduanas
Fr en entrepôt
It sotto vincolo doganale
Pt à ordem da alfândega

unumschränkte Treuhand *(f)*
De
En discretionary trust
Es fideicomiso discrecional
(m)
Fr fidéicommis à apprécia-
tion *(m)*
It fondo fiduciario discrezio-
nale *(m)*
Pt fundação discricionária *(f)*

unverteilte Gewinne *(n pl)* De
En undistributed profits
Es beneficios no distribuidos
(m pl)
Fr bénéfices non répartis
(m pl)
It profitti non distribuiti *(m pl)*
Pt lucros não distribuidos
(m pl)

unvollständig *adj* De
En incomplete
Es incompleto
Fr incomplet
It incompleto
Pt incompleto

unvorteilhaft *adj* De
En unprofitable
Es nada lucrativo
Fr sans profit
It poco proficuo
Pt não lucrativo

unwiderruflicher Kredit-brief *(m)* De
En irrevocable letter of credit
Es carta de crédito irrevocable *(f)*
Fr lettre de crédit irrévocable *(f)*
It lettera di credito irrevocabile *(f)*
Pt carta de crédito irrevogável *(f)*

uomo d' affari *(m)* It
De Geschäftsmann *(m)*
En businessman
Es hombre de negocios *(m)*
Fr homme d'affaires *(m)*
Pt homem de negócios *(m)*

Urheberrecht *(n)* n De
En copyright
Es derechos de autor *(m pl)*
Fr droit d'auteur *(m)*
It diritto d'autore *(m)*
Pt direitos de autor *(m pl)*

Urheberrechtsverletzung *(f)* n De
En infringement of copyright
Es infracción de los derechos de autor *(f)*
Fr contrefaçon líttéraire *(f)*
It infrazione dei diritti d'autore *(f)*
Pt infracção de direitos de autor *(f)*

Urkunde *(f)* n De
En deed; document
Es título; documento *(m)*
Fr titre; document *(m)*
It atto; documento *(m)*
Pt título; documento *(m)*

Urkundenbeweis *(m)* n De
En documentary evidence
Es prueba documental *(f)*
Fr preuve écrite *(f)*
It prova scritta *(f)*
Pt prova documental *(f)*

Ursprung *(m)* n De
En origin
Es origen *(m)*
Fr origine *(f)*
It origine *(f)*
Pt origem *(f)*

Ursprungszeugnis *(n)* n De
En certificate of origin
Es certificado de origen *(m)*
Fr certificat d'origine *(m)*
It certificato d'origine *(m)*
Pt certificado de origem *(m)*

Urteil *(n)* n De
En judgment
Es juicio; adjudicación *(m pl)*
Fr jugement; arrêt *(m)*
It giudizio *(m)*
Pt julgamento *(m)*

urteilen *vb* De
En judge
Es juzgar
Fr juger
It giudicare
Pt julgar

usage commercial *(m)* Fr
De Handelsgebrauch *(m)*
En custom of the trade
Es uso comercial *(m)*
It uso commerciale *(m)*
Pt uso comercial *(m)*

usança *(f)* n Pt
De Usance *(f)*
En usance
Es usanza *(f)*
Fr usance *(f)*
It usanza *(f)*

usance n En, Fr *(f)*
De Usance *(f)*
Es usanza *(f)*
It usanza *(f)*
Pt usança *(f)*

Usance *(f)* n De
En usance
Es usanza *(f)*

Fr usance *(f)*
It usanza *(f)*
Pt usança *(f)*

usanza *(f)* n Es, It
De Usance *(f)*
En usance
Fr usance *(f)*
Pt usança *(f)*

uso comercial *(m)* Es,Pt
De Handelsgebrauch *(m)*
En custom of the trade
Fr usage commercial *(m)*
It uso commerciale *(m)*

uso commerciale *(m)* It
De Handelsgebrauch *(m)*
En custom of the trade
Es uso comercial *(m)*
Fr usage commercial *(m)*
Pt uso comercial *(m)*

uso e desgaste razoável *(m)* Pt
De übliche Abnützung *(f)*
En fair wear and tear
Es uso y desgaste razonable *(m)*
Fr usure normale *(f)*
It usura normale *(f)*

uso y desgaste razonable *(m)* Es
De übliche Abnützung *(f)*
En fair wear and tear
Fr usure normale *(f)*
It usura normale *(f)*
Pt uso e desgaste razoável *(m)*

usufruct n En
De Nießbrauchsrecht *(n)*
Es usufructo *m)*
Fr usufruit *(m)*
It usufrutto *(m)*
Pt usufruto *(m)*

usufructo *(m)* n Es
De Nießbrauchsrecht *(n)*
En usufruct; beneficial interest
Fr usufruit *(m)*
It usufrutto *(m)*
Pt usufruto *(m)*

usufructo vitalicio *(m)* Es
De lebenslängliche
    Nutznießung *(f)*
En life-interest
Fr usufruit viager *(m)*
It usufrutto vitalizio *(m)*
Pt usufruto vitalício *(m)*

usufructuario *(m) n* Es
De Nießbrauchnutzer *(m)*
En beneficial owner
Fr usufruitier *(m)*
It usufruttuario *(m)*
Pt usufrutuário *(m)*

usufruit *(m) n* Fr
De Nießbrauchsrecht *(n)*
En usufruct, beneficial
    interest
Es usufructo *(m)*
It usufrutto *(m)*
Pt usufruto *(m)*

usufruitier *(m) n* Fr
De Nießbrauchnutzer *(m)*
En beneficial owner
Es usufructuario *(m)*
It usufruttuario *(m)*
Pt usufrutuário *(m)*

usufruit viager *(m)* Fr
De lebenslängliche
    Nutznießung *(f)*
En life-interest
Es usufructo vitalicio *(m)*
It usufrutto vitalizio *(m)*
Pt usufruto vitalício *(m)*

usufruto *(m) n* Pt
De Nießbrauchsrecht *(n)*
En usufruct; beneficial
    interest
Es usufructo *(m)*
Fr usufruit *(m)*
It usufrutto *(m)*

usufruto vitalício *(m)* Pt
De lebenslängliche
    Nutznießung *(f)*
En life-interest
Es usufructo vitalicio *(m)*
Fr usufruit viager *(m)*
It usufrutto vitalizio *(m)*

usufrutto *(m) n* It
De Nießbrauchsrecht *(n)*
En usufruct; beneficial
    interest
Es usufructo *(m)*
Fr usufruit *(m)*
Pt usufruto *(m)*

usufrutto vitalizio *(m) n* It
De lebenslängliche
    Nutznießung *(f)*
En life-interest
Es usufructo vitalicio *(m)*
Fr usufruit viager *(m)*
Pt usufruto vitalício *(m)*

usufruttuario *(m) n* It
De Nießbrauchsnutzer *(m)*
En beneficial owner
Es usufructuario *(m)*
Fr usufruitier *(m)*
Pt usufrutuário *(m)*

usufrutuário *(m) n* Pt
De Nießbrauchsnutzer *(m)*
En beneficial owner
Es usufructuario *(m)*
Fr usufruitier *(m)*
It usufruttuario *(m)*

usura *(f) n* Es, It, Pt
De Wucher *(m)*
En usury
Fr usure *(f)*

usuraio *(m) n* It
De Geldverleiher *(m)*
En moneylender *(m)*
Es prestamista *(m)*
Fr prêteur d'argent *(m)*
Pt prestamista *(m)*

usura normale *(f)* It
De übliche Abnützung *(f)*
En fair wear and tear
Es uso y desgaste razonable
    (m)
Fr usure normale *(f)*
Pt uso e desgaste razoável
    (m)

usure *(f) n* Fr
De Wucher *(m)*
En usury
Es usura *(f)*
It usura *(f)*
Pt usura *(f)*

usure normale *(f)* Fr
De übliche Abnützung *(f)*
En fair wear and tear
Es uso y desgaste razonable
    (m)
It usura normale *(f)*
Pt uso e desgaste razoável
    (m)

usury *n* En
De Wucher *(m)*
Es usura *(f)*
Fr usure *(f)*
It usura *(f)*
Pt usura *(f)*

utile *(m) n* It
De Gewinn *(m)*
En profit
Es ganancia; beneficio *(f m)*
Fr bénéfice; profit *(m)*
Pt lucro; benefício *(m)*

utile lordo *(m)* It
De Bruttogewinn *(m)*
En gross profit
Es ganancia bruta *(f)*
Fr bénéfice brut *(m)*
Pt lucro bruto *(m)*

utile netto *(m)* It
De Reingewinn *(m)*
En net profit
Es ganancia net *(m)*
Fr bénéfice net *(m)*
Pt lucro líquido *(m)*

utile sulla carta *(m)* It
De imaginärer Gewinn *(m)*
En paper profit
Es ganancia por realizar *(f)*
Fr profit fictif *(m)*
Pt lucros no papel *(m pl)*

utility company En
De gemeinnütziges Unter-
    nehmen *(n)*
Es empresa de servicios
    públicos *(f)*
Fr entreprise d'utilité publi-
    que *(f)*
It società di servizi pubblici
    (f)
Pt empresa de utilidade
    pública *(f)*

V

vacación *(f)* n Es
De Ferien; Urlaub *(f pl; m)*
En vacation; holiday
Fr vacances *(f pl)*
It vacanza *(f)*
Pt férias *(f pl)*

vacaciones de verano *(f pl)*
Es
De Sommerferien *(f pl)*
En summer holidays
Fr vacances d'été *(f pl)*
It vacanze estive *(f pl)*
Pt férias de verão *(f pl)*

vacaciones retribuidas *(f pl)*
Es
De bezahlter Urlaub *(m)*
En holidays with pay
Fr congés payés *(m pl)*
It vacanze retribuite *(f pl)*
Pt férias pagas *(f pl)*

vacances *(f pl)* n Fr
De Ferien; Urlaub *(f pl; m)*
En vacation; holiday
Es vacación *(f)*
It vacanza *(f)*
Pt férias *(f pl)*

vacances d'été *(f pl)* Fr
De Sommerferien *(f pl)*
En summer-holidays
Es vacaciones de verano;
   veraneo *(f pl; m)*
It vacanze estive *(f pl)*
Pt férias de verão *(f pl)*

vacanza *(f)* n It
De Ferien; Urlaub *(f pl; m)*
En vacation; holiday
Es vacación *(f)*
Fr vacances *(f pl)*
Pt férias *(f pl)*

vacanze estive *(f pl)* It
De Sommerferien *(f pl)*
En summer holidays
Es vacaciones de verano;
   veraneo *(f pl; m)*
Fr vacances d'été *(f pl)*
Pt férias de verão *(f pl)*

vacanze retribuite *(f pl)* It
De bezahlter Urlaub *(m)*
En holidays with pay

Es vacaciones retribuidas
   (f pl)
Fr congés payés *(m pl)*
Pt férias pagas *(f pl)*

vacation n En
De Ferien; Urlaub *(f pl; m)*
Es vacación *(f)*
Fr vacances *(f pl)*
It vacanza *(f)*
Pt férias *(f pl)*

vacío comercial *(m)* Es
De Außenhandelsdefizit *(n)*
En trade gap
Fr déficit du commerce exté-
   rieur *(m)*
It disavanzo della bilancia
   commerciale *(m)*
Pt vazio comercial *(m)*

vagão de caminhos de ferro
   (m) Pt
De Eisenbahnwagen *(m)*
En railway carriage
Am railroad car
Es vagón de ferrocarril *(m)*
Fr wagon de chemin de fer
   (m)
It carrozza ferroviaria *(f)*

vaglia postale *(f)* It
De Postanweisung *(f)*
En postal order
Es giro postal *(m)*
Fr mandat-poste *(m)*
Pt vale postal *(m)*

vagón de ferrocarril *(m)* Es
De Eisenbahnwagen *(m)*
En railway carriage
Am railroad car
Fr wagon de chemin de fer
   (m)
It carrozza ferroviaria *(f)*
Pt vagão de caminhos de ferro
   (m)

valable *adj* Fr
De gültig; gut (für)
En valid; good (for)
Es válido
It valido
Pt válido

vale *(m)* n Pt
De Belegstück; Schuldschein
   (n m)
En voucher; I. O. U.

Es pieza justificativa; pagaré
   (f m)
Fr pièce justificative; fiche *(f)*
It pezza d'appoggio;
   pagherò *(m f)*

vale postal *(m)* Pt
De Postanweisung *(f)*
En postal order
Es giro postal *(m)*
Fr mandat-poste *(m)*
It vaglia postale *(f)*

valeur *(f)* n Fr
De Wert *(m)*
En value
Es valor *(m)*
It valore *(m)*
Pt valor *(m)*

valeur ajoutée *(f)* Fr
De Mehrwert *(f)*
En added value
Es valor agregado *(m)*
It valore aggiunto *(m)*
Pt valor adicionado *(m)*

valeur à revenu fixe *(f)* Fr
De festverzinslíches Wertpa-
   pier *(n)*
En fixed-interest security
Es obligación a interés fijo *(f)*
It titolo a interesse fisso *(m)*
Pt obrigação de juro fixo *(f)*

valeur au porteur *(f)* Fr
De Inhabereffekten *(n pl)*
En bearer security
Es valor al portador *(m)*
It valore al portatore *(f)*
Pt título ao portador *(m)*

valeur capitalisée *(f)* Fr
De kapitalisierter Wert *(m)*
En capitalized value
Es valor capitalizado *(m)*
It valore capitalizzato *(m)*
Pt valor capitalizado *(m)*

valeur comptable *(f)* Fr
De Buchwert *(m)*
En book value
Es valor contable *(m)*
It valore d'inventario *(m)*
Pt valor contabilizado *(m)*

valeur déclarée *(f)* Fr
De angegebener Zollwert *(m)*
En declared value
Es valor declarado *(m)*
It valore dichiarato *(m)*
Pt valor declarado *(m)*

valeur de l'actif *(f)* Fr
De Aktivwert *(m)*
En asset value
Es valor en activo *(m)*
It valore in attivo *(m)*
Pt valor do activo *(m)*

valeur de rachat *(f)* Fr
De Rückkaufswert *(m)*
En surrender value
Es valor de rescate *(m)*
It valore di riscatto *(m)*
Pt valor de resgate *(m)*

valeur intrinsèque *(f)* Fr
De innerlicher Wert *(m)*
En intrinsic value
Es valor intrínseco *(m)*
It valore intrinseco *(m)*
Pt valor intrínseco *(m)*

valeur marchande *(f)* Fr
De Marktwert *(m)*
En market value
Es valor de mercado *(m)*
It valore di mercato *(m)*
Pt valor de mercado *(m)*

valeur nominale *(f)* Fr
De Nennwert; Stückelung *(m f)*
En nominal value; face value; denomination
Es valor; valor nominal *(m)*
It valore nominale; taglio *(m)*
Pt valor nominal *(m)*

valeurs admises à la Bourse *(f pl)* Fr
De an der Börse notierte Wertpapiere *(n pl)*
En listed security
Es valores cotizables *(m pl)*
It titoli quotati (in borsa) *(m pl)*
Pt valor de Bolsa com cotação oficial *(m)*

valeurs aurifères *(f pl)* Fr
De Aktien von Goldbergwerken *(f pl)*
En gold shares

Es acciones auríferas *(f pl)*
It azioni aurifere *(f pl)*
Pt acções de ouro *(f pl)*

valeurs de tout repos *(f pl)* Fr
De mündelsichere Wertpapiere *(n pl)*
En gilt-edged securities
Es valores de toda confianza *(m pl)*
It titoli di assoluta fiducia *(m pl)*
Pt valores de toda confiança *(m pl)*

valeurs non cotées *(f pl)* Fr
De nicht notierte Werte *(m pl)*
En unquoted securities
Es títulos no cotizados *(m pl)*
It titoli non quotati *(m pl)*
Pt títulos não cotados *(m pl)*

valid *adj* En
De gültig
Es válido
Fr valable
It valido
Pt válido

validação testamentária *(f)* Pt
De Testamentseröffnung; Bestätigung *(f)*
En probate
Es validación de los testamentos *(f)*
Fr homologation d'un testament *(f)*
It omologazione di testamento *(f)*

validar por assinatura Pt
De gegenzeichnen
En countersign
Es refrendar
Fr contresigner
It controfirmare

valido *adj* It
De gültig; gut (für)
En valid; good (for)
Es válido
Fr valable
Pt válido

válido *adj* Es, Pt
De gültig; gut (für)
En valid; good (for)
Fr valable
It valido

valioso *adj* Es, Pt
De wertvoll
En valuable
Fr de valeur
It di valore

valor *(m)* n Es, Pt
De Wert; Aktivposten *(m)*
En value; asset
Fr valeur; actif *(f m)*
It valore; attivo *(m)*

valoracion del trabajo *(f)* Es
De Arbeitsbewertung *(f)*
En job evaluation
Fr évaluation du travail *(f)*
It valutazione del lavoro *(f)*
Pt avaliação de tarefa *(f)*

valor adicionado *(m)* Pt
De Mehrwert *(f)*
En added value
Es valor agregado *(m)*
Fr valeur ajoutée *(f)*
It valore aggiunto *(m)*

valor agregado *(m)* Es
De Mehrwert *(f)*
En added value
Fr valeur ajoutée *(f)*
It valore aggiunto *(m)*
Pt valor adicionado *(m)*

valor al portador *(m)* Es
De Inhabereffekten *(n pl)*
En bearer security
Fr valeur au porteur *(f)*
It valore al portatore *(f)*
Pt título ao portador *(m)*

valor capitalizado *(m)* Es, Pt
De kapitalisierter Wert *(m)*
En capitalized value
Fr valeur capitalisée *(f)*
It valore capitalizzato *(m)*

valor contabilizado *(m)* Pt
De Buchwert *(m)*
En book value
Es valor contable *(m)*
Fr valeur comptable *(f)*
It valore d'inventario *(m)*

valor contable *(m)* Es
De Buchwert *(m)*
En book value
Fr valeur comptable *(f)*
It valore d'inventario *(m)*
Pt valor contabilizado *(m)*

valor de Bolsa com cotação oficial *(m)* Pt
De an der Börse notierte Wertpapiere *(n pl)*
En listed security
Es valores cotizables *(m pl)*
Fr valeurs admises à la Bourse *(f pl)*
It titoli quotati (in borsa) *(m pl)*

valor declarado *(m)* Es, Pt
De angegebener Zollwert *(m)*
En declared value
Fr valeur déclarée *(f)*
It valore dichiarato *(m)*

valor de la clientela *(m)* Es
De Geschäftswert *(m)*
En goodwill
Fr bon vouloir *(m)*
It avviamento *(m)*
Pt boa vontade *(f)*

valor de mercado *(m)* Es, Pt
De Marktwert *(m)*
En market value
Fr valeur marchande *(f)*
It valore di mercato *(m)*

valor de rescate *(m)* Es
De Rückkaufswert *(m)*
En surrender value
Fr valeur de rachat *(f)*
It valore di riscatto *(m)*
Pt valor de resgate *(m)*

valor de resgate *(m)* Pt
De Rückkaufswert *(m)*
En surrender value
Es valor de rescate *(m)*
Fr valeur de rachat *(f)*
It valore di riscatto *(m)*

valor do activo *(m)* Pt
De Aktivwert *(m)*
En asset value
Es valor en activo *(m)*
Fr valeur de l'actif *(f)*
It valore in attivo *(m)*

valore *(m)* n It
De Wert *(m)*
En value
Es valor *(m)*
Fr valeur *(f)*
Pt valor *(m)*

valore aggiunto *(m)* It
De Mehrwert *(f)*
En added value
Es valor agregado *(m)*
Fr valeur ajoutée *(f)*
Pt valor adicionado *(m)*

valore al portatore *(f)* It
De Inhabereffekten *(n pl)*
En bearer security
Es valor al portador *(m)*
Fr valeur au porteur *(f)*
Pt título ao portador *(m)*

valore capitalizzato *(m)* It
De kapitalisierter Wert *(m)*
En capitalized value
Es valor capitalizado *(m)*
Fr valeur capitalisée *(f)*
Pt valor capitalizado *(m)*

valore dichiarato *(m)* It
De angegebener Zollwert *(m)*
En declared value
Es valor declarado *(m)*
Fr valeur déclarée *(f)*
Pt valor declarado *(m)*

valore d'inventario *(m)* It
De Buchwert *(m)*
En book value
Es valor contable *(m)*
Fr valeur comptable *(f)*
Pt valor contabilizado *(m)*

valore di mercato *(m)* It
De Marktwert *(m)*
En market value
Es valor de mercado *(m)*
Fr valeur marchande *(f)*
Pt valor de mercado *(m)*

valore di riscatto *(m)* It
De Rückkaufswert *(m)*
En surrender value
Es valor de rescate *(m)*
Fr valeur de rachat *(f)*
Pt valor de resgate *(m)*

valore in attivo *(m)* It
De Aktivwert *(m)*
En asset value
Es valor en activo *(m)*
Fr valeur de l'actif *(f)*
Pt valor do activo *(m)*

valore intrinseco *(m)* It
De innerlicher Wert *(m)*
En intrinsic value

Es valor intrínseco *(m)*
Fr valeur intrinsèque *(f)*
Pt valor intrínseco *(m)*

valor en activo *(m)* Es
De Aktivwert *(m)*
En asset value
Fr valeur de l'actif *(f)*
It valore in attivo *(m)*
Pt valor do activo *(m)*

valore nominale *(m)* It
De Nennwert *(m)*
En face value; nominal value
Es valor nominal *(m)*
Fr valeur nominale *(f)*
Pt valor nominal *(m)*

valores cotizables *(m pl)* Es
De an der Börse notierte Wertpapiere *(m pl)*
En listed security
Fr valeurs admises à la Bourse *(f pl)*
It titoli quotati (in borsa) *(m pl)*
Pt valor de Bolsa com cotação oficial *(m)*

valores de equilíbrio *(m pl)* Pt
De Ausgleichsposten *(m pl)*
En balancing items
Es asientos saldados *(m pl)*
Fr postes rééquilibrants *(m pl)*
It voci di pareggio *(m pl)*

valores de toda confiança *(m pl)* Pt
De mündelsichere Wertpapiere *(n pl)*
En gilt-edged securities
Es valores de toda confianza *(m pl)*
Fr valeurs de tout repos *(f pl)*
It titoli di assoluta fiducia *(m pl)*

valores de toda confianza *(m pl)* Es
De mündelsichere Wertpapiere *(n pl)*
En gilt-edged securities
Fr valeurs de tout repos *(f pl)*
It titoli di assoluta fiducia *(m pl)*
Pt valores de toda confiança *(m pl)*

valores privilegiados cumulativos *(m pl)* Es

De kumulative Vorzugsaktien *(f pl)*
En cumulative preference shares
Fr actions de priorité cumulatives *(f pl)*
It azioni preferenziali cumulative *(f pl)*
Pt acções preferenciais cumulativas *(f pl)*

valores transaccionáveis pelo banco *(m pl)* Pt

De diskontierbare Wechsel *(m pl)*
En bankable bills
Es efectos negociables *(m pl)*
Fr papier bancable *(m)*
It effetti scontabili *(m pl)*

valor intrínseco *(m)* Es, Pt

De innerlicher Wert *(m)*
En intrinsic value
Fr valeur intrinsèque *(f)*
It valore intrinseco *(m)*

valorizzazione *(f)* n It

De Erschließung *(f)*
En development
Es explotación *(f)*
Fr exploitation; lotissement *(f m)*
Pt exploração *(f)*

valor nominal *(m)* Es, Pt

De Nennwert; Stückelung *(m f)*
En nominal value; face value
Fr valeur nominale *(f)*
It valore nominale; taglio *(m)*

valuable *adj* En

De wertvoll
Es valioso
Fr de valeur
It di valore
Pt valioso

valuación *(f)* n Es

De Wertbestimmung *(f)*
En valuation
Fr évaluation *(f)*
It valutazione *(f)*
Pt avaliação *(f)*

valuation *(of assets)* n En

De Wertbestimmung *(f)*
Es valuación *(f)*
Fr évaluation *(f)*
It valutazione *(f)*
Pt avaliação *(f)*

value n En

De Wert *(m)*
Es valor *(m)*
Fr valeur *(f)*
It valore *(m)*
Pt valor *(m)*

value added tax *(VAT)* En

De Mehrwertsteuer *(f)*
Es impuesto sobre valor añadido *(m)*
Fr taxe sur la valeur ajoutée (TVA) *(f)*
It imposta sul valore aggiunto (IVA) *(f)*
Pt imposto sobre valor aduzido *(m)*

valuta *(f)* n It

De Währung *(f)*
En currency
Es moneda *(f)*
Fr monnaie *(f)*
Pt moeda *(f)*

valuta debole *(f)* It

De schwache Währung *(f)*
En soft currency
Es moneda débil *(f)*
Fr monnaie faible *(f)*
Pt moeda fraca *(f)*

valuta di riserva *(f)* It

De Reservewährung *(f)*
En reserve currency
Es moneda de reserva *(f)*
Fr monnaie de réserve *(f)*
Pt moeda de reserva *(f)*

valuta estera *(f)* It

De Devisen *(f pl)*
En foreign currency; foreign exchange
Es divisas extranjeras *(f pl)*
Fr devises *(f pl)*
Pt moeda estrangeira *(f)*

valuta forte *(f)* It

De harte Währung *(f)*
En hard currency
Es moneda fuerta *(f)*
Fr monnaie forte *(f)*
Pt moeda forte *(f)*

valutare *vb* It

De bewerten
En evaluate
Es evaluar
Fr évaluer
Pt avaliar

valutare i danni It

De den Schadenersatzbetrag feststellen
En assess damages
Es evaluar daños
Fr fixer des dommages-intérêts
Pt avaliar os danos

valutazione *(f)* n It

De Wertbestimmung; Abschätzung *(f)*
En valuation; appraisal
Es evaluación; valuación *(f)*
Fr évaluation *(f)*
Pt avaliação *(f)*

valutazione approssimativa *(f)* It

De rohe Schätzung *(f)*
En rough estimate
Es presupuesto aproximado *(m)*
Fr estimation approximative *(f)*
Pt avaliação aproximada *(f)*

valutazione del costo per partita *(f)* It

De Stapelkostenberechnung *(f)*
En batch costing
Es fijación de precio por lotes *(f)*
Fr évaluation du coût des lots *(f)*
Pt fixação do preço por lote *(f)*

valutazione del lavoro *(f)* It

De Arbeitsbewertung *(f)*
En job evaluation
Es valoracion del trabajo *(f)*
Fr évaluation du travail *(f)*
Pt avaliação de tarefa *(f)*

valutazione eccessiva *(f)* It

De Überschätzung *(f)*
En over-estimate
Es presupuesto por exceso *(m)*
Fr surestimation *(f)*
Pt avaliação excessiva *(f)*

valutazione prudente (f) It
De vorsichtige Schätzung (f)
En conservative estimate
Es presupuesto prudente (m)
Fr évaluation prudente (f)
Pt avaliação cautelosa (f)

valute bloccate (f pl) It
De blockierte Devisen (f pl)
En blocked exchange
Es divisas bloqueadas (f pl)
Fr devises bloquées (f pl)
Pt câmbio bloqueado (m)

vantaggi accessori (m pl) It
De Sozialleistungen (f pl)
En fringe benefits
Es beneficios suplementarios
    (m pl)
Fr avantages accessoires
    (m pl)
Pt benefícios extras (m pl)

vapor (m) n Pt
De Dampfer (m)
En steamer
Es buque de vapor (m)
Fr bateau à vapeur (m)
It vapore (m)

vapor de serviço autónomo
    (m) Pt
De Trampschiff (n)
En tramp steamer
Es vapor volandero (m)
Fr navire de tramping (m)
It carretta (f)

vapore (m) n It
De Dampfer (m)
En steamer
Es buque de vapor (m)
Fr bateau à vapeur (m)
Pt vapor (m)

vapor volandero (m) Es
De Trampschiff (n)
En tramp steamer
Fr navire de tramping (m)
It carretta (f)
Pt vapor de serviço autóno-
    mo (m)

variable cost En
De variable Kosten (f pl)
Es coste variable (m)
Fr coût variable (m)
It costo variabile (m)
Pt custo variável (m)

variable Kosten (f pl) n De
En variable cost
Es coste variable (m)
Fr coût variable (m)
It costo variabile (m)
Pt custo variável (m)

variance analysis En
De Varianzanalyse (f)
Es análisis de variaciones (m)
Fr analyse de la variance (f)
It analisi della variazione (f)
Pt análise de variação (f)

Varianzanalyse (f) n De
En variance analysis
Es análisis de variaciones (m)
Fr analyse de la variance (f)
It analisi della variazione (f)
Pt análise de variação (f)

variations saisonnières (f pl)
    Fr
De saisonbedingte Schwan-
    kungen (f pl)
En seasonal fluctuations
Es fluctuaciones estacionales
    (f pl)
It fluttuazioni stagionali (f pl)
Pt flutuações de época (f pl)

vazio comercial (m) Pt
De Außenhandelsdefizit (n)
En trade gap
Es vacío comercial (m)
Fr déficit du commerce exté-
    rieur (m)
It disavanzo della bilancia
    commerciale (m)

véhicule commerciale (f) Fr
De Nutzfahrzeug (n)
En commercial vehicle
Es vehículo comercial (m)
It veicolo commerciale (m)
Pt veiculo comercial (m)

vehiculo comercial (m) Es
De Nutzfahrzeug (n)
En commercial vehicle
Fr véhicule commerciale (f)
It veicolo commerciale (m)
Pt veiculo comercial (m)

veicolo commerciale (m) It
De Nutzfahrzeug (n)
En commercial vehicle

Es vehículo comercial (m)
Fr véhicule commerciale (f)
Pt veículo comercial (m)

veículo comercial (m) Pt
De Nutzfahrzeug (n)
En commercial vehicle
Es vehículo comercial (m)
Fr véhicule commerciale (f)
It veicolo commerciale (m)

vencer vb Es
De fällig sein
En fall due
Fr échoir; venir à échéance
It scadere; essere pagabile
Pt vencer-se

vencer-se vb Pt
De fällig sein
En fall due
Es vencer
Fr échoir; venir à échéance
It scadere; essere pagabile

vencido adj Es, Pt
De rückständig; verfallen
En overdue; expired
Fr arriéré; expiré
It scaduto

vencimento (m) Pt
De Fälligkeit (f)
En maturity
Es vencimiento (m)
Fr échéance (f)
It scadenza (f)

vencimento atrasado (m) Pt
De Lohnnachzahlung (f)
En back pay
Es pago atrasado (m)
Fr rappel de traitement (m)
It arretrati di paga (m pl)

vencimiento (m) n Es
De Fälligkeit (f)
En maturity
Fr échéance (f)
It scadenza (f)
Pt vencimento (m)

venda (f) n Pt
De Verkauf (m)
En sale
Es venta (f)
Fr vente (f)
It vendita (f)

venda a dinheiro *(f)* Pt
De Kassageschäft *(n)*
En cash sale
Es venta al conta *(f)*
Fr vente au comptant *(f)*
It vendita a contanti *(f)*

venda a prestações *(f)* Pt
De Ratenkauf *(m)*
En hire-purchase
Es compra a plazos *(f)*
Fr vente à tempérament *(f)*
It vendita a rate *(f)*

vendable *adj* Fr
De marktfähig
En marketable
Es vendible
It vendibile
Pt comercializável

venda de porta-a-porta *(f)*
Pt
De Haus-zu-Haus-Verkauf
(m)
En door-to-door selling
Es venta a domicilio *(f)*
Fr vente à domicile *(f)*
It vendita a domicilio *(f)*

**venda directa ao
consumidor** *(f)* Pt
De Direktverkauf *(m)*
En direct selling
Es venta directa *(f)*
Fr vente directe *(f)*
It vendita diretta *(f)*

venda em leilão *(f)* Pt
De Versteigerung *(f)*
En sale by auction
Es venta a subasta *(f)*
Fr vente aux enchères *(f)*
It vendita all'asta *(f)*

venda forçada *(f)* Pt
De Zwangsverkauf *(m)*
En forced sale
Es venta forzosa *(f)*
Fr vente forcée *(f)*
It vendita forzosa *(f)*

venda insistente *(f)* Pt
De aufdringliches Verkaufen
(n)
En hard sell
Es venta insistente *(f)*
Fr vente débrouillarde *(f)*
It vendita facendo sforzo *(f)*

venda ou devolução Pt
De Rücksendung wenn un-
verkauft
En sale or return
Es venta o devolución
Fr vente avec faculté de re-
tour
It da vendere o rimandare

venda pelo correio *(f)* Pt
De Auftrag durch die Post *(m)*
En mail order
Es pedido por correo *(m)*
Fr commande par lettre *(f)*
It ordine per corrispondenza
(f)

vendas de exportação *(f pl)* Pt
De Ausfuhrverkäufe *(m pl)*
En export sales
Es ventas de exportación *(f pl)*
Fr ventes d'exportation *(f pl)*
It vendite per esportazione
(f pl)

vendas em pirâmide *(f pl)* Pt
De Schneeballverkauf *(m)*
En pyramid selling
Es venta en pirámide *(f)*
Fr vente en pyramide *(f)*
It vendita a piramide *(f)*

venda subtil *(f)* Pt
De unaufdringliches Verkau-
fen *(n)*
En soft sell
Es venta sencilla *(f)*
Fr vente par des moyens
discrets *(f)*
It vendere senza forzare

vendedor *(m)* n Es, Pt
De Verkäufer *(m)*
En salesman; vender
Fr vendeur *(m)*
It venditore; commesso *(m)*

vendedor por atacado *(m)* Pt
De Großhändler; Grossist *(m)*
En wholesaler
Es mayorista *(m)*
Fr grossiste *(m)*
It grossista *(m)*

vender *vb* Es, Pt
De verkaufen
En sell
Fr vendre
It vendere

vender n En
De Verkäufer *(m)*
Es vendedor *(m)*
Fr vendeur *(m)*
It venditore *(m)*
Pt vendedor *(m)*

vendere *vb* It
De verkaufen
En sell
Es vender
Fr vendre
Pt vender

vendeur *(m)* n Fr
De Verkäufer *(m)*
En salesman; vender
Es vendedor *(m)*
It venditore; commesso *(m)*
Pt vendedor; caixeiro *(m)*

vendibile *adj* It
De marktfähig
En marketable
Es vendible
Fr vendable
Pt comercializável

vendible *adj* Es
De marktfähig
En marketable
Fr vendable
It vendibile
Pt comercializável

vending machine En
De Verkaufsautomat *(m)*
Es máquina expendedora *(f)*
Fr distributeur automatique
(m)
It macchina venditrice au-
tomatica *(f)*
Pt máquina de vendas *(f)*

vendita *(f)* n It
De Verkauf *(m)*
En sale
Es venta *(f)*
Fr vente *(f)*
Pt venda *(f)*

vendita a contanti *(f)* It
De Kassageschäft *(n)*
En cash sale
Es venta al conta *(f)*
Fr vente au comptant *(f)*
Pt venda a dinheiro *(f)*

vendita a domicilio *(f)* It
De Haus-zu-Haus-Verkauf
     (m)
En door-to-door selling
Es venta a domicilio *(f)*
Fr vente à domicile *(f)*
Pt venda de porta-a-porta *(f)*

vendita all'asta *(f)* It
De Versteigerung *(f)*
En sale by auction
Es venta a subasta *(f)*
Fr vente aux enchères *(f)*
Pt venda em leilão *(f)*

vendita a piramide *(f)* It
De Schneeballverkauf *(m)*
En pyramid selling
Es venta en pirámide *(f)*
Fr vente en pyramide *(f)*
Pt vendas em pirâmide *(f pl)*

vendita a rate *(f)* It
De Ratenkauf *(m)*
En hire-purchase
Es compra a plazos *(f)*
Fr location-vente *(f)*
Pt compras a prestações *(f pl)*

vendita diretta *(f)* It
De Direktverkauf *(m)*
En direct selling
Es venta directa *(f)*
Fr vente directe *(f)*
Pt venda directa ao consu-
     midor *(f)*

vendita facendo sforzo *(f)* It
De aufdringliches Verkaufen
     (n)
En hard sell
Es venta insistente *(f)*
Fr vente débrouillarde *(f)*
Pt venda insistente *(f)*

**vendita per giudizio
ipotecario** *(f)* It
De Zwangsvollstreckung *(f)*
En foreclosure
Es venta por juicio hipoteca-
     rio *(f)*
Fr vente de l'immeuble
     hypothéqué *(f)*
Pt execução judicial a uma hi-
     poteca *(f)*

vendita sforzosa *(f)* It
De Zwangsverkauf *(m)*
En forced sale
Es venta forzosa *(f)*
Fr vente forcée *(f)*
Pt venda forçada *(f)*

vendite per esportazione
     (f pl) It
De Ausfuhrverkäufe *(m pl)*
En export sales
Es ventas de exportación *(f pl)*
Fr ventes d'exportation *(f pl)*
Pt vendas de exportação *(f pl)*

venditore *(m)* n It
De Verkäufer *(m)*
En salesman; vender
Es vendedor *(m)*
Fr vendeur *(m)*
Pt vendedor; caixeiro *(m)*

venditore all'asta *(m)* It
De Versteigerer *(m)*
En auctioneer
Es subastador *(m)*
Fr commissaire-priseur *(m)*
Pt leiloeiro *(m)*

vendre vb Fr
De verkaufen
En sell
Es vender
It vendere
Pt vender

venta *(f)* n Es
De Verkauf *(m)*
En sale
Fr vente *(f)*
It vendita *(f)*
Pt venda *(f)*

venta a domicilio *(f)* Es
De Haus-zu-Haus-Verkauf
     (m)
En door-to-door selling
Fr vente à domicile *(f)*
It vendita a domicilio *(f)*
Pt venda de porta-a-porta *(f)*

venta al conta *(f)* Es
De Kassageschäft *(n)*
En cash sale
Fr vente au comptant *(f)*
It vendita a contanti *(f)*
Pt vend a dinheiro *(f)*

venta a subasta *(f)* Es
De Versteigerung *(f)*
En sale by auction
Fr vente aux enchères *(f)*
It vendita all'asta *(f)*
Pt venda em leilão *(f)*

venta directa *(f)* Es
De Direktverkauf *(m)*
En direct selling
Fr vente directe *(f)*
It vendita diretta *(f)*
Pt venda directa ao consu-
     midor *(f)*

venta en pirámide *(f)* Es
De Schneeballverkauf *(m)*
En pyramid selling
Fr vente en pyramide *(f)*
It vendita a piramide *(f)*
Pt vendas em pirâmide *(f pl)*

venta forzosa *(f)* Es
De Zwangsverkauf *(m)*
En forced sale
Fr vente forcée *(f)*
It vendita forzosa *(f)*
Pt venda forçada *(f)*

venta insistente *(f)* Es
De aufdringliches Verkaufen
     (n)
En hard sell
Fr vente débrouillarde *(f)*
It vendita facendo sforzo *(f)*
Pt venda insistente *(f)*

venta o devolución Es
De Rücksendung wenn un-
     verkauft
En sale or return
Fr vente avec faculté de re-
     tour
It da vendere o rimandare
Pt venda ou devolução

venta por juicio hipotecario
     (f) Es
De Zwangsvollstreckung *(f)*
En foreclosure
Fr vente de l'immeuble
     hypothéqué *(f)*
It vendita per giudizio ipote-
     cario *(f)*
Pt execução judicial a uma hi-
     poteca *(f)*

ventas de exportación *(f pl)*
Es
De Ausfuhrverkäufe *(m pl)*
En export sales
Fr ventes d'exportation *(f pl)*
It vendite per esportazione
(f pl)
Pt vendas de exportação *(f pl)*

venta sencilla *(f)* Es
De unaufdringliches Verkaufen *(n)*
En soft sell
Fr vente par des moyens discrets *(f)*
It vendere senza forzare
Pt venda subtil *(f)*

vente *(f)* n Fr
De Verkauf *(m)*
En sale
Es venta *(f)*
It vendita *(f)*
Pt venda *(f)*

vente à domicile *(f)* Fr
De Haus-zu-Haus-Verkauf *(m)*
En door-to-door selling
Es venta a domicilio *(f)*
It vendita a domicilio *(f)*
Pt venda de porta-a-porta *(f)*

vente à tempérament *(f)* Fr
De Ratenverkauf *(m)*
En hire-purchase
Es compra a plazos *(f)*
It vendita a rate *(f)*
Pt venda a prestações *(f)*

vente au comptant *(f)* Fr
De Kassageschäft *(n)*
En cash sale
Es venta al conta *(f)*
It vendita a contanti *(f)*
Pt venda a dinheiro *(f)*

vente aux enchères *(f)* Fr
De Versteigerung *(f)*
En sale by auction
Es venta a subasta *(f)*
It vendita all'asta *(f)*
Pt venda em leilão *(f)*

vente avec faculté de retour
Fr
De Rücksendung wenn unverkauft
En sale or return

Es venta o devolución
It da vendere o rimandare
Pt venda ou devolução

vente débrouillarde *(f)* Fr
De aufdringliches Verkaufen *(n)*
En hard sell
Es venta insistente *(f)*
It vendita facendo sforzo *(f)*
Pt venda insistente *(f)*

vente de l'immeuble hypothéqué *(f)* Fr
De Zwangsvollstreckung *(f)*
En foredosure
Es venta por juicio hipotecario *(f)*
It vendita per giudizio ipotecario *(f)*
Pt execução judicial a uma hipoteca *(f)*

vente directe *(f)* Fr
De Direktverkauf *(m)*
En direct selling
Es venta directa *(f)*
It vendita diretta *(f)*
Pt venda directa ao consumidor *(f)*

vente en pyramide *(f)* Fr
De Schneeballverkauf *(m)*
En pyrarhid selling
Es venta en pirámide *(f)*
It vendita a piramide *(f)*
Pt vendas em pirâmide *(f pl)*

vente forcée *(f)* Fr
De Zwangsverkauf *(m)*
En forced sale
Es venta forzosa *(f)*
It vendita forzosa *(f)*
Pt venda forçada *(f)*

vente par des moyens discrets *(f)* Fr
De unaufdringliches Verkaufen *(n)*
En soft sell
Es venta sencilla *(f)*
It vendere senza forzare
Pt venda subtil *(f)*

ventes d'exportation *(f pl)* Fr
De Ausfuhrverkäufe *(m pl)*
En export sales

Es ventas de exportación *(f pl)*
It vendite per esportazione *(f pl)*
Pt vendas de exportação *(f pl)*

Verabredung *(f)* n De
En appointment
Es entrevista *(f)*
Fr entrevue *(f)*
It appuntamento *(m)*
Pt encontro *(m)*

Verantwortlichkeit *(f)* n De
En accountability; responsibility
Es responsabilidad *(f)*
Fr responsabilité *(f)*
It responsabilità *(f)*
Pt responsabilidade *(f)*

verbale *(m)* n It
De Protokoll *(n)*
En minutes (of a meeting)
Es actas *(f pl)*
Fr procès-verbal *(m)*
Pt minutas de acta *(f pl)*

Verband *(m)* n De
En association
Es asociación *(f)*
Fr association *(f)*
It associazione *(f)*
Pt associação *(f)*

Verbesserung *(f)* n De
En improvement
Es mejora *(f)*
Fr amélioration *(f)*
It miglioramento *(m)*
Pt melhoramento *(m)*

verbindlich *adj* De
En compulsory
Es obligatorio
Fr obligatoire
It obbligatorio
Pt obrigatório

Verbrauch *(m)* n De
En consumption
Es consumición *(f)*
Fr consommation *(f)*
It consumo *(m)*
Pt consumo *(m)*

Verbraucher *(m)* n De
En consumer
Es consumidor *(m)*

Fr consommateur *(m)*
It consumatore *(m)*
Pt consumidor *(m)*

Verbrauchsabgabe *(f)* De
En excise duty
Es impuesto de consumos *(m)*
Fr droit sur la consommation *(m)*
It imposta sul consumo *(f)*
Pt imposto indirecto *(m)*

verderbliche Waren *(f pl)* De
En perishable goods
Es mercancías perecederas *(f pl)*
Fr marchandises périssables *(f pl)*
It merci deperibili *(f pl)*
Pt mercadorias perecíveis *(f pl)*

verdienen *vb* De
En earn
Es ganar
Fr gagner
It guadagnare
Pt ganhar

Verdrängungstonne *(f)* n De
En displacement-ton
Es tonelada de desplazamiento *(f)*
Fr tonneau de déplacement *(m)*
It tonnellata di dislocamento *(f)*
Pt tonelada de deslocação *(f)*

Verdrehung *(f)* n De
En misrepresentation
Es declaración falsa *(f)*
Fr déclaration inexacte *(f)*
It dichiarazione falsa *(f)*
Pt deturpação *(f)*

Vereinbarung *(f)* n De
En settlement
Es acuerdo *(m)*
Fr accord *(m)*
It accordo *(m)*
Pt acordo *(m)*

Verfahren *(n)* n De
En procedure
Es procedimiento *(m)*

Fr procédure *(f)*
It procedura *(f)*
Pt procedimento *(m)*

verfallen *adj* De
En expired; out of date
Es vencido
Fr expiré; périmé
It scaduto
Pt vencido

Verfallstermin *(m)* n De
En deadline
Es fecha tope *(f)*
Fr date limite *(f)*
It ultima data o ora possibile *(f)*
Pt data de vencimento *(f)*

verfügbar *adj* De
En available
Es disponible
Fr disponible
It disponibile
Pt disponível

verfügbarer Saldo *(m)* De
En balance in hand
Es sobrante *(m)*
Fr salde en caisse *(m)*
It saldo in cassa *(m)*
Pt saldo em poder *(m)*

verfügbares Einkommen *(n)* De
En disposable income
Es renta disponible *(f)*
Fr revenu disponible *(m)*
It reddito disponibile *(m)*
Pt receita disponível *(f)*

Verfügung *(f)* n De
En disposal
Es disposición *(f)*
Fr disposition *(f)*
It disposizione *(f)*
Pt disposição *(f)*

Vergleichsabkommen *(n)* n De
En deed of arrangement; deed of composition
Es acta de disposición; concordato *(m f)*

Fr contrat d'arrangement; concordat *(m)*
It atto di accordo; atto di concordato *(m)*
Pt escritura de acordo; concordata (por escrito) *(f)*

vergoldet *adj* De
En gold-plated
Es chapado en oro
Fr plaqué d'or
It placcato in oro
Pt laminado a ouro

vergüten *vb* De
En compensate
Es compensar
Fr compenser
It compensare
Pt compensar

Vergütung *(f)* n De
En remuneration
Es remuneración *(f)*
Fr rémunération *(f)*
It rimunerazione *(f)*
Pt remuneração *(f)*

Verhältnis *(n)* n De
En ratio; proportion
Es razón; relación; proporción *(f)*
Fr rapport; proportion *(m f)*
It rapporto; proporzione *(m f)*
Pt razão; proporção *(f)*

Verhältnis des Aktienkurses zum Reingewinn De
En price-earnings ratio (P/E)
Es proporción precio-ingresos *(f)*
Fr quotient cours-bénéfice *(m)*
It rapporto prezzo-utile *(m)*
Pt taxa custo-ganhos *(f)*

verhandeln *vb* De
En negotiate
Es negociar
Fr négocier
It negoziare
Pt negociar

Verhandlung *(f)* n De
En negotiation
Es negociación *(f)*
Fr négociation *(f)*
It trattativa *(f)*
Pt negaciação *(f)*

**Verhandlungen wiederauf-
nehmen** De
En re-open discussions
Es reabrir la discusión
Fr rouvrir la discussion
It riaprire la discussione
Pt reabrir discussões

Verhandlungslage *(f)* De
En bargaining position
Es situación de negociar *(f)*
Fr situation permettant de
négocier *(f)*
It situazione permettente di
trattare *(f)*
Pt situação de regatear *(f)*

Verhandlungsposition *(f)* De
En bargaining power
Es poder de negociación *(m)*
Fr pouvoir de négociation *(m)*
It potere di contrattare *(m)*
Pt poder de regateio *(m)*

verificação *(f)* n Pt
De Untersuchung *(f)*
En examination; verification
Es verificación *(f)*
Fr vérification *(f)*
It verifica *(f)*

verificação alfandegária
(f) Pt
De zollamtliche Untersuchung
(f)
En customs examination
Es control de aduanas *(m)*
Fr visite douanière *(f)*
It visita doganale *(f)*

**verificación contable
interna** *(f)* Es
De interne Revision *(f)*
En internal audit
Fr vérification interne *(f)*
It verifica contabile interna *(f)*
Pt fiscalização contabilística
interna *(f)*

verifica contabile interna *(f)*
It
De interne Revision *(f)*
En internal audit
Es verificación contable in-
terna *(f)*
Fr vérification interne *(f)*
Pt fiscalização contabilística
interna *(f)*

verificar *vb* Es
De nachprüfen
En verify
Fr vérifier
It verificare
Pt verifica *(f)*

verificar *vb* Pt
De nachprüfen
En verify
Es verificar
Fr vérifier
It verificare

verificare *vb* It
De nachprüfen
En verify
Es verificar
Fr vérifier
Pt verificar

vérificateur des comptes *(m)*
Fr
De Rechnungsprüfer *(m)*
En comptroller
Es interventor *(m)*
It controllore *(m)*
Pt controlador *(m)*

vérification comptable *(f)* Fr
De Bücherrevision *(f)*
En audit
Es revisión (examen) de cuen-
tas *(f)*
It revisione dei conti *(f)*
Pt fiscalização de contas *(f)*

vérification interne *(f)* Fr
De interne Revision *(f)*
En internal audit
Es verificación contable in-
terna *(f)*
It verifica contabile interna *(f)*
Pt fiscalização contabilística
interna *(f)*

vérifier *vb* Fr
De nachprüfen
En verify
Es verificar
It verificare
Pt verificar

vérifier et certifier Fr
De prüfen
En audit
Es revisar
It rivedere
Pt fiscalizar as contas

verify *vb* En
De nachprüfen
Es verificar
Fr vérifier
It verificare
Pt verificar

Verkauf *(m)* n De
En sale
Es venta *(f)*
Fr vente *(f)*
It vendita *(f)*
Pt venda *(f)*

(zum) Verkauf anbieten De
En offer for sale
Es ofrecer en venta
Fr offrir en vente
It offrire in vendita
Pt pôr à venda

verkaufen *vb* De
En sell
Es vender
Fr vendre
It vendere
Pt vender

Verkäufer *(m)* n De
En salesman; vender
Es vendedor *(m)*
Fr vendeur *(m)*
It venditore; commesso *(m)*
Pt vendedor; caixeiro *(m)*

Verkauf mit Zugaben *(m)* De
En premium offer
Es oferta a prima *(f)*
Fr offre à prime *(f)*
It offerta sopra la pari *(f)*
Pt oferta-prémio *(f)*

Verkaufsabteilung *(f)* n De
En sales department
Es departamento de ventas
(m)
Fr service ventes *(m)*
It ufficio vendite *(m)*
Pt departamento de vendas
(m)

Verkaufsagent *(m)* n De
En distributor
Es distribuidor; concesiona-
rio *(m)*

Fr distributeur; concessionnaire *(m)*
It distributore; concessionario *(m)*
Pt distribuidor; concessionário *(m)*

Verkaufsanalyse *(f) n* De
En sales analysis
Es análisis de ventas *(m)*
Fr analyse des ventes *(f)*
It analisi delle vendite *(f)*
Pt análise de vendas *(f)*

Verkaufsautomat *(m) n* De
En vending machine
Es máquina expendedora *(f)*
Fr distributeur automatique
(m)
It macchina venditrice au-
tomatica *(f)*
Pt máquina de vendas *(f)*

Verkaufsgewandtheit *(f) n* De
En salesmanship
Es arte de vender *(m)*
Fr art de vendre *(m)*
It arte della vendita *(f)*
Pt ciência de vender *(f)*

Verkaufskontenbuch *(n) n* De
En sales ledger
Es libro mayor de ventas *(m)*
Fr grand livre des ventes *(m)*
It partitario delle vendite *(f)*
Pt livro-mestre de vendas
(m)

Verkaufskosten *(pl) n* De
En selling cost
Es coste de venta *(m)*
Fr frais de vente *(m)*
It costo di vendita *(m)*
Pt custo de venda *(m)*

Verkaufsleiter *(m) n* De
En sales manager
Es jefe de ventas *(m)*
Fr directeur commercial *(m)*
It direttore commerciale *(m)*
Pt chefe de vendas *(m)*

Verkaufsoption *(f) n* De
En put option
Es opción de venta *(f)*
Fr option à vendre *(f)*
It premio a vendere *(m)*
Pt opção de venda *(f)*

Verkaufspersonal *(n) n* De
En sales force
Es personal de ventas *(m)*
Fr personnel de vente *(m)*
It forze di vendita *(f pl)*
Pt pessoal de vendas *(m)*

Verkaufsvoraussage *(f) n* De
En sales forecast
Es pronóstico de ventas *(m)*
Fr prévision de ventes *(f)*
It previsione delle vendite *(f)*
Pt previsão de vendas *(f)*

Verkehrsspitze *(f) n* De
En peak hours
Es horas punta *(f)*
Fr heures de pointe *(f)*
It ore di punta *(f)*
Pt horas de ponta *(f)*

Verkehrsstockung *(f) n* De
En traffic jam
Es embotellamiento de tráfico
(m)
Fr encombrement de circula-
tion *(m)*
It ingorgo stradale *(m)*
Pt engarrafamento de tráfego
(m)

Verladung *(f) n* De
En shipment
Es embarque *(m)*
Fr embarquement *(m)*
It imbarco *(m)*
Pt embarque *(m)*

Verlag *(m) n* De
En publishing house
Es casa editorial *(f)*
Fr maison d'édition *(f)*
It casa editrice *(f)*
Pt casa editora *(f)*

verlangen *vb* De
En requisition
Es requisar
Fr réquisitionner
It requisire
Pt requisitar

**Verlängerung eines
Kredites** *(f)* De
En extension of credit
Es prórroga de crédito *(f)*
Fr prolongation d'un crédit *(f)*
It proroga di credito *(f)*
Pt prorrogação de crédito *(f)*

**Verlängerung einer
Zahlungsfrist** *(f)* De
En extension of payment time
Es prórroga de pago *(f)*
Fr délai de paiement *(m)*
It proroga di pagamento *(f)*
Pt prorrogação de pagamento
(f)

Verletzte(r) *(m) n* De
En injured party
Es parte lesionada *(f)*
Fr partie lésée *(f)*
It parte lesa *(f)*
Pt parte lesada *(f)*

Verletzung (eines Rechtes,
usw.) *(f) n* De
En infringement
Es infracción *(f)*
Fr infraction *(f)*
It infrazione *(f)*
Pt infracção *(f)*

**Verletzung der Gewähr-
leistungspflicht** *(f)* De
En breach of warranty
Es incumplimiento de la ga-
rantía *(m)*
Fr rupture de garantie *(f)*
It violazione di garanzia *(f)*
Pt violação de garantia *(f)*

Verlust *(m) n* De
En loss
Es pérdida *(f)*
Fr perte *(f)*
It perdita *(f)*
Pt perda *(f)*

(einen) Verlust abschreiben
De
En write off a loss
Es cancelar una pérdida
Fr amortir une perte
It cancellare una perdita
Pt anular um prejuízo

Vermerk *(m) n* De
En memorandum
Es memorando; apunte *(m)*
Fr note *(f)*
It promemoria *(f)*
Pt memorando *(m)*

vermieten *vb* De
En rent
Es alquilar
Fr louer; affermer
It affittare; appigionare
Pt alugar

Vermieter *(m) n* De
En landlord; lessor
Es propietario; arrendador
(m)
Fr propriétaire; bailleur *(m)*
It proprietario; locatore *(m)*
Pt proprietário; arrendador
(m)

vermitteln *vb* De
En mediate
Es intermediar
Fr s'entremettre
It fare da intermediario
Pt intermediar

Vermittlung *(f) n* De
En mediation
Es intermediación *(f)*
Fr médiation *(f)*
It mediazione *(f)*
Pt intermediação *(f)*

Vermögen *(n) n* De
En estate
Es finca *(f)*
Fr bien; propriété *(m f)*
It proprietà *(f)*
Pt bens; propriedade *(m pl; f)*

Vermögensanlage *(f) n* De
En capital asset
Am fixed asset
Es activo fijo *(m)*
Fr actif immobilisé *(m)*
It capitale fisso *(m)*
Pt bens de capital *(m pl)*

Verordnung *(f) n* De
En directive
Es directiva *(f)*
Fr directive *(f)*
It direttivo *(m)*
Pt ordem de serviço *(f)*

Verpachtung *(f) n* De
En lease
Es alquiler *(m)*
Fr bail *(m)*
It affitto *(m)*
Pt aluguer; arrendamento *(m)*

Verpackung *(f) n* De
En packing
Es embalaje; envase *(m)*
Fr emballage *(m)*
It imballaggio *(m)*
Pt embalagem; empacota-
mento *(f m)*

Verpackung inbegriffen De
En including packing
Es franco embalaje
Fr franco d'emballage
It imballaggio incluso
Pt incluindo embalagem

verpfänden *vb* De
En hypothecate
Es hipotecar
Fr hypothéquer
It ipotecare
Pt hipotecar

Verpfändungsurkunde *(f) n*
De
En letter of hypothecation
Es carta de hipoteca *(f)*
Fr lettre hypothécaire *(f)*
It atto ipotecario *(m)*
Pt carta de hipoteca *(f)*

Verpflichtung *(f) n* De
En obligation; liability
Es obligación; responsabili-
dad *(f)*
Fr obligation; responsabilité
(f)
It obbligazione; responsabi-
lità *(f)*
Pt obrigação; responsabilida-
de *(f)*

verre *(m) n* Fr
De Glas *(n)*
En glass
Es vidrio *(m)*
It vetro *(m)*
Pt vidro *(m)*

verre à glaces *(m)* Fr
De Spiegelglas *(n)*
En plate glass
Es vidrio plano pulido *(m)*
It cristallo *(m)*
Pt chapa de vidro *(f)*

verre à vitres *(m)* Fr
De Fensterglas *(n)*
En window glass

Es cristal de ventana *(m)*
It vetro da finestre *(m)*
Pt vidro de montra *(m)*

Verrechnungsscheck *(m) n*
De
En crossed cheque
Es cheque cruzado *(m)*
Fr chèque barré *(m)*
It assegno sbarrato *(m)*
Pt cheque cruzado *(m)*

Verrechnungsstelle *(f) n* De
En clearing house
Es cámara de compensacio-
nes *(f)*
Fr chambre de compensa-
tion *(f)*
It stanza di compensazione
(f)
Pt câmara de compensações
e rateio *(f)*

verre dépoli *(m)* Fr
De Mattscheibe *(f)*
En ground glass
Es cristal deslustrado *(m)*
It vetro smerigliato *(m)*
Pt vidro esmerilado *(m)*

versagen *vb* De
En fail
Es fallar; faltar
Fr échouer; failir
It mancare; fallire
Pt falhar; faltar

Versammlung *(f) n* De
En meeting
Es reunión *(f)*
Fr réunion; assemblée *(f)*
It riunione; assemblea *(f)*
Pt reunião; assembleia *(f)*

**(eine) Versammlung
abhalten** De
En hold a meeting
Es celebrar una reunión
Fr tenir une assemblée
It tenere una riunione
Pt fazer uma reunião

Versand *(m) n* De
En despatch; dispatch
Es despacho; expedición
(m f)
Fr envoi *(m)*
It spedizione; dispaccio *(f m)*
Pt despacho; remessa *(m f)*

Versandschein *(m)* De
En despatch note
Es aviso de expedición *(m)*
Fr bordereau d'expédition;
  bulletin d'envoi *(m)*
It bollettino di spedizione *(m)*
Pt aviso de despacho *(m)*

versare un deposito It
De hinterlegen
En pay a deposit
Es hacer un depósito
Fr donner des arrhes
Pt pagar depósito

verschiedene Ausgaben
  (f pl) De
En sundry expenses
Es gastos varios *(m pl)*
Fr frais divers *(m pl)*
It spese varie *(f pl)*
Pt despesas diversas *(f pl)*

verschiffen *vb* De
En ship
Es embarcar
Fr embarquer
It imbarcare
Pt embarcar

Verschmelzung *(f)* n De
En merger
Es fusión *(f)*
Fr fusion *(f)*
It fusione *(f)*
Pt fusão *(f)*

versement *(m)* n Fr
De Zahlung *(f)*
En payment
Es pago *(m)*
It pagamento *(m)*
Pt pagamento *(m)*

versement à compte *(m)* Fr
De Anzahlung *(f)*
En payment on account
Es pago a cuenta *(m)*
It pagamento in conto *(m)*
Pt pagamento por conta *(m)*

Versendung *(f)* n De
En consignment
Es consignación *(f)*
Fr envoi; expédition *(m f)*
It consegna; spedizione *(f)*
Pt consignação *(f)*

**Versendung vom Ursprungs-
  ort** *(f)* De
En shipment from origin
Es envío desde el punto de
  origen *(m)*
Fr envoi du lieu de départ *(m)*
It spedizione dall'origine *(f)*
Pt carregamento desde a
  origem *(m)*

versicherbar *adj* De
En insurable
Es asegurable
Fr assurable
It assicurabile
Pt susceptível de ser objecto
  de seguro

Versicherer *(m)* n De
En insurer; underwriter
Es asegurador *(m)*
Fr assureur *(m)*
It assicuratore *(m)*
Pt segurador *(m)*

versichern *vb* De
En insure
Es asegurar
Fr assurer
It assicurare
Pt segurar

Versicherte(r) *(m)* n De
En insured
Es asegurado *(m)*
Fr assuré *(m)*
It assicurato *(m)*
Pt titular de seguro *(m)*

Versicherung *(f)* n De
En insurance; assurance
Es seguro *(m)*
Fr assurance *(f)*
It assicurazione *(f)*
Pt seguro *(m)*

**Versicherung auf
  Gegenseitigkeit** *(f)* De
En mutual insurance
Es coaseguro *(m)*
Fr assurance mutuelle *(f)*
It mutua assicurazione *(f)*
Pt seguro mútuo *(m)*

Versicherungsdeckung *(f)* n
  De
En insurance cover
Es cobertura de la póliza de
  seguro *(f)*

Fr garantie d'assurance *(f)*
It copertura assicurativa *(f)*
Pt cobertura de seguro *(f)*

Versicherungsgesellschaft
  (f) n De
En insurance company
Es compañía de seguros *(f)*
Fr compagnie d'assurance *(f)*
It compagnia di assicura-
  zione *(f)*
Pt companhia de seguros *(f)*

Versicherungsmakler *(m)* n
  De
En insurance broker
Es corredor de seguros *(m)*
Fr courtier d'assurance *(m)*
It mediatore di assicurazioni
  (m)
Pt corretor de seguros *(m)*

**versicherungsmathema-
  tisch** *adj* De
En actuarial
Es actuarial
Fr actuariel
It attuariale
Pt actuarial

Versicherungspolice *(f)* n De
En insurance policy
Es póliza de seguro *(f)*
Fr police d'assurance *(f)*
It polizza di assicurazione *(f)*
Pt apólice de seguro *(f)*

Versicherungsprämie *(f)* n
  De
En insurance premium
Es prima de póliza de seguro
  (f)
Fr prime d'assurance *(f)*
It premio di assicurazione
  (m)
Pt prémio de seguro *(m)*

Versicherungsschein *(m)* n
  De
En insurance certificate
Es certificado de seguro *(m)*
Fr certificat d'assurance *(m)*
It certificato di assicurazione
  (m)
Pt certificado de seguro *(m)*

Versicherungssyndikat (n) n
De
En underwriting syndicate
(insurance)
Es sindicato de seguros (m)
Fr syndicat d'assureurs (m)
It sindacato di assicuratori
(m)
Pt consórcio de seguradores
(m)

**Versicherungsverein auf
Gegenseitigkeit** (m) De
En friendly society
Am lodge
Es sociedad de socorro mu-
tuo (f)
Fr société de secours mutuel
(f)
It società di mutuo soccorso
(f)
Pt mutualidade (f)

Versicherungsvertreter
(m) n De
En insurance agent
Es agente de seguros (m)
Fr agent d'assurances (m)
It agente di assicurazioni (f)
Pt agente de seguros (f)

verstaatlichte Industrie
(f) De
En nationalized industry
Es industria nacionalizada (f)
Fr industrie nationalisée (f)
It industria nazionalizzata (f)
Pt indústria nacionalizada (f)

Verstaatlichung (f) n De
En nationalization
Es nacionalización (f)
Fr nationalisation (f)
It nazionalizzazione (f)
Pt nacionalização (f)

verstauen vb De
En stow
Es estibar
Fr arrimer
It stivare
Pt estivar

Verstauung (f) n De
En stowage
Es estiba (f)
Fr arrimage (m)
It stivaggio (m)
Pt estiva (f)

versteckte Belastung (f) De
En hidden tax
Es impuesto latente (m)
Fr imposition latente (f)
It tassa invisibile (f)
Pt imposto ocultado (m)

versteckter Mangel (m) De
En latent defect
Es defecto latente (m)
Fr vice caché (m)
It difetto latente (m)
Pt defeito latente (m)

Versteigerer (m) n De
En auctioneer
Es subastador (m)
Fr commissaire-priseur (m)
It venditore all'asta (m)
Pt leiloeiro (m)

Versteigerung (f) n De
En auction; sale by auction
Es subasta; venta a subasta
(f)
Fr vente aux enchères (f)
It asta; vendita all'asta (f)
Pt leilão; venda em leilão (m f)

vertagen vb De
En adjourn
Es aplazar
Fr ajourner
It aggiornare
Pt adiar

Vertagung (f) n De
En adjournment
Es aplazamiento (m)
Fr ajournement (m)
It aggiornamento (m)
Pt adiamento (m)

verteilen vb De
En distribute; allot
Es repartir; asignar
Fr répartir; attribuer
It ripartire; assegnare
Pt repartir; atribuir

Verteilung (f) n De
En distribution; allotment
Es reparto; adjudicación (m f)
Fr distribution; attribution (f)
It ripartizione (f)
Pt distribuição; aporciona-
mento (f m)

Verteilungsbrief (m) n De
En allotment letter
Es letra de adjudicación (f)
Fr avis d'attribution (m)
It lettera da ripartizione (f)
Pt aviso de aporcionamento
(m)

vertenza di lavoro (f) It
De Arbeitsstreitigkeit (f)
En trade dispute
Es conflicto laboral (m)
Fr conflit du travail (m)
Pt conflito comercial (m)

vertenza operaia (f) It
De Arbeitskonflikt (m)
En industrial dispute
Es conflicto laboral (m)
Fr conflit ouvrier (m)
Pt conflito de trabalho (m)

vertical integration En
De vertikaler Zusammen-
schluß (m)
Es integración vertical (f)
Fr integration verticale (f)
It integrazione verticale (f)
Pt integração vertical (f)

**vertikaler Zusammen-
schluß** (m) De
En vertical integration
Es integración vertical (f)
Fr integration verticale (f)
It integrazione verticale (f)
Pt integração vertical (f)

Vertrag (m) n De
En contract
Es contrato (m)
Fr contrat (m)
It contratto (m)
Pt contrato (m)

(einen) Vertrag formulieren
De
En draw up a contract
Es redactar un contrato
Fr rédiger un contrat
It redigere un contratto
Pt redigir um contrato

vertraglich adj De
En contractual
Es contractual
Fr contractuel
It contrattuale
Pt contratual

Vertragsbeendigung (f) n De
En determination of a con-
tract
Es rescisión de un contrato (f)
Fr résolution d'un contrat (f)
It risoluzione di un contratto
(f)
Pt rescisão de contrato (f)

Vertragsentwurf (m) n De
En draft contract
Es proyecto de contrato (m)
Fr projet de contrat (m)
It progetto di contratto (m)
Pt minuta de contrato (f)

Vertragspreis (m) n De
En contract price
Es precio contractual (m)
Fr prix contractuel (m)
It prezzo contrattuale (m)
Pt preço contratual (m)

Vertragsverletzung (f) n De
En breach of contract
Es incumplimiento del contra-
to (m)
Fr rupture de contrat (f)
It rottura di contratto (f)
Pt rotura de contrato (f)

vertreiben (Waren, usw.) vb
De
En distribute
Es distribuir
Fr distribuer
It distribuire
Pt distribuir

vertreten vb De
En represent
Es representar
Fr représenter
It rappresentare
Pt representar

Vertreter (m) n De
En representative
Es representante (m)
Fr représentant (m)
It rappresentante (m)
Pt representante (m)

Vertrieb (m) n De
En distribution (of goods)
Es distribución (f)
Fr distribution (f)
It distribuzione (f)
Pt distribuição (f)

Veruntreuer (m) n De
En embezzler
Es defalcador (m)
Fr détourneur (m)
It malversatore (m)
Pt desfalcador (m)

vervielfältigen vb De
En multiply
Es multiplicar
Fr multiplier
It moltiplicare
Pt multiplicar

Vervielfältiger (m) n De
En multiplier
Es multiplicador (m)
Fr multiplicateur (m)
It moltiplicatore (m)
Pt multiplicador (m)

**Vervielfältigung der
Produkte** (f) De
En diversification
Es diversificación (f)
Fr diversification (f)
It diversificazione (f)
Pt diversificação (f)

Verwahrer (m) n De
En depositary
Es depositario (m)
Fr dépositaire (m)
It depositario (m)
Pt depositário (m)

Verwahrung in Stahlfach (f)
De
En safe deposit
Es depósito en caja fuerte (m)
Fr dépôt en coffre-fort (m)
It servizio di cassette di sicu-
rezza (m)
Pt depósito em cofre forte (m)

verwalten vb De
En administer
Es administrar
Fr administrer
It amministrare
Pt administrar

Verwalter (m) n De
En administrator
Es administrador (m)
Fr administrateur (m)
It amministratore (m)
Pt administrador (m)

Verwaltung (f) n De
En administration
Es administración (f)
Fr gestion (f)
It gestione (f)
Pt gestão (f)

Verwaltungsrat (m) n De
En director
Es director (m)
Fr administrateur (m)
It amministratore (m)
Pt director (m)

Verzicht (m) n De
En renunciation; waiver
Es renuncia (f)
Fr renonciation (f)
It rinunzia (f)
Pt renúncia (f)

verzollen vb De
En clear through customs
Es retirar de aduanas
Fr dédouaner
It sdoganare
Pt despachar na alfândega

verzollt adj De
En duty-paid; out of bond; ex
bond
Es derechos pagados; des-
pachado de aduanas; fue-
ra de aduanas
Fr acquitté; dédouané; à
l'acquitté
It dazio pagato; sdoganato
Pt direitos pagos; despachado da alfândega

Verzollung (f) n De
En customs clearance
Es despacho de aduana (m)
Fr formalités douanières (f pl)
It sdoganamento (m)
Pt despacho de alfândega
(m)

Verzug (m) n De
En delay
Es retraso (m)
Fr retard; délai (m)
It ritardo (m)
Pt atraso (m)

vested interest En
De festbegründetes Recht (n)
Es interés creado (m)

Fr droit acquis *(m)*
It diritto acquisito *(m)*
Pt interesse adquirido *(m)*

vetro *(m) n* It
De Glas *(n)*
En glass
Es vidrio *(m)*
Fr verre *(m)*
Pt vidro *(m)*

vetro da finestre *(m)* It
De Fensterglas *(n)*
En window glass
Es cristal de ventana *(m)*
Fr verre à vitres *(m)*
Pt vidro de montra *(m)*

vetro smerigliato *(m)* It
De Mattscheibe *(f)*
En ground glass
Es cristal deslustrado *(m)*
Fr verre dépoli *(m)*
Pt vidro esmerilado *(m)*

vettore *(m) n* It
De Spediteur *(m)*
En carrier
Am conveyer
Es transportador *(m)*
Fr expéditeur *(m)*
Pt transportador *(m)*

viabilidade *(f) n* Pt
De Durchführbarkeit *(f)*
En feasibility
Es practicabilidad *(f)*
Fr practicabilité *(f)*
It fattibilità *(f)*

viagem *(f) n* Pt
De Seereise *(f)*
En voyage
Es viaje *(m)*
Fr voyage *(m)*
It viaggio *(m)*

viaggiatore di commercio
  (m) It
De Geschäftsreisende(r);
  Handelsvertreter
En commercial traveller
Es viajante de comercio *(m)*
Fr commis-voyageur *(m)*
Pt caixeiro viajante *(m)*

viaggio *(m) n* It
De Seereise *(f)*
En voyage
Es viaje *(m)*
Fr voyage *(m)*
Pt viagem *(f)*

viajante de comercio *(m)* Es
De Handelsvertreter; Ge-
  schäftsreisende(r) *(m)*
En commercial traveller
Am salesman
Fr commis-voyageur *(m)*
It viaggiatore die commercio
  (m)
Pt caixeiro viajante *(m)*

viaje *(m) n* Es
De Seereise *(f)*
En voyage
Fr voyage *(m)*
It viaggio *(m)*
Pt viagem *(f)*

vice caché *(m)* Fr
De versteckter Mangel *(m)*
En latent defect
Es defecto latente *(m)*
It difetto latente *(m)*
Pt defeito latente *(m)*

vice-chairman *n* En
De stellvertretender Vorsit-
  zende(r) *(m)*
Es vice-presidente *(m)*
Fr vice-président *(m)*
It vicepresidente *(m)*
Pt vice-presidente *(m)*

vice-direttore *(m) n* It
De Unterdirektor *(m)*
En assistant manager
Es sub-director *(m)*
Fr sous-directeur *(m)*
Pt subdirector *(m)*

vice-président *(m) n* Fr
De stellvertretender Vorsit-
  zende(r) *(m)*
En vice-chairman
Es vice-presidente *(m)*
It vicepresidente *(m)*
Pt vice-presidente *(m)*

vice-presidente *(m) n* Es, Pt
De stellvertretender Vorsit-
  zende(r) *(m)*
En vice-chairman

Fr vice-président *(m)*
It vicepresidente *(m)*

vicepresidente *(m) n* It
De stellvertretender Vorsit-
  zende(r) *(m)*
En vice-chairman
Es vice-presidente *(m)*
Fr vice-président *(m)*
Pt vice-presidente *(m)*

vidrio *(m) n* Es
De Glas *(n)*
En glass
Fr verre *(m)*
It vetro *(m)*
Pt vidro *(m)*

vidrio plano pulido *(m)* Es
De Spiegelglas *(n)*
En plate glass
Fr verre à glaces; glace de vi-
  trage *(m f)*
It cristallo *(m)*
Pt chapa de vidro *(f)*

vidro *(m) n* Pt
De Glas *(n)*
En glass
Es vidrio *(m)*
Fr verre *(m)*
It vetro *(m)*

vidro de montra *(m)* Pt
De Fensterglas *(n)*
En window glass
Es cristal de ventana *(m)*
Fr verre à vitres *(m)*
It vetro da finestre *(m)*

vidro esmerilado *(m)* Pt
De Mattscheibe *(f)*
En ground glass
Es cristal deslustrado *(m)*
Fr verre dépoli *(m)*
It vetro smerigliato *(m)*

vierteljährlich *adj* De
En quarterly
Es trimestral
Fr trimestriel
It trimestrale
Pt trimestral

vierteljährliche Zahlungen
  (f pl) De
En quarterly payments
Es pagos trimestrales *(m pl)*

Fr　paiements trimestriels *(m pl)*
It　pagamenti trimestrali *(m pl)*
Pt　pagamentos trimestrais *(m pl)*

vigente *adj* Pt
De　in Kraft
En　in force
Es　en vigor
Fr　en vigueur
It　in vigore

violacão de garantia *(f)* Pt
De　Verletzung der Gewährlei-stungspflicht *(f)*
En　breach of warranty
Es　incumplimiento de la ga-rantía *(m)*
Fr　rupture de garantie *(f)*
It　violazione di garanzia *(f)*

violazione di garanzia *(f)* It
De　Verletzung der Gewährlei-stungspflicht *(f)*
En　breach of warranty
Es　incumplimiento de la ga-rantía *(m)*
Fr　rupture de garantie *(f)*
Pt　violação de garantia *(f)*

virement bancaire *(m)* Fr
De　Banküberweisung *(f)*
En　bank transfer
Es　transferencia bancaria *(f)*
It　trasferimento bancario *(m)*
Pt　transferência bancária *(f)*

virement postal *(m)* Fr
De　Postüberweisung *(f)*
En　mail transfer
Es　transferencia postal *(f)*
It　trasferimento per posta *(m)*
Pt　transferência postal *(f)*

virement télégraphique *(m)* Fr
De　Kabelauszahlung *(f)*
En　telegraphic transfer
Es　giro telegráfico *(m)*
It　rimessa telegrafica *(f)*
Pt　transferência telegráfica *(f)*

visa *n* En; Es *(f)*, Fr *(m)*
De　Visum *(n)*
It　visto *(m)*
Pt　visto *(m)*

visita doganale *(f)* It
De　zollamtliche Untersuchung *(f)*
En　customs examination
Es　control de aduanas *(m)*
Fr　visite douanière *(f)*
Pt　verificação alfandegária *(f)*

visita medica *(f)* It
De　ärztliche Untersuchung *(f)*
En　medical examination
Es　examen médico *(m)*
Fr　examen médical *(m)*
Pt　inspecção médica *(f)*

visite douanière *(f)* Fr
De　zollamtliche Untersuchung *(f)*
En　customs examination
Es　control de aduanas *(m)*
It　visita doganale *(f)*
Pt　verificação alfandegária *(f)*

visto *(m) n* It, Pt
De　Visum *(n)*
En　visa
Es　visa *(f)*
Fr　visa *(m)*

visual-display unit (vdu) En
De　Bildschirmeinheit *(f)*
Es　unidad de visualización *(f)*
Fr　unité de visualisation *(f)*
It　unità di visualizzazione *(f)*
Pt　móvel-montra de expo-sição de visuais *(f)*

Visum *(n) n* De
En　visa
Es　visa *(f)*
Fr　visa *(m)*
It　visto *(m)*
Pt　visto *(m)*

vocational training En
De　Berufsausbildung *(f)*
Es　formación profesional *(f)*
Fr　formation professionelle *(f)*
It　addestramento professio-nale *(m)*
Pt　treino vocacional *(m)*

voci di pareggio *(m pl)* It
De　Ausgleichsposten *(m pl)*
En　balancing items
Es　asientos saldados *(m pl)*
Fr　postes rééquilibrants *(m pl)*
Pt　valores de equilíbrio *(m pl)*

void (of contract, etc.) *adj* En
De　nichtig
Es　nulo
Fr　nul
It　nullo
Pt　nulo

voiture *(f) n* Fr
De　Auto; Wagen *(n m)*
En　car
Es　coche *(m)*
It　automobile; macchina *(f)*
Pt　carro; automóvel *(m)*

voiturier public *(m)* Fr
De　Güterbeförderer *(m)*
En　common carrier
Es　empresa de transportes *(f)*
It　vettore *(m)*
Pt　empresa de transportes *(f)*

voix prépondérante *(f)* Fr
De　entscheidende Stimme *(f)*
En　casting vote
Es　voto decisivo *(m)*
It　voto decisivo *(m)*
Pt　voto decisivo *(m)*

vol *(m) n* Fr
De　Diebstahl; Flug *(m f)*
En　theft; flight
Es　robo; vuelo *(m)*
It　furto; fuga *(m)*
Pt　furto; voo *(m)*

vol avec effraction *(m)* Fr
De　Einbruchdiebstahl *(m)*
En　burglary
Es　robo *(m)*
It　furto con scasso *(m)*
Pt　roubo *(m)*

Volkswirtschaftslehre *(f) n* De
En　economics
Es　economía *(f)*
Fr　économie politique *(f)*
It　economia *(f)*
Pt　economia *(f pl)*

Volkszählung *(f) n* De
En　census
Es　censo *(m)*
Fr　recensement *(m)*
It　censimento *(m)*
Pt　censo *(m)*

voll *adj* De
En full
Es lleno
Fr plein
It pieno
Pt cheio

Vollbeschäftigung *(f)* n De
En full employment
Es pleno empleo *(m)*
Fr plein emploi *(m)*
It piena occupazione *(f)*
Pt pleno emprego *(m)*

volle Zahlung *(f)* De
En payment in full
Es pago en pleno *(m)*
Fr libération intégrale *(f)*
It pagamento in pieno *(m)*
Pt pagamento completo *(m)*

vollgezeichnet *adj* De
En fully subscribed
Es plenamente suscrito
Fr intégralement souscrit
It interamente sottoscritto
Pt totalmente subscrito

Vollmacht *(f)* n De
En authority; power of attorney
Es autoridad; poder *(f m)*
Fr mandat; procuration *(m f)*
It autorità; procura *(f)*
Pt autoridade; poderes de procuração *(f: m pl)*

(eine) Vollmacht erteilen De
En execute a power of attorney
Es otorgar poder notarial
Fr conférer des pleins pouvoirs
It conferire una procura
Pt dar execução a poderes de procuração

Vollmachtgeber *(m)* n De
En principal
Es mandante *(m)*
Fr mandant *(m)*
It mandante *(m)*
Pt mandante *(m)*

vollstrecken *vb* De
En execute
Es ejectuar; legalizar

Fr exécuter; réaliser
It eseguire; effettuare
Pt executar

Vollstrecker *(m)* n De
En executor
Es albacea *(m)*
Fr exécuteur *(m)*
It esecutore *(m)*
Pt executor *(m)*

Vollwertdeckung *(f)* n De
En full cover
Es garantía total *(f)*
Fr garantie totale *(f)*
It garanzia totale *(f)*
Pt cobertura total *(f)*

volontaire *adj* Fr
De freiwillig
En voluntary
Es voluntario
It volontario
Pt voluntário

volontario *adj* It
De freiwillig
En voluntary
Es voluntario
Fr volontaire
Pt voluntário

volume *(m)* Fr, It
De Kubikinhalt *(m)*
En cubic capacity
Es capacidad cúbica *(f)*
Pt capacidade cúbica *(f)*

volumen de ventas *(m)* Es
De Umsatz *(m)*
En turnover
Fr chiffre d'affaires *(m)*
It giro d'affari *(m)*
Pt movimento de dinheiro *(m)*

voluntario *adj* Es
De freiwillig
En voluntary
Fr volontaire
It volontario
Pt voluntário

voluntário *adj* Pt
De freiwillig
En voluntary
Es voluntario
Fr volontaire
It volontario

voluntary *adj* En
De freiwillig
Es voluntario
Fr volontaire
It volontario
Pt voluntário

von Hypothek befreit De
En free from mortgage
Es deshipotecado
Fr déshypothéqué
It libero d'ipoteca
Pt livre de hipoteca

voo *(m)* n Pt
De Flug *(f)*
En flight
Es vuelo *(m)*
Fr vol *(m)*
It fuga *(m)*

Voranschlag *(m)* n De
En estimate
Es presupuesto *(m)*
Fr devis *(m)*
It preventivo *(m)*
Pt previsão *(f)*

Vorarbeiter *(m)* n De
En foreman
Es capataz *(m)*
Fr contremaître; chef d'équipe *(m)*
It capo operaio; capo squadra *(m)*
Pt encarregado; capataz *(m)*

vorausbezahlt *adj* De
En prepaid
Es pagado por adelantado
Fr payé d'avance
It pagato in anticipo
Pt pago adiantadamente

vorausgesetzt De
En on condition
Es a condición
Fr sous réserve
It a condizione
Pt sob condição de

Voraussage *(n)* n De
En forecasting
Es pronóstico *(m)*
Fr prévision *(f)*
It previsione *(f)*
Pt previsão *(f)*

Vorauszahlung *(f)* De
En advance payment; pre-
  payment
Es anticipo *(m)*
Fr paiement par anticipation
  (m)
It pagamento anticipato *(m)*
Pt pagamento adiantado *(m)*

vorbehalten *vb* De
En reserve
Es reservar
Fr réserver
It riservare
Pt reservar

Vorderfront *(f) n* De
En frontage
Es fachada *(f)*
Fr façade *(f)*
It facciata *(f)*
Pt fachada *(f)*

Vordruck *(m)* De
En printed form
Es formulario; impreso *(m)*
Fr formulaire *(m)*
It modulo stampato *(m)*
Pt impresso *(m)*

vorfabrizieren *vb* De
En prefabricate
Es prefabricar
Fr préfabriquer
It prefabbricare
Pt pré-fabricar

vorgestern *adv* De
En day before yesterday
Es anteayer
Fr avant-hier
It avantieri
Pt anteontem

vorhersehen *vb* De
En forecast
Es pronosticar
Fr prévoir
It pronosticare
Pt prognosticar

Vorladung *(f) n* De
En writ
Es auto; orden *(m f)*
Fr assignation *(f)*
It citazione *(f)*
Pt citação; ordem *(f m)*

vorläufig *adj* De
En preliminary
Es preliminar
Fr préliminaire; préalable
It preliminare
Pt preliminar

vorläufige Dividende *(f)* De
En interim dividend
Es dividendo provisional *(m)*
Fr dividende intérimaire *(m)*
It acconto di dividendo *(m)*
Pt dividendo interino *(m)*

Vormund (eines Minderjähri-
  gen) *(m) n* De
En guardian
Es tutor *(m)*
Fr tuteur *(m)*
It tutore *(m)*
Pt tutor *(m)*

Vorrat *(m) n* De
En stock
Es stock; existencias *(m; f pl)*
Fr stock; marchandises
  (m; f pl)
It stock; scorta *(m f)*
Pt existências *(f pl)*

Vorrat auf Lager *(m)* De
En stock in hand
Es mercancías en almacén
  (f pl)
Fr marchandises en magasin
  (f pl)
It merce in magazzino *(f)*
Pt mercadorias em
  existência *(f pl)*

vorrätig De
En in stock; on hand
Es en almacén; disponible
Fr en magasin; disponible
It in magazzino; disponibile
Pt à mão; ao dispôr

vorrätig halten De
En keep in stock
Es guardar en almacén
Fr garder en stock
It tenere in magazzino
Pt reter em armazém

Vorratslager anlegen De
En stockpile
Es acumular existencias

Fr stocker
It ammassare
Pt acumular existências

Vorrecht *(n) n* De
En priority
Es prioridad *(f)*
Fr priorité *(f)*
It priorità *(f)*
Pt prioridade *(f)*

vorschießen *vb* De
En advance (money)
Am prepay
Es anticipar
Fr avancer (de l'argent)
It anticipare
Pt adiantar

Vorschlag *(m) n* De
En proposal
Es propuesta *(f)*
Fr proposition *(f)*
It proposta *(f)*
Pt proposta *(f)*

Vorschuß *(m) n* De
En advance
Am prepayment
Es adelanto *(m)*
Fr avance *(f)*
It anticipazione *(f)*
Pt adiantamento *(m)*

Vorschußkredit *(m) n* De
En bridging loan
Am bridge-over
Es crédito provisional *(m)*
Fr crédit provisoire *(m)*
It credito provvisorio *(m)*
Pt crédito provisório *(m)*

vorsichtige Schätzung *(f)* De
En conservative estimate
Es presupuesto prudente *(m)*
Fr évaluation prudente *(f)*
It valutazione prudente *(f)*
Pt avaliação cautelosa *(f)*

Vorsitzende(r) *(m) n* De
En chairman
Es presidente *(m)*
Fr président *(m)*
It presidente *(m)*
Pt presidente *(m)*

Vorstand *(m) n* De
En management; board of directors
Es dirección; consejo de administración *(f m)*
Fr administration; conseil d'administration *(f m)*
It direzione; consiglio d'amministrazione *(m f)*
Pt gerência; direcção *(f)*

Vorstandsbericht *(m) n* De
En directors' report
Es informe de la administración *(m)*
Fr rapport des administrateurs *(m)*
It relazione degli amministratori *(f)*
Pt relatório de directores *(m)*

Vorstandssitzung *(f) n* De
En board meeting
Es reunión del consejo de administración *(f)*
Fr réunion du conseil d'administration *(f)*
It riunione del consiglio d'amministrazione *(f)*
Pt reunião da administração *(f)*

vorzeitig (bezahlt) De
En anticipated
Es anticipado
Fr anticipé
It anticipato
Pt antecipado

Vorzugsaktie *(f) n* De
En preference share
Es acción preferente *(f)*
Fr action privilégiée *(f)*
It azione privilegiata *(f)*
Pt acção preferencial *(f)*

Vorzugssatz *(m) n* De
En preferential duty
Es derechos preferenciales *(m pl)*
Fr tarif de faveur *(m)*
It tariffa preferenziale *(f)*
Pt direito preferencial *(m)*

votar *vb* Es, Pt
De stimmen
En vote
Fr voter
It votare

votare *vb* It
De stimmen
En vote
Es votar
Fr voter
Pt votar

vote *vb* En
De stimmen
Es votar
Fr voter
It votare
Pt votar

voter *vb* Fr
De stimmen
En vote
Es votar
It votare
Pt votar

voting shares En
De stimmberechtigte Aktien *(f pl)*
Es acciones con derecho de voto *(f pl)*
Fr actions avec droit de vote *(f pl)*
It azioni con diritto di voto *(f pl)*
Pt acções com direito a voto *(f pl)*

voto decisivo *(m)* Es, It, Pt
De entscheidende Stimme *(f)*
En casting vote
Fr voix prépondérante *(f)*

voucher *n* En
De Belegstück *(n)*
Es pieza justificativa *(f)*
Fr pièce justificative; fiche *(f)*
It pezza d'appoggio *(f)*
Pt vale *(m)*

voyage *n* En, Fr *(m)*
De Seereise *(f)*
Es viaje *(m)*
It viaggio *(m)*
Pt viagem *(f)*

vuelo *(m) n* Es
De Flug *(f)*
En flight
Fr vol *(m)*
It fuga *(m)*
Pt voo *(m)*

W

Waage *(f) n* De
En scales
Es balanza *(f)*
Fr balance *(f)*
It bilancia *(f)*
Pt balança *(f)*

wachstumsorientierte Wertpapiere *(n pl)* De
En growth stocks
Es títulos de crecimiento *(m pl)*
Fr titres avec perspectives de croissance *(m pl)*
It titoli di sviluppo *(m pl)*
Pt acções de acréscimo de capital *(f pl)*

wage *n* En
De Lohn *(m)*
Es salario *(m)*
Fr salaire *(m)*
It salario *(m)*
Pt salário *(m)*

wage claim En
De Lohnforderung *(f)*
Es reclamación de salario *(f)*
Fr revendication de salaire *(f)*
It rivendicazione salariale *(f)*
Pt demanda de salário *(f)*

wage earner En
De Lohnempfänger *(m)*
Es asalariado *(m)*
Fr salarié *(m)*
It salariato *(m)*
Pt assalariado *(m)*

wage freeze En
De Lohnstopp *(m)*
Es bloqueo de salarios *(m)*
Fr blocage des salaires *(m)*
It blocco dei salari *(m)*
Pt congelação de salários *(f)*

wage rate En
De Lohnsatz *(m)*
Es tarifa de salarios *(f)*
Fr taux des salaires *(m)*
It tariffa salariale *(f)*
Pt base salarial *(f)*

wage restraint En
De Lohnbeschränkung *(f)*
Es restricción de salario *(f)*
Fr contrainte sur les salaires *(f)*
It restrizioni sui salari *(f pl)*
Pt restrição de salários *(f)*

wages agreement En
De Lohnvereinbarung *(f)*
Es acuerdo sobre salarios *(m)*
Fr convention des salaires *(f)*
It accordo sui salari *(m)*
Pt acordo sobre salários *(m)*

wagon de chemin de fer *(m)* Fr
De Eisenbahnwagen *(m)*
En railway carriage
Am railroad car
Es vagón de ferrocarril *(m)*
It carrozza ferroviaria *(f)*
Pt vagão de caminhos de ferro *(m)*

Wahrscheinlichkeit *(f)* n De
En probability
Es probabilidad *(f)*
Fr probabilité *(f)*
It probabilità *(f)*
Pt probabilidade *(f)*

Währung *(f)* n De
En currency
Es moneda *(f)*
Fr monnaie *(f)*
It valuta *(f)*
Pt moeda *(f)*

Währungsabwertung *(f)* n De
En devaluation
Es devaluación *(f)*
Fr dévaluation *(f)*
It svalutazione *(f)*
Pt desvalorização *(f)*

Währungsausgleichsfonds *(m)* n De
En exchange equalization account
Es cuenta de compensación de cambio *(f)*
Fr fonds de stabilisation des changes *(m pl)*

It conto per la stabilizzazione dei cambi *(m)*
Pt conta de compensação de transacções *(f)*

Währungsgebiet *(n)* n De
En currency area
Es zona monetaria *(f)*
Fr zone monétaire *(f)*
It zona monetaria *(f)*
Pt zona monetária *(f)*

Währungspolitik *(f)* n De
En monetary policy
Es política monetaria *(f)*
Fr politique monétaire *(f)*
It politica monetaria *(f)*
Pt política monetária *(f)*

Währungsreform *(f)* n De
En monetary reform
Es reforma monetaria *(f)*
Fr réforme monétaire *(f)*
It riforma monetaria *(f)*
Pt reforma monetária *(f)*

waiting list En
De Warteliste *(f)*
Es lista de espera *(f)*
Fr liste d'attente *(f)*
It elenco delle prenotazioni *(m)*
Pt lista de espera *(f)*

waiver n En
De Verzicht *(m)*
Es renuncia *(f)*
Fr renonciation *(f)*
It rinunzia *(f)*
Pt renúncia *(f)*

war n En
De Krieg *(m)*
Es guerra *(f)*
Fr guerre *(f)*
It guerra *(f)*
Pt guerra *(f)*

war-risk insurance En
De Kriegsrisikoversicherung *(f)*
Es seguro contra riesgo de guerra *(m)*
Fr assurance du risque de guerre *(f)*
It assicurazione contro i rischi di guerra *(f)*
Pt seguro contra risco de guerra *(m)*

warehouse n En
De Warenlager *(n)*
Es almacén *(m)*
Fr magasin; entrepôt *(m)*
It magazzino *(m)*
Pt armazém *(m)*

Waren *(f pl)* n De
En merchandise
Es mercancía *(f)*
Fr marchandise *(f)*
It merce *(f)*
Pt mercadoria *(f)*

Warenhaus *(n)* n De
En department store
Es grandes almacenes *(m pl)*
Fr grand magasin *(m)*
It grande magazzino *(m)*
Pt armazém *(m)*

Warenlager *(n)* n De
En warehouse
Es almacén *(m)*
Fr magasin; entrepôt *(m)*
It magazzino *(m)*
Pt armazém *(m)*

Warenmarkt *(m)* n De
En produce market
Es mercado de productos *(m)*
Fr marché commercial *(m)*
It mercato commerciale *(m)*
Pt mercado de produtos *(m)*

Warenumsatzsteuer *(f)* n De
En sales tax
Es impuesto sobre la venta *(m)*
Fr taxe de vente *(f)*
It imposta sulle vendite *(f)*
Pt imposto sobre vendas *(m)*

Waren unter Zollverschluß *(f pl)* De
En bonded goods
Es mercancías en aduana *(f pl)*
Fr marchandises en douane *(f pl)*
It merci sotto vincolo doganale *(f pl)*
Pt mercadorias à ordem da alfândega *(f pl)*

Warenzeichen *(n)* n De
En trademark
Es marca de fábrica *(f)*
Fr marque de fabrique *(f)*
It marchio di fabbrica *(m)*
Pt marca de fábrica *(f)*

warrant (for payment) n En
De Befugnis (f)
Es mandato (m)
Fr ordonnance (f)
It mandato (m)
Pt mandato (m)

warrant (for goods) n En
De Lagerschein (m)
Es certificado (m)
Fr certificat (m)
It certificato (m)
Pt certificado (m)

warranty n En
De Garantie (f)
Es garantía (f)
Fr garantie (f)
It garanzia (f)
Pt garantia (f)

Warteliste (f) n De
En waiting list
Es lista de espera (f)
Fr liste d'attente (f)
It elenco delle prenotazioni (m)
Pt lista de espera (f)

Wasserschaden (m) n De
En water damage
Es daño causado por el agua (m)
Fr dégâts des eaux (m pl)
It danno causato dall'acqua (m)
Pt dano causado por água (m)

waste products En
De Abfallprodukte (n pl)
Es desperdicios (m pl)
Fr déchets (m pl)
It prodotto di rifiuto (m)
Pt desperdícios (m pl)

wasting assets En
Am depleting assets
De kurzlebige Aktiva (n pl)
Es activo gastable (m)
Fr actifs défectibles (m pl)
It attività in esaurimento (f pl)
Pt bens em uso ou deterioração (m pl)

water damage En
De Wasserschaden (m)
Es daño causado por el agua (m)

Fr dégâts des eaux (m pl)
It danno causato dall'acqua (m)
Pt dano causado por água (m)

waybill n En
De Frachtbrief (m)
Es guía de carga (f)
Fr lettre de voiture (f)
It lettera di vettura (f)
Pt guia de marcha (f)

wealth n En
De Wohlstand (m)
Es riqueza (f)
Fr richesse (f)
It ricchezza (f)
Pt riqueza (f)

wear and tear En
De natürliche Abnützung (f)
Es desgaste natural (m)
Fr usure normale (f)
It logorio naturale (m)
Pt desgaste (m)

Webware (f) n De
En textile
Es textil (m)
Fr textile (m)
It tessile (m)
Pt textil (m)

Wechsel (m) De
En bill of exchange
Es letra de cambio (f)
Fr lettre de change (f)
It tratta cambiale (f)
Pt letra de câmbio (f)

(einen) Wechsel einlösen De
En retire a bill
Es recoger una letra
Fr payer une lettre de change
It ritirare un effetto
Pt recuperar uma letra

(einen) Wechsel nicht akzeptieren De
En dishonour a bill
Es protestar una letra
Fr ne pas honorer un effet
It non onorare un effetto
Pt protestar uma letra

(einen) Wechsel vorlegen De
En present a bill for acceptance
Es presentar una letra para aceptación
Fr présenter une traite à l'acceptation
It presentare una cambiale per accettazione
Pt apresentar uma letra para aceite

Wechselforderungen (f pl) n De
En bills receivable
Es letras a cobrar (f pl)
Fr effets à recevoir (m pl)
It effetti attivi (m pl)
Pt letras a cobrar (f pl)

Wechselkurs (m) n De
En exchange rate
Es tipo de cambio (m)
Fr cours de change (f)
It corso del cambio (m)
Pt câmbio (m)

Wechselmakler (m) n De
En bill broker
Es corredor de cambios (m)
Fr courtier de bons (m)
It agente di sconto (m)
Pt corretor de câmbios (m)

Wechselschulden (f pl) n De
En bills payable
Es letras pagaderas (f pl)
Fr effets à payer (m pl)
It effetti passivi (m pl)
Pt letras a pagar (f pl)

wegwerfbare Verpackung (f) De
En disposable wrapping
Es envoltura desechable (f)
Fr emballage perdu (m)
It imballaggio a perdere (m)
Pt embalagem a destruir (f)

weigh vb En
De wiegen
Es pesar
Fr peser
It pesare
Pt pesar

weight n En
De Gewicht (n)
Es peso (m)
Fr poids (m)
It peso (m)
Pt peso (m)

weighted average En
De gewogener Durchschnitt (m)
Es media ponderada (f)
Fr moyenne pondérée (f)
It media ponderata (f)
Pt média ponderada (f)

weight note En
De Wiegeschein (m)
Es certificado de pesaje (m)
Fr note de poids (f)
It distinta pesi (f)
Pt certidão de peso (f)

weight or measurement En
De Maß oder Gewicht
Es peso o cubicaje
Fr poids ou mesure
It peso o volume
Pt peso ou medida

weitere Auskunft (f) De
En further information
Es más detalles (m pl)
Fr renseignements complémentaires (m pl)
It ulteriori informazioni (f pl)
Pt informação adicional (f)

weitere Gründe (m pl) De
En further reasons
Es rasones adicionales (f pl)
Fr raisons supplémentaires (f pl)
It ulteriori motivi (m pl)
Pt razões adicionais (f pl)

Weiterüberlegung (f) n De
En further consideration
Es examen más detallado (m)
Fr examen plus attentif (m)
It esame più attento (m)
Pt consideração posterior mais detalhada (f)

weiterverfolgen vb De
En follow up
Es perseguir
Fr poursuivre
It seguitare
Pt perseguir

Weltgesundheitsorganisation (WHO) (f) n De
En World Health Organization (WHO)
Es Organización Mundial de la Salud (OMS) (f)
Fr Organisation Mondiale de la Santé (OMS) (f)
It Organizzazione Mondiale della Sanità (OMS) (f)
Pt Organização Mundial da Saúde (OMS) (f)

Werbeberater (m) De
En advertising consultant
Es consultor de publicidad (m)
Fr conseil en publicité (m)
It consulente di pubblicità (m)
Pt perito de publicidade (m)

Werbebrief (m) n De
En sales letter
Es carta de publicidad de ventas (f)
Fr lettre de publicité ventes (f)
It lettera di pubblicità vendite (f)
Pt carta de publicidade de vendas (f)

Werbebüro (n) n De
En advertising agency
Es agencia de publicidad (f)
Fr agence de publicité (f)
It agenzia pubblicitaria (f)
Pt agência de publicidade (f)

Werbefeldzug (m) n De
En advertising campaign
Es campaña publicitaria (f)
Fr campagne de publicité (f)
It campagna pubblicitaria (f)
Pt campanha publicitária (f)

Werbekosten (f pl) n De
En advertising expenditure
Es gastos publicitarios (m pl)
Fr dépenses de publicité (f pl)
It spese di pubblicità (f pl)
Pt despesa com publicidade (f)

Werbemittel (n) n De
En advertising medium
Es medio de publicidad (m)
Fr support publicitaire (m)
It mezzo pubblicitario (m)
Pt meio publicitário (m)

Werbeplan (m) n De
En advertising schedule
Es plan de propaganda (m)
Fr programme des annonces (m)
It programma delle inserzioni (m)
Pt plano de campanha publicitária (m)

Werbeschrift (f) n De
En advertising brochure
Es folleto publicitario (m)
Fr prospectus publicitaire (m)
It opuscolo pubblicitario (m)
Pt folheto publicitário (m)

Werbetarif (m) n De
En advertising rates
Es tarifa para anuncios (f)
Fr tarifs de publicité (m pl)
It tariffa delle inserzioni (f)
Pt taxas de publicidade (f pl)

Werbetext (m) n De
En advertising copy
Es material publicitario (m)
Fr copie publicitaire (f)
It testo pubblicitario (m)
Pt texto de publicidade (m)

Werbeträger (m pl) n De
En media
Es medios de información (m pl)
Fr supports (m pl)
It canali d'informazione (m pl)
Pt meios de informação (m pl)

Werbung (f) n De
En publicity advertising
Es publicidad (f)
Fr publicité (f)
It pubblicità (f)
Pt publicidade (f)

Werkmeister (m) n De
En head foreman
Es capataz jefe (m)
Fr chef d'atelier (m)
It capo officina (m)
Pt encarregado-chefe (m)

Wert (m) n De
En value
Es valor (m)
Fr valeur (f)
It valore (m)
Pt valor (m)

Wertbestimmung (f) n De
En valuation
Es valuación (f)
Fr évaluation (f)
It valutazione (f)
Pt avaliação (f)

Wertpapiere (n pl) n De
En stock; securities
Es títulos; valores (m pl)
Fr titres; valeurs (m pl, f pl)
It titoli; valore (m pl)
Pt títulos; valores (m pl)

Wertsteigerung (f) n De
En appreciation
Es subida (f)
Fr appréciation (f)
It aumento (m)
Pt aumento (m)

wertvoll adj De
En valuable
Es valioso
Fr de valeur
It di valore
Pt valioso

Wertzuwachs (m) n De
En increment
Es aumento; incremento (m)
Fr accroissement; plus-
    value (m f)
It incremento (m)
Pt aumento; incremento (m)

Wettbewerb (m) n De
En competition
Es competición (f)
Fr concurrence (f)
It concorrenza (f)
Pt competição (f)

wetteifernd adj De
En competitive
Es competidor
Fr compétitif
It in concorrenza
Pt competitivo

wharf n En
De Kai (m)
Es muelle (m)
Fr quai (m)
It scalo (m)
Pt cais (m)

wharfage n En
De Kaigeld (n)
Es muellaje (m)
Fr quayage (m)
It diritto di sosta (m)
Pt atracagem (f)

wholesaler n En
De Großhändler; Grossist (m)
Es mayorista (m)
Fr grossiste (m)
It grossista (m)
Pt grossista (m)

wholesale trade En
De Großhandel (m)
Es comercio al por mayor (m)
Fr commerce en gros (m)
It commercio all' ingrosso
    (m)
Pt comércio por atacado (m)

Widerruf (m) n De
En revocation
Es revocación (f)
Fr révocation (f)
It revoca (f)
Pt revogação (f)

widerrufen vb De
En revoke
Es revocar
Fr révoquer
It revocare
Pt revogar

widerstreitende Interessen
    (n pl) De
En conflict of interest
Es pugna de intereses (f)
Fr opposition d'intérêts (f)
It conflitto d'interessi (m)
Pt conflito de interesses (m)

Wiederanschaffungskosten
    (f pl) n De
En replacement cost
Es coste de repuesto (m)
Fr coût de remplacement (m)
It costo di rimpiazzo (m)
Pt custo de substituição (m)

Wiederaufbau (m) n De
En reconstruction
Es reconstrucción (f)
Fr reconstruction (f)
It ricostruzione (f)
Pt reconstrução (f)

Wiederausfuhr (f) n De
En re-exportation
Es reexportación (f)
Fr réexportation (f)
It riesporto (m)
Pt reexportação (f)

wiederausführen vb De
En re-export
Es reexportar
Fr réexporter
It riesportare
Pt reexportar

Wiederverkaufspreis (m) n
    De
En resale price
Es precio de reventa (m)
Fr prix de revente (m)
It prezzo di rivendita (m)
Pt preço de revenda (m)

wiegen vb De
En weigh
Es pesar
Fr peser
It pesare
Pt pesar

Wiegeschein (m) n De
En weight note
Es certificado de pesaje (m)
Fr note de poids (f)
It distinta pesi (f)
Pt certidão de peso (f)

wildcat strike En
De wilder Streik (m)
Es huelga espontánea (f)
Fr grève sauvage (f)
It sciopero selvaggio (m)
Pt greve não oficializada (f)

wilder Streik (m) De
En wildcat strike
Es huelga espontánea (f)
Fr grève sauvage (f)
It sciopero selvaggio (m)
Pt greve não oficializada (f)

Willenserklärung (f) n De
En declaration of intent
Es declaración de intención
    (f)
Fr déclaration d'intention (f)
It dichiarazione d'intenzione
    (f)
Pt declaração de propósito (f)

window display En
De Fensterauslage *(f)*
Es exhibición en vitrina *(f)*
Fr étalage *(m)*
It mostra in vetrina *(f)*
Pt exposição de montra *(f)*

window dressing En
De Schaufensterdekoration *(f)*
Es preparación de escapara-
tes *(f)*
Fr art de l'étalage *(m)*
It allestimento delle vetrine
(m)
Pt preparação de montras *(f)*

window envelope En
De Fensterbriefumschlag *(m)*
Es sobre de ventanilla *(m)*
Fr enveloppe à fenêtre *(f)*
It busta con finestra *(f)*
Pt envelope de endereço ex-
posto *(m)*

window glass En
De Fensterglas *(n)*
Es cristal de ventana *(m)*
Fr verre à vitres *(m)*
It vetro da finestre *(m)*
Pt vidro de montra *(m)*

wind up a business En
De ein Unternehmen abwik-
keln
Es liquidar un negocio
Fr liquider une entreprise
It liquidare una azienda
Pt liquidar um negócio

wirklicher Totalverlust *(m)*
De
En actual total loss
Es pérdida total efectiva *(f)*
Fr perte totale effective *(f)*
It perdita totale assoluta *(f)*
Pt perda total efectiva *(f)*

wirksam *adj* De
En effective; operative
Es efectivo; eficaz
Fr effectif; actif
It efficace; operativo
Pt efectivo; eficaz

Wirksamkeit *(f)* n De
En effectiveness
Es eficacia *(f)*
Fr efficacité *(f)*
It efficacia *(f)*
Pt eficácia *(f)*

wirksam werden De
En become operative
Es entrar en vigor
Fr entrer en vigueur
It entrare in vigore
Pt entrar em vigor

Wirtschaft *(f)* n De
En (the) economy
Es economía *(f)*
Fr économie *(f)*
It economia *(f)*
Pt economia *(f)*

(die) Wirtschaft neu beleben
De
En reflate the economy
Es reanimar la economía
Fr ranimer l'économie
It ravvivare l'economia
Pt reflacionar a ecónomia

wirtschaftlich *adj* De
En economic
Es económico
Fr économique
It economico
Pt económico

wirtschaftliche Sanktionen
(f pl) De
En economic sanctions
Es sanciones económicas
(f pl)
Fr sanctions économiques
(f pl)
It sanzioni economiche *(f pl)*
Pt sanções económicas *(f pl)*

Wirtschaftlichkeit *(f)* n De
En cost-effectiveness
Es efectividad de coste *(f)*
Fr coût et efficacité
It rendimento della spesa *(m)*
Pt eficiência relativa ao custo
(f)

Wirtschaftskrise *(f)* n De
En depression
Es crisis económica *(f)*
Fr crise économique *(f)*
It crisi *(f)*
Pt depressão *(f)*

Wirtschaftsprüfer *(m)* n De
En qualified accountant
Es contador habilitado *(m)*

Fr expert comptable *(m)*
It ragioniere diplomato *(m)*
Pt guarda-livros diplomado
(m)

Wirtschaftsspionage *(f)* n De
En industrial espionage
Es espionaje industrial *(m)*
Fr espionage industriel *(m)*
It spionaggio industriale *(m)*
Pt espionagem industrial *(f)*

Wirtschaftswachstum *(m)* n
De
En economic growth
Es crecimiento económico
(m)
Fr croissance économique
(m)
It sviluppo economico *(m)*
Pt crescimento económico
(m)

with average (WA) En
De havariert
Es con avería
Fr avarié
It con avaria
Pt com avaria

without prejudice En
Am not binding
De ohne Verbindlichkeit
Es sin prejuicio
Fr sous toutes réserves
It senza pregiudizio
Pt sem prejuízo

without recourse En
De ohne Rückgriff
Es sin recurso
Fr sans droit de recours
It senza ricorso
Pt sem recurso

with-profits policy En
Am participating policy
De Police mit Gewinnberech-
tigung *(f)*
Es póliza con beneficios *(f)*
Fr police avec participation
aux bénéfices *(f)*
It polizza con profitti *(f)*
Pt apólice com participação
nos lucros *(f)*

with recourse
En
De mit Rückgriff
Es con recurso
Fr avec droit de recours
It con ricorso
Pt com recurso

witness n
En
De Zeuge (m)
Es testigo (m)
Fr témoin (m)
It testimone (m)
Pt testemunha (f)

Wohlstand (m) n
De
En wealth
Es riqueza (f)
Fr richesse (f)
It ricchezza (f)
Pt riqueza (f)

Wohnungsgebäude (n) n
De
En block of flats
Am apartment house
Es bloque de pisos (m)
Fr immeuble (m)
It fabbricato di appartamenti (m)
Pt edifício de andares (m)

Wohnungsversicherung (f) n
De
En household insurance
Es seguro de casa (m)
Fr assurance ménagère (f)
It assicurazione domestica (f)
Pt seguro de casa (m)

work n
En
De Arbeit (f)
Es trabajo (m)
Fr travail (m)
It lavoro (m)
Pt trabalho (m)

worker n
En
De Arbeiter (m)
Es trabajador (m)
Fr ouvrier (m)
It lavoratore (m)
Pt trabalhador (m)

work force En
De Belegschaft (f)
Es masa obrera (f)
Fr effectif (m)
It massa lavoratrice (f)
Pt massa trabalhadora (f)

working capital En
De Betriebskapital (n)
Es capital circulante (m)
Fr fonds de roulement (m pl)
It capitale d'esercizio (m)
Pt capital para movimentação (m)

working conditions En
De Arbeitsbedingungen (f pl)
Es condiciones de trabajo (f pl)
Fr conditions de travail (f pl)
It condizioni di lavoro (f pl)
Pt condições de trabalho (f pl)

working day En
De Arbeitstag (m)
Es día laborable (m)
Fr jour ouvrable (m)
It giornata lavorativa (f)
Pt dia de trabalho (m)

working partner En
De aktiver Teilhaber (m)
Es socio activo (m)
Fr associé actif (m)
It socio attivo (m)
Pt sócio actuante (m)

working week En
De Arbeitswoche (f)
Es semana laboral (f)
Fr semaine de travail (f)
It settimana lavorativa (f)
Pt semana de trabalho (f)

work in progress En
Am work in process
De Arbeit in der Ausführung (f)
Es trabajo en curso (m)
Fr travaux en cours (m pl)
It lavoro in corso (m)
Pt trabalho em curso (m)

work on hand En
De in Ausführung begriffene Arbeit (f)
Es trabajo en curso (m)
Fr travail en cours (m)
It lavoro in corso (m)
Pt trabalho em mão (m)

work permit En
De Arbeitserlaubnis (n)
Es permiso de trabajo (m)
Fr permis de travail (m)
It permesso di lavoro (m)
Pt carta de trabalho (f)

work study En
De Arbeitsstudie (f)
Es estudio del trabajo (m)
Fr étude du travail (f)
It studio di lavoro (m)
Pt estudo sobre trabalho (m)

World Health Organization (WHO) En
De Weltgesundheitsorganisation (WHO) (f)
Es Organización Mundial de la Salud (OMS) (f)
Fr Organisation Mondiale de la Santé (OMS) (f)
It Organizzazione Mondiale della Sanità (OMS) (f)
Pt Organização Mundial da Saúde (OMS) (f)

writ n En
De Vorladung (f)
Es auto; orden (m f)
Fr assignation (f)
It citazione (f)
Pt citação; ordem (f m)

write off a debt En
De eine Schuld erlassen
Es cancelar una deuda
Fr amortir une créance
It cancellare un credito
Pt cancelar um débito

write off a loss En
De einen Verlust abschreiben
Es cancelar una pérdida
Fr amortir une perte
It cancellare una perdita
Pt anular um prejuízo

Wucher (m) n De
En usury
Es usura (f)
Fr usure (f)
It usura (f)
Pt usura (f)

Y

yacimiento aurífero *(m)* Es
De Goldgrube *(f)*
En gold fields
Fr régions aurifères *(f pl)*
It terreni auriferi *(m pl)*
Pt jazigos de ouro *(m pl)*

yacimiento de carbón *(m)* Es
De Kohlenrevier *(n)*
En coal field
Fr bassin houiller *(m)*
It bacino carbonífero *(m)*
Pt jazigo de carvão *(m)*

yacimiento de petróleo *(m)*
    En
De Ölfeld *(n)*
En oilfield
Fr gisement petrolifère *(m)*
It giacimento petrolifero *(m)*
Pt jazigo de petróleo *(m)*

yesterday *adv* En
De gestern
Es ayer
Fr hier
It ieri
Pt ontem

yield (on capital, etc.) *n* En
De Rendite *(f)*
Es rédito *(m)*
Fr revenu *(m)*
It reddito *(m)*
Pt rédito *(m)*

Z

Zahl *(f) n* De
En number; figure
Es número; cifra *(m f)*
Fr nombre; chiffre *(m)*
It numero; cifra *(m f)*
Pt número *(m)*

zahlbar *adj* De
En payable
Es pagadero; pagable
Fr payable; remboursable
It pagabile
Pt pagável

zahlbar bei Sicht De
En payable at sight
Es pagadero a la vista
Fr payable à vue
It pagabile a vista
Pt pagável à vista

zahlbar bei Vorlage De
En payable on demand
Es pagadero a presentación
Fr payable sur demande
It pagabile a vista
Pt pagável à vista

zahlen *vb* De
En pay
Es pagar
Fr payer
It pagare
Pt pagar

Zahlmeister *(m) n* De
En purser
Es contador de navio *(m)*
Fr commissaire de la marine
    (m)
It commissario di bordo *(m)*
Pt comissário de bordo *(m)*

Zahltag *(m) n* De
En pay day
Es día de pago *(m)*
Fr jour de paiement *(m)*
It giorno di paga *(m)*
Pt dia de recebimento *(m)*

Zahlung *(f) n* De
En payment
Es pago *(m)*
Fr paiement *(m)*
It pagamento *(m)*
Pt pagamento *(m)*

Zahlungsaufschub *(m) n* De
En moratorium
Es moratorio *(m)*
Fr moratoire *(m)*
It moratoria *(f)*
Pt moratória *(f)*

Zahlungsbedingungen *(f pl)*
    n De
En payment terms
Es condiciones de pago *(f pl)*
Fr conditions de paiement
    (f pl)
It condizioni di pagamento
    (f pl)
Pt condições de pagamento
    (f pl)

Zahlungsberechtigte(r) *(m) n*
    De
En payee
Es beneficiario *(m)*
Fr bénéficiaire *(m)*
It beneficiario *(m)*
Pt beneficiário *(m)*

Zahlungsbilanz *(f) n* De
En balance of payments
Es balanza de pagos *(f)*
Fr balance des paiements *(f)*
It bilancia dei pagamenti *(f)*
Pt balança de pagamentos *(f)*

zahlungsfähig *adj* De
En solvent
Es solvente
Fr solvable
It solvibile
Pt solvente

zahlungsunfähig *adj* De
En insolvent
Es insolvente
Fr insolvable
It insolvente
Pt insolvente

Zahlungsunfähigkeit *(f) n* De
En insolvency
Es insolvencia; quiebra *(f)*
Fr faillite; déconfiture *(f)*
It insolvenza *(f)*
Pt insolvência *(f)*

Zahlung unter Protest *(f) n*
    De
En payment under protest
Es pago sobre protesta *(m)*
Fr paiement sous protêt *(m)*
It pagamento sotto protesto
    (m)
Pt pagamento sob protesto
    (m)

**Zahlung zum vollen Aus-
gleich** *(f)* De
En payment in full discharge
Es pago de liberación *(m)*
Fr paiement libératoire *(m)*
It pagamento a completa ta-
    citazione *(m)*
Pt pagamento contra exe-
    cução completa *(m)*

zavorra (f) n It
De Ballast (m)
En ballast
Es lastre (m)
Fr lest (m)
Pt lastro (m)

zecca (f) n It
De Münze (f)
En mint
Es casa de la moneda (f)
Fr la Monnaie
Pt casa da moeda (f)

Zedent (m) n De
En transferor
Es cesionista (m)
Fr cédant (m)
It cedente (m)
Pt cessionista (m)

Zehnerklub (m) n De
En Group of Ten (Paris Club)
Es Grupo de los Diez (m)
Fr Groupe des Dix (m)
It Gruppo dei Dieci (m)
Pt Grupo dos Dez (m)

Zeichner (m) n De
En designer
Es diseñador (m)
Fr dessinateur (m)
It disegnatore (m)
Pt desenhador (m)

Zeichnung (f) n De
En design
Es diseño (m)
Fr dessein (m)
It disegno (m)
Pt desenho (m)

Zeichnung (einer Anleihe) (f) n
De
En subscription
Es suscripción (f)
Fr souscription (f)
It sottoscrizione (f)
Pt subscrição (f)

Zeitcharter (f) n De
En time charter
Es fletamento de tiempo (m)
Fr affrètement à temps (m)
It contratto di noleggio a tempo (m)
Pt fretamento de tempo (m)

Zeitgeschäfte (n pl) n De
En forward dealings
Es negociaciones a término (f pl)
Fr opérations à terme (f pl)
It operazioni a termine (f pl)
Pt transacções adiantadas (f pl)

Zentralheizung (f) n De
En central heating
Es calefacción central (f)
Fr chauffage central (m)
It riscaldamento centrale (m)
Pt aquecimento central (m)

Zentralisierung (f) n De
En centralization
Es centralización (f)
Fr centralisation (f)
It centralizzazione (f)
Pt centralização (f)

zerbrechlich adj De
En fragile
Es frágil
Fr fragile
It fragile
Pt frágil

zero balance Am
En nil balance
De Nullsaldo (m)
Es saldo nulo (m)
Fr solde nul (m)
It saldo nullo (m)
Pt saldo nulo (m)

Zessionar (m) n De
En transferee; assignee
Es cesionario (m)
Fr cessionaire (m)
It cessionario (m)
Pt cessionário (m)

Zeuge (m) n De
En witness
Es testigo (m)
Fr témoin (m)
It testimone (m)
Pt testemunha (f)

Ziel (n) n De
En goal; target
Es meta; objetivo (f m)
Fr bout; but (m)
It scopo; traguardo (m)
Pt meta; objectivo (f m)

Zinsen (m pl) De
En interest
Es interés (m)

Fr intérêt; prime (m f)
It interesse (m)
Pt juro (m)

Zinseszinsen (m pl) n De
En compound interest
Es interés compuesto (m)
Fr intérêts composés (m pl)
It interesse composto (m)
Pt juro composto (m)

Zinsfuß (m) n De
En interest rate
Es tipo de interés (m)
Fr taux d'intérêt (m)
It tasso d'interesse (m)
Pt taxa de juro (f)

Zinssatz (m) n De
En interest rate
Es tipo de interés (m)
Fr taux d'intérêt (m)
It tasso d'interesse (m)
Pt taxa de juro (f)

zip code Am
En postcode
De Postleitzahl (f)
Es designación postal (f)
Fr indicatif postal (m)
It codice postale (m)
Pt designação postal (f)

Zoll (m) n De
En customs; customs duty
Es aduana; derechos de aduanas (f; m pl)
Fr douane; droit de douane (f m)
It dogana; diritto doganale (f m)
Pt alfândega; direitos alfandegários (f; m pl)

Zollabfertigung (f) n De
En customs clearande
Es paso de aduanas (f)
Fr dédouanement (m)
It sdoganamento (m)
Pt despacho alfandegário (m)

Zollabkommen (n) n De
En tariff agreement
Es acuerdo tarifario (m)
Fr accord tarifaire (m)
It accordo tariffario (m)
Pt acordo de tarifas (m)

zollamtliche Untersuchung
(f) De
En customs examination
Es control de aduanas *(m)*
Fr visite douanière *(f)*
It visita doganale *(f)*
Pt verificação alfandegária *(f)*

Zolleinfuhrschein *(m)* n De
En bill of entry
Es declaración de aduana *(f)*
Fr déclaration en douane *(f)*
It bolletta di entrata *(f)*
Pt declaração alfandegária *(f)*

Zollerklärung *(f)* n De
En customs declaration
Es declaración de aduana *(f)*
Fr déclaration en douane *(f)*
It dichiarazione doganale *(f)*
Pt declaração alfandegária *(f)*

zollfreie Einfuhr *(f)* De
En duty-free admission
Es admisión libre de impuestos *(f)*
Fr admission en franchise *(f)*
It ammissione in franchigia doganale *(f)*
Pt admissão livre de impostos *(f)*

Zollrückvergütung *(f)* n De
En (customs) drawback
Es reembolso de derechos de aduana *(m)*
Fr remboursement des droits d'importation *(m)*
It rimborso d'esportazione *(m)*
Pt reembolso de direitos alfandegários *(m)*

Zollschranke *(f)* n De
En customs barrier
Es barrera aduanera *(f)*
Fr barrière douanière *(f)*
It barriera doganale *(f)*
Pt barreira alfandegária *(f)*

Zollunion *(f)* n De
En customs union
Es unión aduanera *(f)*
Fr union douanière *(f)*
It unione doganale *(f)*
Pt união aduaneira *(f)*

zona *(f)* n Es, It, Pt
De Zone *(f)*
En zone
Fr zone *(f)*

zona de desarrollo *(f)* Es
De Ortsplanungsgebiet *(n)*
En development area
Fr zone de développement *(f)*
It zona di sviluppo *(f)*
Pt zona de desenvolvimento *(f)*

zona de desenvolvimento *(f)* Pt
De Ortsplanungsgebiet *(n)*
En development area
Es zona de desarrollo *(f)*
Fr zone de développement *(f)*
It zona di sviluppo *(f)*

zona degli acquisti *(f)* It
De Geschäftszentrum *(n)*
En shopping centre
Es centro de negocios *(m)*
Fr centre commercial *(m)*
Pt centro de comércio *(m)*

zona de la esterlina *(f)* Es
De Sterlinggebiet *(n)*
En sterling area
Fr zone sterling *(f)*
It zona della sterlina *(f)*
Pt zona esterlina *(f)*

zona della sterlina *(f)* It
De Sterlinggebiet *(n)*
En sterling area
Es zona de la esterlina *(f)*
Fr zone sterling *(f)*
Pt zona esterlina *(f)*

zona deprimida *(f)* Pt
De Notstandsgebiet *(n)*
En distressed area
Es región deprimida *(f)*
Fr région déprimée *(f)*
It area indigente *(f)*

zona di sviluppo *(f)* It
De Ortsplanungsgebiet *(n)*
En development area
Es zona de desarrollo *(f)*
Fr zone de développement *(f)*
It zona de desenvolvimento *(f)*

zona esterlina *(f)* Pt
De Sterlinggebiet *(n)*
En sterling area
Es zona de la esterlina *(f)*
Fr zone sterling *(f)*
It zona della sterlina *(f)*

Zona Europea de Comercio Libre *(f)* Es
De Europäische Freihandelszone *(f)*
En European Free Trade Area (EFTA)
Fr Zone Européenne de Libre Échange *(f)*
It Zona Europea di Libero Scambio *(f)*
Pt Zona Europeia de Comércio Livre *(f)*

Zona Europea di Libero Scambio *(f)* It
De Europäische Freihandelszone *(f)*
En European Free Trade Area (EFTA)
Es Zona Europea de Comercio Libre *(f)*
Fr Zone Européenne de Libre Échange *(f)*
Pt Zona Europeia de Comércio Livre *(f)*

Zona Europeia de Comércio Livre *(f)* Pt
De Europäische Freihandelszone *(f)*
En European Free Trade Area (EFTA)
Es Zona Europea de Comercio Libre *(f)*
Fr Zone Européenne de Libre Échange *(f)*
It Zona Europea dl Libero Scambio *(f)*

zona monetaria *(f)* Es, It
De Währungsgebiet *(n)*
En currency area
Fr zone monétaire *(f)*
Pt zona monetária *(f)*

zona monetária *(f)* Pt
De Währungsgebiet *(n)*
En currency area
Es zona monetaria *(f)*
Fr zone monétaire *(f)*
It zona monetaria *(f)*

zone n En, Fr, *(f)*
De Zone *(f)*
Es zona *(f)*
It zona *(f)*
Pt zona *(f)*

Zone (f) n De
En zone
Es zona (f)
Fr zona (f)
It zona (f)
Pt zona (f)

zone de développement (f)
Fr
De Ortsplanungsgebiet (n)
En development area
Es zona de desarrollo (f)
It zona di sviluppo (f)
Pt zona de desenvolvimento
(f)

**Zone Européenne de Libre
Échange** (f) Fr
De Europäische Freihandels-
zone (f)
En European Free Trade Area
(EFTA)
Es Zona Europea de Com-
mercio Libre (f)
It Zona Europea di Libero
Scambio (f)
Pt Zona Europeia de
Comércio Livre (f)

zone monétaire (f) Fr
De Währungsgebiet (n)
En currency area
Es zona monetaria (f)
It zona monetaria (f)
Pt zona monetária (f)

zone sterling (f) Fr
De Sterlinggebiet (n)
En sterling area
Es zona de la esterlina (f)
It zona della sterlina (f)
Pt zona esterlina (f)

Zufriedenstellung (f) n De
En satisfaction
Es satisfacción (f)
Fr satisfaction (f)
It soddisfazione (f)
Pt satisfação (f)

Zuführung (f) n De
En appropriation
Es apropiación (f)
Fr affectation (f)
It stanziamento (m)
Pt apropriação (f)

Zugang (m) n De
En accrual
Es incremento (m)
Fr augmentation (f)
It incremento (m)
Pt acréscimo (m)

zukünftige Lieferung (f) De
En future delivery
Es futura entrega (f)
Fr livraison à terme (f)
It consegna a termine (f)
Pt futura remessa ou entrega
(f)

zurückstellen vb De
En defer
Es aplazar
Fr différer; ajourner
It differire
Pt adiar

zurücktreten vb De
En resign
Es dimitir
Fr se démettre
It dimettersi
Pt demitir-se

Zusammenarbeit (f) n De
En cooperation
Es cooperación (f)
Fr coopération (f)
It cooperazione (f)
Pt cooperação (f)

Zuschlagsgebühr (f) n De
En extra charge
Es suplemento (m)
Fr supplément (m)
It spesa supplementare (f)
Pt encargo suplementar (m)

zuteilen vb De
En apportion
Es repartir
Fr répartir
It ripartire
Pt atribuir

zu treuen Händen halten De
En hold in trust
Es quardar in fideicomiso
Fr tenir par fidéicommis
It tenere in fidecommesso
Pt reter em custódia

zuverlässig adj De
En reliable
Es digno de confianza
Fr digne de confiance
It fidato; attendibile
Pt digno de confiança

Zwang (m) n De
En duress
Es compulsión (f)
Fr contrainte (f)
It costrizione (f)
Pt coerção (f)

Zwangs- De
En forced
Es forzado
Fr forcé
It forzato
Pt forçado

Zwangsliquidation (f) n De
En compulsory winding-up
Am forced liquidation
Es liquidación forzosa (f)
Fr liquidation forcée (f)
It liquidazione forzata (f)
Pt liquidação forçada (f)

Zwangsverkauf (m) n De
En forced sale
Es venta forzosa (f)
Fr vente forcée (f)
It vendita forzosa (f)
Pt venda forçada (f)

Zwangsvollstreckung (f) n
De
En foreclosure
Es venta por juicio hipoteca-
rio (f)
Fr vente de l'immeuble
hypothéqué (f)
It vendita per giudizio ipote-
cario (f)
Pt execução judicial a uma hi-
poteca (f)

Zweckforschung (f) n De
En research and development
(R & D)
Es investigación y desarrollo
Fr recherche industrielle (f)
It studi e sviluppi
Pt investigação e desenvolvi-
mento

zweifelhafte Forderung *(f)*
De
En doubtful debt
Es deuda de pago dudoso *(f)*
Fr créance douteuse *(f)*
It credito dubbio *(m)*
Pt dívida duvidosa *(f)*

Zweigbüro *(n) n* De
En branch office
Es sucursal *(f)*
Fr succursale *(f)*
It succursale *(f)*
Pt sucursal *(f)*

Zwischenbilanz *(f) n* De
En interim financial statement
Es extracto financiero provi-
    sional *(m)*
Fr bilan intérimaire *(m)*
It rendiconto finanziario
    provvisorio *(m)*
Pt extracto financeiro interino
    (m)

Zwischenhändler *(m) n* De
En middle man
Es intermediario *(m)*
Fr intermédiaire *(m)*

It intermediario *(m)*
Pt intermediário *(m)*

zwischenmenschliche
    Beziehungen *(f pl)* De
En human relations
Es relaciones humanas *(f pl)*
Fr relations humaines *(f pl)*
It relazioni umane *(f pl)*
Pt relações humanas *(f pl)*

THE BRITISH CHAMBERS OF COMMERCE

Recent Publications

- **BRITISH CHAMBERS OF COMMERCE QUARTERLY ECONOMIC SURVEY**
Britain's most extensive business survey. Regionally dis-aggregated and covering service, as well as manufacturing industry, this quarterly survey represents a unique information source for Britain's major economic and industrial trends. Drawn from a sample of over 7,000 companies in 15 regions, the survey follows national and regional trends in such fields as exports, home sales and orders, investment trends, employment trends, skill shortages, capacity utilisation and external business factors.

  Price: £30.00 per copy (incl. p&p)   Annual Subscription: £100.00

- **BUSINESS BRIEFING**
Business Briefing is the business information weekly, launched with the active co-operation of the Department of Trade and Industry and the Central Statistical Office. Published by British Chambers of Commerce, Business Briefing provides a regular monitor of business statistics, news, regulations and information - what businesses need to know in one clear, concise and authoritative package. It brings together information from a wide range of sources in the private sector, Europe, the Department of Trade and Industry, Employment, Environment, Transport, Energy, Treasury, Inland Revenue and Customs & Excise. Completed every Thursday, evening Business Briefing is posted every Friday lunchtime, first class.

  Price: A one year subscription costs £94.00 (UK), £106.00 (Europe) or £120 (Overseas Airmail)

- **BECOMING A DIRECTOR**
A timely and topical publication, in question and answer format and is designed to guide all directors, whatever their background, though the legal maze governing their role. With contributions from lawyers, accountants and insolvency practitioners it will be an indispensable guide to people in business. Published in association with Coopers & Lybrand Deloitte.

  Price: £10.00 (incl. p&p)

- **EXPORT SERVICES 1992-1993**
This guide is designed to assist an exporter to find practical business-oriented help and advice from Chambers of Commerce and Industry (CCIs) throughout the UK. Covering topics from Export Counselling to Export Documentation.

  Price: £8.00 (Incl. p&p)

- **EXPORT TRAINING DIRECTORY**
  The British Chambers of Commerce Directory of Export Training has been designed to give the exporting community an easy-to-read guide to the availability of Export Training courses throughout the UK, covering five basic categories: Introduction to Basic Exporting; Export Procedures and Documentation; Export Finance (including letters of credit); Export Marketing, Selling, Distribution and Negotiation and Importing.

  The Directory gives details of short courses which are normally repeated at regular intervals during the year, where courses are held, course titles and main elements of content, frequency and duration.

  Price: £12.00 (incl. p&p)

- **BRITISH CHAMBERS OF COMMERCE POLICY DOCUMENT - 1st Edition February 1992**
  The Policy document presents a summary of some of the issues upon which the British Chambers of Commerce has made representations in recent months. As such it reflects the on-going concerns of the UK businesses in all sectors and of all sizes across the country. The document provides details on the policy issues concerned with the environments of political, economic, physical, working and regulatory.

  Price £10.00 (incl. p&p)

- **SMALL FIRMS AND CLEARING BANKS**
  An independent report commissioned by British Chambers of Commerce and produced by the University of Birmingham concludes that the relationship between banks and small firms is "sterile, uncommunicative and unimaginative". The report based on a survey of Chamber of Commerce members seeks to provide an unbiased examination of the crucial issue facing small businesses.

  Price £45.00 (incl. p&p)

- **EFFECTIVE BUSINESS SUPPORT: A UK STRATEGY PHASE TWO**
  This 16 page colour brochure details the progress made in the British Chambers of Commerce 4 year development strategy. Chambers of Commerce and Industry (CCIs) are committed to helping British business meet the challenging environment created by the Single European Market by developing a network of CCIs that provide quality assured and a consistent high level of business support services throughout the UK.

  Complimentary

To obtain these and other publications, please send your order, together with a cheque/postal order, made payable to:

> **The Association of British Chambers of Commerce**
> **9 Tufton Street**
> **London   SW1P 3QB**

THE BRITISH CHAMBERS OF COMMERCE

A large and growing network of Chambers of Commerce and Industry, representing 95,000 businesses throughout the UK

We Mean Business To You

- Business information
- Management training
- Export advice and assistance
- Fax and telex facilities
- Industry/education links
- Export documentation
- Databases
- Overseas trade missions and exhibitions

- Product sourcing
- Single Market Assistance
- Conferences and seminars
- Taking your views to government
- Business counselling
- Business contacts
- Local economic development
- An International and European network

For further information, please contact:
The British Chambers of Commerce
9 Tufton Street
London SW1P 3QB
Tel: 071-222-1555   Fax: 071-799-2202

Effective Business Support
from
Britain's Biggest Business Network